Strange Parallels: Southeast Asia in Global Context, c. 800–1830

Volume 1: Integration on the Mainland

Winner of the World History Association Book Prize

"*Strange Parallels* will certainly be seen for decades to come as one of those intellectual enterprises that helped define a generation of thinking about a particular time and place, in novel and often wonderful ways."

Eric Tagliacozzo, Cornell University

"This book thus represents a dramatic new stage in the historiography on early modern Southeast Asia (and Eurasia), setting a demanding agenda for future researchers that makes earlier approaches appear almost Jurassic by comparison."

Michael Charney, School of Oriental and African Studies, University of London

"Let me say again that this [book] is a masterpiece.... It is extremely important and will, I predict, become a landmark not only in the study of Southeast Asia but also in the study of early modern world history."

Li Tana, Australian National University

"A resounding scholarly achievement.... His work integrates Southeast Asian history into the past millennium and puts the region on the global map."

Ben Kiernan, Yale University

"This is the most ambitious and challenging effort any scholar has yet made to bring Southeast Asian history into the mainstream of the human experience in cogently postcolonial terms."

Alexander Woodside, University of British Columbia

"This work...has an originality which readers have come to from Victor Lieberman.... [It] will seal Victor Lieberman's repu as one of the finest historians of South East Asia and, indeed, one most original historians dealing with worldwide comparisons."

M. C. Ricklefs, National University of Sin

Strange Parallels

Southeast Asia in Global Context, c. 800–1830
Volume 2: Mainland Mirrors: Europe, Japan, China, South Asia,
and the Islands

Blending fine-grained case studies with overarching theory, this book seeks both to integrate Southeast Asia into world history and to rethink much of Eurasia's premodern past. It argues that Southeast Asia, Europe, Japan, China, and South Asia all embodied idiosyncratic versions of a Eurasian-wide pattern whereby local isolates cohered to form ever larger, more stable, more complex political and cultural systems. With accelerating force, climatic, commercial, and military stimuli joined to produce patterns of linear-cum-cyclic construction that became remarkably synchronized even between regions that had no contact with one another. Yet this study also distinguishes between two zones of integration, one where indigenous groups remained in control and a second where agency gravitated to external conquest elites. Here, then, is a fundamentally original view of Eurasia during a 1,000-year period that speaks to both historians of individual regions and those interested in global trends.

Both a specialist in precolonial Burma and a comparativist interested in global patterns, Victor Lieberman graduated first in his class from Yale University and obtained his doctorate from the School of Oriental and African Studies of the University of London. His publications include *Burmese Administrative Cycles: Anarchy and Conquest, c. 1580–1760,* which won the Harry J. Benda Prize from the Association for Asian Studies; *Beyond Binary Histories: Re-Imagining Eurasia to c. 1830,* which he edited and an earlier version of which appeared as a special issue of *Modern Asian Studies* devoted to Lieberman's scholarship; and *Strange Parallels: Southeast Asia in Global Context, c. 800–1830, Volume 1: Integration on the Mainland,* which won the World History Association Book Prize. He is the Marvin B. Becker Collegiate Professor of History and Professor of Southeast Asian History at the University of Michigan.

STUDIES IN COMPARATIVE WORLD HISTORY

Editors

Michael Adas, *Rutgers University*

Patrick Manning, *University of Pittsburgh*

Philip D. Curtin, *The Johns Hopkins University*

Other Books in the Series

Michael Adas, *Prophets of Rebellion: Millenarian Protest Movements Against the European Colonial Order* (1979)

Philip D. Curtin, *Cross-Cultural Trade in World History* (1984)

Leo Spitzer, *Lives in Between: Assimilation and Marginality in Austria, Brazil, and West Africa, 1780–1945* (1989)

Philip D. Curtin, *The Rise and Fall of the Plantation Complex: Essays in Atlantic History* (1990; second edition, 1998)

John Thornton, *Africa and Africans in the Making of the Atlantic World, 1400–1800* (1992; second edition, 1998)

Marshall G. S. Hodgson and Edmund Burke III (eds.), *Rethinking World History: Essays on Europe, Islam and World History* (1993)

David Northrup, *Indentured Labor in the Age of Imperialism, 1834–1922* (1995)

Lauren Benton, *Law and Colonial Cultures: Legal Regimes in World History, 1400–1900* (2002)

Victor Lieberman, *Strange Parallels: Southeast Asia in Global Context, c. 800–1830, Vol. 1: Integration on the Mainland* (2003)

Kerry Ward, *Networks of Empire: Forced Migration in the Dutch East India Company* (2009)

Strange Parallels

Southeast Asia in Global Context, c. 800–1830
Volume 2
Mainland Mirrors: Europe, Japan, China, South Asia, and the Islands

VICTOR LIEBERMAN
University of Michigan

CAMBRIDGE UNIVERSITY PRESS

CAMBRIDGE
UNIVERSITY PRESS

32 Avenue of the Americas, New York NY 10013-2473, USA

Cambridge University Press is part of the University of Cambridge.

It furthers the University's mission by disseminating knowledge in the pursuit of education, learning and research at the highest international levels of excellence.
www.cambridge.org
Information on this title: www.cambridge.org/9780521530361

First published 2009
Reprinted 2013

A catalogue record for this publication is available from the British Library

Library of Congress Cataloging in Publication data
Volume 1 was cataloged as:
Lieberman, Victor B., 1945–
Strange parallels : Southeast Asia in global context, c. 800–1830 / Victor Lieberman.
    p. cm. – (Studies in comparative world history)
Includes bibliographical references and index.
ISBN 0-521-80086-2   ISBN 0-521-8049605 (pb.)
1. Asia, Southeastern – Historiography. 2. Asia, Southeastern – History.
I. Title.   II. Series
ds524.4L54   2003
959–dc21   2002071481

ISBN 978-0-521-82352-4 Hardback
ISBN 978-0-521-53036-1 Paperback

To Sharon, forever
Jessica and Brad
Emily and Jeffrey
Marc
Elias
Elijah, Keren, Isaac, Julius, Adira, and Elia

Contents

Contents

List of Figures

xv

Abbreviations Used in the Notes

AC	Anthony Reid, *Southeast Asia in the Age of Commerce*, 2 vols. (New Haven, 1988, 1993)
AHR	*American Historical Review*
BEFEO	*Bulletin de l'Ecole Francaise d'Extreme-Orient*
BKI	*Bijdragen tot de Taal-, Land- en Volkenkunde*
BSOAS	*Bulletin of the School of Oriental and African Studies, University of London*
CASS	*Canadian-American Slavic Studies*
CC	*Climatic Change*
CEHI	Tapan Raychaudhuri and Irfan Habib, eds., *The Cambridge Economic History of India, Vol. 1: c. 1200–c. 1750* (Cambridge, 1982)
CHAC	Michael Loewe and Edward Shaughnessy, eds., *The Cambridge History of Ancient China* (Cambridge, 1999)
CHC, vol. I	Denis Twitchett and Michael Loewe, eds., *The Cambridge History of China, Vol. 1: The Ch'in and Han Empires, 221 BC–AD 220* (Cambridge, 1986)
CHC, vol. III	Denis Twitchett, ed., *The Cambridge History of China, Vol. 3: Sui and T'ang China, 589–906 AD, Part 1* (Cambridge, 1979)
CHC, vol. VI	Herbert Franke and Denis Twitchett, eds., *The Cambridge History of China, Vol. 6: Alien Regimes and Border States, 907–1368* (Cambridge, 1994)
CHC, vol. VII	Frederick Mote and Denis Twitchett, eds., *The Cambridge History of China, Vol. 7: The Ming Dynasty, 1368–1644, Part 1* (Cambridge, 1988)

CHC, vol. VIII	Denis Twitchett and Frederick Mote, eds., *The Cambridge History of China, Vol. 8: The Ming Dynasty, 1368–1644, Part 2* (Cambridge, 1986)
CHC, vol. IX	Willard Peterson, ed., *The Cambridge History of China, Vol. 9, Part 1: The Ch'ing Empire to 1800* (Cambridge, 2002)
CHEIA	Denis Sinor, ed., *The Cambridge History of Early Inner Asia* (Cambridge, 1990)
CHJ, vol. I	Delmer Brown, ed., *The Cambridge History of Japan, Vol. 1: Ancient Japan* (Cambridge, 1993)
CHJ, vol. II	Donald Shively and William McCullough, eds., *The Cambridge History of Japan, Vol. 2: Heian Japan* (Cambridge, 1999)
CHJ, vol. III	Kozo Yamamura, ed., *The Cambridge History of Japan, Vol. 3: Medieval Japan* (Cambridge, 1990)
CHJ, vol. IV	John W. Hall, ed., *The Cambridge History of Japan, Vol. 4: Early Modern Japan* (Cambridge, 1991)
CHJ, vol. V	Marius Jansen, ed., *The Cambridge History of Japan, Vol. 5: The Nineteenth Century* (Cambridge, 1989)
CHSEA	Nicholas Tarling, ed., *The Cambridge History of Southeast Asia, Vol. 1: From Early Times to c. 1800* (Cambridge, 1992)
CIHC	Patricia Buckley Ebrey, *The Cambridge Illustrated History of China* (Cambridge, 1996)
CIHMA, vol. II	Robert Fossier, ed., *The Cambridge Illustrated History of the Middle Ages, Vol. 2: 950–1250* (Cambridge, 1997)
CIHMA, vol. III	Robert Fossier, ed., *The Cambridge Illustrated History of the Middle Ages, Vol. 3: 1250–1520* (Cambridge, 1986)
CSSH	*Comparative Studies in Society and History*
EAH	Ainslie Embree, ed., *Encyclopedia of Asian History*, 4 vols. (New York, 1988)
EHR	*Economic History Review*
FH	*French History*
FHS	*French Historical Studies*
FzOG	*Forschungen zur Osteuropaischen Geschichte*
HJ	Conrad Totman, *A History of Japan* (Walden, MA, 2000)
HJAS	*Harvard Journal of Asiatic Studies*
HM	Barbara Watson Andaya and Leonard Andaya, *A History of Malaysia* (2nd ed., Honolulu, 2001)

HMI	M. C. Ricklefs, *A History of Modern Indonesia Since c. 1200* (3rd ed., Stanford, 2001)
HUS	*Harvard Ukrainian Studies*
IBE	Catherine Asher and Cynthia Talbot, *India Before Europe* (Cambridge, 2006)
IESHR	*Indian Economic and Social History Review*
IHR	*International History Review*
JAH	*Journal of Asian History*
JAOS	*Journal of the American Oriental Society*
JAS	*Journal of Asian Studies*
JEEH	*Journal of European Economic History*
JEH	*Journal of Economic History*
JEMH	*Journal of Early Modern History*
JESHO	*Journal of the Economic and Social History of the Orient*
JfGO	*Jahrbucher für Geschichte Osteuropas*
JGH	*Journal of Global History*
JJS	*Journal of Japanese Studies*
JMBRAS	*Journal of the Malay Branch, Royal Asiatic Society*
JMH	*Journal of Modern History*
JRAS	*Journal of the Royal Asiatic Society*
JSEAH	*Journal of Southeast Asian History*
JSEAS	*Journal of Southeast Asian Studies*
JSH	*Journal of Social History*
JWH	*Journal of World History*
LCH	Sheldon Pollock, ed., *Literary Cultures in History* (Berkeley, 2003)
LIC	*Late Imperial China*
MAS	*Modern Asian Studies*
MN	*Monumenta Nipponica*
ms	manuscript
NCHI	*The New Cambridge History of India*
NCMH, vol. II	Rosamond McKitterick, ed., *The New Cambridge Medieval History*, Vol. 2, *c. 700–c. 900* (Cambridge, 1995)
NCMH, vol. VII	Christopher Allmand, ed., *The New Cambridge Medieval History*, Vol. 7, *c. 1415–c. 1500* (Cambridge, 1998)
n.d.	no date
pers. commun.	personal communication
PP	*Past and Present*

PPP	*Paleogeography, Paleoclimatology, Paleoecology*
RH	*Russian History/Histoire Russe*
RR	*The Russian Review*
SEAR	*South East Asia Research*
SEER	*Slavonic and East European Review*
SP	Victor Lieberman, *Strange Parallels: Southeast Asia in Global Context, c. 800–1830, Vol. 1: Integration on the Mainland* (Cambridge, 2003)
SR	*Slavic Review*
SYMT	Paul Jakov Smith and Richard von Glahn, eds., *The Song-Yuan-Ming Transition* (Cambridge, MA, 2003)

Preface

Not unlike Michel de Montaigne, I found that the more I ate, the bigger my appetite became.[1] Originally I intended to write a one-volume history of mainland Southeast Asia from c. 800 to 1830, with a concluding chapter suggesting similarities to premodern Russia. But as I read, I began to sense that mainland Southeast Asia shared critical developmental features not only with Russia but with other far-flung sectors of Eurasia, and that analysis of those features could help to free Southeast Asia from the historiographic ghetto in which it had long been confined. I resolved therefore to supplement mainland history with Eurasian comparisons. Rather than try to cover Eurasia at large, I decided to develop case studies of Russia, France, and Japan, for it seemed that the history of those regions, focusing on cyclic-cum-linear state consolidation under indigenous elites, stood closest to patterns in mainland Southeast Asia's principal realms, namely, Burma, Siam, and Vietnam.

I still assumed that this would be a one-volume work, albeit a rather long one. But eventually it became clear that a single volume could not contain the necessary argument and documentation. With the deeply appreciated support of Frank Smith, Editorial Director for Academic Books at Cambridge University Press, I therefore separated the comparative material on Europe and Japan to form a second volume.

The matter, however, did not rest there. When Volume 1 appeared in 2003, the Preface said that Volume 2 would cover Russia, France, Japan, and island Southeast Asia. As research for those chapters proceeded, I began to realize that mainland Southeast Asia, most of Europe, and

---

[1] Albert Thibaudet and Maurice Rat, eds., *Montaigne: Oeuvres Completes* (Paris, 1962), 952.

Japan together constituted part of a distinctive Eurasian subcategory that I term "the protected zone" and the coherence of which becomes apparent only when contrasted with another subcategory that I term the "exposed zone." Defined primarily by subjection to Inner Asian conquest elites, the latter zone includes Southeast Asia's principal neighbors, China and South Asia, together with most of Southwest Asia. Accordingly, Volume 2 now has been expanded to include substantial chapters on China and South Asia.

Thus, for better or worse, what began as a modest study of mainland Southeast Asia has become a history of much of the premodern world. In undertaking this expansion, my comparative goals are several. By showing how ostensibly unconnected peoples on the fringes of two continents experienced broadly comparable political and cultural trajectories, governed by a similar constellation of forces, with coordinated rhythms of cyclic and secular construction, I seek to demonstrate that these societies constituted variations on a hitherto unrecognized, thousand-year-long Eurasian pattern. At the same time I argue that the protected zone as a whole differed substantially from China and South Asia, most notably in the relation between indigenous and external agency, but also in developmental chronology. That is to say, because of its position along Eurasia's periphery, the protected zone not only remained more insulated from Inner Asian conquest, but also generated charter civilizations appreciably later than much of the exposed zone. These protected-zone features in turn often were associated with smaller-scale, more manageable demographic and political units. I considered dividing the present volume into two sections, one on the protected zone, and the second on the exposed zone, but ultimately declined to do so for fear that by masking overlapping similarities, such an approach might tell in favor of replacing the old European/non-European dichotomy with a no less deceptively reified bifurcation. Still, I shall be pleased if others are inspired to substantiate, refute, or modify the protected-zone thesis. Finally, I attempt to show – somewhat counterintuitively – that broad Eurasian parallels can enrich local understandings. If we recognize, for example, that for much of the period c. 900 to 1800 mainland Southeast Asia, China, parts of South Asia, and much of Europe experienced coordinated demographic, and by extension political, rhythms, we are obliged to consider what common elements – climatic, epidemiological, commercial, intellectual – were at work. Explanations of local change framed entirely in terms of idiosyncratic cultural or social traits become prima facie suspect. If we consider that Japan's demographic/economic rhythms frequently diverged from those in Europe and Southeast Asia, the isolation of key variables becomes yet more feasible.

Yet although my geographic coverage has mushroomed, the Southeast Asian roots of this project remain much in evidence. Reconceptualizing Eurasia as a coherent, interactive ecumene and assessing Southeast Asia's place within that ecumene I see as complementary tasks. Hence this volume's subtitle: *Mainland Mirrors*. A Southeast Asian focus, in fact, governs three aspects of my presentation. First, specific conceptual categories – including the protected zone, charter civilizations, postcharter collapse, politicized ethnicity, and political cycles punctuated by ever less disruptive interregna – derive initially from my study of the mainland, whose experience in some ways provides an analytic template. By extension, discussions of other realms, particularly in Chapters 2 to 4, regularly consider similarities and differences with mainland Southeast Asia. Second, I have grouped societies in concentric circles defined not by geography, but by thematic proximity to mainland patterns. Volume 1 was specifically about the mainland. The case studies of this volume begin with the protected zone, whose patterns most closely resembled those of the mainland, before moving to exposed-zone regions, whose developmental affiliations were less close. Moreover, my choice of China and South Asia, rather than, say, the Ottoman empire, to illustrate exposed-zone patterns in Chapters 5 and 6 reflects my desire to examine areas in closest physical and cultural proximity to Southeast Asia. Third, having examined non-Southeast Asian realms, I circle back, as it were, in the last chapter to consider archipelagic Southeast Asia's relation to continental patterns. I conclude that for most of their history the islands' role was much like that of the mainland, but that starting in the 16th century and with increasing force to the end of the period under review, European interventions in the archipelago in some ways resembled nomad interventions in Asia's great agrarian heartlands. (Having finally satisfied my comparative appetites, I might add that my forthcoming research will return to precolonial Burma to reexamine some of *Strange Parallels'* larger theses in a controlled local setting.)

If non-Burma specialists helped me with Volume 1, for the current book, given that I have conducted primary research in none of the realms under review, my debts are yet more numerous and substantial. Often I have benefited from the collegiality of historians whom I have yet to meet in person and several of whom volunteered to read Chapter 1 as well as the chapter of their own expertise.

For Russia my chief guide has been my Michigan colleague Valerie Kivelson, whose enthusiasm for all aspects of Russian history infected me some 15 years ago. Her comments on various drafts of Chapters 2 and 3 and her suggestions for further readings proved indispensable. Marshall Poe also advanced my understanding of pre-Petrine military and administrative history, while Richard Hellie provided an extremely helpful line-by-line critique of all pre-1620 Russian material in Chapter 2.

My writing on pre-1350 France profited from perceptive, detailed critiques by Patrick Geary, David Potter, and my Michigan colleague Paolo Squatriti. Paolo has done his best to keep me abreast of developments in medieval research. For help with Renaissance and Reformation France I am grateful for careful, thoughtful commentary by Mack Holt and Michael Wintroub, while my drafts on Bourbon and Revolutionary France benefited from the astute insights not only of my Michigan colleague Dena Goodman but of David Bell, William Beik, and Michael Kwass. The willingness of these non-Michigan scholars to share their knowledge at length with a virtual stranger has been remarkable.

A similar altruism enriched the Japan chapter. Philip Brown, whom I met when he served as a visiting professor in Ann Arbor, carefully critiqued my first draft of Chapter 4 and responded with patient detail to subsequent e-mail inquires. My Michigan colleague Tomi Tonomura also read a draft of Chapter 4 and addressed a stream of e-mail and verbal questions. Conrad Totman (whose *A History of Japan* became my early guide), Lee Butler, Matthew Stavros, Jonathan Zwicker, and Peter Shapinsky provided helpful comments on all or part of early versions of Chapter 4. The final draft drew on generous reviews by Karen Wigen, David Howell, and Anne Walthall, all three of whom went to considerable trouble on my behalf. Professors Brown, Howell, Wigen, Butler, and Stavros also gave me offprints and/or manuscripts of recent and forthcoming publications. William Wayne Farris supplied painstaking commentary on my pre-Tokugawa efforts and graciously allowed me to read in manuscript his forthcoming book *The Population of Ancient Japan*. That work, in combination with his commentary and his recently published *Japan's Medieval Population*, utterly transformed my view of pre-1400 Japan. Ken Ito and Joan Piggott helped me with specific inquiries. Memorable conversations some years ago with Mary Elizabeth Berry informed my early understandings of Japan and alerted me to some of the pitfalls that comparative inquiry into Japanese history was likely to create.

The vastness of Chinese historiography and the multiple incarnations through which Chapter 5 evolved mean that my debts for that chapter are no less extensive. Michigan scholars C. S. Chang – whose two-volume *The Rise of the Chinese Empire* is only the most tangible of his many forms of generous assistance – Marty Powers, Miranda Brown, James Lee, and Ernie Young helped me with both overviews and specific problems. John Wills, Jr. (a man of contagious intellect and affability), Li Bozhong, William Atwell, Tonio Andrade, and Christian Lamouroux carefully critiqued early drafts and reshaped my approach to controversial issues. Li Bozhong kindly let me read several unpublished manuscripts. In addition, Mark Elliott, Peter Perdue, and Patricia Buckley Ebrey each supplied commentary on the penultimate version of Chapter 5, spotting questionable claims and interpretations, alerting me to new publications, and pushing me to a level of historiographic awareness to which I could not have aspired on my own. To say I am deeply grateful is inadequate.

Early drafts of Chapter 6 on South Asia benefited from reviews by my Ann Arbor colleagues Tom Trautmann, Barbara Metcalf, and Farina Mir. Through extended correspondence, Alan Strathern also critiqued this chapter and led me to rethink big issues of cultural transfer and integration in South Asia and Eurasia generally. I benefited from discussions with Richard Eaton on Indian Islam and from conversational insights and an unpublished paper on the Marathas provided by Stewart Gordon. The final version of Chapter 6 reflects penetrating comments by Cynthia Talbot and Sanjay Subrahmanyam, both of whom rescued me from factual errors and challenged me to rethink assumptions and terms of reference.

For Chapter 7 I was fortunate to draw on insightful critiques by Merle Ricklefs, Barbara Watson Andaya, Leonard Andaya, and Will Redfern, each of whom approached island Southeast Asia from a slightly different geographic and thematic perspective. Professors Ricklefs, Watson Andaya, and Andaya also provided forthcoming essays in manuscript. Greg Bankoff kindly reviewed my Philippine material, whereas Jan Wisseman Christie answered inquiries and provided me with invaluable unpublished papers on early Java.

With problems of economic theory, David Hancock; with epidemiology, Marty Pernick; and with Chinese climate reconstructions, Pao K. Wang assisted me. Rudi Lindner answered my quixotic queries on Inner Asian and Ottoman history, as did Juan Cole on Indian and general Muslim history, and Carla Sinopoli on both Asian and European archeology.

Roger Albin, a generous polymath in the University of Michigan Medical School, provided a well-informed critical reading of the entire manuscript. As external reviewer for Volume 2, Barbara Watson Andaya offered welcome suggestions for strengthening my Conclusion and general presentation. I have profited too from editorial assistance by my lifelong friend Charles Berman and from extended historiographic discussions with my close friend and Michigan colleague Todd Endelman.

Strange though it may sound, rarely, if ever, did two readers of the same material offer the same criticisms. I have therefore had an abundance of input from a wide variety of angles. If, despite this multifaceted support, inaccuracies, dubious interpretations, and other deficiencies remain, the fault is entirely my own.

This research benefited from the following grants and fellowships: a Social Science Research Council/American Council of Learned Societies Research Grant; a National Endowment for the Humanities Fellowship for University Teachers; a National Endowment for the Humanities Summer Stipend; and from the University of Michigan, a Horace H. Rackham Faculty Fellowship, an Institute for the Humanities Fellowship, and publication subventions from the Office of the Vice-President for Research to produce maps and charts. The latter were skillfully prepared by Malgorzata Krawczyk. For permission to incorporate their research findings in Figures 2.3a to 2.3f, I thank Michael Aung-Thwin, Bob Hudson, David B. Miller, Hugh D. Clout, and Peter Turchin, and for permission to use material in Figure 6.2, Jillian Luff.

A word finally about sources. With some exceptions, I stopped reading new literature for Chapters 2 and 3 in 2005 or 2006, and for Chapters 4 to 7 in 2006 to 2008. I appreciate as keenly as any scholar the value of a bibliography, and originally I intended to list at the end of Volume 2 all sources cited in the footnotes. It turned out, however, that this would have added 130 pages to an already ponderous text. A bibliography for both volumes is therefore available online at http://www.umich.edu/~eurasia/strangeparallels/bibliography.html. To facilitate identification, the first time each item appears in the footnotes of a new chapter in this volume, it receives a full citation.

V.L.
October 2008

CHAPTER ONE

A Far Promontory

Southeast Asia and Eurasia

1. RETHINKING EURASIA

Between 1240 and 1390 the principal realms of mainland Southeast Asia collapsed. The same was true of France and Kiev, whose political and economic travails merged with a general European crisis. After a political revival that started in most cases in the mid-1400s and continued for a century or so, in the late 1500s the chief kingdoms in what are now Burma (Myanmar), Thailand, Vietnam, France, and Russia again fell apart, this time more briefly. For a second time political fortunes then stabilized, aided in each case by administrative and military reforms. Yet in the second half of the 18th century a third round of warfare and disorder spread across mainland Southeast Asia and, from its French epicenter, across Europe. And once again, in both regions these disturbances ushered in a phase of renewed consolidation and effective reform.

Other than by sheer coincidence, how can we explain these correlations between regions with no obvious cultural or material links? Why in each realm did successive interregna tend to grow less prolonged and dislocating? Conversely, in these far-flung Eurasian areas – as well as in Japan, China, and European states whose chronologies did not match exactly the cyclic pattern just described – why should movements toward administrative integration have become increasingly successful over the long term? And why did sustained consolidation characterize some sectors of Eurasia, but not others?

This is the second book in a two-volume study designed to address these and similar questions. As a specialist in Southeast Asia, I seek in the first instance to connect my region to world history and thus to breach that encapsulation which, I suggested in Volume 1, has long characterized regional historiography. Typically, scholars of the precolonial era saw Southeast Asian development, such as it was, as dependent on external maritime contacts. Either because Southeast Asians lost control over the main lines of trade in the mid-1600s, or because even before that date external stimuli actually had only a superficial impact on intensely conservative cultures, historians posited a high degree of precolonial inertia – which contrasts with the restless dynamism of Europe.[1]

Without eliding differences between regions, I attempt in this volume to balance those differences against overarching, hitherto ignored, traits that linked Southeast Asia to Europe and other sectors of Asia during roughly a thousand years. In so doing, I hope not only to recontextualize Southeast Asian historiography, but to influence far broader discussions that began in the late 20th century about the long-term relation between white-skinned peoples and the rest of the world generally. That is to say, in enfeebling Orientalism, sustained comparisons promise to weaken Orientalism's inseparable twin, European exceptionalism.

A regnant trope from the 1700s until the 1990s and still deeply influential both in the academy and among educated nonspecialists, European exceptionalism claims that Western economic and military dynamism – Europe's escape from a relative immobility that was the fate of the rest of mankind – derived from a distinctive complex of physical and cultural features that, in some versions, appeared as early as the middle ages. As explicated in E. L. Jones' oft-cited *The European Miracle*, Europe, or more accurately its western half, benefited from contingent synergies between advantageous geography – dispersed agrarian cores favoring multistate competition, low man-to-land ratios, extensive coastlines, access to New World wealth – and cultural patterns unusually conducive to innovation.[2] According to David Landes, who places primary stress on cultural entelechy, by the 15th century, if not earlier, a contrast loomed between self-limiting West European regimes and Asian political forms less sympathetic to mercantile and urban autonomy and market competition. Refined in later centuries, the Western emphasis on contractual government, individual and corporate autonomy, secure property rights, and empirical inquiry produced those twin glories of

---

[1] See discussion at *SP*, 5–21.
[2] E. L. Jones, *The European Miracle* (rpt., Cambridge, 1993).

the modern world, political democracy and industrial capitalism.[3] In perhaps the most arresting recent formulation of such views, Jack Goldstone argues that the steam engine, which he sees as the central prerequisite for industrialization and modernity itself, derived not from general European culture, but from a confluence of specifically British factors in the late 1600s. These included the Glorious Revolution's promotion of secular, pluralist, liberal ideals; the triumph of Isaac Newton's epistemology based on experiment and universal laws; the popularization of Newtonian perspectives with support from the Anglican church; and the practical application of such views by British technicians and entrepreneurs within a culture of "engine science" committed to innovation and pragmatic inquiry.[4]

Three Critiques of European Exceptionalism

As an Italian historian quipped long before postmodernists began to theorize subjectivity, ultimately all history is contemporary.[5] The *sine qua non* for European exceptionalism's intellectual appeal – an appeal, by the way, that extended well beyond colonial sympathizers to many

---

[3] David S. Landes, *The Wealth and Poverty of Nations* (New York, 1998). Similar analyses, albeit informed by a more sophisticated knowledge of non-Western cultures, underlie Jan Luiten van Zanden, "The Road to the Industrial Revolution," *JGH* 3 (2008): 337–59; and Tirthankar Roy, "Knowledge and Divergence from the Perspective of Early Modern India," *JGH* 3 (2008): 361–87, which emphasizes the unique ease with which technical knowledge diffused both geographically and socially in early modern western Europe. See too the emphasis on cultural determination in Lawrence Harrison and Samuel Huntingdon, eds., *Culture Matters* (New York, 2000).

[4] Jack Goldstone, "The Rise of the West – or Not? A Revision to Socio-Economic History," *Sociological Theory* 18 (2000): 175–94; idem, "Neither Late Imperial Nor Early Modern," in Lynn Struve, ed., *The Qing Formation in World-Historical Time* (Cambridge, MA, 2004), 242–302; idem, "Europe's Peculiar Path: Would the World Be Modern if William III's Invasion of England in 1688 Had Failed" (ms); idem, *Why Europe? The Rise of the West in World History 1500–1800* (New York, 2008), 150–61. Goldstone's work builds on Margaret Jacob, *The Cultural Meaning of the Scientific Revolution* (Philadelphia, 1988), esp. ch. 5, and Betty Jo Teeter Dobbs and Margaret Jacob, *Newton and the Culture of Newtonianism* (Atlantic Highlands, NJ, 1995). For other recent expressions of European, West European, and/or British exceptionalism by prominent academics, see sources cited in *SP*, 66–69; n. 3 *supra*; David Levine, *At the Dawn of Modernity* (Berkeley, 2001); R. I. Moore, *The First European Revolution* (Oxford, 2002), esp. 193–98; idem, "The Transformation of Europe as a Eurasian Phenomenon," in Johann Arnason and Bjorn Wittrock, eds., *Eurasian Transformations, Tenth to Thirteenth Centuries* (Leiden, 2004), 77–98; Robert Brenner and Christopher Isett, "England's Divergence from China's Yangzi Delta," *JAS* 61 (2002): 609–62; and sources in n. 13 *infra*.

[5] Benedetto Croce, *Theory and History of Historiography* (London, 1921), 11–15.

Marxists and resolute anti-imperialists – was Western political and economic dominance from the late 18th to the late 20th century. But starting as early as the 1940s and with particular force during the last two or three decades, the collapse of European colonialism, Asia's remarkable economic dynamism, and the emergence of India and China as major political/military actors have combined to render the intellectual climate ever less sympathetic to notions of entrenched Asian deficiency. Although by itself this shift in historiographic sensibility has attracted remarkably little analysis, it has given the search for antecedents to contemporary Asian vigor an emotional impetus, an intellectual sanction, an operational space that were quite absent during the era of unquestioned Western dominance. More or less unself-consciously, many historians now seek to do for Asia what Jones, Landes, and others did for Europe, namely to provide a suitable historic pedigree for current success. After all, one could hardly tell a nobleman, even a parvenu, that his ancestors were beggars.

In practice, revisionist views of European exceptionalism's foundational insistence on East-West incomparability have assumed three principal guises. First, scholars have tried to find Asian analogues to specifically European sociopolitical institutions, among which the two most popular candidates, arguably, have been feudalism[6] and the public sphere. On the whole, these inquiries bore modest fruit – and in many cases, have been abandoned – because the terms of reference proved too narrow. As regards the public sphere, for example, although scholars of precolonial India and post-1600 China and Japan have argued for local analogues to that European arena of discourse analyzed by Jurgen Habermas, in no Asian society apparently do we find the same institutional safeguards, the same critical surveillance of government and society, or the same habitual assertion of civic power against the state as were central to Habermas' concept. If after 1600 many of the most advanced sectors of Asia supported a growing density of communications and public commentary on intellectual, aesthetic, and literary issues, such developments said far less about the possibilities of European-style democracy in Asia than about more general, politically neutral processes of commercialization and rising literacy.[7]

---

[6] See, e.g., Edmund Leach et al., *Feudalism: Comparative Studies* (Sydney, 1985); John W. Hall and Marius Jansen, eds., *Studies in the Institutional History of Early Modern Japan* (Princeton, 1968), 3–51; Peter Duus, *Feudalism in Japan* (New York, 1993).

[7] Cf. Jurgen Habermas, *The Structural Transformation of the Public Sphere* (Cambridge, MA, 1989); C. A. Bayly, *Empire and Information* (Cambridge, 1999), ch. 5; "Symposium: 'Public

A second, more promising line of inquiry has sought to compare family structures and demography in Europe and Asia. From Thomas Malthus to John Hajnal to E. L. Jones, many argued that one secret to Western economic success lay in northwestern Europe's system of delayed marriages and frequent celibacy, which depressed childbearing and favored capital accumulation within the stem family. This low fertility, low mortality regime is said to have contrasted with the high fertility, high mortality regimes of China and India. For pre-1800 China, at least, this dichotomy has now collapsed. James Lee and others have shown that, in reality, abortion, female infanticide, adoption, low rates of male marriage, chaste widowhood, and greater spacing between births combined to depress Chinese marital fertility to levels far below those in Europe, while keeping overall Chinese growth rates between 1400 and 1800 at about the same level as in Europe. In other words, whereas the European family system limited fertility by controlling access to marriage, China achieved the same result by controlling fertility within marriage. Furthermore, since Chinese could adjust family size to changing circumstances, mortality responses to short-term pressures were no more, and in many cases less, severe than in northwestern Europe.[8]

Given industrialism's centrality to modern narratives, it is hardly surprising that the third line of inquiry, which compares industrial potential in pre-1850 Europe and Asia, has generated the most lively interest. The thrust of these revisionist efforts has been to expand the lineage of modern economic growth and thus to deny exclusive European parentage. Because Japan was Asia's first success story, it was to be expected that earliest efforts would focus on that island realm, where Tokugawa

---

Sphere'/'Civil Society' in China?" *Modern China* 19 (1993): 107–240; R. Bin Wong, "Great Expectations," *Chugoku Shigakkai* 3 (1993): 7–49; Frederic Wakeman, "Boundaries of the Public Sphere in Ming and Qing China," *Daedalus* 127 (1998): 167–89; Eiko Ikegami, *Bonds of Civility* (Cambridge, 2005); Mary Elizabeth Berry, *Japan in Print* (Berkeley, 2006).

[8] On comparative demography, John Hajnal, "European Marriage Patterns in Perspective," in D. V. Glass and D. E. Eversley, eds., *Population in History* (Chicago, 1965), 101–40; Jones, *European Miracle*, 15–21; James Lee and Wang Feng, *One Quarter of Humanity* (Cambridge, MA, 1999); James Lee et al., "Positive Check or Chinese Checks?" *JAS* 61 (2002): 591–607; Tommy Bengtsson et al., *Life Under Pressure: Mortality and Living Standards in Europe and Asia, 1700–1900* (Cambridge, MA, 2004). But see Philip C. C. Huang, "Development or Involution in Eighteenth-Century Britain and China?" *JAS* 61 (2002): 501–38 for a more Malthusian paradigm. In Japan the importance of fertility control has long been recognized.

organization, once denounced as an impediment to growth, is now generally credited with laying the foundation for Japan's rapid textile-led expansion after 1880.[9] Subsequently, historians of precolonial South Asia also discovered trends toward commodification, agricultural specialization, even protoindustrialization that bore at least a superficial similarity to early modern Europe.[10] Most shocking, given China's geographic and cultural centrality, have been assaults on the venerable notion of Chinese economic failure vis-à-vis Japan and the West, an assault led most ably by Kenneth Pomeranz. According to that brilliant and indefatigable scholar, until c. 1800 labor productivity, living standards, consumer culture, resource constraints, and market efficiency in the Yangzi delta, China's economic core, were actually quite comparable to patterns in England, Europe's most advanced sector. Ultimately England alone escaped from an ecological cul-de-sac as a result of three structural factors, all heavily influenced by geography: a) British trade with Eastern Europe and America favored a higher degree of core–periphery specialization, favorable to industrialization in the core, than was possible in China, where manufacturing advances diffused more easily from advanced districts to outlying areas. b) By providing vast quantities of cheap foodstuffs and timber, the New World's "ghost acreage" allowed Britain to transcend ecological limits in a fashion impossible in China. c) Britain was uniquely blessed with abundant and accessible deposits of coal.[11]

Pomeranz' views have not won universal acceptance. The Europeanist Robert Brenner and China historians Philip Huang and Christopher Isett have disputed his central claim that labor productivity in early modern China and England was comparable. In their view, whereas large farms, mixed cropping, and animal husbandry placed

---

[9] See Thomas C. Smith, *The Agrarian Origins of Modern Japan* (Stanford, 1959); idem, *Native Sources of Japanese Industrialization 1750–1920* (Berkeley, 1988), ch. 1; and sources in Ch. 4 *infra*.

[10] Frank Perlin, "Proto-Industrialization and Pre-Colonial South Asia," *PP* 98 (1983): 30–95; Prasannan Parthasarathi, "Rethinking Wages and Competitiveness in the 18th Century: Britain and South India," *PP* 158 (1998): 79–109; Sanjay Subrahmanyam, ed., *Merchants, Markets and the State in Early Modern India* (Delhi, 1990); Jack Goody, *The East in the West* (Cambridge, 1996). See too discussions of maritime-dependent economic growth in Southeast Asia in *AC*; plus my "Secular Trends in Burmese Economic History, c. 1350–1830," *MAS* 25 (1991): 1–31.

[11] Kenneth Pomeranz, *The Great Divergence* (Princeton, 2000); idem, "Political Economy on the Eve of Industrialization," *AHR* 107 (2002): 425–46; idem, "Beyond the East-West Binary," *JAS* 61 (2002): 539–90. Cf. Andre Gunder Frank, *Re-Orient* (Berkeley, 1998).

England on a path of growing capitalization and declining labor inputs per land unit, which freed labor for an urban-based industrial revolution, the Yangzi basin's small-farms, crops-only regime moved it in the opposite direction toward rural labor intensification and involution.[12] Others have emphasized less geographic and economic than cultural and political differences. C. A. Bayly and Patrick O'Brien, for example, have called attention to the advantages that western Europe in general, not merely Britain, derived from the impersonal, transgenerational character of commercial enterprise; from the peculiarly European ideology of progress and techniques of protoscientific inquiry; and from a vigorously critical and increasingly patriotic public opinion. Such sentiment was a precondition for timely public investments, in particular for those massive Hanoverian commitments to naval and military power that allowed Britain to reap hugely disproportionate rewards from agricultural intensification in Asia and the Americas.[13]

This diversity of opinion among Pomeranz and his critics (to which we shall return in Chapter 5) should not blind us to overarching agreements. Many historians now assign a relatively late date, the 17th or even the late 18th century, to Britain's divergence from "normative" Eurasian patterns, while attributing that escape to contingent, multi-factoral synergies rather than to legacies of medieval origin. Moreover, virtually all scholars now reject binary contrasts between an economically dynamic West and a preternaturally stagnant East. Brenner and Isett do so because they split off the English farmer from his less market-responsive counterparts elsewhere in Europe as well as in China. Most

---

[12] Huang, "Development or Involution"; Brenner and Isett, "England's Divergence." Likewise van Zanden, "Road to Industrial Revolution," 342, 344, 348 argues that appreciably higher interest rates and a far lower incidence of wage labor in China than in western Europe point to less efficient market integration by the 17th century, if not earlier. Cf. Pomeranz' reply to Huang, "Beyond the East-West Binary," and discussion in Ch. 5 *infra*.

[13] C. A. Bayly, *The Birth of the Modern World 1780–1914* (Malden, MA, 2004), 58–83, 312–15; idem, "South Asia and the 'Great Divergence,'" *Itinerario* 24 (2000): 89–103; Patrick O'Brien, "The Reconstruction, Rehabilitation and Reconfiguration of the British Industrial Revolution as a Conjuncture in Global History," *Itinerario* 24 (2000), 117–34; idem, "The Foundations of European Industrialization," in Jose Casas Pardo, ed., *Economic Effects of the European Expansion 1491–1824* (Stuttgart, 1992), 463–502. Also P. H. H. Vries, "Governing Growth," *JWH* 13 (2002): 67–138, esp. 112–14. To be fair, Pomeranz, *Great Divergence*, 194–206 also emphasizes coercion in the Atlantic economy but ties it less closely to broad cultural and political differences.

others do so because they see in various parts of Eurasia not only "extensive growth" but bouts of "Smithian growth" lasting anywhere from 75 to 200 years.

In extensive growth, output expands through the sheer addition of production units, but in Smithian growth wider exchange (instigated by growing demand), greater specialization, and commercial economies of scale reduce transaction costs and thus improve productivity and income within a conservative technological framework.[14] Plausible claims for Smithian growth have been made not only for medieval Europe, early modern England, and Holland, but also *inter alia* for Angkor, Tokugawa Japan, Mughal South Asia, and Song and Qing China.[15] In a word, much recent economic, like demographic, research is inclined to regard premodern Eurasia as a zone not of opposed dichotomies but of potentially comparable sites. The same point has been made by John F. Richards, whose recent study of agrarian and maritime expansion between 1500 and 1800 argues that key sectors of Europe and Asia exhibited similar patterns of frontier settlement, resource scarcity, and energy constraint.[16]

---

[14] Smithian refers to the growth process envisioned by Adam Smith. The other chief types of growth are "involutionary," of the type Huang posits for Qing China, wherein labor productivity and income decline through demographic pressure on a static resource base; and "modern," of the type Britain enjoyed after 1850, in which labor productivity and per capita income grow continuously within a constantly expanding technological frontier. Needless to say, many hybrid cases defy these ideal types. See Victor Lieberman, "Transcending East-West Dichotomies," in Lieberman, ed., *Beyond Binary Histories* (Ann Arbor, MI, 1999), 53–54 and sources therein; O'Brien, "Reconstruction, Rehabilitation," 126–30; and S. R. Epstein, *Freedom and Growth* (London, 2000), 7–11.

[15] Previous notes on Asian economies, plus *SP*, chs. 2, 3; E. L. Jones, *Growth Recurring* (Oxford, 1988); Jack Goldstone, "Efflorescences and Economic Growth in World History," *JWH* 13 (2002): 323–90; Li Bozhong, *Agricultural Development in Jiangnan, 1620–1850* (New York, 1998); Timothy Brooke and Gregory Blue, eds., *China and Historic Capitalism* (Cambridge, 1999).

[16] John F. Richards, *The Unending Frontier* (Berkeley, 2003). All three critiques of European exceptionalism – the search for similarities in sociopolitical institutions, in demography, and in economic/industrial potential – are examples of comparative history, that is to say, investigations of structural similarities between societies regardless of chronology or physical linkages. As such, they may be distinguished from connective history, which may be defined as inquiry into contacts between geographically distinct but contemporary societies regardless of structure. For notable examples of the latter, see Sanjay Subrahmanyam, *Explorations in Connected History: From the Tagus to the Ganges* (New Delhi, 2005); idem, *Explorations in Connected History: Mughals and Franks* (New Delhi, 2005); John Wills, Jr., *1688: A Global History* (New York, 2001); William McNeill, *Plagues and Peoples* (Garden City, NY, 1976); Janet Abu-Lughod, *Before European Hegemony* (New York, 1989); Jerry Bentley, "Cross-Cultural Interaction and Periodization

New Axes of Comparison

Building on Volume 1, this book develops a fourth axis of Eurasian comparison: long-term trends to political and cultural integration. To be sure, we already have a modest comparative literature on pre-1850 Eurasian state formation.[17] But earlier research differs from the present effort in theme, chronology, and geographic scope.

Previous writers have compared the institutional workings and economic impact of early modern states. For example, R. Bin Wong, using Chinese and West European norms to interrogate one another, contrasted Chinese and European policies toward elite autonomy, social welfare, and taxation. Goldstone examined the contribution of ecological strains to state breakdowns in early modern England, France, Turkey, and China. P. H. H. Vries compared European, Qing, Ottoman, and Mughal fiscal policies in order to determine whether, as is often claimed, peculiarly European patterns of mercantilism and warfare boosted early modern economic growth.[18]

Yet no scholar has considered the central questions of this volume: Why during at least a thousand years did regions on the far reaches of Eurasia, with distinctive social and economic systems and little or no contact, experience parallel consolidations? Why not uninterrupted

---

in World History," *AHR* 101 (1996): 749–70; idem, *Old World Encounters* (Oxford, 1993); William Atwell, "Time, Money, and the Weather," *JAS* 61 (2002): 83–114; Geoffrey Gunn, *First Globalization* (Lanham, MD, 2003); J. R. McNeill and William McNeill, *The Human Web* (New York, 2003). On the distinction between comparative and connective histories, see too *SP*, 14. As will be seen, this volume employs both comparative and connective approaches.

[17] Following Charles Tilly, *Coercion, Capital, and European States, AD 990–1900* (Cambridge, MA, 1990), 1, "state" is here defined as a coercion-wielding organization that is distinct from household and kinship groups and that exercises priority over all other organizations within a substantial territory. Insofar as many pre-1800 states, esp. in Southeast Asia and India, necessarily tolerated, in theory as well as deed, the use of force by highly autonomous subordinate groups, the former description seems more widely applicable than Max Weber's definition of the state as a community that claims a monopoly on the legitimate use of force within a territory.

[18] R. Bin Wong, *China Transformed* (Ithaca, 1997), chs. 4–6; Jack Goldstone, *Revolution and Rebellion in the Early Modern World* (Berkeley, 1991); idem, "Efflorescences"; Vries, "Governing Growth." On comparative state formation, see too Cemal Kafadar, "The Ottomans and Europe," in Thomas Brady, Jr., et al., eds., *Handbook of European History 1400–1600* (Grand Rapids, 1994), 589–635; Prasenjit Duara, *Rescuing History from the Nation* (Chicago, 1995), pt. 1; "Early Modernities" issue of *Daedalus* 127 (1998); essays in Lieberman, *Beyond Binary Histories*; Peter Turchin, *War and Peace and War* (New York, 2006), focusing on ethnic competition as a goad to state formation; Peter Turchin and Sergey Nefedov, *Secular Cycles* (forthcoming).

construction in one region, permanent collapse in another, and random, directionless oscillations in yet a third? Why, as noted, did interregna in diverse realms become ever less disruptive (an interregnum I define as the temporary collapse of effective central power), and why did such disorders correlate ever more closely between regions? Why in each realm over several centuries did capital and elite norms of language, religion, social organization, and ethnicity tend to modify and displace provincial and plebeian traditions? In other words, why did local ethnicities and dialects coalesce into more coherent imperial or kingdom-wide cultures? Could political integration proceed in the absence of cultural consolidation – or vice versa? Can we distinguish between uniquely Asian and European political and cultural trajectories, or did intracontinental differences in some respects exceed those between Asia and Europe? Most basic and curious, what factors governed Eurasian coordination? What was the relation, for example, between agrarian growth, long-distance trade, technological diffusion, and interstate pressures – and how did those relations change by time and place? Why in much of Eurasia did the pace of integration accelerate markedly between 1500 or 1600 and 1800 – and does that acceleration in itself justify the term "early modern" as a Eurasian-wide periodization?[19] How shall we relate European, mainland Southeast Asian, and Japanese patterns to the experience of China, Southwest Asia, South Asia, and island Southeast Asia, in all of which integration relied more heavily on external agency and in most cases followed a different chronology? In brief, in what ways and to what extent can we regard premodern Eurasia as a coherent ecumene?

Whereas most other comparative studies have adopted a limited time frame, commonly the 17th to early 19th centuries or some fraction thereof,[20] I am convinced that the sustained character of Eurasian parallels, in particular the declining duration and severity of successive

[19] On use of the term "early modern," cf. John Richards, "Early Modern India and World History," *JWH* 8 (1997): 197–209; Anthony Reid, ed., *Southeast Asia in the Early Modern Era* (Ithaca, 1993); Sanjay Subrahmanyam, *Penumbral Visions* (Ann Arbor, 2001), 261–65; *SP*, 79–80, esp. n. 117; and discussion *infra*.

[20] S. A. M. Adshead, *China in World History* (3rd ed., New York, 2000), and to a lesser extent, Wong, *China Transformed* are exceptions. See too the essays by R. I. Moore, "Transformation of Europe"; idem, "Feudalism and Revolution in the Making of Europe," in M. Barcelo et al., eds., *El Feudalisme Comptat I Debatut* (Valencia, 2003), 19–34. Although concentrating on a more narrow period than my inquiry, Moore considers the same conundrum of far-flung coordination c. 900 to 1300, which he compares *en passant* to the Axial Age of the 6th and 5th centuries B.C.E.

periods of fragmentation, can best appreciated by considering the entire period from the mid- or late first millennium C.E. to the early 19th century.

Finally and most obviously, whereas other comparativists have excluded Southeast Asia, I place that region, or at least its mainland component, at the center of inquiry. *Volume 1: Integration on the Mainland* analyzed secular-cum-cyclic patterns of construction in the territories of Burma, Siam (modern Thailand), Laos, Cambodia, and Vietnam. The present volume uses those patterns as a lens to examine Europe, Japan, China, South Asia, and island Southeast Asia. Rather than impede comparisons, the marginality of mainland Southeast Asia – a distant promontory when viewed from most of Eurasia – actually makes it easier to recognize overarching trajectories and to isolate unifying causes. For example, the sudden, exceptional vigor of the European economy c. 900–1250 becomes less exceptional if we consider that mainland Southeast Asia in those same years exhibited a vitality no less stunning. Given that Europe and Southeast Asia to 1250 had only the most rudimentary institutional similarities, no common cultural legacies, and no direct contact, how much weight should we accord third-party commercial links? Shared epidemiological adjustments? Hemispheric climatic shifts? Parallel, but independent social adaptations?

As a scholar of Burma, I attempt to join Southeast Asian to world history for the first time in serious and sustained fashion. But in so doing, without necessarily rejecting European exceptionalism, I hope to provide fresh perspectives on that phenomenon, to develop novel criteria for intra-Eurasian classification, and to reconceptualize Eurasia as an interactive zone. In short, I seek to modify both Southeast Asian and Eurasian historiography during a thousand years.

2. POLITICAL AND CULTURAL INTEGRATION IN MAINLAND SOUTHEAST ASIA C. 800–1830: A PRÉCIS

Naturally, readers seeking to understand the history of precolonial mainland Southeast Asia are urged to consult the first volume of *Strange Parallels*, but for those unable to do so, this section summarizes that volume's principal arguments.[21] I shall briefly consider in turn territorial consolidation, administrative centralization, and cultural integration,

---

[21] For a more extended but still concise overview, see *SP*, 21–66. Since I completed that volume, a number of publications and manuscripts have appeared, many of which

after which I shall analyze the dynamics underlying those trends. With that framework, indispensable for Eurasian comparisons, in place, this chapter will sketch the main theoretical arguments of Volume 2 and will conclude by assessing the virtues and pitfalls of my methodology.

Territorial Consolidation: Overview of Mainland Southeast Asian Political History

Jungle-clad highlands divide mainland Southeast Asia into three principal north–south corridors, namely, the Irrawaddy basin in the west, the

reinforce my arguments, others of which suggest modifications. For the western mainland, key works include Bob Hudson, "The Origins of Bagan" (Univ. of Sydney, PhD diss., 2004); Bob Hudson and Terry Lustig, "Communities of the Past," *JSEAS* 39 (2008): 269–96; Wil O. Dijk, *Seventeenth-Century Burma and the Dutch East India Company 1634–1680* (Singapore, 2006); Michael Charney, *Powerful Learning* (Ann Arbor, 2006); Michael Aung-Thwin, *The Mists of Ramanna* (Honolulu, 2005); Donald Stadtner, "The Mon of Lower Burma," *Jl. of the Siam Society* 96 (2008): 193–215, critiquing Aung-Thwin. In stressing maternal nurturance, Barbara Watson Andaya, "Localizing the Universal," *JSEAS* 33 (2002): 1–30 reinterprets early Theravada success. For recent work on the central mainland, see Hiram Woodward, *The Art and Architecture of Thailand* (Leiden, 2003); Kennon Breazeale, ed., *From Japan to Arabia: Ayutthaya's Maritime Relations with Asia* (Bangkok, 1999); Mayoury Ngaosrivathana and Kennon Breazeale, eds., *Breaking New Ground in Lao History* (Chiang Mai, 2002); Michael Coe, *Angkor and the Khmer Civilization* (New York, 2003); Greater Angkor Project, "Redefining Angkor," *Udaya* 4 (2003): 107–25; Richard Stone, "The End of Angkor," *Science* 311 (2006): 1364–68; Dan Penny et al., "Vegetation and Land Use at Angkor, Cambodia," *Antiquity* 80 (2006): 599–614; Wilaiwan Khanittanan, "Khmero-Thai: The Great Change in the History of the Thai Language of the Chao Phraya Basin," *Papers from the 11th Annual Meeting of the Southeast Asian Linguistics Society*, S. Burusphat, ed. (Tempe, AZ, n.d.), 375–91. Exploring new approaches to Vietnamese history are Nola Cooke and Li Tana, eds., *Water Frontier* (Lanham, MD, 2004); George Dutton, *The Tay Son Uprising* (Honolulu, 2006); Nhung Tuyet Tran and Anthony Reid, eds., *Vietnam: Borderless Histories* (Madison, WI, 2006); essays by Alexander Woodside and Keith Taylor in Benjamin Elman et al., eds., *Rethinking Confucianism* (Los Angeles, 2002); James Anderson, *The Rebel Den of Nung Tri Cao* (Seattle, 2007); Liam Kelley, *Beyond the Bronze Pillars* (Honolulu, 2005); Olga Dror, *Cult, Culture, and Authority* (Honolulu, 2007). On Vietnam's maritime connections, see Li Tana, "A View from the Sea," *JSEAS* 37 (2006): 83–102; John Whitmore, "The Rise of the Coast," ibid., 103–22; and Charles Wheeler, "Re-thinking the Sea in Vietnamese History," ibid., 123–53. For Chinese influence on the mainland, Sun Laichen, "Military Technology Transfers from Ming China and the Emergence of Northern Mainland Southeast Asia (c. 1390–1527)," *JSEAS* 34 (2003): 495–517; Geoff Wade, "An Early Age of Commerce in Southeast Asia: 900–1300 C.E." (a manuscript version of which the author kindly provided). See too regional overviews in Michael Charney, *Southeast Asian Warfare 1300–1900* (Leiden, 2004); Tony Day, *Fluid Iron: State Formation in Southeast Asia* (Honolulu, 2002); and esp. Barbara Watson Andaya, *The Flaming Womb* (Honolulu, 2006).

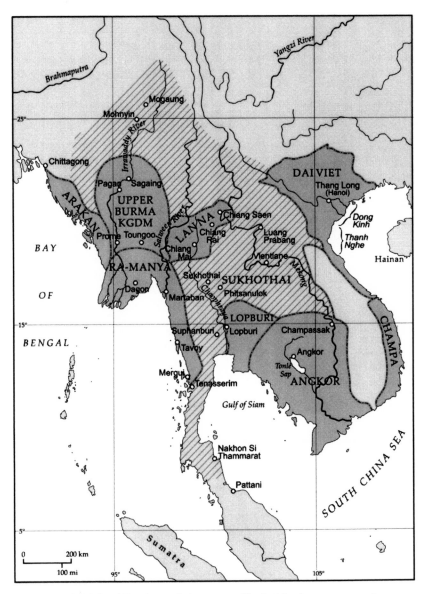

Figure 1.1. Mainland Southeast Asia, c. 1340. The hatched area represents a zone of fluid, generally small-scale Tai polities.

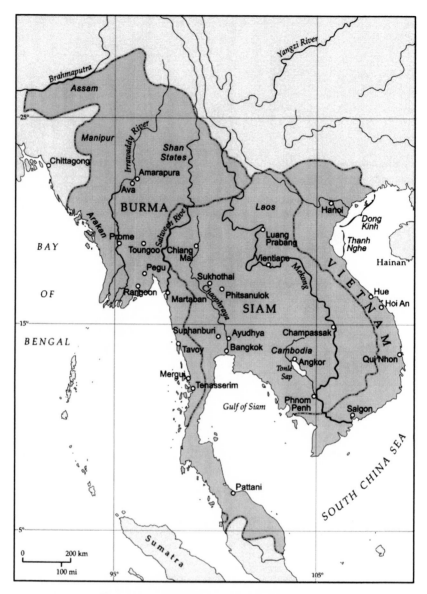

Figure 1.2. Mainland Southeast Asia in 1824.

broad Chaophraya-Mekong lowlands in the center, and the narrow eastern littoral. Given their demographic and economic superiority, these
corridors inevitably served as hubs for imperial consolidation. Consolidation was cyclic insofar as it was repeatedly interrupted by severe

political breakdowns. But it was linear not only because, at least in the west and center, breakdowns grew shorter and less institutionally and culturally disruptive, but also because progressively larger territories were incorporated.

During all or most of the period c. 850 to 1300/1350, four lowland states were preeminent: Pagan in the west, Angkor in the center, and Champa (modern central Vietnam) and Dai Viet (modern north Vietnam) in the east. Low hills and coastal access ensured that northern Vietnam's chief external contacts lay with China. Indeed, for most of the period between 43 and 938, what is now northern Vietnam had been incorporated into Chinese empires, and Chinese norms defined elite Vietnamese aesthetic, literary, religious, and political expression. Elsewhere, however, northern mountains inhibited contact with China, whose imperial authority in any case did not extend to Yunnan until the 1250s. This upland barrier joined easy maritime contacts to orient other cultures across mainland (as well as island) Southeast Asia toward India, ensuring that Indic high culture, that is to say, fluid local syntheses of Hindu, Buddhist, and animist elements, dominated everywhere outside northern Vietnam (and even there Indic elements were not insignificant).

Despite varied external stimuli and divergent founding dates, the mainland's chief polities between c. 850 and 1300/1350 shared a number of defining features. Lying in areas without indigenous writing and open to the seduction of literate arts and world religions from older, more densely settled Eurasian cores, each polity was heir to a process of cultural borrowing and localization that was well underway by the mid-first millennium C.E. but that intensified toward the close of the first and at the start of the second millennium. Through conquest, patronage, and expanding religious networks, Angkor, Pagan, and Dai Viet (and less dramatically, Champa) each yoked together a medley of smaller realms and dispersed population clusters in a movement that Hermann Kulke terms the transition from regional to imperial states.[22] In the western mainland, for example, although competition between city-states may

---

[22] Hermann Kulke, "The Early and the Imperial Kingdom in Southeast Asian History," in David Marr and A.C. Milner, eds., *Southeast Asia in the 9th to 14th Centuries* (Singapore, 1986), 1–22. Evidence for territorial transitions of this sort is weaker for Champa, although the shift of capital from Indrapura to Vijaya in 1000 may have reflected not only Vietnamese pressure, the usual explanation, but a determination to tap growing maritime trade. In the Irrawaddy basin the latest evidence from Upper Burma, summarized in Hudson, "Origins of Bagan"; idem and Lustig, "Communities of the Past";

have begun in the 6th or 7th century, not until Pagan's conquest of the south coast in the mid-1000s was the Irrawaddy basin unified. Likewise, in the Khmer (Cambodian) interior, statelets appeared as early as the 7th century, but only with the ceremonial unification of Khmer lands in 802, the more or less permanent location of the capital at Angkor after c. 900, and mid-10th-century conquests did a unified Khmer kingdom centered on Angkor gain stable expression. In northern Vietnam, although initial unification and literate acculturation proceeded under the aegis of China, after Chinese control collapsed in 938, local experiments culminated in 1009 in the creation of the state that became known as Dai Viet.

As the first extensive indigenous polity in its sector, each of these states provided a political and cultural charter for later generations. In recognition of this legacy, I term these states "charter" polities and the period between c. 850 and 1300 or 1350 the "charter era." In varying local combinations, Pagan, Angkor, and Dai Viet all benefited from new systems of religious endowment; more extensive pacification; stronger, more agriculturally propitious monsoons associated with the Medieval Climate Anomaly 800/850–1250/1300; perhaps from the domestication of smallpox (see below); and from maritime trade. Between 900/1000 and 1250 all three realms saw substantial agrarian and population growth, with a corresponding increase in water control projects, agrarian revenues, and labor services.[23] Yet even at their height, each charter polity dominated only lowland centers and, in some cases, a small

and Aung-Thwin, *Mists of Ramanna*, 13–42, suggests that Pagan's 11th-century unification climaxed processes of political and economic elaboration that began appreciably earlier, and therefore correlated more closely to changes in the Khmer world, than had been recognized.

[23] Apart from Champa, charter political economies appear to have relied far more heavily on agrarian than maritime revenues; *SP*, 93–112, 216–29, 362–65. Recently, Li, "View from the Sea" and Whitmore, "Rise of the Coast" have suggested that coastal trade played a larger role in Dai Viet state formation than earlier scholars appreciated. This view accords with Wade, "Early Age of Commerce," emphasizing Song/international commercial stimuli to Southeast Asian handicrafts, monetization, and entrepots, c. 900–1300. However, there is no indication that such stimuli were responsible for rapid agrarian expansion, esp. in interior locales around Pagan and Angkor and particularly in Pagan, which was largely insulated from those Song impulses that Wade emphasizes. In Dai Viet as for Pagan, Whitmore, ibid., 122, also concludes that "a densely populated, well-irrigated . . . and productive agrarian interior remained dominant," and that Tran kings, despite their coastal origins, concentrated on expanding Dai Viet's agricultural base.

upland perimeter, with extensive upland interior and Malay peninsular areas enjoying an irreducible independence. Thus large swaths of the mainland escaped even nominal imperial control.

Finally, between the late 1200s and the mid-1400s Pagan, Angkor, and Dai Viet all suffered severe internal disorders and external attacks culminating in the sack of each capital, the collapse of central authority, and cultural/ethnic displacements of varying degrees of severity.[24] In large measure, these late charter disorders reflected the strains of sustained economic expansion combined with long-standing institutional weaknesses. After three centuries of growth, as population outstripped irrigable land and, especially at Angkor, as soil erosion and canal siltation further reduced marginal productivity, pressures mounted on both local peasantries and lay and religious elites reliant on agrarian rents. The decentralized, even acephalous character of political organization – in particular, the autonomy of wealthy religious institutions, endemic princely competition, and the quasi-royal pretensions of provincial governors – made it exceedingly difficult for central authorities to curb factionalism or to maintain discipline. To an uncertain but possibly critical degree, drier climate from c. 1250 to 1470, corresponding to the end of the Medieval Climate Anomaly, aggravated agricultural difficulties in imperial cores at the same time as it joined continuous sedimentation to promote coastal settlement far from the inland capitals of Pagan and Angkor. So, too, rising long-distance commerce, an artifact of Southeast Asian, Chinese, and general Eurasian prosperity, accelerated the shift in the political center of gravity from Pagan, Angkor, and Dai Viet to more maritime-oriented sites, including Pegu, Ayudhya, Phnom Penh, and Cham Vijaya.

Compounding internal stresses were external assaults: The Mongols attacked Dai Viet and Pagan in the late 1200s. Chams and then the Ming Dynasty invaded Dai Viet from 1361 to 1427. Most critical, between c. 1100 and 1350, Tai bands from what is now South China, northern Laos, and northwestern Vietnam entered the lowlands in force.[25]

---

[24] *SP*, 119–23, 236–42, 367–42, plus Coe, *Angkor*, 20, 196–201, and Greater Angkor Project, "Redefining Angkor." The latter focuses on climatic shifts and the disastrous agricultural effects of deforestation for land clearance and firewood in the northern hills.

[25] "Tai" languages include Siamese Tai, the chief tongue of modern Thailand; Shan, spoken by Tai-Shans in northern and northeast Burma; and Laotian, spoken in contemporary Laos. On mainland ethnography, see Frank Lebar et al., *Ethnic Groups of*

If some Tai incursions enjoyed Mongol patronage, most basically they reflected an as yet poorly understood synergy between demographic pressures in the uplands and growing Tai involvement in the basins as mercenaries, tributaries, and cultivators. Through such channels Tais acquired the cultural capital, including a knowledge of Buddhism and Indic statecraft, needed to dominate and assimilate to lowland societies. As charter polities split in response to these manifold pressures and as Tai successor states arose, as early as 1340 in lieu of the four great charter empires, the mainland had fragmented into at least 23 independent polities (see Figure 1.1).

In general these disruptions – religious and ethnic as well as territorial – were more wrenching in the central than in the western mainland, which in turn experienced more prolonged traumas than the east. In the center not only was Angkor abandoned at some point between 1350 and 1450 in favor of more coastal-oriented sites at Ayudhya and Phnom Penh, but Khmer and Mon ethnic dominance in much of the interior yielded by 1300 to Tai preeminence, while Angkor's Hindu/Mahayana civilization metamorphosed into Theravada Buddhist forms of ritual, monasticism, literature, art, and architecture. In the west Tai incursions proved less disruptive, and Theravada Buddhism retained, indeed strengthened, its long-standing hegemony. Nonetheless, Burman-led[26] polities not only faced repeated Tai invasions in the northern Irrawaddy basin, but as early as 1300 lost control over coastal Lower Burma, where a newly assertive Mon culture supplanted Burman influence. Even Dai Viet, although spared large-scale Tai incursions and subject to less prolonged collapse than the central or western mainland, wilted under assaults from Champa (which, alone among charter principalities, prospered in the 14th century, only to fall victim to a revived Dai Viet in 1471). Amidst agrarian and social upheavals, Dai Viet also experienced an intellectual/cultural transformation that anticipated the rise

---

Mainland Southeast Asia (New Haven, 1964). Tai incursions in the north may have begun in the late first millennium, but only in the 13th century did Tai states arise in the great basins; David Wyatt, *Thailand: A Short History* (2nd ed., New Haven, 2003), 25–49. The first Mongol attack on Dai Viet actually came in 1257.

[26] "Burman" refers to the principal ethnic group in the Irrawaddy basin, whereas "Burmese" refers either to the language and culture of that group or to the collectivity of peoples, Burman and non-Burman, living in the area of the contemporary Union of Myanmar. In the precolonial era the other principal ethnic groups in the western mainland included Tai-Shans in the north and Mons in the southern lowlands. For a recent reconstruction of Burman–Mon relations in the 13th to 15th centuries, see Aung-Thwin, *Mists of Ramanya*.

of state-sanctioned Neo-Confucianism at the expense of the Mahayana Buddhist[27] aristocratic order of the charter era. These political and cultural shifts during what might be termed "the long 14th century" (c. 1280–1430/1450) constituted the first of three generalized interregna in much of mainland Southeast Asia.

Starting in the mid-1400s, however, fragmentation gradually yielded to a recentralizing phase that by 1540 had compressed the 23 states of 1340 into some 9 or 10 major survivors. Chief among these were Toungoo Burma, which by 1560 had reunified the entire Irrawaddy basin and extended its authority over the surrounding highlands and the northwest Malay peninsula; Ayudhya (Siam), which dominated the Chaophraya basin and the northeast peninsula; Lan Sang, centered in modern Laos, which dominated the middle Mekong; Cambodia, with its capital at or near Phnom Penh; and a revived Dai Viet, which, after recovering from the Ming occupation of 1407–1427, went on to subdue its ancient rival Champa and thus to extend its authority over what is now central Vietnam. We shall return to this grand recentralizing movement, but for now let it suffice to say that territorial reintegration benefited from renewed agricultural reclamation, expanding long-distance trade, movements of religious/cultic reform,[28] the domestication of Ming administrative models in Dai Viet, and the introduction of Chinese and more especially European-style firearms, chiefly from the early 1500s. Most such developments favored lowland polities at the expense of upland and interior rivals. With the partial exception of Dai Viet, each postcharter state based itself on a sector of the lowlands at some distance from the old charter capital. In administrative and cultural terms too, each, we shall find, was substantially innovative.

In the mid- to late 1500s the chief mainland states again collapsed, inaugurating a second generalized interregnum. This second breakdown, like that of the 13th/14th centuries, reflected an excess of good

---

[27] "Theravada" Buddhism, the dominant faith in modern Myanmar, Thailand, Cambodia, and Laos, offers everyone the prospect of improving his/her karma through charity and morality, which in turn will increase happiness in this and future lives; but it promises *nirvana* only to a virtuoso, essentially monastic, elite. "Mahayana" Buddhism, which came to dominate Tibet, Mongolia, China, Korea, Japan, as well as Vietnam, promises everyone a chance of salvation through meditation, mysticism, and/or devotion to past and aspirant Buddhas.

[28] Insofar as Neo-Confucianism was more a doctrine of social harmony than a religion of personal salvation, "cult" seems a more appropriate designation than "religion."

fortune, but in this case it was less obviously a matter of unsustainable economic and demographic growth than of insupportable territorial conquests (although one could argue that by spurring conquests, renewed economic growth inspired political overextension). In a word, the chief empires expanded too rapidly to maintain secure control over outlying dependencies.

In the western and central mainland, that is to say, Burma and Siam, these travails proved quite short lived compared to postcharter dislocations. They also involved neither ethnic/cultural displacements nor geopolitical shifts on the scale of the 14th century, and they yielded to a phase of more judicious territorial conquest and internal reform that would last to the mid-1700s. In the west the Restored Toungoo Dynasty of Burma abandoned unrealistic claims to Siam, but tightened its hold over closer Tai realms north and east of the Irrawaddy basin. In the 17th and early 18th centuries the Siamese kingdom of Ayudhya increased its authority over Cambodian, Lao, and Malay tributaries. Yet amidst this consolidation, Cambodia, Lao, and Malay polities retained far greater freedom of maneuver than they would later enjoy.

In the western and central mainland this cyclic pattern repeated itself a third and final time: between 1752 and 1767 Burma and Siam again collapsed, in this instance through locally specific combinations of exhausting warfare, provincial overtaxation; a rapid, destabilizing expansion of domestic and international trade (with China, in particular); conflict between market-based and hereditary status systems; and an attendant erosion of hereditary military service. With unprecedented speed and efficiency, however, both empires revived under new, more martial dynasties, namely, the Kon-baung kings of Burma and the Chakri kings of Siam, with the latter now based at the new capital of Bangkok. Following indecisive wars against one another, both dynasties turned against weaker regional rivals, thus extending their authority, in the case of Burma over Arakan, Manipur, and Assam to the west, in the case of Siam over Cambodia, Lao, and Malay kingdoms to the east and south. By 1824, following this dramatic acceleration, the entire western and central mainland had been divided for the first time into but two imperial systems.

Along the eastern littoral political evolution was less linear, in part because Chinese influence promoted elite family structures that were more competitive with the crown than their counterparts in Indic Southeast Asia, but more basically because the eastern lowlands lacked a unifying riverine artery comparable in integrative potential to the great

Irrawaddy or Chaophraya.[29] After a brief reunification in the 1590s, the Vietnamese polity again split into warring north–south regimes, led by rival seigniorial families, that remained in place until 1774. To some degree, reunification in 1802 was an accident. One might conclude therefore that devolution along the eastern littoral went in a direction opposite to sustained integration in the western and central mainland.

Yet in four respects, the east conformed to more general integrative patterns across the mainland. First, although hostile to one another, the northern and southern seigneuries, those of Trinh and Nguyen, remained nominally loyal to the same dynasty, the Le, and regarded themselves in some contexts as parts of an overarching polity. Second, despite local accommodations, in terms of objective cultural practices and subjective elite affinities, southerners remained far closer to northern Vietnamese than to the Chams and Khmers whom they displaced. In this sense, the post-1600 *nam tien,* the "southern advance," of Vietnamese-speakers accelerated a tendency toward ethnic-cum-cultural unification in the eastern littoral that began long before 1600, continued well into the 19th century, and paralleled Burmese and Siamese ethnic integration. Third, in expanding against Chams, Khmers, and eventually Siamese, the southern regime responded to many of the same economic and strategic imperatives and adopted many of the same approaches as its Burmese and Siamese counterparts, while entering a specifically Southeast Asian multistate system. Like a thickening spider web stretched across the mainland, this transmitted stimuli from one sector to another with ever greater sensitivity. Thus the implosion and rebirth of the Burmese polity c. 1740–1760 joined commercial strains to shatter the Siamese empire in 1767, whose reintegration contributed to the collapse and revival of Vietnamese power between 1771 and 1802. Fourth, along with Burma and Siam, the Vietnamese polity emerged substantially larger and more powerful from late-18th-century disorders. By 1802 not only had all Vietnamese-speaking areas from China

---

[29] Wheeler, "Re-thinking the Sea" has argued with originality and insight that in Vietnam, especially its central sector, littoral and lagoon traffic compensated for terrestrial fragmentation in a fashion similar to that of a great river. However, if coastal trade and communications have been underestimated, there is little evidence that coastal ties between northern and central Vietnam or between central and southern Vietnam were as ramified as those within central Vietnam itself. Furthermore, if Vietnamese coastal links were truly comparable to those of the Irrawaddy or Chaophraya, why was political fragmentation consistently more pronounced in the eastern than in the western or central lowlands?

to the Gulf of Siam coalesced for the first time into a single realm, but the new state exerted growing pressure over the western uplands and Cambodia. Moreover, in southern Vietnam as in Lower Burma and Siamese-dominated Laos, anticentralizing revolts after 1800 proved deeply counterproductive.

In sum – in lieu of four modest charter polities in 1240, 23 kingdoms in 1340, and 9 or 10 kingdoms in 1540 – mainland Southeast Asia by the second quarter of the 19th century contained three unprecedentedly grand territorial assemblages: those of Burma, Siam, and Vietnam (see Figure 1.2).

Administrative Centralization

As privileged cores extended their territorial writ, they commonly sought to strengthen their systems of patronage, extraction, and coercion. External expansion and internal administrative reform were mutually reinforcing, because larger domains required more efficient control, while the concentration of resources that flowed from better coordination aided conquest and colonization. Much as recurrent collapse gave territorial consolidation a spasmodic, compensatory quality, administrative reform commonly sought to address antecedent disorders.

The typical Southeast Asian realm remained what I term a "solar polity": a system of quasi-sovereign satellites in orbit around a central sun whose gravitational pull, in lieu of fixed borders, ebbed with distance. Insofar as each planet had its own moons, which in turn had their dependencies, each satellite replicated in miniature the organization of the solar system as a whole. Moreover, the most distant tributaries might owe allegiance to more than one overlord, while in the rugged interior scattered hill peoples (including refugees from the valleys) often sought to escape entirely the attention of lowland rulers. Although these patterns persisted throughout the period under review, over time the gravitational pull of each sun increased markedly. That is to say, hill people became more sensitive to the cultural and political influence of lowland centers;[30] distant, once independent states were reduced to tributary status; tributaries were converted to intermediate provinces; intermediate

---

[30] On growing lowland influences on hill people, *SP*, 208–209, 231, 267, 312–13, 350–51, 422–23; Victor Lieberman, *Burmese Administrative Cycles* (Princeton, 1984), 134–37, 203–204, 212, 217–22, 253; Katherine Bowie, "Slavery in Nineteenth-Century Northern Thailand," in E. Paul Durrenberger, ed., *State Power and Culture in Thailand* (New Haven, 1996), 100–38.

provinces assimilated to the status of core districts; and within each core taxation and service arrangements grew more effective.

During the charter era, c. 850–1350, the farthest planets were commonly ruled by hereditary tributary kings; less distant realms, by heads of influential local families or relatives of the High King. All such leaders were tied to the overlord by inherently unstable personal and ritual ties. Possessing their own armies and quasi-sovereign ceremonial pretensions, outlying principalities – many of them formerly independent kingdoms – were in a position, particularly during disputed royal successions, to challenge the capital directly. Within each lowland core, moreover, temples and monasteries performed many functions of social control, land reclamation, and administration later assumed by lay officials. Because these religious institutions, although linked to the throne by family and patronage networks, enjoyed extensive landed wealth and functional autonomy, they tended to compress and to obviate royal administration. The surprising longevity of charter polities reflected a) this decentralized, gelatinous, multicellular structure, which often allowed each polity to survive the malfunction of any of its individual parts; b) the infrequency until at least the mid-1100s of external military challenges, which derived from the fact that major empires did not yet abut one another; c) the cultural gulf that protected capital-centered elites, with an effective monopoly of Indic or Sinic high culture, against challenges by predominantly illiterate, animist commoners.

After charter polities collapsed, beginning in some locales as early as the 1300s and continuing everywhere into the 1800s, religious institutions lost most of their landed wealth, along with a substantial measure of administrative autonomy. In part, this was because new states arose outside those regions where charter religious donations had been concentrated. In part, this was because temples and monasteries proved ill equipped to prevent forcible lay usurpations during postcharter disorders. In part, because more monetized economies undermined the old system of religious landed donations in favor of cash gifts, which reduced monastic capital and manpower. And in part, religious institutions lost power because new intellectual currents and wider literacy favored more effective royal supervision of texts and religious personnel than had been possible in Pagan, Angkor, or early Dai Viet.

If, however, monastic autonomy threatened royal authority less directly than in the charter era, like their charter predecessors, those polities that arose between 1350 and 1600 continued to face challenges from satellite principalities, which were still entrusted to senior princes and local dynasts with independent military forces. As soon as the capital seemed vulnerable, provincial heads typically sought either to seize the capital and place themselves at the head of the imperial system or to break away from the system entirely. In fact, the sustained independence that many former provincial centers enjoyed during postcharter disorders arguably rendered their sovereign pretensions more credible than during the charter era itself. In both Burma and Siam the late-16th-century collapse was precipitated by the joining of ambitious provincial leaders with foreign invaders to attack the capital.

Largely in response to these disasters, in the late 1500s and early 1600s the reconstituted empires of Burma and Siam undertook administrative experiments designed, as it were, to strengthen the gravitational pull of the capital. As negotiated with local power holders, who were among the first to recognize the need for more effective central coordination, and as elaborated by the mid-17th century, these reforms rendered the king more ceremonially remote; replaced august viceroys in the provinces with more docile nonprincely governors; insisted that the crown, rather than governors, appoint subgubernatorial officials at major provincial towns; markedly increased the capital's military superiority over provincial centers; and strengthened patronage links between capital officials and quasi-hereditary local headmen. In close cooperation with the latter, sometimes termed the "gentry," royal officials extended censuses and cadastres into the provinces, multiplied written communications, and used the resultant information to systematize taxes and to enlarge the ranks of hereditary or quasi-hereditary servicemen (*ahmu-dans* in Burma, *phrai luang* in Siam) obliged to provide the crown with specialized military or civilian labor.[31] In the interest of military mobilization and fiscal extraction, service reform in turn required more elaborate efforts at social regulation, extending in Burma to an insistence on endogamy among *ahmu-dan* service units. Burma and Siam also eroded the autonomy of tributaries and retained, in some cases tightened, postcharter curbs on Buddhist monastic landholding and ordination.

In both realms the aforementioned breakdowns of the mid- to late 18th century prompted frantic new efforts, supported by local elites and generally effective, to strengthen service registration and cadastres, tributary controls, firearms supply, and commercial taxation.

---

[31] Burmese *ahmu-dans* tended to be more specialized, esp. militarily, and to display a wider range of status ranks than Siamese *phrai luang*.

In post-1767 Siam, in particular, the crown dramatically expanded its revenues from Chinese domestic and foreign trade. As the scale of operations increased, central and, to some extent, provincial governance in both Burma and Siam grew more routinized and specialized, with more trained scribes, jurists, revenue officers, and military experts. (At the same time, especially in Siam, commercial growth reintroduced unwelcome political and social tensions.) Smaller Lao and Khmer principalities sought to imitate the administrative and military reforms of their great neighbors, but in the face of demographic and maritime constraints, they had at best limited success. (Besides being less populous than Siam or Vietnam, Laos was landlocked, while Cambodia was gradually cut off from the sea by Vietnamese and Chinese coastal settlements.) As befit the solar structure of empire, outlying dependencies in 1820 still enjoyed greater prestige and autonomy than did territories closer to the Burmese or Siamese capital. Some of the most distant tributaries still paid homage to more than one empire and retained trappings of independent sovereignty. Yet within both the western and central mainland, the autonomy of those same polities was less pronounced in 1820 than in 1620 – when in turn it was weaker than in 1420. In short, amidst crises and fluctuations, over several centuries Burmese and Siamese administrations became more stable and penetrating.

At first sight, administrative trends in Vietnam appear less linear than in Burma or Siam. In the late 1400s the Neo-Confucian revolution introduced a full-blooded Chinese-style bureaucracy, complete with civil service exams, elaborate written communications, novel maps and military itineraries, three layers of appointed officials, and increasingly effective curbs on Buddhist landholding. From the late 1500s, however, oligarchic pressures, military exigency, and non-Chinese cultural influences combined periodically to erode Sinic practices in favor of more patrimonial, more characteristically Southeast Asian forms. This was true in the north for long periods and more especially on the southern frontier. Yet even in the latter zone, as the influence of Chinese émigrés and local literati increased, Neo-Confucian techniques gradually acquired normative prestige. In the early 1800s, after unifying the entire Vietnamese-speaking world, the southern-based Nguyen regime again openly embraced Chinese-style provincial administration in an ambitious effort, by no means unsuccessful, to integrate its fissiparous, elongated domain. In this sense, albeit by looking more directly to China than to north Vietnamese precedents, the Nguyen resumed and intensified Sinicizing trends apparent in the 15th and 17th centuries.

Cultural Integration

Along with territorial consolidation and administrative centralization, a third index of integration within each empire was a growing uniformity of religious and social practices, languages, and ethnicity. Such transformations proceeded along two axes: vertically, select practices spread from elites to lower strata, although some exchange normally occurred in the opposite direction as well; and laterally, motifs from the capital and outlying provinces entered into more sustained dialogue, with the capital again tending to enjoy a privileged position. In general, osmotic, capillary local processes rendered cultural evolution more gradual and continuous than territorial or administrative change, even though in this sphere too we find a marked acceleration after 1500 or 1600. Culture is here defined as a system of rules, instructions, and symbolic representation that govern the ways people order their existence and interpret their world.[32]

To the 15th century cultural standardization was quite limited. Not only were capital religious cults in the charter era promiscuously inclusive, with animist, Theravada, Mahayana, Saivite, Vaisnava, and (in Dai Viet) Confucian elements all enjoying official patronage, but the upper classes were essentially indifferent toward the religious practices of their own peasantries. Before 1300, indeed 1600 in many areas, literacy, the *sine qua non* for any concept of orthodoxy, remained rare at the village level. Knowledge of universal sacred languages – Pali, Sanskrit, or Chinese – together with foreign-derived concepts of political space, sanctity, and aesthetics, remained largely the preserve of aristocrats and religious specialists attached to royal courts or elite temples. Economic self-sufficiency rooted in extensive landholdings tended to insulate charter-era monkhoods from regular village contact. Among the peasantry local ethnic and linguistic orientations were only strengthened by charter collapse and Tai irruptions. Thus in 1400 each lowland sector contained at least three major linguistic/cultural systems, each

---

[32] I follow Clifford Geertz, *The Interpretation of Cultures* (New York, 1973). With Geertz, Ernesto Laclau, and Chantal Mouffe, *Hegemony and Socialist Strategy* (London, 1985), and Johannes Fabian, *Language and Colonial Power* (Cambridge, 1986), I regard this system not as a coherently structured whole but as an unsutured complex of negotiated symbols whose interpretation normally fluctuates with locale, class, corporate group, and individual. At the same time within any stable population, by definition, such rules permit a measure of common identifications and implicit understandings. See too *SP*, 37 ff.; Keith Luria, *Territories of Grace* (Berkeley, 1991), 2–3; and John Tomlinson, *Globalization and Culture* (Chicago, 1999), 17–20.

with several subdivisions. The western lowlands supported Burmese, Tai, and Mon cultures. The central lowlands supported Tai, Mon, and Khmer; and the eastern lowlands, Vietnamese, Cham, and Khmer. More difficult communications and transport and far lower population densities meant that the interior uplands contained a yet more kaleidoscopic array of Tibeto-Burman, Karen, Miao-Yao, Austroasiatic, Tai, and Malayo-Polynesian languages and cultures.[33]

However, from the 15th century, and with accelerating force in the 18th and early 19th centuries, the progress of cultural integration is easily demonstrated. In vertical terms, whereas textually based Indic religions once had been the more or less exclusive preserve of capital-based elites, in the western and central mainland Theravada Buddhism became a demotic, village-based religion with a permeable monastic/lay boundary. Not only did Theravada monks, who now depended on alms from village faithful, develop an intimacy with the laity more pronounced than in the charter era, but virtually all males received a basic religious education, primarily in the vernacular language rather than in Pali, so as to obtain at least temporary admission to the monastic order. Officials thus joined local enthusiasts, lay and monastic, to build vast networks of Theravada monasteries, to popularize rituals of merit-making and ordination, to marginalize spirit propitiation, to valorize the Buddhist canon, and to push textually based, elite notions of orthodoxy and orthopraxis deep into the peasant world. In this process, elite concepts were continually redefined to fit local understandings, while certain popular religious practices ascended the social hierarchy. In Vietnam as well, most notably in the north and center from the late 1400s to the mid-1800s, the spread of Neo-Confucianism substantially modified village organizations, peasant status systems, family structures, and gender roles, while marginalizing or redefining animist and non-Confucian beliefs.

Whereas charter-era societies had been overwhelmingly illiterate, by 1830 at least 50 percent of Burmese (and an indeterminate but probably comparable percent of Siamese) males could read simple vernacular-language materials. In Vietnam literacy rates were lower, perhaps 20 percent among males. In part this was because Neo-Confucianism,

---

[33] Cf. LeBar, *Ethnic Groups*. The number of languages in a region often is inversely proportional to its population density, but even in relatively populous coastal sectors of northern Vietnam before 1400, Li, "View from the Sea," 100–102 has called attention to a high degree of ethnic diversity.

being more elitist and lacking a Theravada-style system of ordination, eschewed universal male education, and in part because literacy in Chinese characters or Vietnamese *nom* (quasi-phonetic scripts derived from Chinese but adapted for writing the Vietnamese language) was inherently more difficult than in fully phonetic Indic alphabets. Yet 20 percent represented a major increase over the charter era, when even some leading Vietnamese courtiers could neither read nor write.

Symptom and cause of expanding literacy was the appearance in all three lowland sectors, especially in the 1700s and early 1800s, of ever more popular literatures that were also more thematically, lexically, and stylistically innovative. In the Indic world secular and, in some degree, religious writing now tended to use Burmese, Tai, and Khmer in lieu of Pali and Sanskrit, while in Vietnam *nom* supplemented or replaced Chinese characters. As vehicles of mass literacy, Pali, Sanskrit, and Chinese were no more practical than Latin in 18th-century Europe and, especially in the case of Pali and Sanskrit, suffered a comparable displacement.

No less marked than vertical integration was the horizontal extension of capital-area usages. If in 1400 self-identified Burmans in the Irrawaddy basin were roughly half the total population, concentrated in the north, by 1820 lowlanders who in various contexts identified themselves as Burmans were probably closer to 90 percent. Through majority colonization, minority emigration, intermarriage, voluntary assimilation, and targeted violence, Lower Burma thus evolved from a substantially Mon to an overwhelmingly Burman society – even as provincial customs modified capital usages and Burman identity was redefined in local contexts. Similar shifts toward Burman ethnicity transformed Tai districts in the northern Irrawaddy basin. Outside the basin, Tais rarely accepted Burman ethnicity, and within the empire as a whole, Burmans in 1820 probably were only 60–70 percent. Nonetheless, considerations of practical utility and prestige did lead many interior Tais, especially Tai-Shan tributaries in regular contact with the Burmese court, to adopt Burmese alphabets, architecture, and political and religious usages.

Likewise, in the lower Chaophraya basin in lieu of the 15th-century array of Khmer, Mon, and Tai communities, a new, melded ethnicity and language – Siamese – emerged to dominate the basin and the upper Malay peninsula. By 1650, if not earlier, a plurality of people within Ayudhya's sphere of influence probably regarded themselves as Siamese in many intergroup contexts. Meanwhile, much as non-Burmans copied elements of Burmese culture, peoples in Tai, Malay, and Khmer states tributary to Ayudhya or Bangkok who declined to adopt Siamese ethnicity nonetheless imitated Siamese customs, both at local courts and at a more demotic level of mythology, monastic practice, grammar, and vocabulary.

In the southern half of modern Vietnam the tiny lowland minority that spoke Vietnamese dialects in 1400 had become a substantial majority by 1850, while within the empire as a whole, Vietnamese-speakers surely exceeded 80 percent. With language arrived Vietnamese religious, family, village, and agricultural influences. If the localization of immigrant Vietnamese culture joined residual Cham and Khmer influences to create an array of Vietnamese identities all along the 1,800-kilometer eastern corridor,[34] over the long term Vietnamese acculturation and political integration proved mutually reinforcing. In varying degrees Cham and Khmer communities, like their Mon counterparts in Lower Burma, were ghettoized, assimilated, and displaced.[35] In brief, whereas in 1400 the Irrawaddy, Chaophraya, and eastern lowlands each had supported three major linguistic/cultural traditions, by 1825 each sector supported one incontestably dominant complex.

Admittedly, both the weakness and strength of integration limited uniformity. Integration was too weak in the sense that physical barriers – still rudimentary transport and communications, undeveloped markets, weak monetization – curbed the reach of capital cultures in general and of ethnicity in particular. The mainland's rugged interior remained a cultural mosaic, divided among literate, Buddhist wet-rice-growing Tais in upland valleys and illiterate, pagan slash-and-burn cultivators at higher elevations who supported a vast number of languages and ethnicities. Although hill tribes, as noted, were increasingly influenced by lowland currents, imperial culture and imperial administration resembled one another in that both climbed hills with great difficulty. Even in the lowlands, however, individuals faced choices in defining themselves, and identities remained multiple and situationally specific. In the Chaophraya basin, in particular, the novelty of Siamese culture (which cohered only in the 15th century), the prominence of Chinese traders, and unusually large wartime deportations of minority peoples (needed to compensate for Siam's huge losses to Burma)

---

[34] Keith Taylor, "Surface Orientations in Vietnam," *JAS* 57 (1998): 949–78.

[35] Although Sinic cultural practices diffused less easily than Indic, hill peoples in the eastern mainland also borrowed selectively from Vietnamese culture, as well as from lowland Tai.

combined as late as 1800 to limit to perhaps half of the population those who in censuses or interactions with people from outside the locality would identify themselves as Siamese.

Integrative processes were too strong in the sense that the same dynamics as encouraged amalgamation necessarily nurtured countervailing and crosscutting currents. As central officials imposed new obligations and migrants introduced new cultural norms, subalterns in the heartland and minorities on the frontier often felt obliged to resist marginalization by defiantly championing symbols of local identity. Where assimilation did occur, it typically involved not wholesale but selective imitation and recombination in culturally fluid "middle grounds."[36] Meanwhile the same expansion of communications as favored the domestic circulation of ideas and people could draw elites toward external models and away from their own peasantries, however earnestly the latter sought "to catch up." This was most obvious in Vietnam, where prestigious Chinese norms proved irresistible to wealthy families, encouraging an elite–mass cultural divide persistently wider than that in Indic Southeast Asia. But even in Indic Southeast Asia, especially in tributary states, the prestige of imperial culture could seduce local leaders from allegiance to their own traditions, again creating novel elite–mass tensions. Finally, as the market eroded local self-sufficiency, the market's ability to supply ever more discriminating tastes also encouraged specialization in artistic and literary expression, clothing, housing, handicrafts, and religious practice, all of which also carried the potential for social fracture and disputation. In this ability to support niche specialties alongside overarching commonalities, cultural integration resembled both administrative centralization, with its demand for ever greater fiscal, military, and scribal expertise, and commercialization, which demanded an ever more refined division of economic labor. In this sense, systemic integration and functional specialization were two sides of the same coin.

---

[36] Phrase comes from Richard White, *The Middle Ground: Indians, Empires, and Republics in the Great Lakes Region, 1650–1815* (Cambridge, 1989). See too Michael Banton, "The Direction and Speed of Ethnic Change," in Charles Keyes, ed., *Ethnic Change* (Seattle, 1981), 31–52; and the discussion of frontiers, boundaries, and borders as political and cultural constructs in Bruce Batten, *To the Ends of Japan* (Honolulu, 2003), 6–14, 125–26, 235–41.

The Dynamics of Integration: Overview

In sum, after a period of postcharter fragmentation, starting in the early or mid-15th century and accelerating to the second quarter of the 19th century, the principal states of mainland Southeast Asia expanded their territories, centralized their administrations, and saw their populations adopt more uniform religious and ethnic identities. Burma's early Kon-baung Dynasty, founded in 1752; the Chakri Dynasty that took power in Siam in 1782; and the Nguyen Dynasty of Vietnam, which assumed national control in 1802 all represented the apogee of indigenous achievement. But so far I have said little about underlying dynamics. How shall we explain these long-term trends?

My essential argument is this: Four phenomena – expansion of material resources, new cultural currents, intensifying interstate competition, and diverse state interventions – combined to strengthen privileged lowland districts at the expense of outlying areas. Each phenomenon in this virtuous circle had a certain autonomy, yet all four constantly reinforced and modified one another.

Material expansion, under which rubric I include commercial, demographic, and agrarian expansion as well as the importation of firearms, magnified the physical superiority of emergent political cores over less favored districts. By boosting literacy, opening new avenues of communication, and encouraging frontier colonization, economic growth also enhanced the cultural influence of emergent cores. New cultural currents refer to a) the growth of Theravada and Neo-Confucian orthodoxy, and b) the spread of ethnicities, languages, and other social practices associated with imperial centers. Cultic/religious reform strengthened royal claims to moral authority, civilized rural society, and thus complemented military pacification without requiring a fresh commitment of royal resources. By enhancing popular identification with the throne, royally sanctioned ethnic and social practices had much the same centralizing effect.

As states, nourished by these trends, became more powerful, warfare grew markedly in scale, duration, and expense. If warfare reinforced the appeal of capital cultures by increasing popular dependence on the throne, it also placed growing demands on each state's fiscal and administrative system. At the same time, by eliminating buffer states and incorporating more distant principalities, territorial expansion amplified the twin dangers of foreign invasion and provincial rebellion. Especially after c. 1450, states that would survive these Darwinian pressures were obliged to upgrade their military forces, to develop new provincial and tributary controls, to exalt cultural symbols emblematic of the state, and to expand systematically their economic and manpower base. Meanwhile, independent of deliberate policy and often in fact unnoticed, the sheer growth of the state also tended to promote economic expansion and cultural diffusion.

The eastern corridor lacked a unifying artery along which these processes could unfold. Nonetheless, not only did the Vietnamese lowlands see cultural trends similar to those farther west, but the southern Vietnamese state, as noted, responded to the same basic stimuli and followed much the same chronology as its western neighbors. For these reasons, whether the south ultimately remained independent or joined the north leaves unchanged my basic analysis.

The Dynamics of Integration: Expansion of Material Resources

Let us flesh out these abstractions, starting with the impact of economic change, which had both external and domestic components. Maritime trade, on present evidence, made but a modest contribution to the genesis of charter polities, with the chief exception of Champa;[37] but such trade, buoyed largely by the growth of the Chinese market, increased markedly from the mid-1100s to at least the late 1200s.[38] Between 1460 and 1630 Chinese and Indian Ocean demand for Southeast Asian forest, agricultural, and entrepot goods rose yet more sharply. External trade leveled off or fell in the western and central mainland from 1640, only to pick up, chiefly in response to Chinese demand, after 1720 and more particularly in the late 1700s and early 1800s. We also find a long-term growth in overland trade with South China. Although by no means static, it is doubtful that agriculture grew as rapidly as external trade, especially after 1720. By their very nature, moreover, market taxes, in cash or luxury goods, were easier to collect and redistribute than bulky, perishable in-kind agricultural taxes. For these reasons external trade tended to magnify the income superiority, hence the military and

---

[37] See nn. 22, 23 *supra*.

[38] *SP*, 93–94, 121–22, 145–49, 222–23, 240, 365, 371, and n. 23 *supra*. Thereafter, between c. 1280/1300 and 1400 most sources suggest only modest commercial growth or even contraction, but a minority viewpoint argues for undiminished vitality, esp. of the China trade, from 1280 to 1500. See sources in Ch. 7, n. 89 *infra*.

patronage potential, of lowland authorities in control of ports and frontier bazaars at the expense of more isolated, less commercially favored elites. Maritime contacts also boosted tax revenues indirectly by stimulating domestic commerce and specialization in each of the principal lowland corridors. Although not spatially uniform – its influence was more consistently critical in Siam and southern Vietnam than in Burma or northern Vietnam – over the long term foreign trade favored imperial projects in all three regions.

By virtue of their expense and inaccessibility, foreign firearms had much the same effect. Before c. 1530 Chinese-style guns coming overland may have strengthened interior states disproportionately, but between 1550 and 1830 with the introduction by sea of ever more powerful and reliable European-style weapons, the advantage shifted permanently to authorities in control of the ports. As the percentage of imperial troops equipped with imported or European-style firearms rose in all three empires, with a notable spurt in the late 18th and early 19th centuries, cannon, matchlocks and (in the 1700s) flintlocks transformed naval strategies, stockade fighting, and urban defenses alike. In turn, firearms procurement and training demanded more efficient systems of supply, recruitment, taxation, and command. Landlocked polities were increasingly marginalized. Firearms thus help to explain both the success of pacification in the western and central mainland between 1550 and 1830 and the vigor of Nguyen armies and navies along the southeastern littoral from 1620 to the early 1800s.

Agriculture also exhibited long-term dynamism, the product of several influences. By increasing the reach and force of monsoon flows and minimizing droughts linked to El Nino events, the Medieval Climate Anomaly c. 800/850–1250/1300 contributed in some uncertain but possibly critical degree to that demographic and agricultural vigor, and associated institutional vitality, characteristic of the charter era, two of whose chief polities, Pagan and Angkor, lay in dry zones. The 14th century brought markedly drier weather to much of the mainland, reinforcing a postcharter shift away from the dry zones, but between c. 1470 and 1570 and from 1710/1720 to 1805, heavier monsoons again improved yields and encouraged cultivation of more marginal lands.[39] I speculated that during the charter era local population growth and closer

---

[39] On climatic phases and associated agrarian shifts, see *SP*, 101–12, 121, 142–43, 156–57, 174, 176, 224–26, 239–40, 265, 267, 276, 295, 363–64, 370–71, 385, 396, 420, 438–39, 459, plus nn. 98–107 and discussion *infra*.

contacts with longer-settled areas of Eurasia allowed Southeast Asians to develop immunity to diseases that had once proved uniformly fatal. This too would have favored agrarian expansion in those lowland districts where populations needed to sustain local chains of endemic infection were most dense and where exposure to foreign disease was most common.[40] More certainly, voluntary migrations and military deportations from the hills joined natural increase to expand lowland populations throughout the period under review, and most especially after 1500. On balance, we shall find, the state too aided rural economies. With an effectiveness that varied over time, mainland courts not only organized deportations but promoted frontier colonization, offered some incentives to commercial agriculture, and through pacification created conditions favorable to natural increase.

If most growth was extensive, that is to say, dependent on the mere addition of production units, in some contexts output also rose per land and labor unit. During the charter era, new labor systems associated with magnificent Hindu-Buddhist temples at Pagan and Angkor provided a major initial boost to irrigation and reclamation, not to mention artisanal technique and production. In the postcharter era as well, more individualized landholding systems and new commercial opportunities favored double- and triple-cropping and more labor-intensive systems of planting, irrigation, and harvesting. In circular fashion, the resultant demand for labor encouraged population growth, which made possible further Boserupian intensification.[41] As they extended the agrarian frontier, Burman, Tai, and Vietnamese cultivators typically promoted

---

[40] In fact, local immunities may develop through any or all of the following mechanisms: a) Increased contact, often trade mediated, with external sources of infection can help to convert infrequent but extremely lethal epidemics into endemic diseases of childhood. Once a disease has become endemic, universal childhood exposure precludes the horrendously destructive virgin-soil effects associated with the Black Death in Europe or smallpox in the New World and Oceania. b) Population growth – the result of improved nutrition, cumulative natural increase, more regular exposure to once lethal diseases – can cross the demographic threshold needed to maintain local chains of infection. c) Coevolution can select hosts for resistance and parasites for milder impacts. See *SP*, 50, 97–98, 224, 251, 295, 369, 370, 420; Roger Albin, pers. commun., Oct. 11, 2008; and discussion *infra*.

[41] In addition to *SP* 49–52, 95–101, 141–45, 174–75, 224–28, 248–55, 293–307, 362–65, 385–92, 409–10, 437–40, see Ester Boserup, *The Conditions of Agricultural Growth* (Chicago, 1965); idem, *Population and Technological Change* (Chicago, 1981), arguing that moderate population growth, far from producing Malthusian decline, could generate major improvements in productivity; and David Henley, "Population and the Means of Subsistence," *JSEAS* 36 (2005): 337–72, showing how external commercial demand could collapse subsistence-oriented demographic and agrarian regimes.

water-control systems that were more ecologically varied than those practiced by their Mon, Khmer, and Cham predecessors. The latter groups' resultant demographic weakness presaged ethnic as well as political eclipse. Expansion of buffalo and oxen herds, cumulative refinements in tools and technique, and the selection of rice strains, cotton, and other crops geared to specific niches permitted further gains in rural carrying capacity. The same was true of agricultural processing and the village-based production of metalware, implements, and textiles. Introduced apparently from India in the 14th century, cotton, in particular, spurred all manner of rural handicrafts and domestic trade.

Under these combined influences, population in the western and central mainland probably doubled between 1400 and 1820, while in what is now Vietnam it more than tripled. All things being equal, this meant larger aggregate, and in some contexts per capita, commercial demand and lower distribution costs not only for rice and specialized foodstuffs but for domestic and imported handicrafts and textiles. Evidence of Smithian specialization in agriculture, handicrafts, and retail distribution is readily available, especially in urban hinterlands and particularly after 1720. Foreign traders reinforced domestic pressures to commodification by a) disseminating new crops, most notably Indian cotton and more productive "slender-type" strains of rice, but also New World maize, sweet potatoes, peanuts, and tobacco; b) introducing new agricultural and artisanal techniques; c) supplying large quantities of Japanese copper and silver and New World silver critical to domestic monetization; and d) magnifying the variety and volume of Indian and European textiles and Chinese foodstuffs and handicrafts, which lured producers to the market. Conversely, domestic population and economic growth aided foreign trade by boosting export and import capacity.

In the short or medium term, by creating shortages of irrigable land or bullion and by aggravating center–periphery and intra-elite conflicts, economic and demographic growth repeatedly destabilized mainland polities. Thus, as noted, in the 13th/14th centuries land shortages, ecological strains, and the novel prosperity of poorly controlled maritime peripheries weakened Pagan, Angkor, and Dai Viet. Periodically between 1600 and 1830, the superior dynamism of frontier districts again pitted them against long-settled regions. The late 1500s, late 1700s, and early 1800s also saw severe monetary disturbances, the result of a heating up of the entire South China Sea economy with attendant bullion shortages. We find too, particularly in the 18th and early 19th centuries, a building tension between the market's insistence on social and geographic mobility, on the one hand, and elite determination to preserve hereditary service categories, on the other hand. This conflict between commercial choice and social ascription – which, we shall find, bore a generic resemblance to tensions in Russia, France, and Japan in this same period – weakened the military systems of both Burma and Siam.

Over an extended period, however, as central authorities learned to tap larger manpower and commercial reserves, domestic economic vitality reinforced the centralizing impact of foreign trade and firearms. The political benefits of economic expansion were actually fourfold. First, even if output in lowland cores and in upland dependencies grew at the same rate, the former's larger initial size would have provided a constantly increasing absolute advantage in rice, cash income, manpower, and war animals. But in fact, better pacification, easier access to foreign trade, and centripetal resource transfers (via deportations, tribute, and trade) ensured that, for much of the period under review, economic growth was more vigorous in lowland zones than in upland peripheries.

Second, monetization tended to enhance each capital's ability to extract and allocate resources. With markets affording cultivators easier access to cash, the creation of tax farms and the commutation of notoriously unwieldy in-kind taxes and labor services became more feasible. Hence in all three realms after 1550, but especially in the 1700s and early 1800s, we find movements from services and in-kind levies to cash taxation. Along with maritime income, domestic cash revenues were used to finance military campaigns, to coordinate patronage, and to support more centralized, politically docile forms of religious donations.

Third, by eroding the self-sufficiency of local actors, commercial integration enhanced each capital's coordinating appeal. As specialization boosted reliance on distant markets, traders and landowners looked to the throne to protect long-distance exchange, to standardize weights and measures, and in some instances, to unify legal jurisdictions. Likewise, the growing role of tax commissions and commercial monopolies, the enhanced legal authority of royal courts in trade and land disputes, and the danger of uncontrolled peasant mobility all made it increasingly difficult for local elites to maintain their preeminence without help from the throne. Leading provincial families therefore joined royal officials to negotiate novel arrangements that simultaneously strengthened central prerogatives, enhanced the flow of tax revenues to the capital, provided provincial elites with expanded patronage and tax income, and secured their place in a wider, more inclusive social universe.

Fourth, this same mobility of goods and labor helped to extend the cultural influence of each capital region. On agrarian frontiers after 1500 and more especially after 1650, waves of Burman and Vietnamese colonists swamped minority peoples, spreading the language, ethnicity, and social practices of their home regions. Nearer to each imperial core, urban trade and pilgrimage networks attracted pedlars, seasonal or full-time workers, itinerant monks, actors, and entertainers, all agents of cultural exchange. The proliferation of commercial contracts and legal cases and the growth of cities, with their hybrid milieux, encouraged numeracy and written skills at surprisingly humble levels. Without something approaching mass literacy, the aforementioned blossoming of vernacular-language literatures would have been inconceivable. In institutional terms, the chief spur to popular literacy – and to the erosion of the charter-era divide between elite and popular culture – was new networks of Theravada monasteries and Confucian academies. Expanding rapidly from the 15th century, such facilities, with their complements of manuscripts and scholars, benefited from rural population growth; from rising per capita wealth; from easier commercial contacts with Sri Lanka, India, and China; and in Vietnam, from the scholarly interests of Chinese immigrant families, whose arrival was usually a by-product of trade.[42]

The Dynamics of Integration: New Cultural Currents

If agrarian and commercial expansion thus aided cultural integration, social and psychological forces that cannot be tied so directly to economic stimuli also reshaped culture. Snobbery, the ambition to display the prestigious dialects, art styles, and manners of the court, inspired avid imitation among provincial elites, whose behavior in turn influenced lower strata, whether through mimesis or opposition. To inland communities where literacy was rare, sacred texts exuded mystical power and esoteric knowledge. For women Theravada links between

---

[42] Recent scholarship on Vietnam – see n. 23 *supra* – has emphasized cultural role of such immigrants. Especially from the late 1500s, Vietnamese Confucian studies and preparation for the examinations also drew strength from the growing importation of Chinese printed texts. Li Tana, pers. commun., Feb. 29, 2004. On the procurement of Indian Ocean texts in Theravada Southeast Asia, *SP*, 98–99, 194, 320–22.

motherhood and merit-making offered opportunities to display one's piety and to identify with the monkhood. Above all, religious reform sanctified the emotional journeys of countless individuals. To those who through migration or displacement had lost the protection of natal spirits, or simply to those of anxious temperament, the conviction that meritorious acts would yield karmic rewards in a future existence promised greater predictability and emotional security than spirit propitiation. Conversely and rather ironically, in northern Vietnam during the 14th century and to some extent in the late 1700s, the conviction that Mahayana Buddhism had failed to solve severe social problems led many rural leaders to turn from Buddhism to the less metaphysical, more socially prescriptive teachings of Neo-Confucianism.[43]

The main point is that within each mainland Southeast Asian realm between c. 1400 and 1830 two principal cultural shifts – the rise of religious/cultic orthodoxy and the spread of capital-centered ethnicities, languages, and social and artistic conventions – favored political centralization. Consider each in turn.

Cultic orthodoxy, whether Theravada or Neo-Confucian, favored royal authority in several interrelated ways: a) By idealizing the ruler as font of morality and bulwark against anarchy, Theravada and Neo-Confucian teachings and texts sanctioned central supervision of local personnel, both lay and religious, while devaluing local spirits in favor of supralocal, royally sanctioned sources of sanctity. b) Both Theravada monks and Neo-Confucian scholars depended on royal training and certification. Vietnamese civil service exams, which relied on a state-approved corpus and obliged students to leave their villages to write about issues of imperial governance, offer the most obvious example, but Theravada monks also looked to the throne to define orthodoxy in texts and praxis and to honor provincial talents. c) Both cults lent practical support to administration, indirectly by enlarging the local supply of literate officials, and in Vietnam directly, by providing Chinese bureaucratic blueprints. d) Both created new social infrastructures: schools, monasteries, law codes, community rituals, and models of family organization. By rendering rural life more literate and civilized, these innovations reduced the need for imperial coercion and compensated for

---

[43] On Vietnamese transitions, Whitmore, "Rise of the Coast"; *SP*, 372–73, 377–83, 402–405, 442. On Theravada appeals in the Indic world, ibid., 135–39, 188–92, 258–63, 314–17, 323–24; Andaya, "Localizing the Universal," and idem, *Flaming Womb*, 75–81, emphasizing appeals to women.

the yet limited reach of officialdom. e) Each in its own way, Theravada and Neo-Confucian reform promoted an ethic of self-discipline, moral obligation, and emotional mastery that provided a psychological underpinning for pacification. Although extending over a longer period, c. 1400–1830, and arguably less intense or institutionally creative than European analogues, these transitions recall those autonomous transformations in social control – the "disciplinary revolution" – that Philip Gorski claims was critical to the growth of state power in much of Europe between 1550 and 1750.[44]

Standardization of ethnic, linguistic, and social practices was no less centripetal than religious change, at least potentially. True, as scattered Tai-speakers across the mainland showed, without sustained communications, without a central authority to patrol cultural boundaries, and without a common "other" against whom to define the ingroup, common cultural features like language had no intrinsic political significance. At most, shared traits created a potential community. This potential, however, could be critical in several contexts. Among religious and lay elites, more sustained economic and social interaction opened unified fields for discussion and contestation. Precisely because the same symbols meant different things to different observers, negotiation to determine normative texts and rituals became more frequent.

Moreover, to the extent that cultural motifs became linked to rival political centers, conflict could transform such motifs into a public marker, a badge, of political loyalty. In periods of insecurity, people seized, often arbitrarily, on symbols – language, hairstyle, dress, tattoos, religious emblems – to erect boundaries that could strengthen their common claim to resources in competition with outgroups deemed to be alien and minatory. In Sow-theng Leong's formulation, a cultural group becomes ethnic when its members consciously choose cultural markers to promote internal solidarity and mobilization against rival populations.[45] Because the social structures on which such symbols

---

[44] Philip Gorski, *The Disciplinary Revolution* (Chicago, 2003). For contemporary studies suggesting that religious belief facilitates "prosocial" behavior, that is, altruistic but personally costly behavior, particularly in ingroup contexts, and for the psychology of such behavior, see Ara Norenzayan and Azim Shariff, "The Origin and Evolution of Religious Prosociality," *Science* 322 (2008): 58–62.

[45] Sow-theng Leong, *Migration and Ethnicity in Chinese History* (Stanford, 1997), 20. Cf. Mark Elliott, *The Manchu Way* (Stanford, 2001), 16–20, 353; and *SP*, 37, n. 46, which defines an ethnic group as "a collectivity within a larger society that claims a common name and history and that elevates one or more symbolic elements as the epitome of that common identity and as a boundary against outsiders." On the theory of

relied and the outgroups against whom self-definition was directed might vary, ethnic boundaries also could shift. Over time, however, by yoking the welfare of diverse local groups to that of the sheltering royal capital, a recurrent dread of external attack could combine with thicker communications to popularize ethnic symbols and to reify and standardize identities. In varying degrees in Burma, Siam, Vietnam, and indeed in some smaller states, ethnic pride became enshrined in folk tales, songs, dramas, histories, and kingdom-wide cults of protective spirits. For their part, Burmese, Siamese, Vietnamese, and Khmer rulers patronized majority languages, religions, and ethnicities, especially on the frontier, in part to improve administrative efficiency but more basically to strengthen emotional identification with the throne against rival populations. Modern societies, in short, are by no means the only extensive groups able to generate and mobilize popular loyalties.

To be sure, allegiances of this sort differed from post-1750/1789 European-style nationalism not merely because they were far less socially insistent and uniform, but also because they made distinct intellectual claims. Southeast Asian thought subordinated secular cultures to universal religious loyalties far more rigorously than does modern nationalism. As seen from each Southeast Asian capital, the world was composed not of equal nations, each with its own legitimate culture, but of realms that exhibited varying degrees of adherence to a universal truth, Theravadin or Confucian. By extension, sovereignty resided not in a national secular community, but in a ruler whose cosmically sanctioned authority was proleptically universal. In keeping with the Theravadin World-Ruler (*cakkavatti*) and the Sino-Vietnamese Son of Heaven paradigms, Southeast Asian monarchs often gloried in the heterogeneity of subject populations. Absent rebellion or other direct challenges to majority practices, religious theory and practical necessity alike ensured minority peoples a secure autonomy. If we define "nation" as the political expression of a sovereign secular community, and "empire" as a sovereign state whose possessions include several formerly independent kingdoms and cultures, then Southeast Asian states clearly fell in the latter category. So too, because status was determined by distance from the ruler, hence from the principles of cosmic morality he

ethnicity, see too sources in ibid., 40–41, n. 51; Orlando Patterson, "Context and Choice in Ethnic Allegiance," in Nathan Glazer and Daniel Moynihan, eds., *Ethnicity: Theory and Experience* (Cambridge, MA, 1975), 305–49; Patrick Geary, *The Myth of Nations* (Princeton, 2002).

embodied, the political and legal ethos of Southeast Asia, in contrast to nationalism's insistent civic and legal egalitarianism, was deeply hierarchic. Lacking any concept of popular sovereignty, Southeast Asian political thought had no use for horizontal communication or collective voice among the king's subjects. Without colonialism, there is no reason to imagine that such notions would have evolved into recognizably European-style identities. Given these differences, in lieu of "nationalism," I prefer "politicized ethnicity" to describe precolonial forms of cultural loyalty focused on the state.[46]

Yet, *pace* scholars like Benedict Anderson and Ernest Gellner who posit a unbridgeable divide between premodern political allegiance and European nationalism, we also find at least three similarities between precolonial Southeast Asian political collectivities, on the one hand, and European identities – both before and after 1789 – on the other. Bear in mind that most European nations also began as heterogeneous imperial conglomerates whose provinces served as cultural periphery to the metropole and whose cultural integration was a contested, imperfect, initially undertheorized affair starting in some cases as early as the 12th century, accelerating from the 17th century, and lasting well into the 20th.[47]

---

[46] A similar determination to avoid a) the teleological assumption that pre-20th-century Chinese identities automatically would have evolved into modern nationalism, and b) the assumption of a radical break between premodern and modern notions of identity, led Prasenjit Duara to coin the term "culturalism." See Duara, "Historicizing National Identity, or Who Imagines What and When," in Geoff Eley and Ronald Suny, eds., *Becoming National: A Reader* (Oxford, 1996), 151–57. See too Susan Burns, *Before the Nation: Kokugaku and the Imagining of Community in Early Modern Japan* (Durham, NC, 2003), 9, 224; Joshua Fogel, ed., *The Teleology of the Modern Nation-State* (Philadelphia, 2005); and my reservations about Mary Elizabeth Berry's use of "nation" to describe Tokugawa Japan in Ch. 4, n. 378 *infra*. Although recognizing the danger of teleological projection, in pre-1750 French and Russian contexts I occasionally use "proto-nationalism" as equivalent to "politicized ethnicity."

[47] Whether Europe itself produced instances of "genuine" nationalism before 1750/1789 is debated. Compare, on the one hand, the restrictive definitions in Benedict Anderson, *Imagined Communities* (London, 1991); Ernest Gellner, *Nations and Nationalism* (Ithaca, 1983), arguing that premodern states were inherently hostile to cultural homogeneity; and Eric Hobsbawm, *Nations and Nationalism Since 1780* (Cambridge, 1990), with, on the other hand, the more subtle medieval/early modern understandings of Adrian Hastings, *The Construction of Nationhood* (Cambridge, 1997); Liah Greenfeld, *Nationalism* (Cambridge, MA, 1992); Philip Gorski, "The Mosaic Moment," *The American Jl. of Sociology* 105 (2000): 1428–68; Sheldon Pollock, *The Language of the Gods in the World of Men* (Berkeley, 2006), 562–65; and Aviel Roshwald, *The Endurance of Nationalism* (Cambridge, 2006).

First and most basic, with states growing more coherent and inter-state conflict more intense, we find within major Southeast Asian and European realms an increasingly secure correlation between a core territory, a paramount state organization, and membership in a distinct cultural community as proclaimed by kingdom-specific symbols. Such tendencies, almost by definition, became more pronounced during war than in peacetime, in areas of frontier competition than in interior locales, and in competitive multiethnic than in culturally uniform zones.[48]

Second, contrary to historians who assume that universal religion was incompatible with ethnic/political particularism, in practice in Southeast Asia as in Europe from the 15th well into the 19th century, the two merged without great difficulty.[49] How did Southeast Asians understand this relation? On the one hand, where rival communities upheld different cultic traditions, religious and ethnic loyalty could fuse. We find this in Buddhist Burman attacks against animist Shans in the 1500s and against Hindu Manipuris in the 1700s. This pattern became most evident in what is now southern Vietnam, where Vietnamese settlement and Neo-Confucian "civilizing" projects inspired attacks on Cham and Khmer cultures – to which Khmers responded in the 18th century with what can only be called genocidal massacres of tens of thousands of Vietnamese in the name of their holy Buddhist religion.[50] On the other hand, where rival populations supported the same Theravada doctrine, as on the Burman–Mon and Burman–Siamese frontiers, each community tended to claim that its observances alone were orthodox, that it

---

[48] Cf. the indices of "nation" offered in Berry, *Japan in Print*, 212. Among mainland Southeast Asia's three major empires in 1824, Siam had the smallest percentage of its total population belonging to the central ethnic group. If politicized ethnicity was a source of strength, why then was Siam the most successful early 19th-century military power? The answer is at least threefold: a) Most critical, Siam's cosmopolitan, commercial orientation tended to weaken ethnicity at the same time as it provided a critical source of guns and tax income superior to that available to Burma or Vietnam. b) Bitterly anti-Burmese but militarily valuable Mon refugees in Siam eroded the tie between Siamese ethnicity and loyalty to the Bangkok throne. c) Regardless of their modest percentage in the overall population, Siamese in the Chaophraya basin were sufficiently numerous to provide a cohesive imperial core.

[49] Compare the claim, in Anderson, *Imagined Communities*, that universal religious and national loyalties were incompatible, with Hastings, Greenfeld, and Gorski in n. 47 *supra*; Wolfgang Reinhard, "Introduction," in Reinhard, ed., *Power Elites and State Building* (Oxford, 1996); David Bell, *The Cult of the Nation in France* (Cambridge, MA, 2001); and Linda Colley, *Britons: Forging the Nation 1707–1837* (New Haven, 1992).

[50] See graphic descriptions in Ben Kiernan, *Blood and Soil* (New Haven, 2007), 158–61; *SP*, 412.

alone remained faithful to texts and prophecy. Here too such claims translated easily into ethnic disdain.[51]

Third, in mainland Southeast Asia as in Europe, the slowly increasing proportion of imperial subjects willing to identify ethnically and culturally with each capital in the centuries before 1800 anticipated later trends. In Burma and Dai Viet central ethnicities cohered among political elites during the charter era. In the new Tai realms an analogous process occurred in the 14th and 15th centuries. Modified identities then diffused vertically and laterally, accelerating sharply in the chief lowland zones from the early 1700s. Under European colonial influence, national culture became more secular, egalitarian, and exclusive. Nonetheless, the vertical and lateral extension of Burmese, Siamese, and Vietnamese collectivities built on pre-1850 loyalties in a fashion that was far less artificial and less dependent on intelligentsia interventions than was the 20th-century construction of Malay or Indonesian nationalism. To appreciate this distinction, one need only consider that whereas Europeans created "Malaya," "Indonesia," and the "Philippines" *de novo*, on the mainland they merely modified long-standing Burmese, Siamese, and Vietnamese state forms and identities.

The Dynamics of Integration: Intensifying Interstate Competition

Alongside economic growth and shifting cultural sensibilities, warfare provided a critical spur to Southeast Asian state formation. From the early 1500s and again in the late 1700s and early 1800s, the growing size of infantry forces and the rising cost of guns and firearms-resistant stone or brick forts rendered warfare ever more expensive and administratively taxing. At the same time, as noted, the conquest of ever more geographically and culturally distant communities magnified the danger that restive tributaries and provincial heads would join forces with outside invaders. Such pressures became particularly intense in Indic states, where repeated administrative initiatives between 1550 and 1830 responded to the demands of external warfare and/or domestic revolt. Siam's reorganization of provincial governorships and of the *phrai luang* service system following Ayudhya's humiliation at the hands of the Burmese in 1569, Burma's yet more dramatic expansion of the *ahmu-dan* military service system and provincial government after the First Toungoo state collapsed in 1599, and ambitious fiscal and military changes

---

[51] Lieberman, *Burmese Administrative Cycles*, ch. 5.

in both empires during the exhausting Burmese–Siamese contests of 1759–1819 well illustrate this pattern. Administrative reform thus had a convulsive tendency, with periods of military challenge or collapse followed by intensified reorganization. In Vietnam the programmatic autonomy of Confucianism and literati suspicion of the army weakened the link between warfare and administrative reform. Yet there too, Chinese bureaucracy appealed to Vietnamese literati in part because it promised to curb regionalism in an unpropitious geographic environment and to bolster the state in recurrent conflicts with Champa, Cambodia, and Siam.

As for psychological effects, warfare could strengthen popular identification with the throne by integrating conscripts from different locales and, as I just suggested, by rendering frontier communities more dependent on the capital for security, by nurturing chauvinistic stereotypes, and by generating mythic reminders of communal danger and salvation. Such views became particularly salient after 18th-century breakdowns in Burma and Siam, when acute disorders drove countless thousands to venerate newly risen dynasts as World-Rulers on whom their salvation in this and future lives depended.

The Dynamics of Integration: Intended and Unintended Consequences of State Interventions

In these ways, polities drew strength from an interlocking set of economic, cultural, and military changes on the ground. Yet, surely, the lines of causation ran in the opposite direction as well: as its capacity and ambition increased, each state constantly modified, both deliberately and unintentionally, the economic and cultural milieu in which it operated. If military spurs to government action often were critical, they were never exclusive: court factionalism, religious imperatives, personal eccentricities all had their day. In crafting new policies, elites deployed a mix of charter legacies, Chinese models, trial and error, and one another's best practices as reported by diplomats, merchants, and defectors. Expertise in administration and political economy – like knowledge of new crops, commercial technique, or firearms – was therefore a resource that could accumulate and that further explains the linear, ratchet-like nature of political integration.

To bolster their resource base, rulers not only reformed financial and service administration but welcomed foreign merchants, sponsored overseas trading expeditions, encouraged bullion imports and mining, rationalized riverine tolls, standardized legal jurisdictions, and, in Siam and Vietnam, built major transport canals. In the agrarian sector they coordinated large-scale irrigation, diking, the introduction of new crops, resettlement, and frontier colonization. To suggest that on balance such actions proved beneficial to the economy is neither to deny that other measures (overtaxation, monopolies, warfare) could be ruinous nor to pretend that such inducements approached best-case institutional and legal conditions such as Douglass C. North has postulated for parts of western Europe.[52]

Alongside self-conscious efforts to expand their tax base, the chief states encouraged production through activities whose economic impact was incidental to their original political purpose and, in some cases perhaps, unnoticed. Although a preeminently political act, territorial unification, for example, tended to lower commercial costs by constricting the number of rival tribute-takers, facilitating exchange between zones with unique resource profiles, quelling internal disorder, and thus reducing uncertainty for cultivators and traders alike. Intentionally or not, cash taxation channeled peasant surplus toward the market, with numerous spinoff effects. Likewise, by encouraging family landholding, postcharter tenurial systems may have increased smallholder productivity. Unification of weights and measures, partly intended as a symbolic statement of suzerainty, often had important commercial benefits. Large-scale construction and resettlement around the capitals of Ava, Ayudhya, Bangkok, Thang Long (Hanoi), and Hue powerfully concentrated market demand. Finally, by reducing child mortality and enhancing marriage and fertility, lowland pacification tended to stimulate population growth.[53]

A similar mix of intended and unintended consequences characterized state influences on culture. In keeping with their soteriological raison d'être, Theravada regimes directed considerable resources to purifying the monkhood, standardizing sacred texts, promulgating Buddhist law codes, and supporting an annual cycle of monastic donations. To these religious programs must be added persistent efforts to unify lay

[52] Douglass C. North and Robert Paul Thomas, *The Rise of the Western World* (Cambridge, 1973); North, *Institutions, Institutional Change, and Economic Performance* (Cambridge, 1990).

[53] M. C. Ricklefs, "Some Statistical Evidence on Javanese Social, Economic, and Demographic History in the Later Seventeenth and Eighteenth Centuries," *MAS* 20 (1986): 1–32; Norman Owen, "The Paradox of Nineteenth-Century Population Growth in Southeast Asia," *JSEAS* 18 (1987): 45–57; *AC*, vol. I, 12–18.

status hierarchies, to define aesthetic standards, and to modify select social practices. Through literary and artistic patronage Ava, Ayudhya, Bangkok, and Hue made themselves arbiters of taste and cultural magnets for provincial imitators. By promoting Confucian legal norms of family organization and by regulating social status through civil service examinations, Vietnamese leaders sought with particular vigor to shape lowland village society. In frontier areas as well, I have noted, 15th-century Vietnamese and 18th- and early-19th-century Burmese and Vietnamese rulers periodically attempted to promote majority culture at the expense of restive minorities through a combination of colonization, public display, and targeted repression. Less intentionally, by appealing to a combination of snobbery and practical ambition, political patronage offered local elites an implicit but persistent lure to engage in what might be termed self-Burmanization, self-Vietnamization, and self-Siamization. The growing circulation between provincial and capital agencies of documents and legal decisions had a similar standardizing effect. In Burma and Siam the annual rotation of tens of thousands of provincial servicemen at the capital provided another powerful, if incidental and perhaps unnoticed, vehicle of cultural integration. All in all, outside Vietnam it would be an exaggeration to claim that Southeast Asian states pursued consistently assimilatory language or ethnic policies. In Burma efforts to promote majority culture were normally ad hoc responses to anti-Burman revolts that had invoked ethnic symbols as a sign of resistance. In a larger sense, however, by defining cultural norms – religious, legal, literary, aesthetic, ethnic – by rewarding acceptance of those norms, by widening channels of capital–provincial communication, and by fostering commercial growth that aided cultural circulation, each imperial capital, deliberately and inadvertently, encouraged uniformity.

In sum, long-term integration within each sector of mainland Southeast Asia reflected the interplay of several variables, including foreign trade, imported firearms, agricultural and domestic commercial expansion, wider literacy, movements of religious and cultural reform, intensifying warfare, and multifaceted state initiatives. If most factors had their own etiology, most also modified one another in ways that were both open ended and potentially cumulative, as Figure 1.3 suggests. Thus, for example, economic growth and cultural change bolstered the state, which, responding in part to military imperatives, promoted economic

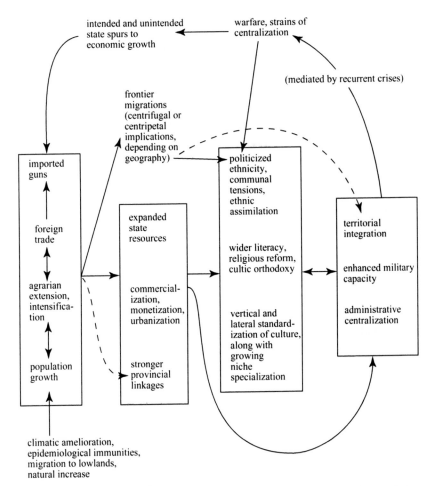

Figure 1.3. Some elements in the integration of mainland Southeast Asian realms to 1824 and their potential interactions. Dashed lines indicate the ambiguous, potentially centrifugal implications of frontier settlement in the eastern lowlands during the 17th and 18th centuries.

growth and cultural integration. All such movements spun webs of material and psychological dependence. It is not far fetched to suggest that the transition from substantially self-sufficient isolates (statelets, subsistence economies, resolutely local cultural systems) in 900 to larger, more internally specialized systems in 1800 resembled the evolution from single-cell organisms to complex, multicellular organisms.[54] In the western and central mainland, in particular, successive interregna became less disruptive precisely because ever greater numbers, having come to depend on large, inclusive systems for their material and emotional well-being, regarded such systems as normative and as worthy of enormous sacrifice to reassemble.

This abstract, synchronic précis should not obscure how widely individual factors and outcomes differed by time and place. Thus, whereas post-1600 frontier settlement consistently strengthened Burma and Siam, in the eastern littoral the effects were more ambiguous, giving at least temporary support to a distinctly southern Vietnamese identity. So too, Vietnam's reliance on Chinese norms after 1450 provided a uniquely sophisticated administrative model, but it engendered elite–mass tensions without close Theravadin parallel. On the other hand, in both the western and eastern lowlands the relative mildness of postcharter disruptions joined frontier tensions to foster a closer link between ethnicity and political loyalty than in Siam. Likewise, in the Irrawaddy basin and northern Vietnam, maritime stimuli were less consistently influential than in the Chaophraya basin. In short, depending on criteria, one can organize the chief mainland realms (and their less successful competitors) into quite different configurations.

Note finally that if more encompassing systems in 1830 than in 900 were "inevitable," territorial and ethnic boundaries themselves long remained uncertain. In the western mainland, had First Toungoo rulers in the late 1500s made different strategic decisions, the political center of gravity could have remained in Lower rather than Upper Burma and Burman ethnicity would not have eclipsed Mon ethnicity as rapidly as it did. In the central mainland, had Khmer leaders developed a more effective maritime policy, they might have retained control over the Chaophraya basin, and Siam might never have consolidated. In the eastern mainland, without a series of substantially fortuitous events in the late 1700s, I suggested that the 150-year old division between northern and southern Vietnamese territories well might have become permanent.

---

[54] For theoretical perspectives on the relation between spatial integration and internal specialization, see *The Sociology of Georg Simmel* (Glencoe, IL, 1950); Mary Elizabeth Berry, "Was Early Modern Japan Culturally Integrated?," in Lieberman, *Beyond Binary Histories*, 103–37; and esp. the biological analogies in David Christian, *Maps of Time* (Berkeley, 2004), 108, 248–52.

3. SYNCHRONIZED TRAJECTORIES IN MAINLAND SOUTHEAST ASIA, EUROPE, AND JAPAN: A PRELIMINARY SURVEY

Idiosyncrasies

We shift now from Southeast Asia to Eurasia at large. Elements of cyclic-cum-linear integration can be found in many parts of Eurasia, not to mention North and West Africa.[55] But Chapters 2 to 4 focus on western Europe, northeastern Europe, and Japan, because major states in these regions shared with those of continental Southeast Asia a number of developmental features that in combination formed a modestly distinct complex.[56] These features included mid- to late first millennium charter states whose high culture derived from older centers of civilization, prolonged postcharter ruptures, a renewal of political and cultural integration from c. 1450 or 1550, with a marked acceleration in most cases during the 18th and early 19th centuries; long-term protection against both nomadic and seaborne invaders; and, outside Vietnam, relatively good internal communications and/or an economic imbalance that favored the capital over outlying areas. To illustrate these patterns, in western Europe I trace the emergence of France. I could have used England, Spain, Portugal, or Sweden, but French political centrality, the sophistication of French historiography, and a political chronology eerily similar to that of mainland Southeast Asia make it more attractive. To the east, although Austria might have served, I focus on Russia as the most successful, best researched long-term actor. In Asia, Korea offers intriguing parallels, especially to Vietnam.[57]

---

[55] On the assimilation of North Africa to Southwest Asian history, see C. A. Bayly, *Imperial Meridian* (London, 1989), chs. 1, 2; Justin McCarthy, *The Ottoman Turks* (London, 1997). On the relation to Eurasia of West Africa, which saw an extension of cavalry-based empires c. 1100–1500 during the same general period as the European high middle ages and the charter states of Southeast Asia, see George Brooks, *Landlords and Strangers: Ecology, Society and Trade in Western Africa 1000–1630* (Oxford, 1996); McNeill, *Human Web*, 94–101, 150–52.

[56] For documentation of claims in this section, see Chs. 2–4 *infra*.

[57] These parallels include Han conquest, 10th-century (re)unification, 13th- to 14th-century political rupture, 15th-century revival accompanied by Neo-Confucian social and political reforms and curbs on Buddhism, and cumulative, if uneven, commercial and agricultural intensification from the late 1300s to the mid-1800s. In turn post-1600 economic growth nourished social mobility, popular culture, and a heightened sense of Korea as an independent polity. See Martina Deuchler, *The Confucian Transformation of Korea* (Cambridge, MA, 1992); Hochol Lee, "Agriculture as a Generator of Change in Late Choson Korea," in Anthony Reid, ed., *The Last Stand of Asian Autonomies* (New

Possibly too the Himalayan foothills could have provided useful analogies, but I examine Japan, because its historiography is most developed. Thus I consider six examples – Burma, Siam, Vietnam, France, Russia, and Japan – of sustained, essentially indigenous-led consolidation during roughly a thousand years.

Obviously, even this select category contained enormously diverse integrative potentials. If all these polities, Russia aside, by the 19th century controlled territories in the same order of magnitude,[58] populations and geographies differed substantially. Whether because of tropical disease, generally poor soils, or low ratios of arable-to-nonarable land, each Southeast Asian realm in 1800 probably held only between 4,000,000 and 7,000,000 people, a number that could not possibly support urban, commercial, or information networks comparable to those in more densely settled regions.[59] Mainland Southeast Asia's north–south mountain ranges and rugged interior further lowered the ceiling for economic synergy, political integration, and cultural diffusion of all sorts. By contrast, France, Japan, and Russia in 1800 each had between 28,000,000 and 42,000,000 people. With at least four major rivers, no major mountain barriers, and an elaborate urban grid, France faced relatively modest problems of communication and political control. What is more, France benefited from exceptionally dense pan-European systems of trade and communications. Whereas in interior Southeast Asia in 1830 pagan hill people were still defying incorporation into lowland political and religious systems, their "raw" counterparts in the Alps and Pyrenees had been "cooked" for several centuries. Although the Japanese islands lacked large navigable rivers and easy external access, those islands, especially from the 16th century, also boasted dense trade networks and a transport/communication axis along the Inland Sea–Kanto corridor that favored economic and political integration. The vastness of the Russian plain and Siberia carried more obvious centrifugal dangers, but these were offset by riverine communications (whether

---

York, 1997), 103–31; James Palais, *Confucian Statecraft and Korean Institutions* (Seattle, 1996), esp. 3–121; Yi Tae-jin, "The Influence of Neo-Confucianism on 14th-16th Century Korean Population Growth," *Korean Journal* 37 (1997): 5–23.

[58] In 1820, Burma exercised some degree of authority over 730,000 square kilometers; Siam, 900,000; Vietnam, 330,000; continental France, 540,000; and Japan, 320,000. However, Russia in 1820 controlled some 18,000,000 square kilometers.

[59] *SP*, 175–76, 295, 420, 438–39; *AC*, vol. I, 13, 14. Chris Baker and Pasuk Phongpaichit, *A History of Thailand* (Cambridge, 2005), 23–24 offer a yet lower population estimate for Siam of 1–2,000,000 in 1800, but they provide no evidence.

by sled in winter or by boat),[60] by the heavy concentration of people and wealth in the western part of the Muscovite and Romanov empires, and by Russia's dramatically improved post-1700 access to European military and administrative technologies.

Reinforcing geographic and demographic differences were widely discrepant cultural and social models, inevitable given these regions' substantial isolation from one another. At least through the mid-16th century Russia's Tatar heritage and Orthodox identity distinguished it from central and western Europe. In the 18th century, Europe at large had only the most circumscribed contact with Japan or mainland Southeast Asia. Nor, although they traded in the 17th century and although both were in some sense Buddhist, did mainland Southeast Asia and Japan enjoy regular intercourse. Within Southeast Asia itself, Indic societies remained surprisingly insulated from Sinicized Vietnam.

In combination, such features yielded critical differences in political form and penetration. If we modify Charles Tilly's European schema to construct a Eurasian continuum from market-intensive, capital-rich to market-deficient, coercion-rich societies, among the six realms under review we find that France, where serfdom effectively disappeared by 1500 (some would say 1150) and where markets increasingly underpinned state operations, lay closest to the former pole. Despite commercial growth in Russia, Burma, and Siam, in 1800 these three realms were still thinly populated and substantially dependent on conscripted or hereditary bound labor for private production and government service; as such they represented a more market-deficient path. Japan and Vietnam lay somewhere in between.[61] In terms of territorial administration, whereas France in 1810 supported an increasingly Weberian

---

[60] Although the major Siberian rivers flow north into the Arctic Sea, Russians crossed Siberia by following their east–west tributaries.

[61] I thus alter the paradigm in Tilly, *Coercion, Capital*, in two important ways: a) In a purely European context, Tilly places France not at one pole, but intermediate between the coercion-dependent path of Russia and the capital-dependent path of the Dutch Republic, Venice, and other city states. b) Tilly's terminology, contrasting "capital-intensive" with "coercion-intensive" states (e.g., p. 28), is somewhat misleading because it suggests greater per capita use of physical force – executions, whippings, torture, military cantonment – in Russia than in France, when in fact, if we could somehow quantify such phenomena, conditions may have been similar, at least in the 17th century. In truth, Tilly's intended distinction is between "market-intensive" and "market-deficient" societies. In the latter, labor of necessity was supplied primarily through conscription, hereditary obligation, and community self-policing. Insofar as Russian and Southeast Asian peasants found hereditary involvement in systems of communal labor the best in a series of bad options, dependency could be entirely voluntary, and physical force,

bureaucracy with three levels of appointed officials in all departments between Paris and the frontiers,[62] Burma and Siam remained solar polities, with patrimonial rather than bureaucratic norms, usually only one layer of appointees even in the central lowlands, and authority over distant tributaries ebbing so gradually as to preclude any notion of fixed frontiers. So far as we can tell, ratios of appointed officials to subjects and of government income to total output were always far lower in Southeast Asia than in France. With some 265 *daimyo* domains, hereditarily ruled principalities in Tokugawa Japan were yet more numerous than in Burma or Siam. Notwithstanding bureaucratic tendencies in internal administration, for most of the period from 1620 to 1802, Vietnam, divided between warring regimes, represented an extreme of territorial fragmentation.

To complicate further Eurasian comparisons, lest one assume that integration in different spheres of activity necessarily correlated, consider that in 1750 Vietnam and Japan were among the most politically decentralized realms, but in ethnic and cultural terms, among the most unified. Among Southeast Asian states in 1820, Siam was the least uniform culturally but the most powerful militarily. In the late 1700s, the Burmese throne was keenly interested in local religious observance but unable to provide up-to-date military forces. In Russia, official priorities were reversed.

Shared Indices of Integration: Territorial, Administrative, and Cultural Trends

In short, we are dealing with deeply idiosyncratic societies. How extraordinary, how puzzling, how demanding of explanation, then, is the fact that all these realms, ranged around the edges of Eurasia and enjoying little or no contact, should have followed broadly comparable integrative trajectories at roughly the same time. Clearly, I do not pretend that the structures or concentrations of power that grew out

---

as opposed to social obligation, was not necessarily central to the political economy. I have benefited from discussions with Valerie Kivelson. See discussion in Ch. 3 *infra*.

[62] Ideal-type Weberian bureaucratic features include a clear chain of command, codified job descriptions, specialized training, full-time vocation, cash salaries, meritocratic preferment, and continuous monitoring. Cf. Max Weber, *Economy and Society*, Guenther Roth and Claus Wittich, eds., 2 vols. (Berkeley, 1978), vol. II, ch. 11; Clive Church, *Revolution and Red Tape* (Oxford, 1981); Isser Woloch, *The New Regime* (New York, 1994).

of these processes were very similar. I do claim, however, that within each region, *judged by local standards*, political and cultural cohesion in 1830 exceeded that in 1600, which exceeded that in 1400, and so forth. In every region, *judged again by local standards*, political and cultural networks in 1830 were unprecedentedly extensive and, other side of the same coin, internally specialized. Innumerable local specificities did not preclude overarching parallels in trajectory, process, and chronology.

To demonstrate these claims, I shall sketch for Russia, France, and Japan, first, the same indices of consolidation as I just used for Southeast Asia, namely territorial unification, administrative centralization, and cultural homogenization; and second, the dynamics of integration. In each Eurasian region I focus on survivors, on states left standing, because I am interested in long-term integration. *En passant* this volume, like Volume 1, also considers the misfortunes of cannibalized states – Chiang Mai, Cambodia, Champa, Tver, Lithuania, Burgundy, Brittany, some *daimyo* domains – whose flesh fed the victors. Because expansion and contraction were two aspects of the same zero-sum game, if one were to trace territorial fluctuations not among victors, but losers, the similarities I am about to describe between far-flung Eurasian regions would be no less pronounced. A consideration of failed states reminds us, finally, that the coherence of local units to form Burma, Siam, Russia, France, and so forth was in no sense preordained and that different territorial configurations remained a live possibility well into the 15th or 16th century.

What parallels, then, do we find between Southeast Asia, northwestern Eurasia, and the Japanese isles? At roughly the same time as charter states began to cohere in mainland Southeast Asia, that is to say during the second half and more especially the last third of the first millennium, the Frankish/Carolingian kingdom redrew the map of western Europe, the Kievan federation arose in Russia, and the charter *ritsuryo* order took hold in Japan. Much as Dai Viet grew out of the collapse of the Tang empire, the Frankish kingdom devolved indirectly from Rome. By contrast, Kiev and *ritsuryo* Japan – like Pagan and Angkor – had never been incorporated into a distant imperium. The latter four societies owed their civilizing impulse not to imperial conquest but to commercial, diplomatic, or military contacts with external powers, in the case of Kiev with Byzantium, in the case of Japan with Tang China and Korea, in the case of Pagan and Angkor with India and Sri Lanka. Nonetheless, lying on the periphery of established civilizations and lacking indigenous literacy, all six regions imported from older Eurasian centers (South Asia, China, the Mediterranean) systems of writing, world religions, and legal and administrative concepts that helped to generate what Barbara Price terms "secondary states."[63] All charter polities climaxed a halting process of local consolidation and experiment that began in the early or mid-first millennium c.e.[64] Charter consolidation was therefore more hesitant and experimental than later efforts at integration, precisely because, by definition, there was no local blueprint. No less axiomatic, each claimed an unprecedentedly extensive regional territory,[65] although by later standards such authority was superficial, unstable, and – outside the sprawling Frankish empire – spatially limited. All relied on religious institutions to provide sacerdotal power and literate skills and, Kiev apart, to serve as nodes of social control and agrarian reclamation.[66] All six realms tolerated a vast gap between literate elites who prided themselves on participation in universal religious domains and illiterate, localized, substantially animist rural populations. Finally, because their religious, dynastic, and territorial traditions were accepted as normative, all provided an inspirational charter – hence my designation – for subsequent generations.

In timing and effects, the disintegration of these six polities varied considerably. One of the earliest of our charter polities to cohere, the territorially impressive but administratively shallow Frankish/Carolingian kingdom, was also first to disintegrate, in this case in the mid- to late 9th century. In its western sector the Frankish/Carolingian empire was reincarnated in the Capetian kingdom, which rested on more solid foundations and achieved considerable success between c. 1110 and the early 1300s, only to founder amidst a multifaceted

---

63 Barbara Price, "Secondary State Formation: An Explanatory Model," in Ronald Cohen and Elman Service, eds., *Origins of the State* (Philadelphia, 1978), 161–86. Cf. the distinction between "primary" and "secondary" civilizations in Bruce Trigger, *Understanding Early Civilizations* (Cambridge, 2003), 28–29; Christopher Scarre and Brian Fagan, *Ancient Civilizations* (Upper Saddle River, NJ, 2003), 10–11; and n. 154 *infra*.

64 On precharter Southeast Asia, n. 22 *supra*; Hudson and Lustig, "Communities of the Past"; Charles Higham, *The Archaeology of Mainland Southeast Asia* (Cambridge, 1989). Kiev's late 10th-century ascendancy built on 8th-century Viking transformations. Competition among Frankish kingdoms started in the late 400s and climaxed with Carolingian triumphs in the 770s. In Japan *ritsuryo* consolidation c. 670–900 capped statemaking experiments that began c. 200–400 c.e.

65 I exclude comparisons with the supraregional Roman and Chinese empires from which the Vietnamese and Frankish states ultimately derived.

66 In Kiev, where the chief monasteries were urban, monastic landholding was insignificant. However, in the 14th century northeast Russian monasteries, aided by princely tax immunities, spearheaded reclamation and accumulated substantial estates.

European crisis from the mid-14th century to the mid-15th century. An "administrative cycle" I define as a three-part oscillation from a phase of growing territorial and political integration, to a phase of maximum integration, to a phase of territorial fragmentation and political collapse. By this definition, between c. 508, when Clovis in effect founded the early Frankish kingdom in northern Gaul, and the 1420s, when French royal fortunes during the Hundred Years War reached their nadir, the lands that would become France experienced two major administrative cycles.[67]

By comparison, the history of Japan's charter polity was exceedingly placid. Although maturing at roughly the same time as the Frankish kingdom, that is to say, the 7th and 8th centuries, Japan's Heian (Kyoto)-centered political order experienced a glacial devolution that began in the late 1200s, accelerated in the mid-1300s, but did not finally consume central authority until 1467. Thus, one could argue, from c. 600 to the late 15th century the Japanese islands knew but a single extended cycle. Japanese development was more leisurely both because demographic and economic growth to c. 1280 was anemic, and because Japan, unlike France, faced no external military threat.[68] Late charter experiences in

---

[67] Precisely because the Merovingian period, c. 500–720, was one of more or less endemic polycentrism, I prefer to see those centuries as the first phase of the charter cycle, rather than as a complete administrative cycle in their own right. By this reckoning, the first French cycle extended roughly from c. 500 to c. 890, whereas the second extended from c. 1110 to 1428. One could argue that the second cycle ended in 1346–1356, with French defeats at Crecy and Poitiers, but in the 1420s French prospects were arguably more dire. Cf. Christopher Allmand, *The Hundred Years War* (Cambridge, 1989), ch. 1; Geary, *Myth of Nations*, 136–41; and Ch. 2 *infra*. The often overworked term "crisis" I define as a period of pervasive, acute uncertainty that prefigures a sustained attempt to assert control and to resolve anxieties. Cf. J. B. Shank, "Crisis," *AHR* 113 (2008): 1090–99.

[68] This thesis of a single prolonged cycle assumes that neither the Genpei War, 1180–1185, nor the period of north–south wars, 1336–1368/1392, qualified as a period of "territorial fragmentation, political and institutional collapse," the first because recent scholarship minimizes the institutional significance of the Genpei War, the second because the Ashikaga shogunate remained militarily and politically dominant throughout most of the 14th century. If, however, one were to define both of these episodes as genuine interregna, one could argue that pre-1550 Japan had three administrative cycles: a) the *ritsuryo*/Heian cycle, c. 600–1180, b) the Kamakura cycle, c. 1192–1333, and c) the early Ashikaga cycle, c. 1338–1467. The prolonged civil wars and severe institutional dislocations of 1467–1603 engendered a period of recentralization from the mid-1500s that culminated in the Tokugawa shogunate. Without getting bogged down in semantic squabbles, the larger point is that – *in contrast to patterns elsewhere* – each political dislocation in Japan until the general collapse of the late 1400s was more severe and prolonged than the previous dislocation. This pattern, to repeat, was largely the result

Kiev, Pagan, Angkor, and Dai Viet stood somewhere between those of France and Japan. Along with Japan but in contrast to France, before 1470 Kiev and each Southeast Asian realm knew only one complete administrative cycle culminating in a generalized collapse. But as in France, so too in Kiev and Southeast Asia external invasions contributed directly to these breakdowns.

These, then, were significant differences in pre-1470 patterns of devolution. Alongside such distinctions I would note four overarching similarities. First, in all six realms, political collapse reflected the interaction of long-standing institutional weaknesses with the destabilizing effects of economic growth, aggravated in some cases by postcharter climatic deterioration. As I have already noted for Southeast Asia but as was also true in varying degrees for Kiev, post-1280 Japan, and Carolingian and Capetian France, economic expansion – rather counterintuitively – was politically debilitating because it strengthened provincial authorities at the expense of the imperial court, widened access to literate skills and wealth once monopolized by imperial elites, and in several cases created severe and growing land shortages. Second, compared to later crises, disorders attending charter breakdown were unusually disruptive. Typically these disorders lasted two to three times longer than the next period of fragmentation;[69] inflicted unequaled physical and in some cases demographic damage; opened the way (outside Japan) to alien penetration; promoted fundamental administrative, social, and in some cases religious change; and helped shift the political center of gravity, temporarily or permanently, from charter heartlands to former peripheries (e.g., from Upper to Lower Burma, from Angkor to Ayudhya and Phnom Penh, from Kiev to the northwest and northeast, from Japan's Heian region to the Kanto plain).[70] Third, for reasons to be considered later, five of six charter breakdowns (all except the Carolingian) occurred in the same period, 1240–1470. If we include France's second fragmentation, ushered in by the Hundred Years War and the Black

---

of lethargic pre-1280 growth and a pacific foreign environment. See discussion in Ch. 4, n. 10 and *passim*.

[69] In the future France this is true whether we consider post-Carolingian collapse, c. 890–1110, or post-Capetian collapse, c. 1337–1428/1453.

[70] And yet more briefly, from Dong Kinh to Than Nghe in Vietnam. In northern France, from at least the 6th century the political center of gravity remained in or near the Paris basin, but there too we find major postcharter geopolitical shifts insofar as the emergent Capetian kingdom embraced only the western sector of the old Carolingian empire.

Death of 1337–1350, the ubiquity of the 14th- to 15th-century crises becomes yet more pronounced.

Finally, in all six regions territorial consolidation resumed at some point between 1430 and 1600 and continued to gain strength, in the face of fresh challenges, well into the 19th century. As noted, France and Russia along with mainland Southeast Asia experienced in the late 1500s a new breakdown, albeit shorter and less severe than postcharter disorders. This yielded to another phase of consolidation and expansion, which, following a relatively brief collapse in Southeast Asia and France in the late 1700s, ushered in a final round of rapid territorial conquest, imitative reform, and massive, high-stakes competition, namely, the Napoleonic Wars and the Burmese–Siamese–Vietnamese wars. Whereas in mainland Southeast Asia by 1825 these conflicts had reduced the 23 states of 1340 to 3, in Europe by 1900 the 500 more or less independent political units of 1450 had collapsed into some 25.[71] Or to describe the same process from a different angle, in Burma, Siam, Russia, and Japan, territories under central authority in 1825 were 2 to 20 times larger than they were in 1500. For Vietnam, which completed its nominal conquest of Champa by 1471, the increase was limited to about 50 percent, and for France, hemmed in by coalitions on the continent, only some 25 percent. On the other hand, if we were to include New World acquisitions (omitted in Figure 1.8), French territories in 1758 would be over three times larger than they were in 1500.

Figures 1.4 to 1.9 seek to capture these tendencies toward a) long-term territorial consolidation, with a notable acceleration in most cases after 1450/1500 and again in the late 1700s and early 1800s, and b) progressively milder periods of fragmentation, as indicated by the decreasing amplitude and length of successive breakdowns (outside Japan).

Given the symbiosis of territorial consolidation and administrative centralization, it is hardly surprising that both processes exhibited a similar rhythm and that administrative evolution in different realms followed broadly comparable trajectories.

As in Southeast Asia, charter polities in northern Europe and Japan tended to be superficial, personalistic, partially dependent on religious institutions for local control, and content with a largely ritualistic overlordship. No less familiar, the longevity of Kiev, the Frankish kingdom,

---

[71] Charles Tilly, ed., *The Formation of National States in Western Europe* (Princeton, 1975), 15, 24; Jones, *European Miracle*, 106. It should be noted, however, that the great majority of European states that disappeared were within the Holy Roman Empire.

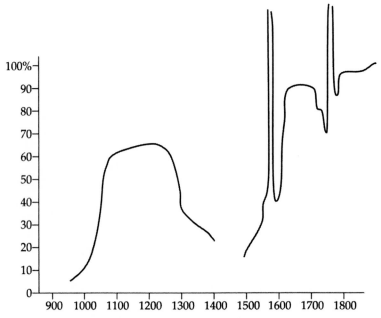

Figure 1.4. Territorial consolidation in western mainland Southeast Asia. This chart shows the amount of territory controlled by the dominant regional power between 900 and 1824. The number of square kilometers held by that power in 1824 defines the 100-percent level on the vertical axis, with earlier formations represented as a percentage of that 1824 figure. Thus, for example, because the empire of Pagan at its peak in the mid-1200s controlled some two-thirds as much territory as the Kon-baung empire in 1824, the graph for 1250 stands at about 67 percent. This same format underlies Figures 1.5 to 1.9 as well. The 15th-century gap in this figure corresponds to the period between the decline of Ava and the rise of Toungoo. Especially in the early periods in this and in Figures 1.5 to 1.9, fluid, overlapping, often ill-defined frontier loyalties make precise territorial calculations difficult. *Sources*: Victor Lieberman, *Strange Parallels: Southeast Asia in Global Context, c. 800–1830. Volume 1: Integration on the Mainland* (Cambridge, 2003), Ch. 2; idem, *Burmese Administrative Cycles* (Princeton, 1984), chs. 1, 4, 5.

and *ritsuryo* Japan owed much to their acceptance of extensive local autonomy, most pronounced of course in outlying areas, and to the monopoly on literacy and high culture that insulated central elites from popular challenges.

For most of the period under review, states remained concentric ring systems, that is, closely administered cores surrounded by provinces whose autonomy increased with distance. If Southeast Asian solar polities represented unusually decentralized versions, this basic description

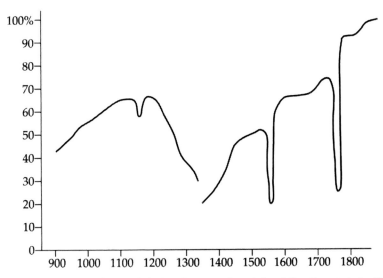

Figure 1.5. Territorial consolidation in central mainland Southeast Asia. The 14th-century gap represents the period separating the decline of Angkor from the early success of Ayudhya. *Source*: Lieberman, *Strange Parallels, Volume 1,* Ch. 3.

applies as well to *ancien régime* France, Muscovy, and Tokugawa Japan. The principal point is that in each polity, after postcharter consolidation resumed, we find a long-term if halting tendency for peripheral zones and autonomous enclaves to assimilate to the status of intermediate or core provinces, and for systems of extraction and coordination in the core to grow more specialized and efficient. In other words, although French resource extraction was far more reliable than Burmese, at a workable level of abstraction the conversion of outlying *pays d'etats* to the status of inner *pays d'elections* paralleled the conversion of Burmese tributary states to appointed governorships.

In this extension of central control, moreover, loosely comparable strategies were at work. In the early stages, centralization normally entailed not the destruction but the subordination of outlying courts and institutions, whose loyalty the capital ensured by appointing senior personnel and/or by subordinating those bodies to an overarching network of royal agencies. If in the short term this mosaic strategy severely limited integration, it reduced the financial costs for the capital and the psychological costs for outlying populations. Moreover, in the long term, central institutions, including new governorships, financial organs, and military agencies, could proliferate as resources permitted

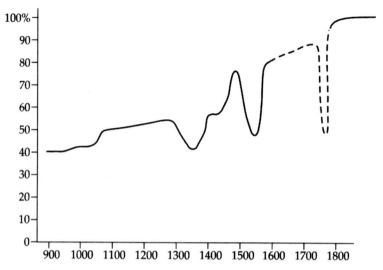

Figure 1.6. Territorial consolidation in eastern mainland Southeast Asia. The dashed line corresponds to the period of division between rival Vietnamese regimes, chiefly the Trinh and Nguyen, followed by the Tayson and the Nguyen. For most of the period c. 1620 to 1744 the Trinh in the north and the Nguyen in the south shared a nominal loyalty to the Le Dynasty. *Source*: Lieberman, *Strange Parallels, Volume 1*, Ch. 4.

and circumstances demanded. Animating and complementing institutional elaboration were expanded systems of patronage. Even in *ancien régime* France, royal officials typically sought not to destroy private patronage, rather to coordinate and manage it through new offices, tax privileges, and concessions of all sorts. By impelling Darwinian flight from earlier weaknesses, interregna often proved extremely creative in promoting such changes. Everywhere between 1450 and 1550, in the aftermath of prolonged disorders, new patronage and fiscal systems improved territorial coordination. Everywhere outside Vietnam in the early 1600s,[72] and everywhere save Japan in the late 1700s and early 1800s, energetic postcrisis central leaderships further strengthened their influence over outlying dependencies.

---

[72] In Vietnam in the early 1600s the Nguyen broke free from northern control, but within its own expanding territory exhibited much of the same institutional creativity and territorial vigor as new dynasties elsewhere; *SP*, 406–19. In Japan, although the country fragmented from 1467 to 1603, local *daimyo* administrations greatly improved administrative/military efficiency and through widening inter-*daimyo* coalitions lay the foundations for the Tokugawa achievement.

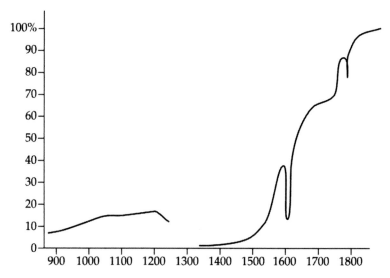

Figure 1.7. Territorial consolidation in Russia. The late-13th-century gap represents the interregnum between the collapse of Kiev and the rise of Moscow. As a relatively short-lived empire whose center of gravity lay outside the Russian heartland, the Mongol empire is excluded. *Sources*: Jerome Blum, *Lord and Peasant in Russia* (Princeton, 1961); John Channon, *The Penguin Historical Atlas of Russia* (London, 1995); Janet Martin, *Medieval Russia 980–1584* (Cambridge, 1995); Martin Gilbert, *Atlas of Russian History* (UK, 1972).

During the charter and immediate postcharter eras, lay authorities in each polity were only too willing to permit religious institutions extensive autonomy and resources, not least because religious networks compensated for as yet weak secular powers of social control. But as the state grew more competent, lay authorities in each realm moved to claim much of that authority and untaxed wealth. Increasingly effective curbs on monastic landholding and religious personnel in Vietnam after c. 1400, in Burma, Siam, Russia, and Japan after c. 1550 or 1600, and insistent French royal claims on church wealth to 1789 illustrate this trend. Thereafter Revolutionary France became unique, surely, in the physical and ideological violence of its anticlerical assault, but not in the principle of growing state supremacy.

Likewise, especially from the early 1600s, in order both to restore social discipline and to improve the flow of royal taxes and services, central authorities sought to extend censuses and cadastres, to develop new mapping techniques and spatial imaginaries, to augment the number of appointed officials, to cement ties to local elites, and to reduce

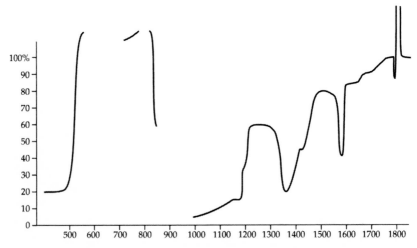

Figure 1.8. Territorial consolidation in France. The gap between the mid-800s and the early 1000s represents the period between Carolingian fragmentation and early Capetian success. Pre-1700 territories refer to the boundaries not of the titular kingdom of France but of the French royal domain. *Sources*: Elizabeth Hallam, *Capetian France 987–1328* (London, 1980); Christopher Allmand, *The Hundred Years War* (Cambridge, 1989); Xavier de Planhol, *An Historical Geography of France* (Cambridge, 1994); Louis Bergeron et al., *Histoire de la France. L'espace Francais* (Paris, 1989); Roland Mousnier, *The Institutions of France Under the Absolute Monarchy 1598–1789. Volume 2: The Organs of State and Society* (Chicago, 1984).

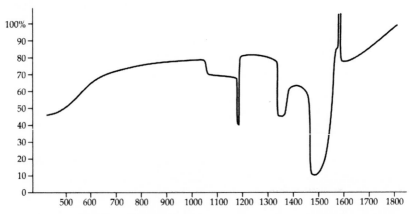

Figure 1.9. Territorial consolidation in Japan. *Sources*: Conrad Totman, *A History of Japan* (Malden, MA, 2000); Bruce Batten, *To the Ends of Japan* (Honolulu, 2003).

rural violence. During the 17th century the elaboration of Russian serf-dom, the aforementioned expansion in the ranks of Burmese servicemen (*ahmu-dans*) and Siamese royal workers (*phrai luang*), Tokugawa curbs on social and geographic mobility, and French Counter-Reformation controls testified to this regulatory trend. In virtually every case, the ensuing increase in central operations, particularly as they focused on revenue and military functions, joined wider literacy to promote written communications, more routinized procedures, and more specialized administrative organs, as well as the ceremonial elevation of the ruler vis-à-vis provincial magnates.

As in Southeast Asia, so in those territories that cohered as Japan, France, and Russia we also find sustained movements toward vertical and horizontal integration of culture, that is to say, of language, artistic styles, religious practices, and ultimately, ethnicity. And as in Southeast Asia, cultural integration, being substantially dependent on barely visible capillary processes, tended to be more gradual and continuous than territorial and administrative consolidation.

In Japan, according to Barbara Ruch, the most prominent feature of postcharter culture was an unprecedented melding of hitherto distinct subcultures, including the vigorous popularization of Buddhism and the diffusion of selected aristocratic and warrior practices among merchants, prosperous farmers, and low-level clerics.[73] Notwithstanding Tokugawa efforts to impede cross-class diffusion, literacy and learning continued to spread among *samurai*, townsmen, and well-to-do peasants, spurred by new schools, trade circuits, commercial publishing, and urban sites of interclass exchange, until in the realm of intellectual production the gap between *samurai* and wealthy commoners virtually disappeared. The Tokugawa period produced an ever more protean demotic literature printed in *kana*, which adapted Chinese characters to express local speech in a fashion loosely comparable to Vietnamese *nom* scripts. Such works combined with popular travel, new markets, and commercial maps to foster a more inclusive Japanese horizontal consciousness, defined implicitly or explicitly vis-à-vis Chinese, Europeans, or Ainu. This consciousness remained insufficiently theorized, too limited spatially and socially, too compromised by Sinic and Buddhist universalism, with an insufficiently visible external "other," to support what I would recognize as "national" identity. Yet by 1830

[73] Barbara Ruch, in *CHJ*, vol. III, ch. 12, esp. 501.

not only was *samurai* culture across the islands substantially uniform, but the spoken dialect, writing, and fashions of Edo set the standard for growing numbers of educated peasants and provincial townsmen.

In France, a polyglot empire whose *pays* and seigneuries long retained their own customs and laws, as late as 1789, by one estimate, only a third of the population regarded Parisian French as their primary language. Yet as in Japan, slowly in the middle ages and accelerating from the late 15th or 16th century, cultural usages from the capital region diffused outward, even as they imbibed provincial traditions. Thus Parisian French moved south along trade arteries on either side of the Massif Central, ousting regional languages in elite speech and local publications. So too, in the spheres of high culture and administration, vernacular French languages, Parisian dialect in particular, displaced Latin, whose waning fortunes, I suggested, paralleled the displacement of Pali, Sanskrit, and (less markedly) Chinese in Japan and in Southeast Asia. Tied to a host of practices ranging from dress, deportment, and literature to nuptiality, Parisian dialect became in effect the key to participation in kingdom-wide culture. Meanwhile within each region of France, schools, migrations, and new commercial circuits combined to disseminate elite linguistic and religious practices among progressively lower social strata, both urban and rural.

In Russia as in western and central mainland Southeast Asia, traumatic 13th- and 14th-century dislocations meant that postcharter cultural systems tended to be more novel than their Japanese, French, or Vietnamese equivalents. Yet with broadly familiar chronology and dynamics, from the 14th through the 17th centuries an emergent Great Russian ethnicity became inextricably linked to a deepening sense of popular Orthodoxy and reverence for the Muscovite tsar. Invigorated by the proliferation of rural churches and monasteries, by royal patronage, population growth, frontier settlement, and conflicts with Muslims in the south and with Catholics to the west, Great Russian ethnicity and Orthodox culture came to embrace, with suitable geographic and class emphases, all groups in the Volga–Oka heartland. Thence Russian Orthodox culture expanded to absorb substantial Finno-Ugric, Baltic, non-Russian Slavic, even Tatar populations. Although in 1795 authorities identified only 49 percent of the population within Russia's imperial frontiers as Great Russians, this was undoubtedly far more than the same geographic area contained in 1500. Only after 1550 in the Volga basin, and after 1650 in the eastern Ukraine, the Don and Ural basins, and Siberia, did Great Russians develop a substantial presence, in some areas forming a large majority by 1800.[74]

What were the political and psychological implications of these cultural trends? As in Southeast Asia, at least three factors limited their standardizing, centralizing thrust. First, these trends were too weak in that they breached geographic and social isolates episodically and unevenly, creating identities that in varying degrees were overlapping, labile, and situationally dependent. As Sudipta Kaviraj reminds us, although premodern spaces and groups did have limits, they shaded off into one another far more easily than in our own world.[75] By extension, without sustained supralocal communications and a clear unifying political framework, objective cultural similarities had little political valence.

Second, these trends were too strong insofar as the same dynamics as encouraged amalgamation nurtured countervailing currents. As in Southeast Asia, efforts to impose official culture and royal taxes could stir anticentralizing revolts and self-willed isolation (by French peasant tax protesters, Russian Pugachevists, Japanese *ikki* leaguers). Even where assimilation prevailed, invariably it produced socially and geographically specific recombinations. Moreover, if new communications circuits weakened parochialism, those same circuits could wean local elites away from the religious traditions, even the language, of their own peasantries. As Chinese norms seduced Vietnamese literati, French language and etiquette led Russian nobles to distance themselves from popular culture. Likewise in post-1670 France, by ensnaring elites far more readily than peasants and laborers, the spread of Parisian norms in the provinces widened, at least temporarily, the gap between local notables and the popular classes. Because metropolitan cultures first attracted local elites, such splits were probably inevitable. So too, especially in urban environments, commercial specialization and an interest in novelty per se automatically nurtured diversity, hence potential fracture, in all manner of consumer habits and of aesthetic and intellectual expression.

---

[74] See Janet Hartley, *A Social History of the Russian Empire* (London, 1999), 7–16 and Ch. 4 *infra*.

[75] Sudipta Kaviraj, "Writing, Speaking, Being," in Dagmar Hellmann-Rajanayagam and Dietmar Rothermund, eds., *Nationalstaat und Sprachkonflikte in Sud-und-sudostasien* (Stuttgart, 1992), 40.

Third, in France at least to the mid-1700s and elsewhere to the end of the period under review, official ideologies in varying degrees remained committed to cosmopolitan over national ideals and to social hierarchy over horizontal unity. Governments continued to conceptualize their authority in primarily dynastic and religious terms that were ostensibly universalist and often indifferent to secular culture. Muscovy's raison d'être was to promote Orthodoxy. The French sovereign styled himself the Most Christian King. Tokugawa intellectuals blended Neo-Confucian and Mahayana with Shinto beliefs. As defenders of universal doctrine, Theravada and Christian rulers, in particular, prided themselves on the diversity of their subject territories, which they annexed in blissful disregard of local culture. At the same time, as guarantors of morally sanctioned social hierarchy, governments felt compelled to prescribe sumptuary insignia, to enforce estate barriers, and thus to oppose, passively if not actively, the notion of generic subject possessed of a standard culture.

And yet in Russia, France, and Japan as in mainland Southeast Asia, not only did universal ideologies coexist with an intensifying, if undertheorized, emphasis on secular culture, but in many contexts ethnic and religious loyalties proved mutually reinforcing. The fact that Muscovites, by definition, were Orthodox while their chief enemies (Poles, Swedes, Tatars) were non-Orthodox encouraged a persistent, if imperfect, fusion of ethnicity, religion, and political loyalty reminiscent of that which divided Khmers and Vietnamese. If the Japanese faced no obvious external enemy, Tokugawa advocates of "nativist learning" (*kokugaku*) nonetheless sought to cultivate a sense of Japanese alterity and superiority to China (and later to Western powers). Catholic universalism proved quite compatible with a conviction that France was the "eldest son of the church" and with pride in French cultural leadership. Louis XIV's motto "un roi, une loi, une foi" was simultaneously an expression of Counter-Reformation fervor and of protonational aspiration. By the same token, although hierarchy surely was inimical to citizenship, it is a modernist conceit to imagine that citizenship was indispensable to community. Not only those Burmese of diverse backgrounds who rallied to Kon-baung kings in struggles against Lower Burma and Siam, but Russians in the Time of Troubles (1598–1613), Frenchmen during recurrent wars with England, and even Japanese *kokugaku*-partisans in the absence of war had no difficulty conceiving of political community as an assemblage of status groups, each with unique privileges and obligations but all dependent on the state to protect their special rights and their common security.[76]

Pressures to Integration

In sum, as in each of mainland Southeast Asia's three principal corridors, so in Russia, Japan, and France after 1500 and more especially 1700, central territories expanded, administrations grew more coherent, and cultures, more uniform. But what dynamics were at work in Europe and Japan? As with Southeast Asia, I shall treat in turn economic factors, cultural forces, military pressures, and state initiatives.[77]

In considering economics, again it is necessary at the outset to emphasize divergent contexts. Vietnam apart, mainland Southeast Asian population densities in 1800 were only 4 to 10 percent those of Japan and France, which limited technical experiment, commercial exchange, and urbanism alike. According to Gilbert Rozman's schema of urban networks, between 1400 and 1800 France, Japan, and Russia all advanced to the highest level of urban/commercial integration, Stage G ("national marketing"). By contrast, Burma, Siam, and Vietnam probably moved only from Stage D ("imperial city") to Stage E ("standard marketing") or possibly Stage F ("intermediate marketing").[78] So too, in Southeast Asia and Russia, the central importance of bound labor, the corresponding weakness of wage labor, the alien ethnicity of merchant enterprise, historically high interest rates, the weakness (or utter absence) of

[76] See Victor Lieberman, "Ethnic Politics in 18th-Century Burma," *MAS* 12 (1978): 455–82, and Chs. 2–4 *infra*.

[77] Cf. the triptych of Marxist models, bellical models, and cultural models for European state formation discussed in Gorski, *Disciplinary Revolution*, ch. 1.

[78] Gilbert Rozman, *Urban Networks in Russia, 1750–1800, and Premodern Periodization* (Princeton, 1976), esp. 33–40, 84–87; *SP*, 148, 177–78, 295. In Rozman's Stage D ("imperial city"), only two to four levels of central places were present, urban population was concentrated in one city, and administrative, rather than commercial, needs dominated urban maturation. With four or five levels of central places, Stage E ("standard marketing") saw an increase in secondary cities, the appearance of periodic markets far removed from administrative centers, and a growing penetration of market forces on the village level. Nonetheless, administrative forces remained dominant in the capital, and intermediate markets were still relatively undeveloped. Stage F ("intermediate marketing") had five or six levels of central places, whereas Stage G ("national marketing") had seven. The latter included more standard marketing towns, which fed new intermediate market towns, which fed larger and more numerous regional cities, which fed the national capital. After Stage E, urban development responded primarily to commercial rather than administrative forces.

banking, and restrictions on land alienation[79] were symptomatic of market systems less complex or integrated than those in western Europe or Japan. Neither in Russia nor Southeast Asia is there particularly strong evidence of the consumer revolution that figures prominently in early modern Japanese, Chinese, and European historiography.[80] Moreover, no Asian society under review had access to frontier resources on anything like the scale of Siberia or the New World, which, along with modest levels of technical innovation, helps to explain why the economy of Japan and possibly Burma lost steam in the late 1700s.

That said, all six realms with which we are concerned experienced cumulative if episodic increases in population, output, and market specialization. Within the boundaries of 1820, between 1300 and 1820 the population of France rose roughly 75 percent, those of Burma and Siam perhaps 100 percent, that of Vietnam some 133 percent, of Japan 433 percent, and of Russia perhaps 900 percent.[81] Everywhere frontier reclamation encouraged extensive growth, but population increase also could enhance per capita productivity, as for example, where such increase permitted the creation of more intensive irrigation networks, led to the opening of areas with novel agricultural or mineral resources, or by swelling demand, raised the rewards for crop and handicraft specialization.[82] Different socioeconomic structures aside, all six realms provide evidence of long-term Smithian specialization and at least limited progress at the margins of technology. Symptom and cause of intensification were trial-and-error improvements in crops, cultivation methods, and transport. Technical and organizational change was not autonomous insofar as it responded to production bottlenecks or higher demand, which in turn might reflect population pressures, political

---

[79] Cf. *SP*, 160, 298; van Zanden, "Road to Industrial Revolution," 342–43, 346, citing archipelagic and Siamese data; Richard Hellie, *The Economy and Material Culture of Russia 1600–1725* (Chicago, 1999), 636.

[80] Pomeranz, *Great Divergence*, ch. 3; Craig Clunas, *Superfluous Things* (Cambridge, MA, 1991); Susan Hanley, *Everyday Things in Premodern Japan* (Berkeley, 1997); Daniel Roche, *A History of Everyday Things* (Cambridge, 2000); Maxine Berg and Elizabeth Eger, eds., *Luxury in the Eighteenth Century* (New York, 2003); Carlo Marco Belfanti, "Was Fashion a European Invention?" *JGH* 3 (2008): 419–43.

[81] For Southeast Asian figures, *SP*, 52, 175–76, 420; on France and Japan, Fig. 4.2 *infra*. Whereas Russia's 1820 population is reliably put at approximately 50,000,000, for the 14th and 15th centuries we have widely varying estimates. See Hartley, *Social History*, 9; Robert Crummey, *The Formation of Muscovy 1304–1613* (London, 1987), 2–3; Richard Hellie, *Enserfment and Military Change in Muscovy* (Chicago, 1971), 305.

[82] Cf. n. 41 *supra*.

crises, or resource depletion. Nonetheless, an increased stock of knowledge permanently transformed each society's production horizon and, along with population increases, helps to account for the cumulative nature of growth and the constantly enhanced mobility of goods and factors of production.

International trade had similar implications. Overland and/or maritime trade expanded in all six realms, particularly from the late 1400s to the early 1600s, and (outside Japan) in the 18th and early 19th centuries. In western Europe and, to a lesser degree, Japan and Southeast Asia, imported foodstuffs and Indian and/or Chinese textiles drew peasant producers to the market, stoking innovation and labor intensification. External contacts also supplied new crops (to which we shall return) as well as bullion and specie, critical to domestic and long-distance trade in all six realms.

Such growth tended to magnify in familiar fashion the political superiority of privileged districts – Southeast Asian lowlands, the Volga–Oka interfluve, the Baltic coast, the Paris basin, the Inland Sea–Kanto axis – over more marginal areas. Even if core and periphery grew at the same pace, the core's initial superiority ensured a self-reproducing absolute advantage, as I have noted for Southeast Asia. Yet, at least to 1650 in most areas, growth in the core exceeded that in outer zones. Furthermore, the development of national markets, which implied a concentration of higher level commercial functions in the capital region, meant that where frontier colonization and overseas trade became a principal engine of growth (as in post-1650 Burma, Siam, Russia, and France), the center retained major benefits. Favored districts could then pyramid their powers both of coercion (military superiority) and attraction (patronage and cultural display).

Not only the scale but the nature of each political economy changed. Wide variations in the extent of commodification notwithstanding, in all six realms we find a gradual movement from subsistence to specialized market production, from in-kind to cash taxes (although in Tokugawa Japan this was limited by rice-based calculation of *samurai* awards), and from land grants to salaries and commercial favors. Everywhere such tendencies became more pronounced from the late 15th and especially in the 18th century. And commonly, such changes helped central authorities to extend their influence. The argument differs from one context to another, but in repeated instances the state's enhanced patronage and regulatory ambition and the growing economic importance of tax revenues, contracts, and market access obliged ambitious provincial notables and peasants to seek alliance with a central apparatus. Thus as in Southeast Asia so in Europe, as S. R. Epstein, William Beik, Sharon Kettering, and Valerie Kivelson have argued, as well as in Japan, one key to centralization lay in the growing inclination of local elites to support, indeed to help create, a coordinating agency that could underwrite privilege, protect long-distance markets, improve commercial regulation, limit transaction costs, simplify jurisdictions, and share tax revenues. In short, centralization was more often a matter of bottom-up initiatives and local–central negotiation than of top-down imposition.[83] More broadly, Steven Pinker has suggested that early modern market integration joined modest improvements in living standards to expand the circle of reciprocity, to magnify the value of human life, and thus to complement efforts by both government officials and religious reformers to pacify society. At least in some West European countries, especially from the early 1600s, such trends produced a sustained reduction in homicides and mayhem.[84]

To be sure, economic and demographic growth could be profoundly destabilizing. By driving minority peoples to rebel against frontier colonization, by stoking price inflation, by allowing population to outstrip good quality land or government posts, by opposing market mobility to hereditary status, economic expansion repeatedly threatened social and political order. In the 13th/14th, late 16th, and late 18th centuries commercial and demographic growth fed political crises in mainland Southeast Asia, France, and Russia alike. From the mid-1700s tension between inherited rank and *arriviste* achievement roiled all six societies. In each case over the long run, however, reforms allowed the central apparatus to harness demographic and economic growth to its own purposes. The cyclic nature of political construction owed much to

---

[83] Epstein, *Freedom and Growth*, esp. chs. 1–3; William Beik, *Absolutism and Society in Seventeenth-Century France* (Cambridge, 1985); Sharon Kettering, *Patrons, Brokers, and Clients in Seventeenth-Century France* (New York, 1986); Valerie Kivelson, *Autocracy in the Provinces* (Stanford, 1996); Philip Brown, *Central Authority and Local Autonomy in the Formation of Early Modern Japan* (Stanford, 1993). A similar emphasis on the role of absolutism in compensating West European nobles for their declining economic power, and in enhancing the role of East European nobles through a "second enserfment" of the peasantry, informs Perry Anderson, *Lineages of the Absolutist State* (London, 1979). See too historiographic discussion at John Hurt, *Louis XIV and the Parlements* (Manchester, 2002), ix–xv.

[84] Steven Pinker, "A History of Violence" (www.edge.org/3rd culture/pinker07/pinker 07 index.html), citing Manuel Eisner, Norbert Elias, Robert Wright, and Peter Singer, and focusing on England and Holland from the early 17th century. Christian, *Maps of Time*, 349 makes a similar point.

this oscillation between institutionally destabilizing economic expansion and postcrisis adjustment.

To the extent that they enhanced popular identification with central norms of language, religion, and ethnicity, I suggested that new cultural currents provided critical, if diffuse, psychological support to political integration. As in Southeast Asia, cultural integration drew strength from central patronage, social emulation, and autonomous religious impulses, as well as from multifaceted economic change, with the latter providing a particularly potent solvent of social and spatial isolates. This was true along agricultural frontiers – in southern Vietnam, southern Russia, northern Japan – where settlers tied more or less closely to imperial culture confronted alien populations. It was yet more obvious in long-settled districts, where towns and fairs served as cultural magnets and where a growing surplus nurtured new trade and communications grids. Of particular significance to cultural circulation, in all six realms (albeit least dramatically in Russia) literacy rose, especially after 1500. Again, pressures were multiple. Governments demanded more local record-keepers. Religious reform could breed a hunger for textual authority. Literacy promised social mobility and relief from tedium. Economic growth provided the wherewithal for schools and teachers, lent numeracy and reading ever greater practical value, and opened paths along which written materials could migrate. Symptom and cause of changing popular attitudes was the appearance, unusually luxuriant in Japan and France but everywhere in bloom by 1700, of kingdom-specific literatures using vernacular languages and/or writing systems. Exploring fictional as well as nonfictional, secular as well as religious themes, and experimenting with an array of genres, early modern writings claimed far wider readerships than charter-era compositions. Ironically, if French and Japanese printing permitted unmatched per capita output of new materials, Theravada monasteries, still reliant on manuscripts, fostered male literacy rates comparable to, if not higher than, those in France and Japan.

Even if they had little ostensible political content, in all six realms local movements of religious socialization also undergirded state formation. Gorski, as noted, argues that the Calvinist "disciplinary revolution," including novel techniques of communal surveillance and a relentless insistence on self-mastery, fostered forms of non-state governance on which more visible official efforts depended. Without Calvinism, the twin political miracles of early modern Europe – Brandenburg–Prussia's assemblage of highly unpromising territories into a military colossus and the Dutch Republic's rise to preeminence despite its surprisingly puny central apparatus – are inexplicable.[85] But, as Gorski concedes, Calvinist reform was merely the most insistent version of a wider early modern shift in European sociability affecting Catholic and Lutheran lands as well. Thus Counter-Reformation France experienced a tightening of clerical regulation, the spread of popular confraternities and sacraments, more demanding systems of poor relief, expanded lay and ecclesiastical roles for women, and a notable expansion in lay education, all of which served to align personal salvation with public discipline, to instill respect for hierarchy without a direct outlay of royal resources, to curb physical assaults, and thus to make governance more feasible.[86] Although at first glance rural isolation, near universal illiteracy, and relative indifference to questions of personal autonomy rendered Russian peasants less promising for this sort of disciplinary revolution than their French counterparts, we shall find that in Muscovy as well during the 16th and 17th centuries, a deepening of popular Orthodox sensibilities joined government tax demands to engender novel systems of communal self-governance and peasant self-policing. These in turn provided a social and attitudinal foundation for serfdom. Likewise in Japan, albeit from an earlier date and with a weaker religious component, corporate villages (*so*) developed an ethic of family obligation and mutual surveillance to curb antisocial behavior and to distribute tax and service burdens. Such self-governing communities became the building blocks of Warring States *daimyo* and Tokugawa power.[87] With due allowance for differences in social categories and effectiveness, these transformations invite comparison with religious socialization in Southeast Asia. In each case, shifts in popular sensibility c. 1500–1830 built on earlier, more elitist projects and thus represented a form of vertical acculturation. Moreover, in each case religious reform complemented state efforts and market inducements to reduce popular violence.

As political systems cohered, as once independent principalities were cannibalized, and as warfare grew in scale and expense, would-be survivors were compelled to overhaul their military, fiscal, and

---

[85] Gorski, *Disciplinary Revolution*, chs. 2, 3.

[86] Ibid., 15–19, 115–37; Luria, *Territories of Grace*; Mack Holt, ed., *Renaissance and Reformation France* (Oxford, 2002), 230–31; and Ch. 3 *infra*. However impressive Prussian and Dutch performances may have been, it is worth remembering that the two most successful European states c. 1550 to 1750 were Catholic Spain and Catholic France.

[87] On Russian and Japanese villages, see Chs. 3, 4.

provincial systems. Although well-nigh universal across Southeast Asia and Europe, military pressures tended to be more sustained in Europe because a) European colonial rivalry and meager intra-European buffer zones magnified opportunities for conflict; b) denser European communications, more mobile mercenaries, and the absence of an internal barrier comparable to the Indic–Sinic divide sped the transmission of best military practices; c) greater commercial and technological sophistication permitted more rapid innovations in firearms manufacture and military training and organization. French administrative overhauls during the Hundred Years War, the Wars of Religion, the wars of Louis XIV, and the Revolutionary–Napoleonic Wars, and a string of Russian reforms from Ivan III (r. 1462–1505) through Peter the Great (r. 1682–1725), testified to the link between warfare and administrative/fiscal reform, a link that demanded attention even in the teeth of economic stagnation.[88]

At least as emphatically as in Southeast Asia, moreover, European war assisted cultural integration by enhancing the need for royal coordination, by mixing youths from different provinces, by encouraging

---

[88] Military pressure to European state formation has inspired a vast literature. For overviews, see Michael Roberts, "The Military Revolution, 1550–1650," reprinted in his *Essays in Swedish History* (London, 1967), setting forth his thesis that in Europe more efficient drill and firepower promoted more ambitious strategies, which mandated larger armies, which in turn encouraged more competent fiscal and administrative institutions and a growing interest in social regulation; Geoffrey Parker, *The Military Revolution* (Cambridge, 1988), arguing *pace* Roberts that the key catalyst to early modern military change was not more ambitious strategies, but the developing science of fortifications; Marshall Poe, *The Russian Moment in World History* (Princeton, 2003); John LeDonne, *The Russian Empire and the World 1700–1917* (New York, 1997); Richard Hellie, *Enserfment and Military Change in Muscovy* (Chicago, 1971); Tilly, *Formation of National States*, idem, *Coercion, Capital*; Brian Downing, *The Military Revolution and Political Change* (Princeton, 1992); Thomas Ertman, *Birth of the Leviathan* (Cambridge, 1997); and sources in Chs. 2, 3 *infra*. For a critique of Tilly, Downing, and Ertman, all of whom seek to explain divergent European constitutional systems by considering the relation of military pressures to local institutions, see Gorski, *Disciplinary Revolution*, 5–15. See too Jeremy Black, *War and the World* (New Haven, 1998); idem, ed., *War in the Early Modern World* (London, 1999); idem, *A Military Revolution?* (Atlantic Highlands, NJ, 1991), esp. 67–82; Guy Rowlands, *The Dynastic State and the Army under Louis XIV* (Cambridge, 2002) and David Parrott, *Richelieu's Army* (Cambridge, 2001). In varying degrees, all three of the latter authors suggest, *pace* earlier research, that more effective civil governance during peacetime was less a consequence than a precondition of army expansion. A close reading of Hellie shows that a similar argument could be made for Russia. However, because the brief eras of peace in Russia and France during the 17th and 18th centuries were widely regarded as preludes to renewed fighting and because military objectives normally informed fiscal experiment, these views modify the chronology of state formation without negating its fundamental sensitivity to military imperatives.

identification with royal norms, and by generating stereotyped images of an alien, minatory "other." If such sentiments were most commonly articulated by the nobility and educated townsmen, sustained conflicts also politicized ethnicity among the popular classes, especially along threatened frontiers, as expressed in songs, prayers, folktales, and public rituals in Russia and France as well as in Burma and Vietnam.

Japan was an exception proving the rule about warfare's centralizing impact: as noted, absence of an external military threat during most of its history contributed to an unusually slow pace of administrative change and, despite dense communication circuits, to a comparatively weak sense of ethnic alterity. Conversely, Japan's period of most rapid administrative change, 1467–1603, was the era of most intense civil war.

Finally, as in Southeast Asia, as administrative capacity grew, each state used that capacity to modify, directly and indirectly, not only its administrative system but its economic and cultural environment. If policy reflected a mix of factors, including court factionalism and autonomous social visions, in the shaping of French and Russian economic policy it is fair to say that military demands were rarely far from the surface. Wars typically absorbed 60 to 90 percent of early modern French and Russian state budgets, and a determination to grow the economy in the interest of national power helps to explain Jean-Baptiste Colbert's mercantilism, Peter the Great's forced industrialization, royal French efforts to upgrade transportation and disseminate technical advances, as well as *laissez faire* policies in both Russia and France from the mid-1700s. "[O]ne cannot help but be struck," Jan de Vries has written of Europe, particularly western Europe, between 1600 and 1750, "by the seemingly symbiotic relationship existing between the state, military power, and the private economy's efficiency."[89]

As in Southeast Asia, consider too the often unintended economic impact of government actions. In Europe and Tokugawa Japan unification and pacification, although preeminently political acts, encouraged trade by linking distant markets, standardizing weights and currency, reducing tolls, and widening judicial jurisdictions. Designed to facilitate official communications and *daimyo* attendance at Edo, Tokugawa road improvements had major commercial spinoffs. By concentrating people and expenditure in capital cities, governments in all six realms, without necessarily planning to do so, offered private producers

---

[89] Jan de Vries, *The Economy of Europe in an Age of Crisis, 1600–1750* (Cambridge, 1976), 242, strongly supported by Tilly, *Coercion, Capital*, esp. ch. 3.

expanded market access. Everywhere cash taxes also had the effect, if not the objective, of boosting commodity production. Much the same could be said of new protections for peasant tenures in 17th-century Burma and Japan.[90] These benefits coexisted with often ruinous effects of other government actions, including wartime impositions and excessive, inequitable taxation.

Similarly, in art, literature, language, dress, and deportment, Paris, Versailles, Moscow, St. Petersburg, Kyoto, and Edo, like Southeast Asian capitals, functioned as arbiters of taste for ambitious provincial elites in ways at times unanticipated. Often the initiative for cultural standardization came not from the throne, content to rule over a polyglot realm, but from provincial figures eager to enhance their prestige by imitating court language and taste. The flow of written documents between provinces and capital could have similar, if unintended, implications. To this must be added the self-consciously integrative effects of official efforts to standardize religious practices, to promote particular literary forms, to unify social hierarchies, and to marginalize communities (Huguenot, Muslim, Cathar, Japanese Christian, Mon, Cham, Khmer) considered politically and/or religiously suspect.

In sum, in France, Russia, Japan as in each of mainland Southeast Asia's three chief sectors, integration reflected a complex synergy between local movements of economic and cultural change, intensifying interstate competition, and wider state interventions. As ties of interdependence and cultural identification grew more dense, polities became more secure, and periods of fragmentation became shorter and less violent. Tethered, the stallion grew accustomed to its restraints.

This is not to claim, of course, that powerful states *never* disappeared, that their legacy was *always* so influential and immediate as to mandate continuous improvements on the original design. Vast realms fragmented permanently once the burden of size exceeded the productivity of the imperial economy, the efficiency of imperial communications, and/or the cohesion of imperial culture.[91] One thinks, for

---

[90] See Epstein, *Freedom and Growth*, ch. 3; and Chs. 3, 4 *infra*. Pomeranz, *Great Divergence*, 194–206 discounts the economic benefits that European warfare provided through technical spillovers, increased demand, and incentives to institutional change. However, he does not address directly the factors I cite, namely, improved pacification, forced industrialization, urban concentration, tax incentives to monetization, and protection of peasant tenures.

[91] See the insights into imperial size in Mark Elvin, *The Pattern of the Chinese Past* (Stanford, 1973), ch. 1. Chs. 5 and 6 *infra* will consider why the Chinese empire, unlike its Roman and Mughal counterparts, proved remarkably durable.

example, of Babylonia, Rome, or the Mongols. Although obviously all left institutional and cultural legacies, those legacies tended to be more diffuse and/or short lived than those of the six charter realms I have sketched. Admittedly, the distinction can be one of degree rather than kind. One could argue, for example, that the 350 years or so that separated Roman decline from early Carolingian vigor were the first in that series of progressively shorter breakdowns that included post-Carolingian disorders, the Hundred Years War, the French Wars of Religion, and the French Revolution. Charlemagne proudly modeled himself on Rome, and Roman law and culture continued to shape French thought to Napoleon and beyond. Nonetheless, in practical terms the religious, institutional, and geopolitical links between the sprawling, Mediterranean-based, pagan Roman empire and the Christian Frankish kingdom were so much more tenuous than those between the Carolingian and Capetian realms as to render Rome's inclusion in the institutional lineage of the French monarchy comparatively artificial.[92] Not surprisingly, except for Russia – whose geography was far more coherent than size alone suggests – all six post-900 realms under review were of modest size.

The combination of accelerating post-1450 administrative centralization, firearms-based warfare, rising literacy and textuality, more popular literatures, more encompassing ethnicities, wider money use, increased market specialization, and more complex international linkages marks the period from the late 15th or early 16th century to the late 18th or mid-19th century as a more or less coherent period in each of the six realms under review. Starting with recovery from 13th–15th-century breakdowns and ending with the French Revolution and European irruptions in mainland Southeast Asia and Japan, this period anticipated, however weakly, more sustained integrative processes in the late 19th and 20th centuries. As such this era has a claim to being called "early modern." Now, as noted, Jack Goldstone, in provocative essays, has argued against use of this term on the grounds that the principal feature of true modernity, namely the use of "engine science" to support industry, was not the inevitable outcome of universal processes, but a highly contingent phenomenon entirely unique to Britain. Yet if modernity would be unrecognizable without industry, it would be no less so without

---

[92] Although proud of Roman legacies, Carolingians and Capetians regarded Clovis as their charter king. Marcus Bull, ed., *France in the Central Middle Ages* (Oxford, 2002), 24, 26, 38, 39, 140. See discussion Ch. 2 *infra*.

efficiently mobilized states, cohesive national territories, collective political identities, popular literacy, and commercialized economies. All these developments the period 1450–1850 clearly adumbrated. If, in the absence of European intervention, we cannot assume that these features would have culminated in an industrial-based order, neither can we see modernity as an externally derived total rupture from prior history everywhere outside Britain. By this logic, I am inclined to characterize all six societies between 1450/1500 and 1789/1858 as "early modern."[93]

Factors Promoting Eurasian Coordination

If I have identified features characteristic of the period c. 1450–1850 in distant sectors of Eurasia, thus far I have said little directly about the reasons for global synchronization. Why was integration in far-flung realms not only progressive but increasingly coordinated? Why did political breakdowns often overlap? The more numerous the parallels, the less satisfying "random coincidence" is likely to be. I would cite nine potential coordinating factors, most already mentioned in passing but whose role now requires more direct consideration.[94]

1. High Cultural Transmissions from Core Civilizations to Secondary Sites. We saw that the florescence of Pagan, Angkor, Dai Viet, Kiev,

---

[93] See n. 19 *supra*, Goldstone citations in n. 4 *supra*, and critiques of Goldstone by James Millward, "The Qing Formation, the Mongol Legacy, and the 'End of History' in Early Modern Central Asia," in Struve, *Qing Formation*, 92–120 (see esp. n. 3 on pp. 93–94 on which I have drawn) and by Evelyn Rawski, "The Qing Formation and the Early Modern Period," ibid., 207–41. On "early modernity," see too Richard von Glahn, "Imagining Pre-modern China," in *SYMT*, 35–70; On-Cho Ng, "The Epochal Concept of 'Early Modernity' and the Intellectual History of Late Imperial China," *JWH* 14 (2003): 37–61; Jerry Bentley, "Early Modern Europe and the Early Modern World," in Charles Parker and Bentley, eds., *Between the Middle Ages and Modernity* (Lanham, MD, 2007), 13–31. Whereas different political and institutional rhythms make "medieval" a largely meaningless category for Southeast Asian realms, for those realms as for Russia, France, and Japan, "early modern" is becoming an accepted convention for the period c. 1500–1750/1820 – which testifies to growing Eurasian coordination after 1450/1500. For Burma, one could argue, the period ends in 1824 (First Anglo-Burmese War), for Siam in 1855 (Bowring Treaty), for Vietnam in 1858 (French invasion), for France in 1789, for Russia in the early 1800s (this is more debatable), and for Japan in 1853 (Perry's arrival). Goldstone's complaint that "early modernity" implies an inevitable progression to "modernity" echoes objections to the use of "proto-nationalism." See n. 46 *supra* and Ch. 4, n. 378 *infra*.

[94] Cf. discussion of spurs to global early modernity in Christian's brilliant *Maps of Time*, ch. 11.

Carolingian/Capetian France, and *ritsuryo* Japan required importation of cultural motifs from Eurasia's long-established urban cores. Insofar as these transmissions were gradual and secondary states cohered at different times, as early as 500 in Gaul and as late as 930 in Kiev, one could argue that transmission from "advanced" to "backward" areas was inevitable. The rise of secondary states around the Eurasian periphery thus requires no further explanation. In an abstract sense, this may be true, but one is struck by the rough coincidence, the relatively narrow time band, of secondary state formation within a much broader range of possibilities. After all, mainland Southeast Asia was in regular contact with India and China by the mid-first millennium B.C.E., as was much of northern Europe with the Mediterranean from a yet earlier date. By the first century C.E. continental influences were pouring into Japan. Why, then, the mid- and late-first-millennium florescence in widely separated perimeters? The "inevitable" spread of civilization rephrases, without solving, the problem of early coordination.

2. Disease. In the late first and early second millennia, accelerating growth around Eurasia's northern and eastern perimeters probably owed something to common disease regimens, especially with those often fatal diseases such as smallpox that confer long-term immunity on survivors. Populations too isolated to gain regular exposure to epidemic disease and/or too small to sustain a local chain of infections normally suffer frightful losses among all age groups, including young adults, whenever exposure does occur. After 1492 Amerindians met this fate, with catastrophic results. However, as exposures become more frequent, as populations become large enough to sustain local chains of infection, and as the number of adult survivors with immunity rises, the disease typically changes from an epidemic killer of all ages to an endemic threat primarily affecting children. Because children are less productive and easier to replace than adults, this transition from near universal to selective mortality can yield major long-term benefits – demographic, economic, and by extension, cultural and political.[95] There is reason to suspect that between c. 800 and 1300 such transitions accelerated population growth in several isolated regions of Eurasia that previously

---

[95] Although this is primarily a matter of survivors acquiring personal life-long immunity, some research suggests that natural selection can enhance genetic resistance in the population at large and/or reduce pathogen lethality. Note 40 *supra* and Marty Pernick, pers. commun., Feb. 5, 2006; July 7, 2006.

had been subject to infrequent and, for that very reason, uniformly dev-astating epidemics of smallpox and measles. These regions included Europe's Celtic, Scandinavian, and Slavic fringes, the main Japanese islands, lowland mainland Southeast Asia, and hitherto isolated sectors of South China and South India. According to this line of reasoning, the expansion of local settlement and a strong post-800 reticulation of Eurasian trade, by both land and sea, put peripheral regions into more sustained contact with older, more urban, more densely settled regions – the Mediterranean, North India, North and coastal China – where smallpox, measles, and enteric fevers had long been endemic. This scenario is frankly speculative for much of Europe and Southeast Asia, but reasonably well documented for post-700 Japan.[96]

Likewise, to the extent that rising European and Chinese demand stimulated world trade, such trade benefited from Europe's post-1450 recovery from bubonic plague and from China's equally well-documented post-1400 recovery from severe depopulation caused by epidemics and political upheaval.[97]

But we are still left asking: Why should local settlement and Eurasian trade have expanded after c. 800?

3. Climate. Volume 1 discussed at some length, and this chapter has alluded to, submillennial modifications in northern hemispheric cli-mate. These were precipitated by interactions involving three principal so-called forcing mechanisms, namely, solar radiation, which correlated

---

[96] Even within a region of endemicity, however, more isolated districts remained vul-nerable, and the constant harvest of children continued to depress long-term pop-ulation growth. Note too that in reverse of the aforementioned civilized-periphery disease gradient, in hitherto lightly settled South China (and South India ?) set-tlement may have accelerated after 800 because northern settlers gained some protection against once prohibitive local diseases, including malaria, dengue fever, and bilharzia. See *SP*, 50, 97–98, 224; Lieberman, "Transcending East-West Dichotomies," 59; *AC*, vol. II, ch. 1; Frank Fenner et al., *Smallpox and Its Eradication* (Geneva, 1988), 209–32; McNeill, *Plagues and Peoples*, chs. 2–4; Linda Newson, "Old World Dis-eases in the Early Colonial Philippines and Spanish America," in Daniel Doeppers and Peter Xenos, eds., *Population and History* (Madison, WI, 1998), 17–36; William Wayne Farris, *Population, Disease and Land in Early Japan, 645–900* (Cambridge, MA, 1995), 71; idem, *Japan's Medieval Population* (Honolulu, 2006), 26–28; and Chs. 2–4 *infra*.

[97] For different views on the extent and causes of 14th-century Chinese epidemics, *CHC*, vol. VI, 585; David Morgan, *The Mongols* (Cambridge, MA, 1986), 133; *SYMT*, 138; McNeill, *Plagues and Peoples*, 144–45, 168; Abu-Lughod, *Before Hegemony*, 170–75, 183, 341–43; Lloyd Eastman, *Families, Fields, and Ancestors* (New York, 1988), 4; Lee, "Positive Check," 600, Table 1.

positively with global warming; volcanism, which correlated negatively; and oscillations in the heat economy of ocean currents, principally the El Nino Southern Oscillation, which also correlated negatively.
As developed initially from European data, the chief post-800 phases
of climate nurtured by these forcing mechanisms were the Medieval
Climate Anomaly (also known as the Medieval Warm Period) 800/850–
1250/1300, which by extending the growing season and drying rich bottom lands in northern latitudes contributed to the rapid demographic
and economic growth characteristic of the European high middle ages;
a more variable, cooler, wetter, and, for northern Europe, less agriculturally propitious phase 1250/1300–1470; a partial reversal of that cooling
trend between c. 1470 and 1560/1570; more intense cooling during the
so-called Little Ice Age 1560/1570–1710; and another, but more modest
warming phase between 1710/1720 and c. 1805. Volume 1 also used
empirical and theoretical studies to argue that the same periods of
hemispheric warming and partial desiccation as aided agriculture in
northern Europe promoted, ironically, stronger monsoons in mainland
Southeast Asia by increasing water vapor in the tropical atmosphere,
by increasing vegetation-dependent convection, and most critically, by
raising spring/summer temperatures in the interior of Asia and thus
magnifying the land–sea thermal contrast on which monsoons rely. The
ensuing increase in the strength and reach of monsoon rains was critical
to boosting rice production in those interior dry zones where Pagan and
Angkor were based.[98]

Recent research has strengthened these claims both by documenting
more clearly phases of Eurasian and European climate[99] and – most

---

[98] *SP*, 101–12, 156–57, and sources therein.

[99] Key reconstructions of historical Eurasian climate that have appeared since *SP*
include Willie Soon, Sallie Baliunas et al., "Reconstructing Climatic and Environmental Changes of the Past 1000 Years: A Reappraisal," *Energy and Environment* 14 (2003):
233–96; Rudolf Brazdil et al., "Historical Climatology in Europe – The State of the
Art," *CC* 70 (2005): 363–430; David Zhang et al., "Global Climate Change, War, and
Population Decline in Recent Human History," *Proceedings of the National Academy
of Sciences* 104 (2007): 19,214–19,219, arguing for close cyclic links between temperature, war, and population trends 1400–1900; Jan Esper et al., "Low-Frequency Signals in
Long Tree-Ring Chronologies for Reconstructing Past Temperature Variability," *Science*
295 (2002): 2250–53; Timothy Osborne and Keith Briffa, "The Spatial Extent of 20th-
Century Warmth in the Context of the Past 1200 Years," *Science* 311 (2006): 841–44;
Anders Moberg et al., "Highly Variable Northern Hemisphere Temperatures Reconstructed from Low- and High-Resolution Proxy Data," *Nature* 433 (2005): 613–17; John
Matthews and Keith Briffa, "The 'Little Ice Age,'" *Geografiska Annaler* 87 A (2005):
17–36; Michael Mann, "Global Surface Temperatures over the Past Two Millennia,"

intriguing – by showing long-term correlations between warmer temperatures in northern Eurasia and stronger monsoon flows in South Asia, South China, and mainland Southeast Asia. Of particular interest, R. H. Kripalani and others have shown consistently high inverse correlations between the depth of winter snow cover in European Russia and Siberia, on the one hand, and the strength of Indian and Southeast Asian summer monsoons, on the other hand. That is to say, the warmer the continental atmosphere, the less snow cover in Russia and the stronger the land–ocean temperature contrast needed to energize Asian monsoon flows. Likewise a research team headed by Pingzhong Zhang recently demonstrated strong positive correlations between the Medieval Climate Anomaly, warmer Chinese temperatures, Alpine glacier retreat, and heavier Asian summer monsoons.[100] There is also evidence during

Geophysical Research Letters 30 (2003): 5-1–5-4; and Emmanuel Le Roy Ladurie, *Histoire Humaine et Comparee du Climat* (Paris, 2004), 7–16, 91–155 and *passim*, arguing for cooling throughout the 15th century. Virtually all of these sources confirm the existence of the Medieval Climate Anomaly, which, depending on locale and definition, started as early as 800 or 850 and extended to 1250/1300 or even 1350. Note, finally, that 10,000 years ago Holocene warming, albeit more pronounced than during the Medieval Climate Anomaly, helped to transform human development by assisting the onset of farming in the Neolithic Revolution. Christian, *Maps of Time*, 222–38.

[100] See R. H. Kripalani et al., "Empirical Study on Nimbus-7 Snow Mass and Indian Summer Monsoon Rainfall," *International Jl. of Climatology* 16 (1996): 23–34, arguing that the snow mass can explain 50 to 80 percent of the variability in Indian monsoon rainfall and suggesting possible links between snow cover and El Nino events. See too supporting work by T. P. Barnett et al., "Effects of Eurasian Snow Cover on Regional and Global Climate Variations," *Jl. of Atmospheric Science* 46 (1989): 661–85, covering Southeast Asia; Tetsuzo Yasunari et al., "Local and Remote Responses to Excessive Snow Mass over Eurasia Appearing in the Northern Spring and Summer Climate," *Jl. of the Meteorological Society of Japan* 69 (1991): 473–87. Geoffrey Parker, "Crisis and Catastrophe," *AHR* 113 (2008): 1053–79 has suggested a similar link between deep Central Asian snow and weak South/Southeast Asian monsoons. On correlations during the past 1,810 years between stronger Asian summer monsoons, rising northern hemispheric and Chinese temperatures, glacier retreat, and Chinese agrarian output, see Pingzhong Zhang et al., "A Test of Climate, Sun, and Culture Relationships from an 1810-Year Chinese Cave Record," *Science* 322 (2008): 940–42. Also of value in establishing climate links between northern Europe and Asia is the recent study by Richard Allan and Brian Soden, "Atmospheric Warming and the Amplification of Precipitation Extremes," *Science Express* (2008), 1–7, which argues that a) global warming increases tropical precipitation far more substantially than was hitherto appreciated, and b) global warming can reduce precipitation in drier temperate zones, such as northern France and Russia, where dry autumns were typically beneficial to medieval harvests. On mechanisms mediating between solar radiation, terrestrial warming, stronger monsoons, and ocean currents (e.g., the El Nino Southern Oscillation), see too David Anderson et al., "Increase in the Asian Southwest Monsoon During the Past Four Centuries," *Science* 297 (2002): 596–99; Anil Gupta et al., "Abrupt Changes in the

the Medieval Climate Anomaly that the melting of Himalayan glaciers augmented the flow of Indochina's chief rivers, again to the benefit of local cultivation.[101] Latest research indicates, finally, that in some locales Medieval Climate Anomaly warming began, albeit modestly, in the 9th or even the 8th century, which is earlier than was long assumed.[102] This is intriguing insofar as economic expansion at Angkor and in much of northern Europe also is now thought to have begun in the late 8th or 9th centuries.

True, global climate change rarely, if ever, yielded uniform effects across Eurasia. In Japan regional circulation systems produced temperature and rainfall patterns periodically out of phase with those of northern Europe, thus contributing to distinctive Japanese demographic rhythms. Even between different sectors of northern Europe, between northern and Mediterranean Europe, North and South China, and Europe and the Mideast, we find lags and disjunctures.[103] Bear in mind, too, that climate change was always mediated, and partly masked, by social, cultural, and technological factors. In some contexts adverse conditions stimulated compensatory adaptation through migration, new agrarian technique, and new cultivars.[104] More generally, as agrarian production grew more diverse and technically advanced, and as the nonagrarian component of each economy assumed greater importance,

---

Asian Southwest Monsoon During the Holocene and Their Links to the North Atlantic Ocean," *Nature* 421 (Jan. 23, 2003): 354–56; Richard Alley, *The Two-Mile Time Machine* (Princeton, 2000), 144–51; Neville Brown, *History and Climate Change* (London, 2001), 57; *SP*, 103–106; Peter Whetton and Ian Rutherfurd, "Historical ENSO Teleconnections in the Eastern Hemisphere," *CC* 28 (1994): 221–53.

[101] Arguing by extension from the claim by Dan Penny, pers. commun., April 14, 2003, that colder temperatures and glacier thickening reduced river flows.

[102] See the state-of-the-art review by Soon, Baliunas et al., "Reconstructing Climatic and Environmental Changes."

[103] In some periods there is also evidence of counterphasic climatic trends in parts of South Asia and mainland Southeast Asia, and in Japan and parts of Southeast Asia. Cf. the observation in Anderson et al., "Increase in the Asian Southwest Monsoon," 597 that a weakening of the Southwest monsoon often coincides with a strengthening of the East Asian monsoon; and the emphasis on local variations in Yasunari et al., "Local and Remote Responses"; Keith Briffa et al., "Unusual Twentieth-Century Summer Warmth in a 1,000-Year Temperature Record from Siberia," *Nature* 376 (1995): 157–58; Henry Pollack et al., "Surface Temperatures in Russia Over the Past Five Centuries Reconstructed from Borehole Temperatures," *Jl. of Geophysical Research* 108 (2003): 2-1–2-12; Brown, *History and Climate Change*, 69, 98, 100, 105, 108, 126–27, 149–53, 170, 215.

[104] This point receives emphasis at Richards, *Unending Frontier*, 115; *SP*, 111–12; and Robert Marks, *Tigers, Rice, Silk, and Silt* (Cambridge, 1998), chs. 6–8.

societies became less vulnerable to climatic fluctuation. Thus whereas climate between c. 900 and 1800 had a cyclic quality or in some locales even deteriorated, during the same centuries across Eurasia population and agricultural output grew notably.

Such qualifications aside, improved climate – in combination with epidemiological adjustments, stronger Eurasian commerce, and new institutional structures – helps to explain why the demographic and agrarian vitality of medieval western Europe and Kiev correlated with that of Pagan, Angkor, and Dai Viet. By promoting population growth in different sectors of Eurasia, more benign climate between 800/850 and 1250/1300 also may have contributed to a) an expansion in market demand, hence long-distance and intraregional trade, in areas as distant as the North Sea and Southeast China; and b) the domestication of smallpox and other epidemic diseases around the Eurasian perimeter through the combined effects of local population growth and intensifying trade contacts.[105] Those more modest climatic ameliorations c. 1470–1560/1570 and 1710/1720–1805, which together bracketed the coldest period of the Little Ice Age, also favored agrarian and demographic expansion.

Conversely, in explaining the wrenching crises that gripped Southeast Asia and Europe c. 1240–1450, one must consider interactions involving a) ecological strains, including land degradation and slowing reclamation, precipitated by the previous 300 to 400 years of rapid climatically assisted agrarian expansion; b) political strains caused by the intersection of institutional weaknesses with land shortages, declining marginal productivity, and falling rents; c) the Black Death, whose transmission owed much to antecedent commercial expansion; d) growing Tai and Mongol activities (see below); and e) the pronounced, increasingly well-documented climatic downturn that afflicted much of Europe and mainland Southeast Asia – colder, wetter summers in the first instance, markedly diminished monsoons (and presumably river flows) in the second – that started with the passing of the Medieval Climate Anomaly.[106] So too between c. 1580 and 1680 recurrent political crises in

---

[105] There is also some suggestion, at least at northern latitudes, that a warmer, more stable climate was associated with a reduction in pathogenic virulence.

[106] Note 99 *supra*; SP, 106, 121, 238–40, 370–71; *CHC*, vol. VI, 585–86; Le Roy Ladurie, *Histoire Humaine*, chs. 2, 3; Anderson et al., "Increase in the Asian Southwest Monsoon," 599, referring to "an abrupt monsoon shift about 1300"; and most esp. Richard Stone, "Tree Rings Tell of Angkor's Dying Days," *Science* 323 (2009): 999, marshaling "indisputable" tree-ring "evidence for pronounced weakening of the monsoon" starting in

much of Europe, China, and Southeast Asia reflected, in some uncertain degree, the effects of Little Ice Age cooling.[107]

4. The Warhorse Revolution. Building on the work of Michael Chamberlain, R. J. Barendse proposed that the 10th to 12th centuries should be seen as the period of the "warhorse revolution," when mounted warriors became militarily and, in varying degrees, politically dominant in western Europe, Byzantium, Russia, the Mideast, North India, North China, and Japan. In each case, specialized cavalrymen overawed free peasants and built more durable, if initially more decentralized, political systems than their predecessors had been able to sustain. Two factors tended to favor this result: a) Expanding agrarian output and exchange allowed mounted warriors with strong rural roots to seize directly the fruits of rising prosperity. b) The breeding of taller, stronger warhorses, known in Europe as destriers, joined with superior armor and equipment to give cavalry lancers across Eurasia a decisive advantage over infantry.[108]

Valid though these arguments surely are in some contexts, alone they cannot solve our larger problem of Eurasian coordination. For one thing, although showing how some warriors exploited rising productivity, they say nothing as to *why* productivity in far-flung areas should have grown between c. 900 and 1250 in the first place. Beyond this, equine determinism simply does not work for tropical Pagan or Angkor, where cavalry was of minor significance.[109] In Japan, mounted warriors did increase their share of the agrarian surplus, while

---

the late 1200s or early 1300s and culminating in exceptionally severe droughts, which wreaked havoc with Angkor's already teetering hydraulic system, from 1362 to 1392 and 1415 to 1440.

[107] See *AC*, vol. II, ch. 5; William Atwell, "Volcanism and Short-Term Climatic Change in East Asian and World History, c. 1200–1699," *JWH* 12 (2001): 29–98; Parker, "Crisis and Catastrophe"; Le Roy Ladurie, *Histoire Humaine*, chs. 5–9; and Ch. 3 *infra*.

[108] See R. J. Barendse, "The Feudal Mutation," *JWH* 14 (2003): 503–29, with fleeting references to Japan, and Michael Chamberlain, *Knowledge and Social Practice in Medieval Damascus, 1190–1350* (Cambridge, 1994), 28–37, paying more attention to Japan. Cf. R. H. C. Davis, *The Medieval Warhorse* (London, 1989). For a critique of Barendse, albeit on grounds other than those which I raise, see Stephen Murillo, "A Feudal Mutation?," *JWH* 14 (2003): 531–50. See too Ch. 6, nn. 152, 248 *infra*.

[109] Gordon Luce, *Old Burma – Early Pagan*, 3 vols. (Locust Valley, NY, 1970), vol. I, 10, 19, 38, 71, 95; Ian Mabbett and David Chandler, *The Khmers* (Oxford, 1995), 76, 156, noting the small size of local horses; Coe, *Angkor*, 185–86; Bin Yang, "Horses, Silver, and Cowries," *JWH* 15 (2004): 299; Michael Charney, *Southeast Asian Warfare 1300–1900* (Leiden, 2004), ch. 7.

supplanting provincial infantry and encroaching on capital elites. But this reflected no European-style technological dynamic. Japanese warhorses remained very small, the size of a modern pony; these were incapable of galloping with an armored rider for any distance, and mounted archers, not lancers, prevailed.[110] So too, although for all or part of the period between c. 1000 and 1300 cavalry exerted growing influence in the Russian steppe, North China, North India, and much of the Muslim world, in these regions cavalry dominance reflected the waxing power of Inner Asian nomads, who embodied a social dynamic quite different from that represented by French and Japanese horsemen. Again in contrast to western Europe, Inner Asian cavalry tended to remain light archers – not lancers – astride small, swift ponies.[111]

5. Mongol and Inner Asian Influences. This discussion of cavalry leads us to consider Mongols and other Inner Asians as a coordinating agent. One of the chief arguments of this book is that "the protected zone" (which occasionally I also term the "protected rimlands"[112]) – including Southeast Asia, Japan, and much of Europe – differed from the "exposed zone" – including China, most of South Asia, and Southwest Asia – in that the former alone escaped long-term occupation by nomadic and seminomadic peoples from Inner Asia. Nonetheless, in the 13th and 14th centuries, Turko-Mongol conquerors, although not occupying directly any part of the protected zone for a substantial period,

---

[110] William Wayne Farris, *Heavenly Warriors* (Cambridge, MA, 1992), 14–18, 57–60; Karl Friday, *Hired Swords* (Stanford, 1992), 35–40, 50–52, 172–73; Thomas Conlan, *State of War: The Violent Order of 14th-Century Japan* (Ann Arbor, 2003), 20–21.

[111] Hellie, *Enserfment*, 21, 25, 30, 151, 160, 285 n. 30; Morgan, *The Mongols*, 90–91; Thomas Barfield, *The Perilous Frontier* (Cambridge, MA, 1989), chs. 5, 6; H. G. Creel, "The Role of the Horse in Chinese History," *AHR* 70 (1965): 647–72; Denis Sinor, "Horse and Pasture in Inner Asian History," *Oriens Extremus* 19 (1972): 171–83; Rudi Lindner, "Nomadism, Horses, and Huns," *PP* 92 (1981): 3–19. Although Turkic armies employed armored cavalry astride big horses, these accompanied a throng of unarmored archers on smaller mounts. Moreover, Turkic heavy cavalry was not a post-1000 innovation but harked back to Parthian practices in the early centuries C.E. McNeill, *Human Web*, 84–85, 130–31.

[112] "Rimlands" refers specifically to mainland Southeast Asia, northern Europe, and Japan, because these areas lay along Eurasia's perimeter. However, as a generic synonym for the "protected zone" – which I contrast with the "exposed zone" – "rimlands" is problematic because a) some areas with protected zone traits such as Nepal, Bhutan, and southern Siberia do not lie along the Eurasian perimeter, and b) some areas that I include in the "exposed zone" such as South India and Southeast China lie not much closer to Inner Asia than do mainland Southeast Asia or Russia. See discussion *infra*.

did subject it to a variety of shocks. These interventions help to explain why during the 13th and 14th centuries the protected zone shared in Eurasia-wide political and economic dislocations. In Southeast Asia, for example, although Turko-Mongol incursions were small scale and short lived, they hastened Pagan's collapse, threatened Angkor, accelerated shifts within Dai Viet, and assisted, if indirectly, Tai penetration in the western and central mainland. In Japan, Mongol attacks intensified strains within the Kamakura shogunate. In Russia, Turko-Mongols not only destroyed the charter polity of Kiev but heavily influenced post-Kievan, that is to say Muscovite, political and military evolution.[113] In central and western Europe, although Mongol armies penetrated no farther than the upper Adriatic, unintentionally they transmitted the Black Death from the Russian steppe to the eastern Mediterranean, whence it spread to western and northern Europe after 1347. Between 30 and 60 percent of Europeans perished.[114] These Mongol-mediated dislocations in Europe, mainland Southeast Asia, and Japan coincided with more direct Inner Asian incursions in Southwest Asia, where Mongols destroyed the Abbasid caliphate at the heart of the Muslim world and wrecked the Seljuk Sultanate; in South Asia, where Turkic invaders founded the Delhi Sultanate; and in China where Mongols founded the Yuan Dynasty on the grave of the Song.[115] To the degree that demographic and political compensation for 14th- and 15th-century upheavals helped to inaugurate the early modern era, Inner Asians contributed indirectly to that Eurasian-wide revival.

In settled areas directly accessible to the steppe, we shall find that Inner Asians continued to shape history well into the 19th century. After 1360, however, they exerted virtually no influence on western Europe,

---

[113] The latest statement on this topic is Donald Ostrowski, *Muscovy and the Mongols* (Cambridge, 1998). See discussion this chapter and Ch. 2 *infra*.

[114] McNeill, *Plagues and Peoples*, 143–50; Adshead, *China in World History*, 148–52; Jack Weatherford, *Genghis Khan and the Making of the Modern World* (New York, 2004), 244–50; and Bin Yang, "Horses, Silver, and Cowries," esp. 320–21 suggest that the Black Death entered the Russian steppe along Mongol caravan routes from North China; whereas Ole Benedictow, "The Black Death," *History Today* 55 (2005): 42–49; idem, *The Black Death, 1346–1353* (Woodbridge, UK, 2004), 44–54 argues that it had long infected the steppe. Benedictow also offers substantially higher mortality estimates than some earlier authors. But see Samuel Cohen Jr.'s scathing review of Benedictow in *The New England Journal of Medicine*, March 10, 2005, and discussion in Ch. 2 *infra*.

[115] Morgan, *The Mongols*, chs. 5, 6; Donald Quataert, *The Ottoman Empire, 1700–1922* (Cambridge, 2000), 17; K. N. Chaudhuri, *Asia Before Europe* (Cambridge, 1990), 246–48; *SYMT*. On c. 1250–1450 as a period of generalized Eurasian crisis, see too Atwell, "Time, Money"; and discussion *infra*.

Japan, or Southeast Asia. Thus never again would they be so ubiquitous an agency of Eurasian coordination as in the 13th and 14th centuries.

6. Commerce as a Multifaceted Coordinating Agency. One can easily exaggerate international influences on local economies: as late as 1846 for most European countries the ratio of exports to total production, and of imports to national consumption, probably remained in the range of 1–2 percent. Local and regional price structures endured well into the second half of the 19th century.[116] And yet by 1500 trade, including the exchange of foodstuffs and bullion, arguably had become the most consistent and direct agency of Eurasian coordination.

Except for Kiev, long-distance commodity flows – as opposed to critical trade-mediated cultural exchanges – seem to have made a limited contribution to charter state genesis, but by the 12th century population growth and agrarian surpluses in one sector of Eurasia after another had joined improved ships and mercantile reorganization to link markets from Flanders to Fujian with novel efficiency. Regional specialization, primarily in luxuries but also in bulk goods, spurred cities and contributed to that urban cultural brilliance that was a central feature not only of medieval Europe, but of charter Southeast Asia, Fatimid/early Mamluk Egypt, medieval South Asia, and Song China.[117] In South China and Japan between c. 1000 and 1400 hardy fast-ripening rice strains from Champa that had been introduced along the trade routes boosted yields and population. In turn, Song demand shaped Southeast Asian exports, while Song coins aided Japanese and Javanese monetization. So too after 1300 Indian cotton plants transformed handicrafts and domestic exchange across East and Southeast Asia.[118]

The severe political, demographic, and economic crises that afflicted much of Eurasia between c. 1240 and 1450 reflected a constellation of forces, many of which, we saw, were a function of commercial expansion

---

[116] Patrick Karl O'Brien, "Intercontinental Trade and the Development of the Third World Since the Industrial Revolution," *JWH* 8 (1997): 77–78.

[117] For overviews of long-distance trade and its role in state and urban formation c. 1000–1400, Abu-Lughod, *Before Hegemony*, esp. chs. 1, 11; William McNeill, *The Pursuit of Power* (Chicago, 1982), esp. 50–55 (I discount McNeill's claim that Chinese economic growth was the primary motor behind all Eurasian growth c. 900–1200); Atwell, "Time, Money"; Hermann Kulke, "Rivalry and Competition in the Bay of Bengal in the 11th Century and Its Bearing on Indian Ocean Studies," in Om Prakash and Denys Lombard, eds., *Commerce and Culture in the Bay of Bengal, 1500–1800* (New Delhi, 1999), 17–20; Jan Wisseman Christie, "The Medieval Tamil-Language Inscriptions in Southeast Asia and China," *JSEAS* 29 (1998): 253.

[118] *SP*, 144–45, 170; and Chs. 4, 7 *infra*.

during the previous 300 to 400 years. Market dislocations and bullion shortages plagued centers in East Asia no less than in Europe and the Mideast.[119]

In the late 15th and 16th centuries, however, the situation again reversed itself. Demographic and political recovery and economic reorganization in key regions joined technical improvements in mining and smelting, a great leap in Japanese and New World silver production, improved ship construction and navigation, and the revolutionary opening of trans-Pacific routes to inaugurate another sustained global increase in monetized exchange. Dennis Flynn and Arturo Giraldez have identified two stages in that process named after the provenance of bullion supplies: the Potosi/Japan Cycle from the 1540s to the 1640s, and the Mexican cycle from c. 1700 to 1750. By raising the price of silver to the point where formerly prohibitively expensive production techniques became feasible, Chinese, and to a lesser extent Indian, demand for the white metal underwrote the early expansion of both Japanese and New World mines. All told, between 1525 and 1800 the annual production of precious metals rose at least tenfold, with the great bulk migrating from Latin America to Europe and from Latin America, via Europe and the Philippines, to India and East Asia. Each silver cycle was marked by a diminishing silver price differential between various sectors of Eurasia, a sustained increase in the volume of commodity exchange, and rising levels of international, regional, and local specialization.[120]

Across Eurasia between 1500 and 1800, these ramified linkages played a major coordinating role. In both Europe and Japan we find

---

[119] See n. 117 *supra*; Ch. 2, n. 160 *infra*; plus Richard von Glahn, *Fountain of Fortune* (Berkeley, 1996), 48–97.

[120] Such movements, however, were rarely linear: between China and Europe, for example, the silver price differential fell to c. 1640, rose in the late 1600s, and fell again after c. 1750. See Dennis Flynn and Arturo Giraldez, "Cycles of Silver," *JWH* 13 (2002): 391–427; idem, "'Born with a Silver Spoon'," *JWH* 6 (1995): 201–21; idem, "Arbitrage, China, and World Trade in the Early Modern Period," *JESHO* 38 (1995): 429–48. After c. 1750 the British-dominated exchange of Bengali opium for Chinese tea generated what Flynn and Giraldez term the "tea and opium cycle." I rely too on Flynn, "Comparing the Tokugawa Shogunate with Hapsburg Spain," in James Tracy, ed., *The Political Economy of Merchant Empires* (Cambridge, 1991), 332–59; Ward Barrett, "World Bullion Flows, 1450–1800," in James Tracy, ed., *The Rise of Merchant Empires* (Cambridge, 1990), 224–54, esp. figures on 238; Clara Eugenia Nunez, ed., *Monetary History in Global Perspective, 1500–1808* (Seville, 1998), esp. essays by Richard von Glahn and Om Prakash; Charles Kindleberger, *Spenders and Hoarders* (Singapore, 1989), esp. Table 7; Artur Attman, *American Bullion in the European World Trade, 1600–1800* (Goteburg, 1986); Andre Gunder Frank, *Re-Orient* (Berkeley, 1998).

a sharp rise in circulating silver, an expansion of Chinese silk (and, in Europe, Indian cotton) imports, and the development in the 18th century of manufactures specifically designed to substitute local for imported Chinese or Indian textiles. In coastal China the influx between c. 1550 and 1820 of silver from Europe, Japan, and Southeast Asia to pay for textiles, tea, and porcelain provided a critical boost to monetization and to the conversion of food-growing land to industrial crops. Many of these same patterns obtained in Southeast Asia, whose rice, mineral, and spice exports to Europe and China rose sharply in tandem with textile imports. Specialization encouraged more efficient land use, which in turn boosted labor demand, hence population growth. By raising caloric returns per labor unit and per land unit, New World maize, peanuts, and, above all, sweet potatoes had similar demographic benefits for China, Vietnam, and Japan.[121] Consider too that in Vietnam and Japan after 1450/1500 a number of mining, engineering, metallurgical, mathematical, and agricultural techniques derived from China, as did early modern Europe's famed technological trinity – compass, gunpowder, and printing – albeit at a earlier date.[122] From the early 1700s Russian industry was no less indebted to central and western Europe.

As we have seen, trade and cities in turn promoted literacy, intellectual experiment, and the spread of capital languages and culture. Between 1500 and 1800 in one Eurasian region after another, local versions of the disciplinary revolution owed much to commercially driven

[121] On maritime spurs to commercial and demographic vitality, see esp. Robert Innes, "The Door Ajar: Japan's Foreign Trade in the 17th Century" (Univ. of Michigan, PhD diss., 1980); K. N. Chaudhuri, *The Trading World of Asia and the English East India Company 1660–1760* (Cambridge, 1978); Marks, *Tigers, Rice*; William Rowe, "Approaches to Modern Chinese Social History," in Olivier Zunz, ed., *Reliving the Past* (Chapel Hill, 1985), 236–96; Richard von Glahn, "Money-use in China and Changing Patterns of Global Trade in Monetary Metals, 1500–1800," in Nunez, *Monetary History*, 51–59; *AC*, vol. II; *SP*, 146–50, 167–70, 179–80, 254–56, 269–70, 286–307, 414–18, 435–37, 442; David Bulbeck et al., comps. *Southeast Asian Exports Since the 14th Century* (Leiden, 1998). On ways in which external commercial demand could erode demographically restrictive subsistence routines, see Henley, "Population and Means of Subsistence." On New World crops, *SP*, 175, 437, 438; Sucheta Mazumdar, "The Impact of New World Crops on the Diet and Economy of China and India, 1600–1900," in Raymond Grew, ed., *Food in Global History* (Boulder, 1999), 58–77; Man-houng Lin, "From Sweet Potato to Silver," in Hans Pohl, ed., *The European Discovery of the World and Its Economic Effects on Pre-Industrial Society, 1500–1800* (Stuttgart, 1990), 304–27. Potatoes also provided a delayed, modest boost to French agriculture.

[122] Pamela Long, *Technology, Society, and Culture in Late Medieval and Renaissance Europe, 1300–1600* (Washington, DC, 2000), 1; Ch. 4 *infra*. European paper also derived from China via the Mideast in the 12th century.

social mobility and vertical communication, and to the premium that new states, themselves beneficiaries of economic growth, placed on social regulation. By facilitating the movement of scholars, clerics, and diplomats, international trade further reconfigured local administrations and cultures (see item 9 *infra*).

As I have argued elsewhere, although intra-Asian exchange in this period exhibited some features reminiscent of Immanuel Wallerstein's schema, on the whole, Wallerstein's theoretical distinction between cores, semiperipheries, and peripheries offers a poor guide to early modern trade. Unlike Wallerstein's peripheral states, mainland Southeast Asian and Japanese governments before 1800 faced no externally imposed political restrictions. Moreover, in lieu of a methodical periphery-to-core transfer of wealth a la Wallerstein, we find systems of multifocal Smithian exchange that strengthened simultaneously the economies and polities of China, Southeast Asia, Japan, and Europe alike.[123]

7. Firearms. Along with expanded global trade, the mid-1500s inaugurated a Eurasian-wide military transformation dominated by European-style guns, both hand-held weapons and artillery. Although European guns derived ultimately from Chinese weapons transmitted probably via the Mongols, and although, as Laichen Sun has shown, mainland Southeast Asia already had experimented with Chinese-derived firearms,[124] by the mid-1500s the latter were markedly inferior to European weapons in range, power, and accuracy. Astonishingly synchronized and foolhardy territorial overextensions in Russia, Burma, and Japan in the mid- and late 1500s [125] reflected a shared hubris inspired in part by European-style guns, borne along commercial routes by merchants and mercenaries. If Japanese military technology then began to stagnate and if Southeast Asia never developed the siege artillery or the infantry drill and tactics that underlay the military revolution in

---

[123] *SP*, 47; Victor Lieberman, "Wallerstein's System and the International Context of Early Modern Southeast Asian History," *JAH* 24 (1990): 70–90. Cf. Markus Vink, "A Match Made in Heaven?," in Ernst van Veen and Leonard Blusse, eds., *Rivalry and Conflict* (Leiden, 2005), 267–314.

[124] Thomas Allsen, "The Circulation of Military Technology in the Mongolian Empire," in Nicola Di Cosmo, ed., *Warfare in Inner Asian History (500–1800)* (Leiden, 2002), 265–93; Laichen Sun, "An 'Age of Gunpowder' (c. 1390–1683) in Asian History" (ms).

[125] Ivan IV's Livonian War (1558–1593), Bayin-naung and Nan-da-bayin's Siamese expeditions (1563–1593), and Hideyoshi's Korean invasion (1592–1598).

Europe,[126] between 1550 and 1830 a succession of technical advances in western Europe did make themselves felt, with varying lag times, in mainland Southeast Asia as well as in Russia. In the latter case, successful entry into the European multistate system hinged on adaptation of flintlocks, artillery, and infantry drill and an associated strategic shift from cavalry to infantry – which reversed the late first millennium change from infantry to cavalry. Likewise in Japan to c. 1630 and in Southeast Asia to 1830 the new weapons encouraged changes in training, finance, and logistics. Together with coastal trade, such shifts, I suggested, underlay the growing power differential between Southeast Asian coast and interior. In short, from Scotland to Honshu and the Gulf of Siam, firearms conferred an advantage on the wealthiest, most flexible polities.

8. Cumulative Political Expertise and Parallel Institutional Initiatives. Progressive centralization also bespoke cumulative improvements in administrative organization, which reflected changes in each state's economic and technical horizon and which responded to what we have seen often were parallel political crises. If European, Southeast Asian, and Japanese leaders struggled with these challenges in isolation, they also followed broadly similar logics that placed a premium on social order and resource control, that chose from a limited range of options, and that self-consciously sought to redress antecedent weaknesses. To the extent that postcrisis reform and pacification spurred economic growth in distant regions, we have another partial explanation for economic coordination, as for example, during post-1450 booms in Europe and Southeast Asia. In turn, to the degree that rapid growth generated fresh political strains, renewed expansion contributed, if indirectly, to the next round of synchronized distress.

9. Intellectual Synergies. Finally, coordinated integration in far-flung regions owed much to intensifying intellectual exchanges. Every charter civilization, we saw, imported religion and literacy from an older Eurasian center. Thereafter the Neo-Confucian revolution in Vietnam and the Tokugawa synthesis of Neo-Confucianism, Buddhism, and Shinto benefited from scholarly, commercial, and diplomatic contacts with China. Similar conduits exposed Russia to Renaissance and Counter-Reformation influences, which yielded in the 1700s to

---

[126] See n. 88 *supra*.

Enlightenment currents. With broad cultural change often came technical advances, as in cartography, accounting, and military organization. In the 17th century, diplomatic and religious cross-fertilization also helps to explain the close coordination of Siamese and Burmese provincial reform.[127]

Sanjay Subrahmanyam has marshaled 16th- and 17th-century evidence to suggest that the writing of global histories in such widely separated locales as the Ottoman empire, India, Portugal, Mexico, and Poland reflected an intensified circulation of textual and visual materials. On the other hand, it is doubtful (nor does Subrahmanyam claim) that such materials testify to genuinely pan-Eurasian intellectual perspectives, with common epistemologies and historiographic assumptions, as opposed to parallel but ultimately self-contained visions. Surely the idea that West Asian millennialism inspired 16th-century imperial projects in Europe, South Asia, and Southeast Asia is empirically untenable.[128]

All nine factors operated in each of our six realms, which helps to explain why their political and cultural chronologies began to mesh more closely. But the local mix of factors and the geographic and cultural contexts differed, which is why we find innumerable specific differences.

4. AREAS OF INNER ASIAN CONQUEST AND PRECOCIOUS CIVILIZATION: PRELIMINARY COMMENTS ON CHINA AND SOUTH ASIA

The Protected Zone and the Exposed Zone

Chapters 2 to 4 consider in some detail Europe and Japan, because there progressive, indigenous-led integration had most in common with mainland Southeast Asia, which provided our initial frame of reference.

---

[127] Cf. Victor Lieberman, "Provincial Reforms in Taung-ngu Burma," *BSOAS* 43 (1980): 548–69.

[128] See Sanjay Subrahmanyam, "On World Historians in the Sixteenth Century," *Representations* 91 (2005): 26–57; idem, "Connected Histories," in Lieberman, *Beyond Binary Histories*, 289–316; idem, "'Persianization' and 'Mercantilism,'" in Prakash and Lombard, *Commerce and Culture*, 47–85; idem, *Penumbral Visions*, 261–65. Not only were millennial 16th-century Burmese, Lao, and Siamese ideologies near-exclusive blends of Theravada and indigenous concepts, but Japan, which exhibited the same late 16th-century expansionary impulse as societies farther west, was yet more insulated against West Asian millennialism. For comparisons of early modern European and Chinese shifts in literary, artistic, and intellectual sensibilities, see Ch. 5, n. 202 *infra*.

These areas – along with Korea and, one might argue, Nepal, Bhutan, Assam, and some coastal areas in South Asia – constituted Eurasia's protected zone.[129] Yet to grasp the coherence of this overarching category, it is necessary to contrast it with regions whose political history for much of the second millennium was shaped substantially by actors, generally Inner Asians, originating outside the regions in question. These latter regions, to repeat, I term the "exposed zone" of Eurasia. By way of illustration, Chapter 5 or 6 could have examined Southwest Asia, but considering the close ties between Southeast Asia and its immediate northern and western neighbors and wary of too extended an inquiry, I chose to focus on China and South Asia. The book finishes by comparing the mainland sector of Southeast Asia with the archipelago, where Europeans played a role analogous in some ways to that of Inner Asians in China and India.[130]

Manifold differences aside, we saw that protected-zone states in western and northeastern Europe, Japan, and mainland Southeast Asia shared a number of basic features. To recapitulate: a) As befit our definitional distinction, in most cases throughout their history and in every case after 1400, all protected-zone polities were effectively sheltered against sustained occupation by nomads from Inner Asia. Political and cultural leadership thus remained in the hands of indigenous elites. b) Lying on the periphery of older city-based civilizations, all began as secondary states in the mid- to late first millennium C.E. c) Internal geography encouraged political and cultural cohesion. Russia apart, all protected-zone realms were of modest size, and with the chief exception of Vietnam, all enjoyed reasonably good internal communications and/or an economic/demographic imbalance markedly favorable to the capital region. d) Between c. 800 and 1830 and especially after c. 1450, in each realm we find movements, with varying degrees of persistence and success, toward territorial consolidation and administrative centralization. e) During this same period, each realm became more culturally integrated, both vertically and horizontally.

Similarities Between the Two Zones

To be sure, the same basic forces as promoted integration in the protected zone – population growth, agrarian expansion, European-style firearms,

---

[129] On other candidates for protected zone status, see nn. 55 and 112 *supra*, and 144 *infra*.
[130] See Chs. 5–7 for documentation of ensuing claims.

local and long-distance trade, wider literacy, military competition, and accumulated institutional and technical expertise – also encouraged integration in China and South Asia. In terms of basic dynamics and a persistent trend toward larger, more complex organizations, I see no fundamental divide between the six realms we have just considered, on the one hand, and China and South Asia, on the other. (I use "China" to designate the area controlled by the Qing empire, essentially the modern People's Republic of China, Mongolia, and Taiwan; "South Asia" refers to the area of contemporary India, Bangladesh, Pakistan, southern Nepal, and eastern Afghanistan.)

For example, in China – *locus classicus* of the dynastic or administrative cycle – successive periods of imperial collapse and provincial independence grew shorter and less institutionally disruptive. In China, as in Burma, Siam, Russia, and France, by far the most prolonged rupture, calling into question the very existence of central authority, came at the end of the charter period, after the first extended unification (in China this lengthy period of fragmentation, after the unifying Han Dynasty collapsed, is known as the Age of Divison, c. 190–589). If in France the lengths of the first three postcharter eras of fragmentation were in the order of 220:116:36, in Burma 252:14:5, and in Russia (which had only two postcharter interregna) 210:15, in China the ratio for the first four major interregna was 399:119:152:17.[131]

---

[131] Of course, all such dates are somewhat arbitrary because central authority normally declined and strengthened gradually. For China, I date the Age of Division from 190 to 589, the Tang–Song transition from 860 to 979, the Southern Song era of fragmentation from 1127 to 1279, and the Yuan–Ming transition from 1351 to 1368. The same logic leads me to omit from this list of major interregna the Qin–Han and Sui–Tang transitions: both were exceedingly brief and involved substantial elite and institutional continuity. In France the first three interregna lasted from c. 890 (severe Carolingian debility) to 1110 (early Capetian vigor), from 1337 (onset of the Hundred Years War) to 1453 (conclusion of the war), and from 1562 (start of the Wars of Religion) to 1598 (Edict of Nantes). While France remained politically fragmented, i.e., in an interregnum, from 1337 to 1453, Valois fortunes arguably reached their lowest point in 1428, which is why the second French administrative cycle as defined in the text preceding n. 67 *supra* ends in 1428. In Burma, the corresponding interregna were 1287 (fall of Pagan) to 1539 (First Toungoo reunification), 1599 (fall of Pegu) to 1613 (Restored Toungoo reunification), and 1752 (fall of Ava) to 1757 (Kon-baung reconquest of Pegu). In Russia, the first two interregna lasted from 1240 (Mongol conquest) to c. 1450 (end to first Muscovite civil war and effective independence from the Tatars) and from 1598 (onset of the Time of Troubles) to 1613 (end of the Time of Troubles). Though locally disruptive, Pugachev's 1773–1774 revolt was not an interregnum. Central mainland Southeast Asian patterns were similar to that of Burma.

In other words, it makes as much (or as little) sense to talk about Carolingian, Capetian, Valois, and Bourbon "dynastic cycles" as about Han, Tang, and Song – and for basically similar regions: in each realm, as political, cultural, and commercial ties between subregions grew tighter, imperial integration became normative, and the state itself grew more stable and effective. Adumbrated in some respects under the Han and Tang and assuming sophisticated form as early as the Song, the late imperial system of civil service examinations, rotated appointments, bureaucratic operations, provincial supervision, civilian supremacy, official–gentry cooperation, and cartography reached its apogee in the 18th century under the Qing.

Between the first unification and 1800, moreover, Chinese imperial territories more than doubled. The most dramatic expansion occurred under the Qing, whose post-1650 conquests paralleled Russia's occupation of Siberia (in effect, Russia and the Qing divided Inner Asia between them), French colonial acquisitions, and Southeast Asian consolidations. So too, over an unusually long period but with a marked acceleration from the 16th to 19th centuries, Han Chinese cultural norms and ethnicity spread into what is now South, Southwest, and West China, while within each region elite and popular cultures entered into more sustained dialogue. The initial diffusion of Chinese culture over a vast area and its stubborn subsequent resistance to regional fragmentation reflected *inter alia* high rates of Chinese frontier colonization, the homogenizing thrust of civil service examinations, the availability of block printing, the standardizing intellectual thrust of a nonphonetic ideographic script, the intensely prescriptive cast of Confucian thought, and a disciplinary revolution, underway by the 10th century, that may have been as successful in maintaining local order and obviating central controls as 16th-century European religious movements.

In material terms, unification drew strength from uniquely efficient water transport focusing on the Yellow and Yangzi rivers, the Grand Canal, and countless smaller linkages – as well as from an eight-fold population increase between 100 and 1800 that reproduced Chinese village culture over a vast landscape. Supporting a Smithian specialization that was regional, interregional, and international, China's demographic/economic vitality in turn benefited from prolonged pacification, New World crops, post-1450 bullion imports, elite patronage of best agrarian practices, and substantially free market policies. If civil service exams, ideographic script, and the Grand Canal lacked

European or Indic Southeast Asian analogues, other broad dynamics we can recognize. Moreover, demographic and economic expansion followed a rhythm curiously similar to that of Europe and mainland Southeast Asia, with growth particularly notable c. 900–1250/1300, c. 1470–1620, and c. 1710–1830.

In South Asia movements of political and cultural integration were far more limited and fragile than in China, but there too certain long-term trends are familiar. Surveying South Asia's principal empires – those of the Mauryas, Guptas, Delhi Sultanate, Mughals, and British – one finds that intervals between successive empires tended to grow shorter, especially if we start our calculations with the collapse of the Guptas in the mid-500s. That is to say, the longest era of polycentrism followed Gupta collapse; the second longest followed the decline of the Delhi Sultanate in the late 1300s; and the shortest era of polycentrism lay between the collapse of the Mughals and the founding of the British Raj. As periods of imperial collapse grew shorter, successive empires secured larger sectors of the subcontinent. Symptom and cause of imperial stability was the enhanced efficiency of military and fiscal organization, with changes particularly notable in the 13th, 16th, and late 18th and early 19th centuries. The southward diffusion, first, of Sanskritic and, then, of Perso-Islamic culture, the northward spread from the Tamil country of *bhakti* devotional cults, the growing post-1650 circulation of brahmanical notions of caste, and the continuous expansion of settled agriculture and commercial circuits encouraged a real, if modest, degree of cultural uniformity across the subcontinent that paralleled, and yet was independent of, political integration. Notwithstanding a post-1700 slowdown that had more in common with Japan than with Europe or Southeast Asia, long-term economic trends in South Asia also followed a recognizable rhythm, including expansion between c. 900 and 1300 and more especially c. 1450 to 1700. Finally, economic and technical spurs to political integration are broadly familiar: improved climate and possible disease adjustments between c. 800 and 1300, long-term increases in population and cultivation, commercial intensification, the post-1500 spread of firearms, and greater institutional sophistication. As an unprecedentedly powerful state that benefited from agrarian colonization, expanding world trade, guns, and successful experiment and that inaugurated within its region what is generally termed the "early modern" era, Mughal India (heyday c. 1560–1707) bears obvious comparison to Toungoo Burma, Late Ayudhya Siam, Romanov

Russia, late Valois/Bourbon France, Tokugawa Japan, and late Ming/ Qing China.[132]

Distinguishing Features of China and South Asia

How, then, did China and South Asia differ from regions examined in Volume 1 and in Chapters 2 to 4 of this volume? I see three major differences: those of Inner Asian exposure, developmental chronology, and physical scale.

First, whereas western and northern Europe, Japan, and mainland Southeast Asia were substantially and increasingly shielded against Inner Asian occupation, China and India lay open to domination by people of nomadic or seminomadic background from the steppes, uplands, deserts, and forests of Inner Asia. Throughout much of the period under review and with increasing force between 900/1100 and 1700/1800, Inner Asians directed political development in China and South Asia – as well as in Transoxania, Persia, and those parts of Southwest Asia, North Africa, and southeastern Europe that came under Seljuk, Mongol, Mamluk, or Ottoman control. Insulation/ vulnerability to Inner Asian occupation is the central criterion of protected zone/exposed zone status.

Following Nicola Di Cosmo, Mark Elliott, Thomas Barfield, and Robert Taaffe, I define "Inner Asia" – a notoriously amorphous concept – as that region lying generally north and east of the Black Sea; north of the Himalayas, Korea, and most of modern Iran; north and west of China proper; and south of the tundra and Siberian forest belt. This region, whose territory fluctuated at the margins with ecological, demographic, and political shifts, included much of southern Russia, parts of Afghanistan and Iran, the modern states of Turkmenistan, Uzbekistan (heart of the region formerly known as Transoxania), Tajikistan, Kyrgyzstan, and Kazakhstan, plus Xinjiang, Mongolia, and Manchuria.[133] Although scattered river valleys and oases from

---

[132] On the "early modern" rubric, see n. 93 *supra* and Ch. 5, n. 165 and Ch. 6, n. 35 *infra*.

[133] Some scholars have resisted including Manchuria in Inner Asia whether because the Manchu language is not closely related to Mongol, because much of Manchuria does not consist of grasslands, or because Manchus under the Qing assimilated to Chinese culture. Cf. Manchuria's exclusion in Svat Soucek, *A History of Inner Asia* (Cambridge, 2000), viii–xii; David Christian, "Inner Eurasia as a Unit of World History," *JWH* 5 (1994): 173–211; idem, *A History of Russia, Central Asia and Mongolia, Volume 1* (Malden,

Turkmenistan to Xinjiang supported advanced agriculture and impressive cities, while eastern forested areas supported mixed farming and hunting, the political economy of Inner Asia at large centered on pastoral nomadism. In the parched southern steppe or desert the chief animal was the Bactrian camel, whereas better-watered grasslands in the northern steppe nourished not only vast flocks of sheep, goats, and cattle but also horses hardier and far more numerous than mounts in agricultural areas. For centuries nonpareil equestrian skills, an ethos focused on hunting and warfare, proficiency with the short double-reflex bow (which allowed volleys from horseback), tactical flexibility, a ruthlessness and stamina demanded by an unforgiving environment, remarkable mobility, and a far larger percentage of men trained for war than in settled societies assured Inner Asian cavalry a recurrent advantage over agrarian state soldiery, that is until the late 1600s when new military and administrative technologies helped the Russian and Qing empires (the latter, of course, in origin Inner Asian) to reverse the tide.[134]

Not surprisingly, warriors from Inner Asia – the "pivot of history," "the heartland of Eurasia"[135] – repeatedly invaded a vast swath of agrarian territories stretching from southeastern Europe and Asia Minor, through Mesopotamia and Iran, to India and China. Although they started as early as the second millennium B.C.E.,[136] such incursions

MA, 1998), xv–xvii, 3. But Mark Elliott, *The Manchu Way* (Stanford, 2001), 6, 57, 358, and *passim*; idem, "The Limits of Tatary," *JAS* 59 (2000): 603–46 emphasizes ecological, cultural, and political links between Manchuria and areas farther west, as do Barfield, *Perilous Frontier*, 12; Denis Sinor and Robert Taaffe in *CHEIA*, 1–40, esp. maps on pp. 6, 29; Peter Perdue, *China Marches West* (Cambridge, MA, 2005), xiii–xiv, 19–40; Perdue, pers. commun., Oct. 20, 2007. Elliott, moreover, has convincingly refuted the Sinicization thesis. See Ch. 5 *infra*. So too Nicola Di Cosmo, "State Formation and Periodization in Inner Asian History," *JWH* 10 (1999): 3, n. 8, and idem, *Ancient China and Its Enemies* (Cambridge, 2002), 13, explicitly includes Manchuria in his definition of "Inner Asia." I basically follow Di Cosmo's definition. Perdue, *China Marches West*, and Denis Sinor, "Central Eurasia," in Sinor, ed., *Orientalism and History* (Bloomington, 1970), 93–119 use "Central Eurasia" for the entire region from the Ukraine to the Pacific, but because the nomadic and seminomadic groups with whom I am concerned originated in Asia, I find "Inner Asia" a more congenial term. For other geographic usages, see Andre Gunder Frank, *The Centrality of Central Asia* (Leiden, 1992), 5–6; Nicola Di Cosmo, "Introduction," in Di Cosmo, *Warfare in Inner Asian History*, 1–2, incl. n. 2.

[134] Joseph Fletcher, "The Mongols: Ecological and Social Perspectives," *HJAS* 46 (1986): 12; Di Cosmo, "Introduction," 3–4; Perdue, *China Marches West*.

[135] Di Cosmo, "Introduction," 1, citing Halford Mackinder. For similar emphases, see Soucek, *History*, ch. 1; Bentley, "Cross-Cultural Interaction," 766.

[136] *CHEIA*, chs. 3–5; Frank, *Centrality of Central Asia*, 9–10, 13; Victor Mair, "The North(west)ern Peoples and the Recurrent Origins of the 'Chinese' State," in Fogel,

became particularly influential in the 5th, 10th to 13th, and 15th to 17th centuries C.E., under a succession of Xiongnu, Khitan, Jurchen, Mongol, Turkic, and Manchu confederations. Inner Asian history has often been reduced to internal cycles governed by climate or by the personality of unifying rulers.[137] Certainly, time and again economic crisis or domestic turmoil inspired the accession of charismatic leaders, more intense militarization, and territorial expansion.[138] Yet Inner Asian, no less than agrarian, history also exhibited strong linear trends influenced by new material horizons and by cumulative organizational and cultural expertise.

Thus, for example, Di Cosmo has defined four principal stages in Inner Asian political history in terms of expanding access to external resources: tribute empires (209 B.C.E.–551 C.E.), trade-tribute empires (551–907), dual-administration empires (907–1259), and direct-taxation empires (1260–1796).[139] Examples of the latter include the Yuan, Manchu, Timurid, Mughal, Uzbek, Safavid, and Ottoman states. Both exogenous and internal dynamics governed this evolution. Particularly after the 9th century C.E., economic growth in areas of sedentary agriculture drew adjacent Inner Asian peoples into more sustained relations, whether as tribute-takers, traders, mercenaries, or objects of missionary outreach. Such contacts increased both the attraction of agrarian conquest and the ability of steppe peoples to dominate settled populations. Inner Asians acquired from agrarians not only the latest siege and weapons technologies[140] but also a growing sophistication in literate culture and administration. Turkic tribes, by embracing Islam, and Khitan, Jurchen, and Manchu peoples, by honoring Confucianism, raised their suitability as rulers in the eyes of sedentary subjects. Hence, ironically, even as sedentary civilizations became more technologically and

Teleology of the Modern Nation-State, 46–84. On the origins of pastoral nomadism and early nomad–Chinese interactions, Di Cosmo, *Ancient China,* pts. 1, 2.

[137] Cf. Barfield, *Perilous Frontier;* A. M. Khazanov, *Nomads and the Outside World* (Cambridge, 1984); and historiographic critiques at Perdue, *China Marches West,* 6–7, 532–36, Di Cosmo, "State Formation," 1–40; idem, "Ancient Inner Asian Nomads," *JAS* 53 (1994): 1092–1112. On climatic influences, Ch. 2, n. 150.

[138] Di Cosmo, "State Formation," 15–26 identifies a recurrent sequence from crisis to militarization to the creation of more centralized structures.

[139] Di Cosmo, "State Formation," 26–40. Barfield, *Perilous Frontier* sought to tie nomad fortunes tightly to those of the Chinese, arguing that interdependence drove Chinese empires and nomadic confederations to rise and fall in tandem in a cyclic-cum-secular trajectory. But Di Cosmo, "State Formation," 12–13 raises a variety of theoretical and empirical objections to the Chinese link. See too Perdue, *China Marches West,* 7.

[140] Allsen, "Circulation of Military Technology"; Elvin, *Pattern of Chinese Past,* 18, 84–90.

economically potent, Inner Asian influence expanded during much of the second millennium. Often before entering sedentary domains, internalized sedentary norms obliged Inner Asians to modify, if not abandon their tribal and shamanic affiliations.[141]

The main point is that while restless peoples of Inner Asian origin, responding to these opportunities, repeatedly invaded the agrarian arc most vulnerable to their cavalry, they could not exert comparable influence on most of Europe, Southeast Asia, or Japan, that is, the protected zone. True, as noted, the Mongols briefly menaced Angkor and attacked Pagan, Dai Viet, and Japan, but insularity in the case of Japan; malaria, dysentery, and limited pasture in mainland Southeast Asia precluded sustained success. After the Mongols withdrew, neither Southeast Asia nor Japan again faced a serious threat from Inner Asia.[142] Western Europe and central Europe, which like mainland Southeast Asia were part of a peninsula shielded from the steppe by distance and inadequate pasture, also lay beyond the effective range of Inner Asian horsemen, at least from the 10th century.[143] With the defeat of the Magyars in 955, central Europe faced no major threat from the east until the Ottomans, who crested outside Vienna in 1683. (Unsuitable cavalry terrain and/or climate also protected what are now Nepal, Bhutan, Assam, and Kerala from Inner Asian occupation.[144])

---

[141] To recall earlier discussion in this chapter, the basic sedentary-frontier scenario that I have outlined for Inner Asians seems to apply to mainland Southeas Asia, where from the 11th to 13th centuries growing Tai–valley interactions increased both the lure of lowland civilization and the capacity of Tais to absorb lowland religious and administrative culture. But whereas after c. 1350 Tai inroads in Southeas Asia ebbed, Inner Asian incursions in the exposed zone intensified during much of the second millennium.

[142] Even if one were to classify 1765–1769 Qing thrusts against Burma and their 1788–1789 incursion into Vietnam as Inner Asian invasions, both attacks were soundly defeated.

[143] On the inadequacy of Hungarian and central European pasture for Inner Asian horsemen, see Sinor, "Horse and Pasture," 181–82; Lindner, "Nomadism, Horses." Cf. Walter Pohl, "The Role of Steppe Peoples in Eastern and Central Europe in the First Millennium A.D.," in P. Urbanczyk, ed., *Origins of Central Europe* (Warsaw, 1997), 65–78; McNeill, *Human Web*, 100–102; and David Morgan, "The Mongols in Syria, 1260–1300," in P. W. Edbury, ed., *Crusade and Settlement* (Cardiff, 1985), 231–35, arguing that inadequate pasture also helped doom Mongol efforts in Syria. To my mind, the argument in Fletcher, "The Mongols," 45–47 that the lone fact of Ogodei's death in 1241 spared Europe from nomad attacks for centuries thereafter makes little sense.

[144] Whether by Manchus or Mughals, although in Nepal Gorkha ascendancy from 1768 introduced a Hindu line of novel ethnic background. Tibet's status was more ambiguous. Although for most of its history Tibet was protected against Inner Asian occupation, under the Yuan Dynasty Mongol rulers patronized Tibet's Sakyapa monastic

Russia, of course, lay more exposed. Not only did Kiev face repeated nomad threats, not only were Russians after 1240 obliged to pay tribute to the Mongol-Tatar Kipchak khanate, but Muscovite reunification benefited extensively from Mongol-Tatar administrative and military techniques and early patronage. In a very real sense, Russian tsars became – and in fact boasted of being – heirs to the Kipchak khans. Nonetheless, along with the rest of the protected zone but unlike China and South Asia, areas of Russian settlement, namely the forested districts, were never occupied for any significant period by Inner Asian forces, who were content to enroll Russian princes as tributaries and who themselves remained confined to the southern steppe. This meant that even in the 14th and 15th centuries, Russians, not steppe nomads, controlled forest-zone administration, that local politics began to reflect indigenous, not Inner Asian priorities, and that in religious and literary expression, if not administrative/military affairs, Russia continued to look to Byzantium, not Inner Asia.[145] Muscovy's unification of the Russian lands proceeded in violent opposition to Inner Asian claims, and the nomad contribution to that process, though substantial, was both indirect and entirely unintentional. Indeed, for Mongol-Tatars, Moscow's rise was an utter catastrophe. In contrast to China, South, and Southwest Asia, after 1450 Russia became ever more secure against nomad military threats, while from 1448 Inner Asian cultural influence also receded rapidly.

What were the practical consequences of the exposed zone's vulnerability? Most basic and obvious, whereas between 1200 and 1800 in the protected zone political development remained in the hands of primarily local elites, in India and China integration relied substantially on

order, while in the late 16th and 17th centuries Mongol patronage was critical in elevating the Gelugpa sect and the Dalai Lama (whose title was originally conferred by a Mongol patron). In 1717 Tibet was invaded by the Zunghars and in 1720 became an autonomous protectorate under the Qing with a Manchu garrison in Lhasa. See *EAH*, vol. I, 159–60, 356–57; vol. III, 104–106, and vol. IV, 96–97; Christopher Beckwith, *The Tibetan Empire in Central Asia* (Princeton, 1987); *CIHC*, 227; Perdue, *China Marches West*, 102–104, 227–68 *passim*. Sri Lanka also may be considered part of the protected zone for much of its history, notwithstanding Tamil invasions/expansion in the 11th and 13th/14th centuries and European involvement from the 16th century, after which Sri Lanka's position paralleled that of island Southeast Asia. See Ch. 7 *infra*.

[145] Thus Morgan, *The Mongols*, 174, 199, suggests that the Golden Horde, which ruled Russia from its capital of Sarai on the lower Volga near the Caspian, lasted longer than Mongol conquest regimes in China or Persia precisely because it remained physically separated from the subject agrarian population. I rely on Ostrowski, *Muscovy and the Mongols*; Richard Hellie, pers. commun., Feb. 28, 2006; and sources in Ch. 2 *infra*.

Inner Asians who altered local trajectories to fit their own requirements. South Asia, for example, between c. 550 and 1200 remained divided among modest regional states whose increasingly coherent personalities suggest that South Asia may have been headed toward a permanent competitive multistate system not unlike that of Europe. But after c. 1200 Muslim Turkic invaders from the northwest, many of nomadic background, with easy access to high-quality horses from Inner Asia and using Inner Asian cavalry tactics, introduced, if not a novel imperial vision, then eminently practical means to achieve that vision. Turkic conquests gave birth to the Delhi Sultanate and assumed their most long-lived and awesome form in the Mughal empire. Sultanate and Mughal success reflected not only superior cavalry but wider commercial linkages and Perso-Islamic administrative traditions, imported from Transoxania, Afghanistan, and Persia, that in many ways were more efficient than earlier South Asian practices.[146] Thus in South Asia, where Inner Asians revolutionized political geography and modified elite culture with growing force from the mid-1500s to early 1700s, arguably they became the principal catalysts of early modernity. Although we shall not consider these areas in any detail, successive Turko-Mongol and Turkic conquerors, whether Seljuk, Ilkhanid, Timurid, Safavid, or Uzbek, also played a critical integrative role in Anatolia, the Levant, the Iranian plateau, and Transoxania, as did the Ottomans in the Balkans, the southern and eastern Mediterranean, and parts of Southwest Asia.[147]

In a startlingly original essay, Victor Mair recently argued that Inner Asians dominated state formation in China for much of its early history, including the Shang Dynasty (c. 1600–1050 B.C.E.), possibly the Qin (221–206 B.C.E.) and early Han (206 B.C.E.–9 C.E.), as well as much of the post-Han Age of Division (190–589) and the early Tang Dynasty (618–907).[148] Be that as it may, in China as in South and Southwest Asia and in clear contrast to the protected zone, Inner Asian influence increased

---

[146] On Turko-Persian-Islamicate political and cultural traditions to which South Asian invaders laid claim, see *IBE*, chs. 2, 5; Carter Vaughn Findley, *The Turks in World History* (Oxford, 2005), chs. 1–3; Robert Canfield, ed., *Turko-Persia in Historical Perspective* (Cambridge, 1991); and Ch. 6 *infra*.

[147] Daniel Goffman, *The Ottoman Empire and Early Modern Europe* (Cambridge, 2002); Cemal Kafadar, *Between Two Worlds* (Berkeley, 1995); Soucek, *History*, chs. 5–11; Roger Savory, *Iran Under the Safavids* (Cambridge, 1980); Findley, *Turks in World History*, ch. 3.

[148] Mair, "North(west)ern Peoples." See discussion in Ch. 5 *infra*.

markedly during the second millennium C.E., as seen most dramatically in the conquests of the Mongol Yuan (1215/1276–1368) and Manchu Qing (1644–1911) Dynasties. Of course, in uniting North and South China in 1279, the Mongols rejoined a cultural area that Khitan and Jurchen invasions from the north had helped to sunder in the 10th to 12th centuries; in effect, some Inner Asians reversed a fragmentation others had fostered. But without the Mongols, whose achievement the Ming inherited, we cannot assume that North and South China, which Marco Polo regarded as separate countries, would have come together again or that the condition of multistate competition that we find in China for most of the period from 900 to 1279 would not have become permanent. (Somewhat the same could be said about the late-6th-century reunification of China. Benefiting from Inner Asian military and administrative legacies, the Sino-foreign Sui Dynasty reversed a fragmentation that Inner Asians had not initiated but that 4th- and 5th-century Inner Asian interventions had helped to perpetuate.) In the 17th and 18th centuries, the Manchus again utterly transformed China's condition by joining China proper with Xinjiang, Qinghai, Tibet, Mongolia, and Manchuria to form a domain over twice as large as the Ming empire. The Mongol empire, of course, also had joined China proper and the steppe, but Qing conquests in Inner Asia proved far more durable. *Mutatis mutandis*, stripped of Taiwan, Outer Mongolia, and trans-Amur/Ussuri territories, the Manchu empire became the People's Republic of China. Furthermore, although the Manchus, lacking a literate tradition comparable to that of the Mughals, copied Chinese precedents wholesale, they brought administration to unprecedented levels of efficiency – not least because they were determined to show skeptical literati that they could operate Chinese systems better than the Chinese themselves.

In cultural and ethnic terms as well, Inner Asian rule in China and South Asia carried signatures that responded to the insecurity of small conquest elites, especially in the early stages of rule. On the one hand, the Manchus, as just noted, strove to win over Chinese literati by demonstrating their Confucian bona fides. On the other hand, like earlier conquest dynasties in China, they simultaneously sought a separate authority that Mark Elliott terms "ethnic sovereignty." A fraction of 1 percent as numerous as their Chinese subjects, the Manchus strove to maintain their cohesion, hence domination, by monopolizing key administrative and military positions, by instilling fear, by allying with other non-Chinese populations, and by maintaining strict legal, residential, institutional – in short, ethnic – distinctions between themselves and the Chinese. Within the empire at large, moreover, they sought to balance Chinese influence by appealing to distinctive Inner Asian cultures: Manchu shamanic, Mongolian Lamaist Buddhist, Turkic Muslim, and Tibetan Budddhist. This policy, far less Sinocentric than Ming or Song policy and rooted in specifically Turko-Mongol traditions, reduced China to one of several imperial audiences and placed the Qing emperor at the apex of a genuinely universal, multicultural domain.[149]

In some respects, one could argue, Mughals remained more culturally distant from their host population than Manchus. Like the latter, the Mughals readily incorporated local elites and patronized local traditions. Yet whereas the Manchus, from a remote impoverished land, perforce adopted Neo-Confucian culture enthusiastically in order to govern China proper, Delhi Sultans and Mughals prided themselves on their mastery of Perso-Islamic culture and presented themselves in official pronouncements as champions of a faith, Islam, which, at least at the elite level and especially in the early stages of Turko-Persian intervention in India, was distinct from the practices of the vast majority of their subjects. Notwithstanding the development of a pan-confessional warrior culture, moderately successful Muslim proselytism, and ever more extensive Hindu-Muslim accommodations at both elite and popular levels, conquest elites in South Asia challenged and modified local traditions far more directly than their counterparts in China. Indeed, in South Asia Perso-Islamic culture can be seen as a second charter dispensation, comparable in its universal claims and north–south transmission to Sanskrit Hindu culture in the mid- and late first millennium. By the same token, although as a percentage of the total population immigrant warrior elites in India may not have been much larger than Manchus in China, the Mughals arguably conceded even less power to non-Muslims than the Manchus accorded Chinese literati.[150]

Whereas protected-zone elites, being of the same ethnicity and religion as most of their subjects, often sought to politicize ethnic loyalty

---

[149] Elliott, *Manchu Way*, 4–6, 209 ff., and *passim*; Rawski, "The Qing Formation," 218–23; Jonathan Hay, "The Diachronics of Early Qing Visual and Material Culture," in Struve, *Qing Formation*, 315.

[150] Ch. 5, nn. 245–251; Ch. 6, nn. 320–327 *infra*; John Wills, Jr., pers. commun., April 8, 2007. Cf. Savory, *Iran Under the Safavids*, 76, 184–85, noting that "the fundamental dichotomy of the Safavid state" was the ethnic split between an aristocracy of Turkic tribal warriors and representatives of sedentary, urbanized Persian culture. Although emphasizing inclusive tendencies rather more than Savory, Andrew Newman, *Safavid Iran* (London, 2006) does not dispute the centrality of Turk–Tajik tensions.

as an aid to governance and wartime effort, in South Asia and more especially China Inner Asian rulers tended to regard such sentiments as deeply subversive. And yet neither Manchu nor Mughal experience supports the assumption, basic to modern nationalism, that ethnic and religious solidarity between rulers and ruled was a necessary precondition for political effectiveness. On the contrary, in these vast exposed-zone realms the superiority of Qing and Mughal over indigenous regimes stemmed precisely from their character as small, cohesive Inner Asian conquest elites.

Admittedly, like most heuristic contrasts, my protected zone versus exposed zone classification risks eliding elements of overlap and indeterminacy. As just noted, although Inner Asian influence in Russia remained more short lived than in China or South Asia, between c. 1240 and 1400/1450 Russia obviously shared with those regions subjection to Inner Asian conquest. Moreover, if western Europe and Southeast Asia were proof against Inner Asian incursions, they still lay exposed to Germanic, Viking/Norman, and Tai assaults, all of which profoundly influenced local political and cultural/linguistic evolution. And yet, whereas in China and India Inner Asian domination grew dramatically after 1526 or 1644, in western Europe Germanic, Muslim, and Viking inroads ceased at various points between 500 and 1000, and Tai incursions in Southeast Asia were concentrated before 1350. This distinctive chronology, plus the fact that Franks, Vikings, and Tais entered the protected zone as modest-sized warbands of illiterate pagans quite willing to assimilate to the dominant local culture – rather than as large, centrally directed confederations determined to maintain cultural/ethnic barriers as an aid to governance – helps to explain why recognizable conquest elites in Europe and Southeast Asia disappeared centuries before their counterparts in China and India.

One could also object to my emphasis on Inner Asian influence by arguing that those conquest elites' use of ethnic and religious markers to buttress their power was merely a peculiar instance of a more universal ruling-class tendency to stress cultural distinctions between themselves and their subjects. In this respect, Sinicized literati in Vietnam, Paris-oriented provincials in *ancien régime* France, and the Francophone nobility of Russia (whose distance from popular culture grew markedly in the 18th century) resembled Mughals and Manchus. This is quite true, but again differences in degree, and probably also in kind, were critical. In Russia the nobility considered themselves and their serfs to be of one ethnicity and one religion. The state self-consciously championed both features at the expense of non-Russian cultures. Russians completely dominated the imperial nobility; and Catherine the Great, precisely because she was of German origin, went to great lengths to identify publicly with Russian language, religion, and culture. If Manchu rulers and Chinese literati had much in common, quotas and markers prejudicial to majority ethnicity also divided them in a fashion without Russian analogue. Elites in France, Japan, and Vietnam were even more homogeneous and rooted in majority culture than in Russia.[151]

Along with different vulnerabilities to Inner Asian cavalry, a second major distinction between the protected zone, on the one hand, and South Asia and China, on the other, is the chronology of

---

[151] Of course, on the expanding frontiers of France, Russia, Japan, Burma, Siam, and Vietnam, local peoples suddenly found themselves subject to imperial rulers of different ethnicity and/or religion than themselves, but this was an invariable feature of annexed peripheries. As such, it differed fundamentally from the imposition of ethnicity or culture by small alien conquest elites at the very core of newly created empires such as occurred in China repeatedly and in India under the Delhi Sultanate and Mughals. The Ottomans approximated Qing and Mughal patterns insofar as they a) originated in the nomadic cavalry cultures of Inner Asia, b) imposed alien ethnicity and culture at the center of an imperial system that they themselves created, c) remained a minority of the total imperial population, d) favored among their subjects a relatively high degree of ethnic/cultural compartmentalization, even if the latter is often exaggerated, and e) were externally derived agents of an unprecedentedly successful early modern political integration. Like the Mughals, the Ottomans also experienced devolutionary strains in the 17th and 18th centuries. On the other hand, the exceptional precocity, longevity (from c. 1300 to 1922), and stability of Ottoman rule compared to Turkic rule in India or Manchu rule in China, and the ensuing centuries-long conversion of Anatolia to Ottoman/Turkic ethnicity and to Islam, provided the Ottoman empire with an expanding ethnic core far larger, relatively, than its Mughal or Qing counterpart. (In 1800 perhaps 25 to 40 percent of Ottoman subjects considered themselves to be Ottomans/Turks compared to a fraction of 1 percent of Qing inhabitants who were Manchu.) In these terms the Ottoman empire, notwithstanding its Inner Asian origins, was not dramatically different from the Austrian or even the Russian empire (where Great Russians in 1800 were only about 50 percent of the total). Other Ottoman features without Mughal or Qing analogue but similar to Russia and Austria included an absence of fresh Inner Asian incursions in the 16th and 17th centuries and constant entanglement in the multistate system of Europe, with attendant pressures to military and fiscal reform. Note 147 *supra*; Quataert, *Ottoman Empire*, chs. 8, 9; McCarthy, *Ottoman Turks*, chs. 4, 7, 8; Halil Inalcik, ed., *An Economic and Social History of the Ottoman Empire*, 2 vols. (Cambridge, 1994); Cem Emrence, "Imperial Paths, Big Comparisons: The Late Ottoman Empire," *JGH* 3 (2008): 289–311; Rudi Lindner, pers. commun., July 4, 2008. Again, therefore, some elements transcended the protected zone/exposed zone distinction. Founded by Turkic tribesmen from eastern Anatolia, the Armenian highlands, northern Syria, and Iraq in the early 1500s, the Safavid empire shared critical features with the Ottomans, but unable to halt fresh incursions by Afghan and Baluchi tribesmen in the early 1700s, never matched Ottoman stability or longevity.

"civilization."[152] In a word, states and literate cultures arose much earlier in the Indo-Gangetic plain and North China than in the protected zone.

Between c. 2600 and 1750/1250 B.C.E. the Indus basin, and between c. 1600 and 1050 B.C.E. the Yellow River plain, supported urbanized, literate, state-level, bronze-age societies, those of Harappa and Shang, respectively. Following the eclipse of those ancient formations, in both North India and North China reclamation outside the original cores, agrarian intensification, the introduction of iron and other novel technologies, and a new phase of urbanization produced a succession of secondary states that culminated during the late first millennium B.C.E. and the early centuries C.E. in "universal" empires. These were the empires of the Mauryas and Guptas in North India and of Han in China. Characterized by unprecedented territories, large armies, complex administrative organs, wider money use, and a partial desacralization of the natural world, these empires – and their local successors – provided a civilizational template for yet more distant sectors of Eurasia without their own literate or state traditions. Included in this latter category, of course, were Southeast Asia, which looked to India for cultural and political models, and Japan, which sought inspiration from Tang China.

Broadly similar patterns obtained in Southwest Asia and the eastern Mediterranean. Between c. 3500 and 2000 B.C.E. southern Mesopotamia and Egypt generated urban, literate, copper- and/or bronze-using states. In these homes of ancient civilization but more particularly in ever widening spheres beyond their frontiers then arose a long series of secondary states (Akkadian, Old Babylonian, Assyrian, Minoan, Mycenaean, classical Greek, Hellenistic) that benefited from centuries of political and intellectual experiment, the diffusion of bronze and iron, agrarian and commercial expansion. Finally, between c. 550 B.C.E. and 400 C.E., Southwest Asia and the Mediterranean created new "universal" empires, including those of Achaemenid Persia and Rome. Like the Maurya, Gupta, and Han empires, Rome in particular provided a model for stateless societies in yet more distant Eurasian regions. Thus,

---

[152] Scarre and Fagan, *Ancient Civilizations*, 4–8 define "civilizations" as "urbanized state-level societies," while Trigger, *Understanding Early Civilizations*, esp. 43–46 defines "early civillization" as "the earliest and simplest form of *class-based* society." See too Charles Maisels, *Early Civilizations of the Old World* (London, 1999), 25–27, 342–48, using V. G. Childe's list of traits for the Urban Revolution. Ensuing discussion relies on these sources: Miriam Stark, ed., *Archaeology of Asia* (Oxford, 2006); specialized sources cited in Chs. 5, 6 *infra*; and Carla Sinopoli, pers. commun., Sept. 4, 2004.

as Southeast Asians borrowed from India and the Japanese from China, Franks looked to Rome and the Rus to Byzantium.[153]

In other words, we may visualize Eurasia and Egypt as consisting of three historic territories: a) relatively small territories, namely the Indus valley, parts of North China, southern Mesopotamia, and the Nile valley, each of which engendered a "primary civilization," which Bruce Trigger defines as a society whose institutions were not "shaped by substantial dependence upon or control by other, more complex societies"; b) those original territories plus far more extensive lands beyond them, which supported a succession of secondary states and civilizations culminating in the universal empires of Maurya, Gupta, Han, and Rome; "secondary civilizations," to follow Trigger and Price, "developed under the influence or tutelage of more advanced neighbors";[154] and c) extensive territories yet farther afield, including Southeast Asia, much of South India, northern Europe, Korea, Japan, and the Himalayan foothills, that also generated secondary states, but usually at a considerably later date as a direct result of contact with states in the second category. The main point is that all of the first and most of the second category constituted my "exposed zone" of Eurasia, which was later subject to Inner Asian conquest; whereas most of the third category constituted the "protected zone," insulated against such incursions.[155] *Not all exposed-zone societies developed primary civilizations, but all societies that developed primary civilizations lay in the exposed zone.*

How, then, were these two features – civilizational precocity and vulnerability to Inner Asian incursions – related? The Indo-Gangetic plain, North China, Mesopotamia, and the Nile valley were first to develop urban state systems, in part because they boasted productive riverine locales capable of supporting large populations, flora and fauna suitable for domestication, easily cleared vegetation, and intense local synergies. By definition, we just saw that primary civilizations did not derive

---

[153] The Achaemenids influenced the Maurya empire as well as the later Parthian and Sasanid empires in Persia itself.

[154] See Trigger, *Understanding Civilizations*, 28–29, 48–49; n. 63 *supra*; and Henry Wright, "Uruk States in Southwestern Iran," in G. M. Feinman and Joyce Marcus, eds., *Archaic States* (Santa Fe, 1998), 173, defining primary states as those that arose from interactions among prestate societies. South China probably belongs in this second category.

[155] Because it developed secondary states at roughly the same time as Southeast Asia and escaped effective control by the Delhi Sultanate and the Mughals, much of South India belongs in this third category. However, the Deccan, which developed states at roughly the same time as Southeast Asia but later came under Turkic rule, occupies a more ambiguous status.

political or cultural institutions from more complex state societies. However, this did not preclude their welcoming crops, animals, and key technologies from afar. Indeed, their position athwart east–west arteries of communication, migration, pastoralism, and trade offered critical access to external ideas and material inputs. Interactions between the Nile valley, the Fertile Crescent, northeastern Iran, Turkmenistan, western Afghanistan, and the Indus valley facilitated the rapid dissemination across this region of crops, domestic animals, writing, bronze metallurgy, and chariots. Within this broad zone, which Gregory Possehl terms an "interaction sphere," "[r]ich communication and sharing of ideas and products were essential ingredients in [the] process of cultural change" and in the genesis of Mesopotamian and Harappan cultures.[156] The external debts that ancient North China incurred are less obvious and have produced a spectrum of scholarly opinion, not uninfluenced by patriotic pressures.[157] Yet, *pace* an earlier emphasis on the immaculate conception of Chinese civilization, most scholars accept that in some degree technological, military, and economic transmissions along what J. R. McNeill and William McNeill term "the Old World Web" also aided state development in North China – from where in turn Chinese animals and crops spread westward in ancient times. To follow Mair again, the early states of Shang and Zhou probably were founded by steppe pastoralists from the northwest who differed from their Chinese subjects not only in ecology and culture, but race. It cannot be entirely accidental, Michael Cook argues, that in both China and South Asia, civilization first appeared in areas that were in easiest contact with the Mideast and that were most similar to it ecologically.[158] As agents of east–west transmission, long-distance traders, oasis farmers, and most especially steppe pastoralists "bound the agrarian heartlands together from the shores of the Mediterranean to the Yellow Sea, persistently tightening the strands of

---

[156] Gregory Possehl, *The Indus Civilization* (Walnut Creek, 2002), 28–29 ("the old Near Eastern hearth of domestication was simply much larger than older hypotheses assumed"), plus 1–9, 23–29, 215–35, 247–50; Nayanjot Lahiri, *The Archaeology of Indian Trade Routes up to c. 200 BC* (Delhi, 1992), 12–143 *passim*, esp. 64–66, 141–43.

[157] On 20th-century political pressures to emphasize the unique originality of Chinese civilization, Ian Glover, "Some National, Regional, and Political Uses of Archaeology in East and Southeast Asia," in Stark, *Archaeology of Asia*, 18–21.

[158] Mair, "The North(west)ern Peoples"; Michael Cook, *A Brief History of the Human Race* (New York, 2003), 149–53, 179–81, and chs. 8, 9.

existing webs, and eventually fusing them together into the Old World Web."[159]

Yet in China, most of India, and Southwest Asia this same physical openness to external influences joined growing ties between sown and steppe, particularly from the start of the second millennium C.E., to render sedentary societies far more vulnerable to nomadic conquest than were the more physically isolated – and culturally laggard – Eurasian peripheries. In other words, the same mountains, seas, jungles, poor pasture, and malarial climates as inhibited Inner Asian assaults slowed cultural and commercial transmissions and contributed to the relatively late date of charter state formation in the protected zone. Thus, for example, the Qin–Han unification of China antedated comparable developments in key sectors of northern Europe, Southeast Asia, and Japan by some 700 to 1,200 years.

On the other hand, once the process of political consolidation in the protected zone got underway, because these areas could import sophisticated, prepackaged technological and religiopolitical (Christian, Hindu, Buddhist, Confucian) complexes, consolidation proceeded far more rapidly, with less laborious trial-and-error, than in older Eurasian cores. This was part of a more general process whereby over three millennia cultural circulation reduced the once yawning gap in organizational capacity between Eurasia's civilizational cores and its protected zone. Within the latter zone itself between c. 1000 and 1830, I argued that similar coordination – commercial, intellectual, military – eroded material differences (for example between French, Russian, and Japanese levels of urbanization) and helped to synchronize political and cultural rhythms ever more closely.

Along with exposure to Inner Asian conquest and civilizational precocity, a third distinctive feature of China and South Asia – though again, not of *all* exposed-zone states – was the enormous size of imperial lands and populations, factors that in turn imposed limits on progressive centralization stricter than in much of the protected zone.[160] Whereas,

---

[159] Quote from McNeill, *Human Web*, 59. Long-distance traders operated both overland and by sea. For views offering varying degrees of support, see previous note; Di Cosmo, *Ancient China*, ch. 1 ("The Steppe Highway") and ch. 2; Jared Diamond, *Guns, Germs and Steel* (New York, 1997), 180–86, 329–30; and specialist sources in Chs. 5, 6 *infra*. Abu-Lughod, *Before Hegemony*, 14 notes that Mongols entered the Mideast along ancient trade routes joining Iraq to Inner Asia.

[160] Within the exposed zone this emphasis on vast size, and an associated tendency to weak interstate incentives, is only selectively applicable. For example, the Safavid and

as noted, Burma, Siam, Vietnam, France, and Japan in 1820 each controlled between 320,000 and 900,000 square kilometers with populations ranging from 4,000,000 to 32,000,000, the Qing empire of over 11,000,000 square kilometers in 1800 held 320–350,000,000 subjects, and the Mughal empire at its height in 1700 spanned some 5,000,000 square kilometers with perhaps 175,000,000 inhabitants.[161] In part, the vast scale of Chinese and Indian empire reflected the power of Inner Asian cavalry. In part, it reflected the openness of the North China and Indo-Gangetic plains, whose internal divisions were less sharp than those geographic features that hemmed in France and more especially Japan and the three chief Southeast Asian realms. More particularly, in China, I have suggested, the size and recurrent coalescence of empire reflected *inter alia* efficient water transport together with the homogenizing power of a nonalphabetic writing system, civil-service examinations based on a standardized corpus, and Confucianism's preoccupation with issues of social and political order. Like Khitans and Jurchens before them, Manchus were quick to avail themselves of these cultural instruments in governing China proper.

Given the dispersal of resources over vast territories, imperial populations many times larger than in the protected zone, and preindustrial limits on communication and transport, it is hardly surprising that Indian and Chinese empires faced unusually daunting challenges to stability and penetration. If, over the long term, Indian empires grew larger and more powerful, political evolution in the subcontinent was far less continuous than in protected-zone states. For much of its history South Asia oscillated between short-lived periods of comparatively weak unification and long eras of polycentrism, which, I noted,

Uzbek polities, both founded by Turkic tribesmen, operated on a territorial scale closer to Southeast Asian kingdoms than to the Qing or Mughal empires. Likewise, warfare involving Ottomans and European powers in the west, and Ottomans, Safavids, and Uzbeks in the east, provided an incentive for fiscal experiment at least as sustained as in Southeast Asia – and considerably more sustained than in either Qing China or Tokugawa Japan. See Marshall Hodgson, *The Venture of Islam. Vol. III: The Gunpowder Empires and Modern Times* (Chicago, 1974), chs. 1–3; Savory, *Iran Under the Safavids*; Newman, *Safavid Iran*; Kathryn Babayan, *Mystics, Monarchs, and Messiahs* (Cambridge, MA, 2002); Soucek, *History*, chs. 10, 11; Virginia Aksan, "Locating the Ottomans Among Early Modern Empires," *JEMH* 3 (1999): 103–33; Goffman, *Ottoman Empire*.

[161] The Ottoman empire at its height c. 1675 controlled some 3,800,000 square kilometers, but probably had only 25,000,000 subjects. The Safavid empire, about half as large as the Ottoman, had only 5,000,000 people. Previous notes, and Colin McEvedy and Richard Jones, *Atlas of World Population History* (New York, 1980), 137, 153.

approximated the condition of Europe at large. Although capable of sweeping initial conquests, neither the Delhi Sultanate nor the Mughal empire succeeded in preventing recurrent, ultimately fatal provincial challenges. Such instabilities ensured that institutional and dynastic links between successive Indian empires were relatively modest. Conversely, postimperial successor states showed considerable vitality, regional literary traditions luxuriated across South Asia, even under the Mughals; and the linguistic and ethnic map of India remained highly fragmented.

In China continuities between successive empires were far more pronounced than in South Asia, interregna were shorter, language patterns at both elite and popular levels were more unified, and regional literary cultures were conspicuously anemic.[162] Yet in contrast once again to protected-zone states, where the ratio of appointed officials to subjects grew between 1000 and 1800, China during the same period was obliged to reduce that ratio drastically and to compensate with cultural instruments of integration and with ad hoc administrative arrangements between centrally appointed officials, local subbureaucrats, and autonomous, unpaid gentry elites. This is not to conclude that in 1800 local governance was less effective in China than in, say, Burma or France. By some yardsticks – elite acculturation, the longevity and effectiveness of rural pacification, the sheer scale of people and lands under unified control – it was far more impressive. Direct administrative penetration is hardly the only metric of early modern integration. But it does argue that in China as in South Asia, size precluded the same long-term progressive centralizing trend that we find in most protected-zone states.

Size also bears on the question of why Chinese authorities were consistently less interested than their protected-zone counterparts in fiscal maximization. By best estimates, the percentage of national wealth collected by the Qing was only half to a fifth as large as that collected in 18th-century France, England, or Russia.[163] In part this low-tax regime reflected Neo-Confucian philosophical commitments; in part, the fact that when China was unified, the isolation that accompanied subcontinental dominion conferred greater freedom from military pressure than European and Southeast Asian states normally enjoyed. But a third

---

[162] On language contrasts between India and China, see the clever observations in Cook, *Brief History*, 184–85.

[163] See Ch. 5, nn. 295, 296 *infra*.

explanation must be that even when military necessity dictated serious tax increases, as in the late Ming and late Qing, extraction beyond this modest level exceeded the state's political and technical capacity. To have raised taxes sharply on trade or unregistered lands would have invited resistance from gentry elites without whose voluntary services local government could not function. If the government had tried to circumvent local elites by enlarging the number of paid provincial posts, the salary bill would have eaten up virtually the entire tax increase and probably would have overwhelmed the center's ability to monitor additional personnel. In the Qing period a major increase in bureaucratic recruitment, which necessarily would have been overwhelmingly Chinese, also might have endangered Manchu dominance.

In other words, by unifying "everything under Heaven" from Xinjiang to the East China and South China Seas, the most successful China-centered empires minimized multistate competition, which permitted a low-tax fiscal regime. In reciprocal fashion, by limiting central demands on local elites, light taxes and limited military demands helped the empire hold together. Only in the absence of chronic large-scale warfare and sustained mobilization, perhaps, could so populous and vast a polity as China have survived. To some extent, Mughal and protected-zone experiences provide counterfactual confirmation of these claims. To recompense military nobles, the Mughals imposed markedly higher taxes than the Qing, but those demands, along with territorial overextension and relatively weak cultural bonds, contributed to imperial disintegration.[164] Protected-zone states combined heavy military demands with territorial stability, in large part because they operated on a more manageable physical scale than either Manchus or Mughals.

Once again, Russia, at first glance, seems to defy protected-zone generalizations: with some 18,000,000 square kilometers in 1820, the Russian empire was appreciably larger than the largest domain ruled by Inner Asians, that of the Qing. Nonetheless, imperial control in Russia proved far easier than in India or China. Russia's population, only 42,000,000 in 1800 or roughly an eighth that of China, was in the same order of magnitude as in other protected zones. Moreover, rather than being evenly dispersed, Russia's population was heavily concentrated in the west and southwest sectors of the empire, in an area appreciably smaller than China proper. Siberia and Russian Inner Asia were basically

---

[164] Ch. 6, nn. 309, 310 *infra*.

empty and after 1600 posed no military threat. Between 1620 and 1830 Russia, along with most other protected-zone states but in contrast to Qing China and especially Mughal India, thus saw a more or less constant pyramiding of central resources and a continuous strengthening of local control mechanisms.

To sum up, protected-zone realms – Burma, Siam, Vietnam, Russia, France, and Japan – differed from China and South Asia in at least three respects, the first two of which derived in part from China and South Asia's greater geographic openness: a) The protected zone was not occupied for any substantial period by peoples from Inner Asia, whereas political development in China and South Asia from 1000/1200 was increasingly dominated by such peoples. b) Charter states appeared in the protected zone 700 to 1,300 years later than in North China and North India. c) In most protected-zone realms modest scale joined sustained interstate competition to favor cultural integration more readily than across India, and accelerating administrative centralization more readily than in either China or India.[165]

Europeans in India and Archipelagic Southeast Asia

This attention to Inner Asian catalysis offers, finally, a novel perspective on the role of Europeans in South Asia and archipelagic Southeast Asia. In essence, Europeans in those areas before 1830 can be seen as exercising an early modern integrative function similar in some respects to that of Inner Asians in China and India.

In India the British, eager to portray themselves as replacing an incompetent Mughal regime, had no difficulty seeing the Raj as successor to the Mughal state, whose territories they in effect reassembled. Similarities were not merely geopoltical. Both British and Mughals derived their power from administrative/fiscal logics that originated beyond the subcontinent, both revolutionized military organization and finance, allied with local commercial interests, fused settled society with more mobile forms of wealth, and introduced substantially novel linguistic and cultural practices that provided new vehicles for elite integration. In these ways Europeans, coming by sea, resembled Inner Asians, coming by land.

---

[165] Tokugawa Japan's pacific environment, which permitted a relatively relaxed fiscal and administrative policy, was a partial exception confirming this general proposition. Note, apropos my earlier comparison, that whereas Qin–Han unification preceded that of Pagan by some 1,200 years, Mauryan unification came 1,300 years earlier.

Yet British interventions to 1830 were even more innovative and efficiently integrative than those of the Mughals. They pursued a novel program of racial rather than religious privilege (in fact, tended to discourage Christian proselytism), extended their imperial boundaries in the east and south well beyond Mughal dominions, squeezed intermediate landholders more effectively than the Mughals, insisted on more penetrating, rule-bound systems of taxation and administration, and re-oriented South Asian warfare from cavalry to artillery, disciplined infantry, and naval support. At the same time the British responded to forces – global struggles with France, demands of British trade and domestic politics, European ideological currents – that lay even farther afield from South Asia than forces in Inner Asia.

Island Southeast Asia, that is to say, the archipelago extending from Sumatra to the Philippines, resembled mainland Southeast Asia in a number of key features. Both sectors of Southeast Asia shared a distinctive sociocultural profile. Both imported Indian culture in the first millennium, generated Hindu-Buddhist charter polities from 900 to 1400, and experienced 14th-century strains that yielded after 1400/1450 to political reintegration, vigorous urbanization, and commercial expansion. Moreover, both remained shielded from Inner Asian incursions, the mainland by climate and northern highlands, the islands by the sea itself.[166]

But island Southeast Asia also differed from the mainland in basic respects. For one, with the partial exception of Java, island demography and geography were less favorable to centralization. Even before Europeans arrived, most island polities, with dispersed populations and widely separated commercial zones, were smaller and more fissiparous than their mainland counterparts.

Most critical, in the archipelago as in China and South Asia, but in contrast to mainland Southeast Asia, early modern political history came to depend substantially on actors from outside the region. If the reunification/expansion of China after 1279 and 1644 was the work of Mongols and Manchus, and if South Asian integration required Turks (and, from the late 1700s, the British), in island Southeast Asia Iberians and Dutchmen played a comparable role. European intervention proved most transformative in what are now the central and northern Philippines, which before the Spanish knew nothing more encompassing than

---

[166] A Mongol attack on Java in 1293, like contemporary attacks on Japan, miscarried.

village confederations. However, between c. 1620 and 1830 the halting unification of coastal and interior Java and the creation of secure political connections between Java, the Spice Islands, and enclaves in Sulawesi and Sumatra also depended on Europeans, in this case the Dutch. In other words, the seas that had long protected island Southeast Asian from external conquest began to invite such conquest, and the archipelago shifted from being part of the protected zone to part of the exposed zone. In this respect, one could argue, the archipelago resembled vast, hitherto self-sufficient coastal zones in Africa and the New World.[167]

In obvious ways, in the island world as in India, European activities differed from Inner Asian interventions. As overseas agents of imperial governments or trading companies rather than as members of vast military confederations, Spanish and Dutch soldiers, traders, and clergy were never more than a tiny fraction of Manchu or Mughal forces. They moved not from interior to coast but from coast to interior, relied on naval rather than cavalry superiority, and remained tied to a distant metropole without remote Inner Asian analogy. At first the Dutch showed far less interest in territorial acquisition than in commercial privilege. If Inner Asian incursions in China and India began in the second millennium B.C.E., Europeans arrived in force in Southeast Asian waters only in 1511.

And yet I shall argue that both European and Inner Asian conquests between c. 1500 and 1800 actually represented the second phase in a process of resource acquisition and institutional experiment whose first phase began with the great Eurasian economic boom of c. 950–1300/1350. More basically, like Inner Asians in China and India (or the

---

[167] As well as Sri Lanka. Note 144 *supra*, Alan Strathern, *Kingship and Conversion in Sixteenth-Century Sri Lanka* (Cambridge, 2007); idem, "Sri Lanka in the Long Early Modern Period" (ms). Accordingly, one could conceptualize Eurasia as divided into four zones: a) Inner Asian nomadic homelands, b) exposed-zone areas subject to Inner Asian occupation, c) protected-zone realms including northern and western Europe, Japan, mainland Southeast Asia, Tibet, the Himalayan foothills, and far South India, and d) archipelagic Southeast Asia, Sri Lanka, and some areas of coastal South India that shifted from protected- to exposed-zone status with the development of European seapower. However, I have declined to adopt this schema for three reasons: a) I am afraid of creating confusion with the three-zone schema discussed in the text accompanying nn. 154, 155 *supra*; b) so conventional an approach would elide hitherto unnoticed similarities between Inner Asians and seaborne Europeans; c) the distinction between the second and fourth zones crumbles with the realization that some of the same areas in zone b as became subject to Inner Asian occupation, namely coastal India, also became subject to European seapower.

British in India), the Spanish and Dutch were externally derived powers, possessed of novel military and administrative advantages, who, by superseding or co-opting indigenous formations, forged unprecedentedly expansive systems. Finally, as alien conquest elites, the Spanish and Dutch tended toward strategies of ethnic privilege, and in the Philippines religious imposition, that bore some resemblance to Manchu and Mughal policies. Indeed, one can arrange Inner Asian and European cultural influences along a loose continuum. At one extreme, an essentially preliterate, shamanic Manchu tradition had virtually no impact on Chinese high culture, but Manchu elites readily imbibed much of the latter. At the other extreme, Spanish Christianity transformed Filipino culture, hitherto illiterate and animist, but quarantined itself against indigenous influences. Synergies between Perso-Islamic and Hindu cultures, between British and Indian conventions, and between Dutch and Indonesian traditions lay somewhere between these poles.

5. CRITIQUES AND CAVEATS

Before substantiating these arguments, I want to address objections that the approach presented in this chapter is likely to inspire.[168]

One potential criticism runs as follows: In my desire to find equivalences between Southeast Asia and more "advanced" parts of the globe, I employ Eurocentric models. Variations occur, but on predetermined grids that derive ultimately from a Whiggish European metanarrative obsessed with the long-term emergence of the nation-state. Integration is deemed both normative and inherently more conducive to the general good than fragmentation. "Collapse" and "chaos" acquire negative connotations. By these criteria, Hindu South Asia, island Southeast Asia, and other regions where indigenous centralization faltered are implicitly dismissed as "failures." However, Burma and mainland Southeast Asia – which, happy coincidence, happen to be the area of my own expertise – emerge as success stories alongside Europe and Japan. For the first time mainland Southeast Asia enters the big leagues. In short, this is a neo-modernization project, driven by a desire to compensate for mainland Southeast Asia's marginality and encumbered with all the weaknesses of modernization theory, including a teleological focus on the nation, a willingness to treat European norms as the acme of

[168] Cf. *SP*, 21–24, 81–84.

achievement, a tendency to take early modern states' self-aggrandizing claims at face value, and a corresponding indifference to the life experiences of provincial populations, subordinate classes, and preliterate peoples.[169]

But if we accept the initial goal of comparing European and non-European development, obviously we must seek uniform criteria. If some of my key categories derive from European historiography, these categories are now part of a universal discourse on which Japanese, Chinese, and South Asian historiography are no less dependent. As provisional topics for inquiry, market integration, political centralization, cultural diffusion, and so forth carry very little culturally specific baggage. At the same time, basic concepts in my interpretation of French and Russian experience – charter polities, administrative cycles, progressively shorter and less disruptive eras of breakdown – derive not from European studies at all, but from my reading of Burmese and Chinese history. In my opinion, patterns of cyclic-cum-linear integration in Pagan, Toungoo, and Kon-baung Burma can tell us more about Capetian, Valois, and Bourbon France than French historiography can tell us about Burma.

Nor do I necessarily treat integration as morally superior to fragmentation. To be sure, by lowering transaction costs, quelling internal disorder, guaranteeing hierarchy, and broadening cultural horizons, state strengthening benefited wide sectors of the population. A deep yearning, by no means restricted to elites, for such benefits helped to drive integration from below in one Eurasian region after another. Inevitably, these same processes exacted a heavy price – in self-respect, cultural security, tax and service demands, and state-sanctioned violence – from those on the social margins. *En passant* I describe both benefits and costs. I am, however, less concerned with drawing up an ethical balance sheet than with solving the central, recurrent conundrum: Why in far-flung sectors of Eurasia over several centuries and with surprising synchronism did interlocking trends toward political, cultural, and commercial integration grow ever more insistent? *This is the intellectual*

---

[169] Cf. views of Barbara Watson Andaya in her review of *SP* in *JESHO* 47 (2004): 488–90; James Scott, *Weapons of the Weak* (New Haven, 1985); Taylor, "Surface Orientations"; Day, *Fluid Iron*, esp. ch. 4; Chris Baker, "Autonomy's Meanings," in Sunait Chutintaranond and Chris Baker, eds., *Recalling Local Pasts* (Chiang Mai, 2002), 167–82.

axis on which the book pivots, besides which cost–benefit calculations are largely irrelevant.

By extension, if a revisionist impulse leads me to examine parallels, I am also at pains to describe differences – in charter experience, social structure, commercial potential, religious and cultural expression, military organization, and so forth. I do so within Southeast Asia, within Asia, within Europe, and between these regions. The excitement of Eurasian comparisons derives not from a spurious superficial identity, but from the juxtaposition of overarching similarities with idiosyncratic local outcomes. The more diverse those outcomes, the more pressing the challenge to explain gross convergences. With those who argue for the peculiar weakness by European or Chinese standards of the precolonial Southeast Asian state – with Tony Day, who argues that Southeast Asian historical formations were "like no other on earth"[170] – I have no real quarrel. I would point out simply that mainland empires in 1830 were less superficial than those of 1600, which in turn were far less superficial than those of 800; that even the most recalcitrant hill peoples were increasingly drawn into webs of cultural, political, and economic significance focusing on the imperial lowlands;[171] and that gross rhythms and dynamics of state and culture formation in Southeast Asia coincided with those in other Eurasian rimlands. To the twinned questions – Why progressive integration? Why Eurasian parallels? – a scholarship that focuses exclusively on idiosyncrasy has no answer. (Lest one exaggerate Southeast Asian weaknesses, note too that the latest research on factionalism and state–local interactions in early modern Europe substantially qualifies earlier emphases on efficient centralization.)

This perspective, I hope, also inoculates me against charges of resurrecting European exceptionalism. One might complain that although the chapter began by critiquing European exceptionalism, at the end of the day I place France atop every ranking. Among the realms under review, France in 1830 (indeed, 1500 or 1700) was the most administratively unified and militarily innovative and, together with Japan, Vietnam, and perhaps China, the most culturally cohesive. France alone replaced dynasticism with nationalism, and clientage with popular mobilization.

---

[170] Day, *Fluid Iron,* 291. Cf. James Scott, "Hill and Valley in Southeast Asia, or . . . Why Civilizations Can't Climb Hills," Paper prepared for "Beyond Borders" Workshop, Paris, June 2000.

[171] See n. 30 *supra.*

How does this tale of European triumph differ from the stories we learned in high school? But in truth, I never promised to dethrone European exceptionalism. My goal has been more modest: merely to chart hitherto ignored but limited similarities between Southeast Asia and other sectors of Eurasia, including Europe. By definition, every early modern integration was in some ways *sui generis*. Tokugawa Japan supported exceptionally coherent cultural and commercial networks but saw little need for military experiment or progressive administrative centralization. The Russian empire in 1800 prioritized military strength and fiscal extraction but was culturally fragmented and commercially limited. Why, then, not also acknowledge western Europe's unusual combination of penetrating administrations, thick commercial linkages, extracontinental engagement, intense interstate competition, and patriotic public spheres? Not a few critiques of European exceptionalism strike me as jejune and exaggerated, happy to throw out the baby with the bath water.[172]

By the same token, I have no desire to glorify Burma's past by artificially conflating Burmese and West European experience. Fundamental differences in political ethos and organization in 1500 only grew more pronounced thereafter. What is more, by inhibiting accommodation to European colonialism, precolonial Burmese culture contributed, if indirectly, to that country's late-20th-century status as home to one of Asia's weakest economies and most isolated regimes.

Nor do I seek to essentialize or naturalize the nation, to present "Burma," "France," "Japan," "China" and so forth as the same entities in 1100 as in 1830. Admittedly, I am more interested in long-term integration than fragmentation, because I seek to show that Southeast Asian experience fit wider trends. Admittedly too, the chances that France or Burma would assume a radically new territorial or ethnic identity were appreciably less in 1700 than in 1500, when they were less than in 1300. But this is hardly the same as essentialism. In 1428 the existence of "France" as a coherent entity remained in grave doubt. As late as 1790 it was unclear whether a single Vietnamese state would emerge. In every region I consider the histories of failed kingdoms and eclipsed cultures and those contingencies that sealed their fates. Likewise, I argue, most early modern ethnicities not only arose late, but even among core populations remained spatially and semiotically fluid. In no two centuries were the external markers, the self-images, the social constituencies of

---

[172] See *SP*, 73–74.

ethnicity precisely the same, so at bottom national continuity is a matter of heuristic convenience.[173]

Another grand objection concedes that I allow for local and temporal variation but argues that the comparisons themselves remain at a such a high level of abstraction as to deracinate history. Both my analogies and distinctions are too abstract, too arid to have much value in understanding the richness of the past.

Value, however, can only be measured against previous understandings. Unexceptional though it may appear in hindsight, the simple fact that mainland Southeast Asia's chief regions, the Japanese islands, and major European realms all moved from extreme fragmentation in 700 to substantial cultural and political integration in 1830 has, to my knowledge, never been noted. Nor has the pattern in Southeast Asian and European realms whereby successive breakdowns tended to become less prolonged and disordered. Nor has synchronized construction and collapse in far-flung sectors of Eurasia. Nor, so far as I know, has the distinction between Eurasia's protected zone and exposed zone. Given this inattention, it is hardly surprising that much remains to be said about the coordinating role of climate, disease, trade, agrarian reclamation, and institutional experiment. Precisely because it promises to wed abstraction to particularity, comparative histories of Eurasia offer some of the same benefits as comparative histories of Europe itself.

Finally, one could object that my comparisons, hinging on restricted criteria, ignore patterns whose analysis would produce classifications within Eurasia very different than those I propose. For example, if we were to compare not political integration, but urbanism, industrial potential, literary production, or consumer culture, the distinction between protected and exposed Eurasian zones would yield quickly to a view in which island and mainland Southeast Asia stood together at some distance from western Europe, China, North India, and Japan. On the other hand, in its high levels of female autonomy and public mixing of the sexes, Southeast Asia showed greater affinities to western Europe than to China or South Asia. A consideration of social hierarchy, spirit propitiation, or images of nature would produce yet other alignments. And so forth.

With these observations I agree fully. Mine is but one of several valid approaches, in the same sense that intellectual, gender, economic, and

---

[173] Cf. Prasenjit Duara, "Bifurcating Linear History," *Positions* 1, 3 (1993): 779–804; idem, *Rescuing History*; Geary, *Myth of Nations*.

diplomatic history all have valid but circumscribed functions. Of course, my approach can claim certain large virtues. A concern with long-term integration can reveal novel connections between ostensibly disparate phenomena: administrative, religious, literary, and economic. These are often treated in isolation, but I submit that all were transformed by a wider, more rapid circulation of goods and people, and I explore feedback loops without which topical inquiries may be inadequate. For good or for ill, unified markets, wider patronage, and rising literacy modified the self-images and material options, in short the life prospects, of all classes and regional groups, not merely capital elites. Most basic, by deploying historiographies from a long neglected peninsula to interrogate other sectors of Eurasia, this approach offers new views of Eurasia as an interactive unit. But if my approach promises certain benefits, I make no claim to an exclusive prerogative.

Accordingly, this volume locates Southeast Asia within Eurasia according to quite specific criteria. To substantiate the thesis that integration in each of mainland Southeast Asia's chief regions paralleled trends elsewhere, Chapters 2 to 4 examine areas of closest affinity, namely Europe and Japan. Chapters 5 and 6 shift to consider externally assisted integration in China and South Asia. The last chapter tries to develop new perspectives on island history while, by way of contrast, highlighting features peculiar to the mainland.

CHAPTER TWO

Varieties of European Experience, I

The Formation of Russia and France to c. 1600

The dominant paradigm in European historiography has been linear innovation, that is to say, the sequential elaboration of distinctive political and social forms. A venerable convention in Chinese and Southeast Asian historiography has been the dynastic or administrative cycle, the recurrent alternation of periods of political strength and debility within a conservative institutional framework. I seek to meld these approaches, while liberating both from regional restriction and wedding political to cultural and economic history.

To investigate the intersection of cyclic and linear trends in Europe, I considered surveying the continent, but in the end I decided it was more practical to focus on Russian and French case studies while referring *en passant* to other realms. To the virtues of these particular examples Chapter 1 already alluded. Russia and France not only boast rich historiographies, but as hegemonic states with different social systems at either end of Europe, they covered a major part of Charles Tilly's continuum between market-intensive and market-deficient states.[1]

---

[1] See my modification of the schema in Charles Tilly, *Coercion, Capital, and European States, AD 900–1990* (Cambridge, MA, 1990) in Ch. 1, n. 61 *supra*. Cf. state typologies developed in Stein Rokkan, "Dimensions of State Formation and Nation-Building," in Charles Tilly, ed., *The Formation of National States in Western Europe* (Princeton, 1975), 562–600, esp. 575 ff.; Hendrik Spruyt, *The Sovereign State and Its Competitors* (Princeton, 1994). One might question Russia's bona fides as a European state by pointing out that Russian social structures were peculiar, even by East European standards; that between c. 1240 and 1450, Russia's political and military orientation lay toward Inner Asia; and that from the mid-1600s most of its imperial holdings also lay east of the Urals. Yet, as Chs. 2 and 3 will show, not only did Russia's political center and the vast bulk of its population always lie in Europe, but as a Christian polity, even under Mongol-Tatar

Moreover, if their precise chronologies were *sui generis*, Russia and France well illustrate a periodization found in much of Southeast Asia and Europe: late first/early second millennium vigor, 13th- to 14th-century collapse, mid-15th- and 16th-century revival halted by fresh disorders in the late 1500s or early 1600s, followed by accelerating integration to 1830 and beyond. Symptom and cause of political integration, in Russia and France as in Southeast Asia, elite religious systems penetrated to lower levels, capital tongues expanded at the expense of sacred languages above and provincial dialects below, while central ethnicities grew more encompassing, clearly delimited, and politicized.

Such comparisons weaken conventional European/Asian dichotomies in two ways. Most basic, they show that societies in Europe and mainland Southeast Asia, peninsulas at the far ends of Eurasia, shared a tendency toward episodic but increasingly durable political and cultural consolidation. At the same time, they suggest that in some contexts neither Europe nor Asia is a decisive category. Kiev and Angkor, for example, shared certain features found neither in France nor Vietnam. In Tilly's schema, for much of the period to 1650 Russia and Burma lay closer to one another than either did to France. Chapter 4, on Japan, will reinforce the view that similarities between Asian and European realms could exceed intra-Asian comparabilities.

Far from camouflaging local differences, I emphasize them both within and between regions. I argue not that central control over provincial officials in France and Burma was comparable, merely that in both realms external zones assimilated over time to a more interior status. I argue not that commercial profiles were similar, only that waves of market integration were broadly coordinated across Eurasia.

Unfortunately, comparative data on trade, climate, disease, and state influences are often too limited to admit confident claims about the contribution to these trends of individual factors. Analysis is further complicated by the fact that apart from climate, each factor was simultaneously independent and dependent variable. Pathogens, for example, had an autonomous dynamic, but their impact was mediated by climate

rule, Russia's early cultural ties ran to Byzantium. After c. 1400 Inner Asian influence on Russia steadily receded, to be replaced from the late 1500s by ever stronger cultural, military, and political links to central and western Europe. By the mid-1600s Russia was acknowledged to be an influential European military power, and by the mid-1700s it had become a pillar of the European interstate system. Thereafter, to the end of the period with which we are concerned, Russia's cultural and political involvement in Europe only deepened.

and commercial openings. By promoting specialization, long-distance trade raised demographic ceilings, but trade cycles remained sensitive to shifts in global population.

The best one can do presently is to delineate stages in the integration of each region and to identify potential coordinating agents. To facilitate comparisons with Southeast Asia, my European inquiry is structured around four periods familiar from Volume 1 but that also embody more or less accepted conventions in Russian and French historiography: a) The period c. 500–1240/1330, conventionally termed "medieval" by Europeanists, but much of which, by analogy to Southeast Asia, I term the "charter era." Russia's charter polity of Kiev functioned from c. 930 to 1240, whereas the Frankish/Carolingian charter state operated much earlier, from c. 500 to the late 800s. Some 220 years after Carolingian collapse, the Capetian Dynasty began to extend its control over modern France and continued to prosper to the early 1300s. Thus, as Chapter 1 suggested, whereas by 1240 Russia had seen the early and middle phase of a single administrative cycle, France already had completed one cycle and had entered a second.[2] b) An extended period of fragmentation in both Russia and France, c. 1240/1337–1450, which was part of a general Eurasian crisis. c) Vigorous early modern consolidation c. 1450–1560, leading to another collapse, albeit far shorter and milder than postcharter interregna. d) The high early modern era of rapidly accelerating integration, which began in the early 1600s and continued in France to 1789 and in Russia to the early 1800s, with a significant subperiodization in Russia from the turn of the 18th century.[3] In varying degrees

---

[2] Recall that Chapter 1 defined an "administrative cycle" as a three-part oscillation from a phase of growing territorial and political integration, to a phase of maximum integration, to a phase of territorial fragmentation, political and institutional collapse.

[3] Among these periodizations, in France the lumping together of Carolingian and Capetian eras is least conventional, whereas 1789 is usually considered a watershed between early modern and modern. I nonetheless take French history to c. 1830 to maintain comparisons with Southeast Asia and Russia. See periodization schemas in Michele Fogel, *L'etat dans la France Moderne de la Fin du XVe Siecle au Milieu du XVIIIe Siecle* (Paris, 1992); Pierre Goubert, *The Course of French History* (London, 1991); Marcus Bull, ed., *France in the Central Middle Ages 900–1200* (Oxford, 2002); David Potter, ed., *France in the Later Middle Ages 1200–1500* (Oxford, 2002); Georges Duby, *France in the Middle Ages 987–1460* (Oxford, 1991); Emmanuel Le Roy Ladurie, *The Royal French State 1460–1610* (Oxford, 1994); idem, *The Ancien Regime 1610–1774* (Oxford, 1996); Nicholas Riasanovsky, *A History of Russia* (4th ed., New York, 1984); Janet Martin, *Medieval Russia 980–1584* (Cambridge, 1995); John Fennell, *The Crisis of Medieval Russia 1200–1304* (London, 1983); Robert Crummey, *The Formation of Muscovy 1304–1613* (London, 1987); and Paul Dukes, *The Making of Russian Absolutism 1613–1801* (London, 1990).

each of these political eras also had a certain cultural coherence. At the outset, therefore, the gap between Russian and French periodization was considerable, but as Russia became subject to the same economic rhythms as western Europe and more open to European military and cultural influences, that gap narrowed dramatically. This chapter will survey the first three periods, whereas Chapter 3 will consider trends from c. 1600 through 1830.

1. CHARTER POLITIES, EARLY AND LATE, C. 500–1240/1330

Introduction: Distinct Heritages, Comparable Rhythms

In the mid-first millennium c.e., the areas that would coalesce as Kievan Rus and as the kingdom of France already differed substantially. By West European standards, the future heartland of Kiev, stretching from the Dnieper basin north to the future Novgorod in a region that had never come under Roman imperial control, was isolated and politically constricted, with a population that consisted overwhelmingly of illiterate slash-and-burn cultivators. Whereas by the 9th century prototypes of the three-field system of crop rotation had begun to appear on demesne lands in northern France, demographic densities in western Russia would not support similar systems until the 15th to 17th centuries.[4] Soviet and some Western historians argued that in what is now western Russia during the 6th and 7th centuries the rearing of horses, cattle, and sheep and the spread of oats and winter rye cultivation joined an expansion in handicrafts, foreign trade, and domestic tribute to encourage the emergence of indigenous "statelets" based on fortified settlements. Containing from a few hundred to a few thousand people each and supporting markets and artisans, these settlements typically controlled strategic positions overlooking river junctions, which suggests an interest in trade, and drew tribute from surrounding communities. Nonetheless Byzantine and early Russian accounts and archeology agree that political authority in these preliterate, proto-urban

---

[4] Klavs Randsborg, *The First Millennium* A.D. *in Europe and the Mediterranean* (Cambridge, 1991), 179; Adriaan Verhulst, "Economic Organization," *NCMH*, vol. II, 483–87; idem, *The Carolingian Economy* (Cambridge, 2002), 61–63; Marc Bloch, *French Rural History* (Berkeley, 1966), 34; R. A. French, "The Introduction of the Three-Field Agricultural System," in James H. Bater and R. A. French, eds., *Studies in Russian Historical Geography*, 2 vols. (London, 1983), vol. I, 65–81; nn. 73, 96, 221 *infra*.

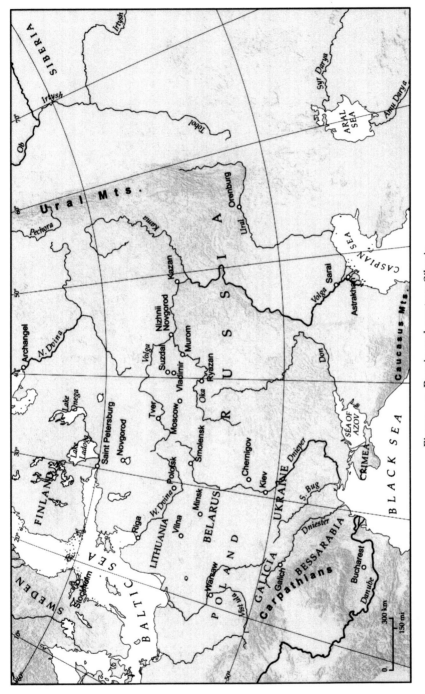

Figure 2.1. Russia and western Siberia.

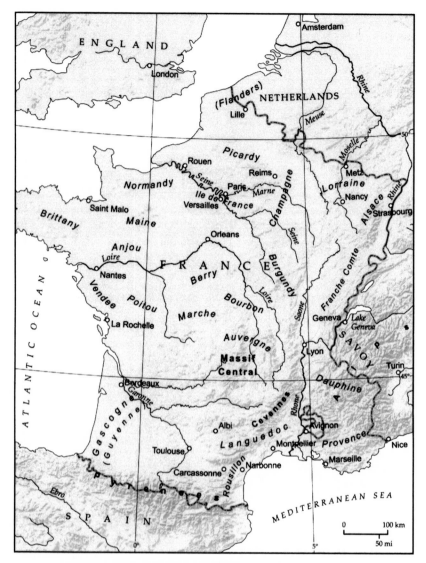

Figure 2.2. France, with boundaries of the kingdom in 1789.

domains remained highly localized.[5] The most ambitious comparative schema of urban development, by Gilbert Rozman, puts western Russia

[5] On pre-Kievan economy and polity, Simon Franklin and Jonathan Shepard, *The Emergence of Rus 750–1200* (London, 1996), 3–27; R. A. French, "The Early and Medieval Russian Town," in Bater and French, *Studies*, vol. II, esp. 249–57; Lawrence Langer,

as late as 900 somewhere between what he terms Stage A ("pre-urban") and Stage B ("tribute city"), the latter with a single administrative center in a thoroughly decentralized political environment.[6]

By comparison, long before the Roman conquest in the first century B.C.E., Gaul, approximating the territory of modern France, had reached Rozman's Stage B. This area benefited from its role as cul-de-sac for westward Eurasian migrations, from soils and climate more agriculturally propitious than in Russia, and from close cultural and economic links to the Mediterranean, which naturally intensified under Roman rule.[7] Even after the prolonged decay of Roman cities, in 750 the future territory of France retained a network of towns that Rozman describes as an advanced form of Stage C ("state city") or possibly Stage D ("imperial city").[8] If Frankish aristocrats and clerics recast both the form and ethos of Mediterranean Christianity, they still imbibed elements of what had been Gallo-Roman culture via the church, nurtured Latin as an aid to church reform, and proudly invoked Roman symbols. In their own inflated estimation, Charlemagne's coronation in 800 showed that the Franks had not merely continued the Roman empire but had superseded it. Denser populations and more elaborate commercial and cultural networks would continue to privilege western Europe well into the 19th century.

If we compare western Russia and France with mainland Southeast Asia during the late first millennium C.E., France resembled most closely the Red River plain of northern Vietnam. In both cases incorporation into a universal empire, that of Rome or China, provided an early conduit for

"The Medieval Russian Town," in Michael Hamm, ed., *The City in Russian History* (Lexington, KY, 1976), 11–13; B. Grekov, *Kiev Rus* (Moscow, 1959), 13, 125–44, 593–606; M. Tikhomirov, *The Towns of Ancient Rus* (Moscow, 1959); B. Rybakov, *Early Centuries of Russian History* (Moscow, 1965), 9–28; David Hill, "Unity and Diversity," in Richard Hodges and Brian Hobley, eds., *The Rebirth of Towns in the West AD 700–1050* (Oxford, 1988), 8–15; and David Christian, *A History of Russia, Central Asia and Mongolia, Volume 1* (Malden, MA, 1998), 328–34.

6 Gilbert Rozman, *Urban Networks in Russia, 1750–1800, and Premodern Periodization* (Princeton, 1976), 34–35, 42–45, 84. Cf. *supra* Ch. 1, n. 78.

7 Rozman, *Urban Network*, 34–35, 84. The sixth-century population of the former Gaul may not have been dramatically less than its Roman peak of 9,000,000, or 16 people per square kilometer, which was certainly greater than in the future territory of Kiev. Jacques Dupaquier et al., *Histoire de la Population Francaise*, 4 vols. (Paris, 1995), vol. I, 90–111; Fernand Braudel, *The Identity of France*, 2 vols. (New York, 1988, 1990), vol. II, 66–67, 83–85, 96–97.

8 Rozman, *Urban Networks*, 34–35, 84. Stage A had no central place levels. Stage B had one level. Stage C had two, consisting of a national administrative center and smaller administrative/satellite centers with 3–10,000 people each.

literacy and associated political traditions, which were localized before and more especially after that empire collapsed. By contrast, the Dnieper basin's thin population and its dependence on commercial, rather than imperial, transmissions bore some resemblance to western and central mainland Southeast Asia. At the same time western Russia remained more isolated than its Southeast Asian counterparts. Whereas by the 4th or 5th century C.E. the Irrawaddy and Mekong basins already boasted Indian alphabets and religions, in 750 the Dnieper basin still lay beyond the orbit of Byzantine, or indeed any, literate civilization.

These distinctive inheritances, not to mention the enormous physical distances and the lack of sustained contact between medieval France and Russia, render all the more puzzling the parallelism of their evolution. Along with other sectors of western and northern Europe, from the 9th or 10th century both societies saw a quickening of economic activity and political experiment. In both regions economic growth and political innovation accelerated to the early or mid-13th century, only to collapse at some point between 1240 and the 1330s.

Kievan Genesis and Prosperity

Consider first the founding and expansion of Kiev. For generations Slavic, Finnic, and Baltic tribes in what is now western Russia had exchanged goods with the Baltic, the Volga, and the Black Sea. From the mid-8th or early 9th century, however, the region's political economy was transformed by the arrival in strength of Viking traders, who enjoyed marked advantages over local peoples in military organization, metal-working tools, riding gear, and perhaps agricultural implements.[9] The Rus, as these adventurers were called in early sources, responded to two stimuli, namely, a strong demand for silver in the expanding North Sea/Baltic economy, and expansionist Abbasid trade policies that suddenly made available in the marts of the lower Volga large quantities of Abbasid silver *dirhams*.[10] The degree to which the Rus attached themselves to preexisting fortified centers is debated, as is the influence

---

[9] Franklin and Shepard, *Emergence*, 47 and ch. 1 *passim*; Neil Price, "Novgorod, Kiev and Their Satellites," in Mogens Herman Hansen, ed., *A Comparative Study of Thirty City-State Cultures* (Copenhagen, 2000), 263–76, esp. 263.

[10] Richard Hodges and David Whitehouse, *Mohammed, Charlemagne & the Origins of Europe* (Ithaca, 1983), 113–22; Franklin and Shepard, *Emergence*, 9–29; Thomas Noonan, "Why the Vikings First Came to Russia," *JfGO* 34 (1986): 321–48.

and ethnicity of those pre-Viking settlements. What seems reasonably clear is that by the mid-800s from the Baltic to the upper Volga stretched an archipelago of small fortified Rus-led trading settlements, each of which offered protection to local tribespeople, many of them Slavic-speakers, in return for tribute (furs, wax, honey, and slaves) that could be exchanged for silver. Gradually these settlements cohered into a militarized network whose unity advanced notably in 862 when, according to a later chronicle, Rus leaders invited a Viking prince named Riurik to rule over them.[11]

Shortly thereafter turmoil along the Volga joined with a sharp reduction in Abbasid silver to redirect Rus interest from the upper Volga toward Constantinople, which was then entering a period of sustained commercial expansion and which could provide the Rus with naval stores, coins, and diverse luxuries prized for domestic patronage and northern transshipment. The focus on Byzantium automatically elevated the importance of the Dnieper trade route and the mid-Dnieper region, in particular the old southern settlement of Kiev, which became the principal Rus political center in the early or mid-10th century. In the 960s, by destroying the Khazar kingdom on the lower Volga, the Rus further enlarged their catchment of tribute-paying Slavs and reinforced the primacy of the north–south Dnieper route. This was the famous road "from the Varangians to the Greeks" – that is, from the Scandinavian north to Constantinople.[12]

During Kiev's so-called Golden Age, variously dated c. 980 to 1054, 1125, or 1132,[13] governance was reorganized, and novel cultural conventions took root. The Riurikid Dynasty – which would govern Russia until 1598 – dominated a vast zone from the mid-Dnieper in the south

---

[11] Franklin and Shepard, *Emergence*, ch. 1; Price, "Novgorod, Kiev," 266; Basil Dmytryshyn, ed., *Medieval Russia: A Source Book, 850–1700* (Ft. Worth, TX, 1991), 2–18.

[12] Janet Martin, *Treasures of the Land of Darkness* (Cambridge, 1986), 111–13; Franklin and Shepard, *Emergence*, 50–138, 142–45; Christian, *History of Russia*, 334–46; Price, "Novgorod, Kiev," 266–68. For evidence that the 9th or 10th to 12th centuries were a period of demographic and economic vitality in Byzantium, see Warren Treadgold, *A History of the Byzantine State and Society* (Stanford, 1997), 402–13, 569–79, 699–706; Michael Angold, *The Byzantine Empire 1025–1204* (London, 1997), 81–89; and esp. Paul Stephenson, "Byzantium Transformed, c. 950–1200," in Johann Arnason and Bjorn Wittrock, eds., *Eurasian Transformations, Tenth to Thirteenth Centuries* (Leiden, 2004), 185–210.

[13] On the dating of Kiev's heyday, see Riasanovsky, *History*, 29–30; Martin, *Medieval Russia*, 77–89.

to Lake Onega in the north and from Murom in the east to Polotsk in the west. These "lands of Rus" were conceived as the collective possession of the dynasty, whose princes distributed provincial seats through a complex, evolving system of rotated appointments. Externally the Riurikids treated with courts as distant as France and England. But given the emphasis on Black Sea routes, Kiev's primary contacts were with Byzantium and Orthodox Bulgaria, which together provided a model for virtually all high culture in pre-Mongol Russia. After years of growing Orthodox influence, the famed Prince Vladimir in 988 authorized Byzantine clergy to baptize the people of his capital. This was at once a political and civilizational foundation, comparable to the contemporary expansion of Theravada Buddhism in Upper Burma or the somewhat earlier spread of Sinic Mahayana Buddhism in *ritsuryo* Japan. As ties developed with Constantinople and Bulgaria, the face of urban Rus was transformed. Kiev and lesser towns sprouted hundreds of churches and monasteries, built mostly by Greek specialists. Byzantine painting, music, church organization, and law also found avid local imitators, while the language of writing, namely Church Slavonic, and the technology of writing apparently derived from Bulgaria. Supplementing older Viking and perhaps Khazar concepts of authority, the new faith provided a novel identity for the Rus political elite, which even before the conversion was becoming more diverse through inclusion of Slavs, Finns, and other non-Vikings.[14]

Economically the 11th and early 12th centuries were boom times for Kiev. At its height the city reportedly contained 36,000 to 50,000 people,[15] which was probably two to four times larger than the second Rus town, Novgorod. Kiev remained the chief transit point to Byzantium, pumping out slaves, furs, and forest products, while importing

---

[14] On Kiev's politics and culture, Martin, *Medieval Russia*, ch. 1; Simon Franklin, *Writing, Society, and Culture in Early Rus, c. 950–1300* (Cambridge, 2002), 10–15, 83–106, 120–27, 187–88; idem, "Dirty Old Books," in Valerie Kivelson and Joan Neuberger, eds., *Picturing Russia* (New Haven, 2008), 12–16; Andrzej Poppe, *The Rise of Christian Russia* (London, 1982); Franklin and Shepard, *Emergence*, ch. 4; John Meyendorff, *Byzantium and the Rise of Russia* (Cambridge, 1981), ch. 1; "Proceedings of the International Congress Commemorating the Millennium of Christianity in Rus'-Ukraine," *HUS* 12–13 (1988–89). On the relation of Kievan to pre-Byzantine political concepts, W. K. Hanak, "Some Conflicting Aspects of Byzantine and Varangian Political and Religious Thought in Early Kievan Rus," *Byzantoslavica* 37 (1976): 46–55.

[15] Martin, *Medieval Russia*, 61, for c. 1200. Franklin and Shepard, *Emergence*, 282, cite estimates ranging from 20,000 to 100,000.

Mediterranean olive oil, wine, and other luxuries. Kiev also served as the hub for intraregional trade and handicraft production, both of which drew strength from elite sedentarization and new ecclesiastical needs. Between 1013 and 1112 elites based in Kiev erected some 83 percent of all masonry, or to use David B. Miller's phrase "monumental," buildings in the lands of Rus.[16] The city and its environs boasted the most numerous and opulent churches, the most sophisticated urban crafts, and an aristocracy who set the fashion for provincial imitators. Kiev's undisputed dominance in this period was symbolized by its hosting both the senior Riurikid, later known as the Grand Prince, and the leader of the newly established Orthodox church, the Metropolitan, whose ecclesiastical province lay under the authority of the Patriarch of Constantinople.[17]

In the course of the 12th century Kiev's relative position weakened, in part because of poor leadership in Kiev; in part, some claim, because Turkic invasions and new Mediterranean routes eroded Constantinople's competitiveness;[18] but most basically because Rus towns on the frontiers, some hitherto inconsequential, became more numerous and prosperous. Miller's study of masonry buildings, which he argues were a sensitive indicator of urban dynamism in general and elite accumulation in particular, shows that in all the lands of Rus between 1013 and 1112 an annual average of 0.48 stone and brick edifices appeared, but from 1113 to 1237 the figure rose to 1.53, and during the peak years of 1188 to 1212 the rate was 2.3. Yet as the overall number swelled, Kiev's percentage of the total plummeted from 83 percent between 1064

---

[16] David B. Miller, "Monumental Building and Its Patrons as Indicators of Economic and Political Trends in Rus, 900–1262," *JfGO* 38 (1990): 321–55, esp. 339, 350. On trade and towns, see too idem, "The Kievan Principality in the Century Before the Mongol Invasion," *HUS* 10 (1986): 215–40; Thomas Noonan, "The Flourishing of Kiev's International and Domestic Trade, c. 1100–c. 1240," in I. S. Koropeckyj, ed., *Ukrainian Economic History* (Cambridge, MA, 1991), 102–46; Franklin and Shepard, *Emergence*, 279–84; Omeljan Pritsak, *The Origins of the Old Rus' Weights and Monetary Systems* (Cambridge, MA, 1998), chs. 4–8.

[17] Andrzej Poppe, "Words That Serve the Authority," *Acta Poloniae Historica* 60 (1989): 159–84; Omeljan Pritsak, "Kiev and All of Rus," *HUS* 10 (1986): 279–300; Franklin and Shepard, *Emergence*, 279–80.

[18] Martin, *Land of Darkness*, 45; Donald Queller and Gerald Day, "Some Arguments in Defense of the Venetians on the Fourth Crusade," *AHR* 81 (1976): 734. But see arguments for generalized Byzantine prosperity thru the late 1100s, n. 12 *supra*. On Turkic incursions from the steppe as a direct threat to Kievan trade, see Franklin and Shepard, *Emergence*, 252–53, 271–73; Riasanovsky, *History*, 39.

and 1112 to less than 17 percent between 1188 and 1237. The biggest increases occurred in new provincial centers in the west, the far north at Novgorod, the northeast, and to a lesser extent in the southwest (see Figure 2.3c).[19] The same provincial dynamism appears if we consider the spread of chronicle writing, large monasteries, or new bishoprics.[20] Each frontier zone relied on foreign trade independent of the old Kiev–Constantinople axis: the west with Poland, Bohemia, and Hungary; Novgorod with the Baltic; and the northeast with the Volga and thence the Abbasid Caliphate.[21] Moreover, each frontier city was supported by a thickening network of secondary towns and local settlements during what, by all indications, was an era of rapid population growth and frontier reclamation. Iu. S. Aseev noted that of 43 known Kievan "towns," 25 were first mentioned in the chronicles between 1150 and 1240.[22] Using a more elastic definition of towns, M. Tikhomirov claimed that 89 such settlements in the 11th century grew to 300 by 1240.[23] At a yet more local level, Simon Franklin and Jonathan Shepard have graphed during the 12th century a "thickening pattern" of small rural settlements, especially along the tributaries of the middle and upper Dnieper and in the valleys of the Dniester, Bug, and upper Volga.[24] Meanwhile, despite its *relative* decline, Kiev continued to prosper by focusing on craft production, local exchange, and the transit trade between central Europe and northern Black Sea ports.[25]

---

[19] Miller, "Monumental Building, 900–1260," esp. charts at 350–55. See too Noonan, "Flourishing of Kiev's Trade," 102–46; and on early Novgorod, Price, "Novgorod, Kiev," 268–72.

[20] Franklin and Shepard, *Emergence*, 305–306; Martin, *Medieval Russia*, 81–88.

[21] Furs and forest products remained important exports to central Europe, but the addition of hides, flax, and hemp points to agricultural expansion in western Rus. In the opposite direction imports from Europe, including Flemish cloth, also grew more diverse. From the Caliphate derived spices, gems, textiles, and steel blades. Martin, *Lands of Darkness*, 43–52; Riasanovsky, *History*, 44; Franklin and Shepard, *Emergence*, 324–39.

[22] Cited in Miller, "Kievan Principality," 223. According to A. V. Kuza, cited in Franklin and Shepard, *Emergence*, 337, whereas in 1150 Rus had about 50 small towns, by 1200 the number was close to 80.

[23] Tikhomirov, *Towns*, pt. 1, ch. 1, and pt. 2. Cf. Martin, *Medieval Russia*, 60–61; French, "Early and Medieval Russian Town," 257–59; Langer, "Medieval Town," 12–13.

[24] Franklin and Shepard, *Emergence*, 406–407. Also ibid., 139, 177–78, 265, 323–39; and R. E. F. Smith, *Peasant Farming in Muscovy* (Cambridge, 1977), 113.

[25] Miller, "Monumental Building, 900–1260," 337–42; idem, "Kievan Principality," 217, 219; Martin, *Medieval Russia*, 64–65; Thomas Noonan, "The Monetary History of Kiev in the Pre-Mongol Period," *HUS* 11 (1987): 409; idem, "Flourishing of Kiev's Trade," 102–46.

In short, whether we consider trade, the elaboration of literate Christian traditions, urbanism, or frontier settlement, sustained Rus expansion began in the 9th century, gained strength in the 10th and 11th centuries, and accelerated sharply in the 12th and early 13th centuries. Although as early as 1136 provincial autonomy – artistic, diplomatic, above all, political – had become marked, outlying towns continued to share a culture emanating from Kiev, and Riurikid princes still regarded Kiev as the premier seat. Thus to talk about the expansive energy of Kievan civilization into the 13th century is perfectly valid.[26]

Is not this basic chronology familiar from Southeast Asia? Pagan was founded in the 9th century and expanded in the 11th, but frontier colonization and temple construction became most vigorous between 1100 and 1280. Although Khmer statelets appeared as early as the 7th century, Angkor's most impressive era of conquest, colonization, and construction extended from the mid-900s to the early 1200s. In northern Vietnam, population growth and reclamation continued throughout the Ly (1010–1225) and early Tran (founded 1225), but crested in the late 1200s.

Nor was Russian development unique within Europe. As we shall see, after modest growth in the 9th century, between c. 950 and 1280 much of western and central Europe enjoyed a phase of demographic, agrarian, and commercial vitality more pronounced than in any period before the late 1700s.[27] Figures 2.3a to 2.3g compare remarkably congruent indices of economic vigor in Burma, Kiev, France, and central Europe. One of the first signs of economic expansion, and of supralocal contacts that such expansion encouraged, was the appearance of essentially new polities. Starting in the 10th or early 11th century, at roughly the same time as Kiev arose, the duchy of Normandy, the County of Flanders, the Duchies of Burgundy and Savoy, the Kingdom of Arles, the Duchy of Swabia, and the principalities of Bavaria, Ostmark (Austria), and Saxony evolved organs of central administration and/or began to expand their territories. Farther afield the 10th and

---

[26] "If one abandons the Kiev-based centralist schema, then there was no rise and fall, but rather a rise and rise, a continued growth and expansion . . . the lands of the Rus flourished economically and culturally not *in spite* of political decay, but in part *because of* political flexibility." Franklin and Shepard, *Emergence*, xix.

[27] Even before the early 11th century, Hill, "Unity and Diversity," esp. Fig. 5, plots a remarkable congruence of urban development in the late first millennium in such far-flung areas as England, Hungary, the Balkans, Russia, Scandinavia, Ireland, and France.

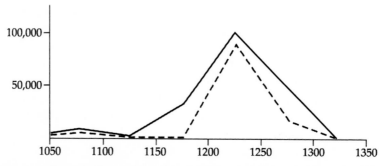

Figure 2.3. Some indices of economic and demographic growth in Southeast Asia and Europe, c. 900–1400. (a) Religious donations at Pagan, 1050–1350. The solid line shows donations to Buddhist institutions of rice land measured in *pe* (1 *pe* = 1.75 acres); the broken line represents donations in silver measured in *kyats* (1 *kyat* = 0.566 oz.) *Source*: Michael Aung-Thwin, *Pagan: The Origins of Modern Burma* (Honolulu, 1985), 187–88.

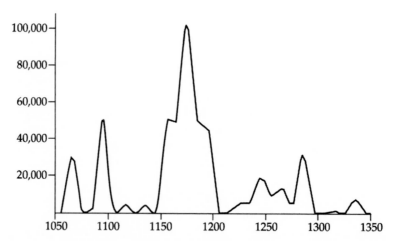

Figure 2.3 (*continued*) b. Religious construction at Pagan, 1050–1350. The vertical axis represents cubic meters of building material used in a sample of 89 epigraphically or historically dated buildings at Pagan. *Source*: Manuscript version of Bob Hudson, Nyein Lwin, and Win Maung, "The Origins of Bagan [sic]," *Asian Perspectives* 40 (2001): Figure 1.

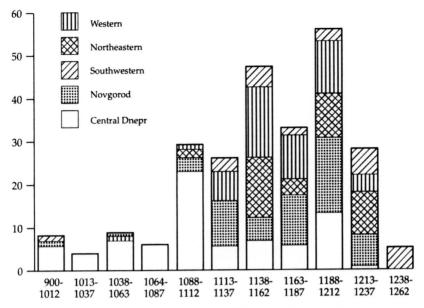

Figure 2.3 (*continued*) c. Monumental building in Rus and its component regions, 900–1262. The vertical axis shows the number of large structures in stone and brick. *Source*: David B. Miller, "Monumental Building and Its Patrons as Indicators of Economic and Political Trends in Rus', 900–1262," *Jahrbucher fur Geschichte Osteuropas* 38 (1990): 350.

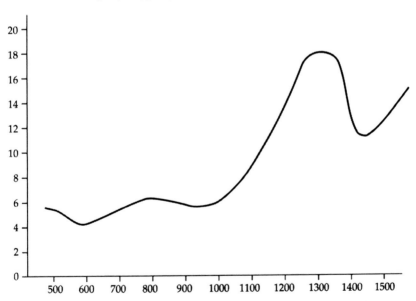

Figure 2.3 (*continued*) d. Estimated population within the territory of contemporary France, 500–1560. The vertical axis represents millions of people. Figures derive from sources listed in this chapter, nn. 98, 291 *infra*.

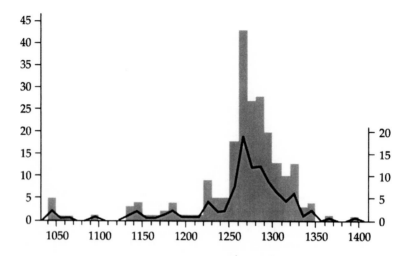

Figure 2.3 (*continued*) e. Medieval town foundations in France, excluding English Gascony, 1040–1400. The left vertical axis represents the number of new towns; the right represents the percentage. *Source*: Hugh D. Clout, ed., *Themes in the Historical Geography of France* (London, 1977), 97.

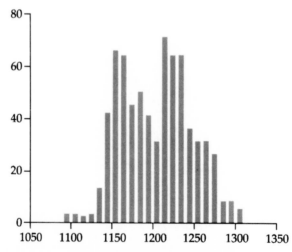

Figure 2.3 (*continued*) f. The number of French assarts, 1050–1350. The vertical axis represents the number of land clearances (assarts) mentioned in contemporary sources. *Source*: Peter Turchin and Sergey Nefedov, *Secular Cycles* (Princeton, forthcoming, available in 2008 on PDF File), 117, Figure 4.3.

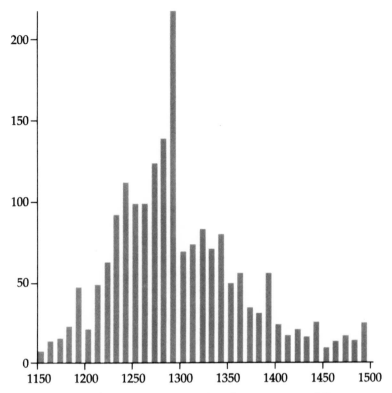

Figure 2.3 *(continued)* g. Dates of town foundations in central Europe, 1150–1500. The vertical axis represents the number of foundations. *Source:* N. J. G. Pounds, *An Economic History of Medieval Europe* (London, 1994), 102.

11th centuries saw the appearance of the Bohemian state, the kingdom of Poland, a Magyar principality on the Hungarian plain, Croat and Serb states, the first Bulgarian empire south of the Danube, as well as the nucleus of a Danish principality on Sjaelland, a Norse state around Trondheim, and a Swedish principality centered on Uppsala. Most such polities centered initially on a fertile agricultural core protected against invasions and capable of supporting a dense population that, through forest clearance and settlement, then spilled out into new districts. Until the 13th or 14th century, kingdoms continued to expand into the open frontiers between them.[28]

[28] N. J. G. Pounds and S. S. Ball, "Core Areas and the Development of the European State System," *Annals of the American Association of Geographers* 54 (1964): 24–40; N. J. G. Pounds, *An Economic History of Medieval Europe* (London, 1994), 92–96; Derek Sayer, *The Coasts of Bohemia* (Princeton, 1998), 29–35.

We shall return to the Eurasian economic boom of 900–1250/1300, but the immediate challenge is to explain Kiev's florescence. At the outset, one must distinguish between different types of economic activity, interconnected though they surely were. If we consider elite income in Kiev, it is obvious from the foregoing account that this depended first and foremost on long-distance trade. The Rus originally came in search of Abbasid silver, then shifted their base to trade with Constantinople, and when that lost some of its glitter, developed new routes to central Europe and Muslim Southwest Asia. As late as the 12th century, Kievan princes owned relatively few large estates and remained more concerned in the countryside with raising war horses and livestock than with tillage.[29] By extension, commerce provided the principal impulse to urbanization and, through the links it forged to Byzantium, shaped every facet of elite religion and culture. At Kiev more plausibly than at Pagan, Angkor, or Dai Viet, one therefore can argue that charter vitality derived from external commercial stimuli, in this case from Byzantium and, to a lesser extent, central Europe and the Mideast.

Yet despite its undeniable virtues, as a total explanation of Kievan prosperity, external demand falls short. For one thing, as Tikhomirov in his critique of V. O. Kliuchevsky's commercial theory of Kievan urban genesis was quick to point out and as later scholars have confirmed, some towns lay at considerable distances from international routes and derived their prosperity primarily from agriculture and local handicrafts, rather than long-distance trade. We find such examples in the 10th-century Kievan heartland,[30] and more especially in later centuries in the southwest and the northeast, where towns became most dense not along river routes per se, but in areas with the best agricultural climate and soil.[31] But even at preeminently commercial cities like Kiev and Novgorod, prosperity required a populous hinterland to supply

[29] On agriculture, livestock-rearing, and trade, see Martin, *Land of Darkness*; idem, *Medieval Russia*, 59–60; Koropeckyj, *Ukrainian Economic History*, 38–46; Riasanovsky, *History*, 45; I. Ia. Froianov, "A New View of the History of Kievan Rus," *Soviet Studies in History* 24 (1986): 9–107, esp. 21–23, 31, 53–67.

[30] Franklin and Shepard, *Emergence*, 173.

[31] Tikhomirov, *Towns*, 53–65, supported by Soviet scholars Rybakov, *Early Centuries*, 17–18; Grekov, *Kiev Rus*, 167–83; and in varying degrees by French, "Early and Medieval Russian Town," 258–59; Miller, "Monumental Building 900–1262," 329; R. E. F. Smith, *The Enserfment of the Russian Peasantry* (Cambridge, 1968), 4, 9; and Paul Dukes, *A History of Russia* (Durham, NC, 1990), 17–21.

foodstuffs, corvées,[32] as well as agricultural (flax, hemp, hides) and forest products and most especially slaves for export.

Of course, insofar as it allowed Riurikid princes to extend their influence over rural society, one could argue that foreign trade stimulated agricultural and population growth indirectly. In order to obtain goods for shipment to western and central Europe, Baghdad, and Constantinople, Riurikid princes encouraged settlement by providing colonists with protection, interim economic support, and leadership. Such was the case in the late 10th and 11th centuries around Kiev itself, and during the 12th to 14th centuries on the northeastern frontier. Indeed, the proliferation of competitive Riurikid lineages impelled ambitious but impoverished princes from long-settled areas to move with their retainers (*druzhina*) to the frontier, where they pacified the local population, welcomed migrants, and in due course began to collect tribute. More generally, princes aided settlement by reducing tribal conflicts and by blunting raids from the steppe, home to Turkic and other nomadic peoples. Although interactions across the steppe frontier could be peaceful, nomad attacks not only impeded Rus settlement of the steppe but periodically threatened Kiev's agrarian base in the great forested zone to the north as well as Kiev's trade links to Byzantium.[33]

It would be wrong, however, to exaggerate the rural penetration of princely elites, to ignore the parasitic element in their interventions, or to minimize autonomous forces in rural society and economy. Stimulated by rising population in core areas and by opportunities for cereal farming and stock-keeping on the frontier, forest clearance and migration often intensified long before the regular presence of a Riurikid prince. Such reclamations were organized not by princely landowners – indeed private landed property into the 12th century remained relatively undeveloped – but by free peasant communities of Slav, Iranian, and Finnic peoples according to procedures and customs that almost certainly antedated Kiev. Rising frontier populations in the southwest, the west, and the northeast in turn attracted mobile "one-horse traders," and small towns and markets arose at key points on their routes – which then drew princes eager to skim off export goods and to develop

---

[32] Corvées were needed both for monumental buildings and the serpentine walls outside Kiev, which were built during "down times" in the agricultural cycle.

[33] Martin, *Land of Darkness*, esp. chs. 4–6; idem, *Medieval Russia*, 88–99; Franklin and Shepard, *Emergence*, 268, 368; and n. 18 *supra*. On steppe–forest geography and Kiev–steppe relations, see too Willard Sunderland, *Taming the Wild Field* (Ithaca, 2004), 5–15.

political and urban structures. In other words, rural development often preceded princely intervention, rather than vice versa, and minimal princely interference could be beneficial.[34] Thus, in keeping with the views of Tikhomirov, Rybakov, and others, Miller has observed that Rus town formation normally began with local agricultural development: "an expanding land fund was the motor of economic development."[35] According to Franklin and Shepard, who, as noted, mapped the proliferation of small rural settlements, early Kievan princes were "riding the tiger of economic growth and, in the northern forests, population growth."[36] For example, Rus princes in the 12th century were attracted to the Dniester in part because of trade routes, but also because this region already was densely populated with Slav agricultural communities. "Princes arrived to find local and transit trade as a going concern, although princes [then] became catalysts for the concentration of wealth." It was this quasi-autonomous, antecedent economic expansion that later enabled northern princes to sit in towns "feeding off a ... spider's web of routes."[37] Likewise, Thomas Noonan emphasized local rather than long-distance spurs to Kievan handicraft production.[38] Note too N. J. G. Pounds' characterization of 10th- and 11th-century state formation across northern and eastern Europe generally: if commerce supplied a valuable ancillary source of wealth, in virtually every instance effective political organization required a preexisting agricultural surplus.[39]

At each node of Kievan trade, therefore, both local supply *and* external demand must be considered; if trade stimulated rural settlement, the reverse was also true. Moreover, to the degree that Kiev's chief trading partners in northern and eastern Europe, Byzantium, and the Caliphate also enjoyed demographic, agrarian, and/or urban vigor at various times between 850 and 1200, long-distance trade reflected a generalized increase in European and West Asian demand.[40]

---

[34] Franklin and Shepard, *Emergence*, 339.
[35] Miller, "Monumental Building 900–1260," 329; ibid., "Kievan Principality," 223. Cf. Tikhomirov, *Towns*, 53–65; Rybakov, *Early Centuries*, 17–18; Grekov, *Kiev Rus*, 167–83; Jerome Blum, *Lord and Peasant in Russia* (Princeton, 1961), 17–21.
[36] Franklin and Shepard, *Emergence*, 177. On the interplay between princely and local initiatives, see too ibid., 170, 178–79, 265, 325–32, 337–39; Smith, *Enserfment*, 9–10.
[37] Franklin and Shepard, *Emergence*, 328, 370. Also Christian, *History of Russia*, 342.
[38] Noonan, "Flourishing of Kiev's Trade," 111, 144 and *passim*.
[39] Pounds, *Economic History*, 93. See too nn. 77–85 *infra*.
[40] In Byzantium from the 10th, possibly the 9th, through the 12th centuries population growth and an increase in urbanism and coinage proved compatible with growing

Alongside external trade and Riurikid patronage, what factors, then, impelled population growth in the Kievan lands? New disease regimens and climate are obvious candidates. Volume 1 and Chapter 1 of this volume suggested that in the late first millennium populations around the Eurasian rim grew, in part, because more regular trade and migratory contacts with older centers transformed smallpox, measles, and other once universally fatal epidemics afflicting all ages into more manageable endemic diseases of childhood. In reciprocal fashion, greater disease resistance helped local populations cross the demographic threshold needed to sustain local chains of infection among children. Beginning in trans-Alpine and central Europe in the 6th or 7th centuries, such adjustments may not have reached the British Isles, Scandinavia, and the Dnieper basin until the late first or early second millennium.[41] But for Russia, hard evidence, as opposed to conjecture, is frankly unavailable.

The Medieval Climate Anomaly, 800/850–1250/1300, also discussed in Chapter 1, may have affected this picture in two ways. First, it may have influenced disease regimens. It is known that long-term changes in temperature or precipitation can modify bacterial and viral agents, change the migratory behavior of disease vectors, and influence human susceptibility. In early modern Europe, periods of low disease mortality historically were associated with warmer, more stable

imperial debility. See n. 12 *supra*, plus Alan Harvey, *Economic Expansion in the Byzantine Empire* (Cambridge, 1989); idem, "The Middle Byzantine Economy: Growth or Stagnation?" *Byzantine and Modern Greek Studies* 19 (1995): 243–61; the deft summary at Michael McCormick, *Origins of the European Economy* (Cambridge, 2001), 587–92. On the economic vigor of central and northern Europe c. 900–1200, nn. 27, 28 *supra* and n. 50 *infra*, plus Hill, "Unity and Diversity"; Robert Bartlett, *The Making of Europe* (Princeton, 1993); McCormick, *Origins*, 11, 606–12, 670–74. The Mideast cycle was more complicated, with Egypt and Iraq showing considerable vigor from the 7th to the 10th centuries. From the late 1000s Iraq languished, but under the Fatimids and early Mamluks Egyptian trade continued to prosper after 1300. Elihayu Ashtor, *A Social and Economic History of the Near East in the Middle Ages* (Princeton, 1976), chs. 1–6; M. Shatzmiller, *Labour in the Medieval Islamic World* (Leiden, 1994), 43–50; Janet Abu-Lughod, *Before European Hegemony* (New York, 1989), 185–247, 356–58; McCormick, *Origins*, 580–86, 612–13, 688–95; Ch. 1, n. 117 *supra*. The increased regularity and volume of long-distance exchange favored more efficient mercantile organization, systems of credit, shipbuilding, and navigation, which in turn stimulated local demand and magnified the local impact of long-distance trade.

[41] An interactive minimum population of approximately 400,000 is generally needed to sustain measles endemicity, and 100,000 to 200,000 for smallpox. See Ch. 1, nn. 95, 96 *supra*; William McNeill, *Plagues and Peoples* (Garden City, NY, 1976), 114–17, 153; *SP*, 251.

weather,[42] which is potentially significant insofar as during much of the period 850 to 1250 Russian climate warmed notably.

Second and somewhat less speculative, by extending the growing season and reducing crop failures, the Medieval Climate Anomaly may have enhanced nuptiality and fertility. Located for the most part north of the 50th parallel, the lands of Rus had a short growing season (130–150 days in the mid-20th century) and as such were especially vulnerable to late and early frosts. Ye. P. Borisenkov calculates that between 950 and 1950 Russia endured over 350 "hungry years," most precipitated by bad weather.[43] Food shortages in premodern Europe not only height-ened mortality (less often through starvation than by obliging people to wander far from home, which exposed them to disease), but also low-ered fertility by increasing amenorrhea and spontaneous abortions and reducing coital frequency. Conversely and unsurprisingly, good har-vests tended to correlate with enhanced fertility, disease resistance, and infant survival.[44] In Russia, in particular, warmer temperatures would have permitted earlier plantings and later harvests at any given latitude, while extending northward the latitude at which cultivation was fea-sible within the vast forested zone stretching from the middle Dnieper to the Baltic. Warmer springs also would have increased survival rates among newborn farm animals. By helping to reach the demographic threshold beyond which local chains of infection could be maintained, agrarian prosperity in turn may have helped to tame smallpox and measles.

Relying on pollen and tree-ring evidence, borehole thermometry, glacier sediments, and chronicles, diverse studies suggest that mid-summer temperatures in much of Russia rose 0.8 °C to 1.5 °C from

---

[42] On climatic influences on disease, J. N. Biraben and Jacques Le Goff, "The Plague in the Early Middle Ages," in R. Foster and O. Ranum, eds., *Biology of Man in History* (Baltimore, 1975), 48–80; Kenneth Kiple, ed., *The Cambridge World History of Human Disease* (Cambridge, 1993), 264–65, 275–84; Jack Goldstone, *Revolution and Rebellion in the Early Modern World* (Berkeley, 1991), 30, 180–83, 356; J. D. Post, *Food Shortage, Climatic Variability, and Epidemic Disease in Preindustrial Europe* (Ithaca, 1985).

[43] Ye. P. Borisenkov, "Documentary Evidence from the U.S.S.R.," in Raymond S. Bradley and Philip D. Jones, eds., *Climate Since A.D. 1500* (London, 1995), 171, 182. See too Martin, *Medieval Russia*, 58–60.

[44] Previous note, plus Philip Hoffman, "Rural, Urban, and Global Economies," in Mack Holt, ed., *Renaissance and Reformation France* (Oxford, 2002), 66; John Walter and Roger Schofield, eds., *Famine, Disease, and the Social Order in Early Modern Society* (Cambridge, 1989), esp. essays by Walter and Schofield and by Jacques Dupaquier. For a minimal-ist view of food shortage mortality, however, see Massimo Livi-Bacci, *Population and Nutrition* (Cambridge, 1991).

the 7th or 9th to the late 11th century, cooled during part of the 11th century, and then rose, amidst continuing fluctuations, for much of the 12th and 13th centuries, during which time average summer temperatures, some claim, were as much as 2 °C warmer than in 500. In most areas markedly colder, wetter, agriculturally unfavorable conditions set in only after 1250/1300.[45] All things being equal, a rise of 0.8 °C to 2 °C would have extended the growing season at any given latitude by three to eight weeks or more, thus raising cereal yields by a very substantial amount,[46] and would have pushed climatic conditions

[45] K. V. Kremenetski et al., "Medieval Climatic Warming and Aridity as Indicated by Multiproxy Evidence from the Kola Peninsula, Russia," *PPP* 209 (2004): 113–25, dating the most pronounced warming to 1000–1200; A. Hiller et al., "Medieval Climatic Warming Recorded by Radiocarbon Dated Alpine Tree-Line Shift on the Kola Peninsula, Russia," *The Holocene* 11 (2001): 491–97, dating maximum warming to 1000 to 1300, when mean summer temperatures were at least 0.8 °C higher than *today* and when pine forests grew at least 100–140 meters above the current tree line in the Khibiny Mountains; H. H. Lamb, *Climate Past, Present and Future*, 2 vols. (London, 1977), vol. II, 564–65; V. A. Klimanov, "Climatic Changes in [the] Little Ice Age on the Plains of the USSR," and M. Chernavskaya, "Botanical Indicators of the Little Ice Age in the Russian Plain," in T. Mikami, ed., *Proceedings of the International Symposium on the Little Ice Age Climate* (Tokyo, 1992), 58–70, suggesting sustained Medieval Climate Anomaly (MCA) temperature increases of 2–3 °C over 6th- to 9th-century levels; A. Graybill and S. G. Shiyatov, "Dendroclimatic Evidence from the Northern Soviet Union," in Bradley and Jones, *Climate*, 393–414, showing 14th-century rises of 0.6 °C over the late 12th century; Keith Briffa et al., "Unusual 20th-Century Summer Warmth in a 1,000-Year Temperature Record from Siberia," *Nature* 376 (1995): 156–59, suggesting 13th-century MCA increases of 1–1.5 °C over the late 10th century; E. A. Vaganov et al., "Reconstruction of Summer Air Temperatures in the Eastern Taimyr over the Last 840 Years," *Russian Jl. of Ecology*, 28 (1997): 355–59; Willie Soon, Sallie Baliunas et al., "Reconstructing Climatic and Environmental Changes of the Past 1000 Years: A Reappraisal," *Energy and Environment* 14 (2003): 233–96, esp. 239, 251–52, 292, suggesting hemispheric MCA rises of 1–2 °C; Timothy Osborne and Keith Briffa, "The Spatial Extent of 20th-Century Warmth in the Context of the Past 1200 Years," *Science* 311 (2006): 841–44; Julia Smith, *Europe After Rome* (Oxford, 2005), 56, claiming that 12th-century northern European temperatures were nearly 2 °C higher than in 500 C.E. Likewise, the Winter Severity Index for Russia, based on Buchinskii, in H. H. Lamb, *The Changing Climate* (London, 1966), 219–20, averaged −0.88 from 1100 to 1280, but −7.4 from 1280 to 1450. But note that Leonid Serebryanny, "Glacioclimatic Features of the Little Ice Age in the Soviet Union," in Mikami, *Proceedings*, 87–93 argues for cold intervals in the 12th to 13th centuries in the Caucasus, as do Vaganov et al., "Reconstruction," 357 and Briffa et al., "Unusual 20th-Century Summer Warmth."

[46] According to Jean M. Grove, *The Little Ice Age* (London, 1988), 413–14, in southern England, at roughly the same latitude as Kiev, a fall of 0.7 °C from 1200 to 1400 shortened the growing season by about three weeks, and a further fall to 1700 cut out another two weeks. Despite modern agricultural methods, in the north Caucasus 1965–1985 weather produced variations in winter wheat yields of up to 32 percent, while on the Baltic coasts, a 1 °C drop lowers agricultural potential 17 to 25 percent.

northward by 320 to 1,280 kilometers.[47] Warming contributed to well-documented agrarian expansion in Poland between 1050 and 1250/1300 – said to have been the most agriculturally propitious in that country's entire history – and in southeast Sweden, both of which areas were subject to the same climatic influences as western Russia.[48]

Of course, climate must be considered alongside political changes, wider trade openings, and disease adjustments. But recall evidence that a) from 800/850 to 1250/1300 heavier monsoons, driven by hemispheric warming, encouraged population growth in mainland Southeast Asia, and b) the milder the winter and the less snow cover in Russia, the stronger are Indian Ocean monsoons.[49] Surely this offers a clue to coordinated agrarian-cum-demographic prosperity in northern Europe and monsoon-dependent areas in Southeast Asia, South Asia, and South China; and indirectly perhaps, to the more or less coordinated domestication of smallpox and measles in hitherto thinly populated Eurasian peripheries. At the same time climatically aided prosperity, hence rising market demand, in Europe, South Asia, Southeast Asia, and South China helps to explain the vitality of Janet Abu-Lughod's eight commercial circuits that extended in the 13th century all the way from the North Sea to the South China Sea.[50]

To sum up: In the 10th century Russia developed its first extensive supralocal political organization. Notwithstanding centrifugal tendencies, the cultural, economic, and dynastic reach of Kievan civilization continued to expand into early 1200s through the interplay of foreign commercial stimuli, princely patronage, and agrarian dynamism. The latter in turn had politicocommercial, climatic, and

Neville Brown, *History and Climate Change* (London, 2001), 14–15. Likewise, according to Geoffrey Parker, *Europe in Crisis 1598–1648* (Brighton, UK, 1980), 22, a 1 °C drop in northern Europe today reduces the farm growing season by 30 days, but in medieval conditions, without fertilizers, pesticides, and scientifically selected seeds, the impact on yields would have been larger. See too Richard Kata, "Assessing the Impact of Climatic Change on Food Production," *CC* 1 (1977): 85–96.

[47] Murray Sayle, "After George W. Bush, the Deluge," *London Review of Books* 23 (June 21, 2001): climatic conditions in the northern hemisphere move northward 125–200 miles for every 0.5 °C rise in air temperature.

[48] Norman Davies, *God's Playground: A History of Poland* (Oxford, 1981), vol. I, 49; Brown, *History and Climate*, 150, 157, 161. The number of Swedish farms tripled or quadrupled 1100–1300.

[49] See Ch. 1, n. 100.

[50] Abu-Lughod, *Before European Hegemony*, ch. 1 and *passim*. The eight circuits were those of western Europe, the eastern Mediterranean, the Eurasian steppe, Muscat to Tabriz, the Red Sea, the Arabian Sea, the eastern Indian Ocean, and Southeast Asia–China.

perhaps epidemiological roots, although on present evidence, there is no easy way to disentangle their contributions.

Integration and Devolution in the Future Area of France: The Frankish/Carolingian Charter State, c. 500–1000

What can an examination of the lands that would cohere as France add to this Eurasian picture? Several large patterns emerge. First, demographic and economic trajectories in France loosely paralleled developments in mainland Southeast Asia and Kiev, with modest growth for much of the 8th and 9th centuries, followed by a marked acceleration from the late 10th through the mid- or late 13th century. Second, more clearly than at Kiev, the primary roots of early medieval French economic vitality were agrarian and independent of long-distance trade. Third, as already indicated, France's long-standing links to Mediterranean civilization and its relatively developed economy supported an indigenous charter polity, the Frankish/Carolingian kingdom, earlier than those of Kiev or mainland Southeast Asia. After prolonged disorders accompanying the collapse of this early polity, France then went on to develop a more territorially modest but institutionally secure kingdom, that of the Capetians, which was roughly contemporary to Kiev, Pagan, Angkor, and Dai Viet. Thus, whereas the lands of Rus between c. 700 and 1240 moved from prestate localism to Kiev-centered integration, France moved from early charter integration (c. 500–720) to unstable Carolingian integration (c. 720–843) to pronounced localism (c. 890–c. 1110) to Capetian recentralization (c. 1110–1328). Yet despite these differences, in a larger sense, in both western Europe and the Russian plain, economic growth during the late first and early second millennia joined Mediterranean influences to inspire novel efforts at political and religious integration.

The western Roman economy had been sliding into local self-sufficiency since the 3rd or 4th century. In the 7th century, after years of recurrent plague, intermittently cold wet weather, and Germanic invasions, western Europe's population may have reached its lowest point since Roman times – by one estimate, Gaul in 700 held only one-eighth as many people as it had in 150 C.E.[51] As the Mediterranean-centered market economy contracted, barter, gifts, plunder, and tribute

---

[51] Xavier de Planhol, *An Historical Geography of France* (Cambridge, 1994), 68, citing Pierre Chaunu.

substantially displaced monetized transactions, technology regressed, and power shifted from urban to rural areas and from control of taxation to landowning.[52] To be sure, one can exaggerate these travails. After 750, we shall see, rural output began edging up once again, and trade in the Baltic (whose links to the Caliphate and Constantinople nurtured Kiev), in the North Sea, and across the Mediterranean showed new life.[53] Nonetheless, cereal yields, which ultimately framed all economic and political options, remained low. Even on royal manors in northern France in the 9th century, seed-to-crop ratios of 1:3 or 1:2 were still common.[54] This then was the constricted economic context in which the Frankish kings arose.

Following the collapse of Roman imperial power, Gaul became a patchwork of states led by Germanic war leaders in alliance with Gallo-Roman aristocrats. During the 5th century Frankish tribes, some of whom had served as Roman allies, entered in strength into northern Gaul, where they founded a number of kingdoms. Among these, the most successful was led by Clovis (r. 481–511), of the Merovingian Dynasty, who – almost 500 years before his Kievan counterparts – embraced Christianity, in Clovis' case Latin-rite Christianity. By the mid-6th century the Merovingians, working with local aristocratic families, had established at least a nominal authority over most of Gaul and had adapted Roman political traditions to their family enterprise. Partible royal inheritance and enduring regional cultures meant that, apart from brief interludes in 558–561 and 613–639, the Frankish lands after Clovis remained divided among three or four kingdoms (*Teilreiche*), often mutually hostile and each subject to internal tensions. From the late 600s, however, the Merovingians were thrust aside by another, more dynamic family of Frankish magnates, the Carolingians, whose

---

[52] Patrick Geary, *Before France and Germany* (New York, 1988), 96–103, 165, 228–29; Georges Duby, *The Early Growth of the European Economy* (Ithaca, 1974), ch. 1; Robert-Henri Bautier, "Haut Moyen Age," in Dupaquier et al., *Histoire de la Population*, vol. I, 119–206; McCormick, *Origins*, 115–19, 782–84; Bryan Ward-Perkins, "The End of the Roman Empire," *History Today* 55 (2005): 12–16; Chris Wickham, *Framing the Early Middle Ages* (Oxford, 2005), 105–15, 123–24, 197, 826, 831.

[53] McCormick, *Origins*, 7–12, 571–798; Hodges and Whitehouse, *Mohammed, Charlemagne*, chs. 5, 6; Verhulst, *Carolingian Economy*; idem, "Economic Organization," 481–509; Mark Blackburn, "Money and Coinage," in *NCMH*, vol. II, 538–559; Edward James, *The Origins of France* (London, 1982), 63, 68; Hodges and Hobley, *Rebirth of Towns*, 1–15, 43–62.

[54] Duby, *Early Growth*, 14, 28–29; *CIHMA*, vol. II, 286; and Verhulst, "Economic Organization," 487, slightly raising earlier figures.

base lay farther north and whose identification with Gallo-Roman civilization was, on the whole, less direct. By reorganizing the army and royal household, massively expanding the royal domain, enhancing supervision of provincial leaders, and reforming ecclesiastical structures, the Carolingians in the 720s and 730s began to reassert authority over the Merovingian core (northern France and the Low Countries) and to bring autonomous dependencies outside that core under more effective control. More dramatically, from the 770s they expanded into fresh territories, chiefly Catalonia, Saxony, Bavaria, and North Italy. Fleeting though it proved to be, the empire at its height under Charlemagne in the early 800s embraced most of what had been Roman territory north of the Alps and the Pyrenees.[55]

As northern Europe's most extensive and powerful barbarian polity, the Frankish/Carolingian kingdom resembled charter states in Southeast Asia and Kiev in several basic respects. Most obvious, the Franks, lacking independent literate traditions, translated and localized the high culture of an earlier universal civilization, in this case Rome. Hence the use of Latin for writing, the reliance on the Roman *civitas* (city-territory) as a basic administrative unit, the conversion of the Roman fisc into the Merovingian royal domain, and the perpetuation/modification of Roman ceremonial, legal, and monetary forms.

No less characteristic of charter states, territorial unification followed a long era of polycentrism and uncertain experiment. Some 250 years separated Clovis' early efforts from Carolingian consolidation. Pagan's 11th-century conquests and Angkor's 10th-century unification climaxed integrative processes that began as early as the 7th century. Although Vietnam inherited Tang provincial structures, some 70 years of competition among Tang successor states still preceded Ly dynastic consolidation in 1009. As we just saw, Kiev's late-10th-century ascendancy followed Viking interventions as early as the

---

[55] Carolingians formally displaced Merovingians as kings of Francia in 751. On Frankish history 450–810, Patrick Geary, *The Myth of Nations* (Princeton, 2002), 135–50; idem, *Before France*; Ian Wood, *The Merovingian Kingdoms, 450–751* (Harlow, UK, 1994); James, *Origins*, chs. 1–6; idem, *The Franks* (Oxford, 1988), esp. 231–35; Richard Fletcher, *The Barbarian Conversion* (Berkeley, 1997); Roger Collins, *Charlemagne* (Toronto, 1998); Rosamond McKitterick, *The Frankish Kingdoms Under the Carolingians* (London, 1983); *NCMH*,vol. II, pts. I, II, IV; Christoph Sonnlechner, "The Establishment of New Units of Production in Carolingian Times," *Viator* 35 (2004): 21–48; James Collins, *From Tribes to Nation* (Toronto, 2002), 4–25; Wickham, *Framing the Middle Ages*, 44–47, 103–105, 123–24, 194–203, 574–76.

mid-700s.[56] In each case, therefore, unification was halting, slow, and uncertain, in part, of course, because economic conditions were primitive, but also because a charter polity, by definition, was unprecedented. Roman and Chinese norms aside, there was no local rule book, no clear blueprint to follow. By this same logic, later reintegrations were easier, in part because local precedents had become available.

In religious terms too, Frankish kingdoms – like Pagan, Angkor, Dai Viet, and Kiev – engendered a reasonably novel identity. Whereas in the 5th century, notwithstanding their nominally Christian affiliations, Gallo-Roman elites were still fixated by classical secular culture, the Franks subordinated that tradition to a culture whose primary sources of language and inspiration were expressly Christian. Through religious donations, patronage of church reform, alliance with the papacy and the episcopacy, and their zeal to expand the faith in the east through both conquest and missionary outreach, Frankish kings, in particular the Carolingians, created an ideal of Christian kingship that later French rulers embraced enthusiastically. Thereafter Capetians appropriated Merovingian and Carolingian legacies, venerated Charlemagne, and honored Clovis, first to adopt Catholicism, as their kingdom's founder.[57] In effect, while glorying in their Roman heritage, Frankish kings joined Catholic bishops and Anglo-Saxon missionaries on the continent to generate trans-Alpine Europe's first independent, expressly Christian civilization.[58] As in Kiev and Southeast Asia, moreover, the pride that charter elites, lay and religious, felt on participating in a universal religious ecumene separated them in some degree from their more resolutely illiterate, pagan, and parochial subjects.

---

[56] In Japan, we shall find, *ritsuryo* consolidation capped a process lasting some four centuries.

[57] Geary, *Before France*, 176–78; Wood, *Merovingian Kingdoms*, 66–73, 184–202, 304–21; Jean Dunbabin, *France in the Making 843–1180* (Oxford, 1985), 256, 264–66; Elizabeth Hallam, *Capetian France 987–1328* (London, 1980), 176–77 (see too the 2nd ed. by Hallam and Judith Everard, Harlow, UK, 2001); Jacques Krynen, "Rex Christianissimus," *History and Anthropology* 4 (1989): esp. 91–92; Bernd Schneidmuller, "Constructing Identities of Medieval France," in Bull, *France in the Central Middle Ages*, 15–42; Janet Nelson, "The Frankish Kingdoms, 814–898: The West," in *NCMH*, vol. II, 141; Bull, *France in the Central Middle Ages*, 24, 26, 38, 39, 140; Colette Beaune, *The Birth of an Ideology* (Ithaca, 1983), 53–60, 70–89.

[58] Previous note, plus Randsborg, *First Millennium*, 17 ("Western Europe was for the first time making an independent attempt at establishing a lasting 'civilization'"); McKitterick, *Frankish Kingdoms*, 140–41 ("The barbarians of the Frankish kingdoms were in fact shaping an entirely new culture and a new society"); James, *The Franks*, 127–28.

Beyond this, in typical charter state fashion the Frankish realm provided an ethnic and territorial foundation for later generations. In
the Frankish heartland north of the Loire, Gallo-Romans gradually
assimilated to the ethnicity – as defined by language, dress, and self-
identification – of their Frankish overlords. In the Merovingian period
"Francia" still referred to the area north of the Loire, but thereafter it
came to provide a canopy for the Carolingian empire's entire western
sector. After Charlemagne's grandsons divided the empire in 843, that
sector became known as "West Francia" (*Francia occidentalis*). By the
late 900s documents referred to this realm simply as "the kingdom of
France" or the "kingdom of the Franks" (*Regnum Francorum*), while in
popular speech the king was probably called the "king of France." Not
all elites within this western realm regarded themselves as Franks, for
regional identities burned fiercely, not least in the south. Still, by 1000 the
meaning of the Latin word *francus*, after various semantic migrations,
had settled down to something approximating *francais*.[59] By contrast, in
the German-speaking eastern sector of Charlemagne's empire, where
his legacy was reborn in 962 as the Ottonian empire, forerunner of
the Holy Roman Empire, the regional term *Germania* began to replace
"East Francia." In institutional terms, one might argue, the Empire,
more directly than France, was heir to the Carolingians. But in ethnic
terms, in the east a process Heinrich Fichtenau termed "defrancization"
encouraged disassociation from Frankish identity. In common usage
"Frank" and "Francia" thus became restricted to the western kingdom,
the core of modern France.[60] Similar processes, I argued, began to yoke
Burman ethnicity to Pagan and Avan authority, Siamese ethnicity to the
Ayudhyan state, and Vietnamese ethnicity to Dai Viet.

Finally, although more impressive than its Merovingian predecessor, the Carolingian empire, like Pagan, Angkor, and most especially
Kiev, remained overextended, subject to pronounced regional tensions,
dependent on a partly or even substantially oral administrative culture,
and thus inherently unstable.[61] As the more enthusiastic interpreters

---

[59] Geary, *Myth of Nations*, 115–18, 135–41, 152–55, 174; James, *The Franks*, 7–10, 108–13,
225–35; Planhol, *Historical Geography*, 90–108, esp. 95–96.

[60] Duby, *France in the Middle Ages*, 15, citing Fichtenau; James, *The Franks*, 234–35. On East
Francia see too Schneidmuller, "Constructing Identities," 25–32. On linguistic evolution
in the western kingdom, see Roger Wright, ed., *Latin and the Romance Languages in the
Early Middle Ages* (London, 1991).

[61] On Frankish Carolingian government, including historiographic debates between optimists and pessimists, see Paul Fouracre, "Frankish Gaul to 814," in *NCMH*, vol. II,

of Carolingian government have emphasized, the crown strenuously sought to revive intellectual activity, to reconstitute aspects of Roman public authority, to standardize units of taxation, and to expand the use of writing for charters, laws, and royal orders. To dominate regional magnates known as counts, Pepin III (r. 751–768) and Charlemange (r. 768–814) sought to place them in areas where they lacked personal connections, to prescribe their duties, and to subject them to traveling circuit inspectors (*missi dominici*, "those sent by the king"). Provided it enlisted an elite consensus, the crown was capable of prodigious short-term mobilization. But such a consensus never extended to reliable, systemic provincial control. Roman trappings and *missi dominici* aside, the Carolingians could not reconstruct a Roman-style system of salaried officials, if only because the long-term decline of cities, coinage, and communications denied them the basic prerequisites. What held together the empire – in essence, a loose solar polity reminiscent of charter Southeast Asian states[62] – were, first, royal prestige; second, wealth accruing from the king's own estates; third, the obligation that members of the imperial aristocracy incurred for provisional land grants; and fourth and perhaps most basic, the prospect that continued conquests would yield yet more rewards. Provisional grants, however, tended to metamorphose into hereditary allods, and when Carolingian conquests ceased and the prospect of fresh spoils evaporated after c. 804, those families who had helped build the empire split into rival camps. Chronic civil wars and the consequent need to buy support with fresh grants dispersed the royal estate and, with it, the material bases of royal power. The deep-rooted Frankish tradition of dividing lands equally among a king's sons further reduced the prospects for sustained coordination. Conceivably too, early stirrings of economic revival magnified the resources of local lords vis-à-vis the center. After Charles the Fat's effort to reunite the empire aborted in 887, disintegration proceeded rapidly.[63]

---

esp. 106–108, and *NCMH*, vol. II, chs. 15–17; McKitterick, *Frankish Kingdoms*, chs. 4, 6; Collins, *Charlemagne*, 102–24; Sonnlechner, "Establishment of New Units," 42–48; Richard Hodges, *Towns and Trade in the Age of Charlemagne* (London, 2000), ch. 4. Cf. Merovingian administration discussed at Wood, *Merovingian Kings*, 55–70, 88–119, 152–54, 221–38, 255–92; James, *The Franks*, 182–99; and Collins, *Charlemagne*, 16–22.

[62] Cf. the description of three zones of authority in McKitterick, *Frankish Kingdoms*, 97, and *SP*, 33.

[63] On Carolingian decline, n. 61 *supra* plus R. I. Moore, *The First European Revolution c. 970–1215* (Oxford, 2000), 39–44; Timothy Reuter, "Plunder and Tribute in the Carolingian

Aggravating these internal strains, 9th-century assaults by Magyars, Saracens, and Vikings helped to transfer authority to progressively smaller, more militarily flexible jurisdictions. Whereas the early Carolingians had extended Frankish power in all directions, now the momentum was reversed. Most destructive were raids by Vikings, whose shallow-draft ships let them sail far up coastal rivers and devastate the European seaboard from the 790s and more especially the 840s well into the 10th century. To buy them off, the West Frankish king in 911 was obliged to let Vikings colonize the mouth of the Seine – whereby pagan Vikings eventually became Christian Normans.[64]

In short, by the late 9th century, even before Kiev became capital of Rus, the Frankish charter state collapsed and Frankish lands entered their first, most prolonged, most chaotic interregnum, which would last to the early 12th century. After the first formal partition of the Carolingian empire in 843, the West Francia successor state (bounded on the north and west by the sea, in the south by the Pyrenees and the Mediterranean, and in the east by four rivers[65]) corresponded to Roman Gaul. But in terms of human geography this entity, in the words of Jean Dunbabin, was "a ragbag of old sub-kingdoms and peoples," without common language, law, or tradition of unity.[66] In addition to the Frankish heartland stretching from the Loire toward the lower Rhine, West Francia included the formidable principalities of Catalonia, Brittany, Aquitaine, Gascony, Gothia, Burgundy, and Flanders. At the same time as these territories devolved from the Carolingian empire, each faced mounting pressures from subordinate units. Thus whereas in 900 we can count 29 separate territories within West Francia, by 1000 the number had risen to 55.[67] Some historians have gone so far as to conclude that the Carolingian empire was a mere interlude of two or three generations in a long-term process of political devolution. In Joseph Strayer's

Empire," *Transactions of the Royal Historical Society*, 5th ser., 35 (1985): 75–94; idem, "The End of Carolingian Military Expansion," in Peter Godman and Roger Collins, eds., *Charlemagne's Heir* (Oxford, 1990), 391–405; Johannes Fried, "The Frankish Kingdoms, 817–911: The East and Middle Kingdoms," in *NCMH*, vol. II, 142–89.

[64] Simon Coupland, "The Vikings in Francia and Anglo-Saxon England to 911," in *NCMH*, vol. II, 190–201.

[65] The Escaut, Meuse, Saone, and Rhone rivers. Planhol, *Historical Geography*, 91, 108–109.

[66] Dunbabin, *France in the Making*, 4. Also Schneidmuller, "Constructing Identities," 15–31.

[67] Geoffrey Barraclough, *The Crucible of Europe: The Ninth and Tenth Centuries in European History* (London, 1976), 94.

words, the empire was a "political miracle," and like all miracles, could halt the natural course of events only temporarily.[68]

Sources of Renewed Vitality, c. 900–1328: The Capetian Achievement

The social and military counterpart to post-Carolingian political devolution was the so-called feudal transformation (or feudal revolution), which involved the cellularization and militarization of rural society. Debate surrounds the extent, legal implications, and chronology of these changes – once dated to the early 1000s, but now increasingly said to have been underway since at least the 9th century – but on their main outlines there is substantial agreement.

Vassalage, that is to say, the formal promise of service in return for land or other gifts, had been a key element of the Carolingian system. Yet alongside lords and servile laborers, in the early 9th century there remained at least a modest free population, possessed of allods and required to swear fidelity to the king and, in many cases, to provide him with taxes and military service; Carolingian levies still had been composed substantially of peasants. Civil wars, Viking invasions, and the use of expensive armor and weaponry now undermined this group by transferring power to local leaders (castellans), usually members of the Carolingian nobility, who controlled strongpoints and professional soldiers. Gradually castellans arrogated to themselves many of those rights of taxation and justice that had once been exercised by the Carolingians and their designated representatives. Although most complete in northern France and southeastern England, feudal reorganization left few areas of western Europe untouched. The seigneury, with castle and lordly domain at its center, now became the chief unit of production as well as administration.[69] To ensure continuity of family landholdings,

---

[68] Joseph Strayer, *Western Europe in the Middle Ages* (Prospect Heights, IL, 1982), 49. So too wrote James, *Origins*, 124: "The history of Gaul from 500 (and earlier) to 1000 is indeed the history of a slow and virtually uninterrupted annexation by the aristocracy of powers of justice, taxation and lordship that had belonged to the [Roman] emperors and then to the Frankish kings . . . so that by 1000 Gaul was a patchwork of scores of petty states." For comparable views, see Pierre Bonnassie, *La Catalogne du Milieu du X a la Fin du XI Siecle* (Paris, 1975), vol. I, 379; Robert Fossier, *Peasant Life in the Medieval West* (Oxford, 1988), 128–29.

[69] For debates on the dating, structures, and significance of the "feudal transformation/revolution," see the emphasis on late 10th-century change in Georges Duby, *The Three Orders* (Chicago, 1980); Jean-Pierre Poly and Eric Bournazel, *The Feudal Transformation, 900–1200* (New York, 1991); Pierre Bonnassie, *From Slavery to Feudalism*

castellans began to strengthen the patriline, commonly by transmitting the patrimony intact to their eldest legitimate son and relegating bastards and younger sons to alternate careers, often in the church. The church thus became critical to feudal reorganization, both because it sanctioned new concepts of legitimacy and because it recruited disproportionately from disinherited sons. The latter were compensated through church endowments – in 1200 religious bodies held up to a third of all land in northern France[70] – but on the proviso that lands controlled by celibate clerics not become a source of hereditary power to rival noble houses. As lordly families consolidated control over land, they used that authority to demand from the peasantry a more complete obedience. Freemen and former slaves now were amalgamated into the

in South-Western Europe (Cambridge, 1991); David Levine, *At the Dawn of Modernity* (Berkeley, 2001), 17–61, 189–233; Moore, *First European Revolution*, 30–111; idem, "The Birth of Europe as a Eurasian Phenomenon," in Victor Lieberman, ed., *Beyond Binary Histories* (Ann Arbor, 1999), 144–46; and the anti-"mutationist" argument for greater continuity between c. 800 and 1100 effectively championed by Dominique Barthelemy, *La Societie dans le Comte de Vendome de l'An Mil au XIVe Siecle* (Paris, 1993), esp. ch. 8; by Constance Bouchard, "Rural Economy and Society," in Bull, *France in the Central Middle Ages*, 77–101; by Stephen White in his trenchant critique of Duby in "Tenth-Century Courts and the Perils of Structuralist History," in Warren Brown and Piotr Gorecki, eds., *Conflict in Medieval Europe* (London, 2003); and by Wickham, *Framing the Middle Ages*, 260–61, 304–306, 398–406, 535–47, 570–88 discussing the early spread c. 700–1000 of the "feudal mode of economic production," as opposed to "peasant modes of economic production" and feudal political relations. See too T. N. Bisson's claim for yet more radical discontinuities starting c. 1000 in "The 'Feudal Revolution,'" *PP* 142 (1994): 6–42; critiques of Bisson by Barthelemy, Stephen White, Timothy Reuter, and Chris Wickham, and Bisson's rejoinder, all in *PP* 152 (1996): 196–223 and 155 (1997): 177–225; and the summary of the debate, with growing sympathy for the gradualist view, in R. I. Moore, "Feudalism and Revolution in the Making of Europe," in M. Barcelo et al., eds., *El Feudalisme Comptat i Debatut* (Valencia, 2003), 19–34. Note too that Susan Reynolds, *Fiefs and Vassals* (Oxford, 1994) argues against the very existence of "feudalism" as a coherent system, at least before c. 1180; and that another line of research, represented by Frederic Cheyette, Stephen White, and William Miller, emphasizes not vertical but horizontal social solidarities. For historiographic overviews, Lester K. Little and Barbara H. Rosenwein, eds., *Debating the Middle Ages: Issues and Readings* (Oxford, 1998), pt. II, esp. 107–13; Collins, *Tribes to Nation*, 35–70.

70 And perhaps a sixth in the south. Moore, *First European Revolution*, 12. This argument linking noble families and landholding to church reorganization follows ibid., 30–111; Moore, "Feudalism and Revolution"; idem, "The Transformation of Europe as a Eurasian Phenomenon," in Arnason and Wittrock, *Eurasian Transformations*, 77–98. Even after 1000 or 1100, however, noble inheritance practices continued to vary by region. Moore, *First European Revolution*, 65–75, 88–91; Constance Bouchard, *Strong of Body, Brave and Noble: Chivalry and Society in Medieval France* (Ithaca, 1998), 67–74; Duby, *France in the Middle Ages*, 62–64; *CIHMA*, vol. II, 51–54; Patrick Geary, pers. commun., Sept. 7, 2006.

enserfed labor force attached to noble manors. Thus, along with the conversion of public into seigniorial justice came a marked drop in the number of independent allodists. Apart from the great territorial princes, many of whom offered at best a grudging obedience, and aside from his own vassals on remaining royal estates, the West Frankish king no longer had any subjects.

Feudalism is often seen as anarchic, but it is more profitable to view it as a reaction against local anarchy and as a more or less successful attempt to stabilize authority on the basis of primary personal loyalties. By wedding economic and social power to local political authority, feudalism strengthened military defenses and, as we shall see, encouraged agricultural intensification. Moreover, by allowing the king to establish himself at the head of a long chain of vassal ties, feudal theory, as developed from the late 1100s, began to provide the crown with far more effective claims to local resources than Carolingians had ever attained.

However, for this potential to be realized, before political recentralization could begin, a demographic and commercial transformation also had to occur. Especially between c. 900 and 1300 in France as in Europe generally, agriculture and commerce became ever more efficient, urban and rural landscapes were transformed, and the population rose sharply. According to Georges Duby, "It is doubtful whether the rate of progress between 1180 and 1220 in the lands which constitute modern France has ever been equalled."[71] The coincidence of this vitality with economic expansion in Kiev and charter Southeast Asia is striking indeed. Before considering the political implications, let us examine the uncertain origins of West European prosperity, particularly as they bear on our problem of Eurasian coordination.

Many historians assumed that cumulative growth, an inevitable progression, simply reached a critical mass in the late 10th and 11th centuries. But for Robert Fossier and others, the contrast between early medieval gradualism and high medieval vigor was too dramatic to support such an explanation. "[I]t would be unreasonable," wrote Fossier, "to make the meagre land clearances of the ninth century the precursors of the explosion of food production in the twelfth century . . . [T]he quantitative difference in effort requires that we look for a cause other

---

[71] Duby, *France in the Middle Ages*, 155. N. J. G. Pounds, *An Historical Geography of Europe* (Cambridge, 1990), 72 argues that the rate of growth exceeded anything until the 19th century. See too Robert Fossier, "The Leap Forward," *CIHMA*, vol. II, 270–329.

than natural progression."[72] More recently, the pendulum has swung back, for research now paints a less gloomy picture of the Carolingian economy than was once common. In advanced areas of northern Europe in the 8th and 9th centuries primitive systems of fallow began yielding to more regular cultivation including the so-called three-course rotation. Admittedly, until the 11th or 12th century yields remained frightfully modest, while in much of the countryside agriculture was still not cereal based, much less market oriented.[73] Yet the new rotations, an associated increase in watermills for grinding corn, and reclamation of forests and wastes lay the foundation for that shift in political power from the Mediterranean north of the Alps that would accelerate throughout the second millennium. By the late 800s, especially between the Loire and Rhine, large bipartite manors were selling surpluses, and monetized exchange was starting to revive.[74] Thus long-term cumulative economic improvements leading to a high medieval explosion now seems plausible.

But in truth, this approach merely shifts the problem of dynamism from the 11th century to the 700s or 800s. Why did the economy begin to revive in those years, rather than in, say, the 6th century? Nor is it obvious why generations of incremental change suddenly should have become transformative in the 11th century.

Similar problems attach to technological theories of takeoff focusing, for example, on the spread of horseshoes, new harnesses, windmills, watermills, and most especially heavy asymmetrical plows with

[72] Robert Fossier, in *CIHMA*, vol. II, 2. Cf. Moore, *First European Revolution*, 39; Patrice Bourdelais, "Le paysage humain," in Andre Burguiere et al., eds., *Histoire de la France: L'espace Francais* (Paris, 1989), 189–93; Guy Bois, *La Mutation de l'An Mil* (Paris, 1989); and the more agnostic position of Bartlett, *Making of Europe*, 110.

[73] Verhulst, *Carolingian Economy*, 61–71; Moore, *First European Revolution*, 38. Three-course rotations began to appear in northern France, but the South, with its lighter soils, developed a two-year cycle of fallow and grain. See n. 96 *infra*.

[74] On the economy c. 650–1000, n. 53 *supra*, esp. Verhulst, *Carolingian Economy*, arguing for economic improvements starting fitfully as early as the mid-7th century and continuing, despite severe periodic dislocations, into the high medieval era (p. 135), plus idem, "The Origins of Towns in the Low Countries and the Pirenne Thesis," *PP* 122 (1989): 3–35; Hodges, *Towns and Trade*; Pierre Toubert, "La part du grand domaine dans le decollage economique de l'Occident (VIIIe–IXe siecles)," in *La Croissance Agricole du Haut Moyen Age* (Auch, 1990), 53–86; Yoshiki Morimoto, "Autour du grand domain carolingien," in Adrian Verhulst and Morimoto, eds., *Economie Rurale et Economie Urbaine au Moyen Age* (Ghent, 1994), 25–79; Sonnlechner, "Establishment of New Units," 42–48; Georges Comet, "Les cereals du bas-Empire au Moyen Age," in Miquel Barcelo and Francois Sigaut, *The Making of Feudal Agricultures?* (Leiden, 2004), 131–76.

moldboards capable of turning western Europe's waterlogged clay soils. Not only did many of these innovations become generalized too late, in the late 900s and 1000s, to explain late-8th- and 9th-century revival, but archeology shows that many had been known long before they began to spread in economically precocious regions like Burgundy and northern Italy; the asymmetrical moldboard plow, for example, had been used since the 2nd century. Like three-course crop rotation, new technologies could accelerate growth, but their spread seems to have reflected an antecedent desire to eliminate bottlenecks – or to increase seigniorial revenues – in economies that were already in transition.[75]

Another potentially critical factor, Viking raids, are said to have encouraged expansion in two ways. First, at their height in the 9th century, Scandinavian incursions stimulated the economy by weakening antiquated estate systems in favor of more efficient labor routines (see below) and by putting booty and specie into circulation. Second and rather paradoxically, the effective end to Viking incursions in the 10th century – Europe's first extended calm since the incessant movement of peoples started in the late Roman era – provided the peace needed for rapid growth. But this approach, merits aside, is not entirely satisfactory because: a) In some areas the restoration of peace reflected not an end to Viking (and Arab) raids, but local political changes. b) The 11th century continued to see fighting in many areas, some of which were economically dynamic. Indeed, the first regions to awaken economically – Spain and northern and peninsular Italy – were not the most peaceful.[76]

What about foreign trade apart from the Vikings? Building on Carolingian developments, by the 10th century European wealth and cities were concentrated along a grand commercial artery running from Italy to the Low Countries and southern Britain. Linking the textiles of the Low Countries to imports from Genoa and Venice, the Champagne fairs were a key node, with secondary centers in southern France; but away

---

[75] Wider availability of iron may have promoted the heavy plow, but this too presupposes antecedent growth. Cf. Lynn White, *Medieval Technology and Social Change* (Oxford, 1966); Frances and Joseph Gies, *Cathedral, Forge, and Waterwheel* (New York, 1995), chs. 3, 5; Duby, *France in the Middle Ages*, 33; Fossier, *CIHMA*, vol. II, 3–4; McCormick, *Origins*, 10; Verhulst, "Economic Organization," 485–86; idem, *Carolingian Economy*, 67–68, 78; Barcelo, *Making of Feudal Agricultures*; J. R. McNeill and William McNeill, *The Human Web* (New York, 2003), 101–102, 141–42.

[76] See Duby, *Early Growth*, 112–20; idem, *France in the Middle Ages*, 32; Fossier, *CIHMA*, vol. II, 5.

from this central spine commercial growth was far weaker.[77] Here, then, is a case for the fructifying impact of long-distance trade, which Michael McCormick shows had a unique ability to create windfall profits and to promote efficient resource allocation.[78] Insofar as the Low Countries-to-Italy route formed the first of Abu-Lughod's eight Eurasian trading circuits,[79] long-distance trade again offers a potential explanation for coordinated post-900 florescence in Southeast Asia and Europe.

Yet if long-distance trade accelerated growth in western Europe, it is even less likely than in Kiev to have been the prime mover. In volume and value West European trade focused overwhelmingly on local foodstuffs, salt, and handicrafts, not Mediterranean or Asian luxuries or even bulk goods from central Europe. Moreover, urban ability to absorb imports and process exports depended on the countryside's ability to supply cities (whose death rates exceeded their birth rates) with migrants and food. While noting trade's stimulatory effects, McCormick readily concedes that commercial vitality rested on agrarian profits.[80] According to Arlette Higounet-Nadal, medieval French "rural overpopulation was certainly the motor of urban development."[81] In the words of Robert Lopez, "Even as demographic growth was a prime motor of agricultural progress, so agricultural progress was an essential prerequisite of the Commercial Revolution . . . it is proper to say that the revolution took off from the manor."[82] "To put the circulation of money before agricultural development," wrote Fossier, is "to put the cart before the horse."[83] R. I. Moore, Duby, Adriaan Verhulst, and others concur fully.[84]

---

[77] Pounds, *Economic History*, 104–15, 364–81, 463–72; Arlette Higounet-Nadal, "La croissance urbaine," in Dupaquier et al., *Histoire de la Population*, vol. I, 267–311; Abu-Lughod, *Before European Hegemony*, 51–101; Malcolm Barber, *The Two Cities* (London, 1992), 61–76; Verhulst, *Carolingian Economy*, ch. 7; McCormick, *Origins*, 778–98 and *passim*.

[78] McCormick, *Origins*, 578.

[79] See nn. 40, 50 *supra*.

[80] McCormick, *Origins*, 578–79.

[81] Higounet-Nadal, "La croissance," 267.

[82] Robert Lopez, *The Commercial Revolution of the Middle Ages, 950–1350* (Englewood Cliffs, NJ, 1971), 56.

[83] Fossier in *CIHMA*, vol. II, 5.

[84] See Moore, *First European Revolution*, 35–36, linking urban growth not to trade but to intensification of agriculture and local exchange ("the cities of medieval Europe 'grew out' of the countryside"); idem, "Transformation of Europe," 97 ("Although these changes occurred in a context of increasing commercial and other inter-civilizational contacts, they arose primarily and predominantly from intensive economic growth and the social tensions to which it gave rise within each civilization."); Duby, *Early Growth,*

Nor can one make the same case for France as for Kiev that profits from trade underlay royal power, which aided pacification, which spurred population growth: not only do Capetian records point to skimpy revenues from foreign commerce,[85] but the foundations of prosperity were laid during the nadir of supralocal authority well before Capetian accession.

Focusing on social and cultural changes associated with the feudal transformation, Moore, Duby, Fossier, Pierre Toubert, and Richard Hodges have emphasized the economic benefits of intensifying lordly competition and new forms of labor organization.[86] As the 9th-century crown lost the ability to award new lands and booty and as the costs of warfare, luxuries, and church construction rose, warriors and churchmen alike sought to raise agrarian productivity so as to augment taxes and rent. With a view to improving work routines, promoting better tools, and reclaiming wastes, lords therefore concentrated the laboring population in villages. The conversion in some areas of slaves – who had little work incentive and whose conditions made childrearing difficult – into serfs combined with lordly interest in labor reproduction and with rural Christianization to lay greater stress on marriage and procreation, while inhibiting infanticide. In turn, population growth and defense needs favored a further aggregation of dispersed tenements. Focused on the parish church, graveyard, and forge, the emergent village promoted at one and the same time Christianization, cereal-based communal agriculture, and new systems of crop rotation. By the 12th century, with market forces inducing money-strapped lords to convert more

10 (Early medieval "economic growth . . . was essentially agricultural"); Verhulst, *Carolingian Economy*, 113 ("The best explanation of this commercial flowering . . . which in the end must have stimulated international exports . . . is the dynamism of the Carolingian manorial economy."); S. R. Epstein, *Freedom and Growth* (London, 2000), 70–71, showing that even in 1500 long-distance trade remained miniscule compared to domestic trade; and Ross Sansom, "Populous Dark Age Towns," *Jl. of European Archaeology* 2 (1994): 97–129.

85 John W. Baldwin, *The Government of Philip Augustus* (Berkeley, 1986), 144–75, esp. Table 4, showing that in 1202 towns and commerce combined yielded only 20 percent of royal revenues, the great bulk of which surely derived from local, rather than long-distance, exchange. See too Joseph Strayer, *The Reign of Philip the Fair* (Princeton, 1980), 142–91, and Pounds, *Economic History*, 93.

86 Moore, *First European Revolution*, 39–64; idem, "Transformation of Europe"; Duby, *France in the Middle Ages*, 33–54; idem, *Early Growth*, 177–86, 229–70; idem, *Three Orders*, 153; Fossier, *Peasant Life*, chs. 2, 4, 5; Toubert, "La part du grand domaine," 53–86; Hodges, *Towns and Trade*; Barcelo, *Making of Feudal Agricultures*, 226.

serfs into dues-paying tenants, peasants gained additional incentives and opportunities to raise output.[87] Here, then, were economic spurs rooted in a culture of lordly acquisition and new village structures. What is more, the surge in aristocratic donations to the church had major economic benefits, for as in Southeast Asia, large capital resources and institutional continuity let religious networks play a disproportionate role in agrarian reclamation and technical innovation.[88]

To the extent that in Europe the feudal transformation, and in Pagan and Angkor new temple complexes, concentrated dispersed populations – in Europe around lordly manors and parish churches, in Southeast Asia around regional temples – one could conclude that in both areas agricultural intensification depended on new systems of labor control. One thinks as well of the stimulus that princely colonization provided on the Kievan frontier. But, accident apart, without a shared etiology, without a common institutional background, how can we explain the broadly synchronized appearance of more productive social arrangements in parts of Eurasia that had no contact with one another? (The mystery deepens if we consider, in anticipation of Chapters 5 and 6, that South China and South India also experienced innovative social systems and marked agrarian expansion after 900 or 1000.) Moreover, if the West European economy took off from the 11th century, how are we to explain preliminary advances in agriculture and trade from the late 8th and 9th centuries, before many argue that the feudal revolution was truly launched? Conversely, if we accept that elements of the feudal mode were in place by the 8th or 9th century, why did growth not accelerate until the 11th?

Shall we again consider changing disease regimens? The Mediterranean plague cycle that began in 541 ended in 767. Because these epidemics spared most of trans-Alpine Europe, they probably contributed

---

[87] Bouchard, "Rural Economy and Society," 90–98, emphasizing the rapid decline of serfdom.

[88] Bull, *France in the Central Middle Ages*, 97–101, 149–62; Moore, *First European Revolution*, 11–12, 45–50, 75–88; idem, "Transformation of Europe"; James, *Origins*, 105–19. Cf. *SP*, 112–14, 228–30. To follow McNeill, *Human Web*, 140–42, another economically productive social pattern in northern France and other areas with moldboard plows was the habit whereby different families joined to form plow teams. Because this inspired cooperation beyond the limits of blood and because townspeople came from the countryside, the transfamilial character of commercial enterprise and the penchant for voluntary corporations owed much to the traditions of rural plow teams.

to the northward shift in Europe's demographic center of gravity.[89] But this says nothing about the absolute, as opposed to the relative, vigor of North European demography in the late first millennium. Nor is there any record in Southeast Asia of the bubonic plague usually associated with Europe's 6th-to-8th-century maladies. McNeill's thesis about acclimation to smallpox and measles in northern Europe and other Eurasian rimlands has greater comparative potential and may, in fact, be of capital significance, but for Europe his theory remains speculative.

On the other hand, there is growing evidence that the same rise in temperatures during all or part of the Medieval Climate Anomaly 800/850–1250/1300 as favored cultivation in Southeast Asia and Kiev also aided agriculture in northern and central France. In combination, documentary, dendroclimatological, hydrological, and vegetation studies show that after some 400 years of markedly cold, wet weather, in the 9th and 10th centuries the climate in France and much of western Europe, albeit still subject to wide annual variation, began to grow warmer and drier. Warming continued, with some fluctuations, to the early 1100s, followed by a colder period to 1180, which ushered in a warming phase to c. 1300. From 1180 to 1299 milder climate (mean extreme minimum temperatures averaged 3.5 °C higher than in 1901–1960) allowed cultivation of subtropical olive and fig trees in the Po and Rhine valleys, where they are not found today.[90] Though possibly

[89] Biraben and Le Goff, "The Plague"; McNeill, *Plagues and Peoples*, ch. 3; Ynez Viole O'Neill, "Diseases of the Middle Ages," in Kiple, *Cambridge World History of Disease*, 270–78; Robert S. Gottfried, *The Black Death* (New York, 1983), 10–13.

[90] Mean January temperatures were about 0.6 °C higher than in 1901–1960. C. Pfister et al., "Winter Air Temperature Variations in Western Europe During the Early and High Middle Ages (AD 750–1300)," *The Holocene* 8 (1998): 535–52, emphasizing solar forcing and multidecadal fluctuations. Pierre Alexandre, *Le Climat en Europe au Moyen Age* (Paris, 1987), esp. 807–808 offers a seminal study of weather notices in medieval chronicles. For proxy reconstructions of climate for France and northern Europe, besides Ch. 1, nn. 99, 100 *supra* and Pfister et al., "Winter Air Temperature," see Thomas Crowley and Thomas Lowery, "How Warm Was the Medieval Warm Period?" *Ambio* 29 (2000): 51–54, suggesting Medieval Climate Anomaly (MCA) rises of approximately 0.8 °C in England and Germany; A. E. J. Ogilvie et al., "North Atlantic Climate c. AD 1000," *Weather* 55 (2000): 34–45, suggesting MCA rises of 1–2 °C in the North Atlantic; Keith Briffa, "Dendroclimatological Reconstructions in Northern Fennoscandia," in Mikami, *Proceedings*, 5–10, suggesting MCA rises of almost 2 °C over 800 levels in northern Sweden; Smith, *Europe After Rome*, 56, suggesting MCA rises of almost 2 °C across northern Europe; Jean Grove and Roy Switsur, "Glacial Geological Evidence for the Medieval Warm Period," *CC* 26 (1994): 143–69, pointing to 1050–1150 cooling; C. Pfister, "Five Centuries of Little Ice Age Climate in Western Europe," ibid., 208–13; H. H. Lamb, *Climate, History, and the Modern World* (London, 1995), chs. 5, 10; Barcelo,

detrimental to Mediterranean agriculture, such conditions were well suited to northern France, where optimal cereal cultivation requires warm sunny springs and dry summers and autumns. Drier climate, moreover, made it possible to farm rich bottom lands along the rivers without worrying that seed would rot or be washed away.[91] Much as in Kiev (roughly the same latitude as Paris), a rise of 0.8 °C to 2 °C would have extended the growing season by some three to eight weeks. In late-20th-century western Europe, with each additional day's ripening cereal yields increase by 63 kilos per hectare.[92] In an era without chemical fertilizers or pesticides to stabilize yields, climate's impact would have been yet greater. Advantageous conditions continued to the early 1300s, when a markedly colder, wetter era set in. To extrapolate from early modern studies, larger harvests and warmer temperatures would have reduced human and animal mortality, while lowering the average female age of marriage and raising fertility.[93]

In these ways from the 9th and 10th centuries improved climate may have combined with antecedent and contemporary experiments in crop rotation and manorial reorganization – and with enhanced immunity to smallpox and measles? – to encourage population growth, which in turn favored denser settlements, more intensive cultivation, market production, and an associated increase in rural carrying capacity. The outlook improved for much of the late 10th to 13th centuries as a result of yet warmer, drier climate in combination with an end to Viking attacks, the full benefits of the feudal revolution, further improvements in agrarian

Making of Feudal Agricultures, 181–87; J. M. Grove, "The Initiation of the 'Little Ice Age' in Regions Round the North Atlantic," *CC* 48 (2001): 53–82; Michael McCormick et al., "Volcanoes and the Climate Forcing of Carolingian Europe, A.D. 750–950," *Speculum* 82 (2007): 865–96, pointing to some years of volcanically induced extreme cold during the early MCA. For a good overview of European and global climate change to c. 1350, see Brown, *History and Climate*, 16, 99–103, 118–40, 147–81, 240–43.

[91] Emmanuel Le Roy Ladurie, *Times of Feast, Times of Famine* (New York, 1971), 288–92; idem, *Histoire Humaine et Comparee du Climat* (Paris, 2004), 7–9; Bouchard, "Rural Economy and Society," 88.

[92] Notes 46, 47 *supra*; Parker, *Europe in Crisis*, 22.

[93] On the relation of climate to population growth, see Duby, *Early Growth*, 5–11; idem, *France in the Middle Ages*, 33; Le Roy Ladurie, *Times of Feast*, chs. 6, 7; Fossier in *CIHMA*, vol. II, 5–7; Bourdelais, "Paysage humain," 189; Gustaf Utterstrom, "Climatic Fluctuations and Population Problems in Early Modern History," in Donald Worster, ed., *The Ends of the Earth* (Cambridge, 1988), 39–79; Grove, *Little Ice Age*, 412–15. On the demographic impact of improved food supplies, also n. 44 *supra*, and W. Bach et al., *Food-Climate Interactions* (Dordrecht, 1981). On the demographic potential of market integration, David Henley, "Population and the Means of Subsistence," *JSEAS* 36 (2005): 337–72.

technique, and more local and long-distance trade. To pursue a theme mooted in the discussion of Kiev, Jack Goldstone, J. D. Post, and Mary Matossian also raise the possibility that drier, warmer weather reduced disease pathology.[94] Constance Bouchard concludes unequivocally: "At its base the agricultural expansion of the central Middle Ages was the result of changes in the climate."[95]

Five caveats, however, bear repeating: a) Synergies with other factors make it impossible to isolate completely climate's contribution. b) The precise degree of medieval warming is still debated. c) Climatic shifts across Eurasia were rarely uniform in timing or degree. d) Adverse climate could stimulate compensatory economic shifts. e) Over time, as crops diversified, techniques improved, and trade and handicrafts expanded, climate's influence diminished. Nonetheless, directly through its influence on agrarian yields and indirectly through its impact on trade and possibly disease, climate in the late first and early second millennia offers potential insights into Eurasian coordination.

Whatever the precise mix of stimuli, in France the contours of medieval economic growth are reasonably clear. Between 950 and 1200 great waves of land reclamations, led by lay lords and monasteries, transformed arable zones, woods, and wetlands alike. Ill-defined tracts once claimed by kin-based warrior groups were now divided into precisely demarcated estates owned by castellans and monks eager to raise output. The ensuing spread of iron moldboard plows drawn by efficiently harnessed horses rather than by oxen, together with drier climate, the three-field system of crop rotations,[96] and better animal breeding, combined to reduce fallow, improve fertilization, distribute work routines more evenly, and thus permit more effective cultivation of the heavy, exceptionally rich soils of northern France. In lieu of the twofold or threefold returns characteristic of the Carolingian era, yields of fivefold now became common, and in favored areas of Picardy, the Ile de France, and Champagne by 1300 the figure had reached eightfold,

---

[94] Yet evidence comes almost entirely after 1300. See n. 42 *supra*, plus Mary Kilbourne Matossian, *Poisons of the Past* (New Haven, 1989).

[95] Bouchard, "Rural Economy," 88.

[96] Whereas in earlier "three-course rotations" three crops rotated in the same field, in the more productive "three-field system" that began to appear on some demesne lands as early as the 9th century, fields corresponded to each of the rotations. See nn. 4, 73 *supra*, plus Pounds, *Economic History*, 59, 132, 191–93; Collins, *Tribes to Nation*, 49–50. However, James Goldsmith, "The Crisis of the Late Middle Ages," *FH* 9 (1995): 417–50, esp. 441 cautions that as late as the 14th century, the fully developed three-field system was still largely restricted to the most advanced areas of northern France.

even twelvefold.[97] Progress was less marked in the west and south-west, where drainage and soil inhibited the system of regular rotation. Nonetheless, symptom and cause of prosperity, within the borders of modern France as a whole, between 1000 and 1300 the population may have tripled to 18,000,000 or more.[98] Common people increased their consumption of protein, vegetables, and wine.[99] Prosperity also let the countryside absorb new technologies; elites, more luxuries; peasants, more cheap textiles and handicrafts. Thus, if per capita consumption remained meager, aggregate demand became formidable. Currency penetrated beyond the dominant strata. Cash dues began to replace in-kind payments. Markets began to eclipse socially embedded reciprocity. Serfs metamorphosed into tenants, and peasant landowners organized village communes.

With wider exchange, with a new infrastructure of roads and bridges, and with a ready supply of migrants and food for the towns, the urban network expanded to Rozman's Stage E ("standard marketing"), characterized by four or five levels of central places.[100] Whereas the Romans left no durable cities north of the Alps, the 11th century created what Moore terms northern Europe's first authentic urbanization.[101] Benefiting from Italian example, French institutions of credit, contract, and banking also matured, and interest rates fell markedly.[102] Gracing this market network, between 1000 and 1300 – in the same

[97] Fossier, "Leap Forward," 286; Dunbabin, *France in the Making*, 143; Levine, *At the Dawn*, 176–80, 404; Moore, "Transformation of Europe," 82–86. On agricultural innovation, including the spread of nitrogen-fixing legumes, see too Bourdelais, "Paysage humain"; Henri Dubois, "L'essor medieval," in Dupaquier et al., *Histoire de la Population*, vol. I, 207–66; Planhol, *Historical Geography*, 135–41; Guy Bois, "Reponse," *Medievales* 21 (1991): 102; McNeill, *Human Web*, 138; Barcelo, *Making of Feudal Agricultures*, 131–76, 226, 240; Verhulst, *Carolingian Economy*, 65.

[98] Some of the following sources offer yet higher 1300 figures: Bourdelais, "Paysage humain," 191, 199; Dubois, "L'essor medieval," 207–20; Braudel, *Identity*, vol. II, 137; Duby, *France in the Middle Ages*, 33, 261; Peter Turchin and Sergey Nefedov, *Secular Cycles* (Princeton, forthcoming), ch. 4, Fig. 1a; Colin McEvedy and Richard Jones, *Atlas of World Population History* (New York, 1980), 57, 59. But see notably smaller population estimates and a more jaundiced view of medieval economic growth at Goldsmith, "Crisis of Late Middle Ages."

[99] Dubois, "L'essor medieval," 237–38; Levine, *At the Dawn*, 180–87.

[100] Rozman, *Urban Networks*, 34–35, 84. On medieval French urbanization, see too Higounet-Nadal, "La croissance urbaine"; Hugh Clout, "Early Urban Development," in Clout, ed., *Themes in the Historical Geography of France* (London, 1977), 84–103.

[101] Moore, *First European Revolution*, 31–35.

[102] From approximately 30 percent per annum in 1170 to 10–12 percent by 1270. Jan Luiten van Zanden, "The Road to the Industrial Revolution," *JGH* 3 (2008): 343, 350–52. On credit, contract, and banking, also Edwin S. Hunt and James M. Murray, *A History*

period as Angkor and Pagan erected their magnificent temples and Rus multiplied stone constructions – the French built 80 new cathedrals, 500 other large churches, and perhaps 10,000 parish churches.[103] As in Pagan and Angkor, religious construction itself became an economic catalyst, spurring advances in technology, transport, and labor organization.

These economic changes and associated cultural shifts provided at least six spurs to political units more solid and stable than the early Frankish and Carolingian kingdoms. First, especially in northern France, in reverse of 9th- to 10th-century patterns, larger surpluses and new technologies began to favor overlords at the expense of local castellans. Only magnates with substantial income from road and riverine tolls, loans, market taxes, justice, as well as from land could afford the massive stone forts, siege engines, warhorses, armor, and crossbowmen that became the *sine qua non* for victory from the 12th century.

Second, the mounting costs of warfare joined with lineage proliferation and the market-reinforced ethic of conspicuous consumption to force many indebted castellans to sell allods to their superiors, who either reinvested them with a fief or paid them conditional fees.

Third, as market-oriented landowners substituted cash payments for military service, cellular structures weakened. Again, this inflicted disproportionate injury on local castellans, because their power typically required personal service, whereas wealthy princes could hire mercenaries.[104]

Fourth, as commerce strengthened supralocal linkages, many nobles, clerics, and townsmen sensed the need for a wider judicial and regulatory authority. To enforce laws over a broad area, to coordinate public works, to provide standard coinage and measures, to protect long-distance trade, and to rationalize exactions, the jurisdiction of the castellany and county had become too narrow.[105]

---

of Business in Medieval Europe (Cambridge, 1999), pt. 1; Lopez, *Commercial Revolution*, chs. 2, 3, 6; Pounds, *Economic History*, esp. chs. 3–9; Fossier, "Leap Forward."

[103] David Hackett Fischer, *The Great Wave* (New York, 1996), 13; Moore, *First European Revolution*, 37.

[104] On the first three changes, see George Holmes, ed., *The Oxford History of Medieval Europe* (Oxford, 1991), 117–21; Duby, *France in the Middle Ages*, 155–60; Dunbabin, *France in the Making*, 286–89; Fossier, *Peasant Life*, 141; Geoffrey Koziol, "Political Culture," in Bull, *France in the Central Middle Ages*, 58–61; Jean Dunbabin, "The Political World of France, c. 1200–c. 1336," in Potter, *France in the Later Middle Ages*, 29–34.

[105] This theme receives emphasis at Spruyt, *Sovereign State*, 92–93, 105–108; and Epstein, *Freedom and Growth*. See too Hallam, *Capetian France*, 112, 138–39, 224–25; Duby, *France*

Fifth, the training of specialized lay administrators and lawyers – often disinherited noble sons – in church schools and universities funded by the new prosperity encouraged the development of archives, financial accounting, and codified Roman-based legal systems. From the late 1200s the substitution of paper for parchment – the "paper revolution" – lowered the costs of information storage, but the basic impetus to expand archives and education in the 12th and 13th centuries derived from the needs of ambitious administrations. The advantage for the aspiring prince of Roman law, whose revival was part of a multifaceted renaissance of classical learning, lay in its bias toward central authority and its sympathy for property in an increasingly commercial world. In reciprocal fashion, the development of written codes joined the growth of legally protected communes, guilds, and corporate bodies to regularize market exchange, to limit state predation, and thus ultimately to enhance commercial resources available to the state.

Finally, with closer contact between the learned milieu of church schools and the nobility, aristocrats began to internalize the value system of *courtoisie*, stressing sexual restraint, emotional moderation, and prudence. If markets held the most unruly elements of the nobility in a net of economic obligations, *courtoisie* and chivalry began to exert a similar psychological effect. Despite their unqualified elitism, these psychological changes adumbrated more socially inclusive cultural shifts, or to use Philip Gorski's phrase "disciplinary revolutions," in 16th- and 17th-century Europe.[106]

The French crown was neither the first nor the only beneficiary from such developments. With its early monopoly on writing, the papacy was in a position to create one of Europe's first centralized monarchies,

---

in the Middle Ages, 162–69; idem, *Early Growth*, 251–56; Joseph Strayer, *Medieval Statecraft and the Perspectives of History* (Princeton, 1971), 77–83.

[106] Norbert Elias, *The Civilizing Process*, 2 vols. (New York, 1978, 1982), focusing on top-down changes imposed on the court nobility; Philip Gorski, *The Disciplinary Revolution* (Chicago, 2003), focusing on bottom-up changes associated with popular Calvinism. On intellectual, literary, legal, and cultural changes favorable to centralization, i.e., the fifth and sixth spurs, see Duby, *France in the Middle Ages*, 174–81; idem, *The Chivalrous Society* (Berkeley, 1980), chs. 6, 13; van Zanden, "Road to Industrial Revolution," 351–59; Robert Benson and Giles Constable, eds., *Renaissance and Renewal in the Twelfth Century* (Cambridge, MA, 1982), pts. II and III; Harold Berman, *Law and Revolution* (Cambridge, MA, 1983), 86–100; M. T. Clanchy, *From Memory to Written Record* (London, 1979); R. I. Moore, *The Formation of a Persecuting Society* (Oxford, 1987); idem, *First European Revolution*, 95, 119–46; Dunbabin, "Political World," 34–45.

inviting emulation by secular princes.[107] Within the nominal territory of West Francia, leaders of regions like Normandy, Flanders, Anjou, and Toulouse during the 11th and 12th centuries also began to quell over-mighty castellans, to employ expert administrators, and to patronize specifically regional cultures. Some of these projects began earlier than their French royal counterparts, and most continued alongside royal efforts. Territorial princes alternately imitated, defied, and ignored the kings of France, whose real power for much of the 1100s was inferior to that of Flanders, a nominal dependency, and especially to that of the newly formed Plantagenet empire spanning Anjou, Normandy, Aquitaine (north of the Garonne), and England. In other words, subsequent events should not blind us to the possibilities that a) a principality other than that of the Paris basin might have united much of modern-day France; b) West Francia might have been permanently divided among two or more consolidated states; c) West Francia might have remained under a nominal, increasingly ineffective suzerain in somewhat the same fashion as did Germany, where in the 12th and 13th centuries the Holy Roman Empire foundered on the shoals of princely particularism and Italian urban autonomy. In fact, in France all three political options remained alive into the 15th century.[108]

Yet if its ultimate triumph was in some ways fortuitous, the French crown, which passed definitively from the Carolingian to the Capetian Dynasty in 987, also enjoyed enduring advantages. Most basic, Geoffrey Koziol has argued, even at the nadir of French royal authority regional magnates looked to Carolingian-derived kingship for a model of legitimate authority, sanctioned by God, that they could imitate in governing their own territories. Just as the king honored his subordinates, so dukes and margraves, co-heirs with the king to Carolingian legitimacy, honored theirs. This fundamentally mimetic quality of French political culture meant that territorial lords could not repudiate the kingly office without repudiating the very basis of their own authority.[109] Central to

---

[107] Andre Vauchez, "A Strict Normalisation," in *CIHMA*, vol. II, 397–401; R. W. Southern, *Western Society and the Church in the Middle Ages* (London, 1970), chs. 4, 5.

[108] Dunbabin, *France in the Making*, chs. 8 (see p. 221), 12; Duby, *France in the Middle Ages*, 194–99; Hallam, *Capetian France*, chs. 3, 4; Karl Ferdinand Werner, "Kingdom and Principality in Twelfth-Century France," in Timothy Reuter, ed., *The Medieval Nobility* (Amsterdam, 1978), 243–90; Koziol, "Political Culture," 43–44.

[109] Koziol, "Political Culture," 47–55; plus Fossier, *CIHMA*, vol. II, 143; Poly and Bournazel, *Feudal Transformation*, 186. Even south of the Loire in the 11th century, charters were still dated by the year of the French king's reign.

this mimetic system, from the late 1100s French kings benefited from the solidification of feudal hierarchies within each subordinate region, and from the concomitant elaboration of doctrines asserting the king's feudal suzerainty over territorial princes. To the degree that concepts of feudal hierarchy gained currency, the princes' achievement of feudal superiority in their own lands increased their theoretical dependence on the crown. The elaboration by the mid-1200s of doctrines, derived from church teachings and Roman law, that treated the kingdom, or *patria*, as an object of semireligious veneration only reinforced these claims to royal preeminence.[110] As heirs to Charlemagne, French kings also enjoyed a privileged relation to the church that obliged them to protect church property outside the Ile de France and that afforded them control over more bishoprics and monasteries than any other lord. For their part, churchmen at spiritual centers associated with the crown were only too eager to develop and propagate new doctrines of royal superiority. Finally and of pivotal practical importance to Capetian success was the fact that the royal heartland of the Ile de France, which was among Europe's richest agriculture zones with excellent communications and an emergent intellectual/commercial hub in Paris, benefited disproportionately from rapid economic growth in the 12th and 13th centuries.

The initial assertion of Capetian authority naturally focused on the Ile de France, where kings gradually subdued castellans and expanded the system of royal estate-managers (*prevots*). By the reign of Louis VI (1108–1137) this work was well under way, and the crown began to intervene farther afield.[111] The turning point in Capetian fortunes came under Philip Augustus (r. 1180–1223), who, asserting his rights over a "derelict" vassal, conquered Plantagenet holdings in Normandy in 1204, followed by Maine and Anjou. Thus he gained access to the sea, thwarted Plantagenet efforts to build a rival empire straddling the Channel, and laid the basis for Capetian advances in the next hundred

[110] On the elaboration of feudal and corporatist theories of royal power, see Reynolds, *Fiefs and Vassals*, 210–14, 258–322, emphasizing the novelty of feudal hierarchy; Hallam, *Capetian France*, 168–69; Spruyt, *Sovereign State*, 106–107; Koziol, "Political Culture," 54–59; Ernst Kantorowicz, *The King's Two Bodies* (Princeton, 1957), 232–72.

[111] Discussion of Capetian expansion relies on Hallam, *Capetian France*; Barber, *Two Cities*, ch. 11; Duby, *France in the Middle Ages*, pt. III; Dunbabin, *France in the Making*, chs. 6–14; Joseph Strayer, *The Albigensian Crusades* (Ann Arbor, 1971); James Given, *State and Society in Medieval Europe: Gwynedd and Languedoc Under Outside Rule* (Ithaca, 1990); and biographies of three principal rulers, Baldwin, *Philip Augustus*; Strayer, *Philip the Fair*; and Jean Richard, *Saint Louis* (Cambridge, 1992).

years. Through war, marriage, inheritance, purchase, and feudal claims, Philip's heirs secured additional northern and central territories. In the course of the 13th century, in the name initially not of feudal rights but of suppressing the Albigensian heresy, the Capetians also conquered Languedoc, a Mediterranean land that, although nominally part of West Francia, had remained culturally and politically independent.[112] If Riurikid holdings in 1240 constituted some 20 percent of the Russian empire of 1800, by 1328 the Capetian royal domain was already over half as large as the French kingdom of 1789.

These territorial gains – and the need to finance wars – joined demographic and commercial vitality and innovative taxation to swell royal revenues between 1180 and 1223 by some 220 percent, and 207 percent from 1202 to 1287.[113] The chief sources were domain revenues, judicial fees, excise taxes, currency manipulations, and commuted feudal dues. Bribes, pensions, and money-fiefs secured the loyalty of key territorial lords, while cash payments supported both mercenaries and an ever more specialized body of officials. Under Philip the Fair (r. 1285–1314) the king's right to supplement his domain income with general taxes for military defense was widely recognized. Thus money facilitated royal expansion through both feudal and postfeudal claims.

To recapitulate French developments between c. 900 and 1328: Post-Carolingian trends were profoundly devolutionary, but by the 12th century a combination of local political reorganization, unprecedented economic growth, and new commercially aided cultural currents had nurtured a monarchical system far more stable and effective than that under Charlemagne. If the precise contributions of climate and other factors to economic revival after c. 900 remain uncertain, the broad correlation of medieval French vigor with that of charter Southeast Asia and of Kiev is clear.

Political and Cultural Cohesion in Kiev and Capetian France

But if economic and political vitality in Southeast Asia, western Russia, and France were broadly coordinated, what can we say about the

---

[112] On north–south cultural differences and the conquest of Languedoc, Planhol, *Historical Geography*, 90–134, 240–44; Linda Paterson, "The South," in Bull, *France in the Central Middle Ages*, 102–33; Strayer, *Albigensian Crusades*.

[113] Calculated from Duby, *France in the Middle Ages*, 176, and Hallam, *Capetian France*, 240, albeit without allowing for inflation. See too Baldwin, *Philip Augustus*, 152–64.

resultant levels of integration? How did Kievan and Capetian patterns compare to one another – and to those in Southeast Asia?

Assessments of Kievan integration have gone through two phases. The long-dominant interpretation, promoted by such scholars as George Vernadsky and John Fennell, emphasized the dysfunctional aspects of the Kievan system and evidence of progressive decline. In their view Kievan princes in the 11th century brought the state to its maximum power. But thereafter endemic feuds ushered in a period of disorder highlighted in 1169 when, to the horror of Kievan chroniclers, rebel princes sacked the capital.[114]

More recently, Franklin, Shepard, and Janet Martin have urged that we look not at the fortunes of the city of Kiev per se, but at the evolution of the realm as a whole. Martin, in particular, has claimed that frequent intradynastic wars illustrated not chaos but an attempt to refine the principles of rotated succession that princes had agreed upon in 1097.[115] The post-1097 multiplication of lineages and the economic strength of peripheral principalities tended to pit revisionists, who wanted to hasten the eligibility of younger princes to key regional seats, against conservatives, who wanted to keep 11th-century rules. But most efforts to redistribute power still assumed the need for recognized principles of accession. In fact, each round of interprincely fighting yielded more precise, more elaborate procedures, so that successive confrontations can be seen as signs of continued systemic coherence. These scholars draw much the same conclusion from the diffusion of Kievan institutions and culture. Provincial bishops remained subject to the Kiev Metropolitan, while provincial architecture, monastic organization, art, law, and chronicles all derived from Kiev and offered a more or less standardized statement of Rus history. At least in the eyes of native ecclesiastical authors, if Orthodoxy joined Kiev and other Orthodox peoples in a religious commonwealth, Orthodoxy also created a civilizational barrier between the Rus and pagan peoples within and without the Kievan

---

[114] See historiographic discussion at Martin, *Medieval Russia*, 92–93; George Vernadsky, *Kievan Russia* (New Haven, 1976), ch. 4; Fennell, *Crisis*, chs. 1–3, plus Omeljan Pritsak, "Kievan Rus' and Sixteenth-Seventeenth-Century Ukraine," in Ivan L. Rudnytsky, ed., *Rethinking Ukrainian History* (Edmonton, Canada, 1983), 98.

[115] Cf. n. 26 *supra*. Those principles included lateral succession within a single generation to specified regional centers, and exclusion from the Grand Princely throne of princes whose fathers had not held the throne. See Martin, *Medieval Russia*, 21–32, 90–124, supported in part by Nancy Shields Kollmann, "Collateral Succession in Kievan Russia," *HUS* 14 (1990): 377–87; and Franklin and Shepard, *Emergence*, chs. 9, 10, esp. 369–71.

sphere. Rus were defined by fealty to the Riurikid dynasty, a common language (albeit with variants), and a common faith.[116]

I indicated that I sympathize with this search for solidarities. Yet such sympathy cannot gainsay the fact that, in comparative terms, the Kievan realm remained extraordinarily decentralized.

Given Kiev's low population densities and limited communications, Grand Princes naturally concentrated their attention on the capital region itself. Courts under the authority of the senior Riurikid prince adjudicated disputes in Kiev and in a circle of nearby towns and fortresses. High-ranking members of the prince's retinue (*boyars*) may have met to discuss political and judicial matters, while the Kievan Metropolitanate maintained its own courts empowered to enforce Christian norms among the laity and to handle administrative issues involving the clergy.[117]

With important local variations, comparable arrangements were found in outlying principalities. Ranging from Galich and Polotsk in the west to Vladimir-Suzdal in the northeast, Kievan princely seats totaled about 12 in 1230.[118] But over these outlying principalities the capital exercised little, if any, substantive control. Although Riurikid princes regarded these lands of Rus as the collective possession of the dynasty and sought to work out principles of territorial succession, there was no stable hierarchy among provincial centers. Nor was there an imperial administration, nor indeed by any normal definition, a unitary state. Each outlying center handled as it saw fit justice, taxes, and military affairs within its own circle. By the 12th century, if not earlier, Galich, Chernigov, Vladimir-Suzdal, and other centers also conducted external relations without reference to Kiev or to one another, except

---

[116] Martin, *Medieval Russia*, 21–25, 78–88, 94, 132–33; Franklin and Shepard, *Emergence*, 315–19, 370–71; D. Obolensky, *Byzantium and the Slavs* (New York, 1994), 75–107. On political self-images in Kiev, Edward Reisman, "Determinants of Collective Identity in Rus', 988–1505" (Univ. of Chicago PhD diss., 1987), chs. 4–7; Franklin and Shepard, *Emergence*, 176–77, 230; Charles Halperin, "The Concept of the *Ruskaia Zemlia* and Medieval National Consciousness from the 10th to 15th Centuries," *Nationalities Papers* 8 (1980): 75–86; Pritsak, "Kiev and All Rus."

[117] Franklin and Shepard, *Emergence*, 221–24; Noonan, "Monetary History"; Martin, *Medieval Russia*, 34–35, 59–60, 70–73; Daniel Kaiser, "Reconsidering Crime and Punishment in Kievan Russia," *RH* 7 (1980): 282–93; Nancy Shields Kollmann, *By Honor Bound: State and Society in Early Modern Russia* (Ithaca, 1999), 183–84, citing I. Ia. Froianov.

[118] A number that, together with Kiev, recalls the roughly 13 tribal centers that existed prior to 882. Hellie, pers. commun., Feb. 28, 2006.

for ad hoc alliances based on temporary mutual advantage.[119] Having become ineligible for the central throne, some branches of the dynasty, like those of Chernigov and Polotsk, effectively withdrew from Kievan succession politics entirely. As with the Carolingians, imperial authority was effective during only a few reigns, namely, those of Vladimir (r. c. 980–1015) and Iaroslav the Wise (r. 1019–1054), plus, some would argue, Vladimir Monomakh (r. 1113–1125) and his son Mstislav (r. 1125–1132). As early as 1136 a revolt at Novgorod established that city's right to select its own ruler rather than accept Kiev's appointee. In 1158, 11 years before he sacked Kiev, the prince of Vladimir-Suzdal sponsored building projects that symbolically challenged the primacy of Kiev,[120] while by century's end the ruler of Vladimir-Suzdal (imitated perhaps by other regional leaders) had arrogated to himself the title of Grand Prince (*velikii kniaz*).[121] In 1203 dissident princes again subjected Kiev to a devastating sack. If we follow Franklin and Shepard, 12th-century sources refer to the Suzdal Land, the Smolensk Land, and so forth, but – in contrast to West Francia – there was in this period no commonly accepted geographic term for the collectivity of principalities.[122] In church architecture too, although Kiev provided the model, after c. 1150 provincial styles became more discernible, partly in response to foreign influences.[123]

In short, the Kievan realm was more decentralized not only than Capetian France but Carolingian France and the chief pre-1500 Southeast Asian realms, for in contrast to those states, the titular leader at Kiev, the Grand Prince, lacked independent, nonconciliar powers of appointment and revocation over subordinate rulers. Nor, since the lands of Kiev's city-based monasteries were limited, did Kiev enjoy the centripetal economic benefits that Angkor and Pagan derived from temple estates. Given these localizing and archaic features, it is perhaps not surprising that Kievan secular, as opposed to church, administration

---

[119] Franklin and Shepard, *Emergence*, 369–71.

[120] Janet Martin, "From Kiev to Muscovy," in Gregory Freeze, ed., *Russia: A History* (Oxford, 1997), 12; idem, *Medieval Rusia*, 112–14.

[121] Poppe, "Words That Serve," 182–84.

[122] "Rus" or "the Rus Land" usually meant only the territory around Kiev itself. Although the "Ile de France" likewise referred to the area around Paris, more inclusive terms like "West Francia" and "Kingdom of France" had no Rus counterpart. Simon and Franklin, *Emergence*, 341 and ch. 9 *passim*. Yet Valerie Kivelson, pers. commun., March 28, 2006 has expressed some misgivings about this view. See too Halperin, "Concept of the *Ruskaia Zemlia*"; Martin, *Medieval Russia*, 35–42, 94–104.

[123] Franklin and Shepard, *Emergence*, 355.

remained substantially preliterate. Although from the mid-11th century writing crept into the margins of law, diplomacy, and domestic dealings, written documents in government retained a primarily symbolic function. These objects might complement memory, but they had not yet begun to replace it. Thus in family conferences feuding princes hurled at one another parchments recording their "cross-kissed oaths" – written artifacts themselves, not the information they contained, buttressed honor. Not until the second half of the 1200s, after Kiev had been eclipsed, do we begin to see signs of a broader but still limited shift to documentary assumptions and habits.[124] Again, Kiev relied on written records less extensively than Pagan, Angkor, Dai Viet, Muscovy (Russia's principal post-1400 polity), or Capetian France.

How culturally integrated was Kiev? The population in the capital and in nearby communities was the first to adopt Christian rituals and motifs, as attested by the spread of Christian burials south and east of Kiev and by the growing use during the 11th century of Christian rather than pre-Christian symbols in dress and decoration. Compared to Southeast Asian or (we shall find) Heian Buddhism, Byzantine-Kievan Christianity, at least at the official level, was far more hostile to heathen survivals. With the senior prince close at hand, brazen acts of pre-Christian veneration thus became rare. As Riurikid princes and Orthodox bishops extended their authority beyond Kiev, modest churches also were built in *pogost* or parish centers, where they exerted pressure on provincial populations to adopt Christian symbols.

Nonetheless, as the presence of pagan priests even in 12th-century Novgorod, a major city, and as the persistence of predominantly pagan burials and ornaments in the provinces suggest, the church long remained a missionary enterprise in an at best nominally Christian land.[125] Overwhelmingly urban in focus and at first heavily Greek in senior personnel, Christianity was preeminently the religion of the ruling social stratum. A church document dated between 1077 and 1089 lamented that although princes and leading families (*boyars*) came to

---

[124] See Simon, *Writing, Society*, 129–228, 275–79; idem, "Literacy and Documentation in Early Medieval Russia," *Speculum* 60 (1985): 1–38; Valerie Kivelson, "Merciful Father, Impersonal State," in Lieberman, *Beyond Binary Histories*, 191–219; and the startlingly original views of Richard Hellie, "Late Medieval and Early Modern Russian Civilization and Modern Neuroscience," in A. M. Kleimola and G. D. Lenhoff, eds., *Culture and Identity in Muscovy, 1359–1584* (Moscow, 1997), 150–51.

[125] Martin, *Medieval Russia*, 74.

the church to "get married with proper ceremony and blessing... the common people do not... [rather] the common people take wives as if by abduction, with much leaping and dancing and hooting."[126] Many Slavic tribes subject to Kiev reportedly still lived in the forest "like beasts," practicing polygamy.[127] Indeed, possibly in reaction to proselytizing efforts, certain tribes, determined to maintain their independence, actually intensified pagan identities as advertised with distinctive ornaments and dress.[128] Before the 14th century, Daniel Kaiser claims, "Christianity had almost no impact outside the towns, and thus the clergy's cultural baggage... could have had no importance in rural society."[129] Likewise in Franklin's view, pre-13th century Christianity had not made "significant inroads into the countryside." Often so-called Christian priests were merely "converted" shamans.[130] Frequent repetition in the 1200s and 1300s of canons against unblessed marriages, ancestor worship, the adoration of fires, trees, and the Slavic thunder god confirm the continued popularity of pre-Christian practices.[131]

Thus, although lower social groups surely became more familiar with elite religion, popular ideas of sanctity remained syncretic, preliterate, and localized. The age of Russian peasant piety lay centuries in the future. By extension, although we lack hard information, it is doubtful that peasants or provincial townspeople – as opposed to church writers – had much sense of an overarching Orthodox or Kievan unity; and at the popular level one can speak confidently only of local identities.[132]

---

[126] Franklin and Shepard, *Emergence*, 230.

[127] Martin, *Medieval Russia*, 74, apparently citing the same source as the previous note. Where Christian burials took place, grave robberies to recover the bones for storage in accord with pre-Christian norms were common. On popular religion in the Kievan era, see ibid., 73–76, 132–33; Franklin and Shepard, *Emergence*, 174–77, 225–30, 370–71; Reisman, "Determinants," 269–93; I. Ia. Froianov et al., "The Introduction of Christianity in Russia and the Pagan Traditions," in Marjorie Balzer, ed., *Russian Traditional Culture* (Armonk, NY, 1992), 3–15; V. G. Vlasov, "The Christianization of the Russian Peasants," ibid., 16–47; David Miller, "Kievan Principality," 215–40.

[128] Franklin and Shepard, *Emergence*, 179.

[129] Daniel Kaiser, *The Growth of the Law in Medieval Russia* (Princeton, 1980), 187; also 168.

[130] Franklin, "Literacy and Documentation," 37, confirmed by Hellie, pers. commun., Feb. 28, 2006.

[131] S. C. Rowell, *Lithuania Ascending* (Cambridge, 1994), 296.

[132] Reisman, "Determinants," 276–77; Henrik Birnbaum, "The Balkan Slavic Component of Medieval Russian Culture," cited ibid., 277, n. 63. But cf. the different emphasis at Franklin and Shepard, *Emergence*, 371.

Turning to French political and cultural life, one immediately senses greater horizontal and vertical coherence.[133] Through texts and communal memory, churchmen and lay elites in France had access to the political and high cultural traditions of Rome, and, more especially, of the Carolingians. If French kings and territorial lords engaged in prolonged contests to determine the meaning of those shared inheritances, the Carolingians provided a set of political precedents, of guiding principles, unavailable to Kiev. These included certain legal usages, the notion of purposive royal intervention on the local level, the hierarchy of territorial lords and titles, a tradition of church–crown cooperation, the ideal of Christian kingship, France's post-843 titular boundaries, and the very concept of "the kingdom of France." In part because Kiev operated in a substantially preliterate milieu, in part because Kiev lacked easy access to Roman legacies, but most basically – and, of course, this was partly a symptom of illiteracy and isolation – because Kiev was a charter polity, Kievan princes were obliged to find their way without guide or blueprint. In this enforced originality, I already suggested, they resembled Frankish leaders 400 or 500 years earlier. And as with the Franks, their experiments brought much instability and violence.

No less critical were geographic and economic differences. Because the boundaries of the Kievan realm were vague, almost limitless, they favored a localism more extreme than in France, pronounced though the latter surely was. Constant frontier reclamation and the opening of trade routes all around the perimeter of Rus were inherently centrifugal, as we saw. The open frontier, plus mediocre soils and a still short (if expanded) growing season also mandated low man-to-land ratios and a low-yield agrarian regime, which constricted resources available to would-be centralizers and cultural innovators alike. But in post-Carolingian France, now hemmed in by the Empire as well as by the North Sea, the Atlantic, the Mediterranean, and the Pyrenees, neither king nor nobles could any longer expand resources by moving easily outside the kingdom, whether for plunder or colonization. It became imperative not only to intensify agrarian productivity, but to work out stable political arrangements within the kingdom. Material differences between Russia and France not only persisted, but may have widened. By 1240 we saw that France was in Rozman's Stage E of urbanization ("standard marketing"), whereas Russia was still only in an advanced

---

[133] I am again indebted for some of the following perspectives to Geary, pers. commun., Sept. 7, 2006.

form of Stage C ("state city").[134] Russian cereal yields recall those of Carolingian France, while overall population densities in 1240 may not have been 10 percent those of France.

These charter horizons defy a simple Asian–European binary. In terms of charter novelty, low man-to-land ratios, and open frontiers, Pagan and Angkor stood closer to Kiev than to Capetian France. On the other hand, elite lay literacy in Indic Southeast Asia by 1200 was comparable to that in France. Moreover, Vietnam resembled Capetian France rather closely in terms of easy access to a sophisticated imperial culture, in Vietnam's case that of China; relatively high man-to-land ratios, and limited frontier expansion, which in Vietnam was blocked by mountains to the west and until 1471 by Cham resistance along the narrow eastern littoral.

A succession of Capetian rulers used these cultural and material advantages to create Europe's most powerful, widely imitated state. Styling themselves "emperors in their kingdom," from the early 12th to 14th centuries they secularized governance, used representative bodies to raise taxes, and claimed the right to judge disputes among their most powerful subjects.[135] Whereas Carolingian rulers had divided their lands among male heirs, the Capetians, as part of the general movement toward noble primogeniture, consistently bestowed the bulk of the royal domain on their eldest son. What is more, to forestall challenges, early Capetians (like 13th-century Vietnamese rulers) were careful to have that son anointed and to associate him with the throne while his father was still alive.[136] And yet, if France became uniquely powerful by 14th-century European standards, by later French standards the Capetian realm even at its height c. 1310 remained a rather fragile mosaic of five more or less distinct zones.

---

[134] See Ch. 1, n. 78; this chapter, nn. 8, 15, 100 *supra*; Rozman, *Urban Networks*, chs. 2–5. But note that Novgorod and some other lower level cities may have held over 10,000 people.

[135] James Collins, *The State in Early Modern France* (Cambridge, 1995), 2–10 refers to the pre-1500 monarchy as the "judicial monarchy." See too idem, *Tribes to Nation*, iv–v, x–xi.

[136] In executing these reforms, which made it unnecessary for royal contenders to bargain away their rights to gain magnate support, the Capetians were biologically blessed insofar as they had a clear male heir in every generation from 987 to 1328. Wood, *Merovingian Kingdoms*, 56–60; Goubert, *Course of French History*, 2, 16; Moore, *First European Revolution*, 70; Robert Fawtier, *The Capetian Kings of France* (New York, 1960), 48–59. On curiously similar succession reforms in 13th-century Dai Viet, see *SP*, 358–61.

The first, most tightly held zone was the Ile de France centered around Paris. Although part of the royal domain, this was distinguished from the rest of the domain by its greater administrative homogeneity and by a tradition of service to the crown that made it the nursery of royal officials. (The royal domain itself may be defined as the collection of jurisdictions supplying the king with revenues and military service and administered by royal agents.[137]) Within the Ile de France, Paris supported an increasingly specialized, if prebureaucratic, administration concerned chiefly with justice (the *parlement* of Paris had appellate jurisdiction for the entire kingdom) and finances. Second was the royal domain outside the Ile de France. Extending in noncontiguous, "Swiss cheese" fashion from the Channel to the Mediterranean and from the Atlantic to the Rhone and in 1328 covering some two-thirds of the titular kingdom of France, this was an administrative pastiche over which the throne had neither the means nor inclination to promote uniformity. Rather, the crown deliberately retained local institutions both to conciliate local sentiment and to build on local advances. At the same time the crown erected a novel overarching structure of salaried officers (*baillis* in the north, *senechaux* in the south), who with their staffs had responsibility for levying troops, executing justice, and collecting taxes. The third zone were royal apanages. Although each king bestowed the bulk of the royal domain on his eldest son, recently acquired lands outside that original patrimony were still given as hereditary fiefs – apanages – to younger sons. But from 1284 apanages began to lose their hereditary character, a change that, together with the grants' declining size, suggests a deliberate policy of further subordinating princely interests to those of the throne.[138] The fourth zone consisted of the great territorial principalities, including Flanders, Brittany, and Aquitaine,

---

[137] Strayer, *Philip the Fair*, 142; Richard, *Saint Louis*, 21–33; and Hallam, *Capetian France*, 247. Analysis of late Capetian administration relies too on Given, *State and Society*, ch. 6; Hallam, *Capetian France*, 159–73, 239–66, 299–308; Strayer, *Philip the Fair*, ch. 5; idem, *On the Medieval Origins of the Modern State* (Princeton, 1979); Baldwin, *Philip Augustus*, 125–37, 220–47; Koziol, "Political Culture," 55–58; John Le Patourel, "The King and the Princes in 14th-Century France," in J. R. Hale et al., eds., *Europe in the Late Middle Ages* (London, 1965), 155–83; David Potter, "Introduction," in Potter, *France in the Later Middle Ages*, 1–22; Michael Jones, "The Crown and the Provinces in the 14th Century," in ibid., 61–89; Dunbabin, "Political World," 23–46.

[138] Hallam, *Capetian France*, 112, 247–66, 299–301; Andrew Lewis, *Royal Succession in Capetian France* (Cambridge, MA, 1982), esp. 174–78, 193–97; idem, "The Capetian Apanages and the Nature of the French Kingdom," *Jl. of Medieval History* 2 (1976): 119–34; Potter, "Introduction," 7, 13.

which lay outside the holdings of the royal family but within the titular boundaries of France. Like apanages, these were held in fief from the crown. Here too Paris sought to assert claims of financial entitlement and judicial appeal. But as hereditary lords of large, cohesive outlying regions whose administrations benefited from the same centralizing trends as the Capetian state itself, the great fief-holders were far more able than leaders in the first three zones to resist royal demands and to pursue independent external policies. Finally, outside France proper some small principalities within the Holy Roman Empire but adjacent to French territory (Lorraine, Savoy, Provence) came under growing Capetian influence.

Capetian centralization drew strength from, even as it impelled, intellectual and symbolic changes sanctifying the Capetians and their realm. By the 12th century vernacular writers were equating "France" with Roman Gaul and identifying its leading inhabitants as *franceis [francais]*. From the 1120s and with ever greater enthusiasm in the 13th century, royalist clerics extolled the Capetians as scourge of Jews and heretics, workers of miracles, Most Christian Kings. The people of France were God's new Chosen People, and "most sweet France" became a symbol of the heavenly kingdom. With royal patronage and military success, such images, at first restricted to narrow scholarly circles in the Paris basin, gained wider currency, albeit chiefly among noble, clerical, and urban elites. Thus, if the tutelary cult of the Capetian saint-king Louis still had not penetrated Burgundy or the southwest, by the mid-1300s it had spread from the capital to Normandy, the Loire valley, even Provence. The partial transfer of sanctity from church to crown appeared too in the rise of Gallican theories championing the liberties of the French church over and against Rome.[139]

Within the northern linguistic zone known as the *langue d'oil*, royal prestige and easier communications also favored the tongue of the Ile de France at the expense of Picard, Norman, Poitevin, and other dialects.

---

[139] On the growth of French/Capetian protopatriotic themes and royal claims, Krynen, "Rex Christianissimus," 7–96; idem, "Genese de l'etat et histoire des idees politiques en France a la fin du Moyen Age," in *Culture et Ideologie dans la Genese de l'Etat Moderne* (Rome, 1985), 395–412; Gabrielle M. Spiegel, "The Cult of Saint Denis and Capetian Kingship," *Jl. of Medieval History* 1 (1975): 43–65; Strayer, *Philip the Fair*, chs. 4–6; Schneidmuller, "Constructing Identities," 34–42; Beaune, *Birth of an Ideology*, esp. chs. 1, 3, 6, 11; Planhol, *Historical Geography*, 93–117; Hallam, *Capetian France*, 178–79, 260–63, 308–17; Kantorowicz, *King's Two Bodies*, 232–72; Potter, "Introduction," 4–7; Collins, *Tribes to Nation*, iv–v, xii, xix, xxiv–xxv.

Among elites Parisian French by 1200 was regarded as most desirable for elevated speech, and in 1254 the royal chancellery began using Parisian French alongside Latin. By pitting nobles throughout the north against Languedoc in the south, the Albigensian crusades further strengthened the equation of the royal court with Ile de France culture. By ranging regional nobilities behind the French king and by inviting distinctions between "Franks" and other Europeans, the Crusades from 1144 to 1270 had much the same effect.[140] In the south the cultural counterpart to northern political dominance was the imposition of Gothic architecture on Albi and Carcassone. But if north-to-south cultural flows dominated, the Ile de France also absorbed provincial currents, as for example, legal scholarship and romantic poetry from the south (where literary Occitan flourished) and monastic influences from Burgundy.[141]

In broad chronology, if not audience, the rural penetration of elite-defined Christianity between 1000 and 1300 paralleled the spread of north French culture. Although the Carolingian era saw the organizational and liturgical unification of Christian microcultures, popular animism retained much of its power. Cloud-flying wizards, moon goddesses, werewolves, and watersnake women were honored in broad daylight only a few miles from great cathedrals.[142] But accelerating prosperity from the 11th century and the attendant proliferation of stable villages, relic cults, cathedrals, and most critical, parish churches allowed French Christianity to breach its urban confines and influence even remote settlements and humble strata. The late 11th to 14th centuries thus saw determined church efforts to standardize rituals and liturgies, to tighten control over parish priests, to bring sacraments closer to the peasantry, to curb pre-Christian survivals, to combat heresy (which, however, tended to grow alongside literacy), and to channel

---

[140] An account of the first crusade, *Gesta Francorum*, saw this event as the ethnogenesis of the "Frankish people." Alan V. Murray, "Ethnic Identity in the Crusader States," in Simon Forde et al., eds., *Concepts of National Identity in the Middle Ages* (Leeds, 1995), 59–73.

[141] On regional cultural trends, n. 112 *supra*, plus Strayer, *Albigensian Crusades*, 163–74; Hallam, *Capetian France*, 257; Peter Rickard, *A History of the French Language* (London, 1989), 25–46; A. Brun, *Recherches Historiques sur l'Introduction du Francais dans les Provinces du Midi* (Paris, 1923), 7–76. For a comparative view of the birth of French as well as Occitan literature, Sheldon Pollock, *The Language of the Gods in the World of Men* (Berkeley, 2006), 447–51, 464–69.

[142] Poly and Bournazel, *Feudal Transformation*, 310–18; Jacques LeGoff, *Pour un Autre Moyen Age* (Paris, 1977), 236–79, 307–31; essays by Alexander Murray and Sofia Boesch Gajano in Little and Rosenwein, *Debating*, 92–103, 330–39; Smith, *Europe After Rome*, 29.

popular piety toward approved cults, the Virgin in particular. An associated tide of religious endowments also served to join local societies to a wider world. In consequence, in France by 1300 – more commonly than in Russia – peasants were baptized and attended church, while some of the most blatantly pagan practices receded.[143]

Lest one exaggerate the solidity or specificity of French cultural integration, however, consider the power of Latin Christian identities above the level of the French kingdom, and the resilience of regional cultures below. As regards the former, some of the same forces – commerce, universities, *courtoisie* – as strengthened the kingdom of France simultaneously nurtured a pervasive Latin high culture. On every European frontier knights were identically organized, trained, and equipped. Most critical, the church promoted uniformity through standardized episcopal structures, European-wide monastic orders, the use of Latin, the concentration of local cults upon the great figures of Christian history, papal assertions of control over everything from liturgy to canonization, long-distance pilgrimages, and the Crusades. In the hostility it bred toward Muslims, Jews, and Orthodox Christians, Latin Christianity actually assumed some of the functions of ethnicity. By the same token, from England to Hungary church leaders and nobles invoked a Latin Christian identity to distinguish themselves from, and at the same time to control, their own peasants, routinely denigrated as "pagani," "heretici," "illitterati."[144] In its elitism, confident universalism, and tension with still weak kingdom-focused loyalties and vernacular cultures, Latin Christianity c. 900 to 1300 resembled Theravada Buddhism, Neo-Confucianism, and Russian Orthodoxy.

Also as in Southeast Asia and Russia, beneath the level of the emergent kingdom regional cultures remained enormously vital. In 1300 French patriotic sentiment and Parisian dialect, though increasingly influential, were still restricted to urban notables, high clerics, and nobles in the orbit of the court. Outside the Paris basin, among petty

---

[143] Andre Vauchez, "The Birth of Christian Europe: 950–1100," in *CIHMA*, vol. I, 80–119; idem, "A Strict Normalisation," 396–443; John Van Engen, "The Christian Middle Ages as an Historiographical Problem," *AHR* 91 (1986): 519–52; Richard Kieckhefer, *Magic in the Middle Ages* (Cambridge, 1990); Rosalind and Christopher Brooke, *Popular Religion in the Middle Ages* (London, 1984); Marie-Dominique Chenu, "The Evangelical Awakening," in Little and Rosenwein, *Debating*, 310–29; Moore, *First European Revolution*, 11–12, 57–64, 82–88, 175; Levine, *At the Dawn*, 61–106; Marcus Bull, "The Church," in Bull, *France in the Central Middle Ages*, 134–66.

[144] Previous note, plus Bartlett, *Making of Europe*; Moore, "Birth of Europe," 149–53.

rural knights – not to mention peasants and common townsmen – loyalties, speech, and cultural usages remained resolutely local. Thus, for example, not only did dialects and law in much of Languedoc retain closer links to Catalonia than to northern France, but the north itself still supported some 12 *langue d'oil* dialects and uncounted subdialects. In few, if any, contexts did common people think of themselves as "French," and in popular parlance "France" still usually referred to the Ile de France.[145] By the same token, although elite urban practices gained ground, as late as 1550 many parish priests were barely literate, and popular religion remained overwhelmingly oral and luxuriantly diverse.[146] Note that the Buddhicization of the Southeast Asian peasantry, drawing strength from new educational and commercial circuits, also made dramatic strides only after the 15th and 16th centuries.

Not surprisingly, local loyalties joined aggrandizing regional administrations to set strict limits to central power. I have noted that reforms in the great fiefs not only preceded but continued alongside the more spectacular Capetian centralization. Brittany's dukes, for example, exploited its Celtic traditions and English connections to resist Capetian demands even as they subordinated local nobles and created new financial institutions. Aquitaine, whose duke was also king of England, began to oppose the very concept of French sovereignty. When in the mid-1300s the monarchy stumbled under the twin burdens of broken succession and the Black Death, satellite leaders threatened to pull down much of the Capetian edifice.

2. FRAGMENTATION, C. 1240–1450

The Poison Fruits of Growth: A Survey of 13th- to Mid-15th-Century Difficulties

Across mainland Southeast Asia, I have argued, charter disintegration between c. 1250 and 1440 reflected the combined effects of institutional

---

[145] See n. 139 *supra*, plus Jones, "Crown and Provinces," 61–89.

[146] Guy Devailly, "L'encadrement paroissial," in *La Religion Populaire en Languedoc du XIIIe Siecle a la Moitie du XIVe Siecle, Cahiers de Fanjeaux* 11 (1976): 387–417; Robert Scribner, "Elements of Popular Belief," in Thomas A. Brady et al., eds., *Handbook of European History 1400–1600*, 2 vols. (Grand Rapids, MI, 1994, 1995), vol. I, 231–62, esp. 239; LeGoff, *Moyen Age*, 307–31. According to Smith, *Europe After Rome*, 223–24, the strength of early medieval Christianity was precisely its ability to ground a universal faith in a multitude of local contexts.

weaknesses; destabilizing economic growth; post-1250/1300 cooling, which weakened monsoon flows; and external assaults.[147] In Upper Burma, Angkor, and Dai Viet, after some 300 years of continuous reclamation, a dearth of fresh cultivable land in long-settled districts joined climatic deterioration and the accumulation of untaxed lands by princes and temples to erode each crown's resource base. By shifting power from inland capitals toward the peripheries, frontier colonization and the expansion of maritime trade – the latter an artifact of economic vitality in Southeast Asia, China, and South Asia – further weakened central authority. In each instance military shocks finally collapsed the system. In the western and central mainland, Mongols to a limited extent, but more particularly Tais were the chief external agents; in Dai Viet Chams and the new Ming Dynasty in China filled that role. But insofar as the Mongols facilitated Tai expansion and indirectly paved the way to the Ming, they influenced charter collapse across the mainland. Note, finally, that in each sector military disorders and frequently adverse weather inhibited recentralization until the mid- or late 15th century.

In genesis and basic chronology, Southeast Asia's postcharter crises found unmistakable echoes in Kiev and France. In 1240 the Kievan polity, and in the second quarter of the 14th century the French kingdom, both disintegrated through the combined effects of a) institutional strains aggravated by two to three centuries of sustained demographic and commercial expansion, and b) Mongol-mediated pressures, direct or indirect. Thereafter in both realms deteriorating weather, warfare, severe epidemics, and bullion shortages took a hideous toll while inhibiting recentralization. But in both regions as in Southeast Asia, by the mid-1400s the long era of fragmentation had yielded to a new phase of state building.

Within this overarching paradigm, differences between Russia and France suggest that the former again resembled mainland Southeast Asia, at least its western and central sectors, rather more closely than it resembled France. Mongol assaults on Kiev were no less jarring than Tai attacks in Southeast Asia. Indeed, because the Mongols were an externally based military power who, unlike the Tais, declined to adapt to local culture, they posed a more alien and systemic threat than Tai warbands. By comparison, France's 14th-century political crisis was essentially internal. The French king's foes were not steppe nomads or "barbarian" hill tribes, rather his own feudatories, who, while seeking

---

[147] *SP*, 119–49, 236–58, 367–93, and Ch. 1, pt. 2 *supra*.

to redistribute power, worked within the same political and cultural paradigm as the king himself. For much of the Hundred Years War even the kings of England sought not to destroy France, merely to place themselves on its throne. As for the Mongols, their influence on France was entirely indirect and invisible, as distant vectors of the Black Death. In an economic sense as well, although long-settled interior districts faced an appalling set of 14th-century disasters, there is no indication that France, lacking an external agrarian frontier, suffered from unusually rapid commercial or agrarian growth *on the periphery* such as weakened Angkor, Pagan, and Kiev.

France and Russia differed from one another too in the severity of their 13th/15th-century crises. In France the upheavals of 1337–1453 were merely the second in a series of progressively shorter eras of fragmentation, the first having followed Carolingian collapse in the 9th century. The sophistication of Capetian/early Valois political and fiscal institutions meant that relatively limited changes were needed between 1429 and 1453 for the system to begin to right itself. But in Russia, both because central controls had been primitive to start, and because the Mongols transformed the political and military environment, Kiev's collapse forced adjustments even more wrenching, one could argue, than those that transformed Southeast Asia in these same centuries.

Kiev's Collapse and the Era of Fragmentation to c. 1450

It is convenient again to pick up the story with Kiev, the first charter realm under consideration to collapse. Striking from western Siberia, between 1237 and 1240 armies of the Kipchak khanate – whose rulers were Mongol heirs to Chinggis Khan but whose rank and file were Turkic Tatars[148] – sacked Kiev and other major Rus cities, massacred the population, and imposed heavy tribute on Rus principalities as distant as Volynia, Galicia, and Novgorod.

I referred earlier to two schools of Kievan historiography, the one emphasizing the progressive decline of central influence over outlying

---

[148] After Chinggis Khan's death in 1227, the westernmost sector of his empire became known as the Kipchak khanate (anachronistically also called the Golden Horde), under whose authority Russia was conquered. "Tatar" refers to the predominantly Turkic population that from an early date provided the bulk of forces attacking Russia under Mongol leadership. Martin, *Medieval Russia*, 134–35; Donald Ostrowski, *Muscovy and the Mongols* (Cambridge, 1998), 32–33, 252–55; David Morgan, *The Mongols* (Malden, MA, 1986), 136–45; *EAH*, vol. IV, 77–78.

areas, the second focusing on vitality and coherence in the Kievan system as a whole. Not surprisingly, the former school, that of "feudal disintegration," sees the events of 1237–1240 primarily as a function of domestic weakness, which in turn reflected the uncertainties of princely succession and the rising agrarian and commercial power of outlying principalities at the expense of the old Kievan heartland. By the early 1200s southern and western principalities were locked in bitter rivalries for succession to the Grand Princely office to which those in the north and east were largely indifferent. The Mongols intensified this leadership crisis, so that when the invaders arrived in Kiev in 1240, Riurikid princes did not even attempt a joint defense. In this view, the Mongols were merely an acceleratory agent, a mallet driving a wedge into already visible fault lines.[149] Even had they not invaded, in two or three generations Kiev would have fragmented formally and irrevocably.

But the second historiographic school is also persuasive insofar as it emphasizes the utter novelty and incomparable power of Mongol assaults. In purely military terms the Mongols were a nontraditional enemy, invincible everywhere from Croatia to South China, whose success must be sought in their nonpareil mounted archery skills, incomparable mobility, innovative tactics, and advanced siege equipment. Against the mightiest war machine of its time, even the most coordinated Rus defense would have been ineffectual. Of course, the Kievan federation, left to its own devices, might have fragmented anyway. But it is also possible, Martin argues, that without the Mongols, the intradynastic conflicts of the early 13th century, like those of the 11th and 12th centuries, would have produced a workable consensus.[150]

---

[149] Metaphor from Martin, *Medieval Russia*, 158, although she herself opposes the feudal disintegration approach. For statements of the latter, Leo de Hartog, *Russia and the Mongol Yoke* (London, 1996), 27, 33–34; Riasanovsky, *History*, 70; Fennell, *Crisis*, 86. On early 13th-century politics, see too Martin Dimnik, *Mikhail, Prince of Chernigov and Grand Prince of Kiev 1224–1246* (Toronto, 1981); Martin, *Medieval Russia*, 118–23, 33–40.

[150] Martin, *Medieval Russia*, 124, plus 91–94, 132–33, 140, 158. Also, Franklin and Shepard, *Emergence*, 367–68. In evaluating the role of the steppe in Kiev decline, note that long before the Mongols, from 1061, Kiev was having trouble keeping at bay Turkic tribes known as Polovtsy or Cumans. To explain the Mongol explosion itself, some have invoked a long phase of warm wet weather, which was ideal for pastures and which boosted Mongol population, followed by a sudden local cold phase in the early 1200s that triggered desperate expansion. But the evidence is weak. See Lamb, *Climate, History*, 184–85, 317; Gareth Jenkins, "A Note on Climatic Cycles and the Rise of Chinggis Khan," *Central Asiatic Jl.* 18 (1974): 217–26; Joseph Fletcher, "The Mongols: Ecological and Social Perspectives," *HJAS* 46 (1986): 22–34; and the convoluted arguments of Brown, *History and Climate*, 211–23, 274. For a graphic account of the Mongol conquest

What is indisputable is that the Kipchak khanate, whose leadership by the mid-1300s had passed from Mongol to Tatar control,[151] radically intensified preexisting devolutionary tendencies and substantially modified the character of that devolution. This Inner Asian contribution to Rus political fragmentation was actually threefold. First and most basic, by devastating the city of Kiev and its environs, the Mongols immediately obliterated the chief symbol of Rus unity and hastened the transfer of power from the Dnieper heartland to outlying areas, in particular the southwestern and northern frontiers of the old Kievan realm. Second, Mongol, or Mongol-Tatar, interventions accelerated a long-term politicocultural split between eastern and western lands of Rus. Originally all the lands of Rus were obliged to pay tribute to the Kipchak khanate. In the course of the 14th century, however, Volynia and the Dnieper basin in the west entered the orbit of Lithuania, while the north and northeast remained politically and economically oriented toward the khanate and the east. In combination with pre-1240 cultural differences and with the subsequent rivalry between Lithuania and Muscovy, this division gradually assumed ethnic and linguistic significance, as we shall see. Third, in northeastern Rus, which they supervised and taxed most scrupulously, Mongols and Tatars weakened Riurikid cohesion by manipulating succession to the Grand Princely throne of Vladimir – would-be institutional successor to the Grand Princedom of Kiev – and by pitting one tributary principality against another. Although Mongols and Tatars did not occupy the northeast directly for a sustained period and although in the long term their actions proved politically self-defeating, until the late 1300s their interventions joined intradynastic rivalries and Riurikid inheritance patterns to forestall Rus challenges to steppe domination.[152]

If early Inner Asian interventions inhibited recentralization, economic difficulties c. 1240–1450 had a similar effect. Now I hasten to note that in Russian as in Southeast Asian historiography, an earlier emphasis on postcharter economic collapse is now balanced by greater sensitivity to elements of continuity. Donald Ostrowski has claimed – albeit not to universal agreement – that as an empire dependent on

of Rus, Jack Weatherford, *Genghis Khan and the Making of the Modern World* (New York, 2004), 138–50.

[151] From the late 1200s Mongols in the khanate began assimilating culturally and biologically to their Tatar subjects, and by the mid-1300s that process was effectively complete. See n. 148 *supra*.

[152] Martin, *Medieval Russia*, ch. 6, esp. 162.

commercial income, the Kipchak khanate directed trade up the Volga through Rus towns like Moscow and Nizhnii Novgorod, which in turn linked up with Baltic markets via Novgorod. Certainly, transit taxes and fur exports aided Moscow and other northeastern principalities. By the late 1300s not only was handicraft production approaching pre-Mongol levels, but from 1363–1387 new masonry constructions in the northeast were only slightly fewer than in northern Rus during the 25 years immediately preceding the Mongol conquest.[153] Agriculture in some locales also progressed, at least to 1400. If Rus penetration of the steppe, anemic to begin with, halted completely before the Tatars, reclamation in the forests of the north and northeast continued under the aegis of princes, peasant communes, and large monasteries, assisted, some argue, by the invention or dissemination of a new plow (*sokha*).[154] According to R. H. Hilton and R. E. F. Smith, the continued availability of good arable land ensured that late medieval economic pressures in Russia were less severe than in western Europe.[155] By the second half of the 14th century, Martin argues, a "general economic recovery" was evident across the Russian lands.[156]

Yet it is also clear that Rus production fell sharply after 1240, so that such late-14th-century growth as did occur started from a very low level. Miller has shown that after Mongol attacks, masonry and brick construction in northern and northeastern Rus virtually ceased and did not fully recover pre-Mongol levels for over 150 years. Much the same was true of artisan output.[157] As late as 1390 towns in the areas once subject to Kiev at its height were still only about half as numerous as in

[153] Ostrowski, *Muscovy and Mongols*, 91, 108–32; David B. Miller, "Monumental Building as an Indicator of Economic Trends in Northern Rus' in the Late Kievan and Mongol Periods, 1138–1462," *AHR* 94 (1989): 360–90, esp. 366, 373; idem, "Monumental Building, 900–1262," 350, 355. For similar views, Richard Halperin, *Russia and the Golden Horde* (Bloomington, IN, 1987), 75–86; Nancy Shields Kollmann, *Kinship and Politics: The Making of the Muscovite Political System, 1345–1547* (Stanford, 1987), 29–30; Martin, *Land of Darkness*, chs. 4–6; Crummey, *Formation of Muscovy*, 16–17. Without necessarily disputing Muscovite prosperity, Hellie, pers. commun., Feb. 28, 2006 has denied that it depended on a Pax Mongolica.

[154] However, Ostowski, *Muscovy and Mongols*, 123 disparages claims for the *sokha* by P. P. Smirnov and D. K. Zelentin.

[155] R. H. Hilton and R. E. F. Smith, "Introduction," in Smith, *Enserfment*, 26 and 13–16; Smith, *Peasant Farming*, 113, 120–21.

[156] Martin, *Medieval Russia*, 222, also 165–69, 222–26. For comparable views, Dukes, *History*, 35–38, and A. M. Sakharov, "Rus and Its Culture in the 13th to 15th Centuries," *Soviet Studies in History* 18 (1979–80), 29–30.

[157] Miller, "Monumental Building, 1138–1462," esp. 368, 383; Ostrowski, *Muscovy and Mongols*, 112–13.

the 1220s, and settlements themselves on average were only about half as large.[158] If the Tatars encouraged trade in the northeast, their tribute demands were certainly heavier than under Kiev, while fragmentation in the former Kievan realm as a whole must have raised the costs of commerce by parcelizing justice, multiplying units of measure, increasing local tolls, and posing chronic risks of warfare and confiscation.

Dramatically compounding these difficulties, in 1351–1353 the first wave of the Black Death hit Russia. Although the origins of the disease are unclear – McNeill believes it began on the China–Burma frontier whence the Mongols spread it via North China and Inner Asian caravan routes to the Russian steppe, whereas Ole Benedictow argues that it had long been endemic in the western steppe – most authors accept that Mongol-Tatars introduced the plague from the steppe to the Crimean port of Kaffa. Thence it raced across the Mediterranean to western and central Europe, only to spread back east along overland trade routes from Germany to Russia. In 1364–1365, if not earlier, a second wave apparently moved up the Volga. Striking perhaps in tandem with influenza and typhus, plague not only crippled Russian towns and trade in the mid-1300s, but continued to afflict Russian commerce at gradually lengthening intervals for a century or more.[159] Also limiting Russian, indeed Eurasian, commercial vitality for much of the 15th century were bullion shortages, which reflected *inter alia* the Black Death's inflation of European labor costs, technical difficulties and lode exhaustion in central European silver mines, problems with African gold supplies, and a mid-1400s collapse in Chinese silver production. Steady debasement of 15th-century Russian coinage testified to the inadequacy of supplies.[160]

---

[158] French, "Early and Medieval Russian Town," 261–63; Blum, *Lord and Peasant*, 61–62; Hellie, pers. commun., Feb. 28, 2006.

[159] See Ch. 1, n. 114 *supra*, plus John T. Alexander, *Bubonic Plague in Early Modern Russia* (Baltimore, 1980), 12–15; Lawrence Langer, "The Black Death in Russia: Its Effects upon Urban Labor," *RH* 2 (1975): 53–67; idem, "Plague and the Russian Countryside: Monastic Estates in the Late 14th and 15th Centuries," *CASS* 10 (1976): 351–68; Miller, "Monumental Building, 1138–1462," 371–72; David Herlihy, *The Black Death and the Transformation of the West* (Cambridge, MA, 1997), 22–25; Ynez Viole O'Neill, "Diseases of the Middle Ages," in Kiple, *Cambridge World History of Disease*, 275–79. Some have queried the traditional identification of the Black Death with bubonic and pneumonic plague. See discussion *infra*.

[160] Blum, *Lord and Peasant*, 118–19, 199; Richard Hellie, "Russia, 1200–1815," in Richard Bonney, ed., *The Rise of the Fiscal State in Europe, c. 1200–1815* (Oxford, 1999), 482, referring to the "coinless period." But for different emphases, see money references in Ostrowski, *Muscovy and Mongols*, 126–27, and Thomas Noonan, "Forging a National

Nor was rural society spared. Between 1352 and 1450 the Black Death and famine claimed at least a quarter, possibly far more, of the Rus population, which, of course, was overwhelmingly rural. The most severe losses apparently occurred not in the mid-14th century, but between 1400 and 1430. Lawrence Langer argues that famines in this period were, in large measure, a function of village disintegration and land abandonment precipitated by plague. The ensuing disorders helped to transfer extensive lands from lay lords and village communes to monasteries whose institutional continuity and wealth helped to compensate for loss of individual members. With depressing frequency, 14th- and 15th-century documents refer to labor shortages and abandoned lands (*pustoshi*). No less indicative of population scarcity were vigorous attempts by landowners to attract settlers and to restrict the freedom of peasants already in place.[161]

Finally, climate reconstructions point to a period of colder, more disturbed conditions starting in the early or late 1200s, intensifying in the late 1300s and early 1400s, and moderating only in the mid- or late 1400s. Such weather must have compressed the short northern growing season, reducing yields and aggravating the disruptive effects of the Black Death. Colder weather and associated famines may have increased susceptibility to influenza and typhus. Some scholars also have speculated that by disturbing rodent colonies or promoting bacterial mutations,

Identity," in Kleimola and Lenhoff, *Culture and Identity*, 495–523. On Eurasian shortages, John Day, *The Medieval Market Economy* (Oxford, 1987), 1–54, 199–215; Harry Miskimin, *The Economy of Early Renaissance Europe, 1300–1460* (Cambridge, 1975), 138–44; idem, *The Economy of Later Renaissance Europe, 1460–1600* (Cambridge, 1977), 28–29, 35–36; David Potter, "The King and His Government Under the Valois, 1328–1498," in Potter, *France in the Later Middle Ages*, 174; William Atwell, "Time, Money, and the Weather," *JAS* 61 (2002): 83–113; Ch. 1, n. 119 *supra*; and essays by Harry Miskimin, John Munro, and John Deyell in John Richards, ed., *Precious Metals in the Later Medieval and Early Modern Worlds* (Durham, NC, 1983).

[161] On rural plague impacts, Langer, "Black Death," 62; idem, "Plague and the Countryside"; 351–68, esp. 357, 367; Crummey, *Formation of Muscovy*, 3, 42; Alexander, *Bubonic Plague*, 13–16; Blum, *Lord and Peasant*, 61; Richard Hellie, *Readings for Introduction to Russian Civilization, Muscovite Society* (Chicago, 1970), 92–104; Martin, *Medieval Russia*, 201, suggesting 25 percent minimum overall plague deaths; and Ole Benedictow, "The Black Death," *History Today* 55 (2005): 42–49; idem, *The Black Death, 1346–1353* (Woodbridge, UK, 2004), Map 1, and 31–34, 211–15, 383, arguing for 60 percent European mortality (he offers no Russian figures) and emphasizing that the Black Death, unlike diseases spread by human cross-infection, produced higher rural than urban mortality. On the latter point, see too Gottfried, *Black Death*, 57–58, 75–76.

climate change helped to generate and/or spread the Black Death itself.[162]

In sum, if colonization and trade showed some vitality, overall material conditions between 1240 and 1450 were less favorable to political expansion than they had been under Kiev, and certainly than they would become when Moscow's "gathering of the Russian lands" took off in the late 15th and 16th centuries. As the pre-1450 political ambition of both Lithuania and Moscow testifies, bullion shortages, plague, and cold weather were not fatal barriers to consolidation. But by later standards, pre-1450 century rulers must have found it exceedingly difficult to obtain cash reserves, to undertake palace and fortification projects, to extract agricultural surplus, and, above all, to maintain large cavalry forces.

Pagan's collapse begot rival states in Upper and Lower Burma, while Angkor generated successor kingdoms at Phnom Penh and Ayudhya. What, then, did Russia's post-Kievan political map look like? Apart from the Kipchak khanate, three regional constellations divided the Kievan inheritance, those of Lithuania, Novgorod, and Riurikid princes in the northeast.

In the mid-1200s, partly in response to military pressure from the Teutonic Knights, pagan tribes in what is now Lithuania and northeast Poland achieved a semblance of unity, and it was from this loose tribal confederation that the principality of Lithuania emerged. As the only Kievan successor state whose nucleus lay outside the Mongol-Tatar zone and as an area that, some claim, suffered limited damage from the Black Death, Lithuania was first to fill the vacuum created by the decline of the Kipchak khanate. By 1377, through war, marriage, and diplomacy, a succession of Lithuanian Grand Dukes had extended their authority from their capital of Vilna almost to the Black Sea. Incorporating the old Kievan heartland of the Dnieper basin, they thus rendered credible their explicit ambition to succeed the Grand Princes of Kiev. Well into the 15th century Lithuania continued to expand east and south, overshadowing both Moscow and Novgorod and dominating the former Kievan

---

[162] On climate, nn. 43–48 *supra*, plus Atwell, "Time, Money, and Weather," 92–96; idem, "Volcanism and Short-Term Climatic Change in East Asian and World History, c. 1200–1699," *JWH* 12 (2001): 44, 52; and Smith, *Peasant Farming*, 120. But for discrepant evidence, see Serebryanny, "Glacioclimatic Features," 87–93; Brown, *History and Climate*, 260. On climate change as precipitant of disease, see Alexander, *Bubonic Plague*, 13–16; n. 42 *supra*.

lands.[163] As a collaborative enterprise of blood-related princes, the early Lithuanian polity in fact resembled Kiev. Lithuania's vast size and substantially preliterate culture – features also familiar from Kiev – joined its openness to foreign influences to render the new realm not only administratively superficial, but culturally diverse. As it expanded into Kievan areas, Orthodox subjects became a substantial majority, and Rus language, law, architecture, and political concepts exercised a growing appeal to Lithuanian elites. After 1385–1386, when Lithuania joined its former rival Poland in a dynastic union and Lithuania's ruler formally accepted Catholicism, Polish Catholic influence began to supplant Russian Orthodox. Yet both Christian traditions, and for a while pagan rites as well, were still honored by Lithuania's Grand Dukes.[164]

In the far north of the old Kievan realm, the principality of Novgorod championed a tradition that was at once more urban and less politically ambitious than that of Lithuania. Continuing the long-standing exchange of Russian furs and forest products for bullion and handicrafts from northcentral Europe, Novgorod after Kiev declined became Russia's most cultured and prosperous city. In contrast to the southwest of the old Kievan realm, where landed magnates (*boyars*) became ascendant, and to the northeast, where princes dominated *boyars*, Novgorod was led by an urban patriciate of merchant-cum-landowning families. There was no hereditary prince. In the 14th and 15th centuries Novgorod sponsored a vast fur-trapping and commercial expansion east to the Urals and north to the Arctic Ocean. But despite the city's wealth, its small population and reliance on imported grain rendered Novgorod the weakest militarily of the three chief successors to Kiev.[165]

The third major regional heir to Kiev was the northeast, whose heartland in the Volga-Oka interfluve included the towns of Vladimir, Suzdal, Tver, and Moscow. Starting in the late Kievan era, notwithstanding indifferent soils, the protection that thick forests afforded against nomad attacks encouraged local settlement. Operating in an environment less

---

[163] Rowell, *Lithuania Ascending*, Map 2 and 49–81, 169–70. Cf. Geoffrey Barraclough, ed., *The Times Atlas of World History* (London, 1978), 141, 43; Riasanovsky, *History*, chs. 10, 14; Oswald Backus, *Motives of West Russian Nobles in Deserting Lithuania for Moscow, 1377–1514* (Lawrence, KA, 1957); Martin, *Medieval Russia*, 162–65, 204–18, 303–308; Reisman, "Determinants," 348–52.

[164] Rowell, *Lithuania Ascending*, chs. 2–6; Martin, *Medieval Russia*, 215–18, 303–304.

[165] On Novgorod, Martin, *Treasure*, chs. 3, 6; idem, *Medieval Russia*, 81–112, 175–93, 210–16 *passim*; Price, "Novgorod, Kiev"; Fennell, *Crisis, passim*; Riasanovsky, *History*, ch. 9; Joel Raba, "Church and Foreign Policy in the 15th-Century Novgorodian State," *CASS* 13 (1979): 52–58.

urban, less attuned to Black Sea culture, and more exposed to Inner Asia than Kiev, northeastern elites necessarily modified their Kievan inheritance. Yet at the same time the princes of Vladimir-Suzdal, as noted, mimicked the Kievan title of Grand Prince long before the Mongols appeared, preserved Kievan law and architecture, and persuaded Kiev's Metropolitan to move to Vladimir in 1289, whence he relocated to Moscow in 1326.[166] Of the three successor zones, only in the northeast did Riurikid rule survive. If we consider mainland Southeast Asia in this period, the relation between Kiev and the northeast resembled most closely that between Pagan and Toungoo Burma. In both cases, a shift in the political center of gravity to the frontier went hand in hand with substantial dynastic and religious continuity.

Riurikids in the northeast were unusually active in promoting rural settlement and trade, with riverine and portage tolls providing key income. In the long term, some have argued,[167] princely traditions in this area supported exceptionally effective resource mobilization. Yet for much of the 13th and 14th centuries these advantages remained of limited avail against economic and epidemiological woes and divisive Mongol-Tatar tactics. Because the Mongol-Tatars lay closer to the northeast than to Lithuania or Novgorod, their influence on local politics was more decisive. At the same time, many northeastern principalities suffered from their own determination to maintain Kievan patterns of joint clan ownership and multiple inheritance. The petty domains that emerged from this tradition were known as *udely*, or "portions," because they represented an allodial share in the joint patrimony; and the era when such hereditary domains proliferated, the 13th to mid-15th centuries, is known as the "apanage period." Although such fissioning occurred in most areas once subject to Kiev, nowhere was it more pervasive than in the northeast. During the 13th century the once-unified, hegemonic principality of Vladimir-Suzdal split into a dozen competing *udely*, which continued to fragment thereafter. All told, some 13 Kievan principalities in 1200 had split into 50 by 1300 and 250 a century later.[168]

---

[166] These dates, different than in some secondary sources, come from Hellie, pers. commun., Feb. 28, 2006.

[167] See, e.g., Richard Pipes, *Russia Under the Old Regime* (New York, 1992), chs. 2–4.

[168] Hellie, "Russia, 1200–1815," 482; John Fennell, *The Emergence of Moscow 1304–1359* (London, 1968); idem, *Crisis*, chs. 5–7; Martin, *Medieval Russia*, chs. 4–6; Crummey, *Formation of Muscovy*, chs. 2, 3.

In a word, notwithstanding Lithuanian expansion, between 1240 and 1450 extensive areas once subject to Kiev entered a period of political fragmentation, demographic and economic decline, and unprecedented vulnerability. Simultaneously, the unity of the Kievan church ended as the rulers of Lithuania sought to create a Metropolitanate for their Orthodox subjects separate from the Metropolitanate now centered in the northeast.

France, c. 1270–1450: A Conjuncture of Calamities

After a long upward trajectory, western Europe – like mainland South-east Asia and the former lands of Rus – also suffered violent, massive ruptures for much of the period between 1240 and 1450. Late medieval France, in particular, experienced an intractable economic depression, an epidemiological crisis, and a century-long civil war that severely tested the nascent French state. Even more obviously than in Kiev or Southeast Asia, many of these difficulties reflected some three centuries of economic and political growth.

As I indicated, the argument that France's late-13th- to 14th-century crisis was an unwelcome artifact of economic expansion focuses less on the centrifugal implications of frontier commercial or agrarian growth, as in Kiev, Pagan, and Angkor, than on production ceilings in established core regions. In fact, this argument has two versions. The most popular interpretation, a neo-Malthusian thesis that in varying degrees underlay analyses by Guy Bois, Emmanuel Le Roy Ladurie, and more recently by William Chester Jordan, David Levine, and Pierre Charbonnier, argues that between c. 950 and 1250 demographic growth exhausted the medieval economy's carrying capacity. After c. 1250, as market pressures encouraged conversion of arable to noncereal uses and as population pressed against quality available land, cultivators through-out France were forced into ever more marginal terrains. Thus both land and labor productivity began falling, and population, although growth leveled off, began to outstrip cereal production. Accordingly, from the 1250s to the 1310s prices for cereal and land rose sharply, and the dreaded *disettes*, that is, the interval that came after the last grain crop had run out and before the new crop came in, grew in frequency, severity, and duration. Underlying this analysis are assumptions that a) existing agrarian technology was incapable of increasing total output and b) nonagrarian technology could not absorb marginal labor more effectively than it did.[169]

Recently, S. R. Epstein, expanding in some respects the work of James Goldsmith, has questioned both assumptions. In Epstein's view, in 1300 neither the agrarian nor the urban sector had fulfilled its productive potential – indeed many of the gains from medieval technology still had not been exhausted by the 1700s. In both countryside and town, the chief barrier to diffusion of best practices, to Smithian specialization, and to maintaining or improving productivity was simply that producers lacked reliable access to competitive markets. In turn the high cost of trade reflected medieval political fragmentation, with its frequent warfare, localized justice, redundant tolls, multiple coinages and units of measure, and poor transport. According to Epstein, the late medieval European economic crisis therefore should be seen largely as a "crisis of integration" to which political unification and better transport ultimately would provide an effective remedy. But while disputing causation, Epstein does not deny the basic contention that by 1270 or 1300 France, along with much of western Europe, had come up against a profound structural impediment to continued growth.[170]

---

[169] For expressions of this view, see Guy Bois, *The Crisis of Feudalism* (Cambridge, 1984), 263–76, 396–99; Emmanuel Le Roy Ladurie, *The French Peasantry 1450–1660* (Berkeley, 1987), ch. 1; idem and Joseph Goy, *Tithe and Agrarian History from the 14th to the 19th Centuries* (Cambridge, 1982), 72–73, 89; William Chester Jordan, *The Great Famine* (Princeton, 1996), 11–12, 28–33, 107; Levine, *At the Dawn*, 160–62, 242–43, 338; Pierre Charbonnier, "The Economy and Society of France in the Later Middle Ages," and "Society and Economy," in Potter, *France in the Later Middle Ages*, 47–60, 117–29; E. Carpentier and M. Le Mene, *La France du XIe Siecle au XVe Siecle: Population, Societe, Economie* (Paris, 1996), 331–36; Robert Fossier, "Clouds Gather in the West," and "The Great Trial," *CIHMA*, vol. III, 17–118.

[170] Epstein also argues that in response to economic conditions, medieval peasants could exert some control over nuptiality and fertility. Epstein, *Freedom and Growth*, esp. ch. 3. Although Epstein does not cite Goldsmith in his index or bibliography, Goldsmith, "Crisis of Late Middle Ages," 417–50 anticipated Epstein's critique of the neo-Malthusian model by arguing that most of France in 1330 remained underpopulated by 18th-century yardsticks, that best agrarian practices had in no way exhausted their potential, and that the region of most dense population, namely the Paris basin and areas to its north, was also the region of greatest dynamism, most rapid immigration, and highest living standards. Goldsmith, however, differs from Epstein in two key respects: a) in the 1330s, he claims, the economy, rather than slowing down, remained vigorous; b) he sees the collapse of mid-century as the result not of institutional and transport restraints, but of entirely exogenous shocks, namely the Black Death and the Hundred Years War. But in my view (see discussion *infra*) Goldsmith exaggerates the externality of both factors. For work more compatible with Epstein, see B. M. S. Campbell on English agriculture in J. M. Duvosquel and E. Thoen, eds., *Peasants and*

Hard-pressed peasants were vulnerable to even moderately adverse climatic fluctuations. But in France as in mainland Southeast Asia and indeed much of the northern hemisphere, after 1250 or 1300 volcanism, reduced solar radiation, oceanic convolutions, and albedo enhancement associated with deforestation combined to ensure that climatic change was anything but mild. Amidst considerable annual and decadal variations, the period c. 1300 to 1450 proved colder than any comparable time-span in northwest Europe since the 8th century. Spring frosts, dangerous to germination, became more common, as did cool, wet summers and autumns, with frequently disastrous harvests on marginal lands, poor harvests even on good land, and increased erosion. From 1314 to 1322 a succession of cold, wet summers produced what Jordan argues was one of the most severe food shortfalls ever to strike northern Europe. The 1340s again saw poor, irregular harvests across France. Climatically induced crises, more localized and less crippling, recurred into the 15th century. By one calculation, between 1150 and 1350 the likelihood of two successive crop failures increased 70-fold.[171]

As if these stresses were insufficient, the Black Death burst upon western Europe in 1347–1350, followed by recurrent waves from 1360 to 1441. In the greater part of the territories of France, losses to 1360 alone may have reached 40 to 50 percent or more.[172] Neo-Malthusians view the Black Death ("that holocaust of the undernourished"[173]) as

---

Townsmen in Medieval Europe (Ghent, 1995), 541–59, and Philip Hoffman, *Growth in a Traditional Society: The French Countryside 1450–1815* (Princeton, 1996).

[171] Levine, *At the Dawn*, 159–62 (with 70-fold estimate), 242–43, also claiming that northern and western Europe grew 4° (Fahrenheit/Centigrade?) colder. On climate and its effects, besides nn. 90–93 *supra*, see Jordan, *Great Famine*, 16–17 and *passim*; Le Roy Ladurie, *Histoire Humaine*, chs. 2, 3; idem, *Times of Feast*, 288–92; Christopher Allmand, *The Hundred Years War* (Cambridge, 1989), 120–21; Bois, *Crisis*, 83, 147, 339; Brown, *History and Climate*, ch. 9, esp. 243–54; Lamb, *Climate, History*, 84–85, 99, 195–99; Alexandre, *Le Climat*, 781–89, 807–808; *CIHMA*, vol. III, 39–40. There is substantial agreement on the trend in annual temperatures, but less on winter temperatures. Albedo refers to the reflection of solar rays from the earth's surface back into space caused by deforestation and unbroken snow cover.

[172] See various estimates at Le Roy Ladurie, *French Peasantry*, 31–32; Henri Dubois, "La depression (XIV et XV siecles)," in Dupaquier et al., *Histoire de la Population*, vol. I, 318–37 (cf. ibid., 515); Bois, *Crisis*, 299, 316; O'Neill, "Diseases of the Middle Ages," 275–78; Allmand, *Hundred Years War*, 165; Benedictow, *Black Death*, 96–109, 308–37, 380–84, denying that losses were less in the north of France than elsewhere.

[173] Emmanuel Le Roy Ladurie, *The Peasants of Languedoc* (Urbana, IL, 1976), 13. For similar views, M. M. Postan, *Essays on Medieval Agriculture and General Problems of the Medieval Economy* (Cambridge, 1973); Pounds, *Economic History*, 138; Bois, *Crisis*, 274. Likewise, according to Roger Albin, pers. commun., Oct. 8, 2008, recent excavations of cemeteries

a logical consequence of urban overcrowding, popular immiseration, poor nutrition, and the movement of hungry rats from empty granaries to human dwellings. Others have seen it as a biological phenomenon with a rhythm largely independent of social context. Not only have they sought to weaken the link between nutrition and mortality, but they have emphasized that some sparsely populated areas – rural Russia, Greenland, and Scandinavia – suffered as much as, if not more than, densely populated zones, while some cities were largely spared.[174]

Nonetheless, two possible links remain between the Black Death and general economic conditions. First, as noted, not only crop failures, but the Black Death – as well as typhus and influenza, to which the plague was sometimes linked in humans, and rinderpest, murrain, and scab among domestic animals – may have been aggravated by colder, wetter weather insofar as those conditions modified the action of pathogens and disease vectors while increasing human and animal vulnerability. In this view, colder weather undermined agrarian prosperity at the same time as it helped spread disease.[175]

Second, if one shifts the argument from overpopulation to the routes of disease transmission, one can make a strong case that medieval prosperity was a necessary precondition for the 14th-century pandemic. McNeill believes that plague spread in saddlebags and grain stores from areas of enzootic rodent infestation in North China to the Crimea along

from the initial wave of the Black Death have revealed a disproportionate number of child and elderly skeletal remains, which is consistent with malnutrition-based vulnerability. But more data are needed to settle this question.

[174] Livi-Bacci, *Population and Nutrition*; Day, *Medieval Market Economy*, 188–91; Ester Boserup, *Population and Technological Change* (Chicago, 1981), 94–95; Herlihy, *Black Death*, 32–38. For recent Black Death scholarship, including debates over identification of the disease rather than the reasons for its virulence, see Norman Cantor, *In the Wake of the Plague* (New York, 2001), 11–25; Susan Scott and Christopher Duncan, *The Biology of Plagues* (Cambridge, 2001); Samuel Cohen, Jr., "The Black Death: End of a Paradigm," *AHR* 107(2002): 703–38; idem, *The Black Death Transformed* (New York, 2003), denying that the 14th-century disease was bubonic. But for reassertions of the bubonic view, see John Kelly, *The Great Mortality* (New York, 2005), 295–304; Michael McCormick, "Rats, Communication, and Plague," in Elizabeth Lehfeldt, ed., *The Black Death* (Boston, 2005), 65–71; Didier Raoutl et al., "Molecular Identification of 'Suicide PCR' of *Yersinia pestis* as the Agent of Medieval Black Death," *Proceedings of the National Academy of Science* 97/23 (Nov. 7, 2000): 12,800–12,803; and esp. Benedictow, *Black Death*, pt. 1.

[175] See nn. 42, 94 *supra*, plus Bruce Campbell, "Britain 1300," *History Today* 50 (2000): 10–12, and Cantor, *In the Wake*, 14–16, both mentioning animal diseases; Jan de Vries, "Population," in Brady, *Handbook*, vol. I, 21; Herlihy, *Black Death*, 21–31; Kelly, *Great Mortality*, 37, 60–64, 303.

Mongol-protected caravan routes whose traffic increased in response to 13th-century demand. But even if we accept that the plague originated in the Russian steppe and spread thence to new Italian outposts in the Crimea, it is clear that ramified maritime links propelled it with astonishing speed, up to 600 kilometers a fortnight. Not only did ships move great quantities of foodstuffs, with their inevitable complement of rats and rat fleas, with novel frequency between the Crimea, Constantinople, Venice, Genoa, and Marseilles, but from the late 1200s better Italian ship design permitted year-round trade between the Mediterranean and the Atlantic, which opened northern Europe to the disease. From coastal footholds in Marseilles, Bordeaux, Rouen, Calais, and the Low Countries, the Black Death metastasized to riverine cities (Paris, Lyon), interior market towns, rural production zones, and eventually even the most isolated hamlets. Because virtually no area was free of market involvement by the mid-1300s, none was immune to the plague. Along the busiest highways the disease moved up to 2 kilometers a day, and along secondary lines of communication about 0.7 kilometers. Thus, before quarantines had been invented, increases in population, market specialization, and trade inaugurated what Benedictow terms Europe's "golden age of bacteria."[176]

For almost a century after 1350 the population of many French districts remained anywhere from 33 to 70 percent below preplague levels.[177] Because these huge losses restored upward pressure on land productivity and wages, and because Malthusian theory predicts that a mortality crisis will yield to a phase of universal and early marriages, the absence of any sustained population recovery for over a century is, at first sight, puzzling. In part, stagnation reflected the fact that new outbreaks of disease, poor weather, and crushing taxes and disorders associated with the Hundred Years War kept mortality high. At the same time, by raising the land threshold needed for economically viable households, collapsing grain markets may have helped to delay

[176] Figures on disease movement from Benedictow, "Black Death," 42–49; idem, *Black Death*, 96–109 and pt. 2 *passim*. See too Abu-Lughod, *Before European Hegemony*, 71–72, 111–13, 154, 170–83. Undeveloped commercial networks in northern and eastern Europe may explain why first-millennium Mediterranean plagues had little or no impact on these frontier zones, and why in the 14th century Iceland, Finland, and perhaps isolated parts of east-central Europe suffered only modest plague damage.

[177] See national and regional estimates at n. 172 *supra*, plus Allmand, *Hundred Years War*, 165; Pierre Chaunu and Richard Gascon, *Histoire Economique et Sociale de la France, Tome 1: De 1450 a 1660, v. 1: L'Etat et la Ville* (Paris, 1977), 42.

rural marriages.[178] Although the price for manufactures fell less than for foodstuffs, the urban sector also suffered, because the ensuing price scissors joined population decline to reduce aggregate, and possibly per capita, rural consumption of non-farm goods. Merchants and artisans responded with cost-cutting measures and technical innovations in transport, manufacture, and finance – what Edwin Hunt and James Murray term a "harvest of adversity."[179] An associated shift from luxuries to cheap manufactures and from grain to more specialized industrial and foodcrops ultimately favored towns over the countryside and, along with a secular decline in interest rates, lay the foundations for a general urban-based recovery late in the 15th century. But at least until the mid-1400s, when the Hundred Years War ended and population growth resumed, the overall volume of French trade almost certainly remained well below its medieval apogee.[180] The aforementioned Eurasian bullion shortage only aggravated this downturn,[181] while from the early 1300s expanding all-water routes between the Mediterranean and the North Sea crippled the famed Champagne fairs.[182] In sum, if compensatory adjustments in France offered some hope for the future, the overall economic picture between c. 1300 and 1450 was at least as bleak as that in Russia.

How did the economic crisis impact politics? And vice versa? According to Bois' classic study of Normandy, presented as representative of

---

[178] De Vries, "Population," 37–40, writing of Europe generally; and in English context, Larry Poos, *A Rural Society after the Black Death: Essex 1350–1525* (Cambridge, 1991). See too Pounds, *Economic History*, 449–50; Day, *Medieval Market Economy*, 195 ff.

[179] Hunt and Murray, *History of Business*. Similar arguments appear at Herlihy, *Black Death*, ch. 2; Collins, *Tribes to Nation*, 143–44; and Epstein, *Freedom and Growth*, 55, 108 ff., which terms the process "Schumpeterian creative destruction."

[180] On war as a major additional cause of market dislocation, Epstein, *Freedom and Growth*, 169, 171; Anne Curry, "France and the Hundred Years War, 1337–1453," in Potter, *France in the Later Middle Ages*, 115. On falling post-1350 interest rates, which reflected declining investment and rising per capita savings, see van Zanden, "Road to the Industrial Revolution," 350–51. However, to the extent that post-1350 demographic decline was merely cyclic, Van Zanden's thesis that the demographic downturn of 1350–1450 helped alter permanently the relation between capital and labor in western Europe is suspect.

[181] See n. 160 *supra*. According to Epstein, *Freedom and Growth*, 60–62, 70, a pronounced secular fall in the price of private capital in some West European countries between 1300 and 1500 argues against the view that bullion shortages slashed credit. Yet Epstein also shows that interest rates fell far less sharply in France than elsewhere. Cf. n. 180 *supra*.

[182] Braudel, *Identity*, vol. II, 161–66. But see Epstein, *Freedom and Growth*, 79 on vitality of Languedoc fairs after 1350 and of those in Brittany and Burgundy after 1400.

northern France, as early as the 1310s falling per capita productivity produced a downward pressure on rental income greater than could be made good by an increase in the number of peasant units. After the Black Death, falling cereal prices and sharply rising labor costs compounded the woes of landed elites. To compensate for plummeting profits, the nobility, especially its impecunious lower ranks, resorted to private pillage and, more especially, warfare – the chief example being the Hundred Years War – in the hope of obtaining ransoms, booty, and royal employment. This dynamic helped to prolong the Hundred Years War, with intermittent fighting from 1337 to 1453. (Reliance on forcible acquisition rather than agrarian intensification, one could argue, reversed the economic logic of the 10th and 11th centuries that helped give birth to medieval expansion.) At the same time the war obliged large territorial lords, most notably the French king, radically to augment their income through taxation in order to pay for war materiele and a standing army and to compensate those nobles who commanded royal forces or brought their own contingents.[183] With the crown and sectors of the nobility thus developing a common interest in higher taxation, taxes began to replace feudal rents as a principal form of elite expropriation.[184] But the resultant tax increases pressed upon a peasantry already reeling from rents, plague, and war.[185] Thus, despite short-lived demographic recoveries, between 1350 and 1450 taxed households in the country as a whole fell by up to half – and by some 70 percent in Normandy, which in Bois' memorable phrase, endured a demographic "Hiroshima."[186] Although the Black Death apparently spared mainland Southeast Asia, between 1280 and 1390 the imperial cores of Pagan, Angkor, and Dai

---

[183] See Bois, *Crisis*, esp. 221 ff., 256, 273–74, 277–81, 345, 401; the summary of his thesis in Herlihy, *Black Death*, 36–37, plus Allmand, *Hundred Years War*, 47–48, 63–64, 70–82, 93–96, 104–105, 127,166; Benedictow, *Black Death*, 6, 391; David Potter, *A History of France, 1460–1560* (New York, 1995), 177; Potter, *France in the Later Middle Ages*, 139–40, 179–80, 194, 197.

[184] This argument is central to Perry Anderson, *Lineages of the Absolutist State* (London, 1974). See too Duby, *France in the Middle Ages*, 266, 272–74; John Bell Henneman, *Royal Taxation in Fourteenth-Century France* (Philadelphia, 1976), esp. ix, 1–17, 274–311; idem, "The Military Class and the French Monarchy in the Late Middle Ages," *AHR* 83 (1978): 946–65.

[185] Royal coin debasements and retaliatory trade embargoes proved no less counterproductive. On the impact of royal policies, Duby, *France in the Middle Ages*, 273; Miskimin, *Economy 1300–1460*, 54; Bois, *Crisis*, 213–14, 335–45.

[186] Bois, *Crisis*, 64–67, 316–45. Le Roy Ladurie, *Royal French State*, ix refers to "apocalyptic disintegration" across France between 1350 and 1430. But see Charbonnier, "Society and Economy," 122–23 for a critique of Bois' pre-1348 tax figures.

Viet also experienced acute social tensions and ecological strains. In the most densely populated zone, northern Dai Viet, from 1340 to 1400 alone, rural uprisings, disease, and warfare claimed over a third of the population.[187] In these ways, in France as in parts of Southeast Asia, exceptional vitality in the 12th and 13th centuries contributed to a generalized collapse in the 14th and early 15th centuries.

This progression characterized another French sphere as well: far from being a random expression of escalating intra-elite violence, the Hundred Years War pivoted on two contradictions that arose from the expansion of the high medieval state.[188] As Plantagenet–Capetian struggles as early as the reign of Philip Augustus (r. 1180–1223) suggested, the early Capetian system of attenuated zones and overlapping spheres of influence was inherently incompatible with the more exclusive and centralized ambitions of both the expanding English and French monarchies. Because they were simultaneously kings in their own right and, in their capacity as dukes of Aquitaine, vassals of the French king, the Plantagenet kings of England occupied an increasingly ambiguous position. After indecisive hostilities, a fresh French attempt to confiscate Aquitaine on the grounds that its English duke had broken his vassalic obligations produced a final rupture in 1337–1340. Setting forth his own quite plausible claim to the French throne, Edward III of England now declared that Philip of Valois, whom French nobles had chosen to succeed the last Capetian in 1328, was a usurper. Thus he severed the feudal bond between the English and French kingdoms. During the ensuing century-long contest, English kings sought either to seize the French crown themselves or to detach and hold in full sovereignty western and northern provinces, particularly those on the coast. Conversely, the Valois were determined to avoid the dismemberment of their patrimony and a return to France's landlocked position of 1200. In brief, state-building projects of the 13th century helped to make the great 14th-century wars not only possible, but necessary.[189]

If the first source of political tension was between the emergent English (or to be more accurate, Anglo-French) and French dynastic

---

[187] *SP*, 119–23, 236–42, 367–72, 420.

[188] Analysis follows Strayer, *Medieval Origins*, 58–61; Allmand, *Hundred Years War*, esp. 7–12, 82–83; Holmes, *Oxford History*, 294–302; P. S. Lewis, *Essays in Later Medieval French History* (London, 1985), 20–21, 236; and Malcolm Vale, *The Angevin Legacy and the Hundred Years War 1250–1340* (Oxford, 1990), 1–8, 175–269.

[189] On such tensions as a general European phenomenon, Epstein, *Freedom and Growth*, 54–55.

states, the second was between, on the one hand, Valois aspirations to exclusive sovereignty within France and, on the other hand, the extensive powers retained by the great apanage princes and non-English territorial princes in what I earlier termed the third and fourth zones of France. We have seen that these princes typically created administrations similar to that of the central state, each with its own law courts and financial machinery. Although before 1350 family ties and the interpenetration of apanage and royal officials ensured apanage subordination, thereafter the economic crisis joined with imprudently generous royal awards, the English war, and intra-Valois feuds to erode those controls. Without at first attempting to separate themselves from the central state in the English fashion, the princes of the blood who held Burgundy, Orleans, Berry, Bourbon, Anjou, and other territories sought to expand those possessions, to centralize their institutions, to imitate royal prerogatives – yet at the same time to capture the central apparatus whose resources they needed to strengthen their regional positions. To those ends, the great princes usurped royal rights to collect taxes, mint coins, hear judicial appeals, award salaries, and grant town charters – even as they colonized the royal machinery with their own protégés. Thus regional lords sought, if not to swallow the central state, then to reorganize it in a system Graeme Small terms "princely polyarchy."[190]

The losers in this high-stakes competition were increasingly tempted to ally with the English, so that war between French and English dynasts fused with wars between noble factions within France. In the most famous such defection, following the 1419 assassination of the duke of Burgundy, the latter's followers helped the English to complete their conquest of northern France. As the saying went, the English entered France through the hole in the head of the duke of Burgundy.[191] Thereafter Burgundy's dukes, with holdings in both France and the Holy Roman Empire, expanded their territory and began acting as independent rulers on the English model. With its rich cities, permanent armies,

---

[190] Graeme Small, "The Crown and the Provinces in the 15th Century," in Potter, *France in the Later Middle Ages*, 140, citing Bernard Chevalier. Cf. ibid., 130–54, discussing too the waxing power of the *bonnes villes* and representative assemblies; and Bernard Chevalier, "France from Charles VII to Henry IV," in Brady, *Handbook*, vol. I, 369–75. For different interpretive emphases, see also E. Perroy, "Feudalism or Principalities in Fifteenth Century France," *Bulletin of the Institute of Historical Studies* 20 (1947): 181–85; Strayer, *Medieval Origins*, 62–63; Jones, "Crown and Provinces," 66–73.

[191] Marina Warner, *Joan of Arc* (Berkeley, 1981), 32–33. Also Desmond Seward, *The Hundred Years War* (New York, 1978), 178–88; Allmand, *Hundred Years War*, 29–33.

law courts, and fiscal machine, 15th-century Burgundy in fact became a power not greatly inferior to England or France, albeit with a discontinuous territory and poorly integrated French, German, and Flemish cultural zones. Supported by England, the dukes of Brittany played a similar game.[192]

Valois fortunes reached low points in 1360, 1419–1422, and 1427–1428. By the later date, with Valois power largely confined south of the Loire and with Burgundy, Brittany, as well as English holdings effectively independent, it seemed that France might splinter on the German model.

Yet however jarring these shocks, in the end they proved less disruptive than those that in this same period ripped apart western and central mainland Southeast Asia and Russia. So seductive had the concept of "France" become that even many Anglo-Burgundian partisans were committed to reunifying the kingdom, albeit under the English king, and thus ending the *"pitie en France."*[193] In any case, French military triumphs led to the collapse of the Anglo-Burgundian alliance in 1435 and of English territorial ambitions. By century's end Burgundy and Brittany also had rejoined the kingdom. French fiscal and military reforms in the 14th and 15th centuries built on solid Capetian foundations and battened on wartime exigency. The Hundred Years War saw no sizable alien settlement, even on the modest scale of earlier Viking incursions. Despite Valois identification with the Loire, Paris – around which a long-distance road network had coalesced in the 12th and 13th centuries – remained the administrative, intellectual, and economic heart of the

---

[192] On Burgundy and Brittany, Hugo de Schepper, "The Burgundian-Habsburg Netherlands," in Brady, *Handbook*, vol. I, 499–533; Jean Richard, "Royal Enclaves and Provincial Boundaries," in P. S. Lewis, ed., *The Recovery of France in the Fifteenth Century* (London, 1971), 216–41; C. A. J. Armstrong, *England, France, and Burgundy in the Fifteenth Century* (London, 1980), esp. chs. 9–11; H. Dubois, "Naissance de la fiscalite dans un etat princier au Moyen Age," in J. Ph. Genet and M. Le Mene, eds., *Genese de l'Etat Moderne* (Paris, 1987), 91–100; P. S. Lewis, *Later Medieval France: The Polity* (London, 1968), 224–34; Allmand, *Hundred Years War*, 142, 166; M. C. E. Jones, "The Breton Nobility and Their Masters from the Civil War of 1341–64 to the Late Fifteenth Century," in J. R. L. Highfield and Robin Jeffs, eds., *The Crown and Local Communities in England and France in the Fifteenth Century* (Gloucester, 1981), 51–71; Patrick Galliou and Michael Jones, *The Bretons* (Oxford, 1991), chs. 10–13.

[193] Warner, *Joan of Arc*, 45, 48. See too Armstrong, *England, France, and Burgundy*, 343–74; Jean-Philippe Genet, "Le roi de France anglais et la nation francaise au XVe siecle," in Rainer Babel and Jean-Marie Moeglin, eds., *Identite Regionale et Conscience Nationale en France et en Allemagne du Moyen Age a l'Epoque Moderne* (Sigmaringen, Germany, 1997), 39–58.

realm.[194] But in Burma in this period Pagan was permanently eclipsed, Upper Burma lost the coast, and Tais entered the lowlands in force. In the central mainland, Angkor's abandonment, the collapse of Hindu civilization, and Tai incursions were yet more dramatic.[195] Likewise, Mongol incursions and Kiev's eclipse constituted fundamental shifts. In what is now France the closest analogue to these massive postcharter dislocations, we saw, occurred not in the 14th or 15th century, but after c. 890 with the collapse of the Frankish/Carolingian charter regime.

Vietnam and France, on the other hand, continued to demonstrate intriguing similarities. Neither Chams nor Tais remained in Vietnam in force after 1390, so in contrast to western and central mainland Southeast Asia, both Dai Viet and France escaped alien settlement. Both had population densities greater than the Indic mainland or Russia, but as yet limited opportunities for frontier colonization, which meant that economic woes focused on long-settled cores. Moreover, in a political sense both heartlands emerged relatively intact. In neither realm did frontier provinces succeed in breaking away, and in neither did the pre-1300 capital, Thang Long (Hanoi) or Paris, lose its preeminence.[196]

Note finally that the economic and political tribulations of France were shared in some degree by much of western Europe between c. 1290 and the mid- or late 1400s. Not only did the region as a whole see economic expansion grind to a halt in the late 1200s, not only did the Black Death kill 30 to 60 percent of all Europeans, but in response to labor shortages and wartime dislocations, popular uprisings in the second half of the 14th century roiled areas from France, England, Flanders, and north Germany to Sicily, Florence, and Spain. Although the 1358 French peasant rebellion known as the *Jacquerie*, sparked by grievances associated with the opening phase of the Hundred Years War, was suppressed with great brutality, from 1363 to 1420 serious peasant revolts continued to break out in the Auvergne, Languedoc, and the Lyon area. The Peasants' Revolt in England of 1381, expressing resentment of wartime taxes, judicial reorganization, and labor restrictions and involving perhaps 100,000 people, was probably the largest single uprising of the medieval period. In Andalusia and Catalonia aristocratic efforts to impose new forms of serfdom joined working-class demands for tax

---

[194] On Paris' evolving centrality, Planhol, *Historical Geography*, 252–56, 273; Clout, "Early Urban Development," 87–91; Potter, "Introduction," 9; Jones, "Crown and Provinces," 88.

[195] *SP*, 123–39, 242–63.

[196] Ibid., 367–83.

relief to precipitate massive urban and peasant uprisings in 1391 that quickly assumed an anti-Semitic character. In this atmosphere of economic retrenchment and anxiety, West European states also faced civil wars and dynastic crises that pitted the throne against aristocracies desperate to regain or to preserve their authority. Between 1369 and c. 1470 the fractious Castilian nobility, like its French counterpart, achieved a new peak of influence and power, including the right to appropriate royal revenues and to raise private armies. In England magnate autonomy joined royal incompetence and the crown's loss of prestige following the Hundred Years War debacle to precipitate the Wars of the Roses (1455–1471/1485) between the ducal houses of York and Lancaster for control of the throne and of local government. Typically, as in France, these disturbances sidetracked centralization projects that had shown great promise in the 12th and 13th centuries. What is more, from the late 1200s tensions between central integration and regional resistance frequently meshed with interstate rivalries, embroiling not only England and France, but Flanders, Naples, Sicily, Iberia, and southern Germany. Thus, for example, the Hundred Years War between England and France had its counterpart in a 90-year conflict between Catalonia-Aragon, Sicily, and Naples.

In much of central and eastern Europe the political situation was less dire, in part perhaps because the Black Death was less pervasive and land pressures were more limited. Yet in Poland and Bohemia promising early efforts at state-building also faltered, in the former because the crown in the late 1300s and 1400s was obliged to make major concessions to the *szlachta* gentry, in the latter because bitter religious and ethnic splits culminated in the devastating Hussite wars of 1420 to 1436.[197]

To summarize this chapter's larger argument thus far: In the second half of the first millennium, economic growth and external contacts encouraged political integration in Southeast Asia and the future

---

[197] On European upheavals c. 1290–1485, n. 189 *supra*; Potter, *France in the Later Middle Ages*, 106, 124; Simon Barton, *A History of Spain* (New York, 2004), 83–92; David Birmingham, *A Concise History of Portugal* (Cambridge, 1993), 21; Barbara Tuchman, *A Distant Mirror: The Calamitous 14th Century* (New York, 1978); John McKay et al., *A History of Western Society* (4th ed., Dallas, 1991), 356–82, 411–12; Davies, *God's Playground*, chs. 3–5; John Bossy, *Christianity in the West 1400–1700* (Oxford, 1985), 81–82; Sayer, *Coasts of Bohemia*, 31–42; Barraclough, *Times Atlas*, 140–43, 150–51; Martin Malia, *History's Locomotive* (New Haven, 2006), 37–59, referring to the destabilizing impact of the plague after 1380.

kingdoms of Russia and France. Favored by Roman legacies and a relatively sophisticated economy, the lands of France were politically precocious. From c. 500 to the mid-1400s they therefore experienced two complete administrative cycles, whereas each Southeast Asian region and Russia experienced but one. Nonetheless, between c. 900 and 1240 all five regions – the three chief sectors of mainland Southeast Asia, Russia, and France – enjoyed extremely rapid economic growth and, for all or part of this period, unprecedentedly effective political systems as measured against *local* precedents. This coordinated upsurge reflected locally variable mixtures of the same basic factors, namely, novel institutional and social arrangements, pacificatory political interventions, markedly better climate, stronger long-distance trade, and possible epidemiological adjustments. At various times between 1240 and 1400 all five states fragmented as a result of tensions that flowed from the previous era of expansion, in combination with the Black Death, climatic downturn, and military challenges.

Whereas at the start of our study, in the 6th or 7th century, the political trajectories of our five regions had diverged quite sharply, Eurasian prosperity from 900 to 1250 produced considerably greater coordination. As the next section will argue, congruencies between Russia and France and between Europe and Southeast Asia would become yet more pronounced after 1450.

3. BROAD RENEWAL, BRIEF COLLAPSE, C. 1450–1613

A New European-Wide Cycle

In Muscovy and France as in each sector of mainland Southeast Asia, after generations of disorder, consolidation resumed in the mid- to late 1400s and remained vigorous for over a century. Obviously, critical differences persisted within and between regions. Roman and Renaissance intellectual currents, a denser population, and a more complex commercial system continued to support a more penetrating, monetized administration in France than in Burma, Siam, or Muscovy. By these same criteria, post-1450 Dai Viet, with its access to Ming models, arguably remained closer to France than to its Indic neighbors or to Russia. On the other hand, in religious and ethnic terms, in 1550 the population of Muscovy was as cohesive as those of France or Dai Viet, and considerably more so than the imperial populations of Burma or Siam. Again, therefore, depending on criteria, Eurasian realms can be grouped into various configurations, few of which fit a neat European/Asian divide.

Against such distinctions, striking indeed are post-1450 similarities in political and economic rhythms. In France and Muscovy as in Southeast Asia, disorders to the mid-1400s bred support for renewed central authority. Each realm's resource base expanded through a mix of post-civil war (and in Europe, postplague) demographic compensation, more effective state interventions, improved weather, diffusion of best agricultural and commercial practices, growing international bullion stocks, and rising long-distance trade. At the same time European-style firearms and an associated intensification of warfare forced each state to enhance its income, military efficiency, and provincial controls. Thus between 1450 and 1600 Russia, France, and the chief Southeast Asian realms all extended their territories and assimilated peripheral zones to an administrative status more closely resembling that of the imperial cores. In each polyglot empire – in which category France must be included – the circulation of capital dialects and cultural motifs became symptom and cause of this limited, incremental integration. And in each realm wider literacy and rural proselytism promoted religious perspectives that provided intellectual and emotional support for royal pacification.

Finally, in Russia and France in the late 1500s and/or early 1600s institutional fragility joined succession crises, military strains, renewed Malthusian pressures, climatic downturn (and in France, a calamitous religious split, whetted by the new print culture) to precipitate yet another round of disorder and invasion. In genesis and chronology, the Muscovite Time of Troubles 1598–1613 and the French Wars of Religion 1562–1598 showed uncanny similarities to the contemporary collapse of Burma, Siam, and Dai Viet. As in Burma and Siam, so in Russia and France late-16th- to early-17th-century breakdowns were appreciably shorter and less destructive than the calamities of the 13th to 15th centuries – yet longer and more wrenching than late-18th-century travails.[198]

As Chapter 1 suggested, in all five realms as well as Japan, this post-1450/1500 mix of accelerating territorial consolidation, greater institutional sophistication, state-focused acculturation, rising literacy, and

---

[198] The French Religious Wars 1562–1598 were longer and more territorially dislocating than French Revolutionary upheavals – but far less institutionally disruptive. See discussion *infra*.

commercial intensification lends the late 15th century some claim to inaugurating "early modernity" in the sense that connections between these features, on the one hand, and post-1800 features, on the other, became unprecedentedly direct and secure.[199]

Before examining renewed consolidation in Muscovy and France, I would emphasize that their trajectories, intriguing in their own right, again assume added value as illustrations of more general European patterns. In eastern Europe after c. 1450 Poland, Habsburg Austria, and the Ottoman empire joined Russia to forge a new regional order. In the 1460s Poland, victorious over the Teutonic Knights, gained direct access to the Baltic, which allowed the Polish nobility to draw enormous profits from the Baltic grain boom and the price revolution of the 16th century. With the link to Lithuania elevated in 1569 to a constitutional union and with dramatic victories over Russia during the latter's Time of Troubles, the Polish-Lithuanian Commonwealth, which came under increasing Polish domination, reached its apogee in the early 1600s. Likewise, the Austrian Habsburgs, benefiting from the 15th-century decline of Bohemia, gained control by the mid-1500s over Bohemia, Moravia, Silesia, and those parts of Hungary salvaged from the Ottomans. Even by 16th-century standards, institutional links among Habsburg possessions remained rudimentary. Nonetheless, modeled at first on Burgundian prototypes but directed substantially against the Ottomans, a cluster of conciliar agencies, including a permanent War Council, succeeded in augmenting substantially the court's fiscal and military resources. The Ottomans arose in the late 1200s as part of Turkic nomadic invasions from Inner Asia that shattered Byzantine power. But it was only after entering the Balkans in the mid-1300s and more especially after capturing Constantinople in 1453 that the Ottomans too entered a phase of uninterrupted expansion, aided by refurbished military and fiscal systems, including the *janissary* infantry corps and the *timar* system of military land grants. By 1600 they had subdued southeastern Europe along with North Africa, the Hejaz, and the Fertile Crescent. Able to shift armies with great speed and to forge a culturally integrated elite, yet at the same time willing to conciliate local traditions, the Ottomans perfected rule over an empire as ethnically diverse as it was extensive.[200]

---

[199] See Ch. 1, nn. 19, 93 *supra*.

[200] See Anderson, *Lineages*, 279–327; Anna Filipczak-Kocur, "Poland-Lithuania Before Partition," in Bonney, *Rise of the Fiscal State*, 443–79; Davies, *God's Playground*, 89, 122–24; R. J. W. Evans, *The Making of the Habsburg Monarchy 1550–1700* (Oxford, 1979),

In this same period what some West European historians are content to call the New Monarchies also exhibited an aggressive territoriality and a penchant for (re)centralization that, together with high levels of cultural uniformity within their core territories, made them a recognizable species within the early modern genus. By and large the New Monarchies, in which category France is usually included, sought to restore late medieval powers that had lapsed during crises of the 14th and 15th centuries, while advancing select fiscal and administrative reforms and staking bolder rhetorical claims.[201] In England, for example, from 1485 the new Tudor Dynasty, capitalizing on postplague economic revival and the political exhaustion that followed a generation of civil war, proceeded to curb rampant magnate power, to increase the royal domain through large-scale land resumptions, to expand the doctrine of taxation to cover more than extraordinary expenditure (although, in practice, revenue increases from 1490 to 1570 were modest), to extend the jurisdiction of royal law courts, and to create a new inner council for policy. By seizing the entire ecclesiastical apparatus and declaring himself head of the English church, Henry VIII further strengthened the crown's fiscal position. Thus fortified, Tudor kings incorporated Wales in 1536 and, despite bitter resistance, imposed direct rule on Ireland.

In the late 1400s Isabella of Castile and Ferdinand of Aragon joined their states in a dynastic union, ended aristocratic challenges that had

---

ch. 5; Cemal Kafadar, "The Ottomans and Europe," in Brady, *Handbook*, vol. I, 589–635; and Ch. 1, nn. 147, 151 on the Ottomans.

[201] Discussion of the so-called New Monarchies of western Europe relies on Anthony Goodman, *The New Monarchy: England 1471–1534* (Oxford, 1988); Patrick O'Brien and Philip Hunt, "England, 1485–1815," in Bonney, *Rise of the Fiscal State*, 53–100; John Merriman, *A History of Modern Europe* (New York, 1996), 28–33, 181–217; Anderson, *Lineages*, 60–142, 172–91; John Brewer, *The Sinews of Power* (Cambridge, MA, 1988), 3–24; Barton, *History of Spain*, ch. 3; Henry Kamen, *Empire: How Spain Became a World Power 1492–1763* (New York, 2003); idem, *Crisis and Change in Early Modern Spain* (Aldershot, UK, 1993); Tobias Green, "Masters of Difference: The Jewish Presence in Cabo Verde, 1497–1672" (Univ. of Birmingham, PhD diss., 2006), 428–33; Subrahmanyam, *The Portuguese Empire in Asia 1500–1700* (London, 1993); Birmingham, *Concise History of Portugal*; Collins, *The State*, 1–27; Michael Roberts, *The Early Vasas: A History of Sweden 1523–1611* (Cambridge, 1968), chs. 1–5; Stewart Oakley, *A Short History of Sweden* (New York, 1966), 62–88; A. F. Upton, *Charles XI and Swedish Absolutism* (Cambridge, 1998), 4–6; Gorski, *Disciplinary Revolution*, 10–15; Anthony Pagden, *Lords of All the World* (New Haven, 1995); Richard Bonney, ed., *Economic Systems and State Finance* (Oxford, 1995), chs. 6–8; and essays by David Sacks, I. A. A. Thompson, and Philip Hoffman in Hoffman and Kathryn Norberg, eds., *Fiscal Crises, Liberty, and Representative Government 1450–1789* (Stanford, 1994).

produced decades of civil conflict, brought centuries of Reconquest from the Muslims to a triumphant conclusion, expelled the Jews, and laid the foundations for Spain's American empire. Although Castile and Aragon remained administratively distinct, within the former territory (far wealthier and more populous than Aragon) the crown constrained the great nobles through a series of conciliar and judicial reforms administered by men drawn largely from the lesser nobility. The Habsburgs, who assumed the Spanish crown in 1516 and who brought with them *inter alia* the Franche Comte, the Netherlands, and dependencies in Italy, transformed their New World territories by moving from the Caribbean to the mainland. In fact, the empire's extraordinary sprawl and a fierce defense of local privilege stymied administrative integration. Even within Spain, the legal unification of Castile and Aragon was not mooted, and the Inquisition remained one of the few unifying institutions. Yet at least to 1648 Habsburg Spain remained the premier European power thanks to Castilian and New World wealth, military innovation, expanded royal councils, Flemish and Italian talent, and a racialized Castilian-centered Spanish identity that fused with Counter-Reformation zeal.

If defense of Catholicism against Muslims and then Protestants gave the Spanish monarchy its sacred purpose and if English attacks during the Hundred Years War honed French identity, in the same period conflicts with Castile and with Muslim powers drove fractious Portuguese elites together, first for defense within Iberia, and then, building on Reconquest experience, for expansion in the Atlantic and Asia. From the late 1400s the Portuguese crown used overseas land grants and commercial privileges to cement noble support. Along with Portugal's modest size and maritime orientation, these projects fostered an elite identity no less cohesive than that in England and considerably more so than that in Spain.

In Sweden it was the Danish attempt at reconquest in 1520 that spurred creation of an effective monarchy under the usurper Vasa Dynasty. The new rulers benefited from iron and copper exports (the political equivalent to Spanish silver and gold) and, more spectacularly than its Tudor contemporaries, from the Protestant confiscation of church wealth. With this independent revenue base, which obviated tax increases, the crown was able to rationalize administration, conciliate the aristocracy, establish a standing army, expand the fleet, and in the 1560s embark on an initially successful program of Baltic expansion.

In what is now Germany and Italy, at first sight political developments look very different from those elsewhere in Europe. True, the Holy
Roman Empire long retained important appellate and arbitrative functions, not to mention symbolic capital. Yet by the mid-1200s, while state-
building in France and England was still in full spate, imperial efforts
to discipline the German nobility and to unify Germany and Italy effectively had collapsed in the face of German princely ambition, northern
Italian urban resistance, and papal opposition. If between 1300 and 1450
German particularism and the continued debility of the Empire bore
some resemblance to devolutionary trends across Europe, the strong
post-1450 revival of central fortunes that we find elsewhere had no
imperial parallel. Indeed, local consolidation gained further legal and
practical force from the Augsburg settlement of 1555, which awarded
each German principality the right to determine whether Catholicism
or Lutheranism would prevail in its territory.

Why, then, this persistent localization in Germany and Italy? The fact
that feudalism came later to Germany and was more territorially limited than in England or France meant that efforts by Hohenstaufen Holy
Roman Emperors to deploy concepts of feudal hierarchy had a weaker
cultural basis. Moreover, whereas in much of France the appearance
of relatively large post-Carolingian regional states preceded the rise
of local castellans and thus inhibited the most extreme forms of fragmentation, in Germany the 11th-century weakening of neo-Carolingian
imperial authority and the rise of castellans coincided, generating a
plethora of extremely small units that as late as 1500 still numbered some
2,400.[202] No less critical, the Empire as a whole was geographically disadvantaged. Whereas in France, England, Portugal, and Sweden, the
seat of royal authority remained near the economic center of gravity,
medieval emperors had no comparable base and no natural communication arteries. The wealthiest sector of the medieval Empire, North
Italy, lay outside the chief imperial holdings, and in fact unsuccessful
12th- and 13th-century Hohenstaufen campaigns to subdue North Italy
gravely weakened the Empire. That the reforming papacy, which energetically opposed its universal vision to that of the Empire, lay adjacent
to North Italy only magnified imperial woes. Yet more basic perhaps,
the Empire ironically was cursed by the fact that Europe's urbanized,
commercial spine, from North Italy to the Netherlands, straddled the

---

[202] Thomas Ertman, *Birth of the Leviathan* (Cambridge, 1997), 232–33.

Empire's western sector. Here urban and commercial density favored city-states and small principalities more stubbornly independent than in kingdoms – including England, Sweden, Spain, and France – the bulk of whose territories lay outside this commercial spine.[203] Finally, on the Slavic frontier the post-1050 pattern of colonization under the auspices of local German lords, rather than the emperor, also promoted centrifugalism. This situation had much in common with Kiev, but contrasted with that in France, where colonization was both limited and internal, and in Spain and Britain, where it remained under royal control.

However, in three respects political developments in Italy and Germany did intersect, even anticipate, developments in Europe at large. First, northern Italian cities, Florence in particular, developed the basic instruments of public finance, debt, statecraft, and diplomacy, as well as a culture of civic participation and secular patriotism, that fueled the growth of sovereign states across Europe in subsequent generations. Second, driven by the same imperative of escalating warfare and benefiting from the same post-1450 economic revival as aided other European realms, many German and Italian states pursued policies of territorial demarcation, fiscal expansion, and administrative rationalization comparable to those of the New Monarchies, albeit on a generally more modest scale. Thus in the 1400s and 1500s German states, whose number contracted, struggled to expand and consolidate their holdings, to establish royal primogeniture, and to create more professional administrative machineries; while in Italy some 250 independent communes in 1200, following a similar logic, yielded by 1480 to six small to medium-size states.[204] Third, from the 1490s even moderately successful Italian and German principalities became vulnerable to great power predators. Particularly in Italy, as massive French and Spanish armies poured into the peninsula, it became clear that western Europe's future lay not with city-states or small principalities but with consolidated territorial entities: by the mid-1500s Lombardy, South Italy, Sardinia, and Sicily all

---

[203] This point receives emphasis in Tilly, *Coercion, Capital*, 9–28, 47–51; Thomas A. Brady, Jr., "The Rise of Merchant Empires, 1400–1700," in James D. Tracy, ed., *The Political Economy of Merchant Empires* (Cambridge, 1991), 117–60; and Anderson, *Lineages*, 168. On the Empire's weakness, see too ibid., 143–72; 224–45; Strayer, *Western Europe*, 91–94; Levine, *At the Dawn*, 27–53.

[204] Florence, Venice, Milan, the Papal state, Naples, and Sicily-Aragon.

had become attached to the Spanish composite monarchy. In these Darwinian contests, therefore, Italian states unwittingly anticipated wider European trends.[205]

Note finally that the problems that convulsed late-16th- to early-17th-century Russia and France may be seen as early manifestations of far more general continental woes. Between 1590 and 1650 England, Scotland, Ireland, Catalonia, Portugal, Naples, Sicily, Bohemia, Holland, Switzerland, several German states, and the Ukraine all suffered upheavals sufficiently severe to engender the rubric "general crisis of the 17th century." According to recent scholarly syntheses, these travails reflected local combinations of population pressure, climatic downturn, institutional blockages, and escalating warfare, problems that in turn fed popular distress and intra-elite competition. And in familiar fashion, disruptions in this period typically were less prolonged or severe than those of the 13th to 15th centuries, but more so than 18th-century disturbances.[206]

Muscovite Construction, c. 1450–1580: Mongol-Tatar Patronage and Decline

Against this European and Eurasian background, let us examine Muscovy's expansion between c. 1450 and 1580.

---

[205] The waning of the Hanseatic League also conforms to this pattern. On German, Baltic, and Italian developments, including the interesting problem of why North Italy on its own did not develop a large consolidated state, see Spruyt, *Sovereign State*, 109–50; Eberhard Isenmann, "The Holy Roman Empire in the Middle Ages," in Bonney, *Rise of the Fiscal State*, 243–80, emphasizing the Holy Roman Empire's surprisingly precocity in state funding; Carlo Capra, "The Italian States in the Early Modern Period," in ibid., 417–42; Tilly, *Capital, Coercion*, 76–80; Barber, *Two Cities*, ch. 8; Geoffrey Barraclough, *The Origins of Modern Germany* (New York, 1984); Garrett Mattingly, *Renaissance Diplomacy* (Boston, 1971), chs. 5, 12–19; Epstein, *Freedom and Growth*, ch. 5; William J. Connell and Andrea Zorzi, eds., *Florentine Tuscany* (Cambridge, 2000).

[206] See the early formulation in Trevor Ashton, ed., *Crisis in Europe, 1560–1660* (London, 1965), superseded by Theodore Rabb, *The Struggle for Stability in Early Modern Europe* (New York, 1975), esp. chs. 1–3; Peter Clark, ed., *The European Crisis of the 1590s* (London, 1985); Goldstone, *Revolution and Rebellion*, esp. 63–169, 343–48; the 17th-century crisis issue of *MAS* 24 (1990): 625–97; Geoffrey Parker and Lesley Smith, eds., *The General Crisis of the Seventeenth Century* (2nd ed., London, 1997); Geoffrey Parker, *Europe in Crisis, 1598–1648* (2nd ed., Oxford, MA, 2001); Robert Crummey, "Muscovy and the 'General Crisis of the Seventeenth Century,'" *JEMH* 2 (1998): 156–80; "AHR Forum: The General Crisis of the Seventeenth Century Revisited," *AHR* 113 (2008): 1029–99. As Ch. 3 will show, between 1648 and 1653 Russia and France also experienced fresh upheavals less severe than those of 1562–1613.

As Nancy Shields Kollmann has emphasized, the period c. 1280–1450 saw developments seminal to Muscow's long-term success, including the founding in Moscow of the Daniilovich line of Riurikids, who would rule until 1598; the Daniilovichi's securing of the Grand Princely throne of Vladimir against local rivals, and the destruction of some major Riurikid competitors. Externally, the realm expanded from a tiny area in 1280 to almost 400,000 square kilometers by 1462.[207] As early as 1380, although his purported victory seems to have had limited practical effect, Moscow's ruler exploited internecine Tatar disputes to lead a mixed Tatar and Russian force against the Kipchak khanate.[208]

Yet despite its early promise, in 1450 Moscow remained but one, and by no means the most formidable, contender within the still highly fragmented former lands of Kiev. If they hesitated to challenge Moscow directly, other Riurikids during the early 1400s showed a marked, indeed growing, independence of Moscow, in some cases styling themselves "Grand Prince" in competition with the Daniilovichi. In the face of Lithuanian expansion, early-15th-century Moscow itself remained strangely inert, frequently passive. Indeed, without the countervailing power of the Tatars, to whom Moscow remained at least nominally tributary, Moscow, most of the Riurikid principalities of the northeast, as well as Novgorod probably would have been swallowed by Lithuania.

Only in the late 15th and the 16th centuries did Moscow gain a decisive advantage over regional competitors. Indeed, Ivan III (r. 1462–1505) may be seen as the true founder of the Muscovite state. Through marriage, inheritance, and warfare, that ruler absorbed or neutralized the remaining independent Riurikid principalities, including Moscow's long-time nemesis Tver, as well as the once mighty commercial center of Novgorod. Conquest of Novgorod in turn brought Moscow into open rivalry with Poland-Lithuania for control of frontier zones and trade routes leading to the Baltic. Much of the 16th century was therefore devoted to western wars during which Moscow seized over a third of Lithuanian territory. To the east, having thrown off Tatar control

---

[207] On pre-1550 Muscovy, see Kollmann, *Kinship and Politics*; idem, *Honor Bound*; idem, "Muscovite Russia, 1450–1598," in Freeze, *Russia*, 27–54; A. E. Presniakov, *The Formation of the Great Russian State* (Chicago, 1970); Fennell, *Crisis*; idem, *Emergence of Moscow*; Crummey, *Formation of Muscovy*, chs. 1–6; Martin, *Medieval Russia*, chs. 7–12. On Muscovite territories, Smith, *Peasant Farming*, 103; John Channon, *The Penguin Historical Atlas of Russia* (London, 1995), 36–37.

[208] For reevaluations of this battle of Kulikovo, traditionally considered a major Russian victory, Ostrowski, *Muscovy and Mongols*, 155–60; Martin, *Medieval Russia*, 211–15.

during the course of the 15th century, Moscow in 1552 and 1556 smashed the Tatar states of Kazan and Astrakhan that had devolved from the Kipchak khanate. Thus Ivan III, his son, and his grandson succeeded in a) enhancing their security by seizing zones intermediate between their own territorial core and those of rival states like Lithuania,[209] b) obtaining prized northeastern furs for export, while improving access to Baltic, Caspian, and Arctic Ocean ports, and c) opening the steppe to eventual Russian settlement. By 1598 Moscow controlled 11 to 12 times more territory than in 1462 and had become the largest European-based state.[210] Internally, notwithstanding continued reliance on Tatar political and military models, this period saw the development of an anti-Tatar Orthodox church ideology that viewed Muscovy as divinely sanctioned successor to Byzantium.[211] In short, although Moscow arose relatively late, its dramatic post-1450 conquests coincided substantially with the reassembly of France and other New Monarchies in western Europe; with the expansion of Polish, Ottoman, and Austrian spheres elsewhere in eastern Europe; and with the post-1450 revival of the Burmese, Siamese, and Vietnamese kingdoms (not to mention with consolidations in Japan and South Asia, which we shall consider in subsequent chapters).

How then shall we explain the timing and progress of Russian integration? I shall consider six factors – Mongol-Tatar patronage, Mongol-Tatar disintegration, multifaceted economic expansion, firearms, imaginative administrative experiments, and cultural changes – the last four of which have obvious parallels in Southeast Asia and elsewhere in Europe.

---

[209] Andrei Pavlov and Maureen Perrie, *Ivan the Terrible* (London, 2003), 12–15, 41–54. On theories of Russian expansion, focusing on the need to create ever more distant client states and buffer zones in a region without natural defenses, see Ostrowski, *Muscovy and Mongols*, 187–88; Marshall Poe and Eric Lohr, "Introduction," in Lohr and Poe, eds., *The Military and Society in Russia 1450–1917* (Leiden, 2002), 5–8; John LeDonne, *The Russian Empire and the World 1700–1917* (New York, 1997), 1–8.

[210] Smith, *Peasant Farming*, 103; Richard Hellie, *Enserfment and Military Change in Muscovy* (Chicago, 1971), 21; Donald Ostrowksi, "Troop Mobilization by the Muscovite Grand Princes," in Lohr and Poe, *Military and Society*, 35–40; Martin, *Medieval Russia*, 312–26; idem, "Muscovy's Northeast Expansion," *Cahiers du Monde Russe et Sovietique* 24 (1983): 459–70.

[211] Ostrowski, *Muscovy and Mongols*. Note that on pp. 16–17, Ostrowski promotes basically the same tripartite Muscovite periodization as I favor, namely 1304–1448, 1448–1589, and 1589–1722. See too the emphasis on the mid-1400s as a watershed in Muscovite development in Richard Hellie, "The Expanding Role of the State in Russia," in Jarmo Kotilaine and Marshall Poe, eds., *Modernizing Muscovy* (London, 2004), 29–55.

The earliest spur derived from Mongol-Tatar intervention, which allowed the Daniilovichi – who were ineligible according to traditional Riurikid rules of succession but whom the Mongols considered more reliable than rival houses – to retain the powerful Grand Princely throne of Vladimir almost continuously after 1328 or 1332. Without the fiscal and military advantages that flowed from this office, the Daniilovichi could never have dominated northeastern principalities as rapidly as they did, if at all. Moreover, as Ostrowski's recent foray into the vexed historiography of Tatar legacies has shown, Tatar practices fundamentally transformed Muscovite administrative and military organization. By interacting with Tatar envoys and commanders within the Rus lands and by visiting regularly the Kipchak capital of Sarai on the lower Volga, 14th-century Muscovite princes became intimately familiar with Tatar territorial administration, advisory councils, noble ranks, censuses, taxation, postal relays, and military land grants, not to mention cavalry weapons and tactics. That they should have borrowed such techniques from one of the largest and most powerful empires of its time, especially as Kievan administration had been deficient in many of these very spheres, is hardly surprising. Thus Tatar-based systems of taxation, which were far more exploitative than earlier Russian practices, allowed Muscovite Grand Princes to grow immensely wealthy both before and, more importantly, after they became independent of the khanate. As late as the early 1600s Muscovite forces continued to center around cavalry archers using Tatar-style composite bows, short-stirrup saddles, helmets, and maneuvers. Muscovite clans may have reorganized themselves according to Mongol norms, while at least through the late 15th century tsars proudly identified as successors to the Kipchak khans.[212]

Note, however, that compared to China, South Asia, and Southwest Asia, in Russia indigenous actors from an early date retained extensive autonomy. Because it was too inhospitable for steppe cavalry and too economically marginal to justify direct administration, the Tatars never stationed large forces in Muscovy; and by the early 1300s such forces as

---

[212] Hellie, *Enserfment*, ch. 9 (this remains the standard work on early modern Russian military change); Poe and Lohr, "Introduction," 3; Ostrowski, "Troop Mobilization," 22–23; idem, *Muscovy and Mongols*, 51–52, 104, 182, 185; idem, "The Mongol Origins of Muscovite Political Institutions," *SR* 49 (1990): 525–42; idem, "Sixteenth-Century Muscovite Cavalrymen," in Kivelson and Neuberger, *Picturing Russia*, 28–32; Chester Dunning, *A Short History of Russia's First Civil War* (University Park, PA, 2004), 15–16; Nancy Shields Kollmann, "The Cap of Monomakh," in Kivelson and Neuberger, *Picturing Russia*, 38–41, esp. 40 on Ivan III as the "white emperor."

did exist under Tatar commanders (*basqaqi*) responsible for Rus tribute and conscripts had been withdrawn in favor of Muscovite princes, who were willing to deliver tribute directly to their Tatar overlords at Sarai. Muscovy thus rose to preeminence under Tatar tutelage, but the Tatars never envisioned Muscovy's success and indeed became the first major victims of that success. Arguably the closest analogy was the relation between Ming China and Dai Viet in the early 1400s. In both instances, a brief alien occupation opened a conduit for local elites to acquire from their neighbor sophisticated administrative and military techniques, which they promptly turned against that neighbor.[213]

After Mongol-Tatar intervention, a second precondition for Russian expansion was, ironically, Mongol-Tatar collapse. Whether, to recall earlier discussion, Inner Asians unwittingly introduced the Black Death to the rodent population of the western steppe or whether an endemic infestation suddenly became more virulent, from 1345 to 1396 a series of plague visitations inflicted crippling losses on cities held by the Kipchak khanate and on those Tatar herdsmen who formed the khanate's demographic base. Although Russians also suffered grievously, the khanate's apparently greater difficulties helped precipitate severe political crises within the khanate from the 1350s.[214] Compounding plague damage, between 1350 and 1410 the Ottomans and the Ming constricted those east–west caravan routes that provided the Kipchak khanate's chief income, while Timur (Tamerlane) demolished much of the khanate's remaining urban centers. With the original Mongol-Tatar synthesis of

[213] Morgan, *Mongols*, 142–44; Ostrowski, *Muscovy and Mongols*, chs. 1, 2; Martin, *Medieval Russia*, 150–51, 156, 175, 199–200, and historiography at 382–85; Fennell, *Emergence of Moscow*; Halperin, *Golden Horde*. After 1450 Tatar refugees provided another cultural conduit. Cf. Dai Viet and the Ming, *SP*, 375–83. A major difference with Dai Viet, however, is that whereas the Mongol-Tatars had little or no cultural/religious influence on Moscow, Ming Neo-Confucianism, building on pre-Ming ties, had a major impact on Vietnam.

[214] On plague and the Tatars, whose smaller absolute numbers and heavier urban/commercial reliance may have left them more vulnerable to plague dislocations than Muscovites, see esp. Uli Schamiloglu, "Preliminary Remarks on the Role of Disease in the History of the Golden Horde," *Central Asian Survey* 12 (1993): 447–57, plus McNeill, *Plagues and Peoples*, 133–34, 168–75, 216; Martin, *Medieval Russia*, 201; Halperin, *Golden Horde*, 29. For analyses of Mongol-Tatar decline, see too ibid., 28–29, 54–70; Hartog, *Mongol Yoke*, chs. 6–10; Crummey, *Formation of Muscovy*, 51–82; 97–101, 152–55; Martin, *Medieval Russia*, chs. 7, 10–12; Edward Keenan, "Muscovy and Kazan," *SR* 26 (1967): 548–58; Michael Khodarkovsky, *Russia's Steppe Frontier* (Bloomington, IN, 2002), chs. 1, 3. Despite or because of steppe debility, 16th-century Muscovy obtained up to 40,000 horses annually, a critical military resource, from the Nogai nomad confederation, one heir to the Kipchak khanate.

city and steppe in tatters, after 1430 the khanate began to fragment, with new khanates arising in the Crimea, at Kazan and Astrakhan on the Volga, and in Siberia. At first Moscow and these polities – all of which, along with a still nomadic Nogai Horde, may be considered heirs to the Kipchak state – competed and allied with one another on more or less equal terms, but in the course of the 15th century Tatar debility joined Moscow's growing economic and organizational strength to tilt the balance. Climaxing decades of interference in Tatar affairs, Moscow's triumphs over Kazan and Astrakhan in the 1550s not only opened new economic vistas and afforded the core greater protection from steppe raids, but signaled Moscow's definitive succession to Kipchak supremacy.

Muscovite Construction, c. 1450–1580: Economic and Military Spurs

Arguably of greater long-term import to the changing power balance than internal Tatar difficulties was a marked expansion in Muscovite population and wealth between 1450 and 1560. According to Richard Hellie, the years 1500–1550 were "probably the most peaceful and most prosperous period in Russian history prior to [1945–1985]."[215]

As elsewhere, growth was overdetermined, that is, spurred by interlaced factors whose individual contributions are difficult to assess. The plague of 1448 (some say 1428) was the last in a series of major countrywide visitations that began in 1351. Whether the waning of the disease reflected changes in rodent hosts or bacteria, climatic warming, acquired immunities, or barriers against nomad transmission is less important than the fact that abatement contributed to a resumption or acceleration of population growth.[216] At roughly the same time, that is, the mid-1400s, Russian climate, like that of Europe generally, entered a modest warming phase, aided by the end of the Sporer Minimum of solar radiation and coinciding with an era of improved rainfall in Southeast Asia.[217] Longer growing seasons can only have aided agriculture

---

[215] Hellie, "Russia, 1200–1815," 485.

[216] Alexander, *Bubonic Plague*, 12–29; McNeill, *Plagues*, ch. 4; Langer, "Black Death," 60–67; Crummey, *Formation of Muscovy*, 3, 42–43.

[217] According to Lamb's Winter Severity Index, whereas Russian winters 1350–1450 averaged –10.8, one of the coldest stretches on record, from 1450 to 1600 they were –3.0, and between 1550 and 1600, warmed to +0.8. Lamb, *Changing Climate*, 220; idem, *Past, Present, and Future*, vol. II, 564. Varying degrees of supportive data appear at Briffa, "Dendroclimatological Reconstructions," 5–10, focusing on spring and summer temperatures; Klimanov, "Climatic Changes," 58–64; Chernavskaya, "Botanical Indicators," 65–70; Borisenkov, "Documentary Evidence," 171–83; Vaganov et al.,

in the Volga–Oka interfluve, which lies a full 5 degrees latitude north of Kiev.[218]

Having returned to preplague levels by 1500, Muscovy's population, some speculate, rose by 1 percent a year to 1560, by which time it may have been in the neighborhood of 6,500,000.[219] With the threat of Crimean Tatar slave raids still inhibiting settlement of the steppe, with virgin lands in the interfluve rapidly disappearing, and with the new class of *pomest'e* landlords (see below) demanding higher payments, pressure grew to adopt more intensive agrarian regimes than the hitherto dominant slash-and-burn and "long fallow"systems. Accordingly, from the late 1400s a three-field system of crop rotations (or three-field prototypes) began to appear on the estates of large monasteries, *boyars* (high nobles), and the crown, whence the new regime spread fitfully and unevenly in the 16th and 17th centuries to the lands of humble servitors and some peasants. (Comparable pressures, we have seen, supported three-field prototypes on some French estates as early as the 8th or 9th century.) Whereas Kievan-era religious bodies had been preeminently urban, from the mid-1300s new monasteries, spurred by princely grants of tax immunity, became wealthy landowning institutions and key agents of rural reclamation.[220] To be sure, Russian yields remained frightfully poor by West European standards, and post-1450 climatic amelioration proved temporary. Nonetheless, the benefits – better integration of pasturage and husbandry, more even year-round distribution of work, reduced fallow, moderately improved fertility – that derived from three-field crop rotations and associated improvements in manuring, weeding, and drainage inaugurated in R. A. French's words, "if not an agrarian revolution, an agrarian transformation and an advance in efficiency" more far reaching than anything Russia would experience until Soviet collectivization.[221]

"Reconstruction," 355–59. Average warming, however, was probably less than 1 °C, and some authors, *pace* Lamb, suggest that cooler, more erratic weather set in c. 1550–1600. Cf. *SP*, 143–44, 253, 385–86.

[218] Cf. Chernavskaya, "Botanical Indicators," 68; Leslie Symons, *The Soviet Union: A Systematic Geography* (London, 1990), chs. 3–4.

[219] For widely varying estimates, see Hellie, *Enserfment*, 87 and 379 n. 93 (citing the 1 percent growth figure), 305 n. 9; Dunning, *Short History*, 13; Crummey, *Formation of Muscovy*, 2–3; idem, "Muscovy and the General Crisis," 166.

[220] Martin, *Medieval Russia*, 224–25, and n. 221 *infra*.

[221] French, "Introduction of Three-field System," 79 (with quote) and 65–79; idem, "Introduction," ibid., 19; Richard Hellie, "The Structure of Russian Imperial History," *History and Theory* 44 (2005): 92. Cf. nn. 4, 73, 96 *supra*. Yet Hellie, pers. commun., March 2,

Agricultural intensification was a precondition for domestic commercial expansion and monetization. Larger rural surpluses, the opening of frontier areas with unique production profiles, a turn to handicrafts among land-scarce peasants, and monastic trading ventures all promoted market exchange. At the same time in the more densely populated core territories, demands for cash rents and taxes obliged peasants to sell crafts and surplus foodstuffs, which facilitated urban growth.[222] By one reckoning, 16th-century towns increased from 130 to 210,[223] and by 1550 may have held 3 percent of the total population. Marketing areas now began to spill outside the gates of walled cities, while within the walls commercial zones became more distinct. According to Rozman, between 1450 and 1600 the urban/commercial network moved from Stage C ("state city") to Stage E ("standard marketing"), with two to three additional levels of central places and qualitatively higher integration.[224]

In this same period Muscovy's foreign trade grew because its Volga conquests improved access to Siberian furs and Southwest Asian markets, and because Muscovy's trading partners in central Europe, Persia, and the Ottoman empire, beneficiaries of a widespread postplague, postcrisis recovery, also were prospering. If, even more clearly than in Southeast Asia, the chief roots of post-1450 vitality in Muscovy were domestic, foreign contacts strengthened the local economy in three ways: a) The three-field system apparently entered Muscovy

---

2006 argues that late-16th-century disorders seriously reduced the incidence of the three-field system. On Muscovite agriculture, see too Janet Martin, "Backwardness in Russian Peasant Culture," in Samuel Baron and Nancy Shields Kollmann, eds., *Religion and Culture in Early Modern Russia and Ukraine* (DeKalb, IL, 1997), 19–33; Smith, *Peasant Farming*, chs. 1–6, 10, and App. 1; Blum, *Lord and Peasant*, chs. 10–12; Michael Confino, *Systemes Agraires et Progres Agricole: L'Assolement Triennal en Russie aux XVIII-XIX Siecles* (Paris, 1969), 19–37, 53. Although his work has been criticized, Slicher van Bath offers diachronic yield estimates in "The Yields of Different Crops (Mainly Cereals) in Relation to the Seed, c. 810–1820," *Acta Historiae Neerlandica* 2 (1967): 94–95.

[222] Richard Hellie, "The Foundation of Russian Capitalism," *SR* 26 (1967), 148–50 calculates that peasants by 1560 sold 42 percent of their harvest. On commercialization, cash dues, and cash taxes, also Crummey, *Formation of Muscovy*, 2–7, 21–22, 156–57; Blum, *Lord and Peasant*, 79, 117–34, 142–43, 181–230; idem, "Prices in Russia in the 16th Century," *JEH* 16 (1956): 182–99; Smith, *Peasant Farming*, 105–108, 223–38; Martin, *Medieval Russia*, 273–80.

[223] French, "Early and Medieval Russian Town," 263–64, excluding annexed towns. Also Blum, *Lord and Peasant*, 123–24.

[224] Rozman, *Urban Networks*, 33–37, 56–66, 83–85. Cf. nn. 6–8, 100 *supra*. On Moscow's population, ibid., 59; Martin, *Medieval Russia*, 273.

via Lithuania and the Baltic.[225] b) European-style firearms and foreign trade revenues promoted settlement and trade indirectly by aiding pacification and frontier defense. c) External trade promoted flax and hemp exports from the northwest, favored urban growth, and provided Moscow with a consistent bullion surplus (up to 50 percent of its European imports) critical for domestic coinage. In response to rising international demand and technical breakthroughs in mining and smelting, central Europe's silver output increased after 1460, to be supplemented from the 1530s by Japanese and more dramatically by New World production.[226]

How did Muscovite policies influence economics? If we follow Epstein's thesis that European economies in the 14th and early 15th centuries faced a crisis of integration in which excessively small jurisdictions and endemic disorder inhibited investment and the spread of best practices,[227] post-1450 growth also owed much to state initiatives, even if the economic benefits of these initiatives were not always intended. The end to civil wars in 1453 and Moscow's rapid absorption thereafter of once-independent Riurikid principalities encouraged trade and reclamation in the core, while from the 1550s new anti-Tatar defenses (*zaseki*) on the southern frontier reduced threats to the core and allowed colonization of the steppe (although this would become demographically significant only in the 17th century). The eclipse of independent Riurikid polities let the crown honor requests from merchants, nobles, and monasteries for more uniform weights, measures, and coinages, and favored efforts at legal integration, as seen in the imperial law codes (*sudebniks*) of 1497 and 1550. These documents sought, albeit with uncertain practical effect, to curb banditry, to regularize land tenures, to limit

---

[225] French, "Introduction of Three-field System," esp. 72–73, 78–79.

[226] Muscovy imported bullion and cloth from Europe and textiles and horses from the Ottoman empire and Persia, while supplying furs, hemp, and naval stores to Europe and textiles and silver to the Muslim world. On foreign trade and bullion flows, Arthur Attman, *The Russian and Polish Markets in International Trade 1500–1650* (Göteburg, 1973); idem, *The Bullion Flow Between Europe and the East 1000–1750* (Göteburg, 1981), ch. 3; John Munro, "Precious Metals and the Origins of the Price Revolution Reconsidered," in Clara Nunez, *Monetary History in Global Perspective, 1500–1808* (Seville, 1998), 35–50; Martin, *Medieval Russia*, 312–26; idem, "Muscovy's Northeast Expansion"; Ward Barrett, "World Bullion Flows, 1450–1800," in James Tracy, ed., *The Rise of Merchant Empires* (Cambridge, 1990), 224–54; Blum, *Lord and Peasant*, 127–34; Nancy Shields Kollmann, "Russia," in *NCMH*, vol. VII, 748–51; Crummey, *Formation of Muscovy*, 16–20; Paul Bushkovitch, *The Merchants of Moscow, 1580–1760* (Cambridge, 1980); Ostrowski, *Muscovy and Mongols*, 122–26, stressing pre-1450 vitality.

[227] Epstein, *Freedom and Growth*, esp. ch. 3, albeit focusing on western Europe.

litigants' court costs, and to provide a degree of judicial probity and uniformity. Royal immunity charters to monasteries that engaged in trade and reclamation, and royal demands for cash taxes, must have further aided market activity. The same was certainly true of large army contracts, the concentration of court and ecclesiastical purchases in Moscow, and massive fortress projects around the Muscovite perimeter that relied substantially on paid labor.[228]

In reciprocal fashion, economic expansion strengthened the emergent state, as Michael Cherniavsky noted when he claimed that the chief difference between the medieval and early modern Russian polity was the "huge increase in resources – demographic and economic," together with an apparatus that learned to feed efficiently on those resources.[229] By permitting a substantial expansion of cavalry levies and by amplifying the incidence and range of royal exactions, the late-15th- to 16th-century boom allowed Moscow – as well as its archrival Poland-Lithuania – to expand force levels and pursue territorial goals with greater consistency. Before 1460 Muscovite rural imposts had been extremely light, with royal income consisting chiefly of trade and transit taxes. No doubt the 16th-century crown continued to derive substantial income from customs receipts, import and export monopolies, and the reminting of imported bullion.[230] But with the help of a class of crown-dependent landholders then in formation, the throne also obliged three categories of subjects – private peasants, tax-paying peasants on crown lands, and townsmen – to accept a mushrooming list of domestic taxes and corvées, including ad hoc military taxes assessed per plow unit and monopoly sales of alcohol and salt. Chiefly in response to military demands, whose share of total tax receipts rose dramatically from

---

[228] On the economic implications of state actions, Hellie, *Enserfment*, 85, 157–59; Denis J. B. Shaw, "Southern Frontiers of Muscovy, 1550–1700," in Bater and French, *Studies*, vol. I, 118–42; Langer, "Plague and the Countryside," 351–68; Noonan, "Forging a National Identity," 495–523; Sunderland, *Wild Field*, 24–31; Hellie, pers. commun., March 2, 2006; idem, "The Costs of Muscovite Military Defense and Expansion," in Lohr and Poe, *Military and Society*, 41–66. On the law codes of 1497 and 1550, see Horace Dewey, "The 1497 Sudebnik – Muscovite Russia's First National Law Code," *American Slavic and East European Review* 15 (1956): 325–38; idem, "The 1550 Sudebnik as an Instrument of Reform," *JfGO* 10 (1962): 161–80, noting, however, that in 1497 commercial regulation still seems to have been primarily a matter of regional codes.

[229] Michael Cherniavsky, "Russia," in Orest Ranum, ed., *National Consciousness, History, and Political Culture in Early-Modern Europe* (Baltimore, 1975), 137.

[230] Ostrowski, *Muscovy and Mongols*, 91, 122–26; Martin, *Land of Darkness*, 169; and Kollmann, "Russia," 748–51 all emphasize such revenues, even though our earliest figures are quite late.

30 percent in 1505 to 84 percent in 1584, direct domestic levies in the 16th century increased, by some accounts, sixfold, *after* allowing for inflation. Although such demands finally became insupportable, Marc Zlotnik and R. E. F. Smith have concluded that at first major increases were feasible both because original levies had been light and because the countryside was enjoying rapid growth.[231]

Not only did revenues rise, but as in Southeast Asia and France heavier reliance on cash enhanced central operations. A number of corvées and in-kind obligations were commuted, and forced monetary loans/confiscations from monasteries probably increased.[232] On the other side of the ledger, as monetary rewards became more feasible, cavalry received stipends to buy horses and weapons, and field commanders and governors received cash to supplement in-kind local exactions. Although land grants remained the chief form of cavalry compensation, in the case of musketeers, foreign mercenaries, and chancellery personnel cash grants became the norm. By the late 1500s fortress construction, as noted, also depended heavily on wage labor and market procurement, which were normally more efficient than corvées and in-kind levies.[233]

Along with Tatar conquest, Tatar decline, and rapid demographic/economic growth, firearms and European-based military changes in the late 15th and 16th centuries provided a fourth, if somewhat tardy, spur to Moscow's "gathering of the Russian lands." Guns and economic growth were linked by the new weapons' high cost and by Russia's growing military and commercial engagement on its western frontier. Indeed, German and Italian gun-founders were critical.

---

[231] On tax increases, Marc Zlotnik, "Muscovite Fiscal Policy: 1462–1584," *RH* 6 (1979): 243–58, esp. 244, 253–54 (note, however, that his data in n. 47 for inflation-based corrections are open to different interpretations); Chester Dunning, "The Preconditions of Modern Russia's First Civil War," *RH* 25 (1998): 123; Smith, *Peasant Farming*, 224–25, 232–38; Kollmann, "Muscovite Russia," 47; Crummey, *Formation of Muscovy*, 20–21; Peter Lyashchenko, *History of the National Economy of Russia to the 1917 Revolution* (New York, 1949), 225–26.

[232] See nn. 230, 231 *supra*, plus Horace Dewey, "Immunities in Old Russia," *SR* 23 (1964): 645; idem, "The Decline of the Muscovite *Namestnik*," *Oxford Slavonic Papers* 12 (1965): 38; Hellie, "Costs of Muscovite Military"; idem, pers. commun., March 2, 2006.

[233] On growing cash operations, previous notes, plus Kollmann, *Honor Bound*, 184; Hellie, *Enserfment*, 24–25, 36–38; Dewey, "Decline of *Namestnik*," 38; Brian Davies, "The Politics of Give and Take," in Kleimola and Lenhoff, *Culture and Identity*, 39–67; Marshall Poe, "The Consequences of the Military Revolution in Muscovy," *CSSH* 38 (1996): 603–18, esp. 608–609; Poe, pers. commun., Aug. 9, 2000; Hellie, "Costs of Muscovite Military."

Cast often in resilient bronze rather than iron and using granular gunpowder, Western-style cannon influenced the outcome of 16 out of 20 Muscovite battles in which they were used between 1470 and 1520. In the mid-1500s further improvements in charge-to-missile ratios, range, and rate of fire joined new military mining techniques to transform utterly Russian fortress design, replacing artillery-vulnerable, contour-hugging structures with much stouter, polygonal, turret-laden forts designed to concentrate defensive artillery fire. From 1492 to 1600 Russia completed more than 30 major European-style fortresses of this type on its western border, including Smolensk, said to be the greatest construction project in the 16th-century world.[234] Both in executing and defending against the new siege techniques, infantry proved more valuable than cavalry, while among infantry, handguns became increasingly common. In 1550 Muscovy's first musketeer units, the *strel'tsy*, numbered 3,000, but 50 years later indigenous musketeers alone numbered some 20,000 and artillerymen, another 3,500.[235] The transition from European mercenaries to indigenous gunners that we find in Burma and Siam in the late 1500s and early 1600s[236] thus began in Russia at least a generation earlier, as did the imposition of special taxes to support the new formations.

To be sure, before 1550 one can easily exaggerate the new weapons' impact. Their great expense and the persistence of serious Tatar threats ensured, as noted, that even after 1600 the military relied chiefly on Tatar-style cavalry. Yet had Moscow not joined the 16th-century gunpowder revolution, Hellie argues, European armies "certainly would have dismembered the newly consolidated state."[237] Conversely, on the southeastern and eastern frontiers, where European weapons began to give Moscow a technological advantage over the Tatars, firearms contributed to the conquest of Kazan, rendered Moscow's forts largely

---

[234] Hellie, *Enserfment*, 157–58; idem, "Costs of Muscovite Military," 48–49.

[235] Hellie, *Enserfment*, 161, 267; Kollmann, "Muscovite Russia," 41.

[236] Victor Lieberman, "Europeans, Trade, and the Unification of Burma, c. 1540–1620," *Oriens Exrtremus* 27 (1980): 203–26.

[237] Hellie, *Enserfment*, 156. Discussion of pre-1600 firearms relies on ibid., 153–66; idem, "Warfare, Changing Military Technology, and the Evolution of Muscovite Society," in John A. Lynn, ed., *Tools of War* (Urbana, IL, 1990), 74–99; Dunning, *Short History*, 25–27; Ostrowski, "Troop Mobilization," 19–40; Thomas Esper, "Military Self-Sufficiency and Weapons Technology in Muscovite Russia," *SR* 28 (1969): 185–208; J. L. H. Keep, *Soldiers of the Tsar* (Oxford, 1985), chs. 1, 2; Gustav Alef, "Muscovite Military Reforms in the Second Half of the 15th Century," *FzOG* 18 (1973): 73–108; Marshall Poe, "The Military Revolution, Administrative Development, and Cultural Change in Early Modern Russia," *JEMH* 2 (1998): 247–73.

immune to Tatar siege, and helped open Siberia, valued as a unique source of furs, to conquest from the late 1500s.[238]

Muscovite Construction, c. 1450–1580: Administrative Creativity

But as the eclipse of Riurikid rivals with access to substantially the same economic and military resources suggests, Moscow's success also reflected an insistent, idiosyncratic political creativity – a fifth precondition for integration. As in Southeast Asia, innovation responded to both interstate and domestic imperatives. Perhaps the most seminal change involved the ruling house itself: apanage princes were subordinated and fractious Kievan-style lateral succession yielded to primogeniture. Having begun fortuitously, lineal succession soon recommended itself on practical grounds, much as in Tran Vietnam and Capetian France in an earlier period. On the one hand, insofar as it curbed succession disputes such as still paralyzed other Riurikid polities, primogeniture strengthened Moscow vis-à-vis those external actors. On the other hand, a smooth succession promised to protect the existing court elite against displacement by rival factions. Between 1425 and 1453 the new system was tested in a great civil war between the son of the previous Grand Prince and apanage princes invoking the rights of that Grand Prince's younger brothers. Not unlike the contemporary Ming occupation of Dai Viet or the Hundred Years War in France, these upheavals liquidated opposition and inclined survivors toward greater cohesion. After the civil war, primogeniturial succession was enshrined, princely apanage armies came under Moscow-appointed lieutenants, and Moscow forbade apanage princes to contract politically dangerous marriages. In thus radically recasting family relations, the Daniilovichi were unique among Riurikid dynasties.[239]

As it disciplined the royal family, Moscow also strove to emasculate newly annexed principalities. Although at first some principalities retained separate courts, their leading nobles were gradually induced

---

[238] Previous note, plus Khodarkovsky, *Steppe Frontier*, 20–21, 113, 127; Peter Perdue, *China Marches West* (Cambridge, MA, 2005), 84–89.

[239] Kollmann, *Kinship and Politics*, 155–59; idem, "The Boyar Clan and Court Politics," *Cahiers du Monde Russe et Sovietique* 23 (1982): 5–31; Martin, *Medieval Russia*, 236–48; Gustave Alef, "The Crisis of the Muscovite Aristocracy," *FzOG* 15 (1970): 15–58; Crummey, *Formation of Muscovy*, 109–14. Cf. n. 136 *supra* on Capetian and Tran changes.

to take service at Moscow and assimilate to a unified imperial hierarchy. Key to controlling the provinces were *namestniki* – "governors" or "lieutenants" – a few of whom were local princes but who were usually Moscow courtiers sent to supervise local defense, justice, and taxes. Appearing in the 14th century, *namestniki* enjoyed a more modest status than the august princely viceroys of pre-1620 Burma and Siam. Yet as plenipotentiaries who "fed" on the provincial population in lieu of salaries, who replaced local dynasts, and who at first were subject to rather nominal supervision, they resembled their Southeast Asian contemporaries. Moreover, like Burmese and Siamese governors at a later date, from the late 1400s *namestniki* began to face more effective curbs on jurisdiction and tenure.[240] Between 1460 and 1530 much of their fiscal authority was transferred to local landlords. Thereafter to 1580, in order to improve criminal and revenue administration, Moscow eliminated most *namestniki* in favor of variegated provincial regimes that included appointees responsible for specific taxes, elected boards, and military governors (*voevody*) whose deputies – unlike those of the early *namestniki* – the capital itself appointed. Eventually military governors would dominate all of the provinces.[241]

With the reduction of princely and provincial rivals, the Muscovite court grew larger and more hierarchical. Through the early 1400s the Grand Prince functioned as *primus inter pares* among leading nobles who kept private military retinues and who, in theory, could leave Moscow for other principalities. By the late 1400s these privileges had ended. A system of status regulation (*mestnichestvo*) for high-ranking servicemen and courtly rituals of self-abasement unusually intense by European (though not Southeast Asian) standards sought to elevate

---

[240] Cf. *SP*, 154–64, 271–72, 275–80.

[241] Comparable to *namestniki* but governing smaller rural communities were so-called *volosteli*. My discussion of the evolving relation between the Muscovite throne and provincial elites relies on Pavlov and Perrie, *Ivan*, 73–77, 199–200; Brian Davies, "The Town Governors in the Reign of Ivan IV," *RH* 14 (1987): 77–143; Crummey, *Formation of Muscovy*, ch. 4; Gustave Alef, *Rulers and Nobles in Fifteenth-Century Muscovy* (London, 1983); Kollmann, "Russia," 761–62; idem, *Kinship and Politics*; idem, *Honor Bound*, Introduction and chs. 4, 5; idem, "Muscovite Russia," 27–54; Edward L. Keenan, "Muscovite Political Folkways," *RR* 45 (1986): 115–81; Hellie, *Enserfment*, 21–74, 267–73; Dewey, "Immunities"; idem, "Decline of *Namestnik*"; idem, "1497 *Sudebnik*"; idem, "1550 Sudebnik"; Janet Martin, "Muscovite Frontier Policy," *RH* 19 (1992): 169–80; Daniel Rowland, "Did Muscovite Literary Ideology Place Limits on the Power of the Tsar (1540s-1660s)?" *RR* 49 (1990): 125–55; Michael S. Flier, "The Iconography of Royal Ritual in Sixteenth-Century Muscovy," in Speros Vyronis, Jr., ed., *Byzantine Studies: Essays on the Slavic World and the Eleventh Century* (New Rochelle, NY, 1992), 53–76.

the Grand Prince. How shall we explain these changes? In part, as in Southeast Asia, growing hierarchy reflected the stark disproportionality between royal and noble resources: with land and trade increasingly state monopolies, with few opportunities for private accumulation in the still backward economy, and with noble – though, pointedly, not royal – lands subject to partible inheritance, royal largesse became a critical determinant of elite fortunes.[242] In part too, these changes, like acceptance of royal primogeniture, expressed an evolving, voluntary consensus. Both constant foreign wars and the 15th-century civil war, which saw spectacular *boyar* defections, argued that if self-lacerating factionalism were to be contained and the system on which they all depended were to survive, nobles would have to accept that the ruler, in theory, was all powerful. Like service to God, service to the ruler became a source of clan and personal pride. Yet *boyars* expected that the Grand Prince would continue to consult them. Far from being incompatible, *boyar* and royal power thus became mutually constitutive, as suggested by the simultaneous growth of the state and of great agnatic noble clans, most of which arose only in the 1400s and 1500s.[243]

As Moscow's military requirements and territory expanded, central agencies had to process an unprecedented flow of written communications, including military pay registers, muster records, land cadastres, and legal documents. Although noble culture remained basically illiterate, from the late 1400s Moscow was able to recruit priests' sons, elite slaves, and merchants to serve as scribes. The "paper revolution" that transformed West European archives from the late 1200s now having reached Russia, the court of Ivan IV (r. 1533–1584) completed the formation of chancelleries focusing on military, financial, and foreign affairs. This was a well compensated, increasingly specialized apparatus whose members were distinctly nonnoble, hence apolitical. Although its size would grow dramatically, until Peter the Great (r. 1682–1725) central administration retained the basic organizational structure of Ivan IV's reign.[244]

[242] Cf. Kollmann, *Honor Bound*, 17, 146; Alef, *Rulers and Nobles*. See too Ostrowski, *Muscovy and Mongols*, 47–48, 104–106, arguing that *mestnichestvo* derived from Mongol-Tatar usages.

[243] Kollmann, *Kinship and Politics*.

[244] Peter Brown, "Muscovite Government Bureaus," *RH* 10 (1983): 269–330, esp. 270–71; Crummey, *Formation of Muscovy*, 106, 150–51; Poe, "Military Revolution," 247–73; idem, "Muscovite Personnel Records, 1475–1550," *JfGO* 45 (1997): 361–77; Hellie, "Russia, 1200–1815," 487–92. The mid-1500s also saw judicial duels and oaths yield to more evidentiary-based systems of judicial inquiry and testimony.

Also reflecting military pressures, but far more numerous and influential than scribes, was a new "middle service class" of provincial cavalrymen.[245] Grand Princely armies traditionally were composed of the prince's own retainers together with the private retinues of princes and nobles, but by the late 1400s these forces, with their divided commands, had proven insufficiently reliable or numerous. Influenced perhaps by Tatar and Muslim precedents,[246] Ivan III created cavalry communities more closely tied to the throne by settling warriors from diverse backgrounds on confiscated tracts that functioned, most scholars believe, as lands (*pomest'e*) held on condition of service rather than as allods with absolute ownership. During the economic upturn, *pomest'e* estates spread throughout Muscovy until by 1570 their holders numbered some 17,500. Supplemented by a similar number of allod-based horsemen and frontier auxiliaries, this permitted a huge increase over mid-1400 cavalry levels and a distinct advantage over Lithuania's more decentralized military system.[247]

In key respects *pomest'e* organization resembled the Burmese *ahmu-dan* system that also cohered in the 15th to 17th centuries. In the more monetized economy of France by this time vassalic military obligations had lost all significance. But in Muscovy as in Burma, still limited monetization required that, in lieu of salaries, the throne award hereditary military personnel specified lands in return for service. And in both Burma and Russia, by assuming responsibility for local taxes and justice, the new servicemen, acting as a hinge between appointed governors and the peasantry, became major props to royal authority in the countryside.[248]

Indeed, the founding of *pomest'e* communities was part of a more general strategy of enlisting local solidarities. It is true that flat terrain and the Dvina, Volga, and Don provided Russia with better internal communications than any Southeast Asian realm. Without serious mountain

---

[245] The "upper service class" were capital nobles, whereas the "lower service class" were chiefly salaried soldiers without service lands. Hellie, *Enserfment*, 21–74, 267–73.

[246] According to Ostrowski, *Muscovy and Mongols*, 48–50, 59–61.

[247] *Pomest'e* referred to the land grant and *pomeshchik* to the recipient. Martin, *Medieval Russia*, 271; Hellie, *Enserfment*, 267; idem, "Structure of Russian Imperial History," 90–94; Kollmann, "Russia," 760–61. See too Donald Ostrowski, "Early *Pomest'e* Grants as a Historical Source," *Oxford Slavonic Papers* 33 (2000): 36–63, questioning the view that the *pomest'e* was distinct from hereditable private property.

[248] On Burma, *SP*, 153, 163; Victor Lieberman, *Burmese Administrative Cycles* (Princeton, 1984), 96–105. Without a service land component, the *phrai luang* system in Siam resembled the *pomest'e* system less closely.

barriers or a theory of multiple sovereignties comparable to *cakkavatti* ideology,[249] Muscovy never accorded tributary rulers anywhere near the prominence they enjoyed in Indic Southeast Asia. Nonetheless, by 1560 Muscovy already was 8 to 10 times larger than either the Burmese or Siamese empire, yet its total number of administrative personnel – central officials, chancellery people, governors and their deputies; merchants, peasants, and military servitors acting in an official capacity – may have been no greater than in these other realms, possibly in the order of 1,000–1,500.[250] Such realities, coupled with still inadequately monetized operations and a still substantially illiterate elite culture, obliged Moscow, like its Southeast Asian counterparts, to enlist whatever rural powers proved amenable. Moscow promised local elites full autonomy, protection against violence by its own armies and those of neighboring states, tax exemptions and commissions, help with controlling peasant labor, ritual honors, and in some cases, access to central offices. In return it demanded a reliable supply of warriors and taxes. Thus in the center and in the northwest private landlords (churches, monasteries, lay allodialists) joined *pomest'e*-holders in overseeing peasant taxes and suppressing brigands. Absent large landlords, in the far north self-governing communes of free tax-paying peasants assumed a similar role. In Baltic areas, Lithuanian nobles and German burghers retained corporate privileges. In the cities of central and northern Russia, merchant guilds supervised tolls and tavern taxes for the crown. Not surprisingly, taxes often were highly localized, and efforts at legal unification made only modest headway. In practice, even Moscow's claim to exclusive sovereignty coexisted with pockets of limited sovereignty, not only in surviving apanages but in quasi-independent Tatar and Lithuanian principalities and in the Stroganov family's vast Urals domain.[251]

Russian Cultural Integration to c. 1600

Alliance with the Orthodox church, whose Metropolitan, as noted, settled in Moscow in 1326, provided another critical aid to Russian

---

[249] *SP*, 154, 201, 261.

[250] Note 244 *supra*, plus Poe, pers. commun., Aug. 9, 2000 ("The total of all these "officials" [if that is the right word] could not have been much above 1000 or 1500 in 1550. But I'm only guessing."); and Hellie, pers. commun., March 2, 2006 ("Poe's guess may be about right, but perhaps it's a bit high.").

[251] Dewey, "Decline of *Namestnik*," 26; Kollmann, *Honor Bound*, 8–17; idem, "Muscovite Russia," 44; idem, "Russia," 748–70; Bushkovitch, *Merchants of Moscow*, 13–24; Davies, "Town Governors," 132–33.

consolidation. Beneficiaries of countless donations, monasteries by 1550 not only owned perhaps a third of Muscovy's populated land but directed major commercial ventures.[252] Although, as in Burma and Latin Europe, religious tax immunities generated periodic tensions with the crown,[253] on balance church support for the Daniilovichi proved invaluable in disputes with other Riurikid princes and in the physical defense of the capital.

Above all, from the mid-1400s church spokesmen began to create a novel ideological rationale for the monarchy that defined Muscovy as an Orthodox Christian bulwark in express opposition to Muslim Tatars and other non-Orthodox peoples. This trend was inspired by a combination of events, including Moscow's spectacular conquests, the disintegration of the Kipchak khanate, and perhaps most seminal, the fall of Constantinople in 1453. Insofar as Byzantium had maintained a pro-Kipchak policy, the Muscovite church was now free to dispense with Byzantine political concerns even as it idealized Byzantine culture and presented Muscovy as heir to that stricken empire. Thus from the mid-1400s anti-Tatar, anti-Muslim doctrines began to displace and mask Tatar legacies. Ironically this transition was made all the easier by the fact that in official culture, especially its religious aspect, as opposed to administrative and military affairs, the Tatars actually had only a limited impact: they neither propagated Islam nor persecuted Christians.[254] But according to the new ideology as elaborated in the 16th century, the Muslim "Tatar yoke" had been an unmitigated disaster, whereas everything of value in Rus came from Byzantium and Kiev. Like their blessed Kievan forbears whose realm they sought to reassemble, so long as they upheld Orthodoxy the Grand Princes of Moscow – from 1474 periodically termed "tsars," in imitation of the Byzantine title – were assured obedience within the realm and victory over heathens and heretics on the frontier. By 1552, in the

---

[252] Paul Bushkovitch, *Religion and Society in Russia: The Sixteenth and Seventeenth Centuries* (New York, 1992), 14; Langer, "Plague and Countryside," 351–68; Kollmann, "Muscovite Russia," 33, 46.

[253] Ostrowski, *Moscow and Mongols*, 227; Hellie, pers. commun., March 2, 2006. Such tensions led to the cancelling of certain church immunities and other privileges by the mid-1500s.

[254] Kollmann, "Cap of Monomakh," 40. Yet she emphasizes that Muscovy deliberately erased such Tatar legacies as had influenced royal self-presentation and regalia. Hellie, pers. commun., Feb. 28, 2006 also notes that Turks influenced Russian popular names and clothing, albeit at an uncertain date.

words of the Metropolitan, Moscow had become the "center of God's world."[255]

What effect did such claims have on vertical integration? Richard Wortman and Edward Keenan argue that the high nobility acknowledged few, if any, vertical bonds with the lower orders. Between 1400 and 1700 the upper service class, that is to say the *boyar* aristocracy, recruited heavily from Tatar, Polish-Lithuanian, and central European warriors, whose dress and customs, not to mention genes, flowed easily into the Muscovite court.[256] Often identifying more closely with fellow nobles at Tatar and Lithuanian courts than with their own peasantry, *boyars* proudly invoked foreign genealogies and images of power. Unlike late medieval claims that the French race *in toto* descended from the Trojans, Russian myths of Trojan descent separated princes from peasantry. Not surprisingly, Ivan IV boasted to envoys that he was no "Russe," but a "German" prince ruling an alien and inferior people.[257]

---

[255] Phrase from Kollmann, *Honor Bound*, 173. From 1505, moreover, Muscovy adopted the Byzantine Agapetos formula: "in his person, the ruler is a man, but in his authority he is like God." Hellie, pers. commun., March 2, 2006. Moscow began choosing prelates without Byzantine control from 1448 and obtained its own Patriarch in 1589. Though used occasionally from 1474, "tsar" became official in 1547. I follow Ostrowski, *Muscovy and Mongols*, which plays down the Third Rome doctrine, as does Daniel Rowland, "Moscow – The Third Rome or the New Israel?" *RR* 55 (1996): 591–614, arguing that Moscow saw a succession of chosen peoples from Israel to Rome to Byzantium to itself. But the literature on ideology is as contentious as it is vast. See Reisman, "Determinants," 339–61; Pavlov and Perrie, *Ivan*, 15–18, 33–36, 49–53; Martin, *Medieval Russia*, 192–98, 224–66, 338–40; John Fennell, *A History of the Russian Church to 1448* (London, 1995), ch. 17; Michael Cherniavsky, "Ivan the Terrible and the Iconography of the Kremlin Cathedral of Archangel Michael," *RH* 2 (1975): 3–28; Jaroslaw Pelenski, "The Origins of the Official Muscovite Claims to the Kievan Inheritance," *HUS* 1 (1977): 29–52; Marc Szeftel, "The Title of the Muscovite Monarch up to the End of the 17th Century," *CASS* 13 (1979): 59–81; Gustave Alef, "The Adoption of the Muscovite Two-Headed Eagle," *Speculum* 41 (1966): 1–21; Michael Flier, "Till the End of Time," in Valerie Kivelson and Robert Greene, eds., *Orthodox Russia* (University Park, PA, 2003), 127–58; idem, "The Throne of Monomakh," in James Cracraft and Daniel Rowland, eds., *Architectures of Russian Identity 1500 to the Present* (Ithaca, 2003), 21–33; idem, "Iconography of Royal Ritual." The Kipchak khanate, against which the church defined itself, converted to Islam in the early 1300s.

[256] By one calculation, Muscovite aristocrats whose names indicated an indigenous Rus origin were barely 23 percent. Ostrowski, *Muscovy and Mongols*, 56–58. Also Pipes, *Russia Under the Old Regime*, 182; Kollmann, *Honor Bound*, 9–10; Richard Hellie, *The Economy and Material Culture of Russia 1600–1725* (Chicago, 1999), 385–86; Hellie, pers. commun., March 2, 2006.

[257] Richard Wortman, *Scenarios of Power: Myth and Ceremony in Russian Monarchy*, vol. I (Princeton, 1995), 14, 26. "German" probably should be glossed as "Viking descended." See too ibid., 5–6, 22–30; Edward Keenan, "Royal Russian Behavior,

Yet it is also clear that before 1600 cultural differences between secular elites and the general populace were more modest than they would
become in the 1700s, and that aristocratic solidarities coexisted, perhaps
uneasily, with powerful vertical affiliations. Despite numerous grada-
tions in status and wealth, throughout central Muscovy all nobles and
peasants spoke Old Russian or Middle Russian, were basically illiterate, and considered themselves Orthodox Christians. If we can project
early- and mid-17th-century patterns to the mid- and late 1500s, the
line between elite and popular culture remained nebulous and permeable: *boyars* consulted folk healers, and even high clergy participated
in rituals of popular origin. Claims to cross-class religious unity and
inclusive moral hierarchy became central to tsarist ideology, as seen
in 16th-century tsarist art and architecture (critical to communicating
ideas in lieu of writing); in royal ceremonies invoking God's blessing
on the entire Orthodox community, great and small; and in traditions
of tsarist consultation not only with *boyars* but, in some contexts, with
leaders of the people at large.[258]

By extension, Muscovites instinctively used religion, and to a lesser
extent language, to define themselves vis-à-vis enemies to the west,
east, and south. Those Catholic Livonian and Tatar Muslim prisoners, even common soldiers, who accepted Orthodoxy often were freed,
much as Catholic and Muslim emigres at court were expected not only
to Russify their names, but to accept Orthodox baptism.[259] According

---

Style, and Self-Image," in Edward Allworth, ed., *Ethnic Russia in the USSR* (New York,
1981), 3–15. Cf. Beaune, *Birth of an Ideology*, 198–99, 226–44, 333–38, showing how the
Trojan myth blessed "everyone [in France] – nobles and non-nobles alike . . . with the
same pure and illustrious blood" (p. 226).

[258] For evidence of vertical Orthodox solidarities, Valerie Kivelson, "Muscovite 'Citizenship': Rights without Freedom," *JMH* 74 (2002): 465–89; idem, "Patrolling the Boundaries," *HUS* 29 (1995): 302–23; idem, "Merciful Father, Impersonal State"; idem, "'The
Souls of the Righteous in a Bright Place,'" *RR* 58 (1999): 1–25; Eve Levin, "Supplicatory
Prayers as a Source for Popular Religious Culture in Muscovite Russia," in Samuel H.
Baron and Nancy Shields Kollmann, eds., *Religion and Culture in Early Modern Russia
and Ukraine* (DeKalb, IL, 1997), 96–114; Paul Bushkovitch, "The Epiphany Ceremony of
the Russian Court in the 16th and 17th Centuries," *RR* 49 (1990): 1–18; George Weick-
hardt, "Political Thought in 17th-Century Russia," *RH* 21 (1994): 316–37; Rowland,
"Did Russian Literary Ideology Place Limits on the Tsar?" 125–55; idem, "Moscow
– Third Rome or New Israel?"; idem, "Two Cultures, One Throne Room," in Kivelson, *Orthodox Russia*, 33–57; Michael Flier, "Church of the Intercession on the Moat/
St. Basil's Cathedral," in Kivelson and Neuberger, *Picturing Russia*, 42–46; Flier, "Till
the End."

[259] Ostrowski, *Muscovy and Mongols*, 21, 55–58; W. M. Reger, "Baptizing Mars," in Lohr
and Poe, *Military and Society*, 389–412; Kollmann, *Honor Bound*, 9–10; Janet Martin,

to church-based accounts, on attacking "Godless and cursed Kazan," Ivan IV urged his forces to die "for our Orthodox faith" against "infidels and enemies of Christ."[260] Sixteenth-century nonecclesiastical sources, reflective of elite lay opinion, also emphasized the state's theological raison d'être and the principled opposition between the entire Orthodox community and the enemies of God, namely Catholics, Lutherans, Muslims, Jews, and pagans.[261]

To what degree did peasants share the outlook of royal officials and churchmen? The starting point must be Kaiser's aforementioned observation that until the 14th century, Christian legal, ritual, and social systems had minimal impact outside the towns of Rus.

Thereafter three developments eroded rural encapsulation. First, a network of religious institutions, once exclusively urban, spread across the countryside. Between 1350 and 1450 princely patronage, Greek

"Mobility, Forced Resettlement and Regional Identity in Muscovy," in Kleimola and Lenhoff, *Culture and Identity*, 442–43; Reisman, "Determinants," 358–67; Crummey, *Formation of Muscovy*, 86–87; Kollmann, "Russia," 758; Michael Khodarkovsky, "Ignoble Savages and Unfaithful Subjects," in Daniel Brower and Edward Lazzerini, eds., *Russia's Orient* (Bloomington, IN, 1997), 9–26; idem, "Not By Word Alone," *CSSH* 38 (1996): 267–75; idem, "Four Degrees of Separation," in Kleimola and Lenhoff, *Culture and Identity*, 261–64, the latter emphasizing the very different prospects of noble and nonnoble converts. But on postconversion barriers to assimilation, see Janet Martin, "The Novokshcheny of Novgorod," *Central Asian Survey* 19 (1990): 13–38; idem, "Tatars in the Livonian Army During the Livonian War," in Lohr and Poe, *Military and Society*, 365–87.

[260] See Paul Bushkovitch, "The Formation of a National Consciousness in Early Modern Russia," *HUS* 10 (1986): 366–67, 370; Khodarkovsky, *Steppe Frontier*, 35; Jaroslaw Pelenski, *Russia and Kazan: Conquest and Imperial Ideology (1438–1560s)* (The Hague, 1974); Rowland, "Moscow – Third Rome or New Israel?," 607–608; idem, "Blessed Is the Host of the Heavenly Tsar," in Kivelson and Neuberger, *Picturing Russia*, 33–37. Perdue, *China Marches West*, 81–83, following Edward Keenan, suggest that these accounts reflected an ideology that developed only after Kazan fell, but several sources in this note and n. 261 *infra* indicate much earlier origins.

[261] Sergei Bogatyrev, "Battle for Divine Wisdom," in Lohr and Poe, *Military and Society*, 325–63; the late-16th-century *Stroganov Chronicle* quoted in Peter Turchin, *War and Peace and War* (New York, 2006), 17–21; Pavlov and Perrie, *Ivan*, 51–52. This emphasis on the interpenetration of literate ecclesiastical and largely illiterate secular elite cultures in the mid-1500s departs somewhat from Ostrowski, *Muscovy and Mongols*, and yet more emphatically from Edward Keenan's two-culture theory, as in Keenan's "Response to Halperin," *JfGO* 46 (1998): 404–18, esp. 413–14. On the other hand, it is consistent with Khodarkovsky's work, with Pelenski, *Russia and Kazan*, 291 *et passim*; and most sources in n. 259 *supra*. Religious rhetoric aside, note that in practice Muslim resistance, strategic calculations, and the notion that all social groups, even non-Orthodox, had claims to tsarist protection produced a fluid array of transconfessional accommodations. See Khodarkovsky, "Four Degrees," 257–64; idem, *Steppe Frontier*, 114–17, 190–91; and Kivelson, "Muscovite Citizenship," 473–74.

inspiration, and local initiatives combined to found some 150 rural monasteries, which by recruiting peasant monks and disseminating Christian norms outside monastery walls provided a beachhead for folk Christianity.[262] After monastic influence waned in the late 15th century, the Metropolitan and bishops worked with local communities, or perhaps one should say, with cooperative local elites, to fill the gap by promoting the building of parish churches. As late as 1400, V. G. Vlasov argues, there were virtually no churches for the peasantry. Thereafter we find a gradual proliferation of such edifices sporting the so-called "hipped roof," which may have derived from pagan temples and which, in Vlasov's view, testified to the relative novelty of rural Christianity.[263] Although in contrast to Theravada monasteries, Muscovite churches did not teach peasant literacy, which in consequence remained very limited,[264] icons and ritual complexes opened new spiritual and symbolic perspectives. The ensuing dissemination of elite doctrines, however partial, however subject to local variation, paralleled the transformation of Theravada Buddhism into a genuinely peasant religion in 15th- and 16th-century Southeast Asia, the more limited rural proliferation of Neo-Confucian academies in post-1450 Vietnam, and, as we shall see, the dissemination of normative Catholicism in Counter-Reformation France.

Second, although less easily demonstrated, economic and demographic growth must have promoted elite and supralocal norms by drawing peasants to markets and fairs, by thickening intervillage contacts, and by swelling the number of itinerant traders, entertainers, and minstrels.[265] Insofar as it depended on denser, wealthier communities, church construction itself testified to a measure of rural prosperity.

Third, both intentionally and unintentionally, diverse state actions promoted central elite norms. As tsarist courts and chanceries extended

---

[262] Bushkovitch, *Religion*, 11–19; Martin, *Medieval Russia*, 224–25; Kivelson, pers. commun., July 30, 2003.

[263] V. G. Vlasov, "The Christianization of the Russian Peasants," in Balzer, *Russian Traditional Culture*, 16–33, citing N. M. Nikol'skii. See too T. A. Bernshtam, "Russian Folk Culture and Folk Religion," ibid., 34–47; Levin, "Supplicatory Prayers"; Kollmann, "Muscovite Russia," 37–40; Bushkovitch, *Religion*, 19–20; Fennell, *Russian Church*, 89–90; Eve Levin, "*Dvoeverie* and Popular Religion," in Stephen Batalden, ed., *Seeking God* (DeKalb, IL, 1993), 31–52.

[264] Probably well below 3 percent, judging from the 1600s. Gary Marker, "Literacy and Literary Texts in Muscovy: A Reconsideration," *SR* 49 (1990): 89.

[265] See Russell Zguta, *Russian Minstrels* (Philadelphia, 1978), chs. 2, 3; Dukes, *Making of Russian Absolutism*, 27; and previous notes on 16th-century trade.

their writ, rural landholders and peasants were obliged to come to terms with notions of non-kin hierarchy, written reports, and routinized procedure. Ad hoc consultative bodies known as "Assemblies of the Land" allowed the tsar to communicate directly with provincial *pomest'e*-holders, merchants, even free peasants, and gave physical expression to the "God-dependent" community that was central to Muscovite self-image. Petitions to the tsar from servitors and urban estates provided another channel of center–periphery as well as vertical exchange. Much the same may be said of rituals that engaged commoners and provincial landholders beyond the confines of the Kremlin: royal pilgrimages, entries into outlying cities, and alms distributions to provincial poor. By transforming the Kremlin into a magnificent architecture assemblage and by founding provincial churches on Kremlin models, Muscovite rulers worked to implant visual images of their authority. The 16th-century court also sought to create sacral links to the provinces by venerating miracle-working icons from the hinterlands, by working to standardize liturgy, and by promoting the canonization and unification of provincial saints in what was in effect a kingdom-specific pantheon reminiscent of those in France, Burma, and Vietnam. As in Burma and Siam, moreover, the regular rotation from the provinces to the capital of hundreds of military servicemen (*vybornye dvoriane*) and the substitution of imperial service categories for regional designations worked to implant a standardized imperial ethos. Intentionally or not, large-scale deportations and *pomest'e* resettlement also must have eroded local attachments.[266]

Evidence that these combined pressures modified the religious culture of peasants and resident rural landholders lies not only in the proliferation of rural churches, but in the disappearance of pre-Christian mound (*kurgan*) burials, the growth of peasant miracle cults, the novel prominence of rural clergy, and rural acceptance of the Julian church

---

[266] On the homogenizing potential of state actions, Dunning, *Short History*, 24 (cf. *SP*, 192–93; 317–18); Hellie, *Economy and Material Culture*, 638, 642; Pavlov and Perrie, *Ivan*, 198–99; Ann Kleimola, "Justice in Medieval Russia," in Daniel Kaiser and Gary Marker, eds., *Reinterpreting Russian History* (New York, 1994), 117–22; Kaiser, *Law*, chs. 4–6; Crummey, *Formation of Muscovy*, 106; Bushkovitch, *Religion*, 22, 74–89; Kollmann, *Honor Bound*, 12–16, 186–202; idem, "Russia," 766–67; Dewey, "1550 Sudebnik"; Martin, "Mobility, Forced Resettlement," 431–49; Noonan, "Forging a National Identity," focusing on the pre-1425 era; Rowland, "Two Cultures," 33–57; and n. 258 *supra*. On kingdom-specific pantheons in France, Burma, and Vietnam, nn. 139 *supra*, 332 *infra*, and *SP*, 116, 192, 357–58.

calendar, which in turn regulated popular festivals. The 16th century also saw the early triumph among peasants of the Christian naming system.[267] Popular exposure to elite norms is suggested too by the impressive erudition of some rural priests and by the reliance of popular prayers on official sources. In the same vein, Michael Flier argues, from the late 1400s apocalyptic concerns, hitherto an elite affair, began to enter popular consciousness, albeit in part because notions of the Resurrection harmonized with pre-Christian ancestor cults.[268] Admittedly, church attendance was still infrequent, many peasants remained innocent of rudimentary Orthodox notions, and recognizably pagan elements persisted for centuries.[269] Still, as in Burma, Siam, and Dai Viet, so in Russia it is reasonable to argue that culture was far more vertically connected in 1600 than in 1300. The same Orthodox worldview, the same resolutely Christian self-identification, albeit with important variations in vocabulary and sophistication, influenced all classes.[270]

Horizontal culture showed similar integrative tendencies. True, legal and administrative usages continued to distinguish once independent principalities from one another.[271] But over the long term, differences between the heartland and outer areas eroded as military servitors merged into a unified hierarchy, defined in its upper reaches by the *mestnichestvo* system of rankings; as standardizing administrative and liturgical reforms began to take hold; and as servitors sought to internalize and reproduce linguistic and cultural norms from the Muscovite court.[272] At a lower social level, horizontal exchange drew strength not only from aforementioned state actions but from the cumulative entry of Muscovite settlers, traders, and priests into frontier districts and from

---

[267] Daniel H. Kaiser, "Quotidian Orthodoxy in Muscovite Family Life" (ms, 1999); idem, "The Seasonality of Family Life in Early Modern Russia," *FzOG* 46 (1992): 21–50; Vlasov, "Christianization"; Bushkovitch, *Religion*, 31, 50, 74–127.

[268] Flier, "Till the End," 146–52.

[269] In the 1660s archpriest Avvakum detailed the persistence of numerous pagan practices. Previous note, plus R. E. F. Smith, *Bread and Salt* (Cambridge, 1984), 6, 95–97; Hellie, pers. commun., Feb. 28, 2006.

[270] Cf. Valerie Kivelson, "The Devil Stole His Mind," *AHR* 98 (1993): 734, referring to 1648; Kivelson, pers. commun., 2007.

[271] So too, some Muslim converts and even relocated Russian servitors and townsmen continued to identify themselves by regional origins. Martin, "Mobility, Forced Resettlement"; idem, "Novokshcheny of Novgorod."

[272] See, e.g., Pavlov and Perrie, *Ivan*, 68–71; Martin, "Muscovy's Northeast Expansion," 462, 464.

the ensuing inclination of hitherto pagan Finnic and Baltic peoples to accept elements of Russian religion and culture.[273]

The political benefits for Moscow of cultural integration were considerable. Without embracing Slavophile clichés, one can accept that identification with the imperial court made it an irresistible magnet for ambitious elites and accorded tsarist tax and conscription demands an intrinsic legitimacy. As Moscow – now the only major Orthodox land not controlled by infidels – expanded in all directions, provincial servicemen, townsmen, and peasants alike began to imbibe, however imperfectly, tsarist claims that Moscow had become the New Jerusalem and Muscovites, God's new Chosen People (thus duplicating, independently apparently, claims made on behalf of the French as early as the Capetian period). Victories, real and imagined, over Muslims inspired a profusion of popular miracle cults, songs, and folklore.[274] Along with incantations and legal petitions, such sources suggest that by the late 1500s people of diverse statuses in a region extending from the Arctic Ocean to the Caspian Sea and from the borders of Poland-Lithuania to the Volga basin thought of themselves as part of a politicoreligious community that was rigidly hierarchical but in which, Valerie Kivelson has shown, all groups had secure legal rights, as well as duties, acknowledged by the throne. Many regarded the tsar with cult-like veneration, believing that their salvation – and perhaps that of the world – depended on the tsar's piety.[275] During the Time of Troubles (1598–1613), when the Daniilovich Dynasty collapsed, apocalyptic fears joined anti-Polish, anti-Catholic xenophobia to inspire, we shall see, a broadly based, popularly assisted royal revival in the name of Orthodoxy.

---

[273] Hellie, "Russia, 1200–1815," 483; Martin, *Medieval Russia*, 226–27; Crummey, *Formation of Muscovy*, 121; Khodarkovsky, *Steppe Frontier*, 190; A. V. Chernetsov, "The Crosier of St. Stefan or Perm," in Kivelson and Neuberger, *Picturing Russia*, 21–27.

[274] Flier, "Till the End," 128, 154–58; idem, "Church of the Intercession"; Dunning, *Short History*, 81; Bushkovitch, *Religion*, 111–13; Maureen Perrie, *The Image of Ivan the Terrible in Russian Folklore* (Cambridge, 1987), 66–72, 181–88; Pavlov and Perrie, *Ivan*, 51; Rowland, "Moscow – Third Rome or New Israel?"; idem, "Two Cultures."

[275] Writing of a slightly later period, Kivelson, "Muscovite Citizenship," 465–89; idem, "Bitter Slavery and Pious Servitude," in Robert Crummey et al., eds., *Russische und Ukrainische Geschichte vom 16.–18. Jahrhundert* (Wiesbaden, 2001), 110–19. Cf. Dunning, *Short History*, 79–82, 302; Marshall Poe, "*A People Born to Slavery*": Russia in Early Modern European Ethnography, 1476-1748 (Ithaca, 2000).

In sum, of the six elements that were simultaneously cause and symptom of Muscovite expansion from 1300 to 1600 – Mongol-Tatar patronage, Mongol-Tatar disintegration, economic growth, firearms, political innovation, and growing religious-cum-cultural unity – the last five became particularly prominent from the second half of the 15th century. Which factors, then, were most influential? Wherein lay the basic sources of dynamism?

However critical a precondition for Russian centralization nomad intervention may have been, by 1450 the Tatars no longer exercised a major constraint on Russian politics. In itself, therefore, Tatar decline cannot easily explain the rapid acceleration of Russian power *after* 1450, all the more so as that expansion was directed westward as much as against the steppe. On the other hand, before 1550, although their potential is apparent in hindsight, firearms made only a modest contribution to an already remarkably successful program of territorial expansion. If Mongol influence peaked too early and guns appeared too late to explain Moscow's takeoff, the insistent creativity of the court merits attention. Changes began in the 14th century, received a major boost from the 1425–1453 civil wars, and gathered strength thereafter. Yet without sustained economic growth after 1450, I think it unlikely that *pomest'e* expansion, tax reforms, and fortress construction could have continued. Economic growth aided reform directly, by boosting state resources, and indirectly, by raising the cost of warfare, the intensity of interstate competition, and the need for administrative and fiscal experiment. At the same time, by strengthening the central apparatus, encouraging the circulation of goods and people, and expanding local wealth, economic growth promoted the spread of Christian and tsarist motifs.

A further tantalizing question for those seeking ultimate causes: Did Tatar decline, Russian economic expansion, and 15th-century changes in court organization all depend to a significant degree on the Black Death? I have noted that the plague seems to have inflicted on the Tatars disproportionate demographic and political damage, while Gustave Alef, Lawrence Langer, and others have suggested that Russian recovery from the same devastation underlay the growth in population and tillage after 1450. Alef has also argued that the plague helped Muscovite political reform in two ways: a) By pruning the dynasty from 1350 to 1450, it allowed Daniilovich primogeniture to take hold. b) Demographic recovery after 1450 combined with partible inheritance to render noble families more economically dependent on Moscow.[276] But Kollmann has questioned noble economic dependence,[277] and the Black Death alone can explain neither economic correlations with Southeast Asia, which apparently escaped the plague, nor the sustained nature of Russian growth during most of the 1500s. On the other hand, insofar as parts of China and Southeast Asia also recovered from brutal 14th-to 15th-century population losses (if not to the Black Death, then to warfare and other epidemics), while post-1450 Chinese and Southeast Asian demand stimulated trade between those regions and throughout the Indian Ocean, global demographic shifts may help to explain Russian–Southeast Asian correlations.[278]

Muscovite Crisis and Disintegration, c. 1560–1613

Mainland Southeast Asia's principal empires collapsed between 1568 and 1613 in large part because they were overextended and exercised weak control over outlying principalities. Aided by foreign armies, tributary and provincial revolts placed insupportable tax and service burdens on imperial cores, where – most clearly in Burma – ever more peasants sought to escape their obligations to the throne. By stoking price inflation and causing the number of elite claimants for government posts to rise more rapidly than the number of such posts, 16th-century population growth magnified these tensions. Between 1580 and 1610 the mainland also endured severe droughts and famines as a result of hemispheric cooling and heightened El Nino activity. External invasion, frontier revolt, and debility in the core fed on one another to the point of utter desolation. Yet most clearly in Burma and Siam, collapse ushered in a new leadership whose early 17th-century reforms sought, more or less successfully, both to resurrect and to improve upon precrisis structures.[279]

Allowing for obvious differences in institutions and scale, a similar tale of overexuberant expansion, taxpayer flight, revolt on the imperial

---

[276] Alef, *Rulers and Nobles*, esp. his essays "The Crisis of the Muscovite Aristocracy," "Muscovite Military Reforms in the Second Half of the 15th Century," and "Aristocratic Politics and Royal Policy in Muscovy in the Late 15th and Early 16th Centuries." On the Black Death's effects, see too nn. 159–61 *supra*.

[277] Kollmann, *Kinship and Politics*, 39.

[278] See Chs. 5, 7 *infra*.

[279] Post-1600 Dai Viet, however, failed to contain southern centrifugalism. See *SP*, 154–64, 274–82, 394–400.

periphery, foreign invasion, dynastic collapse, and political restoration captured Muscovy's fate between 1560 and 1613. In Muscovy as in Toungoo Burma and Dai Viet, the earliest, many would argue most basic, problem was territorial overextension. In 1558 Ivan IV sought to widen access to Baltic trade by capturing Livonia, corresponding roughly to modern Estonia and Lithuania, but Russian forces were stymied by the technical superiority of Polish-Lithuanian and Swedish armies. Dragging on to 1583, these campaigns imposed crushing tax and corvée demands on the peasantry and weakened the Muscovite core. As in Southeast Asia, strong population growth ironically may have aggravated vulnerabilities by swelling the ranks of frustrated elites seeking offices and by combining with bullion imports to erode the value of government income through price inflation.[280] A psychopath acknowledging neither institutional nor religious restraints, Ivan IV spawned a terrorist regime, the *oprichnina*, whose arbitrary depredations further burdened the economy.[281] In order to maintain themselves and to meet their obligations to the government, *pomest'e*-holders began to squeeze ever harder those peasants tilling their land. But as in Southeast Asia, peasants responded by resisting passively, becoming private slaves, or fleeing to the frontier, in this case the newly opened steppe, where rich soils and the absence of landlords were powerful magnets. Government efforts to stabilize the situation by restricting movement among peasants and urban taxpayers had little success. As early as the 1580s only 17 percent of arable land around Moscow was being cultivated, and the capital was collecting less than 7 percent of normal urban revenues

---

[280] Dunning, "Preconditions," 124–28; idem, *Short History*, 12, adapting models of state breakdown developed in Goldstone, *Revolution and Rebellion*. On 16th-century price inflation, which probably reflected both rising bullion imports and the fact that rising local exchange velocities outpaced increases in local productivity, see Hellie, "Russia, 1200–1815," 494; Munro, "Precious Metals," 35–50; Crummey, "Muscovy and the General Crisis," 167–68; Blum, "Prices in Russia"; Dunning, *Short History*, 8, 11–13; Bushkovitch, *Merchants of Moscow*, 52, 54. Cf. Fischer, *Great Wave*, 65–91; *SP*, 157, 276–77, 395.

[281] Interpretations of the *oprichnina* fall into four categories: a) those stressing the tsar's paranoid psychosis; b) those stressing genuine threats to Ivan's position, whether by the boyar elite, apanage princes, Novgorod, or the church; c) those combining the first two explanations; d) Ostrowski's theory that the *oprichnina* reflected unresolved tension between Byzantine and Tatar cultural traditions. See Richard Hellie, "What Happened? How Did He Get Away with It? Ivan Groznyi's Paranoia and the Problem of Institutional Restraints," *RH* 14 (1987): 199–224; Pavlov and Perrie, *Ivan*, 107–68, esp. 118–25; Dunning, *Short History*, 28–39; Ostrowski, *Muscovy and Mongols*, 189–98.

from the northwest.[282] Severely compounding these difficulties, exceptionally cold, wet weather in the early 1570s, 1588, and 1601 to 1603 – part of the same dramatic climatic shift as afflicted Southeast Asia and most of Europe – produced horrendous famines that in 1601 to 1603 alone may have claimed a third of the Russian population.[283]

After the death of the last Daniilovich ruler in 1598 followed by that of his brother-in-law and successor in 1605, the economic crisis fused with an unprecedented political crisis. With the extinction of the sacred dynasty, no other source of legitimacy was readily available. Pretenders claiming to be Ivan IV's son[284] succeeded only in stoking factional and regional strife. In 1606, united by resentment of tsarist demands, an array of southern frontier peoples – fugitive peasants, Cossacks, non-Russian minorities (Tatars, Mordva, Chuvash) – launched the first steppe revolt in Russian history. As in Southeast Asia, precisely because newly acquired frontier regions were least well integrated into the emerging state, they were first to explode. Finally, again in familiar fashion, paralysis in the core invited foreign invasion, in this case by the Poles, who occupied Moscow from 1610 to 1612, and by Swedes, who seized much of the northwest. Some doubted Russia would survive as an independent state. Aptly, the anarchy of 1598 to 1613 is known as the Time of Troubles.[285]

Yet as in Burma and Siam, the shock of foreign occupation stimulated effective remedies in a political and cultural system whose inherent strength was by no means exhausted. The Time of Troubles, one might say, was more purgative than toxic. Accordingly, as in western and central mainland Southeast Asia, the collapse of the late 1500s proved

---

[282] Blum, *Lord and Peasant*, 153; Martin, *Medieval Russia*, 370. On 1580–1613, see esp. Pavlov and Perrie, Ivan; Dunning, *Short History*; Hellie, *Enserfment*, ch. 5; Crummey, *Formation of Muscovy*, ch. 8; idem, " The Reconstitution of the Boiar Aristocracy, 1613–1645," *FzOG* 18 (1973): 187–220; S. F. Platonov, *Ivan the Terrible* (Gulf Breeze, FL, 1986), esp. Richard Hellie's introduction.

[283] Dunning, *Short History*, 11–13, 35, 43, 68–73, with fatality estimates; C. Pfister and R. Brazdil, "Climatic Variability in 16th-Century Europe and Its Social Dimensions," *CC* 43 (1999): 5–53; *SP*, 156–57; Briffa et al., "Unusual 20th-Century Summer Warmth"; V. Kozlov and M. Kisternaya, "Architectural Wooden Monuments as a Source of Information for Past Environmental Changes in Northern Russia," *PPP* 209 (2004): 103–11.

[284] However, Dunning, *Short History*, ch. 8 treats seriously the first Dmitrii's claims.

[285] The Time of Troubles has also been dated, more broadly, 1582–1619, and more narrowly, 1605–1613. The Union of Lublin in 1569 between Poland and Lithuania led to Polish ascendancy, and it was Polish forces that led the invasion of Muscovy.

to be far shorter and less disruptive than that of the 13th to 15th centuries. Particularly noteworthy was the fact that in contrast to the late Kievan era, the main frontier revolt, by the Cossack Bolotnikov, fed on deep-felt grievances but did not seek to secede from Muscovy. Indeed, some Cossacks eventually assisted the restoration of central authority. In 1612–1613 a broad-based resistance made up of high nobles, *pomest'e*-holders, Cossacks, churchmen, and townsmen succeeded in expelling the Poles and installing a government under Mikhail Romanov, member of a leading *boyar* family. The chief symbols of Russian identity remained religious: Catholic Poles were "accursed heretics," "who had abandoned the Christian faith" and against whom "Orthodox Christians in love and unity" now fought for their "Orthodox sovereign."[286] By instinct and social origins, the new dynasty therefore was profoundly conservative. But to restore order and forestall fresh external attacks, like its Burmese and Siamese counterparts, the new dynasty had to address the intertwined issues of peasant flight and military reform – to which we shall return.

Factors Promoting the Revival of France, c. 1450–1560

In the same period as Toungoo Burma, Ayudhya, and Dai Viet lay the foundations for imperial grandeur and Muscovy transformed itself from a modest post-Kievan contender into Europe's largest state and preeminent Orthodox power, France fled the terrors of the Hundred Years War to enter what French historians term the "beautiful 16th century," c. 1460–1560.[287]

The Hundred Years War itself provided the earliest spur to revival. After Burgundy in 1435 made peace with Charles VII (r. 1422–1461), the English lost their main ally and within 20 years had been expelled from all continental holdings apart from Calais. From the 1430s, revulsion at wartime devastation and Charles VII's improving fortunes inspired among parish clergy, townsmen, and at least some peasants in ever

---

[286] Dmytryshyn, *Medieval Russia*, 365–72; Serge Zenkovsky, *Medieval Russia's Epics, Chronicles, and Tales* (New York, 1963), 379–87; Kivelson, "Bitter Slavery," 117–18; idem, "Muscovite Citizenship," 471–72, 478–79. Also Geoffrey Hosking, *Russia: People and Empire 1552–1917* (Cambridge, MA, 1997), 62; Dunning, *Short History*, chs. 22, 23; Rowland, "Moscow – Third Rome or New Israel?," 605; Paul Avrich, *Russian Rebels 1600–1800* (New York, 1972), 10–47.

[287] Janine Garrisson, *A History of Sixteenth-Century France, 1483–1598* (London, 1995), 427; Goubert, *Course of French History*, ch. 5, focusing on 1494–1552.

wider regions an ardent identification with the French crown and its patron saints; in the 13th century such sentiments had been primarily the preserve of the high nobility and urban notables in the Paris basin. Building on earlier notions of commonwealth (*res publica*) and father-land (*communis patria*), Valois partisans gradually changed the war's rationale from dynastic right to promoting the security and honor of the French community, under its heaven-ordained king, against English outsiders.[288]

If enhanced royalist sentiment was the conflict's chief emotional legacy, its principal institutional gifts included regular taxation and a permanent army, both of which also reflected the developing ideol-ogy of "the common good." Although the old idea that the king should live off his own domain remained influential, early French defeats and uncontrolled brigandage led growing numbers to accept the notion that to defend the realm, the crown should be entitled to regular taxes even in peacetime. By 1380 the basic triumvirate of taxes that would last to 1790 – a direct tax (*taille*), levied on unprivileged persons in the north but on nonnoble land in the south; a salt tax (*gabelle*); and sales taxes (*aides*) – was in place, together with an expanded network of tax officials. Nonetheless, the crown's military weakness and bullion shortages made it impossible to operate the system effectively until the last years of the Hundred Years War. The creation between 1439 and 1445 of a standing cavalry force in the provinces, the so-called *compagnies d'ordonnances*, built upon changes introduced in the 1360s but followed much the same delayed chronology as tax reform, which was in fact designed to fund the army. Henceforth, at least in theory, the crown was the only body in France legally empowered to levy taxes.[289] In order to win the acquiescence of vocal elements for these and other initiatives and to bind localities more closely to the throne, Charles VII promoted a policy of strategic decentralization, creating sovereign courts outside of Paris and acknowledging the right of local representative bodies to approve

---

[288] Strayer, *Medieval Origins*, 90–91; Lewis, *Later Medieval France*, 59–77, 373–74, 380; idem, *Essays in Later Medieval French History*, 5–6; Allmand, *Hundred Years War*, 53, 136–50, 171; Potter, *History*, 177; idem, "Introduction," 5; Curry, "France and the Hundred Years War," 115–16.

[289] On 14th- to 15th-century tax and military reforms, Henneman, *Royal Taxation*, esp. ch. 8; Martin Wolfe, *The Fiscal System of Renaissance France* (New Haven, 1972), chs. 1, 2; Potter, "King and His Government," 172–78; James Collins, *Fiscal Limits of Absolutism* (Berkeley, 1988), 18–31; idem, *Tribes to Nation*, 162–70; Le Roy Ladurie, *Royal French State*, 60–66.

taxation. These basic military and judicial structures also survived well into the 17th century.[290] In short, the latter stage of the Hundred Years War produced a watershed in sentiment and governance no less decisive than the mid-15th-century civil war in Muscovy.

After the Hundred Years War, a second, more sustained spur to political recovery was the demographic-cum-economic revival that began, depending on region, between 1440 and 1480 and continued in most areas into the 1550s or 1560s. If population within the modern borders of France in 1435 had fallen to 11,000,000 or less, by 1560 it was again approaching the putative medieval peak of 18,000,000. This basic level would continue until the 18th century, when the historic ceiling began to lift. After 1450, therefore, France never again suffered what Le Roy Ladurie terms a "first-order fluctuation."[291] Hence Fernand Braudel's memorable verdict: "1450 was a watershed of which no remotely comparable example exists throughout the rest of French history."[292] For reasons by no means accidental, demographic stability paralleled political stability: neither the crisis of the late 1500s nor late 1700s threatened the state as profoundly, or lasted as long, as 14th- to 15th-century collapse.

How, then, shall we explain this post-1450 economic recovery, whose correlation with post-1450 expansion in Russia and Southeast Asia needs no further emphasis? As in Russia, warmer winters and drier summers and autumns, especially c. 1500–1560, improved harvests, although less markedly perhaps than during the Medieval Climate Anomaly.[293] In mainland Southeast Asia, recall, post-1450 warming correlated with stronger monsoons. In France as in Russia plague abatement, whether through acquired immunity, vector control, or bacterial

---

[290] J. Russell Major, *From Renaissance Monarchy to Absolute Monarchy* (Baltimore, 1994), chs. 1, 2; Potter, "King and His Government," 155–81.

[291] Whereas the first-order fluctuation of 1340–1540/60 lasted some 200 years and lost a minimum of 30 percent, and possibly 60 percent of the population, subsequent second-order fluctuations lasted only 10–30 years and involved population losses of 10–20 percent. Le Roy Ladurie, *French Peasantry*, 232–33, and 98, 101; Arlette Higounet-Nadal, "Le relevement," in Dupaquier et al., *Histoire de la Population*, vol. I, 367–73; Potter, *History*, 7–13; Hoffman, "Rural, Urban, and Global," 70–71.

[292] Braudel, *Identity*, vol. II, 128.

[293] Le Roy Ladurie, *Histoire Humaine*, ch. 4; Lamb, *Changing Climate*, 10, 94–102; Pfister, "Five Centuries," 208–13; P. D. Jones and R. S. Bradley, "Climatic Variations over the Last 500 Years" and "Recent Developments in the Studies of Climate Since A.D. 1500," in Bradley and Jones, *Climate Since 1500*, esp. 652–53, 674–75; H. H. M. Salmon, *Society in Crisis: France in the Sixteenth Century* (London, 1975), 34; and nn. 90–93 *supra*.

mutation, also accounts for the recovery to preplague population levels. Until those levels returned in the mid-1500s and less valuable lands again came under the plow, productivity remained higher than in the pre-1347 era, contributing to a cyclic upswing. As new state structures and rising urban influence suggest, however, economic recovery also entailed genuinely novel features, particularly in the urban economy where, we saw, labor shortages stimulated cost-cutting measures and technological innovation.

External contacts were valuable insofar as they a) introduced fresh techniques in textiles, metallurgy, navigation, paper-making, clocks, printing, banking, and finance;[294] b) supplemented French calories with Baltic cereals and Atlantic fish; and c) supplied central European silver and, from the mid-1500s, large quantities of New World bullion that was needed for both market expansion and government operations. By 1600 French state income, measured in tons of silver-equivalent, was more than four times greater than in the early 1300s. This growth in bullion stocks made possible the fiscal revolution that the Hundred Years War and later military demands merely set in motion.[295] Yet while acknowledging the value of foreign trade, one may question the primary role Braudel and Immanuel Wallerstein accord it as an engine of growth. Philip Hoffman, Bartolome Yun, Robert Duplessis, and Epstein argue that in this as in earlier periods, the key to economic performance remained local institutions, market structures, and transport, which governed the demand for bullion and the response to foreign commercial opportunities. Even by late-17th-century standards, in the 1550s foreign trade as a proportion of domestic trade and output remained extremely limited.[296]

---

[294] Pamela Long, *Technology, Society, and Culture in Late Medieval and Renaissance Europe, 1300–1600* (Washington, DC, 2000), chs. 1–3, 5, 8, 9; Collins, *Tribes to Nation*, 143–44; Marie-Therese Boyer-Xambeu et al., *Private Money and Public Currencies* (Armonk, NY, 1994), esp. 43–128. Bills of exchange became particularly important for private trade.

[295] On bullion flows and state finance, Le Roy Ladurie, *Royal French State*, 28–30; Miskimin, *Economy, 1460–1600*, 28–43; Fischer, *Great Wave*, 70–91. For narratives emphasizing the post-1450 impact of foreign trade, Fernand Braudel, *The Wheels of Commerce* (New York, 1986); Immanuel Wallerstein, *The Modern World System*, vol. I (Orlando, FL, 1974).

[296] See Hoffman, "Rural, Urban, and Global," 80–85; idem, *Growth in a Traditional Society*; Bartolome Yun, "Economic Cycles and Structural Changes," in Brady, *Handbook*, vol. I, 113–42, esp. 128–29; Robert Duplessis, *Transitions to Capitalism in Early Modern Europe* (Cambridge, 1997), 90; Epstein, *Freedom and Growth*, 71; Le Roy Ladurie, *Royal French State*, 42–43. Discussion of rural and urban economic history 1450–1600 also follows Le Roy Ladurie, *French Peasantry*, ch. 2; Higounet-Nadal, "Le relevement,"

Arguably more critical than external commerce after 1450 were the economic benefits, at times unintended, of novel state actions. Recall again Epstein's analysis of the 14th-century downturn: fragmented, noncompetitive markets reduced the incentive to disseminate best practices and thus to realize the potential of existing technologies. Once the Hundred Years War ended, the crown improved jurisdictional integration by reducing apanages and autonomous principalities, limiting seigniorial impediments to trade, monopolizing coinage, standardizing weights and measures, encouraging trade fairs, and extending the scope of royal courts. If many of these actions had an express political objective, they still served the economic needs of merchants and peasants by lowering transaction costs and encouraging specialization. That markets were becoming more unified and investment funds more available is suggested by the falling cost of private capital between 1300 and 1550.[297] By the same token, the return of domestic peace after 1453 – although obviously a political event whose benefits would be reduced by post-1494 Italian campaigns and post-1562 religious wars – helped to restore confidence, which translated into accelerated reclamation, earlier marriages, and heavier investment.[298] In varying degrees, we have seen, political unification in Burma, Siam, Dai Viet, and Russia after 1450 produced similar, if unquantifiable, advantages.

France in this period still had no genuinely national economy, rather a series of regional economies, some of which were drawn into the orbit of neighboring countries. But with fairs and markets proliferating, production in most regions gradually became more monetized and dependent on urban credit. Whereas agricultural growth beyond urban hinterlands tended to be more extensive than intensive, in the cities

367–420; Chaunu and Gascon, *L'Etat et la Ville* (esp. pt. 2, "La France du mouvement"); Garrisson, *History*, pt. 1; Philip Benedict, ed., *Cities and Social Change in Early Modern France* (London, 1989); Bernard Chevalier and Philippe Contamine, eds., *La France de la Fin du XV Siecle* (Tours, 1985), esp. pt. 1.

[297] However, still inadequate systems of transport, banking, and coinage kept the decline in France appreciably less than in England, Germany, or Flanders. Epstein, *Freedom and Growth*, 36–44, 54–72, esp. Fig. 3.1, and chs. 4, 5; van Zanden, "Road to Industrial Revolution," 342–43; Howell Lloyd, *The State, France, and the Sixteenth Century* (London, 1983), 112; Boyer-Xambeu et al., *Private Money*, 111–23; Jonathan Dewald, "Social Groups and Cultural Practices," in Holt, *Renaissance and Reformation*, 45–48; Wolfe, *Fiscal System*, 57; R. J. Knecht, *Francis I* (Cambridge, 1988), 316–21; Spruyt, *Sovereign State*, 160–67.

[298] Robert Boutruche, "The Devastation of Rural Areas During the Hundred Years War and the Agricultural Recovery of France," in Lewis, *Recovery of France*, 40–42; Potter, *History*, 2.

changes in taxation, handicrafts, and education allowed this round of growth to start at a higher level of skills and capital than the medieval expansion. By 1560 French town-dwellers were probably 10 percent of the total, compared to some 3 percent in Russia and perhaps 5 percent in Burma and Siam. In Rozman's schema, whereas Russian urbanism in 1550 was at Stage E, France had entered an advanced form of Stage F ("intermediate marketing").[299]

Commercialization accelerated the movement, underway since at least the 1200s, from hereditary obligation to contract and cash relations. This was true at both the level of peasant agriculture and of elite politics. By 1500 market and credit opportunities had converted extensive domain lands and servile tenements to legally protected private property, had eclipsed the seigneury as a social unit, and effectively had destroyed serfdom. Lordship, once based on seigniorial rights, now operated chiefly through land rents. Likewise, as feudal cavalry declined in favor of professional infantry, commutation of service became more widespread, and vassalage crumbled as a basis of political organization. Men now agreed to serve kings or magnates in return for wages, pensions, appointments, or generalized preferment. Misleadingly called "bastard feudalism," the system was actually one of clientage mediated by cash.[300]

As the political unit with the most developed powers of taxation and patronage, the monarchy was best placed to profit from these trends. In France as in Russia, a combination of military and inflationary pressures drove tax demands, which were heavy by medieval standards but still quite tame by those of the 17th century. Measured in terms of grain equivalent, gross regular tax revenue climbed sharply under Louis XI – whose reign (1461–1483) in fact marked a turning point in royal taxation – declined during the first half of the 16th century, and rose again to 1581.[301] Yet military demands meant that whatever was raised

---

[299] Rozman, *Urban Networks*, 34–36, 66, 84–87. Urban estimates of 10–15 percent appear at Benedict, *Cities*, 7, and Ladurie, *Royal French State*, 47 (wherein towns are defined as places with over 2,000), but Higounet-Nadal, "Relevement," 394 cites claims of only 6.5 percent. Cf. Hoffman, "Rural, Urban, and Global," 90–92, discussing the late 1500s shift of resources from countryside to towns; Collins, *Tribes to Nation*, 217–18.

[300] Lewis, *Essays*, chs. 2, 5; Potter, *History*, ch. 6; Major, *From Renaissance Monarchy*, 61–68; Robert Harding, *Anatomy of a Power Elite* (New Haven, 1978), 76, 214; Bruce Lyon, *From Fief to Indenture* (Cambridge, MA, 1957). Cf. n. 87 *supra*.

[301] Potter, *History*, 144; Richard Bonney, "France, 1494–1815," in Bonney, *Rise of the Fiscal State*, 140–41; Philip Hoffman, "Early Modern France, 1450–1700," in Hoffman and Norberg, *Fiscal Crises*, 239. By 1581 revenues in grain equivalents were somewhat

was never sufficient. Sixteenth-century rulers therefore developed three additional strategies: a) They strengthened control over church lands as a source of patronage, imposed the first permanent tax on the clergy, and periodically obliged the church to sell property to benefit the crown.[302] b) They radically expanded venality, that is, the highly lucrative sale of judicial and other royal offices (see below). c) They resorted ever more heavily to borrowing – loans from office-holders and towns, bond issues on the security of Paris revenues, and borrowings from foreign bankers. Neither Russian nor Southeast Asian monarchies in 1750, let alone 1500, had comparable access to capital. Along with France's heavier reliance on cash taxes and the decline of hereditary service – even as hereditary service was growing in Burma, Siam, and Russia – these features again testify to the sophistication of the French economy.

Such revenues simultaneously boosted the crown's influence over traditional elites and widened its base of recruitment. With the continued decay of feudal networks, the habit among high nobles – already developed in the late medieval era – of looking to the royal treasury for pensions, gifts, and tax assignments grew apace. By and large, leading nobles embraced the crown not as a distant competitor, but as a source of much needed income.[303] For its part the court was only too eager to purchase the cooperation of powerful magnates. Under Louis XI a third of royal income went directly to noble pensions and another half to the army, itself a major source of employment for the traditional, so-called sword nobility. In the 1500s the throne let senior nobles dispose of whole blocks of royal offices. Provincial assemblies, dominated by churchmen and nobles, also retained a sizeable portion of the new taxes, which can be considered royal only in a nominal sense.[304] By the same token,

below maximum levels under Louis XI, but in labor equivalents were substantially higher. On taxes, venality, loans, and the corrosive impact of inflation, Hoffman, "Rural, Urban, and Global," 86–89; Chaunu and Gascon, *L'Etat et la Ville*, 146–76; Emmanuel Le Roy Ladurie and Michel Morineau, *Histoire Economique et Sociale de la France, Tome 1: De 1450 a 1660, v. 2: Paysannerie et Croissance* (Paris, 1977), esp. 978–82; Collins, *Fiscal Limits*, 18–64; Garrisson, *History*, 198; Holt, *Renaissance and Reformation*, 131; David Potter, pers. commun., June 30, 2006.

[302] See Frederic Baumgartner, *Change and Continuity in the French Episcopate* (Durham, NC, 1986), 4–12, 55–83. French kings, an ambassador claimed in 1569, "deal in bishoprics and abbeys as elsewhere in pepper and cinnamon" (p. 4).

[303] Potter, *History*, 177, 287 and ch. 6; Major, *From Renaissance Monarchy*, ch. 3.

[304] Ladurie, *French Royal State*, 59; Peter Lewis, "Les pensionnaires des Louis XI," in Chevalier and Contamine, *La France*; Potter, *History*, 198–206; idem, "King and His Government," 179–80; James B. Wood, *The Nobility of the Election of Bayeux 1463–1666* (Princeton, 1980); Jonathan Dewald, *Pont-St-Pierre 1398–1789* (Berkeley, 1987).

loans, tax farms, and venality lured municipal oligarchs toward a closer identification with the throne, and it was largely from successful urban families that there emerged an expanded class of legal officers, with the so-called robe nobility at its apex.

A variety of urban-based technological innovations extended the efficiency and reach of the revived administration. To be sure, these were also available to princely and ducal courts, but the crown's larger resources allowed it to pyramid advantages. Italian banking strengthened royal finances. Novel maps and spatial concepts, also indebted in part to Italian example, addressed endemic boundary confusion. Although eventually it would prove deeply destabilizing, the post-1470 introduction of printing spread royal ordinances and propaganda. And by reducing the cost of books, printing and cheaper paper fueled that expansion of schools and universities whose graduates dominated the robe nobility, the liberal professions, and a new humanist culture.[305] Neither the introduction of woodblock printing in Vietnam in the 1400s, nor the debut of movable type in Russia in the 1550s, nor the transition from epigraphic to palm-leaf orthography in Burma had so dramatic an impact. Along with those French cities that formed its administrative ganglia, the 16th-century French state thus operated from a higher technical level than its medieval predecessor.

This was yet more obviously true of weaponry. Cannon played a key role in reducing English strong points during the last phase of the Hundred Years War. In the early 1500s the *trace italienne* bastion, designed to ward off artillery, returned the advantage to the defense but vastly magnified expenses for defenders and attackers alike. Meanwhile cavalry yielded substantially to disciplined infantry, which the Swiss had pioneered but whose value and numbers increased with more effective systems of drill and with the adoption of arquebuses in the late 1400s and heavy muskets from the 1540s. Whereas in the early 1300s the French peacetime army, chiefly cavalry, had been only 2,000, by the mid-1500s standing forces, extensively equipped with firearms, numbered 18,000 and wartime, mercenary-led armies could total 40,000

---

[305] On technical innovations, Long, *Technology, Society*; Bernard Guenee, *States and Rulers in Later Medieval Europe* (Oxford, 1985), 25–31; Potter, *History*, 24–28; Ladurie, *Royal French State*, 26–27, 68–69, 143–45; Rickard, *History of French Language*, 62–63; George Huppert, *Les Bourgeois Gentilshommes* (Chicago, 1977), 60 ff.; Natalie Zemon Davis, *Society and Culture in Early Modern France* (Stanford, 1975), ch. 7; Lucien Febvre, *Life in Renaissance France* (Cambridge, MA, 1977), ch. 2. On French maps c. 1450–1610, David Buisseret, ed., *Monarchs, Ministers, and Maps* (Chicago, 1992), 99–113.

to 50,000. If such forces remained subject to divided commands and too small to coerce the general population, they afforded the crown a decisive advantage over individual magnates or towns. Between 1480 and 1650, and more particularly 1540 to 1560, this complex of changes (siege artillery, handguns, fortified bastions; larger, better trained infantries) – which Geoffrey Parker, following Michael Roberts, terms the "military revolution" – dramatically increased military costs and, by extension, the burden on systems of taxation, logistics, command, and recruitment.[306] As in Southeast Asia and Russia, the wealthiest, most efficient and innovative states thus reaped enormous benefits. The new era was fairly inaugurated in 1494, when France's Italian invasion sparked a frightfully expensive struggle with the Habsburgs, lasting to 1559, to control Italy and France's eastern and northern frontiers.[307]

At a more subtle level, consider finally the contribution to integration of fresh cultural and legal currents. Throughout much of Latin Europe 16th-century elites, under the influence of Renaissance humanism, began to place yet heavier emphasis on civil order and to exchange feudal valor for the ideals of self-cultivation and *politesse*. Relying on Italian models, the court's self-proclaimed civilizing function under Francis I (r. 1515–1547) and Henry II (r. 1547–1559) recommended these ideals to the high nobility, whose familiarity with Italian concepts of refinement grew during the Italian campaigns. Admittedly, these trends remained limited – Louis XIV's courtiers would recoil in horror at tales of their noble ancestors' brutishness and license[308] – but the tone of the medieval court altered. Meanwhile a new network of urban schools, colleges, and universities introduced humanist views to educated,

---

[306] On force sizes, Ladurie, *Royal French State*, 26, 53, 60; Garrisson, *History*, 153–58, 210; J. R. Hale, *War and Society in Renaissance Europe, 1450–1620* (New York, 1985), 63; Potter, *History*, 261–64; John Lynn, *Giant of the Grand Siecle* (Cambridge, 1997), 55; David Parrott, *Richelieu's Army* (Cambridge, 2001), 164, 548–49. On military change and its wider impact, see Ch. 1, n. 88 *supra*, esp. Geoffrey Parker, *The Military Revolution* (Cambridge, 1988), chs. 1–3, arguing *pace* earlier views that the critical factor in the growth of army size and cost was not firearms per se, but fortifications; plus Clifford Rogers, ed., *The Military Revolution Debate* (Boulder, 1995); R. J. Knecht, *French Renaissance Monarchy* (London, 1984), 47–49; Kenneth Chase, *Firearms* (Cambridge, 2003), 56–82, 224 n. 31; Peter Wilson, "European Warfare, 1450–1815," in Jeremy Black, ed., *War in the Early Modern World* (London, 1999), 177–206.

[307] On French foreign policy 1460–1560, Potter, *History*, ch. 8; Garrisson, *History*, chs. 4, 5. Cf. the role of guns in Southeast Asia in this period, *SP*, 59–61, 146, 152–53, 256–58, 270, 285, 393, 406.

[308] Ronald Asch, *Nobilities in Transition 1550–1700* (London, 2003), 70; Jonathan Dewald, *Aristocratic Experience and the Origins of Modern Culture* (Berkeley, 1993), 137–39.

largely nonnoble circles, chiefly in the towns. Renaissance humanism was less explicitly political than Neo-Confucianism, and compared to Theravada Buddhism or Russian Orthodoxy, its social base was far more narrow. But like those other 15th- to 17th-century awakenings, which in Southeast Asia also benefited from wider literacy, Renaissance humanism strengthened the yearning for a more universal civilizing authority – a role the French crown was happy to assume.[309] At the same time the development of absolute property rights and the money economy multiplied litigation at all levels. Royal offers of relatively impartial justice appealed to peasants, traders, and petty lords who had lost faith in seigniorial and ecclesiastical courts and who were willing to pay higher taxes to support an effective supralocal judicial authority.[310]

In sum, between 1450 and 1560 the legacies of the Hundred Years War joined demographic/economic renewal, commercial and technical innovation, rising military expenses, and new cultural movements to strengthen the French monarchy. The institutional building blocks of the Renaissance state, David Potter reminds us, had been in place since the early 1300s, and in many respects change was one of degree, rather than of kind.[311] Still, the net transformation was at least as critical as the divide separating Toungoo Burma, early Ayudhya, Le Vietnam, and post-1460 Muscovy from an earlier world. But precisely how did these pressures modify French administration? What new structures emerged?

Novel French Political Structures, c. 1450–1560: Comparisons with Southeast Asia

As in Southeast Asia and Russia, the most obvious change was territorial. By 1453, English holdings in Normandy and Aquitaine had been

---

[309] Of course, as Gorski, *Disciplinary Revolution* shows, this role also could be filled by autonomous religious and social organizations. On pacifying 16th-century culture change, see too Elias, *Civilizing Process*; Marvin Becker, *Civility and Society in Western Europe 1300–1600* (Bloomington, IN, 1988); Asch, *Nobilities in Transition*, 70–100; Huppert, *Bourgeois*, esp. ch. 7; Kristen Neuschel, *Word of Honor* (Ithaca, 1989), esp. 108–13, 186–208; Garrisson, *History*, 40–46; Knecht, *Francis I*, ch. 17; John Hale, *The Civilization of Europe in the Renaissance* (New York, 1994), 360–422, 490–500. See too Ellery Schalk, "The Court as 'Civilizer' of the Nobility," in Ronald Asch and Adolf Birke, eds., *Princes, Patronage, and the Nobility* (Oxford, 1991), 245–63, cautioning that court culture was not emulated by most provincial nobles before the early 1600s.

[310] See Dewald, *Pont-St-Pierre*, 148–56, on the surprising enthusiasm with which 16th-century Norman villagers used royal courts.

[311] Potter, "King and His Government," 181.

reconquered. In 1477 the crown absorbed ducal Burgundy and in 1491 extinguished Brittany's long-cherished independence. Other annexations, acquired through inheritance, war, purchase, and confiscation – and aided initially by fortuitous die-offs in collateral branches of the Valois royal family – included Anjou, Maine, Provence, and the Bourbon territories. As the failed attempt to annex Italian areas suggests, the crown was motivated not by a modern vision of the French "national hexagon" but by a mix of dynastic claims, strategic calculation, and opportunism that was largely indifferent to language and culture. All told, despite the Italian failure, French territory, which had fallen from a nominal 400,000 square kilometers in 1320 to 250,000 in 1425, rose to over 450,000 in 1600.[312]

But this was much more than a reassembly insofar as nominal authority yielded to a more credible royal influence. Step by step, almost imperceptibly, the annexed duchies, reconquered fiefs, and great apanages were dismantled, and France evolved from a family-run collection of principalities into a more coherent, if still vulnerable, kingdom. Although the specter of fragmentation was not finally exorcised until the 17th century, as early as 1465–1468, when Brittany, Burgundy, and other princely houses failed in a bid to increase their autonomy, the unifying verdict of the Hundred Years War was confirmed. In Potter's words, the 1460s and 1470s saw "the last major fling of princely independence" and the "definite affirmation of royal power in binding the country together."[313] Whereas as late as 1461 the French royal domain accounted for 60 percent of the nominal kingdom, by 1610 it represented virtually the entire area. In other words, the third and fourth zones of late medieval French administration were assimilated to the royal domain.

A principal figure in this transformation was the governor (*gouverneur*), to whom the king assigned authority over specific regions, chiefly frontier principalities and apanages absorbed by the crown. Though present as early as the 1330s, governors became a regular fixture only from the late 1400s. Chosen from princes of the blood or powerful provincial families and enjoying quasi-royal dignities, governors sought to fill the vacuum created by the eclipse of dukes and apanage princes.

---

[312] Chaunu and Gascon, *L'Etat et la Ville*, 20, 25; Galliou and Jones, *Bretons*, 247–52.
[313] Potter, *History*, 2, 134. See too Ladurie, *Royal French State*, 34–35, 61–78, 104–108; Salmon, *Society*, 20–21; Small, "Crown and Provinces"; Collins, *Tribes to Nation*, 188–94.

Essentially, they mediated central–provincial relations by serving both as clients to the king or to great families at court, and as patrons to local elites, for whom they secured titles, perks, and positions.[314] Insofar as they received fixed emoluments, often resided at court, and did not rival the king directly, 16th-century French governors were less formidable than Burmese viceroys (*bayins*). By and large they also enjoyed less autonomy than Russian *namestniki*. But as viceregal plenipotentiaries sent by the crown to replace hereditary dynasts in newly annexed areas between 1450 and 1600, French governors, Burmese *bayins*, Siamese viceroys, and Russian *namestniki* exhibited unmistakable similarities.

With the eclipse of rival principalities, the royal court grew more elaborate.[315] Whereas until the late 1400s great princely households had rivaled that of the king, the 16th-century royal court had no domestic peer. Its chief functions were to present ritualized claims to supremacy and to coordinate patronage. Tied closely to the court was the chief executive agency, the Royal Council (*conseil du roi*), which included an intimate committee for high policy and a larger body for routine administration. The early and mid-1500s saw the rise of legal experts who linked major departments and whose senior members, with policy discretion, prefigured royal ministers. As transactions mushroomed, chiefly in response to war demands, executive organs grew more specialized, routinized, and dependent on archives.[316]

Alongside this executive elaboration, we find throughout the 1500s a marked expansion of the judicial and fiscal machinery, which meant that venality in office, hitherto on a modest scale and often criticized,

[314] At first governors' terms of office were limited, but after 1483 lifetime appointments became common. Not until the 1550s did short-term commissioners (*maitres de requetes*) raise the possibility, not fully realized until the mid-1600s, of close central control in the provinces. In other words, if governors extended royal influence, they still shared with former apanage princes and great fief-holders extensive ceremonial rights and practical autonomy. See Potter, *History*, xiii, 117–23; Bernard Chevalier, "Governeurs et governements en France entre 1450 et 1520," *Francia* 9 (1980): 291–307; Knecht, *Francis I*, 345–48; Small, "Crown and Provinces," 153–54; and esp. Harding, *Anatomy of Power Elite*, pts. 1, 2.

[315] Notwithstanding its semiperipatetic character. Potter, *History*, 4, 38–89, 285; Schalk, "Court as Civilizer"; Garrisson, *History*, ch. 7; R. J. Knecht, "The Court of Francis I," *European Studies Review* 8 (1978); 1–22.

[316] On administration, Collins, *The State*, 1–21; Chaunu and Gascon, *L'Etat et la Ville*, pt. 1; Potter, *History*, chs. 3–5; idem, "King and His Government"; Major, *From Renaissance Monarchy*, chs. 1–3; Salmon, *Society*, ch. 4; Ladurie, *Royal French State*, pts. 1, 2; Garrisson, *History*, 170–208, 240–44; Knecht, *French Renaissance Monarchy*; David Parker, *The Making of French Absolutism* (New York, 1983),1–27; Potter, pers. commun., June 30, 2006.

now mushroomed and gained more formal sanction. The principle of venality was simple: the king sold to qualified buyers quasi-hereditary membership in existing or newly created agencies concerned chiefly with justice and taxation. Buyers were attracted not only by annual wages and tax exemptions, but by the status enhancement that venal office conferred, including in some cases entrée to the nobility. Along with royal courts of first instance, a network of intermediate presidial courts and the superior law courts known as *parlements* (including the *parlement* of Paris and by 1554 seven provincial *parlements*) expanded their authority at the expense of ecclesiastical and seigniorial courts. Parallel to the judicial system, a complex fiscal organization, with its own multilevel jurisdictions and venal office-holders, "grew exponentially" in the 16th century.[317] By expanding the infrastructure of governance at a very low initial cost, venality not only provided the crown with substantial income, but began to compensate for the kingdom's habitual underadministration and to address demands for wider, more reliable adjudication in a society still rife with crime and violence. At the same time, venality extended royal influence in the provinces and, along with crown's new borrowing techniques, gave provincial elites, including urban merchants who dominated the tax system, a strong vested interest in the preservation of central authority. All told, whereas in 1460 royal officials, excluding minor functionaries, had totaled some 2,000, and in 1515 some 4,000–5,000, by 1560 France had at least 10,000 such personnel.[318] The Venetian ambassador reported in 1546, "offices are infinite in number and grow daily . . . half of which would suffice."[319] Despite or because of the turmoil of the late 1500s, the ranks of financial and judicial officials continued to rise markedly under Henry III (r. 1574–1589).

---

[317] Phrase from Collins, *The State*, 17. See too idem, *Fiscal Limits*, ch. 1; idem, *Tribes to Nation*, 290–94; Salmon, *Society*, 70–79, 160–62; Dewald, "Social Groups," 45–48. The six provincial *parlements* of 1501 and seven by 1554 later increased to 17. On venality, classes of royal functionaries, and the role of venal office-holders, see too Roland Mousnier, *The Institutions of France Under the Absolute Monarchy, 1598–1789*, 2 vols. (Chicago, 1984), vol. II, 27–59; William Doyle, *Venality* (Oxford, 1996), 2–10; Le Roy Ladurie, *Royal French State*, 16–25.

[318] Figures at Potter, "King and His Government," 157, 160; idem, *History*, 123–24; Ladurie, *Royal French State*, 17, 139; Salmon, *Society*, 79; Chaunu and Gascon, *L'Etat et la Ville*, 37–39; Collins, *The State*, 21; idem, *Tribes to Nation*, 293–94; Doyle, *Venality*, 6. On the need for more effective adjudication in a deeply insecure, violent society, Potter, *History*, 132–34, and Ch. 1, n. 84 *supra*.

[319] Quoted in Knecht, *Renaissance Monarchy*, 15.

By what yardsticks shall we measure French governance? Among major European kingdoms in the early 1500s, France, it is generally accepted, was most effectively taxed and had the largest per capita administrative cadre.[320] By the standards of Indic Southeast Asia, its system was yet more impressive. France's 10,000 functionaries of 1560 meant one for about 1,800 people. By contrast, in Burma in 1560, if we include all central officials (*ahmu-ahmat*), tributary rulers, and township (*myo*) headmen with royal appointment orders, the total was only 1,000–1,500, or about one official per 3,000–4,500 inhabitants.[321]

But even this comparison overstates French–Burmese equivalence for six reasons: a) French officials were more professional and specialized. Judicial officers, including venal office-holders, faced specific educational requirements and often worked for the state on a daily basis.[322] By contrast, Burmese officials lacked professional training, and quasi-hereditary headmen exercised official duties only occasionally. French officials, moreover, were supported by more full-time clerks, sergeants, and collectors than their Burmese counterparts. b) Burmese headmen attended annual ceremonies at the capital and submitted periodic census reports, but otherwise had no regular contact with capital agencies. By contrast, most French judicial officers were enmeshed in hierarchies with written procedures and formal channels of appeal. c) *Compagnies d'ordonnances* gave Valois rulers greater military leverage in the provinces than was available to their Burmese counterparts. d) Because French government operations, resting on a tripod of taxes, venal sales, and loans, were fully monetized, the crown could tap resources and centralize rewards far more efficiently than in Burma, where in-kind goods, with their fatal problems of transport and storage, still comprised 79 percent of all taxes.[323] Likewise, in Burma tax farms, popular in France since the late 1100s, took hold only in the late 1700s, and grants of land and people, inherently entropic, remained the chief form of remuneration even as French feudal grants lost all significance.

---

[320] Potter, *History*, xii, 253.

[321] J. S. Furnivall and Pe Maung Tin, eds., *Zam-bu-dipa ok-hsaung kyan* (Rangoon, 1960), 41; Frank Trager and William Koenig, *Burmese Sit-tans, 1724–1826* (Tucson, 1979), ch. 7; and Lieberman, *Administrative Cycles*, 20–21. Siamese, Lao, and Burmese patterns were similar.

[322] Salmon, *Society*, 77; Dewald, "Social Groups," 48–49.

[323] That is, between 1350 and 1550. Victor Lieberman, "Secular Trends in Burmese Economic History, c. 1350–1830, and Their Implications for State Formation," *MAS* 25 (1991): 24.

Again, one is reminded of Tilly's distinction between market-intensive and market-deficient environments. e) Whereas Burmese kings interpreted traditional Buddhist law but claimed no power of original legislation, and whereas medieval French kings had claimed that they merely *discovered* the law in strict accordance with custom, early 16th-century French kings, eager to create new fiscal and military structures, claimed an absolute right to make positive law.[324] f) Although hardly uniform, royal authority in France was far more territorially pervasive than in Burma. By 1550 the French monarchy had eliminated hereditary dynasts in favor of governors in apanages and other great fiefs. But First Toungoo kings appointed officials only around the capital, while quasi-hereditary *bayin* viceroys controlled the rest of the lowlands, and Tai vassal kings occupied upland wet-rice valleys. In vast interior areas unsuitable for wet-rice cultivation, preliterate hill peoples remained beyond the administrative gaze, if not cultural influence, of the lowlands. Thus, whereas France had one appointee for every 45 square kilometers, in 1560 the Burmese empire had one for every 470–700 square kilometers. And whereas the French crown received substantial income from throughout the kingdom, early Toungoo taxes (as opposed to tribute) were largely confined to Lower Burma.

In formal complexity, administrations in 16th-century Dai Viet and France may have been comparable. Senior Vietnamese officials passed Chinese-style examinations as selective as any French educational tests, while written procedures and operational norms were arguably as nomothetic as in France. No fewer than three levels of appointed officials lay between the Vietnamese court and hereditary headmen, while the ratio of officials to population – provided we include village officials (*xa quan*) along with those of province, prefecture, and district – was in the order of 1:500, much higher than that in France.[325] On the other

[324] Cf. R. Lingat, "Evolution of the Conception of Law in Burma and Siam," *Jl. of the Siam Society* 38 (1950): 9–31; Collins, *The State*, 2–12; David Parker, "Sovereignty, Absolutism and the Function of the Law in 17th-Century France," *PP* 122 (1989): 36–74.

[325] Assuming a capital bureaucracy of approximately 1,000, plus appointees to 13 provinces, 30 prefectures, 100 districts, 9,000 villages, and a population of 5,500,000. John K. Whitmore, "The Development of Le Government in 15th Century Vietnam" (Cornell Univ., PhD diss., 1968), 169–70; Insun Yu, "Law and Family in 17th and 18th Century Vietnam" (Univ. of Michigan, PhD diss., 1978), 19–27; Alexander B. Woodside, *Vietnam and the Chinese Model* (Cambridge, MA, 1971), 143; John K. Whitmore, pers. commun., August 15, 2000.

hand, Chinese administration was grafted to a poorly commercialized Southeast Asian economy: in telling contrast to France, official emoluments even in Dong Kinh were chiefly in land and grain. Moreover, if we remove village officials – whose positions did not require professional training or examinations – from the list of Vietnamese officers, we lose some nine-tenths of the total.

Let us shift perspective once again, to use as our yardstick not 16th-century Southeast Asia but 19th-century France. By these lights, obviously, the state appears extremely superficial. An earlier historiographic emphasis on the "absolutism" of Francis I has yielded to a view of the Renaissance monarchy as basically decentralized and consultative.[326] In part, decentralization reflected a peculiar West European legal tradition, derivative from Roman law and feudalism, that emphasized inviolable corporate privilege, private property, and formal limits on sovereign power.[327] But more basically, 16th-century France followed a familiar early modern logic: in an age of still weak central staffs and armies of questionable loyalty, royal success lay not in combating but in co-opting local structures. In France the chief institutional beneficiaries included the aforementioned provincial *parlements* (law courts) and assemblies and town corporations. Growing generally out of law courts that existed in the great fiefs before their incorporation into the kingdom, each *parlement* retained sovereign judicial authority within its territory. Likewise, the most powerful provincial estates, in Brittany, Guyenne, Burgundy, Dauphine, Provence, and Languedoc, lay on the periphery, in the so-called *pays d'etats*, where the crown swore to maintain local privileges after annexation. As guardians of those liberties, estates could negotiate, collect, and disburse royal taxes. By contrast, in the inner, more closely governed regions of the kingdom, the so-called *pays d'elections*, the crown raised taxes directly through its own officials

---

[326] See historiographic discussion in Potter, *History*, Preface; and the views in idem, "King and His Government"; Small, "Crown and Provinces"; Major, *From Renaissance Monarchy*; idem, *Representative Government in Early Modern France* (New Haven, 1980), pt. I; Le Roy Ladurie, *Royal French State*, pts. 1, 2; and Mack Holt, "The Kingdom of France in the 16th Century," in Holt, *Renaissance and Reformation*, 5–26. On the other hand, much recent work also emphasizes localization in 18th-century French administration. See discussion *infra*.

[327] For various formulations of this argument, see Downing, *Military Revolution*; David Landes, *The Wealth and Poverty of Nations* (New York, 1998); Berman, *Law and Revolution*; van Zanden, "Road to Industrial Revolution," 351–57. Cf. Kollmann's views on West European exceptionalism, *Honor Bound*, 17–20, 175–76.

(*elus*).[328] Given this jurisdictional complexity, it is hardly surprising that taxation remained numbingly diverse and that royal efforts at legal codification proceeded on the basis not of the kingdom, but of provinces and *pays*.[329]

In short, if the great territorial fiefs disappeared, France – like 16th-century Muscovy and Southeast Asian empires – remained a messy assemblage of zones and enclaves whose autonomy tended to increase with distance from the capital. The crown's not infrequent resort to extreme brutality advertised its continued weakness. By the same token, two of the chief centralizing institutions of the Renaissance monarchy, namely, governorships and venal office-holding, also proved to be superb instruments of local power. Governors and other magnates absorbed into their own networks numerous royal officials, including military officers, who were loyal primarily to their patron. A king who manipulated ties to relatives and magnates could make the system work, but if privilege were violated or if patronage fell into the hands of an independent faction, offended groups often revolted. After 1560, we shall see, such revolts helped tear the monarchy apart.

French Political Identities and Cultural Integration, c. 1400–1600

Theories of royal power reflected this tension between local privilege and royal pretensions to a more complete authority. Like other European rulers, French kings laid great stress on legality, both because arbitrary action – "tyranny " – was abhorrent to the medieval and Renaissance mind and because feudal law, with its hierarchy of privileges, provided a basis for fresh territorial acquisitions. Yet with the erosion of feudalism, kings, their supporters, and eventually their opponents also were driven to consider wider claims to royal authority. Such claims derived from diverse sources, including Roman legal doctrines of public power, the Ciceronian notion of the common good, and Christian images of the king as God's viceregent.[330]

---

[328] Yet the operation in Normandy and elsewhere of assemblies and *elus* blurs the distinction and highlights the lack of uniformity. See Knecht, *Renaissance Monarchy*, 109; Major, *From Renaissance Monarchy*, ch. 2; Klaus Malettke, "Pays d'election [sic] et pays d'etats en France a l'epoque moderne," in Babel and Moeglin, *Identite Regionale*, 73–88.

[329] Holt, "Kingdom of France," 21–23.

[330] Already beloved of Renaissance French propagandists, the slogan "one king, one faith, one law" reflected this aspiration for a more effective unity. Holt, "Kingdom

To be sure, popular loyalties still focused commonly on the *pays*, the region, rather than on "France." The Hundred Years War bred a spectrum of political responses, only a fraction of which could be termed patriotic. Yet between 1400 and 1600 royal claims reflected and encouraged modifications in both popular and elite sentiment. During the later phase of the war, I suggested, anti-English insurrections and a flurry of ballads, histories, and artistic propaganda show that anti-English stereotypes, supported by a generally royalist parish clergy, circulated in many areas of the country, primarily among politically active elites, of course, but with some impact on the peasantry.[331] As in all prenational formations, sovereignty flowed not from the people up, rather from God/the cosmos down (although ideas of mutual obligation between king and people might be present). The population was thus bound to the ruler by a religious commitment that, in France as in Theravada Southeast Asia, somehow distinguished the people of each kingdom from adherents of the same faith in adjacent realms. Thus Colette Beaune has traced the post-1400 spread of what she terms the French "royal religion," a complex of images, symbols, and saint cults, Capetian in origin, which stressed the unique Christian sanctity of France embodied in its ruler. The Most Christian King, as the French sovereign was termed from the 14th century, automatically ascended to heaven; his holy blood allowed him to cure scrofula; the royal fleur-de-lys and regalia were sanctified by God. Although by the 1330s veneration of Capetian patron saints had moved beyond the Paris basin, in the 15th century cults of those saints and others who protected France against the English – especially Saints Catherine, Martialis, and the military archangel Michael – spread far more widely in the Loire and along France's threatened borders in the east, southwest, and southeast. (Recall that the Burmese, Vietnamese, and Muscovite courts also venerated protective spirits/saints specific

---

of France," 21; Jacques Krynen, "Genese de l'etat et histoire des idees politiques en France a la fin du Moyen Ages," in J. P. Genet, ed., *Culture et Ideologie dans la Genese de l'Etat Moderne* (Rome, 1985); Potter, *History*, 32–37; Lewis, *Later Medieval France*, 72–101; Knecht, *Renaissance Monarchy*, 13–24.

[331] See nn. 139, 288 *supra*, plus essays by B. Ditcham, G. Thompson, C. Reynolds, E. Danbury, and K. Daly in Christopher Allmond, ed., *Power, Culture, and Religion in France c. 1350–c. 1550* (Woodbridge, UK, 1989); Warner, *Joan of Arc*, pt. 1; Iris Black, "Accidental Tourist in the Hundred Years War," in Simon Forde et al., eds., *Concepts of National Identity in the Middle Ages* (Leeds, 1995), 171–87; Ladurie, *Royal French State*, 280. On regional and kingdom-wide identities in Europe c. 1300–1700, see too essays by J. Ehlers, J.-P. Genet, H. Neveux, P. Contamine, J. Kerherve, B. Guenee, and F. Collard, in Babel and Moeglin, *Identite Regionale*.

to each realm.) "All those who fight against the holy kingdom of France fight against King Jesus...and they will win nothing," explained the royal religion's most famous commoner exponent, Joan of Arc.[332]

The conviction that France was "the eldest son of the church" inspired in the 15th and 16th centuries new legal writings on the "Gallican liberties," emphasizing limits to papal authority in France and the king's right to tax the French clergy. Gallicans harped on the religious deficiencies of Venice, England, and Spain, all the while accepting a basic allegiance to Rome. As an erudite distillation of popular sensibilities, 16th-century Gallicanism expressed what Alain Tallon calls a "national" religious consciousness.[333]

Royalist sentiment became manifest as well in an expanded legal literature on royal prerogatives outside the church, in learned histories of France's Trojan origins, in poetry on patriotic sacrifice, and in elaborate pageants and urban *entrees* that sought to make the monarchy more visible to its subjects.[334] Symptomatic of changing perspectives, new terminology tended to flatten personal and territorial distinctions in favor of a shared subordination to the crown. Thus from the late 1400s some local chronicles as well as royal documents began to replace "vassal" with "subject" in describing leading princes and to use "province" alongside or in lieu of *pays* and *terre* to designate different parts of the realm.[335]

How did language relate to political integration? When asked in which language Saint Margaret spoke to her, Joan of Arc replied that she spoke in French, "For how could she have spoken English, since she was not on the English side?"[336] In fact, educated Frenchmen in the

---

[332] Beaune, *Birth*, 193. On post-1400 French royal religion, ibid., pt. 1; Planhol, *Geography*, 100. Cf. n. 266 *supra*.

[333] Alain Tallon, *Conscience Nationale et Sentiment Religieux en France au XVIe Siecle* (Paris, 2002), 1–24, 165–235. Cf. Jotham Parsons, *The Church in the Republic: Gallicanism and Political Ideology in Renaissance France* (Washington, DC, 2004), paying rather more attention to divisions within the French church; Potter, *History*, 218–24.

[334] Beaune, *Birth*, chs. 6–11; Allan Ellenius, ed., *Iconography, Propaganda, and Legitimation* (Oxford, 1998); Lawrence Bryant, *The King and the City in the Parisian Royal Entry Ceremony* (Geneva, 1986); idem, "Making History," in Michael Wolfe, ed., *Changing Identities in Early Modern France* (Durham, NC, 1996), 46–77; Michele Fogel, *L'Etat dans la France Moderne de la Fin du XV Siecle au Milieu du XVIII Siecle* (Paris, 1992), 39–61; Potter, *History*, 24, 29–56, 277; Garrisson, *History*, ch. 7.

[335] Small, "Crown and Provinces," 130–31; Holt, "Kingdom of France," 17–18.

[336] Beaune, *Birth*, 272–73. On language ibid., ch. 10; Ladurie, *Peasants of Languedoc*, 149–52; Rickard, *History of French Language*, chs. 4, 5; Potter, *History*, 6; and nn. *infra*.

16th century conceived of their kingdom as a polyglot realm wherein languages filled different social and geographic niches and in which travelers and men of affairs were expected to be multilingual.[337] Not only did Latin retain its liturgical monopoly and scholarly prestige, but at least seven principal vernaculars were still spoken (the *langue d'oil*, the *langue d'oc*, Franco-Provençal, Basque, Breton, Flemish, and German), each with numerous dialects (of which that of the Ile de France was the leading *langue d'oil* dialect). Yet if multilingualism was regarded as natural, it is also true that during the late 1400s and 1500s the dialect of the Ile de France (which henceforth I shall term "French") accelerated its medieval expansion and assumed ever greater prominence as both an objective and subjective marker of identification with the Paris-based political order. By 1500 in the northern plains, French had become the only accepted literary vehicle and had compressed other *langue d'oil* dialects in elite speech. The Breton–French boundary advanced westwards, and even in western Brittany a growing minority could speak French. In the south French made rapid inroads east and west of the Massif Central, converting first royal officials, then lesser notables and townsmen. The *parlements* of Bordeaux and Toulouse adopted French, which spread as well down the Rhone to the Mediterranean, so that by 1490 the French of bilingual Provençal notables contrasted with the exclusive *langue d'oc* dialects of commoners. The last time a poem in the *langue d'oc* won a prize in the Floral Games at Toulouse was 1513. By 1550 French had reached Landes, and by 1600 the Pyrenees. In short, although Occitan (*langue d'oc*) literature enjoyed an Indian summer in the late 1500s and bilingualism remained common, in one region after another elites began to adopt French for polite conversation, while scribes, poets, playwrights, and printers forsook both Latin and local vernaculars for French.[338]

What dynamics underlay these changes? The royal court, like its Southeast Asian and Russian counterparts, became a more powerful magnet. As royal patronage and litigation before royal justices

---

[337] See the exhaustive study by Paul Cohen, "Courtly French, Learned Latin, and Peasant Patois" (Princeton Univ., PhD diss., 2001), esp. 28–386, describing how multilingualism was conceived and accommodated within "the Kingdom of Babel." Also Tallon, *Conscience Nationale*, 4–5; Adrian Hastings, *The Construction of Nationhood* (Cambridge, 1997), 103–104.

[338] Potter, *History*, 6; Cohen, "Courtly French," 464–65, 475–563, 694–712, 723–39; Planhol, *Historical Geography*, 122–34, 243–44, 313–17; Brun, *Recherches Historiques*, 77 ff.; Robert Schneider, *Public Life in Toulouse 1463–1789* (Ithaca, 1989), 45–47, 85–89.

increased, the incentive for provincial nobles to dwell near the king grew apace. At the same time, particularly under Francis I, Italian notions of noble refinement and Renaissance urbanity enhanced the role of the court (whether in Paris or the Loire) as a hub of fashion, refined tastes, and social contacts. Whereas leading nobles seldom resided in medieval cities and even in 1550 many avoided lengthy stays in Paris, by 1600 prolonged residence in Paris mansions had become more common. Lower down the scale, Paris' commercial and intellectual renown – in 1500 the University of Paris alone had some 11,000 students, chiefly from official families – drew a constant stream of provincial youths, aided by improved transport. No less than the great nobles, when these men returned to the provinces, they spread Parisian speech and fashion.[339]

Meanwhile within the provinces, 16th-century prosperity and the associated demand for scribes, notaries, and lawyers swelled the number of urban schools, colleges, and universities, most offering instruction in French as well as Latin. The privileged position of French in royal administration recommended that those training for judicial office anywhere in the kingdom be able to read and speak it. Commercial printing had a similar impact, for both prestige and profitability favored French. Paris had its first press by 1470, Lyon three years later, after which presses sprang up in many provincial cities. By flooding the south with French-language books and periodicals to the growing exclusion of the *langue d'oc*, the presses of Lyon and Toulouse, in particular, promoted French fluency as well as literacy, because the latter was normally a precondition for acquiring the former. So too Basque, Breton, Poitevin, Picard, and so forth appeared in print less frequently, especially for upmarket audiences, and even Latin declined. Thus whereas 77 percent of pre-1500 books were in Latin and dealt with predominantly religious topics, after 1575 a growing majority were in French, covering an array of topics and genres.[340]

---

[339] Dewald, "Social Groups," 40–42, 50, 59; Harding, *Anatomy of Power Elite*, ch. 12; Planhol, *Historical Geography*, 270–75; Garrisson, *History*, 232–44; Collins, *Tribes to Nation*, 200–210. Although Francis I spent much of his time in the Loire, he returned to Paris in the 1520s.

[340] Despite the growth of provincial publishing, Paris long dominated the industry. On education and printing, Cohen, "Courtly French," 173–81, 603–604; Ladurie, *Royal French State*, 69; Garrisson, *History*, 40–46; Huppert, *Bourgeois*, ch. 7; Davis, *Society*, 197; Dominique Julia and Daniel Milo, "Les ressources culturelles," in Burguiere et al., *Histoire: L'Espace Francais*, 379–82; Lucien Febvre and Henri-Jean Martin, *The Coming of the Book* (London, 1976), 248–49, 319–21.

Historians long assumed that the monarchy itself eagerly sought to unify language.[341] To be sure, the government did accord French a unique prestige by employing it at court, patronizing French literature, and promoting vernaculars in lieu of Latin for legal proceedings.[342] But as Paul Cohen recently has shown, not only did the 16th-century throne make no systematic effort to impose French on the provinces, whose linguistic luxuriance, like vegetative fecundity, was often cited as a sign of vitality, but in the interests of social control the crown, along with local elites, actually sought to deny the lower orders opportunities to acquire polished French. Moreover, at the elite level the chief impetus for linguistic unification derived not from the crown, but from two intertwined groups of local actors: a) provincial officials, lawyers, urban notables, and merchants, who sought to fashion the language of the royal court into an idiom of elite sociability that would set them off from the lower orders; and b) poets, historians, and grammarians, both those patronized at court and provincial scholars in Normandy and elsewhere, who, under the influence of Italian humanist and classical models, strove to develop a literary medium above *patois* and below Latin that could glorify the monarchy many of them served.[343] Not surprisingly, as they adopted the language of the court and high nobility, aspiring provincials also imitated their dress, manners, artistic and architectural tastes, perhaps even their patterns of nuptiality. The fact that territories outside the kingdom also adopted French for administration reinforces the view that the spread of French was less the result of royal fiat than of substantially autonomous social and cultural processes.[344]

---

[341] See, e.g., Piero Fiorelli, "Pour l'interpretation de l'ordonnance de Villers-Cotterets," *Le Francaise Moderne* 18 (1950): 77–88; Paul Allies, *L'Invention du Territoire* (Grenoble, 1980), 66–67.

[342] Vernaculars obviously included, but were not restricted to, French. Cohen, "Courtly French," 683–701; Garrisson, *History*, 237–40.

[343] In other words, as usual, the relation between capital and provincial culture was dialogic. Cohen, "Courtly French," 75–98, 456–563, 647–747, esp. 730–34; idem, "L'imaginaire d'une Langue Nationale," *Histoire Epistemologie Langage* 25 (2003): 19–69; idem, "Linguistic Politics on the Periphery," in Brian Joseph et al., eds., *When Languages Collide* (Columbus, OH, 2003), 165–200; Garrisson, *History*, 236–40; Michael Wintroub, pers. commun., Nov. 30, 2000. On French feelings of inferiority vis-à-vis Italian culture, Michael Wintroub, "Civilizing the Savage and Making a King," *Sixteenth Century Jl.* 29 (1998): 465–94. Note that many provincial scholars celebrated the *langue d'oc* for regional expression at the same time as they promoted French as a national idiom. Cohen, "Courtly French," 564–721.

[344] Cohen, "Courtly French," 470–71; Planhol, *Historical Geography*, 243, plus 128–34. On the link between language and broader cultural trends, see also Susan Cotts Watkins,

But if the throne lacked the will and the means to impose French, it also lacked the ability to stop its dissemination down the social scale. This was particularly clear in provincial towns, many of which became islands of French-language print culture in which almost all townsmen participated to some degree. By 1575 a mixture of economic self-interest and social emulation ensured that most urban men in the north and 67 to 75 percent of artisans in the southern cities of Lyon, Narbonne, and Montpellier were literate, overwhelmingly in French. Through workplace readings, religious assemblies, and festivals, even illiterates gained information about national events. Accordingly, city-dwellers were most likely to understand French, to adopt northern social usages, and to think of themselves as French.[345] It was also in the towns, aided by schools and emboldened by the transparency, hence vulnerability, of urban religious practices, that church reformers launched their most successful attacks on religious "impurities" by disciplining popular festivals and youth societies. Not surprisingly, given the urban focus of reform, towns became the chief bastions of both Calvinism and radical Catholicism.[346]

Rural culture remained more conservative, a mosaic of substantially preliterate capsules. In Languedoc in 1575, as opposed to 67–75 percent of artisans, only about 3 percent of agricultural workers and 10 percent of even the better-off peasants could sign their names. Thus French language and national culture influenced only the very highest levels of rural society.[347] This urban–rural gap reflected the countryside's inability to support extensive schooling, the town's growing economic dominance, and urban reformers' initial failure to adapt their message to peasant worldviews. In the early 1500s peasant Christianity, many argue, remained preliterate, inclusive rather than dualistic, preoccupied with prophylaxis and fecundity, inclined to regard priests as magicians and the consecrated host as a source of healing power. Although most people probably attended mass regularly, in many areas the church still had no control over such basic activities as marriage. This divide

"Regional Patterns of Nuptiality in Western Europe, 1870–1960," in Ansley Coale and Watkins, *The Decline of Fertility in Europe* (Princeton, 1986), 333–35.

[345] Ladurie, *Peasants of Languedoc*, 149–50; idem, *Royal French State*, 49; Davis, *Society*, 209–225; Dewald, "Social Groups," 54.

[346] Salmon, Society, 132; Robert Muchembled, Popular Culture and Elite Culture in France 1400–1750 (Baton Rouge, 1985), ch. 3.

[347] Davis, *Society*, 195, following Ladurie; Salmon, *Society*, 30, and n. 345 *supra*.

between an educated urban-based minority and the mass of the population would not begin to close until the great "Christianization offensive" of the 17th century.[348]

Yet in a broader sense, by implanting French language in provincial cities and by preparing printing and other urban technologies to penetrate the countryside, cultural change between 1400 and 1600 was proleptically national. That rural France eventually would respond to urban elite prescriptions was foreshadowed in the peasantry's embrace of the "royal religion," in growing attendance at weekly church services, the founding of some village schools, the appearance of rural pockets of textually based Protestantism, and in the early rural dissemination of printed materials.[349]

Having attempted a balance sheet for administrative integration in France and Southeast Asia c. 1400–1600, let us do the same for cultural circulation. I see five major differences, of which the first four favored circulation in France, and the fifth, in Southeast Asia. First, as I emphasized, Southeast Asia's rugged mountain interior had no true French analogue. Nowhere in France do we find groups as culturally insulated as preliterate, *swidden* hill peoples in Southeast Asia.

Second, because continuities of every sort – dynastic, institutional, religious – were greater in France, French subjects had more stable models for internalization. Notwithstanding Hundred Years War traumas, the Valois Dynasty, royal institutions, above all, the language, ethnicity, and religion of the court remained unchanged from 1328 to 1589. But mainland Southeast Asia in these years suffered frequent dynastic shifts, Tai irruptions, and seesaw political/cultural contests between Burman and Mon, Siamese and Khmer, Vietnamese and Cham. Likewise, the Neo-Confucian revolution in Dai Viet was deeply innovative. Of course, as we shall see shortly, the Protestant Reformation was also disruptive, the occasion for over three decades of civil war. But unlike Theravada Buddhism and Neo-Confucianism, Calvinism remained a

---

[348] John Delameau, *Between Luther and Voltaire* (London, 1977), 154–74; Muchembled, *Popular Culture*, pt. 1; Yves-Marie Berce, *Fete et Revolte* (Paris, 1976), chs. 1–2; Dewald, "Social Groups," 37–38; Collins, *Tribes to Nation*, 220–23. For more attention to the complex interplay between official rituals and teachings and popular understandings, see Bossy, *Christianity in the West*, pt. 1; Robin Briggs, *Communities of Belief* (Oxford, 1989), 7–65, 381–413; Philip Benedict and Virginia Reinburg, "Religion and the Sacred," in Holt, *Renaissance and Reformation*, 119–46.

[349] Briggs, *Communities*, 21; Garrisson, *History*, 41, 46; Ladurie, *Peasants of Languedoc*, 150–51; Davis, *Society*, 200–209; and previous note.

strictly minority movement. Moreover, unlike Theravada Buddhism or Neo-Confucianism, it took root not in the mid-1400s but a century later, after the French monarchy had consolidated its position; and in fact, most Huguenots shared with Catholics strong protopatriotic loyalties.

Third, although woodblock printing entered Dai Viet in the mid-1400s, shortly before printing entered France, manuscripts continued to dominate there as across the mainland. Along with looser commercial links, weaker urbanization, smaller reading publics, and more centrifugal geographies, this prevented Southeast Asian kingdoms from supporting the same density of kingdom-wide communications as Renaissance France. Not even in Dai Viet do we find the same outpouring of protopatriotic histories, poetry, and pictorial representations as in France.

Fourth, the greater absolute and relative number of royal officials in France and their more even spatial distribution bred greater receptivity to capital norms.

Finally, however, whereas in western and eastern mainland Southeast Asia sustained frontier colonization by settlers championing majority ethnicity powerfully aided integration, frontier settlement was insignificant in France (although seasonal migrations of farm workers in the opposite direction, from peripheries to the lowlands and back, had a more modest homogenizing effect).[350]

Set against these differences, consider the following overarching parallels. In France as in each Southeast Asian realm, cultural integration from 1400 to 1600 benefited from the resurrection of a central political authority that lent its prestige to particular cults, languages, literatures, social and aesthetic norms. Within the provinces elite mimicry joined rising prosperity and market linkages to disseminate capital usages. Notwithstanding the uniqueness of European printing, between c. 1450 and 1600 Burma, Siam, Dai Viet, and France all saw textual-based cultic reforms (Theravada, Neo-Confucian, Protestant, Counter-Reformation), a proliferation of schools, and a flourishing of vernacular literatures at the expense of sacred languages above (Pali, Sanskrit, Chinese, Latin) and of provincial languages below. In each realm the throne continued to base its authority on universal doctrines, even as it invoked the protection of kingdom-specific spirits or saints, claimed religious superiority to other peoples of the same nominal faith, and promoted secular cultures that lay in uneasy tension with universal claims.

---

[350] Ladurie, *French Peasantry*, 11–12, 407, 410.

In each case politicized ethnicity moved from elite strata downward and from the capital region outward. And in every case cultural integration accelerated in the 16th century. As we just saw, Russia, despite lower levels of literacy, can be assimilated to these same patterns.

French Collapse, 1562–1598: The Wars of Religion

In the last four decades of the 16th century, at approximately the same time as Russia, Burma, Siam, and Dai Viet collapsed to the delight of predatory neighbors, France fell apart during the Wars of Religion. Grievous though they were, France's afflictions fit our by now familiar schema of progressively shorter, less severe breakdowns. The Wars of Religion lasted not 220 or 116 years, but 36. Except for 1590–1592, the Spanish never played the intrusive role of the English during the Hundred Years War or of Vikings in the 9th century. And, on the whole, royal institutions held up better than during the 14th and 15th centuries, not to mention the 9th to 12th.

Much is familiar too about the mechanics of decline.[351] A basic problem was the throne's attempt to manipulate noble factions through patronage, an arrangement that remained vulnerable to a failure of leadership or a reduction in funds. Until 1559 these problems had been contained by strong royal personalities, the prospect that the Habsburg wars still might yield new spoils, and favorable economic trends. Thereafter all three supports crumbled. From 1559 to 1589 weak kings and minority rule, a vacuum at the center, encouraged leaders at court to pursue vicious feuds and those in the provinces to magnify their autonomy. Climaxing decades of rising military costs, Valois defeat at the hands of the Habsburgs in 1559 raised the factional stakes by bankrupting the state, depriving many of military employment, and forcing a sharp reduction in pensions. In effect, more actors – a function of 16th-century population growth – were forced to compete for a shrinking pie. In addition, economic trends became unfavorable. Renewed

---

[351] Discussion of the 16th-century crisis relies on Mack Holt, *The French Wars of Religion, 1562–1629* (Cambridge, 1995); idem, "Putting Religion Back into the Wars of Religion," *FHS* 18 (1993): 524–51; plus Salmon, *Society*, pt. 2; Harding, *Anatomy of Power Elite,* 46–67, 86, 98–100, 214–15; Garrisson, *History*, pt. 3; Myriam Yardeni, *La Conscience Nationale en France pendant les Guerres de Religion (1559–1598)* (Louvain, 1971); Mark Greengrass, *France in the Age of Henri IV* (London, 1995); Stuart Carroll, *Noble Power During the French Wars of Religion* (Cambridge, 1998); Philip Benedict, "The Wars of Religion, 1562–1598," in Holt, *Renaissance and Reformation*, 147–75.

Malthusian pressures in the second half of the century – reminiscent of the early 1300s – weakened collective disciplines in crop rotation and pasturage, lowered productivity, and imposed a ceiling on grain production. This in turn squeezed rents and depressed living standards, with predictable consequences for social peace and rational discourse. As in Southeast Asia and Russia, the Little Ice Age climate deteriorated from the 1550s, dramatically so in the 1580s and 1590s. Finally, after 1560 rising inflation – a function of population pressure, stagnating productivity, rising urban exchange velocities, currency devaluation, and massive imports of New World bullion – magnified the woes of the government and fixed-income elites alike.[352]

Late-16th-century crises in France, Russia, and mainland Southeast Asia therefore involved the following common elements: military overextension, unstable systems of patronage, weak provincial controls; a century of rapid, ultimately destabilizing economic and demographic growth, including price inflation; and climatic downturn. Within this mix of factors, foreign military pressures arguably were less critical in France than in Burma, Siam, or Muscovy, but overpopulation and inflation, on present evidence, were more severe.

More or less unique to France and of central import, however, was the sea change in religious sensibilities that produced the Catholic–Huguenot rupture. If religious passions drew strength from general economic immiseration, the new print culture gave religious claims an unprecedentedly popular audience, while extremism followed a peculiar internal logic. French Huguenots embraced John Calvin's views that biblical authority was to be set above church tradition, that the sacraments were of value but not essential, that salvation was predestined, in short, that basic doctrines of the church of Rome were false. Because French kings had pledged to defend their people from heresy, Calvinism, in the eyes of French Catholics, challenged the most fundamental and cherished understandings of the realm. In particular, because it rejected conventional notions of free will, grace, and purity, Calvinism confronted all Frenchmen with irreversible, utterly terrifying choices between truth and error, eternal salvation and damnation.

---

[352] Cf. Goldstone's model of state breakdown and 16th-century inflation, in n. 280 *supra* and discussion in *SP*, 68, 277, 301, 395. On French economic and climate trends, Hoffman, "Rural, Urban, and Global," 89–90; Dewald, "Social Groups," 27–44; Le Roy Ladurie, *French Peasantry*, ch. 3; Bois, *Crisis*, ch. 15; Lloyd, *The State, France*, 94–96; Le Roy Ladurie, *Histoire Humaine*, chs. 5, 6; Pfister and Brazdil, "Climatic Variability"; William Atwell, "Volcanism and Climatic Change," 56–62.

Given a widespread sense that the Last Judgment was at hand, this made compromise exceedingly difficult and rendered religious violence a sacred imperative. A visceral compulsion to cleanse the community from "Catholic idolatry" or "Huguenot filth," an "eschatological anguish"[353] had few parallels in the generally more tolerant, reincarnationist religious milieu of Southeast Asia, although perhaps one could develop analogies to apocalyptic fears during Muscovy's Time of Troubles.

With the failure of negotiations and the outbreak of Catholic–Huguenot fighting in 1562 and more especially after 1574, governors, commanders, and office-holders nominally loyal to the crown tended to align themselves with high noble patrons. As magnate-led networks with distinct religious identities supplanted royal authority in many regions, the kingdom fragmented, and a seemingly interminable cycle of war, truce, and more war began. To enhance their military and political prospects and to provide discipline no longer available in royal service, local commanders appealed to foreign powers, most notably Spain, and enlisted popular religious organizations, whose obsessions only intensified popular anxieties. By the time the last Valois ruler, Henry III, was assassinated in 1589, he held little more than Bordeaux and the cities of the Loire and Normandy.

But however severe France's paralysis may have been, it was, to repeat, less total than in earlier periods. More consistently than their counterparts during the post-Carolingian era, during the aristocratic reaction of 1314–1315, or during the Hundred Years War, provincial leaders, with minor exceptions (most notably in Brittany), now sought less to subvert than to dominate the central government. Too many people had a stake in royally funded networks in the army, the judiciary, and fiscal administration to abandon the system of central finance that had been so painfully constructed since 1440. Nor could one dismiss the increasingly coherent French national identity that insecurity in general, and Spanish invasions from 1590–1592 in particular, served only to stimulate among Catholics and Huguenots alike. In reaction against domestic anarchy and foreign intervention, in the 1590s weary Protestants and moderate Catholics groped their way uneasily to unite behind

---

[353] A theme central to Denis Crouzet, *Les Guerriers de Dieu*, 2 vols. (Paris, 1990). On the internal logic of religious conflict and extremism, see too Holt, "Putting Religion Back"; Natalie Zemon Davis, "The Rites of Violence," *PP* 59 (1973): 51–91; Barbara Diefendorf, *Beneath the Cross* (Oxford, 1991).

Henry IV, founder of the Bourbon Dynasty, who proceeded to marginalize the extremists and to reestablish an unambiguously Catholic monarchy with a semiautonomous church, along with protections for the small Protestant minority. By reviving a sacral monarchy as the only barrier to renewed anarchy and by discrediting a range of ideas hostile to royal initiatives, the Wars of Religion prepared the way for the so-called absolutist monarchy of the 17th century.[354] Thus in the aftermath of 16th-century breakdowns, Burma, Siam, Russia, and France all obtained new dynasties and embarked on efforts at recentralization.

INTERIM CONCLUSION

The conclusion to Chapter 3 will summarize Russian and French history from the 6th to the 19th century, but for now I would offer the following interim synopsis.

The Franks jerry-built an extensive state earlier than their counterparts in Indic Southeast Asia or Russia, because Gaul boasted a more complex economy and more direct access to external models of high culture and governance, namely, those of imperial Rome. The Frankish/Carolingian kingdom c. 500 to c. 890 provided a cultural and institutional inspiration for the later kingdom of France (and the Holy Roman Empire) in much the same way that Pagan, Angkor, Dai Viet, and Kiev provided charters to regional heirs. But by the time Kiev and most Southeast Asian charter states cohered, the Carolingian empire was already a memory.

Between c. 900 and 1250 the fortunes of France, Russia, and mainland Southeast Asia began to intersect more closely, primarily as a result of a coordinated economic upsurge. This far-flung vitality sprang from locally specific combinations of the same factors, namely, agriculturally propitious climate, putative disease adjustments, economically beneficial social innovations, and expanding long-distance trade. In every case, prosperity promoted unprecedentedly effective political systems, so that the heyday of the Capetian Dynasty (c. 1110–1328) overlapped with the apogee of charter polities in Russia and in each of

---

[354] Holt, *Wars of Religion*, 210–16; idem, "Redrawing the Lines of Authority," in Holt, *Renaissance and Reformation*, 202–28; Barbara Diefendorf and Virginia Reinburg, "Catholic Reform and Religious Coexistence," in ibid., 176–201; Major, *Renaissance Monarchy*, ch. 5; Greengrass, *Age of Henri IV*. On the generalized xenophobia, reminiscent of Russia's Time of Troubles, gripping many Frenchmen in this period, see Collins, *Tribes to Nation*, 258–59.

mainland Southeast Asia's chief regions. What is more, at various points between 1240 and 1400 all five states splintered. Each collapse reflected the ecological and political strains of long-term growth combined with Mongol mediation (military or epidemiological) and deteriorating post-1250/1300 climate.

Fragmentation persisted to the mid-15th century, when a new phase of economic/demographic expansion and political integration got underway. As "cycles" are wont to do, in many ways this phase merely returned to the *status quo ante*. But post-1450 economies and states also exhibited genuinely novel features that allowed each society to achieve higher levels of productivity and greater institutional coherence. Such advances benefited from cumulative technical expertise, improved climate, growing Smithian specialization both local and international, expanding bullion flows, from the deliberate and unintended economic consequences of state interventions, and from the diffusion of new technologies among which European-style firearms were most influential. Everywhere warfare provided a major catalyst to innovation.

Accordingly, not only were post-1450 polities typically more powerful than their pre-1300 predecessors, but a new round of fragmentation in Russia, France, and Southeast Asia in the late 1500s and early 1600s proved shorter and less disruptive than the collapse of the 13th to 15th centuries. (At least this was true outside Vietnam, whose conquest of what is now central and southern Vietnam precipitated a north–south split after 1620.) At each stage the polities on which I focus differed widely in solidity and efficiency, but my longitudinal comparisons are place specific. By the same token, within each realm centrally defined linguistic, religious, and ethnic norms diffused horizontally and to some extent vertically, with recognized symbols becoming a marker of political allegiance. Enhanced state patronage propelled cultural integration, as did new religious and educational networks, fresh market linkages, the mimetic impact of social snobbery, and, in France, the introduction of printing. Ultimately, each realm's coherence embodied a psychology of interdependence that was simultaneously commercial, political, and cultural. As we shall see in Chapter 3, these processes would accelerate markedly after 1600.

CHAPTER THREE

Varieties of European Experience, II

A Great Acceleration, c. 1600–1830

1. OVERVIEW: WIDER DIFFERENCES, CLOSER PARALLELS

From the early 1600s to the early 1800s, political and cultural integration in the chief states of both Europe and mainland Southeast Asia showed unprecedented dynamism. Yet, ironically, in this very period the physical capacities of European and Southeast Asian states diverged ever more widely.

Consider first the growing power differential. In 1520, recall, although royal authority in France already was more uniform and penetrating than in Burma, Siam, and probably Vietnam, all four realms, along with Muscovy, retained strong patrimonial and solar polity features. Three hundred years later, similarities were less obvious. True, the gravitational pull of Southeast Asian capitals had increased markedly. But tributaries still enjoyed extensive autonomy, and imperial authority still debouched in attenuated zones, not fixed frontiers. Even in the lowland cores of Burma and Siam, royal personality suffused central administration, and tax collections still depended on long patron–client chains that typically pocketed a third or more of total collections.[1] But by 1825 France and other West European states, with Russia in train, had developed increasingly bureaucratic, impersonal systems that operated with growing uniformity within well-demarcated frontiers. European travelers in the 16th century had marveled at Southeast Asian wealth and power. "This King of Pegu hath not any Armie or power by Sea,"

---

[1] *SP*, 158–209, 302–35, 399–454; Victor Lieberman, *Burmese Administrative Cycles* (Princeton, 1984), ch. 2.

declared Cesare Fedrici, an Italian visitor to Burma in 1567, "but in the Land, for People, Dominions, Gold and Silver he farre exceeds the power of the great Turke in treasure and strength."[2] By contrast, among late-18th- and early-19th-century European visitors a common reaction was bemused contempt. And whereas Burmese and Vietnamese armies in the 1500s had elicited European admiration, 300 years later they were often seen as a joke.[3] Thus even as the three main Southeast Asian empires annexed more distant territories, they themselves began to suffer Western encroachments. From 1770 to 1848 Burma, Siam, and Vietnam subdued Manipur, Assam, Laos, and Cambodia, but between 1824 and 1858 Great Britain started the conquest of Burma, France invaded Vietnam, and Europeans began colonizing Siam's economy.

Identifying reasons for this divergence is not particularly difficult. Like Europe, Southeast Asia had a multistate system involving polities of comparable power whose rivalry spurred administrative and military experiment; indeed Europe and mainland Southeast Asia were among the few Eurasian regions to support such systems for long periods. But weaknesses in metallurgy and mining and relative isolation meant that the full European revolution in artillery, fortifications, infantry training, and weapons had no purchase in Southeast Asia. More basically, Southeast Asia remained too thinly populated, too compartmentalized, too lacking in core–periphery specialization to approach the most advanced economies in Asia, much less Europe. Beyond this, as Chapters 5 and 6 will argue, between c. 1700 and 1830 West European states and economies capitalized on a variety of institutional and cultural advantages over all Asian rivals, including a) market mechanisms that permitted historically low interest rates, low transaction costs, and high levels of wage labor; b) legal and social conventions that afforded commercial enterprise unusual transgenerational continuity and security from political interference;[4] c) patriotic publics, operating through

---

[2] Samuel Purchas, ed., *Hakluytus Posthumus or Purchas His Pilgrimes*, vol. X (Glasgow, 1905), 125. See too accounts by Gasparo Balbi and Ralph Fitch in ibid., 143–204; Donald Lach, *Southeast Asia in the Eyes of Europe* (Chicago, 1968), 543 ff.; Armando Cortesao, ed., *The Suma Oriental of Tome Pires and The Book of Francisco Rodriques*, 2 vols. (London, 1944), vol. I, 97–115.

[3] See, e.g., accounts by Hiram Cox, *Journal of a Residence in the Burmhan Empire* (rpt., London, 1971); John Crawfurd, *Journal of an Embassy from the Governor General of India to the Court of Ava*, 2 vols. (London, 1834); idem, *Journal of an Embassy to the Courts of Siam and Cochin China* (rpt., Singapore, 1987).

[4] On Europe's low interest rates, low transaction costs, frequent wage labor, and protection against predation, see Jan Luiten van Zanden, "The Road to the Industrial

civil society institutions, which critiqued performance in the name of national power; d) activist states, responsive to public opinion, which sought at all costs to augment economic and military strength;[5] e) the scientific revolution, particularly its Newtonian expression, which encouraged technical experiment and, along with more general Enlightenment perspectives, destabilized intellectual conventions;[6] and f) a unique preoccupation with maritime power, which awarded Europe disproportionate profits from global agrarian intensification and ensured that Europe's "ghost acres" in the New World had no Chinese counterpart, for example, in Southeast Asia.[7] In this constellation of forces, rather than any single attribute, Europe's growing commercial and military superiority probably resided.

Given these discrepancies, intriguing indeed were post-1600 parallels between political trajectories in Southeast Asia and Europe. Between 1613 and 1824 all five realms under review – Burma, Siam, Vietnam, Russia, and France – expanded their territories. Burma's zones of control (remember, there were no demarcated frontiers) grew by about 15 percent, Siam's by almost 50 percent, and Russia's by 150 percent. Vietnam split, but after a quasi-fortuitous (re)unification in 1800, the Nguyen Dynasty accelerated the historic push south and west. If most Bourbon overseas conquests and Napoleonic gains proved to be as

Revolution," *JGH* 3 (2008): 337–59, arguing for superiority over China and India by 1500, if not earlier; K. N. Chaudhuri, *Trade and Civilisation in the Indian Ocean* (Cambridge, 1985), 209–15, 226–28; idem, *Asia Before Europe* (Cambridge, 1990), 385–86; C. A. Bayly, *The Birth of the Modern World 1780–1914* (Malden, MA, 2004), 60–64; idem, "South Asia and the 'Great Divergence,'" *Itinerario* 24 (2000): 89–103; Harold Berman, *Law and Revolution* (Cambridge, MA, 1983); Brian Downing, *The Military Revolution and Political Change* (Princeton, 1992), chs. 1–2. On Europe's penchant for organizations independent of the family, Ch. 2, n. 88. But for a vigorous dissent from the view that property in Europe enjoyed greater transgenerational continuity or legal security than in China, see Kenneth Pomeranz, *The Great Divergence* (Princeton, 2000), 169–72, 195–98.

[5] See sources in Ch. 1, n. 13.

[6] Daniel Roche, *France in the Enlightenment* (Cambridge, MA, 1998), 19–26, 75–78, 88, 485–673; Joel Mokyr, *The Lever of Riches* (Oxford, 1990), chs. 9, 10; Jack Goldstone, "Introduction: Economic Growth, Cultural Change, and the Making of the Modern World" (ms); Jonathan Israel, *Radical Enlightenment* (Oxford, 2001), esp. pts. III–V; Ch. 1, n. 4 *supra*; David Bell, pers. commun., Feb. 22, 2006; and discussion *infra*.

[7] E. L. Jones, *The European Miracle* (2nd ed., Cambridge, 1987), 70–84; Pomeranz, *Great Divergence*, ch. 6. In addition, any Chinese attempt to colonize Southeast Asia – rather than merely to impose favorable terms of trade – would have been far more difficult than European colonization of the New World, both because Southeast Asian states were more formidable than Amerindian polities and because the Chinese had no epidemiological superiority such as collapsed New World societies on European contact. We shall return to these comparisons in Ch. 5.

temporary as they were spectacular, the 1815 Vienna settlement still left metropolitan France some 25 percent larger than in 1600. By 1820, *judged by local standards*, administration in all five realms was far more stable and effective than in 1520, and revolts, where they did not cease entirely, grew less formidable.[8] Each polity expanded its tax base and administrative cadre, curbed both provincial governors and religious organizations, gathered more local information, expanded the army, and widened the use of firearms. Meanwhile, with the partial exception of Russia,[9] cultural consolidation, both horizontal and vertical, increased, even as commercialization and literacy encouraged niche specialization. Thus Burman culture eclipsed Mon; Siamese culture infiltrated the Lao, Malay, and Khmer periphery; Vietnamese usages swamped Cham and Khmer; Russian ethnicity and Orthodoxy expanded in all directions; and Parisian culture continued its horizontal and vertical extension.

During these two centuries, c. 1600–1830, moreover, we find a number of synchronized subperiods. In all five realms, in response to recent breakdowns, the early or mid-1600s saw vigorous reforms designed to reassert central authority. As Theodore Rabb argued for Europe but as was also true in much of Southeast Asia, the success of those efforts joined economic amelioration to promote an era of stability and cultural assurance from the mid- or late 1600s well into the 18th century.[10] But

---

[8] This claim holds true for France, where from the 16th to 18th centuries the territorial scale and violence associated with municipal and peasant anti-tax revolts declined markedly. Paradoxically, however, from 1660 to 1789, the *frequency* of anti-tax protests increased as smugglers targeted the crown's salt and tobacco monopolies through relatively nonviolent small-scale incidents. Jean Nicolas, *La Rebellion Francaise* (Paris, 2002), esp. 44–63; Michael Kwass, pers. commun., June 21, 2006. In post-1802 Vietnam uprisings remained frequent, large scale, and troubling. But this too is an exception proving the rule insofar as the sudden doubling of Vietnamese territory by 1802 created novel problems of coordination without parallel in realms whose territories were more stable.

[9] Growing French influence on the nobility after 1750 opened a gap with the peasantry more marked than in the Muscovite era. See discussion *infra*.

[10] Theodore Rabb, *The Struggle for Stability in Early Modern Europe* (New York, 1975). For France, Michele Fogel, *L'Etat dans la France Moderne de la Fin du XVe Siecle au Milieu du XVIIIe Siecle* (Paris, 1992) also emphasizes the coherence of the era 1661–1749, characterized as a period of "incorporation and integration." In Vietnam, although the Trinh regime faced serious internal difficulties, the failure of its southern campaigns by 1672 permitted the Nguyen to consolidate and expand for another century. In Burma the era 1662–1736, and in Ayudhya the first four reigns after the 1688 coup, were relatively placid and successful. In Russia the resolution of mid-17th-century disorders solidified a system of serfdom and landholder privilege that endured into the 1800s.

if economic expansion continued to favor integration over the long term, between 1750 and 1793 instabilities associated with rapid growth combined with military weakness to collapse four of the five states under review.[11] In other words, the French Revolution may be seen as a uniquely innovative ideological variant on a more widespread late-18th-century crisis. In both France and Southeast Asia these disorders constituted the last and shortest interregnum, after disruptions during all or part of the periods 890–1110 (for France alone), 1240–1450, and 1562–1613. Not merely in chronology, but also in their scale, chronology, pressures to innovate, and Darwinian intolerance of the weak, the wars that transformed Southeast Asia in the late 1700s and early 1800s[12] resembled the French Revolutionary and Napoleonic conflicts. Whereas in Europe between 1750 and 1830 the number of independent states fell from some 370 to 57,[13] in mainland Southeast Asia some nine major states in 1750 had collapsed into three by 1824. What is more, as in France and Russia, so in the Southeast Asian lowlands, cultural and linguistic integration accelerated markedly from the mid- or late 1600s.

In short, as Chapter 2 suggested, in mainland Southeast Asia and some major European realms, over *la longue duree* chronologies of cohesion and fracture meshed ever more closely. In the early 9th century not only did maximum conquests by the Frankish/Carolingian kingdom precede by at least 400 years comparable achievements by Pagan, Angkor, early Dai Viet, and Kiev, but the latter four charter realms followed rhythms moderately distinct from one another. However, starting with the mid-15th century political revival of all five areas and continuing through the reforms of the early 1600s to the epochal wars of the late 1700s and early 1800s, developments became more closely synchronized across mainland Southeast Asia, between major European realms, and between Southeast Asia and Europe. Figures 1.4 to 1.8 capture some of these maturing parallels.

That coordination should have grown *within* Europe and *within* mainland Southeast Asia is hardly surprising. Within each region, denser trade and communication circuits and intensifying warfare provided

---

[11] Or five out of six, if we include the two Vietnamese states, the others being Burma, Siam, and France.

[12] See *SP*, 184–87, 299–313, 419–33.

[13] Note, however, that the great bulk of these reductions occurred in Germany, chiefly as a result of French interventions.

obvious links. Across Southeast Asia, the tremendous pull of the Chinese market from the late 1500s and more especially the 1720s, and a flood of Chinese immigrants, further strengthened coordination.

But given the fact that mainland Southeast Asia and Europe had minimal contact, why should gross coordination *between* these regions also have increased? We shall return to this conundrum, but in preliminary fashion I would point to four harmonizing factors. First, widespread political collapse in the late 1500s and/or early 1600s was itself a major spur to synchronization insofar as it prompted independent but parallel reforms. Second, from the 15th or 16th century, and with rising force in the 18th, improved firearms joined cumulative institutional expertise to fortify central authorities in Southeast Asia and Europe alike. Third, in both regions better post-1710 climate and improved pacification invigorated population growth and Smithian specialization. Fourth, after 1550 and more especially 1720, international trade – by disseminating Chinese and Indian textiles, New World crops, New World bullion, and novel technologies – became an ever more insistent agent of simultaneity. Although these processes yielded more powerful states in Europe, until European armies arrived, the only relevant yardstick for Southeast Asian actors was the strength of local opponents. In Southeast Asia itself interstate inequality, hence predation and the impetus to reform, was no less marked than in Europe.

Note finally that accelerating coordination across Europe boosts our confidence that France and Russia can stand as emblems for the continent. Until 1648 alternatives to the unified territorial state – city-states, urban leagues, the Holy Roman Empire – retained some plausibility. Russia in many ways was still an outlier to Europe. But the Thirty Years War (1618–1648) – in which, the Swedish king Gustavus Adolphus noted, "all the wars of Europe are now blended into one" – signaled both the triumph of the sovereign territorial state, of which France became the 17th century's most successful example, and the creation of a diplomatic-cum-military system composed of sovereign states and spanning much of the continent.[14] The Seven Years War (1756–1763) fully extended the system to Russia, whose armies by the 1630s already had come to depend on central and western European models and whose nobles under Peter the Great had begun to regard themselves as Europeans culturally. To be sure, Russian serfdom and social

---

[14] Cf. Hendrik Spruyt, *The Sovereign State and Its Competitors* (Princeton, 1994).

ethics remained peculiar – Russia lay at one extreme of Charles Tilly's market-intensive/market-deficient continuum – and Russian periodization preserved distinctive features: the Petrine revolution was unusually dislocating, and until the 1860s Russian political structures remained exceptionally conservative. Yet no one can doubt that 18th-century Russia was a major European power, and that between c. 1600 and 1830 Russian administrative and territorial consolidation, if not the social context in which it occurred, paralleled consolidations in France and other major European realms. Nor, amidst local idiosyncrasies, were trends to cultural integration in Russia and France without broad European analogy. Another brief European *tour d'horizon* may confirm these claims and serve as background for our final installment of Russian and French history.

In 17th-century England the Stuart monarchy's flirtation with French-style "absolutism" joined population pressure and religious discord to spark civil war. Those conflicts and the Glorious Revolution of 1688–1689 confirmed that a Protestant crown would have to rule in cooperation with Parliament and demonstrated the strength of a national system of governance reliant on local dignitaries. Britain's early centralization, which facilitated uniform national tax rates, and an absence of venality constituted further unique advantages. From 1688 to 1815 a substantial growth in the size, probity, and efficiency of public administration, astounding increases in deficit financing and indirect taxation, and the growing professionalism of the army and more especially of the navy dramatically enhanced Britain's position around the globe and in Europe. The commercial economy facilitated cheap war finance through the Bank of England, while Parliament fostered financial accountability, political legitimacy, and national over provincial loyalties. Able to collect in taxes by the late 1700s almost twice the share of national income that France collected, yet with minimal opposition, Britain developed an unusually participatory and efficient version of what John Brewer terms the "fiscal-military state." Meanwhile, nurtured by an aggressively anti-Catholic (alternately anti-Spanish, anti-French, anti-Irish) patriotism with roots in the 16th century and buoyed by the expansion of printed media and of the home market, London culture gained greater salience within England, even as English culture became hegemonic within Great Britain and English identity was reconfigured in an emergent British identity. Following Welsh precedent, the incorporation of Scotland and Ireland into what contemporaries termed "the British empire in Europe" had cultural correlates. Whereas in 1000 the British Isles supported 200 distinct languages, as early as the 16th century the hybrid tongue that would evolve into modern English became supreme, with the vast majority of the others headed for extinction.[15]

The Dutch Republic, which in truth was less a republic than a mercantile oligarchy, resembled England in that it benefited during the 17th century from a Protestant culture of social discipline, a precocious nationalism, a buoyant, highly urbanized commercial economy, and a limited but real political representation that fostered consensus and encouraged bourgeois investment in the public debt. By securing unusually low-cost loans to finance the armed forces and by regulating a range of economic activities, the state, even though it controlled a small population and was neither particularly centralized nor bureaucratic, was able not only to win independence from Spain by 1648, but to build a global empire in America, South Africa, and Indonesia that survived, amidst growing difficulties, to the Napoleonic era. Key to this success, Philip Gorski argues, were powerful institutions of local self-governance that obviated a large central apparatus but that also ensured efficient military mobilization and fiscal extraction and a remarkable degree of social order. Shaped by its Calvinist heritage and by bitter struggles against Spain and later France, Dutch culture, at least until the triumph of French classicism in the late 1600s, gloried in its distinction from the Catholic south.[16]

---

[15] On British languages, David Northrup, "Globalization and the Great Convergence," *JWH* 16 (2005): 256; Richard Bailey, *Images of English* (Ann Arbor, 1991), 20–37. On British political/fiscal evolution, John Brewer, *The Sinews of Power* (Cambridge, MA, 1988), with tax data on 22, 89–91; Patrick O'Brien and Philip Hunt, "England, 1485–1815," in Richard Bonney, ed., *The Rise of the Fiscal State in Europe, c. 1200–1815* (Oxford, 1999), 53–100; Philip Gorski, *The Disciplinary Revolution* (Chicago, 2003), 152–59; idem, "The Mosaic Moment," *American Jl. of Sociology* 105 (2000): esp. 1452–56; Adrian Hastings, *The Construction of Nationhood* (Cambridge, 1997), chs. 2, 3; Linda Colley, *Britons, Forging the Nation 1707–1837* (New Haven, 1992); J. A. Sharpe, *Early Modern England: A Social History. 1550–1760* (London, 1987), 4–31, 99–123; C. A. Bayly, *The Imperial Meridian* (London, 1989), chs. 3, 4; John Miller, "Britain," in Miller, ed., *Absolutism in Seventeenth-Century Europe* (New York, 1990), 195–224; Jack Goldstone, *Revolution and Rebellion in the Early Modern World* (Berkeley, 1991), ch. 2; John Merriman, *A History of Modern Europe* (New York, 1996), 232–60, 442–80; Roger Albin, pers. commun., Oct. 8, 2008.
[16] On the Netherlands, Gorski, *Disciplinary Revolution*, 39–77; idem, "Mosaic Moment," 1428–68; Marjolein 't Hart, "The United Provinces, 1579–1806," in Bonney, *Rise of the Fiscal State*, 309–25; Jonathan Israel, *Dutch Primacy in World Trade 1585–1740* (Oxford, 1989); idem, *The Dutch Republic* (Oxford, 1995); Simon Schama, *An Embarrassment of Riches* (London, 1987), esp. 15–125; J. C. H. Blom and E. Lamberts, eds., *History of the Low Countries* (New York, 2006), ch. 4; and discussion in Ch. 7 *infra*.

In Sweden continued metal exports and Gustavus Adolphus' sweeping military reforms paved the way to conquests along the Baltic littoral, which peaked in 1661. In the long term, Sweden's demographic base proved too weak to hold these areas against Danish, Prussian, and Russian counterattacks. Nonetheless, during the 17th and early 18th centuries support from the lesser nobility, low-level officials, clergymen, and peasants allowed the crown to resume lands formerly alienated to leading nobles, and on that basis, despite periodic magnate challenges, to develop and retain what A. F. Upton termed "probably the most efficient military-bureaucratic machine in Europe."[17] This included a cost-effective system of cantonal military allotments and a precocious audit system designed to ensure balanced budgets. Together, administrative centralization, an effective clerical monopoly on education, and the printing of dictionaries, literary works, and university lectures in Swedish encouraged cultural and linguistic standardization, so that by 1650 religious dissent was virtually unknown, and Sweden's core population was one of the most homogenous in Europe.

In 17th-century Spain pride in past military glories combined with commercial weakness, a fierce defense of magnate, clerical, and local privilege, and a consequent emphasis on ad hoc improvisation to forestall effective reform on the English or Swedish model. Impelled by Dutch and French military challenges, between 1622 and 1643 the chief minister, the Count of Olivares – whose motto was "one king, one law, one money" – sought to tax all sectors in proportion to their resources and thus to integrate the realm fiscally and militarily; but those efforts withered before open insurrections in Catalonia and Portugal. After 1700 the new Bourbon monarchy, inspired by kindred French dynastic example and relying on administrators recruited from the lesser nobility, crafted fresh plans to enhance the legal authority and income of the state, to curb the church, reduce Catalan autonomy, and safeguard Spain's still vast New World holdings. In full spate by 1740, this self-conscious modernizing program continued, with mixed results, to the Napoleonic era. The Bourbons also promoted Castilian speech at the expense of Catalan in local administration, but widespread illiteracy,

---

[17] A. F. Upton, "Sweden," in Miller, *Absolutism in Seventeenth-Century Europe*, 99. On Swedish development, ibid., 99–121; A. F. Upton, *Charles XI and Swedish Absolutism* (Cambridge, 1998), esp. 1–11, 251–61; Paul Monod, *The Power of Kings* (New Haven, 1999), 300; Perry Anderson, *Lineages of the Absolutist State* (London, 1974), 173–91; Stewart Oakley, *A Short History of Sweden* (New York, 1966), 89–183; Gorski, *Disciplinary Revolution*, 13–15, 150–52.

poor market integration, and Bourbon deference to custom in non-Catalan areas of proven loyalty meant that by French, not to mention English, Dutch, or Swedish standards, cultural integration remained limited. After recovering its independence from Spain, Portugal under the ultraregalist Marquis of Pombal (in power 1750–1777) launched reforms, broadly reminiscent of those in Spain, designed to develop the mercantilist economy of both the metropole and its overseas possessions and to enhance royal authority at the expense of the church and the great noble families.[18]

Although what are now Germany and Italy remained fragmented, we find a continuing trend toward local consolidation, in Italy, for example in Piedmont-Savoy, and more especially across Germany. In Germany the Holy Roman Empire survived, but imperial institutions, including a permanent Reichstag, proved cumbersome, ineffectual, and increasingly anomalous, certainly by the 18th century. At the subimperial level, however, Austria, Prussia, Saxony, Bavaria, and some lesser states succeeded in developing more cohesive territories, professional armies, and effective tax systems on the general European model. Indeed, nothing threatened the political vitality and intellectual underpinning of the Empire more than the struggle between the Prussian and Austrian ruling houses. Habsburg Austria, whose ruler retained the imperial title, controlled extensive lands both within the Empire and without, the latter including Hungary, parts of Italy, Croatia, the southern Netherlands, and from 1772 southwest Poland. Although, as was true of Spanish holdings, this was a polyglot agglomeration ruled not through a single administration, rather through autonomous local institutions, the Thirty Years War did produce a standing army, a substantially new, more crown-dependent nobility in the Czech lands, and a fervent Counter-Reformation imperial ideology that sought to compensate for political localism. During the second half of the 18th century, in response to

---

[18] On Spain, Ruth Mackay, *The Limits of Royal Authority: Resistance and Obedience in 17th-Century Castile* (Cambridge, 1999); Simon Barton, *A History of Spain* (New York, 2004), 119–71; I. A. A. Thompson, "Castile: Polity, Fiscality, and Fiscal Crisis," and idem, "Castile: Absolutism, Constitutionalism, and Liberty," in Philip Hoffman and Kathryn Norberg, eds., *Fiscal Crises, Liberty, and Representative Government 1450–1789* (Stanford, 1994), 140–225; idem, "Castile," in Miller, *Absolutism in Seventeenth-Century Europe*, 69–98; Juan Gelabert, "Castile, 1504–1808," in Bonney, *Rise of the Fiscal State*, 201–41; Merriman, *History*, 219–31. On Portugal, C. R. Boxer, *The Portuguese Seaborne Empire 1415–1825* (London, 1969), ch. 8; David Birmingham, *A Concise History of Portugal* (Cambridge, 1993), 65–95.

Prussian challenges and Enlightenment currents, Austrian rulers made yet more vigorous efforts, with mixed results, to centralize administration in Bohemia and Austria, to unify legal practices in those lands, to end serfdom, limit church autonomy, and strengthen the army, all the while promoting German as the language of imperial administration.

Austria's principal German rival, Prussia, whose rise represented the quintessential triumph of dynastic ambition and efficient administration over what seemed to be hopelessly unfavorable geography, acquired East Prussia in 1618, Eastern Pomerania in 1648, and Silesia, seized from Austria, in 1742. In defending and imposing order on these scattered lands, Prussia evolved institutions devoted overwhelmingly to the army and a culture that laid unique stress on Calvinist-Pietist social discipline, military primacy, and noble domination, albeit with a service nobility dependent on the crown and with medieval corporate institutions emasculated. By 1740 Prussia, with about 4 percent of its people in arms, had Europe's largest standing army relative to its population and perhaps the most centralized administration. Yet the state's vulnerability was shown by its collapse before Napoleon, a defeat that inspired military and social reforms more ambitious than in Austria.[19]

One might conclude from Prussian, other German, and Dutch examples that early modern Europe nourished more novel polities, with weaker pre-1600 territorial and political roots, than Southeast Asia. But this ignores the upstart Nguyen state – Southeast Asia's Prussia – that rose in southern Vietnam more or less *de novo* in the early 1600s and went on to become one of the mainland's principal powers. Like Prussia, Nguyen Vietnam was far removed from the metropolitan sources of its civilization, bent every effort to wring strength from a sparsely settled frontier, and through its powerful army, created the nucleus for regional recentralization in the 19th century.[20]

---

[19] On Italian and German states, Olwen Hufton, *Europe: Privilege and Protest 1730–1789* (London, 1980), chs. 5–7; Merriman, *History*, 299–307, 432–34, 448–51, 575; Carlo Capra, "The Italian States in the Early Modern Period," in Bonney, *Rise of the Fiscal State*, 417–42; Gorski, *Disciplinary Revolution*, 11, 79–113; R. J. W. Evans, *The Making of the Habsburg Monarchy 1550–1700* (Oxford, 1979), pts. 1, 2; Anderson, *Lineages*, 236–78, 299–327; H. W. Koch, "Brandenburg-Prussia," and Jean Berenger, "The Austrian Lands," in Miller, *Absolutism in Seventeenth-Century Europe*, 123–74; Derek Sayer, *The Coasts of Bohemia* (Princeton, 1998), 44–52.

[20] For some of these views I am indebted to Alexander Woodside, pers. commun., Sept. 14, 1999.

2. RUSSIAN POLITICAL AND CULTURAL TRENDS TO C. 1830

Stabilization and Renewal to c. 1650

In brief, there is every indication that in basic trajectory and chronology, consolidation across Europe between 1600 and 1830 paralleled developments in mainland Southeast Asia. In this context, let us examine more closely tsarism's early 17th-century revival and reform.

After the Time of Troubles the new Romanov Dynasty struggled to restore domestic order and to forestall fresh external assaults. In Southeast Asia as in Russia, the most prized resource was people, not land. After unauthorized peasant movements in the late 1500s opened the door to disastrous invasions, restorationist regimes in Burma and Siam made one of their highest priorities the strengthening of manpower control. Accordingly, the *ahmu-dan* system in Burma (overhauled 11 years prior to the imposition of serfdom in Russia) and the *phrai luang* system in Siam, both of which systematized rules evolving since the early 1400s, sought to curb social and geographic mobility.[21]

Now in fact, the Romanov court faced conflicting interests in this regard. Because they often sheltered fugitive peasants, large monasteries, frontier officials, and *boyars* tended to oppose restrictions on movement. Yet demands by the middle service class of *pomest'e*-holders for a secure labor force could not be ignored, both because *pomest'e* cavalrymen, many impoverished by the Time of Troubles, remained militarily valuable, and because they had become the chief bulwark against rural upheaval. At the same time the government's own fiscal needs required that agrarian production in the core be stabilized and that taxpayers be fixed and monitored. Between 1613 and 1649 those demanding new labor controls won out. By defining all cultivators of private land as "serfs," the *Ulozhenie* of 1649 – the most comprehensive law code since 1550 – bound Russian tillers to the soil. In thus formalizing serfdom, it extended curbs on movement that began as early as 1455 and had become notably more onerous during the disorders of the 1580s and 1590s. At the request of urban communes, who feared per capita tax increases if local residents fled, the government in 1649 imposed similar controls on townsmen. Whereas before 1600 most Muscovites had little contact with the state aside from tax payments, now officials assigned

---

[21] Lieberman, *Administrative Cycles*, 92–105, 288–92; *SP*, 163, 182, 280.

people to hereditary categories – serf, state peasant, crown peasant, townsman – and joined landlords and local leaders in hunting down fugitives.[22]

Given the still modest size of the central apparatus, how could so ambitious a system of social control succeed? In part, it worked because tsarist officials committed greater resources to record-keeping and finding absconders. In part, because the 1649 political compact enlisted the natural leaders of rural society, namely, provincial cavalrymen, who were transformed into a landlord class that Valerie Kivelson terms "the gentry."[23] In the course of the 17th century, this class gained not only increased authority over peasant labor, but a reduction in their own service requirements and the effective conversion of *pomest'e* lands into allodial property. In part too, the new labor controls proved effective because, as just indicated, economic self-interest led communities to police themselves: as in Burma, the fact that state demands fell on collectivities rather than individual households created powerful incentives to keep neighbors from running away.

At the same time and by extension from the previous point, serfdom appealed to widely shared assumptions about collective well-being and group obligation. Although Russian social estates were profoundly unequal, all people enjoyed some dignity by virtue of their Christian identity, their membership in a local status group (e.g., village, clan), and their claims to tsarist legal protection. Muscovites valued not personal freedom, which they equated with vulnerability, but the security that stemmed from inclusion in a stable, hierarchical, God-centered community. Deeply rooted in 16th-century tsarist and church teachings, discussed in Chapter 2, such sentiments received powerful reinforcement during the Time of Troubles. Thus not only did the *Ulozhenie*, an elite

---

[22] On the evolution of 16th- to 17th-century social controls and center–provincial relations, Richard Hellie, *Enserfment and Military Change in Muscovy* (Chicago, 1971), pts. I and II; idem, "The Stratification of Muscovite Society: The Townsmen," *RH* 5 (1978): 119–75; idem, "Warfare, Changing Military Technology, and the Evolution of Muscovite Society," in John Lynn, ed., *Tools of War* (Urbana, IL, 1990), 85–90; Valerie Kivelson, "The Effects of Partible Inheritance," *RR* 53 (1994): 197–212; idem, *Autocracy in the Provinces* (Stanford, 1996); idem, "The Devil Stole His Mind," *AHR* 98 (1993), 749–50; Carol Stevens, *Soldiers on the Steppe* (DeKalb, IL, 1995), chs. 4–7; Nancy Shields Kollmann, *By Honor Bound* (Ithaca, 1999), 203–21; J. Michael Hittle, *The Service City* (Cambridge, MA, 1979), chs. 1–3. On *boyar* roles from the late 1500s to mid-1600s, Robert O. Crummey, "The Reconstitution of the Boiar Aristocracy, 1613–1645," *FzOG* 18 (1973): 187–220; idem, *Aristocrats and Servitors* (Princeton, 1983), esp. chs. 1, 2.

[23] See Kivelson references in previous note.

document, exhibit a pervasive fear of mobility and noncomformity, but 17th-century legal cases revealed widespread enthusiasm among peasants and poor townsmen themselves to repress all manner of deviance, from unauthorized movement to unfamiliar religious practices to petty insubordination. In practical terms, moreover, if serfs could not leave the land, neither could access to land be denied them so long as they fulfilled their labor obligations, which ensured access to a resource critical to sustain their families. Although subject to gentry supervision in many districts, the self-regulating village commune (*mir*), to which we shall return, became responsible for redistributing peasant allotments, allocating taxes, and settling disputes. *Pace* Tilly, in such a world self-enserfment could be an attractive, even morally correct option, and elite coercion, though surely widespread, may not have been the principal instrument of social order.[24]

In post-1600 Theravada Southeast Asia (Burma, Siam, Cambodia, and Laos), I argued that village monasticism joined self-regulating service organizations to provide a rural infrastructure outside direct royal control that nonetheless aided the state by helping to pacify society.[25] Theravada monasteries were arguably thicker on the ground, and certainly had a more critical educative function, than Russian parish churches. Yet Russian rural communes and churches resembled Southeast Asian institutions insofar as they inculcated respect for hierarchy, devalued local sources of sanctity, promoted social discipline of a sort, and facilitated tax collections – without extensive provision of scarce state resources.[26] All this reinforces my suggestion that Calvinism – although promoting discipline to an extraordinary degree – was but

---

[24] See my comment on Tilly in Ch. 1, n. 61 *supra*. On the cultural roots of serfdom, Ch. 2, n. 258 *supra*, plus Valerie Kivelson, "Male Witches and Gendered Categories in 17th-Century Russia," *CSSH* 45 (2003): 606–31; idem, "Bitter Slavery and Pious Servitude," in Robert Crummey et al., eds., *Russische und Ukrainische Geschichte vom 16.-18. Jahrhundert* (Wiesbaden, 2001), 110–19; idem, "Mapping Serfdom," in Valerie Kivelson and Joan Neuberger, eds., *Picturing Russia* (New Haven, 2008), 47–50, citing Steven Hoch; Kivelson, "Community Harmony/Community Strife" (ms); idem, "Witchcraft Accusations and Social Stratification in 17th-Century Russia" (ms). See too sensitive analyses of hierarchy and honor in Nancy Shields Kollmann, "Society, Identity and Modernity in 17th-Century Russia," in Jarmo Kotilaine and Marshall Poe, eds., *Modernizing Muscovy* (London, 2004), 417–31; Kollmann, *Honor Bound*, ch. 5 and *passim*. On the *mir*'s communal functions, Steven Hoch, *Serfdom and Social Control in Russia* (Chicago, 1986), 133–59.

[25] *SP*, 135–39, 200–202, 259–63, 314–24.

[26] Comparable benefits flowed from Neo-Confucianism, which had the added advantage of providing bureaucratic models. Cf. *SP*, 377–83 and Gorski, *Disciplinary Revolution*, 34 ff., 138–59, on Calvinist spurs to bureaucracy.

one in a series of early modern regulatory doctrines that supplemented new state structures.

In administrative terms the chief link between the countryside and the court were military governors, *voevody*, whose ranks expanded during and after the Time of Troubles. Like the old *namestniki* discussed in Chapter 2, *voevody* triangulated their personal interests with those of the crown and the gentry. Still, *voevody* typically enjoyed shorter tenures than *namestniki* and, unlike *namestniki*, were obliged to share provincial responsibilities with other civil and military appointees. Along with the reworking of capital–gentry ties, these changes paralleled the early-17th-century shift in Burma and Siam from august viceroys to dependent governors now subject to term limits, crosscutting jurisdictions, and new reporting procedures.[27]

The first half of the 17th century also saw major military reforms that recall contemporary Burmese efforts to train *ahmu-dan* musketeers and Nguyen efforts to plant military colonies, but that relied far more heavily on foreign models and were more technologically innovative. Its very foundation an act of defiance against Poland, the Romanov Dynasty sensed that if it were to defend itself, much less go onto the offensive in the west, it would have to accelerate the transition from steppe cavalry to European infantry and create a standing army on western lines. Under the eye of Dutch, Swedish, Scottish, and other foreign advisers, Russians were therefore trained to use imported handguns and to employ the latest linear infantry tactics. As early as 1632–1634, during renewed fighting around Smolensk, these "new formation regiments," which constituted about half of Russian theater forces, were said to be "vastly superior" to their Polish foes.[28]

---

[27] On Russian governors, Ch. 2, n. 241 *supra*, plus Kivelson, *Autocracy*, 133–43, 268, and *passim*; idem, "Cartography, Autocracy, and State Powerlessness," *Imago Mundi* 51 (1999): 83–105; Hellie, *Enserfment*, 67–71; idem, "Russia, 1200–1815," in Bonney, *Rise of the Fiscal State*, 490; Hittle, *Service City*, 48–53. On Burma, where more humble *myo-wuns* replaced *bayin* viceroys, and on Siam, see *SP*, 161–63, 278–80.

[28] Hellie, *Enserfment*, 172. On military changes to the 1650s, ibid., 167–80; idem, "Warfare, Changing Military Technology," 85–88; idem, "The Costs of Muscovite Military Defense and Expansion," in Eric Lohr and Marshall Poe, eds., *The Military and Society in Russia 1450–1917* (Leiden, 2002), 41–66; Denis J. B. Shaw, "Southern Frontiers of Muscovy, 1550–1700," in James Bater and R. A. French, *Studies in Russian Historical Geography*, 2 vols. (London, 1983), vol. I, 126–34; Paul Dukes, "The Thirty Years War, the Smolensk War and the Modernization of International Relations in Europe," in Kotilaine and Poe, *Modernizing Muscovy*, 203–22; William Reger IV, "European Mercenary Officers and the Reception of Military Reform in the 17th-Century Russian Army," in ibid., 223–45.

Pressures to Territorial Expansion and Administrative Integration:
Warfare, New Intellectual Currents, and Economic Growth,
c. 1650–1830

In sum, by strengthening social controls, reorganizing provincial administration, and modernizing its army, Moscow by 1650, not unlike Burma,
Siam, and France in the early 1600s, had mastered its most serious
domestic and external challenges since the 14th century. Thereafter,
although Russian reforms grew unusually insistent and socially disruptive, in terms of broad timing and basic dynamics, integration continued to parallel that in Southeast Asian and other European realms.
Indeed, of the three principal goads to Russian expansion and internal
reform between 1650 and 1830 – intensifying warfare, novel intellectual
currents, and economic-cum-demographic growth – the first and third
are quite familiar.

Consider first military competition. Territorial acquisition in Russia
and Southeast Asia from 1650 to 1830 exhibited the following generic
similarities: a) In part, success reflected the ability of political cores to
magnify their physical ascendancy through demographic intensification and/or frontier colonization. Thus Burmese demographic superiority increased in the western, Siamese in the central, and Vietnamese
in the eastern mainland; while Russia's population enjoyed a growing
advantage over the Tatar steppe, the Caucasus, Siberia, Sweden, and
much of the Baltic.[29] b) If demographic growth favored the eventual
victors, it is also true that inept policy weakened states whose material resources in the early 1600s were still reasonably competitive. In
1620 Cambodia, for example, was still a credible rival to Ayudhya, as
were Poland and Ottoman Turkey to Russia. Cambodia crumbled in
part because it failed to curb endemic factionalism. Turkey and Poland
were slower to embrace the military revolution than Russia, a failure
that in the case of Poland was compounded by the suicidal implications
of *szlachta* (noble) democracy and a remarkable insouciance about interstate imperatives.[30] c) Southeast Asian empires and Russia followed
a comparable strategic logic: border zones were set up outside the

---

[29] I follow John LeDonne, *The Russian Empire and the World 1700–1917* (New York, 1997),
1–20 and *passim*. Also Willard Sunderland, *Taming the Wild Field* (Ithaca, 2004), 35–134.

[30] Geoffrey Parker, *The Military Revolution* (Cambridge, 1988), 37–38, 126–28; David Kirby,
Northern Europe in the Early Modern Period: The Baltic World 1492–1777 (London, 1990);
Anderson, *Lineages*, 288–98; Anna Filipczak-Kocur, "Poland-Lithuania Before Parti-
tion," in Bonney, *Rise of the Fiscal* State, esp. 473–77.

main defensive perimeter, but as those zones became integrated into the empire through settlement and patronage, they not infrequently demanded creation of yet more distant buffers.[31] d) As the post-1600 expansion of the service systems in Burma and Siam and the extension of Russian serfdom suggest, military concerns dominated social policy. e) In Southeast Asia as in Russia, imperial expansion climaxed after large-scale early-19th-century warfare. Burma achieved its maximum influence in the 1820s, Vietnam in the 1830s, Siam in the 1840s. In John LeDonne's view, Russia reached its apogee in strategic, if not territorial, terms between 1797 and 1831, when it humbled France, Sweden, and Persia and annexed Finland, Bessarabia, Poland, and most of the Caucasus.[32]

And yet in basic ways, Russia's geopolitical options also differed from those of mainland Southeast Asia. Burma, Siam, and, to a lesser extent, Vietnam enjoyed formidable natural defenses – east–west mountains in the far north and north–south uplands extending to the coast – that afforded substantial security. Not surprisingly, across much of the mainland large-scale warfare was episodic. A great upsurge in the second half of the 16th century was followed in the west and center by a century and a half of rather more pacific conditions as each state consolidated itself within new frontiers. Dynastic collapse then ushered in a fresh phase of attempted expansion and intensified conflict from 1759 to 1848. Administrative reform naturally coincided with these periods of sustained fighting.

But Russia, lying on a plain that ran from the Rhine to the Urals, which themselves were a barrier of no significance en route to Inner Asia, could never dream of "natural" frontiers. As such, Russia remained far more vulnerable to attack, more inclined to destroy hostile concentrations on its borders through offensive operations, and thus more often at war than its Southeast Asian counterparts. To summarize two centuries of strategic advance: During the Thirteen Years War of 1654–1667, in order to avenge Polish attacks during the Time of Troubles, extend its

---

[31] Chiang Mai illustrated this tendency in the Siamese realm, as did the Mekong delta in the Nguyen. All around the Muscovite core we find examples, from Smolensk to the Left Bank Ukraine to the Crimea to the Volga basin. *SP*, chs. 2–4; Marshall Poe and Eric Lohr, "Introduction," in Lohr and Poe, *Military and Society*, 5–6; John LeDonne, "The Grand Strategy of the Russian Empire, 1650–1831," in ibid., 175–95; William C. Fuller, Jr., *Strategy and Power in Russia 1600–1914* (New York, 1992), chs. 1–5.

[32] LeDonne, "Grand Strategy," 188–95, claiming, with some exaggeration, in my view, that Persia, Sweden, and Prussia became Russian "client states."

western defenses, and exploit anti-Polish disturbances in the Ukraine, Russia seized Smolensk, Kiev, and the Left Bank Ukraine. In the face of Swedish resistance Russia took the entire Baltic coast to Riga during the Northern War of 1700–1721. In the late 18th century Russia joined Austria and Prussia in dismembering Poland. To the south, after a century of conflict with the Ottomans, Russia from 1774 to 1812 captured the Crimea, the north shore of the Black Sea, and Bessarabia, while between 1801 and 1813 Russia also occupied Caucasian areas to the discomfiture of Turkey and Persia. Far to the east, throughout the 17th and 18th centuries Russian power flowed into Siberia, Kazakhstan, and Alaska. Finally, from 1805 to 1815 wars against Napoleon led to the acquisition of Finland and the formation of a Russian-dominated Kingdom of Poland. Or to restate the difference, whereas between 1613 and 1825 Burmese armies took the field against external foes one year out of five, with the great bulk of those efforts concentrated between 1759 and 1811, from 1613 to 1825 Russian armies were on campaign almost one year in two, often on more than one front.[33]

Of course, as this litany of advances suggests, the flip side of Russia's early-17th-century vulnerability was the opportunity for open-ended expansion: when victorious, its armies faced few obvious limits. Hence the extraordinary size of the empire, over 18,000,000 square kilometers by 1825, some 25 times larger than Burma and 33 times larger than France. Russia's destruction of rival cores all along its western flank, the heavy concentration of population and wealth in the western sector of the empire, Siberia's relative emptiness, the steppe's growing post-1600 military obsolescence, good riverine communications in both Europe and Siberia,[34] and brilliant strategic planning meant that, until the Crimean War, disintegrative forces were kept at bay.

European involvement meant, furthermore, that from 1650 to 1820 Russia continued to face far more persistent pressures than mainland Southeast Asia to upgrade its military. In the latter region a low-level technological parity between major states, the lesser frequency of

---

[33] Burmese forces were so engaged in 42 years out of 212. *U Kala, Maha-ya-zawin-gyi*; vols. I, II, Saya Pwa, ed. (Rangoon, 1926, 1932); vol. III, Hsaya U Kin So, ed. (Rangoon, 1961); U Tin, comp., *Kon-baung-zet maha-ya-zawin-daw-gyi*, vols. I, II (rpt. London, 1967–1968). But Russian forces were so engaged in 99 years out of 212. Nicholas Riasanovsky, *A History of Russia* (4th ed., New York, 1984); Arcadius Kahan, *The Plow, the Hammer, and the Knout* (Chicago, 1985), 8, Table 1.3; John Channon, *The Penguin Historical Atlas of Russia* (London, 1995), 50–55.

[34] See Ch. 1, n. 60.

conflict, and a limited cash economy bred relative conservatism. Even in the early 1800s after a period of unusually intense competition, only Vietnam kept a large standing army and supplemented in-kind military support with substantial cash salaries. Although the Nguyen also built European-style citadels, as late as 1822 about half of regular troops did not have firearms. Arms manufacture across the mainland remained limited – the best guns were all imported – and European-style tactical innovations remained minimal.[35]

However, as early perhaps as the mid-1600s Russian elites, the first in world history, self-consciously began to define themselves as leaders of a "backward" realm that had to "catch up" with central and western Europe militarily and, by extension, economically.[36] During the Thirteen Years War Russia resumed large-scale arms imports from the Netherlands and the training, under Western officers, of additional "new formation regiments," that is to say, semistanding units with some cash salaries and with infantry far outnumbering cavalry. Flintlocks, rather than cumbersome matchlocks, and bronze artillery made notable advances. An ad hoc household-based draft, instituted in 1647, facilitated infantry expansion.[37]

New formation regiments tended to decay in the late 1600s, probably for cost reasons, so that with the start of the Northern War in 1700, Peter the Great, that historic eccentric, was forced to renew as well as to innovate. This he did with manic zeal. Peter's regular army grew to 200,000, second only to that of France. Whereas in the 1650s, over 80 percent of command positions had been held by non-Russians, by 1720, 88 percent of the officer corps were Russians. Uniforms, line tactics, drill, flintlocks, bayonets, and cannon all followed western or central European models,

[35] *SP*, 48, 60–61, 65 ff., 79, 146–53, 164–67, 256–58, 268–79, 285, 309–10, 406, 426, 454; and Crawfurd, *Journal of an Embassy to Siam and Cochin China*, 492–95, estimating Vietnam's 1822 standing army at 40,000 to 50,000. In part, Vietnam's relative sophistication reflected the more continuous nature of warfare in the eastern corridor, which involved both intra-Vietnamese contests and campaigns against Cambodia.

[36] At least this is the claim of Poe and Lohr, "Introduction," 3. However, Valerie Kivelson, pers. commun., April 3, 2006, has expressed reservations about the view that Muscovites saw themselves as "backwards" and suggests that this attitude may have taken root only with Peter the Great.

[37] Hellie, *Enserfment*, 181–201; idem, "Warfare, Changing Military Technology," 90–94; J. L. H. Keep, *Soldiers of the Tsar* (Oxford, 1985), 89–92; Stevens, *Soldiers*, 8–9, 83, 160; Fuller, *Strategy and Power*, 1–34, and sources in n. 28 *supra*. On the growth of military chancelleries and personnel, Kollmann, *Honor Bound*, 204–205; Marshall Poe, "The Consequences of the Military Revolution in Muscovy," *CSSH* 38 (1996): 263.

as did the fledgling navy.[38] After Peter the army continued to grow, reaching 303,000 in 1765 and 597,000 in 1812, by which time Russia had become the strongest land power in Europe.[39] (On a per capita basis, the 1812 figure was roughly twice as large as Vietnam's standing army in 1822.) Despite this post-Petrine expansion, Peter's basic system of military finance – focusing on trade taxes, salt and vodka monopolies, and the poll (soul) tax – continued into the early 1800s. During the most difficult years of the 18th century the military consumed 60 to 80 percent of state expenditure, a proportion that fell to 40 to 60 percent during and after the Napoleonic Wars. But as the empire's resource base grew from 1701 to 1825, real military outlays, adjusted for inflation, probably rose at least 20-fold.[40] Peter also introduced Europe's first systematic conscription, backed by an imperial census. Whereas in the 1600s peasants had been "borrowed" temporarily for the army, now they were recruited for permanent service. And whereas in the early 1600s peasants had been responsible for provisioning individual servitors directly, now they supplied taxes to the government, which in turn paid the army.

[38] For various estimates of French and Russian army size, see Jeremy Black, *A Military Revolution?* (Atlantic Highlands, NJ, 1991), 6–7, 29; Janet Hartley, *A Social History of the Russian Empire 1650–1825* (London, 1999), 26; and n. 141 *infra*. On Russian military reforms, Keep, *Soldiers*, chs. 5, 6; Hellie, "Warfare, Changing Military Technology," 94–97; Eugenii V. Anisimov, *The Reforms of Peter the Great* (Armonk, NY), 1993), 57–69; Lindsey Hughes, *Russia in the Age of Peter the Great* (New Haven, 1998), chs. 2, 3; Carol Stevens, "Evaluating Peter's Army," in Lohr and Poe, *Military and Society*, 170 and 147–71. On Peter's struggles to implement reforms, esp. Paul Bushkovitch, *Peter the Great* (Cambridge, 2001).

[39] I follow Hartley, *Social History*, 26, which agrees broadly with Kahan, *Plow*, p. 9, Table 1.5 note. Cf. Black, *Military Revolution*, in previous note.

[40] On military expenses in absolute and proportional terms (again figures differ), see Geoffrey Hosking, *Russia: People and Empire, 1552–1917* (Cambridge, MA, 1997), 191; Gary Marker, "The Age of Enlightenment 1740–1801," in Gregory Freeze, ed., *Russia: A History* (Oxford, 1997), 116; John P. LeDonne, *Absolutism and Ruling Class* (New York, 1991), 258–81, esp. Tables 15.1 and 15.5. Inflation clearly reduced the value of nominal outlays, but was nothing like the 9,600 percent nominal increase captured in LeDonne's tables. Marker, "Age of Enlightenment," 133 suggests that from 1710 to 1800 prices rose approximately 400 percent, whereas Ian Blanchard, *Russia's 'Age of Silver'* (London, 1989), 282, claims 225 percent from 1700 to 1807. I have found no inflation figures for 1807 to 1825, so the estimate of 20-fold is a very conservative guess; if inflation from 1701 to 1825 were only 225 percent, the real increase would have been over 42-fold. On inflation, see too B. N. Mironov, "The Price Revolution of the 18th Century," in Daniel Kaiser and Gary Marker, eds., *Reinterpreting Russian History* (New York, 1994), 281–85; Kahan, *Plow*, 68, 239–41, 322; Jerome Blum, *Lord and Peasant in Russia* (Princeton, 1961), 305–307; Richard Hellie, *The Economy and Material Culture of Russia, 1600–1725* (Chicago, 1999), 8, 642; and n. 73 *infra*.

In other words, military requirements on the western frontier – "keeping up with the Swedes," in Hellie's phrase – demanded a thorough rationalization of the state and militarization of society. Under the terms of 18th-century censuses, which provided the basis for both poll taxes and conscription, a variety of groups, some hitherto exempt, were lumped along with serfs, state peasants, Cossacks, and former slaves into a single category of rural taxpayers.[41] More than demographic pressures, state demands, which as noted were levied on communities rather than individual households, were responsible for the development from the 17th through 19th centuries of communal peasant tenures and periodic land redistribution.[42] Given Russia's relative poverty, there was no obvious alternative to building a competitive European-style army on the backs of an unfree peasantry.

On the steppe European arms paid Russia even greater dividends than on the western frontier, because there the technological gap told heavily in Russia's favor. As early as 1653, with the help of French Huguenot and Dutch fortification engineers, Moscow sealed off its southern frontier against renewed steppe incursions. Thereafter nomad armies proved increasingly helpless against flintlock-wielding infantry, riverboats armed with cannon, light field artillery, and the relentless march of Russian settlement and fortified lines.[43]

The effort to Europeanize the armed forces extended as well to strategic economic ventures. Beginning with a Dutch-directed arsenal in 1632, the state built and operated armories, textile, mining, and metallurgical enterprises that as early as 1721 had made Russia self-sufficient in gunpowder and nearly so in the production of world-class flintlocks and artillery.[44]

If European warfare demanded administrative and economic reform, European contacts also modified the intellectual and cultural environment in which such changes took root. During the 15th and 16th

---

[41] Hellie, "Warfare, Changing Military Technology," 96–97; idem, *Enserfment*, 189–95; Poe, "Consequences"; Poe and Lohr, "Introduction," 9–10; Hartley, *Social History*, 19–23. On changing real tax burdens, also David Moon, *The Russian Peasantry 1600–1930* (London, 1999), 79–88.

[42] See discussion at Moon, *Russian Peasantry*, 212–22, and Hartley, *Social History*, 78–79.

[43] These resources were directed first against the Kalmyks and later the Kazakhs. Shaw, "Southern Frontiers"; Michael Khodarkovsky, *Russia's Steppe Frontier* (Bloomington, IN, 2002), 20–21, 131–83, 223; Sunderland, *Wild Field*, 24–134 *passim*.

[44] Moreover, some private enterprises that depended on army contracts adopted Western technology. See Hellie, *Enserfment*, 181, 183; Jarmo Kotilaine, "In Defense of the Realm," in Lohr and Poe, *Military and Society*, 67–95; Kahan, *Plow*, 95–105; and discussion *infra*.

centuries, we saw that Russian nobles had looked to the steppe for models of warfare, dress, taxation, even political organization.[45] But within leading circles in the 1600s European ideas grew increasingly influential and, from the early 1700s, incontestably dominant. As Kivelson, Nancy Shields Kollmann, Paul Bushkovitch, Marc Raeff, and others have shown, by the third quarter of the 17th century the Muscovite political order already was under strain as a result not of military defeat, but of continuous expansion and Western exposure.[46] In fact, the sources of instability were several. Territorial extension, military demands, the growth of serfdom, and the sheer volume of transactions joined to encourage a degree of administrative standardization. Most Muscovites were loath to see traditions of personal intercession yield to nomothetic treatment. But as high officials began to view the state as a self-sufficient organism, they sought new legal and cultural concepts to guide their work. At the same time, alienated from popular devotion, some high nobles welcomed Jesuit-influenced religious ideas entering via the Ukraine and Belarus that sought to elevate morality over ritualism, charity over miracle cults, and public service over asceticism. Print technology, which probably arrived from Germany in the 1550s, and new schools helped to disseminate these views, albeit in an Orthodox idiom and at first within a very restricted social milieu.

Between Peter's effective accession in 1689 and the early 1800s the most obvious innovation was not the wholesale rejection, but the further modification and partial displacement of Orthodox culture in favor of more expressly secular concepts as derived from diverse European sources.[47] At first Protestant countries inspired efforts to create what Raeff terms a "well-ordered police state." By the mid- and late 1700s

---

[45] Ostrowski, *Muscovy and Mongols*, pt. 1 and Ch. 2, Pt. 3 *supra*.

[46] Discussion of 17th-century thought relies on Kivelson, *Autocracy*; idem, "Devil Stole His Mind"; Kollmann, *Honor Bound*, 203–21; Paul Bushkovitch, *Religion and Society in Russia: The Sixteenth and Seventeenth Centuries* (New York, 1992), esp. chs. 3, 6, 7; Marc Raeff, *Understanding Imperial Russia* (New York, 1984), 10–33; Lindsey Hughes, *Sophia, Regent of Russia 1657–1704* (New Haven, 1990), ch. 7; Douglas J. Bennet, Jr., "The Beginnings of Enlightened Absolutism in Russia," in Nancy Shields Kollmann, ed., *Major Problems in Early Modern Russian History* (Armonk, NY, 1992), 385–420; and Hans-Joachim Torke, "From Muscovy Towards St. Petersburg 1598–1689," in Freeze, *Russia*, 55–86.

[47] Marc Raeff, *The Well-Ordered Police State* (New Haven, 1983); Hughes, *Age of Peter the Great*, chs. 4, 7–10; Cynthia Whittaker, "The Reforming Tsar," *SR* 51 (1991): 77–98; idem, *Russian Monarchy: Eighteenth Century Rulers and Writers in Political Dialogue* (DeKalb, IL, 2003); idem, "The Idea of Autocracy Among 18th-Century Russian Historians,"

Russian thinkers were borrowing from French *philosophes* to present the sovereign as part of a European community of enlightened reforming rulers. Under Catherine II, the Great (r. 1762–1796), economic policy and plans for a society of "orders" followed French and German norms, while Alexander I (r. 1801–1825) used a Napoleonic template for ministerial and legal reform.[48] Starting with Peter, therefore, rulers presented themselves less as guardians of Orthodox tradition than as agents of self-nurturing state power and social progress along Western lines. Earthly well-being, not eternal salvation, now provided the state's primary raison d'être. But to succeed, this program required an educated, forward-looking elite, for whose benefit the crown founded European-style schools, promoted European cultural norms, and encouraged foreign specialists in both official and private employ. For its part, the nobility readily accepted changes that made sense within its cultural framework – for example, they assimilated civil society to the tradition of tsar–*boyar* consultation – while ignoring themes with less resonance. Peter's 1703 transfer of the capital from Moscow to St. Petersburg, his new Western-style city on the Baltic, heralded and facilitated these cultural shifts.

By this time what Hellie terms "a literacy revolution" was well under-way. An early stimulus derived from the aforementioned development in the mid-1500s of paper archives by chancellery scribes and from the ensuing demand that officials in communication with the chancelleries be literate. Absent state schools, education in this period depended on clerical and private tuition. By 1649 literacy – involving perhaps 3 per-cent of the total population – was sufficient for the government to print 2,400 copies of the new *Ulozhenie* law code, followed by 300,000 ABC primers. As in France, albeit in Russia at a later date, printing naturally lowered the cost of written material.[49] By the early 1700s Russia was manufacturing its own paper, and the government was demanding

in Jane Burbank and David Ransel, eds., *Imperial Russia* (Bloomington, IN, 1998), 32–59; Valerie Kivelson, "Kinship Politics/Autocratic Politics," in ibid., 5–31; Isabel de Madariaga, *Russia in the Age of Catherine the Great* (New Haven, 1981), pts. 6, 9.

[48] Madariaga, *Catherine*, pts. 1–7; Richard Wortman, *Scenarios of Power: Myth and Ceremony in Russian Monarchy*, vol. I (Princeton, 1995), 202; Hartley, *Social History*, chs. 6, 8, 9.

[49] On literacy and the introduction and impact of printing, see Richard Hellie, "Late Medieval and Early Modern Russian Civilization and Modern Neuroscience," in A. M. Kleimola and G. D. Lenhoff, eds., *Culture and Identity in Muscovy, 1359–1584* (Moscow, 1997), 152–55; Gary Marker, *Publishing, Printing, and the Origins of Intellectual Life in Russia, 1700–1800* (Princeton, 1985), 17–69.

with fresh insistence that officials be able to read and write. From early technical institutions founded by Peter, government-sponsored schools expanded to include by 1804 a network of parish schools, elite gymnasia, military academies, and six European-style universities. As nobles came to value education as a path to social prestige as well as career success, the foundations were laid for more efficient governance.[50]

We shall return to 18th-century cultural shifts, but now I would examine – after warfare and European cultural currents – a third principal spur to post-1650 political integration, namely, economic growth. Some historians of Russia – whose views run curiously parallel to an earlier tradition of Southeast Asian and Tokugawa historiography – have argued wistfully that 17th-century upheavals cut short a commercial revolution on the West European model.[51] Admittedly, the Time of Troubles brought severe dislocations, which higher taxes in the mid-1600s probably compounded. During the second half of the century the urban population appears to have fallen in absolute as well as relative terms.[52] So too, serfdom slowed frontier settlement, while from 1590 to 1730 generally cold spring temperatures compressed the growing season.[53] Yet on the whole the 17th century, especially the second half, was an era of modest vitality, not least because, despite the imposition of serfdom, the receding Tatar danger encouraged southern colonization (both illegal and state sanctioned), which helped to counter the effects of climatic cooling while opening up chernozem soils superior to those of the forest heartland. Thus frontier fortress-cities and smaller towns

---

[50] Hartley, *Social History*, 125–45.

[51] E.g., Alexander Yanov, *The Origins of Autocracy* (Berkeley, 1981); Chester Dunning, *A Short History of Russia's First Civil War* (University Park, PA, 2004), 316–17; Richard Hellie, "The Foundations of Russian Capitalism," *SR* 26 (1967): 148–54. Cf. *AC* vol. II, ch. 5, and Ch. 4 *infra*.

[52] David Miller, "State and City in 17th-Century Muscovy," in Michael Hamm, ed., *The City in Russian History* (Lexington, KY, 1976), 49; Henry Eaton, "Decline and Recovery of the Russian Cities from 1500 to 1700," *CASS* 11 (1977): 223; Dunning, *Short History*, 316–17.

[53] Hellie, *Economy*, 641; H. H. Lamb, *The Changing Climate* (London, 1966), 221; R. E. F. Smith and David Christian, *Bread and Salt* (Cambridge, 1984), 109–10; Ye. P. Borisenkov, "Documentary Evidence from the U.S.S.R.," in Raymond Bradley and Philip Jones, eds., *Climate Since A.D. 1500* (London, 1995), 171–83; M. Chernavskaya, "Botanical Indicators of the Little Ice Age in the Russian Plain," in T. Mikami, ed., *Proceedings of the International Symposium on the Little Ice Age Climate* (Tokyo, 1992), 65–70; idem, "Weather Conditions of 1695–96 in European Russia," *Jl. of Applied Meteorology* 35 (1996): 1059–62; A. Graybill and S. G. Shiyatov, "Dendroclimatic Evidence from the Northern Soviet Union," in Bradley and Jones, *Climate Since 1500*, 393–414.

in the south and west defied the bleak urban trend elsewhere. But even in the heartland, post-1650 demographic growth helps to explain the revival of the three-field system, the growing replacement of oxen by more efficient horses, and the stirrings of a land market.[54]

Between 1725 and 1825 the imperial population grew rapidly, from perhaps 16,000,000 to 50,000,000; only about a third of this increase consisted of annexed peoples. In explaining a post-1750 drop in famine-related mortality, Arcadius Kahan gives some credit to climatic warming[55] – which, recall, correlated with stronger Southeast Asian monsoons and improved harvests in northwestern Europe. In addition, better inland shipping allowed Russian grain to reach areas of local shortage, typhoid and plague diminished, and smallpox vaccinations began to yield results. Above all, land pressures in the core joined with better frontier defenses to draw millions of legal serfs and illegal runaways to the fertile lands of the Ukraine, the north Pontic shore, the Don and Volga basins. In the 18th century – at roughly the same time as the Irrawaddy delta, the Mekong delta, and the frontier below Ayudhya were converted into major rice zones – Russian cultivated acreage expanded by some 250 percent, chiefly on the steppe frontier.[56] Even more dramatically than in Burma or Vietnam, Russian colonization encouraged a regional division of labor. The black-earth frontier, given over almost exclusively to agriculture, supplied vast quantities of foodstuffs and raw materials to central and northern Russia. In the latter regions, many serfs, encouraged by their masters, found trading, wage

---

[54] Hellie, *Enserfment*, 305 n. 9; idem, *Economy*, 9–10, 636; Michael Confino, *Systemes Agraires et Progres Agricole: L'Assolement Triennal en Russie aux XVIII-XIX Siecles* (Paris, 1969), 26–55, 133 ff.; R. E. F. Smith, *Peasant Farming in Muscovy* (Cambridge, 1977), 229–31; Moon, *Russian Peasantry*, 121–26; Hartley, *Social History*, 9; Blum, *Lord and Peasant*, 161–67, 205–11. Moreover, Khodarkovsky, *Steppe Frontier*, 19, 22, 223 argues that an end to Tatar raids freed up resources in the core.

[55] Kahan, *Plow*, 11–14, 46; cf. Hartley, *Social History*, 150. On population trends, Kahan, *Plow*, 7–8, ch. 1 *passim*, and 364; Blum, *Lord and Peasant*, 277–81; Hartley, *Social History*, 9–12 (whose figures exclude the Caucasus, Poland, and Finland); Gary Marker, "Age of Enlightenment," 119, 130. Although surely the population grew somewhat from 1820 to 1825, we lack detailed figures; so both here (1825) and in Ch. 1, n. 81 *supra* (1820) the total is rounded off to 50,000,000. On frontier settlement and economic expansion 1700–1825, Kahan, *Plow*, esp. chs. 2–6; Michael Khodarkovsky, *Where Two Worlds Met* (Ithaca, NY, 1992), 224–34; Blum, *Lord and Peasant*, chs. 15–17; Edgar Melton, "Proto-Industrialization, Serf Agriculture, and Agrarian Social Structure," *PP* 115 (1987): 69–106; Wilson Augustine, "Notes Towards a Portrait of the 18th-Century Russian Nobility," *CASS* 4 (1970): 373–425; Hellie, *Economy*, 625–45; Moon, *Russian Peasantry*, 49–65.

[56] Kahan, *Plow*, 364; Moon, *Russian Peasantry*, 56.

labor, and handicrafts more profitable than agriculture, and industry became concentrated.

From this combination of extensive and intensive growth flowed stronger market linkages and undeniable productivity gains. From 1755 to 1795 alone the number of periodic fairs increased by a remarkable 550 percent, exclusive of new territories.[57] This growth in fairs, a 740 percent increase in the per capita money supply between 1700 and 1800, falling price differentials within and among regions, declining real prices for iron, steel, and other key commodities, and the growth of manorial manufacturing and commercial farming all point to specialization and market unification.[58] Gilbert Rozman claims that Russia's urban/commercial network in the 18th century finally entered the highest level, Stage G ("national marketing"), a transition comparable to that which occurred in England from 1525 to 1675 and in France and Japan from 1500/1520 to 1700/1720.[59] By one calculation, between 1720 and 1807 internal growth and external annexations increased Russian national income almost fivefold.[60]

Admittedly, by West European standards, these achievements remained modest. Harsh climate, mediocre podzolic soils in the heartland, still weak urban demand, expensive overland transport, anemic rural investment, and the risk-averse orientation of the repartitional peasant land system combined to inhibit agrarian experiment and to permit cereal yields in the early 1800s that not only were among the lowest in Europe, but substantially unchanged since the late 1500s.[61] In the commercial sector the key role of fairs and pedlars was itself a sign

[57] Kahan, *Plow*, 269, Table 5.1. On commerce, ibid., chs. 4–6; Mironov, "Price Revolution," 281–85; Gilbert Rozman, *Urban Networks in Russia, 1750–1800, and Premodern Periodization* (Princeton, 1976), 41–220, 244, 254, 283; William Blackwell, ed., *Russian Economic Development from Peter the Great to Stalin* (New York, 1974), 4–158.

[58] Kahan, *Plow*, 275, Mironov, "Price Revolution," 281; Hellie, *Economy*, 641.

[59] Rozman, *Urban Networks*, 66, 86–87. Yet it is unclear whether townsmen grew as a percentage of the population. Rozman, *Urban Networks*, 84–88; J. Michael Hittle, "The Service City in the 18th Century," in Hamm, *City*, 62, and Blum, *Lord and Peasant*, 281 paint a far rosier urban picture than do Mironov, "Revolution," 282, or Hosking, *Russia*, 256.

[60] Blanchard, *Age of Silver*, 281; ibid., 282–83, 294 argues that for a brief period in the late 1700s per capita income approached that of England.

[61] This was per land unit, but per capita yields were more respectable. See Hellie, *Economy*, 1–2; Blum, *Lord and Peasant*, 330; Hartley, *Social History*, 150–56; Steven Hoch, "The Serf Economy, the Peasant Family, and the Social Order," in Burbank and Ransel, *Imperial Russia*, 199–209; and esp. Moon, *Russian Peasantry*, 126–39.

of backwardness. The superior acumen of foreign traders joined with patriarchal education, status anxiety, weak financial mechanisms, and competition from tax-exempt nobles, monasteries, and trading peasants to hobble the merchant class. Nor did the state help matters by declining to enforce contracts.[62] Most basically, Hellie argues, caste-like impediments to mobility and a nearly universal reliance on the state to inaugurate economic activity and to allocate rewards weakened innovation.[63]

Again, however, if we triangulate Russia with western Europe and mainland Southeast Asia, several considerations suggest that Russia occupied an intermediate position. First, cash operations, though modest by European standards, were more extensive than in Southeast Asia. This was true not only of taxes and salaries, but credit: whereas loans sustained the French crown as early as the 1520s and whereas by 1830 mainland Southeast Asia still lacked any institutionalized state debt, the Russian crown secured substantial, primarily foreign, loans from the 1770s.[64] Second, whereas in 1800 urban networks in both France and Russia were in Rozman's Stage G, Southeast Asian systems were in Stage E or F. Third, the scale and technical level of metal and textile industries in Russia, though behind best West European practices, exceeded anything in Southeast Asia.[65] Fourth, royal retail/wholesale monopolies, often a sign of underdevelopment, were less extensive than in Indic Southeast Asia but more critical than in *ancien régime* France.[66]

How did foreign contacts influence the Russian economy? And what does this say about our abiding concern with Eurasian coordination? In origin, frontier colonization – arguably the chief engine of Russian growth – responded to local population pressure and strategic calculation far more than to the lure of foreign markets.[67] Nor were New World

---

[62] Alfred J. Rieber, *Merchants and Entrepreneurs in Imperial Russia* (Chapel Hill, NC, 1982), chs. 1–3; Elise Wirtschafter, *Social Identity in Imperial Russia* (De Kalb, IL, 1997), 71–86; Hellie, *Economy*, 637–38, 642; Hartley, *Social History*, 159–68. On periodic redistribution of peasant plowlands by the *mir*, and the ensuing emphasis on household equality and non-innovation, see Hoch, *Serfdom*, 15–16, 134, 151, 158.

[63] Hellie, *Economy*, 636–45. A similar argument informs Marshall Poe, *Russia's Moment in World History* (Princeton, 2003).

[64] LeDonne, *Absolutism*, 280–83; Kahan, *Plow*, 321.

[65] By 1800 Russia was the world's largest producer of pig iron. See Kahan, *Plow*, ch. 3; LeDonne, *Absolutism*, 268; Hartley, *Social History*, 156–63.

[66] The tsar monopolized trade in a limited range of luxuries, but after 1762, earlier than in Siam, these were phased out. Cf. Hellie, *Economy*, 636, 640–41; Kahan, *Plow*, 187–90.

[67] On this point, LeDonne, *Russian Empire*, 89–90, 107; idem, *Absolutism*, 268; Blum, *Lord and Peasant*, 287–88.

crops like maize and potatoes, which had a notable demographic impact in Asia, significant in Russia before the 1840s. On the other hand, once Russia broke through to the Baltic and the Black Seas, foreign trade grew rapidly, which in turn stimulated urbanization, new transport links, and all manner of domestic exchange. Whereas from 1720 to 1820 mainland Southeast Asia's trade with China, its principal partner, rose perhaps fourfold, 18th-century Russian trade with the rest of Europe expanded, according to different estimates, 15-fold to 26-fold.[68] Russia imported arms, luxuries, dyestuffs, and silver, while exporting hemp, flax, linen, iron, naval stores, timber, and cereals. Although not initially reliant on foreign markets, from the 1780s cereal producers on the southern frontier became major suppliers to Mediterranean and northern European cities. Starting with Peter, Russia systematically recruited West European and German experts – in finance, mining, architecture, textile, glass, paper, and coin production, as well as military affairs – who permanently upgraded the country's technological capacity.[69] Moreover, western and central Europe compensated for consistent trade deficits with Russia by supplying silver bullion and specie, often 40 percent of the value of Russian imports. With domestic bullion output rising but still inadequate, these supplies underpinned monetization and specialization in both the heartland and on the frontier.[70] Russia had no trade with Southeast Asia and only modest trade with China,[71] but from 1720 to 1830 all three regions benefited from European demand, the growth in world bullion stocks, and the enhanced efficiency of maritime craft.

Insofar as the Romanov state was restructured along Western lines, one also can make a case for indirect foreign influences on the economy by considering the economic effects of government action. As just noted, between 1650 and 1825 the government transformed trade, industry, and finance by developing Baltic and Black Sea ports, recruiting specialists, and founding schools and banks. The most advanced

---

[68] Mironov, "Price Revolution," 280–81; Kahan, *Plow*, 163, giving the lower estimate. The difference centers on currency values. On foreign trade, ibid., ch. 4; Walther Kirchner, *Commercial Relations Between Russia and Europe 1400–1800* (Bloomington, IN, 1966).

[69] Hellie, *Economy*, 641; Kahan, *Plow*, 124, 136–38, 163. On industry generally, ibid., ch. 3.

[70] Kahan, *Plow*, 163–66, 192–93; Blanchard, *Age of Silver*, chs. 3–6; Hartley, *Social History*, 157; Arthur Attman, *The Bullion Flow Between Europe and the East 1000–1750* (Göteburg, 1981), 74–83, 104–24.

[71] See figures at Kahan, *Plow*, 232–35, 164–65.

sectors of the economy all depended on government sponsorship and contracts, if not ownership. The state promoted agriculture, albeit at a low level of efficiency, by regulating labor mobility and facilitating frontier settlement. Uniform weights and measures, a generally stable currency, some new canals and bridges, and one of Europe's best systems of post roads lowered transaction and information costs. In line with theories of domestic laissez-faire, the 1753 abolition of custom houses in European Russia (except along the borders with Baltic provinces) powerfully encouraged the internal market, which was protected by high tariffs in 1757 and 1793.[72]

The reciprocal political impact of all this was fairly obvious. Demographic and commercial growth made possible a self-sustaining material superiority over rival power centers in the steppe, the Baltic, and the Black Sea region. To cite the most conspicuous index of growth, poll taxes, quitrent (*obrok*), the salt monopoly, vodka sales, and trade taxes together rose from a mere 8,500,000 rubles in 1724 to 393,000,000 in 1825, only a modest fraction of which, on present evidence, can be attributed to price inflation.[73] Larger revenues fed the army, state-run industries, Western-style schools, infrastructural upgrades, and an increasingly professional civil service, while the aforementioned tripling of population from 1725 to 1825 magnified the army's recruiting base.

In short, although in Russia foreign influences were stronger and military demands more importunate than in Southeast Asia, in both regions between 1650 and 1825 we find intensifying synergies between warfare, domestic economic growth, wider external linkages, and state interventions in the economy.

Strengthening the Central State, c. 1650–1830; Frontier Revolts as a Sign of Success – Comparisons with Southeast Asia

Let us analyze more closely the impact of these diverse forces on civilian political structures. One of the most curious features of Romanov rule in the 18th century was the contrast between the chaos of royal succession and the growing solidity of administration. After Peter abolished

---

[72] On government economic policy, Hellie, *Economy*, 10, 628–45; LeDonne, *Absolutism*, 267–68; Moon, *Russian Peasantry*, 49–54; Hartley, *Social History*, 158–59.

[73] LeDonne, *Absolutism*, Tables 15.2 (p. 278) and 15.6 (p. 282). This represents a nominal increase of 4,624 percent, but estimates of 18th-century price inflation range only from 225 percent to 400 percent. See n. 40 *supra*.

primogeniture, from 1725 to 1801 women ruled more often than men, two tsars were murdered, and the throne became the plaything of guard regiments. Yet palace turmoil failed to destabilize the state, in part because usurpers invoked the myth of the "reforming tsar" that stressed achievement over hereditary claims, but more basically because the polity was undergirded by a more secure elite/court consensus and an increasingly complex administration.[74]

The most obvious indication of the latter trend was the growing size of the civil apparatus. In the 1600s the number of civilian officials of all classes may have tripled to 4,000. By 1755 the corresponding figure was 10,500; by 1800, 38,000; by 1856, 114,000.[75] Whereas Russia in 1800 thus had roughly one official per 1,100 subjects (and by 1850 one per 500), the corresponding Burmese ratio in 1800 was probably no more than 1:2,500 or 1:3,000. Real cash outlays on civil administration expanded even more rapidly than personnel registers, reflecting a combination of population growth, territorial acquisitions, rising per capita tax demands, conversion of in-kind and service obligations to cash, heavier reliance on loans and tax farms, and a partial shift from military to civilian priorities.[76]

Physical growth and better funding encouraged long-term shifts in government organization and ethos. From the mid-1600s the *boyar duma* ceased to be the seat of major decisions or routine administration, much of which devolved on proliferating chancelleries. The social distance between *boyars* and chancellery heads narrowed, as did that between princely and nontitled servitors. Thus the capital elite evolved into a larger, more fluid, and to some extent a more parvenu body, as symbolized by the destruction of *mestnichestvo* family registers in 1682. Symptomatic of the government's growing interest in communications and accurate local information, the mid- and late 1600s saw an unprecedented expansion in mapmaking, both local and imperial. As chancellery operations became more routine and inclined to red tape, they also became more open to bribery and corruption. Such

---

[74] See Wortman, *Scenarios*, 81–146; Brenda Meehan-Waters, "Catherine the Great and the Problem of Female Rule," *RR* 34 (1975): 293–307; Whittaker, "Reforming Tsar."

[75] These figures include judges, clerks, scribes, and gubernatorial assistants. Hittle, *Service City*, 48; Kivelson, *Autocracy*, 19; Kollmann, *Honor Bound*, 204–205; Walter Pintner, "The Evolution of Civil Officialdom, 1755–1855," in Pintner and Don Rowney, eds., *Russian Officialdom* (Chapel Hill, 1980), 192. Cf. Ch. 2, n. 250 *supra*.

[76] LeDonne, *Absolutism*, chs. 14, 15, esp. Tables 15.1 and 15.5, which again must be offset against inflation.

shifts bred popular resentment. But insofar as administrative change still responded more to exigency than imported doctrine, what Kivelson terms the "official discourse" of paternalism, mercy, and Orthodox piety remained in place.[77]

Starting with Peter, impersonal bureaucracy became official, while the old discourse of personal patronage became submerged. Southeast Asia never knew so abrupt a change, both because the scale of operations, hence the incentives to routinization, remained more modest, and because Indic lands lacked access to a prepackaged meritocratic ideology. Thus Peter, relying heavily on Swedish models, established a quasi-meritocratic Table of Ranks, swept away overlapping chancelleries in favor of functional colleges, and created more standardized provincial jurisdictions.[78] In practice, much of this remained a dead letter – or worse. Borivoj Plavsic and Hellie argue that Petrine innovations actually bred confusion and massive corruption.[79] According to LeDonne, well into the 19th century no Russian government was bureaucratic in the sense that formal prevailed over personal criteria.[80] According to Walter Pintner and Don Rowney, provincial administration before Catherine was "as close to nonexistent as the political and fiscal survival of the empire would tolerate."[81] Yet the new patrimonial-institutional mix also provided flexibility: a bribe here and there let local elites soften the system's hard edges. Over the long term, moreover, salaries and pensions began to moderate corruption, Western cartographic and organizational procedures became more fully assimilated, and education favored

---

[77] Kivelson, "Devil Stole His Mind," 751–53; idem, *Autocracy*, 264–65; idem, "Merciful Father, Impersonal State," in Victor Lieberman, ed., *Beyond Binary Histories* (Ann Arbor, 1999), 216–19. On administrative expansion and routinization, see too Valerie Kivelson, *Cartographies of Tsardom: Maps and Political-Geographic Imagination in 17th-Century Russia* (Ithaca, 2006), 1–56 and *passim*; Leo Bagrow, *A History of the Cartography of Russia up to 1800* (Wolfe Island, Ont., 1975), chs. 1–3; Peter Brown, "Bureaucratic Administration in 17th-Century Russia," in Kotilaine and Poe, *Modernizing Muscovy*, 57–78; George Weickhardt, "Modernization of Law in 17th- Century Russia," in ibid., 79–95; Marshall Poe, "Absolutism and the New Men of 17th-Century Russia," in ibid., 97–115; Crummey, *Aristocrats*; Bushkovitch, *Religion*, 129; Kollmann, *Honor Bound*, 138–39, 226–35; Marker, *Publishing, Printing*, 19–20.

[78] Hughes, *Age of Peter the Great*, 100–21, 180–85.

[79] Borivoj Plavsic, "Seventeenth-Century Chanceries and Their Staffs," in Pintner, *Russian Officialdom*, 21–23; Hellie, "Russia, 1200–1815," 499.

[80] LeDonne, *Absolutism*, ix, 88, 306. See too Stephen Velychenko, "Identities, Loyalties and Service in Imperial Russia: Who Administered the Borderlands?" *RR* 54 (1995): 189–90, 201.

[81] Pintner, *Russian Officialdom*, 106.

professionalism: whereas in 1755, 75 percent of Russian officials had no formal education, a century later their training substantially resembled that of their Western counterparts.[82]

Accordingly, the late 18th and early 19th centuries saw a further rationalization of activity, not least at the local level.[83] Catherine created a new framework of provinces (*gubernii*) and districts (*uezdy*), while doubling the number of provincial posts. Each provincial capital had a salaried staff headed by a governor of fixed term who served alongside the local military commander. New courts and boards of public welfare also arose, with responsibility for staffing them divided between central authorities and the provincial nobility. At the lowest level the village commune (*mir*), regarded by provincial officials and landowners alike as indispensable agency of social control, remained responsible for land reallocations, tax and draft burdens, petty justice, and suppressing rural violence. Judged by professional training and official-to-subject ratios, provincial government in Russia in the 1830s may not have been more effective than in Vietnam – in training, it was probably inferior – but it was surely more ambitious than in Burma or Siam.

Provincial reform in turn required new compacts between the throne and rural elites. The advantages that the Russian nobility (*dvorianstvo*) derived from 18th-century government expansion were threefold. First, as a price for participating in the new structures and supporting insecure rulers, noble landholders demanded and won a monopoly on serfs, a further strengthening of serf controls, and freedom from obligatory state service. Second, expansion of the army and civil apparatus offered invaluable career openings for many hard-pressed provincial nobles.[84] Third, Western education, simultaneously a precondition and by-product of political reform, afforded nobles new and exclusive status markers.

---

[82] Kivelson, *Autocracy*, 130–80, 266–78; Hittle, *Service City*, 203–204; LeDonne, *Absolutism*, 47, 262, 271; Pintner, "Evolution of Officialdom," 190–226; Hartley, *Social History*, 111–22; Kivelson, *Cartographies*, 39–41.

[83] Discussion of local administration and noble organization follows previous note, plus Madariaga, *Catherine*, 79–89, 277–307, 555; Edward Thaden, *Russia's Western Borderlands, 1710–1870* (Princeton, 1984), esp. 23; Michael Confino, *Societe et Mentalites Collectives en Russie sous l'Ancien Regime* (Paris, 1991), 345–87; Robert Jones, *The Emancipation of the Russian Nobility 1762–1785* (Princeton, 1973); Augustine, "Notes"; Raeff, *Understanding*, 94–131; John Armstrong, "Old-Regime Governors: Bureaucratic and Patrimonial Attributes," *CSSH* 14 (1972): 2–29; Hoch, *Serfdom*, esp. 133–59, 187–90.

[84] See essays by Brenda Meehan-Waters and Robert Givens in Pintner, *Russian Officialdom*, 76–129.

As in Southeast Asia and France, state aggrandizement also led to a marked reduction in the autonomy of religious organizations. Eager to placate *pomest'e*-holders whose peasants were escaping in alarming numbers to ecclesiastical properties, Ivan IV forbade the church to acquire new lands and restricted its tax immunities.[85] In the mid-1600s the state sought to centralize control over parishes and monasteries. Determined to obtain yet wider access to church resources and responding in part to Western models, Peter replaced the Patriarchate with a more tractable Holy Synod, reduced the number of monks and nuns, and limited entry into the parish clergy, whose members, like all churchmen, were poll-tax exempt. In 1764 Catherine went a step further, secularizing all religious lands and converting almost a million church peasants into state peasants. Meanwhile, officials conscripted supernumerary churchmen and supported renewed church efforts to strengthen internal administration. If, as Gregory Freeze has argued, religious bodies retained greater independence than is often acknowledged, this reduction in autonomy and income was certainly as dramatic as anything in postcharter Burma or Vietnam, all the more so since in Russia the time frame for these changes was more compressed.[86]

To appreciate the state's expanding influence, consider finally changing patterns of revolt. In Southeast Asia novel tax and manpower demands precipitated bitter anticentralizing rebellions, particularly in frontier areas of minority ethnicity. The two most spectacular such uprisings, the Mon insurgency of 1740–1752 and the Tayson revolt of 1771, smashed, respectively, the Burmese and Vietnamese states.[87] In Russia as well, groups along the periphery protested imperial impositions. The western frontier, for example, saw a pro-Swedish revolt by the Ukrainian Cossack Hetman in 1709 and a major Polish rebellion in

---

[85] These curbs were promulgated even though as individuals, Ivan IV and many private landholders continued to donate lands to monasteries.

[86] Moscow had its own Patriarch from 1589. Ch. 2, n. 255. On changing church–state and church–society relations, Donald Ostrowski, "Church Polemics and Monastic Land Acquisition in 16th-Century Muscovy," *SEER* 64 (1986): 355–79; Kollmann, *Honor Bound*, 218; Robert Crummey, *The Formation of Muscovy 1304–1613* (London, 1987), 130–31; Bushkovitch, *Religion*, 20–21, 122–23; Hellie, *Enserfment*, 42–44; Blum, *Lord and Peasant*, 362–66; Georg Michels, *At War with the Church* (Stanford, 1997), 188 ff., 227; Hughes, *Age of Peter the Great*, 337–43; Madariaga, *Catherine*, 111–22; Gregory Freeze, "Handmaiden of the State?," *Jl. of Ecclesiastical History* 36 (1985): 82–102; idem, "Institutionalizing Piety," in Burbank and Ransel, *Imperial Russia*, 210–49. Cf. *SP*, 159–60, 181, 373, 377 ff., 388–89.

[87] *SP*, 183–84, 202–205, 310–12, 319, 328–35, 419–26.

1830–1831. No less dangerous were risings in the southern borderlands, where colonization threatened the autonomy of both Russian frontiersmen and non-Russian peoples. As tsarist authority widened, southern resistance tended to move ever farther afield where military controls and serfdom were less secure.[88]

As early as the Time of Troubles a revolt originating near the Polish border, only 500 kilometers from the capital, won support from Russian Cossacks as well as Finnic and Tatar peoples in the middle Volga. Massive frontier revolts again engulfed much of the Volga and Don basins in 1670–1671 and 1707–1708. These trends culminated in 1773–1774 in the most extensive rebellion in Russian history before 1905, that of Emelyan Pugachev. This Don Cossack sought to enlist alienated Russians, including serfs, fugitive peasants, industrial workers, and fellow Cossacks, by vowing to replace the entire Petrine system – Westernizing nobles, serfdom, the poll tax, conscription – with the Cossack way of life "so that all men will be equal."[89] But ironically, Pugachev also won support from Bashkirs, Tatars, Kazakhs, and other tribal peoples embittered by their growing marginalization at the hands of Slavic settlers. At its height, the revolt inflamed a huge southeastern area, including the Ural and Volga basins.

Pugachev's rebellion thus resembled the great 18th-century Mon and Tayson revolts in Southeast Asia in several respects: a) The Mon revolt of 1740, the Tayson revolt of 1771, and Pugachev's movement all originated in peripheral zones subject to economic and administrative pressure from an expanding imperial core. b) All arose during a globally synchronized era of demographic and commercial growth, which fueled frontier settlement, imperial consolidation, and by extension, frontier resistance. c) More specifically, each followed interstate wars – Burmese wars against Manipur, Vietnamese wars against Siam, and the Russo-Turkish War of 1768–1774 – that sharply raised frontier taxes and diverted imperial troops from internal pacification.[90] d) Each

---

[88] Ensuing discussion follows Paul Avrich, *Russian Rebels 1600–1800* (New York, 1972); Marc Raeff, "Pugachev's Rebellion," in Robert Foster and Jack Greene, eds., *Preconditions of Revolution in Early Modern Europe* (Baltimore, 1970), 161–201; Michael Khodarkovsky, *Two Worlds*, chs. 6, 7; idem, *Steppe Frontier*, 172–74; Dunning, *Short History*, 29, 58, 175 ff., 326–28; Moon, *Russian Peasantry*, 240–54.

[89] Moon, *Russian Peasantry*, 244. Most Cossacks in origin were ethnically Ukrainian or Russian. On Bolotnikov's Time of Troubles revolt, see Ch. 2, n. 286 *supra*.

[90] By the same token, Bolotnikov's revolt of 1606–1607 came during the Time of Troubles, Razin's revolt of 1670–1671 came in the wake of the Thirteen Years War, and Bulavin's revolt of 1707–1708 came during the Great Northern War.

constructed an unstable alliance of ethnic minorities and disgruntled members of the dominant ethnicity. e) Each revolt countered the ideological power of central elites with a combination of rival dynastic claims and localized cultural statements, often with millennial overtones.[91] f) Each proved deeply counterproductive, paving the way to accelerated centralization and colonization. Thus Pugachev's defeat led to Catherine's 1775 provincial reforms, the full incorporation of the southeastern steppe within that new provincial system, and a strengthening of Russian military forces in the region.[92]

There was, however, a crucial overarching difference: whereas in Burma and Vietnam imperial renewal came only after provincial revolts destroyed the reigning dynasty and inaugurated late 18th-century interregna, Pugachev's rising never moved beyond the southeast frontier. Why then was Russia's version of the late-18th-century crisis – if we may so dignify Pugachev's enterprise – so much tamer than its Burmese or Vietnamese counterparts?

In each Southeast Asian realm, challenges from the periphery became fatal only in combination with disorders in long-settled areas. But peasants in the Muscovite core – *pace* an earlier Marxist emphasis on the class, rather than regional basis of Pugachev's following – generally remained deaf to his frontier-oriented appeals to fugitive peasants, Cossacks, and minority peoples. In other words, where it had long been established, Russian serfdom proved more stable than Southeast Asian systems of manpower control. At the same time, the scale of empire worked in Russia's favor: whereas St. Petersburg could safely concentrate forces from a vast area against distant frontiers, in the far smaller imperial worlds of Southeast Asia, each capital lacked the same territorial margin of safety. Western training, organization, and flintlocks also gave imperial forces an advantage over untrained frontiersmen in Russia more decisive than in Burma or Vietnam. Finally, Manipuri victories over Burma and Siamese challenges to Vietnam had sapped imperial morale before the revolts broke out. But at the time of Pugachev's revolt, recent or impending victories over Russia's historic foes, the Ottomans

---

[91] Like Pugachev and other Russian rebels, the leader of the Mon revolt of 1740 sought legitimacy by claiming to be a scion of the ruling dynasty. On these claims and the invocation of local prophecies, cf. Victor Lieberman, "Ethnic Politics in 18th-Century Burma," *MAS* 12 (1978): 455–82; idem, *Burmese Administrative Cycles*, 216-20; Li Tana, *Nguyen Cochinchina* (Ithaca, 1998), 148–54.

[92] On this point, see esp. Moon, *Russian Peasantry*, 252–54; Sunderland, *Wild Field*, 57–60.

and Poland, afforded the Romanovs unbounded confidence and prestige.[93]

Cultural Fracture and Integration in the Russian Imperial Core, c. 1650–1830

As the empire expanded, culture within its Great Russian[94] core – basically the area controlled by Moscow in 1550 – experienced fundamentally contradictory trends. What might be termed the dominant rhythm split noble from peasant culture. The subordinate trend offered precisely the opposite, a promise of renewed elite–mass integration.

Let us first explore signs of cultural rupture, which derived chiefly from the nobility's ever more enthusiastic embrace of Western norms. As we saw in Chapter 2, in the 16th century, wide sectors of society shared a worldview emphasizing the unity of Muscovy's God-centered community under its Orthodox sovereign. Reinforced by the Time of Troubles, xenophobic expressions of all-class solidarity gained additional strength, at least temporarily, from church efforts to reform local practices.[95] Yet ironically over the long term, these very events had a destabilizing component, both because the church's reforming zeal eventually inspired a popular backlash and because the moral issues raised in acute form by the Time of Troubles and enserfment led more thoughtful members of the elite to rethink religious assumptions.[96] A more skeptical outlook, more tolerant of individual sensibilities, began to influence sectors of the nobility. From the mid-1600s this trend drew inspiration, as noted, from religious currents in the Ukraine and Belarus and the founding of schools on the Jesuit model, as well as from an influx of European traders and mercenaries and the printing, under aegis of tsar and church, of some historical, scientific, and literary works.[97] In these ways, without rejecting Orthodoxy, sectors of the nobility began to develop a more European outlook that distinguished them from

---

[93] In this sense, Russia in 1773 was comparable to Siam in 1827, when the ever-victorious Chakri Dynasty suppressed a major anticentralizing Lao revolt at Vientiane. *SP*, 312–33 *passim*. Not until the Crimean War would military defeat generate a major internal crisis in Russia.

[94] Great Russians as distinct from other Orthodox eastern Slavs, Belarussians, and Ukrainians. See discussion *infra*.

[95] Dunning, *Short History*, 320–24.

[96] Bushkovitch, *Religion*, 131 ff.

[97] Kollmann, *Honor Bound*, 210–15.

their own peasantry and adumbrated more wrenching changes under Peter.

It was, in fact, in the religious sphere that new tensions first appeared. From the circle of learned reformers known as the Zealots of Piety came Nikon, who as Patriarch from 1652 sought to bring Russian texts and practices in line with Greek Orthodoxy and to purge "corrupt" churches and monasteries. Imbued with the same impulse to standardization and surveillance as favored serfdom and secular centralization, in 1666 the church, with the tsar's support, therefore launched a campaign to enforce Nikonian worship, upgrade clerical training, repress pagan elements, and bring sacraments closer to the peasantry.[98] These efforts not only had limited success, but precipitated a popular opposition known as the Schism or *raskol*. Those resisters best known to historians were nativist priests and laymen called Old Believers who sought to preserve church ritual and linguistic practices from foreign innovation. "Spit on [the foreigners]! You are Russian, Alexis, not Greek. Speak your mother tongue; don't be ashamed of it," one Old Believer wrote Tsar Alexis (r. 1645–1676).[99] But as Georg Michels and others have shown, a wider circle of dissidents were less interested in ritual issues than in defending their organizational and social autonomy from central interference, whether by the church or the crown. Thus a determination to preserve their independence led some monasteries and hermitages that had remained outside the church's institutional structure into open revolt, while among many laymen religious concerns fused with struggles to preserve traditional secular entitlements against tsarist tax and service demands.[100] If dissenters came from diverse backgrounds, the most

---

[98] Sources in n. 100 *infra*, plus Debra Coulter, "Church Reform and the 'White Clergy' in 17th-Century Russia," in Kotilaine and Poe, *Modernizing Muscovy*, 291–316. On 17th-century peasant Christianity, also Michels, *At War*, 188–216, 227–28.

[99] Pierre Pascal, *Avvakum et Les Debuts du Raskol* (Paris, 1963), 511.

[100] On church–society and church–state relations, Michels, *At War*; idem, "The Solovki Uprising" (ms); idem, "The Patriarch's Rivals," in Kotilaine and Poe, *Modernizing Muscovy*, 317–41; Pascal, *Avvakum*; Robert Crummey, *The Old Believers and the World of Antichrist* (Madison, WI, 1970); idem, "Old Belief as Popular Religion," *SR* 52 (1993): 700–12; idem, "Religious Radicalism in 17th-Century Russia," *FzOG* 46 (1992): 171–85; idem, "Interpreting the Fate of Old Believer Communities in the 18th and 19th Centuries," in Stephen Batalden, ed., *Seeking God* (DeKalb, IL, 1993), 144–59; Boris Uspensky, "The Schism and Cultural Conflict in the 17th Century," in ibid., 106–43; Bushkovitch, *Religion*, chs. 3, 7; Michael Cherniavsky, "The Old Believers and the New Religion," *SR* 25 (1966): 1–39; Eve Levin, "From Corpse to Cult in Early Modern Russia," in Valerie Kivelson and Robert Greene, eds., *Orthodox Russia* (University Park, PA, 2003), 81–103; Daniel Kaiser, "Quotidian Orthodoxy," ibid., 179–92.

socially vulnerable groups – Cossacks and Siberian peasants defending their liberties, downwardly mobile soldiers, townsmen, and state peasants – tended to be most hostile to official religion. The ever more enthusiastic embrace of serfdom and of foreign culture by the state and its noble supporters only widened the gap. From 1668 until Pugachev, virtually every revolt included schismatics who rejected Petrine Westernization – shaved beards, Western dress and calendar, the poll tax – as works of the Antichrist. Peter himself was assailed as a German, a Swede, a Muslim in disguise. Thus the xenophobia of the Time of Troubles reappeared. But whereas in 1612 it had united Muscovites of different strata against foreigners, now embittered Russians directed that sentiment against an indigenous ruling class deemed alien and illegitimate.

Even after 18th-century rulers eased persecution, religious sectarianism persisted under the umbrella of Old Belief, which from the early 1700s developed a sacred canon, founded schools, promoted missionary outreach, and thus institutionalized itself as a "textual community." By the 1820s Old Believers may have constituted 20 percent of adult Great Russians.[101] Moreover, the Old Belief expressed in extreme form the alienation of many who still attended official churches. True, in some respects Old Believers stood apart: not only were their rituals distinct, but whereas Old Believers denied the tsar's legitimacy, most peasants nursed a "naive monarchist" image of the ruler as paternal benefactor. Yet whatever their sectarian affiliation, peasants and poor townsmen differed from the nobility in that they tended to exhibit a deep conservatism, even petrification (no pun on Peter intended), in dress, ritual, art, and music; to cherish a communal economic ethic; and to retain religion as the defining criterion of community. Thus peasants tended to be hostile to "educated society" (*obshchestvo*).[102]

Noble distance from popular culture was therefore proportionate to the former's European identity, which strengthened dramatically in the 18th century. Whereas Peter had literally forced reluctant nobles to shave their beards and adopt Western dress, from the mid-1700s social emulation and the expansion of education, publications, foreign travel, and other contacts began to give European customs a life of

---

[101] Hosking, *Russia*, 73; Crummey, "Interpreting," 151; idem, "Old Belief as Popular Religion," 707; Michels, *At War*, 220, 228–29.

[102] Daniel Field, *Rebels in the Name of the Tsar* (Boston, 1989); Moon, *Russian Peasantry*, 278; Kaiser and Marker, *Reinterpreting*, chs. 17, 18; Hosking, *Russia*, pt. 3; Hoch, *Serfdom*, 1–14, 91–159; Crummey, *Old Believers*, chs. 6, 7; Hartley, *Social History*, ch. 8.

their own, chiefly among the high nobility, of course, but increasingly among rural gentry as well. As in France, wealthy nobles educated their sons and maintained at least one house in the capital, while from the late 1700s European entertainments, architecture, and literature spread to the provinces.[103] If Hungarian and German culture enjoyed an early cachet and if Russian scholarship continued to look to Germany, the language of polite society became increasingly French. An English visitor thought it foolish for wealthy Russians to fight Napoleon "when they can't eat their dinners without a French cook to dress it, when they can't educate their children without . . . [French] tutors and governesses . . . – in a word when every association of fashion, luxury, elegance, and fascination is drawn from France . . . "[104] The nobility, particularly its upper ranks, thus became estranged not only from their own peasants – high nobles tended to see their rural estates as outposts of civilization in a semibarbarous world – but from most Russian merchants, who, if they knew any foreign language, were likely to know German. The triumph by the early 1800s of a written Russian that avoided Old Church Slavonic and religious terminology and that borrowed from French syntax encouraged a literary florescence, but did little to lessen the rift between elite and popular culture.

Such horizontal cleavages exceeded cultural splits in central Burma or Siam, each of which knew but one religious system and one language (not counting deportee tongues and sacred scripts). The situation in Vietnam was closer insofar as both Russian and Vietnamese elites employed languages (Chinese or French) inaccessible to the general populace, imbibed foreign norms, and supported alien, rationalist philosophies that contrasted with the peasantry's more deist/magical preoccupations. In Russia as in Vietnam in 1800 male literacy, a major vehicle of cross-class exchange, probably still was only some 10–20 percent.[105] But the cultural split in Russia in 1800 was more polarizing

---

[103] Hartley, *Social History*, 155–56, 192–94; essays by Dmitri Shvidkovsky and Priscilla Roosevelt in James Cracraft and Daniel Rowland, eds., *Architectures of Russian Identity 1500 to the Present* (Ithaca, 2003), 51–79. On Peter as cultural reformer, Hughes, *Age of Peter the Great*, chs. 9, 10; essays by Lindsey Hughes and Ernest Zitser in Kivelson and Neuberger, *Picturing Russia*, 51–62.

[104] Quoted in Blum, *Lord and Peasant*, 350. On the changing relation of noble to peasant and popular urban culture, see esp. Hartley, *Social History*, chs. 6–10; Confino, *Societe et Mentalites*, 345–87; Wortman, *Scenarios*, vol. I, 81–214; Hosking, *Russia*, 115–18, 164–71, 286–96.

[105] See scanty data, which must be extrapolated to 1800, in Marker, "Literacy and Literary Texts in Muscovy: A Reconsideration," *Slavic Review* 49 (1990): 74–89; Jeffrey Brooks,

than in Vietnam for three reasons: a) The Petrine revolution began much later. Whereas in Dong Kinh Chinese norms were introduced in the first millennium and dominated by the 1460s, in Russia Western norms influenced provincial nobles only in the early to mid-1700s and by the mid-1800s had barely touched the peasantry. Old Believers joined Pugachev in 1773, but Buddhist anti-Confucian revolts in Dong Kinh had reached a dead end as early as 1520. b) Whereas Vietnamese society lacked large ascriptive groups and Neo-Confucianism was expressly meritocratic, Russia's caste-like system severely inhibited vertical exchange. c) In the small-scale world of Vietnam, town–rural communication was easier than in the vast Russian plain, where many serfs lived in what may fairly be called rural ghettos.

Yet alongside these horizontal cleavages, the Russian core also knew cultural trends that created a bridge, potential or actual, between social estates. Secular trends notwithstanding, Orthodoxy remained central to official ideology, to popular self-images, and indeed to the life rituals of most nobles as well as townsmen and peasants. From the mid-1700s, as part of the ongoing reform of ecclesiastical organization, the church made fresh efforts to upgrade the knowledge of its flock and to reduce a bewildering array of local practices (Freeze's "Russian Heterodoxy"), although as ever, success proved easier among elites and townspeople than in the countryside.[106] Despite or because of her German origins and Francophile Enlightenment interests, Catherine went to great lengths to promote Orthodoxy at the expense of other creeds as well as to acquire excellent Russian speech and to present herself to her subjects as "Mother of All the Russias." During the invasion by Napoleon, who was pilloried in church propaganda as a godless infidel, manifestos urged "Orthodox peasants [to] take up arms for the faith and [fight] for your Tsar!" – which they did in large numbers. The postwar period saw a renewed official emphasis on Orthodoxy and social paternalism.[107]

When Russia Learned to Read (Princeton, 1985), 4; Richard Hellie, *Slavery in Russia 1450–1725* (Chicago, 1982), 237–40, 603–604; and Moon, *Russian Peasantry*, 348. On the Neo-Confucian revolution and literacy in Vietnam, *SP*, 377–99, 427–54.

[106] Gregory Freeze, "The Rechristianization of Russia," *Studia Slavica Finlandensia* 7 (1990): 101–36; idem, "Institutionalizing Piety"; LeDonne, *Absolutism*, 142–43; Hartley, *Social History*, 236–44, 256; Gary Marker, "God of Our Mothers," in Kivelson and Greene, *Orthodox Russia*, 193–209.

[107] Quote in Hosking, *Russia*, 134. See too Alexander Martin, "The Response of the Population of Moscow to the Napoleonic Occupation of 1812," in Lohr and Poe, *Military and Society*, 470–89; Hartley, *Social History*, 259–61; Marc Raeff, *Political Ideas and Institutions in Imperial Russia* (Boulder, 1994), 65–75. On Catherine's public and private cultural

At the same time, ironically, Western-derived nationalism inspired among educated elites a new quasi-secular vision of social solidarity. For much of the 18th century Russian theorists sought to assert equality with other Europeans, but by the turn of the 19th century as that goal proved elusive, many invoked the West as an antimodel, claiming that the spirituality and innocence of the "Russian people" were far superior to the superficial rationalism of their Western counterparts. Such concepts posited an ethnic, all-class Russian nation to replace or to supplement the prenational community of Orthodox imagination.[108]

Economic activity fostered less cerebral, more practical challenges to social compartmentalization. The mid-17th-century goal of a static caste-like society, in which only nobles owned serfs and townsmen enjoyed a monopoly on trade and manufacture, proved impossible to achieve, in part because boundaries between social estates (*soslovie*) were always permeable at the margins, but more basically because towns attracted illegal immigrants, the growing peasant population became too dispersed for town traders to supply, and freedom from guild restrictions and urban taxes gave rural industry an advantage over the towns. Enterprising peasants and people of diverse origins (*raznochintsy*) began trading outside the towns and, along with nobles, founding manufactures. In Russia as in Southeast Asia – and, we shall see, France and Japan – between 1750 and 1830, both *de jure* and *de facto* social barriers therefore began to erode in favor of a somewhat more fluid, market-oriented order.[109] As J. Michael Hittle observed, "All this was clearly a case of the law, always a step or two behind, trying to catch up with life."[110] After 1745, for example, peasants were allowed to trade in villages. Between 1801 and 1817 the nobility's legal monopoly on land crumbled, while its monopoly on serfs, though legally intact, was often violated.

identities, Valerie Kivelson, pers. commun., Feb. 20 and April 12, 2007; Madariaga, *Catherine*, chs. 21, 32 and *passim*; John Alexander, *Catherine the Great* (New York, 1989), 17–60.

[108] James Cracraft, "Empire Versus Nation," *HUS* 10 (1986): 527–32; Liah Greenfeld, *Nationalism* (Cambridge, MA, 1992), ch. 3; Hans Rogger, *National Consciousness in 18th-Century Russia* (Cambridge, MA, 1960); Hosking, *Russia*, 133 ff., 171–72; Michael Cherniavsky, *Tsar and People* (New Haven, 1961), 128–34.

[109] Cf. *SP*, 296, 300–301, 316, 441–42.

[110] Hittle, *Service City*, 171. On cross-class enterprise and eroding controls, ibid., 66–69, 168–88, 200–202; Blum, *Lord and Peasant*, 281–303, 358–62, 489–91; William Blackwell, *The Beginning of Russian Industrialization, 1800–1860* (Princeton, 1968), 205–11; Elise Wirtschafter, *Stuctures of Society* (DeKalb, IL, 1994), esp. ch. 4; Moon, *Russian Peasantry*, 143–50; Hartley, *Social History*, 159–71.

Meanwhile, the expansion of business and government service nurtured literate professionals – teachers, doctors, technicians, middle-grade officials – who lacked noble status but had some access to noble culture. The proliferation of such groups joined more relaxed censorship and a rise in elite literacy to popularize periodicals, books, and private associations, which in turn spread novel views of politics and culture. Alongside devotional and utilitarian books, markets developed for belles lettres, adventure, even science.[111] Printing, European contacts, and the sheer size of the urban network favored greater innovation than in Southeast Asian realms, none of which could match the 500 new works appearing annually in Russia by the 1780s. Yet in both regions wider literacy and more diverse literary genres stimulated one another.[112]

Nor was the peasantry, 85–90 percent of the Great Russian population,[113] untouched by new cultural currents. Self-tuition, especially in the far north, had long allowed some peasants to read, even write. But after 1750, especially in central Russia and among state peasants, literacy grew through Old Believer networks, contacts with clergy and government clerks, the dissemination of urban prints and chap books, trade and part-time work in the cities. Elements of high culture also continued to filter into the peasant world through oral channels: Raeff, for example, suggests that demobilized soldiers brought to the villages a knowledge of Western ways and gentry norms. Especially in the south and in the Ukraine, a growing corpus of calendars, laws, and decrees that peasants painstakingly copied and used for petitions, as well as prayers, histories, and folktales, many written by peasants themselves, showed unmistakable awareness of elite usages, including a surprisingly detailed knowledge of palace politics. Likewise, whether through woodblock prints or oral literature, in some areas by the 19th century the supposedly isolated peasantry had altered their image of witches to accord with the most up-to-date Western ideas.[114]

---

[111] Marker, "Enlightenment," 139; idem, *Publishing*, 70–236; Raeff, *Understanding*, 100–111, 129–45; idem, *Origins of the Russian Intelligentsia* (New York, 1966), 122–71; Kaiser and Marker, *Reinterpreting*, 386–427.

[112] On Southeast Asian literary florescence from 1650 to 1830, SP, 188–98, 313–23, 443–49.

[113] Moon, *Russian Peasantry*, 21.

[114] Raeff, *Understanding*, 71–78; Kaiser and Marker, *Reinterpreting*, 388, 394–99; Brooks, *Learned To Read*, ch. 3; Wirtschafter, *Structures*, 8, 66–67; Crummey, "Religious Radicalism," 172; Valerie Kivelson, review of Georg Michels, *JMH* 74 (2002): 208; idem, "'The Souls of the Righteous in a Bright Place,'" *RR* 58 (1999): 3; idem, "Witchcraft in Russia, 1467–1850" (ms).

Culture and Control on the Imperial Periphery, c. 1650–1830

As cultural practices in the imperial core grew more complex, the empire as a whole became ever more ethnically and religiously variegated. This was the inevitable result not of imperial debility, but of rapid expansion into new ethnic territories. Until the conquest of Kazan in 1552, the population had been overwhelmingly Orthodox in religion and Great Russian in ethnicity. Pagan Finnic and Baltic peoples were few and, in many cases, assimilable. But in the latter half of the 16th and in the 17th century Muscovy incorporated the ancestors of today's Ukrainians and Belarussians, in varying degrees distinct from Great Russians, as well as numerous non-Slavic peoples in the Volga basin, both animists and Muslims, and scattered indigenes in Siberia. In the early 1700s Germans, Estonians, and Latvians on the Baltic littoral entered Russia's orbit. Polish partitions then brought in large numbers of Jews, Lithuanians, more Belarussians, and Poles, followed by peoples in the Crimea, Caucasus, Kazakhstan, Finland, and Bessarabia. As early as 1782, Great Russians had become less than 49 percent of the total imperial population, a figure that fell thereafter.[115] If this was larger than the percentage of Siamese in the Siamese empire, it was considerably smaller than that of Burmans in the Burmese empire or Vietnamese in the reunified Nguyen domain.[116] What is more, most of Russia's post-1550 additions proved indigestible. Muslims, Catholics, Lutherans, Jews, and Buddhists all boasted rich religious and literary traditions distinct from those of Orthodoxy, and their social structures often differed profoundly. In short, Russia's post-1650 military success let political control rapidly outrun cultural bonds.

How, then, was so vast and variegated a realm held together? Most obviously, through military and administrative means. Frontier regions had little autonomy, and such freedom as they did enjoy waned in the 18th and 19th centuries. True, communications between St. Petersburg and Kamchatka were at least six times slower than between the Burmese capital and its farthest tributaries. But whereas the latter were hereditary Tai dynasts, St. Petersburg's agents were Russian garrison commanders. In Siberia and the steppe, clan and tribal leaders answered directly to army commands, tribute payments went to the imperial fisc, and imperial law took precedence over indigenous custom. Unable to resist the heavy machine of Russian armies and colonization, subject to

---

[115] Hartley, *Social History*, 10–13.
[116] *SP*, 329–30, 433.

simultaneous military pressure from Qing China, denied profits of agrarian raiding, and increasingly dependent on Russia for access to their traditional pasturelands, Kazakhs, Kalmyks, and other nomads in the late 1700s and early 1800s faced deepening poverty and political emasculation. In an ironic reversal of the relation between steppe and sown in the 14th century, Russian officials now manipulated steppe politics so as to fragment opposition – while laying plans to refashion nomadic societies in the Russian image.[117] As "civilized" Christian areas, Russia's western borderlands faced less intrusive policies than the steppe or Siberia, but in the west as well, over the long term, centralizing trends became unmistakable. After its 1709 revolt to preserve the Ukraine's "rights and liberties" failed, the Cossack Hetmanate was drastically curtailed. In 1764 the Hetmanate was abolished altogether, after which the region was incorporated into the Russian provincial system and peasants were effectively enserfed. Under Catherine similar changes transformed much of Belarus and Lithuania. The Baltic provinces, Finland, and Poland retained special privileges by virtue of their "advanced" European character and international treaties, but none boasted an independent princely house or (apart from Poland) its own army. After the failed revolt of 1830–1831, the new Kingdom of Poland lost most of its distinctive institutions, including its army and legislature.[118]

In tandem with administrative pressures, the empire advanced ideological claims that varied with time and context. Sometimes it sought to inculcate loyalty by promoting a universal, supraconfessional self-image. Even in the 17th century we find a tendency to conceptualize the realm not as a unified patrimony, but as an agglomeration of once separate realms under a single ruler.[119] In Siberia Russian settlers and officials accepted that they lived in an irreducibly polyethnic world in which all subjects had some claims to tsarist protection.[120] With the

---

[117] Khodarkovsky, *Steppe Frontier*, chs. 1, 4, 5; idem, *Worlds Met*, chs. 5–7; Hosking, *Russia*, 10–18, 39; Peter Perdue, *China Marches West* (Cambridge, MA, 2004), chs. 4, 7, 15. On Siberia, Yuri Slezkine, *Arctic Mirrors* (Ithaca, 1994), chs. 1–3; David Collins, "Subjugation and Settlement in 17th- and 18th-Century Siberia," in Alan Wood, ed., *The History of Siberia* (London, 1991), 37–56.

[118] Orest Subtelny, *Ukraine: A History* (Toronto, 1988), chs. 10, 12; Zenon Kohut, *Russian Centralism and Ukrainian Autonomy* (Cambridge, MA, 1988), chs. 3–7; Thaden, *Western Borderlands*, pts. 1, 2; Hosking, *Russia*, 23–41.

[119] Wortman, *Scenarios*, 32; Cracraft, "Empire Versus Nation," 524–41; Michael Khodarkovsky, "From Frontier to Empire," *RH* 19 (1992): 115–28.

[120] Kivelson, *Cartographies*, chs. 6–8.

conquest of additional non-Orthodox areas by Peter – first to use the title "emperor" – and with the growth of Western secularism, officials placed yet greater emphasis on universalist, sometimes vaguely Christian visions of disparate peoples and cultures united by personal loyalty to the ruler and by appreciation of his/her civilizing mission. Within the nobility, participation in a multiethnic enterprise created an imperial consciousness far more tolerant than the narrow Russianness of peasants, merchants, and most clergy. In such a milieu Georgian, Tatar, Ukrainian, and Polish elites could find an honorable place, and the Baltic German K. V. Nessel'rode could serve as foreign minister for 30 years, although he scarcely spoke Russian.[121] Imperial pride reflected not only victories and size, but variety itself, as suggested by the words of the early 19th-century historian Nikolai Karamzin: "If we look at the expanse of this unique state, our minds are stunned: Rome in its greatness never equaled it . . . One need not be a Russian . . . to read with admiration accounts . . . of a nation which . . . won dominion over one-ninth of the world, opened up countries hitherto unknown, brought them into the universal system of geography and history, and enlightened them in the Divine Faith."[122]

Yet as Karamzin's paean also shows, even as it emphasized diversity, the state remained committed to Orthodox primacy as symbol and instrument of imperial unity. In 17th-century Siberia, where large-scale native conversion proved impractical, Russians still conceived of their conquests as expressly theodictic. If not by converting the natives en masse, then by planting Russian colonists and building churches, Muscovy sought to Christianize the landscape and spread God's glory to the ends of the earth.[123] As the 17th century progressed, efforts to convert Muslims and animists on the imperial periphery grew more systematic and penal.[124] During the more secular Enlightenment era, notwithstanding Catherine's commitment to religious toleration and

---

[121] Hosking, *Russia*, 160. On multiethnic tolerance, ibid., 26–41, 158–62; Wortman, *Scenarios*, 136–37; Andreas Kappeler, *La Russie, Empire Multiethnique* (Paris, 1994), esp. 141–45; Thaden, *Western Borderlands*, 80, 231–42; Khodarkovsky, *Steppe Frontier*, 176, 195–96.

[122] From Karmazin's *History of the Russian State* quoted in Hosking, *Russia*, 41. On the popularization of such images, Willard Sunderland, "Shop Signs, Monuments, Souvenirs," in Kivelson and Neuberger, *Picturing Russia*, 104–108.

[123] Kivelson, *Cartographies*, ch. 6, discussing both actual practices in 17th-century Siberia and historiographic debates concerning them.

[124] Hughes, *Age of Peter the Great*, 353; Michael Khodarkovsky, "The Conversion of Non-Christians in Early Modern Russia," in Robert Geraci and Khodarkovsky, eds.,

her courting of Muslim clerics, state support for Orthodoxy remained strong, both because Enlightenment theories placed Christian Europeans at the apex of unilinear development, and because in popular imagination Orthodoxy remained fused with Russian political hegemony. Thus in Poland, Lithuania, Belarus, and the Ukraine, Catherine brought almost 2,000,000 Uniates – adherents to Orthodox ritual who, under Polish influence, had affiliated to Rome – back under the authority of the Russian Orthodox hierarchy.[125] Likewise, against a background of rivalry with the Ottomans and the Crimean khanate, in the 18th century St. Petersburg promoted Orthodoxy among Muslims and pagans in the Volga and Kama region, and to a lesser extent in the Caucasus and the steppe. In Michael Khodarkovsky's formulation, after Russian military and civil officials, Orthodox missions became a third-tier political institution. Frequently proselytism was accompanied by sustained efforts, justified by Enlightenment unilinearism, to transform hunters and nomads into agriculturalists, which also promised to hasten Russification of laws and culture.[126]

How successful were these efforts? Officials claimed vast numbers of animist converts, but while some, like the Siberian Buryats, did enter the lower rungs of Russian society, many animist conversions were temporary and nominal. Among Muslims in the North Caucasus and the Volga basin and among Buddhist Kalmyks in the steppe, proselytism could be counterproductive, contributing to revolts, emigration, and Islamic revivalism. Orthodox conversion and Russian culture had the greatest allure not to commoners, but to non-Russian elites, and for obvious reasons. Whereas families of commoners who converted often found themselves isolated from both former kin and new coreligionists and gained at best temporary material advantages, elite converts

Of Religion and Empire (Ithaca, 2001), 125; Georg Michels, "Rescuing the Orthodox," in ibid., 19–37.

[125] Thaden, *Western Borderlands*, 46–53, 67; Michael Khodarkovsky, "Of Christianity, Enlightenment, and Colonialism," *JMH* 71 (1999), 394–430; idem, *Steppe Frontier*, 186–88; Yuri Slezkine, "Naturalists Versus Nations," in Daniel Brower and Edward Lazzerini, eds., *Russia's Orient* (Bloomington, IN, 1997), 27–57; Madariaga, *Catherine*, 503–18; LeDonne, *Absolutism*, 142–43.

[126] Michael Khodarkovsky, "Not By Word Alone," *CSSH* 38 (1996): 267–75, esp. 292; idem, "Conversion of Non-Christians," 115–43; idem, *Steppe Frontier*, 130, 142, 171, 186–220; Raeff, *Political Ideas*, 135–36; Sunderland, *Wild Field*, 62–64, 79, 102–104. On conversion policies and practices, see also essays by Sergei Kan and Firouzeh Mostashari in Geraci and Khodarkovsky, *Of Religion*; Hartley, *Social History*, 15; Paul Werth, "Orthodoxy as Ascription (and Beyond)," in Kivelson and Greene, *Orthodox Russia*, 239–51; Slezkine, *Mirrors*, chs. 1, 2.

not only retained their original privileges, but typically intermarried with Russian nobles and became fully assimilated within two or three generations.[127] Catherine saw elite Russification as an inevitable and highly desirable by-product of institutional and social integration. The borderlands, she declared, must "be Russified in the easiest way possible, so that they should cease looking like wolves to the forest."[128] To that end, St. Petersburg supported Russian-language education for noble youths in non-Russian areas, made Russian the language of provincial and clerical administration, admitted non-Russians to elite schools in the capital, and welcomed an array of non-Russian chiefs, elders, and princes into the nobility. Not surprisingly, such policies had the strongest impact in those Slavic, substantially Orthodox areas whose preannexation cultures were most similar to Russia's. By the early 1800s Ukrainian nobles and even gentry to all intents and purposes had become Russian, while Russification also spread among the clergy and part of the urban population. Similar patterns affected parts of Belarus and Lithuania. In the steppe and the Caucasus assimilation was far less common, but there too elite Russification joined rising tsarist exactions to widen the gap between elites and commoners and thus to weaken local resistance.[129]

Finally, imperial integration benefited from large-scale frontier colonization, chiefly by Russians and Ukrainians. Such settlement reflected the combined effects of state-sponsored migration and of illegal flight from serfdom, epidemics, and famine. If official efforts to induce landowners to move their serfs to the periphery bore little fruit, grants, loans, tax exemptions, and other inducements to state peasants had the desired effect. While the proportion of Great Russians within the borders of 1719 remained fairly constant at about 69 percent, the Slavic population on the north shore of the Black Sea, so-called New Russia, rose dramatically. In Siberia as well, Russians grew from a negligible proportion in 1600 to 70 percent by 1800, and in the North Caucasus, from 15 percent in 1762 to over 50 percent by 1795. Overall, the percentage of Russian peasants located on the steppe climbed

[127] Khodarkovsky, "Conversion of Non-Christians," 140; idem, *Steppe Frontier*, 144.

[128] Referring specifically to western areas. Kohut, *Russian Centralism*, 104. Also ibid., 81.

[129] Hartley, *Social History*, 18, 72, 76, 143; Kohut, *Russian Centralism*, 294–303; Velychenko, "Identities, Loyalties," 198–99; Hosking, *Russia*, 40; Khodarkovsky, *Steppe Frontier*, 144, 162–83, 200, 226; Madariaga, *Catherine*, 61, 582–83; Marc Raeff, "Patterns of Imperial Policy Towards the Nationalities," in Edward Allworth, ed., *Soviet Nationality Problems* (New York, 1971), 22–42.

from 29 percent in 1678 to 46 percent by 1811.[130] Because Russian settlers – much like their Burman and Vietnamese counterparts – occupied
ecological-cum-economic niches distinct from those of indigenes, cultural cross-fertilization often was limited. Yet, precisely because Russian
and Ukrainian settlers tended to identify with Orthodox tsarist culture,
such settlement strengthened central political control, as advocates of
colonization themselves were quick to argue. Conversely, by constricting pastures and rendering nomads ever more economically dependent
on Russian towns and garrisons, Russian settlement crippled the capacity of nonagrarian peoples for independent action.[131]

To summarize cultural change in the Romanov empire: By 1830,
largely as a result of growing European influence, key usages – language, religious beliefs, domestic styles – were more horizontally lay-
ered in the old Muscovite core than in either Daniilovich Russia or
the cores of Southeast Asian empires. Yet at the same time, intellectual
shifts and commerce opened new vertical avenues of exchange within
the Great Russian heartland. And because noble assimilation and colonization extended Russian culture itself from the Baltic to the Pacific,
way beyond the original Muscovite heartland, that culture, like the
state with whose fortunes it was inextricably twined, was vastly more
influential across Eurasia in 1830 than it had been in 1613.

3. FRANCE DURING AND AFTER THE BOURBONS

The Construction of French "Absolutism," c. 1600–1720:
Renewed Integrative Pressures

Absolutism was traditionally defined as a species of monarchy, represented most famously by Louis XIV's France, which encroached on
subjects' privileges, overrode local bodies committed to defend those
privileges, and through its control of bureaucrats and other "new men"
dependent on the crown, substantially decoupled itself from society. As
recent scholars have shown, none of these generalizations can easily
be defended: France's so-called absolutist state, much like its Romanov

---

[130] Hartley, *Social History*, 10–13; Sunderland, *Wild Field*, 73–95, 113–34; Moon, *Russian Peasantry*, 56. See too ibid., 49–65; Khodarkovsky, *Steppe Frontier*, 146, 161–62. Under Catherine, 100,000 foreign migrants also were welcomed on the frontier.

[131] Khodarkovsky, *Steppe Frontier*, 30, 141–42, 161, 165–74 and n. 117 *supra*. To some extent Russian mercantile penetration had a similar effect on Ukrainian autonomy. Kohut, *Russian Centralism*, 285–92.

counterpart, remained less an agency of unilateral dictation than of improved coordination among sectors of the elite whose privileges the crown, supporting essentially patrimonial structures, was eager to maintain.[132] On the other hand, in France as in Burma, Siam, and Russia, political organization by 1720 clearly had become more effective than in 1600, with royal authorities acquiring new military, fiscal, and patronage powers, greater influence over provincial affairs, a novel interest in social and economic regulation, and new theoretical claims.

In part, as in Russia, these trends reflected subtle social and psychological shifts conducive to projects of integration and pacification in which the crown necessarily played a leading role. Although, as we shall see, the 17th-century French economy was generally sluggish, stronger financial links between Paris and the provinces and the growing importance of royal patronage drew high nobles from their rural estates to the capital. Similarly, the city's cultural and social preeminence rendered Paris – in a movement Robert Harding terms "social centralization" – ever more irresistible to provincial nobles pursuing litigation, advantageous marriages, or cultural stimulation. Such developments, apparent during the 1500s, intensified in the 17th century even before Louis in 1682 made Versailles, southwest of Paris, his magnificently centripetal residence and seat of government.[133] In part, a 17th-century

---

[132] The historiography of French "absolutism" is vast. See evolving perspectives in William Beik, *Absolutism and Society in Seventeenth-Century France* (Cambridge, 1985), esp. 10–12, 17; Nicholas Henshall, *The Myth of Absolutism* (London, 1992); Peter Campbell, *The Ancien Regime in France* (Oxford, 1988); idem, *Power and Politics in Old Regime France 1720–1745* (London, 1996), 1–35, 177–90, 296–318; James Collins, *The State in Early Modern France* (Cambridge, 1995), 116–19; idem, *Classes, Estates and Order in Early Modern Brittany* (Cambridge, 1994), esp. 271–88, critiquing Marxist views and stressing intra-elite differences; idem, *From Tribes to Nation* (Toronto, 2002), v–vi, xi–xii; Sharon Kettering, *Patrons, Brokers, and Clients in Seventeenth-Century France* (New York, 1986); Roger Mettam, *Power and Faction in Louis XIV's France* (Oxford, 1988), esp. 24–29; Francois-Xavier Emmanuelli, *Un Mythe de l'Absolutism Bourbonien* (Aix-en-Provence, 1981); David Parker, *The Making of French Absolutism* (New York, 1983); idem, *Class and State in Ancien Regime France* (London, 1996), esp. ch. 1; idem, "Absolutism," in *Encyclopedia of European Social History*, vol. III (2001): 439–48; Guy Rowlands, *The Dynastic State and the Army Under Louis XIV* (Cambridge, 2002), 2–17, 340–49; and Julian Swann, "The State and Political Culture," idem, "Politics: Louis XV," William Doyle, "Politics: Louis XIV," and Munro Price, "Politics: Louis XVI," all in William Doyle, ed., *Old Regime France* (Oxford, 2001), 139–248.

[133] Robert Harding, *Anatomy of a Power Elite* (New Haven, 1978), esp. 171–79, 216; Beik, *Absolutism and Society*, 245–78. On the role of Versailles, Peter Burke, *The Fabrication of Louis XIV* (New Haven, 1992), chs. 4–6; Swann, "State and Political Culture," 143–45; and discussion *infra*.

passion for systemic order – a passion intrinsically sympathetic to royal coordination that encouraged tighter control of everything from laws and military affairs to language and theater – drew inspiration from the standardizing epistemological thrust of printing and cartography. It has been suggested, for example, that cartographic advances instilled in both statesmen and informed readers a more bounded, uniform, and linear image of the monarchy's territorial destiny (an image, I would note, that had analogues in Petrine and post-Petrine Russia as well as Japan, but not Southeast Asia, where power was conceptualized as ebbing gradually from a central point).[134] By promoting *politesse* and *honnetete* (civility and propriety), printing, theater, and new royal academies joined local emulation of courtly manners to disseminate an elite ethos of self-restraint and to reduce the once formidable cultural gap between courtiers and country nobles.[135] At a lower social level the growth of market relations and commercial disputes continued to nourish an interest in litigation and a willingness to use royal law courts. Likewise, Steven Pinker suggests that by widening feelings of social interdependence and empathy, commercial ties joined religious reform and state interventions to dampen public violence and brutality.[136]

More certainly and dramatically, recurrent political crises shaped elite and popular sympathies. After the calamities of the late 16th century, Frenchmen – not unlike their Burmese and Russian contemporaries – were increasingly apt to see the crown as a providential institution

---

[134] I follow Michael Biggs, "Putting the State on the Map," *CSSH* 41 (1999): 374–405; Daniel Nordman, *Frontieres de France* (Paris, 1998), 89–104, 515, 525; and Peter Sahlins, "Natural Frontiers Revisited," *AHR* 95 (1990): 1423–51. On French cartography c. 1500–1790, see too Roger Kain and Elizabeth Baigent, *The Cadastral Map in the Service of the State* (Chicago, 1992), ch. 6; David Buisseret, ed., *Monarchs, Ministers, and Maps* (Chicago, 1992), ch. 4. On general epistemological changes, Jay Smith, *The Culture of Merit* (Ann Arbor, 1996), ch. 4; Michael Foucault, *The Order of Things* (New York, 1973), 27–28, 57–63. On Japan see Ch. 4, n. 306.

[135] Ellery Schalk, "The Court as 'Civilizer' of the Nobility," in Ronald Asch and Adolf Birke, eds., *Princes, Patronage, and the Nobility* (Oxford, 1991), 245–63; idem, *From Valor to Pedigree* (Princeton, 1986); Parker, *Class and State*, 144–57, 269–70; Rowlands, *Dynastic State*, 7–9, 178–86, 232–38. On changing noble roles, see too idem, "The Ethos of Blood and Changing Values?," *Seventeenth-Century French Studies* 19 (1997): 95–108; Jonathan Dewald, *The European Nobility 1400–1800* (Cambridge, 1996), 151–62; James Wood, *The Nobility of the Election of Bayeux 1463–1666* (Princeton, 1980); and Norbert Elias' classic *The Civilizing Process*, 2 vols. (New York, 1978, 1982).

[136] Jonathan Dewald, *Pont-St-Pierre 1398–1789* (Berkeley, 1987), 183–89, 251–63; Steven Pinker, in Ch. 1, n. 84 *supra*, suggesting that public sadism endorsed even by the French court in the 16th century had lost some of its acceptability by the late 1700s.

offering stability in a deeply dangerous, potentially anarchic world. An intense yearning for renewed harmony and order became manifest in xenophobia, misogyny, and noble determination to curb fresh admissions to their ranks, but most critically, in renewed support for royal prerogatives.[137] Thus, although in fact the Wars of Religion had stimulated theories in two opposite directions, the one seeking to limit, the other to extend royal authority, the latter trend predominated, as seen in the growing influence of Jean Bodin's theory of royal power as an inalienable sovereignty that alone was entitled to make public law. Royal authority gained further support from the Counter-Reformation, which sought to discipline a restive population and to instill a renewed reverence for divinely constituted authority.[138] By bringing France once again to the edge of anarchy, a series of noble and popular revolts from 1648 to 1653 known as the Fronde reinforced the too-easily forgotten lessons of the 1590s and implanted in Louis XIV (r. 1643–1715), his ministers, and growing sectors of the educated public a fresh commitment to social order, royal service, and unchallenged royal leadership.

But in France as in Russia, arguably the most consistent spur to political reform in the 17th and 18th centuries was military. This was true even though in France as in Russia, the most militarily significant reforms typically cohered not during wartime itself, when chaos threatened to overwhelm planning, but after peace was restored, when more measured efforts became feasible. The fact that from 1661 to 1789 France, like Russia, was at war almost one year in two, and in most other years was preparing for war, meant that military considerations were rarely far from the thinking of key statesmen.[139] Bourbon campaigns to 1714

---

[137] Cf. early-17th-century images of the Burmese crown as a barrier against renewed anarchy, Lieberman, *Administrative Cycles*, 129. On growing hostility to social mobility and efforts, continuing through Louis XIV, to define noble status more carefully, see Schalk, *Valor to Pedigree*, 90–93, 107–34, 202–14; Mack Holt, ed., *Renaissance and Reformation France 1500–1648* (Oxford, 2002), 58; Ronald Asch, *Nobilities in Transition 1550–1700* (London, 2003), 16–19.

[138] See Mack Holt, "Redrawing the Lines of Authority," in Holt, *Renaissance and Reformation*; Greengrass, *Age of Henri IV*; William F. Church, *Richelieu and Reason of State* (Princeton, 1972), esp. 24–37; Parker, *Making*, 50–59; Schalk, *Valor to Pedigree*, chs. 4–8; Black, *Military Revolution*, 71–77; Collins, *Tribes to Nation*, 258–74; and discussion of the Counter-Reformation *infra*.

[139] "The *end goal* of [all royal action] was to strengthen the hold of the Bourbon dynasty on the realm and enhance its prestige on the international stage." Rowlands, *Dynastic State*, 10. "Absolute monarchs also had at their disposal armies of ever greater size and firepower – to finance them was the essential reason for the expansion of the machinery

fell into two principal phases, the great anti-Habsburg, anti-Spanish struggles of 1635–1659 and Louis XIV's wars of 1667 to 1714. During the first phase, France sought both to block the emergence of a powerful German state dominated by Habsburg Austria and to arrest the progress of Habsburg Spain, then Europe's preeminent power whose holdings in the Mediterranean, the Franche Comte, and the southern Netherlands practically surrounded France. France emerged triumphant – its new status symbolized by the use of French rather than Latin in the final treaties – with strategic acquisitions in the northeast and southeast. In the second set of wars Louis XIV sought at first to extend his north-eastern frontiers, still dangerously close to Paris, and to subordinate the prosperous Dutch state. Notwithstanding ever more effective anti-French coalitions led by Holland, Austria, and England and the erosion of French superiority as other states emulated French military organiza-tion, France by 1714 had achieved today's basic hexagonal shape, minus Lorraine, Savoy, Nice, Avignon, and the Comtat. Meanwhile if France's continental domain remained modest by Russian standards, in the New World – in Quebec, the Mississippi valley, Louisiana, the Caribbean – the 17th century saw French acquisitions on a scale more reminiscent of eastern Siberia.[140]

Military expansion overburdened fiscal institutions, not to mention the long-suffering peasantry. Whereas 16th-century French royal armies peaked at 50,000, by 1635–1642 the government was fielding 70,000–80,000, and by the 1690s, a remarkable 300,000–350,000.[141] Moreover, per soldier costs rose rapidly for weapons, professional training, barracks,

---

of state." Parker, "Absolutism," 439. David Parrott, *Richelieu's Army* (Cambridge, 2001) demonstrates convincingly that Richelieu's reforms were far more traditional, improvised, ineffective, and socially disruptive than most scholars have assumed. Yet if the chronology of effective reform was surprisingly late and if the relation between warfare and administrative reform was synergistic, the larger thesis that warfare over the long term nourished administrative centralization remains valid. I draw similar conclusions from my reading of Rowlands, *Dynastic State*, 17–23, 336-62 and *passim*; Black, *Military Revolution*, 67–82; Parker, *Class and State*, 158 ff.; and John Lynn, *Giant of the Grand Siecle: The French Army 1610–1715* (Cambridge, 1997). See too Ch. 1, n. 88 *supra* and discussion *infra*.

[140] Pierre Boulle and D. Gillian Thompson, "France Overseas," in Doyle, *Old Regime France*, 105–38. Lorraine in 1766 and Corsica in 1768 were the last *ancien régime* acqui-sitions in Europe.

[141] I follow Parrott, *Richelieu's Army*, 164, 178, 182-83, 194, 220, 222, who offers pre-1650 figures lower than such authors as Black, *Military Revolution*, 6–7; Geoffrey Parker, "The Military Revolution, 1550–1660 – A Myth?," *JMH* 48 (1976): 195–214; Wilson, "European Warfare," 196; or Lynn, *Giant*, 33, 55.

fortifications, and pensions – to which were added huge capital costs for the navy. Whereas even in peacetime French armed forces for most of the 17th and the entire 18th century never took less than 60 percent of annual nondebt expenditures, in wartime they absorbed over 80 percent – again exclusive of debt, which itself was heavily military in origin.[142]

New Political Structures

What structures emerged from this mix of cultural, political, and military pressures? How did government change between the Wars of Religion and the death of Louis XIV?

As the only king whose statue the Paris crowd initially spared in 1789, Henry IV (r. 1589–1610), founder of the Bourbon Dynasty, was long revered as the ruler who set the world to rights after the Wars of Religion. He sought to satisfy influential constituencies less through structural reform than by reducing direct taxes, revitalizing existing institutions, and dispensing well-publicized patronage. The Catholic majority he won over by himself converting from Protestantism, but he protected Huguenot worship through the Edict of Nantes (1598). Royal office-holders welcomed his creation of the *paulette*, which guaranteed hereditary office in return for an annual fee and which had the added advantage for the crown of reducing the patronage powers of the great nobles.[143]

More ambitious were changes under Louis XIII (r. 1610–1643) and his chief minister, Cardinal Richelieu, changes that responded primarily to the crushing pressures of the anti-Habsburg wars.[144] The years 1627 to 1642 saw the following departures: a) The king suppressed the Protestants' fortified places, a virtual state within a state, in effect concluding the Wars of Religion. b) The throne sought to enhance control over its own military by abolishing some senior posts and appointing governors

---

[142] David Bien, "Old Regime Origins of Democratic Liberty," in Dale Van Kley, ed., *The French Idea of Freedom* (Stanford, 1994), 29 .

[143] Collins, *The State*, 24–25; idem, *Tribes to Nation*, 281–90, 294–97; Kettering, *Patrons, Brokers*, 178–79.

[144] Collins, *The State*, 29–30, 50–58, emphasizing the years 1627–1635. See too Richard Bonney, *Political Change in France Under Richelieu and Mazarin 1624–1661* (Oxford, 1978), ch. 2; A. Lloyd Moote, *Louis XIII, The Just* (Berkeley, 1989); R. J. Knecht, *Richelieu* (London, 1991); Daniel Hickey, *The Coming of French Absolutism* (Toronto, 1986); and Kettering, *Patrons, Brokers*.

directly loyal to Richelieu and the king. This was not a question of eliminating clientage per se – new governors promptly built fresh networks – but of trying to join networks into a single line of command. c) To help collect taxes and to aid the war effort, Paris sent to the provinces more nonvenal, short-term appointees known as *intendants*. d) With the same objective, the throne sought to extend revenue jurisdictions known as *elections* from the *pays d'elections* to some of the outlying *pays d'etats*. e) To expand cash income, the throne also sold ever more offices, relied more heavily on tax farms, and on the strength of future collections secured loans from tax farmers and *parlementaires*. By 1650 central treasury receipts, measured in grain or labor equivalent, were almost five times larger than in 1590 and constituted about an eighth of France's gross domestic product.[145]

Traditionally, Richelieu's reforms have been seen as a decisive advance toward centralization.[146] More recently David Parrott has argued that these measures were ill conceived and ill executed, that they proceeded on a more traditional basis than most have appreciated, that rising taxes aided a narrow group of financiers far more than the army, and that on the whole, rather than strengthen central influence, such measures aggravated problems of control and authority in French society.[147] Certainly, between 1624 and 1645 tax demands sparked a series of bitter revolts, particularly in outlying provinces, and then contributed to the most desperate upheaval between the Wars of Religion and the Revolution, the aforementioned Fronde of 1648 to 1653. This was less an antiroyalist movement per se than a struggle between individuals and factions eager to protect their position during a period of great economic stress and political uncertainty caused chiefly by the strains of the anti-Habsburg struggle. The Fronde fed on popular hatred of wartime exactions, the resentment that members of the Paris *parlement* and other office-holders felt against fiscally driven threats

---

[145] In nominal terms, direct taxes receipts rose from 10,000,000 livres in 1610 to 72,600,000 in 1643. Francoise Bayard, *Le Monde des Financiers au XVIIe Siecle* (Paris, 1988), 30; Philip Hoffman, "Rural, Urban, and Global Economies," in Mack Holt, ed., *Renaissance and Reformation France* (Oxford, 2002), 87; Parker, *Making*, 64; James Collins, *Fiscal Limits of Absolutism* (Berkeley, 1988), 214–22.

[146] Cf. Collins, *The State*; idem, *Classes, Estates*, 184–95; Lynn, *Giant*; and sources in n. 144 *supra*.

[147] See Parrott, *Richelieu's Army*, pts. 2, 3, esp. pp. 547–56, for whose argument minimalist estimates of army size prior to 1650 are central, and n. 139 *supra*. Parrott's work has received consistently favorable reviews.

to their privileges, the disintegration of Richelieu's patronage network after his death, and the minority of Louis XIV.[148]

Ultimately, however, the Fronde – like the Hundred Years War and the Wars of Religion – strengthened the monarchy. The revolt collapsed because insurgents lacked a coordinated program, and because the throne, playing on renewed fear of anarchy, adopted polices that proved to be at once more firm, more conciliatory, and more imaginative. Never again did the nobility and *parlements* join in serious rebellion. As usual, new policies reflected a grand centralizing vision less than cumulative improvisation. On the one hand, the court relied no longer on local forces to quell tax protests, but a standing army of 55,000 to 60,000 quite willing to shoot down protesters. Eventually the court also abandoned unruly Paris for more secure Versailles. On the other hand, the throne developed new strategies to accommodate oligarchic interests. From provincial estates (assemblies), towns, and office-holders, Versailles wanted obedience, easy loans, and taxes. In return it strengthened elite privilege by giving the *pays d'etats* greater freedom in allocating taxes, by adjudicating disputes, and by integrating local leaders into a larger network of personal contacts leading to the king. Whereas in the 16th and early 17th centuries great noble families, led by provincial governors, had run autonomous networks, Louis XIV's ministers, expanding the plans of Richelieu and of Richelieu's successor as chief minister Cardinal Mazarin, shifted resources, especially in frontier provinces, to what Sharon Kettering calls "provincial brokers." Responsible to senior ministers at court and thus ultimately to the king, brokers were locally based dignitaries with influence both at court and in the region, where they organized provincial and municipal clienteles. To those willing to support the crown, brokers awarded civil and military appointments, pensions, and opportunities to invest in lucrative tax farms. Thus they attached local institutions to the crown more firmly, clientage became

[148] Orest Ranum, *The Fronde* (New York, 1993); Collins, *The State*, 65–78; Parker, *Class and State*, ch. 3; Francois Bluche, *Louis XIV* (New York, 1990), chs. 3, 4; and Geoffrey Parker, "Crisis and Catastrophe," *AHR* 113 (2008): 1053–79, emphasizing climatic factors and assimilating the Fronde to a more general 17th-century European/global conjuncture. Some sources refer to the "Frondes" plural. I have chosen not to include the Fronde in the litany of major state breakdowns, but if one were to do so, the pattern of decreasingly lengthy periods of disorder would still hold. On 17th-century protest in general, see too Charles Tilly, *The Contentious French* (Cambridge, MA, 1986), chs. 4, 5; and William Beik's incisive *Urban Protest in Seventeenth-Century France* (Cambridge, 1997).

more unified, and provincial notables gained an interest in expanding the public debt, whether for war or domestic works. Peasants and townsmen paid the tax bill, of course, but in some measure, one could argue, they too benefited from the strengthening of social order.[149]

As national patronage grew more coordinated, at the highest social level the great titled aristocrats, the *grands*, abandoned their local power bases to reside at or near Versailles, where they joined leading ministers and financiers in an increasingly consolidated national elite, totaling perhaps 600 families, under personal supervision of the king. As in the provinces so at Versailles, Louis XIV sought not to repress elites, but to balance rival interests more effectively. And again, throne–elite relations remained deeply reciprocal. The crown still relied on the *grands*, to whom it was intimately bound by education and sentiment, to lead the army, to serve as governors, and to influence provincial affairs through local clienteles. Aristocrats also became the chief subscribers to government loans. But for their part, titled nobles could not maintain their lifestyle without such investments, plus royal gifts, pensions, and salaries, which might comprise half their total income and which created what Michael Kwass has termed "a type of welfare state for the privileged."[150] Reinforcing Versailles' practical seduction was an unprecedentedly elaborate system of royal propaganda, artistic patronage, and stylized etiquette that portrayed the king as social arbiter and sacral pivot.[151]

These reforms simultaneously impeded and encouraged standardization. On the one hand, royal support for local privileges – whose legal elaboration paralleled the growth of written culture and of the

---

[149] Kettering, *Patrons, Brokers*, esp. 44–237; Beik, *Absolutism and Society*, esp. 3–55, 223–339; Swann, "State and Political Culture." William Beik, pers. commun., June, 2006. But see Collins, *Classes, Estates*, 23–29, 60–70, 229–77, emphasizing the Breton nobility's interest in low direct taxes.

[150] Michael Kwass, *Privilege and the Politics of Taxation in Eighteenth-Century France* (Cambridge, 2000), 24. On the evolving position of the nobility and its component parts, previous note, plus Dewald, *Pont-St-Pierre*, 175–76; Parker, *Class and State*, chs. 4–6; Bayard, *Le Monde des Financiers*, 297–455.

[151] On Versailles and the nobility, previous note plus Mettam, *Power and Faction*; Collins, *The State*, 135–39 and *passim*; Rowlands, *Dynastic State*, 340–64, defining the *grands* and critiquing Mettam's thesis of "the king's faction"; Daniel Dessert, *Argent, Pouvoir et Societe au Grand Siecle* (Paris, 1984), exploring links between financial and mercantile activities; Bluche, *Louis XIV*, 347–80; Peter Burke, *Fabrication of Louis XIV*; Smith, *Culture of Merit*, 185–90; Paul Sonnino, ed., *The Reign of Louis XIV* (Atlantic Highlands, NJ, 1990); Emmanuel Le Roy Ladurie, *The Ancien Regime 1610–1774* (Oxford, 1996), chs. 4–6.

state itself – ensured that tax immunities were legion, that the church remained a state within the state, and that the realm remained divided into what Clive Church calls "a mad mosaic of fiscal, legal, and administrative jurisdictions."[152] A traveler, it was said, changed legal systems as often as he changed horses. The northern heartland remained far more closely governed than peripheral provinces, while as late as 1700 the realm was still conceived more as a dynastic collection of territories than as a bounded, unified entity.[153] Nor, despite frequent criticism and short-lived efforts at suppression, did venality weaken. Indeed, to fund his wars Louis XIV expanded the sale of offices; as early as 1665 France had 46,000 venal officials, compared to 4,000–5,000 in 1515.[154] As revocable nonvenal functionaries, the 30-odd *intendants* (who were gradually reinstalled after the Fronde) adumbrated later trends,[155] but even they remained helpless without cooperation from local elites. In Peter Campbell's view, the "baroque state" tried to rise above society, but "inevitably had to compromise. It endowed itself with grandiose schemes, indulged in flamboyant display, but retained most of those *trompe-l'oeil* features that promised more than they could deliver."[156]

Yet at the same time, more obviously perhaps than in Russia and certainly than in Southeast Asia, the growing scale of state operations favored a degree of standardization. During the post-1660 transition from what has been termed a judicial and legislative to an administrative monarchy, ministries mingled patrimonial traditions with more nomothetic, protobureaucratic practices. If the focus of politics remained the court, the magnates who dominated the court socially were largely excluded from executive power: magistrates and career administrators formed the backbone of ministries, and administration came to rely less on royal favorites than on self-regulating institutions. In the provinces as well, power devolved from high nobles to *intendants*, royal

---

[152] Clive Church, *Revolution and Red Tape* (Oxford, 1981), 21. Cf. Gail Bossenga, "Society," in Doyle, *Old Regime France*, 52.

[153] Sahlins, "Natural Frontiers," esp. 1427–38.

[154] Le Roy Ladurie, *Ancien Regime*, 470; Collins, *The State*, 93; William Doyle, *Venality* (Oxford, 1996), 10–48; and Ch. 2, n. 318 *supra*. Parker, "Absolutism," 441 cites a figure of 70,000 or more venal officers including those in tax farms, municipalities, and the army in 1715.

[155] Doyle, *Venality*, 15–16, 62.

[156] Campbell, *Power and Politics*, 4, referring to the state that took shape by 1650 and persisted in essential features to the mid-1700s. Cf. characterizations at Parker, *Class and State*, 173–87.

judges, and office-holders of the *parlements*.[157] In lieu of seigniorial and municipal jurisdictions, peasants in many regions sought out royal law courts, whose caseloads mushroomed. If a unified legal code did not emerge until Napoleon, late-17th-century edicts helped to normalize procedures of criminal and civil law, administered within a kingdom-wide framework of royal jurists.[158] In this same period, that is 1660 to 1720, *intendants*, Versailles, and a large standing army blew apart the system of military clientage that had fed the religious wars and the Fronde. Previously, high nobles who recruited regiments had retained proprietary authority, but now career officers began to look to the ministry of war for commissions, promotion, and finance.[159] Significantly, in the 1690s all French infantry began to wear white or grey uniforms in lieu of regimental medley, even as long-term employment, wider contacts, and more reliable central funding slowly transformed the provincial outlook of many officers to a genuinely national perspective. A stronger sense of decorum became evident as well in the decline of noble dueling and private violence.[160] In the financial sphere the crown consolidated indirect tax farms, instituted the first direct tax to which all laymen were subject, and eliminated some of the worst financial abuses. Not only were nominal treasury receipts, measured in grain equivalents, in 1720–1729 almost 50 percent higher than in 1650–1659,[161] but the proportion of collections that remained in private hands fell. To guide financial and military planning, the state, aided by parish priests, collected local information to an extent inconceivable in earlier generations.

The success of these structural changes, which commonly had a military objective, may be judged not only in military expansion and

---

[157] Doyle, "Politics: Louis XIV," 173–74, 193–94; Collins, *Tribes to Nation*, 403–14, 456–57; Hilton Root, *Peasants and King in Burgundy* (Berkeley, 1987), ch. 2, and Kettering, *Patrons, Brokers*, 224–37, discussing "bureaucratic" features. On the transition from the judicial or legislative to the administrative monarchy, Peter Sahlins, *Unnaturally French* (Ithaca, 2004), 7; Collins, *The State*, 3; idem, *Tribes to Nation*, 404–405.

[158] Collins, *The State*, 146–47; idem, *Classes, Estates*, 13–15; Xavier de Planhol, *An Historical Geography of France* (Cambridge, 1994), 243–44; Dewald, *Pont-St-Pierre*, 251–63. On royal disciplining of regional tribunals, John Hunt, *Louis XIV and the Parlements* (Manchester, 2002). Yet Anthony Crubaugh, *Balancing the Scales of Justice* (University Park, PA, 2001) argues that seigniorial courts of high justice remained surprisingly vital.

[159] Rowlands, *Dynastic State*, 349–60; Parrott, *Richelieu's Army*, 554–56.

[160] Francois Billacois, *The Duel* (New Haven, 1990), esp. ch. 15; Kettering, *Patrons, Brokers*, 213; Rowlands, *Dynastic State*, 354; Lynn, *Giant*, 169–76; Monod, *Power of Kings*, 307.

[161] Philip Hoffman, "Early Modern France, 1450–1700," in Hoffman and Norberg, *Fiscal Crises*, 238 Table 1; Rowlands, *Dynastic State*, 111, 117.

improved systems of training, garrison, and supply, but in the maintenance of a peacetime force not much smaller than Richelieu's wartime army and in the recruitment of wartime forces in the 1690s four times larger than in the 1630s. Although the War of the Spanish Succession (1701–1714) shook the new edifice, for the first time the dynasty could realize the huge military potential of its subjects.[162]

Economic Trends c. 1620–1780 and the Problem of French–Southeast Asian Correlations

Before resuming the political narrative, let us consider French economic trends both as prelude to 18th-century upheavals and as a clue to political correlations with Southeast Asia.

French state formation between c. 1620 and 1720 was hypertrophic in the sense that the state – as measured by revenues, soldiers, or civilian personnel – expanded far more rapidly than population or output. Admittedly, an earlier emphasis on economic stagnation has yielded to a more nuanced picture that acknowledges the deepening of 16th-century trends, including growth in rural manufacture and Atlantic trade, financial specialization, and agricultural productivity in the Paris basin, Normandy, and parts of the southeast. Yet by later standards, these achievements remained modest. Grain yields for the country as a whole in 1700 still averaged only about 5:1 or 6:1, with 25–50 percent of arable still left fallow.[163] From 1633 to 1653 and again from 1689 to 1713 the economy, in Le Roy Ladurie's words, "touched rock-bottom." Not surprisingly, population grew far more slowly than in the 16th century, from some 19,000,000 (within current frontiers) in 1610 to only 21,500,000 in 1700.[164]

How can we account for this weakness, which was more marked than in 17th-century Russia and probably (although statistics are poor) most

[162] Parrott, *Richelieu's Army*, 276, 399, 555; Rowlands, *Dynastic State*, 3, 23, 109–60, 336–62; Lynne, *Giant*, pts. 2, 5; Collins, *Tribes to Nation*, 407–409.

[163] Thomas Schaeper, "The Economic History of the Reign," in Sonnino, ed., *Louis XIV*, 27; Joel Felix, "The Economy," in Doyle, *Old Regime France*, 16–17.

[164] Le Roy Ladurie, *Ancien Regime*, 303, with quoted phrase. On demographic and economic patterns, Schaeper, "Economic History," 27–43; idem, *The Economy of France in the Second Half of the Reign of Louis XIV* (Montreal, 1980); Jacques Dupaquier et al., *Histoire de la Population Francaise*, 4 vols. (Paris, 1995), vol. II, esp. chs. 5, 6, 9; Daniel Hickey, "Innovation and Obstacles to Growth in the Agriculture of Early Modern France," *FHS* 15 (1987): 208–14; Hoffman, "Rural, Urban, and Global," esp. 71; Bossenga, "Society," 42; Felix, "Economy," 7–41; Robert Duplessis, *Transitions to Capitalism in Early Modern Europe* (Cambridge, 1997), 142–43, 164–71.

of lowland Southeast Asia? Bullionist explanations fail, since supplies from Latin America continued to rise throughout the 1600s.[165] Robert Brenner and Hilton Root have argued that to maintain its base of tax-paying peasants, the crown protected inefficient smallholders and communal systems against English-style enclosure, inhibiting productivity gains.[166] But according to Philip Hoffman, not did only enclosures boost productivity far less than has been assumed, but in many French districts the same smallholder regime as floundered in the mid-1600s proved quite vital a century later.[167] In part, population growth by 1560 had come up against a new ceiling that could not be breached without some combination of better transport, new urban stimuli, and more efficient credit on the English or Dutch model. The late-16th- to 17th-century demographic pause was therefore a cyclic adjustment comparable to that of the 14th century, but without the Black Death and far more moderate. Furthermore, after 1590 and more especially from 1683 to 1710, France, along with Southeast Asia and Russia, suffered from Little Ice Age climatic deterioration. According to Thomas Schaeper, this was probably the chief reason French yields 1620–1720 declined by 10 percent, a decline that in turn raised mortality and depressed fertility.[168] Also critical in limiting consumption and investment were heavy wartime taxes, whose incidence seems to have correlated closely with economic difficulties. Finally, French trade suffered from the general European slump of 1620 to 1720.[169]

---

[165] Ward Barrett, "World Bullion Flows, 1450–1800," in James Tracy, ed., *The Rise of Merchant Empires* (Cambridge, 1990), 224–54.

[166] T. H. Aston and C. H. E. Philpin, eds., *The Brenner Debate* (Cambridge, 1987), esp. ch. 1; Root, *Peasants and King*, 13–15, 105–54. Also Emmanuel Le Roy Ladurie, *The French Peasantry 1450–1660* (Berkeley, 1987), 408–11.

[167] Philip Hoffman, *Growth in a Traditional Society: The French Countryside 1450–1815* (Princeton, 1996), 15–16, 27–34, 165–70, 189–92, 203–204; idem, "Rural, Urban and Global," 71–98.

[168] Schaeper, "Economic History," 31; Jacques Dupaquier, "Demographic Crises and Subsistence Crises in France, 1650–1725," in John Walter and Roger Schofield, eds., *Famine, Disease, and the Social Order in Early Modern Society* (Cambridge, 1989), 189–99; Felix, "Economy," 11–12. Yet Collins, *Tribes to Nation*, 426, also notes many good harvests between 1660 and 1715. On cooling in northern Europe, which correlated with weaker Southeast Asian monsoons, Bradley and Jones, *Climate Since 1500*, 246–68, 652–53, 674; Le Roy Ladurie, *Ancien Regime*, 214–16; Emmanuel Le Roy Ladurie, *Histoire Humaine et Comparee du Climat* (Paris, 2004), chs. 6–9; Ch. 1, n. 99 *supra*.

[169] Jan De Vries, *The Economy of Europe in an Age of Crisis, 1600–1750* (Cambridge, 1976), chs. 1, 4; Peter Kriedte, *Peasants, Landlords and Merchant Capitalists* (Cambridge, 1983), ch. 2.

Logically enough, the upturn that began in the second or third decade of the 18th century benefited from a reversal of these same trends. The mid-1710s opened a phase of warmer temperatures and drier summers, especially pronounced in mid-century, which raised harvests notably and reduced winter mortality in non-Mediterranean France.[170] Mortality decline after 1740 benefited too from a retreat of smallpox, typhus, plague, and other pandemics, although in each case it is unclear to what extent we should credit warmer weather, better nutrition, pathogen mutations, government actions (quarantines, famine relief), or the hygienic benefits of cheap linen underwear and clothing.[171] Economic growth and a modest reduction in the incidence of warfare meant that real per capita taxes rose far more slowly in the 18th than in the 17th century – which, along with the hexagon's novel security from invasion, reduced war's economic cost.[172]

Yet arguably the most critical spur to 18th-century growth was a synergy between state interventions, a new urban consumer culture, and multifaceted Smithian specialization. As regards state policy, the monarchy's deficiencies are glaring enough, including a failure to divert noble funds from rentier activities to productive investment, to suppress more effectively guilds and commercial regulation, to curb military and court expenses, to allocate taxes more equitably, or to reduce debt charges to English levels. Yet after 1720/1730 we also see positive signs, aided by a pragmatic, if partial, shift away from Colbertian regulation. From the

[170] Annual average temperatures rose 1–1.5° C from 1720–1760 over 1680–1710. See Lamb, *Climate, History*, 242–49; C. Pfister, "Monthly Temperature and Precipitation in Central Europe from 1525 to 1979," in Bradley and Jones, *Climate Since 1500*, 118–42; plus the emphasis on climatic stimuli to agrarian growth at Felix, "Economy," 16 (in the 18th century "the principal factor benefiting the economy was the more temperate climate"); Le Roy Ladurie, *Histoire Humaine*, 16–17, 531–71; David Weir, "Markets and Mortality in France, 1600–1789," in Walter and Schofield, *Famine, Disease*, 231–32; Gwynne Lewis, *The French Revolution: Rethinking the Debate* (London, 1993), 8.

[171] Stephen Kunitz, "Diseases and the European Morality Decline, 1700–1900," in Kenneth Kiple, ed., *The Cambridge World History of Human Diseases* (Cambridge, 1993), 287–92; Bossenga, "Society," 42; Weir, "Markets and Mortality," 201–34; Roche, *Enlightenment*, 494–96; idem, *The Culture of Clothing* (Cambridge, 1994), 151–220; Roger Price, *The Economic Modernization of France* (New York, 1975), 203–209; Goldstone, *Revolution and Rebellion*, 180–83; Roger Schofield et al., eds., *The Decline of Mortality in Europe* (Oxford, 1991).

[172] Pierre Chaunu and Richard Gascon, *Histoire Economique et Sociale de la France, Tome 1: De 1450 a 1660, v. 1: L'Etat et la Ville* (Paris, 1977), 42; Le Roy Ladurie, *Ancien Regime*, 303–307, 381, 401–404; Hoffman, "Early Modern France," 238; Felix, "Economy," 12–13.

mid-1700s officials reduced barriers to trade in foodstuffs (insofar as this was compatible with public order), eased agriculture's fiscal burden, promoted the latest manufacturing and agrarian techniques, and built Europe's most impressive arterial road network. If some 30,000 kilometers of new highways from 1738 to 1789 were designed more for strategic than commercial ends, they nonetheless reduced transaction costs by speeding the circulation of goods, people, and commercial information.[173]

Nourished by better transport, as well as by public spending, noble urbanization, and colonial trade, in 1790 French towns (places with 2,000 or more residents) contained some 20 percent of the population.[174] Paris alone may have had 700,000. In the towns arose a consumer culture, more dynamic and broadly based than in Southeast Asia or Russia, which devalued the stationary economy in favor of circulation, individualism, emulation, and acquisition. Thus even urban artisans, shopkeepers, wage earners, and servants began to buy not only cheap clothes, but crockery, soap, mirrors, books, furniture, clocks, sugar, coffee, tobacco, and other items once associated with elite status. The value of textiles, for example, in the average Parisian household rose from 1700 to 1789 by a factor of 3.5, and even in the poorest sectors of Paris, 2.7.[175]

---

[173] Mercantilist regulation had been preeminently associated with Louis XIV's controller-general of finance, Jean-Baptiste Colbert (1619–1683). On roads, Le Roy Ladurie, *Ancien Regime*, 358–59; Bossenga, "Society," 42; Felix, "Economy," 17–26; Fernand Braudel, *The Identity of France*, 2 vols. (New York, 1988, 1990), vol. II, 466–67, 480–85; Price, *Economic Modernization*, 4–7. Moreover, the government-assisted Canal du Midi linked the Mediterranean and Atlantic from 1682. On government policies and their philosophical foundations, Roche, *Enlightenment*, 122–24, 153–58; Elizabeth Fox-Genovese, *The Origins of Physiocracy* (Ithaca, 1976); Philippe Minard, *La Fortune du Colbertisme* (Paris, 1998), emphasizing the continued appeal of regulation; Michael Kwass, pers. commun., June 21, 2006; Hoffman, "Rural, Urban, and Global," 64–66, 92–98; idem, *Growth in a Traditional Society*, 201–205; Felix, "Economy," 27–41; Vivian Gruder, "Whither Revisionism? Political Perspectives on the Ancien Regime," *FHS* 20 (1997): 283; James Riley, *The Seven Years War and the Old Regime in France* (Princeton, 1986), 162–91, 223–39.

[174] Peter McPhee, *A Social History of France 1789–1914* (New York, 2004), 7. Major cities grew, but many middle and smaller towns declined. On urban trends, also Rozman, *Urban Networks*, 66, 84–87; Collins, *Tribes to Nation*, 470–81; Bossenga, "Society," 69; Roche, *Enlightenment*, 179–80; idem, *The People of Paris* (Berkeley, 1987), 9–35; idem, *A History of Everyday Things* (Cambridge, 2000), 33–39; Philip Benedict, ed., *Cities and Social Change in Early Modern France* (London, 1989), 24–25, 39–48.

[175] Felix, "The Economy," 27. On French consumer culture, Roche, *Enlightenment*, 548–77, 626–27; idem, *Everyday Things*, chs. 7–9; idem, *Culture of Clothing*; idem, *People of Paris*, esp. pt. 2; Maxine Berg and Elizabeth Eger, eds., *Luxury in the Eighteenth Century* (New York, 2003), pts. 2, 5; Colin Jones and Rebecca Spring, "Sans-culottes,

Although consumerism in the countryside remained more restricted, there too, at least among prosperous peasant landowners, purchase of consumer goods and tools increased.

Easier market access in turn stimulated production. According to Jan de Vries' "industrious revolution" thesis, those addicted to the market were far more willing than subsistence producers to innovate and to work intensively for long periods.[176] In urban hinterlands, most dramatically in the Paris basin, demand for foodstuffs joined improved transport to reduce fallow and to encourage crop specialization, better seeds, tools, and fertilizers, as well as peasant stratification. Rising consumer demand and surplus rural labor also promoted rural cottage industries and systems of urban manufacture that, although still heavy artisanal, tended to become more specialized and concentrated. Whereas from 1700 to 1789 agricultural output grew by 25 percent, industry and trade rose by almost 70 percent. By the latter date, some scholars estimate, nonagrarian activities produced at least half of French wealth.[177] To be sure, before the 1840s one can hardly talk of either an

---

Sans Café, and Sans Tabac," in Maxine Berg and Helen Clifford, eds., *Consumers and Luxury* (Manchester, 1999), 37–62; Cissie Fairchilds, "The Production and Marketing of Populuxe Goods in 18th-Century Paris," in John Brewer and Roy Porter, eds., *Consumption and the World of Goods* (New York, 1993), 228–48; Collins, *Tribes to Nation*, 438–43.

[176] Jan de Vries, "The Industrious Revolution and the Industrial Revolution," *JEH* 53 (1994): 249–70. For hints of a consumer-cum-industrious revolution elsewhere in Eurasia, Pomeranz, *Great Divergence*, chs. 2, 3; Chs. 4, 5 *infra*; *SP*, 175–79, 304–308, 436–37.

[177] Agrarian and nonagrarian growth rates are calculated in bushels of wheat at Goldstone, *Revolution and Rebellion*, 190, 204, 221, but the sectoral discrepancy is appreciably less if measured in *livres*, ibid., 204 and Felix, "Economy," 20. When foreign trade is included, Felix claims that nonagrarian activities represented more than 50 percent of national wealth in 1789. Le Roy Ladurie, *Ancien Regime*, 307–308, 363 sees agrarian and non-agrarian production as equal, although Goldstone, *Revolution and Rebellion*, 190 and Roche, *Enlightenment*, 553 treat agriculture more generously. On industry and trade, see too Roche, *Culture of Clothing*, 259–329; Liana Vardi, *The Land and the Loom* (Durham, NC, 1993), 110–232; Collins, *Tribes to Nation*, 444–50; Kriedte, *Peasants, Landlords*, 101–61, esp. 131; Duplessis, *Transitions*, 237–43; Roger Price, *An Economic History of Modern France 1730–1914* (London, 1981), chs. 1, 3; Planhol, *Historical Geography*, 233–40; Bossenga, "Society," 69–70; Felix, "Economy," 25 ff.; Parker, *Class and State*, 28–47; Ernest Labrousse et al., *Histoire Economique et Sociale de la France*, Tome 2 (Paris, 1970), 217–66, 499–528. On agriculture, ibid., 417–71; Vardi, *Land and Loom*, 49–109; Duplessis, *Transitions*, 164–71; Dewald, *Pont-St-Pierre*, 74–89; McPhee, *Social History*, ch. 1; and esp. Hoffman, *Growth in a Traditional Society*, ch. 5. An earlier emphasis on stark French economic deficiency vis-à-vis England has yielded to a rather more positive view of French performance. See previous sources plus Francois Crouzet, *Britain Ascendant* (Cambridge, 1985), esp. chs. 1, 2; Patrick O'Brien, "Path Dependency, or Why

agricultural or industrial revolution. Agrarian change left much of the countryside untouched; and without the example of British industrialization, it is unclear whether France would have escaped from a new involutionary equilibrium.[178] Nonetheless, from 1700 to 1790 rural and urban manufacture, local agrarian advances, better weather, and epidemic regression combined to sustain a 30 percent population increase, to some 28,000,000.[179] If France as a whole still had no genuinely national market, regional markets became more integrated, and the amplitude of cyclic price movements declined.[180]

Although data are limited, it is doubtful that in any mainland Southeast Asian realm in 1790 the value of manufactures and services equaled that of agriculture, that 30 percent of food production was marketed,[181] or that cities contained 20 percent of the population. Domestic markets were more constricted than in France, communications more difficult, access to foreign technology far more limited, foreign traders more prominent, and the emphasis on entourage and clientage less supportive of consumerism. Nonetheless, Volume 1 provided ample evidence that across mainland Southeast Asia after 1710/1720 money use, frontier settlement, foreign trade, agricultural, craft, and regional specialization all registered notable advances that continued, indeed accelerated, to the early 1800s.[182] A comparable transformation, we just saw, occurred in Russia. Why, then, this broad coordination between European and Southeast Asian economies?[183]

First, North European warming after 1710/1720 coincided with improved rainfall in mainland Southeast Asia, with marked agricultural benefits in both cases. Second, states in both regions promoted

---

Britain Became an Industrialized and Urbanized Economy Long Before France," *EHR* 49 (1996): 213–49; Colin Jones, *The Great Nation* (London, 2002), xxiii, 160–70; Sarah Maza, "Luxury, Morality, and Social Change," *JMH* 69 (1997): 213–14 and sources in her nn. 38–41.

[178] Cf. Pomeranz, *Great Divergence*, 206–207 *et passim*; Crouzet, *Britain Ascendant*, 42–43.

[179] Bossenga, "Society," 42; Le Roy Ladurie, *French Peasantry*, 406; P. M. Jones, *The Peasantry in the French Revolution* (Cambridge, 1988), 1–6; Parker, *Class and State*, 211; Dupaquier et al., *Histoire de la Population*, vol. II, chs. 2, 6, 9; Fig. 4.2 *infra*.

[180] Yet as late as 1789 only the Cinq Grosses Fermes of northern France constituted an organized market run as a single unit, and trade between this area and extra-French regions often was as important as trade with the south. See Planhol, *Historical Geography*, 241–42; Parker, *Class and State*, 32–35.

[181] As was true in France, Braudel, *Identity*, vol. II, 489.

[182] See Ch. 1 *supra* and *SP*, 167–79, 286–99, 303–309, 435–40.

[183] Cf. discussion of synchroniziing agents in the text accompanying Ch. 1, nn. 94–128 *supra*.

growth by reducing rural disorders, externalizing warfare, reducing tolls and multiple jurisdictions, opening new transport links, demanding cash rather than in-kind taxes, and concentrating demand around each capital. In turn, French and Southeast Asian states drew strength from European-style firearms and institutional refinements that followed late-16th-century breakdowns. Third, in each kingdom population growth and lower transaction costs boosted demand for foodstuffs and handicrafts – which called forth more specialized production, which strengthened markets, which aided state operations. Frontier colonization in Southeast Asia may have been no less supportive of demographic expansion than was French protoindustry.

Consider finally the coordinating role of international trade, which we touched upon in discussing Russia but which deserves further treatment. Synchronization between France and mainland Southeast Asia owed virtually nothing to bilateral trade.[184] Rather, Europe and Southeast Asia were two among many zones benefiting from a specialization which was at once national, regional, and global and in which Asia played a vital coordinating role. It was Asian, especially Chinese, demand for silver that kept the mines of the New World profitable after their first decades, permitting a more or less continuous increase in American silver exports to both Europe and Asia. From 1533 to 1660 Chinese demand also drew Japanese silver into international circuits.[185] China's hunger for the white metal – between 1560 and 1800 China absorbed 25 to 50 percent of all world production[186] – reflected, first, the Ming turn to uncoined silver as the basis of its monetary system; and second, the rapid growth of China's population and economy from c. 1500 to 1630 and from c. 1700 to 1830. If, as usual, the primary roots of China's vitality were domestic and if bronze coin (better suited to rural marketing) replaced silver in much of the interior in the 18th century,

---

[184] On French involvement in Southeast Asia, David Wyatt, *Thailand: A Short History* (New Haven, 2003), 97–103. If French profits from trade with China in 1745 were less than 0.5 percent of French GNP (computed from Le Roy Ladurie, *Ancien Regime*, 360; Campbell, *Ancien Regime*, 35; Felix, "Economy," 20), French trade with Southeast Asia probably did not equal 5 percent of that with China.

[185] See Ch. 1, n. 120 *supra*.

[186] See various estimates at Barrett, "World Bullion Flows," 224–54; Andre Gunder Frank, *Re-Orient* (Berkeley, 1998), 142–49; Richard von Glahn, "Myth and Reality of China's 17th-Century Monetary Crisis," *JEH* 56 (1996): 429–54; Pomeranz, *Great Divergence*, 190; Kenneth Pomeranz and Steven Topik, *The World That Trade Created* (Armonk, NY, 1999), 16; Artur Attman, *American Bullion in the European World Trade, 1600–1800* (Göteburg, 1986), 33.

over the long term silver powerfully stimulated coastal–hinterland exchange and exports of sugar, tea, and silk.[187] In turn exports joined widespread domestic intensification and state-sponsored reclamation to enhance labor demand, to erode fertility controls, and thus to stoke an historic population boom – along with demand for yet more foreign silver.[188] India had a smaller population than China and used more varied monetary media. Yet there too between 1550 and 1800 and especially after 1700 growing money use, not least among humble urban and rural strata, relied on imported copper, cowries, and New World silver. The latter arrived overland and via the Indian and Pacific Oceans for exchange against raw silk, cotton, and finished textiles. Indian cloths had long been popular in Southeast Asia and West Asia but from the late 17th century became the rage in western Europe.[189]

How, then, did these types of multilateral exchange help to coordinate growth in France and Southeast Asia? The benefits to France of rising global trade were as follows.[190] a) In France as in Europe generally, American silver became the *sine qua non* for marketization. Spain, with a weak manufacturing base, ran a consistent deficit with France and other European countries, which allowed France to obtain from

---

[187] Thus in Lingnan in southeast China from 1550 to 1820 the economy was restructured in part to meet European demand for porcelain, sugar, tea, and especially silk, all purchased chiefly with Spanish and Japanese silver. Robert Marks, *Tigers, Rice, Silk, and Silt* (Cambridge, 1997), 119, 127–33, 176–84. On the impact of China's overseas trade, also Richard von Glahn, *Fountain of Fortune* (Berkeley, 1998), chs. 3–7; Pomeranz, *Great Divergence*, 159, 189–94, 269–74; Sucheta Mazumdar, *Sugar and Society in China* (Cambridge, MA, 1998), ch. 2; and Ch. 1, n. 121 *supra*. China's turn to silver started in the Yuan period.

[188] James Lee and Wang Feng, *One Quarter of Humanity* (Cambridge, MA, 1999), 113–18. Also Thomas Buoye, *Manslaughter, Markets, and Moral Economy* (Cambridge, 2000), 60–66.

[189] An uncertain fraction of silver imports to India flowed out to China, where the silver-to-gold ratio was often lower. See *CEHI*, 382–407; Frank Perlin, "Money-use in Late Pre-colonial India and the International Trade in Currency Media," in John F. Richards, ed., *The Imperial Monetary System of Mughal India* (Delhi, 1987), 232–373; Om Prakash, "Precious Metals Flows into India in the Early Modern Period," in Clara Eugenia Nunez, ed., *Monetary History in Global Perspective, 1500–1808* (Seville, 1998), 73–84; Susil Chaudhury, "The Inflow of Silver to Bengal in the Global Perspective, c. 1650–1757," in ibid., 85–95.

[190] On French foreign trade, n. 177 *supra*, plus Labrousse et al., *Histoire Economique*, 186–201, 499–511; John Clark, *New Rochelle and the Atlantic Economy During the Eighteenth Century* (Baltimore, 1981); Le Roy Ladurie, *Ancien Regime*, 307, 360–65; Lakshmi Subramanian, ed., *The French East India Company and the Trade of the Indian Ocean* (Calcutta, 1999); Jean Tarrade, *Le Commerce Colonial de la France a la Fin de l'Ancien Regime*, 2 vols. (Paris, 1972), esp. vol. II, 495–97, 506–509, 676–87.

Spain itself, from Spanish colonies (to which France was the leading supplier of manufactures), and from Spain's European trading partners New World bullion whose value rested ultimately on Asian silver demand. In Europe as a whole between 1600 and 1800, by one estimate, overall silver stocks rose 179 percent and per capita stocks, 55 percent.[191] b) Besides silver, France imported tropical "drug foods" (tea, tobacco, coffee, cocoa, and sugar) from Asia and the Caribbean, Asian textiles, as well as North Atlantic fish and Baltic timber and grain. By transcending local ecological limits, imported food and fiber provided "ghost acreage" that was functionally equivalent to frontier reclamation in Russia and Southeast Asia. c) Along with tropical foods, Asian textiles – which were cheaper and more colorful than European textiles – and porcelain drew French consumers to the market, aiding de Vries' industrious revolution. d) Asian silks and cottons prompted successful 18th-century efforts at import substitution, that is, local manufacture.[192] e) After c. 1760 French exports – local goods and colonial re-exports as well as imitations of Asian products – to Latin America, Spain, Italy, Africa, the Mideast, and central Europe grew far more rapidly than any other sector of non-farm production, with particular benefit to the rural textile industry.[193] f) In the 18th century New World maize and potatoes permitted rapid population growth in some poor French regions.[194] g) The latest Dutch and English techniques aided French agronomy and manufacture. All told, 18th-century French foreign trade – in 1775 still primarily intra-European, but shifting steadily toward the Atlantic – rose threefold in value, and overseas trade, a remarkable eightfold.[195] Maritime trade thus served to concentrate population and wealth along the coasts, which joined the northern textile/agricultural belt as the most vital sector. "All the wealth of France has moved toward its frontiers; all its great, opulent cities are on its borders; the interior

---

[191] Barrett, "World Bullion Flows," Table 7.8.

[192] On consumer tastes and import substitution, Felix, "Economy," 27–28; Pomeranz, *Great Divergence*, 193, 242; Duplessis, *Transitions*, 204; Maxine Berg, "Asian Luxuries and the Making of the European Consumer Revolution," in Berg, *Luxury in the Eighteenth Century*, 228–44; and Roche, *Culture of Clothing*, 126, 198–99, 260–61, 446, noting that of 198 textile types in the *Encyclopedie*, 131 originated in Asia.

[193] Duplessis, *Transitions*, 240; Price, *Economic Modernization*, 132–33; Schaeper, "Economic History," 40.

[194] Felix, "Economy," 16; Roche, *Everyday Things*, 243–44; Robert Schneider, *Public Life in Toulouse 1463–1789* (Ithaca, 1989), 288.

[195] Figures from Labrousse et al., *Histoire Economique*, 503, 509; Duplessis, *Transitions*, 240; Le Roy Ladurie, *Ancien Regime*, 360.

is frightfully thin," observed an Italian in 1770.[196] But if two economies emerged, one dynamic and outward looking, the other basically stagnant, the former was sufficient to inaugurate for France as a whole in the 1720s an era of growth arguably as impressive as the high middle ages and more so than the long 16th century. Between 1720 and 1760, James Collins concludes, a "new France" arose.[197]

Comparable benefits accrued to 18th-century Southeast Asia. Notwithstanding a persistent silver drain to China, substantial American and Japanese bullion remained in Southeast Asia to lubricate trade, while American maize and sweet potatoes enhanced the value of hitherto marginal soils. Chinese, Indian, and European manufactures drew producers to the market, encouraging a more tentative version of the European consumer revolution.[198] At the same time Dutch and English traders raised the demand for entrepot and local goods from Burma, Siam, Cambodia, and Vietnam. A growth in Indian merchant capital, partly the result of European investments, also led to a marked increase in Indian shipping to Burma and Siam.[199] Yet more basic, China's demographic revolution, which, to repeat, had local roots but which benefited from European bullion and demand for sugar, tea, and silk, spilled over into Southeast Asia. Volume 1 described the dramatic increase in Chinese immigration, mining, and agricultural enterprise in Southeast Asia, designed chiefly to supply the Chinese home market, during what Anthony Reid termed the "Chinese century" 1740–1840. As in France, trade-mediated technological transfers, in this case from China to Southeast Asia, also became influential. Not surprisingly, after the crises of 1767–1802 Chinese traders were critical to the political revival of both Siam and Vietnam.[200]

Can we quantify the contribution to coordinated French–Southeast Asian prosperity that derived from Asian–European trade – as distinct

---

[196] Quoted in Roche, *Enlightenment*, 143.

[197] Collins, *The State*, ch. 5 ("A New France, 1720s–1750s").

[198] On New World bullion and crops and Indian textiles in mainland Southeast Asia, *SP*, 46, 47, 51–52, 72, 112, 145–49, 157, 168, 170–78, 252–56, 285–96, 415, 420, 436–38; Wil O. Dijk, *Seventeenth-Century Burma and the Dutch East India Company 1634–1680* (Singapore, 2006).

[199] Previous note, plus K. N. Chaudhuri, *The Trading World of Asia and the English East India Company 1660–1760* (Cambridge, 1978), ch. 9; P. J. Marshall, *East Indian Fortunes* (Oxford, 1976), 29, 86; Lieberman, *Administrative Cycles*, 156–59; *SP*, 167–72.

[200] Anthony Reid, ed., *The Last Stand of Asian Autonomies* (New York, 1997), 11–14, 57–82; *SP*, 170–71, 286–94, 302–305, 426, 435–37; and Ch. 7 *infra*.

from non-Asian trade, climate, and domestic factors? Given the synergistic nature of domestic and external stimuli, the task is exceedingly difficult. In France we know that the ratio of foreign trade to agricultural output between 1700 and 1790 narrowed from 1:6 to 2:5, but that Europe in 1775 still absorbed 63 percent of all external French trade and that commerce with Asia represented well under 5 percent of non-European trade.[201] By these lights, Asia's impact seems very limited. But no one, so far as I know, has quantified the extent to which French domestic and external trade relied ultimately on Chinese silver demand, or how extensively Asian trade modified French consumer habits and manufacturing.[202] For mainland Southeast Asia we also lack reliable statistics on the economic contribution of New World crops, foreign demand, and bullion-dependent liquidity. Nor can we say with any precision how extensively South China's commercial upsurge in the 1700s, that great northern engine for Southeast Asia, depended on European links.

In the face of such imponderables, one can only conclude – modestly and baldly – that between 1710 and 1800 direct and indirect trade ties between Europe and East Asia impacted both regions more extensively than during the previous period of rapid growth from 1450 to 1620, when the New World–South China Sea connection was either unformed or in its infancy. In turn, European/Asian linkages c. 1450–1620 were far more influential than during the economic boom of the 11th to 14th centuries, when climate, disease, and parallel social changes seem to have been the chief agents of Eurasian coordination.

---

[201] See n. 184 *supra*, plus Labrousse et al., *Histoire Economique*, 502–509, Figs. 52 and 53. Cf. Hoffman, "Rural, Urban, and Global," 80–85; Duplessis, *Transitions*, 202; Tarrade, *Commerce Colonial*, vol. II, 738–39.

[202] Of some relevance are studies of England, where Patrick O'Brien suggests that extracontinental trade funded 16–20 percent of gross capital formation. O'Brien, "European Economic Development: The Contribution of the Periphery," *EHR* 35 (1982): 1–18; idem, "European Industrialization," in Hans Pohl, ed., *The European Discovery of the World and Its Economic Effects on Pre-Industrial Society, 1500–1800* (Stuttgart, 1990), 154–77. David Richardson, "The Slave Trade, Sugar, and British Economic Growth, 1748–1776," *Jl. of Interdisciplinary History* 17 (1987): 739–69 argues that Caribbean demand accounted for 12 percent of the growth of British industrial output 1748–1776. But insofar as Britain in 1751 imported three-quarters as much from Jamaica as from the whole of Asia (M. N. Pearson, *Before Colonialism*, Delhi, 1988, 46) and insofar as in 1775 only 8 percent of British exports went to Asia (Duplessis, *Transitions*, 202), Asia's direct contribution to British growth seems very modest.

The French Revolution and Its Aftermath

The relation between economic vitality and the fortunes of the French monarchy after 1720 was ironic. On one level, economic and technical progress combined with military pressures to accelerate Bourbon centralization. In the countryside *intendants* continued to absorb the judicial functions of many seigneuries and to attempt more direct control of villages, thus replacing the lord as intermediary between king and community.[203] Alongside the traditional spheres of justice and finance, *intendants* and their assistants also assumed responsibility for the great tasks of a new age of commerce – for town building, urban police, public health, education, poor relief, and market unification. As temporary, closely monitored appointees, *intendants* typified the ascent of *commis*, precursors of modern civil servants (albeit within a system still dominated by personal loyalties whose essential ethos could not yet be termed "bureaucratic"). If fiscal necessity obliged the crown to abandon plans to reduce the number of venal office-holders, some 70,000 by 1715, after c. 1740 their numbers grew more slowly and their influence waned vis-à-vis that of *commis*, whose upper echelons trained at the new technical institutes, the *grandes ecoles*. From the 1720s until the early 1750s the ministerial system exhibited a growing stability and professionalism.[204] Higher technical standards likewise permeated the army and navy. To repress military desertion and fiscal fraud and to create a unified economic space, the crown sought to demarcate external boundaries more clearly and to rid itself of territorial enclaves and exclaves.[205] Most telling, as Kwass has shown, recurrent military expenses and practical limits to peasant taxation compelled the monarchy to create wartime taxes, the *dixieme* in 1710 and the *vingtieme* in 1749, which attempted to strike all subjects, including formerly tax-exempt categories, regardless of rank and which in the case of the *vingtieme* became permanent in 1751.

---

[203] Root, *Peasants and King*, 45–65; Dewald, *Pont-St-Pierre*, 148–56, 181–89, 251–63; Schneider, *Public Life*, 282–84.

[204] Although representative of *commis*, *intendants* usually also owned a venal office. Doyle, *Venality*, 15–16, 62, 89–151; Mousnier, *Institutions*, vol. II, 60–64, 502–80, 634–71; and n. 154 *supra*. On 18th-century government in general, see too Francois Furet, *Revolutionary France 1770–1880* (Oxford, 1992), 9–10; Swann, "State and Political Culture," 150; Le Roy Ladurie, *Ancien Regime*, 359, 366, 417–19 (on pre-1789 *grandes ecoles*); 470; Collins, *The State*, 93, 111, 165 and chs. 5–7; idem, *Tribes to Nation*, 426, 451–57, 481–88; Church, *Revolution and Red Tape*, chs. 1–2; Campbell, *Power and Politics*, 1–35, 296–318, emphasizing patrimonialism.

[205] Sahlins, "Natural Frontiers," 1438–40.

To justify universal taxation, whose incidence increased from the 1760s, the crown promoted, albeit hesitantly, appeals to patriotic duty and fiscal equality; and to collect the new imposts, it shifted responsibility from judicial and communal bodies to a more centralized administration capable of targeting individuals as well as groups.[206]

Yet at the same time as the monarchy's claims and capacities expanded, contradictions inherent in its evolving ideology joined the effects of socioeconomic change and military competition to erode its intellectual and moral authority. Some of the same trends as enhanced its technical level eroded its moral appeal, so that the monarchy managed simultaneously to grow stronger and more vulnerable. If French political discourse was unique, certain political and social strains resembled, at a reasonable level of abstraction, tensions in mainland Southeast Asia. Comparable too were the phoenix-like collapse and rapid reassembly of French and Southeast Asian states in the late 1700s, the rejuvenated states' passionate embrace of warfare, and the ensuing imperative to further administrative reform and ethnic unification.

In the chief Southeast Asian realms commercial and population growth in the second and third quarters of the 18th century contributed to unwelcome tensions, including (in diverse local combinations) land shortages, inflationary pressures, an exodus from royal to private service, the rise of commerce over manpower as a source of ministerial income, a corresponding conflict between nominal rank and real economic power, and intensifying factionalism. In both Burma and Vietnam maritime commercial expansion also aggravated north–south tensions. But if such problems created the potential for political collapse, in each case that potential was realized, the system burst apart, only as a result of inept political leadership and disastrous military reverses: Manipuri raids into Burma, Burmese invasions into Siam, and Siamese challenges to Vietnam's position in Cambodia and the Gulf.[207]

France's 18th-century difficulties may be seen in a similar light. An entire generation of historians have eviscerated Marxist claims that

---

[206] The first nominally universal tax, the capitation, was levied in 1695. Kwass, *Privilege and Politics*, 33–115, 314; idem, "A Kingdom of Taxpayers," *JMH* (1998): 295–339; Chaunu and Gascon, *L'Etat et la Ville*, 47; Benedict, *Cities*, 40. Clearly, the gross imbalance between slow economic growth and hypertrophic state expansion c. 1620–1720 ended, but I am uncertain whether state growth c. 1720–1789 continued to outstrip increases in GNP. On shifting patterns of anti-tax protest c. 1660–1789, see n. 8 *supra*.

[207] On 18th-century political and military crises, see *supra* Ch. 1, and *SP*, 182–87, 299–313, 419–35.

the French Revolution heralded the triumph of capitalism or the bour-geoisie. Conflicts precipitating revolution are now seen as the result of specifically French institutional and cultural pressures; there was little essential economic difference between the bourgeoisie (whose defini-tion, many now argue, is problematic) and the nobility; and the revo-lution's chief legacy lay not in economics, but political culture.[208] This emphasis on peculiarly French discursive and institutional forms is inherently unsympathetic to comparison. Yet, while rejecting Marxist actors, these same historians, intentionally or not, offer ample evidence that the cyclic-cum-secular growth of the 18th-century economy was itself a major source of instability and discursive innovation. If French political thought was *sui generis*, the revolution was one in a series of upheavals that extended to Asia. And in both France and Southeast Asia, crises in the late 1700s exhibited generic similarities to state break-downs in the 14th and late 16th centuries.

In 18th-century France the strains of demographic and commercial expansion – at once familiar and unrecognizable to Southeast Asianists – were at least fivefold.

First, as in Upper Burma and more especially Dong Kinh, there is evidence for Jack Goldstone's thesis that population growth intensified both popular distress and intra-elite competition. On the one hand, the proportion of French peasants with midget plots or no land at all grew, while supply and demand decreed that between the 1730s and 1789 food prices rose over twice as fast as wages. Thus, notwithstanding the econ-omy's overall vitality, much of the population actually was consuming

---

[208] For interpretive approaches to 1789 emphasizing culture and politics, see Francois Furet, *Interpreting the French Revolution* (Cambridge, 1981); idem, *Revolutionary France*; Lynn Hunt, *Politics, Culture, and Class in the French Revolution* (Berkeley, 1984); idem, *The Family Romance of the French Revolution* (Berkeley, 1992); Mona Ozouf, *Festivals and the French Revolution* (Cambridge, MA, 1988); Keith Michael Baker, *Inventing the French Revolution* (Cambridge, 1990); Roger Chartier, *The Cultural Origins of the French Revolu-tion* (Durham, NC, 1991); Robert Darnton, *The Forbidden Best-Sellers of Pre-Revolutionary France* (New York, 1996); and Sophia Rosenfeld, *A Revolution in Language* (Stanford, 2001). For historiographic overviews, see William Doyle, *The Origins of the French Rev-olution* (3rd ed., Oxford, 1999), esp. pt. 1; Lewis, *French Revolution*; Ron Schechter, ed., *The French Revolution: The Essential Readings* (Oxford, 2001); Kwass, *Privilege and Poli-tics*, 3–4; Gruder, "Whither Revisionism?" 245–85; Lynn Hunt, "The World We Have Gained: The Future of the French Revolution," *AHR* 108 (2003): 1–19; Rebecca Spang, "Paradigms and Paranoia: How Modern Is the French Revolution?" ibid., 119–47. Doyle, *Origins*; McPhee, *Social History*, and other works retain the term "bourgeoisie," but Maza, "Luxury, Morality" decries its imprecision.

less per capita in 1789 than in 1700.[209] During the revolution's early and middle phases, 1789–1793, land hunger in the countryside and fear of urban food shortages utterly transformed politics by bringing the lower classes onto the stage for the first time.

On the other hand, growing numbers of what Goldstone terms marginal elites came up against relatively inflexible limits to mobility. During the 1700s, as a result of commercial expansion, what may be termed the middle strata – commoners who were neither laborers nor peasants – grew over seven times more rapidly than the general population, with particularly rapid increases from 1740 to 1780.[210] After 1770 most aspiring merchants and lawyers thus found it increasingly difficult to acquire offices that conferred noble status; only the wealthiest financiers and traders could be accommodated in this way.[211] Along with a growing cultural emphasis on utility and rationality, this frustration contributed to a vigorous critique of the privileged orders and those values – immorality, indolence, and violence – that the aristocracy allegedly embodied. Among all educated groups, including liberal nobles, such views proved surprisingly popular.[212] In 1789 the Estates General split, and the Revolution began, precisely over the question of whether the nobility (0.52 percent of the population) and clergy were entitled to separate status and disproportionate authority over the rest of society. This "clogging" of the channels of social promotion seems to have affected with particular severity lawyers without cases and writers without jobs. Adumbrating upheavals in 20th-century Africa and Asia, this alienated intelligentsia played a decisive role in the prerevolutionary process by churning out reams of libelous

---

[209] At the same time, rents outstripped income. On economic trends and social tensions, Lewis, *French Revolution*, 18; Kwass, *Privilege and Politics*, 114; Florin Aftalion, *The French Revolution: An Economic Interpretation* (Cambridge, 1990), 36–40; Jones, *Peasantry in the Revolution*, 1–123, esp. 32–33; Goldstone, *Revolution and Rebellion*, 184, 249–68. On Goldstone's model of revolution, see Ch. 2, nn. 280, 352 *supra* and *SP*, 68, 277, 301, 395.

[210] Doyle, *Origins*, 122.

[211] Thus prices for noble offices rose far more rapidly than general prices. See Guy Chaussinand-Nogaret, *The French Nobility in the Eighteenth Century* (Cambridge, 1985), 129 and *passim*; Colin Lucas, "Nobles, Bourgeois and the Origins of the French Revolution," *PP* 60 (1973): 84–126; Goldstone, *Revolution and Rebellion*, 225–49; Hunt, *Politics, Culture*, 173–76, 204–205, 217–33.

[212] See McPhee, *Social History*, 26–27; Sarah Maza, *Private Lives and Public Affairs* (Berkeley, 1993), 1–67, 94–97, 313–24 and *passim*; and idem, "Luxury, Morality," emphasizing antinoble critiques, yet denying that middle strata had a coherent class consciousness.

anti-establishment pamphlets and by leading agitation preparatory to the Estates General.[213]

Second and related to the previous point, by blurring estate and corporate identities in favor of a more individualistic, meritocratic ethos, the rapid circulation of goods and ideas joined government demands to weaken the social foundations of the *ancien régime*. Noble privilege became vulnerable not merely because the number of frustrated would-be entrants grew, but also because those lifestyle markers and sumptuary privileges that once had distinguished the nobility (and other groups) were eroding. Consumerism and mass production, by definition, confused traditional understandings of rank. The wives of merchants could now buy, if not the same goods, then passable imitations of those purchased by a marquise. Upper-class food, utensils, and dishes gradually made their way down the social scale. By privileging personal achievement, academies, salons, and masonic lodges further crosscut estate (and in some cases, gender) divisions. With privilege itself – including titles and jurisdictions – convertible to commercial property, noble claims to respect based on notions of honor and service rang increasingly hollow.[214] Royal insistence on universal taxation had a comparable, if unintended, homogenizing effect.[215] Admittedly, in late-18th-century Vietnam and Siam, upper-class observers also lamented that money was undermining proper hierarchy; particularly in Siam, the irresistible lure of maritime profits vitiated bans on noble

---

[213] See esp. Darnton, *Best-Sellers*; Chartier, *Cultural Origins*, 189–92; Doyle, *Origins*, ch. 11; Arlette Farge, *Subversive Words* (University Park, PA, 1994); Gruder, "Whither Revisionism?" 254–77. The claim that French nobles were 0.52 percent appears at Dewald, *European Nobility*, 22–23.

[214] By the same token, noble involvement in trade and manufacturing defied ideas of derogation. On eroding barriers and the incipient fusion of noble and nonnoble elites, see Chaussinand-Nogaret, *Nobility*, which probably exaggerates noble economic initiatives but draws attention to lifestyle convergence; Georges Lefebvre, "Urban Society in the Orleanais in the Late 18th Century," *PP* 19 (1961): 46–75; Roche, *Culture of Clothing*, 39, 299, 504; idem, *Enlightenment*, 555–561; idem, *Everyday Things*, 202–20; Maza, "Luxury, Morality," 216–21; Robert Darnton, *The Great Cat Massacre* (New York, 1984), 131, 136; Bailey Stone, *The Genesis of the French Revolution* (Cambridge, 1994), 95–99; and Smith, *Culture of Merit*, showing that even in the late-18th-century army, a noble bastion, professional competence became the overriding criterion of preferment. But see too McPhee, *Social History*, 16, 24–29, 33, arguing that a wide gulf in values, privileges, and sources of wealth continued to divide most educated nonnobles from the nobility, esp. in the provinces. On salon culture and female roles, I rely on Dena Goodman, *The Republic of Letters* (Ithaca, 1994); idem, "Public Sphere and Private Life," *History and Theory* 31 (1992): 1–20; idem, "Becoming a Woman in the Age of Letters" (ms).

[215] Kwass, *Privilege and Politics*, 41–42, 213–52, 297, 314.

(*khunnang*) trade.[216] But whereas in Southeast Asia merchants infiltrated elites whose formal status remained unchanged, in France commercialization joined resentments among the middle strata and some of the lesser nobility to encourage a reconceptualization of the entire notion of privilege. It was this incipient, yet still uncertain fusion of affluent nonnobles and nobles into a new elite whose authority rested less on hereditary claims than on money, consumption, and informal markers that both stoked ambition and made surviving noble privileges all the more galling. Precisely because the monarchy, even as it toyed with ideas of fiscal equality and patriotic community, continued to trumpet hierarchy, inequality, and privilege, such currents critically weakened its credibility. More immediately, conflict between corporate privilege and ever more insistent calls for fiscal reform created the political impasse that set the stage for 1789.

Third, by helping to invent "public opinion," new communication networks made possible a transfer of authority from the crown to the "people" or the "nation." Absolutist theory regarded the king as the only public person. But after c. 1750 growing literacy, the expansion of the book trade, pamphlets, and periodicals (much of it disrespectful of authority, some in fact smuggled in from abroad), and the mushrooming of libraries, reading rooms, salons, literary societies, clubs, and cafes combined to invite discussion of cultural, political, and economic theories and problems among educated people of all classes, to create a public sphere separate from the royal court, in short, to elevate public opinion as arbiter of legitimacy. Royal ministers sought not merely to censor, but to manipulate public opinion and to curry favor from this new "queen of the world."[217] To follow Roger Chartier and Jonathan Sheehan, it was less the new books' actual content than their inculcated habit of private reading and critical distancing that seduced Frenchmen from traditional allegiances.[218] Impassioned debates over such topics

---

[216] *SP*, 296, 300–301, 316, 441–42; Chris Baker and Pasuk Phongpaichit, *A History of Thailand* (Cambridge, 2005), 17–23.

[217] Doyle, *Origins*, 80. Cf. David Bell, *The Cult of the Nation in France* (Cambridge, MA, 2001), 91; James van Horn Melton, *The Rise of the Public in Enlightenment Europe* (Cambridge, 2001), 56–59. See too Jonathan Sheehan, "Enlightenment, Religion, and the Enigma of Secularization," *AHR* 108 (2003): 1061–80 defining the Enlightenment as a set not of ideas, but of technical institutions and practices – philosophical argument, salons, reading circles, scholarly bodies, newspapers, dictionaries, encyclopedias – that bore no fixed relation to religion or other pressing social questions.

[218] Chartier, *Cultural Origins*, chs. 2–4, 7, 8; Sheehan, "Enlightenment, Religion." On public opinion, its origins, and impact, see too David Bell, "Culture and Religion," in

as Jansenism (a quasi-Augustinian reform current within Catholicism), financial reform, the rights of judicial bodies, and the proper remedies for French economic and military inferiority to England nurtured the idea that the French people, or at least their educated leaders, were the ultimate source of authority. Although such terms as "fatherland" (*la patrie*) and "nation" (*la nation*) appeared long before 1750, usually they had been subsumed within the king's person. Thereafter, and especially after 1770, not only did use of these terms increase dramatically, but they referred to an abstract community independent of the monarchy. Well before the Revolution, therefore, concepts of "nation," "general will," and "citizen" had begun to displace the discursive emphasis on "corporations," "estates," and "families."[219]

Why was there no Asian counterpart to this horizontally conceived political collectivity? Southeast Asia was an unpromising site for thought of this sort. Even Vietnam, whose Neo-Confucian emphasis on politically conscious elites rendered it the most likely Southeast Asian realm to encourage civic participation, lacked the requisite infrastructure of printing, mass communications, and urban space. As Chapters 5 and 6 will argue, China and South Asia boasted commercial densities and urban information networks more comparable to Europe. But the vast size of the Qing and Mughal empires, the absence or weakness in both realms of protected public spheres, above all perhaps, the hostility of alien conquest elites toward nativist thought rendered horizontal, popular political loyalties extremely problematic. Japan resembled France more closely in size, communications networks, and the indigenous character of local leadership. In fact, Chapter 4 will

Doyle, *Old Regime France*, 89–99; Goodman, *Republic of Letters*; idem, "Public Sphere," tracing the 18th-century intersection of private and public lives; Baker, *Inventing*, esp. ch. 8, further complicating the relation of ideas to action; Roche, *Enlightenment*, ch. 13; Doyle, *Origins*, ch. 7; Maza, *Private Lives*; Jack Censer and Jeremy Popkin, eds., *Press and Politics in Pre-Revolutionary France* (Berkeley, 1987); Farge, *Subversive Words*; Lisa Graham, *If the King Only Knew* (Charlottesville, 2000); Swann, "State and Political Culture," 164–67; Mona Ozouf, "L'opinion publique," in Keith Michael Baker, ed., *The French Revolution and the Creation of Modern Political Culture*, vol. 1: *The Political Culture of the Old Regime* (Oxford, 1987), 419–34; Melton, *Rise of the Public*, esp. 1–15, 45–77, 205–11.

[219] Naturalization laws also reflected this evolution. On the transformation of subjects into citizens, see in addition to previous note, Sahlins, *Unnaturally French*, esp. 215–24; Bell, *Cult of the Nation*, 9–15, 24–77 and *passim*; Kwass, *Privilege and Politics*, 6–18, 41–42, 248–323; Doyle, *Old Regime France*, 139–252; Dale Van Kley, *The Religious Origins of the French Revolution* (New Haven, 1996), chs. 2–3; Simon Schama, *Citizens* (New York, 1989).

show, the Tokugawa period gave birth to public commentary in certain spheres, as well as a political doctrine (*kokugaku*, "nativist learning") that bore some resemblance to early European nationalism. Educated Japanese, however, lacked the constant goad to patriotic alterity and horizontal community that well-publicized interstate warfare provided Frenchmen.[220] Nor, obviously, was Japan's political imagination stirred by British or American example or other unsettling, readily accessible ideas from afar. What is more, because Japan's social divisions were more rigid – entry into the *samurai* class, for example, was far more difficult than entry into the French nobility – status anxieties of the type associated with French social mobility were less pronounced. In France alone, non-noble critiques of inequality reflected the frustrated ambition of the middle strata, whose lively fear of lower-class entree invited a symmetical resentment from below. Whetted by the rapid erosion of estate markers, such insecurity bred demands for a new transcendent entity – the "nation" – that could harmonize discordant groups into a unified whole.[221] Consider too French institutional peculiarities. As recurrent crises intensified debates on financial and constitutional reform, the legal right of *parlements*, provincial estates, and the Estates General (and the de facto right of individuals and private bodies) to discuss such issues let them operate openly and independently of the crown in a political fashion quite unknown in Asia. In their internal operations, moreover, France's honeycomb of corporate bodies (not only *parlements* and provincial estates, but corps of office-holders, guilds, professional groups, and eventually masonic lodges) espoused political principles – equality, liberty as protection from arbitrary authority, and liberty as participation – that had no Asian parallel and that, David Bien argues, moved effortlessly onto the national stage.[222]

Commercial growth was a necessary, if insufficient, precondition for a fourth, no less idiosyncratic French cultural shift, namely secularization. The de-Christianization campaigns of 1793–1794 climaxed two to three

---

[220] Cf. Schneider, *Public Life*, 353–54 and Ch. 4, Pt. 4 *infra*.

[221] See Alexis de Tocqueville, *The Old Regime and the French Revolution* (New York, 1955), 81–107; McPhee, *Social History*, 55, 61; Hunt, *Politics, Culture*, 222; Le Roy Ladurie, *Ancien Regime*, 485–86; Greenfeld, *Nationalism*, 133–88; Sahlins, *Unnaturally French*, 221–23; and esp. Maza, "Luxury, Morality," 221–29.

[222] I follow Bien, "Old Regime Origins," 23–71, who emphasizes the ubiquity of such corporate groups in France. Cf. Bell, *Cult of the Nation*, ch. 2; Merriman, *History*, 518; and Chartier, *Cultural Origins*, 162–66, discussing "democratic sociability" among masons.

generations of waning religious authority – present in some degree in most locales, but more pronounced in urban than rural milieux and in central and northcentral districts than in the northwest and northeast, the far north, or much of southern France – as shown by a decline in masses for the dead, a crisis in religious vocations, a dramatic increase in secular over religious books,[223] peasant refusals to pay the tithe, a drop in urban confraternities, and a rise in both illegitimate births and contraception. Such changes reflected intensifying market pressures, as migration, urbanization, consumerism, and the circulation of printed matter opened closed peasant worlds and weakened the parish as the vital framework of people's lives. Also corrosive of church authority were Enlightenment appeals to reason or sensate experience at the expense of dogma; bitter intra-church disputes, as between Jansenists and their foes, which sullied the image of both church and crown; and ironically, Counter-Reformation militance, which in some sectors sparked a popular backlash. Thus, although some research suggests religion retained greater appeal than is often recognized, many influential and humble Frenchmen alike became indifferent to church doctrine and transferred sacrality from the Christian king, God's anointed agent, to new icons of state and nation.[224]

In a brilliant exposition of this thesis, David Bell has argued that in the late 1600s God withdrew from management of the world, leaving humans to work out their own affairs. If French people did not necessarily become secular, they privatized religion and thought of themselves less as Catholics than as members of a self-sufficient nation, inhabiting an increasingly homogenous space, which assumed some of the aura formerly associated with the deity. In an ill-judged effort to capitalize on this shift, the monarchy in its last decades deliberately stoked patriotic sentiment. After 1789 revolutionaries not only continued this project, but came to believe that constructing the nation – as defined by culture,

---

[223] Religious publications fell from 50 percent of the total in 1700 to 10 percent in the 1780s. Chartier, *Cultural Origins*, 70–71, 158–59. See map of religious attitudes in Planhol, *Historical Geography*, 326–28.

[224] Chartier, *Cultural Origins*, chs. 5, 6; Roche, *Enlightenment*, 266–68, 578–607; Collins, *The State*, 101–102, 173–74, 208–14, 249–50; Jeffrey Merrick, *The Desacralization of the French Monarchy in the Eighteenth Century* (Baton Rouge, 1990), esp. 49–169; David Garrioch, *The Making of Revolutionary Paris* (Berkeley, 2002), 184–206. But on the complexities of religious influence, see too Timothy Tackett, *Religion, Revolution, and Regional Culture in 18th Century France* (Princeton, 1986), esp. 52–56, 287–300; Van Kley, *Religious Origins*; Suzanne Desan, *Reclaiming the Sacred* (Ithaca, 1990); Sheehan, "Enlightenment, Religion."

sentiment, and territory – was the central task of political life.[225] In popularizing this message, they drew instinctively on Counter-Reformation missionary models; and indeed, French patriotism resembled French Christianity in its simultaneous insistence on universalism and French preeminence, its goal of moral regeneration, and its claims to transcendent power.[226] But in its terrestrial focus, popular sovereignty, civic equality, and division of the world into comparable nation-states, French patriotism (and those based on French example) truly was unique.

In Theravada Southeast Asian realms like Burma and Siam, notwithstanding a relative decline in religious literature, not only were communications circuits too weak, but the monkhood was too acephalous, too tolerant, and too ascetic to present a political target comparable to French Catholicism. In Vietnam Neo-Confucian's partial displacement of Mahayana Buddhism after 1460 in some ways resembled later French secularization: both movements drew strength from rising literacy, both promoted social doctrines at the expense of theistic systems, both preached social redemption through cultural reform. Again, however, the gradualism of these shifts, the continued vitality of Mahayana, and the more unqualified universalism of both Neo-Confucianism and Mahayana left a smaller space for national identities in Vietnam than in post-Christian France and precluded a rupture on the same scale.[227] In short, different religious inheritances offer yet another explanation for the strength of French patriotism.

Where 18th-century France and mainland Southeast Asia meshed most closely was their sensitivity to intensifying military pressure. Insofar as European conflicts fed on colonial commercial rivalries, new systems of finance, and the dissemination of technical expertise, they represented a fifth destabilizing response to economic growth. During the 18th century France's strategic position deteriorated in competition with countries on both its flanks, namely, Britain and the rising continental powers of Prussia and Russia.[228] It was France's misfortune to

---

[225] Bell, *Cult of the Nation*, chs. 5, 6 and *passim*.
[226] Bell, *Cult of the Nation*, 22–49, 102–103, 119, 143 ff., 161–67, 182–201; Hunt, "The World We Have Gained"; Ozouf, *Festivals*, esp. ch. 10; Albert Soboul, "Sentiment religieux et cultes populaires pendant la Revolution," *Annales Historiques de la Revolution Francaise* 29 (1957): 193–213.
[227] *SP*, 187–209, 313–35, 440–54.
[228] Discussion of international context follows Theda Skocpol, *States and Social Revolutions* (Cambridge, 1979), ch. 2; Stone, *Genesis*, chs. 1, 3; Goldstone, *Revolution and Rebellion*, ch. 3; Greenfeld, *Nationalism*, 182–84; and Riley, *Seven Years War*.

choose – or be forced to choose – an "amphibious" strategy on sea and land, dissipating its resources between two theaters but dominating neither. Compared to Britain it lacked efficient tax and credit mechanisms as well as a single-minded focus on seapower. Compared to Prussia and Russia, France lacked not only an exclusively continental focus, but a rapidly expanding agricultural sector, the self-confidence of aristocracies whose middle strata were too anemic to challenge them, and the sudden advantage that latecomers derived from copying the organizational strengths of established powers. If the Wars of the Spanish Succession (1701–1714) and Austrian Succession (1740–1748) produced frustrations that contrasted with Louis XIV's early glory, the Seven Years War (1756–1763) was an unmitigated disaster that effectively expelled France from North America and India. In Europe itself from 1757 to 1788 France was humiliated by Prussia and forced to watch the decline of its allies, Poland, Sweden, and Turkey.

The political costs of these conflicts were twofold. On the one hand, victory in the American War (1778–1783) notwithstanding, defeats antagonized an increasingly assertive patriotic public opinion and seriously tarnished the monarchy's image.[229] On the other hand and more critical, the financial burdens of the Seven Years War – and more especially and ironically, the only 18th-century war that France clearly won, the American War – joined with price inflation, a cyclic economic downturn from the 1770s, dislocations in foreign trade, and persistent opposition to tax reform to precipitate a severe, ultimately fatal fiscal crisis. France's national (though not per capita) product was actually far larger than Britain's, but elite exemptions and agricultural overtaxation limited rural investment, tax yields, and military potential alike. After disastrous weather ruined the 1788 harvest, which in turn depressed the textile industry, popular distress and fiscal calamity generated the political crisis of the following year.

Although demographic growth was producing an uncomfortable imbalance between resources and demands in much of Europe, such growth was perfectly compatible with successful foreign and domestic policies, as Russia, Britain, and Prussia demonstrated. France's collapse – like those of Burma, Siam, and Vietnam between 1752 and 1786 – reflected economic, social, and institutional strains *in combination* with a string of short-term military and political miscalculations. Whether ultimately the monarchy could have assimilated the new concepts of

---

[229] Stone, *Genesis*, 57–62, 141–47; Collins, *Tribes to Nation*, 482–88.

nation and citizen is debatable, but surely its prospects for survival were reduced by the refusal of Louis XV and his successor to chose decisively between fiscal necessity and solidarity with aristocratic privilege, by Louis XVI's American venture, and by the latter's failure to forge a consensus behind moderate political reform.[230] As late as 1792, one could argue, a constitutional monarchy could have been saved were it not for war-induced paranoia and royal vacillation.

We need not linger over the ensuing radicalization of the revolution, the centrist corrections of the Directory and Napoleon, or Bourbon policies after Napoleon's overthrow, all of which employed a vocabulary alien to Southeast Asian experience. Whereas Siamese and French envoys under Louis XIV had found nothing very shocking at one another's courts, French political discourse from 1789 to 1830, revolving around such notions as secularism, republicanism, and popular sovereignty, veered into a different conceptual universe.[231] Yet if we compare not political culture, but interregna, military expansion, administrative and social trends c. 1760–1830, once again several broad patterns are familiar.

Most obvious was the relative brevity of 18th-century political collapse. In western and central mainland Southeast Asia we saw that disorders in the 14th and 15th centuries exceeded in duration, polycentricity, and ethnic displacement those of 1568–1613, which exceeded those of the mid- or late 1700s. (A similar progression, of course, characterized Russian interregna.) Now in France the overthrow of the monarchy and the church – although deeply innovative in institutional and discursive terms – did not yield territorial losses or central debility as prolonged or intense as during the Wars of Religion, whose problems were less intractable than those of the Hundred Years War, which were mild compared to post-Carolingian travails.[232] True, in 1793 Marseilles, Bordeaux, upper Brittany, and much of the Rhone valley turned against Paris, while in the Vendee in the west peasant armies fought fervently for return of priests and king. The death toll in the Vendee may have reached 250,000; as late as 1799, 40 percent of France remained under

---

[230] See discussion at Campbell, *Power and Politics*, 305–18; Collins, *The State*, chs. 6, 7; Furet, *Revolutionary France*, ch. 1.

[231] For analysis of the Revolution's transformation of popular political culture, see James Livesey, *Making Democracy in the French Revolution* (Cambridge, MA, 2001).

[232] As n. 148 *supra* observes, in temporal duration if not territorial dislocation, one could fit the Fronde of 1648–1653 into this schema.

effective military rule.[233] Yet within a year all major military challenges on the periphery had been quelled. France emerged intact. As in Southeast Asia, the center's victory reflected its administrative and coercive superiority, which the Revolution dramatically enhanced; the pull of protonational or kingdom-wide culture, and an exhilarating sense of cyclic renewal.

Also like its Southeast Asian contemporaries, the new French regime promptly launched a series of transformative regional wars. Whereas in the mid- to late 1700s Burmese, Siamese, Nguyen, and Bourbon armies had all proven feckless, their heirs drew strength from a new cadre of self-selected, battle-tested warriors, as well as from new tactics, new systems of supply and conscription, and a contagious, even messianic élan.[234] To the extent that unprecedented numbers of provincials and men of modest background led the new regime and staffed its officer corps, Republican and Napoleonic armies may be compared fairly to the contemporaneous forces of Alaung-hpaya in Burma, Taksin in Siam, and the Taysons in Vietnam.[235] Within a few years each of these new armies, and those of the reunified Nguyen, had recast the strategic equation, slicing through hitherto invincible enemies and collapsing hitherto sacrosanct principalities. Whereas, we saw, mainland Southeast Asia in 1750 still had at least nine independent states, by 1820 but three remained. Unable to defeat the maritime-continental pincers that had bedeviled 18th-century French strategists, Napoleon, unlike his Southeast Asian contemporaries, achieved only short-term territorial gains. Yet outside France itself in modern Italy and Germany, he dramatically consolidated jurisdictions. Thus about half of the 294 principalities that constituted the Holy Roman Empire disappeared under Napoleon, while the German Confederation that replaced Napoleon's regime had only 39 states.[236] Moreover, much as Burmese invasions unintentionally

---

[233] Furet, *Revolutionary France*, 89–92, 122–40, 152–54, 161; Donald Sutherland, *Les Chouans* (Rennes, 1990); Planhol, *Historical Geography*, 326–28, 340–44; Tackett, *Religion, Revolution*, 52–56, 287–300; David Bell, pers. commun., Feb. 22, 2006.

[234] This could be secular – see John Lynn, "Toward an Army of Honor: The Moral Evolution of the French Army, 1789–1815," *FHS* 16 (1989) – or religious, on which see Lieberman, *Administrative Cycles*, 233–37, 244–48; Li, *Nguyen Cochinchina*, ch. 7.

[235] On the social composition of the French officer corps, Geoffrey Ellis, *The Napoleonic Empire* (London, 1991), 54–58; Martyn Lyons, *Napoleon Bonaparte and the Legacy of the French Revolution* (New York, 1994), 167–68; McPhee, *Social History*, chs. 4, 5. On new armies and leaders in 18th-century Southeast Asia, Lieberman, *Administrative Cycles*, ch. 5; *SP*, 299–304, 422–28.

[236] Hufton, *Europe*, 143–54, referring to 294 German states; Lyons, *Bonaparte*, 203–207, 257–59, referring to "more than 350"; Merriman, *History*, 299, 594–95.

revitalized Siam by stimulating military reforms and elevating more effective leaders, and Siamese pressures aided the Nguyen, so after 1806 in Austria and especially Prussia French victories unwittingly catalysed far-reaching reforms, including in Prussia the appointment of bourgeois officers, creation of a ministry of war, and an end to serfdom.[237]

Within France itself the Jacobins and, more particularly, the Directory (1795–1799) and Napoleon (1799–1814) radically intensified the *ancien régime's* centralizing thrust.[238] In terms of intellectual coherence and programmatic novelty, I have readily conceded that French determination to recast every aspect of public and institutional life according to Enlightenment principles of rationality, uniformity, and efficiency lacked Indic analogue. At a stroke the Revolution swept away legal distinctions between the three social estates, together with ecclesiastical independence, seigniorial justice, venal office, fiscal privilege, internal tariffs, and Bourbon administrative units. In their place came (male) legal/fiscal equality, centrally administered taxes, uniform law courts, uniform decimal weights, measures, and currency; a dramatically larger central administration; an increasingly bureaucratic ethos; elections; and a rationalized framework of some 83 departments, 600 districts, and 44,000 communes. To efface earlier identities, departments were artificially drawn and named for geographic rather than historic features. Napoleon not only substituted appointment for election of departmental, district, and commune officials, but he endowed Parisian ministries with new authority, renewed church–state relations, and standardized law in the Civil Code of 1804. Thus he drew on both *ancien régime* and Revolutionary experience, but without the regional diversity of the former or the popular sovereignty of the latter.[239] Reactionary symbolism

---

[237] Walter Simon, *The Failure of the Prussian Reform Movement, 1807–1819* (New York, 1971); Merriman, *Europe*, 575, and n. 19 *supra*. A principal difference was that whereas Europe's more unified interstate system concentrated military pressures between 1792 and 1815, in Southeast Asia the separation of the western and eastern theaters produced a more drawn out, two-stage process: Burma's 1767 invasion revitalized Siam, after which Siamese challenges unwittingly helped to revitalize Vietnam and sparked intermittent warfare in the east from 1811 to 1848.

[238] Through 1792 the National and Legislative Assemblies were actually decentralizing, and thereafter the Jacobins followed centralizing policies mostly on an ad hoc basis. Systematic centralization thus came only with the Directory and Napoleon. I follow David Bell, pers. commun., Feb. 22, 2006; Church, *Revolution and Red Tape*, chs. 2–9; Ellis, *Empire*, ch. 3; Furet, *Revolutionary France*, chs. 2–6; Lyons, *Bonaparte*, chs. 6–12; McPhee, *Social History*, chs. 2–5; Collins, *Tribes to Nation*, chs. 13–15; and esp. Isser Woloch, *The New Regime* (New York, 1994), 26–39, 114–43, 339, 427–33 and *passim*.

[239] McPhee, *Social History*, 81, 97.

aside, the restored Bourbon monarchy of 1814–1830 retained key Revolutionary and Napoleonic changes, including legal equality, the new
territorial jurisdictions, the Civil Code, freedom of worship, and loss of
church lands.

To recall earlier comparisons, significant though the gap between
French and Southeast Asian administrations was in 1520, it was considerably wider by 1825. Although France, Burma, and Siam were of
comparable size, only Southeast Asian realms retained vassal kings,
independent upland enclaves, hereditary local officials, unabashedly
patrimonial systems of fiscality, and a single layer of provincial
appointees. Whereas in France the ratio of full-time officials to people in 1825 probably was in the order of 1:213,[240] in Burma it still could
not have been much below 1:2,500.

Yet if we use *local* yardsticks, the integrative logic of late 18th- and
early-19th-century changes was no less obvious in mainland Southeast Asia than in France (or, indeed, Russia). Thus in Burma, Siam, and
Vietnam vigorous new dynasties in the late 1700s or early 1800s reduced
the prerogatives of tributaries and hereditary officials, increased the
number of appointed officials, strengthened provincial supervision,
improved censuses and written communications, expanded cash taxes
and commercial monopolies, upgraded military procurement, and in
some cases, tightened controls on monastic wealth. Within 11 years of
Napoleon's Civil Code, Siam's Three Seals Law Code and the Gia-Long
Code of Vietnam offered each regime a unifying legal and symbolic
charter. Nor, at least on paper, was the standardizing thrust of Minh-
mang's provincial reorganization in Vietnam in the 1830s dramatically
inferior to that of French territorial changes in 1789–1790.[241]

With the abolition of hereditary privilege in France, the tentative
pre-1789 fusion of successful commoners and nobles into a unified elite
became more secure, with a corresponding acceptance of wealth – still
chiefly landed – as the final arbiter of status. If the Revolution and
the Napoleonic wars depressed sectors of the economy, peace joined
favorable Revolutionary legacies – sale of church lands, greater fiscal
equity, an end to seigniorial dues and tithes – to create more propitious
conditions. Thus, optimists argue, the 1800s to 1830s saw significant

---

[240] This figure uses widely variant estimates of officials in 1845 to posit 150,000 salaried
personnel, central and provincial, in 1825. But given the spread of estimates, it is
difficult to have full confidence in this ratio. See Church, *Revolution and Red Tape*,
72–73, 298.

[241] *SP*, 185–87, 302–13, 426–35, 447.

improvements in agricultural wages, transport, and agrarian specialization. Yet, even optimists concede, in most of France high transport
costs still favored low-yield agrarian regimes and artisan manufacture
geared to local markets or subsistence – features that would ebb with
the introduction of railroads only from the mid-1800s.[242] Indeed, early-
19th-century commercialization may have modified social structures no
more dramatically in France than in mainland Southeast Asia, especially
Siam, where Chinese trade boosted elite income and forced the crown
to abandon a centuries-old system of monopolies in favor of indirect
commercial taxation.[243]

French Cultural Integration and Fracture, c. 1600–1830

Finally, in France as in each Southeast Asian realm, the late 18th and
early 19th centuries accelerated long-term trends toward cultural and
linguistic integration. During the monarchy's last two centuries the
implications of cultural change were neither unidirectional nor totally
predictable: the Counter-Reformation bred secularism, Parisian hauteur inspired regional resistance, unification of elite practices widened
the gap with popular local customs. Yet if new cultural options arose,
they tended to function within an increasingly coherent national grid
whose symbols became explicitly politicized. By 1830 French culture
was more uniform than that of any Southeast Asian realm, except possibly Vietnam.

Through its precise rituals and meticulous behavior, the 17th-century
court, in particular that of Louis XIV, redefined elite civility. As had
been true since the late Valois period, processes of "social centralization" focusing on cultural affiliation, political patronage, and family
ties continued to disseminate codes of etiquette and speech from the
royal court to the houses of fashionable Parisians, and from the capital
region to status-conscious provincial nobles and wealthy bourgeois.[244]

---

[242] On social and economic trends 1800–1830, cf. the emphasis on growth at McPhee, *Social History*, chs. 4–8; Paul Spagnoli, "The Unique Decline of Mortality in Revolutionary France," *Jl. of Family History* 22 (1997): 425–61; and Livesey, *Making Democracy*, 127–30, 164–66, with the less optimistic views of Hoffman, *Growth in a Traditional Society*, 184–98; Price, *Economic History*, chs. 1, 2; Furet, *Interpreting*, 24 ("nothing resembled French society under Louis XVI more than French society under Louis-Philippe"); Louis Bergeron, *France Under Napoleon* (Princeton, 1981), chs. 5–7.

[243] *SP*, 302–309.

[244] On the spread of court culture and on royal patronage of arts and sciences, see nn. 133, 151 *supra*, including references to Harding's notion of "social centralization," plus

By attracting leading painters, sculptors, musicians, and playwrights to Versailles and by creating royal academies for the fine arts, sciences, and the French language (the latter academy in 1694 published the first official dictionary), the Bourbon court self-consciously sought to refashion a broad spectrum of high cultural practices. If these academies focused on Paris, subsequent royal support for provincial academies of arts and sciences testified to concern with a wider elite audience. So did royal visits to the provinces, the provincial circulation of official journals, and a concentration of royal statues and public works in frontier cities whose allegiance was insecure. Thus in Roussillon, annexed from Spain in 1659, French authorities sought to weaken ties to Catalonia in much the same way as they tried – with mixed results – to modify elite culture in Provence, Languedoc, Franche Comte, and Alsace, namely, by promoting French language in schools and courts, requiring French for lay and church records, and in some cases, encouraging French immigration. If Gallicization in Roussillon ebbed with distance and altitude, it also created opportunities for advancement that ambitious families were quick to exploit.[245]

From the 1630s well into the 18th century the state exhibited an aggressive intolerance toward deviance among the lower orders, as manifest in the policing of prostitutes and vagrants and confinement in poorhouses of indigent children and old people. From the 1580s to the 1670s such concerns joined misogyny, an extension of the criminal law system, religious divisions, and popular insecurity to spur three waves of judicial witch hunts.[246] Because as in most of Reformation and Counter-Reformation Europe, social regulation, religious reform, and state-building went hand in hand,[247] it is hardly surprising that

Elias, *Civilizing Process*; Michael Wieviorka et al., "The Work of Norbert Elias," *Thesis Eleven* 54 (1998): 89–103; Burke, *Fabrication of Louis XIV*, 50–59, 153–58; Bluche, *Louis XIV*, ch. 24; McPhee, *Social History*, 16; Collins, *The State*, 119–22; Schneider, *Public Life*, ch. 8.

[245] Sahlins, *Boundaries*, 116–27. See too discussion of language/culture policy in annexed areas in Ferdinand Brunot, *Histoire de la Langue Francaise des Origines a Nos Jours*, t. 5 (Paris, 1966), 89–103.

[246] Robert Schwartz, *Policing the Poor in Eighteenth-Century France* (Chapel Hill, 1988); Robert Jutte, *Poverty and Deviance in Early Modern Europe* (Cambridge, 1994), 17, 164–76; Collins, *The State*, 34–35, 105, 149–56, 188–91; Robin Briggs, *Communities of Belief* (Oxford, 1989), 21–87, 250, 395–97; idem, *Witches and Neighbors* (New York, 1996), esp. 397–411; Robert Muchembled, *Popular Culture and Elite Culture in France 1400–1750* (Baton Rouge, 1985) 237, 252–71.

[247] See the "confessionalization paradigm" in Gorski, *Disciplinary Revolution*, 16–19, 114–19. Also Collins, *Classes, Estates*, 249–70.

these same years also saw restrictions on French Protestants, culminating in Louis XIV's 1685 revocation of tolerance promised by the Edict of Nantes. Although 200,000 Protestants, many with valuable economic skills, were forced out of the kingdom, this popular measure strengthened the throne, particularly in Languedoc and newly annexed provinces like the Franche Comte.[248] Thus did Louis XIV give expression to the motto "un roi, une loi, une foi."

The French church enthusiastically supported the emphasis on hierarchy and order by providing *intendants* with critical demographic data, controlling poor relief, and in general using its power to launch what Robin Briggs terms, "with only slight exaggeration . . . one of the greatest repressive enterprises in European history," namely the Counter-Reformation.[249] To be sure, campaigns against paganism stretched back to the early middle ages. But only in the 17th century did confessional rivalry, improvements in education, and the colonization of the church by legal and commercial families with a markedly rational, urban, prudential outlook engender a campaign of thoroughgoing rural Christianization. Thus at the same time as the crown worked to ensure social order, the church strove to dominate particularist religious loyalties.

The first step was to upgrade religious personnel, which meant founding new missionary orders and sodalities and reforming the lower clergy, some of whose lifestyles scarcely differed from those of laymen. After 1650 diocesan seminaries joined enhanced priestly income, episcopal visitations, and wider use of cassock and tonsure to raise the stature of some 30,000 local *cures*. With these shock troops, the church then attacked systematically popular religious culture, attempting to ban dubious pilgrimages, healing shrines, ancestral cults, *veillees* (winter evening social gatherings), female-mediated magic and medicine, and sexual license. In a more positive vein, through catechism classes, songs, parables, and a greatly enlarged network of primary

---

[248] Bluche, *Louis XIV*, 413–14; Le Roy Ladurie, *Ancien Regime*, 193–94; Collins, *Tribes to Nation*, 398.

[249] Briggs, *Communities*, 230. Discussion of Tridentine Catholicism follows ibid., 235–413; Dominique Julia and Daniel Milo, "Les ressources culturelles," in Andre Burguiere et al., eds., *Histoire de la France: L'Espace Francais* (Paris, 1989), 382–88; Jean Delumeau, *Catholicism Between Luther and Voltaire* (London, 1977); Muchembled's rather reductionist *Popular Culture*, pt. 2; Pierre Goubert, *The French Peasantry in the Seventeenth Century* (Cambridge, 1986), ch. 12; Yves-Marie Berce, *Fete et Revolte* (Paris, 1976), 127–62; Barbara Diefendorf and Virginia Reinburg, "Catholic Reform and Religious Coexistence," in Holt, *Renaissance and Reformation*, 176–201; Bell, *Cult of the Nation*, 161–97; and esp. Keith Luria, *Territories of Grace* (Berkeley, 1991).

schools,[250] clerics sought – often in local dialect – to teach peasants basic doctrine and to enforce baptism, marriage, Easter duties, attendance at mass, and confession. (This same evangelization offensive sped French-led missions to North America and Asia, including a remarkably successful mission to Vietnam by an Avignon Jesuit.[251])

How successful were these projects? As noted, we find geographic differences, with cities tending to exhibit less enthusiasm than rural areas, and with central and northcentral France less fervent than much of the northwest and northeast, the far north, the Basque country, and the Massif Central.[252] Even in devout regions proscribed practices continued, while everywhere commoners modified missionary messages to suit their own purposes and understandings. "[L]et us regard ourselves," a parish priest from Nantes wrote to a colleague in 1731, "as if we were in China or in Turkey . . . where one sees practically nought but pagans."[253] Such tensions aside, in most of France by 1720 baptism, confirmation, extreme unction, confession, and especially marriage had became more common than in 1600, attendance at Sunday mass had changed from pious habit to strict obligation, while to neglect Easter communion was virtually unknown.[254] The liturgical calendar thus provided a common framework within which French people defined themselves and made sense of time. If French Catholicism was universal, it was also specifically French in that it continued to portray France as a uniquely devout Christian land, used the pulpit to disseminate royal propaganda, spread notions of France's "natural frontiers" in its schools, and employed systems of episcopal organization and clerical education that were effectively separate from Rome and much influenced by Gallicanism.[255] Bell is not alone in suggesting that French

---

[250] Previous notes, plus Brunot, *Histoire de la Langue Francaise*, 32–43, discussing the *petites ecoles*.

[251] Delumeau, *Catholicism*, 65–67, 74–76.

[252] See n. 223 *supra*; Roche, *Enlightenment*, 583; Desan, *Reclaiming the Sacred*, 21, 28. This same geographic split would later govern reactions for and against the Civil Constitution of the Clergy of 1790.

[253] Quote from Chartier, *Cultural Origins*, 104. For assessments of Counter-Reformation success, previous note plus Luria, *Territories of Grace*, 203–209; Roger Chartier, *The Cultural Uses of Print in Early Modern France* (Princeton, 1987), 8–24, 93–99; Delumeau, *Catholicism*, 174, 196, 215–19; Briggs, *Communities*, 266–67, 326–27, 392; Bell, "Culture and Religion," 85–89; Muchembled, *Popular Culture*, 221, 269, 277, 300–307; Roche, *Enlightenment*, 426, 582–84; Collins, *Tribes to Nation*, 221.

[254] Delumeau, *Catholicism*, 196; Roche, *Enlightenment*, 582–83.

[255] Hastings, *Construction of Nationhood*, 100–101; Nordman, *Frontieres de France*, 98–104; Melton, *Rise of the Public*, 68–69; Desan, *Reclaiming the Sacred*, 2–3.

religious unification created both an emotional foundation and a programmatic template for secular nationalism.[256]

French evangelization in the 17th century was far more effective than Russian, because it boasted a more extensive rural infrastructure, a higher literacy base, and more exacting clerical standards.[257] It was also more centralized, sustained, and ambitious than Theravada reform in Burma and Siam or Neo-Confucian reform in Vietnam. Yet we find in France as in these other early modern realms the following common elements: attempts to impose textual norms on illiterate local cultures; the rural extension of elite urban models via schools, texts, and expanded ecclesiastical/scholarly networks; the elevation of male religious power over female sources of knowledge; a heightened emphasis on social hierarchy; and support for the crown as guarantor of hierarchy, cultic orthodoxy, and military power. To the extent that cultic/religious reform provided a psychological underpinning for political pacification, I have suggested that Catholic, Orthodox, Theravada, and Neo-Confucian proselytism after 1500 all may be seen as examples of Gorski's "disciplinary revolution." So too, because in each case an expanded central apparatus worked with local elites to crush religious minorities, the expulsion of the Huguenots paralleled persecution of Old Believers in 17th-century Russia, of Chams and Khmers in post-1500 Vietnam, of Mons in Burma, and of Christians in Tokugawa Japan.

In France the Counter-Reformation remained vigorous between c. 1630 and 1720. But thereafter, as the discussion of de-Christianizing trends indicated, it lost momentum, especially in the center and the north and to a lesser extent in the southeast. By contrast, commercial spurs to secular forms of cultural integration intensified with the economic boom that began c. 1720. This inverse proportionality was hardly accidental, for as noted, market mobility tended to weaken royal and clerical disciplines. And yet secular patterns of integration were never so neat, so uniform as those master blueprints favored by throne and altar.

More intensely than in Southeast Asia or Russia, the commercial circulation of people and goods pried open self-sufficient worlds. French women as well as men took to the roads in search of work, moving from threadbare uplands to the plains, from villages to towns, and back again. Exogamy grew apace: whereas in 1675 only 20 percent of women married outside their own parish, by 1750 roughly half did

---

[256] Bell, *Cult of the Nation*. Cf. Van Kley, *Religious Origins*, chs. 5, 6 and n. 226 *supra*.

[257] My elaboration of Georg Michels, *At War with the Church* (Stanford, 1999), 225.

so.[258] Itinerant workers and tradesmen refined the so-called Tour of France, linking the Paris-Loire region to the south; French popular song essentially arose in the 18th century along the royal roads that they traveled.[259] Pedlars, retail shops, and fairs also joined local to national circuits, introducing articles from the urban world of fashion and gallantry to the countryside, as shown by the ever closer coordination of Parisian and provincial styles in clothing, furniture, ceramics, pious images, and popular art. Moreover, lag times between new Parisian styles and provincial imitation grew progressively shorter: whereas for furniture styles the lag originally was over a century, by the mid-1700s the great royal highways had shrunk it to virtually nothing.[260] As Jonathan Dewald has shown, consumerism joined cottage industry both to weaken seigniorial authority and to create a heightened sense of provincial and rural dependence on major towns.[261] At the same time, recall, by blurring estate distinctions, consumerism and social emulation – in which servants and rich wage earners played a key intermediary role – permitted a degree of vertical acculturation.[262]

Horizontal exchanges flowed yet more obviously from an expansion in Paris-centered intellectual and communication networks. During the Renaissance, Lyon and Bordeaux still competed with Paris for cultural preeminence. But from the late 1600s the definitive installation of the court near Paris; the development there of royal academies, private salons, and schools; the associated flowering of Parisian theater, visual arts, and philosophy; and the circulation in the provinces of books, newspapers, and periodicals reporting on all these activities reduced provincial cities to interlocutors and disseminators. To follow Robert Schneider's analysis of Toulouse, the more provincial elites sought royal approval for their cultural endeavors and forsook local concerns to cultivate the ways of Paris, the easier political centralization became.[263] Literary production in regional dialects, still significant in some areas to the mid- or late 1600s, now collapsed.[264] For fashion

---

[258] Collins, *The State*, 156, 181. Idem, "Geographic and Social Mobility in Early-Modern France," *JSH* 24 (1991): 564–68 corroborates and complicates these figures.

[259] Planhol, *Historical Geography*, 276–77, 285–91.

[260] Planhol, *Historical Geography*, 293–307; Roche, *Everyday Things*, 204–205, 213–20; idem, *Culture of Clothing*, 39, 504.

[261] Dewald, *Pont-St-Pierre*, 39–46, 190–96.

[262] Roche, *People of Paris*, 151, 276–77.

[263] Schneider, *Public Life*, 255–70, 276–92, 325–29, 359.

[264] Pierre Barriere, *La Vie Intellectuelle en France du XVIe Siecle a l'Epoque Contemporaine* (Paris, 1961), 152; Planhol, *Historical Geography*, 273–74, 313–18; Benedict, *Cities*, 37–38;

and ideas as well as language, the whole notion of *comme il faut* focused on the capital. In the 1650s, observed Alexis de Tocqueville, "Paris was still no more than the largest town in France. But by 1789 . . . Paris *was* France."[265]

If printing was somewhat less concentrated in Paris than other forms of intellectual production, it too was decidedly urban centered and corrosive of local cultures. Whereas in the 16th and 17th centuries the presses of Paris, Lyon, Toulouse, and other cities were producing 500 to 1,000 titles annually, by the 1780s the figure was 2,000, overwhelmingly in French rather than dialect and covering increasingly secular and diverse topics.[266] In the 18th century cheap mass-produced books finally escaped the cities to conquer rural areas in the north and east. Alongside books, French-language newspapers, periodicals, pamphlets, broadsides, and ephemera also percolated in the cities through booksellers, cafes, libraries, *cabinets de lecture*, and subscriptions, and in small towns and villages via fairs, pedlars, and mail order.

Symptom and cause of expanded literacy – and thus a major spur to vertical as well as horizontal acculturation – was a growth in primary schools. Institutionally and financially, these owed more to the church than to the state (whose efforts focused on secondary schools and colleges). Sociologically, village schools reflected the vocational demands of the market and the spread of urban patrician models down the social scale and across advanced economic regions. Thus those districts most likely to support schools were precisely those that enjoyed easiest access to urban markets. In geographic terms this meant that the France of large villages and open fields north of a line running from

Bell, *Cult of the Nation*, 35; Emmanuel Le Roy Ladurie, "Les minorites peripheriques," in Andre Burguiere et al., eds., *Histoire de la France: Les Conflits* (Paris, 1990), 459–630 *passim*; Collins, *Tribes to Nation*, 352–68, 375–81. Whereas many fine 16th-century writers stayed in the provinces, by the mid-1600s anyone with ambition had but one destination. Jonathan Dewald, "Social Groups and Cultural Practices," in Holt, *Renaissance and Reformation*, 56.

[265] Tocqueville, *Old Regime*, 72.

[266] On publishing and literacy, Roger Chartier, "Frenchness in the History of the Book," *American Antiquarian Society Proceedings* 97 (1987): 299–329; idem, *Cultural Uses*; idem, *Cultural Origins*, esp. chs. 3, 4; Holt, *Renaissance and Reformation*, 38–39, 185–86; Henry D. Smith II, "The History of the Book in Edo and Paris," in James McClain et al., eds., *Edo and Paris* (Ithaca, 1994), 332–52; Francois Furet and Jacques Ozouf, *Reading and Writing: Literacy in France from Calvin to Jules Ferry* (Cambridge, 1982); Roche, *Enlightenment*, 131–39; idem, *People of Paris*, 197–233; Woloch, *New Regime*, 173–77; Darnton, *Best-Sellers*, 181–97. Meanwhile oral networks spread ballads, folklore, rumor, and simplified versions of written works.

Saint Malo to Geneva was, broadly speaking, more literate – as well as better fed and healthier – than the France of isolated farms and hamlets in the west and south. Within any given region, literacy made easiest headway among servants, trades people, artisans, and rich peasants, with wage laborers and lower peasants far less responsive. All told, between 1688 and 1788 male literacy rose from 29 to 47 percent, and female literacy from 14 to 27 percent.[267] Although these rates were similar to, if not lower than, those in Burma and Siam, French printing and the size of the market ensured greater diversity of materials and more pointed cultural instruction. By the mid-1700s schools and cheap pedlar-borne books were making aristocratic notions of *civilité* and good manners familiar to relatively modest strata. Those who could not read listened to those who could, so the influence of new materials was wider yet.

Given the overwhelmingly French character of printing, the use of French in school curricula, and the north's economic dynamism, it is also hardly surprising that the centuries-long retreat of non-Parisian dialects accelerated. For anyone doing business outside his home district, French now became indispensable. Whereas in the 16th century non-French speakers had been an overwhelming majority, one source claimed that by 1790 some 16,000,000 spoke one of several *langue d'oil* dialects, among which French was by far most common; another 7,000,000–8,000,000 had as their primary tongue a *langue d'oc* dialect, while the rest used Flemish, Breton, Basque, Catalan, or German dialects.[268] But, as David Bell has argued, even in dialect areas diglossia had become so common that nearly the entire population had some understanding of standard French, even if they did not speak it at home. Thus another source from 1792 claimed that out of 28,000,000, only 3,000,000 had no ability whatever to speak French.[269]

---

[267] Figures from Planhol, *Historical Geography*, 151–58; Chartier, *Cultural Origins*, 69–70; Furet and Ozouf, *Reading*, 25–27, 149–52; Nordman, *Frontieres de France*, 453–61. Cf. Roche, *People of Paris*, 199–216. Literacy usually was defined by the ability to sign one's name. On the utility of this criterion, Briggs, *Communities*, 400; Furet and Ozouf, *Reading*, 11–18.

[268] Roche, *Enlightenment*, 239–41. Cf. Planhol, *Historical Geography*, 150–53; Collins, *The State*, 194–95; Braudel, *Identity*, vol. I, 94–95; Daniel Nordman and Jacques Revel, "La formation de l'espace francais," in Burguiere et al., *Histoire: L'Espace Francais*, 155–62; Eugen Weber, *Peasants into Frenchmen* (Stanford, 1976), 70–72. Many of these sources relied on the Abbe Gregoire's study.

[269] Bell, *Cult of the Nation*, 177–79, citing Yves Castan, Claire Asselin, and Anne McLaughlin; David Bell, pers. commun., Feb. 22, 2006; Yves Castan, "Les languedociens du

In sum, codes of civility, religious practices, consumerism, intellectual production, literacy, and language all point to more rapid horizontal and vertical circulation after 1600 and especially after 1720. Yet several familiar considerations warn against exaggerating the resultant homogeneity.

First, by later standards these integrative pressures were still quite weak. If Parisian French was increasingly accessible, in 1790 up to two-thirds of French subjects still may have regarded another *langue d'oil* dialect or another language as their primary tongue, which in turn inhibited acquisition of written French, literacy, and the spread of national sentiment. Louis XIV reportedly could not understand the language of a hungry crowd in Picardy, barely 80 kilometers from the capital; and as late as 1780, widespread diglossia notwithstanding, a French-speaker in the Auvergne complained, "I was never able to make myself understood by the peasants I met on the road. I spoke to them in French, I spoke to them in my native *patois*, I even tried to speak to them in Latin, but all to no avail."[270]

Second, the same pressures as favored integration could promote anti-Parisian regionalism. In some outlying areas resentment of what Francois Furet and Jacques Ozouf term north French economic and cultural "colonialism" led popular strata to reject Parisian styles, French literacy and language, and to distance themselves from local elites who championed those trends. In varying degrees, a Protestant revolt in the Cevennes 1702–1710, the Vendee revolt of 1793–1794, and clerical opposition to the Civil Constitution of the Clergy of 1790 reflected such sentiments.[271] One is reminded of anticentralizing cultural and political movements on the Burmese, Vietnamese, and Russian peripheries.

Third and by extension from the previous point, if in hindsight unification of elite culture was a precondition for unification of popular culture, in the short or medium term throughout France, and not merely along the periphery, elite acceptance of Parisian culture often widened the gap between the laboring classes – peasants, artisans, and servants – and their noble, clerical, and bourgeois superiors. Of course, the latter always had boasted unique forms of language and deportment, but

18e siecle et l'obstacle de la langue ecrite," *96e Congres National des Societes Savantes, Toulouse, 1971: Section d'Histoire Moderne et Contemporaine* (Paris, 1976), vol. I, 73–84. Also Nordman, *Frontieres de France*, 462–85, 497–526.

[270] Bell, "Culture and Religion," 82; McPhee, *Social History*, 9.

[271] Furet and Ozouf, *Reading and Writing*, 297–99; Planhol, *Historical Geography*, 326–44; Sahlins, *Boundaries*, 127–32.

regional elites also had participated in demotic culture by attending popular festivals, joining popular processions, and engaging in other forms of sociability that routinely crosscut class divisions, sometimes with surprising intimacy. After c. 1660, however, a growing class division became visible in several spheres:[272] in the aforementioned disdain that Counter-Reformation missions evinced for popular religion; in the collapse of godparenting, confraternities, and other cross-class activities; in the growing split between Parisian French and local languages, which were now derided as mere *patois* (from *patte*, an animal's paw); in the literary conversion of peasant customs from objects of sympathetic description to objects of satire (or in some cases, patronizing sentimentality); in obsessive bourgeois and noble displays of Parisian styles as a sign of superior status; and in the proliferation of provincial theaters, societies, and informational networks geared to Paris from which commoners were in varying degrees excluded. What is more, the elite's capacity for protean self-redefinition meant that for many aspiring commoners, the goal posts were constantly moving. Precisely because aristocratic notions of *civilité* were becoming familiar to lower strata, many nobles and well-to-do merchants began to consider such customs "vulgar" and to reject them in favor of more "natural," unstudied manners. Likewise, whereas throughout the 18th century peasants in western and southcentral France continued to deepen their attachment to Tridentine Catholicism, we have seen that many city dwellers, office-holders, and educated burghers, as well as artisans, turned away from organized religion. This split between an anticlerical political leadership and what in many areas remained a devoutly Catholic peasantry helped to fuel the social and regional violence of 1789 to 1794.[273]

In essence, the elite's impulse to separate itself from popular practices was the same in 18th-century France as in Russia, and indeed much of Europe. Insofar as capital cultures necessarily attracted provincial elites long before the general population, such provincial splits, as I noted, were an inevitable by-product of cultural diffusion. Yet two critical differences still distinguished vertical acculturation in France

---

[272] Discussion relies on Bell, "Culture and Religion," 82–85; Schneider, *Public Life,* pt. 4; Michael Kwass, pers. commun., June 21, 2006. Cf. Furet and Ozouf, *Reading and Writing,* 297.

[273] Chartier, *Cultural Uses,* 91–99, 180–81, 347; Collins, *Tribes to Nation,* 441, 462–63, 510, 537, 578–80, 642–49. On elite–popular cultural gaps, see too Collins, *The State,* 218; Robin Briggs, *Early Modern France, 1560–1715* (Oxford, 1977), 198, 210; idem, *Communities,* 398–99; and for the 19th century, Weber, *Peasants into Frenchmen.*

and Russia: a) In France far higher levels of literacy, commercialization, and urbanization permitted a cultural and social convergence of nobles and prosperous commoners without close Russian parallel. In other words, although noble percentages per se in France and Russia were comparable, the French educated elite as a whole was far more open and inclusive.[274] b) By the same token, the cultural gap between educated Frenchmen in the broadest sense and the laboring classes, many of whom also could read, was smaller than that between Russian nobles and their illiterate, Russian-speaking peasants. Recall that whereas French male literacy in 1790 was about 47 percent, Russian was 10–20 percent, and whereas most French elites and commoners spoke varieties of the same language, the Russian nobility spoke a language, namely French, truly unintelligible to Russian peasants.

Fourth, at the same time as provincial elites throughout France became more Paris oriented and homogeneous, the proliferation of consumer goods and information magnified horizontal niche specialization within the elite and indeed, the general population. That is to say, constantly multiplying differences in clothes, furniture, housing, food, recreation, music, art, literature, religious sensibility, philosophy, aesthetics, and politics created subjective distinctions and allegiances that, although an inevitable artifact of market refinement, could mask the integrative thrust of the market.[275]

Finally, as cultural ties grew stronger within France, so did pan-European linkages. As the supranational character of the Enlightenment suggests, publications, travel, and correspondence favored all manner of cross-fertilization between thinkers in France, Holland, England, Italy, Germany, Iberia, even distant Russia. Within France many were attracted to the Parisian tongue because they looked not to Paris per se, but to Europe at large, where French provided the prestige language of Enlightenment in Weimar, Potsdam, and St. Petersburg no less than in Paris. At least until the Revolution, secular Enlightenment nationalism and cosmopolitanism were intertwined, somewhat as Gallican loyalties and Latin Christian universalism had been joined. Thus if French culture enjoyed an originality within its sector of Eurasia that neither Russia nor Vietnam – those profligate borrowers – could match, the

---

[274] In 1782 nobles in Russia represented 0.79 percent of the population, compared to some 0.52 percent in France. Hartley, *Social History*, 18 and n. 213 *supra*.

[275] On culture wars and market-related changes in aristocratic sensibility, Joan Dejean, *Ancients Against Moderns* (Chicago, 1997); Jonathan Dewald, *Aristocratic Experience and the Origins of Modern Culture* (Berkeley, 1993).

difference in national self-sufficiency was one of degree rather than of kind.

Yet national culture and national consciousness in the 18th century continued to deepen, aided by new communications, new institutions of public opinion, and by political crises on which the latter battened. Competition with Britain, especially during the Seven Years War, produced a flood of xenophobic French writings, songs, and art, together with a pantheon of national heroes. Although initially sponsored by the crown, by portraying contests with England not as dynastic wars but as conflicts between essentialized peoples, this literature led many to think of themselves as members of a nation capable of mobilizing itself.[276] By impairing royal leadership, constitutional impasses in 1748–1756, 1771–1774, and 1787–1789 also bred images of a self-sufficient political community distinct from the king.[277] Late-18th-century writers boasted that France had become the new Rome, destined to uplift all of Europe. Under neoclassical republican influence, French patriotism (or one version thereof) in the 1780s became a masculine creed of sacrifice and altruism.[278] Thus were adumbrated some of the main themes of 1789.

The Revolutionary and Napoleonic eras intensified cultural integration, while accentuating its political character. Determined to defend the *patrie* and yet fearful that patriotic sentiment was as yet insufficiently widespread, the Revolution sought, with an ardor hitherto unknown outside the sphere of religion, to purge France of subnational loyalties, now equated with weakness and moral corruption. To create the "new man," France had to destroy particularism. This purifying logic sought not only to transform political institutions, but to sever the link between political reaction and church-supported *patois* by promoting "pure" French as the national language. "Counter-Revolution speak[s] low Breton... fanaticism speaks Basque," a Jacobin leader warned ominously. "The unity of the Republic demands the unity of speech."[279] Although in practice state-sponsored schools to 1814, which focused on secondary and higher education, had little impact on popular language practices, repeated elections and referenda and sweeping

---

[276] Bell, *Cult of the Nation*, chs. 3, 4.

[277] Bell, *Cult of the Nation*, 54 ff.; Swann, "Politics," 195–222, and Price, "Politics," 223–48.

[278] Bell, "Culture and Religion," 101–103; idem, *Cult of the Nation*, 91–106, 143–55; Goodman, *Republic of Letters*, 11, 233–80.

[279] Jean-Yves Lartichaux, "Linguistic Politics During the French Revolution," *Diogenes* 97 (1977): 69 and 65–84; Weber, *Peasants into Frenchmen*, 72; Hunt, *Politics, Culture*, 123–24; and esp. Bell, *Cult of the Nation*, ch. 6.

administrative and legal changes between 1789 and 1814 did inspire in millions a stronger French identity that was intertwined, to follow James Livesey, with a novel commitment to free markets, small-scale property, and political equality. This new patriotism did not destroy regional traditions so much as it overlay, modified, and complemented them.[280] Military mobilization against Britain from 1792 to 1815 reinforced such shifts by reifying national differences, by exposing recruits to the discourse of *patrie* and "careers open to talent," and by mixing draftees from different regions.[281] Whereas Louis XIV's armies had widened the sociopolitical horizons of the officer corps, the armies of 1792–1815 did much the same for the common soldier, not least by deliberately pairing non-Francophone recruits with French-speaking compatriots. Henceforth French language did become a symbol of 1789 nationalism, while local tongues came to be associated with backwardness and reaction. During the Napoleonic Wars the fusion of language and patriotism – and, conversely, the erosion of French as a universal civilizing tongue – was reinforced on a European scale by German and Italian reaction against French as the language of aggression and domination. Entangled during the Enlightenment, French virtue (a would-be universal quality) and French power (a national quality) now became easier to separate.[282] I have pointed to similar cultural dynamics in Burma, Siam, and Vietnam during their epic wars of the late 18th and early 19th centuries.[283]

After 1815, amidst competing Bourbon, Orleanist, and Republican versions, the image of the nation was refined and its practical reach extended. If regional affiliations and peasant conservatism endured and if the episcopate dreamed of spiritual reconquest,[284] there was no mass support for a return to *ancien régime* political culture or practices. Even

---

[280] Livesey, *Making Democracy*, 165–66, 246–47, and 127–247, substantially supported by McPhee, *Social History*, 96–97, 106–107, and Jones, *Peasantry in the Revolution*, 251–70. On pre-1814 education, Bergeron, *France Under Napoleon*, 32–36; Furet, *Revolutionary France*, 193–95, 229. On the surprising compatibility of Catholic and Revolutionary commitment in Burgundy and elsewhere, see Desan, *Reclaiming the Sacred*, esp. chs. 1, 6.

[281] McPhee, *Social History*, 94–97, 106–107; Bell, *Cult of the Nation*, 98–106.

[282] Rowlands, *Dynastic State*, 354–55, McPhee, *Social History*, 85, 95; Collins, *Tribes to Nation*, 695; Dena Goodman, pers. commun., Jan. 16, 2006.

[283] *SP*, 199–206, 318, 327–29, 430–34, 450–52; idem, "Ethnic Politics," 455–82; idem, *Administrative Cycles*, ch. 5.

[284] Bergeron, *France Under Napoleon*, 191–99; Furet, *Revolutionary France*, ch. 6; and Weber, *Peasants into Frenchmen*, emphasizing peasant conservatism.

the Bourbons sought to preserve, in Catholic guise, Napoleon's patriotic legacy. From the 1830s the urban-based cultural conquest of the country-side progressed through the Guizot law mandating primary education, as well as through further market integration, postal improvements, the spread of newspapers and journals in French, and the beginning of railroads. By mid-century national literacy had advanced to about 60 percent, with the old illiteracy triangle based on the Atlantic coast much reduced, and with French-speakers in 1863 constituting some three-quarters of the population.[285]

CONCLUSION: EUROPE AND SOUTHEAST ASIA DURING A THOUSAND YEARS

In 1830 France, Russia, Burma, Siam, and Vietnam did not look very much alike. France and Russia had destroyed hereditary local dynasts, had imposed uniform systems of agrarian governance and taxation, and supported first-class military machines. By contrast, Burma and Siam remained concentric ring systems, with long patron–client chains, skeletal provincial administrations, and armies that by European standards were noncompetitive. In its nominally bureaucratic procedures, Vietnam resembled France as closely as its Indic neighbors, but the Nguyen's Sinic-style system remained vulnerable to patrimonial appropriation and regional challenges without French analogue. All in all, the gap in power capacities between Europe and Southeast Asia was far wider in 1830 than in 1500. Southeast Asia's condition reflected a host of limiting factors, including small populations, modest market impulses, and formidable barriers to intraregional and extraregional communication.

And yet, despite these differences, over the long term all five realms showed unmistakable similarities in political strategy, chronology, and trajectory. In Russia and *ancien régime* France no less than in Southeast Asia, royal officials typically sought less to destroy than to co-opt and to supplement provincial elites, gradually assimilating outlying zones to a status similar to that of more closely governed cores. Testimony to a secular improvement in military and extractive capacities, central

---

[285] Planhol, *Historical Geography*, 150–53, 280; Nordman, *Frontieres de France*, 497–508; Peter Rickard, *A History of the French Language* (London, 1989), 121–22; Weber, *Peasants into Frenchmen*, 67–94; Furet, *Revolutionary France*, ch. 7; Woloch, *New Regime*, chs. 4–7; Furet and Ozouf, *Reading and Writing*, chs. 3–7.

authority in each realm in 1830 was stronger than in 1600, when it was more formidable than in 1200. Conversely, in Russia, France, Burma, and Siam eras of fragmentation grew progressively shorter and less territorially disruptive. At the same time cycles of collapse and regeneration grew more synchronized across Eurasia. Post-Carolingian French disorders had no contemporary analogue, but France's 14th- to 15th-, late-16th, and late-18th-century crises found clear echoes in Southeast Asia and Russia. Of course, Europe also knew chronologies different from those of France or Russia, not to mention the appearance of new states (for example, Prussia and the Dutch Republic, reminiscent of Nguyen Vietnam). Yet across Europe, progressive consolidation, punctuated by late medieval and late-16th- to mid-17th-century disorders and by a marked post-1650 acceleration, was reasonably widespread.

Finally, all five realms saw a politically charged consolidation of religious practices, language, and ethnicity. Whereas in 1000 C.E. each area had contained a medley of peoples, and elite religion had been substantially divorced from popular practices, by 1800 in each territory a single ethnic/linguistic/cultic complex associated with the capital enjoyed unchallenged hegemony. This was true even though cultural self-sufficiency still tended to increase with physical and social distance from capital elites. And it was true despite efforts by Russian and Vietnamese elites to distinguish themselves from commoners by privileging foreign elements. The forging of a sovereign "nation" of French citizens after 1789 was merely the most bizarre example of a general tendency for central identities to become more inclusive and for kingdom-specific cultures to modify and displace universal allegiances. So too, although the mix varied, the instruments of cultural integration were everywhere comparable, including new commercial and educational networks, agrarian reclamation, state patronage, and competitive social emulation. If the fit between political cycles and cultural trends was not particularly close, everywhere cultural integration accelerated from the 17th to early 19th centuries.

Why, then, these loose, but increasingly close parallels over a thousand years? On current evidence, the synchronized florescence of Kiev, charter Southeast Asia, and Capetian France owed more to parallel social experiments and especially to the Medieval Climate Anomaly than to long-distance trade. Political collapse in the 13th and 14th centuries reflected the intersection of institutional weakness with resource constraints caused by centuries of sustained growth, strains that were aggravated by post-1250/1300 climatic deterioration, shifting trade routes, Tai irruptions in Southeast Asia, and Mongol-Tatar mediations. The latter could be either military (in Burma, Angkor, and Kiev) or epidemiological (across Europe). Political revival after c. 1450 in all five realms reflected, in part, compensatory, counterphasic trends: institutional responses to antecedent weaknesses, demographic recovery, and climatic amelioration. But post-1450 reintegration also relied on substantially novel technological and organizational factors, so that each polity started from a higher level than its 10th-century predecessor.

This pattern continued to the end of the period with which we are concerned. That is to say, political collapse in the late 1500s/early 1600s and late 1700s again reflected the strains of rapid economic and territorial expansion and escalating warfare, aggravated in France by novel cultural currents (Protestantism in the 1500s, anticlericalism and secular patriotism in the 1700s). And again renewal drew strength from an expansion in each society's administrative, technical, and material repertoire. After 1550, in particular, European–Southeast Asian coordination benefited from European-style weapons and from expanding maritime trade as seen in the Asia-dependent circulation of New World bullion and the increased flow of Asian commodities to Europe.

If Smithian economic specialization was simultaneously local, "national," and global, everywhere in the protected zone the intermediate-level polity – below the universal empire and above the locality – was the chief beneficiary, because it was the most efficient coordinating agency for military and economic tasks. What is more, in all five realms not only were political and cultural integration mutually supportive, but political, cultural, and commercial systems were isomorphic in the sense that each used internal specialization to create more encompassing overarching structures. Finally, despite Tai and Mongol irruptions, in all five realms integration over a thousand years, especially after 1350, proceeded under indigenous leadership.

As we shall see in Chapter 4, comparable patterns, again with peculiar twists, characterized another Eurasian periphery, Japan.

CHAPTER FOUR

Creating Japan

1. OVERVIEW

Seeking to validate early Japanese history by connecting it to European norms, 20th-century historians developed four strategies. They posited an essentialist Japanese identity at least as old as that of most European nations.[1] They segmented Japan's pre-1870 past into approved European categories of ancient, medieval, and early modern.[2] They explored similarities between western European and Japanese feudalism.[3] And they emphasized a pre-1850 Western-style economic dynamism that anticipated Japan's 20th-century industrial success and that, according

---

[1] See George Sansom, *A History of Japan to 1334* (Stanford, 1958), 9; *CHJ*, vol. I, 6–10, 505–506; and historiographic discussion in Oyama Kyohei, "The Fourteenth Century in Twentieth-Century Perspective," in Jeffrey Mass, ed., *The Origins of Japan's Medieval World* (Stanford, 1997), 345–65.

[2] See Thomas Kierstead, *The Geography of Power in Medieval Japan* (Princeton, 1992), 3; Pierre Souyri, *The World Turned Upside Down: Medieval Japanese Society* (New York, 2001), 2; "ancient," "medieval," and "early modern" designations for *CHJ*, vols. I, III, IV; Bruce Batten, *To the Ends of Japan* (Honolulu, 2003), ch. 1; Sebastian Conrad, "What Time Is Japan?" *History and Theory* 39 (1999): 67–83.

[3] Archibald Lewis, *Knights and Samurai* (London, 1974); John W. Hall, "Feudalism in Japan – A Reassessment," in Hall and Marius Jansen, eds., *Studies in the Institutional History of Early Modern Japan* (Princeton, 1968), 3–51; Peter Duus, *Feudalism in Japan* (3rd ed., New York, 1993); S. N. Eisenstadt, *Japanese Civilization: A Comparative View* (Chicago, 1996), ch. 7; William Wayne Farris, *Heavenly Warriors* (Cambridge, MA, 1992), 2–3, 311–400 *passim*; Jeffrey Mass, "The Early Bakufu and Feudalism," in Mass, ed., *Court and Bakufu in Japan* (Stanford, 1982), 123–42; Eiko Ikegami, *The Taming of the Samurai* (Cambridge, MA, 1995), 177–81; and n. 119 *infra*.

to some authors, rendered early modern Japan and western Europe blessed exceptions to normal human experience.[4]

With the less self-congratulatory of these approaches I have no quarrel. My own periodization is basically tripartite and my approach, linear. Naturally, I employ the scholarship on Japanese feudal organization and Tokugawa dynamism. Yet, like most contemporary scholars, I am wary of essentialism. Moreover, rather than oppose the Japanese archipelago and western Europe to the rest of the world, I argue that these areas shared with Southeast Asia, Russia, and other parts of Europe developmental features characteristic of Eurasia's protected zone.

Let me outline some of these common elements. Extending from the Inland Sea transportation corridor to the Kinai and Nobi basins to the Kanto plain, the east–west axis of west-central Honshu gave Japan a political center of gravity comparable to the Irrawaddy and Chaophraya valleys, the Volga–Oka interfluve, or the Seine–Loire basins. Along this axis agrarian and climatic conditions were generally benign, at least compared to eastern Honshu and Hokkaido; populations were correspondingly dense, and communications and trade were comparatively easy.[5] Although control of outlying zones was by no means assured and although the Kinai and Kanto plains – much like Lower and Upper Burma – tended to compete, Japan's political center always remained within this central zone, first at Nara and Heian (Kyoto), later at Edo (Tokyo). This militated against long-term fragmentation and favored a polity on the same demographic and (Russia aside) territorial scale as other protected zone realms.

In west-central Japan as in other parts of the protected zone, the second half of the first millennium C.E. saw the emergence of a complex state whose leaders looked to older Eurasian civilizations, in this case China mediated by Korea, for literary, religious, and administrative norms. Charter culture was not only derivative, but profoundly elitist insofar as mastery of imported arts, religion, and a sacred written language (Chinese, equivalent to Pali, Sanskrit, or Latin elsewhere) tended

[4] See Thomas Smith, *The Agrarian Origins of Modern Japan* (Stanford, 1959); idem, *Native Sources of Japanese Industrialization, 1750–1920* (Berkeley, 1988); Chie Nakane and Shinzaburo Oishi, eds., *Tokugawa Japan* (Tokyo, 1991); Akira Hayami, "A Great Transformation," *Bonner Zeitschrift fur Japanologie* 8 (1986): 3–13; E. L. Jones, *Growth Recurring* (Oxford, 1988); John Lee, "Trade and Economy in Preindustrial East Asia, c. 1500–c. 1800," *JAS* 58 (1999): 2–26.

[5] *HJ*, 12; Conrad Totman, *Early Modern Japan* (Berkeley, 1993), 6–8; Smith, *Agrarian Origins*, 4.

Figure 4.1. Japan.

to wall off courtiers from the vast bulk of the population. Again in typical charter fashion, early administration was superficial and territorially limited. Finally, even more clearly than with Pagan, Angkor, Dai Viet, Kiev, or the Frankish/Carolingian empire, this charter sociopolitical system, centered at Heian and known to c. 900 as the *ritsuryo* order, conditioned concepts of administration, law, and sacred authority for centuries after the charter polity itself had disappeared.[6]

The transformation and ultimate eclipse of the Heian-centered political order was a fitful, gradual process. By the late 1100s warriors, whose services had become indispensable to Heian patrons, had carved out for themselves a substantial share of the power formerly monopolized by the imperial house, court nobles, and elite temples. The warrior-led shogunates of Kamakura (1192–1333) and Ashikaga (1338–1467/1573)[7] simultaneously preserved and displaced Heian institutions, while benefiting from the diffusion of skills once the preserve of Heian charter elites. But the latter shogunate itself proved vulnerable to the continued growth of local social and military networks. If in Southeast Asia, Russia, and France, the 13th to 16th centuries engendered more dynamic economic and political systems, so in Japan the period from c. 1280 to 1600 yielded more efficient agrarian routines, more stable village structures, and more tightly controlled military machines. In 1467 these currents finally overwhelmed the fragile Ashikaga regime, inaugurating generations of warfare between local domains headed by self-made magnates known as *daimyo*. In its mounting post-1300 woes and its inability to control nominally subordinate centers that drew strength from rapid economic change, the Ashikaga shogunate therefore resembled Pagan, Angkor, Dai Viet, and Capetian France.

Following Ashikaga collapse, *daimyo* domains became in effect both the ultimate heirs of the Heian-centered order and the principal building blocks of a fundamentally novel system. As in Southeast Asia, Russia, and France, late-16th- to early-17th-century recentralization drew strength from stronger international trade, European-style firearms, and military incentives to administrative experiment. In Japan

---

[6] See, e.g., John W. Hall, *Japan from Prehistory to Modern Times* (New York, 1971), 48; Joan Piggott, *The Emergence of Japanese Kingship* (Stanford, 1997).

[7] The administration of the Ashikaga shogunate (*bakufu*) was set up in 1336, but the title of "shogun" was granted only in 1338. Named after the family of its founder, the Ashikaga shogunate is also known as the Muromachi shogunate, after the section of Heian/Kyoto where it was based. Although it lasted officially to 1573, its effective power ended in the 1460s.

increasingly expensive, large-scale inter-*daimyo* conflicts dominated the period 1467–1603. The Tokugawa shogunate (1603–1868) that emerged from these contests was an "early modern" polity comparable to the Restored Toungoo/Kon-baung polity in Burma, the Late Ayudhya/ Bangkok polity in Siam, the Romanov and Bourbon states insofar as all cohered in the late 1500s or early 1600s, all endured to the 19th century (or in France, to 1792), and all achieved a novel territorial and administrative control. As such, all represented the apogee of pre-1830 local state development.

In familiar fashion, political cohesion mirrored and encouraged cultural integration. Starting in the late *ritsuryo* era and with gradually accelerating force thereafter, the profound charter-era gap between elite and mass culture eroded – and was transmogrified. Between c. 1100 and 1600, literacy and elements of aristocratic cultivation spread vertically to warriors and other intermediate strata. Most critical, Buddhism developed a mass base and a genuinely popular character. During the Tokugawa era the culture of the elite – which now meant essentially warriors – and of plebeians nourished one another yet more vigorously. But as in Southeast Asian and European realms, cultural integration was also horizontal: after the Tokugawa shifted the center of Japanese life from the Kinai to their new capital of Edo, the dialect, learning, and entertainments of Edo gradually spread to the provinces, at first among high-ranking warriors and then among well-to-do merchants and peasants. Agencies – and indices – of cultural integration, especially from the early 1600s, included a dramatic rise in literacy and commercial publishing, an associated reliance on vernacular scripts, more integrated commercial circuits, easier travel, and an upsurge in consumerism reminiscent of France. No less familiar, the market eroded hereditary divisions between status groups enshrined during the early-17th-century political settlement.

Note finally that throughout the centuries under review, in Japan even more clearly than in other sectors of Eurasia's protected zone, cultural as well as political leadership remained in indigenous hands. Despite a substantial Korean element in the early *ritsuryo* state, after c. 700 there was no displacement or supplementation of local elites by people from outside the archipelago even on the modest scale of Viking intrusions in western Europe or Tai inroads in Southeast Asia.

If these features in varying degrees are familiar from Chapters 2 and 3, how did Japanese trajectories diverge from those in other protected zone realms? To be sure, Japan's isolation is a cliché easily exhausted: even when external contacts were most limited, immigration, trade, tourism, and cultural exchange with Korea and China remained substantial. And yet, *compared to the other Eurasian areas under review*, Japan, by virtue of its island geography on Asia's eastern extremity beyond the chief international trade routes, was exceptionally well protected against unwanted cultural, commercial, and most particularly, military incursions. Notwithstanding 7th-century continental wars and 13th-century Mongol thrusts, Japan's freedom from foreign invasion – in combination with an economic and demographic stability between c. 730 and 1280 highly unusual by Southeast Asian and European standards – helps to explain the gradual character of institutional, social, and cultural change in general and of *ritsuryo* and post-*ritsuryo* decay, in particular. Indeed, without an external military assault such as collapsed other charter systems, when the "classical," or in my terminology charter, era of Japanese history ended and the "medieval" era began has long been debated and has given birth to a confusing variety of periodization schemas.[8] To the extent that warfare remained a matter not of viscerally threatening alien invasion but of competition between interdependent elites, power struggles commonly ended not in wholesale displacement, but in carefully calibrated compromise and substantial institutional continuity. Seemingly contradictory organizations long endured symbiotically, as was the case with warrior alliances and the ultimate source of sovereignty, the imperial court, whose symbolic importance substantially defied fluctuations in practical power from the 7th to the mid-19th century.[9] Nowhere in Southeast Asia, France, or Russia do we find such continuity in political symbolism.

By extension, political collapse and restoration proceeded far more leisurely than in other protected zone states. Between c. 800 and 1830 France, Russia, and each sector of mainland Southeast Asia experienced two to four well-defined administrative cycles. Each cycle, we saw, produced an unprecedented political consolidation and each ended with a severe, generalized political and military collapse. But by this definition, one could argue, between c. 670 and 1467 Japan knew only one complete

---

[8] See, for example, *HJ*, pts. II and III, which date the end of the *ritsuryo* era and the start of the "medieval" period to c. 1250; essays in Joan Piggott, ed., *Capital and Countryside in Japan, 300–1180* (Ithaca, 2006), several of which terminate the *ritsuryo* period c. 900 and start the medieval era in the late 1100s; William Wayne Farris, *Japan's Medieval Population* (Honolulu, 2006), 1, 114, which dates the medieval period from 1150/1185 to 1600; and medieval onset dates and criteria for periodization in n. 52 *infra*.

[9] Hall, "Feudalism in Japan," 50.

cycle – *ritsuryo* and post-*ritsuryo* florescence c. 670–1280, followed by an exceedingly slow motion devolution leading to Ashikaga implosion in 1467. Thereafter civil wars to 1603, representing Japan's most sustained country-wide interregnum, produced a fresh consolidation under the *daimyo* coalition headed by the Tokugawa. Earlier breakdowns, including fighting in the 1180s that ushered in the Kamakura shogunate, and conflict between northern and southern courts in the early Ashikaga period, may be seen as precursors, rehearsals, for the great collapse of 1467 to 1603. The length and violence of the latter interregnum reflected the fact that only in the 15th century did available models of island-wide governance finally prove unworkable. Thereafter, as in post-Carolingian France or post-Kievan Russia, time was needed to construct a new political system through trial and error from the ground up.

In short, Japan's insularity combined with the solidity and prestige of its charter system – and with distinctive economic trajectories – to produce a devolutionary pattern to 1603 opposite to that in other rimlands. Whereas in Southeast Asia, Russia, and France, successive political breakdowns grew shorter and less disruptive as political institutions grew more efficient, in Japan between 1180 and 1603 dislocations grew progressively longer and more severe as Heian and post-Heian institutions decayed. Conversely, between 1180 and 1467 revivals of Japanese central power – first under the Kamakura and then under the Ashikaga – grew ever less secure. Figure 1.9 seeks to capture these trends.[10]

Civil war from 1467 to 1603 fostered all manner of fiscal and administrative experiment by contending *daimyo*. But this was an exception proving the rule that during most of Japanese history, and particularly during the Tokugawa era, an absence of credible military threats minimized pressures for administrative penetration, while affording authorities a relatively thick cushion against popular and regional disaffection. If the Tokugawa era was distinctly "early modern" in its chronology, enabling dynamics, and levels of territorial and cultural integration, the Tokugawa regime also showed an insouciance to problems of resource mobilization quite peculiar among early modern protected zone states.

---

[10] In this scenario, neither the 1180–85 Genpei War nor the split between northern and southern courts 1336–1368/1392 constituted a watershed comparable to postcharter breakdowns elsewhere in Eurasia, because the Genpei War was short lived and institutionally relatively nondislocating, and because for most of the period to 1467 the Ashikaga shogunate remained *primus inter pares* among warrior groups. On the onset of post-1467 disorders, see esp. Mary Elizabeth Berry, *The Culture of Civil War in Kyoto* (Berkeley, 1994).

Between 1600 and 1830 in every other realm so far considered, the rhythm of reform was heavily influenced by outside military pressure. But not until Americans and Europeans broke open the system after 1853 did Japan face comparably insistent external demands.

What is more, Japan's comparative isolation inhibited what was actually a remarkable degree of objective cultural homogeneity from becoming overtly political, especially during the Tokugawa period. Notwithstanding the spur to a sense of Japanese collectivity that commercial publishing offered as early as the 1600s and that "nativist" schools of thought (*kokugaku*) provided in the 1700s, without a visible and consistent external foe, an obvious "other" against whom the Japanese could define themselves, Tokugawa culture carried relatively weak claims to political solidarity.[11]

Such features hardly exhausted Japan's unique inheritance. For at least part of the period under review, Japan's position off the coast of Northeast Asia exposed it to climatic rhythms moderately distinct from those in mainland Southeast Asia and Europe. Moreover, by inhibiting exposure to smallpox, pre-1280 barriers to migration and trade seem to have delayed domestication of that dreaded disease until considerably later than in much of Europe and coastal Southeast Asia.

Japan's subsequent accommodation to smallpox joined with biodiversity, temperate climate, and increasingly efficient cultivation to support rapid, sustained post-1280 economic/demographic growth. By 1720 population densities were three times greater than in north and central Vietnam, and roughly twice those of France.[12] Such concentrations permitted and reflected impressive levels of commercial and

---

[11] The fluidity of Japanese self-images may have been reinforced by the fact that Japanese religion, fragmented among a half dozen or so schools that one scholar termed a "doctrinal multitude" (cited in Karl Friday, *Samurai, Warfare and the State in Early Medieval Japan*, New York, 2004, 156) was more eclectic and tolerant than Catholicism, Russian Orthodoxy, even Theravada Buddhism. Anti-Christian campaigns aside, Japanese officials made few demands for religious conformity.

[12] Because a larger percentage of total land is cultivable in France than in Japan, the latter's population was even more tightly concentrated than population-to-land ratios alone suggest. To be sure, because yield-to-seed ratios for rice are higher than for wheat, rye, or barley, and because rice does not require extensive fallow or pasturing, rice normally supports greater population densities. *SP*, 175; Francesca Bray, *The Rice Economies* (Berkeley, 1986), 1–5, 198–201. Yet sharp differences between Japan and Southeast Asia, both dependent on wet rice, show how decisive factors other than cereal type could be: although Burma's 1720 territory was almost twice as large and only 12–17 percent of land is suitable for cultivation there as in Japan, Japan's population in 1720 was almost eight times larger than that of Burma.

urban development, particularly along the central axis. Yet the closure after c. 1720 of Japan's agricultural frontier under the weight of these numbers, Japan's modest energy base, and its foreign trade policies – less isolationist than once thought, but still restrictive – also favored an intensive, if not involutionary, agrarian system and a self-limiting demographic regime that contrasted with the more trade-oriented, expansive, land-rich systems of Southeast Asia, Russia, and France.

As a result of these climatic, epidemiological, and political distinctions, demographic growth in Japan often not only diverged from, but was actually counterphasic to, what we know of Southeast Asian, French, and Russian cycles. To recall the situation in France, for example, population stabilized at a low level between c. 500 and 750, rose sharply c. 950–1300, collapsed c.1300–1450, revived from 1450–1630, and then, bursting the medieval ceiling, continued to climb into the 19th century. But according to the latest reconstructions by William Wayne Farris, Japan's population grew from c. 300 to 730 and then, along with agrarian output, fluctuated with little net gain for some 550 years until the late 13th or early 14th century. At that point, as France's population was about to collapse, Japan's began a sharp ascent that continued to the start of the 18th century. In the face of resource constraints, Japanese numbers then stabilized from 1720 to the mid-1800s (see Figure 4.2).[13]

Along with security from invasion, these rhythms contributed to four more or less distinct developmental patterns. First, as noted, agrarian and demographic stability c. 730 to 1280 helps to explain the remarkable conservatism of *ritsuryo* and post-*ritsuryo* institutions. Second, by nurturing local power networks, 14th- and 15th-century growth then helped to collapse those same institutions. If this latter dynamic resembled the collapse of other charter states, in Japan it occurred anywhere from 80 to 600 years later. Third, although reunification by 1603 drew on some of the same commercial and technological currents as aided other early modern states, in Japan the 17th century saw a demographic

---

[13] On Japanese population, I rely on Farris, *Medieval Population*, Table E.1, p. 262 and *passim*; plus idem, *The Population of Ancient Japan* (Ann Arbor, forthcoming), 1–20, 173–79 (citations for this source are to ms pages); idem, *Population, Disease, and Land in Early Japan, 645–900* (Cambridge, MA, 1995), 3, 7, 8, 44; Laurel Cornell, "Infanticide in Early Modern Japan?" *JAS* 55 (1996): 24–25; Ochiai Emiko, "The Reproductive Revolution at the End of the Tokugawa Period," in Hitomi Tonomura, Anne Walthall, and Wakita Haruko, eds., *Women and Class in Japanese History* (Ann Arbor, 1999), 211; *HJ*, 7, 232, 247. See discussion of alternate estimates for the period to c. 1280 in *HJ*, 7, 41, 84, 110; and for the period 1280–1600 in n. 151 *infra*.

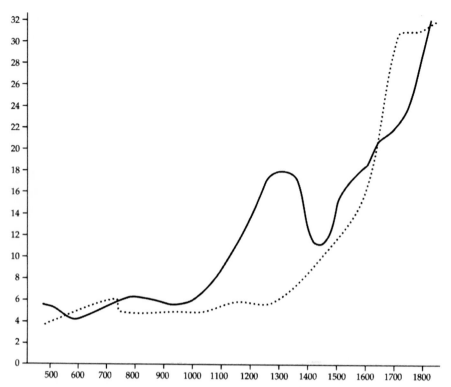

Figure 4.2. Estimated populations within the territories of contemporary Japan and France, 500–1830. The vertical axis represents millions of people; the dotted line represents Japan, the solid line, France. *Sources:* Ch. 2, nn. 98, 291; Ch. 3, nn. 164, 179 *supra;* Colin McEvedy and Richard Jones, *Atlas of World Population History* (New York, 1980), 57; and this chapter, n. 13 *supra* and n. 151 *infra.*

and commercial acceleration without Southeast Asian or European ana-logue. Fourth, however, from c. 1720 to 1840 and beyond, an economic slowdown imposed social and political strains that again lacked close European or Southeast Asian parallel. I hasten to add that insofar as Japan's climatic and epidemiological peculiarities underlay its idiosyn-cratic political fortunes, especially between c. 730 and 1450 and c. 1720 and 1840, they strengthen my larger argument about the coordinating implications elsewhere in Eurasia of climate and disease.

In brief, in cultural and commercial terms Japan became one of the most effectively integrated realms among those under review, but polit-ically it tended to follow a distinctive logic according to an often discrete chronology. Note finally that differences between Japanese political and demographic rhythms and those in Southeast Asia, Russia, and France again show the limited utility in some contexts of Asia and Europe as categories of analysis.

To the fuller explication and documentation of these claims we now turn.

2. THE FORMATION AND EVOLUTION OF AN INTEGRATED POLITY, C. 600–1280

Charter Civilization: The Ritsuryo *Order to c. 900*

In seeking to explain the florescence of Pagan, Angkor, early Dai Viet, Kiev, and Frankish/Carolingian France, we examined locally variable interactions among at least four factors: modifications in agricultural regime, climatic shifts, new disease patterns, and widening cultural and political contacts with Eurasian core civilizations. Although the *ritsuryo* state arose somewhat earlier than its Southeast Asian or Russian counterparts, the same factors command attention. In this case, archeological and documentary evidence is unusually rich.

In the early centuries C.E. a mixed regime of marine products, wild plants, dry crops, and irrigated rice permitted substantial population growth in the three chief islands of Kyushu, Shikoku, and Honshu.[14] Hardy varieties of short-grain rice (*Oryza sativa japonica*) almost certainly were brought by migrants from Korea, while in the 5th century Korean dike expertise contributed to an expansion of rice cultivation in the Kinai region. Likewise, although still not widely distributed, iron goods with the potential to aid land clearance, cultivation, and warfare either arrived from the continent in finished form or were cast from imported pig iron. Phenological and historical records from Honshu suggest that for much of the first millennium the climate, by comparison with both earlier and later periods, was unusually warm.[15] (By contrast, in northern Europe and mainland Southeast Asia

---

[14] Discussion of first-millennium economy and demography relies on Farris, *Population, Disease*; idem, *Medieval Population*, 8–9; *HJ*, 28–31, 38–47; *CHJ*, vol. I, 85–97, 124–40, 151–52; Charlotte von Verschuer, *Le Riz dans la Culture de Heian, Mythe et Realitie* (Paris, 2003); Piggott, *Emergence*, chs. 1–3 *passim*; Gary Crawford, "East Asian Plant Domestication," in Miriam Stark, ed., *Archaeology of Asia* (Malden, MA, 2006), 89–90.

[15] Farris, *Medieval Population*, 39, Table 1.4. In addition, unpublished studies of late Holocene mass accumulation rates for phosphorous and organic carbon in Lake Biwa, which were provided by Philip A. Meyers, Geological Sciences, Univ. of Michigan

the period c. 500 to 800/850 was generally cool.) Although, at least from 697, warmer climate produced an unwelcome increase in droughts,[16] it also may have aided agrarian expansion from southern Honshu to areas farther north. So too, epidemics seem to have been less lethal than they would become after c. 700 when exposure to continental diseases increased and state actions unintentionally widened avenues for transmission. Still concentrated in the south and west, the population of the Japanese islands, by current estimates, rose from 1,000,000 in 1 C.E. to between 5,800,000 and 6,400,000 in 730.[17]

As aggregate wealth expanded and competition for Korean iron intensified, more broadly based political systems sought to manage conflict and to control resources. Thus in the late 5th and 6th centuries a confederation of powerful militarized families centered on the Yamato basin in the Kinai came to dominate much of the area from northern Kyushu to central Honshu. If their polity still lacked stable transgenerational structures, early Yamato rulers coordinated cultic patronage, used hypergamous marriages and foreign luxuries to attract local chieftains, and began to adopt Chinese writing. After a Yamato naval expedition to defend a Korean ally against Tang China and the Korean kingdom of Silla ended disastrously in the 660s, some Yamato lineages concluded that the best way to defend against threats from abroad and to strengthen their position at home was to intensify the use of Chinese techniques, whose prestige had risen with the historic Sui–Tang reunification. As Chinese and Korean refugees brought additional skills and

---

and which point to warmer climate c. 300–500 and c. 650–1050, correlate broadly with H. Arakawa, "Climatic Change as Revealed by the Data from the Far East," *Weather* 12 (1957): 46–51; idem, "Climatic Change as Revealed by the Blooming Dates of the Cherry Blossoms at Kyoto," *Jl. of Meteorology* 13 (1956): 599–600; Hitoshi Fukusawa, "High-Resolution Reconstruction of Environmental Changes from the Last 2,000 Years Varved Sediments in Lake Suigetsu, Central Japan," in Takehiko Mikami, ed., *Paleoclimate and Environmental Variability in Austral-Asian Transect During the Past 2000 Years* (Nagoya, 1995), 84–89; Neville Brown, *History and Climate Change* (London, 2001), 143–44, 154, 155. Cf. Ikuo Maejima and Yoshio Tagami, "Climate Change During Historical Times in Japan," *Geographical Reports: Tokyo Metropolitan University* 21 (1986): 157–71, citing a cold interlude c. 800–910 unreported elsewhere.

[16] Farris, *Medieval Population*, 39. For possible explanations of Japanese–European climate discrepancies, cf. n. 60 *infra*.

[17] The first figure comes from *HJ*, 7, 41; the second from Farris, *Medieval Population*, 8. On early population growth, including the putative role of disease, see too n. 14 *supra*, plus Farris, *Population of Ancient Japan*, 11, 15; idem, "Diseases of the Premodern Period in Japan," in Kenneth Kiple, ed., *The Cambridge World History of Human Disease* (Cambridge, 1993), 376–85. Cf. Verschuer, *Le Riz*, 20; Dana Morris, "Land and Society," in *CHJ*, vol. II, 219.

as official missions began visiting China, access to continental culture, including Mahayana Buddhism, widened.[18]

This halting, drawn-out process of consolidation, typical of charter states, culminated between the 7th and 9th centuries in a sustained drive to build a Chinese-style, literate, Buddhist state.[19] In lieu of a conglomerate of powerful families, 7th-century reforms envisioned a unified realm under a Tang-style Heavenly Sovereign (*tenno*) who would serve simultaneously as law giver, realm protector, and Buddhist savior-king and whose bureaucrats would collect taxes and keep the peace according to standardized written procedures. As refined by the Chinese-inspired Taiho (702) and Yoro (718) administrative codes, many of these goals were realized in central Japan, where the court established a graded system of noble ranks and supervised the registration of population and the regular redistribution of rice lands, over which it claimed a monopoly. In lieu of a moveable court, elegant Chinese-style capitals arose in 710 at Nara and in 794 at Heian; at the latter site the capital would remain for centuries. The term for this new sociopolitical order, *ritsuryo*, refers to the "penal and administrative codes" by which the Heavenly Sovereign sought to rule. As "a hierarchical political formation with a reasonably centered command structure and unified culture," the early-8th-century polity, Joan Piggott argues, was the archipelago's first genuine state.[20] By 750 in the capital alone an inspectorate and eight ministries, under a Council of State, supported 7,000 to 10,000 officials, clerks, technicians, and menial assistants,[21] a figure greater in both per capita and absolute terms than in most European or Southeast Asian charter states. Seven royal highways facilitated the flow of taxes from the hinterland and the two-way movement of officials between the capital and some 66 provinces.

[18] On pre-Yamato formations, the Yamato state, and continental influences to 700, Piggott, *Emergence*, 12–13, 44–126; idem, *Capital and Countryside*, 13–53, 128–29; Walter Edwards, "Japan's New Past," *Archaeology* 50 (1997): 32–41; Bruce Batten, *Gateway to Japan* (Honolulu, 2006), ch. 1; idem, *Ends of Japan*, 91–92, 147–49; Farris, *Population, Disease*, 8–17; idem, *Heavenly Warriors*, chs. 1, 2; idem, *Sacred Texts and Buried Treasures* (Honolulu, 1998), ch. 2; *HJ*, ch. 3; *CHJ*, vol. I, chs. 1–5, 8.

[19] Early *ritsuryo* discussion follows Piggott, *Emergence*; idem, *Capital and Countryside*, 1–11, 103–208; *CHJ*, vol. I, chs. 3–5, 8; Cornelius Kiley, "Provincial Administration and Land Tenure in Early Heian," in *CHJ*, vol. II, 236–340; *HJ*, chs. 3, 4; Kozo Yamamura, "The Decline of the *Ritsuryo* System," *JJS* 1 (1974): 3–37; Farris, *Heavenly Warriors*, 33–119.

[20] Piggott, *Emergence*, 232, 168, invoking criteria set forth by Suzuki Yasutami. Cf. *SP*, 33.

[21] Farris, *Population, Disease*, 15; *HJ*, 76–77; William Wayne Farris, pers. commun., Aug. 11, 2006.

Court aristocrats monopolized both central posts and provincial governorships, with the latter responsible for registering the population, supervising shrines, and transmitting revenues. But rural power lay less with these four-year governors than with some 550 subprovincial district magistrates, who received sizeable land grants, held for life what were in effect heritable posts, and usually hailed from influential, long-established families of local chieftains. The *ritsuryo* military, modeled initially on that of Tang China, included capital guards and provincial militia, both dominated by a mix of low-level central aristocrats and local strong men. Essentially the early *ritsuryo* system was an alliance between the capital aristocracy and these powerful local families.[22]

In terms of internal complexity and local penetration, the *ritsuryo* state by 750 was at least as developed as Angkor, Pagan, or Dai Viet in the 13th century, and far more sophisticated than 13th-century Kiev. This precocity reflected idiosyncrasies in the donor and recipient cultures and in the transmission process itself. Not only was the Tang in the 7th and 8th centuries in its heyday and thus likely to inspire imitation, not only did Korean modifications of Chinese culture facilitate Japanese absorption, but Chinese and Korean political systems were eminently practical and portable. Southeast Asian links to India before 700 arguably were less sustained than those between Japan and the continent, and by 500 Indian Buddhism was in decline. In any case, Indic statecraft lacked the specificity or utility of its Sinic-Korean counterpart. Northern Vietnam, of course, had more direct access to Sinic culture than Japan, but as a Tang province, Vietnam before 939 was hardly in a position to establish an independent state. The Japan–continental relation resembled that between Kiev and Byzantium in that both Japan and Kiev dealt with donor states in full glory and both took care to avoid formal incorporation. Kiev's economy, however, could not support a society as literate or a polity as complex as the *ritsuryo* order. Perhaps the closest analogue is the Frankish/Carolingian kingdom, whose 6th- to early-9th-century maturation overlapped with that of *ritsuryo* Japan. Admittedly, Rome's glory had faded, and the Frankish enterprise ultimately proved quite fragile. Yet Gallo-Roman, like Chinese, administrative tradition was practical and accessible, while the urban

---

[22] Piggott, *Emergence*, 283; Farris, pers. commun., Aug. 11, 2006; idem, *Heavenly Warriors*, 81–119, 357–60, 370–72; John W. Hall, *Government and Local Power in Japan 500 to 1700* (Princeton, 1966), 73–76, 127; Yamamura, "Decline," 9–11; Bruce Batten, "Provincial Administration in Early Japan," *HJAS* 53 (1993): 103–34, esp. 106–14.

and commercial infrastructure of post-Roman Gaul was still relatively advanced.[23]

Despite its sophistication, the *ritsuryo* polity, along with other charter polities, remained an essentially solar or segmentary system. Even in western Honshu imperial authority receded with distance, while sparse settlement and poor communications left southern Kyushu and eastern Honshu effectively independent. The new codes did not superimpose Chinese law so much as they sought to systematize and modify pre-existing relationships, including the role of provincial families and the relatively prominent position of women.[24] Yet it is also clear that new channels did open between a glorious center and an expanding periphery, and that some leading families shifted from control of contiguous territories to imperially sanctioned control of more widely dispersed properties. For their part, local notables often were only too willing to support the new order both because they gained access to prestigious imperial posts and because the new legal and tax machinery reinforced their local authority. This consensual element appears in the fact that *ritsuryo* rulers deployed force frequently against "barbarians" on Honshu's northern frontier, but rarely against prominent local families within Heian's sphere.[25]

Peasants and bound laborers, especially in the core, were profoundly affected by two aspects of the new order: a) increased demands for taxes and services, and b) greater exposure to killer diseases, chiefly smallpox and measles, but also mumps and influenza, which entered Japan from the continent and were transmitted by messengers, corvée laborers, and conscript battalions moving along the new royal highways. A smallpox epidemic in 735–737, one in a series lasting at least to the mid-1100s, may have killed 25 to 35 percent of the population. Although by the 9th century coastal Southeast Asia, Pontine Russia, and northern Europe probably had begun to acquire immunities, Japanese contact with the

---

[23] Cf. Marius Jansen, "On Foreign Borrowing," in Albert Craig, ed., *Japan: A Comparative View* (Princeton, 1979), 18–48 and Ch. 2 *supra*.

[24] See, Piggott, *Emergence*, 39–40, 78–82, 149 (referring to a "segmentary" polity), 183–84, 230–31, 252–58; Farris, *Heavenly Warriors*, chs. 1, 2; Souyri, *World Upside Down*, 14–15. On women, see esp. Fukuto Sanae, "From Female Sovereign to Mother of the Nation," in Mikael Adolphson, Edward Kamens, and Stacie Matsumoto, eds., *Heian Japan, Centers and Peripheries* (Honolulu, 2007), 15–34; Barbara Ruch, ed., *Engendering Faith* (Ann Arbor, 2002); essays by Joan Piggott and Takeda Sachiko in Tonomura et al., *Women and Class*, 17–66.

[25] Piggott, *Emergence*, 13, 125–26, 168–69, 232; Mimi Hall Yiengpruksawan, *Hiraizumi* (Cambridge, MA, 1998), 9–27; Philip Brown, pers. commun., May 10, 2004.

continent was still too infrequent to convert smallpox into a merely endemic threat.[26]

Such demographic crises were all the more insupportable because agrarian productivity remained low. Waterwheels, fertilizers, and iron tools were yet scarce, while dry cropping, slash-and-burn farming, and the collection of wild plants – elements in what Charlotte von Verschuer terms agrarian polyculture – were far more critical than they would later become.[27] Not only did rice yields average a mere 40 to 50 percent of late Tokugawa yields, but few *ritsuryo* lands were double-cropped.[28] Despite the primacy of rice in elite mythology, among popular strata that grain may have provided only a quarter of the food supply.[29] In turn, scarce labor and slash-and-burn mandated a fluid settlement pattern of dispersed hamlets and isolated homesteads rather than the more compact villages of later centuries.[30]

Low productivity also meant that despite Heian's soaring ambition, economic linkages to the provinces were, by later standards, quite limited. Nara, with a peak population of 70,000 to 100,000, and then Heian with 100,000,[31] drew substantial corvées and in-kind tribute from the countryside, but returned little of material value. The court minted bronze cash between 708 and 958, but monetization decreased in the 9th and 10th centuries, with attendant difficulties for collecting and distributing revenues. Rice, rather than coin, was the chief unit of account, and barter, the principal mode of exchange. Although, to be sure, a falling population and commercial growth could coexist – as in

---

[26] See n. 17 *supra*, plus Shoji Tatsukawa, "Diseases of Antiquity in Japan," in Kiple, *Cambridge World History of Disease*, 375, pointing to the arrival of smallpox and/or measles and influenza with Buddhist missionaries in 552; Ann Bowman Jannetta, *Epidemics and Mortality in Early Modern Japan* (Princeton, 1987), 65–68; Farris, *Heavenly Warriors*, 123–24, 211.

[27] Verschuer, *Le Riz*, 20, 263, 291, 300–11, 341–42. My understanding of the *ritsuryo* economy relies heavily on Farris, *Medieval Population*, chs. 1–3; idem, "Famine, Climate, and Farming in Japan, 670–1100," in Adolphson et al., *Heian Japan*, 275–304; idem, *Population, Disease*, chs. 4, 5; supported by *HJ*, 81–86, and Anne Walthall, *Japan: A Cultural, Social, and Political History* (Boston, 2006), 22, 31, 34, 44. Cf. Morris, "Land and Society," 184–94, and idem, "Peasant Economy in Early Japan, 650–950" (UC-Berkeley PhD diss., 1980), 133–62, painting a far rosier picture of pre-1000 productivity; and see discussion *infra*.

[28] Yamamura, "Decline," 12; Farris, *Medieval Population*, 263, Table E.3; idem, pers. commun., Aug. 11, 2006.

[29] Verschuer, *Le Riz*, 261–94, 341.

[30] Farris, *Medieval Population*, 78–79; idem, *Population, Disease*, 131–40; Morris, "Peasant Economy," 106–32; *CHJ*, vol. II, 194–99.

[31] *CHJ*, vol. I, 244; Piggott, *Emergence*, 193; Farris, pers. commun., Aug. 11, 2006.

post-1350 Europe, for example – in *ritsuryo* Japan demonetization and falling exchange velocities seem to have been symptom and cause of demographic retreat.[32] Not surprisingly, the elite remained sharply split between a handful of wealthy aristocratic families chiefly in the capital and a mass of far less affluent officials in the capital and the provinces.[33]

Particularly at Heian, development of the *ritsuryo* system remained inseparable from the domestication of continental high culture. As early as the 8th century writing in Chinese had become common among aristocrats. Chinese astronomy, calendars, art, painting, dance, and music also found avid students, although from the end of the 9th century we find an indigenizing trend facilitated by the development of a writing system known as *kana*, which adapted Chinese characters to Japanese sounds so as to write the spoken language.[34] Imported Sinic doctrines included Confucianism – which shaped administration, law, and the emperor's official persona – Daoism, *yin-yang* beliefs, and Mahayana Buddhism, among which Buddhism was preeminent by virtue of its sophisticated artistic and architectonic repertoire, its grand textual corpus, the prestige of Buddhist state cults in Tang China and Korea, and Buddhism's ability to accommodate indigenous spirits and other sources of supernatural power (*kami*) associated with specific places or families. The court preserved shamanic rites, and the system of *kami* worship, or Shinto, deeply influenced the imported faith in a complex symbiosis known as *kami*-Buddha fusion.[35]

---

[32] Farris, *Population of Ancient Japan*, 130–34; idem, *Medieval Population*, 10, 85. Cf. William McCullough, "The Capital and Its Society," in *CHJ*, vol. II, esp. 161–64; Amino Yoshihiko, "Emperor, Rice, and Commoners," in Donald Denoon et al., eds., *Multicultural Japan* (Cambridge, 1996), 238–39. On cash taxes (chiefly in the Kinai) and in-kind taxes, *CHJ*, vol. II, 206; Batten, "Provincial Administration," 117–18; Yamamura, "Decline," 7–8. *HJ*, 223 estimates that whereas Tokugawa rulers took 25–33 percent of yield as tribute, Heian managed only 6 percent, although Farris, pers. commun., Aug. 11, 2006 notes that the latter figure represented rice to the exclusion of important tribute items like salt, fish, iron, and silk, for which I have found no tax rates. Cf. n. 254 *infra*.

[33] Farris, *Heavenly Warriors*, 125–26; McCullough, "The Capital," 133–34; Conrad Totman, *Japan Before Perry* (Berkeley, 1981), 68–69.

[34] Christopher Seeley, *A History of Japanese Writing* (Honolulu, 1991), 59; Thomas LaMarre, *Uncovering Heian Japan* (Durham, NC, 2000), ch. 2 and *passim*; Walthall, *Japan*, 32–33, 37–39. On early Japanese responses to Chinese culture, see too David Pollack, *The Fracture of Meaning* (Princeton, 1986), chs. 1–3; Edwin Cranston, "Asuka and Nara Culture," in *CHJ*, vol. I, 453–503; Marian Ury, "Chinese Learning and Intellectual Life," in *CHJ*, vol. II, 341–89.

[35] On Heian religion, Sonoda Koyu, "Early Buddha Worship," in *CHJ*, vol. I, 359–414; Stanley Weinstein, "Aristocratic Buddhism" and Allan Grapard, "Religious Practices," in *CHJ*, vol II, 449–575, the latter emphasizing differentiation rather than synthesis;

This relation between imported and domestic cults recalls that in Pagan, where local *nat* spirits had specific jurisdictions subordinate to the Buddha, or in Ly Vietnam, where Buddhist and court leaders put the "Buddha Law" under the protection of indigenous deities. One can also draw analogies to Angkor, where rulers propitiated Hindu gods even as local communities were expected to honor their own *nak ta* spirits.[36] Both Buddhism and Hinduism thus showed a greater tolerance of indigenous tradition than did normative charter Christianity, whether Kievan or Frankish, with its morbid dread of paganism and heresy.

As in other charter states, official culture was not only eclectic, but substantially cosmopolitan and deeply elitist. The embrace of Chinese and Korean models meant that Heian courtiers inhabited a prenational ecumene, what Thomas LaMarre terms an "interimperial" order.[37] Versed in Chinese poetics and Buddhist metaphysics, the Heian elite – about a third of whom in 800 were of recent Korean ancestry[38] – were bound to their peers on the continent by many of the same cultural affiliations as separated them from low-ranking members of their own society. If we follow Takeda Sachiko, so absorbed was the ruling class in Chinese culture, so eager were they to impress foreign visitors with their adherence to classical norms, that they erected Chinese-style buildings by which to hide local "huts of board and grass" from foreign envoys.[39] Theirs was a universal imaginary comparable to the Theravada world of Pagan, Sri Lanka, and early Tai states; to the Hindu universe of Angkorian and Indian imagination, the Sinic ecumene of early Dai Viet and China, or the Catholic and Orthodox worlds of Frankish and Kievan elites. By emphasizing secret formulae, textual study, and gorgeous ceremonies, the court-favored schools of Tendai and Shingon Buddhism, which were controlled by leading court lineages, appealed to an expressly aristocratic sensibility.

Piggott, *Emergence*, 93–101, 231–79; Mikael Adolphson, *The Gates of Power* (Honolulu, 2000), ch. 2; Kazuo Kasahara, ed., *A History of Japanese Religion* (Tokyo, 2001), ch. 3; Samuel Morse, "The Buddhist Transformation of Japan in the Ninth Century," in Adolphson et al., *Heian Japan*, 153–76.

[36] *SP*, 115–18, 231–32, 357–58.

[37] LaMarre, *Uncovering*, 174, plus 3–9, 15, 22, 31–33, 148, 155, 160. Also Souyri, *World Upside Down*, 224 n. 37; Batten, *Ends of Japan*, 93.

[38] Farris, pers. commun., Aug. 11, 2006.

[39] En route to and within the capital. Takeda Sachiko, "Roads in the *Tenno*-Centered Polity," in Piggott, *Capital and Countryside*, 148–65, esp. 154 and 160. There were few "common cultural denominator[s] between the Nara-period ruling class . . . and commoners." Ibid., 154.

This is not to deny that mass and elite culture could intersect, especially in religion. Village shrines mobilized cultivators for *ritsuryo* labor services. Both aristocrat and peasant went on pilgrimage and through prayer and ritual sought good harvests, protection from disease, safe childbirth, longevity. As early as the 8th century, albeit to official disquiet, some residents left their Buddhist monasteries and nunneries to work among Kinai commoners; while in the 11th and 12th centuries itinerant monks, nuns, and "holy men" (*hijiri*) joined Shinto priests, mountain ascetics, and other members of the so-called "wandering world" to offer peasants a variety of services and soteriological doctrines, including those of the Buddhist cults of Amida and Jizo. *Hijiri* proselytism anticipated a more extensive convergence of patrician and plebeian practices during the Kamakura era.[40] And yet throughout the Heian period (794–1185) the unlettered world of folk wisdom, magical arts, and sorcery remained recognizably distinct from the institutional and ceremonial forms of capital-focused Sinic Buddhism. Class differences were obviously more stark in dress, housing, deportment, and – given near universal peasant illiteracy – the arts and literature, which in Heian meant Chinese-style poetry, historiography, and calligraphy. If this cultural gap was no greater than that between Angkor's authors of exquisite Sanskrit poetry and their illiterate *nak ta*-worshipping subjects, it was at least as wide as that in early Dai Viet, Pagan, Kiev, or the Frankish kingdom. Unlike Heian Buddhism, Frankish Christianity, in particular, remained formally committed to peasant proselytism.

By the same token, from the early 700s the emergence within this cosmopolitan culture of a specifically Japanese political identity – which responded to continental wars and which gained expression in the new name for Japan ("Nihon") and in the birth of Japanese histories – remained preeminently the preserve of capital and high-ranking provincial elites. We have little direct evidence, but to judge by later evidence, it seems extremely unlikely that commoners in this period had any consciousness of being ethnically "Japanese."[41]

[40] On Heian Buddhist cross-class commonalities, Janet Goodwin, *Alms and Vagabonds* (Honolulu, 1994), 13–14, 27–45; Piggott, *Capital and Countryside*, 171, 345; Piggott, *Emergence*, 222–26; HJ, 83; Kasahara, *History*, 97–98, 150–56; Morse, "Buddhist Transformation"; Ian Reader and George Tanabe, Jr., *Practically Religious* (Honolulu, 1998), 24–25.

[41] Batten, *Ends of Japan*, 28–34, 90–95. For an 11th-century example of Japanese-cum-cosmopolitan elite consciousness, Robert Borgen, "Jojin's Travels from Center to Center," in Adolphson et al., *Heian Japan*, 384–413.

In Heian Japan, two specific *ritsuryo* features reinforced the distinction between class and mass. First, by tying both civil and military offices to hereditary rank, the system severely inhibited mobility and elite–mass interaction. Second, by mandating periodic redistribution of lands, *ritsuryo* laws, initially at least, joined with chronically low productivity to constrain ambitious peasants from accumulating wealth sufficient to achieve literacy or access to elite culture.

Horizontally divided by class, culture across what we now call Japan also remained geographically fragmented. Not only did the Ryukyu islands and Hokkaido lie outside the sphere of the Heian state, but northern and eastern Honshu, home to the "barbarian" *emishi*, was pacified, at best imperfectly, only in the 8th and 9th centuries. Reflecting a Sinic distinction between "civilized" and "barbarian," Heian promoted colonization ever farther north and the assimilation of *emishi* communities by settlers from more southern districts.[42] But in the late 11th and 12th centuries unassimilated frontier peoples still dominated the northern tip of Honshu as well as Hokkaido. If we may extrapolate from medieval patterns, ethnic boundaries remained porous, with no stable distinction between people loyal to Heian and *emishi*.[43] At the other end of the archipelago, the culture of Ryukyu seems to have been closer to that of coastal China than of Heian.[44] Even within Heian's sphere, southern Kyushu, the Tohoku region of eastern Honshu, and the Kanto remained in varying degrees alien to capital elites. With limited links to Heian and virtually no urban tradition, the Kanto, for example, supported a peculiarly martial ethos, stemming from its role as a frontier staging zone, and a language that to Kinai ears sounded harsh and strange.[45] Indeed, Heian courtiers often described distant

[42] On the aristocratic image of Japan as a "divine nation" (*shinkoku*) and ethnic conflicts in the north, Mark Hudson, *Ruins of Identity* (Honolulu, 1999), 193–205, 239; Okada Shoji, "The Development of State Ritual in Ancient Japan," *Acta Asiatica* 51 (1987): 22–41, Yiengpruksawan, *Hiraizumi*, chs. 1, 2; William McCullough, "The Heian Court, 794–1070," in *CHJ*, vol. II, 28–32.

[43] Some have termed "proto-Ainu" the Satsumon culture of *emishi* in this period. See Brett Walker, *The Conquest of Ainu Lands* (Berkeley, 2001), 20–27; David Howell, "Ainu Ethnicity and the Boundaries of the Early Modern Japanese State," *PP* 142 (1994): 78–79; Souyri, *World Upside Down*, 9–16; Takahashi Tomio, "The Classical Polity and Its Frontier," in Piggott, *Capital and Countryside*, 128–45; Yiengpruksawan, *Hiraizumi*, ch. 2.

[44] Souyri, *World Upside Down*, 15. Through the mid-700s the Hayato people of southern Kyushu also resisted Yamato civilization. Walthall, *Japan*, 17.

[45] Takeuchi Rizo, "The Rise of the Warriors," in *CHJ*, vol. II, 653 ff.; Souyri, *World Upside Down*, 11–13, 18, 23, 55; Farris, *Heavenly Warriors*, 127; John Lie, *Multiethnic Japan* (Cambridge, MA, 2001), 115.

regions as areas of unintelligible babble and darkness threatening to overwhelm the radiance of the center.[46] To the 14th century and beyond, Amino Yoshihiko concludes, eastern Honshu, coastal regions along the Sea of Japan and the Pacific, and the southern islands all retained distinctive, often mutually unintelligible dialects and subdialects and the potential to evolve separate cultures, even polities.[47]

Although our knowledge of popular practices is limited, given popular illiteracy, occupational diversity, and the weakness of trade, we may assume that cultural differences among commoners were far greater than among *ritsuryo* elites. Not only rice, but agriculture itself did not dominate the economy as it would in the Tokugawa era. Relatively large populations of hunters, loggers, mountain folk, fishermen, sailors, salt-makers, and other marine peoples maintained cultural and social traditions distinct from one another as well as from lowland peasants. Even the chief agricultural areas supported significant populations of itinerant artisans, traders, and entertainers divorced in varying degrees from the lifestyles of cultivators. As Amino again has emphasized, in this archaic world homogenizing myths had yet to constrict village imaginations, rice growing had yet to assume ideological primacy, and foreigners, pariahs, pedlars, fisherfolk, and prostitutes enjoyed considerably higher status than they would later do.[48]

In short, in Heian as in other charter states, imperial culture remained explicitly and proudly derivative, markedly elitist, and necessarily tolerant of what, by later standards, was enormous regional and social diversity.

The Stability and Longevity of the Charter Order

In the historiography of other charter polities we found a movement from what might be called "catastrophe theory" to "continuity theory." In Burma, Volume 1 argued, scholars now emphasize the limited impact of late-1200s Mongol invasions and the persistence of Pagan social and

---

[46] LaMarre, *Uncovering*, 138.

[47] On regional, occupational, and ethnic diversity to 950 and beyond, Oyama, "Fourteenth Century," 361–63, citing Amino Yoshihiko; Amino Yoshihiko, "Rereading Japanese History" (translation by Alan Christy of chs. 1, 2, 4 of *Zoku Nihon no rekishi o yominaosu*); idem, "Emperor, Rice, and Commoners," 235–44; *CHJ*, vol. II, 28–32; Farris, *Heavenly Warriors*, 156–57, 161, 223, 289; and Hudson, *Ruins of Identity*, 24–33, 175–244, emphasizing less the preservation than the generation of cultural differences.

[48] Previous note, plus Souyri, *World Upside Down*, 14–15, 91–99, citing Amino.

economic structures well into the 14th century. In the central mainland, recent work argues that Angkorian institutions, far from disappearing with Angkor's eclipse, profoundly influenced Ayudhya and Phnom Penh.[49] In Kievan studies, we saw that an earlier focus on political dysfunctionality has yielded to an emphasis on continuing systemic coherence.[50]

Comparable shifts have influenced Japanese historiography. Whereas scholars once portrayed post-9th-century evolution as so many steps in the lamentable disintegration of an efficient, Sinic state, the latest research emphasizes Heian's political longevity and the continued role of Chinese-style structures as a source of legitimacy. For over six centuries charter elites succeeded in retaining enormous wealth and power and in preventing a rupture between capital and countryside.[51] And whereas the founding of the Kamakura shogunate in 1192 once was seen as separating the classical from the "medieval" eras, many scholars – looking not only at political institutions, but state–temple relations, social hierarchy, and village organization – now postpone that transition to 1280–1350.[52] To be sure, Heian institutions evolved: from the early 900s we shall find that the legal-bureaucratic apparatus of the *ritsuryo* codes yielded to private networks. But if we regard the Heian-centered order as a political, social, and cultural complex – rather than merely as a legal system – one could argue that although Japan's charter order arose earlier than its Southeast Asian or Russian

[49] See *SP*, 119–23, 236–46; Michael Aung-Thwin, *Myth and History in the Historiography of Early Burma* (Athens, OH, 1998), ch. 3; Michael Vickery, "Cambodia After Angkor" (Yale Univ., PhD diss., 1978); and discussion of Southeast Asian charter longevity in Ch. 1 *supra*.

[50] Ch. 2 *supra*.

[51] See historiographic discussions at Hall, *Government and Local Power*, 99–128; Karl Friday, *Hired Swords* (Stanford, 1992), 167–77; idem, *Samurai, Warfare*, 43–44; Batten, "Provincial Administration"; Kierstead, *Geography*, 92–101, 151–52; Jeffrey Mass, "Epilogue," in John W. Hall and Mass, eds., *Medieval Japan* (Stanford, 1974), 248–54; Farris, *Heavenly Warriors*, xix–xx, 297–98; essays in Adolphson et al., *Heian Japan*; and next note.

[52] For arguments that the Kamakura shogunate (1192–1333) inaugurated the "medieval" or "feudal" phase of Japanese history, see *CHJ*, vol. II, 19, 700; *CHJ*, vol. III, 1, 301–302; W. G. Beasley, *The Japanese Experience* (Berkeley, 1999), ch. 5; Berry, *Culture of War*, xv. But for an emphasis on late-13th- and 14th-century departures, Farris, *Medieval Population*, chs. 3, 4; idem, *Heavenly Warriors*, ch. 8; Souyri, *World Upside Down*, ch. 7, distinguishing between the first Middle Ages and the second Middle Ages, with 1280–1350 the transition; Friday, *Hired Swords*, 168–71; G. Cameron Hurst's review of Farris, *Heavenly Warriors*, in *JAS* 53 (1994): 197–98; Adolphson, *Gates*, chs. 1–5, 8, esp. pp. 352–54; Thomas Conlan, *State of War* (Ann Arbor, 2003), 4–5; Mass, *Origins*.

counterparts, they all ended in the same general period, c. 1240–1470.[53]

How, then, shall we explain the durability of this Heian-centered aristocratic dispensation? How could a system of geographic and social privilege that cohered in the late 600s or early 700s endure for six centuries? I would point to four strengths, some shared with other charter states in Southeast Asia and Europe, but others clearly unique to Japan.

First, the court was unusually adept in preserving clear lines of authority and tempering intra-elite disputes. Admittedly, factionalism was endemic, while between c. 800 and 1280 policy control gravitated from emperors to noble regents and back to retired emperors before settling among leaders of a court–warrior dyarchy. Nonetheless, the peculiar Japanese separation between sacred imperial authority and hard political power preserved the imperial family, descended from the Sun Goddess, as the sole source of legitimacy. Within that lineage imperial inheritance patterns, including frequent abdication in favor of designated successors, proved far less disruptive than practices in Indic Southeast Asia or Kiev. Likewise, Heian precluded princely claims to independent territorial sovereignty such as encumbered Pagan and Dai Viet and repeatedly tore at the fabric of Angkor, France, and Kiev. Until the late 1100s Heian faced no rival center, and malcontents found few opportunities to play higher authorities off against one another.[54]

Second and closely related to the previous point, cultural and social elitism encouraged stability. Even more obviously than in Pagan and Dai Viet, the educational chasm between court families and illiterate commoners joined noble claims to godly descent (which had no mainland Southeast Asian analogue) and Buddhist karma to ensure a perfect fit between religious merit and aristocratic birth. Intra-noble rivalries notwithstanding, an esprit de corps walled off the nobility as a whole and excluded unauthorized groups from participating in capital politics. The fit between birth and office-holding, a feature of the *ritsuryo* polity from the outset, only grew more pronounced with time. Ironically,

---

[53] Although the Capetian kingdom represented the second, rather than the first, French consolidation, recall that it too ended in 1328, and that the early Valois reached their nadir in 1428.

[54] On succession patterns and the separation between sacerdotal and political power, G. Cameron Hurst, "*Insei*," in *CHJ*, vol. II, 576–618. On post-938 territorial challenges, Takeuchi, "Rise of the Warriors."

rigid stratification favored vertical cooperation, because each party in a vertical faction could help the other obtain rewards for which he himself was ineligible. Since local landholders, for example, could not aspire to noble status, alliance between them and court nobles to protect their separate economic interests became mutually attractive.[55] In a more proactive sense, by exiling or proscribing dissidents, major temples like the Enryakuji marginalized movements that challenged the ideological premises of elite supremacy.[56]

Economic stability provided a third major prop to the charter order. Here too historiography has shifted. A school of thought popular from the 1960s and promoted as recently as 1999 by Dana Morris argued for agrarian expansion. In this view, more iron plows, improved animal husbandry, reclamation, reduced fallow, and double-cropping permitted output and population to rise during much of the Heian period. From 740 to 900 alone, both of the latter elements allegedly increased by a third.[57]

As already indicated, these views run contrary to those of Verschuer, who believes that a low-productivity regime of slash and burn, wild crops, dry crops, and rice remained substantially unchanged from the 8th through at least the 12th century.[58] But they have been challenged most systematically and convincingly by Farris, who argues that before 1280 evidence for iron plow diffusion, animal husbandry, and double-cropping is sparse, and that most references to new acreage actually described the cyclic reclamation of abandoned, marginal lands. In his view, in the late 600s and early 700s adverse climate, epidemics, and excessive elite exactions combined to shift agriculture and population from a long period of growth to an era of stasis and chronic deficiency that did not begin to lift until the late 1200s.[59] Specifically, from c. 670 to 1100 an excessively hot dry climate, and from 1150 to 1300 a no less

---

[55] Friday, *Samurai, Warfare*, 7, 40–41; *HJ*, 97–98; Mass, "Epilogue," 249. Thus, we find in Heian no counterpart to novel literati influence in Tran Dai Viet or artisanal influence in Pagan.

[56] Piggott, *Emergence*, 224–25; *HJ*, 98, 105–106; Goodwin, *Alms and Vagabonds*, 11. On links between major temples in the capital region and provincial shrines, see Adolphson, *Gates*, 53–63; *HJ*, 105; Hitomi Tonomura, *Community and Commerce in Late Medieval Japan* (Stanford, 1992), 21–26; Adolphson et al., *Heian Japan*, 5–6, 8, 51–53, 132, 212–40.

[57] Morris, "Land and Society," 183–220; idem, "Peasant Economy," chs. 5, 6.

[58] Verschuer, *Le Riz*, esp. chs. 2–4, and nn. 27–29 *supra*.

[59] Farris' research is set forth in *Population, Disease*; "Famine, Climate," including a critique of Morris on 275–78; *Medieval Population*, chs. 1, 2; and *Population of Ancient Japan*.

agriculturally unfavorable shift to cold wet weather, generated repeated and severe famines, of which those in 1180–1182, 1229–1232, and 1257–1260 were particularly lethal. The contrast with agriculturally propitious climate and population growth in northern Europe and mainland Southeast Asia during much of the period c. 850–1250 is as curious as it is marked.[60] As if these afflictions were inadequate, after the disastrous smallpox visitation of 735–737, fresh epidemics, also probably smallpox, struck in 865–866 and 993–995.[61] Famine and epidemics were closely joined – the correlation coefficient from 697 to 758 was 0.88 – because disease felled cultivators, while hunger lowered disease resistance.[62] Nor could the economy readily adapt. Not only was trade lethargic, but until at least the 15th century limited manpower and modest technology obliged agriculture to focus on easily cultivated, but constricted and relatively infertile mountain valleys rather than on more productive, difficult-to-work alluvial basins.[63] (Not coincidentally, early mainland Southeast Asian agriculture also concentrated on easily cleared, but comparatively unproductive dry zones before demographic and technical advances allowed the conquest of richer, more difficult-to-tame alluvial deltas after 1500.[64])

---

[60] Japanese mortality during the 1229–1232 famine alone was at least 16–37 percent. See Farris, *Medieval Population*, 31–59, suggesting that some years of cold, wet weather reflected an upsurge in volcanism (38, 51). But it is unclear why this should not also have affected western Europe (at roughly the same latitude as Japan) and Southeast Asia. H. H. Lamb, *Climate, History and the Modern World* (2nd ed., London, 1995), 171–72, acknowledging the contrast between climate trends in the North Atlantic/European zone and the North Pacific/Japan zone c. 1150–1300, suggests that this period saw "a persistent tilt of the whole circumpolar vortex (and of the climatic zones which it defines) away from the Atlantic and towards the Pacific sector, which was rather frequently affected by outbreaks of polar air." Zonal discrepancies apparently persisted, in less severe form, for much of the period to c. 1830. See discussion *infra*. Brown, *History and Climate Change*, 144 seems to endorse a similar explanation for Japanese–European discrepancy, referring to alterations in Rossby standing waves that "locked" Japan more tightly to a cold oceanic front for "two or three centuries." I confess, however, that I find these explanations opaque.

[61] Killing 34 percent and 20–23 percent of identifiable populations, respectively. Farris, *Population of Ancient Japan*, 66–67.

[62] Farris, "Famine, Climate," 292.

[63] Farris, "Famine, Climate," 286–88, 291; idem, *Medieval Population*, 68–86; idem, *Population of Ancient Japan*, ch. 3; Kozo Yamamura, "Returns on Unification," in John W. Hall, Nagaraha Keiji, and Kozo Yamamura, eds., *Japan Before Tokugawa* (Princeton, 1981), 329–30.

[64] *SP*, 91–112, 141–44, 173–75, 224–28, 248–54, 294–95, 305–306, 409–11, 438–39. One thinks as well of the antecedent move from the more easily cultivated but less productive North China plain to the Yangzi basin.

Over so extensive an area and so long a period, naturally we find some variations. In part because climatic warming was kinder to the north and in part because these were still frontier zones, between 930 and 1150 the population of northern and eastern Honshu grew, while that in the Kinai heartland and western Honshu stagnated or fell.[65] Chronologically, the period c. 670–830 – which suffered famines roughly one year in three – was more difficult than the 10th to 13th centuries. After c. 1050, in particular, we find more dry-cropping of soybeans, buckwheat, millet, and barley, some conversion of dry lands to paddy, more attention to water supply, and somewhat enhanced rice yields.[66] Yet despite these portents of future progress, for the islands as a whole, Farris shows, plague, famine, and post-1180 warfare ensured that population was roughly the same in 1280 as in 730, that is to say, between 5,700,000 and 6,400,000, and that total arable was virtually unchanged. To 1280 and beyond, peasants endured chronic malnutrition, primitive housing and sanitation, and frightful infant mortality rates of 50–60 percent, with a life expectancy at birth of 25 years at most. Recurrent subsistence crises also ensured high levels of family dissolution, female-headed households, and residential instability, patterns that further inhibited demographic growth. Some landowners sought to control the labor force through systems of tied and bonded labor, again with generally negative demographic effects.[67]

Of course, Heian had to pay a political price for this economic sluggishness, which overstrained the tax system, fed zero-sum competition, and inhibited rural penetration. Yet on balance, such stability worked to preserve Heian's political monopoly because a) provincial elites, including governors, tax farmers, and estate managers, could not easily amass sufficient wealth to threaten capital preeminence; b) new social groups, including warriors, traders, artisans, mendicant preachers, and peasants, also remained unable to gain sufficient resources – and self-respect – to challenge the status quo.[68] Conversely, precisely because

[65] Farris, *Population of Ancient Japan*, Map 1 and p. 45–53; idem, *Medieval Population*, 22–25, 33, 274 n. 50.

[66] Farris, "Famine, Climate," 275; idem, *Population of Ancient Japan*, 88–90, 108–18, 129–34; idem, "Diseases of the Premodern Period," 382, 384; idem, *Medieval Population*, 10, 67–78, 234, 263.

[67] Farris, *Medieval Population*, 9–10 (with infant mortality and life expectancy from the early 700s), 47–49, 79–92, 116–17, 153, 256, 262–63; idem, *Population of Ancient Japan*, 2, 119–30.

[68] Cf. *HJ*, 98, 102–103; Farris, *Population, Disease*, 144–47.

post-1280 growth bolstered insurgent elites, we shall find that it accelerated decay of the Heian-centered order. These rhythms, to repeat, had no close analogue in Southeast Asia, France, or Kiev, all of which between 950 and 1250 experienced rapid – and ultimately destabilizing – demographic and commercial growth.[69]

A fourth factor promoting Heian stability was the relative weakness of external contacts. If elite appetites for continental luxuries and high culture ensured that some commercial and scholarly exchanges continued,[70] policing the entry of foreign information and goods was far easier in Japan than along the open land frontiers of Southeast Asia, Kiev, or France. Large-scale immigration from the continent ceased after the 7th century; while Heian's diplomatic insecurity and fear that foreign contacts might stoke provincial autonomy led it to cancel its last mission to China in 894 and to rebuff 10th-century requests from China, Korea, and Manchuria to resume relations.[71] Private trade with the continent began c. 830, but was long confined to an area near the future port of Hakata in Kyushu. Not until the late 12th century, after the split between Heian and Kamakura led to a relaxation of central control, did new ports proliferate and the volume of trade (which until c. 1110, Bruce Batten suggests, was as low as one foreign merchant vessel a year[72]) rise significantly. But even then, compared to Europe or Southeast Asia, trade remained modest. Heian thus prevented the sort of commercial centrifugalism that enfeebled Pagan, Angkor, Dai Viet, and Kiev alike.[73]

---

[69] In part, these differences must have been a function of later smallpox and measles domestication in Japan, and in part, a function of climate. See *SP*, 104–12, 121, 142–43, 224–27, 238–41, 253, 363–64, 370–71, 385; and n. 60 *supra*.

[70] Borgen, "Jojin's Travels," 384–414; Charlotte von Verschuer, "Looking from Within and Without," *MN* 55 (2000): 537–66; Bruce Batten, "Cross-Border Traffic on the Kyushu Coast, 794–1086," in Adolphson et al., *Heian Japan*, 357–83; Piggott, *Capital and Countryside*, 362–402.

[71] *HJ*, 98–99; Batten, *Gateway*, ch. 2; idem, "Cross-Border Traffic," 363–72; *CHJ*, vol. II, 390; McCullough, "Heian Court," 80–96.

[72] Batten, *Gateway*, 119–23.

[73] In other words, provincial centrifugalism in Japan preceded, rather than followed, an expansion in frontier trade. See Batten, *Gateway*, 68–69, 105–23; 136–40, with diachronic statistics on sites yielding Chinese porcelain; idem, "Cross-Border Traffic"; Hurst, "*Insei*," 632–37; idem, "*Kugyo* and *Zuryo*," in Adolphson et al., *Heian Japan*, 93; Mikael Adolphson and Edward Kamens, "Between and Beyond Centers and Peripheries," in ibid., 6–7; and Piggott, *Capital and Countryside*, 363, 389. This last source and Hurst suggest a somewhat earlier date than Batten for the opening of new ports. Cf. trade references in *SP*, 93–94, 121–22, 240, 371.

By the same token, Japan's withdrawal from continental affairs removed the twin dangers of overseas military entanglement and foreign invasion. Recall that Pagan wilted before Mongol and Shan attacks, Tais tore away Angkor's outer provinces, Dai Viet fell to Chams and Chinese, Mongols smashed Kiev, Vikings harried the Carolingians, and English attacks fractured Valois France. But with *emishi* in the north neutralized and continental armies unable or unwilling to invade, Heian's internal fissures, such as they were, could not be widened from without. If Southeast Asia, northern Europe, and Japan were part of the protected zone, Japan was the most protected of all.

Evolution of the Heian-Centered Polity, c. 900 to 1280

In sum, ruling-class cohesion, cultural elitism, economic conservatism, and relative isolation afforded Japan's charter civilization unusual stability and longevity. Stability, however, was not the same as stasis. Between c. 900 and 1280 the *ritsuryo* system of bureaucratic centralization yielded to more private networks at court, in religious administration, and in provincial and military organization.

Several theories have been developed to explain these transitions. Prewar Japanese scholars and a line of Western historians starting with George Sansom and John W. Hall suggested that from the start, the Chinese bureaucratic system was simply too alien and unwieldy for Japan, making a return to more indigenous forms of family authority a foregone conclusion. An intrusive, Tang-style state had been necessary to overcome domestic and foreign problems in the 7th century, but once the position of the emperor and allied elites had been secured and the danger of invasion had subsided, it was no longer needed. In this view, the post-900 accession of the Fujiwara family to a dominant position at court, the conversion of the royal house itself into a private entity, and the retreat from direct to indirect rule in the provinces were, at least in part, reversions to pre-*ritsuryo* traditions.[74]

Other historians have suggested that administrative interventions by the state itself unintentionally engendered social changes that undermined *ritsuryo* structures. In the provinces, for example, by allowing

---

[74] See Sansom, *History to 1334*, chs. 7, 8; Hall, *Government and Local Power*, ch. 4, esp. pp. 99–104; and more recent formulations in Batten, "Cross-Border Traffic," 361; idem, "Provincial Administration," 124; McCullough, "Heian Court," 50, 74–75. See too historiographic references in Piggott, *Emergence*, 283, 389 n. 6; Farris, *Population, Disease*, 141; Adolphson and Kamens, "Between and Beyond," 9.

wealthy farmers to manage tax collections, Heian nurtured a new class of magnates outside the system of district magistrates. At the same time, frequently rotated, often absentee governors found it expedient to delegate ever more responsibility to provincial assistants. The net result was a secular shift in power from Heian to the provinces, and within the provinces from central appointees to newly risen local families whose *de facto* power lacked formal recognition.[75]

Largely independent of government actions, economic growth, some claim, also strengthened local tax managers and landowners, who used their control over land and people to constrict the flow of revenues to Heian. In this view, society got richer as capital elites grew poorer.[76] But if we accept the above evidence that economic growth before c. 1280 remained very modest, this hypothesis becomes implausible.[77]

To my mind, the most cogent single explanation for *ritsuryo* devolution is Farris' thesis, which, contrary to the theory of growth, argues that the economy was simply too poor to sustain an elaborate Chinese-style system over the long term. Recurrent epidemics, lapsed cultivation, and floating populations sabotaged *ritsuryo* efforts to register people and redistribute lands on a regular basis. By overburdening a weakened population, spiraling rounds of monumental building and ritual display only aggravated chronic shortfalls in taxes and corvées.[78] In response, the court began to cut back on expenditures and converted provincial governors into tax farmers obliged to meet set quotas. But with tax revenue still problematic, Heian aristocrats and temples, in cooperation with local elites, also developed private, generally tax-exempt estates – *shoen* – and engaged warriors to protect those private assets. In these ways, especially from the mid-1000s, centralized structures atrophied, but capital elites themselves retained access to provincial surpluses.[79] Batten has tried to argue against this theory of poverty by

---

75 With few exceptions, these new elites were not descended from families who had monopolized district posts in the early *ritsuryo* period. Batten, "Cross-Border Traffic," 361; idem, "Provincial Administration," 114–34; Piggott, *Capital and Countryside*, 193–97; Morris, "Land and Society," 233–35. But see too Farris, *Population, Disease*, 141–42, and idem, *Population of Ancient Japan*, 89–90, critiquing this approach.

76 See n. 57 *supra*, plus Batten, "Provincial Administration," 130–32; McCullough, "Heian Court," 37–38; *HJ*, 107–10.

77 See nn. 58–63 *supra*, esp. *Population of Ancient Japan*, 90.

78 Farris, *Population of Ancient Japan*, 88; idem, pers. commun., Aug. 11, 2006; plus *CHJ*, vol. II, 37, 38, 44, 72; Piggott, *Emergence*, 282.

79 At the same time, because only senior courtiers were still receiving official salaries, junior officials became ever more dependent on the great households for sustenance.

noting that although Japan was as poor in the 7th as in later centuries, 7th-century elites succeeded in implementing the *ritsuryo* system with impressive results.[80] Yet severe smallpox epidemics, as well perhaps as climatic deterioration, seem to have been post-700 features. Moreover, the weaker the initial economic base, the more likely cumulative strains were to undermine a system that showed early promise.

In any case, to explain a phenomenon covering many provinces and lasting centuries, are we not forced to consider multiple factors? Farris' theory of economic constriction, for example, seems compatible both with a partial reversion to pre-Chinese traditions and with the idea that administrative changes unintentionally aided local elites.[81]

What is indisputable is that from the late 9th century the use of extragovernmental mechanisms and the incorporation of power centers outside the *ritsuryo* bureaucracy gradually transformed the state at all levels.[82] At the court itself, emperors retained effective authority to 842, but thereafter and most especially from c. 970 to 1070 the heads of the Northern Fujiwara family, an old noble line, dominated affairs. The secret to Fujiwara ascendancy lay in providing consorts to young emperors who were then eased into retirement as soon as a Fujiwara-mothered successor was available. Acting as regents on behalf of their young and pliant grandsons, Fujiwara ministers colonized imperial administration with relatives and clients. But to ensure adequate income, from the late 900s they also transferred some public lands as *shoen* to themselves, their allies at court, and allied temples. And they revised *ritsuryo* statutes so as to grant the increasingly elaborate administrative organs (*mandokoro*) of aristocratic households greater authority over these estates. Fujiwara power thus came to rest on both bureaucratic and extrabureaucratic structures.[83]

Privatization continued from 1086 to 1185, during which time a series of energetic retired emperors displaced the Fujiwara at court. Although

---

Farris, *Population, Disease*, 142–46; idem, *Heavenly Warriors*, 122–26; idem, "Famine, Climate," 299–300. For supporting views, see Mikael Adolphson, "Institutional Diversity and Religious Integration," in Adolphson et al., *Heian Japan*, 212–44, esp. 227; Joan Piggott, "Court and Provinces Under Regent Fujiwara no Tadahira," in ibid., 35–65.

[80] Batten, "Provincial Administration," 115–16.

[81] Yamamura, "Decline" implicitly combines elements of the first, second, and fourth theories.

[82] Adolphson and Kamens, "Between and Beyond," 9–10.

[83] *HJ*, 88–92; McCullough, "Heian Court," 20–80; Morris, "Land and Society," 227–32; Kiley, "Provincial Administration," 245; Farris, *Population of Ancient Japan*, 89; Piggott, "Court and Provinces"; Adolphson, "Institutional Diversity," 227.

politically this period represented a reassertion of imperial authority, in institutional terms it further eroded *ritsuryo* norms. Like Fujiwara regents, abdicated emperors set pliant young relatives on the throne, but exercised real power through both statutory bodies and their own household organs. After unsuccessful efforts to halt the growth of *shoen*, the imperial house switched course completely and began converting large chunks of public land into *shoen* of its own and of its allies. Whether under Fujiwara or imperial auspices, *shoen* embodied a reciprocal relation between capital and provincial elites. On the one hand, courtiers sought assured income outside the tax system. On the other, local landowners and tax managers sought protection against rivals, immunity from civil or criminal prosecution, and a reduction or elimination of taxes that only Heian courtiers could guarantee. Especially after c. 1050 when a modest reclamation of abandoned lands got underway, provincial elites commended ever more lands under their charge as *shoen* to a variety of high-ranking capital patrons. In a world where most public functions and much public land had been privatized, the retired emperors' primary role was to settle disputes among noble houses and to suppress revolts that might upset the factional balance. To accomplish those tasks and to protect their own interests, retired emperors, like other Heian actors, engaged career warriors whom they rewarded with offices and land rights.[84]

Parallel developments transformed religious institutions. The early *ritsuryo* court helped to finance major temples in Heian and central Japan.[85] But as imperial finances declined in the 10th and 11th centuries, such temples were obliged to seek independent sources of income. Like lay aristocrats, they therefore accumulated *shoen*, which were donated by aristocrats seeking spiritual or political help and by provincial landholders seeking protection and tax reduction.[86] At the same time major fanes converted provincial temples into branch affiliates, to which they offered tax exemptions and political protection in return for military help and yearly dues.[87] Like *shoen*, temple networks therefore bypassed the state, but kept resources flowing to the capital. Along

---

[84] Hurst, "*Insei*," 614–18, 640–42, and 576–643 *passim*; *HJ*, 92–94.

[85] See n. 56 *supra*, plus Adolphson, "Institutional Diversity," 213–27.

[86] Thus, for example, the powerful Enryakuji temple came to control some 300 estates. Adolphson, *Gates*, 57; Tonomura, *Community and Commerce*, 22.

[87] Adolphson, "Institutional Diversity," 227–40; idem, *Gates*, chs. 3, 4. Actually, there were two stages in this incorporation of provincial shrines, that of *betsuin*, or detached cloisters, and *matsuji*, or branch temples.

with noble and imperial houses and (somewhat later) leading warrior families, the great temples thus emerged as one of those private power blocs – known as "gates of power" (*kenmon*) – that cooperated to maintain one another's status and to govern the realm under nominal imperial authority.[88]

Nor was provincial governance unaffected by *ritsuryo* evolution.[89] On the one hand, in lieu of the original system of variable assessments levied directly on cultivators, after c. 900 I noted that Heian subjected provincial governors to fixed tax quotas in a generally successful effort to stabilize its income in an era of economic difficulty. On the other hand, as *shoen* proliferated from c. 1050 to 1300, provincial elites joined Heian patrons in acquiring interlocking revenue rights – *shiki* – in *shoen* at the expense of the public fisc. Agricultural lands thus became divided into two broad categories: "provincial lands" (*kokugaryo*) still subject to taxation and comprising some 50–60 percent of the total; and tax-exempt *shoen*. With many governors now no longer even visiting their provinces and treating their appointments as mere sources of absentee income, militarized local elites began to deal with the capital directly.

In many ways, these adjustments proved advantageous, a source of Heian's longevity and a testament to its flexibility. In linking leading courtiers and major temples more directly to the most dynamic elements of provincial society and to multiple sources of local authority, post-1050 innovations widened the political and financial base of court elites and enhanced capital–provincial integration. More responsive to shifts in power than *ritsuryo* administration, the system of *shiki* revenue rights proved to be an eminently flexible instrument, while Heian's ability to play off *shoen*-holders against *kokugaryo*-managers gave it additional leverage in the provinces.[90]

---

[88] Accordingly the 11th to 15th centuries are often termed the *kenmon* era. Adolphson, *Gates*, 10–20 and *passim*.

[89] Ensuing discussion relies on Morris, "Land and Society," 199–235; Takeuchi, "Rise of the Warriors," esp. 644–53; Kiley, "Provincial Administration," 236–340; Hurst, "*Kugyo* and *Zuryo*," 66–101; Batten, "Provincial Administration"; Charlotte van Verschuer, "Life of Commoners in the Provinces," in Adolphson et al., *Heian Japan*, 305–28; Kierstead, *Geography of Power*, chs. 1–3; Sasaki Muneo, "The Court-Centered Polity," in Piggott, *Capital and Countryside*, 227–44; Toda Yoshimi, "Kyoto and the Estate System in the Heian Period," ibid., 245–79; Farris, *Population of Ancient Japan*, 89–90, 112, 117.

[90] Adolphson and Kamens, "Between and Beyond," 1–10; Adolphson, "Institutional Diversity," 240.

And yet by the mid-12th century changes in landholding and provincial organization also posed three long-term threats to court authority and domestic order: a) With the decline of gubernatorial authority, with the rise of private economic networks, and with no universally accepted system of adjudication, claimants were increasingly tempted to use force to collect rents and to settle disputes over *shoen* income. b) Career warriors began to exploit these cleavages to carve out an independent role. In an era of slow growth and bitterly contested claims, capital elites became ever more dependent on such enforcers to collect revenues. c) By freezing not only provincial taxes but in many cases *shoen* rents at the level of about 900,[91] Heian elites ensured that any increase in production would be captured not by themselves but by provincial elites. In effect, while enhancing their short-term financial security, they surrendered claims to future growth and invited new forces to contest Heian's ancient monopoly of power and privilege.

Notwithstanding the sluggishness of the overall economy, in the late 11th and 12th centuries there were already signs that economic shifts between regions could be politically destabilizing. The most demographically vital regions between 930 and 1150, we saw, were outlying areas like the Kanto, Tohoku in the far north, the northwest coast of Honshu, and to a lesser extent Kyushu, areas where fresh land and woodlands were more abundant than in the Kinai. From the 1080s a breakaway regional regime led by military families in northern Tohoku defied Heian rule for a century, while in the 1180s the Kamakura shogunate rose from the Kanto to challenge Heian directly.[92]

Socially, as both of those challenges also showed, the most dynamic element in the late Heian period were career warriors – *bushi* or *samurai*, the "teeth and claws" of their capital patrons – whose services became ever more prized as rival groups resorted to violence to acquire land, exact rents, and settle disputes. These warriors, chiefly mounted archers, came from two strata. Most numerous were those of local origins, descended from a mixture of pre-*ritsuryo* chieftains, tax managers, and resident provincial officials. With court aristocrats inclined to disdain death and blood as sources of pollution and with raw power an increasingly indispensable adjunct of landownership, men of violence

---

[91] *CHJ*, vol. II, 214–15; *HJ*, 107.
[92] On provincial shifts, n. 65 *supra*, plus Yiengpruksawan, *Hiraizumi*, chs. 2–6; *HJ*, 93–96; Friday, *Hired Swords*, 91; Ikegami, *Taming Samurai*, 69–70; Kiley, "Provincial Administration," 255–56, 335–36.

built networks that became a key element of provincial life by the 10th century. This was especially true in eastern Honshu, where gentry lived in palisaded manors and developed clan-like military hierarchies that bore at least a superficial similarity to post-Carolingian developments in Europe.[93] The second, more influential group, principally members of the Taira and Minamoto clans, proudly claimed descent from cadet branches of the imperial family. Having originally left Heian to seek their fortunes in the provinces, these men enjoyed enormous local prestige even as ancestral associations and military functions let them retain or extend their influence at the capital.[94]

With the help of court patrons, leading warriors acquired titles, offices, and substantial revenue rights. Well into the 12th century, Karl Friday suggests, the relation between the warrior class as a whole and their aristocratic benefactors resembled that between a ferocious, but obedient dog and its owner. As yet warriors showed scant inclination to act as a coherent interest group.[95] However, from mid-century violent disputes between aristocratic factions at court gave high-placed military nobles opportunity to assume an increasingly independent and prominent role. After a Taira chieftain at Heian overplayed his hand, full-scale fighting, the Genpei War of 1180 to 1185, broke out between Taira armies and Minamoto forces, the latter centered in the Kanto, to determine which warrior alliance would dominate at court. As campaigns raged from Kyushu to Tohoku, the Genpei War proved far more wrenching and territorially extensive than provincial disturbances in the 10th and 11th centuries. Emerging victorious from this epic encounter (which engendered a rich literature of war tales), Minamoto no Yoritomo, leader of Minamoto forces, now declared his camp competent to join the imperial court in governing the entire realm. Rather

---

[93] See n. 3 *supra*. Whereas *buke* ("military house") refers to patrilineages of high-status warriors, *bushi* and *samurai* are generic terms for warriors. More specifically, according to Farris, *Heavenly Warriors*, 6–7, *bushi* were "lightly armored, mounted archers" after c. 1100, while *samurai* were "the lightly armored, mounted archer of the twelfth century and after."

[94] On *bushi* origins and roles to c. 1150, Takeuchi, "Rise of the Warriors," 644–709; Farris, *Heavenly Warriors*, esp. chs. 6–8; Friday, *Hired Swords*, esp. 70–177; idem, *Samurai, Warfare and the State*, 5–14, 36–62, 104; idem, "Lordship Interdicted," in Adolphson et al., *Heian Japan*, 329–54; Jeffrey Mass, "The Kamakura Bakufu," in *CHJ*, vol. III, 46–58; *HJ*, 103–104; Ikegami, *Taming Samurai*, 47–117, emphasizing cultural differences between aristocrats and *bushi*; and Souyri, *World Upside Down*, 17–28, 36–43, emphasizing differences between western and eastern Japan.

[95] Friday, *Hired Swords*, 176. Also idem, "Lordship Interdicted"; idem, *Samurai, Warfare*, 10; Mass, "Kamakura Bakufu," 48–51.

than at Heian, he set up his headquarters in the Kanto at the coastal town of Kamakura, which gave its name to the period of warrior-led government from 1192 to 1333. Yoritomo proceeded to pacify the countryside and to guarantee the income of cooperative aristocrats, temples, and warriors alike. The Kamakura shogunate, as it became known, was therefore revolutionary in two respects: a) For the first time a provincial authority led by men not of the most exalted social ranks patronized the imperial court; this reversed age-old relations and foreshadowed an era of warrior domination. b) A warrior was able to grant favored *bushi* followers their most fervent desire, something Heian had been unwilling to concede, namely, a formal guarantee of landholdings outside Heian's purview.[96]

One must not exaggerate Kamakura novelty, because the dominance of the Kinai and of the civil nobility continued to erode only gradually, and Heian's authority remained far more than symbolic. As Lee Butler observed, for over 30 years historians have been retrieving power from medieval warriors to whom they too readily conceded such authority.[97] Indeed, for most of its history the Kamakura shogunate should be seen as a dyarchy, in which two chief power blocs, courtiers centered in Heian and warriors in Kamakura and the east, shared governance and privilege. (Although the power of religious institutions was more limited and their interests less coordinated, if we include those institutions, the Kamakura state, like its late Heian predecessor, was composed of three power blocs.[98]) Yoritomo, who served as *shogun* or "generalissimo," and his regental successors based their power on their own extensive *shoen* and on the expanded ranks of their personal vassals.[99] Kamakura appointed such men to serve as "military governors" (*shugo*), who were responsible for suppressing lawless elements

---

[96] Mass, "Kamakura Bakufu," 47–58; Kozo Yamamura, "Introduction," in *CHJ*, vol. III, 13; Adolphson, *Gates*, 125, 183–84; G. Cameron Hurst, "The Kobu Polity," in Mass, *Court and Bakufu*, 3–28. Kamakura discussion relies too on Jeffrey Mass, *Yoritomo and the Founding of the First Bakufu* (Stanford, 1999); Edwin Reischauer and Albert Craig, *Japan: Tradition and Transformation* (Sydney, 1973), 39–49; essays by Cornelius Kiley, Jeffrey Mass, Paul Varley, Lorraine Harrington, and Takeuchi Rizo in Mass, *Court and Bakufu*; Adolphson, *Gates*, ch. 5; Souyri, *World Upside Down*, chs. 3, 4, 6; and Friday, *Samurai, Warfare, and the State*, 44–62.

[97] Lee Butler, *Emperor and Aristocracy in Japan, 1467–1680* (Cambridge, MA, 2002), 7 and 7–12.

[98] See Adolphson's modification of the *kenmon* thesis of Kuroda Toshio. Adolphson, *Gates*, esp. 10–20, 352–55; idem, "Enryakuji – An Old Power in a New Era," in Mass, *Origins*, 237–60; Jeffrey Mass, "Introduction," ibid., 10.

[99] Known as *gokenin* or "housemen."

and marshalling warriors at the provincial level, and as "military land stewards," who were charged with maintaining peace and collecting rents for absentee landlords on private estates. Buttressed by warrior notions of honor and reciprocal obligation, a lord–vassal network tied to the *shogun* (or his regent) thus came to control a substantial number of estates and to exercise supreme military power. Yet in the early Kamakura era not only were Kamakura vassals thin on the ground outside the *bushi* heartland of eastern Japan, but most of these arrangements were outgrowths of Minamoto family governance. As such, they were comparable to arrangements employed by aristocratic houses and religious shrines for centuries.

Moreover, in a compromise typical of much of Japanese history, Kamakura institutions did not replace so much as supplement or parallel Heian institutions. The court's incomparable prestige, the shogunate's reliance on the court to sanction appointments, and the strength of nonwarrior *shoen* in western Japan precluded a systematic assault on the old order. The shogunate's main responsibilities were to maintain peace and to control the warrior class.[100] Even after a failed imperial revolt in 1221 led Kamakura to tighten its supervision of Heian and to colonize western and central Japan with military land stewards from the Kanto, Kamakura honored much of the court's customary authority over tax lands and nonwarrior *shoen*. Throughout most of the Kamakura period, as had been true for centuries, warriors in the Kanto held the lion's share of revenue and land, but in western Japan they controlled only about a third of the harvest and less than 10 percent of the land.[101] Especially in western Japan, most artisans, marine peoples, and mountain folk remained under the protection of the imperial court, and capital shrines remained outside warrior control.[102] In the religious sphere too, despite the rise of popular Buddhist sects (see below), Mikael Adolphson and others have shown that the ideology of the late Heian period and the institutional prerogatives of elite temples continued substantially into the 14th century.[103]

---

[100] Jeffrey Mass, "What Can We Not Know About the Kamakura Bakufu?," in Mass and William Hauser, eds., *The Bakufu in Japanese History* (Stanford, 1985), 29; Jeffrey Mass, *Antiquity and Anachronism in Japanese History* (Stanford, 1992), ch. 7; Adolphson, *Gates*, 14; Duus, *Feudalism*, 47–48; *CHJ*, vol. III, 196.

[101] Farris, *Heavenly Warriors*, 312–13, 349.

[102] Souyri, *World Upside Down*, 93–95, 214.

[103] Adolphson, *Gates*, esp. 10–11, 18–19, 185–239, 346–55. Also Osumi Kazuo, "Buddhism in the Kamakura Period," in *CHJ*, vol. III, 544–82; Peter Arnesen, "Suo Province in

3. DEVOLUTION AND REINTEGRATION, C. 1280–1603

Late Kamakura and Ashikaga Political Tensions, c. 1280–1467

In a word, the Kamakura shogunate was simultaneously the last stage of Heian court power and the beginning of warrior dominance. Warrior muscle let Kamakura exploit the long-term privatization of Heian governance and ensuing aristocratic splits to increase *bushi* power. But neither the Kamakura shogunate nor its successor, that of the Ashikaga, retained sufficient control over warrior networks to prevent fresh disorders. From the late 1200s to the early 1500s devolution therefore continued until the islands had fragmented utterly. While placing them in Eurasian context, let us examine these ongoing localizing trends – as well as the grand phoenix-like countermovement that rose in the 16th century from the ruins of the Ashikaga regime.

In part because demographic-cum-economic growth quickened after c. 1280, the late Kamakura system faced strains more severe than those that confronted Heian. We shall return to the effects of post-1280 expansion, but for now consider that as money use and debt increased among Kamakura's vassals, those trends reinforced conflicts between civil and military claims to *shoen* revenues. The fragmentation of once ample warrior patrimonies into slender inheritances – partly a function of growth in the warrior population – had much the same effect. In essence, although agricultural wealth was expanding, elite claimants to usufruct were proliferating more rapidly. At a lower social level, particularly in the Kinai, commercialization gave rise to a new mobility, brigandage, and a further tendency to solve disputes by violence.

Compounding internal stresses, in 1274 and 1281 the Mongols invaded Kyushu after the shogunate had spurned their demands for tribute. Although the Mongols by 1279 had vanquished the Southern Song and their second invasion involved no less than 140,000 (mostly Chinese) troops, both assaults miscarried, with the second succumbing to *samurai* resistance, an epidemic, and a typhoon (the "divine wind" or *kamikaze*). By comparison with Kiev, even Pagan, these invasions caused minimal damage. Still, they fed elite unhappiness, because

the Age of Kamakura," in Mass, *Court and Bakufu*, 92–120. *Ritsuryo* provincial names, road systems, and titles were yet more long lived. Not surprisingly, this multiplicity of power centers supported a juridical system of exceptional complexity. Souyri, *World Upside Down*, 59.

the Kamakura regental family monopolized prized commands, and because unlike domestic triumphs, victory over seaborne invaders yielded no estate spoils to compensate warrior houses for lost blood and treasure.[104]

As factionalism festered over such issues and over the imperial succession, in the early 1300s parts of Kyushu and Tohoku slipped beyond the control of either Kyoto (the postcharter name for Heian) or Kamakura. Exploiting this poisonous atmosphere, in the early 1330s the emperor Go-Daigo led a revolt that at last destroyed the Kamakura shogunate.

Although Go-Daigo dreamed of restoring imperial rule, in fact his schemes paved the way to the second shogunate, that of the Ashikaga (1338–1573). Naturally, the Ashikaga retained features from preceding eras. The emperor was still sovereign, and in theory, the office of *shogun* remained an imperial appointment. Yet Ashikaga government came to differ from the Kamakura in a number of practical respects that together highlighted the ultimate disintegration of the *ritsuryo* system, the transfer of power from courtiers to warriors, and the final eclipse of central by local power.

Whereas for most of its history the Kamakura regime had been a genuine dyarchy between Heian courtiers and warrior households, under the Ashikaga the imperial family and the community of aristocratic and religious proprietors at Kyoto suffered an accelerating loss of power and income.[105] Whereas the first shogunate had remained in Kamakura, Ashikaga *shogun* established their primary seat in Kyoto

---

[104] In truth, the Mongol impact was ambiguous insofar as their invasions allowed Kamakura to extend its authority into Kyushu; but the debt amnesties and confirmation of existing rights that Kamakura granted Kyushu warriors were paltry compared to estate spoils that domestic wars usually produced. Kyotsu Hori, "The Economic and Political Effects of the Mongol Wars," in Hall, and Mass, *Medieval Japan*, 184–98; Kawazoe Shoji, "Japan and East Asia," in *CHJ*, vol. III, 411–23; Hitomi Tonomura and Anne Walthall, "Introduction," in Tonomura et al., *Women and Class*, 7. On Kamakura decline, see too *HJ*, 158–63; Souyri, *World Upside Down*, 61–64, 101–20; Andrew Goble, *Kenmu: Go-Daigo's Revolution* (Cambridge, MA, 1996), ch. 4; Ishii Susumu, "The Decline of the Kamakura Bakufu," in *CHJ*, vol. III, 128–74; Nagahara Keiji, "The Decline of the *Shoen* System," in ibid., 260–300.

[105] On the Ashikaga (Muromachi) regime, Adolphson, *Gates*, 288–345, 354–55; John W. Hall, "The Muromachi Bakufu," in *CHJ*, vol. III, 175–230; Imatani Akira, "Muromachi Local Government," in ibid., 231–59; Nagahara, "Decline of *Shoen*," 260–300; John W. Hall and Toyoda Takeshi, eds., *Japan in the Muromachi Age* (Berkeley, 1977), esp. essays by Kawai Masaharu and Cornelius Kiley; Souyri, *World Upside Down*, chs. 8–10; *HJ*, 144, 158–71; *EAH*, vol. III, 52–58; Lorraine Harrington, "Regional Outposts of Muromachi Bakufu Rule," in Mass and Hauser, *The Bakufu*, 66–98; Prescott Wintersteen,

itself and assumed privileges once reserved for the emperor, including the right to issue orders in the imperial name. At the same time, with the eclipse of imperial structures, *shogun* necessarily devised new administrative arrangements, foremost of which was an expanded network of military governors, or *shugo*. As these governors, intensifying a trend apparent in the Kamakura era, usurped the powers of the old civilian governors, the chain of command running from *shogun* to *shugo* to provincial warriors carried almost the entire weight of central and local government.

By building warrior coalitions, the Ashikaga achieved stints of stability, most notably between 1368 and 1416. The *shogun* manipulated *shugo* by appointing them to noncontiguous provinces and obliging many to reside at Kyoto. After decades of intermittent fighting between the so-called northern and southern imperial courts, in 1392 the shogunate also succeeded in obtaining the surrender of the breakaway southern court that had been founded by Go-Daigo in the 1330s. Although the northern court in Kyoto under the Ashikaga always had the upper hand, these conflicts between rival courts, especially between 1336 and 1368, were by far the most serious disturbances since the Genpei War of 1180–1185, which the new hostilities obviously dwarfed in duration, if not intensity. Such successes aside, respect for central authority remained weaker than under Kamakura, and the Ashikaga shogunate never became more than an alliance of convenience among powerful military houses in which the *shogun* served as *primus inter pares*. At its zenith in the early 1400s, the Ashikaga exercised effective control only over central and western Japan. Even there *shugo* acquired the right to transmit offices to their heirs, to levy new taxes, to convert provincial lands (*kokugaryo*) to personal holdings, and to absorb the functions and income of the old military land stewards. Once they were accepted as primary lawgivers in the provinces, *shugo* were in a position to incorporate more local warriors into their own lord–vassal networks.

I hasten to emphasize, however, that the trend toward local consolidation remained imperfect, and for this reason *shugo* should be seen as transitional between the more centralized structures of Kamakura and

"The Muromachi *Shugo* and *Hanzei*," in Hall and Mass, *Medieval Japan*, 210–20; Tonomura, *Community and Commerce*, 8–9; Conlan, *State of War*, chs. 4, 5, 7, 8; Paul Varley, "Cultural Life of the Warrior Elite in the Fourteenth Century," in Mass, *Origins*, 192–208; and Berry, *Culture of Civil War*, xxx, terming the Ashikaga a "complex corporatist state."

the fully autonomous *daimyo* domains of the 16th century. Many a *shugo* held estates outside the province he administered, while within each province lands under direct *shugo* control usually represented only a fraction of the total territory. Moreover, some provincial warriors maintained ties to the *shogun* over the heads of the *shugo*. Of necessity, therefore, military governors continued to look to the *shogun* and to Kyoto for support. Ultimately this proved fatal to many *shugo* houses, because during the disorders of the late 15th century their immersion in shogunal politics, symbolized by their residence in Kyoto, led them to lose touch with the provinces. Ironically, although a shift among warriors from partible to unitary male inheritance, starting as early as the mid-1200s, stemmed estate fragmentation, by fomenting disputes among rival claimants within the same warrior clan, this change further weakened some *shugo* houses.[106]

But most basically, *shugo*, and by extension the shogunate itself, became vulnerable because they could not curb the energy of local actors who benefited more directly than *shugo* from agricultural and commercial expansion, to which we shall turn shortly. Whereas the *ritsuryo* regime had protected a small and relatively homogeneous elite in a period of anemic growth, the early shogunates tried – with diminishing success – to accommodate far more numerous and diverse constituencies in a period of rapid economic and social change. If Kamakura and Ashikaga warriors represented a challenge to Heian imperial elites from below, in the end those warriors themselves fell victim to yet more humble insurgents in more direct control of local wealth. In pursuit of political and economic advantage, local warriors – calling themselves *kokujin*, "provincials," to distinguish themselves from "outsiders" – as well as local merchants, villagers, and religious sectarians mounted increasingly effective challenges, playing one sector of the capital elite against another. Menaced from below, the court, major shrines, the *shogun*, and *shugo* fell to quarreling with one another. By the 1460s the Ashikaga regime had been reduced to little more than a Kyoto city administration. Temples and courtiers lost their chief sources of income. Bandits infested the countryside. Pirates roamed the coasts and the Inland Sea. The *shogun* had minimal control over *shugo*, whose families were rent by factional disputes and threatened by their own deputies. In Conrad

---

[106] Goble, *Kenmu*, 119; Souyri, *World Upside Down*, 124, 166–69; Walthall, *Japan*, 61, 74; Ikegami, *Taming Samurai*, 123–27. On Ashikaga decline, previous note, plus Miyagawa Mitsuru, "From *Shoen* to *Chigyo*," in Hall and Takeshi, *Muromachi Age*, 89–105.

Totman's words, "A condition of perfect political *laissez faire* seemed at hand."[107]

The Warring States Era and Reunification, c. 1467–1603

A succession dispute within the shogunal house finally collapsed the Ashikaga system. During the ensuing Onin War of 1467 to 1477 the *shugo* of central Japan split into two camps whose massive battles ravaged Kyoto and left the shogunate nearly as powerless as the imperial court.

With the capital's evisceration, many *shugo* now returned to their provinces in an attempt to build independent military bases. But most found, in Hall's words, "that the times had already passed them by."[108] Local organizations that had been gathering strength inconspicuously throughout the Ashikaga era now rushed to fill the vacuum created by the shogunate's collapse. In economically advanced areas of the Kinai as early as the 13th or 14th century and in other provinces thereafter, nucleated villages evolved into self-governing corporations (*so*). Larger, more stable populations, the growing economic value of the commons, wider commercial opportunities, struggles with landlords and bandits, the transformation of dependents into free peasants eager to participate in village affairs – in varying local combinations, all these factors favored autonomous village organizations, which in some areas forged supralocal networks. Although not without internal tensions, peasant communities, including at first resident warriors, often showed considerable cohesion, maintaining their own laws and irrigation procedures and organizing to ward off outsiders and to demand rent reductions from higher authorities.[109] In some areas village self-government fused with Buddhist devotionalism to create military leagues able to compete with secular armies. Thus the Honganji branch of the True Pure Land sect of Buddhism developed a territorial administration and organized armies that fought across central Japan in the 1520s and

---

[107] *HJ*, 168. Ashikaga fortunes deteriorated rapidly after the death in 1441 of Yoshinori, who was succeeded by two successive youthful, far less effective *shogun*.

[108] Hall, "Muromachi Bakufu," 229.

[109] On the evolution of corporate villages, Tonomura, *Community and Commerce*, 3–13, 37–187; idem, "Re-Envisioning Women in the Post-Kamakura Age," in Mass, *Origins*, 138–69; Kristina Kade Troost, "Peasants, Elites, and Villages in the Fourteenth Century," in ibid, 91–109; Farris, *Medieval Population*, 137–39, 246–52, 264; Nagahara Keiji, "Village Communities and Daimyo Power," in Hall and Takeshi, *Muromachi Age*, 107–23; idem, "The Medieval Peasant," in *CHJ*, vol. III, 330–37; Souyri, *World Upside Down*, 128–35, 161–66, 183–88; Ikegami, *Taming Samurai*, 121–34.

early 1530s. Temples attached to the Lotus (Hokke) sect were similarly active.[110] Particularly after the Onin War we also find merchant-led urban communities, some with self-defense organizations, at Kyoto, Hakata, Sakai, and elsewhere, as well as pirate networks along the Inland Sea.[111]

But the primary victors from post-Onin upheavals and economic growth were neither religious leagues, independent cities, nor pirates, but warrior hierarchies more cohesive than the old *shugo* networks. Emerging usually from the ranks of *shugo* retainers, charismatic warriors succeeded in overthrowing *shugo* houses, or in obliging *shugo* survivors to compete in radically new circumstances. The process by which such leaders established independent authority is termed the "overthrow of those above by those below," and the period of more or less continuous conflict between the outbreak of the Onin War and the start of Japan's reunification is known as the Warring States period (1467–1568). Coming after the Genpei War of 1180–1185 and the struggle between the northern and southern courts in the 14th century, this period, together with the unification wars of 1568–1603, became the most prolonged, disruptive, and institutionally creative of successive breakdowns, precisely because in this period the inutility of earlier administrative models had become most obvious and the need for innovation most keenly felt.

Responding to the incessant need to raise and supply armies, regional magnates – *daimyo* – now deepened a process of consolidation from the bottom up, as it were, that had begun fitfully before the Onin War. Whereas *shugo* domains had been based on the old imperial provinces, *daimyo* domains centered on strongpoints and natural defenses and reflected local military realities. Whereas *shugo* held only a portion of their jurisdictions as direct proprietorship, Warring States *daimyo* converted most local warriors into vassals and thus succeeded eventually in forging consolidated proprietary domains. Key to this transformation, Pierre Souyri argues, was a deepening split between landowning village warriors, on the one hand, and more humble peasant smallholders

---

[110] Nagahara, "Medieval Peasant," 338–41; *HJ*, 149, 170–71; Hall, *Japan*, 133–34; Berry, *Culture of War*, 39, 145–70; Souyri, *World Upside Down*, 192–95, 198–200; David Davis, "*Ikki* in Late Medieval Japan," in Hall and Mass, *Medieval Japan*, 221–47.

[111] On merchant organizations, Hall, *Japan*, 123; Souyri, *World Upside Down*, 195–98, 200–201. On pirate networks, Peter Shapinsky, "Lords of the Sea: Pirates, Violence, and Exchange in Medieval Japan" (Univ. of Michigan, PhD diss., 2005), chs. 3–5.

and tenants, on the other. By buying off village warriors with secure fiefs or stipends and by encouraging, and later requiring, fighters to live in castle towns, *daimyo* deprived the peasantry of their most effective leaders. Thus they neutralized local resistance. Where necessary, co-optation was supplemented by brutal repression of hostile villages, religious leagues, and "free towns."[112] With the countryside thus pacified, *daimyo* readily accepted village self-government – but on the proviso that village corporations maintain order, halt peasant movement, and meet tax demands, whose per capita burden, recorded in cadastral surveys, may have risen substantially in the first half of the 16th century.[113] Such surveys also helped *daimyo* recruit corvées for fort construction, camp duty, supply, and transport. Likewise, artisan and trade guilds were replaced by organizations of "official merchants" serving *daimyo* armies and courts, while independent Buddhist and Shinto sects fell under the surveillance of *daimyo* magistrates. To systematize control over their domains, many *daimyo* issued legal codes or "house laws." Whereas *shugo* had derived authority from the *shogun*, these codes portrayed each territory as an organic entity (*kokka*) to be ruled by the *daimyo* in the name of public welfare and authority (*kogi*).[114]

Daimyo retainers led armies of peasant footsoldiers who stood midway between common cultivators and professional warriors and whose ranks swelled with intensifying warfare. In lieu of relatively uncoordinated fights in which mounted archers enjoyed pride of place, in the late 1400s and more especially during the 16th century, battles became well organized contests between massed units of pike- and bow-wielding infantry trained for coordinated maneuver. Whereas in the late 1100s an

[112] Souyri, *World Upside Down*, 185–201, 214–16. Recent research confirms that settlement of *samurai* in castle downs after 1591 was anticipated on a more modest scale from the mid-1500s. See, besides Souryi, Totman, *Early Modern Japan*, 63; Philip Brown, *Central Authority and Local Autonomy in the Formation of Early Modern Japan* (Stanford, 1993), 20.

[113] Souyri, *World Upside Down*, 212; Nagahara Keiji, "The Sengoku Daimyo and the Kandaka System," in Hall et al., *Japan Before Tokugawa*, 27–63, esp. 36–43; *HJ*, 201, and Farris, *Medieval Population*, 236 all suggest real tax burdens increased 1500–1550. But Brown, pers. commun., May 10, 2004 is more skeptical. See too Mary Elizabeth Berry, *Hideyoshi* (Cambridge, MA, 1982), 32.

[114] On *daimyo* evolution, Miyagawa, "*Shoen* to *Chigyo*"; Hall, "Muromachi Bakufu," 225–30; Nagahara, "Decline of *Shoen*," 289–300; idem, "Medieval Peasant," esp. 341–43; Souyri, *World Upside Down*, ch. 12; Hall et al., *Japan Before Tokugawa*, esp. Introduction and chs. 1–4; John W. Hall, "The Castle Town and Japan's Modern Urbanization," in Hall, *Studies in Institutional History*, 169–88; Ikegami, *Taming Samurai*, 135–48.

army of 10,000 was considered large, by the early 1500s armies reached 30,000 to 60,000, and by the late 16th century 250,000 to 280,000.[115] In the 1500s for the first time, capture or control of territory, rather than destruction of enemy forces, became the chief objective. And as in Europe (albeit in Japan until 1543 without the spur of firearms), victory went to those best able to amass troops, extract revenues, and organize administrative support.[116]

Thus a new class of magnates channeled local resources into the single-minded pursuit of military power. It is no accident that by far the most sustained era of warfare in Japanese history, in particular the second half of the 16th century, also was the era of most rapid, far-reaching administrative experiment. *Daimyo*, of whom some 250 remained as late as 1550, formed ever larger regional leagues, and it was from these grueling contests involving some of the largest armies in the 16th-century world that the unifiers of Japan finally emerged. Building on one another's work, Oda Nobunaga (1534–1582), Toyotomi Hideyoshi (1536–1598), and Tokugawa Ieyasu (1542–1616) each sought first to solidify his regional position, then to seize Kyoto with its aura of imperial legitimacy, and finally to extend his authority over distant coalitions. Notwithstanding new concepts of *daimyo* authority, neither the ideal of a unified state nor the ultimate locus of sovereignty in the emperor had ever been displaced.[117] In this sense, charter legacies inspired post-14th-century reunification more directly than in Indic Southeast Asia, where the heritage of Pagan and Angkor lacked dynastic focus, or in Russia, where Tatar political influences modified those of Kiev.

---

[115] Japanese trends thus anticipated those in France. See Ch. 3, n. 141 *supra*. On the growing size of *daimyo* armies, Paul Varley, "Warfare in Japan, 1467–1600," in Jeremy Black, ed., *War in the Early Modern World* (London, 1999), 53–85, esp. 57, 70, 76; Hall, *Government and Local Power*, 283; Mary Elizabeth Berry, "Public Peace and Private Attachment," *JJS* 12 (1986): 237–71, esp. 242; idem, *Hideyoshi*, 94; idem, *Japan in Print* (Berkeley, 2006), 33; Farris, *Medieval Population*, 191.

[116] Conlan, *State of War*, 69–77, 229 contrasts relatively conservative military tactics and organization to 1477 with accelerated change thereafter (even before the post-1543 dissemination of guns), but also points to gradual military rationalization after 1350. Friday, *Samurai, Warfare, and the State*, 102–34, 166–68 also acknowledges a) the primacy of "horse and bow" warfare 900–1400, b) expanding army size and associated changes in recruitment, tactics, and weapons before 1400, c) rapidly accelerating change after 1477. Varley, "Warfare in Japan," refers to the growing role of footsoldiers even in the 14th century. On firearms, *infra*.

[117] Butler, *Emperor and Aristocracy*, esp. chs. 1–5, plus *CHJ*, vol. III, 226; *CHJ*, vol. IV, 40.

But more basically, Japanese reunification drew on intense contemporary anxieties. As the rapid and complete destruction of some of the most eminent *daimyo* houses showed, no one any longer could feel safe from attacks by other *daimyo*, family rivals, opportunistic vassals, even commoners. To escape such shared terrors, Hideyoshi and more especially Ieyasu offered fellow *daimyo* a federalist compromise that gradually won support: in return for accepting subordination within a unified hierarchy, each would receive promises of autonomy, support against hostile subjects, and nonaggression guarantees from his peers. Individual ambition would yield to collective security. We have met comparable state-strengthening accommodations – for example, at the end of Muscovy's 15th-century civil wars or in early Restored Toungoo Burma.[118] With Hideyoshi's triumph in the Kanto and the north in 1590, followed by Ieyasu's victory over a western coalition in 1600 and his founding in 1603 of the third and final shogunate, that of the Tokugawa, a new territorial and political system began to cohere.[119]

[118] Analogies also come to mind with France at the end of the Hundred Years War. Cf. Berry, *Japan in Print*, 82–83; Ch. 2, nn. 193, 243, 246, 288–90 *supra*; Victor Lieberman, *Burmese Administrative Cycles, 1580–1760* (Princeton, 1984), chs. 1, 2.

[119] That is to say, the third shogunate after Kamakura and Ashikaga. See Berry, *Hideyoshi*; Hall, *Japan*, 142–65; Asao Naohiro, "The Sixteenth-Century Unification," in *CHJ*, vol. IV, 40–95; Totman, *Early Modern Japan*, 39–58; idem, *Tokugawa Ieyasu: Shogun* (San Francisco, 1983), pt. 1; Hall, *Government and Local Power*, 238–95. The new *daimyo* territories are routinely termed "feudal" insofar as they, like medieval European polities, embodied the devolution of public authority to private lords, the social dominance of mounted warriors, and a military system in which each overlord, in return for military service, provided vassals with carefully graded land rights or income. As the Carolingian collapse promoted a warrior class whose power rested on local strongpoints and agrarian control, Kamakura and Ashikaga disorders nurtured *kokujin* and *daimyo*. And as feudal competition and economic growth culminated in Capetian consolidation, in Japan similar forces paved the way to the Tokugawa. See *supra* n. 3. Of course, it is easy to find structural differences between these two "feudalisms": Capetian France had weaker social segmentation than Tokugawa Japan, no sacrosanct emperor, and no systematic removal of warriors from the countryside. Japanese vassalage precluded multiple overlordships, accorded a lesser role to oral and written contract, and relied more heavily on kinship terminology. Japan lacked a European-style manorial economy, Japanese villages were more administratively self-sufficient, the Tokugawa system proved more stable than the Capetian, and so forth. But the most obvious difference is chronological. Because Tokugawa unification occurred 400 years after Capetian unification and benefited from many of the same global economic and technological currents as transformed early modern Europe, I have already suggested that Tokugawa Japan is most profitably compared not to Capetian, but to Bourbon France. See the distinction between "comparative" and "connective" histories at *SP*, 14, and discussion *infra*.

Explaining and Correlating Japanese Reunification, c. 1450–1600

Japan's reunification raises several questions for the comparativist: Why, after centuries of divergent rhythms in Japan, Europe, and mainland Southeast Asia, did economic activity and population growth in all these areas accelerate markedly from 1450 to 1600? If economic growth helped to destabilize the Ashikaga, why did subsequent growth promote reintegration? What exactly was the relation between *daimyo* power and economic change? And why did disorder yield to reunification at roughly the same time in Japan as in Burma under the Toungoo dynasties (1558, 1613), Siam under Late Ayudhya kings (1569–1605), France under Henry IV (r. 1589–1610), and Russia under the Romanovs?

As usual, complex synergies make it difficult to assign priority among a host of factors. I shall first treat the most palpable candidates for growing Eurasian coordination – disease, climate, maritime trade, firearms – before considering specifically Japanese factors whose relation to other Eurasian rimlands was less obvious. Finally, I shall consider how economic changes in Japan between c. 1280 and 1600 influenced both political fragmentation and reintegration.

After c. 1280 less frequent epidemics and references to smallpox as a malady chiefly of children suggest that in the most densely settled parts of Honshu, the long-term conversion of that dreaded minister of adult death into a sometimes nonlethal affliction of children was well underway. Particularly from c. 1370 to 1450 an abatement in both epidemics and warfare has led Farris to identify a "Muromachi Optimum" as the true start of Japan's medieval growth cycle.[120] From 1452 to 1537 fresh smallpox flare-ups not only were relatively short lived, but tended to kill mainly children, perhaps helping to explain a 16th-century Jesuit observation that nearly all adult Japanese bore pockmarks from the virus. This transition probably drew strength from antecedent population growth sufficient to sustain local chains of infection, from expanding internal trade and travel, as well as from more regular continental contacts. Although, as noted, domestication of smallpox (and perhaps measles, on which we have less information) apparently started earlier in Southeast Asia and northern Europe than in Japan, the acceleration of that process in remote sectors of all three regions may have contributed to loosely coordinated demographic vitality between c. 1200

[120] Farris, *Medieval Population*, 6, 101, 110, 127, 146.

and 1600.[121] More certainly, Japan's smallpox acclimatization coincided substantially with Europe's economically pregnant post-1450 adjustment to the Black Death.[122]

On present evidence, improved climate also aided Japanese agrarian expansion and thus helped promote a novel synchronization with Southeast Asian and European economies. Latest research holds that the climate remained cold and wet to c. 1370 or 1400, but then warmed to c. 1500 save for a severe mid-1400s downturn. In the 16th century some scholars claim that cold, wet weather resumed, but the conventional interpretation sees the 16th century gradually becoming much warmer, except for another brief mid-century trough.[123] This had the potential to raise yields on established fields and again to permit cultivation of more marginal lands, particularly in northern Honshu.[124] Recall that the period c. 1450–1630 also was favorable to agriculture in northern Europe and mainland Southeast Asia, in the first region by extending the

---

[121] Ibid., 100–102, 171–72 (with Jesuit observation). Also Jannetta, *Epidemics*, 67–70, 188–98; idem, "Diseases of the Early Modern Period in Japan," in Kiple, *Cambridge World History of Disease*, 385–86; Batten, *Ends of Japan*, 254, 257–58. Cf. *SP*, 50, 97–98, 224, 251–52, 295. Perhaps because the measles virus is more fragile and requires larger host populations than smallpox to become endemic, in both Japan and Southeast Asia the former probably remained an epidemic threat longer. See Farris, *Medieval Population*, 100, and Ch. 1, n. 95 *supra*.

[122] Although some believe that the Black Death ravaged 14th-century North China, Japan almost certainly escaped. Jannetta, *Epidemics*, 191–96; Alan Macfarlane, *The Savage Wars of Peace* (Oxford, 1997), ch. 10 *passim*, esp. 183–90, 381. Influenza struck Japan periodically, and from 1512 syphilis (the "Chinese pox") ravaged a surprisingly large percentage. Yet it is thought that neither of these latter maladies had more than a short-term impact on fertility or mortality. Farris, *Medieval Population*, 171–74.

[123] I benefited from Farris, pers. commun., Aug. 11, 2006, and his judicious discussion in *Medieval Population*, 102–17, 174–90. Ibid., 177–78 tends to favor the cold, wet view of 16th-century weather, but the following sources argue for warming: Minoru Tanaka and Masatoshi Yoshino, "Re-Examination of the Climatic Changes in Central Japan Based on Freezing Dates of Lake Suwa," *Weather* 37 (1982): 252–59, suggesting a rise of 0.6 °C from 1470 to 1580; Takeo Yamamoto, "On the Climatic Change in XV and XVI Centuries in Japan," *Geophysical Magazine* 35 (1971): 187–206, claiming an average rise of 2.4 (sic) °C; Takeshi Kawamura, "Estimation of Climate in the Little Ice Age Using Phenological Data in Japan," in Takehiko Mikami, ed., *Proceedings of the International Symposium on the Little Ice Age Climate* (Tokyo, 1992), 54; Fukusawa, "High-Resolution Reconstruction," esp. 87, 88; Maejima and Tagami, "Climate Change," esp. 163; and Arakawa in n. 15 *supra*. Cf. discussion of mid-15th-century difficulties at William Atwell, "Volcanism and Short-Term Climatic Change in East Asian and World History, c. 1200–1699," *JWH* 12 (2001), 54–55; idem, "Time, Money, and Weather," *JAS* 61 (2002): 83–113.

[124] A decline of 2–3 °C or more is not unusual for the *yamase* effect, which, by bringing cool air from the Sea of Okhotsk in the summer, can depress rice yields in northern Honshu by 30–50 percent. Totman, *Early Modern Japan*, 6.

growing season, in the latter by strengthening monsoons.[125] Lest we exaggerate climate's coordinating impact, however, consider: a) Much of the Japanese record remains disputed. b) Despite generally poor weather, the era c. 1280–1370 also saw agricultural advances in Japan. c) Stimuli across Eurasia largely independent of climate became more potent between 1300 and 1600.

Maritime trade was a pregnant source of such stimuli. From the 13th through the 15th centuries Korean and Chinese trade expanded, with Japan exchanging gold, sulfur, and swords for silk, cotton, porcelain, books, and – critical to Japanese monetization – Chinese bronze coins.[126] The Ashikaga *shogun's* acceptance of Ming vassalage in 1402–1403, a concession needed to pursue tributary trade, in fact set the stage for a disorderly competition among Ashikaga vassals to access continental goods. In periods of central debility, such rivalries favored the opening of new ports and an end to close commercial regulation such as had characterized the Heian period and would resume under the Tokugawa.[127] For its part the Ming economy, whose domestic silver output and production of bronze coins fell even as its need for monetary instruments to lubricate trade and tax payments mushroomed, developed from the late 15th century a nearly insatiable appetite for Japanese silver.[128] Responding to this demand, the introduction by 1533 of Chinese/Korean silver smelting and refining techniques known as *haifuki* suddenly transformed Japan into one of the world's great silver producers.[129] From the early 1500s domestic silver – whose production

---

[125] See *SP*, 49, 101–12, 142–43, 156–57, 224–26, 239–40, 363–64, 370–71, 438–39, 459–60; Ch. 2 *supra*.

[126] Large quantities of Chinese bronze coins entered Japan from the mid-1100s to the early 1500s. On bullion flows and trade fluctuations 1200–1600, Shapinsky, "Lords of the Sea," ch. 4; Souyri, *World Upside Down*, 146–53; Batten, *Gateway*, 137–40; Kozo Yamamura, "The Growth of Commerce in Medieval Japan," in *CHJ*, vol. III, 358–60; Robert Innes, "The Door Ajar: Japan's Foreign Trade in the 17th Century" (Univ. of Michigan, PhD diss., 1980), 21–76, 619–23; Kozo Yamamura and Tetsuo Kamiki, "Silver Mines and Sung Coins," in John Richards, ed., *Precious Metals in the Late Medieval and Early Modern Worlds* (Durham, NC, 1983), 329–62; Richard von Glahn, *Fountain of Fortune* (Berkeley, 1996), 53–54, 83–84, 88–97.

[127] Kawazoe Shoji, "Japan and East Asia," in *CHJ*, vol. III, 432–40, discussing Ashikaga motives; Batten, *Ends of Japan*, 171–72, 189–205; Verschuer, "Looking from Within," 538–40.

[128] Atwell, "Time, Money, and Weather," 84–103; Lee, "Trade and Economy," 15–16; Ch. 3, nn. 185–87 *supra*.

[129] The new *haifuki* cupellation process also aided gold extraction. Innes, "Door Ajar," 23–41; Nagahara Keiji and Kozo Yamamura, "Shaping the Process of Unification," *JJS* 14 (1988): 77–109; von Glahn, *Fountain of Fortune*, 88–97, 128–33.

hinged on high Chinese prices as well as on continental technology – supplemented Chinese coins in local markets while permitting a major expansion of imported continental goods. Nor were Chinese economic influences limited to currency: in the 16th century Chinese floss supplied Japan's silk industry; the abacus revolutionized practical mathematics, with numerous engineering and construction applications; while other Chinese technologies aided shipbuilding and ceramics.[130] Maritime revenues enriched not only Kyushu *daimyo*, but those who controlled Kyoto and Sakai, the chief termini for continental trade.[131] Between the late Heian period and the Meiji restoration, arguably no period saw more intense interest in overseas trade and foreign contacts than the 16th century.

Japan's maritime-assisted prosperity thus intersected with that of Southeast Asia and Europe in three ways. First, during much of the 15th and 16th centuries China's burgeoning population provided a commercial pump for all of East Asia, sucking in not only silver from Japan but spices, minerals, and marine and forest exotica from Southeast Asia, while exporting to those same areas streams of bronze cash, silk, and porcelain, along with new production techniques. Given the early Ming ban on private trade, such exchanges at first depended on official missions, Ryukyuan intermediaries, and smuggling by Chinese and Japanese merchants-cum-pirates. But after the Ming in 1567 allowed trade with countries other than Japan, South Chinese and Japanese merchants resorted increasingly to third-country ports in Ayudhya, Cambodia, Malaya, Vietnam, and the Philippines.[132] If exchange of Chinese silk for Japanese silver was the chief draw, significant quantities of Southeast Asian forest and agricultural products as well as Southeast Asian imitations of Chinese goods also entered Japan. Chinese nautical, metallurgical, ceramic, and textile technologies aided Southeast Asia as well as Japan,[133] while China served as a conduit for the introduction

---

[130] Previous note, plus Farris, *Medieval Population*, 259.

[131] Innes, "Door Ajar," 12–13, 623–24; Wakita Osamu, "The Commercial and Urban Policies of Oda Nobunaga and Toyotomi Hideyoshi," in Hall et al., *Japan Before Tokugawa*, 226; Dennis Flynn, "Comparing the Tokugawa Shogunate with Hapsburg Spain," in James Tracy, ed., *The Political Economy of Merchant Empires* (Cambridge, 1991), 350; James McClain and Wakita Osamu, eds., *Osaka* (Ithaca, 1999), chs. 1, 2; Souyri, *World Upside Down*, 148. On the evolving relation between pirate bands and *daimyo* lords, Shapinsky, "Lords of the Sea," ch. 8.

[132] See *SP*, 254–56, 270, 365, 383–84 and discussion in Ch. 7 *infra*.

[133] Innes, "Door Ajar," 30–41, 51–66. On 15th- to 18th-century Japan-Ryukyu-Southeast Asian trade, Yonei Ishii, ed., *The Junk Trade from Southeast Asia* (Singapore, 1998);

from Southeast Asia to Japan of highly productive Champa rice (see below). In these ways, China helped to coordinate Southeast Asian and Japanese production.

Second, Japan along with much of Eurasia improved monetary liquidity, hence commercial efficiency. As we saw, between c. 1430 and 1460 a reduction in the international supply of precious metals (the result of technical difficulties and mine exhaustion in Europe and China and temporary blockages of key trade routes) created severe coin shortages in one region after another.[134] But thereafter new technologies joined rising bullion prices generated by demographic and commercial expansion in much of Eurasia to stimulate not only Japanese, but New World silver production. In 1557, a mere 24 years after *haifuki* techniques entered Japan, the mercury-amalgam "patio process" was developed in Mexico and, along with other innovations, by the last quarter of the century had increased Spanish American silver output sixfold over the first quarter.[135] Hence Dennis Flynn and Arturo Giraldez' designation of this phase in the global silver market as the Potosi/Japan Cycle.[136] Difficult though it is to quantify silver's contribution to individual regions, clearly the 16th-century flood from Japan and Latin America (supplemented by West African gold) spurred bulk trade, credit, and monetization in Europe, China, Southeast Asia, and Japan alike. Thus, for example, in Lingnan in Southeast China large post-1550 imports of Japanese and New World silver to pay for silk encouraged Pearl River peasants to convert extensive ricelands to mulberry cultivation. To feed those peasants, more peripheral areas commercialized rice, while Lingnan silk fed the triangular trade between China, Japan, and Southeast Asia.[137] What is more, in regions with advanced labor markets, if eventually inflation

idem, "Siam and Japan in Pre-Modern Times," in Denoon, *Multicultural Japan*, 153–59; Thomas Elson, "Japan in the Life of Early Ryukyu," *JJS* 32 (2006): 367–92.

[134] On bullion shortages, Ch. 2, nn. 160, 181; this chapter n. 128 *supra*; *CEHI*, 99, 360.

[135] Ward Barrett, "World Bullion Flows, 1450–1800," in James Tracy, ed., *The Rise of Merchant Empires* (Cambridge, 1990), 238, 242; Dennis Flynn and Arturo Giraldez, "Born with a 'Silver Spoon,'" *JWH* 6 (1995): 201–21, esp. 209; Jurgen Schneider in Wolfram Fischer et al., eds., *The Emergence of a World Economy 1500–1914* (Nurnburg, 1985), 21. New World silver shipments to Asia from 1560 to 1640 were some two-and-a-half times larger than Japanese silver exports to China. Flynn, "Comparing Tokugawa Shogunate," 336; idem, 'Silver Spoon," 202.

[136] Dennis Flynn and Arturo Giraldez, "Cycles of Silver," *JWH* 13 (2002): 391–427, esp. 392. Cf. Ch. 1, n. 120.

[137] See n. 132 *supra*; Ch. 3, n. 187 *supra*, plus Yamamura, "Growth of Commerce," 361; Lee, "Trade and Economy," 16; Kenneth Pomeranz, *The Great Divergence* (Princeton,

proved destabilizing, at first the 16th-century fall in silver's purchasing value encouraged capital accumulation and investment by pushing up commodity prices faster than wages.[138]

Third, wider trade circuits linked Japan to other sectors of Eurasia by facilitating entry of the Portuguese, followed by the Spanish and Dutch. In economic terms, by exchanging Chinese raw silk for Japanese silver, the Portuguese, who landed on an island off Kyushu in 1543 and developed a base at Nagasaki in 1571, anticipated the intermediary role between China and Japan that Southeast Asian ports soon would play. Moreover, from the late 1500s European smelting, excavation, and land survey techniques complemented Chinese technology in transforming Japan's mining and metal-refining industries.[139]

But arguably Europe's chief contribution to pre-1603 Japanese history was military. While Japanese had known of gunpowder weapons since the Mongol invasions, the first effective firearms they saw were Portuguese matchlocks in 1543. Almost at once far-sighted western *daimyo* began not only importing them, but commissioning metalsmiths to produce replicas, a task made easier by Japan's sophisticated sword technology. The Japanese in fact made technical improvements and in 1575, some 20 years before similar techniques appeared in Europe, had three lines of musketeers fire in alternating sequence so as to overcome the matchlock's chief weakness, namely, the length of time needed to reload. Admittedly, this problem, plus the guns' inutility in wet weather, their relative inaccuracy, and Japan's need to import saltpeter, meant that matchlocks never replaced bows and spears. And yet muskets' superior range and penetration and the fact that infantry could master the musket far more easily than the bow ensured, in Paul Varley's words, that "gun units soon became the central features" of *daimyo* armies. After the 1575 battle of Nagashino, where Oda Nobunaga first used alternating salvos with good effect against cavalry, other *daimyo* rushed to increase their supply, deploying up to 3,000 matchlocks on a side, and to improve training and coordination of spearmen and archers, on whom gunners

---

2000), 191–92. On bullionist spurs to Russian and French growth c. 1470–1600, Ch. 2. nn. 226, 295 *supra.*

[138] Cf. David Hackett Fisher, *The Great Wave* (Oxford, 1996), 76–79; Lee, "Trade and Economy," 16; and von Glahn, *Fountain of Fortune*, 213–14, focusing on the 17th century.

[139] Innes, "Door Ajar," 620; Tessa Morris-Suzuki, *The Technological Transformation of Japan* (Cambridge, 1994), 16. Some sources date the Portuguese arrival to 1542. The Spanish arrived in Japan in 1592, the Dutch in 1600.

relied for protection.[140] But the cost of production joined manufacturing challenges to favor the most powerful lords in control of urban markets and technicians, creating a virtuous circle of centralization. So too traditional forts' vulnerability to matchlocks and early cannon may have reinforced a tendency to abandon scattered strongpoints in favor of central citadels.[141] More broadly, firearms, which were generally used not by *samurai* but by footsoldiers, intensified long-standing trends, apparent in much of Eurasia, toward infantry expansion, tactical experiment, weapons specialization, and more lethal conflicts. In Hall's summary view, European firearms "probably hastened by several decades the ultimate unification of the country" – a judgment no less applicable to 16th-century Burma and Siam (where Portuguese mercenaries introduced firearms in the 1520s) and Russia.[142]

The political implications of continued economic growth we shall explore more fully, but already one senses that epidemiological adjustments, climate, expanding maritime exchange, and firearms began to coordinate political developments in Japan and other sectors of Eurasia far more closely after c. 1500 than in previous centuries.

Do internal Japanese dynamics also bear comparison with other Eurasian realms? In Southeast Asia, Russia, and France I argued that

---

[140] On Japanese firearms, fortifications, and military organization 1500–1610, Varley, "Warfare in Japan, " 66–70 (with quoted phrase p. 67); Samuel Hawley, *The Imjin War* (Berkeley, 2005), 4–11, 81–82, 100–103, 114, 138, 157, 266, 309, 578–79 and *passim*, emphasizing muskets' value in late *sengoku* wars and Hideyoshi's 1590s Korean invasions; Geoffrey Parker, *The Military Revolution* (Cambridge, 1988), 140–45, 211–12; Stephen Morillo, "Guns and Gunpowder," *JWH* 6 (1995): 75–106; Souyri, *World Upside Down*, 6; Matthew Stavros, "Military Revolution in Early Modern Japan" (ms, 2005); Shinzaburo Oishi, "The Bakuhan System," in Nakane and Oishi, *Tokugawa Japan*, 17–18; Farris, pers. commun., Aug. 11, 2006; Anne Walthall, pers. commun., 2006.

[141] This is the claim at Hall, *Japan*, 138; idem, "Castle Town," 176–77; supported by Parker, *Military Revolution*, 142–43; by Totman, *Early Modern Japan*, 63; and by accounts of citadel fighting in Korea in the 1590s in Hawley, *Imjin War*, 138, 165, 282, 289, 313, 325, 511. But Brown, pers. commun., May 10, 2004, notes that inability to move artillery overland left many interior castles immune. Varley, "Warfare in Japan," 64, 70 and Lee Butler, pers. commun., Dec., 2006 also suggest that many castles were symbols of grandeur in an age when fighting had largely ceased. William Coaldrake, *Architecture and Authority in Japan* (London, 1996), 104–37, esp. 125, accepts that firearms influenced castle construction to 1639, but denies that artillery ever posed a major threat.

[142] Hall, *Japan*, 138. Likewise Hawley, *Imjin War*, 9 claims, "The introduction of the musket . . . gave a significant advantage to those daimyo who embraced it, doomed their less foresighted rivals, and ultimately hastened the advent of national unification." See also *HJ*, 202; and Stavros, "Military Revolution"; Farris, *Medieval Population*, 191–92, 198. On firearms in Burma and Siam, *SP*, 152–53, 256–58, 270. On Russia, Ch. 2 *supra*.

between 1350 and 1600 state actions intentionally and unintentionally encouraged some forms of economic activity. In medieval France and postcharter Burma, Siam, and Vietnam, I also suggested that individual peasant tenures proved more productive than servile or communal labor.[143] In Japan as well between 1350 and 1600, we find evidence for both types of economic incentive – that is, beneficial political interventions and new forms of peasant organization.

On the one hand, unrestrained warfare led *daimyo* to promote growth more consistently than their *shugo* predecessors. Now I acknowledge that during the north–south wars of 1331 to 1363, and more particularly during the 1467 to 1603 interregnum, large-scale military operations inflicted major damage by ruining crops and infrastructure, spreading disease, and inhibiting population growth. A focus on *daimyo* depredations has come to supplement an earlier focus on *daimyo* as agents of economic expansion.[144] Yet it is also clear that in some contexts *daimyo* succeeded in raising output, both because self-interest required expanding the tax base, and because as consolidation progressed, ever larger areas fell under *daimyo* protection – anticipating the spur to productivity that countrywide pacification would produce after 1603. Compared to unwieldy *shugo* domains whose lords lived in Kyoto, compact *daimyo* jurisdictions were better able to mobilize resources. If local peasants and merchants supplied the know-how, tools, and labor, it was *daimyo*, especially from the mid-1500s, who often coordinated reclamation and water control efforts, accelerating the historic shift from small tributary valleys to the more productive sedimentary basins of Japan's largest rivers. Likewise, because commerce provided a major source of revenue and because urban producers supplied guns, uniforms, and other military goods, 16th-century *daimyo* sought to expand overseas trade, to improve domestic transport, reduce tolls, open mines, stabilize coinage, and standardize measurement. At the same time their relocation of vassals, merchants, artisans, and support personnel to castle towns dramatically boosted urban market demand, while cash taxes, probably inadvertently, stimulated rural commodification.[145]

---

[143] *SP*, 141–49, 248–58, 298, 383–93; and Ch. 2 *supra*.

[144] On the economic costs of warfare in the 14th century and 1467–1603, Farris, *Medieval Population*, 117–27, 190–220, 223; idem, pers. commun., Aug. 11, 2006.

[145] The latter stimulus was particularly important in eastern Honshu. On *daimyo* economic policies and impacts, Farris, *Medieval Population*, 163, 210–12, 222–30, 235–42; Hall et al., *Japan Before Tokugawa*, 46, 52–57, 125–48, 224–47, 327–71 (with agrarian project figures on 329–30); Matao Miyamoto, "Quantitative Aspects of the Tokugawa Economy," in Akira Hayami, Osamu Saito, and Ronald Toby, eds., *The Economic*

On the other hand – here the argument is more conjectural – at the level of individual cultivators, novel landholding arrangements also may have enhanced productivity. Well into the 17th century a substantial, if indeterminate, part of the population still labored in conditions of marked dependency, whether as slaves, serfs, or indentured freemen, with limited opportunities to raise their own families or expand output.[146] However, starting in the 13th or 14th century in the Kinai and continuing in outlying areas into the Tokugawa era, peasant members of corporate villages escaped subjection to landowners and patriarchal heads. Why the change? In part, because increasing man-to-land ratios and market opportunities required more motivated labor that only a smallholder regime could ensure. In part, because withdrawal of warriors to castle towns weakened external control of village labor. In part perhaps, because *daimyo* sensed that smallholders were more fiscally valuable than bonded labor. Kozo Yamamura speculates that by helping to convert bound cultivators into smallholders and tenants with more or less secure land rights, *daimyo* cadastral surveys c. 1500–1650 convinced many cultivators that they could keep the gains from reclamation and intensification. Thus they found reason to maximize family labor and bring more land under the hoe.[147] Philip Brown doubts that cadastres strengthened ownership rights, which he believes were stable over the long term. In his view, new tax systems, relying on village self-governance, shielded rural conditions from close urban scrutiny, cut administrative costs, and minimized disruptive interactions between tax collectors and villagers. The actual burden on the peasantry therefore declined, and it was this organizational change, rather than novel landholding rights, that nurtured peasant incentives.[148] In a larger sense, however, Yamamura and Brown concur

History of Japan: 1600–1990, vol. 1 (Oxford, 2004), 40, Table 1.2; Nagahara and Yamamura, "Shaping the Process," 77–109; *CHJ*, vol. III, 391–93; Hall, *Government and Local Power*, 276–77; Souyri, *World Upside Down*, 212–13.

[146] See discussion at Farris, *Medieval Population*, 10, 47–49, 79–90, 159, 256–57; Souyri, *World Upside Down*, 84–91, 129; Yamamura, "Returns on Unification," 339–41; Nagahara, "Sengoku Daimyo and Kandaka," 33–34.

[147] Yamamura, "Returns on Unification," 339–57, supported in varying degrees by Souyri, *World Upside Down*, 84–91, 102, 119–20, 128–35, 161, 185; Harold Bolitho, "The *Han*," in *CHJ*, vol. IV, 189–90; Akira Hayami and Hiroshi Kito, "Demography and Living Standards," in Hayami et al., *Economic History*, 218–20.

[148] Philip; Brown, "Practical Constraints on Early Tokugawa Land Taxation," *JSS* 14 (1988): 369–401, focusing on Kaga domain and denying that *daimyo* income rose substantially in the late 1500s; idem, *Central Authority*, 58–112, 147–67, 178–240 *passim*; idem, pers. commun., May 10, 2004.

that *daimyo* initiatives at the village level, intentionally or not, extended cultivation and enhanced productivity.

In itself, moreover, the spread among the peasantry of corporate villages (*so*) and stem families (*ie*) may have favored economic expansion. Starting again in the Kinai in the late 1200s and spreading slowly to western and then eastern Japan, corporate villages benefited from antecedent population increases and sedentarization of mobile cultivators. But in turn such villages probably encouraged population growth by protecting against warrior and bandit abuse, managing forests and irrigation in the interests of the community, and encouraging child nurturance.[149] Similar putative benefits derived from peasant stem families, which starting in the Kinai after c. 1450 became basic to village organization. Because such families, adapting *samurai* norms, emphasized stable patrilocal residence, female subordination to lineage priorities, children as guarantors of lineage continuity, and unigeniturial inheritance, Farris suggests that they too reduced child mortality, while promoting family accumulation of property and economic planning.[150]

In combination, then, disease immunities, better climate, maritime influences, *daimyo* initiatives, and new social forms raised population and output between c. 1280 and 1600. But what is the evidence for such growth? Latest estimates, summarized in Figure 4.2, put the Japanese population in 1280 at 5,700,000 to 6,200,000, in 1450 at 9,600,000 to 10,500,000, and in 1600 at 15,000,000 to 17,000,000. This post-1280 upsurge, I emphasized, ended centuries of stasis.[151] By one count, three-quarters of all present-day Japanese villages appeared in Ashikaga

---

[149] I follow Farris, *Medieval Population*. See too n. 109 *supra*.

[150] Farris, *Medieval Population*, 87, 153–60, 252–57, 260. On early *samurai ie*, Ikegami, *Taming Samurai*, 70–72, 96, 123–27. On the changing family role of women c. 1200–1600, see Tonomura and Walthall, "Introduction," and essays by Wakita Haruko, Tabata Yasuko, Kato Mieko, and Hitomi Tonomura in Tonomura et al., *Women and Class*, 1–16, 81–152.

[151] Farris, *Medieval Population*, 262 and 26, 91, 95–100, 164–71, excluding Hokkaido and Ryukyu. My Fig. 4.2 averages Farris' estimates for each date. Cf. Akira Hayami's 1600 estimate of only 12,000,000, which is set forth in his *The Historical Demography of Pre-Modern Japan* (Tokyo, 1997), 41–46; Hayami and Kito, "Demography and Living Standards," 215–22. Hayami's figure is accepted by Matao Miyamato, "Quantitative Aspects of Tokugawa Economy," in Hayami et al., *Economic History*, 36–48; Nakai Nobuhiko, "Commercial Change and Urban Growth in Early Modern Japan," in *CHJ*, vol. IV, 539, and *HJ*, 232; but is critiqued in Farris, *Medieval Population*, 165–72, 231–34 and also has come under recent criticism in Japan (Farris, pers. commun., Aug. 11, 2006). Recall my suggestion that population growth to some degree both facilitated and reflected epidemiological adjustment. Cf. n. 121 *supra*.

Date	Arable (in pre-1600 *cho*)
1150	956,000
1280	977,000
1450	1,241,379
1600	1,588,462
1721	2,251,539

Source: William Wayne Farris, *Japan's Medieval Population* (Honolulu, 2006), p. 263, Table E.2, which substantially agrees with Charlotte von Verschuer, *Le Riz dans la Culture de Heian, Mythe et Realite* (Paris, 2003), 99. On early land units (the *cho* now equals 0.99 hectares), Farris, *Medieval Population*, 231–32. Cf. John W. Hall, Nagahara Keiji, and Kozo Yamamura, eds., *Japan Before Tokugawa* (Princeton, 1981), 334 on changing rice acreage 930–1874; and Matao Miyamoto, "Quantitative Aspects of Tokugawa Economy," in Akira Hayami, Osamu Saito, and Ronald Toby, eds., *The Economic History of Japan: 1600–1990*, vol. 1 (Oxford, 2004), 38, Table 1.1 on post-1600 total arable.

Figure 4.3. Estimates of Japan's total arable.

times.[152] At the same time, as Figure 4.3 shows, total arable rose, albeit less dramatically than, and not always synchronized with, population. A major part of this expansion involved rice land in alluvial plains: whereas previous efforts, recall, focused on tributary valleys, from 1467 to 1651 at least 49 reclamation projects concentrated on more expansive and fertile sedimentary basins.[153] If the degree to which rice yields themselves improved between 1280 and 1600 is uncertain – estimates range all the way from 12 to 200 percent – progress exceeded glacial changes characteristic of the period 700 to 1280.[154] Accordingly, rice assumed a larger role in the overall economy. In Totman's formulation,

---

[152] Troost, "Peasants, Elites," 93, citing Amino Yoshihiko.

[153] Yamamura, "Returns on Unification," 329–34.

[154] See Farris, *Medieval Population*, 230–35, 260, 263, discussing difficulties of computation and offering 1280–1600 estimates ranging from 12 percent (p. 263, Table E.3, column 3) to 45 percent (same Table, column 2, averaging 1600 figures); and Reischauer and Craig, *Japan*, 62–63, claiming "a doubling or tripling of production per acre in parts of the country" in the 14th–16th centuries, although not solely in rice.

the late 13th and 14th centuries inaugurated a transition from the "age of dispersed agriculturalists" to the "age of intensive agriculture."[155]

In fact, many advanced techniques had been known in the Heian period, but only from the late 1200s did labor become sufficiently plentiful, and good land sufficiently scarce, to accelerate diffusion of best practices. Thus especially from the mid-1300s farmers converted extensive dry fields to paddy; evened out low-lying fields with drought-prone elevated lands; and used labor-intensive water control techniques – dikes, sluice-channels, waterwheels, saucer ponds – to grow two crops a year in alluvial basins. By the 1500s some 20 to 30 percent of paddy in central and western Japan was double-cropped.[156] More specialized rice also appeared, the most celebrated being the aforementioned high yield, early ripening, drought-, flood-, and insect-resistant Champa strain from Vietnam that arrived via China and after 1400 became critical to lowland reclamation. In addition, fertilizers (green manure, ashes, excrement) were used more widely, draft animals became more common, and improved smelting and market linkages made iron plows, hoes, and other implements more widely available. With Korean cotton imports no longer sufficient, by 1480 – a century after cotton cultivation became common in Burma – that crop was being grown in the Kinai, and by 1580 in the Kanto.[157]

In turn, larger surpluses and denser population joined foreign stimuli, better transport, and *daimyo* policies to quicken specialization and urban growth.[158] Rising cereal production permitted an increase in the ranks of non-cereal producers: miners, traders, craftsmen, petty manufacturers, and urban laborers. Technical innovations, many as noted from the continent, transformed engineering, metallurgy, ceramics,

---

[155] *HJ* headings for pts. II and III, in substantial agreement with Troost, "Peasants, Elites," 83–95; Farris, *Medieval Population*, chs. 3–6; Tonomura, *Community and Commerce*, 7.

[156] Troost, "Peasants, Elites," 94. Dry lands were also double-cropped. Discussion of agrarian intensification follows ibid., 92–96; Tonomura, *Community and Commerce*, 7; Farris, *Medieval Population*, 129–36, 222–30, 242–43; Farris, pers. commun., Aug. 11, 2006; *CHJ*, vol. III, 313, 330, 355, 376–77; Verschuer, *Le Riz*, 96–106.

[157] Tea and oil-producing plants further diversified the crop profile. Satoru Nakamura, "The Development of Rural Industry," in Nakane and Oishi, *Tokugawa Japan*, 82–83; Farris, *Medieval Population*, 160; Susan Hanley, "Tokugawa Society," in *CHJ*, vol. IV, 689–93; Hayami and Kito, "Demography," 244; Walthall, pers. commun., 2006. On Burmese cotton, *SP*, 144–45, 170–76.

[158] Discussion of trade and manufacture relies on Tonomura, *Community and Commerce*, chs. 4, 5; Yamamura, "Growth of Commerce," esp. 351–95; *HJ*, 152–58; Wakita Haruko, "Dimensions of Development," in Hall et al., *Japan Before Tokugawa*, 295–326; Souyri, *World Upside Down*, 153–56; Farris, *Medieval Population*, 142–53, 235–46.

construction, and textiles. Whereas *ritsuryo* goods usually were denominated in rice or cloth, by the 1500s goods were commonly valued in coin. Credit, money lending, and commutation of service and in-kind taxes grew apace,[159] as did market variety. From c. 1250 to 1500 lists of urban commodities expanded sixfold, and wealthy peasants upgraded their housing, utensils, clothing, and diet.[160] Population growth aided markets, but the reverse also was true: commercial food distribution alleviated the worst effects of famine[161] and, along with industrial crops, provided novel sources of peasant income. Although the Kinai was still Japan's commercial hub, rural and urban markets proliferated most rapidly in less developed regions like eastern Honshu.[162] If in 1450 inhabitants of towns with at least 5,000 people totaled just under 4 percent of the population, by 1600 Farris puts them at 5 percent, that is to say, 750,000 to 850,000. Tardy through it may have been by French standards, Japanese urbanization was approaching Gilbert Rozman's penultimate early modern stage, Stage F ("intermediate marketing").[163]

[159] *HJ*, 153; Farris, *Medieval Population*, 146–47; Sasaki Gin'ya, "Sengoku Daimyo Rule and Commerce," in Hall et al., *Japan Before Tokugawa*, 133–37; *CHJ*, vol. III, 367–68; Suzanne Gay, *The Moneylenders of Late Medieval Kyoto* (Honolulu, 2001), 47–55, 220–21.

[160] According to household inventories and archeology. On consumer goods, including growing use of cotton for clothing and bedding, Tonomura, "Re-envisioning Women," 158, with sixfold figure; Lee Butler, "'Washing Off the Dust'," *MN* 60 (2005): 1–41, esp. 35; Amino Yoshihiko, "Some Problems Concerning the History of Popular Life in Medieval Japan," *Acta Asiatica* 44 (1988): 84–88; Farris, *Medieval Population*, 143–44, 257–61.

[161] Cf. Farris, *Medieval Population*, 111, 181–82; and David Henley, "Population and the Means of Subsistence," *JSEAS* 36 (2005): 337–72, arguing that escape from subsistence-based demographic stagnation in colonial Southeast Asia relied chiefly on market expansion. On rising living standards among wealthy peasants, see the previous note.

[162] The prosperity of the Kanto and the east c. 1450–1600 recalls an earlier expansion c. 930–1150, but contrasts with demographic collapse in at least some parts of that region c. 1150–1300 that probably owed something to colder climate. See nn. 65, 124 *supra*; Farris, *Medieval Population*, 22–25 (on 1150–1300) and 236 (on 1450–1600); and Kozo Yamamura, "From Coins to Rice," *JJS* 14 (1988): 341–67, esp. 353–57.

[163] Characterized by a national administrative center, elevated regional centers, and at least three subordinate marketing levels. Gilbert Rozman, *Urban Networks in Russia, 1750–1800, and Premodern Periodization* (Princeton, 1976), 30–35, 73–87. French–Japanese urban comparisons are complicated by the fact that French towns are commonly defined in the literature as places with at least 2,000 people, whereas Japanese towns, as just noted, had 5,000 people. On urban sizes and functions, Farris, *Medieval Population*, 151–53, 245–46 (with cited figures and percentages); *HJ*, 154–58; Souyri, *World Upside Down*, 99 ("The urbanization of Japan began, hesitantly, only in the fifteenth century."). Again, the claim in Berry, *Japan in Print*, 27 that in 1590 Japanese cities held only 3 percent may reflect a higher definitional threshold than Farris employed.

With Heian-centered political systems in decay, rising output invigorated a variety of decidedly local actors, including corporate villages, religious leagues, and merchant-led political groupings. But above all, as feedback loops between economic growth and *daimyo* policy suggest, expansion translated into larger *daimyo* resources. Reflecting the new strategic emphasis on footsoldiers as well as population increase, late-16th-century armies, recall, could be 25 times larger than their early Kamakura counterparts.[164] By pre-1450 standards, *daimyo* also obtained a large portion of their income from export revenues, merchant and transport taxes, and monetized land taxes. Much as in Europe and Southeast Asia, cash, which was easier to manage than in-kind tribute, became critical to obtain provisions, support retainers, patronize shrines, and employ labor on irrigation, mining, and construction projects. One system of land registration, *kandaka*, sought to calculate all land taxes and warrior services in uniform cash equivalents. If ultimately this system foundered – because the economy remained inadequately monetized – it nonetheless helped some of the greatest 16th-century *daimyo* to penetrate village resources.[165]

Of itself, the geographically uneven nature of commerce offered yet another spur to political integration. Notwithstanding novel commercial vitality in the Kanto and eastern Honshu, 16th-century Kyoto, Sakai, and then Osaka remained the chief termini for trade with the continent and what Wakita Osamu terms "the nucleus of a national economy."[166] Whoever controlled the Kinai enjoyed a major advantage over outlying *daimyo* who depended on Kinai cities to dispose of surpluses and to obtain cotton and other specialized commodities.[167] Having emerged from the rich Owari region near the Kinai, Nobunaga and Hideyoshi moved quickly to seize the Kinai and its commercial

---

[164] Note 115 *supra*, plus figures at Souyri, *World Upside Down*, 30; Conlan, *State of War*, 9 n. 20; Friday, *Samurai, Warfare and the State*, 130.

[165] Ironically, this proved easier in eastern than western Honshu, because the former area's agrarian character meant that novel commercial impulses were more easily manipulated by political authorities. See nn. 159, 162 *supra*, plus Nagahara, "Sengoku Daimyo and Kandaka," 27–63; Sasaki, "Sengoku Daimyo," 133 ("From the fifteenth century on, monetary payments increased with the rapid development of a monetized commodity economy and the gradual increase in the proportion of monetary disbursements."); Souryi, *World Upside Down*, 213.

[166] Wakita, "Commercial and Urban Policies," 226; Yamamura, "Returns on Unification," 327, 358, 366.

[167] See essays by Wakita, Sasaki, and Yamamura in Hall et al., *Japan Before Tokugawa*, 127–133, 226–240, and (taking the story to 1650) 327–72; and Asao, "Sixteenth-Century Unification," 41.

hubs. Conceivably, therefore, the *daimyo* consensus that emerged in the late 1500s and early 1600s recognized that political coordination could ensure not only their collective physical security, but by enhancing market integration, their collective economic welfare as well.[168] Recall from Chapter 2 S. R. Epstein's argument that by reducing disorder and rationalizing coinages, measures, and legal jurisdictions, post-1450 political unification in Europe reduced transaction costs and promoted market efficiency.[169]

To recapitulate this chapter's argument thus far, Japanese patterns to 1600 both diverged from and paralleled those in Russia, France, and mainland Southeast Asia's three chief regions. Each of these latter five areas between c. 700 and 1650 experienced three to four periods of political construction punctuated by two to three distinct interregna. Especially between c. 950 and 1350 rapid economic growth was a source of both creativity and rising tension. Japan's economic lethargy to 1280, together with high levels of elite cohesion and limited external contacts, yielded a far more gradual evolution. Central authority in Japan did not finally collapse until the mid- to late 1400s. Only with Ashigaka implosion, with no central blueprint to follow, did Japanese begin the arduous, generations-long task – equivalent to postcharter efforts starting in France as early as the 9th century and in Russia in the 13th – of building local networks that eventually would culminate in a new islands-wide system.

And yet, between 1450 and 1600 Japan and these other Eurasian regions shared basic features. Between c.1450 and 1600 all moved from political fragmentation to sustained, unprecedentedly effective reintegration. Earlier economic differences aside, in each case rapid economic and demographic growth after 1450 and firearms aided recentralization. In each realm post-1450 economic expansion itself profited from locally specific combinations of epidemiological adjustment, improved climate, social reorganization, expanding local and long-distance trade, agrarian intensification, and military imperatives to revenue extraction. Finally, although still limited in 1600, the waxing fortunes of the Kanto vis-à-vis the Kinai bear comparison to shifts from Kiev to Moscow and from charter to postcharter capitals in Southeast Asia.

---

[168] See comments along these lines at Yamamura, "Returns on Unification," 362, 366–67, 370–72; Bolitho, "The *Han*," 202; Batten, *Ends of Japan*, 172.

[169] See Ch. 2, nn. 170, 227, 296 *supra*.

Warrior Arts, Buddhist Sects, and Oral Literature: Cultural Trends, c. 1200–1600

The diffusive, integrative thrust of demographic and commercial growth was no less apparent in culture than in politics.[170] New interior and frontier markets, the rise of provincial towns, and self-conscious imitation carried Kyoto culture across the islands. With intermediate strata increasing in numbers and influence, with aristocratic art forms gaining warrior and merchant patronage, with literacy broadening, and with Buddhism spreading among even the most humble folk, the once yawning gap between elite and commoner culture narrowed. Thus cohered what Barbara Ruch (with a touch of anachronism?) terms Japan's "first national literature" and a "national" culture.[171] Sectarianism and a penchant for doctrinal innovation encouraged greater religious competition in Japan than in Theravada, not to mention Christian, lands. Then too, commercial circuits were more developed than in Southeast Asia. Such differences aside, in its reliance on denser communications, new educational structures, and popular versions of textual religion, Japanese cultural integration from 1200 to 1600 anticipated the post-1400 advance of cultic orthodoxy and majority ethnicity in Burma, Siam, and Vietnam. After 1400 or 1450 we also saw that parish churches and tsarist loyalties spread among Russian peasants, while the "royal religion" and Parisian dialect won over growing numbers of French peasants and townsmen.

One clear sign of the shrinking social space between nobility and inferior strata was warrior participation in Kyoto high culture. Although few enough when set against the total population, warriors were far more numerous and geographically diverse than the *ritsuryo* aristocracy. In the Kamakura period, especially with the colonization of western Japan by shogunal personnel, Kyoto courtiers provided leading warriors with behavioral models, literacy, and other technical skills.[172] By

---

[170] Ensuing analysis relies *inter alia* on Butler, "Washing Off Dust"; Totman, *Japan Before Perry*, 85–117; *HJ*, 172–98, 243–45; Varley, "Cultural Life," 192–208; idem, "Cultural Life in Medieval Japan," in *CHJ*, vol. III, 447–99; G. Cameron Hurst III, "The Warrior as Ideal for a New Age," in Mass, *Origins*, 209–33; Walthall, *Japan*, 79–81; Souyri, *World Upside Down*, 65–83, 170–95.

[171] Barbara Ruch, "Medieval Jongleurs and the Making of a National Literature," in Hall and Takeshi, *Muromachi Age*, 279–309, esp. 286–91; idem, "The Other Side of Culture in Medieval Japan," in *CHJ*, vol. III, 500–43, esp. 542–43. On the problematic use of "national," see n. 378 *infra*.

[172] Souyri, *World Upside Down*, 55.

the Ashikaga period leading *bushi* dominated much of the capital's cultural life as patrons, spectators, and creators, helping not only to preserve *ritsuryo* traditions, but to move them in new directions. Innovation, for example, appeared in certain types of poetry, performance arts like *noh* theater, tea ceremonies, domestic architecture and decoration known as *shoin* culture, in the growing influence of Zen Buddhism and Confucianism, and most especially, in the writing down and artistic elaboration of war tales, which became the formative texts of *bushi*-led society. In contrast to the Heian aristocratic stress on precedent, lineage, and multiform elegance, the new war tales, and indeed many new art forms patronized by warriors, emphasized self-discipline, the moral autonomy of the individual, simplicity, the unity of aesthetic experience, and the superiority of individual effort over inherited status. New artistic forms spread from the Kinai to outlying domains as territorial lords from northern Honshu to Kyushu sought to create "little Kyotos," and as provincial warriors, as well as priests and merchants, aped – and at the same time further modified – the architecture, theater, garden designs, painting, and literature of the capital. In 15th- and 16th-century Kyoto wealthy merchants also contributed to the elaboration of the tea ceremony, linked-verse, book collecting, and scholarship.[173]

Whether through schools or informal tuition, literacy in some degree spread too among well-to-do peasants, artisans, and common traders. Village self-government required that at least a few grasp the essentials of reading and arithmetic to maintain tax records and to compose village regulations. Temples became *de facto* schools for the offspring of village notables and wealthy cultivators, and as village corporations spread first into western and then eastern Japan, literacy kept pace. In the cities commerce and, less frequently, legal demands also put a premium on reading and computation, especially in merchant families, whose literacy rate in 1600 may have exceeded that among warriors.[174] To represent Japanese sounds, the aforementioned *kana* writing system was created from abstracted Chinese character forms. Although literacy in classical Chinese remained a prized elite attribute to the late 1800s, in the Kamakura era official documents and literature were increasingly written in a combination of Chinese characters and *kana* script, while

---

[173] On merchant culture, Gay, *Moneylenders*, 189–200. On *bushi* as distinct from aristocratic culture, Ikegami, *Taming Samurai*, chs. 2–4.

[174] David Howell, pers. commun., Nov. 3, 2006. See too Amino, "History of Popular Life," 78–79; Gay, *Moneylenders*, 189; Ruch, "Medieval Jongleurs," 282–307; Tonomura, *Community and Commerce*, 61; Farris, *Medieval Population*, 138–39, 259.

village regulations were typically in *kana*. Reminiscent of the partial displacement of Chinese by *nom* in Vietnam, the development of this more flexible writing medium was an obvious precondition for middle strata literacy.[175]

Yet, because such skills remained relatively rare, the post-Heian popularization of Buddhism relied primarily on oral and visual, rather than written, techniques. In essence this was a process of spiritual mobilization by itinerant proselytizers,[176] many from privileged backgrounds who now sought to transmit to a broad cross section textually derived doctrines once restricted to the elite. If recent scholarship – paralleling research into the political shift from aristocrats to warriors – has emphasized the Heian origins of many Kamakura religious practices and has postponed the eclipse of *ritsuryo* forms,[177] over the long term Buddhist organization and popular sensibility clearly were transformed. As elite Heian temples lost ground, a social space opened for experiment both by new sects and by older organizations eager to broaden their base. Thus between 1200 and 1600 urban and rural wealth supported thousands of new temples and nunneries[178] whose influence radiated along new pilgrimage routes. For many upwardly mobile groups – warriors, merchants, wealthy peasants – Buddhism offered social validation. At the same time, growing political disorder and economic change fed soteriological pietism among diverse constituencies. Whereas Heian Buddhism focused on capital temples and cultivated aristocratic patrons, Kamakura temples developed more self-sufficient local organizations and vigorously sought humble converts. Amulets, dances, songs, simple sermons, and pastoral letters stocked the proselytizer's repertoire. Whereas charter religion had been doctrinally tolerant, many

---

[175] Seeley, *History of Writing*, chs. 5–7; Reischauer and Craig, *Japan*, 35; Roy Andrew Miller, *The Japanese Language* (Chicago, 1967), 33–49, 112–20; Ruch, "Medieval Jongleurs," 282; *HJ*, 114–15, 132–33, 176; Farris, *Medieval Population*, 139; Piggott, *Capital and Countryside*, 328–48, 426; Matthew Stavros, pers. commun., Jan. 14, 2004; Jonathan Zwicker, pers. commun., June 8, 2006.

[176] *HJ*, 187. On Kamakura and Ashikaga Buddhism, Janet Goodwin, *Alms and Vagabonds*, idem, "Alms for Kasagi Temple," *JAS* 46 (1987): 827–41; Kasahara, *History*, chs. 5–10; Berry, *Culture of War*, 145–70; Osumi, "Buddhism," 544–82; Martin Collcutt, "Zen and the *Gozan*," in *CHJ*, vol. III, 583–652; Richard Payne, ed., *Re-Visioning Kamakura Buddhism* (Honolulu, 1998).

[177] Goodwin, *Alms and Vagabonds*, 6–14; James Dobbins, "Envisioning Kamakura Buddhism," in Payne, *Re-Visioning*, 24–42; George Tanabe, "*Koyasan* in the Countryside," in ibid., 43–54; Jacqueline Stone, "Chanting the August Title of the *Lotus Sutra*," in ibid., 116–66.

[178] Collcutt, "Zen and *Gozan*," 583–84 offers figures for Zen temples.

new sects were exclusive. Yet because they sought to maximize their followings, new sects also eschewed the complex doctrines and ceremonies of Heian Buddhism in favor of easy devotional practices and simple faith. According to the Pure Land and Lotus sects, salvation awaited all – including sinners, beggars, and women – who threw themselves on the Buddha's infinite mercy. Even as the legal status of women deteriorated, the True Pure Land sect, for example, welcomed females into its communal life.[179] Zen also took root, winning warrior support and shogunal patronage, although its austere insistence that enlightenment derived from self-cultivation, not faith, precluded a truly mass following.[180]

The oral transmission of Buddhism by itinerant preachers was part of a larger vocal literature directed at commoners and propagated by itinerant specialists. Male and female, these performers filled diverse niches as blind bards, preachers, healers, actors, jugglers, prostitutes, pilgrims, and monks. Yet most shared a Buddhist identity, as conveyed by robes or tonsures or names, and all, intentionally or not, transmitted elements of court culture to the provinces.[181] Traveling the length of the country, singly or in groups – Kyoto alone in 1462 had 500 to 600 "lute priests"[182] – they performed on city streets, at crossroads, and in the small temples that now dotted the countryside. Their performances generally derived from written texts – sutras, chronicles, war tales – but they sang, chanted, danced, and used pictures and puppets so as to reach a mass audience.

Originally such performances had an exclusively religious purpose. It was through itinerant teachings about the suffering of the damned and the possibility of salvation that Buddhism first gained a mass following. In the eyes of the populace, vocal literature remained effective as a means to intimidate ghosts and improve karma. However, by the

---

[179] It also introduced women and family into temple life by allowing priests to marry, *HJ*, 193–94. On popular sects, Tonomura, "Re-Envisoning Women," 138–69; Goodwin, *Alms and Vagabonds*; Kasahara, *History*, 157–71, 285–98; Souyri, *World Upside Down*, 73, 193; Stone, "Chanting the August Title." The transformation of burial rituals from the 1400s also illustrates popular Buddhism's rural penetration.

[180] See sectarian social and geographic profiles in Osumi, "Buddhism," 580.

[181] Ruch, "Medieval Jongleurs"; idem, "Other Side of Culture," esp. 542–43; *HJ*, 194–98, 242, 244; Souyri, *World Upside Down*, 96; Mary Elizabeth Berry, "Was Early Modern Japan Culturally Integrated?" in Victor Lieberman, ed., *Beyond Binary Histories* (Ann Arbor, 1999), 110; Goodwin, *Alms and Vagabonds*.

[182] Ruch, "Other Side of Culture," 539–40. These were itinerant performers, generally blind, who chanted vocal literature to the accompaniment of a lute.

16th century – in part because performers, having lost the financial support of shrines, were forced to make a living in the market place – such narratives had come to focus more on entertainment than prose-lytism; and an early concern with the spiritual quests of monks had yielded to an abiding interest in warriors and other lay characters, whose tribulations informed hundred of oral tales. The repertoire of heroes, battles, miracle tales, and ethical dilemmas embodied in these works endeared themselves to men and women across class lines. Between 1300 and 1600 monks and storytellers thus joined with grow-ing travel and trade, the expansion of intermediate strata, and wider literacy to diffuse, and at the same time to simplify and reconfigure, both *bushi* and *ritsuryo* motifs. Curiously, despite this oral emphasis, the habit of some Ashikaga-era entertainers of distributing talismanic or souvenir booklets stimulated literacy, encouraged rudimentary pub-lishing, and may have provided a bridge to the full-blown publishing industry of the Tokugawa period.[183]

Starting in the Ashikaga era, cultural integration – in this case, more class specific than interclass – also drew strength from spread of cor-porate villages (*so*). Originally set up in part to shield its members against external predation but later enlisted by higher authorities as an agency of taxation and control, the *so* assigned tax burdens, super-vised labor exchanges, maintained shrines, administered irrigation and village property, issued ordinances, enforced family norms, and disci-plined miscreants. If the village's tax and arbitration functions bear com-parison to later Russian and French villages, its range of responsibilities seems to have been broader, and its emphasis on social conformity more insistent, than in either European realm. Thus, although or because by Christian standards they had weak institutional links to religious high culture, village collectivities encouraged horizontal cohesion.[184]

In sum, how unified was Japanese culture by 1600? Focusing on con-vergences in attitude and ritual, Ruch claims, "[I]f there is one marked characteristic of the medieval years, it is the clear sense of a coming

---

[183] Note 181 *supra*, esp. Ruch, "Medieval Jongleurs."

[184] Institutional links to high culture were weak in the sense that there was no uniform, elite-controlled system of churches, clergy, and liturgy as in Christian Europe. Note 109 *supra*, plus Hitomi Tonomura, pers. commun., Aug. 30, 2005; Harumi Befu, "Village Autonomy and Articulation with the State," in Hall, *Studies in Institutional History*, 301–14. On Russian and French villages, Ch. 3, nn. 24, 83 *supra*; Hilton Root, *Peasants and King in Burgundy* (Berkeley, 1987); William Doyle, ed., *Old Regime France 1648–1788* (Oxford, 2001).

together for the first time, of a sense of national community."[185] Along
with Buddhism and an archipelago-wide elite literature, she argues, a
variety of social rituals – the tonsure, pilgrimage, wine and song ceremonies, rites to activate good and to thwart evil forces, communication
with spirits of the dead, rituals to ensure a pleasant afterlife – and a complex of basic values and attitudes – including belief in the compassion
and efficacy of deities in this life, confidence in the talismanic power
of felicitous words, an assumption that suffering is normal and necessary, the conviction that sublimation can yield happiness – cohered in
the 14th to 16th centuries among Japanese of all classes. Such elements
became "national through the social rituals of song, dance, festival,
and vocalized myth."[186] Butler's study of bathing enriches this theme
of vertical and horizontal exchange. Originally a monopoly of a tiny
Heian elite, bathing after c. 1400 was imitated and modified by ever
wider social and geographic sectors until by 1600 it embodied a set of
values and practices accepted by people of diverse standing across the
archipelago.[187]

Yet without a powerful political center or a recognizable alien population against whom peoples in scattered areas could unify, there is no
reason to imagine – nor does Ruch or Butler claim – that these affinities translated into a sense of Japanese community, either cultural or
political. Admittedly, threats from abroad, including epidemics, Mongol invasions, and wars with northern "barbarians," led some medieval
writers to conceive of their world as a series of circles, with the imperial capital Kyoto the center of purity, and with hopelessly polluted
distant regions inhabited by devils, not humans.[188] Admittedly too, we
find occasional elite references to Japan as a "divine land" (*shinkoku*). A
politically oriented history text of 1339 began with the famous sentence,
"Greater Japan is the land of the gods"; it was therefore superior to all
other countries. In decrees outlawing Christianity and in letters to the
Iberians and Ryukyu, Hideyoshi repeated that "our country" alone had
divine sanction.[189] Among 16th-century *samurai* intellectuals, European

[185] Ruch, "Other Side of Culture," 501.
[186] Ibid., 542–43.
[187] Butler, "Washing Off Dust."
[188] Conversely, with the weakening of central authority after c. 1350, frontier zones seem
       to have become more culturally fluid. Batten, *Ends of Japan*, 34–42, 85–86, 109–10, 258;
       idem, "Frontiers and Boundaries of Pre-Modern Japan," *Jl. of Historical Geography* 25
       (1999): 166, 172–75.
[189] Souyri, *World Upside Down*, 7, 135–36; Totman, *Japan Before Perry*, 104–105; Berry, *Japan
       in Print*, 97; Herman Ooms, *Tokugawa Ideology* (Princeton, 1985), 45–47; Hudson, *Ruins*

contacts dramatically heightened awareness of "international" diversity, as suggested by artistic portrayals of Iberians and by the fact that Japanese maps based on European prototypes began to depict various countries as distinctive, unified blocks of primary colors.[190]

Revealingly, however, to the 1630s many of these same maps failed to imbue the Japanese islands themselves with a coherent character: what we now call Japan remained partitioned into differently colored blocks, representing the vanished provinces of the 8th century. Although a *ritsuryo*-era map of the three main islands was occasionally reproduced, from c. 900 to 1591 there is no evidence of resumed pan-Japanese surveys or efforts to revise the *ritsuryo* prototype. Rather, new maps offered relentlessly local, fragmented perspectives.[191] No doubt this was because among most warriors, not to mention the vast majority of commoners, *daimyo* domains, *ritsuryo*-era regions, or indeed villages provided the primary foci of identity. In the mid-Tokugawa era, when integration was far more advanced than in pre-Tokugawa times, the word *kuni* ("country") still referred less often to Japan as a whole than to one's region.[192] In the mid-1500s even along the Hokkaido frontier, where warfare between settlers from Honshu and northern Ainu tribesmen (heirs, some argue, to the *emishi* "barbarians" of an earlier age) was starting to produce cohesive identities on both sides, ethnicity seems to have been more situational and political than enduringly cultural. That is to say, regardless of language, dress, or other markers, anyone loyal to territorial lords who acknowledged the Kyoto court was "Japanese." Individuals could readily enter or leave that category.[193] Despite Hideyoshi's pride in Japanese culture, his madcap

---

of Identity, 236–42; Asao, "Sixteenth-Century Unification," 74–78; Matthew Stavros, pers. commun., Jan. 14, 2004.

[190] Tessa Morris-Suzuki, "The Frontiers of Japanese Identity," in Stein Tonnesson and Hans Antlov, eds., *Asian Forms of the Nation* (Richmond, UK, 1996), 46–47; Ronald Toby, "Imaging and Imagining," *Visual Anthropology Review* 14 (1998): 19–44; idem, "The 'Indianness' of Iberia and Changing Japanese Iconographies of Other," in Stuart Schwartz, ed., *Implicit Understandings* (Cambridge, 1994), 323–51; Batten, *Ends of Japan*, 95–96.

[191] Berry, *Japan in Print*, 24, 56, 69–77, 84–98.

[192] Morris-Suzuki, "Frontiers of Identity," 46; Karen Wigen, pers. commun., Sept. 13, 2006; Mark Ravina, "State-Building and Political Economy in Early-Modern Japan," *JAS* 54 (1995): 997–1022. See the map of 72 "Pre-Modern Country (*kuni*) Divisions" at Miller, *Japanese Language*, 165, and discussion *infra*.

[193] Howell, "Ainu Ethnicity," 76–79; idem, *Geographies of Identity* (Berkeley, 2005), 128; Walker, *Conquest of Ainu*, 24–27; and Batten, *Ends of Japan*, 85–86, 109–10, discussing Ainu ethnic formation.

scheme to subdue the Philippines, Korea, and China and move the Japanese emperor to Beijing[194] suggests a peculiarly universal, prenational elite vision – which, as usual, overlay multiform, intensely local popular identities. Even as rice cultivation expanded, maritime and mountain peoples across the islands maintained cultures in varying degrees distinct from those of lowland agricultural villages.[195] Moreover, within the lowlands, although elite merchant and *bushi* prosperity enhanced access to high culture, warrior withdrawal from the countryside and the elaboration of a specifically military culture sharpened distinctions between status groups. These would intensify in the Tokugawa era, to which we now turn.

4. TOKUGAWA IDIOSYNCRASIES, 1603–1854

Early Political Vigor

In theory and structure the Tokugawa shogunate may be distinguished readily both from the "absolutist" regimes of Europe – as Mary Elizabeth Berry has emphasized[196] – and from Indic Southeast Asia. In contrast to those other protected zone realms, authority was divided between the emperor, with symbolic primacy, and the *shogun*, who exercised practical power.[197] Unlike European or Southeast Asian rulers, the *shogun* claimed no paramount loyalty from his subjects and made no effort – through ritual, myth, or political institutions – to cultivate popular attachment to his person. Leading *daimyo* retained extensive autonomy within a system of multiple territorial lordships distinct from the more unitary systems of post-1600 Russia, France, and Vietnam. Accordingly, there was no imperial code of administrative law, no imperial

---

[194] Some sources claim he also planned to conquer India. See Berry, *Hideyoshi*, 207–17; idem, *Japan in Print*, 97; Varley, "Warfare in Japan," 78; Ooms, *Tokugawa Ideology*, 45–46; Hawley, *Imjin War*, 75–77.

[195] Amino, "History of Popular Life"; Souyri, *World Upside Down*, 91–99; Peter Shapinsky, "*Kaizo* and the Maritime Systems of Japan's Seto Inland Sea in the 15th and 16th Centuries" (ms).

[196] Berry, "Public Peace," esp. 240, 255; idem, *Japan in Print*, 228–50. For Tokugawa–European comparisons, see too Mark Ravina, *Land and Lordship in Early Modern Japan* (Stanford, 1999), 194 ff.; Ikegami, *Taming Samurai*, 35–36, 85, 89,177–94; James McClain et al., eds., *Edo and Paris* (Ithaca, 1994); James White, *Ikki* (Ithaca, 1995), 31–32; Conrad Totman, *Politics in the Tokugawa Bakufu, 1600–1843* (Berkeley, 1967), 238–43.

[197] On the other hand, although without parallel in Indic Southeast Asia, this division bore at least a superficial resemblance to that in 17th- and 18th-century Vietnam between the Le sovereigns and the Trinh and Nguyen territorial lords. *SP*, 399–419.

bureaucracy, no monopoly of standing soldiery, no general levy for revenue or conscripts. To these organizational contrasts, one can add three developmental differences. First, whereas the Bourbons, Romanovs, and their post-1600 Burmese and Siamese counterparts all came to power after brief interregna, the Tokugawa shogunate reversed some three centuries of devolution and over 130 years of civil war to provide after the *ritsuryo*/Heian/Kamakura era only the second period of sustained unification in Japanese history. Second, foreign invasions helped catapult the new Russian, French, Burmese, and Siamese regimes to power, but in Japan the foreign component was completely absent. And whereas between 1600 and 1830, in Russia, France, Burma, Siam, and Vietnam, each administration, buoyed by accelerating economic growth, grew more penetrating, in Japan after 1700 the central apparatus, by some measures, weakened, and the economic and demographic vigor of the 17th century ebbed.

Yet in a larger sense – and this, of course, is my main brief – all six country histories may be seen as variations on a common theme of sustained, unprecedented post-1600 integration. As Berry insisted, to declare Japanese political institutions deficient because they failed to match elements on a British or French checklist is to miss broader patterns. This is especially true if, as in Chapters 5 to 7, these polities are contrasted with states where extraregional actors displaced indigenous elites. Moreover, if we consider cultural trends, similarities between early modern Japan, Southeast Asian, and European realms become yet more marked.

Consider first territorial reorganization. In Southeast Asia, Russia, and France, each empire expanded from the 17th to early 19th centuries. Although the plan by Hideyoshi – whose hubris exceeded that of his fellow 16th-century megalomaniac Bayin-naung of Burma – to invade Korea preparatory to conquering China got nowhere, the Tokugawa regime, drawing on Sinocentric traditions of international order, did succeed in organizing unprecedentedly extensive, well-defined zones of influence around its own civilizing center.[198] To the south, Ieyasu

---

[198] Ronald Toby, *State and Diplomacy in Early Modern Japan* (Stanford, 1984), chs. 1, 5, and *passim*, discussing Japanese manipulation of relations with *inter alia* Korea, Ryukyu, Chinese, and Dutch merchants. Also Batten, "Frontiers and Boundaries," 175–78; Morris-Suzuki, "Frontiers of Identity," 46–49; Kato Eiichi, "Research Trends in the Study of the History of Japanese Foreign Relations at the Start of the Early Modern Period," *Acta Asiatica* 67 (1994): 1–29. On Bayin-naung, Lieberman, *Administrative Cycles*, ch. 1.

in 1609 permitted the *daimyo* of Satsuma in Kyushu to conquer the Ryukyu islands, whose rulers, serving as commercial intermediaries between China and Japan, henceforth paid tribute to Satsuma and the shogunate as well as to China.[199] To the north, Ieyasu authorized the Matsumae *daimyo* to develop the marine-products and fur trade of an ill-defined realm known as Ezo, home to Ainu communities that included most of Hokkaido, Sakhalin, and the Kuriles. Not unlike anticentralizing revolts in Southeast Asian and Russia, a 1669 Ainu uprising proved deeply counterproductive, with the Ainu relegated thereafter to economic dependency in a constricted Hokkaido homeland. In the late 1700s concerns about Russia prompted the shogunate to mount exploratory missions in the north, and from 1799/1807 to 1821 to place Hokkaido, the southern Kuriles, and southern Sakhalin under direct rule.[200]

As the Tokugawa regime extended its influence beyond the three main islands of Honshu, Shikoku, and Kyushu, it transformed the map of those same islands and southern Hokkaido. No pre-Tokugawa regime had defined "Japan" with any precision, much less obtained steady support from outlying provinces. Heian and the first two shogunates lacked reliable authority over northern Honshu, southern Kyushu, at times even the Kanto. The essential early Tokugawa achievement was to establish frontiers around Matsumae in the far north, Satsuma in the south, and Tsushima in the southwest, and to render all magnates confined by those boundaries subordinate to the *shogun*.[201] Shortly after

---

[199] Actually, northern Ryukyu was annexed to Satsuma, while the southern nominally independent sector paid tribute. Gregory Smits, *Visions of Ryukyu* (Honolulu, 1999), 15–49; Toby, *State and Diplomacy*, 45–52, 57, 115–16, 147–49; *HJ*, 217–18; Morris-Suzuki, "Frontiers of Identity," 49–50.

[200] From 1799 East Hokkaido and the southern Kuriles, and from 1807 West Hokkaido and southern Sakhalin came under shogunal rule. The 18th-century development of commercial fishing greatly exacerbated Ainu economic dependence. Morris-Suzuki, "Frontiers of Identity," 44–53; Batten, "Frontiers and Boundaries," 178; idem, *Ends of Japan*, 47–48, 174–76, 251–57; David Howell, *Capitalism from Within* (Berkeley, 1995), 27–35; idem, *Geographies*, 123, 130, 141; Walker, *Conquest of Ainu*, 227–29.

[201] Ensuing discussion of the Tokugawa polity relies on Oishi, "Bakuhan System," 11–36; Hall, "Introduction," *CHJ*, vol. IV, 1–39; Bolitho, "The *Han*"; Reischauer and Craig, *Japan*, 80–87; John W. Hall, "The *Bakuhan* System," *CHJ*, vol. IV, 128–82; Totman, *Early Modern Japan*, ch. 7; idem, *Politics*, 32–63; Ravina, *Land and Lordship*, esp. ch. 1; idem, "State-Building," 997–1022; Ronald Toby, "Rescuing the Nation from History," *MN* 56 (2001): 197–237; Walthall, *Japan*, ch. 5. Despite Tokugawa interest in territorial demarcation, in fact Tsushima, with ties of dependency to both Korea and Japan, and Ryukyu, with ties to China and Japan, occupied a somewhat intermediate status between empires. In the north too, not only did actual Japanese authority tend to ebb

his victory of 1600, Ieyasu seized the lands of 91 *daimyo* who had opposed him. Along with other confiscated holdings, these allowed him to construct a super-*daimyo* domain, based on the Kanto–Kyoto axis, which eventually controlled over a quarter of Japan's agricultural production.[202] In addition, major cities (such as Edo, Kyoto, Nagasaki, Osaka) and the chief mines came under shogunal control. Buttressing this great central (albeit not fully contiguous) bloc were domains controlled by 20 collateral Tokugawa families (*shinpan daimyo*) and 115 "house *daimyo*" (*fudai*) families, who generally had demonstrated their loyalty to the Tokugawa before 1600.[203] Located at strategic points in and around shogunal territory, collateral and "house *daimyo*" between them controlled an agricultural output some 37 percent greater than that of the shogunal domain. Finally, in peripheral areas where they could not directly threaten shogunal authority, including northern Honshu, southern Kyushu, and eastern Shikoku, resided powerful "outer *daimyo*" (*tozama*), about 105 in the 1690s, most descended from established lords who became vassals of the Tokugawa only after 1600.[204]

All *daimyo* faced novel restrictions. Without authorization, none could treat with foreign powers, build new fortifications, adjudicate inter-*daimyo* disputes, or, in obvious contrast to the 16th century, undertake military action. Each was obliged to support shogunal construction projects, supply information for Japan-wide censuses, obtain permission to marry, and when conflicts arose, "follow the laws of Edo in all things."[205] To the *shogun* alone fell the minting of currency, control of imperial highways, and oversight of religious institutions. *Daimyo* could be transferred and their lands could be confiscated; and in fact the first half of the 17th century saw many such shifts. Most critical perhaps was the requirement, fully instituted by 1642, that all *daimyo* leave wives and children as hostages at the shogunal capital of Edo and

with distance, but the formal boundary between Japanese and Ainu territory shifted. See nn. 199, 200 *supra* plus Kazui Tashiro, "Foreign Relations During the Edo Period," *JJS* 8 (1982): 305–306; Howell, *Geographies*, 110–11.

[202] This refers to agricultural land controlled directly by the *shogun*, which was almost 16 percent of the total in 1700, and by his liege vassals (*hatamoto* and *gokenin*), which was almost 10 percent. *HJ*, 223–24; Hall, *Government and Local Power*, 343; Reischauer and Craig, *Japan*, 81–85. Because the shogunate to the early 1700s expanded its holdings at *daimyo* expense, these figures were somewhat larger than in 1600. Harold Bolitho, *Treasures Among Men* (New Haven, 1974), 34, 37; Berry, *Japan in Print*, 80.

[203] These figures were for the 1690s.

[204] See map at Reischauer and Craig, *Japan*, 84–85; *HJ*, 223.

[205] Bolitho, "The *Han*," 195.

that they, along with extensive retinues, spend stipulated periods (most commonly, alternate years) at Edo – an arrangement known as *sankin-kotai*, or alternate attendance. Besides diverting *daimyo* income from potentially dangerous projects, such demands bred emotional attachments that in effect uprooted an entire aristocracy. Whereas in the early 1600s many *daimyo* probably regarded residence in Edo as exile, to their grandsons in 1690 (by which time five of six incumbent *daimyo* had been born in the city) it was a welcome return home – an attraction reinforced by Edo's growing commercial and cultural vitality.[206] One is reminded of the social magnetism of Ava, Ayudhya, Versailles, and St. Petersburg.

Nor was Edo's appeal the only positive inducement to loyalty. As I suggested, most *daimyo* realized early on that the new system enhanced their physical and economic security, while allowing them to retain considerable autonomy. Benefiting from Edo's introduction of all-Japan coinage and from islands-wide pacification, *daimyo* found it easier to sell domain products in distant markets. Aside from *sankin-kotai* and ad hoc financial and corvée demands (which, however, could be quite considerable), the shogunate made no regular claims on *daimyo* income. Above all, each *daimyo* continued to provide the soldiers, magistrates, and clerks to govern his own territory. *En masse*, Japanese officials were numerous: if Burma in 1665 had roughly one official for every 3,000 inhabitants and France one for every 470, Japan as a whole in 1610 may have had one for every 314.[207] But Japanese officials served some 240 separate jurisdictions, the most powerful of which were still often regarded as distinct "states" (*kokka*).[208] While historians debate how much autonomy *daimyo* domains (*han*) retained, it is clear that despite

---

[206] On *daimyo* controls, including the hostage system (to 1665) and *sankin-kotai*, see Bolitho, "The *Han*," 185–206, 220–21; Toshio Tsukahira, *Feudal Control in Tokugawa Japan* (Cambridge, MA, 1966), esp. ch. 3; Totman, *Early Modern Japan*, 108–11.

[207] I have found no comprehensive figures. Totman, *Politics*, 40 indicates the early shogunate – which controlled almost a third of the population (see n. 211 *infra*) – had 17,000 supravillage officials. Assuming *daimyo* administrations were comparably dense, this suggests 51,000 officials for 16,000,000 people. Howell, pers. commun., Nov. 3, 2006 notes that because village headmen acted as agents of the shogunate or the domain, and because some *samurai* with titular posts were officials in name only, calculation is extremely difficult. But on balance, he suggests that my figure of 51,000 may be a bit low. Cf. text accompanying Ch. 3, nn. 76, 154 *supra*.

[208] Likewise, a *daimyo* could still style himself a "public authority" (*kogi*), albeit generally subordinate to the shogun's "great public authority" (*o kogi*). Ikegami, *Taming Samurai*, 159; Ravina, "State-Building," 998–1012; idem, *Land and Lordship*, 14, 22, 29–31, 196; Philip Brown, pers. commun., May 10, 2004. The figure of 240 is from the 1690s.

growing conformity to Tokugawa norms, considerable variation persisted in village organization, *samurai* roles, taxation, and land tenure, and that shogunal leadership relied heavily on exhortation, example, and negotiation.[209] The distinction between shogunal lands, intermediate *daimyo* domains, and outer *daimyo* domains recalls the division between nuclear zone, lowland provinces, and tributaries in Burma and Siam, and between the inner *pays d'elections* and outer *pays d'etats* in France. Not without reason has early Tokugawa political structure been termed a "concentric ring" system.[210] Compared to other protected zone realms, however, territorial lords retained extensive power indeed. If *daimyo* in 1720 ruled two-thirds of the population,[211] Burmese and Siamese tributaries – functionally comparable to *daimyo* – governed only 20 to 30 percent. In Vietnam the figure was negligible, while by 1650 Russia and France had eliminated hereditary autonomous territorial rulers entirely.[212]

Two factors explain this relatively high degree of autonomy. First, the fact that by the early 1600s Japan had been fragmented for 130 years

---

[209] Thus the Tokugawa system has been called "centralized feudalism," a collection of "client states," a "federal union of semi-autonomous domains," and a "compound state." See Ravina, "State-Building," 999–1000; idem, *Land and Lordship*, 27–28, 196; Berry, *Hideyoshi*, 147–67; Ikegami, *Taming Samurai*, 160. In general, Ronald Toby, John W. Hall, David Howell (*Geographies*; idem, Review of Brown, *Central Authority*, in *Canadian Journal of History* 30, 1995, 402–404), Daniel Botsman (*Punishment and Power in the Making of Modern Japan*, Princeton, 2005, 80–83), James White (*Ikki*), and Japanese scholars like Sugimoto Fumiko and Yamamoto Hirofumi emphasize centralization; while Ravina, Philip Brown (*Central Authority*, 147–240; idem, "State, Cultivator, Land," *JAS* 56, 1997, 421–44; idem, pers. commun., May 10, 2004), Luke Roberts (*Mercantilism in a Japanese Domain*, Cambridge, 1998, 80–83), Timon Screech (*The Shogun's Painted Culture*, London, 2000, 10, referring to "the Japanese states"), and Japanese scholars like Mizubayashi Takeshi focus on local autonomy, pragmatism, and diversity. Brown, who characterizes the Tokugawa state as "flamboyant" because it joined high nominal authority to low central administrative capability (*Central Authority*, 232–33), also emphasizes that *daimyo* autonomy from the *shogun* paralleled village autonomy from the *daimyo*. For a summary of the debate and a seminal essay in its own right, see Toby, "Rescuing the Nation."

[210] Totman, *Politics*, 237.

[211] To the figure of 7,825,000 people (i.e., 25 percent of 31,300,000, which correlates to 25 percent of agricultural output) ruled by the *shogun* and his liege vassals, must be added over 2,000,000 people in *shogun*-ruled cities. The rest lay under the authority of various *daimyo*.

[212] *SP*, Chs. 2–4; Ch. 3 *supra*; Valerie Kivelson, pers. commun., Jan. 11, 2009; Dena Goodman, pers. commun., Jan. 11, 2009; Sara Chapman, pers. commun., Jan. 12, 2009. On the other hand, *sankin-kotai* and Tokugawa censuses were more territorially uniform than their Southeast Asian Indic equivalents, and minority ethnicity lent Southeast Asian tributaries a cultural uniqueness more pronounced than in Japan.

compared to a mere 15 to 30 years for Burma, Siam, Russia, or France allowed local sovereignties to take stronger institutional and psychological root. This in turn obliged Japan's unifiers to assemble coalitions of *daimyo* whose prerogatives they reduced, but whom they never dreamed of displacing, both because they lacked theoretical models for so radical a change, and because Ieyasu's concern for the future of his yet insecure house required allies.[213] His compromise recalls earlier accommodations after comparable periods of disorder by Tabin-shwei-hti (r. 1531–1550) in Burma, Trailok (1448–1448) in Siam, Louis XI (r. 1461–1483) in France, and Ivan III (r. 1462–1505) in Russia.[214] In each of the latter realms, hereditary lords were eliminated only after generations of further conflict and negotiation. Second, whereas in Europe and Southeast Asia chronic warfare from 1600 to 1815 created ongoing pressure for centralization, Japan (especially after the threat of renewed civil strife receded after 1638) faced no comparable imperative. Ironically, the Tokugawa era, which accorded warriors unprecedented authority, proved to be one of the most peaceful in Japanese history.

Japan's distinctive mix of integrative features notwithstanding, Harold Bolitho's succinct judgment of the early Tokugawa era – that never before "had so much violence been done to local autonomy"[215] – may stand as well for early-17th-century Burma, Siam, Russia, and France.

Daimyo were hardly the only group to fall under closer regulation. Although, as the source of shogunal legitimacy, the emperor and his court at Kyoto were rescued from poverty and treated with deference, to forestall any possibility of political resistance the court was confined to a ceremonial ghetto more restricted than under the Ashikaga.

Yet more dramatically, Buddhist military and economic power, which had posed a major challenge to *daimyo* ambition, was broken. After late-16th-century unification campaigns killed large numbers of recalcitrant clerics, religious organizations came under close control by four shogunal Commissioners of Temples and Shrines. By 1640 a system obliging non-*samurai* to register with parish Buddhist temples made those temples agents of anti-Christian policy and popular supervision. At the same time, the early shogunate reduced the total landholdings of

---

[213] Brown, *Central Authority*, 239; Hall, "Introduction," 14–15; Totman, *Politics*, 235–38.
[214] See *SP*, 151, 270; and *supra*, Ch. 2.
[215] Bolitho, "The *Han*," 196, supported by Toby, "Rescuing the Nation," and Walthall, *Japan*, 96: "The shogunal and domainal governments developed the most complex, sophisticated, and coherent administrative systems Japan had ever seen."

Buddhist and Shinto shrines to the level of a single large *daimyo*.[216] Along with territorial controls, the transformation of religious organizations into a docile arm of the state was one of the most salient commonalities of post-1500 Japanese, Southeast Asian, and European state building. In Southeast Asia after 1500 we saw that Buddhist orders lost the extensive lands and autonomy of the charter era. The Russian Orthodox church suffered a comparable fate, albeit somewhat later, while the French throne gradually strengthened control over church patronage until the Revolution, when church lands were confiscated *in toto*.[217]

A similar determination to prevent a recrudescence of 16th-century turmoil led the Tokugawa to strengthen divisions within the general population. In Bourbon France reaction against social upheaval contributed to new curbs on noble entry and to Counter-Reformation projects,[218] while in 17th-century Burma, Siam, and Russia bitter memories of peasant flight and military collapse generated novel programs of manpower control.[219] Now in Japan as well, revulsion against the mobility and disorder of the Warring States period – a revulsion rooted partly perhaps in the unifiers' own *arriviste* status – was reinforced by the need for reliable finance. The result was an unprecedented Neo-Confucian-sanctioned effort by both *shogun* and *daimyo* to minimize horizontal and vertical mobility among occupational-cum-status groups on whose taxes elite income and state operations rested. Although Japanese realities belied Confucian four-class norms (officials, peasants, artisans, and merchants), and although (apart from the tiny imperial household and, to a lesser extent, pariahs) one cannot speak of a true caste ideology, hierarchy grew far more encompassing and systematic. Whereas before the Tokugawa era social groups had evolved partly to shield their members against state power, now they were validated and defined by the state itself. Dependent on shogunal leadership and example, this system, David Howell shows, operated more or less uniformly across Japan, in shogunal and *daimyo* territories alike, becoming the central institution of Tokugawa order. Reminiscent of Philip Gorski's Calvinist/Protestant Europe, self-policing hierarchies, once established, minimized the need for state intervention. But unlike Gorski's categories, these were not

---

[216] Kasahara, *History*, 333–45; Hall, "*Bakuhan* System," 160; Berry, "Public Peace," 239, 243–44; Tonomura, *Community and Commerce*, 175; Ikegami, *Taming Samurai*, 186–90; Howell, pers. commun., Nov. 3, 2006.

[217] *SP*, 34, 35, 64, 127, 130, 159–60, 246, 316–17, 373, 381; Chs. 2, 3 *supra*.

[218] Ch. 3, nn. 137, 249–56 *supra*.

[219] Ch. 3, nn. 21, 22 *supra*; *SP*, 280-81.

vertical religious communities, rather horizontal status groupings rooted in occupational distinctions. Such divisions required unusual attention to sumptuary markers, as between *samurai* and commoners or commoners and pariahs. Covering everything from food and housing to clothing and personal adornment, sumptuary regulations sought to control not the acquisition of wealth, rather its public display.[220]

The *samurai*, who with their families comprised 6 to 8 percent of the population, constituted the highest principal status category.[221] Although meticulously divided by internal ranks, *samurai* as a class were distinguished by their right to serve as administrators, to receive fiefs or stipends, to use surnames, and to enjoy such sumptuary privileges as the right to carry two swords. If *samurai* were at least 12 times more numerous proportionately than French nobles, entry into their ranks, ironically, was far more difficult than into the French nobility.[222] But while *samurai* enjoyed unique privileges, their 16th-century role as agents of rural rebellion ensured that they too faced novel restraints. Starting with Hideyoshi in 1591 and continuing well into the 1600s, central officials and subordinate *daimyo* obliged vast

---

[220] Howell, *Geographies*, chs. 1–3, esp. 20–23, 42–43, emphasizing the self-policing character of status hierarchies. Cf. Eurasian analogies referenced in Ch. 1, nn. 84–87; Ch. 3, nn. 16, 136, 249–57. On Tokugawa social reorganization, also Souyri, *World Upside Down*, 216; Berry, "Public Peace," 246 ("initiatives in this area [should] be perceived as a systematic attack upon the roots of disorder."); idem, "Was Early Modern Japan Integrated"; Brown, *Central Authority*, 19–20, 88–167, 194, 223–37; Ikegami, *Taming Samurai*, 164–94; White, *Ikki*, 38 ff.; Tsuneo Sato, "Tokugawa Villages and Agriculture," in Nakane and Oishi, *Tokugawa Japan*, 37–62; Chie Nakane, "Tokugawa Society," in ibid., 213–31; Furushima Toshio, "The Village and Agriculture During the Edo Period," in *CHJ*, vol. IV, 478–98; Gilbert Rozman, "Social Change," in *CHJ*, vol. V, 516–28. On sumptuary insignia, Howell, *Geographies*, 16, 39, 64–65, 135–40; Berry, *Japan in Print*, 170; Donald Shively, "Sumptuary Regulation and Status in Early Tokugawa Japan," *Harvard Jl. of Asiatic Studies* 25 (1964–65): 123–64; Eiko Ikegami, *Bonds of Civility* (Cambridge, 2005), 257–60, 273–75, comparing Japan with Europe.

[221] Ikegami, *Taming Samurai*, 162; Berry, *Japan in Print*, 27–28; Howell, *Geographies*, 28, 55–61 all cite figures of 6–8 percent, but other estimates range from 5–10 percent. On the terms *bushi*, *samurai*, and *buke*, n. 93 *supra*.

[222] Howell, *Geographies*, 57–61 cites three reasons for minimal entry to *samurai* ranks: a) domain obligations to existing *samurai*, whose large numbers meant that many of them already were underemployed, b) the continued allure that local political power held for many non-*samurai*, c) the likelihood that wealthy commoners who became *samurai* would have to relinquish their wealth in a system based on the separation of warriors from the land. On the other hand, wealthy commoner families often sought prestigious marriages with impoverished *samurai*. Moreover, esp. in the 19th century, successful merchants, financiers, and farmers could purchase individual *samurai* attributes and, in some cases, even formal entry into the lower ranks of the warrior class. See ibid., 58, 60; Walthall, *Japan*, 121. On the French nobility's size, Ch. 3, n. 213 *supra*.

additional numbers of warriors to relocate from the countryside to shogunal and *daimyo*-controlled towns. There, in return for stipends, they not only surrendered those landholdings that had permitted a dangerous independence, but they evolved from fighting men into educated, brush-wielding functionaries running shogunal and *han* administration. In some respects the ensuing tension between warrior traditions of personal autonomy and the new regimentation recalls the condition of European nobles domesticated at absolutist courts. But on the whole *samurai* feelings of autonomy may have been more fragile – hence more psychologically disruptive – because they lacked both the landed independence and military opportunities of their European counterparts.[223]

With warriors in most domains removed from the countryside and with villages subject to official sword-hunts, 17th-century rural communities lost their capacity for self-defense, but retained pre-Tokugawa traditions of self-governance. Containing some 85 percent of the population, villages were typically divided between a landowning elite who dominated village affairs, and an increasingly influential body of independent small farmers. Village corporations remained responsible for taxes, shrines, irrigation works, local laws, and social discipline, as illustrated by the spread within villages of the so-called five-family unit, which held families collectively liable for one another's tax obligations and conduct.[224]

Below the peasantry in normative status, though not necessarily in wealth, were artisans and merchants, both of whom in practice tended to form a single category of townsmen (*chonin*). With declining foreign trade, no opportunity for venal office, no open real estate market, no war contracts, and limited urban autonomy, Japanese traders and artisans were more circumscribed, in some respects,[225] than their West European,

---

[223] This is my idiosyncratic reading of Ikegami, *Taming Samurai*, esp. 39–42, 241–360. Cf. references to French noble domestication in Ch. 3 *supra*. On pre-1591 *samurai* removal to towns, n. 112 *supra*, and on post-1591 removal, Ikegami, *Taming Samurai*, 160–63; Berry, *Japan in Print*, 27–28; Brown, *Central Authority*, ch. 9; idem, "Practical Constraints."

[224] On Tokugawa village governance, Tonomura, *Community and Commerce*, 169–87; Ikegami, *Taming Samurai*, 166–68; Brown, *Central Authority*, 3–4, 94–112, 134, 222–24.

[225] But trade restrictions were balanced by low tax policies, domestic peace, and rising consumer demand. On towns and merchants, James McClain, *Kanazawa* (New Haven, 1982), 56–63 and *passim*; Berry, *Japan in Print*, 170–73; Akira Hayami, "Introduction," in Hayami et al., *Economic History*, 23–24; Ikegami, *Taming Samurai*, 175, 180–81, 190–94, 338; Totman, *Early Modern Japan*, 64–65, 157–59, 301–303, 329–34; Donald Shively, "Popular Culture," in *CHJ*, vol. IV, 765–68; and discussion *infra*.

if not Russian, counterparts. Merchant and craft associations and town wards – like village organizations – bore collective responsibility for taxes, services, and social order, and in the case of trade associations, for prices and product quality.

At the bottom of the status hierarchy lay a variety of outcastes and pariahs, perhaps 2 percent in all, whose status deteriorated with the general tightening of social boundaries. Forbidden sometimes to wear footwear in the presence of commoners or to bind their hair, these groups too were organized into corporate bodies responsible for internal discipline, mutual assistance, and state obligations.[226] As with *daimyo* domains and villages, so with merchant associations, craft guilds, and pariahs, by relying on self-governing communities, the shogunate deflected grievances to intermediary bodies, effectively melding stability with flexibility.[227]

How did Tokugawa leaders conceptualize their rule over society? If the unifiers were oriented more toward pragmatic management than ideology, even among partisans of Nobunaga, Hideyoshi, and the early Tokugawa we find frequent references to *kogi* – the common good or public interest. In contrast to the faction and violence of the 16th century, *kogi* represented harmony, impartiality, stable hierarchy. Although Warring States *daimyo* also had invoked *kogi* and although in the Tokugawa era individual *daimyo* continued to do so, the rhetoric of benevolent custodianship focused preeminently on the *shogun*, allowing him to rationalize his position within the military elite.[228]

Tokugawa Economic Vitality to c. 1720

But to appreciate early Tokugawa strength, one also must consider economic trends. In contrast again to much of Europe and Southeast

---

[226] The two major outcaste groups were *eta* and *hinin*. Souyri, *World Upside Down*, 98–100; Howell, *Geographies*, 25–38, 65–66, 136–37; Ikegami, *Taming Samurai*, 113–16, 168–71. One is reminded of the deteriorating post-1500 status of Burmese religious slaves (*hpaya-kyun*). Victor Lieberman, "The Political Significance of Religious Wealth in Burmese History," *JAS* 39 (1980): 753–69.

[227] The system of self-governing disciplinary units extended as well to priests, monks, blind people, and the like. On the theory and practice of Tokugawa social organization, see n. 220 *supra*, esp. Howell, *Geographies*, and Ikegami, *Taming Samurai*, 164–71.

[228] See n. 208 *supra*, plus Berry, "Public Peace," esp. 258, 269–71; Totman, *Early Modern Japan*, 80, 95–97; *HJ*, 220–21; White, *Ikki*, 35–38; Butler, *Emperor and Aristocracy*, 289–92; Ooms, *Tokugawa Ideology*, chs. 1–3, and idem, "Neo-Confucianism and the Foundation of Early Tokugawa Ideology," in Peter Nosco, ed., *Confucianism and Tokugawa Culture* (Princeton, 1984), 27–61, emphasizing Tokugawa disinterest in ideology.

Asia – where between c. 1630 and 1710 growth slowed or stopped entirely – in Japan the momentum of the 14th to 16th centuries carried into the early 18th century.

As Figure 4.3 shows, the total arable between 1600 and 1721 rose from some 1,588,000 to 2,252,000 *cho*. New water-control projects drained the lower reaches of large river basins, intensifying that shift from highlands to plains that started in the 15th century. However, in the late 1600s as suitable virgin lands receded and as demand for foodstuffs rose, many peasants turned from reclamation to more intensive techniques. Specifically, they raised labor inputs, developed more specialized hoes, threshers, winnowing, and irrigation gear; expanded fertilizers; and developed rice strains suited to particular locales. Fast-ripening rice spread cultivation into marginal lands in the northeast and encouraged double-cropping farther south. In many districts yields rose continuously, if not dramatically.[229] We find too an expansion in non-rice cash crops, including tea, mulberry, indigo, rapeseed, and especially cotton, which replaced hemp as Japan's chief textile. As in France in the 1700s and Burma from the 1500s, cotton transformed clothing for elites and commoners alike, spurred handicrafts and trade, and influenced manners, even aesthetics.[230] Seventeenth-century changes in housing and diet as well as in clothing and bedding point to improved rural living standards primarily, but not exclusively, among the upper peasantry.[231]

That per capita wealth, as opposed to total output, did not rise yet more dramatically reflected unusually rapid demographic growth. Together, agricultural extension and intensification supported a doubling of population, from recent estimates of 15–17,000,000 in 1600 to

---

[229] Cf. yield data at Susan Hanley and Kozo Yamamura, *Economic and Demographic Change in Preindustrial Japan 1600–1868* (Princeton, 1977), 103; Miyamoto, "Quantitative Aspects," Table 1.1 and 36–45; Farris, *Medieval Population*, 263, Table E.3.

[230] On agrarian change, including crops, implements, and routines c. 1600–1720, Verschuer, *Le Riz*, 20, 96–119; Nakamura, "Development of Rural Industry," 81–85; Sato, "Tokugawa Villages," 62–80; Yamamura, "Returns on Unification," 327–72; Furushima, "The Village and Agriculture," esp. 498–515; Smith, *Agrarian Origins*, chs. 6, 7; Conrad Totman, "Preindustrial River Conservancy," *MN* 47 (1992): 56–76; Walthall, *Japan*, 99–101; Miyamato, "Quantitative Aspects," 36–48; Hayami, "Introduction," 5–6. On cotton in Japan, Susan Hanley, *Everyday Things in Premodern Japan* (Berkeley, 1997), 94–96 and n. 157 *supra*; in Southeast Asia, *SP*, 144–45, 170–76, 251, 416; in France, Daniel Roche, *A History of Everyday Things* (Cambridge. 2000), ch. 8.

[231] Hayami, "Introduction," 27–28; Nakai, "Commercial Change," 538; Miyamato, "Quantitative Aspects," 43; Hayami and Kito, "Demography," 227–46, esp. 231; Hanley, *Everyday Things*, chs. 1-4. Cf. n. 160 *supra*.

31,300,000 by 1721.[232] Villages expanded and spun off satellite settlements, while over 200 castle towns appeared within an extremely short period. Notwithstanding a decline in some castle towns in the late 1600s, the proportion of Japanese in cities grew from an estimated 5 percent in 1600 to 15 percent by the century's end. Twenty castle towns had populations of over 70,000 each, while Osaka and Kyoto each supported 350,000–400,000, and the shogunal capital Edo, probably the world's largest city, neared a million. According to Rozman, Japanese urbanization by 1700 had entered the highest level, Stage G ("national marketing"), characterized by seven levels of central places.[233]

Inevitably, economic intensification spurred and profited from better transport and falling unit costs. The Western Circuit shipping route to northern and western Honshu enriched Osaka. Expanded maritime circuits also circumnavigated Honshu, joined Nagasaki, Osaka, and Edo, and advanced the incorporation of southern Hokkaido.[234] In addition, the shogunate upgraded five major highways, which, although designed for official transport, came to support a swelling volume of commercial traffic.[235] Along the great road from Kyoto to Edo, some 500 kilometers, delivery time for express commercial letters fell from six to two days.[236] By 1650 large regional differences in the price of rice and other goods characteristic of the medieval era had narrowed substantially or disappeared.[237] In both *daimyo* and shogunal cities, licensed

---

[232] See lower estimates for 1600 at n. 151 *supra*, which naturally imply more rapid Tokugawa-era growth. By contrast, the 1721 figure of approximately 31.3 million is generally accepted.

[233] Rozman, *Urban Networks*, 34–35, 73–85, 245. The 15 percent figure, apparently using 5,000 as the urban threshold, appears in Hayami, "Introduction," 23; idem, *Historical Demography*, 52; Hiroshi Shimbo and Akira Hasegawa, "The Dynamics of Market Economy and Production," in Hayami et al., *Economic History*, 162–66; and Berry, *Japan in Print*, 27. On urban growth to c. 1720, see too Hayami and Kito, "Demography," 218; Katsuhisa Moriya, "Urban Networks and Information Networks," in Nakane and Oishi, *Tokugawa Japan*, 97–106; McClain, *Osaka*, 58–67; Nakai, "Commercial Change," 519–79; Lee Butler, "Patronage and the Building Arts in Tokugawa Japan," *Early Modern Japan* (Fall-Winter, 2004): 39–52.

[234] Moriya, "Urban Networks," 100–101, 106–107.

[235] Moriya, "Urban Networks," 100–109; Hall, *Japan*, 210–11; Constantine Vaporis, *Breaking Barriers* (Cambridge, MA, 1994), ch. 1 and *passim*; Hayami, "Introduction," 5–7.

[236] Albeit between 1650 and the early 1800s. Moriya, "Urban Networks," 109–12.

[237] Yamamura, "Returns on Unification," 369–70; Hayami, "Great Transformation," 9; Brown, pers. commun., May 10, 2004. On regional specialization, Shimbo and Hasegawa, "Dynamics," 169–79.

wholesale merchants[238] formed quasi-official trade associations to facilitate long-distance cooperation.

Why, then, this further expansion? As we saw, the legacy of the Warring States period was mixed. Warfare ravaged crops and diverted labor to nonremunerative purposes, even as *daimyo* efforts to widen their tax base aided the economy. Now Japan achieved the best of both worlds – universal pacification and economically beneficial political initiatives – in a process that Yamamura terms "returns on unification."[239]

On the one hand, some two centuries of domestic and external peace – unique among the lands under review – improved the economic climate. Physical destruction ceased. Tens of thousands of military support personnel returned home. Peasants, townsmen, and *daimyo* grew more confident that long-term investments would bear fruit.[240] On the other hand, a variety of *daimyo* and shogunal policies spurred growth. Accelerated removal of virtually the entire *samurai* class from the countryside to cities was the chief reason that the urban population tripled in a few decades. As town-based stipendiaries, *samurai* and their families became consumers *par excellence*, attracting all manner of traders, builders, and craftsmen. The obligation that tens of thousands of provincial *samurai* reside on a regular basis in Edo through the alternate attendance (*sankin-kotai*) system – which could absorb half of domain revenues – also served wonderfully to concentrate market demand. Inter-*daimyo* rivalries now bred not warfare, but conspicuous consumption in Edo. Within *daimyo* domains local versions of *sankin-kotai* had a similar impact – even though there, as in Edo, such results were incidental to the system's political *raison d'être*.[241] With clearer economic intent, 17th-century *daimyo* reduced tolls, standardized local measurements, and promoted reclamation, irrigation, and cash crops.[242] For

---

[238] *Ton'ya*, reminiscent of Russian *gosti*. On early Tokugawa merchants, n. 225 *supra* plus *HJ*, 235–36; Nakai, "Commercial Change," 545–46.

[239] Yamamura, "Returns on Unification," 327–72.

[240] Previous note, plus Masaru Iwahashi, "The Institutional Framework of the Tokugawa Economy," in Hayami et al., *Economic History*, 85–104; Totman, *Early Modern Japan*, 60–61.

[241] Berry, *Japan in Print*, 27–28; 247; Nakai, "Commercial Change," 525–26; Iwahashi, "Institutional Framework," 93–95; Ravina, *Land and Lordship*, 67; Hayami, "Great Transformation," 9–12; McClain, *Kanazawa*, 46–56.

[242] On domain economics, Karen Wigen, *The Making of a Japanese Periphery, 1750–1920* (Berkeley, 1995), 1–3, 68–69, 79, 87, 97–98; Miyamoto, "Quantitative Aspects," 68–79; Shunsaku Nishikawa and Masatoshi Amano, "Domains and Their Economic

its part, the shogunate not only helped to coordinate riparian works, but, as noted, improved transport, met demands for more uniform weights and measures, and used its control over Japan's richest mines to mint the first post-*ritsuryo* coins (in gold, silver, and copper/bronze). With local currencies no longer valid outside the domains, *daimyo* seeking coins with which to pay for imports, *sankin-kotai*, and shogunal construction projects were driven to maximize sales of domain products in *shogun*-controlled Osaka and Edo.[243]

No less critical perhaps were rising productivity incentives in the countryside. Contrary to earlier scholars who saw early Tokugawa taxation as ruthlessly confiscatory, Brown, supported in part by Masaru Iwahashi, argues that the continued withdrawal of *samurai* from villages actually limited their knowledge of agrarian conditions and reduced effective tax rates. By allowing peasants, especially wealthy cultivators, to retain the difference between underestimated yields and true output, such conditions provided a powerful, if unplanned, inducement to reclamation and intensification.[244] More deliberately, as the demand grew for labor-intensive cash crops and handicrafts, domain authorities and landlords in outlying provinces – continuing a trend observed in central regions in earlier centuries – found it profitable to convert hereditary bound laborers into contract workers or tenants, with the latter having more or less secure access to smallholdings. Both of the latter groups could establish their own families and benefit from rising output more readily than servile workers. At the same time, also continuing earlier trends, peasants imitated *samurai* in developing stable stem families (*ie*), which became a principal vehicle for economic planning. This evolving social regime, Hayami and others suggest, was

---

Policies," in Hayami et al., *Economic History*, 247–67; Brown, *Central Authority*, xv, 77–88; McClain, *Kanazawa*, 46–56, 152–53; Roberts, *Mercantilism*, esp. 17–21, 32–102; Furushima, "The Village and Agriculture," 498–501; Ravina, *Land and Lordship*, chs. 2–5; Wigen, pers. commun., Sept. 13, 2006.

[243] Nakai, "Commercial Change," 527–28; Iwahashi, "Institutional Framework," 96–98; Miyamato, "Quantitative Aspects," 58–59; Yamamura, "Returns on Unification," 359–70; *CHJ*, vol. IV, 160, 211; Enomoto Soji, "Domain Coins in the Early Edo Period," *Acta Asiatica* 39 (1980): 42–60; Matao Miyamoto and Yoshiaki Shikano, "The Emergence of the Tokugawa Monetary System in East Asian International Perspective," in Dennis O. Flynn et al., eds., *Monetary History in Global Perspective, 1500–1808* (Seville, 1998), 135–41.

[244] Brown, "Practical Constraints"; idem, *Central Authority*, 147–240; Iwahashi, "Institutional Framework," 99–102. For other versions of the argument that tax changes boosted incentives, Totman, *Early Modern Japan*, 60–62; Innes, "Door Ajar," 9; and Thomas Smith, "The Land Tax in the Tokugawa Period," *JAS* 18 (1958): 3–19.

largely responsible for the moral emphasis peasants placed on industrious family labor and for associated increases in output.[245]

Apart from cold rainy summers that contributed to the Kan'ei famine of the early 1630s to 1642, studies of cherry blooming dates suggest that Tokugawa climate to 1730 – in contrast to Europe and mainland Southeast Asia – remained generally favorable. Although less consistent, lake sediments and freezing dates also indicate more propitious weather to 1730 than for much of the period from 1730 to 1840. Such patterns were critical in the northeast, vulnerable to the *yamase* cooling effect.[246]

In addition, foreign contacts continued to aid the economy. To centralize commercial income and to curb Christian and other potentially destabilizing influences, from 1635 to 1641 the shogunate forbade Japanese travel overseas and ended Iberian trade, while regulating more closely Dutch and Chinese commerce at Nagasaki. This policy, however, did not halt official trade per se, with imports at Nagasaki and at smaller official ports at Satsuma and Tsushima rising in the late 1630s, the early 1660s, and again in the late 1690s. Smuggling further swelled the total.[247]

Admittedly, from the 1660s lower Chinese silver prices and falling mine output led the shogunate to curb sharply silver exports, which

---

[245] On the economic/cultural implications of changing peasant social organization, Hayami, "Introduction," 27–28; Smith, *Agrarian Origins*, chs. 8, 9; Robert Bellah, *Tokugawa Religion* (New York, 1985), 126–31; Miyamoto, "Quantitative Aspects," 43–44; Yamamura, "Returns on Unification," 340–72; Hanley, *Everyday Things*, 26, 38, 137; Rozman, "Social Change," 521–22, 553; Kaoru Sugihara, "Agriculture and Industrialization," in Peter Mathias and John Davis, eds., *Agriculture and Economic Growth* (Oxford, 1996), 151; Ikegami, *Taming Samurai*, 166–68. On the evolution of the *ie* system, n. 150 *supra*, plus Bito Masahide, "Thought and Religion, 1550–1700," *CHJ*, vol. IV, 373–74; Nakane, "Tokugawa Society," 216–26; Susan Hanley, "Tokugawa Society," 700–701.

[246] Compare Arakawa, "Climatic Change as Revealed by the Data," Table 1; idem, "Climatic Change As Revealed by the Blooming Dates"; Hanley and Yamamura, *Economic and Demographic Change*, 321, with Maejima and Tagami, "Climate Change"; Tanaka and Yoshino, "Re-Examination"; Fukusawa, "High-Resolution Reconstruction"; Takehiko Mikami, "Summer and Winter Temperature Reconstructions in Japan," *Pages News* 10 (2002): 17–18; Atwell, "Volcanism," 60–67; idem, "Some Observations on the 'Seventeenth-Century Crisis' in China and Japan," *JAS* 45 (1986): 223–44; Totman, *Early Modern Japan*, 6–7, 110–16, 231, 236–45. On the *yamase* effect, see n. 124 *supra*.

[247] Innes, "Door Ajar," 629, and 1–15, 427–32, 619–33, and *passim*. Satsuma supervised trade with Ryukyu, while Tsushima did so with Korea. See too Marius Jansen, *China in the Tokugawa World* (Cambridge, MA, 1992), ch. 1; Tashiro, "Foreign Relations," 293–94; Lee, "Trade and Economy"; Atwell, "Some Observations," 223–44; Yamamura and Kamiki, "Silver Mines," 329–62. On the inaccuracy of the concept of Tokugawa seclusion (*sekoku*), see the classic study Toby, *State and Diplomacy*, esp. ch. 1. On anti-Christian policies, Jurgis Elisonas, "Christianity and the Daimyo," *CHJ*, vol. IV, 359–72.

had underlain trade with China. Gold and more especially copper still flowed out, but from 1715 rising domestic needs joined mine exhaustion to inspire a more comprehensive policy of trade restriction, accompanied by efforts at import substitution. In 1700 Totman estimates foreign trade already represented less than 1.5 percent of the value of agriculture, quite modest by 18th-century French or Siamese standards. Thereafter, as restrictions took effect and Japan's overall economy grew, foreign trade declined in both relative and absolute terms.[248]

Yet if we remember that for much of the 17th century such trade was more substantial and if we consider indirect benefits, we sense that, on balance, external stimuli between 1600 and 1720 remained quite influential. Even in 1700 the silk industry of Kyoto, which employed 100,000, the metal trades of Osaka, and virtually the entire population of Nagasaki relied on foreign raw materials or markets. Chinese technology continued to aid mining, sugar, ceramic, shipbuilding, and textile industries. Restrictions notwithstanding, Japan also borrowed continental and eventually Dutch techniques in mathematics, cartography, optics, medicine, and botany.[249] After Japanese leaders successfully promoted import substitution in silk and sugar, Chinese goods and technologies still provided the standard for imitation. Yet more basic, in Japan as in the New World, by exerting upward pressure on the domestic price of silver and copper, Chinese demand ultimately made profitable the extraction of those metals, which together formed the basis of early Tokugawa monetization.[250] Consider too the impact of the New World sweet potato, which was grown in upland zones unsuitable for rice and provided exceptionally high calories per acre. Although the full benefits did not begin to appear until the 18th century, the sweet potato helped to protect against famine, especially in western Japan, and along with sugarcane – derived from Taiwan – helps to explain why population rose more rapidly in that region than in the

---

[248] Totman, *Early Modern Japan*, 148, plus Hayami, "Introduction," 14–18; Shimbo and Hasegawa, "Dynamics," 166–69, offering diachronic trade figures; Kazui Tashiro, "Foreign Trade in the Tokugawa Period," in Hayami et al., *Economic History*, 105–18.

[249] Innes, "Door Ajar," 619–26; Morris-Suzuki, *Technological Transformation*, 17–18, 30, 42; Jansen, *China in Tokugawa World*, 25–41; Marcia Yonemoto, *Mapping Early Modern Japan* (Berkeley, 2003), 105 and 197 n. 9.

[250] Note 129 *supra*, Flynn, "Comparing the Tokugawa Shogunate"; Innes, "Door Ajar," 620.

east.[251] Likewise, flood-resistant rice strains from China continued to aid the development of major deltas.[252]

How, specifically, did economic expansion strengthen the early Tokugawa political system? Tokugawa tax rates varied widely by time and place, and we know little about *ritsuryo* taxes on non-rice production. Nonetheless, if we compare a modest average land tax estimate for 1720, namely 33 percent,[253] with the estimated yield of 6 percent from rice tribute and seed-loan interest for the *ritsuryo* period, and if we consider increases in total acreage and yields, we conclude that the Tokugawa state in 1700 drew vastly more wealth – perhaps 20 times more? – from the agrarian sector than its *ritsuryo* antecedent.[254] This discrepancy cannot have been dramatically smaller if we compare Tokugawa agrarian revenues with those of the Kamakura and Ashigaka shogunates. Such income supported powerful armies, lavish construction projects, cultural patronage, *daimyo* awards, and *samurai* stipends, all of which encouraged intra-elite harmony in the 17th century. At the same time,

---

[251] On these and other new crops, mostly from the Americas, including green beans, corn, red peppers, pumpkins, and spinach, see Hanley, *Everyday Things*, 80–82; idem, "Tokugawa Society," 682; Totman, *Early Modern Japan*, 312–13; Jansen, *China in Tokugawa World*, 39; Hayami and Kito, "Demography," 236.

[252] Sugihara, "Agriculture and Industrialization," 151; *HJ*, 108; n. 157 *supra*. Chinese models also aided agricultural implements.

[253] Estimated average land tax rates: Brown, pers. commun., Nov. 13, 2006 ("25–30% of taxable yields" and at most 30 percent of GNP); Sato, "Tokugawa Villages," 43 (60 percent in the 17th century, 33 percent in the 18th); *CHJ*, vol. V, 3 (50 percent in early Tokugawa); Conrad Totman, "Tokugawa Peasants: Win, Lose, or Draw?," *MN* 41 (1986): 464 (average *de facto* rates "well above" the basic 30–35 percent); *HJ*, 223 (the state "skimmed perhaps 25–35% of yield as tribute"); Beasley, *Japanese Experience*, 162–63 (30–35 percent on shogunal lands, nearer 40 percent on *daimyo* domains); Ravina, *Land and Lordship*, 53 (40 percent common for period as a whole); Brown, "Practical Constraints," 383 (46.2 percent mean for selected areas 1625–1640); Penelope Francks, *Rural Economic Development in Japan* (London, 2006), 46 (50–60 percent c. 1600, 33 percent in 1868). Corvées were additional.

[254] That is, rice tax rates increased roughly fivefold (see estimated *ritsuryo* rate at *HJ*, 82, 223), while between 930 and 1720 arable acreage rose by a factor of 2.35 (Fig. 4.3 *supra*; Farris sees no significant acreage increase from 930 to 1150), and rice yields between 730 and 1720, by a factor of 2.27 (Farris, *Medieval Population*, 263, Table E.3). On the other hand, it is worth recalling that between 900 and 1720 Japan's population – which offers a rough indication of the land's carrying capacity – increased only about sixfold (Farris, *Medieval Population*, 8–9, 262; idem, *Japan's Ancient Population*, 42, 46, 80, 174). Of course, as Farris, pers. commun., Aug. 11, 2006 cautions, without statistics on rice vs. non-rice production, non-rice tax rates, nonagrarian tax rates, supplemental levies, and corvées in the *ritsuryo* era, global tax comparisons with the Tokugawa era must remain highly speculative. Cf. n. 32 *supra*.

relatively heavy taxes were accepted by commoners, in part of course because of coercion, but also because improved productivity permitted living standards to stabilize, or rise modestly, even as government exactions increased. Not only did textiles and foods once reserved for *samurai* become more widely available, but longevity in some locales seems to have increased.[255]

Notwithstanding the primacy of agricultural taxes, consider too the political implications of commercial expansion. Contrary to received wisdom that the "outer *daimyo*" in western Japan had most to gain, and the Tokugawa most to lose, from foreign trade, Robert Innes has argued that by concentrating foreign commerce in shogunate-ruled Nagasaki, by awarding international trade and sailing licenses to allied merchants, by requiring that all export copper be refined in Osaka, and by exporting bullion from shogunal mines, central authorities drew considerably greater profit from maritime trade than did peripheral *daimyo*.[256]

The shogunate also profited from the licensing of internal commerce and from control of coinage. More indirectly, as noted, the growth of all-Japan markets centered at first on Osaka gave *daimyo* a vested interest in political unity. Private and government demand joined abundant mulberry bark and water resources to produce low-priced paper, permitting an astounding expansion of official record-keeping.[257] Finally, as we shall see, commerce, travel, and rising literacy encouraged multifaceted cultural exchange, which created its own bias toward political integration.

In brief, in Japan as in Russia, France, and Southeast Asia, 17th-century consolidation derived from acute disorders in the late 1500s that favored administrative experiment and restored social discipline, from diverse maritime influences, and from feedback loops between government action, social reorganization, and economic growth. Until

---

[255] See n. 231 *supra*, plus Hayami, "Introduction," 28, arguing for a 5- to 10-year increase in early modern longevity; Hanley, *Everyday Things*, esp. 13, 26–46 *passim*, 94–96, 178; Alan Macfarlane, *The Savage Wars of Peace* (Oxford, 1997), pts. 3–6; Noriko Tsuya and Satomi Kurosu, "Mortality and Household in Two Ou Villages, 1716–1870," in Tommy Bengtsson et al., eds., *Life Under Pressure* (Cambridge, MA, 2004), 253–92.

[256] Innes, "Door Ajar," 631–33. Cf. Totman, *Early Modern Japan*, 75, 76, 138, 143, 145. However, I cannot accept at face value the suggestion at Flynn, "Comparing the Tokugawa Shogunate," 349–50 that silver profits underpinned Tokugawa unification, not least because Flynn makes no effort to compare commercial with agricultural revenues.

[257] On the production and impact of paper, Hayami, "Introduction," 7; Ikegami, *Taming Samurai*, 274; Wigen, pers. commun., Sept. 13, 2006.

1720 expansion of the state and expansion of the economy were more evenly balanced in Japan than in France, where economic weakness and military demands favored state hypertrophy. Nonetheless in both of these realms as in Southeast Asia and Russia, 17th-century regimes achieved unprecedented internal stability and, in most cases, external strength.

Political and Economic Strains, c. 1720–1840; Overarching Similarities to Other Eurasian Realms

After 1720, one could argue, the parallels end. Every other state thus far reviewed was substantially stronger in 1820 than a century earlier. In Japan the reverse was true. As a percentage of total wealth, shogunal and domain revenues were smaller in 1830 than in 1720. Unable to tax effectively the most dynamic sectors of the economy or to control price movements, leaders failed to maintain the value of *samurai* stipends. The real income of lower and middle warriors thus fell, along with their confidence in the political order. As economic pressures mounted and shogunal supervision waned, *daimyo* grew more independent. Tensions between *samurai* ranks, between domains and the shogunate, and between rival domains eroded the ability of the Tokugawa system to deal with a range of issues, extending from fiscal crisis to new social currents to military obsolescence.[258]

Why these novel difficulties? In part, obviously, the initial division of authority between shogunate and *daimyo* limited the potential for coordination.[259] To some degree as well, shogunal difficulties reflected a generational transition, hardly unique to Japan, from self-made, ambitious early rulers to less vigorous men circumscribed by entrenched ministerial interests.[260] But perhaps the chief bar to reform was the aforementioned fact that Japan, alone after 1638, knew neither serious external threats nor domestic military challenges.[261] Thus the polity

---

[258] On political and fiscal problems, Bolitho, "The *Han*," 206–13, 233–34; Sydney Crawcour, "Economic Change in the Nineteenth Century," in *CHJ*, vol. V, 571–600; *HJ*, 273–74; Totman, *Early Modern Japan*, chs. 14, 15, 20–21. On military obsolescence, ibid., 534–39; Jansen, "Japan in the Early Nineteenth Century," in *CHJ*, vol. V, 63–64.

[259] Totman, *Politics*, 241 emphasizes this contrast with Tudor England.

[260] See discussion at Totman, *Politics*, 204–33.

[261] Lingering fears that the Manchus might repeat Mongol attacks stimulated Tokugawa intelligence-gathering, but never translated into serious defensive preparations. Toby, *State and Diplomacy*, 117–67, 223–25; Smits, *Visions of Ryukyu*, 20–21; Lynne Struve, ed., *The Qing Formation in World-Historical Time* (Cambridge, MA, 2004), 3, 39.

remained largely innocent of two creative dynamics: a) persistent pressure to increase central revenues; and b) dramatic demonstrations, such as military defeat alone could provide, that far-reaching change was necessary. In Burma, Siam, the two Vietnams, Russia, and France, I have emphasized that warfare in general, and anticipated or actual state collapse in particular, provided the main spur to penetrate local society.

In addition, Japan between 1720 and 1840 faced economic constraints more severe than in mainland Southeast Asia or Russia, with their still open agricultural frontiers and vigorous international trade, or France, with its access to both maritime wealth and New World ghost acres. Starting c. 1720, after roughly 450 years of sustained expansion, Japan effectively ran out of fresh cultivable lands and new sources of irrigation.[262] From the late 1600s Japan's timber reserves also showed signs of exhaustion – with attendant problems of soil erosion – as did its copper, gold, and silver mines.[263] Reinforcing, and in some measure reflecting, internal problems were new curbs on maritime trade, which, as noted, were largely inspired by bullion scarcities. Trade with Korea all but ended by the 1750s, and the number of Chinese and Dutch vessels visiting Nagasaki fell to a trickle. Admittedly, by offering the same sort of protectionism as high tariffs in a later age, restrictions spurred import substitution in silk and sugar. As Karen Wigen has pointed out, Tokugawa curbs also succeeded in excluding Europeans at a time they were causing havoc elsewhere in Asia.[264] Yet in cutting Japan off from foreign markets, Tokugawa policy discouraged the growth of great port cities such as provided a principal engine of West European expansion. Relative isolation also made it impossible to overcome domestic scarcities with imported timber and foodstuffs, inhibited economies of scale, and sharply reduced technology transfers compared not only to Europe, but to Japan's own 16th- and 17th-century experience.[265]

---

[262] Yamamura, "Returns on Unification," 334, Table 11.2; Miyamoto, "Quantitative Aspects," 38, Table 1.1 and 36–56; *HJ*, 247.

[263] See *HJ*, 247–52; idem, *Early Modern Japan*, chs. 12, 13, emphasizing ecological strains; Miyamoto, "Quantitative Aspects," 53–55; Tashiro, "Foreign Trade," 113–17.

[264] Wigen, *Making of Periphery*, 82, 97–98, 136; idem, pers. commun., Sept. 13, 2006; plus Lee, "Trade and Economy," 10–11; Innes, "Door Ajar," 474–523, 629–32; Shimbo and Hasegawa, "Dynamics," 166–69; Tashiro, "Foreign Trade," 105–18; Hayami, "Introduction," 12–18. On trade 1700–1840, see too Miyamoto and Shikano, "Emergence of the Monetary System," 143–51; *CHJ*, vol. V, 3–4; Totman, *Early Modern Japan*, 311–13, 343, 485–99 *passim*.

[265] Cf. Thomas Smith, *Native Sources*, 32–36; Reischauer and Craig, *Japan*, 90–91; Berry, *Japan in Print*, 171–72.

By impeding the spread of typhus, typhoid fever, cholera, and plague from the continent, Japan's insularity joined with her rapidly running rivers, efficient waste disposal, and boiling of drinking water to sustain exceptionally high population densities.[266] Welcome though this obviously was for the survivors, without greater productivity, it meant additional pressures on per capita resources.

Add to these constraints adverse weather – in severity, frequency, and geographic scale, most argue that weather-related famines between 1730 and 1840 exceeded 17th-century shortages [267] – and one can appreciate Japan's difficulties compared to France, Russia, or mainland Southeast Asia, whose 18th-century climate was generally favorable. After 1710 neither France nor Russia experienced famine on the scale of Japan, where between 1783 and 1787 alone volcanic- and climate-related crop failures and disease, some claim, killed over 900,000.[268] In other words, whereas in much of Europe and Southeast Asia economic constraints typical of the 17th century eased after 1720, in Japan the chronology of growth was more or less reversed.

Japanese responded to these challenges with generally successful strategies of conservation, intensification, diversification, and population control. Especially from about 1700 a stream of horticultural treatises, government edicts, village, family, and business codes admonished people to nurture resources and to maximize productivity. Increased efficiencies, sanctioned by an aesthetic of simplicity, came to characterize cooking, heating, construction, diet, and clothing.[269] To augment and protect their resource base, the Japanese expanded whaling and fisheries, exploited Hokkaido, experimented with ground coal, and developed precocious programs of forest conservancy. By the late 1700s nearly all forested areas were subject to some degree of purposeful management.[270] Likewise, in the face of domestic bullion shortages,

---

[266] Jannetta, *Epidemics*, 188–207 and *passim*; Hanley, "Tokugawa Society," 698.

[267] Totman, *Early Modern Japan*, 236–45, 343–44, 522; *CHJ*, vol. IV, 592; Maejima and Tagami, "Climatic Change"; Miyamoto, "Quantitative Aspects," 49–50. On the other hand, 17th-century statistics are poor, so this comparison is somewhat provisional.

[268] Walthall, *Japan*, 109 ("It is said that the population declined" by 920,000, apparently from 1783 to 1787); Susan Burns, *Before the Nation* (Durham, NC, 2003), 24–25, citing Kikuchi Isao's estimate of 300,000 deaths for 1783 to 1784 alone.

[269] *HJ*, 248–59; Totman, *Early Modern Japan*, ch. 13; idem, *The Green Archipelago* (Berkeley, 1989); 116–29, 184; Hanley, *Everyday Things*, esp. chs. 2–5; idem, "Tokugawa Society," 693–94. But see Lee Butler's critique of Hanley, "A Book for Believers?," *Early Modern Japan* (Nov., 1998): 3–6.

[270] *HJ*, 256–57; idem, *Green Archipelago*, 1–6, 171–90 and *passim*.

the shogunate restricted bullion exports and imposed nominal currency values, in effect isolating Japan from world metal markets.[271] With best agricultural practices disseminated by texts and word of mouth, farmers selected seeds and prepared the soil with increased care; used yet more fishmeal, industrial by-product, and nightsoil fertilizers; and extended double- and triple-cropping in a pattern that, if not involutionary, was clearly more labor intensive than in most of Europe and Southeast Asia. As people replaced animals in pulling carts and plows, fodder-growing areas were freed up to produce fuel and food for human use.[272] In response to market incentives and to heavier taxes on rice than on non-food crops, peasants switched from rice to tobacco, tea, safflower, cotton, mulberry, indigo, and other industrial crops. Benefiting from resilient consumer demand and the diffusion of Kinai technologies, the mid- and late Tokugawa era also saw a marked rural expansion in agricultural processing and in the manufacture of textiles, pottery, *sake*, soy sauce, lacquerware, and paper. Such activities not only provided a critical supplement to peasant income, but along with urban guild restrictions, declining foreign trade, and discriminatory taxation, encouraged a shift in manufacture from central coastal cities to small towns, rural marketing centers, and villages, especially in peripheral provinces. What urban and population growth did occur after 1720 was concentrated in outlying areas, while established castle towns – with the notable exception of Edo – stagnated or lost population.[273]

---

[271] Miyamoto and Shikano, "Emergence of the Monetary System," 143–50; Hayami, "Introduction," 12–18; Tashiro, "Foreign Trade," 108–109, 113–17. *Daimyo* also issued domain paper scrip (*hansatsu*).

[272] This shift was reinforced by a reduced need for cavalry mounts. Miyamoto, "Quantitative Aspects," 46–48; Totman, *Green Archipelago*, 188. Cf. Kenneth Pomeranz, "Is There an East Asian Development Path?," *JESHO* 44 (2001): 323–24. In the late 1800s, when figures first become available, per hectare rice yields in Japan were 1.8 times greater than in Siam. Hanley, *Everyday Things*, 189; M. Tanaka, "Synoptic Study on the Recent Climate Change in Monsoon Asia and Its Influence on Agricultural Production," in Koichiro Takahashi and Masatoshi Yoshino, eds., *Climatic Change and Food Production* (Tokyo, 1978), 83, Table 2. Cf. n. 12 *supra*.

[273] On rural diversification, protoindustrialization, and shifting urban and provincial patterns 1720–1840, Wigen, *Making of Periphery*, esp. chs. 2–4; idem, "The Geographic Imagination in Early Modern Japanese History," *JAS* 51 (1992): 3–29; David Howell, "Proto-Industrial Origins of Japanese Capitalism," *JAS* 51 (1992): 269–86; idem, *Capitalism from Within*, chs. 1–2; Hayami, *Historical Demography*, 46–57; CHJ, vol. IV, 214–15; Crawcour, "Economic Change," 578–92; Smith, *Agrarian Origins*, pt. 2; idem, *Native Sources*, 17–44; Furushima, "The Village and Agriculture"; Sato, "Tokugawa Villages"; Miyamoto, "Quantitative Aspects," 45–56; Hayami and Kito, "Demography," 213–33; Nobuhiko, "Commercial Change," 519–95; Jansen, "Japan in Nineteenth Century,"

As declining median holdings increased pressure on family resources, abortion, infanticide, and delayed marriage contributed to what may have been new reproductive norms. The depressive demographic effects of such practices were magnified by labor migration, hence spousal separation; by high urban mortality; and perhaps by the market-based spread of childhood diseases.[274] Thus, although acreage virtually stagnated, a novel demographic stability joined conservation, improved crop yields, protoindustry, and labor shortages to permit a modest rise in per capita income after 1720, and a more notable improvement from 1800.[275]

True, rates of overall (and perhaps per capita) growth remained far more limited than in the 17th century.[276] And because the benefits were uneven, burdening laborers and poor peasants while enriching farmers-cum-protoindustrial innovators, growth spawned novel social tensions.[277] Yet such expansion as did occur can be seen as a triumph over resource restraints considerably more severe than in 18th-century Europe or Southeast Asia. Eager to link this performance to Japan's late-20th-century economic success, celebratory cultural histories explain both patterns in terms of Japan's penchant for group solidarity, planning, and self-discipline. Robert Bellah, for one, has sought

53–87; Edward Pratt, *Japan's Protoindustrial Elite* (Cambridge, MA, 1999), 48–77; Totman, *Early Modern Japan*, chs. 12, 13, 20, 21; Morris-Suzuki, *Technological Transformation*, ch. 2.

[274] All agree that late Tokugawa population stabilized, but it is unclear to what degree this reflected a) deliberate efforts at family limitation, b) the essentially unintended effects of economic and cultural change. Insofar as limitation was intentional, scholars also debate to what extent it reflected severe hardship among the poor or self-improvement strategies among relatively secure families. See n. 255 *supra*, plus Miyamoto, "Quantitative Aspects," 49–56; Hayami and Kito, "Demography"; Totman, *Early Modern Japan*, 249–59; Hanley, *Everyday Things*, 133–50; Cornell, "Infanticide," 22–50; Ochiai, "Reproductive Revolution," 187–215.

[275] See different interpretive emphases at Yasukichi Yasuba, "Standard of Living in Japan Before Industrialization," *Journal of Economic History* 56 (1986), 217–26; Wigen, *Making of Periphery*, 99; Totman, "Tokugawa Peasants"; idem, *Early Modern Japan*, 398; Rozman, "Social Change," 522–23, 559, 563; Hanley, *Everyday Things*; idem, "Tokugawa Society," 694 ff.; Miyamoto, "Quantitative Aspects," 45–56; Hayami and Kito, "Demography," 233–35.

[276] Miyamoto, "Quantitative Aspects," 36–82, esp. Table 1.1. It was also more modest than in most of western Europe, some of whose late-19th-century visitors were shocked at the malnourished, impoverished appearance of the Japanese. See income comparisons and European views of Japan in Hayami and Kito, "Demography," 233, 239–40.

[277] On the new 18th- to 19th-century elite of *gono* ("rich farmers") and their relation to Tokugawa authorities, Howell, *Geographies*, 48–49, 69–70, 100; Pratt, *Protoindustrial Elite*. On social tensions, see discussion *infra*.

Tokugawa analogies to Weberian Protestantism, although one could summon Gorski alongside Weber.[278] More contingent explanations of Tokugawa performance stress a) the incentives that proliferating consumer goods offered producers to expand labor inputs (the "industrious revolution") and to enhance efficiency, b) rapid technical diffusion along Japan's dense information networks, and c) the fact that political fragmentation created lightly taxed interstitial spaces where trade could flourish. The latter three factors, all of which continued 17th-century trends, invite comparison to northwestern Europe.[279]

But to return to the principal thesis: whatever benefits economic growth between 1720 and 1840 conferred on segments of the population, for the Tokugawa political system, it proved profoundly destabilizing. The most obvious problem, as noted, was the failure of both *shogun* and individual *daimyo* to tax adequately protoindustry, trade, even many agrarian sectors.[280] In part, this failure reflected institutional inertia and perhaps a naïve precommercial bias.[281] In part, as just noted, slippage between large economic regions, on the one hand, and limited *daimyo* jurisdictions, on the other, created openings for tax avoidance that small, mobile enterprises were quick to exploit. But more basically, the removal of *samurai* from the land in the 17th century and the concomitant investiture of villages with administrative responsibilities – including tax collections – deprived political leaders of rural leverage. *Shogun* and *daimyo* could suppress uprisings, but in day-to-day affairs could not enforce their will on the countryside without support from the very people they wanted to tax. With little incentive to cooperate, village headmen, themselves usually wealthy farmers and entrepreneurs, used their freedom to underreport yields, to keep fresh

---

[278] See Bellah, *Tokugawa Religion*, 2, 7–10, 126, 196, and chs. 5, 6, plus nn. 220, 245 *supra*.

[279] See discussion at Wigen, *Making of Periphery*, 71, 97–98, 190; Morris-Suzuki, *Technological Transformation*, 3–4, 7ff.; Rozman, "Social Change," 566–67; idem, ed., *The East Asian Region* (Princeton, 1991), chs. 3, 4; Hanley, *Everyday Things*; Michio Morishima, *Why Has Japan "Succeeded"?* (Cambridge, 1982); Totman, *Green Archipelago*, 116–29, 171–90, 84. Cf. Pomeranz, *Great Divergence*, 114–65; Ch. 3, n. 176 *supra*. But if political fragmentation and interstitial openings were a necessary condition for commercial initiative, this was hardly sufficient, as Southeast Asia suggests.

[280] Yet undertaxation of nonagrarian pursuits was especially marked: in Choshu in 1842, which Crawcour, "Economic Change," *CHJ*, vol. V, 588-89 takes as representative, agricultural tax rates were 39 percent, but nonagricultural rates less than 10 percent. See too Bolitho, "The Han," 214-15.

[281] *CHJ*, vol. IV, 710; Berry, "Was Early Modern Japan Integrated?" 125; Totman, *Politics*, 64–65.

cultivation off the registers, and to hide the full extent of local trade and manufacture.[282]

To be sure, Burma, Siam, Vietnam, Russia, and France faced similar problems, and without comparative tax data we cannot make dogmatic distinctions. Yet the following considerations suggest that in the other five realms such problems tended to be less severe: a) In contrast to Japan, in Indic Southeast Asia and France rural elites profited from central taxation either directly through commissions or indirectly through provincial patronage, and thus had less incentive to cheat. b) In France, Russia, and Vietnam, resident rural elites, at least in the 18th century, also tended to be more socially distant from the peasantry and more closely tied to superior officials by statutory privilege, culture, and patronage than their Japanese counterparts. c) Outside Japan, I have emphasized that warfare applied ineluctable pressure to improve extraction. But in Japan by one estimate, whereas mid-17th-century effective tax rates reached 60 percent, in the next century they declined to 33 percent, and in the 1800s, 20 percent.[283] d) A secular fall in the price of rice vis-à-vis other consumer goods – which probably reflected more elastic demand for manufactures than for foodstuffs[284] – highlighted an institutional vulnerability unique to Japan: whereas other countries monetized operations, taxes and *samurai* stipends were calculated in nominal volumes of rice. Both shogunal and *daimyo* income thus fell as

---

[282] See n. 244 *supra*, plus Smith, *Native Sources*, 39–41; Bolitho, "The *Han*," 214–19; Yujiro Oguchi, "The Finances of the Tokugawa Shogunate," in Hayami et al., *Economic History*, 198–201; Jansen, "Japan in Nineteenth Century," 75.

[283] Sato, "Agricultural Villages," 43, referring to shogunate taxes. See n. 253 *supra*, plus Oguchi, "Finances," 199–200; Thomas Smith, "The Land Tax in the Tokugawa Period," in Hall, *Studies in Institutional History*, 283–99; idem, *Native Sources*, 39–40, showing real government revenues in 1850 roughly the same as in 1700.

[284] In Japan as in France, the output of manufactured goods grew more rapidly than the output of agricultural goods. One might assume therefore that in both countries the price of manufactures would decline more sharply than that of foodstuffs. This was indeed true in France – but in Japan the opposite obtained. Why? Whereas the 18th-century French population rose 30 percent, Japan's was virtually flat. For obvious biological reasons, people could more easily increase consumption of manufactures than food, especially if income distribution was weighted heavily toward the upper classes – which suggests that Japanese demand for food remained more or less constant, and that increases in per capita income led primarily to higher demand for manufactures. See following note, plus Miyamoto, "Quantitative Aspects," 67, and discussion in Jack Goldstone, *Revolution and Rebellion in the Early Modern World* (Berkeley, 1991), 184–89.

a proportion of the gross product and in real purchasing power.[285] In a word, as Japan became richer, the government grew poorer.

The shogunate and the domains struggled to escape this scissors through a variety of expedients.[286] Even as it resorted to inflationary currency debasements, the shogunate sought, in time honored fashion, to control demand and prices by fiat, wage fixing, compulsory procurement, and marketing through licensed traders who acted in effect as government agents. *Shogun* and *daimyo* exhorted commoners to surrender more, borrowed heavily, imposed special levies on merchants and wealthy villagers, and sought to prevent sumptuary infractions. Particularly from the 1790s, they cut the stipends of *samurai* retainers, which constituted the largest single government obligation. From the mid-to-late 1700s various *daimyo* officials, championing a mercantilist philosophy of domain prosperity (*kokueki*), also promoted industrial crops and other specialized products whose sale they sought to monopolize in competition with traders licensed by the shogunate.

On the whole, these efforts bore little fruit. Exhortations proved ineffectual and debasement and borrowing, self-defeating. Some mercantilist schemes enjoyed an initial success, but in the face of widespread evasion, few *daimyo* improved their finances substantially. By the 1830s (admittedly a period of severe famine) almost all domains owed heavy debts, in one case 33 times its annual income.[287] Recognizing the ineffectuality of earlier approaches, by the second quarter of the 19th century many domains had eased restrictions on rural industry and commerce in favor of license fees and a *daimyo* share in private profits.[288] Shogunal finances exhibited similar strains, both because the agricultural tax base was too narrow and because, insofar as *daimyo* monopolies and markets diverted goods from shogunate-ruled cities, commercial gains for *daimyo* and rural producers threatened shogunal procurement.[289] Not surprisingly, *shogun* and *daimyo* repeatedly clashed over economic issues. On three occasions – during the Kyoho Reform of the 1720s,

---

[285] Smith, *Native Sources*, 39–41; Totman, *Early Modern Japan*, 295; Crawcour, "Economic Change," 575–76; Ravina, *Land and Lordship*, 62; Miyamoto and Shikano, "Emergence of the Monetary System," esp. Fig. 1; Goldstone, *Revolution and Rebellion*, 404–15.

[286] Crawcour, "Economic Change," 573–80, 585–600; Nishikawa and Amano, "Domains," 247–67; Oguchi, "Finances," 192–212; *HJ*, 254–56; Pratt, *Protoindustrial Elite*, 21–27; Howell, *Geographies*, 39, 64–65, 135–37; and esp. Roberts, *Mercantilism*.

[287] The Satsuma domain. Crawcour, "Economic Change," 588.

[288] Crawcour, "Economic Change," 578–92; Roberts, *Mercantilism*, ch. 8; Nakamura, "Development of Rural Industry"; Bolitho, "The Han," 220–25.

[289] Crawcour, "Economic Change," 588–92.

the Kansei Reform of 1787–1793, and the Tempo Reform of the 1830s–1840s – the shogunate and certain *daimyo* made determined efforts to return to the martial simplicity, agrarian primacy, and trade regulation of earlier times. While the Kyoho Reform enjoyed some success, later efforts showed how far commercialization and consumer demand had advanced. By the 1840s villages in advanced regions were served by shops selling a full range of once circumscribed consumer goods. In essence, a polity based on ascription and obedience could not tame a market based on competition and choice.[290]

The social counterpart to growing financial disorder was a blurring of 17th-century status divisions, along with social tensions and a growing climate of disaffection. On the one hand, efforts at fiscal retrenchment often took 20 to 30 percent of *samurai* real income, impoverishing middle and lower grades and driving many into humiliating personal economies, debt, and non-*samurai* by-employments. Whereas in the 17th century warrior consumption had spearheaded cultural innovation, that vitality now ebbed. Aggravating *samurai* self-doubt was their persistently anomalous functionality: they were soldiers without a military role and administrators in a system whose excess of candidates over posts meant that many now had limited hopes of active service.[291]

On the other hand, the prosperity of urban and more especially rural merchants, landlords, and protoindustrialists allowed them to pursue a material lifestyle that was the envy of lower *samurai*, and in the case of some merchants, equal to that of petty *daimyo*. A vibrant urban culture fused *samurai* and commoner contributions. Commercial enterprise permeated rural districts, while farmers entered the towns. In short, although actual practice had diverged from normative ideals even in the 17th century, by the early 1800s two centuries of market expansion had eroded the barrier between city and countryside and had produced an unprecedented lifestyle convergence among townspeople, wealthy peasants, and lower and middle *samurai*. In all these groups, albeit most grudgingly among *samurai*, we find growing involvement in labor markets and a partial shift in the criteria of status from birth

---

[290] Berry, *Japan in Print*, 173. See too Crawcour, "Economic Change," 590–600; Totman, *Early Modern Japan*, 296–315, 467 ff.; White, *Ikki*, 43–45; Tsuji Tatsuya, "Politics in the Eighteenth Century," in *CHJ*, vol. IV, 425–77; Marius Jansen, "Introduction," in *CHJ*, vol. V, 5–8; Harold Bolitho, "The Tempo Crisis," in *CHJ*, vol. V, 116–67.

[291] Crawcour, "Economic Change," 575–76; Totman, *Early Modern Japan*, 380–81; Mary Elizabeth Berry, "Public Life in Authoritarian Japan," *Daedalus* 127 (1998): 142–44. On evolving *samurai* roles and frustrations, also Ikegami, *Taming Samurai*, pts. 4–7.

to achievement.[292] Meanwhile, the autonomy of village corporations and urban neighborhoods joined *samurai* disengagement from routine commercial management to enhance the administrative role of village headmen and urban merchants, converting them into what Berry calls "nonsamurai near-officials."[293]

If political and social tensions fluctuated, by and large in the late Tokugawa era they were notably more acute than during the 17th century. Many *samurai* responded to their declining fortunes with bitter parodies of merchant pretensions, intellectual critiques of government legitimacy, and a growing interest in domain politics. Reinforced from the late 1820s by a sense of European menace, the conviction spread that the political order, as currently managed, was deeply inadequate.[294] In the 1860s *samurai* resentment became among the most potent domestic causes of Tokugawa collapse.

Meanwhile villages grew more turbulent. Whereas the 17th century saw an average of 4.9 protests per year, from 1750 to 1800 – as dislocations associated with commodity production and weather-related famines became more severe – protests rose to an average of 14.4 per year, and from 1801 to 1850 to 16.3. Moreover, whereas early protests appealed peacefully for benevolence from *samurai* officials, after c. 1750 they became larger and more violent. Commonly they also targeted not *samurai* outside the villages, who lost salience, but merchants and village leaders. Hailing from the emergent class of landowners-cum-usurers-cum-entrepreneurs, the latter often were accused of unfair tax allocations. At the same time popular resentment of price fluctuations, tax demands, and food shortages contributed to unauthorized millennial religious movements.[295] More often than their European counterparts,

---

[292] There is also evidence of more frequent *samurai*–commoner marriages. On threats to the status system, see discussion of culture *infra*, plus Berry, *Japan in Print*, 240–51; Nobuhiko, "Commercial Change," 593–95; Jansen, "Japan in Nineteenth Century," 50–51, 66–79, 111; Gary Leupp, *Servants, Shophands, and Laborers in the Cities of Tokugawa Japan* (Princeton, 1992); Hanley, *Everyday Things*, 13–61; Smith, *Native Sources*, 40–41, 156–72; Rozman, "Social Change," 528–33, 563; Howell, *Geographies*, 46–58, 77.

[293] Berry, "Public Life," 143–44. On the "de-samuraization" of Edo and commoners' reluctant "appropriation" of the city, see too William Kelly, "Incendiary Actions," in McClain, *Edo and Paris*, 310–31.

[294] H. D. Harootunian, "Late Tokugawa Culture and Thought," in *CHJ*, vol. V, 182–215, 231–58; Totman, *Early Modern Japan*, 379, 398. 429, 450–64, 504–18.

[295] On village conflict, religious dissent, as well as urban unrest, Bolitho, "The *Han*," 214–16; Hayami and Kito, "Demography," 235; Harootunian, "Late Tokugawa Culture," 215–31; Eiko Ikegami and Charles Tilly, "State Formation and Contention in Japan and France," in McClain, *Edo and Paris*, 446–54; Herman Ooms, *Tokugawa Village Practice*

samurai officials tended to quell rural unrest by buying off peasants with tax reductions, in part because they, unlike the French or Russians, faced no iron military imperative.

To claim it was sliding into paralysis is too dire a judgment on a regime that retained considerable vitality and, absent Western intervention, probably could have continued for some time. Clearly, however, while other Eurasian realms grew more cohesive and ambitious, the Tokugawa regime became hostage to fiscal crisis and accepted a growing dissonance between administrative norms and actual practice. In Berry's words, it made its peace with "chronic indebtedness and insults to the status system."[296]

And yet further reflection suggests that Japanese evolution between c. 1600 and 1830 did parallel that of other Eurasian realms in five critical respects. First and most obvious, post-1600 integration – as in Burma, Siam, Russia, France, and other protected zone polities, but in contrast to, say, Mughal India – remained secure. For well over two centuries *shogun* and *daimyo* maintained the most effective polity Japan had ever known, regional rebellions ceased, and the shogunate extended its authority across the three main islands and to the north and south.

Second, shogunal administrative history after 1650 cannot be reduced to a story of simple regression. Notwithstanding a reluctance to raise taxes, in the 18th and early 19th centuries peasant protest led the shogunate to expand its powers of coercion and intervention across the islands in a development James White terms the "nationalization of contention." Thus the shogunate established a judicial system with self-arrogated islands-wide authority and, when necessary, showed no hesitation following that jurisdiction straight into the domains. From the 1730s the shogunate also required *daimyo* to furnish troops against protests in neighboring domains, and itself intervened in domains to prevent excessive concessions.[297] So too between c. 1700 and 1850, as deforestation and reclamation created severe problems of flooding and erosion that transcended the capacities of individual domains, the

---

(Berkeley, 1996), esp. ch. 2; White, *Ikki*, incl. chart on 128 and 183–91; Stephen Vlastos, *Peasant Protests and Uprisings in Tokugawa Japan* (Berkeley, 1986); Herbert Bix, *Peasant Protest in Japan, 1590–1884* (New Haven, 1986); Burns, *Before the Nation*, 23–24, citing peasant protest figures from Aoki Koji; Walthall, pers. commun., 2006.

[296] Berry, *Japan in Print*, 172.

[297] James White, "State Growth and Popular Protest in Tokugawa Japan," *JJS* 14 (1988), 1–25; idem, *Ikki*, 51; Botsman, *Punishment and Power*, 80–83; Toby, "Rescuing the Nation," 202, 208.

shogunate took responsibility for coordinating river conservancy in the Kinai, Nobi, and Kanto plains, commandeering *daimyo* labor on a grand scale and, when possible, providing additional resources.[298] Nor were internal structures static. Within the shogunate expanded ritual and administrative goals, the need to support additional vassals, and growing Neo-Confucian influence encouraged a notable multiplication of offices, a rationalization and routinization of administrative services, and greater professionalism. These trends were accompanied by the development of an informal power structure, the vertical clique, that enabled a single group to control political and administrative functions, while also allowing the shogunate periodically to renew its leadership and, within limits, to change policies. If not genuinely bureaucratic, by 1830 the shogunate, not unlike its Southeast Asian and European counterparts, had become a "vastly more complex political instrument" than in the early 1600s. Similar developments in domain administration strengthened the capacity of the Tokugawa system as a whole.[299]

Third, to the extent that they had a commercial root, Tokugawa geopolitical and social tensions are familiar from Southeast Asia and Europe. This is not to deny deeply idiosyncratic features, including Japan's peculiar difficulty tapping non-cereal production and its demographic stability; the latter moderated the problem of marginal elites identified by Jack Goldstone in other societies and encouraged the aforementioned fall in the real price of cereals.[300] Yet price inflation – albeit in this case in non-cereal goods – arguably was no less politically destabilizing in late Tokugawa Japan than in Restored Toungoo Burma, Nguyen Vietnam, or late Bourbon France. So too, the benefits that rapid growth afforded the Irrawaddy and Mekong deltas vis-à-vis their imperial cores offer dramatic versions of the competitive advantage that outlying *daimyo* derived vis-à-vis the Kinai–Kanto axis from protoindustry and local population growth after 1720.[301] Yet more broadly, in Japan as elsewhere social and geographic mobility, rooted in commercial expansion, eroded the regime's foundational insistence

---

[298] Oguchi, "Finances," 204–206; Totman, "Preindustrial River Conservancy," 59–76.

[299] Quote from Totman, *Politics*, 234. On administrative expansion and routinization, ibid, 204–61; Berry, "Public Peace," 255–61; White, "State Growth"; and Ikegami, *Taming Samurai*, 241–64, 299–325, discussing Neo-Confucian influence.

[300] On Goldstone's theory of marginal elites, *SP*, 68, 277, 301, 305, and discussion *supra*, Chs. 2, 3. On falling rice prices, n. 284 *supra*.

[301] Cf. *SP*, 173–78, 406–26; Ch. 3 *supra*; Innes, "Door Ajar," 631–33.

on status group segmentation.[302] Given sharper initial divisions, more formidable legal and practical barriers to subsequent mobility, and the absence of any generic notion of "citizen," the threat to estate divisions remained far less potent in Japan than in *ancien régime* France. But tensions between an ideology of hereditary status and the reality of growing mobility were at least as pronounced as in Southeast Asia – where 18th- to early-19th-century commercial growth favored an exodus from royal to private service – or in Russia, where market forces also nourished interstitial groups and permitted a modest erosion of early Romanov social divisions.[303]

Fourth, if we extend our vision to the third quarter of the 19th century, Japan's political trajectory is also broadly familiar. In Burma, Siam, Vietnam, and France, we saw, internal difficulties became overwhelming in the second half of the 18th century only because war invited devastating invasions or imposed unsustainable tax and conscription burdens. Notwithstanding Russian probes from the 1780s and the appearance of English and American vessels, Japan's location long sheltered the regime. But with Commodore Matthew Perry's mission of 1853–1854, followed by European demands for treaty concessions, foreign requests for trade yielded to systematic impositions. Along with the steep costs of military defense, these humiliations stoked long simmering critiques of Tokugawa rule, ushering in the Meiji Restoration, which revolutionized – even as it rested upon – Tokugawa legacies.[304] Insofar as they destroyed the early-17th-century settlement and engendered a more effective political order, American and European demands on Tokugawa Japan therefore recall those interstate pressures that toppled the chief Southeast Asian regimes and Bourbon France roughly a century earlier.[305]

The Dynamics of Cultural Integration Under the Tokugawa

Finally, Japan resembled the other five realms in its accelerating cultural integration, which drew strength from the country's post-1590 political settlement and from its dense commercial and urban networks. I shall

---

[302] See nn. 291–93 *supra*.

[303] See n. 222 *supra*; Ch. 3, n. 221 *supra*; and SP, 182–85, 300–308, 441–45.

[304] W. G. Beasley, "The Foreign Threat and the Opening of the Ports," in *CHJ*, vol. V, ch. 4; Marius Jansen, "The Meiji Restoration," in ibid., ch. 5.

[305] Japan's predicament also recalls pressures for reform that Russia faced following its defeat in the Crimean War.

sketch the dynamics of cultural change before assessing their intellectual and political implications.

After centuries of disorder, state interventions in the 1590s and early 1600s provided the Japanese with what Berry argues was a novel framework in which to visualize their islands. Building on 16th-century projects, the unifiers and their successors sponsored cadastral inquests whose results were used to construct an islands-wide grid in which disparate communities were conceived uniformly as "villages," each with an assessed yield computed in standard units of rice equivalent. All *daimyo* domains and *samurai* stipends now could be assigned according to formalized, consistent principles. What is more, four cartographic surveys in the 17th century and others to 1805 permitted construction of the first pan-Japanese maps since the *ritsuryo* era. Reproduced and elaborated by commercial publishers, to whom the shogunate released copies, these overviews also encouraged the literate public as well as officials to think holistically about the realm. Unity derived not merely from the maps' self-designations – "Japan" (*Nihon*), "Great Japan" (*Dai Nihon*), "our realm," "the entire country" – but from their uniform presentation of *daimyo* domains, the prominence of shogunal cities and the imperial capital, a focus on unifying highways, and the invocation of Heian-era provinces. To all they proclaimed: A united body of *shogun* and *daimyo* now rules an ancient and prosperous realm of shared culture.[306]

A standardizing, integrative cultural logic informed other official acts, including the persecution of sects deemed hostile to Tokugawa rule (notably Christianity and the Fujufuse sect of Hokke Buddhism), the requirement that all commoners register with Buddhist temples, periodic efforts by the shogunate and some domains to make Zhu Xi Neo-Confucianism a semi-official ideology, publications censorship, and policies of Ainu assimilation (see below). More broadly, the status system as a Japan-wide legal and social institution originated in the sword-hunts, land surveys, and censuses of the unification period and continued to draw strength from shogunal example and exhortation.[307]

---

[306] I follow Berry, *Japan in Print*, 22–25, 39–45, 60, 81–100, 209–11, which in varying degrees concurs with Yonemoto, *Mapping*, 1–43 (with map titles on 1, 42); Morris-Suzuki, "Frontiers of Identity," 46–47, 56. Cf. newly bounded spatial imaginaries in France, Ch. 3, n. 134 *supra*.

[307] Toby, "Rescuing the Nation," 208–209; Burns, *Before the Nation*, 30–33; Totman, *Early Modern Japan*, 449–51, 469–73; Howell, *Geographies*, 16, 30–37; Howell, pers. commun., Nov. 3, 2006.

Although the shogunate designed *sankin-kotai* more as a vehicle of political than cultural integration, I have already suggested that the stationing of *daimyo* families in Edo and the constant to-and-fro of a large portion of the ruling class between capital and provinces worked marvelously well to nurture an Edo-centered status hierarchy that crosscut *daimyo* polycentrism, to promote intellectual/cultural conformity, and to disseminate Edo *samurai* dialect (a process aided by manuals expressly designed to teach *daimyo* retinues the Edo tongue). Lengthy residence at the capital elevated *daimyo* leaders, like their European and Southeast Asian counterparts, from provincial warriors to refined courtiers. In the eyes of Edo *samurai*, their rustic peers still stuck in castle towns had become "mountain apes."[308] Within each domain, miniature versions of the alternate attendance system added a second level of horizontal exchange. Late Tokugawa programs of sending youths to study at respected schools in other domains further eroded regional barriers.[309]

Paralleling political spurs to lateral communication were economic pressures. By spreading Edo customs to the provinces, late Tokugawa commerce joined "alternate attendance" to encourage a process – still in progress in the 21st century – that might be termed the "Edo-ization" or "Tokyo-ization" of Japan.[310] During the 17th century, as Edo became Japan's political center, Kyoto remained culturally preeminent and Osaka served as commercial hub. In the 18th and 19th centuries, however, a combination of rural protoindustry, new marketing networks, and shogunal policy weakened Kyoto, Osaka, and many castle towns, while Edo grew rapidly in population, wealth, and cultural brilliance. The implications were captured in the phrase "culture's march eastward." If cultural integration lacked the same official sanction as in Louis XIV's France, Japan, like France, became more of a unicentric cultural zone focused on the capital.[311] Letters, news bills, pamphlets, plays, and word of mouth information circulated from Edo to smaller towns, post stations, markets, and villages, spreading capital customs

[308] Totman, *Early Modern Japan*, 477–78. Also n. 206 *supra*; Reischauer and Craig, *Japan*, 86; Bolitho, "The *Han*," 201; H. B. D. Clarke, "The Development of Edo Language," in C. Andrew Gerstle, ed., *18th Century Japan: Culture and Society* (Sydney, 1989), 63, 70–71.

[309] Richard Rubinger, *Private Academies of Tokugawa Japan* (Princeton, 1982), 24–38.

[310] Henry D. Smith II, "The History of the Book in Edo and Paris," in McClain, *Edo and Paris*, 350–51, citing Peter Kornicki.

[311] Totman, *Early Modern Japan*, 382, 401–403, 477–81.

as well as dialect.[312] Likewise from Edo colporteurs carried not only farming manuals and practical publications, but novels to rent to avid rural readers. Since literary characters were often Edo folk, after 1750 Edo dialect gradually surpassed that of Kyoto and Osaka for fictional dialogue. By the early 1800s printed books from Edo were read almost everywhere, as stamps in provincial lending libraries confirm.[313] Linguistic and cultural centripetalism, at least in parts of Honshu, was further aided by itinerant troupes of actors and singers using Edo colloquial, as well as by peasant migrants and rural entrepreneurs with ties to urban traders.[314]

Improved living standards, new confraternities, and better roads also permitted the transformation of religious pilgrimages into essentially secular recreation, an opportunity to sight-see and escape deadening routine, which Constantine Vaporis claims became a "national obsession."[315] Whereas medieval pilgrimage had attracted primarily warriors and wealthy farmers, in the late Tokugawa era travel became – despite official discouragement – a mass activity, with the famous Ise Shrine alone attracting as many as 5,000,000 (sic) pilgrims in 1830.[316] Melding women as well as men from diverse social and geographic backgrounds, pilgrimage allowed an "Edo man [to] make acquaintance with the Satsuma sweet potato [a man from the far south]."[317]

---

[312] By the early 1800s "Japan was flooded with [urban-derived] information." Moriya, "Urban Networks," 122. See too Anne Walthall, "Peripheries: Rural Culture in Tokugawa Japan," *MN* 39 (1984): 371–92, esp. 379–85; Totman, *Early Modern Japan*, 87, 383, 388, 395, 401–402; Jansen, "Japan in Nineteenth Century," 80; Sato, "Tokugawa Villages," 60.

[313] Clarke, "Development of Edo Language," 63, 71 claims that Edo dialect began to serve as "a lingua franca for the entire country" and to assume "the role of a national language." On the rise of Edo language (which itself contained dialect differences) and its relation to publishing, also Sato, "Tokugawa Villages," 75–77; Totman, *Early Modern Japan*, 382–83, 417; Hiroko Quackenbush, "Edo and Tokyo Dialects," in Gerstle, *18th Century Japan*, 73–84; Zwicker, pers. commun., June 27, 2006.

[314] Clarke, "Development of Edo Language," 63, 70.

[315] Discussion of pilgrimages and travel follows Vaporis, *Breaking Barriers*, 217–61 (quoted phrase p. 259); Jansen, "Japan in Nineteenth Century," 64–65; Moriya, "Urban Networks," 97–123; Berry, "Was Early Modern Japan Integrated?" 131–32; James Foard, "The Boundaries of Compassion," *JAS* 41 (1982): 231–51; Rubinger, *Private Academies*, 19–23.

[316] In more normal years 200,000 to 500,000 visited Ise. Vaporis, *Breaking Barriers*, 242–44. This is not to deny that from the 1100s some poor peasants, even beggars, also went on pilgrimage. Farris, pers. commun., Aug. 11, 2006.

[317] Vaporis, *Breaking Barriers*, 260.

Consider too the impact of the prose style known as *sorobun*, a form of literary Japanese more Sinicized than most popular writing. Notwithstanding the aforementioned trends to linguistic circulation, what is now standard Japanese speech (*hyojungo*), which derived chiefly from the *samurai* dialect of Edo in much the same way as modern French grew from elite Parisian speech, became truly standardized only through radio and television in the mid-1900s. In the Tokugawa era the tongue of an official from Kyushu still might be barely comprehensible to his counterparts in central Honshu, and even between Edo and Kyoto verbal communication could pose problems. Yet these same officials had no difficulty reading one another's documents, for officials everywhere down to the village level wrote in *sorobun* and employed a standard calligraphic style known as *oieryu*. So too, literary and scholarly writing, either in elevated Japanese or classical Chinese, was standardized. More obviously than in France, where Occitan and Provencal exhibited a stubborn vitality, or in Burma, where Mon and Shan literatures flourished, a uniform written language thus weakened barriers to interregional communication (even as it created a common medium in which to express regional identities).[318]

So far I have focused on horizontal acculturation, but the market also sped vertical exchange. Because commercial vitality to 1700 benefited most directly urban commoners (*chonin*) – merchants, shopkeepers, and craftsmen – these strata were well placed to experiment as cultural producers and consumers. From 17th-century cities emerged that vibrant, risqué complex of arts, drama, and writing known as *ukiyo*, "floating world" culture. Focused on the life of brothels and theaters, sites that Tokugawa rulers sought to quarantine as socially polluting, *ukiyo* culture generated a host of innovations, including *kabuki* theater and new forms of popular fiction, poetry, puppet theater, painting, prints, and fashionable dress. As such, it appealed to status groups officially excluded from political life and championed a boisterous, hedonistic ethic that contrasted with Confucian norms. By the 19th century, urban entertainment was addressing a yet more plebian

[318] I rely on Howell, *Geographies*, 199–200; Lie, *Multiethnic Japan*, 186–87; *HJ*, 245; Clarke, "Development of Edo Language"; Quackenbush, "Edo and Tokyo Dialects," 74–78; Berry, "Was Early Modern Japan Integrated?"; Wigen, pers. commun., Sept. 2, 2002; Ken Ito, pers. commun., Oct. 8, 2002; Zwicker, pers. commun., June 8, 2006; Seeley, *History of Writing*, 105, 112, 114, 117, 127, 129, 197; Miller, *Japanese Language*, 141–71; and Smith, "History of the Book," 337–38, noting that the very complexity of Japanese writing tended to encourage reliance on set forms and higher authorities.

audience.[319] Yet "the floating world" was never an exclusively commoner affair, for some of its principal creators were of *samurai* origin,
and its audience from the start was mixed, whether in Kyoto, where
ukiyo culture flourished most brilliantly to the late 1600s, or in Osaka,
Edo, and provincial towns. In the late Tokugawa era as the economic
position of *samurai* declined and as wealth allowed successful *chonin* to
defy sumptuary restrictions, such mixing became yet more pronounced.
Official efforts to enforce status-group distinctions served only to throt-
tle *samurai* creativity, further enhancing the "floating world's" appeal
to many warrior aesthetes.[320] For the first time, according to Donald
Shively, commoners, the nonelite, assumed a critical cultural role.[321]

If commoner practices thus influenced *samurai* and even imperial
courtiers, the reverse was also true. Not only did *ukiyo* culture draw on
upper-class literary and artistic conventions, but *samurai* prestige, merchant aspirations, a yearning for moral certitude, and new cultural vehicles (schools, plays, novels, the work of Buddhist missionaries skilled
in Confucian learning) combined to disseminate elite Neo-Confucian
ideals throughout society.[322] Much as French provincial nobles and
ambitious bourgeois copied elite Parisian speech and fashion, successful Japanese merchants demonstrated their arrival by acquiring skills
indicative of *samurai* status: the tea ceremony, flower arranging, poetic
forms, Chinese philosophy, writing, arts and crafts. So too, the speech of
Edo merchants began to imitate *samurai* literary language.[323] Observed
a scholar of merchant origin as early as 1719:

---

[319] Totman, *Early Modern Japan*, 102–103, 183–88, 195–222, 382–95, 401–27; *HJ*, 260–63;
McClain and Wakita, *Osaka*, ch. 5; Donald Jenkins, ed., *The Floating World Revisited*
(Honolulu, 1993), esp. the essay by Henry Smith II. See too Carlo Marco Belfanti,
"Was Fashion a European Invention?" *JGH* 3 (2008): 435–43, comparing Tokugawa
and European commercial fashion. On artistic styles opposed to *ukiyo* culture, Screech,
Shogun's Painted Culture.

[320] Shively, "Popular Culture," 706–15; Totman, *Early Modern Japan*, 378–95.

[321] Shively, "Popular Culture," 706, and 706–69 *passim*, concentrating on the 17th century.

[322] George Sansom, *Japan: A Short Cultural History* (Stanford, 1952), 481, 483; Bito,
"Thought and Religion," 397–404; Shively, "Popular Culture," 717–32; Harold Bolitho,
"Tokugawa Japan: The China Connection" (ms), 4; Nishiyama Matsunosuke, *Edo Culture* (Honolulu, 1997), pts. 1, 2; Bellah, *Tokugawa Religion*, 54–55, 69, 142–43, 155,
182–83.

[323] Quackenbush, "Edo and Tokyo Dialects," 80–81; Nishiyama, *Edo Culture*, 35–37, noting
how *chonin* female servants in *samurai* Edo households provided a channel of linguistic
transmission; Patricia Graham, *Tea of the Sages* (Honolulu, 1998), 3, 42–49, 66, 97, 100,
138–67; Ikegami, *Bonds of Civility*, 149–53. Yet the tea ceremony and flower arranging
were relatively new arts some of whose early creators were themselves of merchant
origin. Butler, pers. commun., Dec. 2, 2006.

For a long time the merchants have been regarded as inferior to the peasants, but ever since the money economy grew to country-wide proportions, everyone has been borrowing money from them.... Nowadays the peasants and even the samurai, engage in commercial activities. Moreover, most [professionals] – Confucian scholars, doctors, poets, tea-ceremony masters – are *chonin*.[324]

As lower strata appropriated and modified elite conventions, the *samurai* ideal of "gentlemanly accomplishments" (*yugei*) was gradually emptied of class content. In imitation of, and in defensive reaction against, *samurai* pretensions, some businessmen drafted merchant house laws and patriarchal admonitions, founded merchant academies, and developed Neo-Confucian-style teachings stressing the inherent dignity and moral value of their labor.[325] Reacting to 18th-century economic difficulties, *chonin* also pioneered the mercantilist philosophy of *kokueki*, which although eventually appropriated by *samurai* administrators, accorded merchants, consumers, and other elevated male commoners an unprecedented public worth.[326] On a more prosaic level the aristocratic *shoin* style of architecture, along with elements of *samurai* hairstyle, diet, clothing, and sanitation, diffused to lower urban strata in what Susan Hanley terms the "samurai-zation" of material culture.[327]

Nor, especially from the late 1700s, were such currents restricted to city milieux. Greater wealth and easier market access, accompanied by the growing popularity of books and travel, let well-to-do villagers in the late Tokugawa era acquire many of the same physical amenities and genteel accomplishments – the Chinese classics, *noh* drama, drum playing, the tea ceremony, poetry – as successful *chonin*. Rich peasants not only pursued scholarly and artistic activities, but in the teeth of official policy, sometimes ignored sumptuary rules, sponsored *kabuki* performances, built houses to mimic *samurai* residences, even studied

[324] Totman, *Early Modern Japan*, 358. Also ibid., 186, 371, 380; Graham, *Tea*, 100.

[325] On merchant adaptation of *samurai* and Neo-Confucian norms, Shively, "Popular Culture," 765–68; Totman, *Early Modern Japan*, 357–62, 453; *HJ*, 267–70; Tetsuo Najita, *Visions of Virtue in Tokugawa Japan* (Chicago, 1987) on the Osaka Merchant Academy; Bellah, *Tokugawa Religion*, ch. 6. See too Jennifer Robertson, "The Shingaku Woman," in Gail Bernstein, ed., *Recreating Japanese Women, 1600–1945* (Berkeley, 1991), 88–107, showing how merchant teachings, despite their emancipatory potential for men, remained deeply misogynist.

[326] Roberts, *Mercantilism*, 1–31, 103–53, 198–204.

[327] Hanley, *Everyday Things*, 178, and 30–31, 58–61, 154, 166; idem, "Tokugawa Society," 662, 664–70, 692, 704.

martial arts.[328] Nor was it unknown for wealthy farmers to purchase *samurai* status.[329] Revealingly, whereas 18th-century spokesmen championed the inherent worth of *chonin* lives, in the 1800s some thinkers began to make the same claims for rural commoners.

Partial unification of culture meant, furthermore, that, despite a proliferation of Buddhist temples, *chonin* and many educated peasants joined *samurai* in adopting a more secular, rationalist outlook. In part because Buddhist temples came under state control, and in part because Neo-Confucianism, relative prosperity, and *ukiyo* hedonism, each in its own way, favored more secular perspectives, Tokugawa religion softened the preoccupation with escaping the world characteristic of medieval Buddhism. Priests now devoted themselves to civil registration tasks demanded by lay authorities, to cultivating ritual ties between the living and departed relatives, and to commercial syntheses of prayer and secular entertainments.[330] While less hostile to formal religion than some Enlightenment currents (in part, no doubt, because Tokugawa Buddhism, unlike European Christianity, made few claims to institutional or doctrinal exclusivity), this reorientation bears at least a superficial likeness to 18th-century secularizing trends among Russian and French elites.

Again as in France and Southeast Asia and, less obviously, Russia, schools and literacy provided some of the principal avenues of both vertical and horizontal exchange. Familiar too were the dynamics of educational expansion. Urban life and trade required some degree of writing and numeracy, while wealth provided the wherewithal for buildings and teachers. Routinized administration produced a flood of documents that village leaders as well as *samurai* had to read; indeed, in the early Tokugawa era literacy already was a prerequisite for village

---

[328] Walthall, "Peripheries," 371–92; idem, *The Weak Body of a Useless Woman* (Chicago, 1998), chs. 1, 3, 5, 6; Ikegami, *Bonds of Civility*, 204–16; Totman, *Early Modern Japan*, 360–61, 436–42; Hanley, "Tokugawa Society," 664, 670.

[329] And attributes of *samurai* status. See n. 222 *supra*; Jansen, "Japan in Nineteenth Century," 77; Walthall, *Weak Body*, 11. At a lower social level, market integration of mountain and seaside communities further eroded cultural isolates.

[330] Many of the emotional benefits once provided by Buddhist priests now were provided by low-status diviners and unofficial pledge-book priests. On post-1600 religious shifts, some adumbrated as early as the 15th century, Nam-lin Hur, *Prayer and Play in Late Tokugawa Japan* (Cambridge, MA, 2000); Kasahara, *History*, 335, 344–45; Bito, "Thought and Religion," 374–87; Beasley, *Japanese Experience*, 172–73; Hayami, "Great Transformation," 5; Reader and Tanabe, *Practically Religious*; Karen Wigen, pers. commun., Sept. 13, 2006. Cf. comparable shifts in Dai Viet, *SP*, 442–49.

headmen.[331] By 1800 some domains were promoting popular instruction both to inculcate morality and to teach production skills. For their part, ambitious commoners as well as *samurai* valued education as an aid to upward mobility and as a form of cultural capital, prestigious for the family.[332]

Until the late 18th century the chief schools were private academies (*shijuku*) run for *samurai* and wealthy *chonin*. Urban at first, by the early 19th century *shijuku* were tutoring sons of rural traders, village headmen, and well-to-do farmers. From the 1780s and more especially the 1820s three other types of schools also proliferated: official domain academies, chiefly for *samurai* and thoroughly Confucian in outlook; small parish elementary schools (*terakoya*), which community leaders founded to provide basic skills for local youths; and schools tied to particular religious sects, whose clientele was also plebian.[333] Supplemented by home tuition, these institutions by 1850 had produced a male literacy rate of 40 to 50 percent and a female rate of perhaps 15 percent. Although these levels were similar to Indic Southeast Asia, unlike those societies but as in France and Russia, in Japan the ability to read remained far less common in the countryside than in cities, where in fact male literacy became normative.[334]

Rising literacy supported an urban publishing industry in a push–pull relation reminiscent of France. With similar populations and literacy rates, France in the 1770s and Japan in the 1840s produced annual titles in the same order of magnitude.[335] And in both countries

---

[331] R. P. Dore, *Education in Tokugawa Japan* (Berkeley, 1965), 21; Ikegami, *Taming Samurai*, 274.

[332] This was true even for daughters. On spurs to education, Brian Platt, *Burning and Building* (Cambridge, MA, 2004), 34–65, 71; Rozman, "Social Change," 560; Jansen, "Japan in Nineteenth Century," 55–62; Walthall, "Peripheries," 383; Karen Wigen, pers. commun., Sept. 13, 2006.

[333] Platt, *Burning and Building*, 1, 25 says Tokugawa commoners in towns and villages may have established 40,000 to 50,000 (sic) schools, of which 15,000 to 20,000 operated at any given moment from 1848 to 1868. On Tokugawa schools, ibid, chs. 1, 2; Totman, *Early Modern Japan*, 351–55, 429–36; Jansen, "Japan in Nineteenth Century," 57; Rubinger, *Private Academies*; Shively, "Popular Culture," 715–25.

[334] Male literacy among *samurai* and peasant officials was virtually 100 percent, but perhaps only 20 percent among isolated farmers. On the sociology and geography of literacy, Platt, *Burning and Building*, 33–34, emphasizing different types of literacy; Totman, *Early Modern Japan*, 435–36; Hanley, *Everyday Things*, 190; Yonemoto, *Mapping*, 185 n. 26; Moriya, "Urban Networks," 118–21; Ikegami, *Bonds of Civility*, 300–306; Walthall, pers. commun., 2006.

[335] Some 1,500 titles a year in France and 1,000 in Japan, with editions of 500–1,000 in both cases, according to Smith, "History of the Book," 335–36. However, Yonemoto,

printing was symbiotic with market intensification. From 1690 to 1840 the number of new Japanese titles rose over fivefold, while print runs and the number of bookstores, rental libraries, and itinerant lenders also increased markedly. Edo in 1808 had as many lending libraries as barbershops and bathhouses.[336] But if Japanese publishing resembled France in its urban focus, Japan's print revolution relied not on movable type, but woodblocks (which proved more economical and better able to reproduce Japanese script[337]) and took root in the 1590s, almost a century after comparable developments in Europe. Japan's chronology reflected, above all, rapid urban growth associated with unification.

At first subjects close to *samurai* interests – family and military histories, for example – dominated, but from the mid-1600s publishers brought out ever more middle- and low-brow works: travel accounts, almanacs, calendars, maps, urban directories, shopping guides, encyclopedias, dictionaries; manuals for everything from farming and forestry to music, etiquette, and medicine; poetry and art books; school primers; and especially from the 18th century, popular romances, historical and sentimental fiction, humorous tales, and comic books.[338] Written for the most part in a combination of *kana* script and Chinese characters, such publications arguably involved less linguistic displacement than did the rise of French at the expense of Latin. Nonetheless, to maximize audience, the more plebeian of the new works used simple *kana* with minimal Chinese characters, and from the late 1700s most fiction insisted on using colloquial dialogue.[339] As in Siam, Vietnam, and France, the

---

Mapping, 15 suggests that on average over 3,000 titles per year were published during the entire Tokugawa period. Berry, *Japan in Print*, 31 refers to 7,000 titles in print in Kyoto alone in 1692. Discussion of commercial publishing, including French comparisons, draws on these three sources, esp. Berry, *Japan in Print*, chs. 2, 6, plus Berry, "Was Early Modern Japan Integrated?" 116–35; Peter Kornicki, *The Book in Japan* (Leiden, 1998), chs. 1, 4–9; Ikegami, *Bonds of Civility*, esp. ch. 11; Moriya, "Urban Networks," 114–18; Shively, "Popular Culture," 725–33.

[336] Kornicki, *The Book*, 258.

[337] And to integrate text with illustrations. Ikegami, *Bonds of Civility*, 291–97; Berry, *Japan in Print*, 29–31.

[338] Berry, *Japan in Print*, 32–33, 14–15; Ikegami, *Bonds of Civility*, 141, 177, 327–30.

[339] This was particularly true of the prose fictional genre known as *gesaku* ("playful work"). Zwicker, pers. commun., June 8, 2006; Smith, "History of the Book," 337–38; Miller, *Japanese Language*, 50–53; Shively, "Popular Culture," 726–31; Totman, *Early Modern Japan*, 417–22; Clarke, "Development of Edo Language," 66. Yet Brown, pers. commun., May 10, 2004, cautions that our vision of Tokugawa literature remains skewed by the limited number of subjects reviewed in English.

infiltration of popular styles encouraged a more realistic, quotidian literary orientation and a transcendence/modification of "proper" female roles.[340] But surely publishing's most subversive message was the assumption that any educated reader, regardless of status, could access what Berry terms "the library of public information." Skills and insights were open to all. Given sufficient resources and self-discipline, anyone could become learned in poetry, music, philosophy, or medicine – and thus become a gentleperson.[341]

In combination, then, post-1590 political initiatives, market integration, popular travel, *sorobun*, wider literacy, and commercial publishing promoted both an expanding geographic consciousness[342] and new forms of vertical exchange.

Admittedly, one easily can exaggerate the resultant uniformity, for as elsewhere, integration faced formidable limits and countervailing pressures. One barrier to integration was more apparent than real. In Japan no less than in Vietnam or France, market forces bred not only cultural exchange, but specialization. In one field after another – literature, music, painting, furnishings, food, clothing, theater, travel, commercial sex – the market rewarded novelty, and options exploded. One might imagine that this proliferation of possibilities opposed the erosion of difference, which was true in a limited and subjective sense. Yet, as always, specialization was less a barrier to integration than a necessary correlate. Whereas in earlier centuries differences had been primarily a function of social and geographic isolation, in the Tokugawa era, genres arose as subdivisions within ever more complex, overarching taxonomies. The interdependence of subspecialties appeared both in the tendency for innovation to define itself vis-à-vis earlier usages and in the sharing of language, production sites, and distribution networks.[343] As elsewhere, this dialectic of integration-cum-specialization implicated not only culture, but economics (growing markets meant more specialized producers and retailers) and administration (more encompassing organizations required more technically competent functionaries).

---

[340] Patricia Fister, *Japanese Women Artists, 1600–1900* (Lawrence, KA, 1988), 97–100; Zwicker, pers. commun., June 8, 2006; Walthall, *Weak Body*.

[341] Berry, *Japan in Print*, 50–51 and 13–53 *passim*. Also, Ikegami, *Bonds of Civility*, ch. 11 *passim*.

[342] Burns, *Before the Nation*, 28, 34, citing Konta Yozo.

[343] Cf. Berry, "Was Early Modern Japan Integrated?"; idem, *Japan in Print*, 241–42; Hanley, "Tokugawa Society," 660–705; Clarke, "Development of Edo Language," 63; Belfanti, "Was Fashion a European Invention," 435–43. Cf. Ch. 3, n. 275 on France.

A second, more genuine impediment to cultural coherence derived from the continued weakness and unevenness of integrative pressures. Rural illiteracy and yet poor communications ensured that localities, often with distinctive folklore, songs, dress, and speech, continued to provide a primary focus of identity. When explaining where they were from, Tokugawa peasants, Howell points out, habitually identified themselves as coming from village A in province B, with the latter usually derived from Heian-era units. They might also identify their *daimyo* domain, but only when it seemed germane, as when officials from neighboring domains were negotiating with local officials. Being better educated and more widely traveled, *samurai* knew more about Edo culture, but for them the domain was of overwhelmingly emotional and practical importance, and they always invoked that affiliation.[344] Early-19th-century guidebooks warned those venturing outside their home area not to laugh at local customs or accents; and travelogues appealed to urban readers by emphasizing the exoticism of the hinterland.[345] The fact that the same terms for "country" (*kuni*) and "state" (*kokka*) still applied either to *daimyo* domains or to Japan at large suggests how nested were identities and how indistinct, sources of legitimacy.[346] Desperate efforts by leaders in the Meiji era (1868–1912) to design a public education system, to construct a standardized national language, to instill reverence for the emperor, and to develop schools and national communications show that in their view the work of cultural unification had barely begun.[347]

---

[344] Howell, pers. commun., Nov. 3, 2006. Howell, moreover, suggests that a focus on large, powerful domains and on *samurai* sources has led scholars to exaggerate the importance of domains at the expense of smaller units in the affective identities of the general population. Walthall, pers. commun., 2006 concurs that peasant loyalty was directed first to the village, second to the domain, and to a *kuni* (province) only if it overlapped substantially with a domain. But for emphases on domain loyalty, sometimes termed *"han* nationalism," see Bolitho, "The *Han*," 183–84; Roberts, *Mercantilism*, 4–9, 22–23, 196–97, 201–204; Ravina, *Land and Lordship*, 16–45, 194–210. Cf. Toby, "Rescuing the Nation," 203, 212–15; Yonemoto, *Mapping*, 63. Note too the claim in White, "State Growth," 23–24; idem, *Ikki*, 36, that some 19th-century peasant petitions identified the principals as "honorable peasants of the realm," in other words, of the overarching polity.

[345] Morris-Suzuki, "Frontiers of Japanese Identity," 46; Lie, *Multiethnic Japan*, 117, 187; Yonemoto, *Mapping*, 6, 63, 67, 95–98; Ito, pers. commun., Feb. 17, 2003.

[346] Ravina, *Land and Lordship*, 28–45, 196–97; Roberts, *Mercantilism*, 5–6; Toby, "Rescuing the Nation," 219–22.

[347] Berry, "Was Early Modern Japan Integrated?" 111.

Third, even where local communities lay exposed to Edo-centered culture, selectivity and willful recombination ensured that local patterns were anything but a copy of the central template. As Anne Walthall has shown, in refashioning urban and official forms, late Tokugawa peasants could profoundly subvert elite conventions. Peasant drama, art, fables, and song often lionized those who resisted unjust official demands. But even within the same village, class and gender differences structured the understanding of festivals and village history, pitting, for example, tenants and peasant farmers against well-to-do landowners.[348] As in 18th-century France, the fact that provincial elites, both *samurai* and village based, enjoyed easier access than poor commoners to capital culture only widened these cleavages.

Fourth, official influences were ambiguous. As noted, some interventions powerfully favored cultural integration. But other policies passively or actively encouraged diversity. With its mix of Confucian, Shinto, and Buddhist elements, Tokugawa political thought remained relatively eclectic; and as a rule, officials were less interested in intellectual conformity than quiescence. Notwithstanding growing Neo-Confucian influence, shogunal and domain authorities promoted that doctrine less energetically than their counterparts in China, Korea, or Vietnam, not least because without civil service examinations there was less need for an orthodox canon.[349] Spatially too, *daimyo* polycentrism inhibited deliberate efforts at cultural unification such as we find in pre-1830 France, Russia, and Vietnam. In social terms – although here Japan had much in common with Russia, *ancien régime* France, and Southeast Asia – the official emphasis on occupational/status segregation also favored diversity of a most fundamental sort. There was no legal concept of equality, no generic category of "Japanese." Frayed though the status system obviously had become, lifestyles in 1830 still divided *samurai*, townsmen, and poor peasants; while even in Edo *samurai* speech tended to remain distinct from that of ordinary townsmen.[350]

[348] Walthall, "Peripheries," 371–92; idem, *Social Protest and Popular Culture in Eighteenth-Century Japan* (Tucson, 1986), 39–48, 96–119, 173–204 and *passim*; Ooms, *Tokugawa Village Practice*; Hur, *Prayer and Play*, 214–25; Smith, "History of the Book," 350. Cf. n. 295 *supra*.

[349] Bito, "Thought and Religion," 401; Totman, *Early Modern Japan*, 357. On Tokugawa thought generally, Ooms, *Tokugawa Ideology*; Totman, *Early Modern Japan*, chs. 9, 10, 16–19; Ikegami, *Taming Samurai*, ch. 15.

[350] Howell, *Geographies*, 24–44; Hall, *Japan*, 214; Donald Shively, "Popular Culture," *CHJ*, vol. IV, 711; Quackenbush, "Edo and Tokyo Dialects," 73–74, 80–81.

The Implications of Cultural Change for Japanese Self-Images and Political Expression

Given these contradictory currents, by what criteria shall we measure long-term cultural change? Pitifully limited though integration surely was by late-20th-century Japanese standards, by *ritsuryo*, Kamakura, or Ashikaga standards, it was extensive. Virtually all scholars concur that by 1830 writing, speech, literature, and social practices were more spatially and socially uniform than in the pre-Tokugawa period. According to Marius Jansen, for example, by the early 1800s "urban culture was gradually becoming national." "More and more a single culture was informing all status groups throughout Japan."[351] "By the end of the Edo period," Shively wrote, "the urban popular culture became the popular culture of the country."[352] According to Katsuhisa Moriya, "the rising intellectual level of the samurai, townsfolk, and peasantry played a crucial role in the creation of a national culture."[353]

Such shifts modified intellectual/aesthetic sensibilities, political engagement, collective self-images, and attitudes to the world beyond Japan. Consider these changes in turn.

To pursue further Berry's argument, the market in general and publishing in particular encouraged more activist and holistic intellectual perspectives. Censorship and self-censorship precluded frontal challenges to the status system. But the novel assumption that Japanese, regardless of birth, stood to benefit from multiplying choices transformed passive subjects defined by hereditary occupation into active self-fashioners. Consumers, above all readers, now learned that they had options – what interests to pursue, what skills to acquire, how to present themselves – that cut across status lines. By transforming *samurai* and *chonin* into fellow aesthetes, private poetry and art circles – representative of what Eiko Ikegami calls "enclave publics" because they existed outside the status system – opened similar possibilities, while encouraging a supra-estate culture of refinement. As access to public information led individuals of disparate origins to a shared sensibility,

---

[351] Jansen, "Japan in Nineteenth Century," 65; idem, "Introduction," 3.

[352] Shively, "Popular Culture," 769.

[353] Moriya, "Urban Networks," 121. According to Totman, *Early Modern Japan*, 477, "By 1800 countrywide economic and demographic changes were transforming Japan into an essentially unicentric society." For similar comments, see Bito, "Thought and Religion," 378 ff.; Smith, "History of the Book," 350–51; Beasley, *Japanese Experience*, 171; Batten, *Ends of Japan*, 5–6; and esp. Berry, *Japan in Print*, ch. 7.

it also inclined them to view the world itself in more unified terms, because publishing – as if in homage to the dialectic of integration-cum-specialization that spawned it – developed a pervasive interest in codification and taxonomy. An outpouring not only of all-Japan and local maps, but of encyclopedias, dictionaries, and compendia developed generic codes to accommodate the endless specificity that was a cardinal feature of urban commercial life.[354]

Rising literacy and new information systems in turn supported a more broadly based interest in issues of proper governance.[355] True, Tokugawa Japan never knew open debate comparable to that of 18th-century France. As Chapter 3 suggested, if French and Japanese levels of literacy, publishing, and urbanization were comparable, Japan lacked easy exposure to unsettling ideas from abroad, an array of cafes, newspapers, and periodicals expressly concerned with current events, and the patriotic goad of frequent warfare. Add the French/European tradition of corporate bodies and sanctioned liberties, and the peculiarities of French political sociability become more intelligible. [356]

But if Japan did not support a Habermasian public sphere openly skeptical of authority, the late Tokugawa era did foster what H. D. Harootunian terms a new sense of "public opinion" and a "new political space" concerned with issues of general welfare. First in the cities and then in the countryside, the view spread that the stark opposition between ruler and ruled could no longer accommodate the complexity of social life and was exhausting its utility.[357] While over the long term such views fed on new communications systems and commercial dislocation, more immediately they responded to severe famines in the

---

[354] Note 341 *supra*; Berry, *Japan in Print*, 49–52, 250–51 and chs. 2, 5, 6 *passim*; idem, "Was Early Modern Japan Integrated?"; idem, "The Codification of Space and Society" (ms); Eiko Ikegami, "The Emergence of Aesthetic Japan," in Joshua Fogel, ed., *The Teleology of the Modern Nation-State* (Philadelphia, 2005), 11–45; Ikegami, *Bonds of Civility*, 1–18, 39–43, 140–64, 187–90, and chs. 5–11 *passim*, focusing on art and poetry circles.

[355] Harootunian, "Late Tokugawa Culture," 254.

[356] Cf. Ch. 3, nn. 217–22 *supra*; Smith, "History of the Book," 338–52; Ikegami and Tilly, "State Formation," 434–39. Yet Ikegami, *Bonds of Civility*, 12 suggests that private art and poetry circles, although apolitical, had an associational character comparable to the salons, cafes, and reading circles of 18th-century Europe; while Gregory Smits, "Shaking Up Japan," *JSH* 39 (2006): 1045–78 describes expressly political broadsheets from the 1850s.

[357] Harootunian, "Late Tokugawa Culture," 170–77, 253–55. See too Berry, "Public Life," 133–65, emphasizing "public actors" and idiosyncratic intellectual exchanges that she does not hesitate to call a "public sphere"; and Burns, *Before the Nation*, 26–34, 98–99, 129–30, 186, and *passim*.

1780s and 1830s and the perceived failure of authorities to relieve popular suffering. Thus publications and academies began venturing commentary, often indirect, on public issues. At the same time, somewhat
as in Russia, most intellectuals and artists prudently eschewed frontal
critiques in favor of subtle satire and artistic exploration. Among the
chief exemplars of late Tokugawa thought were advocates of melior-
ist creeds who focused on rural hardship and merchant validation;
students of so-called Dutch learning, interested in European technical writings; "nativist" (*kokugaku*) scholars who sought to revitalize the
country by elevating Japan's indigenous legacy over its continental heritage; as well as Neo-Confucian moralists who sought to defend the
regime against its critics. Such discussions tended to shift the criteria of
legitimacy from cosmic laws favored by the authorities to more concrete
measures of performance. Moreover, with their assumption that men
of virtue, whether merchant or *samurai*, had rightful access to officials,
these exchanges eroded the division between ruler and ruled, elevated
learning over blood, and sanctioned discussion of issues affecting society as a whole.[358]

Among literate elites, political engagement of this sort fed and drew
strength from a heightened sense of collectivity to which historians
have attached different labels. Susan Burns refers to late-18th-century
Japanese "culturalism."[359] According to Mark Hudson, Tokugawa
Japan exhibited a high degree of "ethnic solidarity."[360] Jansen refers
to local expressions of "imperial loyalty,"[361] while Berry as early as
the 17th century and Rozman in the early 19th century find evidence of
a Japanese "nation."[362] This collectivity was cultural in the sense that
myriad artifacts – histories, political offices, sacred sites, rituals – bound

---

[358] Previous note, plus Totman, *Early Modern Japan*, 355–79; 450–64 and chs. 16, 19 *passim*;
Berry, *Japan in Print*, 249–51; Toshinobu Yasunaga, *Ando Shoeki* (New York, 1992);
Janine Sawada, *Practical Pursuits* (Honolulu, 2004), chs. 1–3, discussing late Tokugawa
practitioners of personal cultivation.

[359] Burns, *Before the Nation*, 224, building on Prasenjit Duara, "Historicizing National
Identity, or Who Imagines What and When," in Geoff Eley and Ronald Suny, eds.,
Becoming National (New York, 1996), esp. 152–57.

[360] Hudson, *Ruins of Identity*, 243.

[361] Jansen, "Japan in Nineteenth Century," 112. Cf. Bellah, *Tokugawa Religion*, 104–105;
Totman, *Early Modern Japan*, 505–506; Walthall, "Peripheries," 385.

[362] Berry, *Japan in Print*, 211–12 and 209–51 *passim*; Rozman, "Social Change," 560–61.
Similar characterizations appear at Beasley, *Japanese Experience*, 196 ("Among *samurai*,
at least, there was already an incipient national consciousness"); Moriya, "Urban Networks," 121–22 ("national culture," "national consciousness"); Morris-Suzuki, "Frontiers of Identity," 46.

the islands together and created what writers, with more than a trace of chauvinistic pride, repeatedly referred to as "our country," "our Japan," "our people."[363] The collectivity was territorial insofar as the new maps rendered "Great Japan" and the "entire realm" unprecedentedly visible and concrete. If the extent of *Nihon* (Japan) in the north remained fuzzy, to the west and south maps clearly distinguished it from China, Korea, and Ryukyu.[364]

As Howell has shown, the creation of a state with borders separating the zone of "civilization," that is, the three chief islands and the southern tip of Hokkaido, from less fortunate areas meant that everyone living within that state was, by definition, Japanese. Of course, Japanese themselves remained divided into status groups, because hierarchy itself was an attribute of civilization; but the customs of these groups as a whole differed from those of non-Japanese. Reinforced by fear of foreign encroachment, a determination to impose homogenous "civilization" inspired 19th-century campaigns to assimilate Ainu and Ryukyuans in areas that fell under Japanese political control. Thus in 1807 a Japanese magistrate wrote of the Ainu in parts of Hokkaido that had just come under shogunal rule, "We have no choice but to instruct them in such a way that they bind their hearts as one and are not susceptible to the blandishments of foreign countries [i.e., Russia]. . . . [We must encourage them to adopt] the customs of our Country . . . so that after a hundred years, all of Ezo will have been completely transformed to be just like our Country."[365] To eradicate "barbarian" survivals in the northern domain of Nanbu, early-19th-century officials toured the countryside, razor and whetstone in hand, obliging peasant women to shave their eyebrows in Edo fashion.[366] Conversely, all those outside Japan's boundaries – most notably, Ainu not subject to direct rule by the Matsumae *daimyo* or by the *shogun* as well as inhabitants of nominally independent Ryukyu – were forbidden to adopt Japanese clothing, hairstyle, names, or language. In theory, Japan became a culturally uniform realm.[367]

---

[363] Berry, *Japan in Print*, 185, 193, 208, 209, 220–21, 228, 243.

[364] Berry, *Japan in Print*, 39–43, 218–28, 241.

[365] Toby, "Rescuing the Nation," 221.

[366] Howell, *Geographies*, 138–39, noting that distinctive provincial customs had been perfectly acceptable to officials until Russian ships appeared in the area. Morris-Suzuki, "Frontiers of Identity," 56–57.

[367] In other words, in official thinking no middle ground was possible, although in practice cultural exchanges were common. By the same token, diplomatic dealings sought to exaggerate the alien quality of both Ryukyuan and Ainu envoys; and within Japan, because outcastes were part of the domestic status hierarchy, Japanese leaders resisted

This distinctive sense of self began to influence perceptions of China. Many, perhaps most, learned Japanese remained broadly Sinophilic: as a source of cultural inspiration or an idealized template against which to measure their own government's deficiencies, the Middle Kingdom remained an "ideal land of sages and tranquility."[368] But other intellectuals evinced a novel determination to avoid "deracination" by distancing themselves from their ancient cultural model. Such thought evolved through three stages. Initially, many strove to show that the way of Confucius, far from being exclusively Chinese, was universal. Subsequently, some argued that by the standards of Chinese classical learning itself, their country was superior: Japan alone had escaped barbarian control, and its decentralized polity conformed to classical norms more closely than China's unitary empire. Finally, from the late 1700s certain thinkers repudiated Chinese culture altogether in favor of indigenous forms, to which they assigned a unique primordialism and sanctity. Such scholars continued to differ in the degree of Sinophobia. *Kokugaku* ("nativist learning") advocates, for example, rejected both Confucianism and Buddhism, whereas partisans of the Mito school rejected only Buddhism. Yet most such thinkers revered Shinto as the highest truth, directed allegiance to the emperor and the "national body" (*kokutai*), and rejected the corrosive formalism of Chinese thought for Japanese spontaneity and natural virtue.[369]

---

attempts to assign them a non-Japanese racial origin. In the north, so long as most of Hokkaido was defined as lying outside Matsumae's direct rule, Ainu assimilation in those areas was forbidden; but from 1799 to 1821 when the shogunate took over direct rule in Hokkaido, Ainu assimilation was actively pursued. On the theory of Tokugawa ethnicity/culture, and on shifting policies of Ainu segregation under the Matsumae domain and of Ainu assimilation under shogunal rule, see esp. Howell, "Ainu Ethnicity," 69–93; idem, *Geographies*, 1–44, 110–53, 197–204; Morris-Suzuki, "Frontiers of Identity," 50–57; Walker, *Conquest of Ainu*, 204–26; Yonemoto, *Mapping*, 96–107. In Ryukyu, insistence on cultural difference primarily reflected Tokugawa determination to preserve the islands' profitable role as an "independent" Chinese tributary. Smits, *Visions of Ryukyu*, ch. 1.

[368] Jansen, *China in Tokugawa World*, 82; Bolitho, "Tokugawa Japan"; Graham, *Tea*, 3 ff., 38–45, 66, 97, 100; Wigen, pers. commun., Sept. 13, 2006; Jonathan Zwicker, *Practices of the Sentimental Imagination* (Cambridge, MA, 2006), ch. 3; James Bartholomew, *The Formation of Science in Japan* (New Haven, 1989), 8, 16, 21, 26 on Chinese influence on astronomy and mathematics.

[369] On the evolution of *kokugaku*, *Mitogaku*, and other forms of nativist thought, Burns, *Before the Nation*; Bellah, *Tokugawa Religion*, 98–106; Bito, "Thought and Religion," 409–12; Tetsuo Najita, "History and Nature in Eighteenth-Century Tokugawa Thought," in *CHJ*, vol. IV, 639–44; Harootunian, "Late Tokugawa Culture"; Jansen, "Japan in

Emphasizing the link between ethnicity and speech, nativist scholars promoted a conception of Japaneseness that transcended distinctions between status groups, between Edo and the domains, west and east, city and village.[370]

Some Tokugawa nativists professed to see in China a military threat. But arguably the chief spur to self-redefinition derived from Europe. Iberians from the mid-1500s, and more especially Dutch contacts after 1720 (when bans on the import of non-Christian Dutch books were lifted), transformed Japanese understandings of human diversity and fostered a new, more vulnerable sense of Japan's place in the world. Not only did Tokugawa artists assimilate alien Asians to a category of "other" created in the first instance by Iberians, but European contacts led Japanese cartographers and encyclopedists to depict the Japanese as one category amidst a great welter of global ethnicities. "If one inspects European maps," the late-18th-century scholar Ueda Akinari concluded, "it is clear that Japan is a small land, so how could anyone believe that this land was formed before all the others and that the sun and moon emerged from it?"[371] Of more strategic import, from the 1780s through 1820s British, American, and especially Russian incursions in and around Japanese waters, coupled with an awareness of Western military advances elsewhere in Asia, inspired calls to "expel the Western barbarians" – at least among concerned intellectuals.[372] The shogunate firmly rejected foreign requests for trade, and from the 1840s made desultory efforts to improve coastal defenses. It was fear of growing Russian influence, as noted, that led Edo to take direct control over

---

Nineteenth Century," 87–116; Totman, *Early Modern Japan*, 168–76, 284–87, 366–77, 437, 456–64, 504–18; Bob Tadashi Wakabayashi, *Anti-Foreignism and Western Learning in Early-Modern Japan* (Cambridge, MA, 1986), esp. chs. 1, 2; Ryusaku Tsunoda et al., comps., *Sources of Japanese Tradition* (New York, 1958), ch. 22.

[370] Burns, *Before the Nation*, 99, 133, 146, 156–59, 183–86, 220–23; LaMarre, *Understanding Heian Japan*, 4, 7; Naoki Sakai, *Voices of the Past* (Ithaca, 1991), 262–66.

[371] To which his fellow nativist Motoori Norinaga replied that Japan's superiority derived not from size, but from its unique creation by the gods and the unbroken continuity of its imperial line. Burns, *Before the Nation*, 112–13. On changing world views, too Morris-Suzuki, "Frontiers of Identity," 46–47, 56; Berry, "Was Early Modern Japan Integrated?" 128, 136; Toby, "Indianness of Iberia"; idem, "Carnival of the Aliens," *MN* 41 (1986): 415–56; idem, "Rescuing the Nation," 226–27. On "Dutch learning" and European influence, Yonemoto, *Mapping*, 74–76, 86–87, 93; Berry, *Japan in Print*, 225; Donald Keene, *The Japanese Discovery of Europe* (New York, 1954).

[372] Wakabayashi, *Anti-Foreignism*, 39.

the far north from 1799/1807 to 1821 and to reverse, albeit temporarily, Ainu segregation in favor of systematic Japanification.[373]

Nor were late Tokugawa sentiments of cultural/political interconnectedness unknown on the popular level. In response less to foreign threats than to widening domestic travel and cultural circuits, Moriya argues that travel diaries by diverse observers, including peasants and merchants, reveal "the ferment of a developing national consciousness," as they compared customs in their home provinces with those in other areas and became more aware of differences and similarities.[374] If popular views of China generally remained favorable, dramas contrasting Japanese courage with Chinese pusillanimity could elicit enthusiastic responses; and in the late Tokugawa era the term *tojin*, originally associated with Chinese traders, became a pejorative label for all non-Japanese "outsiders."[375] Despite semantic overlap between the terms for *daimyo* domain and the country at large, Ronald Toby argues that late Tokugawa commoners readily acknowledged that only "the country of Japan," not its constituent domains, was equivalent to realms like Korea and China.[376]

Yet for all this evidence of growing collectivity, the tendency to characterize pre-1850 Japan as a "nation" deserves far more circumspect treatment than it often receives. Bounded territorial dominion, a paramount state institution, and conscious membership in a cultural community are necessary ingredients for a "nation"[377] – but they are hardly sufficient. Otherwise, 14th-century France and 18th-century Burma would be of a piece with 20th-century France. So capacious a category risks the same inflation of usage and erosion of precision as plagued Marxist attempts to lump together medieval European and 20th-century Latin American societies as "feudal." "Nations" require as well a shared history, a sovereign horizontally conceived political community, efforts at popular mobilization or political involvement, legal equality, an interstate system composed of similar units, and policies to enhance competitiveness with like units. While bits and pieces can be found in many places and times before 1789, this total complex

---

[373] See nn. 200, 365, 366 *supra*.

[374] Moriya, "Urban Networks," 122.

[375] Jansen, *China in the Tokugawa World*, 84–86.

[376] Toby, "Rescuing the Nation," 223–25, and 202.

[377] See Berry, *Japan in Print*, 212, ibid., ch. 7 *passim*; and n. 362 *supra*.

is sufficiently unique to separate "nations" from expressions of what throughout this book I prefer to term "politicized ethnicity."[378]

These caveats are particularly apt for Japan, whose geography permitted only a weak sense of alterity. Hideyoshi's Korean invasion briefly unified rival *daimyo* against an external foe, but with the collapse of that quixotic venture, Tokugawa Japan knew nothing comparable to the struggles that helped to define Southeast Asian and European states and cultures from 1550 to 1830. That is to say, there was no Japanese analogue to the impact on popular consciousness that protracted wars against England had in France, that anti-Muslim, anti-Polish, and anti-Napoleonic struggles had in Russia, that anti-Mon and anti-Siamese conflicts had in Burma, and so forth. If some Japanese decried barbarians at the gate, *kokugaku* "nativist" thinking remained but one of several contending schools, and until 1853 the episodic, distant nature of European, including Russian, threats failed to spark deep public concern. When the Russian danger receded by 1821, shogunal rule over the far north ended too, along with official efforts to assimilate the Ainu in most of Hokkaido. In practical terms, as Howell pointed out, this infrequency of external contact meant that although many Japanese became aware that the world was filled with countries other than Japan and that as a group they differed from, say, Koreans and Dutch, this was an intellectual construct with little emotional or quotidian significance.[379] Operating almost entirely in intra-Japanese contexts, they routinely invoked whatever identities distinguished them from their peers. Thus, as noted, peasants referred to themselves as members of such and such a locality, while *samurai* identified with those domain or shogunal categories that structured their careers. In 1813 shipwrecked Japanese sailors, on

---

[378] Or simply "ethnicity." "Proto-nationalism" carries more teleological implications than does "politicized ethnicity," as Berry, *Japan in Print*, 212 argues in rejecting "proto-nation" to describe Tokugawa Japan: the term "proto-nation," she warns, "implies stages of development connecting incipience to ripeness," thus "conjoining the histories of the Tokugawa and Meiji periods as necessary complements." But this is also true of the terms "early modern" and "modern," both of which Berry uses freely – presumably because she senses that to describe both Tokugawa and Meiji as fully "modern" would elide crucial differences. Her invocation of "nation" to describe Japan in both periods – e.g., pp. 211-12, 248 – is open to precisely the same objection. Cf. Ch. 1, nn. 46, 47.

[379] Howell, *Geographies*, 27. Toby, "Carnival of the Aliens" makes a somewhat similar point by showing how the infrequency of foreign embassies inspired their exotic representation. Also Berry, *Japan in Print*, 224–25.

being rescued by Americans, referred to themselves as Japanese, but on returning to Japan, immediately resumed local personae.[380]

So too, whereas military and fiscal need drove early modern European and Southeast Asian states not only to maximize resources, but to emphasize religious and ethnic links between rulers and subjects, the Tokugawa regime was largely exempt. From the public the shogunate sought not fervent allegiance, but political disengagement. Thus, in contrast to post-1500 Burma, Siam, Vietnam, Russia, and France, there were no ceremonies of membership in the collectivity, no metanarrative of ethnic genesis or dynastic salvation, indeed no claims by the hegemon to exemplary morality or religious virtue. The only constituency the *shogun* sought to cultivate was the martial elite, for whose benefit he emphasized hierarchy and Tokugawa pedigree.[381] Nor without large-scale foreign conflicts, do we find insistent, bitter demands from below to ethnicize politics such as transformed our other five rimlands. Of course, once Americans and Europeans subverted the status quo in the third quarter of the 19th century, a pan-Japanese identity rooted in cultural distinctiveness and loyalty to the emperor allowed the country to transform its ideological structures and to join the circle of imperialist powers with remarkable success. But absent Western impositions, there is no reason to imagine that local ideologies would have evolved into European-style nationalism. In short, if dense trade and communications favored a high degree of cultural integration and a growing sense of collectivity, to 1853 there was still only modest pressure to see that collectivity as competing with similar bodies for control of resources, in other words, to define the community in explicitly political terms.

CONCLUSION

Japan combined broad developmental analogies to Southeast Asia and Europe with frequently distinct economic and political rhythms.

The accessibility and sophistication of Tang models and a relatively dense population allowed Japan to sustain a precocious and

---

[380] Toby, "Rescuing the Nation," 222–23. Likewise, whereas European travelogues typically sought to tame "uncivilized" foreign peoples, Tokugawa travel writing perforce sought to measure strangeness within the homeland. Yonemoto, *Mapping*, 67–68. On the relative weakness of pre-Meiji "national" identities, see too Mark Ravina, "State-Making in Global Context," in Fogel, *Teleology*, 87–104; David Howell, "Civilization and Enlightenment," ibid., 117–37.

[381] I follow Berry, *Japan in Print*, 228–41.

unusually complex charter system. But the *ritsuryo* polity resembled those of Pagan, Angkor, Dai Viet, Kiev, and Frankish Gaul in that all were secondary states that achieved a novel unification in the second half of the first or the early second millennium. By later standards, all were territorially and administratively limited. All distinguished sharply between an elite immersed in universal literate cultures and an illiterate commoner population. And all provided a territorial, religious, and in Japan's case dynastic, charter that later generations regarded as normative.

Aristocratic cohesion, centuries of economic/demographic stability after 730, and reduced foreign contacts long insulated the Heian-centered regime from domestic and external challenge and ensured that change was exceptionally gradual. Despite the growing conversion after 1050 of public into private resources, well into the Kamakura period (1192–1333) *ritsuryo* social features and institutions remained vital.

Nonetheless, by the late 1200s – as European and some Southeast Asian economies began to slow notably – smallpox domestication, new social conventions, and new rice strains helped to initiate a long period of demographic/economic expansion in Japan. Exercising more direct control over agrarian resources than Heian aristocrats had achieved, warriors became the chief beneficiaries of renewed growth. Whereas the Kamakura shogunate had been essentially a dyarchy between Heian imperial elites and warrior houses, by the Ashikaga shogunate (1338–1467/1573) the balance had shifted decisively in favor of the latter. Yet in the face of ever more assertive local challenges, the Ashikaga regime itself could not enforce an authority even as effective as that of the Kamakura. In the late 1400s and 1500s the islands dissolved into a medley of power networks, among which domains headed by resolutely local warriors proved most viable.

The evolution of central authority in Japan thus may be distinguished from patterns in France, Southeast Asia, and Russia. In France between c. 890 and 1110 and in each of the other regions between 1240 and 1390 charter collapse inaugurated the first and longest interregnum. As local states then expanded their resources and improved their technical machinery, subsequent interregna grew shorter and less disruptive. But in Japan, successive crises – the Genpei War, the north–south civil war of the 14th century, the Warring States period – became longer and more disruptive, as central authority, although terminally ill, refused to die. Not until the great interregnum that began in 1467 was the patient finally laid to rest, some 80 to 600 years after the first breakdown of central power in other protected zone realms. As a uniquely extended era when local actors, bereft of workable models, groped blindly toward a new order, the collapse of 1467 to 1603, the last in a series in Japan, therefore resembled the initial postcharter crisis, the first in a series, elsewhere. Again we see how differences within Asia could exceed those between Asia and Europe.

Over the long term, however, post-1300 economic growth in Japan proved no less corrosive of established institutions than did growth in other regions between c. 1150 and 1350. So too the fundamental progression from charter superficiality to more efficient, resource-rich administrations that we find elsewhere between 1400 and 1600 characterized Japan. Familiar as well were those 16th-century spurs to political reintegration that derived from renewed population growth, vigorous international trade, European firearms, and intensifying warfare. In novelty and seminal experiment, Japan's 1467–1603 interregnum, I just suggested, recalls postcharter breakdowns in 9th-century France, 13th-century Russia, and so forth. But in technology and resources, late-16th-century actors in Japan as elsewhere inhabited a different world than pre-1300 generations.

Analogous to Japanese political devolution, and equally gradual, was the decay of the charter elite's monopoly on Sinic high culture and literacy. Between c. 1200 and 1600 warriors, merchants, and some well-to-do peasants absorbed – at the same time as they transformed and displaced – aristocratic religious, literary, and artistic conventions. Buddhist proselytism and oral literature, in particular, drew strength from new commercial circuits and proliferating exchanges between city and countryside. In its demotic thrust and its reliance on new social and educational networks, the popularization of Buddhism may be likened to the dissemination of textually derived religious doctrines in Southeast Asia and Europe after 1400 or 1450.

Finally, as an unprecedentedly powerful and socially prescriptive formation that arose from 16th-century disorders and persevered for two and a half centuries, the Tokugawa regime resembled Toungoo/ Kon-baung Burma, Late Ayudhya/early Bangkok Siam, Romanov Russia, and Bourbon France. To be sure, in contrast to those polities, the legacy of Warring Sates polycentrism joined a pacific international environment to inhibit progressive centralization and fiscal penetration. Such policies persisted despite a post-1720 economic/demographic slowdown that contrasted with trends in Southeast Asia and Europe and that also owed something to Japan's relative insularity. By the same token, absence of a minatory external foe weakened the tendency for objectively dense cultural circuits to become subjectively political. And yet the novel domestic strength and territorial writ of the Tokugawa shogunate, its rich resource base, its command over religious institutions, its passion for social regulation and pacification, its increasing administrative complexity, its spurs to cultural unity, as well as its ultimate collapse before external pressures – all these patterns, in varying degrees, are familiar. Tensions between hereditary status and market-based mobility recall conflicts in Southeast Asia, Russia, and France. Broadly similar too were rising literacy, an irrepressibly innovative popular culture, the horizontal and vertical diffusion of capital-centered dialects, texts, and performance arts, and a growing sense of collectivity that was cultural and territorial, if not expressly political.

Tokugawa freedom from external military challenge to 1853 reminds us that Japan shared with mainland Southeast Asia, Russia, and France yet another critical feature: unbroken indigenous leadership. That this was by no means universal across Eurasia becomes apparent from a consideration of exposed zone realms, to which we now turn.

CHAPTER FIVE

Integration Under Expanding Inner Asian Influence, I

China: A Precocious and Durable Unity

WHY CHINA AND SOUTH ASIA?

Previous chapters argued that, amidst innumerable discrepancies and peculiarities, mainland Southeast Asian realms, Russia, France, and Japan shared broadly comparable trajectories. To recapitulate: Lying on the periphery of older civilizations, each region imported a world religion and developed a charter polity in the latter half of the first or the early second millennium C.E. Each was substantially protected against occupation from Inner Asia, in recognition of which I have termed these areas part of Eurasia's protected zone. Russia apart, all these states controlled what by Qing or Mughal standards were modest domains. Starting in the late first millennium, resuming at some point between 1450 and 1650, and accelerating in the 18th and 19th centuries, each state expanded territorially and centralized administration. So too, and again with notable acceleration after 1700, linguistic and cultural practices became more horizontally and vertically uniform even as cultural production grew more specialized. Symptomatic of cumulative integration was the tendency everywhere but Japan for successive interregna to grow shorter and less disruptive.

Because I sought to establish that mainland Southeast Asia participated in wider Eurasian trends, I have concentrated thus far on regions whose political chronologies approximated those of the mainland most closely. But several considerations oblige us now to extend our gaze in this and the following chapter to China and to South Asia, both part of what I term the "exposed zone" of Eurasia. First, differences in scale and external vulnerabilities aside, hitherto ignored similarities between protected-zone realms, China, and South Asia between 800 and 1800 confirm how genuinely widespread were the developmental patterns we have considered. Second and in no way contradicting the previous point, much as ethnic categories become salient only when contrasted with a perceived "other," the classificatory significance of the protected zone becomes obvious only when that category is compared to areas of less easily defended and manageable geography. To illustrate exposed-zone patterns, the Ottoman or Safavid empires perhaps could have served, but proximity to Southeast Asia, my own training, and the instructively contrasting fates of Ming/Qing China and Mughal India – accelerating integration in the first case, 18th-century devolution in the second – recommend these particular choices. Third, additional case studies further improve our ability to isolate variables responsible for particular local outcomes. This is true of comparisons between the protected zone and the exposed zone and, as just noted, between China and South Asia. Finally, a consideration of Inner Asian conquest regimes in China and South Asia promises new perspectives on Europeans in island Southeast Asia, a region that I, as a Southeast Asianist, also am eager to place in global context. In effect, this chapter and Chapter 6 provide a bridge between mainland and island Southeast Asia.

What features, then, joined China and South Asia to the regions we have already examined? In both China and South Asia, although more vigorously and sustainedly in China, we find a broadly familiar cyclic-cum-linear administrative rhythm, with successive periods of polycentrism tending to grow shorter and less disordered. In both China and South Asia, albeit again more persistently in China, elite religious and cultural norms radiated from charter heartland to outlying areas, even as local populations modified those legacies. So too, for much of the period c. 800–1800 economic and demographic rhythms in China and South Asia followed a broadly familiar chronology, with a marked intensification in the late first millennium and again from the early or mid-1500s. As beneficiaries of sustained population growth, Smithian specialization, rising world bullion stocks, firearms, and cumulative administrative expertise, the Mughal and Qing empires may be seen as peculiar species within the same genus as protected-zone states between c. 1550 and 1830.

How, then, did China and South Asia differ from mainland Southeast Asia, Europe, and Japan? China and South Asia were patently precocious, creating charter states some 800 to 1,300 years earlier than protected-zone realms, several of which looked eagerly to China and

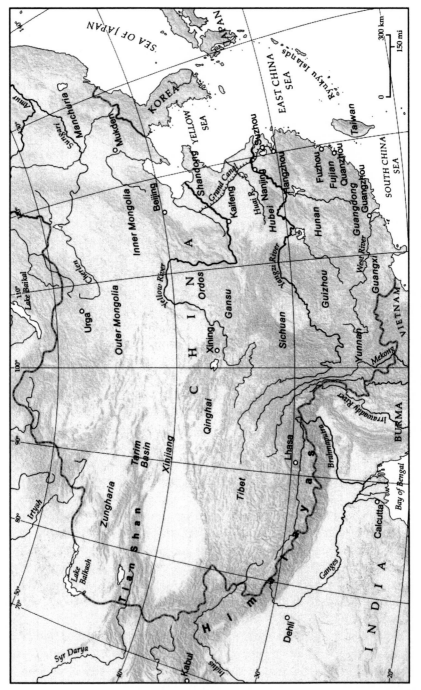

Figure 5.1. China, with Qing imperial boundary c. 1820.

India for cultural models. (Or to use China and India as the norm, we may say that the protected zone was patently tardy.) As befit the definitional distinction between the protected zone and areas subject to external domination, both China and South Asia lay open to ever more insistent incursions by Inner Asian warriors, especially after 1100. In both realms alien conquest in turn produced a) accelerated territorial integration; b) enhanced administrative efficiency, especially after c. 1560 in India and 1660 in China; and c) ethnic/cultural distinctions between conquest elites and host population without clear parallel in the protected zone. Finally, Chinese and South Asian empires also operated on a unique physical and demographic scale, which posed problems of coordination and cultural penetration more daunting than in most of the realms we have considered, including Russia.

1. SIMILARITIES BETWEEN CHINA AND THE PROTECTED ZONE

Progressively Shorter Interregna: A Précis of Chinese Political History

Fleshing out this schema, I submit that China's evolution resembled that in mainland Southeast Asia, Russia, France, and Japan in six basic respects, which we shall consider in turn and all of which testify to increasingly effective integration: a) progressively shorter interregna, b) long-term administrative centralization, c) long-term territorial expansion, d) horizontal cultural integration, e) increased vertical cultural exchange, and f) rhythms of economic and demographic growth that helped to govern political and cultural change and that, from the late first millennium C.E., correlated broadly with economic and demographic rhythms in the protected zone.

To be sure, in China – home to the historiographic trope of the "dynastic cycle" – recurrent political collapse and resurrection operated over a far longer period than in Eurasian peripheries, with a correspondingly larger number of interregna.[1] Yet in China as elsewhere, not only

---

[1] If one were to assume that the shift in the economic and political center of gravity from the Mediterranean to northern Europe in the second half of the first millennium C.E. resembled the contemporaneous shift from North to South China (although in the opposite direction), and if one were to assume further that French civilization was in some fundamental sense heir to Roman civilization, one could argue that Carolingian and Capetian France stood in a similar relation to Rome as did Tang and Song to Han China. By this generous view of European chronology, Valois, Bourbon, and post-1789 French regimes were no less successive incarnations of a charter legacy than

did successive postcharter interregna grow shorter and less destructive, but between c. 900 and 1830 political consolidation in China, mainland Southeast Asia, Russia, and France proved remarkably synchronized. Thus, in each realm, we find what by local standards was a brilliant institutional florescence between c. 900 and 1250, followed by severe dislocations for much of the 13th and 14th centuries, which yielded to growing solidity from the mid-1500s to the early 1800s.

In charter function, if not chronology, the short-lived Qin unification of 221 to 206 B.C.E., and the more durable Han empire of 202 B.C.E. to 220 C.E., were China's equivalent to Pagan, Angkor, early Dai Viet, Kiev, the Frankish/Carolingian kingdom, and *ritsuryo* Japan. Like these other charter consolidations, Qin–Han unification was an unprecedented achievement that climaxed generations, in this case centuries, of intensifying competition. In the 6th century B.C.E. what is now North and northcentral China contained about 170 states, many devolved from the nominally superordinate Zhou Dynasty.[2] These realms engaged in a diplomatic-cum-military free-for-all during the late Spring and Autumn and the early Warring States periods (656–221 B.C.E.), until by 300 B.C.E. only seven major states remained. Consolidation was driven by military innovation, in particular, the development of crossbows, new siege techniques, and massed infantry and cavalry to replace aristocratic chariots; by the growing use of iron for tools as well as weapons; by an associated increase in agricultural output, population, and trade; by new philosophies and systems of governance; and by diverse state initiatives – water works, law codes, new systems of taxation, colonization –

---

were the Tang, Song, Yuan, Ming, and Qing regimes in China. Yet, while one must be sensitive to major long-term shifts and resist essentialist images of China, by several measures – cultic and ethnic identities, political institutions, and most esp. boundaries – the connections between the Roman empire and Christian France were so much weaker than between the Han and later Chinese dynasties as to undermine this analogy. See discussion attending Ch. 1, n. 92 and Ch. 2 *infra*. Ensuing discussion of Chinese political history relies on *CIHC*; *SYMT*; F. W. Mote, *Imperial China 900–1800* (Cambridge, MA, 1999); John K. Fairbank and Merle Goldman, *China: A New History* (Cambridge, MA, 1998); and specialist sources cited below.

[2] About 1050 B.C.E., the Zhou state centered in modern Shaanxi and Henan gained control of much of North China, in some sense anticipating the Qin–Han unification. But the Zhou polity was too decentralized, its institutional and intellectual structures too distinct from those of the Han, and the temporal gap between Zhou and Qin too prolonged to assign the Zhou Dynasty the sort of charter role that is usually attributed to the Qin and the Han. See David Keightley, "The Shang: China's First Historical Dynasty," *CHAC*, 232–91; and Edward Shaughnessy, "Western Zhou History," ibid., 292–351; *SP*, 89–91, 216–18.

that reflected and accelerated economic growth. In 221 B.C.E. the Qin ruler finally brought the Warring States period to a close by uniting the entire North China plain (centered on the Yellow River), the Yangzi basin, and Sichuan. After his dynasty fell, the Han Dynasty not only revived the empire, but eventually refined those administrative ideals – civil supremacy, official literacy, extensive reporting requirements; provincial administration by officials subject to central appointment, transfer, and discipline; demilitarization of the interior – and fostered that Legalist-Confucian ideological amalgam to which all later dynasties would look for inspiration. Between c. 140 B.C.E. and 9 C.E. the Han also extended imperial territory in the northwest, northeast, and most especially the south. Thus, in true charter state fashion, the Han began to define China's essential political and institutional geography and revealed the possibilities of enduring unification.[3]

The Han empire survived turmoil and usurpation from 9 to 25 C.E., but in the late second and early third centuries C.E. succumbed to a mix of peasant revolts, magnate autonomy, and usurpation by military commanders. Ultimately, Valerie Hansen has suggested, many of these problems reflected economic growth in the countryside that widened the gulf between rich and poor but that the center was unable to tap.[4] Han collapse inaugurated the so-called Age of Division, which is formally dated from 220 to 589 but which was foreshadowed by the Yellow Turban peasant uprising of 184 and civil wars among the generals sent to put down that revolt.[5] As in western and central mainland Southeast

---

[3] Chun-shu Chang, *The Rise of the Chinese Empire*, 2 vols. (Ann Arbor, 2006), esp. vol. I, pt. 1; *CIHC*, chs. 2, 3; Valerie Hansen, *The Open Empire* (New York, 2000), chs. 2, 3; Charles Holcombe, *The Genesis of East Asia 221 B.C.– A.D. 907* (Honolulu, 2001), 8–29; Mark Edward Lewis, *The Early Chinese Empires* (Cambridge, MA, 2007), 1–4, 30–46, 206–52, and *passim*; idem, "Warring States: Political History," in *CHAC*, 587–650; Victoria Tinbor Hui, *War and State Formation in Ancient China and Early Modern Europe* (Cambridge, 2005), ch. 2; David Graff, *Medieval Chinese Warfare, 300–900* (London, 2002), 21–31; Michael Loewe, "The Former Han Dynasty," *CHC*, vol. I, 103–222. The assumption that Confucianism became well-defined orthodoxy in the Former Han Dynasty (206 B.C.E.–9 C.E.) has been questioned by Michael Nylan, "A Problematic Model," in Kaiwing Chow et al., eds., *Imagining Boundaries: Changing Confucian Doctrines, Texts, and Hermeneutics* (Albany, 1999), 17–56.

[4] Hansen, *Open Empire*, 146–47. See too Lewis, *Early Chinese Empires*, 21–29, 69–70, 103–51, 253–64, emphasizing the destabilizing effects of Han tax policies, productivity changes, great family power, and "barbarian" resettlement within the empire; Hans Bielenstein, "Wang Mang, the Restoration of the Han Dynasty, and Later Han," *CHC*, vol. I, 223–90; and n. 97 *infra*.

[5] Previous note, plus B. J. Mansvelt Beck, "The Fall of Han," *CHC*, vol. I, 317–76. The interregnum of the "usurper" Wang Mang from 9 to 25 C.E., between the Former Han

Asia, Russia, and France, this first postcharter interregnum was by far the longest and most disruptive. In China it was characterized by territorial fragmentation; consolidation of aristocratic privilege at the expense of central authority; the growth of private estates dependent on semi-servile labor; monetary and fiscal contraction; the flowering of Daoism and the new religion of Mahayana Buddhism at the expense of Confucianism; Inner Asian invasions and domination in the north; rule by transplanted émigré aristocrats in the south; and growing north–south cultural and social differences.[6] This prolonged split well might have become permanent, but for reasons to be examined, the Han legacy of unified empire revived in the late 6th century under the short-lived Sui Dynasty (581–617) and inspired the exceptionally dynamic, cosmopolitan empire of the Tang (618–907).

The Tang, whose first capital at Chang'an became the largest city in the world, recentralized administration and maintained the Grand Canal, which had been developed by the Sui to link North China to the rich Yangzi valley farther south. The early Tang saw an expansion of international as well as domestic trade and a marked receptivity to foreign culture entering via Inner Asia, a receptivity that nurtured among Tang elites a pronounced Buddhist identity. From the mid-700s, however, the Tang, not unlike the Han, had difficulty controlling provincial military leaders and large landholders. China's second major interregnum is usually dated from the formal collapse of the Tang in 907 to the founding of the Song Dynasty in 960, yet in truth the rise of regional warlords after the great An Lushan rebellion of 755 created problems from which the Tang never fully recovered. These same difficulties eroded Chinese control over the trade routes of Inner Asia and weakened elite Buddhist affiliations. From 860 the capital failed to maintain even a modicum of order among local military commanders, who eventually helped to produce some 15 short-lived regional kingdoms between final Tang collapse in 907 and imperial reconsolidation under the Song half a century later.[7]

---

and Later Han Dynasties, was not comparable to dislocations in the late 2nd, 8th, 10th, 13th, or 14th centuries.

[6] *CIHC*, 86–105; Mark Edward Lewis, *China Between Empires* (Cambridge, MA, 2009); Hansen, *Open Empire*, 159–89, 193, 195, 213–14; Richard Davis, *Court and Family in Sung China, 960–1279* (Durham, NC, 1986), 4–5; Graff, *Medieval Chinese Warfare*, chs. 2–6.

[7] For Tang overviews, Denis Twitchett, "Introduction," *CHC*, vol. III, 1–47; C. A. Peterson, "Court and Province in Mid- and Late T'ang," ibid., 464–560; *CIHC*, 127–30; Graff, *Medieval Chinese Warfare*, chs. 8–11; Hansen, *Open Empire*, chs. 5, 6. I have relied too

During the Song Dynasty (960–1276) commercial changes that began in the late Tang accelerated, the Yangzi basin surpassed North China economically, administration grew more bureaucratic, civil service examinations assumed unprecedented importance, and as society became more mobile, the base of government recruitment widened. Along with the rise of Daoxue (Learning of the Way) Neo-Confucianism as an ideology of elite activism, these developments promised the state fresh avenues of local influence. At the same time Neo-Confucianism joined threats on the northern frontier and a further reduction in western contacts to foster more expressly Chinese, post-Buddhist cultural identities.[8]

The Song's remarkable economic and cultural vitality, however, never translated into military strength sufficient to halt the encroachment of tribal peoples from the periphery, including the mountains of eastern Manchuria, the uplands of what are now Tibet, Qinghai, and Sichuan, and most especially, the Mongolian steppe. The invasion and subsequent retreat of these groups therefore produced two further major political ruptures before 1400: a) the two-stage disintegration of the Song state, which lost North China to Jurchens from Manchuria in 1127, and which lost the rest of China to the Mongols in 1275–1279; and b) the collapse between 1351 and 1368 of the Mongol Yuan Dynasty (1215/1276–1368) and its replacement by the Chinese-led Ming Dynasty (1368–1644). Taken together, the disorders of the late Song and late Yuan periods produced severe economic and demographic losses – population may have fallen 38 percent over 171 years – and thus may be assimilated to the notion of a generalized Eurasian crisis between c. 1250 and 1400.[9]

---

on Christian Lamouroux, pers. commun., Aug., 2000; Yang Lu, "The Emperor and His Enemies in Ninth-Century China: A Study of Tang Xianzong and His Time" (ms). I omit from the list of major interregna the Sui–Tang transition for the same reasons as I omit the Qin–Han transition. Cf. Ch. 1, n. 131 *supra*.

[8] On Song political, social, and cultural transitions, see nn. 29–38 *infra*. Although increasingly influential, Daoxue Neo-Confucianism became state orthodoxy only in the late Southern Song and Yuan periods. See Paul Jakov Smith, "Eurasian Transformations of the Tenth to Thirteenth Centuries," in Johann Arnason and Bjorn Wittrock, eds., *Eurasian Transformations, Tenth to Thirteenth Centuries* (Leiden, 2004), 305–308.

[9] Paul Jakov Smith, "Introduction," *SYMT*, 8–10, citing a paper by Robert Hymes to argue that from Song to Yuan population fell by 30 percent, and after renewed growth in the Yuan, fell from the late Yuan to Ming by 23 percent, for a total decline of 38 percent over 171 years, i.e., 1210–1381. By comparison, although pre-Song figures are less reliable, population may have fallen 20 percent from the height of the Han to the early Tang, but appreciably more from the height of the Han to the 5th century. Lloyd Eastman, *Family, Fields, and Ancestors* (Oxford, 1988), 4. On 13th- to 14th-century dislocations, also

Yet, in keeping with the paradigm of increasingly mild interregna, it is also worth noting, first, that the retreat of Song and the advance of Jurchen and Mongol power from 1127 to 1279 lasted longer and arguably produced more serious demographic and economic losses than the Yuan–Ming transition;[10] and second, that neither of these interregna lasted as long or created ruptures – institutional, cultural, or economic – as profound as during the Age of Division. Although the Mongols suspended and downgraded civil service examinations and mixed Inner Asian with Chinese patrimonial practices, they redrew the provincial map along the same lines as the Jurchen-led Jin Dynasty, kept the Chinese tripartite division of authority (civil, military, censorial), and by making Daoxue Neo-Confucianism the basis for examinations, continued the late Song elevation of that doctrine to imperial orthodoxy. The Ming not only patterned its early military and administrative apparatus substantially on the Yuan, but retained the Yuan's provincial borders and educational curriculum.[11] Notwithstanding major population losses, the 13th and 14th centuries also maintained trends toward agricultural specialization, commercialization, and cross-class acculturation that would gather strength to the 1800s. Spreading throughout China from the Yangzi delta – whose economy, Li Bozhong argues,

Herbert Franke and Denis Twitchett, "Introduction," *CHC*, vol. VI, 36–42; Thomas Allsen, "The Rise of the Mongolian Empire and Mongolian Rule in North China," ibid., 321–413; Morris Rossabi, "The Reign of Khubilai Khan," ibid., 414–89; John Dardess, "Shun-ti and the End of Yuan Rule in China," ibid., 561–86, esp. 585–86; Mark Elvin, *The Pattern of the Chinese Past* (Stanford, 1973), ch. 14; G. William Skinner, "Presidential Address," *JAS* 44 (1985): 271–92; Robert Marks, *Tigers, Rice, Silk, and Silt* (Cambridge, 1998), 65, 85–86; *SYMT*, 8–14, 140, 176–211.

[10] Smith, "Introduction," 8–12; showing population losses were concentrated 1210-1292 and 1351–1381 and arguing for more or less continuous agrarian development of the Yangzi delta from Song to Ming; Li Bozhong, "Was There a '14th-Century Turning Point'?" *SYMT*, 136–40, also refuting the thesis of a 14th-century collapse in Jiangnan. On the other hand, Richard von Glahn, "Towns and Temples: Urban Growth and Decline in the Yangzi Delta, 1100–1400," *SYMT*, 176–211 argues that after the Ming took power, their early commercial policies profoundly depressed Yangzi delta market towns for a century or more.

[11] On Yuan–Ming transitions and Yuan legacies, Paul Jakov Smith, "Impressions of the Song-Yuan-Ming Transition," *SYMT*, 82; Hansen, *Open Empire*, 367, 372–73; Rossabi, "Reign of Khubilai Khan," 465–71; *CIHC*, 153–54; Elizabeth Endicott-West, "The Yuan Government and Society," *CHC*, vol. VI, 587–615; Benjamin Elman, "Changes in Confucian Civil Service Examinations from the Ming to the Ch'ing Dynasty," in Benjamin Elman and Alexander Woodside, eds., *Education and Society in Late Imperial China, 1600–1900* (Berkeley, 1994), 112–13; David Robinson, "Politics, Force and Ethnicity in Ming China," *HJAS* 59 (1999): 79–123, esp. 81; Michael Chang, *A Court on Horseback* (Cambridge, MA, 2007), 16–17.

emerged from the 14th-century crisis surprisingly vital – all such trends favored political stability and integration.[12] Thus, whereas after the Han fell Chinese territories remained divided for the better part of the next thousand years, after 1279 Chinese territories remained more or less permanently united.

Accordingly, the fifth and last dynastic transition, that from the Ming to the Manchu-led Qing Dynasty (1644–1911), was the briefest and least dislocating, at least within China proper.[13] Although, or more likely because, the Manchus came from beyond the frontier, they strengthened Ming administrative legacies, while taking more activist approaches to orthodox culture, the economy, frontiers, and social regulation.

For argument's sake, let us focus on political events and let us assume that a) the first postcharter interregnum extended from the three-way division of power among leading Han generals in 190 C.E. to the Sui Dynasty's reconquest of the south in 589, b) the second lasted effectively from severe Tang debility in 860 to the Song reconquest of the south in 979,[14] c) the third lasted from the collapse of the Northern Song in 1127 to the Yuan conquest of the south in 1279,[15] d) the fourth interregnum lasted from the outbreak of serious anti-Yuan revolts in 1351 to the Ming accession in 1368,[16] e) the fifth major interregnum lasted from the mushrooming of anti-Ming rebellions in 1642 to the Manchu conquest of Yunnan in 1659. The resultant ratio of major postcharter

---

[12] On economic and social changes c. 1200–1400, n. 10 *supra*, plus Smith, "Introduction," 1–34; idem, "Impressions," 71–110; Richard von Glahn, "Imagining Pre-modern China," *SYMT*, 35–70; John Dardess, "Did the Mongols Matter?', ibid., 111–34; Lucille Chia, "*Mashaben*," ibid., 284–328.

[13] Jonathan Spence and John Wills, Jr., eds., *From Ming to Ch'ing* (New Haven, 1979); *CIHC*, 212–24.

[14] My date of 860 follows Patricia Buckley Ebrey, Anne Walthall, and James Palais, *East Asia* (Boston, 2006), 108–109, and *CIHC*, 129, 136; but see n. 18 *infra*.

[15] One might question how useful it is to describe as an interregnum, i.e., as a temporary aberration, the era of the Southern Song, which during most of its 150 years was the largest, richest, and most populous state in eastern Eurasia. But my definition of interregnum pivots not on the longevity or vitality of successor regimes, rather on their control of core territories only a fraction as large as those controlled by antecedent and later regimes. Whereas the Han, Tang, Northern Song, Yuan, Ming, and Qing controlled all or almost all of China proper, the Southern Song controlled only the central and southern sectors. Objectively, therefore, the Southern Song was an interlude between prior and subsequent unifications of the Chinese cultural zone; while subjectively Song thinkers themselves regarded the loss of the northern cradle of Chinese civilization as a deeply lamentable anomaly, a condition to be rectified.

[16] Dardess, "Shun-ti," 576–87.

interregna therefore was 399:119:152:17:17, whereas in France the ratio was 220:116:36, in Burma 252:14:5, and in Russia 210:15.[17]

Of course, one can argue about when "effective" central authority over this region or that ended. One could claim, for example, that Tang collapse began only in 874 or 880, which were key dates in the massive rebellion of Huang Chao;[18] or one could terminate the Ming–Qing transition as early as 1655, when Guangxi and Guangdong were incorporated, or as late as 1681, when the Qing crushed the revolt of the Three Feudatories in the south. But the main point seems indisputable: in China as in mainland Southeast Asia, Russia, France, and Japan, political integration grew more secure and the prospect of permanent fragmentation increasingly remote until by 1279 in China (1613 in Burma, 1500 in Siam, 1453 in Russia, 1453 in France, 1603 in Japan) the latter prospect had effectively vanished.

Administrative Integration

A second structural similarity between China and the protected zone was a sustained movement toward administrative integration. As elsewhere, this was both symptom and – along with movements of cultural and economic integration – cause of progressively milder interregna. Yet in China the trend not only was exceptionally precocious, but yielded a system with unusually strong bureaucratic features.

In its early and middle phases the Han Dynasty (202 B.C.E. – 220 C.E.) employed a significant number of officials from non-aristocratic backgrounds and permitted a culture of scholarly criticism and collective action that had few parallels in the later, so-called medieval period. Starting in the late Han, however, and with growing force from the Age of Division through the Tang (618–907), an aristocratic formation, "a conglomeration of great families," came to dominate the imperial court and provincial governments.[19] If military careers still conferred power

---

[17] Cf. Ch. 1, n. 131 *supra*. I am grateful to William Atwell, pers. commun., Dec. 29, 2003, for comments on successive interregna.

[18] The revolt that Huang Chao came to lead began in 874, while in 880/881 he took the Tang capital of Chang'an and founded his own dynasty. See *CIHC*, 129–30; Robert Somers, "The End of the T'ang," *CHC*, vol. VI, 682–789, esp. 682, cataloguing disasters from 820 to 907 and concluding that the Tang "finally abandoned its attempt to control all of China proper" in 884; plus Graff, *Medieval Chinese Warfare*, 244 (citing 979 for Song reunification); and Richard von Glahn, *Fountain of Fortune* (Berkeley, 1996), 49 (citing 978).

[19] Charles Hucker, *China's Imperial Past* (London, 1975), 149, 155–59, 176–80; Lewis, *Early Chinese Empires*, 1–29, 51–74; T'ung-tsu Ch'u, *Han Social Structure* (Seattle, 1972),

on some men of modest origins, high civilian posts were effectively monopolized by sons and protégés of prominent Buddhist-Confucian clans – David Johnson's "medieval Chinese oligarchy" – who benefited from extensive private landholding and from government commercial regulation and whose composition showed surprising stability from 400 to 900.[20] So dependent on powerful courtiers and kinsmen were many emperors, so similar in lifestyle and prestige were the sovereign and his chief supporters, that toward the end of the Later Han Dynasty (25–220 C.E.), in the Age of Division, and for much of the Tang the ruler served as *primus inter pares*.[21] After Han collapse magnates in both North and South China not only built semi-autonomous estates with large servile populations and independent military forces, but strengthened their hereditary claims to office and sanctioned customary, even legal, barriers to social mobility. The Later Han, the Age of Division, and the mid- and late Tang also saw military commanders and provincial governors develop regional bases from which some attempted either to usurp the throne or to found independent kingdoms.[22]

chs. 4, 5; Loewe, "Former Han," 103–222; idem, "The Structure and Practice of Government," *CHC*, vol. I, 463–90; Hans Bielenstein, "The Institutions of Later Han," ibid., 491–519; Yang Lu, "Emperor and His Enemies"; Arthur Wright and Denis Twitchett, eds., *Perspectives on the T'ang* (New Haven, 1973); Albert Dien, ed., *State and Society in Early Medieval China*, (Stanford, 1990); Peterson, "Court and Province," 464–560; Michael Dalby, "Court Politics in Late T'ang Times," *CHC*, vol. III, 561–681; David McMullen, *State and Scholars in T'ang China* (Cambridge, 1988); Lewis, *China Between Empires*, chs. 2, 3; Marty Powers, pers. commun., July 31, 2009.

[20] Previous note, plus David Johnson, *The Medieval Chinese Oligarchy* (Boulder, 1977), chs. 3–4, 6–7, esp. pp. 2–3, 124–26, with statistics; idem, "The Last Years of a Great Clan," *HJAS* 37 (1977): 5–102; Rafe de Crespigny, "Political Protest in Imperial China," *Papers on Far Eastern History* 11 (1975): 1–36.

[21] Denis Twitchett, "The Composition of the T'ang Ruling Class," in Wright and Twitchett, *Perspectives on the T'ang*, 47–85, esp. 47–48; idem, "Introduction," 9; Johnson, *Medieval Chinese Oligarchy*, 121–62; Christian Lamouroux, pers. commun., Aug., 2000; Lewis, *Early Chinese Empires*, 21–29, 51–74, 261–64, emphasizing the throne's theoretical monopoly of authority; idem, *China Between Empires*, 28–85, 250. The Han is divided into the Former Han Dynasty (202 B.C.E. – 9 C.E.) and the Later Han Dynasty (25–220 C.E.)

[22] See nn. 19–21 *supra*. Early imperial and medieval China also saw a recurrent shift in power from the "outer court" of imperial officials to the "inner court" of imperial consorts, eunuchs, and attendants, which could lead to the installation of figurehead emperors. But unlike challenges by magnates and military dynasts, eunuch power was not confined to the pre-Song era. Lewis, *Early Chinese Empires*, 25, 63–64, 162–70, 261–64; *CIHC*, 116, 121; Twitchett, "Introduction," 15–16, 20; Hansen, *Open Empire*, 139–41, 231–33, 402; Patricia Buckley Ebrey, pers. commun., April 10, 2007.

Yet if competing power centers thus circumscribed royal authority, the pre-Song era also knew halting experiments that provided a theoretical and practical basis for later centralization. Normative Han political discourse rested not on privilege, but on law, and insisted on a principled distinction between the private sphere of the court and the public sphere of the state. The Han, moreover, articulated an official hierarchy with clearly defined jurisdictions, while transforming some two-thirds of the empire that originally lay under autonomous kings into provinces (commanderies) whose governors became subject to central appointment and dismissal. Admittedly, provincial leaders drew their subordinates from local elites, local clans dominated the office of county magistrate below the province, while in the capital itself various posts remained open to purchase or inheritance. The requirement that candidates for office be recommended by provincial or central officials narrowed the field to men with elite connections and encouraged patron–client ties throughout the administration. An effort in the mid-second century to introduce a literacy requirement for officials proved highly unpopular. Nonetheless, in some cases Han-era candidates were required to take oral or written tests at the capital. Newly appointed officials served on probation for a year, after which they faced triennial ratings on which salary adjustments and promotions depended. According to the "rule of avoidance," governors and county magistrates could not serve in their native areas. This emphasis on centrally monitored office-holding as a source of income and prestige joined with equal male inheritance of family property to leave Chinese elites more dependent on state support than European noble practitioners of primogeniturial inheritance. With the partial exception of the recommendation system, most elements of Han personnel administration continued during the Age of Division both because they were the only models at hand, and because they provided valued marks of legitimacy.[23]

---

[23] On great family office holding and partible inheritance, *CIHC*, 74–75, 93–95; Hucker, *China's Imperial Past*, 155–59; Lewis, *Early Chinese Empires*, 3–4; idem, *China Between Empires*, 44; Bettine Birge, "Women and Confucianism from Song to Ming," *SYMT*, 213–14; Johnson, *Medieval Chinese Oligarchy*, 112–19. On pre-581 administrative evolution, ibid., 19–43, 121–47; *CIHC*, 75–79; Chang, *Rise of the Chinese Empire*, vol. I, 69–74; Hansen, *Open Empire*, 126–30, 136, 142; Patricia Buckley Ebrey, "The Economic and Social History of Later Han," *CHC*, vol. I, 626–48; idem, "Toward a Better Understanding of the Later Han Upper Class," in Dien, *State and Society*, 49–72; Franklin Houn, "Civil Service Recruitment System of the Han Dynasty," *Tsing Hua Journal of Chinese*

Responding to the manifest weaknesses of post-Han governance, yet also building on experiments under Sino-foreign dynasties in the Age of Division and under the Sui, the Tang adopted several novel personnel procedures, of which the most historically significant was the competitive civil service examination. A modest expansion in manuscript production (serviceable paper was available by the Later Han, but printing would not become common until the Song), government sponsorship of schools, a growth in monastery schools, and the stirrings of commercial vitality combined to enlarge the number of examination hopefuls. In practice, Tang examinations did not radically transform the government's social makeup, because aristocratic candidates, enjoying superior education and contacts, dominated these contests. Moreover, a degree by itself did not entitle one to office, while sons of high officials could hold office without competitive tests. Indeed, only 6 to 16 percent of all Tang officials entered service through examinations, while the proportion of high officials from major national clans, just under 60 percent, was not dramatically lower than during the Age of Division or the Sui.[24] Nonetheless, because examinations elevated some men from lesser families and because they sought to discriminate between aristocratic candidates on the basis of scholarly achievement, examinations strengthened the principle that office-holding, hence wealth and status, should reflect personal performance rather than family prerogative alone. Meritocratic tendencies would gain fresh emphasis in the Song.[25]

A second Tang personnel innovation, which also foreshadowed later changes but which probably did more than examinations in the short term to open government service, derived from the introduction of commercial levies. In order to compensate for the collapse of direct taxes and labor services after the aforementioned An Lushan rebellion

Studies n.s.1 (1956): 138–64; Miranda Brown, pers. commun., Dec. 10, 2003; Martin Powers, *Art and Political Expression in Early China* (New Haven, 1991), esp. chs. 2, 4, 9, 10; and n. 19 *supra*.

[24] See figures and analysis at John Chaffee, *The Thorny Gates of Learning in Sung China* (2nd ed., Cambridge, 1995), 15; Johnson, *Medieval Chinese Oligarchy*, 3, 124–25, 132–36, 149–50; Twitchett, "Introduction," 20–22. On Sui experiments, Tang examinations, and state-supported scholarship, see too Lewis, *China Between Empires*, 250–51; McMullen, *State and Scholars*, 13–26, 92–97, 206–62.

[25] On Tang elite composition and recruitment, Twitchett, "Introduction," 19–22, 28; idem, "Composition of Ruling Class," 82–83 and *passim*; Johnson, *Medieval Chinese Oligarchy*, 49–58, 112–14, 150–52. Already in the late Tang there was pressure to open examinations to descendants of merchants and artisans, historically low-status groups.

of 755, the Tang began to tax mining and trade and created monopolies on the sale of salt, tea, and wine. Financial commissions set up to run these operations relied on men, including merchants, from backgrounds unheard of in government service in the Age of Division or the early Tang; many of these recruits were later confirmed as members of the regular bureaucracy.[26]

In the same centralizing spirit the Sui and/or the Tang abolished the system of recommendations that had favored established families for entry-level court positions, transformed permanent appointments into three-year terms, expanded the system of efficiency ratings, and sought to weaken the hold of local families on provincial (now termed prefectural) appointments by enforcing rules of avoidance and forbidding more than one term in any locale. The Tang organized six functional ministries, with an array of specialized sub-bureaus, that remained the heart of every government until 1900. To provide a channel of information outside the regular bureaucracy, late Tang rulers created a new secretariat, and to meet threats from the imperial family, curbed the power of the Heir Apparent and left the position of empress vacant for decades. Thus Tang administration resembled an imperial household less than had that of the Han.[27]

In military terms, Sui and early Tang success also rested on a relatively new institution, derived in part from the Sino-foreign Northern Zhou Dynasty (557–581), namely, the divisional militia (*fubing*) of tax-exempt farmer-soldiers. This differed from early Han militias in that it provided not universal peasant conscripts, but elite soldier-cultivators who, in return for allocations of farmland, rotated in garrisons at the capital, at provincial centers, and along the frontier. Starting in the mid-Tang Inner Asian military pressures helped

---

[26] Twitchett, "Introduction," 19, 21; *CIHC*, 128. As we shall see, post-An Lushan difficulties also required abandoning close government regulation of urban markets along with the "equal-field" system of government land ownership. Although, in fact, the apex of state economic activism did not come until the New Policies of minister Wang Anshi c. 1070–1086, the retreat from economic management in favor of market forces resumed thereafter. See nn. 135, 137 and discussion *infra*.

[27] On Tang administration and Sui precedents, Benjamin Elman, *A Cultural History of Civil Examinations in Late Imperial China* (Berkeley, 2000), 5–12; *CIHC*, 110–14; Lewis, *China Between Empires*, 248–58; Hucker, *China's Imperial Past*, 153–61; D. C. Twitchett, *Financial Administration Under the T'ang Dynasty* (2nd ed., Cambridge, 1970); idem, "Composition of Ruling Class," 78–79, 82–83; Yang Lu, "Emperor and His Enemies," 33–36, 212–35, which partly supersedes John Chaffee, *Branches of Heaven* (Cambridge, MA, 1999), 7–9.

to eclipse the *fubing* militia in favor of large professional standing armies, often with a sizeable non-Chinese component, concentrated in frontier garrisons under military governors. As the frontier general An Lushan showed all too clearly, once the *fubing* militia decayed, central authorities had little force with which to counter such military figures. And yet by opening political careers to men of relatively humble backgrounds, the governors' extensive personal followings reinforced the mobility implications of examinations and financial commissions.[28]

In another development that reached full fruition under later dynasties and that had generic parallels – albeit centuries later – in Southeast Asia, Russia, France, and Japan, the Tang subjected the religious establishment, in this case the Buddhist church, to closer regulation. Again, Tang policies built on practices during the Age of Division, when the Northern Wei (386/439–534) and Northern Zhou Dynasties had sought to stem the loss of taxable land and people to religion. Tang controls included limits on tax-exempt lands and in 842–845 the disrobing of large numbers of clerics and a sell-off of monastic lands by the state. Although these measures had limited immediate effect, as substantive restrictions multiplied during the Song and Ming, the Buddhist church, whose wealth had grown dramatically during the Age of Division, ceased to be a major factor in China's political economy. In mature form these changes coincided with and in a sense depended upon the development of Daoxue Neo-Confucianism as a philosophy that, unlike Mahayana Buddhism and Tang cosmopolitanism, was preeminently and resolutely Chinese. Emerging from social and intellectual shifts of the 11th and 12th centuries and associated with the great Southern Song scholar Zhu Xi (1130–1200), Neo-Confucianism sought, in essence, to reconcile the Confucian emphasis on personal morality as the foundation for social order with the Buddhist- and Daoist-influenced search for metaphysical principles underlying the cosmos.[29]

---

[28] Peterson, "Court and Province," 464–560; *CIHC*, 93, 111; Hucker, *China's Imperial Past*, 165–69; Twitchett, "Introduction," 16, 33–38; Robert Hymes, *Statesmen and Gentlemen* (Cambridge, 1986), 3; Graff, *Medieval Chinese Warfare*, 12–14, 109–11, 140, 189–247 *passim*; Edwin Pulleyblank, "The An Lu-Shan Rebellion and the Origins of Chronic Militarism in Late T'ang China," in John Perry and Bardwell Smith, eds., *Essays on T'ang Society* (Leiden, 1976), 33–60.

[29] Twitchett, "Introduction," 26; Dalby, "Court Politics," 666–69; Hansen, *Open Empire*, 241–42; Kenneth Ch'en, *Buddhism in China* (Princeton, 1964), chs. 14–16; von Glahn, "Towns and Temples," 209; Hucker, *China's Imperial Past*, 362–72; and esp. Peter Bol, *"This Culture of Ours"* (Stanford, 1992), 129–31 and *passim*; idem, "Neo-Confucianism

In mainland Southeast Asia, Russia, and France we saw that rapid economic growth between c. 950 and 1250 favored novel political experiments. In China a host of factors – complex early legacies, dense communications, a remarkably literate elite culture preoccupied with issues of social stability – ensured that administration by 750 already was far more sophisticated than in most protected-zone realms centuries later. The Song Dynasty (960–1276) produced a yet more routinized, literate, and permeative political order that showed only limited substantive similarities to pre-1300 systems in the protected zone.[30] Yet Song-era changes resembled those in the protected zone insofar as all achieved what by *local standards* were unprecedented levels of integration, all cohered in the late first and early second millennia, and all endured in basic respects to the 18th century. One is reminded of Georges Duby's memorable claim for France that "the various elements that constituted the political system . . . until the end of the ancien regime were all in place [by 1220]."[31]

If recent research presents a less rosy view of examination-based social mobility than was once popular, it is still accepted that the chief Song innovation was to elevate civil service examinations into, at least during the 11th century, the principal method of bureaucratic recruitment. To this end early Song leaders awarded far more degrees

and Local Society, 12th to 16th Century," *SYMT*, 241–83. The "Way" in Daoxue (Learning of the Way) referred to the path by which all people could learn to be moral.

[30] This distinction includes Dai Viet, whose Ly era administration (1010–1225), in particular, had only nominal Sinic features. Ensuing discussion of Song to Qing administrative evolution follows *inter alia* Mote, *Imperial China*, 20, 109–44, 354–64, 474–97, 636–46, 728–29, 774–75, 861–68, 892–96, 943–48, and *passim*; Hucker, *China's Imperial Past*, ch. 11; Chaffee, *Thorny Gates*; Hymes, *Statesmen and Gentlemen*; Beverly Bossler, *Powerful Relations* (Cambridge, MA, 1998); Hansen, *Open Empire*, pt. 3; Brian McKnight, *Village and Bureaucracy in Southern Sung China* (Chicago, 1971); R. Bin Wong, *China Transformed* (Ithaca, 1997), pt. 2; Charles Hucker, ed., *Chinese Government in Ming Times* (New York, 1969); Edward Farmer, *Zhu Yuanzhang and Early Ming Legislation* (Leiden, 1995); Ray Huang, *Taxation and Governmental Finance in Sixteenth-Century Ming China* (New York, 1974); Albert Feuerwerker, *State and Society in Eighteenth-Century China* (Ann Arbor, 1976), chs 2, 3; Beatrice Bartlett, *Monarchs and Ministers* (Berkeley, 1991); Evelyn Rawski, *The Last Emperors* (Berkeley, 1998); Elman, *Cultural History*; Lynn Struve, ed., *The Qing Formation in World-Historical Time* (Cambridge, MA, 2004); Pierre-Etienne Will and R. Bin Wong, *Nourish the People* (Ann Arbor, 1991); Thomas Buoye, *Manslaughter, Markets, and Moral Economy* (Cambridge, 2000); Elman and Woodside, *Education and Society*, pt. 2; Bradly Reed, *Talons and Teeth* (Stanford, 2000); Seunghyun Han, "Re-Inventing Local Tradition: Politics, Culture, and Identity in Early 19th Century Suzhou" (Harvard Univ., PhD diss., 2005); Chang, *Court on Horseback*, 11–14 and *passim*, employing the concept of "patrimonial-bureaucratic" empire.

[31] Georges Duby, *France in the Middle Ages 987–1460* (Oxford, 1991), 298.

than the Tang, created a second level of examinations (the Ming later would add a third), sought to ensure candidate anonymity, and funded more schools to prepare worthy youths. To be sure, the vast majority of candidates still came from bureaucratic families, relatives of officials still could take easier tests, and the portion of officials entering the bureaucracy through open tests fell steadily after c. 1100.[32] Yet Song innovations were critical both because they reinforced the principle of meritocracy, and because the ever growing number of examination hopefuls brought local elites more securely within the cultural orbit of the state. Symptomatic of this more inclusive, popular ethos were novel social and cultural practices: student and literary protests became common, ordinary citizens participated in governance to an extraordinary degree, and the aristocracy lost hegemony over cultural production.

On an intellectual level, examination culture in the Northern Song (960–1127) drew strength from confidence in the state's socially transformative potential; and in the Southern Song (1127–1276) from a Neo-Confucian scholarship that, while insisting on the value of learning independent of government careers, nonetheless aspired to transform the state and supplied material for the examination curriculum.[33] On a social level, early Song examinations militated against the return of aristocratic clans such as had dominated the late Tang and post-Tang eras.[34] In place of the great Tang families now rose two substantially new groups: first in the Northern Song a small, wealthy, tightly knit, endogamous "professional elite" who resided in the capital region and concentrated on acquiring national office through examinations; and second, a far larger, more dispersed, more complex elite who became prominent in the Southern Song (although they undoubtedly originated

[32] Bossler, *Powerful Relations*, 52–53. Largely through wider use of the *yin* or shadow privilege for relatives of officials, the portion of officials who passed open examinations declined from 57 percent in 1046 to 45 percent in 1119 to 27 percent in 1213. Fairbank and Goldman, *China*, 95. See too Hansen, *Open Empire*, 267–68, 293–97; Chaffee, *Thorny Gates*, xxii, 9–43, 95–115, 182–84; Hymes, *Statesmen and Gentlemen*, 1–4; Peter Bol, "The Sung Examination System and the *Shih*," *Asia Major*, 3rd series, 3 (1992): 149–71; Davis, *Court and Family*, 1–14, 169–87. Overall, Fairbank and Goldman, *China*, 94, and Li Bozhong, "Late Imperial Times" (ms), 7 estimate that some 30 percent of Song officials were recruited via examinations.

[33] Hymes, *Statesmen and Gentlemen*, 5–6, 132–35, 214–16; Bossler, *Powerful Relations*, 205–208; Chaffee, *Thorny Gates*, 90–94, 185–86; Mote, *Imperial China*, 144–49; Elman, *Cultural History*, 12–19, 25–29; Smith, "Introduction," in *SYMT*, 2–3, 20–26; Bol, *This Culture*, 300–42.

[34] Cf. Nicolas Tackett, "The Transformation of Medieval Chinese Elites (850–1000 CE)" (Columbia Univ., PhD diss., 2006).

earlier) and who focused on gaining local power as much as national office. Especially in their heartland of the lower Yangzi, this elite is often termed the "gentry." Economically, examinations and the new political order rested on an extraordinary post-900 growth of population, rice acreage, cities, and markets, again most notable in the south, and from an associated increase in schools, literacy, and printed materials that prepared students for examinations. As the market economy burst the confines of Tang regulation, already moribund from the 750s, the Song witnessed what has been termed China's "first commercial revolution."[35]

So numerous had examination candidates become that whereas in 1023 one out of two examination candidates passed, by 1275 only one out of 200 did so.[36] These lengthening odds joined with military debacles, in particular the loss of North China in 1127, and with crippling factionalism to promote a partial withdrawal from imperial politics and a more local orientation among many gentry figures. Inspired by the decentralizing emphasis of Neo-Confucianism, they consoled themselves with the belief that gaining a low-level degree without right to hold office, or taking examinations, or indeed the mere acquisition of a classical education (of the type needed for examinations), with its potential for moral transformation, were sufficient status markers in themselves. The sheer increase in the size of the Southern Song educated elite reinforced this localism, for it became ever easier to find suitable affines close by, to build a shared local sense of elite community, and to gain prestige through local philanthropy. For landholders, family heads, and informal public servants alike, regardless of whether they ever achieved office, status as "gentlemen" thus came to be defined by a combination of local achievement and commitment to notions of cultural excellence that were generated locally, but sanctioned by the court. In the long run, this combination pointed to a novel integration of national and local hierarchies, and by implication, to a more secure base for imperial authority. In other words, starting in the Southern Song and continuing through the mid-Ming and Qing, that is to say, throughout the late imperial era, local elites became influential

---

[35] Following Smith, "Introduction," 24, I define the "gentry" as an elite that combined landownership with the access to office and the prestige that derived from preparation and participation in civil service examinations. On relaxation of Tang economic controls, n. 26 *supra*. On the first commercial revolution, n. 135 and discussion *infra*.

[36] See figures at Fairbank and Goldman, *China*, 95; Chaffee, *Thorny Gates*, 35 ff.

precisely because they became more closely involved with supralocal institutions, cultural markers, and social networks.[37]

In the Song, then, provincial governance developed some of the basic features that would later characterize the Ming and Qing periods. Local elites cultivated access to county magistrates (the lowest rung of imperial officials) and held fast to the conviction that a man's worth was best measured by his potential for scholarly, if not official, success. Among Ming and Qing as among Song gentry, the persistence of equal male inheritance limited the role of landed estates in favor of examinations, lineage organizations, and diversified career strategies.[38] Late imperial elites also continued to patronize such resolutely local projects as famine relief, militias, public works, religious shrines, and community compacts (associations aimed at promoting order through mutual exhortation and aid). Beginning in the Song but with greater vigor between c. 1550 and 1850, orthodox concepts of family, gender, and social obligation diffused below the ranks of formally educated people into ever wider sectors of the peasantry. Indeed, it is fair to say that by implanting in local elites social norms that then spread to more plebeian strata, Song Neo-Confucianism set in motion a peculiarly gradual and powerful version of Philip Gorski's "disciplinary revolution." In China even more clearly than in most protected-zone societies, cultural reform joined market integration to "civilize" the countryside without a large commitment of scarce central resources, and thus to offset the state's weak local presence. By the same token and again more obviously in China than in smaller realms, gentry willingness to provide unremunerated services – what Susan Mann and Ramon Myers term "liturgical" functions – helped to compensate for the state's habitually inadequate paid local cadre.[39]

[37] See nn. 32–36 *supra*, plus Bossler, *Powerful Relations*, 1–8, 51–60, 93–94; Bol, *This Culture*, 32–75; Robert Hartwell, "Demographic, Political, and Social Transformations of China, 750–1550," *HJAS* 42 (1982): 365–442; Patricia Buckley Ebrey, "The Dynamics of Elite Domination in Sung China," *HJAS* 48 (1988): 493–519; Robert Hymes and Conrad Shirokauer, eds., *Ordering the World* (Berkeley, 1993); John Wills, Jr., *Mountain of Fame* (Princeton, 1994), 149–80; Paul Jakov Smith, *Taxing Heaven's Storehouse* (Cambridge, MA, 1991) 4–6, 306–308; idem, "Eurasian Transformations," 303–308.

[38] On inheritance practices, see Birge, "Women and Confucianism," 212–40; William Rowe, "Success Stories," in Joseph Esherick and Mary Rankin, eds., *Chinese Local Elites and Patterns of Dominance* (Berkeley, 1993), 51–81.

[39] Susan Mann, *Local Merchants and the Chinese Bureaucracy, 1750–1950* (Stanford, 1987), 12–13; Ramon Myers and Yeh-chien Wang, "Economic Developments, 1644–1800,"

What principally distinguished late imperial society, c. 1500/1550 to 1850, from that of the Song, I shall argue in due course, were: a) higher commercial velocities in core regions and an expansion of market relations in peripheral locales; commercial intensification in turn favored a stronger urban orientation among well-to-do provincials, closer interpenetration of mercantile and landholding interests, and a marked increase in social mobility;[40] b) a corresponding relaxation of social divisions and closer peasant identification with Confucian social norms; c) an expanded role in the late Ming and Qing for subbureaucratic administrative personnel (clerks, runners, guards, secretaries, accountants), whose services became ever more necessary as population growth lowered the ratio of officials to subjects and as the work load of county governments increased;[41] d) a marked rise in the proportion of men with low-level degrees that carried prestige and corvée exemption,

CHC, vol. IX, 578 ff., 642, 645. Cf. Philip Gorski, *The Disciplinary Revolution* (Chicago, 2003); discussion of Gorski in Chs. 1–4 *supra*; and Steven Pinker, "A History of Violence" (www.edge.org/3rd_culture/pinker07/pinker07index.html). On the evolving relation between local elites and the state, Mann, *Local Merchants*, chs. 1–4; McKnight, *Village and Bureaucracy*; Smith, "Introduction," 23–25; Hymes, *Statesmen and Gentlemen*, chs. 4–8 and p. 216; Bossler, *Powerful Relations*, 203–12 and *passim*; Chaffee, *Thorny Gates*, 186; Bol, "Neo-Confucianism and Local Society," 241–83; Shigeta Atsushi, "The Origins and Structure of Gentry Rule," in Linda Grove and Christian Daniels, eds., *State and Society in China* (Tokyo, 1984), 335–85; Lien-sheng Yang, "Ming Local Administration," in Hucker, *Chinese Government*, 1–21; Reed, *Talons and Teeth*; Kwang-Ching Liu, ed., *Orthodoxy in Late Imperial China* (Berkeley, 1990); Rowe, "Success Stories" and other essays in Esherick and Rankin, *Chinese Local Elites*; William Rowe, "Ancestral Rites and Political Authority in Late Imperial China," *Modern China* 24 (1998): 378–407; Edwin Reischauer and John Fairbank, *East Asia: The Great Tradition* (Boston, 1960), 303, 309–13, 374; and my discussion of the burden of size *infra*. My quick administrative survey ignores the Yuan, in part because it was short lived, in part because its Inner Asian origins created tensions not fully reproduced in Ming or even Qing government. Suffice it to say that in lieu of the once popular view of Mongol autocracy, most scholars now regard Yuan administration not only as distinctly Inner Asian/North Chinese, but as highly factionalized, even by Song standards, and not particularly centralized. In this sense, Smith, "Eurasian Transformations," 302–304, argues that the Yuan continued a policy of limited state activism that began in the Southern Song and carried into the Ming. On Yuan government, Hsiao Ch'i-ch'ing, "Mid-Yuan Politics," *CHC*, vol. VI, 490–560; Dardess, "Shun-ti," 561–86; Endicott-West, "Yuan Government and Society"; David Farquhar, "Structure and Function in the Yuan Imperial Government," in John Langlois, ed., *China Under Mongol Rule* (Princeton, 1981), 25–55; and esp. Nicola Di Cosmo's perceptive "Review of *The Cambridge History of China*, vol. VI," in *HJAS* 56 (1996): 493–508.

40 See previous note; Myers and Wang, "Economic Developments, 577–78; and discussion *infra*.

41 See Reed, *Talons and Teeth*, 3–4, 124, 262, and *passim*, superseding T'ung-tsu Ch'u, *Local Government in China Under the Ch'ing* (Stanford, 1962); the Weberian theses of John

but no prospect of imperial office;[42] e) a sharing among subbureaucrats, lineage heads, merchants, landowners, and local brokers of police, welfare, and other functions that in the Song had been handled by county officials and a narrow class of village officers drawn from large landowners;[43] f) a more ambitious, wide-ranging state activism under the Qing than under the Southern Song, Yuan, or Ming; the latter dynasties had yielded substantial control over local culture and institutions to the gentry. In some degree, all six trends presaged more effective capital–local and elite–mass integration.

With improved cultural circulation and the rise of officials dependent on state certification rather than clan prerogative came a long-term strengthening of central bureaucratic authority and a reduction of autonomous power centers such as threatened earlier dynasties. Whereas pre-Song rulers often differed little from the heads of other great aristocratic families, Song and post-Song emperors were separated from their courtiers – in law and theory and generally in practice – by an unbridgeable social gap. Notwithstanding the recrudescence, especially under the Ming, of ministerial and/or eunuch factionalism, new protocols captured this changed atmosphere: Tang councilors customarily sat alongside the ruler to discuss policy, but Song officials stood at attention before the emperor, while by the Ming they were obliged to kneel before the ruler, perched on an elevated dais. Jurisdictions were fragmented to reduce threats from individual ministers, promotion and demotion followed increasingly routinized procedures, while finance and other services benefited from a growing professionalism. Seeking to erase the late Ming legacy of weak emperors and to gather decision-making powers firmly in their own hands, Qing rulers streamlined paperwork, increased routine inspections, created a confidential

---

Watt, *The District Magistrate in Late Imperial China* (New York, 1972); and discussion *infra*.

[42] Whereas in 1400 there was one such man for every 2,200 people, by 1700 the ratio was 1:300. What is more, by the early 1800s fully one-third of low-level degree-holders obtained their degree not by scholarship, but by purchase, a major increase over Ming and early Qing levels. Elman, "Changes in Confucian Civil Service Examinations," 117; Reischauer and Fairbank, *East Asia*, 304–11; Joseph Esherick and Mary Rankin, "Introduction," in Esherick and Rankin, *Chinese Local Elites*, 4; Yeh-chien Wang, *Land Taxation in Imperial China, 1750–1911* (Cambridge, MA, 1972), 8–9; David Robinson, *Bandits, Eunuchs, and the Son of Heaven* (Honolulu, 2001), 166–67. Cf. Bossler, *Powerful Relations*, 211–12, 327 n. 17. But at the upper end of the scale, the ratio of men with *jinshi* degrees relative to the general population was only one-eighth in 1800 what it had been in the Song. Hucker, *China's Imperial Past*, 318–19, 341.

[43] See McKnight, *Village and Bureaucracy*, 5–6, 178–85. Cf. Reed, *Talons and Teeth*, 259–66.

system of palace memorials, focused decisionmaking in a new agency, the Grand Council; created the Court of Colonial Affairs (Lifan Yuan) for Inner Asian relations; relied on imperial bondservants and Manchu nobles to check the Chinese-dominated civil service; and controlled Manchus themselves through an administrative-cum-military organization known as the Eight Banners.[44] Hence, in part, the greater internal stability of the Ming and more especially the Qing compared to earlier dynasties.

What is more, while supporting imperial relatives with generous stipends, the Northern Song, the Ming from the early 1400s, and the Qing more episodically, excluded princes from major administrative posts, in some cases even keeping them at a distance from the capital. With relatives thus neutralized, usurpations became far less common.[45] So too, late Tang and post-Tang warlordism fed a growing elite distrust of military careers. The intermediate sphere between prefectures and the capital – the trouble zone in which warlords and separatist governors repeatedly had based themselves – now came under firm central direction, although it is often said that the Song and Ming purchased

[44] The personal competence of Qing emperors was not entirely accidental, owing much to the practice of tanistry (see n. 252 *infra*), but the stabilizing longevity of Kangxi and Qianlong was fortuitous. On late imperial structural changes, see James Parsons, "The Ming Dynasty Bureaucracy," in Hucker, *Chinese Government*, 175–231; Evelyn Rawski, "The Qing Formation and the Early Modern Period," in Struve, *Qing Formation*, 223–26; Rawski, *Last Emperors*, 8–10, 59–194; Hucker, *China's Imperial Past*, 303–10, 321–23; Bartlett, *Monarchs and Ministers*, 1–11, 135–228; Willard Peterson, "Introduction," *CHC*, vol. IX, 6–7; and esp. Mark Elliott, *The Manchu Way* (Stanford, 2001), pts. 1, 2 on Banner organization. According to Sugiyama Kiyohiko, "The Ch'ing Empire as a Manchu Khanate," *Acta Asiatica* 88 (2005): 21–48, despite formal continuity between Ming and Qing, in practice the early Qing inner circle was a confederation of powerful families similar to those in other Inner Asian states and perhaps in Han and Tang China, but quite distinct from the Ming. On Inner Asian features during the Qing, see also discussion *infra*. On late Ming ministerial domination, James Geiss, "The Chia-ching Reign, 1522–1566," *CHC*, vol. VII, 482–507; Ray Huang, "The Lun-ch'ing and Wan-li Reigns, 1567–1620," ibid., 514–58 *passim*.

[45] The Han generally excluded princes from meaningful roles, but their influence grew thereafter until the Song. The Qing relied heavily on imperial kinsmen for policy formation and leadership, but barred princes of the blood from the Grand Council and by the 1730s eliminated their power base in the Banners. See Hucker, *China's Imperial Past*, 305, 322; Chaffee, *Branches of Heaven*, vii, 1–12, 16–20, 271–75, and *passim*; Peter Lorge, *War, Politics and Society in Early Modern China 900–1795* (London, 2005), 112–17; Bartlett, *Monarchs and Ministers*, 139, 178; Rawski, *Last Emperors*, chs. 2, 3; Elliott, *Manchu Way*, 138; Susan Naquin and Evelyn Rawski, *Chinese Society in the Eighteenth Century* (New Haven, 1987), 52; Sugiyama, "Ch'ing Empire," again emphasizing the power of the Qing imperial clan.

military obedience at the price of military effectiveness. New controls included deliberately fragmented military jurisdictions, capital-frontier troop rotation, bars to personalized ties between commanders and their troops, and civilian supremacy under literati or eunuch command.[46]

Post-Tang curbs on military governors were part of a more general reform of local administration. Tang-style counties and, atop counties, prefectures remained the base of the pyramid, but early Song rulers, fearful of Tang-style regional revolts, tried to eliminate all agencies between prefecture and capital. Problems of coordination eventually obliged the Song to install over prefectures a network of intendancies that anticipated provincial jurisdictions. Provinces became more well defined under the Ming, which divided the realm into two metropolitan areas and 13 provinces. The Qing retained the basic Ming setup, while adding subprovincial jurisdictions and placing governors-general, two-thirds of whom were Manchus, above provincial governors. Civil administration was extended from China proper to Gansu and Qing-hai, although the northeast, Mongolia, Tibet, and Xinjiang remained outside the provincial system. After the Tang we also find a long-term trend for counties and prefectures to forward more funds to provincial authorities and, beyond, to the central government.[47]

As regards the tax system itself, the so-called "two-tax" reform of 780 persisted in its essentials under later dynasties. Under this Tang arrangement various levies were amalgamated into a tax payable in two installments and comprising two elements, namely, a household service levy apportioned on the basis of property and a land tax proper on all cultivation. Song administrators consolidated the service levy with the land tax and hastened commutation into bronze coin, uncoined silver, or paper money. As Japanese and New World silver poured into China in the 1500s, the simplification and commutation of land taxes resumed with ad hoc local measures, collectively called the Single-Whip reform. Notwithstanding anomalies that reflected both inadequate currency and Ming administrative disorder, the Single-Whip system, in which

---

[46] On evolving military controls, Dardess, "Did the Mongols Matter?" 118; Fairbank and Goldman, *China*, 108–10; Graff, *Medieval Chinese Warfare*, 238–47; Smith, "Eurasian Transformations," 283–84, 286.

[47] Yang, "Ming Local Administration," 18 and *passim*; Rawski, "Qing Formation," 224–26; Hucker, *China's Imperial Past*, 310–15; John Wills, Jr., "Contingent Connections," in Struve, *Qing Formation*, 168–70; Reischauer and Fairbank, *East Asia*, 367–68; Mote, *Imperial China*, 485–86, 639–40, 750–51, 943–45; Peter Perdue, *China Marches West* (Cambridge, MA, 2005), 519.

many cumbersome small items were consolidated into one payment in silver at fixed intervals, generally proved more efficient than earlier systems; and the government, in principle, became better able to hire labor, award salaries, and buy supplies. Substantial additional revenues derived from licensing monopoly goods like salt and precious metals.[48] Not surprisingly, the Qing preserved the main lines of Ming taxation, while improving coordination. Evelyn Rawski claims that growth in the privy purse substantially supplemented Qing public revenues. Be that as it may, a voluntary freeze in 1713 of commuted household service levies, which represented a major portion of the land tax, hobbled later budgets. At the same time, as G. William Skinner and others have argued, because population growth outstripped state capacity to monitor localities, the state's share of the economic surplus gradually declined. We shall return to this devolutionary tendency, which lacked close parallel in the protected zone.[49]

And yet, by winning over gentry and merchants via examinations, tax concessions, lavish cultural patronage, and support against popular disturbances; by enlisting those same unremunerated elites to promote public works and Confucian education; and by encouraging agrarian reclamation and intensification, the Qing succeeded in producing a remarkably prosperous and stable rural order. In pursuit of this goal the Qing perfected the whole panoply of techniques inherited from the Song, Yuan, and Ming – examinations, local schools, public granaries, the *baojia* system of mutual surveillance (wherein households assumed responsibility for one another's behavior), community compacts, biweekly village lectures – while rationalizing selective aspects

---

[48] The "two-tax" reform of 780 referred not to fiscal categories, but to the two seasonal payments. On Single-Whip reform, Ray Huang, "The Ming Fiscal Administration," *CHC*, vol. VIII, 155–59; Mote, *Imperial China*, 731–32; Timothy Brook, *The Confusions of Pleasure* (Berkeley, 1998), xxi, 81, 88–89; Reischauer and Fairbank, *East Asia*, 217, 337–40. On taxation c. 780–1650, see too Hucker, *China's Imperial Past*, 185–86, 347–48, 354–55; *CHC*, vol. III, 498–500; Ray Huang, "Fiscal Administration During the Ming Dynasty," in Hucker, *Chinese Government*, 73–128; Hansen, *Open Empire*, 269–72, 405; Guanglin Liu, "Research Statement" (ms); von Glahn, *Fountain of Fortune*, 8–10, 146, 157–61 and chs. 2–5 *passim*. On the unhappy history of paper money and the growing post-1300 importance of silver, ibid., 43–141, 247–49. Note that commutation had both a secular and cyclic dimension, having also grown in the late phase of dynasties before the Ming.

[49] On Qing fiscal patterns, Rawski, "Qing Formation," 213–18; G. William Skinner, "Introduction," in Skinner, ed., *The City in Late Imperial China* (Stanford, 1977), 20–28; Mann, *Local Merchants*, 14–18, 36–69; Wang, *Land Taxation*, esp. ch. 1; and discussion *infra* on Chinese vs. protected zone differences.

of central administration. To the early 1800s at least, the Qing achieved unprecedented control over grain prices, food reserves, education, and society generally. As R. Bin Wong has argued, the political economy of China in general, and the Qing in particular, evinced the sort of concern for popular welfare that we find in most European states only in the 19th and 20th centuries.[50] With good reason, Paul Jakov Smith concludes, the Qing represented "the culmination of traditional governance" and "the epitome of a statecraft tradition that goes back to the twelfth century."[51] I have made precisely the same claim for 18th to early-19th-century administration in Burma, Siam, Vietnam, Russia, France, and Japan.

Territorial Expansion

Along with shorter interregna and administrative integration, a third macrohistorical parallel to which I have alluded but that now requires more direct treatment is the long-term expansion of imperial territory. Admittedly, until the mid-1600s – in contrast to Southeast Asian states, Russia, and France – the territorial fortunes of successive China-centered empires showed no strong linear trend. That is to say, although imperial authority expanded in the southwest after 1253, losses elsewhere produced an oscillatory pattern from Han to Ming, with little, if any, net gain. The Qing, however, transformed the situation by joining agrarian China to steppe Inner Asia in a durable polity for the first time. This achievement thus corresponded to dramatic Russian conquests in Inner Asia (on which Qing success depended in part), as well as to extensive post-1650 acquisitions by Vietnam, Burma, and Siam and, less notably, Japan and France.[52]

---

[50] Wong, *China Transformed*, 101 and 73–126 *passim*. Note too the claim at Naquin and Rawski, *Chinese Society*, 8–9 that in the 18th century "Chinese officialdom was probably the most highly bureaucratized in the world."

[51] Smith, "Introduction," 34. My discussion follows Wong, *China Transformed*, ch. 5; Smith, "Introduction," 19–23, 30–34, 86–104; William Rowe, *Saving the World* (Stanford, 2001), pts, 2, 3; Naquin and Rawski, *Chinese Society*, 6–14, 223–29; and n. 44 *supra*.

[52] Moreover, as Ch. 3 noted, if we consider (temporary) French acquisitions in North America and India during the 17th and 18th centuries, the parallels with Russia, Southeast Asia, and China are stronger. Discussion of Chinese territorial fortunes follows *CIHC*, 65–70, 82–83, 87, 110–11, 137–38, 169–73, 194–98, 223–28; Chang, *Rise of the Chinese Empire*; *CHC*, vol. I, 377–462; *CHC*, vol. III, *passim*; Perdue, *China Marches West*; Geoffrey Baraclough, ed., *The Times Atlas of World History* (London, 1979), 80–81, 126–29, 168–69, 174–75; Graff, *Medieval Chinese Warfare*.

The Han empire at its height stretched from modern Gansu, the southern frontiers of Inner Mongolia, and central Korea in the north to Hainan island, northern Vietnam, Guangxi, and parts of Sichuan and Yunnan in the south. In order to combat the Xiongnu confederation of Inner Asian tribes, who in 166 B.C.E. had sent 140,000 horsemen to within 100 miles of the capital, the Han not only cultivated nomad allies, but outflanked the Xiongnu in the northeast, founding provinces in parts of modern Korea, and in the northwest, where a million colonists were sent to settle Gansu. What is more, to obtain horses and to secure anti-Xiongngu allies in the far west, Han forces established a protectorate that endured to the early first century C.E. in the southern part of modern Xinjiang.[53]

This vast domain enjoyed only a modest organic unity. Large parallel river systems facilitate east–west communications, but much of West and South China is mountainous. Areas north and west of China proper are either completely unsuited or marginally suited for agriculture and thus incapable of supporting a Chinese-style social order. That the Han could hold together China proper, northern Korea, northern Vietnam, and areas in Xinjiang as long as it did speaks, we shall see, to cultural symbolism and administrative standardization as well as to early military prowess.

With the fragmentation that accompanied the collapse of the Later Han, non-Chinese tribal power flowed into North China, producing through the late 6th century a series of unstable Sino-foreign regimes and generating a political culture that embraced both the steppe frontier and much of North China, but that grew increasingly distinct from that of South China.[54] It was, in fact, from the mixed blood Sino-foreign northwest military aristocracy that the founders of the Sui and Tang dynasties emerged to reassemble the basic Han ecumene. After wresting control of much of what is now Inner Mongolia from Turkic peoples, Tang forces recreated a short-lived protectorate in modern Xinjiang and reasserted control over northern Vietnam. But in Korea and Southwest

---

[53] The protectorate also included districts immediately west of modern Xinjiang. See Yu Ying-shih, "Han Foreign Relations," *CHC*, vol. I, 405–21, 436–60; *CIHC*, 65–70; Lewis, *Early Chinese Empires*, 129–51; Nicola Di Cosmo, *Ancient China and Its Enemies* (Cambridge, 2002), chs. 5, 6; Chang, *Rise of the Chinese Empire*, vol. I, 215–65, vol. II, esp. 107–77.

[54] Di Cosmo, "Review," 503–505; Graff, *Medieval Chinese Warfare*, chs. 2–4; *EAH*, vol. III, 135–38. More particularly, steppe influence in North China increased after the fall of the short-lived reunifying Western Jin Dynasty (265–316).

China newly risen local states excluded the Tang from areas once dominated by the Han. Tang authority in Inner Asia was also unstable, with frequent challenges by early Turks and Tibetan-related groups.[55]

In part because its ruling family was at least half Turkic and had access to both Inner Asian and Chinese traditions, the Tang was the last dynasty until the Mongol Yuan to control both South China and significant areas in Inner Asia. All along its northern frontier the Song faced foes it was unable to dislodge and to whom indeed it began to pay heavy tribute. In the northwest the Xi Xia state of the Tanguts, a semisedentary people related to the Tibetans, and in the northeast the Liao state of the Khitans, who were pastoral nomads, ruled mixed populations of Inner Asians and Chinese. The Liao state fell to Jurchen tribes from Manchuria, whose Jin Dynasty, as noted, expelled the Song from all of North China in 1127. In turn, the Mongols destroyed both the Jin and the Southern Song. While it is true that the Song held out against the Mongols longer than any other power – no mean feat, surely – their military power was never commensurate with their demographic and commercial superiority. Whether because of the chronic northern threat or internal weakness, the Song also were obliged to accept the independence of Vietnam and of the kingdom of Dali in Yunnan.[56]

The last Chinese-led dynasty, the Ming, improved on Song performance insofar as the early Ming expelled the Mongols from China proper, pushed briefly into the steppe, and regained substantial territories formerly held by the Xi Xia and Liao polities. The Ming also took over southwest areas once controlled by Dali. Although it would later contract, Ming territory in 1470 was appreciably larger than Northern Song territory in 1102.[57] But in truth neither of the last two Chinese-led

---

[55] In Korea, Silla, and in Southwest China, Nanzhao frustrated Tang projects. Nicola Di Cosmo, "Qing Colonial Administration in Inner Asia," *IHR* 20 (1998): 287–309; David Wyatt, *Thailand: A Short History* (2nd ed., New Haven, 2003), 10–13.

[56] From 934 Dali succeeded Nanzhao. Denis Twitchett and Klaus-Peter Tietze, "The Liao," *CHC*, vol. VI, 43–153; Ruth Dunnell, "The Hsi Hsia," ibid., 154–214; Herbert Franke, "The Chin Dynasty," ibid., 215–320; Thomas Allsen, "The Rise of the Mongolian Empire and Mongolian Rule in North China," ibid., 321–413; Naomi Standen, *Unbounded Loyalty: Frontier Crossing in Liao China* (Honolulu, 2007), *CIHC*, chs. 6, 7; John Herman, "The Cant of Conquest," in Pamela Crossley, Helen Siu, and Donald Sutton, eds., *Empire at the Margins* (Berkeley, 2006), 136.

[57] Extrapolations from territorial figures at John Dardess, "Did the Mongols Matter?" 117, and Alastair Johnston, *Cultural Realism: Strategic Culture and Grand Strategy in Chinese History* (Princeton, 1995), 236 suggest an 80 percent increase, but Ebrey, pers. commun., April 10, 2007 and John Wills, Jr., pers. commun., April 1, 2007 both doubt so large an increase, which also seems to exceed the maps at *CIHC*, 137, 196. Cf. Mote, *Imperial*

dynasties, the Song or the Ming, could compete effectively with Inner Asian cavalry. This weakness became manifest not only in Song failures vis-à-vis Xi Xia, Liao, and Jin and in Song extinction at the hands of the Mongols, but in the Ming's increasingly defensive posture. After early victories against the Mongols, the Ming suffered humiliating reverses – in 1449 the emperor himself was captured on campaign in the steppe – after which Ming strategy stressed static defense. This was the true origin of the Great Wall.[58] Internecine Mongol strife subsequently reduced dangers in the north, but that was replaced by an ultimately fatal Manchu threat in the northeast.[59] Even the Ming's improved territorial performance vis-à-vis the Song reflected, in large part, the fact that the Mongols had temporarily obliterated other Inner Asian powers – Xi Xia and Jin – that could threaten China proper and, in order to outflank the Southern Song, had destroyed Dali. As John Dardess quipped, by eliminating non-Chinese regimes all along the frontier, the Mongols did China a favor that it had been unable to do for itself.[60]

In other words, the major post-Han territorial extensions occurred not under Chinese, but Inner Asian-dominated regimes that, by wedding tribal military organization to Inner Asian and Chinese political traditions, softened the divide between frontier and sown. The Manchus continued these earlier patterns in two respects: First – like Tanguts, Khitans, Mongols, and Jurchens (from whom Manchus claimed descent) – Manchus were a non-Chinese conquest elite who emphasized clan-based politics, ethnic domination, polyglot administration, and the power of the military class.[61] Second, almost four centuries after the Mongols tried to join all of China and vast stretches of Inner Asia in a single empire, the Qing resumed that project.

China, 685–722. The early Ming also smashed the Tai state of Mong Mao straddling the current Burma–Yunnan border.

[58] Arthur Waldron, *The Great Wall of China* (Cambridge, 1990), esp. 53–164; Kenneth Chase, *Firearms: A Global History to 1700* (Cambridge, 2003), 158–69. Victor Mair, "The North(west)ern Peoples and the Recurrent Origins of the 'Chinese' State," in Joshua Fogel, ed., *The Teleology of the Modern Nation-State* (Philadelphia, 2005), 67 claims that if Timur, who was known in the West as Tamerlane and who died in 1405, had lived another year or two, "he would undoubtedly have reestablished Turko-Mongol Islamic rule" over North China.

[59] Johnston, *Cultural Realism*, 59, 183–86, 216–47; Waldron, *Great Wall*, pt. 2.

[60] Dardess, "Did the Mongols Matter?" 117.

[61] Di Cosmo, "Review," 503–505; James Millward, "The Qing Formation, the Mongol Legacy, and the 'End of History' in Early Modern Central Eurasia," in Struve, *Qing Formation*, 92–120; Morris Rossabi, "The Ming and Inner Asia," *CHC*, vol. VIII, 258; and discussion *infra*.

The central difference, of course, was that whereas Mongol unification lasted barely 90 years, Manchu conquests survived to the end of the imperial era in 1911. What is more, insofar as the bulk of Qing annexations were retained by 20th-century governments, the Qing lay the foundations of the modern Chinese nation-state. All told the Qing more than doubled Ming territory through acquisitions in Manchuria, Mongolia, Xinjiang, Qinghai, Tibet, and Taiwan.[62] Although Manchus, like other Inner Asians, were inspired by Mongol example, their expansion north and west of China proper responded more directly to concerns about Russian encroachment and to fear that the Zunghar, or Western, Mongols might effect an anti-Qing alliance with Tibet.

Ultimately, to follow Peter Perdue, Qing conquests proved more durable than those of either the Mongols or the Ming for four reasons. First, in contrast to the Ming, whose Chinese ethnicity and lower Yangzi base partially isolated them from Inner Asia, Manchus were intimately familiar with the steppe. China's perennially inadequate supply of horses meant that imperial power could extend beyond the Great Wall only with the help of Mongol cavalry, whom the Qing won over through a mix of religious patronage, marriage alliances, diplomacy, economic lures, and force.[63] Second, Chinese economic expansion provided the Qing with greater internal resources. The Ming, like the Song, tried to supply grain and horses to frontier garrisons by providing merchant incentives, but the economy was insufficiently monetized to make this work. By the mid-1700s, however, Qing officials could purchase large supplies on the markets of northwest China and ship them out to Xinjiang. And when prices in the northwest rose sharply, the civilian state granary system, another essentially mid-Qing innovation, could relieve

---

[62] The chief Qing acquisitions lost by 20th-century governments were Taiwan, Outer Mongolia, northwest Xinjiang, trans-Amur and trans-Ussuri territories. On Qing expansion in Inner Asia, Perdue, *China Marches West*; idem, "Military Mobilization in Seventeenth and Eighteenth-Century China, Russia, and Mongolia," *MAS* 30 (1996): 757–93; idem, "Boundaries, Maps, and Movement," *IHR* 20 (1998): 263–86; James Millward's excellent *Beyond the Pass* (Stanford, 1998); idem, "Qing Formation, Mongol Legacy"; Di Cosmo, "Qing Colonial Administration," 287–309. On Qing expansion elsewhere, Laura Hostetler, "Qing Connections to the Early Modern World," *MAS* 34 (2000): 623–62; John Herman, "Empire in the Southwest," *JAS* 56 (1997): 47–74; John Shepherd, *Statecraft and Political Economy on the Taiwan Frontier 1600–1800* (Stanford, 1993); Tonio Andrade, "Commerce, Culture, and Conflict: Taiwan Under European Rule, 1623–1662" (Yale Univ., PhD diss., 2001); Rawski, "Qing Formation," 218–23.

[63] Perdue, *China Marches West*, 68–74, 519, 535, 543–44; Nicola Di Cosmo, "Did Guns Matter?" in Struve, *Qing Formation*, 121–66; and Johan Elverskog, *Our Great Qing* (Honolulu, 2006) on Qing policies and Mongol reactions.

local distress. The Qing also strengthened ties between newly conquered territories, principally Xinjiang, and China proper through large-scale Chinese settlement.[64] Third, the new civilian granary system was symptomatic of a general increase, both secular and cyclic, in administrative efficiency during the early and mid-Qing. The aforementioned reforms, in particular the Grand Council and the system of palace memorials, allowed the Qing to respond more quickly to frontier problems and mobilize resources more efficiently than the Ming. By the same token, Jesuit cartography produced more accurate maps, while Western-style artillery figured in some of the Qing's Inner Asian campaigns.[65]

Finally, Qing expansion benefited from simultaneous Russian advances. Even if they could defeat the Mongols, the Ming could never close off escape routes into the steppe. As Russia and China, who signed frontier treaties in 1689 and 1727, divided much of Inner Asia between them, however, the space for nomad maneuver contracted. For three generations the Zunghar Mongols of Xinjiang strove with astounding energy and imagination to construct an independent empire, but trapped between the Qing hammer and Romanov anvil, their project collapsed in the 1750s. For their part, the Russians were motivated to join the Qing both by security considerations and by the lure of the China market.[66]

Thus by 1760 the Qing could boast something no previous dynasty had achieved: ending the two-millennia threat from the Inner Asian steppe.[67]

Horizontal Cultural Integration

A fourth parallel with Southeast Asian realms, Russia, France, and Japan was the horizontal extension, and simultaneous redefinition, of imperial culture and ethnicity. In familiar fashion, albeit starting far earlier

---

[64] Perdue, *China Marches West*, 70–74, 179, 184, 205, 305, 336, 342–57, 374–400, 519–23, 529, 548–51; Will and Wong, *Nourish the People*, chs. 2, 3; Ebrey, pers. commun., April 10, 2007.

[65] Perdue, *China Marches West*, 73, 184, 204, 305, 446–60, 519, 549–51; Di Cosmo, "Did Guns Matter?" On Qing cartography and territorial expansion, see too Mark Elliott, "The Limits of Tatary," *JAS* 59 (2000): 603–46; Laura Hostetler, *Qing Colonial Enterprise* (Chicago, 2001), 1–80; and n. 330 *infra*.

[66] Perdue, *China Marches West*, 133–73 (esp. 161), 256–99, 518–23, 535–36, 544, 565; Millward, "Qing Formation, Mongol Legacy."

[67] Perdue, *China Marches West*, 551.

in (what we now call) China, cultural integration both reflected and encouraged political consolidation.

During the late Zhou era of the sixth to third centuries B.C.E., competition between polities on the North China plain and between those polities and surrounding populations seems to have stimulated thought about issues of inclusion and identity. The idea took hold that despite their endemic rivalry, the states of the North China plain, an area once loyal to the Zhou king and in theory still subject to a true Son of Heaven, collectively constituted the "realm of civilization." The plain thus became known as "All Under Heaven" (*tianxia*) or the "Central States" (*zhongguo*). The people of this region were Hua or Xia – ethnic terms for Chinese – while peoples on the periphery – Yue, Dian, Yi, Man, Di, Rong, and so forth – were deficient to the degree that they diverged from Chinese culture, in particular from the ritual norms of the Zhou Dynasty. In the late Zhou and more especially the early Han era, educated Chinese often contrasted their culture with that of "barbarians" – some of whose humanity was so suspect that they allegedly ate their eldest sons, slept with their mothers, and tattooed their bodies to look like water creatures.[68]

In truth, the distinction between people of the plain and outsiders remained politically contingent and subject to fluid, ad hoc application. At one time or another various states in the plain itself were branded by their enemies as "barbarian" because they violated accepted norms.[69] What is more, "barbarian" was often (although not invariably) considered a function of learning, not biology, so that the first millennium B.C.E. saw the culture of the North China plain expand north, west, and south through both emigration and voluntary but selective acculturation by frontier peoples eager to share in the plain's prestige. The fact that motifs

---

[68] See the "Chinese" vs. "barbarian" opposition described in Mark Edward Lewis, *The Construction of Space in Early China* (Albany, 2006), 34, 71–72, 182, 206–12, 235, 241–43, 253, 256, 264, 267, 271–80, 297–302, 427–28; idem, *China Between Empires*, 17–18; *CIHC*, 26–59 (esp. 55–59); Constance Cook and John Major, eds., *Defining Chu* (Honolulu, 1999); and Yuri Pines, "Beasts or Humans: Pre-Imperial Origins of the 'Sino-Barbarian' Dichotomy," in Reuven Amitai and Michal Biran, eds., *Mongols, Turks, and Others* (Leiden, 2005), 59–102.

[69] Di Cosmo, *Ancient China*, 93–107. Lydia Liu, *The Clash of Empires* (Cambridge, MA, 2004) has gone further to argue that the Western term "Chinese" had no stable referent in Chinese texts themselves and that "barbarian" also had more itinerant meanings than is usually acknowledged. But sources in the previous note plus Marc Abramson, "Deep Eyes and High Noses: Constructing Ethnicity in Tang China" (Princeton Univ., PhD diss., 2001) agree on the persistent, if qualified, utility of the Sino-barbarian dichotomy in widely separated periods.

flowed in the opposite direction as well, that is to say, from outlying kingdoms to the North China plain, ensured that North Chinese culture constantly mutated even as it expanded. Under the centralized empires of Qin and Han, settlers continued to push outward, especially to the south, assimilating indigenes and opening new channels of communication. Between 2 and 140 C.E. alone, an estimated 5 to 10 million migrants moved from North China into the Yangzi valley and points south. The Han empire incorporated outlying areas most obviously through conquest, military garrisons, and colonization (in the northwest and Inner Asia as well as in the south), but also by strengthening administration in areas like Fujian, Guangdong, and Guangxi, which retained large unassimilated populations; by enrolling the sons of frontier elites in Chinese-style schools; by exploiting Chinese culture's monopoly on literacy; and by creating economic incentives to Sinicization. As always, cultural exchange remained geographically and socially uneven, with subethnic and new ethnic groups forming and reforming, especially on the frontiers. Yet in the middle Yangzi region, for example, where Yueh tribes long had been distinct, by the first century C.E. erstwhile Yueh had begun wearing Chinese-style clothing.[70]

During the postcharter era in at least five of the six Eurasian regions we have examined – western, central, and eastern mainland Southeast Asia, the Russian plains, and Japan – frontier colonization encouraged a substantial shift in the economic and political center of gravity from the charter heartland to what had been the periphery.[71] In the centuries that followed the collapse of the Han, China experienced a prolonged version of the same phenomenon, which might be termed "postcharter

---

[70] Holcombe, *Genesis*, 21, 28. On pre-300 C.E. demographic and cultural shifts, ibid., 18–29; Francis Allard, "Frontiers and Boundaries," in Miriam Stark, ed., *Archaeology of Asia* (Malden, MA, 2006), 233–54; *CIHC*, 82–83; Chang, *Rise of the Chinese Empire*, vol. II, chs. 2–5; Michele Pirazzoli-T'Serstevens, *The Han Dynasty* (New York, 1982), 79–89, 154–59; Marks, *Tigers, Rice*, ch. 2; James Lee, "Migration and Expansion in Chinese History," in William McNeill and Ruth Adams, eds., *Human Migrations* (Bloomington, IN, 1978), 20–47; Abramson, "Deep Eyes and High Noses," 69–72. On ethnicity and assimilation c. 300–600 C.E., Lewis, *China Between Empires*, 167–69, 217–20.

[71] At various times between c. 1300 and 1600 we find a shift from the Upper Irrawaddy heartland to middle and Lower Burma, from Angkor to the Chaophraya basin and Phnom Penh, from Dong Kinh to Thanh Nghe, from Kiev to Lithuania and the northeast, and from the Kinai to the Kanto. Parallels with (what would become) France are less dramatic, because colonization was more limited. Yet the Viking-assisted collapse of the Carolingian empire, whose center of gravity had been the modern Low Countries, did help to shift authority to the Paris basin, on the one hand, and to Saxony and eastern Germany, on the other.

peripheralization"[72]: pushed by nomadic invasions and, to a lesser extent, agrarian exhaustion in the north, and pulled by the rich agricultural potential of the south, migrants and their descendants gradually shifted China's economic and demographic center of gravity from the North China plain to the Yangzi basin and beyond. Despite generations of settlement, in 310 the area south of the Yangzi still had only about 10 percent of China's registered population, and local inhabitants remained overwhelmingly non-Chinese.[73] By the early 7th century the south contained about a quarter of the empire's registered population, by 742 almost half, by 1200 over 60 percent, and by 1290, 85 percent (although the latter figure, reflecting Mongol depredations and statistical anomalies, later declined).[74] By the latter date, despite fluid ethnic boundaries and the persistence of substantial communities beyond state control, Chinese – "Han"– subjects of the state had become a majority in most of the lower and middle Yangzi, southern Sichuan, Guangdong, and the southeast coast.[75]

Although population grew all around the perimeter, the expansion of the Chinese culture zone and the prosperity of the empire thus came to rest heavily on the agricultural wealth – chiefly irrigated rice, supplemented by silk, tea, and other commercial crops – of the Yangzi basin and areas farther south. Ideally suited to the semitropical climate and ample

---

[72] But peripheralization was not confined to this era: during the late Warring States period polities on the edge of the North China plain – Jin, Chu, and most dramatically Qin – gained at the expense of older states, in part because peripheral kingdoms had larger reserves of virgin land to bring under cultivation.

[73] *CIHC*, 87, 91; Holcombe, *Genesis*, 25. Non-Han, i.e., non-Chinese, peoples known as Yue, Minyue, Miao, and so forth generally were not registered.

[74] *CIHC*, 120 (referring to "the south"), and maps on 159; Fairbank and Goldman, *China*, 89 (referring to the area "along the Yangzi and southward"), 90–91; Brook, *Confusions of Pleasure*, 28–29 (referring to the area "south of the Yangzi"); and Elvin, *Pattern of the Past*, 204 Fig. 2, referring to "South" and "North China." Cf. similar figures at Smith, *Taxing Heaven's Storehouse*, 3; idem, "Eurasian Transformations," 280; Valerie Hansen, *Changing Gods in Medieval China 1127–1276* (Princeton, 1990), 4. On southern colonization, see too Richard von Glahn's study of the Song-era Sichuan frontier, *The Country of Streams and Grottoes* (Cambridge, MA, 1987), esp. pts. 2, 3; Hartwell, "Demographic, Political, and Social Transformations," 365–66, 383–85; James Lee, "The Legacy of Immigration in Southwest China, 1250–1850," *Annales de Demographie Historique* (1982): 279–304; Hans Bielenstein, "The Chinese Colonization of Fukien Until the End of the T'ang," in *Studia Serica Bernhard Karlgren Dedicata* (Copenhagen, 1959), 98–122.

[75] Thus in 12th-century Sichuan indigenes, termed "new subjects" (*xinmin*), were distinguished from "the common folk of Han [Chinese] families" (*Hanjia baixing*). Von Glahn, *Country of Streams and Grottoes*, 118. Likewise, Ming officials distinguished between *min*, people considered subjects of the state, and *man*, non-Chinese "beyond the pale." Leo Shin, *The Making of the Chinese State* (Cambridge, 2006), 12.

water of the south and aided by new strains and double-cropping, wet rice supported considerably denser populations than the millet/wheat regime of North China (or indeed, the cereal regimes of western Europe and Russia). By the Sui Dynasty the once marginal Yangzi already had become China's rice basket. Spurred by agrarian intensification and rural handicrafts, and later by New World sweet potatoes, peanuts, and maize, between 1500 and 1850 population growth pushed Chinese migrants yet farther afield. From the North China plain and the southern lowlands they moved into the hilly peripheries of long-settled regions and into substantially new areas in the northwest, the upper Yangzi, the southwest, and Taiwan, areas that supported both subsistence agriculture and specialized production of raw materials for interprovincial trade.

The ensuing process of frontier Sinicization is particularly well documented during the Ming and Qing Dynasties in the arc extending from southern Sichuan, Yunnan, Guizhou, and western Hunan through Guangxi and Guangdong.[76] Indigenes in this region, including tribal speakers of Miao-Yao, Tai-Kadai, Austroasiatic, and Tibeto-Burman languages, faced two intertwined pressures. First, imperial officials strove to demarcate such groups, to incorporate their lands into the standard provincial system, and to transform them from "raw" (barbarian) to

---

[76] On cultural and ethnic change on the southern frontier as well as in Taiwan, nn. 62, 74 *supra*, plus R. Bin Wong, "The Social and Political Construction of Identities in the Qing Empire," in Leonard Blusse and Felipe Fernandez-Armesto, eds., *Shifting Communities and Identity Formation in Early Modern Asia* (Leiden, 2003), 61–72; CIHC, 195–98; Hostetler, *Qing Colonial Enterprise*; Naquin and Rawski, *Chinese Society*, 17–18, 127–33, 199–205; Donald Sutton, "Violence and Ethnicity on a Qing Colonial Frontier," *MAS* 37 (2003): 41–80; C. Patterson Giersch, *Asian Borderlands* (Cambridge, MA, 2006), on Yunnan; Shin, *Making of the Chinese State*, on Ming borderlands; Claudine Lombard-Salmon, *Un Exemple d'Acculturation Chinoise: La Province du Gui Zhou au XVIIIe Siecle* (Paris, 1972); William Rowe, *Saving the World*, 312–17, 417–26, 448; idem, "Social Stability and Social Change," *CHC*, vol. IX, 502–11; idem, "Education and Empire in Southwest China," in Elman and Woodside, *Education and Society*, 417–57; Chuan-Kang Shih, "Genesis of Marriage Among the Moso and Empire-Building in Late Imperial China," *JAS* 60 (2001): 381–412; Herman, "Cant of Conquest," 135–68; David Faure, "The Yao Wars of the Mid-Qing and Their Effect on Yao Ethnicity," in Crossley, *Empire at the Margins*, 171–89; Donald Sutton, "Ethnicity and the Miao Frontier in the 18th Century," ibid., 190–228; Anne Csete, "Ethnicity, Conflict, and the State in the Early to Mid-Qing," ibid., 229–52; Alexander Woodside, "The Ch'ien-lung Reign," *CHC*, vol. IX, 252–60; essays by Stevan Harrell and Norma Diamond in Harrell, ed., *Cultural Encounters on China's Frontiers* (Seattle, 1995); Mark Elvin, *The Retreat of the Elephants* (New Haven, 2004), 216–72; Jared Diamond, *Guns, Germs, and Steel* (New York, 1997), 324–29; Nicola Di Cosmo and Don Wyatt, eds., *Political Frontiers, Ethnic Boundaries, and Human Geographies in Chinese History* (London, 2004).

"cooked" (subjects of the state, civilized, Chinese). To be sure, this project was constantly forced to compromise with inadequate resources, fear of instability, and a special sensitivity among Manchu policymakers, themselves an ethnic minority, to guard against the eradication of difference. Qing frontier policy on the local, not to mention the imperial, level was rarely consistent or single-minded.[77] Nonetheless, in areas of heavy Chinese settlement, fiscal necessity and sincere "civilizing" impulses led some Qing officials (Chinese more often than Manchus), like their Ming and indeed Song, Tang, and Han predecessors, not merely to countenance, but actively to encourage, Sinicization. The state suppressed revolts, at times with near-genocidal ferocity, fostered permanent settlements, and co-opted native power structures, which yielded fitfully to direct rule. Officials sponsored Chinese agricultural techniques and charity elementary schools (*yixue*) and pressured tribal elites to adopt Chinese family norms and dress. Such efforts reflected the "one body" doctrine advocated by the Ming philosopher Wang Yangming, namely, that non-Chinese peoples were no less educable than Chinese.[78] To promote fiscal autonomy and immediate Sinicization – which, it was assumed, translated into political loyalty – the Ming also settled in the southwest almost a million Chinese immigrants, mostly demobilized military families; while the Qing supported a far larger, but primarily voluntary migration to the same region through tax remissions, travel funds, and land grants.

Second, particularly from the early 1700s, rising demand for frontier mineral, forest, and agricultural products joined Chinese immigration to create a sphere of social relations that was partly beyond government control but that also circumscribed the autonomy of southwestern peoples. Even as Chinese settlers displaced some tribesmen to more remote areas or higher elevations, new employment opportunities and trade converted others into debtors, clients, and tenants of the newcomers, who readily appropriated native lands. Chinese Muslims and Chinese merchants, troops, and frontiersmen, some with native wives, provided a principal conduit for cultural transmission (although this was never one way). Ambitious indigenes built Chinese-style houses

---

[77] Perdue, *China Marches West*, 338, 427; Mark Elliott, "Ethnicity in the Qing Eight Banners," in Crossley, *Empire at the Margins*, 33; Shin, *Making of the Chinese State*, chs. 3–5; Sutton, "Ethnicity and the Miao."

[78] Alexander Woodside and Benjamin Elman, "Afterword: The Expansion of Education in Ch'ing China," in Elman and Woodside, *Education and Society*, 528; Rowe, *Saving the World*, 417–26.

and ancestral halls, adopted elements of immigrant dress and coiffure, accepted patrilineality in appointments, copied Chinese farming and trading techniques, and learned to speak, even write Chinese. In these ways some local peoples, particularly elites, "became Chinese," and areas of Austroasiatic, Tai-Kadai, and Miao-Yao speech in South China contracted. But if Sinic acculturation was widespread, usually it also remained selective, which meant that immigrant-indigene boundaries in behavior, dress, and ritual persisted and mutated. For their part, Han newcomers, by virtue of their common vulnerability in an alien environment, tended to congregate in garrison towns and to embrace pan-Chinese identities that masked their often diverse origins. Not unlike European colonial encounters, settler–native interactions gave birth to an ethnographic literature emphasizing the latter's exoticism, primitiveness, and sexuality.[79]

In Qing Manchuria, Mongolia, and Xinjiang a mix of factors – limited agricultural potential, the prior adoption of literate world religions, political ties between Manchus and Mongols, an associated Qing desire to protect Inner Asia in general and Manchuria in particular against Chinese settlement – provided a buffer against dislocation more effective than in the southwest. But in much of Inner Asia too, Qing policies – including fiscal demands, restrictions on nomad movement, military colonies, juridical centralization – joined Chinese migration (legal and illegal), commercial expansion, and growing indebtedness among Mongol aristocrats to sedentarize local peoples and to increase their dependence on the Chinese world.[80]

---

[79] On frontier cultural dynamics, besides previous notes, Rowe, *Saving the World*, 419–26; Shin, *Making of the Chinese State*, esp. 12–13, 125–26, 140–57, 167–70, 181–92; Giersch, *Asian Borderlands*, 187–217; Faure, "Yao Wars"; Sutton, "Ethnicity and the Miao Frontier"; Csete, "Ethnicity, Conflict."

[80] Elverskog, *Our Great Qing*, describing Qing efforts to unify Mongol communities and generally supportive Mongol noble responses; Perdue, *China Marches West*, 338–57; Di Cosmo, "Qing Colonial Administration"; Naquin and Rawski, *Chinese Society*, 17–18, 127–33, 184–93; Evelyn Rawski, "Problems and Prospects," in David Johnson et al., eds., *Popular Culture in Late Imperial China* (Berkeley, 1985), 415; Evelyn Rawski, "Presidential Address," *JAS* 55 (1996): 836; Perdue, "Military Mobilization"; Jonathan Lipman, *Familiar Strangers* (Seattle, 1997), chs. 2–4; Millward, *Beyond the Pass*; Rowe, "Social Stability," 502–503; Dorothea Heuschert, "Legal Pluralism in the Qing Empire," *IHR* 20 (1998): 310–24. Within Xinjiang, where between c. 1760 and 1800 some 200,000 Chinese settled the Ili valley, Qing policy grew yet more pro-immigration after non-Chinese revolts in 1830–31. On frontier commercialization from the 1500s, see esp. Iwai Shigeki, "China's Frontier Society in the 16th and 17th Centuries," *Acta Asiatica* 88 (2005): 1–20.

To be sure, even in China proper the cultures that emerged from these processes were anything but uniform. Major regions varied not only in levels of literacy and urbanization, but in external exposure. From an early date North China, for example, although exhibiting less subethnic and dialect differences than other regions, was drawn into a hybrid steppe-agrarian environment distinct from that of South China. To 14th-century Europeans, the northern country of "Cathay" (a term derived from the "Khitan" tribal name) was a different kingdom than South China, which Marco Polo called "Manzi."[81] If Inner Asian influences were substantial in the north, in the southwest aboriginal customs influenced newcomers to the point where as many Chinese may have become Miao, Tai, and so forth as aborigines became Chinese.[82] Moreover, Chinese migrants themselves varied in provenance, dialect, and social and religious practices.[83] From these idiosyncratic mixtures emerged new provincial dialects and identities – which then interacted with metropolitan customs so as to redefine continuously what "China" was.

Yet however fluid local syntheses may have been, conquest and migration inevitably tended to reduce cultural distance between imperial heartlands and peripheries. Consider, for example, Yunnan. From the 8th to the mid-13th centuries Yunnan's rugged territory supported independent states, Nanzhao and then Dali, which dominated some 30 non-Chinese ethnic groups and blended Indic, indigenous, and Chinese cultural elements. By 1850, however, through assimilation but more especially through six centuries of immigration, self-identified Han Chinese constituted 60 percent of the population. Speaking a substantially new dialect called Southwestern Mandarin, generations of immigrants built a provincial identity increasingly attuned to cultural trends and market demands elsewhere in China. In Yunnan as in Sichuan, Manchuria, and other frontier areas, rising success in

---

[81] Franke and Twitchett, "Introduction," 21; *The Travels of Marco Polo* (New York, n.d.), 179–80; *EAH*, vol. I, 233; Di Cosmo, "Review," 507; *CIHC*, 102–104. The Khitans' Liao Dynasty in North China and Inner Asia lasted from 907 to 1125.

[82] Rowe, *Saving the World*, 420; Sutton, "Violence and Ethnicity," 58; C. Patterson Giersch, "Qing China's Reluctant Subjects" (Yale Univ., PhD diss., 1998, basis of his *Asian Borderlands*), 36, 52, 226. In much the same way, some Vietnamese settlers became Cham or Khmer.

[83] Emily Honig, "Native Place and the Making of Chinese Ethnicity," in Gail Hershatter et al., eds., *Remapping China* (Stanford, 1996), 143–56; Naquin and Rawski, *Chinese Society*, 160, 211, 214; Sow-theng Leong, *Migration and Ethnicity in Chinese History* (Stanford, 1997), chs. 1–3.

examinations mirrored and promoted the local literati's integration into the imperial system.[84]

Such acculturation was driven chiefly by interior population pressure and the ensuing demand for frontier minerals and raw materials. We shall return to rising interregional trade when we consider the "first" and "second commercial revolutions." For now note merely that within China proper improved transport, trade, and communication spurred all manner of lateral cultural exchange, among which migration from interior provinces to the frontier was only the most visible element. Travel for employment, study, or pleasure; the circulation of traders and entertainers, especially drama troupes; and religious pilgrimage all expanded. As early as the Southern Song shrines to worthy men shed their local character, and traders, boatmen, and officials spread the worship of formerly local deities throughout South China. Among Song peasants commercially adept gods began replacing zoomorphic deities in precisely those areas most closely tied to urban transportation routes.[85] In the late Ming and Qing periods, cultic and educational practices, cuisines, apparel, housing styles, and entertainment became the common patrimony of a genuinely empire-wide elite. Urban and rural cultures interpenetrated, aided by the expansion and proliferation of market towns. Cosmopolitan cities hosted quasi-permanent colonies of sojourners from distant areas. The high Qing, in particular, saw a notable increase in the interregional circulation of scholarly and scientific works, educational critiques by people of diverse backgrounds, and letters by intellectuals, all of which, it has been suggested, resembled at least superficially the "republic of letters" of 18th-century Europe.[86]

[84] Wyatt, *Thailand*, 10–15, 33; Charles Backus, *The Nanchao Kingdom and T'ang China's Southwestern Frontier* (New York, 1982); Sun Laichen, pers. commun., 2003; *CIHC*, 197–98; Lee, "Legacy of Immigration," 285, 303–304; Naquin and Rawski, *Chinese Society*, 197–98, 201, 204, 208, 215.

[85] Hansen, *Changing Gods*, 28, 105–27; Lamouroux, pers. commun., August, 2000. On Ming-era travel, Timothy Brook, "Communications and Commerce," *CHC*, VIII, 619–35.

[86] C. A. Bayly, *The Birth of the Modern World 1780–1914* (Malden, MA, 2004), 78. On horizontal acculturation in general, Johnson, "Communication, Class, and Consciousness in Late Imperial China," in Johnson, *Popular Culture*, 34–72; Naquin and Rawski *Chinese Society*, 55–79, 230–32; *CIHC*, 41, 43, 155, 158; Shin, *Making of the Chinese State*, 170–78; Rowe, "Social Stability," 561 and *passim*. On the religious dimension, Peter Gregory and Patricia Buckley Ebrey, "The Religious and Historical Landscape," in Ebrey and Gregory, eds., *Religion and Society in T'ang and Sung China* (Honolulu, 1993), 1–44; Terry Kleeman, "The Expansion of the Wen-Ch'ang Cult," ibid., 45–73; Valerie

Particularly important to intellectual production and lateral communication was the expansion of block printing, which created books since at least the 9th century but dramatically lowered book prices only during the Song. By the 1100s printed books included not only literati classics and belles lettres, but examination primers – for which Song examinations created enormous demand – as well as histories, diverse handbooks, and practical guides. Thus esoteric knowledge became available for popular appropriation and provincial elites gained easier access to official culture. Wider Song and Yuan literacy and an "oversupply" of educated men boosted not only readership, but the number of provincials qualified to print and publish scholarly works. From the mid-Ming, rural and urban audiences for classics, examination primers, novels, dramas, dictionaries, almanacs, and printed materials of all sorts again expanded notably, nurturing an educated public bound by common cultural and aesthetic conventions. Reminiscent of post-1550 France and Tokugawa Japan, these trends would intensify under the Qing.[87]

For its part, the state took a variety of spatial homogenizing initiatives in addition to the aforementioned effort to assimilate frontier peoples. From the Song period on, officials worked with provincial gentry to merge major spirit cults, at least nominally, into regional, and in the case of a few deities, national pantheons replete with quasi-bureaucratic titles. In this sense religious consolidation paralleled the extension of imperial administration itself, although recent work suggests that cultic unity was to some extent illusory, masking persistent local categories and attachments.[88] Recall comparable attempts to organize

---

Hansen, "Gods on Walls," ibid., 75–113; idem, *Changing Gods*, 3–10, 128–65; David Johnson, "The City-God Cults of T'ang and Sung China," *HJAS* 45 (1985): 363–457; Susan Naquin and Chun-fang Yu, eds., *Pilgrims and Sacred Sites in China* (Berkeley, 1992).

[87] On printing, the book trade, and commercially driven horizontal acculturation, Hymes, *Statesmen and Gentlemen*, 2–3; Chia, "Mashaben," 284–328; idem, *Printing for Profit* (Cambridge, MA, 2002); idem, "The Development of the Jianyang Book Trade, Song-Yuan" *LIC* 17 (1996): 10–48; Cynthia Brokaw, "Commercial Publishing in Late Imperial China," *LIC* 17 (1996): 49–92; Evelyn Rawski, "Economic and Social Foundations of Late Imperial Culture," in Johnson, *Popular Culture*, 3–33; Brook, *Confusions of Pleasure*, 58–65, 129–31, 167–89; idem, "Communications and Commerce," 662–67; Kai-wing Chow, "Writing for Success," *LIC* 17 (1996): 120–57; Mote, *Imperial China*, 7–8, 21; *CIHC*, 158, 201–202.

[88] See Judith Bolz, "Not by the Seal of Office Alone," in Ebrey and Gregory, *Religion and Society*, 241–305; James Watson, "Standardizing the Gods," in Johnson, *Popular Culture*, 292–324; Prasenjit Duara, "Superscribing Symbols," *JAS* 47 (1988): 778–95; Romeyn Taylor's essay in Liu, *Orthodoxy in Late Imperial China*, 126–57; Wong, *China Transformed*,

translocal hierarchies of spirits and saints in Burma, Vietnam, Russia, and France.[89] In the Song, the Ming, and most especially the Qing, official–literati coalitions also sought to expand state and private elementary schools, to promote cultural exchanges between North China and the lower Yangzi, and through laws, regular lectures, and ritual displays, to indoctrinate outlying peasantries and non-Chinese villagers in Neo-Confucian orthopraxy. Although again official teachings and local understandings did not necessarily mesh, such measures, and especially the proliferation of private academies and quasi-public charity elementary schools, carried Confucian teachings beyond the confines of prefectural seats to rural districts, and beyond the southeastern commercial heartland to frontier provinces like Gansu, Yunnan, and Xinjiang.[90]

We have met generic equivalents to many of these integrative dynamics in Indic Southeast Asia and Europe, and we shall do so again in South Asia. At least two superb spatial homogenizing instruments, however, remained unique to China (and its cultural offshoots, Vietnam and Korea). First, civil service examinations, and the system of study associated with preparation for the examinations, created marvelous mechanisms of intellectual – and by extension, political – exchange and coordination, if not conformity. Notwithstanding substantial, often passionate diversity of scholarly opinion, examinations required knowledge of a state-approved corpus that was transmitted through substantially standardized school curricula across the empire. Examinations obliged candidates from whatever region to master stylized modes of composition,

96. On the persistence of local understandings, based on the efficacy of unique deities and rituals, alongside, even in opposition to, official views, see Michael Szonyi, "The Illusion of Standardizing the Gods," *JAS* 56 (1997): 113–35; Kenneth Pomeranz, "Water to Iron, Widows to Warlords," *LIC* 12 (1991): 62–99; Robert Hymes, *Way and Byway* (Berkeley, 2002).

[89] *SP*, 116, 192, 357–58; and Ch. 2, nn. 139, 266, 332 *supra*.

[90] Whereas Ming China had some 1,200 academies, Qing China had 1,900, far more widely dispersed. Woodside and Elman, "Afterword," 526–28. On state actions favorable to horizontal cultural integration, I rely on Smith, "Impressions of the Song-Yuan-Ming Transition," *SYMT*, 33; Davis, *Court and Family*, 177–80; R. Bin Wong, "Confucian Agendas for Material and Ideological Control in Modern China," in Theodore Huters, R. Bin Wong, and Pauline Yu, eds., *Culture and State in Chinese History* (Stanford, 1997), 303–25; Victor Mair, "Language and Ideology in the Written Popularizations of the *Sacred Edict*," in Johnson, *Popular Culture*, 325–59; essays by Angela Leung, William Rowe, Alexander Woodside, and Benjamin Elman in Elman and Woodside, *Education and Society*, 381–457, 525–60; Fairbank and Goldman, *China*, 94; Han, "Reinventing Local Tradition," 7–12, 94–154; and Mark Elliott, pers. commun., Jan. 5, 2008, emphasizing both two-way exchanges and the continuing gap between official and popular understandings.

to participate in a three-tiered testing system, to write about issues of imperial, rather than local, governance, and thus to accept an imperial psychology that regarded unified empire as a prerequisite for human welfare. As John Wills, Jr. has shown, this normative vision of empire in turn was linked to an assumption that worthy scholars from diverse locales all were morally obliged to offer services to the ruler. Not only did the same criteria – studying for and taking imperial examinations – come to define elite status from Gansu to Guangdong, but examinations had affirmative action quotas that sought, quite successfully, to prevent poorer, less cultured regions from becoming marginalized.[91] In Europe the arrival of printing led through the vernacular Bible to the Reformation, religious wars, and the fragmentation of Latin Christendom. But in China printing led through the classics to examinations and substantial political and cultural unity.[92]

Second, Chinese writing – nonalphabetic and logographic – permitted intra-elite communication in the face of often mutually incomprehensible spoken dialects. Because Chinese script did not change to reflect differences in pronunciation, scholars, would-be officials, and officials throughout the empire all read the same texts, while at the same time the script inhibited regional languages and cultures within China from gaining independent written expression. Likewise people outside the empire and newly subdued frontier populations who lacked writing systems of their own were more easily drawn into the Chinese political orbit. A stable logographic script also encouraged identification with writers of earlier centuries, reinforcing China's historiographic preoccupation with a central succession of emperors and dynasties.[93] One

---

[91] See Chaffee, *Thorny Gates*, 142 ("the cultural unity created, in large part, by schools and examinations was an important contributing factor to the political unity of late imperial China"), 183; Hansen, *Changing Gods*, 7; Bossler, *Powerful Relations*, 207–208; Elman, *Cultural History*, chs. 1–5 (esp. pp. 256–60), and chs. 7–9 (esp. pp. 442–43, 503–20). On "The Way of the Ruler and the Ministers" as a moral spur to universal recruitment, see Wills, *Mountain of Fame*; idem, "Why Is China So Big?" (ms.).

[92] Cf. Chaffee, *Thorny Gates*, 14.

[93] "The script, identical through space and time, permanent and absolute, inhibits the development of local linguistically defined loyalties because they cannot be written down." W. J. F. Jenner, *The Tyranny of History* (London, 1992), 225. "It was the intellectual commitment of local elites to the text-based dream of empire . . . that both secured the longevity of the imperial system and led to the omnipresence of the written graph in Chinese culture." Mark Edward Lewis, *Writing and Authority in Early China* (Albany, 1999), 4. Also ibid., 10–11, 338–39, 360–65; idem, *Early Chinese Empires*, 53–54; *CIHC*, 28, 85; Ebrey, pers. commun., April 10, 2007; Holcombe, *Genesis*, 60–69, 75, 100–103, 225; Woodside and Elman, "Afterword," 538, 546–51. Admittedly, changes in linguistic

is reminded of the integrative role of *sorobun* prose and *oieryu* calligraphy in Japan. The obvious contrast is with the Roman Empire, South Asia, and Southeast Asia, where – despite the universal aspirations of Latin and Sanskrit and the towering prestige of classical cultures – phonetic alphabets encouraged independent writing systems able to express regional, and eventually national, identities. Thus, to extend Victor Mair's observations, there was no flourishing literary tradition for Cantonese, Fujianese, and other regional vernaculars in China as there was for French, Italian, English, Burmese, Shan, Siamese, Khmer, and various South Asian tongues.[94]

Of course, in explaining why China – unlike post-Roman Europe – repeatedly reassembled as a single polity, civil service examinations and logographic writing were hardly the only factors. As noted, partible inheritance and elite dependence on office holding fragmented aristocratic power bases more readily in China than in Europe.[95] The ratio of settled invaders to former imperial subjects was probably higher in post-Roman northern Europe than in post-Han northern China, which

idiom and usage complicated the task of Qing scholars in reading, say, Tang materials. Note too that before c. 100 C.E. oral may have been more important than written transmission, for only in the Later Han do we find rhetorical claims for the superiority of written texts and long texts without memorization devices. Michael Nylan, "Textual Authority in Pre-Han and Han," *Early China* 25 (2000): 205–58. On Inner Asians' use of Chinese and more esp. non-Chinese writing systems to develop their own scripts, see *CHC*, vol. VI, 282–83, 465–67, 630, 643–44; Herbert Franke, "The Role of the State as a Structural Element in Polyethnic Societies," in Stuart Schram, ed., *Foundations and Limits of State Power in China* (London, 1987), 110–11, *CIHC*, 169; Perdue, *China Marches West*, 126; Morris Rossabi, *Khubilai Khan* (Berkeley, 1988), 154–60; Elliott, *Manchu Way*, 70; Hansen, *Open Empire*, 350–51; Mote, *Imperial China*, 219; and Victor Mair in n. 94 *infra*.

94 This is not to deny that Vietnam (*nom*), Korea (*han'gul*), and Japan (*kana*) developed semiphonetic writing systems from Chinese, that the imperial period saw some Cantonese literature, or that Inner Asian peoples created national scripts (cf. previous note). But the latter often were based on Indic-derived alphabets. Within China proper scripts for regional languages had little impact, and even in Vietnam, Korea, and Japan, Chinese was never displaced in the manner of Latin in the West. To cite Mair, again, the "amount of unadulterated writing in [non-Mandarin] vernacular Sinitic topolects and languages is so pathetically small as to be virtually nonexistent." Victor Mair, "Buddhism and the Rise of the Written Vernacular in East Asia," *JAS* 53 (1994): 707–51, esp. 707, 725 (source of quote), 730, 738. Cf. Ch. 4, n. 318 on *sorobun* and *oieryu*; Sheldon Pollock, *The Language of the Gods in the World of Men* (Berkeley, 2006), pt. 2; and Ch. 6 *infra*.

95 Even in the Tang, a notably aristocratic era, only noble titles, not property, were subject to primogeniture. See n. 23 *supra*. Elvin, *Pattern of the Past*, ch. 1 seeks to explain imperial size in terms of the balance between superior central resources and the rising costs of coordinating ever more distant units. But since the same principles apply to all empires, this tells us little about China's unique longevity. I am indebted to Patricia

inhibited continuity. As we shall see, Chinese geography was inherently more centripetal than European, for China had a much smoother coastline, fewer internal mountain barriers, and more encompassing, easily linked river systems. No less critical, China's vulnerability to the steppe meant that powerful Inner Asian armies could (re)unite imperial territories in a fashion without European analogue. Inner Asian unifiers and would-be unifiers of Chinese territory often had little or no knowledge of Chinese writing, while loyalty to China's logographic corpus could inspire opposition to Inner Asian-led reunification. And yet it is also clear that in the Mediterranean world Greek, Arabic, Hebrew, and Latin alphabets nurtured distinctly local identities in a fashion quite unknown in China, notwithstanding the comparably hypnotic appeal of Roman and Han imperial legacies. Conversely, although geography was not dramatically more sympathetic to empire in China than in South Asia, examinations, scripts, and a politicized, universal syllabus helped China resist political and cultural fragmentation far more effectively than India.

Vertical Cultural Exchange

Horizontal cultural exchange was entwined with a fifth generic parallel to protected zone patterns, namely, vertical cultural integration. Again, this was unusually prolonged in China, but there too it provided a psychological prop to political integration and accelerated from the 16th and more especially the 18th century.

During most of the early imperial period, that is to say, the Han through the Tang, aristocratic political monopoly was paralleled by an elite–mass cultural divide broadly reminiscent of charter-era patterns in Southeast Asia, France, Russia, and Japan. True, Martin Powers has shown that during the middle Han some prosperous members of intermediate strata began to imbibe elements of aristocratic culture. After the throne ordered that schools be built and public offices be filled by men who exemplified Confucian values, there was a "rush for a classical education and other marks of bureaucratic eligibility." In this same period elements of funerary art and luxury consumption once restricted to the high nobility spread to "lower-level bureaucrats," "sub-bureaucrats,"

Buckley Ebrey, pers. commun., April 10, 2007; Ebrey, "Pondering China's Size" (ms); and John Wills, Jr., pers. commun., April 1, 2007 for insights on the problem of China's size, to which we shall return.

and "middle income" families.[96] However, Patricia Buckley Ebrey and others have argued that by favoring economies of scale, iron plows, oxen, and commercial marketing benefited large landowners far more than smallholders, and that this trend, plus population growth and magnate tax abuses encouraged after c. 100 B.C.E. not widespread social mobility, but land concentration and growing stratification.[97]

In any case, even if, as seems likely the Han elite broadened, the cultural gap between what Ebrey terms the "upper class" as a whole – generally synonymous with "cultured gentlemen" (*shi*) – and the masses remained formidable. An estimated 100,000–150,000 *shi* in the late Han period may have constituted something like 0.7 to 1 percent of the adult male population.[98] *Shi* were distinguished from most plebeians not only by fiscal privileges, distinctive family organization, *de facto* endogamy, and escape from a world of subsistence insecurity, but also by aesthetic and ritual perspectives far removed from those of the peasantry.[99] Although paper slowly became available, the rarity, high price, and bulk of most texts ensured that to the end of the Han and beyond, books and literacy remained the preserve of a tiny minority.[100]

During the Age of Division, as a result of strong steppe influences, substantial economic autarky, and magnate power, elite–commoner

---

[96] Powers, *Art and Political Expression*, 108, 129, 136–37; also ibid., 73–85, 93, 106–10, 123–38 *passim*. Ebrey, "Economic and Social History," 631 concurs that the Later Han imperial elite expanded by incorporating more local notables.

[97] On late Han socioeconomic trends, n. 4 *supra*; Ebrey, "Economic and Social History," 617–26; Michael Nylan, "Style, Patronage, and Confucian Ideals in Han Dynasty Art," *Early China* 18 (1993): 227–47; Francesca Bray, *Science and Civilization in China. Volume 6. Biology and Biological Technology, Part II: Agriculture* (Cambridge, 1984), esp. 587–97; Miranda Brown, pers. commun., Dec. 10, 2003; Hansen, *Open Empire*, 147; CIHC, 73–75; Nishijima Sadao, "The Economic and Social History of Former Han," CHC, vol. I, 545–607; Lewis, *China Between Empires*, 29 ("actual cases of [Late Han] upward social mobility were extremely rare").

[98] Ebrey, "Toward a Better Understanding ," 61 cites approvingly an estimate of 100,000 men "capable of being officials," that is *shi*, out of a total population of 55,000,000, of whom perhaps 14,000,000 were adult males (Eastman, *Family, Fields*, 4; Miranda Brown, pers. commun., Aug. 29, 2006). But Miranda Brown, pers. commun., Dec. 10, 2003, also suggests that many *shi* could not seek a bureaucratic career, and that 150,000 may be a more useful figure. Cf. Ebrey, "Economic and Social History," 630–40, referring to five grades of *shi*; Ch'u, *Han Social Structure*, 63–66 and ch. 4 *passim*.

[99] Johnson, *Medieval Chinese Oligarchy*, 5; Hucker, *China's Imperial Past*, 158; Michael Loewe, *Everyday Life in Early Imperial China* (London, 1968), 92–94 and chs. 1–4, 7 *passim*.

[100] Nylan, "Textual Authority," 244.

cultural distinctions and aristocratic insularity became, if anything, more pronounced. As noted, aristocratic clans, who represented the upper end of the *shi* elite and who developed large manorial estates, routinely monopolized official posts; while at the other end of the scale servile groups – clients, retainers, serfs, and slaves – grew at the expense of both the free peasantry and government tax rolls. As more people became immobilized geographically and occupationally, society was said to be divided into three strata: the *shi*, free commoners (*shu min* or, in later periods, *liang min*), and debased people (*jian min*, including tenant farmers as well as servile people, entertainers, and hereditary pariahs). Each had specific legal attributes, and marriage between *shi* and commoners was expressly forbidden.[101] Aristocratic dominance persisted during the Tang Dynasty, when society in its higher levels, according to Denis Twitchett, was more stratified than during any subsequent period.[102] The normally private character of education inevitably reinforced this elitist outlook.[103] Although *shi* and lower groups certainly shared broad traits – kinship patterns, language, attitudes to the supernatural – which defined them vis-à-vis non-Chinese, and although Confucian, Buddhist, and Daoist literati sought to implant their values in the countryside, peasants remained preliterate and substantially local in loyalties and outlook. So far as they can be reconstructed, pre-Tang popular religious cults were oral, shamanic, frequently ecstatic, and devoted to local household and agrarian deities who bestowed good harvests and health in return for animal sacrifices.[104]

Beginning in the Song, however, and accelerating during the Ming and more especially the Qing, the cultural gap narrowed, even as it

---

[101] Twitchett, "Composition of Ruling Class," 49; Johnson, *Medieval Chinese Oligarchy*, 5; Bray, *Agriculture*, 596–97; Graff, *Medieval Chinese Warfare*, 19.

[102] Twitchett, "Composition of Ruling Class," 82. On Age of Division and Tang social organization, ibid., 49 ff., 79–83; Johnson, *Medieval Chinese Oligarchy*, chs. 1–3; Matthew Sommer, *Sex, Law, and Society in Late Imperial China* (Stanford, 2000), 5–6; McMullen, *State and Scholars*, 251; *CIHC*, 88–95; Tang Changru, "Clients and Bound Retainers in the Six Dynasties Period," in Dien, *State and Society*, 111–38; Richard Mather, "Intermarriage as a Gauge of Family Status in the Southern Dynasties," ibid., 211–28. Under the Tang the aforementioned threefold classification coexisted with a classical fourfold division in the law code between scholar-officials, farmers, artisans, and merchants.

[103] Davis, *Court and Family*, 179.

[104] Ebrey, "Toward a Better Understanding," 49–72; Michael Loewe, *Chinese Ideas of Life and Death* (London, 1982), 17; Jacques Gernet, *Everyday Life in China on the Eve of the Mongol Invasion 1250–1276* (Stanford, 1962), 60; Hansen, *Changing Gods*, 13, 31, 78; idem, "Gods on Walls," 76, 77, 100; Gregory and Ebrey, "The Religious and Historical Landscape," in Ebrey and Gregory, *Religion and Society*, esp. 24–34.

assumed new forms. With vertical as with horizontal integration, a principal catalyst was the Song commercial revolution, which dramatically broadened the ranks of the educated, widened avenues of communication, and encouraged social mobility, particularly in the Yangzi basin and other favored areas of South China. The Mongol Yuan and to some extent the early Ming sought to freeze essentially hereditary categories, but such efforts flew in the face of continued market forces. As commercialization in the late Ming and Qing opened gentry ranks to *nouveaux riches* landowners and merchants, permeable class boundaries and shifting terms of entry generated intense insecurity, snobbery, and competition between upwardly mobile groups and those threatened from below. Yet these same competitive pressures, this same blurring of status lines, worked to diffuse gentry fashions among ambitious, but less well-educated groups and to supplement the traditional emphasis on degrees with a new respect for men of leisure whose wealth, however acquired, allowed them to adopt cultured life-styles. Accordingly, the Ming removed bans that prevented merchants from taking civil service examinations. Compared to Tokugawa Japan, Petrine Russia, and *ancien régime* France, all of which had closed nobilities, in China legal barriers to merchant entrée into the sociocultural elite were therefore modest and informal. Johnson claims that classically educated males comprised 10 percent of the adult male population in 1700 and (after a period of rapid population growth) 5 percent in 1800[105] – figures that contrast with the 1 percent or fewer who qualified as literate "cultured gentlemen" in the Han period.

The influence of China's educated elite derived not merely from expanded numbers, but also from closer, more structured interactions

---

[105] Johnson, "Communication, Class," 53–60, esp. 59–60. Cf. n. 42 *supra* referring to the far smaller group who actually obtained a degree via examination or purchase. On the size of the French nobility and the Japanese *samurai* estate, see Ch. 3, n. 213; Ch. 4, nn. 221, 222. Woodside and Elman, "Afterword," 546 put the Chinese gentry at only 1.6–1.9 percent of the *total* population during the "late empire" – but if we exclude women and children, this figure would approximate Johnson's 1800 estimate. In the 13th century, Ebrey, "Dynamics of Elite Domination," 501 says that 2.5 percent of adult males had the education and ambition to take the examinations; *CHC*, vol. VI, 638 says approximately 5 percent of the population in 1300 were "educated." On changing elite composition and size, see too Hansen, *Changing Gods*, 7; Naquin and Rawski, *Chinese Society*, chs. 2–4; Brook, *Confusions of Pleasure*; Craig Clunas, *Superfluous Things* (Cambridge, 1991); Cynthia Brokaw, *The Ledgers of Merit and Demerit* (Princeton, 1991), 3–27; Woodside and Elman, "Afterword," 544–50; Esherick and Rankin, "Introduction"; Rowe, "Success Stories"; Timothy Brook, "Family Continuity and Cultural Hegemony," in Esherick and Rankin, *Chinese Local Elites*, 27–50.

with the general population. If the absolute number of candidates for examinations rose continuously from Song to Qing, relative stasis in the size of the bureaucracy meant that the chance of obtaining an official post became ever more remote, as we saw.[106] Fortunately, new rural and town markets offered educated men a growing range of suitable employments outside government service, as teachers, letter writers, calligraphers, private secretaries, diviners, geomancers, ritual experts, or informal public servants. Converting necessity into virtue, Daoxue Neo-Confucianism accorded projects of local service and cultural patronage a transcendent moral value.[107]

Thus a mycelium of gentry-led organizations continued to expand: schools, community granaries, fraternal and philanthropic organizations, irrigation associations, militias, community compacts, and, perhaps most influential as a vehicle of cross-class interaction, lineage organizations. Complete with corporate landholding and ancestral shrines, the latter sought to join people from different strata on the basis of putative ancestry. Descent groups had been organized sporadically since Song times, but later centuries saw a marked increase, as the economics of landholding, periodic disorders, and Confucian notions of family solidarity encouraged kinsmen to join forces. Like philanthropy and community compacts, lineage organizations relied on classically educated leaders, promoted elite–mass interaction through patronage and ritual, and thus helped to diffuse elite understandings of family obligation and civilized conduct across class lines – even as they forced lower-class participants to reinterpret those norms to meet their own needs. To the extent that a Gorski-style "disciplinary revolution" influenced wide sectors of society, such cross-class associations provided critical institutional support.[108] In the sense that acceptance of

---

[106] Thus the ratio of *jinshi*-degree-holders to the general population fell from about 1:500,000 in the Song to 1:1,000,000 in mid-Ming to 1:4,000,000 in the Qing. Again cf. n. 42 *supra*. My discussion of vertical cultural exchange draws on Naquin and Rawski, *Chinese Society*, chs. 3, 4; Fairbank and Goldman, *China*, 94–101; Hymes, *Statesmen and Gentlemen*, chs. 4–7; Ebrey and Gregory, *Religion and Society*; CIHC, 206–209; Christian De Pee, *The Writing of Weddings in Middle Period China* (Albany, 2007); Brooke, *Confusions of Pleasure*; Janet Theiss, "The Construction and Practice of Local Moral Community" (ms); Johnson, *Popular Culture*, esp. essays by Johnson, James Hayes, Susan Naquin, Victor Mair, and Evelyn Rawski.

[107] Bol, *This Culture*, ch. 9; Bossler, *Powerful Relations*, 205–207; Hymes, *Statesmen and Gentlemen*.

[108] On the definition of "gentry," see n. 35. *supra* and on gentry activities, n. 39 *supra*. On the post-Tang expansion of lineage organizations, Johnson, *Medieval Chinese Oligarchy*,

official norms promised to enhance one's self-image and social standing, self-Confucianization, first by local gentry and then by more plebeian strata, recalls self-Burmanization, self-Siamization, self-Francification, and so on.

Commercial expansion also encouraged peasant acculturation in ways that did not depend directly on elite mediation. The infiltration of money into the countryside, the proliferation of market towns, and the commodification of land and labor enhanced social and geographic mobility not only among merchants, but sectors of the peasantry. In the most commercially advanced areas hereditary legal distinctions eroded as early as the 9th century. If during the Ming Dynasty the lower Yangzi region saw a temporary increase in bonded labor, by the mid-Qing period servile categories of all types had largely disappeared throughout China proper. In lieu of estate owners and bound workers emerged a more fluid, interactive mix of absentee landlords, managerial landlords, independent owners, contractual tenant farmers, and hired workers. Accordingly, legal barriers between the gentry and respectable commoners (*liang min*) effectively disappeared, along with formerly extensive sumptuary distinctions. In other words, as intermediate grades bridged the once-formidable divide, as people moved up and down the scale more rapidly, as wealth rather than birth became the major determinant of status, society grew more egalitarian and cultural motifs circulated more easily.[109]

At the same time, commercialization enhanced the value of literacy and numeracy and magnified resources for popular education. Although few officials advocated truly universal schooling, the early Ming did attempt, with mixed success, to promote community schools

114, 147; Smith, "Introduction," 24–25; Esherick and Rankin, "Introduction," 14, 20–21; Timothy Brook, "Family Continuity and Cultural Hegemony," in Esherick and Rankin, *Chinese Local Elites*, 33ff., 47; idem, "Funerary Ritual and the Building of Lineages in Late Imperial China," *HJAS* 49 (1989): 465–99; Rowe, "Ancestral Rites"; idem, "Social Stability," 531–37; *CIHC*, 206–209; James Watson, "Chinese Kinship Reconsidered," *China Quarterly* 92 (1982): 589–622; Hilary Beattie, "The Alternative to Resistance," in Spence and Wills, *From Ming to Ch'ing*, 239–76.

[109] On the changing social relations and their cultural implications, Smith, "Introduction," 3–4, 33; Brook, *Confusions of Pleasure*, 85, 255–57; Clunas, *Superfluous Things*, ch. 6; Xu Dixin and Wu Chengming, *Chinese Capitalism, 1522–1840* (New York, 2000), 22–43, 130–47, 376; Naquin and Rawski, *Chinese Society*, 99, 114–27; Rowe, "Social Stability," 485–502; idem, "Approaches to Modern Chinese Social History," in Oliver Zunz, ed., *Reliving the Past* (Chapel Hill, 1987), 241–55; Elvin, *Pattern of the Past*, ch. 15; Bossler, *Powerful Relations*, 208–10; Kenneth Pomeranz, *The Great Divergence* (Princeton, 2000), 80–87; Sucheta Mazumdar, *Sugar and Society in China* (Cambridge, MA, 1998), 211–17.

(*shexue*) alongside earlier private academies. The high Qing saw a notable increase in the number and variety of schools, including the aforementioned charity elementary schools aimed at worthy sons of poor Chinese and ethnic minorities.[110] Likewise, especially from the mid-Ming onward, the printing of mass-circulation works reflected and stimulated popular literacy. Only the highly educated could read books written in the terse, allusive literary language of the classics and of government reports. But, as our discussion of horizontal acculturation suggested, for materials written with the grammar and vocabulary of daily speech there was a much larger audience. Building on Song and Yuan precedents, Chinese publishers – like their French and Japanese counterparts – produced ever more diverse popular works, until by the late 1700s presses were turning out how-to books on everything from farming, letter writing, and medical care to funerals and sexual gratification, not to mention proliferating genres of middle- and low-brow fiction, plays, poetry, religious tracts, almanacs, maps, and travelers' guides. The intended audience included merchants, shop clerks, low-level functionaries, women in well-to-do households, anyone with a basic education. Despite or because of this social variety, most commercial works retained a broadly didactic Confucian ethos.[111] One could argue that the growth of popular literature at the expense of the literary classical language represented a Chinese version of the more general shift from universal classical tongues (Latin, Sanskrit, Pali) to vernaculars that we find in Europe, Southeast Asia, and South Asia starting in the early second millennium and accelerating into the 1800s.[112] Estimates for late Qing male literacy range all the way from 15 to 50 percent, with lower levels for elite women. Alexander Woodside argues that without Southeast Asian-style monasteries, Chinese rates could not

---

[110] Rowe, *Saving the World*, 408–17, noting that Chen Hongmou did advocate mass literary training; Woodside and Elman, "Afterword," 526–27; Hucker, *China's Imperial Past*, 318, 335–36; Wong, *China Transformed*, 114–15; Angela Leung, "Elementary Education in the Lower Yangtze Region in the 17th and 18th Centuries," in Elman and Woodside, *Education and Society*, 381–416.

[111] On publishing and schools, nn. 87, 90 *supra*; *CIHC*, 202; Robert Hegel, "Distinguishing Levels of Audience for Ming-Ch'ing Vernacular Literature," in Johnson, *Popular Culture*, 112–42; Rowe, "Social Stability," 487; Evelyn Rawski, *Education and Popular Literacy in Ch'ing China* (Ann Arbor, 1979); *CIHC*, 201–203; Elman and Woodside, *Education and Society*, pt. 4; Mair, "Buddhism and the Rise of the Vernacular," 738. On drama as an agency of popular acculturation, Tanaka Issei, "The Social and Historical Context of Ming-Ch'ing Local Drama," in Johnson, *Popular Culture*, 143–60.

[112] Cf. Sheldon Pollock, "India in the Vernacular Millennium," *Daedalus* 127 (1998): 41–74; idem, *Language of the Gods*, pt. 2.

match those of Burma. But even the lower figure suggests a sea change from the pre-Song era.[113] Testimony to the grassroots value of literate communications was the Qing-era profusion of contracts for renting, mortgaging, and selling land, hiring labor, and arranging marriages.[114]

By continuously defining and disseminating cultural norms, the state helped to coordinate vertical exchange. The Yuan, as noted, elevated a simplified version of Daoxue Neo-Confucianism to imperial orthodoxy; Daoxue activists under the Yuan also sought to make marriage and property law conform to their notions of patrilineal descent.[115] The early Ming broadened those efforts with propaganda and legal coercion, and in fact, by the late Ming, partly through state efforts, Daoxue proscriptions against widow remarriage, female inheritance, and uxorilocal marriage had permeated gentry practice, while corporate lineages, with state blessing, had expanded at the expense of Buddhist and other non-kin organizations.[116] It was only under Manchu rule, however, that officials addressed a Confucian agenda directly to the masses and, in Paul Jakov Smith's words, "transformed Daoxue rules and rituals from the particularized ideological system of the local gentry to a universalized blueprint for society as a whole."[117] Mid-Qing ambition reflected the intersection of those autonomous commercial and cultural trends favorable to integration that I just described with self-conscious dynastic activism. In order to saturate all social levels with orthodox norms, the Qing, for example, promulgated sacred edicts with novel rigor in the countryside, targeted peasant households to honor chaste widows, and promoted lineage organizations, not least in areas of recent class-based disorder. Likewise, the throne sought to enlarge the population of legally free commoners (*liang min*) at the expense of servile and debased groups on the assumption that free commoners were more likely to be

---

[113] On literacy definitions and estimates, Alexander Woodside, "Some Mid-Qing Theorists of Popular Schools," *Modern China* 9 (1983): 5–6; Woodside and Elman, "Afterword," 530–31; Hansen, *Changing Gods*, 11–13; Leung, "Elementary Education"; Rawski, *Education and Popular Literacy*, 24–41, 81–95, 183–93; Johnson, *Popular Culture*, 55–67; Rowe, "Social Stability," 487 n. 45.

[114] Rowe, "Social Stability," 487. Kon-baung Burma saw a similar profusion. *SP*, 178–79, 185–89. On the other hand, lots of contracts, most of Tang date, also were preserved at Dunhuang.

[115] Sommer, *Sex, Law,* 308; Smith, "Eurasian Transformations," 307; Birge, "Women and Confucianism," 212–40.

[116] Smith, "Eurasian Transformations," 307; idem , "Introduction," 24–25; Katherine Carlitz, "Shrines, Governing-Class Identity, and the Cult of Widow Fidelity in Mid-Ming Jiangnan," *JAS* 56 (1997): 612–40.

[117] Smith, "Introduction," 30.

culturally "responsible" and economically secure. Prophylactically, officials suppressed books, plays, and religious sects that threatened their social vision.[118]

Nor, by any means, was cross-class exchange all one way. Adrift in a sea of popular urban culture, literati arts in Ming and Qing China – much like their Tokugawa counterparts – fortified themselves with vigorous, increasingly plebeian styles. Popular religious cults continuously infiltrated gentry beliefs. And, as we shall see shortly, Qing law codes mirrored popular practices, anxieties, and expectations.

Of course, in China as elsewhere vertical integration faced countervailing trends and critical limits. Three such patterns deserve mention. First, as a familiar and inevitable attribute of market specialization, the same commercial pressures as encouraged circulation promoted ever more refined niches not only in literature and scholarship, but in consumption ranging from clothes, food, furniture, and art to sexual services and entertainment. According to Craig Clunas, the market-driven "invention of taste" and the commodification of culture were not much less characteristic of late Ming than of early modern European (and I would add, Tokugawa) cities. As status markers in an increasingly mobile society anxious to shore up its threatened sense of hierarchy, consumer goods brought with them a degree of individuation and social fracture. Starting in the Song period commercialization also led to more frequent sales of impoverished women as concubines and prostitutes. To follow Hansen, the ensuing accentuation of gender roles, dramatically illustrated by the spread of footbinding among both elite and servile women, itself became a pronounced form of cultural cleavage.[119]

---

[118] At the same time, Johnson's characterization ("Communication, Class," 69) of late imperial officials as "a quasi-priestly class, one of whose chief duties was the rectification of ideological deviations and the extirpation of heresy" seems overdrawn, because unlike Counter-Reformation clergy, for example, Chinese officials had limited interest in popular religion. Szonyi and Hymes in n. 88 *supra*; Elliott, pers. commun., Jan. 5, 2008. On state support for social mobility, see too Rowe, *Saving the World*, 448 and *passim*; Mazumdar, *Sugar and Society*, 211–17.

[119] On the implications of growing consumerism, Clunas, *Superfluous Things*, 3–9, 37–38, 42–48, 73–74, 117–28, 150–73, suggesting that urban consumerism retreated under the Qing; Kai-wing Chow, "Writing for Success"; Carlo Marco Belfanti, "Was Fashion a European Invention?" *JGH* 3 (2008): 426–35, 442–43, noting Chinese–European similarities but conceding that in China the "culture of fashion" remained far less pervasive. On women's changing roles, Hansen, *Open Empire*, 286–89; Ebrey, pers. commun., April 10, 2007.

Second, reminiscent of 18th-century France, Russia, and Vietnam, if elite language and culture were marvelous instruments of horizontal integration, that same utility could widen vertical differences. While Qing officials generally could communicate through the official spoken language (Mandarin), often they – like Louis XIV in Picardy – could not speak or understand the popular dialect of the districts where they were posted. Likewise, imperial edicts appeared in the classical language (*wen-yen*), but not in vernaculars. Thus gentry and officials in distant provinces often had more in common with one another than with local plebeians.[120]

Third, poverty, illiteracy, and isolation not only preserved, but raised fresh, impediments to cross-class exchange. Peasants stubbornly retained distinctive religious customs, deities, eschatologies, and organizations, some of which, like the quasi-Buddhist White Lotus sects, with their female supreme deity and disturbingly egalitarian ideas about age and gender, were regarded by authorities, with or without justification, as deeply subversive. Friction between official values and the pathetically limited options available to economically marginal groups helps to explain the appeal of such sects in the mid- and late Qing. Among the landless underclass of young unattached males – so-called "bare sticks" and "rootless rascals" – and among impoverished couples, immiseration promoted sexual patterns, including homosexuality and shared female access, that made a mockery of official efforts to universalize Confucian family norms.[121]

And yet among the population at large, clearly the cultural chasm of the early imperial era had closed substantially by 1830, as seen not only in enhanced mobility and literacy, but in peasant religion and social outlook. Starting in the Song and continuing into the Qing, popular religion – in keeping with elite expectations and with state efforts to replace "superstitious" elements with ideologically acceptable ones – became

---

[120] Woodside and Elman, "Afterword," 546–50; Johnson, *Popular Culture*, 340–41, 400; Chaffee, *Thorny Gates*, 188; Mair, "Buddhism and the Rise of the Vernacular," 726, 728. The spoken language of officialdom, *guan hua* or Mandarin, was based on the speech of the capital region, i.e., usually Beijing, but Nanjing in the late Ming. Cf. Ch. 3, n. 270.

[121] On religious and social deviance, Susan Naquin, "The Transmission of White Lotus Sectarianism in Late Imperial China," in Johnson, *Popular Culture*, 255–91; Judith Berling, "Religion and Popular Culture," ibid., 188–218; Sommer, *Sex, Law*, 12–17, 306–20; Romeyn Taylor, "Official and Popular Religion and the Political Organization of Chinese Society in the Ming," in Liu, *Orthodoxy in Late Imperial China*, 126–57; Woodside and Elman, "Afterword," 539–42.

less amoral and pessimistic, more territorially unified, and more bureaucratic. Indeed, Daoist and popular pantheons came to constitute vast bureaucracies whose jurisdictions, rituals, corruption, and architectural and sculptural representation mirrored those of state officials. Even White Lotus sectarians expounded Confucian ethics.[122] Lineage organizations drew upon and reinforced similar processes of vertical exchange. Likewise, Matthew Sommer argues that the transition from rigid pre-Song caste-like distinctions in sexual morality and law to the more egalitarian order of the Qing reflected not only elite prescriptions, but the needs of a settled peasant community that had come to embrace Confucianism as an emblem of its own worth. Beset by rapid population growth and economic stress, embattled peasants seized upon Confucian norms of sexual propriety and family obligation in order to defend themselves against the moral dangers of downward mobility and against predatory threats stemming from the yet more impoverished underclass of "rogue" males without regular access to women.[123] As Qing officials responded to popular anxieties, for example, by extending upper-class legal protections to peasant women, and as Neo-Confucian norms permeated the countryside, Qing legislation exhibited what Kathryn Bernhardt has termed "peasantization," namely a shift from elite priorities toward those of common peasants.[124] One of the chief features of late Ming and Qing culture, Johnson concluded, was the "extraordinary degree" to which values and beliefs once associated with ruling class interests came to permeate popular consciousness.[125]

In short, over some two millennia as successive interregna became shorter and less disruptive, as imperial administration became more centralized, and as the empire expanded its territorial writ, Chinese culture grew more uniform, both vertically and horizontally.

---

[122] See *supra* nn. 86, 88, 104, plus Stephen Teiser, "The Growth of Purgatory," in Ebrey and Gregory, *Religion and Society*, 115–45; Naquin and Rawski, *Chinese Society*, 230–31.

[123] Sommer, *Sex, Law*, esp. chs. 1, 2, 8, and n. 109 *supra*.

[124] Kathryn Bernhardt, "A Ming-Qing Transition in Chinese Women's History?" in Hershatter et al., *Remapping China*, 42–58, esp. 56–58. Also Sommer, *Sex, Law*, 260–320, 357 n. 3; Theiss, "Construction and Practice"; Brook, *Confusions*, 218–22, 257–59; Naquin and Rawski, *Chinese Society*, 125; Patricia Buckley Ebrey, "The Early Stages of Development in Descent Group Organization," in Ebrey and James Watson, eds., *Kinship Organization in Late Imperial China, 1000–1940* (Berkeley, 1986); Charlotte Furth, "The Patriarch's Legacy," in Liu, *Orthodoxy in Late Imperial China*, 187–211. Cf. peasant acceptance of orthodox family norms in Dong Kinh in *SP*, 448–49.

[125] Johnson, "Communication, Class," 46.

Economic and Demographic Cycles Coordinated with Other Sectors of Eurasia: Explaining Synchronization

A final similarity between China and Eurasian peripheries – a most seminal parallel that in varying degrees shaped the first five trends – was broadly coordinated economic growth. In a word, cycles of economic/demographic expansion and contraction in mainland Southeast Asia, Europe, and China ran loosely parallel, with growth particularly notable from 800/900 to 1270, 1470/1500 to 1640, and 1700 to 1830.[126]

Unless we are content to invoke sheer coincidence, the earliest of these synchronized phases, 800/900–1270, is also most difficult to explain. Again, the most obvious candidate for Eurasian coordination, namely, long-distance trade, cannot suffice. Volume 1 argued against such links as a principal spur to economic or political change in the opening phase of Pagan, Angkor, or Dai Viet, although by the 12th and 13th centuries such contacts had a significant acceleratory effect.[127] Chapter 2 of this volume invoked a similar logic for medieval France and, less confidently, Kiev.

In China as early as the 8th century, it is true that Guangzhou (Canton) and northern Vietnam (then part of the empire) carried on a lively commerce with the Nan-yang (the Southern Ocean), what we call Southeast Asia. In the 11th and 12th centuries, with access to Central Asian routes endangered by Inner Asian inroads in the north, the Song, desperate for revenue, encouraged a further expansion in maritime trade. Thus, aided by the compass (first reported in 1119) and other technical innovations, ships from ports like Fuzhou, Quanzhou, and Guangzhou joined South Asian and Malay vessels on routes leading from Southeast Asia to the China coast. For much of the 13th and even into the 14th century, trade remained vigorous to Korea and Japan as well as the Nan-yang, with Chinese ceramics, textiles, foodstuffs, and bronze cash exchanged for foreign exotica, timber, and other raw materials.[128]

---

[126] Japanese rhythms, of course, were more idiosyncratic. Demographic and economic expansion during the Former Han (206 b.c.e.– 9 c.e.) suggests parallels to early Rome, but their marginal relevance to the history of Southeast Asia and other Eurasian rimlands – not to mention daunting problem of explanation – leads me to neglect these earlier parallels.

[127] *SP*, 88–112, 216–28, 352–65.

[128] Angela Schottenhammer, ed., *The Emporium of the World* (Leiden, 2001), 1–2; von Glahn, *Fountain of Fortune*, 53–56; idem, "Towns and Temples," 187–88, correcting his earlier claim of a post-1160 downturn in trade; Billy K. L. So, *Prosperity, Region, and Institutions in Maritime China* (Cambridge, MA, 2000), esp. pt. 1; Skinner, "Introduction,"

Yet if maritime trade stimulated coastal cities and manufacture, encouraged interregional trade, and provided the state with needed revenues, as an explanation of Song economic and demographic vigor, there is general agreement, for the empire at large if not all districts, that such spurs paled beside domestic factors.[129] In analyzing administrative and cultural integration, this chapter already argued that progress between c. 800 and 1270 drew strength primarily from the colonization of Central and South China, with its vast rice potential. Taming the dense forests and malarial swamps of the Yangzi basin and areas farther south was more difficult than bringing under cultivation the unforested loess soils of the North China plain. No doubt this helps to explain the historic primacy of the north in much the same way that charter agriculture in mainland Southeast Asia began not in the deltas of the Irrawaddy, Chaophraya, and Mekong, with their malarial jungles and difficult-to-turn soils, but in more salubrious, lightly vegetated interior dry zones around Pagan and Angkor. Yet as in Southeast Asia during the 18th and 19th centuries, so in China during the late Tang and Song, once the preliminary work of reclamation had been completed, the south's lush climate and soils proved irresistible. Semitropical South China is far more agriculturally propitious than the north, which despite sophisticated dry-farming techniques for millet and wheat, had never been able to produce truly major grain surpluses. Hence not only did Tang capitals depend on southern rice via the Grand Canal, but from the mid-700s the south, as noted, supported an ever larger portion of China's people. Whereas for centuries China's population had grown very slightly, if at all, between the 8th and 11th centuries it more than doubled. Outside the late Tang and Northern Song capital regions, virtually all growth was in the south, especially the middle and lower Yangzi.[130]

27–28; Hugh Clark, *Community, Trade, and Networks* (Cambridge, 1991), arguing that maritime trade, esp. with the Indian Ocean, drove prosperity in Quanzhou and much of southern Fujian; *HJ*, 99, 108–109, 152–57; Michel Jacq-Hergoualc'h, *The Malay Peninsula* (Leiden, 2002), chs. 9–14; *SP*, 94 n. 16; Ch. 1, nn. 117–18 and Ch. 2, n. 40 *supra*; Ch. 7, nn. 31, 89 *infra*.

[129] See analyses of Song growth in sources in n. 134 *infra*, plus Sufumi So and Billy K. L. So, "Population Growth and Maritime Prosperity," *JESHO* 45 (2002): 96–127, arguing against a strong link between population change and maritime activity in Song/Yuan China.

[130] Twitchett, "Introduction," 23–24; Hymes, *Statesmen and Gentlemen*, 1; n. 74 *supra*. On the ecological transformation of the south, where northern colonization began as early as the Han Dynasty, see esp. Elvin, *Retreat of the Elephants*, 9–114.

Along with large-scale migration from North China, the key elements in this agrarian upsurge were the opening of private estates capable of marshalling tenants and bondsmen for massive reclamation; the development of better cultivation and fertilization techniques; the introduction of flood- and drought-resistant, quick-ripening rice strains from Champa, which permitted double- and even triple-cropping; the dissemination of advanced hydraulic technology, including square-pallet chain pumps, treadle water pumps, norias, improved dams and sluice gates; and the creation of ever more ramified canal, inland waterway, and coastal-shipping networks along which agricultural surpluses and handicrafts could move to market. By one calculation, during the Song grain yields per acre in the Yangzi delta rose 63 percent over the Tang.[131] Larger grain surpluses in turn freed regions and producers to specialize in non-subsistence crops – tea, silk, sugar cane, vegetables, hemp, and by the late Song, cotton – as well as in the production of textiles, iron, salt, ceramics, ships, paper, and books. Textiles, in particular, benefited from new manufacturing processes, practical manifestations, Mark Elvin argues, of Song technical and scientific ferment.[132] Together with improved crop yields, agrarian and handicraft specialization encouraged and reflected rising population densities. In this multifaceted commercial expansion overseas trade played an important, but clearly subsidiary role. Whereas the Tang minted an average of 10 bronze coins per head per year, by 1080/1085 the Song was minting 20 times that figure, some six billion coins a year, from primarily domestic copper and for overwhelmingly domestic consumption. This output, which was never again matched by a Chinese imperial government, was supplemented by uncoined silver, again largely of domestic provenance, and especially from the 1160s, by paper money.[133] Swelling commercial velocities and a sheer increase in the size of the consumer population contributed as well to new credit procedures, retail and wholesale specialization, proliferating provincial markets, and a handful of huge cities that completely outgrew Tang regulations. To recall

---

[131] Chen Jiaqi, "Historical Climate Change and Little Ice Age in Changjiang Delta Area," in T. Mikami, ed., *Proceedings of the International Symposium on the Little Ice Age Climate* (Tokyo, 1992), 151. On water technologies, Elvin, *Pattern of the Past*, 113, 124–28. Champa rice later spread from South China to Japan.

[132] Elvin, *Pattern of the Past*, 179–99, esp. 194–99.

[133] Hansen, *Open Empire*, 266; *CIHC*, 142; Richard von Glahn, "Revisiting the Song Monetary Revolution," *International Jl. of Asian Studies* 1 (2004): 159–78; idem, *Fountain of Fortune*, 43–70, 247–49; and n. 129 *supra*.

Gilbert Rozman's urbanization schema, China during the Song moved from Stage E, "standard marketing," to Stage F, "intermediate marketing," the penultimate level.[134]

In combination, these features, some of which anticipated post-1500 patterns elsewhere in Eurasia, constituted what William Rowe terms the "first commercial revolution" and Elvin terms "the medieval economic revolution."[135] Although by 1270 Chinese agriculture and trade may have been the world's most sophisticated, this expansion coincided with what we have seen were, *by local standards*, comparably dramatic economic advances in Southeast Asia, western Europe, and Kiev.[136] To repeat, then, the basic problem: without exaggerating the impact or the autonomy of long-distance trade, how can we explain this economic coordination in far-flung sectors of Eurasia between 800/900 and 1270?

Changes in state policy were surely significant. The Tang to 755 tried to retain the "equal-field" system of land allocations, over which it claimed a monopoly, and to subject urban markets to tight control. After mid-8th-century upheavals, however, the Tang was obliged to abandon both systems of regulation, so that a private market in land rapidly expanded, along with rural and urban trade. The Song provided tax incentives for land reclamation, disseminated new seeds and

---

[134] Gilbert Rozman, *Urban Networks in Russia, 1750–1800, and Premodern Periodization* (Princeton, 1976), 29–36, 75–77, 83–85. Cf. Ch. 1, n. 78. For overviews of late Tang and Song economic vigor, see Elvin, *Pattern of the Past*, pt. 2; Rowe, "Approaches," 271–72; Hansen, *Open Empire*, ch. 7; *CIHC*, 141–44, 161; Twitchett, "Introduction," 22–31; Hymes, *Statesmen and Gentlemen*, 1–3; von Glahn, "Towns and Temples," 176–211; Smith, "Introduction," 2–7; Marks, *Tigers, Rice*, 53–83; Clark, *Community, Trade, and Networks*, esp. chs. 5–7; the analysis in So, *Prosperity, Region*, 27–127; and n. 129 *supra*.

[135] Rowe, "Approaches," 271, dating the revolution from the 9th to the 13th centuries; and Elvin, *Pattern of the Past*, 203–204 and pt. 2, dating it c. 900–1300. Works, apparently as yet untranslated, in 1998 and 1999 by Miyazawa Tomoyuki and Gao Congming have sought not to reject, but to qualify this thesis, long dominant in both Japanese and Western historiography, that the Song ushered in a precociously dynamic market economy. According to Miyazawa, the Song state dominated the economy through its fiscal and monetary powers, and "administrative money" was oriented to state requirements; not until the 16th-century inflow of New World silver and the development of a genuinely autonomous market did "market money" come into being. Gao attributes to the Song state less monetary control and economic influence than Miyazawa, but also calls attention to the limitations of the pre-1300 market economy and the relative immaturity of private commerce. See critiques of these views in von Glahn, "Revisiting the Song Monetary Revolution"; idem, *Fountain of Fortune*, 9–11. On the other hand, according to Guanglin Liu, "Research Statement," the size of the late-11th-century market economy was only exceeded in the 1770s.

[136] But in Japan, recall, growth was slow or nonexistent c. 700 to 1280, then vigorous to c. 1720.

techniques, sent trade missions to Southeast Asia, and promoted monetization by requiring money for state payments. Some Japanese scholars have argued – albeit, not without challenge – that the integration of local markets into an empire-wide network depended chiefly on Song fiscal and monetary interventions.[137]

Likewise, between 800/900 and 1250/1300 I have emphasized the economic benefits that derived from new state-allied temple foundations in Southeast Asia, from princely competition and frontier colonization in Kiev, and from the "feudal revolution" in northwestern Europe. The European medievalist R. I. Moore sees these and similarly novel political regimes across Eurasia both as a response and a catalyst to economic expansion. By discrediting strategies that had sustained authority for centuries, rapid economic growth after c. 900 engendered wrenching crises in one region after another that obliged "clerical" (by which Moore means essentially "literate") elites to reformulate the role of government – whose enhanced effectiveness facilitated still more intensive development. Although this occurred in an age of "increasing commercial and other inter-civilizational contacts," Moore insists that in every instance change reflected primarily "local and domestic" dynamics, rather than long-distance trade. In this emphasis on domestic causation he and I concur.[138] Yet one is still left to ponder: a) *Why* should economic growth have resumed or accelerated in unconnected regions at roughly the same time, that is to say, in the 9th to 11th centuries? Moore's essay rephrases this problem, without solving it. b) Why in every case should growth have precipitated a series of crises – for which, even with an elastic definition of "crisis," there is scant evidence in 11th-century Southeast Asia? c) Why should so motley an array of political institutions – an intensely literate, monetized Chinese bureaucracy; autonomous

---

[137] On Tang economic regulation and its post-755 decay, Twitchett, *Financial Administration*, esp. chs. 1–3; idem, "Introduction"; Graff, *Medieval Chinese Warfare*, 240–41; *CIHC*, 128; *EAH*, vol. III, 136–38; and n. 26 *supra*. On Japanese historiography of Song expansion, for which von Glahn has limited sympathy, n. 135 *supra*. On the Song state's economic impact and the failure of Wang Anshi's New Policies of economic activism, von Glahn, *Fountain of Fortune*, ch. 2; Hansen, *Open Empire*, ch. 7; Francesca Bray, "Towards a Critical History of Non-Western Technology," in Timothy Brook and Gregory Blue, eds., *China and Historical Capitalism* (Cambridge, 1999), 172–73; and esp. Smith, *Taxing Heaven's Storehouse*, pt. 2 and Conclusion.

[138] R. I. Moore, "The Transformation of Europe as a Eurasian Phenomenon," in Arnason and Wittrock, *Eurasian Transformations*, 77–98 (quotes p. 97). See too idem, "Feudalism and Revolution in the Making of Europe," in M. Barcelo et al., eds., *El Feudalisme Comptat I Debatut* (Valencia, 2003), 19–34; and Ch. 1, n. 20 *supra*.

temple complexes in Indic Southeast Asia; a preliterate princely federation in Rus; fragmented warrior estates in 11th-century France –
why should all have responded to "crises" c. 900–1100 in such a way
as to intensify growth in the 12th and 13th centuries? Moore concedes
modestly, "I have in conclusion, no suggestion to offer as to the reasons for the chronological coincidences... which are striking though
not always precise."[139]

Taking a more long-term perspective, in both post-Roman Europe
and post-Han China one could argue that imperial collapse, by empowering peoples from beyond the frontier, encouraged a shift in the political center of gravity to potentially productive but hitherto neglected
frontier zones, from the Mediterranean to Northwest Europe and from
North to South China. New frontier environments in turn called forth
innovative technologies – moldboard plows, horseshoes, and watermills in Europe; the aforementioned water technologies and new rice
strains in China – along with new estate and manorial systems.[140]

However, this view cannot solve our larger puzzle of coordinated
growth across Eurasia, including Southeast Asia, between c. 850 and
1270 for four reasons: a) In post-Roman Europe and post-Han China
some 500–650 years separated imperial collapse from rapid frontier
reclamation. The link therefore between these phenomena was at best
indirect, and subject to numerous intervening variables. b) Although
in Europe an elite descended from Germanic "barbarians" did indeed
direct post-850 expansion, in China Inner Asians generally remained
confined to the least dynamic agrarian region, that of North China. c) In
the Khmer lands rapid economic growth c. 850–1270 required opening
a new ecological zone, as in Europe and China, but in contrast to those
areas had nothing to do with antecedent imperial collapse or a new
postimperial leadership.[141] d) In Japan between c. 500 and 730, and
in the Irrawaddy basin and Rus, c. 850 to 1240/1300, economic growth
had no connection to either new ecological zones or antecedent imperial
collapse.[142]

What about epidemiological change as a spur to Chinese growth?
Two possibilities arise. First, as Chinese settlers moved from the continental, relatively arid climate of the north to the semitropical south,

[139] Moore, "Transformation of Europe," 97.
[140] Cf. n. 131 *supra*; Janet Abu-Lughod, *Before European Hegemony* (Oxford, 1989), 319; and
Ch. 2 *supra*.
[141] *SP*, 224–28.
[142] *SP*, 90–93, and Chs. 2, 4 *supra*.

they encountered malaria, dengue fever, bilharzia, and other forms of parasitism to which even limited immunological resistances took centuries to develop. Yet this still begs the question why progress should have coincided with intensified colonization in Pagan, Angkor, and Europe. Second, growing overland trade with Central Asia and India in the 6th and 7th centuries, and maritime trade with the Nan-yang from the 8th century, may have exposed Chinese more regularly to measles and smallpox, permitting lethal epidemics to become endemic childhood diseases and contributing to Song demographic vigor. As previous chapters suggested, to the extent that long-distance trade after 800 allowed Northwest Europe, Russia, Southeast Asia, and Japan to make comparable adjustments, we may have an agency of coordination. But – leaving aside the highly speculative nature of most early disease reconstructions – the problem remains why trade in far-flung regions should have expanded at roughly the same time.[143]

What role might climate have played in promoting Chinese expansion to the late 1200s? In China as in Europe warmer climate tended to raise yields and expand acreage by lengthening the growing season and extending northern crop limits.[144] Even in Guangxi and Guangdong in the south, where crops were normally planted all year around, by reducing early and late frosts and by strengthening the summer monsoon, warming ironically could have a more beneficial impact on yields than in North and Central China.[145] In Central and South China for much of the period c. 500–850 and c. 940–1100, as colonization accelerated, several studies point to warmer temperatures and generally higher

[143] See William McNeill, *Plagues and Peoples* (Garden City, NY, 1976), 76–80, 97, 102–103, 116–23, 259–69; Denis Twitchett, "Population and Pestilence in T'ang China," in Wolfgang Bauer, ed., *Studia Sino-Mongolica* (Wiesbaden, 1979), 39–52; Holcombe, *Genesis*, 21; Shoji Tatsukawa, "Diseases of Antiquity in Japan" (sic) in Kenneth Kiple, ed., *The Cambridge World History of Human Disease* (Cambridge, 1993), 375, and Angela Leung, "Diseases of the Pre-Modern Period in China," ibid., 354–62. The latter two sources suggest smallpox and measles arrived in China in the late 400s C.E., with smallpox becoming endemic by the 11th century. For early Europe and Japan, Chs. 2, 4 *supra*; and for Southeast Asia, SP, 50, 97–98, 224.

[144] Li Bozhong, "Changes in Climate, Land, and Human Efforts," in Mark Elvin and Liu Ts'ui-jung, eds., *Sediments of Time* (Cambridge, 1998), 447–86, esp. 468, 471–72 shows that a rise of 1 °C could raise rice yields in the Yangzi delta by 20 percent. See too Twitchett, "Population and Pestilence," 39–40; William Atwell, "Time, Money, and the Weather," *JAS* 61 (2002): 101.

[145] Robert Marks, "'It Never Used to Snow'," in Elvin, *Sediments of Time*, 411–46; idem, *Tigers, Rice*, esp. 224, plus 50, 125–27, 139–40, 196–225.

precipitation.[146] Contrary to earlier views, the latest research also argues that this trend continued into the 13th century, now said to have been the warmest period during the last 1,000 years, when subtropical citrus fruits flourished in areas in Central China that no longer support them. A research team headed by Pingzhong Zhang examining the period from c. 960 to 1340 not only has established strong correlations between increased solar radiation, warmer Chinese climate, glacier retreat, and more powerful Asian summer monsoons, but has argued that warmer, wetter conditions substantially underlay the rapid agrarian and demographic expansion characteristic of the Song. Conversely, periods of cooling and reduced monsoon flows, in the late Tang, late Yuan, and late Ming, tended to be periods of economic stress and popular unrest.[147] During the Medieval Climate Anomaly 800/850–1250/1300, we saw that warming also aided agricultural and demographic growth in Southeast Asia and northern Europe. That Japan suffered both poor weather

---

[146] Pao K. Wang and Zhang De'er, "Recent Studies of the Reconstruction of East Asian Monsoon Climate in the Past Using Historical Literature of China," *Jl. of the Meteorological Society of Japan* 70 (1992): 423–46; Chu Ko-chen, "A Preliminary Study on the Climatic Fluctuations During the Last 5,000 Years in China," *Scientia Sinica* 16 (1973): 226–56; Neville Brown, *History and Climate Change* (London, 2001), 140–42, 156; and Pingzhong Zhang et al., "A Test of Climate, Sun, and Culture Relationships from an 1810-Year Chinese Cave Record," *Science* 322 (2008): 940–42. This latter study points to a phase of colder temperatures and weaker monsoons c. 850–940, followed by dramatic reversals. One would assume warm humid conditions encouraged southern colonization, but Brown, *History and Climate Change*, 141 raises the possibility that they impeded it by expanding forest and marsh and pushing northward the limits of rice cultivation.

[147] Zhang De'er, "Evidence for the Existence of the Medieval Warm Period in China," *CC* 26 (1994): 289–97 offers evidence, including fruit tree locations, not only that mean January temperatures in the 13th century were 0.9–1.0 °C. higher and mean extreme minimum temperatures were 0.6–3.5 °C higher than at present, but also that Hangzhou temperatures for 1131–1264 were appreciably warmer than was hitherto realized. The exhaustive 2008 study of warming and stronger monsoon flows c. 960–1340 in Pingzhong Zhang et al., "A Test of Climate," was compiled by a research team of 17 scientists. For supporting evidence, see C. Pfister et al., "Winter Air Temperature Variations in Western Europe During the Early and High Middle Ages (AD 750–1300)," *The Holocene* 8 (1998): 535–52, esp. 549; Brown, *History and Climate Change*, 151, 154; Thomas Crowley and Thomas Lowery, "How Warm Was the Medieval Warm Period?" *Ambio* 29 (2000): 51–54; and Chen Guangming, "The Climatic Change in Tumo Plain, Nei Mongol (Inner Mongolia)," in Zhang Jiacheng, ed., *The Reconstruction of Climate in China in Historical Times* (Beijing, 1988), 100–13, esp. 106, discussing "the second major warm age (700–1249 AD)." See too recent evidence linking the end of the Medieval Climate Anomaly to severe droughts in eastern mainland Southeast Asia, Ch. 1., n. 106.

and anemic growth for much of the 11th and 12th centuries reinforces the appeal of climatic theories.[148]

Again, however, bear in mind that because climate oscillated whereas long-term demographic change was linear, climatic effects can be understood only in combination with social forces. Almost certainly, climate was less critical to post-850 growth than the permanent shift in the center of gravity from the arid, continental north to the well-watered, semitropical south. Moreover, although as a rule warming correlated with increased precipitation,[149] some local Chinese studies point to a combination of higher temperatures and recurrent drought during part of the 12th and 13th centuries, as well as a frequently inverse relation between rainfall in Central and South China.[150]

In sum, all one can say at present is that Chinese economic expansion between c. 850 and 1270 benefited from an uncertain interplay between higher productivity associated with a rich frontier zone, technical and organizational advances, novel political patronage, maritime trade, epidemiological adjustment, and improved climate, among which the latter three factors offer the strongest possibilities for Eurasian coordination.

In much of China – as in Southeast Asia and Europe – the period c. 1270 to 1450 saw a savage mix of wretched weather, plagues, famines, invasions, and depopulation.[151] Admittedly, political disorders

---

[148] *SP*, 101–12, 224–28, 362–64; Ch. 2, n. 90 *supra*; Ch. 4, n. 60 *supra*; Wang and Zhang, "Recent Studies," Fig. 26; Malcolm Hughes and Henry Diaz, "Was There a 'Medieval Warm Period,' and If So, Where and When?" *CC* 26 (1994): 109–42.

[149] On climate–precipitation correlations, Wang and Zhang, "Recent Studies," 442–43, acknowledging exceptions to the cool–dry link; Marks, *Tigers, Rice*, ch. 6, esp. 199–202; idem, "It Never Used to Snow," 432; Hughes and Diaz, "Was There a Medieval Warm Period," 132; Pao K. Wang, pers. commun., March 2001; Jiachen Zhang and Thomas Crowley, "Historical Climate Records in China and Reconstruction of Past Climates," *Jl. of Climate* 2 (1989): 833–49.

[150] Hymes, *Statesmen and Gentlemen*, 201; Brown, *History and Climate Change*, 69, 154, 212 (but the latter data conflict with ibid., 68); R. H. Kripalani and S. V. Singh, "Large Scale Aspects of India-China Summer Monsoon Rainfall," *Advances in Atmospheric Science* 10 (1993): 71–84. See too Li, "Changes in Climate," 452–53, correlating cooler temperatures with increased rain and destructive flooding in Jiangnan. To complicate things further, Brown, *History and Climate Change*, 68–69, 216 cites studies showing cooling and dryness in Central and North China in the 1200s, which agrees with Wang and Zang, "Recent Studies," 429–30, 442–43.

[151] Discussion follows Smith, "Introduction," 5–11; Dardess, "Shun-ti," 585–86; Brook, *Confusions of Pleasure*, 18; *CIHC*, 174, 184–85; Skinner, "Introduction," 27–28; idem, "Presidential Address," 276–79, 285–86; Li "14th-Century Turning Point," 137–38; and Elvin, *Pattern of the Past*, 203–34, analyzing the "14th-century turning point," when medieval economic dynamism allegedly disappeared.

associated with these events were less prolonged or disruptive than during the Age of Division. Moreover, Li Bozhong and others have denied claims that output in the Yangzi delta, core of the imperial economy, collapsed after 1270. Substantially shielded against political upheaval, this region in fact saw a continuation of Song advances in agrarian productivity, technology, and cotton production, many of which elements spread to the rest of China after 1450.[152] But virtually every other region did suffer major die-offs, with the empire as a whole, as noted, losing some 38 percent of its population between 1210 and 1381, losses that approached those of Europe in this same period.[153]

Again, if we discount coincidence, how shall we explain Eurasian synchronization? In mainland Southeast Asia and France I have argued that by reducing per capita income and stoking intra-elite competition, shortages of quality arable after 300 to 400 years of sustained reclamation contributed to the catastrophes of the 14th and early 15th centuries. In China too, Elvin suggests that the filling up of the southern frontier after 1300 had a depressive economic impact; but even he claims no causal link between diminishing agrarian returns and 14th-century political disorders.[154] On the other hand, in late-13th-century China the Mongols disrupted the economy and reduced the population more dramatically than in Southeast Asia or Japan and at least as severely as in Russia. After a brief Yuan recovery, disorders attending Ming campaigns against the Mongols, followed by highly restrictive early Ming economic policies, inflicted further damage.[155] Along with western Europe and Russia, China also endured major 14th-century epidemics, which contributed to the turmoil that brought down the Yuan Dynasty in 1368. Although it is unclear whether these diseases included the Black Death, most historians accept that in the 1340s Mongols

---

[152] Li, "14th-Century Turning Point," 135–75; von Glahn, "Towns and Temples," 176–211; idem, *Fountain of Fortune*, 10; Bray, "Towards a Critical History," 180–82; Smith, "Introduction," 6.

[153] Smith, "Introduction," 8–11, referring to a two-stage "Great Dying"; Frederick Mote, "Chinese Society Under Mongol Rule, 1215–1368," *CHC*, vol. VI, 620–22, referring to "the most extreme" and "catastrophic" population reduction in Chinese history; Marks, *Tigers, Rice*, 56–57; Clark, *Community, Trade, and Networks*, 175–76; So, "Population Growth and Maritime Prosperity," 96–127; and nn. 9, 151 *supra*. Virtually all these authors, including Li, accept that for China at large 1250–1450 was economically and demographically highly disruptive.

[154] Elvin, *Pattern of the Past*, 204–15, 285–316.

[155] Skinner, "Introduction," 27; von Glahn, "Towns and Temples," 205–11.

introduced that dreaded contagion to the Crimea, thence Europe.[156] In these ways, directly and indirectly, the Mongols helped to coordinate severe 13th- and 14th-century dislocations across Europe, Southeast Asia, and China.

At the same time China, like much of Eurasia, experienced recurrent monetary disorders. Silver shortages in West Asia seem to have drained that metal from China. The Yuan tried to compensate with paper currency, but (as had also been true under the Song) this produced catastrophic inflation that continued until the Ming finally abandoned paper in the 1430s. Thereafter to c. 1470, William Atwell has argued, severe shortages of bronze cash, falling silver production, and a consequent hoarding of silver subjected China to the same "bullion famine," with deleterious effects on investment and trade, as afflicted Europe, the Mideast, Southeast Asia, Korea, and Japan. Indeed, because maritime Asia relied on Chinese cash, Chinese shortages substantially underlay difficulties across East Asia.[157]

Finally, in China as elsewhere, long intervals between c. 1250 and 1495 saw unusually cold weather and disastrous pluvial oscillations: in China no fewer than 36 years in the 14th century had exceptionally severe winters, more than in any other century on record, and major floods and droughts hit the Yellow River region with unprecedented frequency. In Li's view, climatic deterioration was the most influential single factor behind the general downturn of the late 13th to the mid- or late 15th century.[158]

After this contraction, Chinese economic and demographic rhythms remained broadly similar to those in mainland Southeast Asia and much of Europe: a fitful revival toward the close of the 15th century that gathered steam in the early and mid-1500s and lasted to 1630/1640, followed by a mid- to late-17th-century slowdown, followed by renewed

---

[156] On 13th- to 14th-century Chinese epidemics, possibly including the Black Death, Jack Weatherford, *Genghis Khan and the Making of the Modern World* (New York, 2004), 241–45; Dardess, "Shun-ti," 585; *SYMT*, 10, 63, 138; Fairbank and Goldman, *China*, 124; Hansen, *Open Empire*, 336; Leung, "Diseases of Premodern China," 355, 357. On the Mongol-mediated entry of plague to Europe, Ch. 2, nn. 159–60 *supra*.

[157] Von Glahn, *Fountain of Fortune*, 10, 60–89; Atwell, "Time, Money," 83–113, esp. 87, 96–97; Hansen, *Open Empire*, 271, 290, 357, 400; *SP*, 140, 254, 387.

[158] On climatic downturn, nn. 146–49 *supra*, plus Li Bozhong, "Early Imperial Times: Environment and Society" (ms); idem, "14th-Century Turning Point," 137; Dardess, "Shun-ti," 585 (with data on severe winters, floods, and droughts); Chen, "Climatic Change in Tumo Plain," 103–104, referring to the "second major cold age (1250–1399)"; Skinner, "Presidential Address," 285–86; *SYMT*, 137; Atwell, "Time, Money," 92–96.

expansion to the early 1800s. While early Chinese population figures are notoriously uncertain, three recent estimates put the Ming population in 1600 at between 1.4 to 2.2 times larger than the peak Song population; a fourth sees an increase of 73 to 102 percent between 1500 and 1650 alone. All such computations indicate not merely a post-1500 revival of earlier patterns, but sustained advances in agriculture, handicrafts, and commercial organization.[159]

By the mid-1500s peasants throughout China were selling at least a portion of their crop in order to obtain cash with which to buy textiles, implements, and – especially where land was given over almost entirely to industrial crops – foodstuffs. Substantial interregional trade in staples had existed in the Song and Yuan periods, if only to address temporary shortfalls, but now long-distance exchange of high bulk, low unit-cost items became more routinized, as more regions focused on commodities in which they had a comparative advantage. Thus, for example, Henan and Shandong produced cotton, and Zhejiang and Sichuan supplied silk, for processing in coastal centers. Fujian specialized in sugar, Hunan and Guangdong in commercial rice, Guizhou in timber. In particular, cotton textile production skyrocketed shortly before, or at the same time as, cotton took off in Burma, Japan, and Korea. Merchants filled more specialized roles as brokers, wholesalers, commission agents, itinerant buyers, retailers, and bankers, while local-origin merchant groups created empire-wide diasporas to manage long-distance exchange. Pre-1500 urbanization had seen vast numbers of people clustered in a few huge cities, but now provincial towns became better integrated into a national hierarchy, the urban population became more evenly distributed, and nonadministrative market towns proliferated on the

---

[159] The four estimates are as follows: a) Eastman, *Family, Fields*, 4, Table 1.1, claims 108,000,000 for 1086 and 160,000,000 for 1600 (while accepting 65,000,000–80,000,000 for 1400, which is close to Hymes' figure of 67,000,000 for 1400 at *SYMT*, 9); Eastman's increase from 1086 to 1600 is therefore 1.48. b) Peter Perdue, pers. commun., Oct. 20, 2007 argues for 115,000,000 in 1250 and 150,000,000–175,000,000 in 1600 for an average increase of 1.41. c) James Lee, Cameron Campbell, and Wang Feng, "Positive Check or Chinese Checks?" *JAS* 61 (2002): 600 Table 1, Column 4, claim 90,000,000 for 1250 and 200,000,000 for 1600, for an increase of 2.22. d) Martin Heijdra, "The Socio-Economic Development of Rural China During the Ming," *CHC*, vol. VIII, 438 estimates that between 1500 and 1650 population grew either from 155,000,000 to 268,000,000 or from 175,000,000 to 353,000,000, for increases, respectively, of 1.73 and 2.02. Heijdra considers implausibly low a third estimated increase from 137,000,000 to 204,000,000, although those figures accord with estimates a) and b), as well as with Brook, *Confusions of Pleasure*, 162, which claims that between 1370 and 1600 population "certainly more than doubled" to approximately 175,000,000.

subcounty level. According to Rozman, in the late Ming – anywhere from 100 to 200 years before France, Japan, and Russia – China entered Stage G urbanization, "national marketing," the most advanced stage.[160] Such trends sped horizontal and vertical cultural exchange. Meanwhile the agrarian frontier continued to advance in the south and in upland interiors, again to the benefit of Sinic acculturation.

These economic shifts drew strength from improved climate for much of the period 1495 to 1620,[161] but more basically from postcrisis pacification and demographic compensation, a fiscally mandated relaxation of early Ming curbs on trade, further refinements in agrarian and manufacturing technique, and the dissemination of best practices with the help of printing and wider literacy. In varying combinations, of course, many of these same factors transformed post-1450 Southeast Asia, Europe, and Japan.

Nor, despite early Ming curbs, were maritime influences unimportant. With unslaked demand for precious metals encouraging higher bullion prices and, by extension, technical advances in mining and smelting, the international bullion famine ended, slowly in the late 15th century and with a vengeance in the 16th. Southeast Asian, Japanese, and Iberian demand stimulated porcelain, silk, and sugar production on the South China coast, which encouraged food commodification to feed specialty producers. Maritime trade's more basic contribution, however, was to accelerate the shift, beginning in the 13th century, from bronze coin and paper money to uncoined silver, which became the

[160] This stage is characterized by seven levels of central places. Rozman, *Urban Networks,* 34–35, 77, 84–85. Rozman's text p. 77, which I follow, does not seem to agree with his graph, p. 84. Discussion of Ming economic change follows Heijdra, "Socio-Economic Development," 417–578; Brook, "Communications and Commerce," 579–707; idem, *Confusions of Pleasure,* 65–79, 101–39, 190–218; Rowe, "Approaches," 272–83; Xu and Wu, *Chinese Capitalism,* pts. 1–2; Smith, "Introduction," 3–7, 30; von Glahn, "Imagining Pre-modern China," 44–45, 55, 68–70; Marks, *Tigers, Rice,* ch. 3; Chun-shu Chang and Shelley Hsueh-lun Chang, *Crisis and Transformation in Seventeenth-Century China* (Ann Arbor, 1998), 147–52; Bray, "Towards a Critical History," 178–83; Shin, *Making of the Chinese State,* 171; Skinner, "Introduction," 26–28. On cotton, cf. *SP,* 144–45.

[161] Notwithstanding severe droughts and floods in some areas in the 1530s, 1540s, and 1580s. On climate c. 1450–1850, Brook, *Confusions of Pleasure,* 104–107, 163; Marks, *Tigers, Rice,* 114, 125–27; Heijdra, "Socio-Economic Development," 425–27; Wang Shao-wu, "Reconstruction of Temperature Series of North China from 1380s to 1980s," *Science in China,* Ser. B, 34 (1991): 752–59; Zhang, *Reconstruction of Climate,* 31–65, 100–13, 138–45; Myers and Wang, "Economic Developments," 641; Quansheng Ge et al., "2000 Years of Temperature History in China," *Pages News* 10 (2002): 18–19; and nn. 146–49 *supra.*

basic medium of exchange, especially for long-distance trade. Recall that silver flowed in first from Japan and Southeast Asia, and then from the New World via the Indian Ocean and Spanish Manila. All told, as Chapter 3 noted, China became the final destination for a quarter to half of world silver output.[162] Such imports supported not only the Single-Whip reform, the first major tax overhaul since the 8th century, but commutation of labor services and a marked quickening of domestic trade. Thus Chinese prosperity became tied to trade with West Eurasia, Japan, and Southeast Asia. But as usual, China's massive post-1550 imports of bullion must be seen not merely as a precondition for growth, but more basically, as a symptom of rising domestic demand for exchange media.[163]

To what extent should Ming collapse in the 1640s be attributed to inept leadership? To superior Manchu military and administrative organization? To a sudden drop in silver imports, to which Atwell has drawn renewed attention? To social and political strains associated with poor climate and rapid population growth such as helped to destabilize late-16th- and 17th-century regimes in Southeast Asia, Russia, and France? To sheer accident? Whatever weight one accords individual factors, it is clear that upheavals attending the Ming–Qing transition joined disease and colder climate to inaugurate in the 1640s an economic and demographic contraction that did not begin to lift, depending on region and sector, until the 1680s or 1690s.[164]

---

[162] On the growth of a silver-based economy, esp. during "the silver century" c. 1550–1650, see Ch. 3, n. 186; Ch. 4, nn. 135–37 *supra*, plus von Glahn, *Fountain of Fortune*, 44, 48–82, 250–51 and 83–172 *passim*; idem, "Money-use in China and Changing Patterns of Global Trade in Monetary Metals, 1500–1800," in Clara Nunez, ed., *Monetary History in Global Perspective* (Seville, 1998), 51–59; William Atwell, "Ming China and the Emerging World Economy, c. 1470–1650," *CHC*, vol. VIII, 376–416; Kuroda Akinobu, "Copper Coins Chosen and Silver Differentiated," *Acta Asiatica* 88 (2005): 65–86.

[163] On Ming domestic and maritime expansion, see nn. 160, 162 *supra*, plus Mazumdar, *Sugar and Society*, chs. 1–5; Atwell, "Time, Money," 98–103; *AC*, vol. II, ch. 1; *HJ*, 152–58; Evelyn Rawski, *Agricultural Change and the Peasant Economy of South China* (Cambridge, MA, 1972).

[164] From the 1660s China also suffered severe deflation. On the contentious historiography of Ming decline, William Atwell, "Some Observations on the '17th-Century Crisis' in China and Japan," *JAS* 45 (1986): 223–44; idem, "A Seventeenth-Century 'General Crisis" in East Asia?" *MAS* 24 (1990): 661–82; Brian Moloughney and Wenzhong Xia, "Silver and the Fall of the Ming," *Papers on Far Eastern History* 40 (1989): 51–78; von Glahn, *Fountain of Fortune*, 207–45; idem, "Myth and Reality of China's 17th-Century Monetary Crisis," *JEH* 56 (1996): 429–54; Jack Goldstone, *Revolution and Rebellion in the Early Modern World* (Berkeley, 1991), 362–90; Atwell's response to critics, "Another

By 1700/1710, however, in China as in much of Southeast Asia and Europe, growth had resumed. Insofar as the mid-Qing era intensified and broadened social and economic tendencies from the late Ming, many argue that the entire period c. 1500/1550 to 1800/1830 should be regarded as a distinctive phase, that of "early modern China" and of the "second commercial revolution," as opposed to the first commercial revolution of the Song.[165] Eighteenth-century trends included the final eclipse of bonded labor in favor of a mobile, competitive, market-oriented peasantry; the opening of new lands on the imperial frontier and of upriver areas within each of China's eight or nine macroregions; further regional specialization in foodstuffs, fibers, minerals, and handicrafts; a corresponding routinization of bulk interregional trade and a growth in trade diasporas; occupational diversification among the elite and further niche-seeking at all levels; expansion of paper notes and other credit instruments; the continued proliferation of rural markets, where bronze coins began to enjoy a premium over uncoined silver because coins were more useful for petty transactions; and a population boom, from perhaps 150,000,000-200,000,000 in 1700 to 320,000,000-350,000,000 in 1800.[166] In Rowe's formulation, for a thousand years per capita levels of commercialization and long-range trade had been expanding, but only in the early or mid-18th century did interregional exchange finally dominate both local and intraregional trade.[167]

Look at Silver Imports into China, c. 1635–1644," *JWH* 16 (2005): 457–89; idem, "Ming China and World Economy," 407–16; Myers and Wang, "Economic Developments," 564–73, 593; Perdue, *China Marches West*, 383–87; Michael Marme, "Locating Linkages or Painting Bull's Eyes around Bullet Holes?" *AHR* 113 (2008): 1080–89.

[165] See Rowe, "Approaches," 240–41, 272 ff.

[166] Obviously, the larger the figure for late Ming/early Qing population one accepts from the menu of estimates in n. 159 *supra*, the more impressive Ming, and the less impressive Qing, growth appears. See Peterson's formulation of the problem in his "Introduction," 5. Rowe, "Social Stability," 474–75 cites approvingly Ping-ti Ho's estimate of 150,000,000 for 1600 and 1700. James Lee and Wang Feng, *One Quarter of Humanity* (Cambridge, MA, 1999), 28, Fig. 3.1 claim 175,000,000 for 1700. Lee et al., "Positive Check," 600, Table 1, Column 4 claim 200,000,000 for 1700, while Mote, *Imperial China*, 905 claims 250,000,000 for 1650. But all accept an 1800 figure of 320,000,000–350,000,000.

[167] William Rowe, "Domestic Interregional Trade in Eighteenth-Century China," in Leonard Blusse and Femme Gaastra, eds., *On the Eighteenth Century as a Category of Asian History* (Aldershot, UK, 1998), 186–87; Rowe, "Approaches," 273. The suggestion in Clark, *Community, Trade, and Networks*, 6, 179–80 and *passim*, that the Song supported the same basic routinization of bulk interregional trade as the late Ming and Qing is not supported by some recent research. Besides Rowe, see n. 135 *supra* and n. 171 *infra*.

Thus prices in urban grain markets increasingly converged.[168] According to Kenneth Pomeranz, 18th-century health, longevity, and living standards in China and England were comparable, while in both countries – to which I would add France, Japan, and a few advanced locales in Southeast Asia – the greater variety and accessibility of market goods spurred a version of Jan de Vries' industrious revolution, whereby labor, leisure, and consumption were increasingly oriented toward the market.[169]

In the late 1700s the economy began to slow, burdened by a decline in frontier settlement, by the spread of handicraft techniques from the lower Yangzi to outlying provinces – which inhibited core–periphery differentiation – and by a consequent weakening of interregional trade. As Perdue has pointed out, commercial integration between China proper and peripheral regions remained tenuous, and in fact would regress in the 19th century.[170] Yet to mid-century population itself continued to rise, along with monetization and literacy. Such developments, as noted, aided social mobility, cultural circulation, and imperial expansion alike.[171]

High Qing prosperity benefited from Qing pacification, which, by design or serendipity, restored confidence and encouraged investment

---

[168] Li Bozhong, "China's National Market, 1550–1840" (Paper presented to the 8th Annual World History Association International Conference, 1999) argues for a mid-Qing "national market" in which goods, labor, technologies, capital, and information moved relatively freely and price movements were synchronized. See too Naquin and Rawski, *Chinese Society*, 215.

[169] Pomeranz, *Great Divergence*, 17, 32–40, 49, 98, 114–65, 243, 281, supported by von Glahn, "Money-Use in China," 58; Li Bozhong, "'The Countrymen Are Well Fed'" (ms); Belfanti, "Was Fashion a European Invention." See Ch. 3, nn. 175, 176; Ch. 4, nn. 279, 292, 320 *supra*.

[170] Perdue, *China Marches West*, 390–91.

[171] For overviews of the Qing economy, Myers and Wang, "Economic Developments," 563–645; Wong, *China Transformed*, chs. 1–3; Pomeranz, *Great Divergence*; idem, "Re-Thinking the Late Imperial Chinese Economy," *Itinerario* 24 (2000): 29–74; Marks, *Tigers, Rice*, chs. 4–10; Li Bozhong, *Agricultural Development in Jiangnan, 1620–1850* (New York, 1998); idem, "China's National Market"; Philip Huang, *The Peasant Family and Rural Development in the Yangzi Delta, 1350–1988* (Stanford, 1990), pt. 1; S. A. M. Adshead, *Material Culture in Europe and China, 1400–1800* (New York, 1997); Rowe, "Domestic Interregional Trade," 173–92; Elvin, *Pattern of the Past*, chs. 15, 16. Note that although new towns arose, urbanization rates remained far lower than in France (20 percent in towns of over 2,000 people in 1790 – see Ch. 3, n. 174 *supra*), England (24 percent in towns of over 10,000 people in 1800 – *JAS*, 61, 2002, 636), or Burma (15 percent in towns of over 2,000 people in 1800). In China in 1800 residents of towns with 2,000 people or more were only 5–7 percent of the total. Rowe, "Social Stability," 537–38; Myers and Wang, "Economic Developments," 578–79, citing Gilbert Rozman.

after the disorders of the mid-1600s; from post-1680s demographic recovery; from distinctly warmer climate c. 1710 to 1830;[172] from the continued diffusion, aided by commercial printing, of best techniques; and from a post-1684 rise in global trade. As Chapter 3 suggested, by boosting demand for Chinese textiles, porcelain, sugar, and tea, trade with the Nan-yang and, from the early 1700s, with Europe and America stimulated commodification at least as effectively as during the late Ming. Until the early 1800s when opium began to draw bullion out of China, the empire imported some two-thirds of its silver, which (despite the popularity of bronze coin in the countryside) remained critical to domestic commerce.[173] What is more, by feeding lowland peasants whose rice was market bound, and upland peasants unable to grow wet rice, New World sweet potatoes aided population growth.[174] We have met similar domestic–maritime synergies in protected zone economies after 1700.

Finally 18th-century prosperity reflected the fact that the Qing, in Rowe's estimation, was "perhaps the most pro-commercial regime in imperial Chinese history."[175] Committed to enhancing agrarian and commercial productivity, but convinced that the resultant surplus should remain in societal rather than government hands, the Qing combined paternalist interventions with a principled respect for domestic

---

[172] Yangzi delta 18th-century temperatures probably averaged at least 1 °C higher than in the 17th century. Li, "Changes in Climate," 452. Also Quansheng Ge et al., "2000 Years"; Zhang and Crowley, "Historical Climate Records"; Wang, "Reconstruction of Temperature"; *CHC*, vol. IX, 641.

[173] Li, "China's National Market," 12–13 puts total silver imports at 15,500,000 *taels* from 1650 to 1699; 56,200,000 *taels* from 1700 to 1749; and 95,900,000 *taels* from 1750 to 1799, followed by a net export of 29,400,000 *taels* from 1800 to 1833. Cf. figures at Myers and Wang, "Economic Developments," 589–90, 626 ff. On Qing maritime trade and relations, also Marks, *Tigers, Rice*, chs. 5–9; idem, "Maritime Trade and the Agro-Ecology of South China, 1685–1850," in Dennis Flynn et al., eds., *Pacific Centuries* (London, 1999), 85–109; Rowe, "Domestic Interregional Trade," 178; John Wills, Jr., "Maritime Asia, 1500–1800," *AHR* 98 (1993): 83–105; idem, *Pepper, Guns, and Parleys* (Cambridge, MA, 1974); idem, "Contingent Connections," 167–203; idem, "Maritime China from Wang Chih to Shih Lang," in Spence and Wills, *From Ming to Ch'ing*, 201–38; Andre Gundar Frank, *ReOrient* (Berkeley, 1998).

[174] Man-houng Lin, "From Sweet Potato to Silver," in Hans Pohl, ed., *The European Discovery of the World and Its Economic Effects on Pre-Industrial Society, 1500–1800* (Stuttgart, 1990): 304–27; Sucheta Mazumdar, "The Impact of New World Food Crops on the Diet and Economy of China and India, 1600–1900," in Raymond Grew, ed., *Food in Global History* (Boulder, 1999), 62–70; Hansen, *Open Empire*, 410, referring also to maize and peanuts.

[175] Rowe, "Domestic Interregional Trade," 184 and 184–87.

markets and private property. Thus the Qing awarded settlers tax remissions and travel grants, worked to popularize new crops and techniques, sponsored water control projects, enhanced market access by supporting social mobility and legal equality, attuned the system of civilian granaries to market forces, offered economic incentives for merchants in target areas like Xinjiang, and thus pushed the commercial economy to the farthest frontiers of empire. In Rowe's view these policies resembled *laissez faire* less than 18th-century French Physiocracy, with its commitment to self-regulating economic laws, its belief in agricultural primacy, and its sense of responsibility for popular welfare.[176]

Comparative Views of the High Qing Economy

If the high Qing economy was so dynamic, why did China fail to achieve modern economic growth in the manner of western Europe or, more specifically, England? As Chapter 1 hinted, this is an enormously vexed question to which at least four broad answers, in varying degrees competitive and complementary, have been offered. In truth, this literature is only marginally relevant to our inquiry, both because it normally compares China not to France, but to England – birthplace of industrialization – and because even in England industrial manufacture became socially transformative only from the mid-1800s, after the period with which we are concerned. Still, the following overview may be useful for what it has to say about the long-term potential of Eurasia's largest economy.

a) *The Pomeranz Thesis.*[177] Appearing in 2000, *The Great Divergence* re-ignited a debate that seemed to have been resolved a generation

---

[176] Rowe, "Domestic Interregional Trade," 185–86; idem, *Saving the World*, 213–14 and pt. 2 *passim*; and discussion *infra*. Perdue, *China Marches West*, 383–86 makes a similar point. On state policies, see too Myers and Wang, "Economic Developments," 591–604, 631; Helen Dunstan, *State or Merchant?* (Cambridge, MA, 2006), dissecting political economy debates in the 1740s; Buoye, *Manslaughter, Markets*, chs. 1, 6; Mazumdar, *Sugar and Society*, 211–17. On French Physiocracy, which decried mercantilist regulation and argued that agriculture, not trade, was the true basis of wealth, see Ch. 3, n. 173.

[177] Pomeranz, *Great Divergence*; idem, "Political Economy and Ecology on the Eve of Industrialization," *AHR* 107 (2002): 425–46; idem, "Re-Thinking Economy"; idem, "Beyond the East-West Binary," *JAS* 61 (2002): 539–90. Cf. Ch. 1, n. 11. In addition to the four answers I discuss, one could argue that the question of why China failed to industrialize is the wrong question to ask, because it regards England as normative, when in fact, European and Chinese histories should be made to interrogate one another on the assumption that in some respects Chinese society may have been more "advanced" than European. No doubt such an approach has its uses, but to preclude

earlier. Whereas by the late 1970s a consensus had emerged on the deficiencies by European standards of China's premodern economy, Pomeranz suddenly, boldly, and brilliantly insisted on the equivalence of Chinese and European development to the late 1700s.

At the core of his argument was his claim – incorporated in my preceding analysis – that in both western Europe and China centuries-long population growth boosted market demand for foodstuffs and handicrafts, which promoted a Smithian division of labor, which improved efficiency and productivity, which in turn raised general living standards. Until the mid- or late 1700s, Pomeranz claims that growth patterns in England, core of the West European economy, did not differ radically from those in the Yangzi delta, core of the Chinese economy. Institutional and legal barriers to growth, for example, were no higher in China than in England, because labor, land, and commodity markets were equally unencumbered, private property was equally well protected, and state commercial policies were comparably sympathetic.[178] In response to fluctuating economic conditions, Chinese families, as James Lee has shown, regulated fertility as well as their English counterparts, which meant that Malthusian barriers to growth were similar.[179] Nor, on balance, was English technology superior, because its industrial advantage was outweighed by Chinese advantages in agriculture, which probably had the highest yields in the world, both per acre and in seed-to-crop ratios. As a result, by most measures – longevity, nutrition, consumer goods – Chinese residents of the Yangzi delta and Englishmen in 1750 were comparably well off.[180] What is more, in both locales shortages of natural resources, primarily land, grew more pressing. In parts of Europe as well as China by the mid-1700s such constraints were mandating more labor-intensive strategies and imperiling continued expansion. "Overall," Pomeranz argues, "both ends of Eurasia were in serious trouble."[181]

---

investigating the most critical distinction – "the Great Divergence" – in modern world history out of a concern for cultural equivalence strikes me as arbitrarily self-limiting.

[178] Pomeranz, *Great Divergence*, 14–17, 69–91, 166–86, substantially supported by Rowe, *Saving the World*, 191–92.

[179] See Ch. 1, n. 8 *supra*, and Pomeranz, *Great Divergence*, 10–17, 40–41, 107, 206–207, 216.

[180] Pomeranz, *Great Divergence*, 1–165, 216–27; idem, "Political Economy," 429–31. This synchronic view of income and land productivity c. 1750 receives support from Robert Allen, "Agricultural Productivity and Rural Income in England and the Yangtze Delta, c. 1620–1820" (ms, Nuffield College, Oxford, 2003), 14–15, although Allen has a different take on long-term trends. See discussion *infra*.

[181] Pomeranz, *Great Divergence*, 241. Also 13, 207, 225–42.

Why, then, did England, but not China escape this dilemma? Pomeranz cites three critical differences. First, relations between core and peripheries were more conducive to core industrialization in the Atlantic/European world than in China. England's chief peripheries – Ireland, Eastern Europe, the slave-labor systems of North America and the Caribbean – purchased growing quantities of English manufactures in return for foodstuffs and raw materials, but were themselves, for political and social reasons, incapable of industrialization. Thus core–periphery trade favored the continuous expansion of English industry. But in China, the ease with which textile and other technologies diffused from the Yangzi core to outlying areas meant that the latter could easily copy the delta's best protoindustrial practices. Ironically, this ease of diffusion reflected the fact that market mechanisms were less politically encumbered, and more closely approximated the classical liberal ideal, in China than in the Atlantic/European world. At one and the same time this pattern began to inhibit Chinese interregional trade, core–periphery specialization, and Yangzi industrialization.[182] Second, geographic access to vast New World resources removed the land constraint on the English economy in a way that China, with its far more limited resource base and its diminishing incentives to interregional trade, could never duplicate. New World imports of cotton, sugar, and timber in 1830 freed up 25,000,000 to 30,000,000 English acres that would have been needed to produce equivalent goods.[183] American "ghost acres" therefore allowed England to transfer laborers from farm to industry and to specialize further in manufactures. Third, the unique availability in England of coal in easy proximity to manufacturing centers provided a critical domestic source of energy, equivalent to another 15,000,000 acres of forest, that also was unavailable in China. English coal proved essential not only to replace wood fuel, but to support, directly or indirectly, a range of new manufactures, including dye-making, iron, steel, steam engines, and railroads.[184] In short, international trade, New World access, and coal spelled the difference between English industrialization and Chinese conservatism.

b) *High-Level Equilibrium Traps and Agricultural Involution.* The orthodoxy against which Pomeranz directed his work was best represented

---

[182] Ibid., 242–53; Pomeranz, "Beyond East-West Binary," 578.

[183] Pomeranz, *Great Divergence*, 275–76; idem, "Political Economy," 442.

[184] Pomeranz, *Great Divergence*, 59–62, 276, 283. Pomeranz' emphasis on China's pre-1750 productivity by European standards meshes closely with Li , "China's National Market"; idem, *Agricultural Development*; Lee et al., "Positive Check."

by Mark Elvin's 1973 theory of the "high-level equilibrium trap." According to Elvin, by the late 1700s the Chinese economy had reached the limits of traditional technology. Without modern industrial-scientific inputs, no further major improvements in productivity or aggregate output were possible, so any increase in population reduced the surplus above what was needed for subsistence. This in turn meant that the cost of labor was constantly falling vis-à-vis capital. In such an environment, the rational strategy for peasant and merchant alike was not to introduce labor-saving machinery, but to increase labor inputs. Thus China became trapped in a relatively efficient, but labor-intensive regime: yields per acre were high and unit costs for transport and manufacture were low, but output and income per capita were declining, which limited market demand, hence incentives for innovation.[185] In response to Pomeranz, the Europeanist Robert Brenner and the China historians Christopher Isett and Philip Huang in effect revived Elvin's thesis, while exploring Chinese–English disparities that Pomeranz, in their view, had either minimized or ignored.[186]

According to Brenner and Isett, the principal difference between Chinese and English trajectories was this: whereas Yangzi delta peasants in the early Qing, having gained secure control of land along with more or less fixed rents, were effectively immune to competitive market pressures, English tenant farmers in the 17th century, having no such security, were forced to produce competitively to survive. Whereas Chinese partible inheritance led to land fragmentation among ever more numerous and small-scale cultivators, in England unitary inheritance and economies of scale promoted farm consolidation and wage labor. Output per acre may have risen in both countries – in the Yangzi delta in 1800, as a result of double-cropping and rice's unique productivity, grain output per acre was still at least 2.7 times larger than in England – but not only were long-term increases of this sort dramatically larger in England than in China, but they followed very different logics.[187] In the Yangzi

---

[185] Elvin, *Pattern of the Past*, esp. ch. 17. See too Kang Chao, *Man and Land in Chinese History* (Stanford, 1986), elaborating Elvin's approach.

[186] Philip Huang, "Development or Involution in 18th-Century Britain and China," *JAS* 61 (2002): 501–38, building on his earlier *Peasant Family and Rural Development*; Robert Brenner and Christopher Isett, "England's Divergence from China's Yangzi Delta," *JAS* 61 (2002): 609–62. Cf. Ch. 1, n. 12. I attempt to weave these somewhat discrete essays into a unified argument.

[187] Huang, "Development or Involution," 508, 511; Brenner and Isett, "England's Divergence," 624–28, 651–52. Allen, "Agricultural Productivity," 11, 23 claims that in the early 19th century, days worked per acre were 8 times higher in the Yangzi delta than

delta land productivity benefited, Pomeranz claims, from expanded use of beancake fertilizer, but far more basically, his critics argue, from rising labor inputs per acre. By contrast, English advances depended entirely on raising capital inputs, chiefly land and animals, per worker. By 1800 the average English agricultural worker had 45 times more land at his disposal than his Chinese counterpart and marked advantages in animal power and manure.[188] As a result of these and other technical differences, labor (as opposed to land) productivity in the Yangzi delta, Huang contends, *fell* throughout the Qing period in a process he terms "involution"; but in England farm output per head between 1700 and 1800 *rose* 75–100 percent. Whereas in the Yangzi delta low per capita productivity obliged some 85 percent (and in China at large, 95 percent) of the population to remain in the countryside, in England just over one-third was able to feed the rest of the population. Accordingly, whereas in late Ming China only 1–2 percent of the rural population engaged in wage labor, in Britain the figure already was 30–60 percent.[189]

These patterns, Pomeranz' critics claim, had decisive implications for urbanization and industrialization. Chinese protoindustry, chiefly textiles, remained embedded in the countryside as a subsistence-level, primarily female supplement to family farming income. Yangzi cities themselves never became manufacturing centers on the English pattern

in England, while output per acre was 6 times higher (cf. 2.7 times in Huang, "Development or Involution," 511). More critical, however, output per acre in China from 1620 to 1820 rose only marginally, if at all. The latter claim is supported by Dwight Perkins, *Agricultural Development in China 1368–1968* (Chicago, 1969), 16–17; Elvin, *Pattern of the Past*, 307; and Yong Xue, "A 'Fertilizer Revolution'?" *Modern China* 33 (2007): 216.

[188] Huang, "Development or Involution," 503, 511.

[189] Ibid., 502, 508–13; Philip Huang, "Further Thoughts on 18th-Century Britain and China," *JAS* 62 (2003): 160; Brenner and Isett, "England's Divergence," 636, which agree substantially with Myers and Wang, "Economic Developments," 579–80, Xu and Wu, *Chinese Capitalism*, xxiv–xxvii, 37, 375–84; Allen, "Agricultural Productivity." Figures on rural wage labor come from Jan Luiten van Zanden, "The Road to the Industrial Revolution," *JGH* 3 (2008): 348. The thesis that China's system of peasant smallholders inhibited productivity finds broad support in Mazumdar, *Sugar and Society*, 387–409 and *passim*. But see Pomeranz' spirited replies to Huang, "Beyond the East-West Binary"; idem, "Facts Are Stubborn Things," *JAS* 62 (2003): 167–81; and arguments for rising Chinese labor productivity in Li, *Agricultural Development*, 133–55. Moreover, Allen, "Agricultural Productivity," 15 makes the critical point that since 40 percent of rural labor in the Yangzi delta in 1850 was protoindustrial, only 43 percent of work time in the delta was truly agricultural. Despite low urbanization rates, the latter figure was not much higher than England's 36 percent overall. Perdue, pers. commun., Oct. 20, 2007 also suggests, *pace* Huang's decline thesis, that per capita returns on labor may have been constant.

and conducted only limited trade with the countryside, whose per capita purchasing power was falling. But in England the agricultural revolution supported a large off-farm population, rising household consumption, and a handicraft industry that became increasingly urban centered – and that thus anticipated industrial capitalism.[190] According to the anti-Pomeranz camp, although New World resources and markets accelerated growth, domestic and intra-European dynamism are entirely sufficient to explain the rising productivity of English agriculture and manufacture. Both sectors of the English economy relied far more heavily on domestic than on overseas markets, and on European than on New World food imports (in any case, food imports of any sort remained negligible until the 1820s). In the late 18th century, these scholars stress, there was no evidence of a looming Malthusian crisis on the Chinese pattern, let alone a crisis from which New World resources saved England. Nor, Huang insists, were English coal endowments superior or more accessible; Chinese coal never developed simply because there was no industrial demand.[191] According to Brenner and Isett, the same distinction as separated England from China also separated England from much of France and continental Europe, for there too, they suggest, small farmers were substantially insulated from competitive market pressures.[192]

Two recent contributions also emphasize differences between China and northwestern Europe, including but not restricted to England. Stephen Broadberry and Bishnupriya Gupta argue that in advanced parts of China (and India), although grain wages were comparable to those in northwestern Europe, by 1600 silver wages, which assured access to tradable goods and services and provided the best index to labor productivity, already were lower, comparable in fact to stagnating southern and eastern Europe. Thereafter the gap between China and

---

[190] Brenner and Isett, "England's Divergence," 628–36, 647; Huang, "Development or Involution," 518–21. On China's low urbanization rates, see n. 171 *supra*. Cf. Fairbank and Goldman, *China*, 180–81; Xu and Wu, *Chinese Capitalism*, 375.

[191] Huang, "Development or Involution," 531–33; idem, "Further Thoughts," 164. Also Brenner and Isett, "England's Divergence," 642–47. The emphasis in these writings on the domestic and intra-European roots of English growth receives support from Patrick O'Brien, "The Foundations of European Industrialization," in Jose Casas Pardo, ed., *Economic Effects of the European Expansion 1492–1824* (Stuttgart, 1992), 463–502. On 18th-century Chinese interest rates, normally 4–12 (sic) times higher than in the UK, van Zanden, "Road to Industrial Revolution," 342–44.

[192] Brenner and Isett, "England's Divergence," 613, 644–45, 650–51; and Brenner's essays in T. H. Ashton and C. H. E. Philpin, eds., *The Brenner Debate* (Cambridge, 1985).

northwestern Europe only widened. Likewise, Yong Xue has argued, *pace* Pomeranz and Li Bozhong, that the Qing Yangzi delta failed to exploit Manchurian beancake to create a true fertilizer revolution on the European model. This failure reflected not geographic bad luck, not an absence of New World-style "ghost acres," but commercial fragmentation and inertia, along with Manchu resistance to Han settlement in Manchuria.[193]

c) *European Institutional and Cultural Features Favorable to Growth.* While Pomeranz and his critics focused on agrarian and commercial structures, others have approached these patterns more indirectly by considering the economic implications of social and political institutions and of culture.

Without addressing Pomeranz explicitly, Ramon Myers, Yeh-chien Wang, and C. A. Bayly qualify his claim that Chinese institutions were as favorable to commerce as their English or West European counterparts. In Myers' and Wang's view the high Qing economy meshed three components: a vast, primarily local customary economy that was partly monetized; a market economy, fully monetized, urban oriented, and fiercely competitive, whose relatively free operation the state encouraged; and a command economy, based on liturgical organizations and hybrid state–merchant enterprises including salt monopolies, public granaries, and import–export monopolies. Whereas in western Europe by 1550 the market economy had begun to displace the customary economy, in China in 1800 this trend was more limited. In Europe by 1800 impersonal, permanent joint-stock companies could raise capital, generate new technologies, and coordinate production and marketing; but private Chinese firms, notwithstanding the transgenerational character of lineage enterprises, tended to be more transient, smaller, more family dependent, less innovative. And whereas West European enterprise

---

[193] Stephen Broadberry and Bishnupriya Gupta, "The Early Modern Great Divergence," *EHR* 59 (2006): 2–31, showing that a gap appeared in urbanization as well as wages; Xue, "Fertilizer Revolution," 195–229, suggesting that Manchuria also could have supplied coal and food. See too Richard Duchesne, "On the Rise of the West," *Review of Radical Political Economics* 36 (2004): 52–81, seconding the idea that new Qing territories offered a potential New World-style "ecological windfall"; and P. H. H. Vries, "Are Coal and Colonies Really Crucial?" *JWH* 12 (2001): 407–46. Citing Jesuit accounts, Elvin also has reentered the fray to argue that by the late 1700s China's ever more labor-intensive systems of hydraulic maintenance and soil replenishment had degraded the environment far more severely than in Europe. Elvin, *Retreat of the Elephants,* 454–70, largely supported by Pierre-Etienne Will, *Bureaucracy and Famine in Eighteenth-Century China* (Stanford, 1990), 311–18.

enjoyed growing immunity from regulation, the command economy let the Qing retain substantial leverage over some segments of the market to the obvious detriment, for example, of maritime trade.[194]

Precisely because they were wary of maritime trade's centrifugal political potential, the Qing never considered providing the overseas military and naval support that hyperaggressive European states offered their merchants. This was true even though Southeast Asia, for example, offered potential ghost acreage reminiscent of the New World. European access to global resources was less a function of geographic luck, therefore, than of deliberate policy. To follow Bayly, massive French, Dutch, and most especially British naval expenditures let European trading companies and private merchants capture up to 90 percent of value added in the trade of tropical tea, coffee, tobacco, sugar, and opium. This provided valuable – if often exaggerated – benefits through ecological relief, capital formation, new industries, and goads to Jan de Vries' "industrious revolution." Another artifact of war, the national debt spurred financial innovation and gave European public accounts a transparency unknown in China.[195]

What is more, as Chapter 3 argued for France, sustained rivalries between mid-size states that were more ethnically coherent and far less populous than the Qing empire – hence more easily imagined as homes

---

[194] On domestic commercial regulation, Myers and Wang, "Economic Developments," 576–92, 610, 624–26, 641–45, probably written well before appearance of Pomeranz' work; Ramon Myers, "Customary Law, Markets, and Resource Transactions in Late Imperial China," in Roger Ranson, ed., *Explorations in the New Economic History* (New York, 1982), 273–98, noting both customary law incentives to market expansion and disincentives to labor-saving innovation; C. A. Bayly, "South Asia and the 'Great Divergence,'" *Itinerario* 24 (2000): 96–97; idem, *Birth of the Modern World*, 58–64, 81–82. Also Rowe, *Saving the World*, 447–49; Smith, *Taxing Heaven's Storehouse*, 314–16; and Dunstan, *State or Merchant*, esp. 404–79, analyzing tensions between a Sino-Manchu version of "grain liberalism" and more interventionist approaches, with the former gaining in influence. On lineage and family enterprises, n. 108 *supra*; Rowe, "Social Stability," 536–37, 561; Brokaw, "Commercial Publishing"; Pomeranz, *Great Divergence*, 14–17, 69–91, 166–86. Cf. Ch. 2, n. 88 *supra*. At the coast, even after the 1727 lifting of Qing bans on private shipping to the Nan-yang, English trade remained in the hands of government-recognized monopolies. *CIHC*, 234 ff.; Anthony Reid, "Flows and Seepages in the Long-term Chinese Interaction with Southeast Asia," in Reid, ed., *Sojourners and Settlers* (St. Leonards, Australia, 1996), 15–49.

[195] Bayly, "South Asia and the Great Divergence," 98–99; idem, *Birth of the Modern World*, 52, 58–64, 71, 81; Ch. 1, n. 13 *supra*. Of course, Pomeranz, *Great Divergence*, 194–207, 264–87 also emphasizes British projects in the Americas, but he is generally less interested in cultural and institutional peculiarities that gave birth to such projects than in their economic effects.

to discrete political communities – joined with European legal protections for the public sphere to generate patriotic civil societies without clear Chinese parallel. By allowing people openly to critique state and private institutions in the name of national greatness, public opinion, inspired by Enlightenment notions of linear progress and empirical inquiry, sought, often successfully, to enhance those institutions' ability to accumulate wealth, power, and knowledge. It was, Bayly concludes, no single feature, rather this combination of entrepreneurial autonomy and longevity, medium-sized polities, intense global involvement, sustained interstate competition, and a culture of vigorous public critique that accounts for Europe's early modern ascendancy.[196]

d) *British "Engine Science."* If Myers and Bayly emphasize institutional and cultural idiosyncrasy, Jack Goldstone's theory of British industrialization takes that concern with European specificity to an entirely new level.[197]

At the outset Goldstone distinguishes between, on the one hand, modern economic growth, founded on the conscious application of science and technology to generate continuous, ever accelerating increases in output; and, on the other hand, Smithian growth, which was driven by market specialization, but rarely exceeded 1 percent a year, and after 75 to 200 years usually reached a new production ceiling. Operating within a conservative technological context, the latter type of expansion was followed by stagnation or decline, and as such, offered no escape from an agrarian-centered world.[198]

Smithian growth occurred many times and many places, including Song and late Ming and Qing China. But modern growth, Goldstone argues, began only once, in Britain, because only there by 1830 was the steam engine perfected. That singular achievement in turn rested on a complex, highly contingent chain of events, including the triumph after 1688 in England, but not on the continent until much later, of

---

[196] Bayly, *Birth of the Modern World*, 64–83, and Ch. 3, nn. 4–7 *supra*. But on "civil society-like" institutions in Asia, see Ch. 1, n. 7 *supra*. See too Gregory Clark, *A Farewell to Alms* (Princeton, 2007), ch. 13, speculating that England's advantage over China and Japan derived primarily from a demographic system that accorded greater reproductive advantage to the wealthy, which encouraged downward mobility, which favored the cultural and perhaps genetic diffusion throughout society c. 1200–1800 of the values of the most economically successful strata.

[197] See Ch. 1, n. 4, plus Jack Goldstone, "Efflorescences and Economic Growth in World History," *JWH* 13 (2002): 323–90. As noted, Goldstone's work derives in part from that of Margaret Jacob.

[198] Cf. Ch. 1, nn. 14, 15 *supra*.

Newtonian physics; the Anglican church's consequent support for notions of uniform, universal laws; the increasingly experimental, pragmatic, and commercial orientation of British science, which contrasted with the more deductive orientation of continental research; the ensuing infiltration into middle-class British culture of an interest in mechanical demonstration and physical laws; and the rise of an engineering subculture that specialized in turning principles of natural philosophy into mechanisms useful to entrepreneurs. This subculture spawned the engineers and engine-makers who perfected and applied not only the steam engine – which in a single generation gave the average Englishman more than 10 times the fuel energy available to any other human – but a host of inventions that also depended on precise measurement. Only with the deployment of the steam engine in British manufacturing from the 1790s and more especially the 1830s, Goldstone concludes, was modernity possible.

In conclusion, what can we make of these very different comparative approaches to Qing economic history? Several observations come to mind. The attention that Bayly and others pay to European institutional, political, and cultural factors strikes me as entirely salutary, even if measuring the economic impact of such factors is problematic. On the other hand, the debates between Pomeranz and his critics remain exceedingly technical, and do not permit easy judgment by nonspecialists like myself. As yet, no consensus has emerged. When such a consensus does develop, however, it may approximate the views outlined by the economic historian of England Robert Allen. In a brief but impressively documented and argued paper, Allen supports claims by Pomeranz and Li that England in 1800 had only a modest lead over the Yangzi delta in agricultural labor productivity and virtually no advantage in standard of living. Yet Allen agrees with the involutionists that while English labor productivity rose sharply between 1600 and 1750, labor productivity in the Yangzi delta stagnated. Under the impact of population growth, moreover, the real income of the average Yangzi peasant family fell 38 percent from 1620 to 1820, and China by 1750 seemed headed for a Malthusian crash without English analogue.[199]

Such long-term prospects aside, I also sense that the radical pre-1800 divide between England and the rest of Europe so dear to Brenner, Isett, and especially Goldstone is overdrawn. My reading of Philip Hoffman

---

[199] Allen, "Agricultural Productivity," 13–15 and Table 6, presenting a view accepted also by Sommer, *Sex, Law,* 12. Cf. nn. 180, 187, 189 *supra.*

indicates, and Chapter 3 argued, that the key impediment to agricultural modernization in France was neither social structure nor farm size, but fiscal exactions, poor transport, and limited market access; and that such barriers to trade, especially in transportation, eased throughout the 18th century.[200] Likewise my instinctive suspicion is that cultural and social structures in Britain, northern France, and the Low Countries were sufficiently similar that if the English had not invented the steam engine, within a century or so the energy bottleneck would have been broken elsewhere in northwestern Europe.

Finally, whatever China's structural weaknesses vis-à-vis northwestern Europe may have been, the impressive growth in Chinese output, population, and market specialization from c. 1500 to 1640 and more especially between c. 1700 and 1830 paralleled expansions in mainland Southeast Asia – whose trade with China, of course, grew markedly[201] – in France, Russia, and less consistently, Japan. Admittedly, Rowe's thesis that in China and Europe comparable 18th-century commercial and social pressures produced comparable modifications in elite consciousness has not won universal favor among intellectual historians of the Qing, at least some of whom see little of that psychic disjuncture, that sense of the autonomous individual agency, that transcending of antiquity which were hallmarks of early modern European thought.[202] Assimilating Southeast Asian thought to a generic early modern intellectual category is far more problematic.[203] But in a more general sense, late Ming and Qing trends toward commercial intensification, urban–rural and interregional cultural circulation, a more egalitarian and mobile social order, popular literacy and vernacular literatures, and toward a more centralized, territorially expansive, and

---

[200] Philip Hoffman, *Growth in a Traditional Economy* (Princeton, 1996); and Ch. 3, Pt. 3 *supra*.

[201] *SP*, 170–71, 286–94, 303–309, 408–410, 415–18, 435–37.

[202] Compare compelling arguments for Chinese–European intellectual comparabilities in Rowe, *Saving the World*, 191–92, 322–25, 446–47, 453–56 with the more skeptical views of On-cho Ng, "The Epochal Concept of 'Early Modernity' and the Intellectual History of Late Imperial China," *JWH* 14 (2003): 37–61; Rawski, "The Qing Formation," 208; and Lynn Struve, "Chimerical Early Modernity," in Struve, *Qing Formation*, 335–80. On the other hand, Rowe's emphasis on individual subjectivity and responsibility finds varying degrees of corroboration in Wm. Theodore de Bary, "Individualism and Humanitarianism in Late Ming Thought," in de Bary, ed., *Self and Society in Ming Thought* (New York, 1970), 145–248; Clunas, *Superfluous Things*, 170–71; Jonathan Hay, "The Diachronics of Early Qing Visual and Material Culture," in Struve, *Qing Formation*, 303–34; idem, *Shitao* (Cambridge, 2001), esp. 18–25.

[203] Cf. Ch. 1, n. 128 *supra*, and Michael Charney, *Powerful Learning* (Ann Arbor, 2006).

militarily powerful state are thoroughly familiar. On the basis of such criteria, I have noted that many scholars see the late Ming–Qing era as a coherent period to which "late imperial" and "early modern" labels are often applied.[204] Judged in terms not of specific institutions or intellectual trends, nor of absolute levels of wealth or power, but of these insistent integrative tendencies, China between 1500 and 1850 therefore bears comparison to Burma, Siam, Trinh/Nguyen Vietnam, late Muscovite and Romanov Russia, Bourbon France, and Tokugawa Japan.

2. DIFFERENCES BETWEEN CHINA AND THE PROTECTED ZONE

Distinctive Chinese Features: Civilizational Precocity

Given these broad parallels, how did the main lines of Chinese development differ from those in mainland Southeast Asia, Europe, and Japan? I shall concentrate on four interrelated distinctions that bear most directly on my theme of sustained integration: civilizational precocity, growing Inner Asian domination, the vast scale of empire, and modest fiscal and military imperatives.

The first difference is as basic as it is obvious: because China was one of Eurasia's few "primary civilizations," political integration began appreciably earlier than in the Eurasian peripheries considered in Volume 1 and in Chapters 2 to 4 of this volume. A "primary" or "pristine civilization" may be defined as a literate, urban-centered complex whose institutions and high culture were not shaped by substantial dependence upon or control by more complex external societies. If "substantial" is open to a degree of subjectivity, there is near universal agreement that along with the Indus valley and Mesopotamia, North China was the site of a primary Eurasian civilization.[205]

---

[204] See n. 165 *supra*, plus Frederic Wakeman, "Introduction," in Wakeman and Carolyn Grant, eds., *Conflict and Control in Late Imperial China* (Berkeley, 1975), 2–3; *SYMT*, 5, 30, 44–55; Rawski, "Economic and Social Foundations," 3–11; Rowe, *Saving the World*, 446–56; idem, "Domestic Interregional Trade," 184; Perdue, *China Marches West*, 8; Hay, "Diachronics," 308.

[205] On distinctions between "primary" and "secondary" states and civilizations, Ch. 1, nn. 63, 154 *supra*. The distinction between "states" and "civilizations" collapses insofar as standard sources like Christopher Scarre and Brian Fagan, *Ancient Civilizations* (Upper Saddle River, NJ, 2003), 4–8 define "civilization" as "urbanized state-level societies." Discussion of civilizational genesis in China follows ibid.; Bruce Trigger, *Understanding Early Civilizations* (Cambridge, 2003); Charles Maisels, *Early Civilizations of the Old World* (London, 1999); Anne Underhill and Junko Habu, "Early Communities

Because recent archeology has revealed a number of late neolithic and early bronze-age centers of social complexity and original culture outside the Yellow River plain, including sites in Manchuria, Gansu, the middle and lower Yangzi, and Sichuan, a mononuclear thesis of Chinese cultural origins is no longer tenable. Yet, while drawing on elements from an extended "interaction sphere" that embraced much of North and East Central China, it was the Yellow River plain in the north that engendered Shang civilization (c. 1600–1050 B.C.E.), whose heirs eventually would dominate all of China. North China shared with other sites of primary civilization a relatively dry salubrious climate, fertile easily worked soils, domesticable flora and fauna, a river system capable of supporting sizeable populations, access to key raw materials, and a correspondingly rich synergy between multiple sites. After c. 1900 B.C.E. apparently two principal factors, namely, population growth and a drive to control salt supplies and the supply of metals needed for weapons and ritual objects, spurred endemic warfare between numerous walled centers on the North China plain, which in turn propelled state formation and social stratification. By 1400 B.C.E. Shang rulers exercised peripatetic control/influence over a confederation of territories, each apparently ruled by a patrilineal descent group, which were centered in modern Henan and western Shandong. The chief Shang urban centers supported monumental architecture, elaborate ritual cycles, sophisticated bronze metallurgy, logographic writing, and perhaps small standing armies.[206]

in East Asia," in Stark, *Archaeology*, 121–34; Li Liu and Xingcan Chen, "Sociopolitical Change from Neolithic to Bronze Age China," in ibid., 149–76; David Keightly, "Marks and Labels," in ibid., 177–201; Sarah Allan, ed., *The Formation of Chinese Civilization* (New Haven, 2005), esp. chs. 4–6; Michael Puett, "China in Early Eurasian History," in Victor Mair, ed., *The Bronze Age and Early Iron Age Peoples of Eastern Central* Asia, 2 vols. (Washington, DC, 1998), vol. II, 699–714; J. P. Mallory, "A European Perspective on Indo-Europeans in Asia," ibid., vol. I, 175–201; Michael Cook, *A Brief History of the Human Race* (New York, 2003), 132–34, 148–60, 210–19, 267–68; Diamond, *Guns, Germs, and Steel*, 176–86, 323–33; McNeill, *Human Web*, 41–81, 121; and n. 206 *infra*. My list of protected zone/exposed zone differences in this chapter, starting with civilizational "precocity" rather than Inner Asian domination, reverses the order in Ch. 1, partly for variety's sake, and partly because this chapter has a more chronological thrust.

[206] On the Shang and on early Chinese state formation generally, see the previous note, plus David Keightley, *Ancestral Landscapes* (Berkeley, 2000), chs. 2, 5, 7; idem, "The Shang," esp. 258–92; *CIHC*, 16–30, 59; Li Liu and Xingcan Chen, *State Formation in Early China* (London, 2003), focusing on pre-Shang and early Shang; Kwang-chih Chang, *The Archaeology of Ancient China* (4th ed., New Haven, 1986), chs. 5, 6; idem, "The Rise of Kings and the Formation of City-States," in Allan, *Formation*, 125–39; Lu Liancheng and Yan Wenming, "Society During the Three Dynasties," in ibid., 140–201; Gideon

Among primary Old World civilizations, China was arguably the most isolated and original, as suggested by the idiosyncrasy of Chinese writing, cosmology, and metallurgy and by nontheistic strains in early philosophy. Yet to acknowledge that the essential dynamics of state and culture formation, and of the agrarian economy, were indigenous is not to preclude the likelihood that China also benefited from external contacts. Along with the Indus and Nile valleys and Mesopotamia, North China had access to material and cultural elements transmitted by traders, migrating cultivators, and especially by pastoral warriors moving along east–west axes of communication and exchange. From the late third through the first millennium B.C.E. the North China plain, in particular its northwest extension, received from West Asia via the steppe and the oases of Xinjiang the following material and cultural features, the probability of whose diffusion from points west I list in order of decreasing scholarly consensus: chariots and spoked wheels, wheat and barley; horses, horse riding, and cavalry tactics; the compound bow and other weapons; cows, sheep, and goats; bronze metallurgy, iron metallurgy, and the concept of writing. In return Chinese animals and crops (including probably millet, pigs, chickens, and ducks) spread westward along these same east–west axes.[207] That classical Chinese civilization arose not in the Yangzi basin, but on the North China plain, reflected in some uncertain measure this privileged access to external contacts – along with the critical fact that North China's lightly

---

Shelach and Yuri Pines, "Secondary State Formation and the Development of Local Identity," in Stark, *Archaeology*, 202–30; Bruce Trigger, "Shang Political Organization," *Jl. of East Asian Archaeology* 1 (1999): 43–62.

[207] Mair, *Bronze Age and Early Iron Age Peoples*, vol. I, 4–44, 94–113, 222–36, 264–79, and vol. II, 581–643, 659–60, 683–715, esp. Puett, "China in Early Eurasian History," reviewing the recent shift from "processual" to "diffusionist" emphases in Chinese archeology; Mair, "North(west)ern Peoples"; Cook, *Brief History*, 179–83; McNeill, *Human Web*, 43–44, 55, 65, 121; Diamond, *Guns, Germs, and Steel*, 329–30; Hansen, *Open Empire*, 39, 40, 173; Di Cosmo, *Ancient China*, 27–30 and *CHAC*, 86–87 on chariots and other Tocharian influences; ibid., 136–58, 203–208, 221–26, 578–80 on bronze; ibid., 400, 468, 474–75, 534, 542, 578–80, 891–92, 913–14, 946–47 on iron; ibid., 886 on the horse; *CIHC*, 24, 35; J. P. Mallory and Victor Mair, *The Tarim Mummies* (London, 2000), 7, 135–36, 147, 324–32 and *passim*; Fredrik Hiebert, *Origins of the Bronze Age Civilization in Central Asia* (Cambridge, MA, 1994); idem, *A Central Asian Village at the Dawn of Civilization* (Philadelphia, 2003), exploring early Near East-South Asia-Turkmenistan links; and Gary Crawfurd, "East Asian Plant Domestication," in Stark, *Archaeology*, 78–81, 91, emphasizing the key role in the early Chinese economy of crops originating outside China and noting that even for broomcorn and foxtail millet evidence of original Chinese domestication is lacking.

vegetated loess soils, as noted, were easier to clear and cultivate than those of subtropical South China.

Development potentials in Eurasia's protected zone were more circumscribed. Although often enjoying fine water resources and an array, particularly in Southeast Asia, of domesticable plants and animals, during the second and first millennia B.C.E. Southeast Asia, northern Europe, and Japan still supported relatively small, isolated populations. Heavy, often waterlogged soils and a short growing season in northern Europe, indifferent soils and a short growing season in Russia, limited arable land in Japan, and tropical malarial forests in Southeast Asia (and South China) depressed demographic ceilings.

At the same time rimland civilizations had only limited access to pan-Eurasian circuits of communication, migration, and trade, the result again of ocean barriers, jungle-clad mountains, difficult climate, disease, low commercial attraction, and sheer distance. This location at the edge of the world, so to speak, had major political and cultural implications. On the one hand, Southeast Asia, northern Europe, and Japan obtained writing and other "high civilizational" features only after such elements had been elaborated elsewhere. To be sure, both primary civilizations, as I just argued for North China, and secondary civilizations borrowed, but in the former, such borrowings involved individual technological and material elements, rather than cohesive, literate cultural complexes. By definition, only secondary civilizations imported fully formed cosmologies, religious hierarchies, law codes, administrative models, literatures, and systems of art, architecture, and writing. In this sense, the relation of charter Southeast Asia to India, of the Franks and Rus to Rome/Byzantium, of *ritsuryo* Japan to Tang China (and indeed of South India to North India and South China to North China) differed qualitatively from that of prehistoric North China to West Asia or of the Indus valley to Mesopotamia.

What is more, when basic technological features did appear in protected-zone societies, they normally did so long after being refined in primary civilizations. Use of iron for weapons and implements, for example, began in the Near East and southeastern Europe by 1200 B.C.E., in India by 1200–600 B.C.E., and in China between 800 and 600 B.C.E., but in Southeast Asia, whose forging and smelting techniques derived primarily from India, iron appeared only between 500 B.C.E. and 500 C.E. In Kyushu, which depended on Korean ore and metalworkers, small smithing operations date from the first century C.E., while in Honshu,

579

firm evidence of smelting is available only from the 5th or 6th century C.E.[208] By extension, political integration, dependent on a mix of local and external stimuli, began appreciably later in the protected zone. As novel unifications that provided a charter for subsequent polities, the rise of Pagan (c. 1000–1060 C.E.), Angkor (c. 800–950 C.E.), Dai Viet (939–1010 C.E.), Kiev (c. 900–950 C.E.), the Frankish/Carolingian empire (c. 500–770 C.E.), and *ritsuryo* Japan (c. 650–750 C.E.) resembled the Qin–Han revolution in China – but all began some 700 to 1,200 years later.

On the other hand, once economic intensification and its correlate, political consolidation, did get underway, state formation proceeded far more rapidly than in older Eurasian cores, precisely because secondary civilizations could access prepackaged, demonstrably effective cultural and political systems, whether Hindu, Buddhist, Confucian, or Christian. Lacking elaborate outside blueprints, primary civilizations had been obliged to proceed through many centuries of trial and error. Thus, for example, in China some 1,400 years separated the founding of the first extensive polity, the Shang, from Qin–Han unification, but in Japan less than 200 years separated the Yamato polity – arguably equivalent to the Shang in unifying ambition and superficial authority – from *ritsuryo* consolidation.[209] Because long-distance communications and trade grew ever more intense, the lag time between political innovation in Eurasian cores and protected-zone realms would continue to

---

[208] This is not to claim that single-point diffusion always trumped multipoint local invention, for in Europe and elsewhere recent archeology has emphasized the latter, but across Eurasia migrations and trade provided a broad chronological framework within which local experiment and external importation/imitation could proceed in tandem. On the appearance of iron technologies, Carla Sinopoli, pers. commun., Sept. 4, 2008; Puett, "China in Early Eurasian History"; F. R. Allchin, *The Archaeology of Early Historic South Asia* (Cambridge, 1995), 39, 65–66, 71, 76, 83–84; Romila Thapar, *Early India* (Berkeley, 2002), 79–80, 143 (note that in India the relation between domestic and imported technologies is particularly debated); R. F. Tylecote, *The Early History of Metallurgy in Europe* (London, 1987); Donald Wagner, *Iron and Steel in Ancient China* (New York, 1993), chs. 1–3, taking an antidiffusionist stance; *CIHC*, 39, 41; Ian Glover and Peter Bellwood, eds., *Southeast Asia From Prehistory to History* (London, 2004), 36–41, 57–64, 70–71, 91, 156–57, 263–77, 320–22; Joan Piggott, *The Emergence of Japanese Kingship* (Stanford, 1997), 25–34, 45, 51–52, 98; *The New Encyclopedia Britannica* (Chicago, 2007), vol. XVIII, 596–98. Different dates for the same region often reflect the distinction between iron's introduction and functional availability. Note, however, that iron appeared in northern Europe earlier than in most of the protected zone. For a diffusionary schema of agrarian intensification between 3000 and 300 B.C.E. in China, Korea, and Japan, see Crawfurd, "East Asian Plant Domestication," 89–90.

[209] A substantial gap remains even if one were to argue that the Zhou polity of 1050 B.C.E. resembled the Yamato state more closely than did the Shang.

shrink, along with differences in technology and urbanization. By the same token, within the protected zone itself, notwithstanding France's early advantages, we saw that political and economic changes in France and Russia became more closely coordinated.[210]

Distinctive Chinese Features: Inner Asian Domination

A second major distinction between China and the protected zone, a distinction captured in the titles of this and the next chapter, also revolved around differential exposure. The same insularity as delayed state formation in the protected zone helped to shelter those areas from Inner Asian conquest. Conversely, the same openness to influences moving along the trade and migratory corridors of Inner Asia as favored early civilizations in China and other exposed realms left them vulnerable to nomadic domination.

China's relation to Inner Asia was as protean as it was durable. Mair suggests that peoples from the northwestern steppe were instrumental in founding the Shang (c. 1600–1050 B.C.E.) and perhaps the early Zhou (c. 1050–771 B.C.E.) states as well as those of Qin (221–206 B.C.E.) and Han (202 B.C.E.–220 C.E.). Thereafter Inner Asian pastoralists, many of whom seem to have been distinguished from North China cultivators by Indo-European physical features (deep-set eyes, prominent noses, heavy beards) as well as by access to steppe culture and military technique, continued to wield influence far in excess of their numbers. Most unifying dynasties in Chinese history and some of the most long lived were led by peoples with strong north(west)ern steppe associations. The greatest imperial extensions, those of Yuan and Qing, occurred under Inner Asian auspices; while Sinitic dynasties following expansive non-Sinitic dynasties invariably lost territories.[211] Chinese historians

---

[210] See introduction to Ch. 3 and Conclusions to Chs. 2, 3 *supra*. Thus too Rozman, *Urban Networks*, 55, 83–85, and *passim* argues forcefully that although urbanization in Russia began much later than in China or western Europe, the gap between Russian patterns and those in more precocious regions constantly diminished.

[211] E.g., the Ming, the Northern and Southern Song. Mair, "North(west)ern Peoples." The Northern Song, in fact, held the smallest territory of any major ruling house. Smith, *Taxing Heaven's Storehouse*, 7. Thus too Lewis, *China Between Empires*, 151 notes, "... all Chinese dynasties were established by military power, [and] from the [Later] Han onward foreign troops and culture were fundamental to that power." However, lest we assimilate Shang and Zhou history too readily to that of Inner Asian pastoral nomads, note that according to Di Cosmo, *Ancient China*, chs. 1, 2, 4, 6, true pastoral nomadism on the steppe cohered only c. 1000–500 B.C.E.

habitually portrayed north(west)ern peoples as threats to the stability of states on the Yellow River plain, but in truth the relation was the
opposite: such groups were among the chief catalysts of state formation.
Repeatedly Inner Asians drew together North China and the steppe to
create substantially new societies, while revitalizing governance, recasting ethnic relations, and generating imperial ideologies that were both
unusually cosmopolitan and unusually segmented.

Now at first glance, the distinction between Eurasian realms protected from Inner Asian incursion and areas open to such incursions
may seem suspect. After all, the Mongols invaded Kamakura Japan,
pressured Angkor and Dai Viet, conquered Pagan as well as Kiev, and
obliged Russian princes to pay tribute for some two centuries. In truth,
however, these interventions were limited. Mongol attacks on Japan
failed, and their influence on Southeast Asia proved ephemeral. In
any case, in neither Japan nor Southeast Asia did Inner Asians exert
influence after 1300.[212] In Russia, we have seen, Mongol-Tatars (Turks)
clearly did alter the main lines of political development. Yet Tatar overlordship was never accompanied by settlement in the forested zone or
attempts at direct rule. Local authority thus remained in the hands of
Russian princes whose cultural and social identification with the population they ruled was far more intense than that of Inner Asians. Even
at the height of Mongol-Tatar power, Muscovy proudly identified as an
Orthodox Christian polity. In any case, Moscow threw off Tatar control
by the mid-1400s, after which Inner Asian influence receded sharply.

But in China between c. 900 and 1800, with the obvious exception of
the Ming era, Inner Asian influence not only persisted, but grew more
territorially extensive and institutionally secure. Indeed, the growth
of Inner Asian influence constituted a major linear dynamic that propelled at least two of the six trends examined in Part 1 of this chapter, namely, territorial expansion and administrative centralization. If
the latter trends were well nigh universal, in no protected-zone realm
after 1400 did they depend on alien conquest elites. In this sense, China
resembled both South Asia and island Southeast Asia, for political innovation in post-1200 South Asia relied substantially on Turkic, and in
island Southeast Asia after 1571/1670 on Iberian and Dutch, conquest
elites.

---

[212] Unless we consider as examples of Inner Asian influence the unsuccessful 1788–1789
Qing invasion of Vietnam or the Qing–Burmese wars of 1765–1769, which the Qing
also lost.

Here, then, lies a central puzzle of Chinese history, also apparent in Southwest and South Asia: How could conquest elites dominate societies incomparably larger and wealthier? In China the proportion of Inner Asian elites to subjects grew ever more skewed: In 1100 some 750,000 Khitans who founded the Liao Dynasty ruled two to three million Chinese, a ratio of roughly 1:3. A century later 6,000,000 Jurchens ruled some 35,000,000 North Chinese, a ratio of approximately 1:6. In 1300 perhaps one and a half million Mongols controlled 75,000,000 Chinese, a ratio of 1:50. But in 1648 the proportion of Manchus to Chinese subjects was 1:350.[213] Particularly curious is the fact that exceptionally robust economic and demographic growth during the Song and the late Ming eras failed to translate into military success; indeed, both periods culminated in Inner Asian conquest.

Of course, one must guard against assumptions of "inevitability." In 1644, for example, the Manchus came to power in a fluid competition involving *inter alia* themselves, Ming generals, and two Chinese rebel leaders. Although the military and administrative machine the Manchus had built beyond the Great Wall gave them a major advantage, if the chief rebel Li Zicheng had been more capable, or if Ming generals had decided to throw their support behind him rather than the Manchus, it is quite possible that Sinic dominance could have continued. On the other hand, if we are considering counterfactuals, it is also possible that if Timur had not died in 1405, he would have reestablished Turko-Mongol rule over North China and the Ming Dynasty, shortened to 40 years, would have been relegated to a historical footnote![214]

Most obviously, long-term Inner Asian success reflected cavalry superiority. If the old saw that Chinese officials elevated civilized (*wen*) over martial (*wu*) virtues elides numerous exceptions, it is also true that bitter memories of rampant militarism during the period 755–960

---

[213] Computed from *CIHC*, 166 (Khitans), 171 (Mongols); Peter Bol, "Seeking Common Ground: Han Literati Under Jurchen Rule," *HJAS* 47 (1987): 461–62 and Fairbank and Goldman, *China*, 115 (Jurchens); n. 159 *supra*; Eastman, *Family, Fields*, 4; *SYMT*, 9. On Manchus, Elliott, *Manchu Way*, 3 (with 1:350 ratio), 117, 363–64. Each comparison omits steppe confederates of the dominant minority. In the 5th century the ratio of Xianbei and allied tribesmen to subject Chinese was 1:10 or 1:15; *CIHC*, 92.

[214] On 1644 events, in which Beijing bureaucrats of Yangzi delta origins represented a fifth, albeit nonmilitary force, see Gertraude Roth, "The Manchu-Chinese Relationship, 1618–1636," in Spence and Wills, *From Ming to Ch'ing*, 32–33; Frederic Wakeman, Jr. "The Shun Interregnum of 1644," in ibid., 39–87; *CIHC*, 214–15, 221; Frederic Wakeman, *The Great Enterprise*, 2 vols. (Berkeley, 1985), vol. I, 225–318. On Timur, n. 58 *supra*.

joined with the Song Neo-Confucian revival to foster enduring literati suspicion of the professional military – along with institutional curbs on military initiative – that contrasted not only with the full-blooded warrior ethos of Inner Asian tribes, but with the more militarized traditions of the Sui and Tang Dynasties, whose founders were of mixed Chinese and Xianbei descent.[215] Likewise, the premium that steppe and forest environments placed on male aggression, physical stamina, hunting (which required quasi-military coordination), and equestrian expertise, especially mounted archery skills, contrasted with the more sedentary ethos of most agricultural villages. What is more, these traits' universality ensured that among Inner Asians a far larger percentage of adult males, virtually the entire population, were available as warriors, so that the numerical gap between Inner Asian and Chinese forces was always dramatically smaller than that between general populations. Ecological differences between Manchuria and Mongolia notwithstanding, these same advantages aided Jurchens and Manchus no less than Mongols, all of whom must be considered exemplars of Inner Asian military culture.

One could also argue that by facilitating long-distance interactions with diverse peoples, nomadism promoted effective strategies for controlling the logistical and cultural challenges typical of large-scale empires. By contrast, Song (and to a lesser extent Ming) cultural and physical distance from the steppe left them less able than their Sui and Tang, not to mention Mongol and Manchu, counterparts to forge extensive tribal alliances in general, and to acquire desperately needed cavalry mounts in particular. Without steppe allies or reliable purchase of frontier horses (China proper could never compete with the steppe as an environment for breeding and raising horses), Chinese dynasties were obliged to surrender strategic control of the steppe frontier. We shall find that a similar dependence on imported horses disadvantaged agrarian India. [216]

---

[215] On post-755 military controls, n. 46 *supra*. On Sui and Tang Sino-foreign military ancestry, *CIHC*, 109, 111. The Xianbei, originally from southern Manchuria, founded the Northern Wei Dynasty (386/439–534).

[216] On steppe military and political strengths, Ch. 1, n. 134 *supra*, David Christian, "Inner Asia as a Unit of World History," *JWH* 5 (1994): 173–211; idem, *A History of Russia, Central Asia, and Mongolia, vol. 1* (Malden, MA, 1998), 235–429; Perdue, *China Marches West*, 33–36, 51–93, 354; Graff, *Medieval Chinese Warfare*, 228; David Morgan, *The Mongols* (1986), 84–91. On the enduring problem of horse supply, esp. in the Song, see Smith, *Taxing Heaven's Storehouse*, 8, 13–47, 277–81. But Robinson, *Bandits, Eunuchs*, offers a more positive view than many scholars of Ming military capacity and knowledge of steppe affairs. On the legitimacy of defining Jurchens and Manchus as Inner Asians,

Yet as in Southwest and South Asia, cavalry would have been inadequate to ensure Inner Asian dominance were it not combined with systematic borrowing from agrarian cultures. In explaining the success of the most durable Inner Asian empires, Thomas Barfield was surely justified in emphasizing the combinative role of mixed ecological and cultural zones, what he termed "Manchurian" states, on the interface between Inner Asia and China proper. Here, beyond the reach of Chinese armies, frontier polities like that of the Qing could experiment with elements from both worlds, wedding Inner Asian cavalry and tribal organization to Chinese economy, military techniques, administration, and ideology.[217] Now, as Nicola Di Cosmo has shown, in part Inner Asian state formation reflected internal rhythms – he posits a recurrent progression from economic crisis to charismatic leadership to centralized organizations to a search for revenues to sustain those organizations – that did not depend directly on developments in sedentary societies. We find powerful Inner Asian confederations during periods of Chinese political cohesion as well as fragmentation, of economic expansion as well as contraction.[218] But over the long run Inner Asian resources and cultural repertoires also benefited substantially from a secular expansion of trade and population along the Chinese/Inner Asian frontier. During China's first commercial revolution, c. 800/900– 1270, for example, the growth of Chinese settlement and trade provided Tanguts, Khitans, Jurchens, and Mongols with invaluable revenues, administrative and financial expertise.[219] Shortly after the start of the second commercial revolution, Iwai Shikegi argues that Manchu power

Ch. 1, n. 133 *supra*, Perdue, pers. commun., Oct. 20, 2007. On nomadism as a spur to successful imperial strategies, William Honeychurch and Chunag Amartuvshin, "States on Horseback," in Stark, *Archaeology*, 255–78.

[217] On North China frontiers as a zone of Inner Asian experiment, Thomas Barfield, *The Perilous Frontier* (Cambridge, MA, 1989), chs. 1, 5, and *passim*; Rawski, "Presidential Address," 836–38; and the seminal discussion of hybridity in Owen Lattimore, *Inner Asian Frontiers of China* (New York, 1940).

[218] Nicola Di Cosmo, "State Formation and Periodization in Inner Asian History," *JWH* 10 (1999): 1–40. Cf. Christian, *History of Russia, Central Asia, and Mongolia*, pts. 3–5.

[219] Not only Chinese, but Inner Asian frontier populations may have expanded in this period, although I find no statistics. On commercial spurs to pre-1300 Tangut, Khitan, Jurchen, and Mongol state formation, see Elvin, *Pattern of the Past*, 88; Mote, *Imperial China*, 270, 285–88, 391–94; Thomas Allsen, "Mongolian Princes and Their Merchant Partners, 1200–1260," *Asia Major*, 2 (1989): 83–126; Elizabeth Endicott-West, "Merchant Associations in Yuan China," ibid., 127–54; Christian, *History of Russia, Central Asia, and Mongolia*, 385, 387, 400, 416, 426; Thomas Allsen, *Culture and Conquest in Mongol Eurasia* (Cambridge, 2001), esp. 189–211; Nicola Di Cosmo, "Mongols and Merchants on the Black Sea Frontier in the 13th and 14th Centuries," in Amitai and Biran, *Mongols,*

fed on the booming exchange of Inner Asian horses, livestock, furs, and ginseng for Chinese textiles, farm implements, grain, and silver. Because New World silver entering at the coast flowed disproportionately to the northern frontier to pay Ming garrisons, commerce was actually far livelier in this sector than in much of the Chinese interior. Early Manchu commercial monopolies not only provided income, but allowed Manchu leaders to bring within their political orbit a mixed population of Jurchens (amalgamated to form "Manchus" in 1635), Koreans, Mongols, and Chinese. In somewhat similar fashion, I suggested, Tai entry into Southeast Asian lowlands in the 12th and 13th centuries owed much to growing commercial and cultural exchange across charter-era frontiers, while in South Asia between c. 1000 and 1300 and again between 1550 and 1700 we shall find that economic expansion drew together arid-zone warriors and arable-zone cultivators both within the subcontinent and along the interface between India and Inner Asia.[220]

By the same logic, Khitans, Jurchens, and Mongols succeeded in neutralizing their foes' superiority in armaments and military technology by enticing or forcing into their service North Chinese ironworkers, crossbowmen, catapultiers, gunpowder manufacturers, and military engineers. In other words, even as they kept Song cavalry from obtaining quality horses, Inner Asians mastered every one of China's own defensive arts. Against the Northern Song capital of Kaifeng, for example, the Jurchens sent siege engines and mobile towers able to fire Chinese-style incendiary bombs. To subdue the Southern Song, the Mongols, who as late as the mid-1200s were still using inflated skins and rafts to cross rivers, assimilated Chinese shipbuilding and naval warfare. (Mongols also used Chinese ironworkers in their conquest of Russia.) Within 14 years of their naval victory over the Song in 1279, the Mongols had impressed Chinese and Korean sailors and vessels to invade Japan, Champa, and Java. Likewise, to neutralize Ming artillery (which had entered from Europe and West Asia via multiple routes), the Manchus developed new siege tactics, used captured prototypes

Turks, and Others, 391–424; *CHC*, vol. VI, 72, 110, 122, 141, 170, 178, 180, 205, 218–19, 234, 261, 449–50, 658–59; Smith, *Taxing Heaven's Storehouse*, 17, 29.
[220] On commercial contributions to Inner Asian and Manchu power c. 1550–1650, Iwai, "China's Frontier Society," 1–20, arguing that such a frontier enterprise would have been possible in no other period; and Kishimoto Mio, "The Ch'ing Dynasty and the East Asian World," *Acta Asiatica* 88 (2005), 87–109. On the Tais in Southeast Asia, *SP*, 122–23, 242–46; Wyatt, *Thailand*, chs. 2, 3; and on South Asia, Ch. 6 *infra*.

to make their own high-quality Western-style cannon, and organized Chinese and Korean artillerymen and cannoneers in specialized corps. By reducing Ming fortifications, pinning down enemy forces, and minimizing Manchu casualties, Chinese specialists and Western armaments transformed a Manchu-Mongol force of mounted archers into a far more flexible military instrument and contributed directly to early Manchu victories.[221]

More subtle, and in the long term critical to Inner Asian success, was their co-optation of Chinese administration. As Di Cosmo's four-stage model of Inner Asian administrative evolution suggests, political evolution among Inner Asians – no less than among Europeans, Southeast Asians, Japanese, or Chinese – had a cumulative, linear character based on long-term trial and error.[222]

During Di Cosmo's first stage (209 B.C.E.–550 C.E.), that of tribute empires, steppe-based nomadic confederations like that of the Xiongnu extorted tribute from sedentary peoples, whether in China or the city-states of the Tarim basin, but tended to avoid direct involvement with those populations. Administrative borrowing was therefore minimal. To be sure, the Sinicizing policies of the Northern Wei Dynasty (386/439–534), which was founded by the Xianbei people from southern Manchuria, adumbrated later developments. Yet because Northern Wei leaders turned their state into a full-fledged Chinese polity, they were unrepresentative of Inner Asian tradition in this period.

In the second stage, that of trade-and-tribute empires (551–907), Inner Asian peoples supplemented tribute with the profits of commerce with China and the Tarim basin. They developed new forms of control over such trade, but because these empires still avoided direct rule over China proper, both their administrative debts to China and their revenue base remained limited. Representative polities in this period included those of the Turks, Tibetans, and Uighurs. The growth of Inner Asian

---

[221] Di Cosmo, "Did Guns Matter?" 121–66; Smith, *Taxing Heaven's Storehouse*, 304; Elvin, *Pattern of the Past*, 18, 87–90; *CIHC*, 138, 168, 172, 221; Geoffrey Parker, *The Military Revolution* (Cambridge, 1988), 83–84, 136–44; Chase, *Firearms*, 141–71; Rossabi, "Ming and Inner Asia," 270–71. As Ch. 4 noted, the Mongols in fact invaded Japan twice, in 1274 and 1281.

[222] Di Cosmo, "State Formation," whose presentation I modify (cf. Ch. 1, n. 131 *supra*); and Honeychurch and Amartuvshin, "States on Horseback." Cf. schemas of Inner Asian development in Perdue, *China Marches West*, 7; Barfield, *Perilous Frontier*, offering a typology distinct from Di Cosmo; *CHEIA*, chs. 11–15; Franke, "Role of the State," 87–112; and Michal Biran, "The Mongol Transformation," in Arnason and Wittrock, *Eurasian Transformations*, 339–61.

influence in North China is suggested by the fact that after the An Lushan revolt of 755, it was Uighurs, determined to maintain Chinese tribute, who intervened to keep the Tang Dynasty alive, while in the late 800s Shatuo Turks from the steppe replaced Uighurs as the dynasty's last prop.[223]

Final Tang collapse in 907 inaugurated the third stage, that of dual-administration empires (907–1259), whose defining feature was the combination of traditional tribal rule over Inner Asian steppe and forest zones with Chinese-style rule over zones of sedentary cultivation. The appeal of Chinese administration was actually twofold. Most obvious, to supplement tribute from the Song Dynasty, Inner Asians in this period began to tax directly Chinese cultivators, which required sophisticated record-keeping. At the same time, centralized bureaucratic institutions provided Inner Asian rulers with a potent weapon in contests with their own fractious aristocracies. In varying degrees the Liao empire (907–1125) of Khitans, the Jin empire (1115–1234) of Jurchens, and the early Mongol empire all adopted Chinese techniques, albeit often through the filter of previous Inner Asian accommodations. In keeping with Barfield's typology, both Khitans and Jurchens rose to power by straddling the frontier; yet it was the Jurchens, no doubt because their Chinese territories were more extensive, who embraced Chinese models most enthusiastically, with Jin government and law in agrarian areas becoming almost indistinguishable from Tang and Song patterns, and with many settled Jurchens adopting Chinese language, dress, and rituals.[224] Whereas non-Chinese regimes of the 3rd to 6th centuries had seized power because civil wars had torn the Chinese state apart, Khitans, Jurchens, and Mongols wrested power from a strong dynasty, the Song, willing to devote vast resources to defense. Thus their triumphs testified to a quantum increase in Inner Asian capacity. Yet, as befit dual administrations, intratribal tensions between Sinicizing and non-Sinicized partisans could be profoundly debilitating. Moreover, no empire in this period exerted sufficient control over Inner Asia to prevent fresh, ultimately fatal military challenges from that quarter: the Liao fell to the Jin, which along with the Xi Xia state of the Tanguts in the northwest fell to the Mongols.

---

[223] *CIHC*, 109–11; Twitchett, "Introduction," 4, 8–9; Perdue, *China Marches West*, 521; Graff, *Medieval Chinese Warfare*, 228–29, 242–43; Carter Vaughn Findley, *The Turks in World History* (Oxford, 2005), 49, 53–54.

[224] See n. 56 *supra*, plus Jing-shen Tao, *The Jurchen in Twelfth-Century China* (Seattle, 1976), chs. 3–6; Mote, *Imperial China*, chs. 9, 10.

In the fourth and final phase of Inner Asian political evolution, that of direct-taxation empires (1260 to 1830 and beyond), revenues extracted from settled peoples completely displaced tribute, the imperial center of gravity moved more deeply into settled areas, while Inner Asia itself was effectively pacified. Attempted with mixed results by the Yuan Dynasty, direct taxation reached its apogee under the Qing. Unlike the Mongols, who were steppe nomads, but in common with their Jurchen ancestors, Manchus practiced a mix of pastoralism, hunting, fishing, agriculture, and trade. Access to Chinese expertise, particularly in the Liaodong area northwest of Korea, allowed them to build an independent state outside Ming control, which, as noted, conferred a critical advantage during the 1640s struggle for power.[225] The Qing shift from tribal to bureaucratic organization required wholesale imitation of Ming administrative practices. But the engine of expansion and the mainstay of Qing power, the military Eight Banner system, was a uniquely Manchu institution. By the mid-1700s, we have seen, Qing military power had joined intensifying trade along the northern frontier, social changes associated with Mongol conversions to Buddhism, and Russian conquests to eliminate once and for all Inner Asian threats to sedentary civilization. Frontier commercialization thus helped the Manchus to seize power within China initially and then to extend their control beyond. Whereas the Ming had sought to protect themselves by building the Great Wall, the Qing effectively abolished it. And whereas the Mongol regime had held all of China for less than a century, Qing rule lasted 267 years. In Di Cosmo's view, the Qing "came very close to achieving a perfect balance" between steppe and sown, conqueror and conquered, social integration and cultural preservation.[226]

Intertwined with administrative evolution was extensive ideological and cultural adaptation. In elite Tang discourse, the opposition between "Chinese" and "barbarian" – as defined by descent, physiognomy, hair, clothing, and political attitudes – tended to fuse culture with ethnicity.[227] After the Tang fell, however, with the help of compliant

---

[225] For contrasts between preconquest Mongol and Manchu understandings of Chinese culture, see Elizabeth Endicott, "The Mongols and China," in Amitai and Biran, *Mongols, Turks, and Others*, 461–81. On early Manchu state organization, Elliott, *Manchu Way*, ch. 1.

[226] Di Cosmo, "State Formation," 37. Cf. Smith, "Introduction," 31; Roth, "Manchu-Chinese Relationship," 1–38; and Perdue's analysis in nn. 63–65 *supra*.

[227] Abramson, "Deep Eyes and High Noses," iii–iv, 444–99, and *passim*, whose physiognomic distinctions parallel those discussed in Mair, "North(west)ern Peoples";

Chinese literati, Khitans and more especially Jurchens worked to dis-
connect historically Chinese culture from Chinese ethnicity. Even as
they and other Inner Asians sought to safeguard their own identity by
creating separate scripts for non-Chinese languages[228] and by erecting
comprehensive ethnic barriers (see below), Jurchens patronized Confucian learning, sponsored civil service examinations, and translated
Confucian classics into their own language. Indeed, the Jin Dynasty
claimed that it, not the Southern Song, was the true heir to the Tang
and the Northern Song. In these ways alien rulers and their Chinese literati supporters sought to give Confucian thought a universal
character, and to treat it as a sign of civilization – not Sinicization.
This separation of dominion from ethnicity, which received further
impetus in the late Yuan and flowered most brilliantly under the
Qing, lay the ideological foundations for successive alien–Chinese dyarchies.[229]

Why was the Inner Asian learning curve, so to speak, easier than that
of the Chinese? Chinese dynasties repeatedly tried to turn the tables,
to co-opt Inner Asian advantages and exploit their weaknesses, for
example, by employing nomadic auxiliaries, playing tribes against one
another, or manipulating trade. Why did these efforts bear such modest fruit? Why did Inner Asians find it easier to master the secrets of
Chinese strength than vice versa? In part, of course, such asymme-
tries reflected the military advantages of steppe and forest ecology, but
more basically, to cite Barfield, it reflected the fact that successful non-
Chinese dynasties, including the Northern Wei, Liao, Jin, and Qing, originated in mixed ecological, commercial, and cultural zones, spanning
sown and steppe or sown and forest. Such zones favored experimental
combinations of Chinese and Inner Asian features and an instinctive

---

Jing-shen Tao, *Two Sons of Heaven* (Tucson, 1988). Tang elites, while acknowledging
that barbarians could develop a "Chinese heart," politicized the Chinese–barbarian
distinction and thus lay the groundwork for Song elite "protonationalist" sentiment.
See too Jonathan Skaff, "Survival in the Frontier Zone," *JWH* 15 (2004), and idem,
"Straddling Steppe and Sown" (Univ. of Michigan, PhD. diss., 1998), arguing that
among Sui–Tang commoners on the Inner Asian frontier, elite categories had limited
resonance and popular identities remained fluid and pragmatic.

[228] These were based variously on Chinese, Syriac, Tibetan, Mongol, and Uighur models.
See n. 93 *supra*.

[229] Franke, "The Chin," 319–20; Fairbank and Goldman, *China*, 115–18; Tao, *The Jurchen*,
chs. 4, 8; Hansen, *Open Empire*, 322–23, 332; Bol, "Seeking Common Ground," 461–538;
Abramson, "Deep Eyes and High Noses," ch. 1; Mote, *Imperial China*, chs. 3–4, 9–12,
17–20.

understanding of both traditions. The Great Wall/North China region was intrinsically multiethnic, multicultural, multilingual. By the same logic, we saw, the most militarily successful post-Han Chinese-led dynasty, with greatest influence in Inner Asia, namely the Tang, was founded by Sino-Xianbei northwest aristocrats who were heir to both Chinese and Inner Asian traditions.[230] On the other side of the ledger, the Mongols, though invincible in the 13th century, proved politically less adroit in China than the Manchus, primarily because the Mongols' strong steppe/Inner Asian orientation left them relatively isolated from Chinese culture. The Southern Song, one could argue, was China's equivalent to the Mongols: based not on the steppe, but in the monoethnic world of watery South China, Song elites also were far removed from the creative Sino-foreign frontier zone. In part, Neo-Confucian literati prejudice against military professionalism reflected this interior orientation.

One must not imagine, however, that increasingly successful Inner Asian efforts to meld cultures, to "civilize" their rule, eliminated ethnic tensions. On the contrary, within China proper we find throughout the second millennium recurrent conflicts between host population and conquest elites without close analogue in the more ethnically unified realms of Eurasia's protected zone.

In general, Chinese attitudes toward outsiders fell into two schools. On the one hand, the "relativist" or "culturalist" school acknowledged that "barbarians" could become "civilized." This inspired efforts at Sinicization of minority peoples in the southwest and gave birth to the supra-ethnic views of Confucianism just discussed, views that led countless Chinese officials to serve alien rulers. (A similar logic induced Vietnamese literati to support the Ming occupation of the early 1400s.[231]) As the refusal of North Chinese to aid an irredentist Song invasion of Jin territories in 1206 showed quite dramatically, pragmatic accommodation, rationalized by "culturalist" views, was the default position for many under alien rule, especially in North China. By diluting Chinese ethnic pride, Confucian universalism, some have claimed, made it

---

[230] The same was true of the preceding Sui Dynasty. "Although the Tang and . . . Sui were not conquest dynasties, their founding elites and much of their ethos were the direct inheritors and in many cases the direct descendants of the ethnically and culturally mixed elites of the first long-lasting conquest dynasty . . . the Northern Wei, and its [non-Chinese dynastic successors]." Abramson, "Deep Eyes and High Noses," 65. Also *CIHC*, 109–11; Di Cosmo, "Review," 503–504.

[231] *SP*, 375–77.

difficult for Chinese to fight off the more ethnically conscious tribal peoples of Inner Asia.[232]

On the other hand, an "exclusivist" school continued to insist that non-Chinese were preternaturally different. When, as during the Song and Ming, independent Chinese leaders felt threatened by Inner Asian power, this outlook could generate stark expressions of alterity. Although it is hard to know how such ideas resonated on the popular level, eminent Song scholars described Inner Asians not as potential members of a Chinese world order, but as implacable threats and sources of contamination. Having their own way or *dao*, their own inner essence, "barbarians" could never hold to civilized standards. The "offensive odor of [their] sheep and goats," one Southern Song writer lamented, had fouled the "pure air" of the North China heartland.[233] Likewise, when debating steppe strategy, anti-accommodationist Ming officials repeatedly used racialist language to warn that Mongols were subhuman "dogs and sheep," "wild animals at heart," whose insatiable appetites and crude natures made them uneducable as well as untrustworthy. Whereas during the more self-confident Tang era substantial elements of foreign music, clothing, art, and furnishings had entered Chinese culture, during the Song and Ming defining and protecting what was distinctly Chinese assumed higher priority. Revitalizing Confucianism was viewed by many Song intellectuals as the surest route to this goal, and the search for a metaphysic that could respond to the Buddhist challenge helped inspire Neo-Confucianism. The fact that Tanguts, Khitans, and Jurchens were all fervent Buddhists only

---

[232] On Chinese accommodations to Inner Asian-led dynasties, Standen, *Unbounded Loyalty*, emphasizing the contingency of post-Tang Chinese reunification and distinguishing fluid, pragmatic, personalized 10th-century notions of political loyalty, in which culture/ethnicity counted for rather little, from later, more culturally and territorially defined attitudes; plus Fairbank and Goldman, *China*, 109–10; Elliott, *Manchu Way*, 22–23, and Waldron, *Great Wall*, 109, 179–81, discussing different approaches to outsiders; Skaff, "Survival," 140–42; John Langlois, Jr., "Introduction," in Langlois, *China Under Mongol Rule*, 11, 17; Yingcong Dai, "To Nourish a Strong Military," *War and Society*: 18 (2000): 75–76.

[233] Writings of Ch'en Liang quoted in Hoyt Tillman, "Proto-Nationalism in Twelfth-Century China?" *HJAS* 39 (1979): 403–28, quote 408. See too Rolf Trauzettel, "Sung Patriotism as a First Step Toward Chinese Nationalism," in J. W. Hager, ed., *Crisis and Prosperity in Sung China* (Tucson, 1975); Ebrey and Gregory, *Religion and Society*, 32–33; Tao, *Two Sons*, chs. 1, 4, 5, 9; Bol, *This Culture*; *SYMT*, 84–86; *CIHC*, 150–54, 179–85; historiography in Pines, "Beasts or Humans," 50–63, incl. nn. 2–12; and Naomi Standen, "(Re)constructing the Frontiers of Tenth-Century North China," in Daniel Power and Naomi Standen, eds., *Frontiers in Question* (New York, 1999), 55–79, discussing the late-10th- to 11th-century turn to ethnic exclusiveness.

underscored Buddhism's alien unsuitability for China in a post-Tang world.[234]

When China came under alien rule, this sense of cultural opposition, reinforced by immediate grievance, targeted the conquerors, albeit more often through caustic comment than practical action. By denying Chinese access to major posts, the Mongols – who were typically illiterate and whose original cultural orientation was toward Inner Asia – and those West Asian intermediaries, many of them Muslim, on whom the Mongols relied for commercial and fiscal expertise, stirred bitter resentment. Chinese complained that Mongols stank so bad that they could be smelled downwind. Muslims, even when they bathed, still reeked, a Yuan-era scholar averred.[235] According to Marco Polo, "All the Cathaians [North Chinese] detested the rule of the great khan because he set over them Tartars [Mongols] or still more frequently Saracens [Muslims], whom they could not endure, for they treated them just like slaves."[236] During the next period of alien rule, that of the Qing, particularly during liminal moments like the White Lotus Rebellion (1796–1804), the Opium War (1840–1842), and the massive Taiping Rebellion (1851–1864), Elliott finds evidence that despite harmonious public accommodations, large numbers of Chinese still rejected the Manchus in essentialized ethnic terms as irremediably alien and illegitimate.[237] Growing their hair long to reject the Manchu-imposed hairstyle,

---

[234] Johnston, *Cultural Realism*, 187, 228, 230, 243–47, quoting racialist Ming diatribes against the Mongols; *SYMT*, 120–22; Millward, *Beyond the Pass*, 36–43; Waldron, *Great Wall*, 179–83; Hansen, *Open Empire*, 371; *CIHC*, 150–54. So too Ming officials could be heard to complain, "They [Mongols] are not of our kind, and their minds are certainly different." Robinson, "Politics, Force and Ethnicity," 85. On Ming attitudes toward Mongols within China, ibid., 79–123; Robinson, *Bandits, Eunuchs*, 32, 61–62, 79, 84, 91, 158.

[235] Fairbank and Goldman, *China*, 122; Lipman, *Familiar Strangers*, 36–37.

[236] Quoted in *CIHC*, 174. On Yuan-era social and ethnic tensions, which could pit southern against northern Chinese as well as against Inner Asians, Endicott-West, "Yuan Government and Society," esp. 610–15; Mote, "Chinese Society," 616–64; Yan-shuan Lao, "Southern Chinese Scholars and Educational Institutions in Early Yuan," in Langlois, *China Under Mongol Rule*, 107–33; John Langlois, "Political Thought in Chin-hua Under Mongol Rule," ibid., 137–85; Morris Rossabi, "The Muslims in the Early Yuan Dynasty," ibid., 257–95; *CIHC*, 174, 182; Biran, "Mongol Transformation," esp. 344–46. Note too that when the Jin fell, Chinese massacred large groups of Jurchens. *CIHC*, 180.

[237] Elliot, *Manchu Way*, 22–35, 168–71, 207–33, 349–50. I have added the White Lotus to Elliott's list. For similar evidence, see Alexander Woodside, "State, Scholars, and Orthodoxy," in Liu, *Orthodoxy in Late Imperial China*, 160, 171; Woodside and Elman, "Afterword," 552–53; *CIHC*, 242; Rowe, *Saving the World*, 294–95; Fairbank and Goldman, *China*, 118, noting Korean reports that while Chinese scholars might hate the

Taiping leaders branded Manchus "barbarian dogs" and "rank foxes," who forced Chinese to wear monkey headdresses and polluted Chinese women.[238] Paranoid Manchu inquisitions against writings ridiculing any non-Chinese dynasty, endemic Manchu versus Chinese factionalism within Qing administration, altercations between Manchu and Chinese troops and between Manchu troops and Chinese civilians (which had no counterpart between Chinese troops and Chinese civilians) – such patterns also point to endemic, if normally manageable, tensions in which ethnicity was not merely a cloak for economic concerns, but a fundamental constituent of identity.[239] According to Susan Naquin and Evelyn Rawski, during the Qing a distinctive "sense of Chineseness," an equation of Chinese culture with civilization and a contempt for non-Han peoples, circulated broadly from officials to peasants.[240]

Manchu leaders, like the Jurchens before them, naturally sought to counter these sentiments by stressing culturalist interpretations of Confucianism and by professing strict impartiality. Chinese and Manchus, they declared, were "one family." Such professions were frequent and, no doubt, heartfelt, for to have forsaken Neo-Confucian legitimacy would have antagonized the literati whose backing was critical to dynastic survival.[241] In reply to anti-Manchu nativist writings, the Yongzheng emperor (r. 1722–1736) himself wrote a text, assigned for study in every county school, which argued that Qing rule embodied the Confucian obligation to spread civilization to all peoples. Only by practicing Confucian benevolence had the Qing won allegiance within and without China.[242] To give concrete expression to the principle of

Manchus, they dared not record those feelings, and ibid., 159–60, 189–90; Chang, *Court on Horseback*, 303, 395–402.

[238] Daphne Pi-Wei Lei, "Envisioning New Borders for the Old China in Late Qing Fiction and Local Drama," in Di Cosmo and Wyatt, *Political Frontiers*, 381. Also Jonathan Spence, *Treason by the Book* (New York, 2001), detailing 1720s anti-Manchu writings, e.g., 7 ("The barbarians are a different species from us, like animals; it is the Chinese who should stay in this land, and the barbarians who should be driven out."), 88–89, 236.

[239] Previous note, plus Elliott, *Manchu Way*, 216–33; Chang, *Court on Horseback*, 433–34.

[240] Naquin and Rawski, *Chinese Society*, 90–91, notwithstanding subethnicities within the Chinese population and the contextual vagaries of ethnicity. See too Mi Chu Wiens, "Anti-Manchu Thought During the Early Ch'ing," *Papers on China* 22A (1969): 1–24; Prasenjit Duara, *Rescuing History from the Nation* (Chicago, 1995), 51–65; Chang, *Court on Horseback*, 435–36.

[241] Elliott, *Manchu Way*, 22–28, 210–16, 346–47.

[242] Perdue, *China Marches West*, 470–76; Spence, *Treason by the Book*, 128–30, 159–60, 221–22.

inclusion, from the start of their anti-Ming offensive the Qing admitted loyal Chinese to positions of trust. Unlike the Yuan, the Qing made civil service examinations, dominated by Chinese, into the centerpiece of personnel recruitment, and conspicuously patronized Chinese literature, art, and high culture. Such studied appeals go far to explain how the Qing enlisted the Chinese gentry to suppress the Taiping and other mid-19th-century rebellions. Also indicative of interethnic accommodation, although surely not official policy, was the pattern whereby most Manchus came to speak and write Chinese better than Manchu and to adopt diverse Chinese traits.[243]

Yet just as the Chinese population displayed contradictory attitudes to foreigners, conquest dynasties had to navigate between conflicting, at times irreconcilable, interests. To abandon Neo-Confucian legitimacy would undermine civil order, but to lower the walls that separated Manchus from indigenes would drown the former in a Chinese sea. During the Qing as during all conquest dynasties, an inescapable logic mandated preferential treatment for the dominant minority. Thus Peter Bol observed of the Jurchen Jin, "[A]s a conquering minority it was clearly in their political interest to remain distinct. In [the Jin state], after all, power and privilege were distributed in the first place along ethnic lines. For the Jurchens to forsake a distinct political identity would have entailed accepting other criteria for the distribution of privileges and threatened the Jurchen elite."[244] Under alien dynasties administration invariably followed ethnic principles, engendering what Herbert Franke has termed "dual and plural systems."[245] In contrast therefore to post-Tang Chinese legal and political systems that tended toward inclusion and uniformity, the Liao, Jin, and Yuan systems codified ethnic divisions so as to preserve the conquerors' privileges. In some contexts the rulers' chief concern was to prevent their own people from assimilating to Chinese culture; in others, to prevent Chinese from

---

[243] On Manchu Sinicization and Manchu–Chinese cooperation, Elliott, *Manchu Way*, 276–304, 339, 342, 346–47, 352; Fairbank and Goldman, *China*, 146–47, 206–16; Chang, *Court on Horseback*, chs. 5, 6; Wong, "Social and Political Construction of Identities," 61–91, esp. 68–69; Mary Wright, *The Last Stand of Chinese Conservatism* (New York, 1969).

[244] Bol, "Seeking Common Ground," 485. See too Elliott, *Manchu Way*, 13, 346–47; Graff, *Medieval Chinese Warfare*, 58–59.

[245] Franke, "Role of the State," esp. 99–104. See too idem "The Chin," 267–77; Dardess, "Shun-ti," 563–66; Endicott-West, "Yuan Government," 610–14; Joseph Fletcher, "Turco-Mongolian Monarchic Tradition in the Ottoman Empire," in Fletcher, *Studies on Chinese and Islamic Inner Asia* (Aldershot, UK, 1997), ch. 7; Graff, *Medieval Chinese Warfare*, 55–59, 72–73.

adopting the conquerors' identity. The Yuan, for example, divided the population into four hereditary categories – in descending rank, Mongols, Western Asians, North Chinese, and South Chinese – each with specific tax obligations, civil and criminal jurisdictions, and rights to office-holding. Albeit with limited success, the Mongols discouraged Chinese–Mongol intermarriage. For their part, the Jin Dynasty sought to prevent Jurchens from adopting Chinese dress or names or speaking Chinese in the palace.[246]

Even under the Qing, which was unusually sympathetic to Chinese interests, although Manchus were but a fraction of 1 percent of the population, they held 38 percent of provincial posts and 58 percent of governor-generalships and governorships in China proper. In Beijing each of the six boards had a Chinese and a Manchu minister, while some 70 percent of all capital officials were Manchus. Within central administration, factionalism often followed ethnic lines, with Chinese on one side of policy issues and Manchus on the other.[247] According to Elliott, all Qing emperors at least to 1796 shared a pervasive mistrust and contempt for the host population. "[W]hat I am saying here is very important: Learned Chinese officials do not want us Manchus to endure a long time," the Kangxi emperor warned fellow Manchus in a 1707 rescript. "[D]o not let yourself be deceived by the Chinese."[248] To prevent acculturation and to maintain the Banners, Manchu women were forbidden to marry Chinese civilians, Manchus received substantial legal, educational, and occupational privileges, and Manchu garrisons followed a pattern of urban residential segregation that has been termed "Manchu apartheid."[249] Likewise, to preserve ethnic solidarity, Qing emperors, like Khubilai Khan before them and indeed the Qing imperial family generally, refused, in theory at least, to take Han

---

[246] Mote, "Chinese Society," 627–38, 644–48; Rossabi, *Khubilai Khan*, 172–73; Hansen, *Open Empire*, 352, 357–58, 365; *CIHC*, 173, 175; Twitchett, "The Liao," 79; Franke, "The Chin," 269–83.

[247] Figures and analysis from Elliott, *Manchu Way*, 217–19; *CIHC*, 224; Hucker, *China's Imperial Past*, 322; Rawski, "Qing Formation," 223–26; Ebrey et al., *East Asia*, 322–23; Bartlett, *Monarchs and Ministers*, 25–31, 37, 64, 208, 254, 260–67. Moreover, Sugiyama, "Ch'ing Empire," 30, cites a 1725 Jesuit account claiming that within the six boards Manchus tended to reduce their Chinese counterparts to mere figureheads.

[248] Elliott, *Manchu Way*, 169. For other expressions of Qing mistrust/disdain toward the Chinese, ibid., 76; Chang, *Court on Horseback*, 105–106.

[249] Wakeman, *Great Enterprise*, vol. I, 476–82; Elliott, *Manchu Way*, 98, 175–209 *passim*, 255. Cf. *CIHC*, 173; Rawski, *Last Emperors*, 130–31. On Manchu–Chinese intermarriage in violation of prohibitions, Wakeman, *Great Enterprise*, 478; Elliott, *Manchu Way*, 254–55, 339, 353, 473 n. 91.

civilian women as concubines or consorts.[250] Most basic, the Eight Banners, the institutional foundation of the dynasty in which all Manchus were enrolled and which provided cradle-to-grave benefits, became ever more exclusively Manchu. Although originally 35 percent of Bannermen were Chinese, the latter were always treated as inferior to their Manchu and Mongol counterparts. And when in the mid-1700s rising costs and a concern to safeguard Manchu ethnicity led the Qing to purge Banner ranks, most men of Chinese origin were expelled. Convinced that Sinicization had vitiated their Jurchen ancestors, the Qing encouraged Bannermen to preserve the "Old Way of the Manchus"; and in fact, recognizably Manchu linguistic, familial, religious, equestrian, toxophilic, and female customs survived, albeit ever less distinctly, to the mid-1800s and beyond. Such institutional and cultural differentiation in the interests of a conquest elite Elliott terms "ethnic sovereignty" and Michael Chang terms "ethno-dynastic rule."[251]

This is certainly not to claim that ethnic tensions vitiated Qing administration. On the contrary, here as in South Asia and Southwest Asia, Inner Asians proved to be the most potent agents of, if not "early modernity," then certainly of pre-1800 integration. If Inner Asians helped to splinter China after the Han, it was, recall, the Mongols who put China together again after the Song. In terms of territorial conquest, internal

---

[250] Rawski, *Last Emperors*, 9, 127–59; Rossabi, *Khubilai Khan*, 174–75; *CIHC*, 173; Chang, *Court on Horseback*, 390–95; Chaffee, *Branches of Heaven*, 274. In fact, Qianlong, for one, violated palace regulations in this regard.

[251] I am esp. grateful to Mark Elliott, pers. commun., Jan. 5, 2008 for his many insights on Qing ethnicity and imperial affairs generally. See his *Manchu Way*, 4–35, 77–78, 89, 117, 168–70, 210–364 (364 has the number of Manchu, Mongol, and Chinese Bannermen); idem, "Ethnicity in the Eight Banners," 27–57. Those non-Manchus remaining in the Banners were subject to steady Manjurification pressures. See too Elliott, "The Limits of Tartary," *JAS* 59 (2000): 603–46, showing how Manchuria gained added prominence as an idealized reservoir of Manchu culture during the 18th-century struggle against assimilation. "Female customs" refers to distinctive hairstyles and avoidance of Chinese-style footbinding. On Manchu–Han ethnic relations, which Michael Chang puts at the center of Qianlong's imperial tours of South China, see his *Court on Horseback*, 8–9, 14–27, 111–12, 119–20, 185–86, 303–304, 356–65, 432–38, and *passim*. Chang differs from Elliott chiefly in that he focuses not on the Banners, but on imperial tours as an ideological strategy to combine ethnic domination with accommodation of Han literati and merchant interests. Cf. Philip Kuhn, *Soulstealers* (Cambridge, MA, 1990), 66–69; and Pamela Crossley, "The Conquest Elite of the Ch'ing Empire," *CHC*, vol. IX, 310–59; idem, "Thinking About Ethnicity in Early Modern China," *LIC* 11 (1990): 1–35; idem, *The Manchus* (Oxford, 1997). In partial opposition to Elliott, Crossley argues that Manchu identity was originally political and relatively weak, but strengthened over time, becoming cultural and finally "ethnic" in the 19th century.

stability, cultural circulation, and economic output, the Qing may have been the world's most successful early modern dynasty. The Manchus' tiny numbers and fear of being overwhelmed seem to have bred an unusual *esprit de corps*, an acute sensitivity to disorder, and a compensatory determination to demonstrate their Confucian *bona fides*. Perhaps because they adhered not to Chinese primogenitural succession, but to the Altaic system of "tanistry," which allowed them to choose the most capable heir, the Manchus also enjoyed a greater share of effective monarchs than the Ming. What is more, to follow Sugiyama Kiyohiko, within the administrative system inherited from the Ming, the early Qing inserted a network of personalized loyalties focused on Manchu grandees that derived from their specifically Inner Asian background.[252] In combination, these features let the Qing revitalize a system that had shown serious signs of exhaustion.

Earlier generations of both Chinese and Western historians, representing what Elliott terms the "Sinicization School," argued that China invariably swallowed its conquerors. In this view, which focuses on processes internal to Chinese society such as gentrification, urbanization, and commercial expansion, the Manchus succeeded only because they became as Chinese as their subjects and availed themselves of China's internal strengths. By contrast, without denying the importance of Sinocentric processes, advocates of the approach I have just outlined, the so-called Altaic School, emphasize that "Manchuness" was as important a feature of Qing rule as "Chineseness" and that, in large part, the Qing succeeded precisely because they were outsiders.[253] With iconoclastic originality, Di Cosmo goes so far as to argue that after c. 1000 Inner Asian-dominated dyarchies in North China grew ever more normative. By these lights, if Mongol and Manchu rule over South China was anomalous, the same may be said of Song and Ming rule in the north.[254]

[252] Sugiyama, "Ch'ing Empire," focusing on parallels to Mongol patterns. On "tanistry" as an eminently practical Altaic legacy, Fletcher, "Turco-Mongolian Monarchic Tradition"; Elliott, *Manchu Way*, 356.

[253] See historiographic discussion at Elliott, *Manchu Way*, 26–35, 355–60; Chang, *Court on Horseback*, 9–10; and Perdue, *China Marches West*, 536–46, the latter contrasting the Altaic and the Eurasian Similarity Theses. See too Kent Guy, "Who Were the Manchus?" *JAS* 61 (2002): 151–64; Millward, *Beyond the Pass*, 13–15; Rawski, "Presidential Address"; and Ping-ti Ho's polemical attack on Rawski, "In Defense of Sinicization," *JAS* 57 (1998): 123–55.

[254] Di Cosmo, "Review," 503–504. See too Mark Elliott's review of *CHC*, vol. VI in *JAS* 55 (1996): 146–49.

But did the relation between Manchus and Chinese differ fundamentally from that between rulers and subjects in realms not subject
to Inner Asian domination? Surely, as Chapter 1 already indicated, one
can find similarities and overlap. Insofar as at various times between
500 and 1100 what are now England, France, and Russia were occupied by Scandinavians (Danes, Vikings, Normans, Rus) and/or Franks,
and the Chaophraya basin in the 13th and 14th centuries became subject to Tai newcomers who at first differed in speech and culture from
their Mon and Khmer subjects,[255] one could attempt comparisons with
Khitans, Jurchens, Mongols, and Manchus. In a later period, on the
periphery of the expanding Romanov and Habsburg empires, the central imperial elite may have appeared no less alien to newly subjugated peoples (Kazakhs, Poles, Ruthenians) than Manchus appeared to
17th-century Chinese. Moreover, even within the Russian core of the
Romanov empire, we have seen that the nobility's wholesale embrace
after c. 1720 of West European culture magnified differences with commoners to the point where nobles and peasants became, in the eyes
of some observers, almost separate peoples. (Pugachev's men, in fact,
accused Peter of being a German, a Swede, or a Muslim in disguise.)
More broadly yet, to the degree that local elites everywhere, including
Japan, used sartorial, linguistic, and deportment markers to distinguish
themselves from subalterns as emphatically as possible, their behavior
could be said to resemble that of Inner Asian conquest elites in China.

And yet differences between China and the protected Eurasian
peripheries remain pronounced. Tai and more especially Germanic and
Scandinavian incursions occurred near the start of our period and thereafter exercised an ever receding influence, whereas in China Inner Asian
incursions intensified from 900 to 1800. In addition, Danes, Vikings,
and Tais entered as dispersed, illiterate bands of warriors ill prepared
to resist assimilation, whereas Inner Asian conquests were coordinated
by elites determined to institutionalize ethnic superiority. In France
and Russia, the two European realms on which I focus, the distinction between Franks and Gallo-Romans, and between Rus and Slavs,
although originally of capital importance, by 1200 had become a faded
memory. The subsequent expansion of European, especially East European, empires to incorporate ethnically distinct minority populations
along their peripheries obviously created tensions, but such situations
differed fundamentally from that in China where a small, nomadic, alien

---

[255] Chs. 1, 2 *supra*, and *SP*, 241–47, 271–74, 313–30.

elite suddenly seized control of a vast imperial heartland and erected systematic barriers between themselves and the ethnic majority core population.[256]

Nor, it follows from this last observation, was the visible distinction, common to all societies, between aristocrats and commoners fully comparable to that between Inner Asians and Chinese. Jurchen, Mongol, and Manchu conquests were known to every Chinese subject and along with garrisons and impositions provided constant reminders of alien domination. Most resented in the Qing period was the demand that all Chinese men adopt as a sign of submission the Manchu custom of shaved foreheads and pigtails.[257] If, to take a protected-zone analogy, post-1587 Japanese sumptuary distinctions between *samurai*, peasants, merchants, outcastes, and so forth shared with Manchu decrees an element of visible coercive demarcation, no one ever regarded *samurai* as foreign to the Japanese body politic. On the contrary, as Chapter 4 argued, the spatial understanding of Japan's place in East Asia became inseparable from the *samurai*-led classification of status groups within the home population. In turn, because weak local networks and miniscule numbers left Inner Asian elites more vulnerable than leaderships of ancient local pedigree, cultural self-segregation assumed a different guise. The Qing promoted Confucian norms among Chinese peasants, and Chinese culture among southwestern tribes. But, apart from a feckless 12th-century experiment with "Jurchen-ization,"[258] neither Khitans, Jurchens, Mongols, nor Manchus *sought to spread their own culture among the Chinese*. (Qing demands that Chinese wear pigtails sought not to convert Chinese into Manchus, rather to make visible

---

[256] To reformulate the problematic: one could argue that the Qing empire, based in modern Manchuria, simply annexed China, which then became an imperial periphery comparable to, say, Polish territories in the Austrian or Russian empire. By these lights, both Polish-speakers and Chinese-speakers became subjugated peripheral ethnicities. But the disproportionality between Chinese, some 97 percent of the Qing imperial population, and Polish-speakers, some 6 percent of the Russian imperial population after the third partition in 1795, is so enormous as to destroy the analogy. Accordingly, the Qing (while retaining a summer capital at Chengde oriented toward Inner Asia) made Beijing their primary residence and administrative center, but no Russian or Austrian ruler ever dreamed of moving his imperial capital to Polish territory. Some of these points I addressed in Ch. 1 in the text preceding n. 151.

[257] Wakeman, *Great Enterprise*, vol. I, 646–50; Jerry Dennerline, *The Chia-ting Loyalists* (New Haven, 1981), 2, 4; Spence, *Treason by the Book*, 90; Elliott, *Manchu Way*, 89, 247, 400 n. 104.

[258] The Jurchens at first sought to impose their costume and hairstyle on the Chinese. Franke and Twitchett, "Introduction," 40; Franke, "The Chin Dynasty," 281.

Chinese subordination to Manchus.) Indeed, Mongols tried to prevent Chinese from learning their tongue, while the Qing court reportedly sought to reserve Manchu for secret military communications.[259] No conquest elite pushed its shamanic or Buddhist practices on the Chinese population. By contrast, in Burma, Siam, Vietnam, France, Russia, and Japan, central officials worked to disseminate their linguistic, ethnic, and religious practices among core commoners, provincial elites, and frontier peoples alike. Ingroup membership in the protected zone thus had an expansive elasticity entirely absent in Qing China. Likewise, whereas the Yuan and Qing proscribed as deeply subversive nativist writings that called for Chinese unity, in protected-zone societies expressions of politicized ethnicity normally enjoyed strong official support because they preached unity of court and people against aliens beyond the frontier. And whereas Chinese Taiping rebels brought a virulent anti-Manchu strain to the Chinese heartland, in Southeast Asia, Russia, France, and Japan revolts preaching ethnic hatred were invariably minority-led frontier phenomena with no purchase in the core.[260] Nor, of course, did Inner Asian systems of ethnically reserved posts in central administration have a protected zone counterpart.

Consider finally not China proper, but the segmented organization of the Qing empire as a whole. In Burma, Siam, Vietnam, Russia, France, and Japan, the core ethnicity's power monopoly ensured that no minority enjoyed comparable prestige;[261] and in every case leaders privileged that culture in dealing with outlying minority peoples. But in Inner Asian empires the same conflicting imperatives as mandated ethnic barriers in China proper required patronage of different cultural traditions within the empire at large. On the one hand, inner Asian rulers could hardly fail to honor the culture of the Chinese, who represented, in the case of the Qing, some 97 percent of their subjects. On the other hand, to promote Chinese culture at the expense of Manchu or Mongol traditions would weaken those military groups on whom the

---

[259] This is the claim at Pamela Crossley and Evelyn Rawski, "A Profile of the Manchu Language in Ch'ing History," *HJAS* 53 (1993): 70–74, 80, and 63–102 *passim*; but Elliott, pers. commun., Jan. 5, 2008 finds such claims "problematic" and notes that Chinese in the Hanlin Academy were required to study Manchu. On language/culture policy under the Qing, see too Elliot, *Manchu Way*, 216–19, 290–304. Under the Mongols, Rossabi, *Khubilai Khan*, 154, 172. Under the Jin, Franke, "The Chin Dynasty," 281–82.

[260] See *SP*, 202–206, 312, 328–29, 412, 431–32; and Chs. 2–4 *supra*.

[261] A partial exception: in Russia, Baltic German culture enjoyed prestige as great as that of Russian, but miniscule numbers rendered Baltic Germans a completely negligible factor in the empire as a whole.

entire imperial project rested. (The latter consideration did not apply in the southwest, where non-Chinese tribesmen offered the Qing little military benefit.)

The Manchu emperor therefore bestrode a realm of multiple constituencies based on regionally distinctive concepts of authority. To each he appeared in a different but equally "authentic" guise. If the emperor sponsored literary compilations, promoted Confucian morality, and wrote refined poetry to the delight of Chinese literati, he also supported shamanism, martial traditions, and Manchu language to preserve the Manchu way; laid claim to the Mongol legacy of Chinggis and Khubilai Khan; and used Yellow-Hat Lamaism to project a model of Buddhist kingship with deep resonance in Tibet and Mongolia.

Much like protected-zone officials, Ming literati reportedly conceived of their empire as a series of concentric circles, with civilization at the center and with outlying zones embodying progressively attenuated versions of true culture. By contrast, Qing rhetoric, ritual, and symbolism envisioned an empire composed of five blocs, "five peoples" (Manchus, Mongols, Tibetans, Muslim Turkic, and Chinese), who existed not in a stark hierarchy, but in a more or less parallel relation. At the center lay neither "Chinese civilization" nor a Confucian "Son of Heaven," merely the Qing imperial house. And whereas the Ming assumed all peoples would inevitably gravitate toward Chinese norms, Qing policies sought, in principle, to maintain boundaries between these five literate peoples, each with their own language, script, laws, and customs.[262] The administrative counterparts to polyethnicity were separate political jurisdictions in Xinjiang, Qinghai, Mongolia, and Tibet. Led by indigenous elites and responsive to local traditions but supervised by

---

[262] I follow Millward, *Beyond the Pass*, 197–203, idem, "Qing Formation, Mongol Legacy"; plus Perdue, *China Marches West*, 122–27, 205–206, 227, 237, 284, 429–42, 459–60, 472–76, 488, 542; Elliott, *Manchu Way*, 4–5; Hay, "Diachronics," 311–15; Rawski, "Presidential Address," 833–36; idem, *Last Emperors*, 6–11, 197–263; Pamela Crossley, "The Rulerships of China," *AHR* 97 (1992): 1468–83; idem, *A Translucent Mirror* (Berkeley, 1999), 221–22, 312, 320–27; Guy, "Who Were the Manchus?" 154–57; Heuschert, "Legal Pluralism," 310–24; Joanna Waley-Cohen, "Religion, War, and Empire-Building in 18th-Century China," *IHR* 20 (1998): 336–52; idem, "Commemorating War in 18th-Century China," *MAS* 30 (1996): 869–99; Ishihama Yumiko, "The Image of Ch'ienlung's Kingship as Seen from the World of Tibetan Buddhism," *Acta Asiatica* 88 (2005): 49–64, noting that Qianlong claimed to be a *cakravartin*, an incarnation of the Bodhisattva Manjusri, and a reincarnation of Khubilai Khan; Elverskog, *Our Great Qing*, analyzing the Qing impact on Mongol self-images. For Sinocentric images of empire as a civilizing influence on ever more distant spheres, see John Fairbank, ed., *The Chinese World Order* (Cambridge, MA, 1968).

imperial residents in Xining, Urga, and Lhasa who in turn were subject to the Court of Colonial Affairs (Lifan Yuan) in Beijing, these administrations remained separate from that of China proper.[263] To protect Manchu livelihood and culture, the Qing forbade Chinese immigration to the northeast. Moreover, although in Xinjiang the Qing sponsored settlement, they structured it in such a way as to reinscribe differences between Chinese, Chinese Muslims, Turkic peoples, Manchus, and Mongols.[264]

Qing rulers may thus be distinguished from Russian tsars who, in theory and practice, upheld Orthodoxy as superior to all other faiths and energetically promoted Russification of the imperial periphery; from Burmese rulers, who were flamboyantly Burman, exclusively Theravadin, and committed to Burman domination of the formerly Mon Irrawaddy delta; from Louis XIV, who was both "most Christian king" and triumphalist patron of a specifically French political culture; even from those Qing partial imitators, the Nguyen of Vietnam, who strove mightily to Vietnamize their Cham and Khmer frontiers. Suffice it to say that Qing segmentation of subject peoples refined an imperial pattern evolving among Inner Asian conquest elites in China since at least the 11th century.[265]

Distinctive Chinese Features: The Burdens of Size

Along with civilizational precocity and waxing Inner Asian influence, China's extraordinary scale also distinguished it from the protected zone. At every stage the Chinese empire was far larger and more populous than its European, Southeast Asian, or Japanese counterparts, with the partial exception of Russia. By 1800, recall, the Qing controlled over

---

[263] Indeed, in the Court of Colonial Affairs Chinese were excluded from positions higher than clerk-translator. On Inner Asian administration, Di Cosmo, "Qing Colonial Administration," 287–309; Perdue, *China Marches West*, 276–86, 310–23, 338–42, and *passim*; Lorge, *War, Politics, and Society*, 59–60; Ning Chia, "The Lifanyuan and the Inner Asian Rituals in the Early Qing," *LIC* 14 (1993): 60–92.

[264] Elliott, *Manchu Way*, 67–68; Perdue, *China Marches West*, 338–52.

[265] On earlier models of imperial segmentation under Inner Asian conquest dynasties, see *CIHC*, 166–69; Twitchett, "The Liao," 76–80, 91–98; Franke, "The Chin," 267–83; Herbert Franke, "Tibetans in Yuan China," in Langlois, *China Under Mongol Rule*, 307; Rossabi, *Khubilai Khan*, 141–76. Yuan rulers, for example, used Chinese writing and historical imagery to appeal to Sinicized subjects, but staunchly defended Mongol traditions, while identifying themselves as *cakravartins* to appeal to Tibetans and many Uighurs.

11,000,000 square kilometers and 320,000,000–350,000,000 people. The Russian empire encompassed 18,000,000 square kilometers, but fewer than an eighth as many people (42,000,000). Russia's population, moreover, was concentrated in a southwestern sector of the empire smaller than China proper, a configuration that – together with the absence of post-1571 military threats from the steppe – meant that Russia faced far less daunting problems of coordination and control than the Qing. The chief Southeast Asian realms in 1800 ranged between 330,000 and 900,000 square kilometers, with modest populations of four to seven million. About 31,000,000 Japanese inhabited some 320,000 square kilometers, while on the eve of the Revolution 28,000,000 Frenchmen held 528,000 square kilometers. In short, even including Russia, protected-zone realms operated on a different scale than China. The most apt scalar comparison is actually the continent of Europe, which in 1800 was both smaller (9,600,000 square kilometers) and far less populous (180,000,000) than the Qing empire.[266]

I have already emphasized those nonpareil cultural assets that helped successive governments hold together so extraordinary a territory and population: a) a precocious bureaucracy that, along with partible inheritance, was inimical to the development of regional power bases, b) a nonalphabetic, logographic script that permitted written communication among literati unable to talk to one another, while inhibiting the expression of regional cultures, c) Confucianism's intensely prescriptive focus on social control and political order, d) civil service examinations, which, together with a standardized curriculum, imbued local literati with expressly supralocal values and ambitions.

These factors, however, hardly exhausted China's integrative advantages. Tortuous though the mountainous geography of western and much of South China surely is, and modest though the North China plain is measured against the North European plain, compared to Europe or mainland Southeast Asia, the overall geography of China proper was reasonably centripetal. Until the railroad, no land-based transport system could rival China's coastal shipping and inland waterways for efficient linkages between large productive spaces. These networks included a mycelium of canals and rivers in the south and four

---

[266] Sources in Figs. 1.8 and 4.2 *supra*; *SP*, 52 n. 70, 420 Fig. 4.2; Janet Hartley, *A Social History of the Russian Empire* (London, 1999), 11–12; Barraclough, *Times Atlas*, 230–31; Lee, "Positive Check," 600, Table 1; Colin McEvedy and Richard Jones, *Atlas of World Population History* (New York, 1980), 18–19.

major east–west rivers – the Yellow, Huai, Yangzi, and West Rivers – the first three of which were traversed by the Grand Canal. Developed during the Sui and Tang, rebuilt and extended by the Yuan to their new capital of Beijing, and renewed under the Ming, by the 1430s the Grand Canal supplied Beijing each year with up to 15,000,000 bushels of rice tax from the lower Yangzi, thus allowing the capital to remain in the north to monitor Inner Asia.[267] If the canal, like cultural assets, was both cause and symptom of integration, the fact remains that China's water systems had no counterpart in Europe, where the Rhine and Danube are less easily joined and drain smaller regions than the Yellow and Yangzi, not to mention in Southeast Asia, where north–south valleys promoted rigid compartmentalization. Water transport also underwrote China's private interregional trade, which in the 18th century boasted a volume considerably larger than that of Europe and captured a greater share of the cereal harvest than in Europe.[268] Moreover, compared to Southeast Asia or especially Europe, China had a remarkably smooth coastline, with few large islands or peninsulas, and a correspondingly low ratio of coast to interior, all of which aided central control. Europe's major islands and peninsulas typically evolved independent languages, ethnicities, and states. To the extent that relative isolation long sheltered them against Chinese invasion, Taiwan and Korea were exceptions proving the rule about China's lack of protected maritime enclaves.

Finally, as we have just seen, the incomparable power of Inner Asian military machines was itself a critical force for unification without European or Southeast Asian analogue. At the same time, because they were more credible, Inner Asian threats seem to have stimulated a pan-Chinese identity, at least among elites, more effectively than Ottoman threats encouraged a pan-European sensibility.[269]

Preventing imperial fragmentation, however, was not the same as preventing political devolution. Over 30 years ago, in essays still widely cited, G. William Skinner explored the devolutionary implications of

[267] English bushels, equal to 5,000,000 Chinese piculs. Reischauer and Fairbank, *East Asia*, 161–63, 201, 333–34; Elvin, *Retreat of the Elephants*, 130; *CIHC*, 114, 116, 119, 175, 194; Hansen, *Open Empire*, 195–96; Lewis, *China Between Empires*, 254–56.

[268] Pomeranz, *Great Divergence*, 34–35, 185 citing Wu Chengming; Rowe, "Domestic Interregional Trade," 178–79 and *passim*; Perkins, *Agricultural Development*, 136; Li, pers. commun., Nov. 1, 2005; Li, "China's National Market." On centripetal Chinese geographic features, see too Diamond, *Guns, Germs, and Steel*, 413–16.

[269] Notwithstanding claims that Confucian universalism impeded Chinese resistance to more ethnically cohesive Inner Asia tribal peoples. See nn. 232–40 *supra*, plus Di Cosmo, *Ancient China*, chs. 3, 7, 8.

size when he noted that although China's population was some seven times larger in 1850 than in 180 C.E., the number of county-level administrative units remained virtually unchanged (1,180 in the heyday of the Han, 1,360 during the Qing). Likewise, there were about 18,000 officially listed posts in the Tang, 20,000 in the Song, and 20,000 in the Qing.[270] This surprising stasis in formal structure Skinner attributed to two iron constraints: a) A multiplication of field administration units on the same scale as the growth of population would have overwhelmed the communication and coordination capacity of the premodern state. Rule making and policy implementation were difficult enough for 1,300 diverse units without moving to a new order of complexity. b) An expansion on that scale would have required such heavy supportive taxation as to depress elite as well as popular living standards and thus spark recurrent revolts. In response to these pressures, the state decided to concentrate resources on the expanding frontier, where strategic threats required close attention, and to consolidate jurisdictions in more secure interior provinces. Thus between the heyday of the Han and that of the Qing, the geographic size of interior counties expanded sharply, and the number of people in each county-level unit rose from 50,000 to well over 300,000. Officials in the imperial core necessarily focused their energies on revenue collection, while delegating substantial authority in spheres of societal management once considered under the government's legitimate purview – firefighting, water control, public works, famine relief, public security, and moral indoctrination – to unremunerated local gentry and merchants. Thus, whereas in early modern Europe responsibility for public services ascended to progressively higher governmental levels,[271] in China it tended to devolve. The retreat from officially administered trade and land redistribution after the 750s Skinner saw as part of this same retrenchment. From the mid-Tang to the end of the imperial era, Skinner concluded, the Chinese state survived only by systematically reducing the scope of basic-level functions and by accepting a secular, irreversible decline in its local effectiveness. Hence the imperial core has been termed "the inhibited political center."[272]

---

[270] Here I follow Li, "Late Imperial Times," 7–8.

[271] E. L. Jones, *The European Miracle* (Cambridge, 1987), 147–48.

[272] Phrase coined by Thomas Metzger and cited in Myers and Wang, "Economic Developments," 591 n. 71 and 572. For G. William Skinner's theses see his "Introduction," and "Cities and the Hierarchy of Local Systems," in Skinner, *The City*, esp. 18–26, 301–46. His interpretation finds varying degrees of support in Li, "Late Imperial Times"; Hartwell, "Demographic, Political, and Social Transformations," 394–405, 425; Rowe,

All accept that official bureaucratic coverage measured against population contracted, but Skinner's conclusion that state influence on the local level declined is open to several objections. First, to recall our discussion of cultural integration, the long-term horizontal extension of imperial culture and ethnicity, and the simultaneous compression of the once enormous divide between elite and peasant norms, provided an element of social cohesion that could compensate to some extent for contracting official coverage. State support for peasant indoctrination and legal reform suggests that policy makers were well aware of the advantages of this "disciplinary revolution."

Second, as a matter of principle, retreat from economic regulation *ipso facto* was hardly a sign of government incapacity, insofar as a similar retreat characterized postmercantilist Europe, where, by any measure, state power increased markedly.

Third, although the total number of officials remained more or less constant from Tang to Qing, internal reorganization enhanced efficiency. A massive increase in written communications – itself a function of printing, cheap paper, wider literacy, and mushrooming commercialization and litigation – strengthened capital–local linkages, while civil service examinations improved professional recruitment and bureaucratic socialization. Whereas the Tang got only 6 to 16 percent of its officials from examinations, the Song recruited on average 30 percent, and the Qing, a sizeable majority.[273] Likewise, the Qing massively codified regulations; rationalized record keeping, tax collections, and accounting; opened more direct communications between the emperor and provincial officials; concentrated powers in the Grand Council; sought to provide more realistic levels of local finance; and appointed assistant and subdeputy magistrates in some counties to improve local coordination.[274]

Fourth, relative stagnation in the overall number of centrally appointed county-level officials masked an increase in the number of

"Approaches," 267–70; Wong, *China Transformed*, 108; Naquin and Rawski, *Chinese Society*, 11, 26, 44–46, 57–58, 150–51, 164–65, 222–29; *SYMT*, 30–34, 122–23; Elman, *Cultural History*, 129–30; Esherick and Rankin, *Chinese Local Elites*, 3ff., 17–24, 44–48; Mann, *Local Merchants*, 12, 23–29, 62; Madeline Zelin, *The Magistrate's Tael* (Berkeley, 1984), 306–308; Fairbank and Goldman, *China*, 105–106; Shepherd, *Statecraft and Political Economy*, 4–5, 422–36; Hucker, *Chinas Imperial Past*, 311.

[273] Notes 24, 32 *supra*; Li, "Late Imperial Times," 7.

[274] See n. 44 *supra*, plus Naquin and Rawski, *Chinese Society*, 6–9, 224, 229–31; Zelin, *Magistrate's Tael*, chs. 3–5.

private secretaries and subbureaucrats responsible to the county magistrate – his so-called "talons and teeth." Although most such employees lacked statutory authority and although their reliance on ill-regulated perks and fees created tension with both magistrates and the public, subbureaucrats possessed technical skills and connections on which local government increasingly relied. Brian McKnight estimates that the average Song county employed 100 to 150 runners, clerks, guards, accountants, and scribes; whereas according to Bradly Reed, a Sichuan county, where 28 runners, lictors, constables, and associated personnel were authorized, actually employed some 400 in the 1880s.[275] A Yangzi delta county c. 1800 was entitled to 230 subbureaucrats, but engaged about 1,000.[276] It is uncertain how typical these unauthorized increases were for Qing counties at large, but clearly subbureaucratic ranks could expand in response to rising administrative demands, which in turn were driven by demographic and commercial growth and the progressive monetization of the tax system.[277]

Fifth, no more than subbureaucrats were local gentry, merchants, and guilds in any basic sense hostile to effective central control. If gentry abuses, particularly as regards taxes, sometimes compromised imperial interests, local elites also cooperated enthusiastically with officials in promoting public works, welfare activities, and Neo-Confucian teachings. Central authorities kept control of local affairs by enforcing rules of avoidance among appointed officials, drawing jurisdictions so as to fragment potential foes, manipulating exams and cherished status symbols, and stressing those elements of education and taste that they and the gentry shared. No less critical, the Qing bought elite support by limiting taxes (see below) and by enforcing landlord rights to garner rents, which in the Yangzi delta represented 30 to 40 percent of annual output.[278]

Sixth, formal structures should not blind us to the often critical role of conjuncture and personality. According to Smith, the declining ratio

[275] McKnight, *Village and Bureaucracy*, 9; Reed, *Talons and Teeth*, 148–49. For similar examples, see ibid., 13–25, 45–75, 144–48, 160 ff., 246–66; Wang, *Land Taxation*, 58; and n. 41 *supra*.
[276] Li Bozhong, "Some Ideas on the Penetration of the State into the Countryside in Imperial China" (ms), 13.
[277] Reed, *Talons and Teeth*, 4, 29.
[278] See Skinner, "Cities and the Hierarchy," 339–44; and Huang, *Peasant Family and Rural Development*, 42, 103; Brenner and Isett, "England's Divergence," 615. But at the same time the state sought to protect smallholders and tenants from falling into servile dependency characteristic of the Ming. Mazumdar, *Sugar and Society*, 211–17.

of officials to subjects joined with alien conquest and Daoxue ideology to encourage a shift in power from throne to gentry that lasted from the Southern Song to the late Ming. But in the 17th century, peasant unrest threw the gentry into the arms of the Ming and Qing; while for their part, early Qing rulers, men of exceptional ability who were fearful of disorder and eager to demonstrate their Confucian credentials, energetically enlisted gentry and merchant support for granaries, schools, and popular Confucianization. In these ways, partially and temporarily at least, politics could transcend the technical limits of bureaucratic size.[279]

However, if we compare China to more manageable protected-zone states, Skinner's larger point surely remains valid. In China, the ratio of subjects to officials appointed and paid by the central government *rose* sharply, from roughly 5,000:1 in 1100, to 9,000:1 in 1600, to 21,750:1 in 1850.[280] By contrast, the ratio *fell* dramatically in Russia from perhaps 5,200:1 in 1560 to 500:1 in 1850; and in France from 1,800:1 in 1560 to 213:1 in 1825.[281] Burma and Siam offer fewer statistics, but the post-1600 conversion of viceregal and tributary posts to appointed governorships and central selection of provincial deputies point in the same direction. Such changes made possible a host of novel interventions, from serfdom and urban controls in Russia, to radical fiscal reforms and the reduction of urban privilege in France, to service expansion in Burma and Siam.[282] In Vietnam the transposition of China's awesome superstructure to a country the size of a single Chinese province produced after 1450 a marked decline in subject-to-official ratios that almost certainly exceeded that anywhere else in the mainland, and that duplicated the experience of China itself during the Age of Division, when small successor states, suddenly freed from the crushing weight of subcontinental coordination, multiplied county units.[283] In Japan too I have called attention to

[279] On shifting gentry–state relations and local governance, nn. 39–43 *supra*, plus Smith, "Introduction," 32–34; idem, "Eurasian Transformations," 302–308; Wong, *China Transformed*, chs. 4–6; Zelin, *Magistrate's Tael*; William Rowe, "The Public Sphere in Modern China," *Modern China* 16 (1990): 309–29.

[280] Assuming 20,000 officials for 100,000,000 subjects in 1100, for 180,000,000 in 1600, and for 435,000,000 in 1850. See nn. 159, 166, 270, 272 *supra*; Lee et al., "Positive Check," 600, Table 1; McEvedy and Jones, *Atlas*, 166.

[281] See *supra* Ch. 2, nn. 219, 250, 321; Ch. 3, nn. 75, 240, plus McEvedy and Jones, *Atlas*, 79, 157–63; Walter Pintner and Don Rowney, eds., *Russian Officialdom* (Chapel Hill, 1980), 192.

[282] Chs. 2, 3 *supra*, plus SP, 158–64, 185–86, 278–82, 302–13.

[283] See SP, ch. 4; Alexander Woodside, *Vietnam and the Chinese Model* (Cambridge, MA, 1971), 141–52, arguing that Vietnamese administration was more finely grained than

the innovative, closely woven texture of *daimyo* administrations and the Tokugawa system that built upon them.

What about the centralizing implications, then, of China's subbureaucratic expansion and gentry activism? We do not know if subbureaucrats increased as quickly as the general population. But even if they did, as men who were hired locally rather than by the central government, who generally lacked a classical education, and who lived primarily by irregular fees and perks, they were poorly socialized to official culture, weakly responsive to central direction – and routinely vilified by their superiors as greedy vermin. To be sure, clerks and runners sought to safeguard their livelihood by developing their own rationalized procedures and by claiming, especially in the case of clerks, a modicum of Confucian honor. But because their operations often had little or no legal authority and as such remained hidden from imperial view, there developed an entire system of local government about which central officials had only a vague knowledge and over which they exercised even less practical control or policy direction. Such a system could compensate for contracting official coverage to only a limited degree.[284]

Much the same may be said of the benefits that derived from gentry and merchant cooperation with the state, benefits that, though real enough, remained circumscribed by self-interest and local loyalties. In the late Ming period, gentry tax evasion through false land registration, passive resistance, and irregular practices of all sorts, aided by officials and subbureaucrats, contributed to Ming collapse.[285] Notwithstanding initially strengthened central control under the Qing, in the 1660s and again in the late 1700s Qing efforts to obtain accurate acreage information also faltered before resistance by local elites, subbureaucrats, and officials. Without a vastly expanded bureaucracy, sustained reform was impossible. Or to restate the problem, insofar as Qing–gentry

that of either China or Indic Southeast Asia; and Skinner, "Introduction," 21, discussing Age of Division administrative proliferation.

[284] Reed, *Talons and Teeth*, 4, 17, 22, 70–77, 159, 192, and chs. 1–2, 4–7 *passim*; Wang, *Land Taxation*, 131; Zelin, *Magistrate's Tael*, 223–30, 239–48, 257–61, 306–307.

[285] Huang, "Fiscal Administration," 73–128; idem, "The Ming Fiscal Administration," 110–13, 148–71, arguing that concessions to gentry power in the early Ming proved impossible to reverse later; Goldstone, *Revolution and Rebellion*, 368–71; N. Tsurumi, "Rural Control in the Ming Dynasty," in Grove and Daniels, *State and Society in China*, 245–77; and the case study by Beattie, "Alternative to Resistance," 241–50.

cooperation relied more on royal initiatives than institutional change, such cooperation remained hostage to dynastic vigor.[286]

In fact, during the late 1700s and early 1800s declining imperial ambition joined economic growth to abrade the social fabric and over-strain state capacities. Population pressure and unprecedented market dependence increased peasant vulnerability to natural disaster at the same time as novel fiscal deficits – the result of administrative rigidity, domestic revolts, long-term price inflation, and accelerating declines in real per capita income – left the state less able to deal with flood control and famine.[287] Thus, whereas from 1736 to 1780 the Qing had developed an exceptionally ambitious network of state granaries, in the 1780s and 1790s popular demand began to exceed organizational capacity. Without abandoning state granaries entirely, the Qing shifted to encourage community and charity granaries under private control. Originally these were subject to official monitoring, but in the course of the 19th century even this ceased. Nothing could better illustrate Qing difficulties in building stable institutions below the county level.[288] Like-wise, whereas the early and mid-1700s saw intensified efforts to con-trol local finances and to police local culture, often to the benefit of North over South China, from the turn of the next century – two gen-erations before the Taiping revolt, which is often seen as precipitating Qing decline – bureaucratic strains joined financial deficits to force a volte-face. After 1800 the Qing was obliged to reward more members of the rich southern elite for contributions to infrastructure and philan-thropies and to devolve authority over water conservancy, schools, and

---

[286] "[S]o long as tax collections remained the purview of clerks and runners, so long as local gentry and wealthy households held a monopoly of [local] power . . . so long as communications remained poor . . . the ability of the imperial government to institute rationalizing reforms would always be limited." Zelin, *Magistrate's Tael*, 261–62. Thus registered taxable land remained flat from 1753 to 1910, even though real acreage rose an estimated 33 percent. Perdue, *China Marches West*, 337. See too Wang, *Land Taxation*, 26–28, 53; Huang, "Fiscal Administration," 122; Fairbank and Goldman, *China*, 150; *CHC*, vol. IX, 114, 382, 594; Mazumdar, *Sugar and Society*, 214; Beattie, "Alternative to Resistance," 241–42, 263–66; Wills, *Mountain of Fame*, 239–41.

[287] See nn. 185–88 *supra*; Allen, "Agricultural Productivity," 13, 15; Wang, *Land Taxation*, chs. 2, 3; Han, "Re-inventing Local Tradition," ch. 1; Will, *Bureaucracy and Famine*, 269–318; Naquin and Rawski, *Chinese Society*, 219–24. On 18th-century inflation, in the order of 200–300 percent, Zelin, *Magistrate's Tael*, 297–98; Naquin and Rawski, *Chinese Society*, 222.

[288] Will and Wong, *Nourish the People*, esp. 40–42, 69–98; Will, *Bureaucracy and Famine*, 314–17.

dispute mediation to those same elites. Perforce, the Qing relaxed its hold on distinctively southern cultural expressions, as shown, for example, by an increase in the number of enshrined local worthies. In major cities as well, merchants assumed responsibility for hitherto public functions. Resembling in some ways late Ming conditions, the new relation between state and local society again underlined systemic constraints on Qing activism – constraints now reinforced by rapid demographic and commercial growth.[289]

More dramatically indicative of popular distress and government limitation, however, was a series of revolts that between them spanned the better part of a century, including tribal revolts in the southwest, the White Lotus revolt of 1796 to 1804, a Xinjiang rebellion from 1826 to 1835, the great Taiping movement, which convulsed much of South China from 1851 to 1864; the Nien rebellion in North China of 1851 to 1863; and Muslim revolts in the northwest and southwest from 1855 to 1874. With few exceptions, these uprisings – which between them claimed an estimated 60,000,000 (sic) lives[290] – began either on imperial frontiers or in inaccessible, mountainous interior regions, areas of immigration and social instability where imperial authority and cultural orthodoxy were weakest and ethnic and religious minorities, most numerous.[291] Again this points to problems of administrative overextension and inadequate frontier integration that we simply do not see after 1800, certainly not to the same degree, in more easily policed, less populous realms like France, Russia, Japan, Burma, and Siam.

Although the problem of China's 19th-century collapse lies beyond the scope of this book, one senses from this litany of upheavals that some of the same trends as encouraged integration to c. 1820 contributed to subsequent difficulties.[292] Frontier reclamation and rapid population

---

[289] Han, "Re-inventing Local Tradition," esp. chs. 1–3; Naquin and Rawski, *Chinese Society*, 228–29, discussing the rapid shift to private management; William Rowe, *Hankow: Conflict and Community in a Chinese City, 1796–1895* (Stanford, 1989), pt. 2.

[290] Fairbank and Goldman, *China*, 216.

[291] Of course, these were the preferred sites for revolt from Han Dynasty rebellions to the 1940s Communist insurgency. See Fairbank and Goldman, *China*, chs. 9, 10; Naquin and Rawski, *Chinese Society*, 226–28; Philip Kuhn, *Rebellion and Its Enemies in Late Imperial China* (Cambridge, MA, 1970), 6, 9, 38–39, 106–22; Elizabeth Perry, *Rebels and Revolutionaries in North China, 1845–1945* (Stanford, 1980), 7–21, 62, 96–151; Jen Yu-wen, *The Taiping Revolutionary Movement* (New Haven, 1973), 21, 30–58, 63 *passim*; Susan Naquin, *Millenarian Rebellion in China* (New Haven, 1976).

[292] My views have benefited from exchanges with Peter Perdue, 2007.

growth, while aiding imperial expansion, also created ecological strains and ethnic conflicts, particularly on the periphery. Rising literacy and commercialization favored cultural circulation, but those very forces empowered local elites and stoked demands for wider participation in decision making. And as social conditions deteriorated, Manchu ethnic separation, initially a source of strength, left them vulnerable to Chinese racial attacks.

Distinctive Chinese Features: Modest Fiscal and Military Imperatives

Remarkable size and population help to explain, directly and indirectly, a fourth, closely related distinction between China and protected-zone societies in Europe and Southeast Asia (this distinction applies less well to Japan): Chinese governments tended to be less interested in fiscal maximization.

Virtually every major administrative reform between c. 1400 and 1830 in Burma, Siam, Vietnam, Russia, and France sought to enhance the state's military strength by improving resource extraction. This objective explains in Burma and Siam the overhaul of *ahmu-dan* and *phrai luang* service in the 16th and 17th centuries; in Vietnam, the regularization of land taxes under the early Le and the turn to maritime revenues under the Nguyen; in Russia, the late-15th-century *pomest'e* system followed by 17th-century serfdom and Petrine reforms; in France, the start of regular taxation during the Hundred Years War, the 16th-century growth of venality, and the subsequent turn to tax farming and universal taxation. In Japan too, although more episodic, military pressures inspired Warring States and early Tokugawa cadastral surveys and village reorganization.

In China, to be sure, some regimes also put great store on improving tax yields. Yet to a degree extraordinary by Burmese, Russian, or French standards, especially between c. 1368 and 1840, most Chinese governments were satisfied with only a modest income. Because early Ming land registers were not regularly updated to fix new tax quotas, the amount that most districts paid in the 1390s remained the basis for all subsequent exactions, even though population and cultivated acreage grew dramatically thereafter, and military expenses rose sharply. By the second quarter of the 15th century the Ming already had lost much of its ability to collect revenues, and authorized collections were appreciably smaller than those of the Song 400 years earlier.[293] After consolidating control, the new Qing government granted such lavish tax remissions that by 1711 those grants exceeded the central government's total annual revenue. The Kangxi emperor, in effect duplicating early Ming policy, magnanimously decreed in 1713 that commuted corvée tax quotas should remain frozen "in perpetuity." In combination with a decision not to update Ming cadastres, with permanent exemption for newly reclaimed land, and with widespread tax evasion, this ensured that the Qing too would derive minimal benefit from very substantial increases in population and arable. Nor, in contrast to Europe, did the Qing raise taxes sharply on trade, resort to large-scale loans, or initiate centralized tax farming.[294] Although, given available data, the following terms of comparison are not fully equivalent, best estimates are that during the second half of the 18th century imperial taxes captured only 5 percent of the gross national product in China,[295] compared to 12–15 percent in Russia, 9–13 percent of national commodity production in France, and 16–24 percent of national commodity production in Britain.[296] During the 18th century in Russia, moreover, corvées and

---

[293] Note 285 *supra*, esp. Huang, "Fiscal Administration," 86; plus Hansen, *Open Empire*, 374–75; Ebrey, pers. commun., April 10, 2007; Huang, "The Ming Fiscal Administration," 107–11, 126–48, noting that the Ming founder in 1385 had regional land tax quotas inscribed in stone to establish a permanent ceiling. Moreover, salt monopoly aside, Ming domestic and foreign trade was taxed lightly, if at all.

[294] See nn. 49, 286 *supra*, plus Wong, *China Transformed*, 133–34, noting that domestic transit taxes in 1766 accounted for only 11 percent of total revenues; Wang, *Land Taxation*, 10, 29–35, 42, 47, 53, 131, discussing the long-term implementation of Kangxi's decree; Naquin and Rawski, *Chinese Society*, 22, 150, 218–22; Rowe, *Saving the World*, 47, 159; Mann, *Local Merchants*, 43; Goldstone, *Revolution and Rebellion*, 395; Myers and Wang, "Economic Developments," 594–96; Han, "Re-inventing Local Tradition," 22, 57–59, 69.

[295] Naquin and Rawski, *Chinese Society*, 219 ("There is no doubt...that the tax structure...garnered less than 5 percent of the gross national product"); Albert Feuerwerker, "State and Economy in Late Imperial China," *Theory and Society* 13 (1984): 298–307 (4–8 percent); P. H. H. Vries, "Governing Growth," *JWH* 13 (2002): 95 ("about five percent"); Frederic Wakeman, Jr., "China and the Seventeenth-Century Crisis," *LIC* 7 (1986): 21 ("less than six percent" in the late 1800s, including new customs revenues); Fairbank and Goldman, *China*, 150 (both Ming and Qing collected "less than five percent of the gross national product"). See too Mote, *Imperial China*, 908; Immanuel Hsu, *The Rise of Modern China* (6th ed., Oxford, 2000), 59–73; Wang, *Land Taxation*, chs. 1–4; and Rawski, "Qing Formation," 213–18, whose best case for Qing tax increases is rather threadbare.

[296] For Russia, see Arcadius Kahan, *The Plow, the Hammer, and the Knout* (Chicago, 1985), 345 (national taxes "did not exceed" 12–15 percent of per capita income for Russia c. 1720–1800; presumably aggregate per capita income approximated GNP), and

military service were far more onerous than in China, where most labor services had been commuted. If we consider that under the Northern Song in 1080, imperial revenue averaged about 13 percent of national income, and under the Ming in 1550 6–8 percent, we find some support for Skinner's thesis that percentage of the surplus captured in imperial taxes shrank steadily relative to the share retained by local systems.[297]

Why, then, this peculiarly low-tax Chinese regime? Three explanations, by no means mutually exclusive, merit attention. First, successive governments expressed a philosophical commitment to low taxes, in part, as James Lee points out, because early governments relied more on labor than material appropriation,[298] but most basically because, long after corvées had been commuted, Neo-Confucian thought and economic theory alike argued that the government should limits its appetites and that low taxes were indispensable to agrarian prosperity. As an inherently moral institution, the Confucian state was committed

Richard Hellie, "The Costs of Muscovite Military Defense and Expansion," in Eric Lohr and Marshall Poe, eds., *The Military and Society in Russia 1450–1917* (Leiden, 2002), 66 (approximately 12.5 percent of GNP in the 1650s was used to pay for the army alone). British and French figures, which derive from Peter Mathias and Patrick O'Brien, "Taxation in Britain and France, 1715–1810," *JEEH* 5 (1976): 601–50, esp. 607–609, represent the share of commodity output taken as taxes c. 1750–1800. In Britain this figure rose to a whopping 35 percent in 1803–1812. I assume that if services and taxes on services were factored in, ratios of taxes to output would approximate taxes on commodity output alone, but for every country save Britain we have either no statistics or inadequate statistics on the service sector. See too Ch. 3, n. 145 *supra*; Francois Crouzet, *La Grande Inflation* (Paris, 1993), 60; Vries, "Governing Growth," 94–95; John Brewer, *The Sinews of Power* (Cambridge, MA, 1988), 91; Philip Hoffman and Kathryn Norberg, eds., *Fiscal Crises, Liberty, and Representative Government 1450–1789* (Stanford, 1994), 299–302. For Southeast Asia we lack statistics on either total tax yields or national income. For Japan, comparisons are also difficult because *bakuhan* levies included both taxes and (what had been) rents, and because commercial wealth was excluded from gross rural product; but several sources suggest that a pacific environment, rapid commercial expansion, and late Tokugawa inertia allowed effective tax rates on rural incomes (very different, of course, from taxes on crop yields) to fall notably, to something in the range of 20–30 percent. Ch. 4, nn. 253, 283; Penelope Francks, *Rural Economic Development in Japan* (London, 2006), 45–47, 79 ff.; Philip Brown, pers. commun., Nov. 13, 2006. Given that Yangzi delta private rents were only 30-40 percent of the crop (n. 278 *supra*) and that tenantry was far less common in North than in South China, supralocal extraction by Qing and Tokugawa elites – both largely exempt from military fiscal pressures – would seem to have been comparably modest.

[297] Feuerwerker, "State and Economy," 300; Skinner, *The City*, 20–21, 29; Vries, "Governing Growth," 94–95; Huang, 'The Ming Fiscal Administration," 107, 113, 124, 134 (the Ming land tax, including commuted labor services, averaged only 5–10 percent of the crop), 138, 144–48, 166.

[298] Lee, *One Quarter of Humanity*, 128.

not only to realize the full potential of China's resources, but to leave the ensuing surplus as much as possible in societal rather than government hands – as expressed in the formula "storing wealth among the people"(*cang fu yu min*). Thus light taxation became a golden canon, and conscientious officials equated the Confucian admonition to "benevolent governance" with low fiscal demands.[299]

A second explanation for low taxation, however, surely must be that statesmen could afford the moral luxury of fiscal restraint – and such restraint could become a cultural icon – more easily than in Southeast Asia or Europe because Chinese rulers faced less sustained external threats. Ultimately this too was a function of size: When China was unified, the isolation that accompanied subcontinental dominion conferred a *relative* freedom from military pressure. That is to say, for long periods the Chinese state, unlike its Southeast Asian and European contemporaries, did not participate in a multistate system, composed of units of comparable size and strength, in which extinction was a live possibility and in which success could be purchased only by continuous imitative improvements in fiscal and military organization.

Admittedly, as much recent scholarship insists, China's exemption from military pressures was hardly absolute.[300] The Age of Division saw rivalries between more or less coherent states eager to buttress themselves through ambitious military and tax reforms. Thus the Sino-foreign Northern Wei Dynasty asserted its power to assign land and expand cultivation by initiating the aforementioned "equal-field" system, while the Northern Zhou created *fubing* militias to encourage professionalism while holding down military costs. Both institutions flourished into the early Tang.[301] Competition among regional successor states also characterized the period between the fall of the Tang and the

---

[299] Rowe, "Domestic Interregional Trade," 185; idem, *Saving the World*, 331–32, plus 46–47, 159, 170–73, 189–91, 222, 347–48, 365–67, 448; Dunstan, *State or Merchant*; Wang, *Land Taxation*, 28–29; Bol, *This Culture*, ch. 9; Zelin, *Magistrate's Tael*, 113.

[300] For literature emphasizing military demands and values, see Perdue, *China Marches West*; Lorge, *War, Politics and Society*; idem, ed., *Warfare in China to 1600* (Aldershot, UK, 2005); idem, "The Northern Song Military Aristocracy and the Royal Family," *War and Society* 18 (2000): 37–47; Jonathan Skaff, "Barbarians at the Gate?" ibid., 23–35; Kenneth Swope, "Civil-Military Coordination in the Bozhou Campaign of the Wanli Era," ibid., 49–70; Dai, "To Nourish a Strong Military," 71–91; Graff, *Medieval Chinese Warfare*; Johnston, *Cultural Realism*; Joanna Waley-Cohen, "Changing Spaces of Empire in 18th-Century Qing China," in Di Cosmo and Wyatt, *Political Frontiers*, 324–50; idem, "Commemorating War."

[301] Twitchett, *Financial Administration*, 1–17; CIHC, 92; Graff, *Medieval Chinese Warfare*, 12–14, 109–11, 140, 189–247 *passim*; and nn. 26, 137 *supra*.

founding of the Song, while the Song Dynasty repeatedly found itself on the defensive against northern polities, first the Xi Xia and Liao, then the Jin – with whom Song diplomats signed a humiliating 1141 treaty referring to their own as "an insignificant state" and to the Jin as a "superior state"[302] – and finally the Mongols. Not unlike the interstate system of early modern Europe, that of the Song era was replete with treaties, formal borders, alliances, military preparation, and an incessant search for military revenues.[303] To support an army of 1,250,000 soldiers, whose iron weapons were forged in large-scale government arsenals and who in 1065 consumed 83 percent of state cash income,[304] the Northern Song initiated commercial monopolies, encouraged maritime trade, and succeeded, as noted, in garnering some 13 percent of national income. The bitter debate between those supporting and opposing Wang Anshi's New Policies, a debate that dominated the last half-century of the Northern Song, focused on the most practical way to mobilize Chinese resources so as to reconquer northern areas lost to the Xi Xia and Liao.[305]

The main point, however, is that these sort of existential threats and military imperatives were not typical of other, rather longer phases of imperial history. During the middle Han period Xiongnu incursions contributed to the eclipse of universal conscript infantries in favor of increasingly professional standing frontier armies. But by 100 C.E. the latter had helped to collapse Xiongnu power, after which threats by Inner Asian military confederacies became marginal to Later Han history and to final Han disintegration.[306] In some ways Tang military

---

[302] Franke, "The Chin," 234; Hansen, *Open Empire*, 318. On Song military preparation, fiscal policies, and interstate rivalries, ibid., 264–72, 306–309, 313–33; Graff, *Medieval Chinese Warfare*, 239–47; Lorge, *War, Politics and Society*, chs. 1–3; Tao, *Two Sons*; and n. 56 *supra*.

[303] Morris Rossabi, ed., *China Among Equals* (Berkeley, 1983). Cf. Hui, *War and State Formation*, chs. 2, 3, comparing China during the Warring States period of the mid- and late first millennium B.C.E. to early modern Europe.

[304] Hansen, *Open Empire*, 269.

[305] Ibid., 269–72; Bol, *This Culture*, 212–53; Smith, "Eurasian Transformation," 292–99; idem, *Taxing Heaven's Storehouse*; von Glahn, "Revisiting the Song Monetary Revolution," 167, 174, 177.

[306] On the other hand, localized revolts by "barbarians" like the Qiang, who had been settled *within* the empire to strengthen its western defenses, posed major headaches for the Later Han. See esp. Lewis, *Early Chinese Empires*, 26, 129–51, 253–64; idem, *China Between Empires*, 31–33, 150–51; plus Graff, *Medieval Chinese Warfare*, 11, 26–31; *CIHC*, 66–75, 84–85; Yu, "Han Foreign Relations," 377–405, 422–35; and n. 4 *supra*.

history recapitulated that of the Han. From the late 600s external pressures, by Tibetans, Eastern Turks, and Khitans, obliged the Tang to downgrade militias in favor of more full-time professional armies on the frontiers, which created conditions for An Lushan's revolt. But although to the mid-800s Tibetans and Uighurs continued to capitalize on Tang difficulties, the first to seize western lands, the second to demand heavy subsidies, neither group contributed directly to Tang collapse, whose dynamics were primarily domestic.[307]

If military pressures from beyond China proper had limited import for Han and Tang, they were yet less relevant to the political economy of the Yuan, which dominated Mongolia, Manchuria, and Tibet, and which lost China proper, I suggested, because Mongol ties to local society were excessively shallow.

What is true of military pressures under the Yuan applies substantially to the Qing as well. To be sure, as Perdue has shown, from their initial campaigns of conquest, through their 1690–1759 victories in Zungharia and Muslim Xinjiang, to later police actions around the imperial periphery, Qing military mobilization had broad impact: the fiscal system, the bureaucracy, state granaries, commercial networks, and agrarian societies in the northwest all were affected. Manchu leaders, in particular the Qianlong emperor, never tired of flooding China with memorials to their military exploits, which he hoped would "stiffen the sinews" of flaccid Chinese culture.[308]

Yet Qing military patterns differed from those in Russia and France, our European exemplars, and in mainland Southeast Asia in critical respects: a) As Perdue observed, Qing military mobilization effectively ended in the mid-1700s, by which time no credible Inner Asian authority remained beyond imperial control.[309] By contrast, European and Southeast Asian warfare intensified to 1815 and 1847, respectively. b) After the main stage of their conquest of China was complete in 1650, the Qing, notwithstanding Russian skirmishes along the Amur, never faced a sustained enemy remotely comparable to themselves in resources or organization. The Zunghars, whose leaders aspired to unite the

---

[307] See n. 7 *supra*, plus Somers, "End of the T'ang," 682–789. Nanzhao attacks 829–875 were also more symptom than cause of imperial debility.

[308] See Perdue, *China Marches West*, 426, 442–43, 518–51, 564–65; Waley-Cohen, "Commemorating War"; idem, "Military Ritual and the Qing Empire," in Nicola Di Cosmo, ed., *Warfare in Inner Asian History* (Leiden, 2002), 405–44; Chang, *Court on Horseback*, 216.

[309] Perdue, *China Marches West*, 526–27.

Mongols and who humiliated a Qing army, remained a threat for a relatively brief period from the late 1670s to the early 1730s. By and large they were a serious, but not deadly rival, protected chiefly by their inaccessibility, and thus distinct from the threats that the Hapsburgs and Britain posed to France for generations, Burma posed to Siam for 250 years, and Siam presented to Vietnam.[310] If, as fellow conquerors of Inner Asia, Romanov Russia and Qing China resembled one another, their overall strategic situations would have been truly comparable only had Russia lacked a western military frontier. From 1478 to 1945, Russian history was shaped by pressures not from the steppe, but Europe. By contrast, until the Opium War of 1840–1842, China knew no sustained European threat. c) Because Qing China faced no major competitor, war exerted only limited pressure on the political economy. Between 1736 and 1784, a period of relatively heavy military activity, an initial Qing treasury surplus of 24,000,000 *taels* actually tripled, permitting the government to sustain a tax policy whose utter insouciance could not be more different from the grim determination of wartime Southeast Asian, Russian, and French leaders to capture every ounce of silver and every recruit.[311] As Rowe concludes, "Eighteenth-century China faced few of the war-related fiscal pressures of contemporary Europe, and the prevailing political situation, Confucian ideology, and economic theory all combined to dictate that state financial comfort be translated as fully as possible into a policy of low taxation."[312] Of the realms under review, China's relaxed strategic and fiscal posture 1650–1840 resembled most closely that of Japan, where effective Tokugawa rates also declined.[313]

But the third explanation for low taxation in post-1400 China must be that even when necessity dictated, extraction beyond some 6 to 8 percent of national wealth was beyond the state's political and technical capacity. Here Ming experience is instructive. Facing no critical threat until its last decades, the Ming felt it could operate, in Ray Huang's

---

[310] Ibid., 133–299, esp. 223, 225, 209, 254–55, plus 463; Perdue, pers. commun., Aug. 11, 2008. On confrontations with Russian forces, Perdue, *China Marches West*, 138, 166, 169.

[311] Naquin and Rawski, *Chinese Society*, 219 and nn. 293, 294 *supra*. The first Zunghar campaign of 1690 cost only 6 percent of treasury holdings for a year. Perdue, *China Marches West*, 161. Some of Qianlong's so-called Ten Complete Military Victories were little more than self-indulgent vainglory, as Waley-Cohen, "Commemorating War" concedes.

[312] Rowe, *Saving the World*, 159; also 332.

[313] See Ch. 4, n. 283 *supra*.

words, "on a non-competitive basis," which meant that "[t]here was no need to take administrative efficiency seriously."[314] In fact, however, the dynasty, as we saw, remained vulnerable to Inner Asian pressure and was forced after 1450 to move to a defensive posture centered on Great Wall fortifications. Defense already was taking 60 to 70 percent of government outlays by the 1570s,[315] after which war with Japan in Korea, domestic revolts, royal clan expenses, inflation, a shift from hereditary to paid military service,[316] and Manchu attacks only aggravated Ming financial woes. Yet the Ming still failed to execute a new national land survey or to pursue systematic fiscal reform. This inertia reflected ideological bias, a chaotic fiscal structure, too few local personnel – plus a fear that major tax increases would ignite opposition from small and large landowners alike.[317] By the early 1600s a sizeable surplus had become a yawning deficit. With military pay months in arrears and Manchu attacks ever more menacing, from 1618 to 1639 the court finally imposed a series of land tax surcharges. But these efforts too faltered through inefficiency, corruption, and local opposition that the state proved powerless to break. If on paper the new taxes took 10–15 percent of the yield, by the 1640s not even half of that was being collected. Revenue shortfalls starved not only the army, but water control projects, intensifying popular unrest. In short, even when raising taxes became a matter of dynastic survival, the Ming proved politically and organizationally incapable of doing so beyond a modest level.[318]

Much the same may be said of the late Qing, which like the Ming some two centuries earlier, moved from revenue surplus in the 1780s to deficit because of rising military costs (in this case, chiefly to suppress domestic revolts), long-term inflation, post-1840 Western indemnities,

---

[314] Huang, "The Ming Fiscal Administration," 165.

[315] Johnston, *Cultural Realism*, 235. Pirates on the southeast coast also had become a problem. Discussion of Ming military and fiscal woes follows ibid., 183–86, 227–50; Ray Huang, *1587: A Year of No Significance* (New Haven, 1981), 61–63, 89–91, 134, 143–45; idem, "Fiscal Administration"; idem, "The Ming Fiscal Administration," 148–71; Hansen, *Open Empire*, 374–75; Chase, *Firearms*, 166–69; Waldron, *Great Wall*, 53–164; Rossabi, "Ming and Inner Asia," 221–71; Kenneth Swope, "The Three Great Campaigns of the Wanli Emperor, 1592–1600" (Univ. of Michigan, PhD diss., 2001).

[316] Huang, "Fiscal Administration," 115; idem, "The Ming Fiscal Administration," 152–53.

[317] Huang, "Fiscal Administration," 107–25; idem, "The Ming Fiscal Administration," 148–64; idem, *1587: A Year of No Significance*, 62; Hansen, *Open Empire*, 374–75.

[318] Notes 285, 317 *supra*.

and fiscal inability to capture increases in acreage or trade. New post-Taiping Rebellion taxes on trade (*li jin*) swelled provincial revenues, but not those of the central government, which in 1900 actually obtained less of the national product than in 1753.[319] According to Naquin, Rawski, and Madeleine Zelin, two Skinnerian limitations familiar from the Ming were in play. First, to have raised taxes sharply on the commercial economy or on unregistered lands would have invited resistance from those elites without whose liturgical services county and subcounty government simply could not function. Second, if Beijing had tried to circumvent its dependence on local elites by raising the number of paid provincial bureaucrats to keep pace with population, virtually the entire land tax would have gone to pay the new salaries, leaving little for higher-level administrative units, the army, or the palace. At the same time the resultant increase in personnel almost certainly would have overwhelmed the center's ability to monitor and control them. Although its communications and technology obviously were preindustrial, in size and population China in 1800 already was larger than the United States in 2000. If such generic Skinnerian restraints were familiar from the Ming, the Qing faced the additional concern that a major increase in bureaucratic recruitment would have been overwhelmingly Chinese and thus might have endangered Manchu ethnic dominance. Sensing its own limitations perhaps, the government made no effort at structural reform. Accordingly, as just indicated, when taxes did rise in the mid-1800s, provincial governments, whose scale let them manage collections more directly, became the chief beneficiaries.[320]

In sum, much as civilizational precocity and exposure to Inner Asian conquest appear to have been organically related, China's vast size

---

[319] Naquin and Rawski, *Chinese Society*, 219–20; Wang, *Land Taxation*, 11–16, 76–77. On post-Taiping political and fiscal devolution, see too Wright, *Last Stand*; Fairbank and Goldman, *China*, 212–14.

[320] See Naquin and Rawski, *Chinese Society*, 225–26; Zelin, *Magistrate's Tael*, 305–308; Wang, *Land Taxation*, 8–9, 30, 26–35, 131; and n. 286 *supra*. According to McKnight, *Village and Bureaucracy*, 21, even in the Southern Song, when the population was a fraction that of the Qing, expansion of hired clerks on the local level soon exceeded the government's control capacity. By the same logic, graft and extortion by local officials and gentry under the Ming and Qing did not threaten the system because a) by definition, such practices did not engender local elite resistance, b) they did not overstrain central capacities for administrative coordination. Perdue, pers. commun., Oct. 20, 2007 informs me that a recent MIT doctoral dissertation by He Winkai (a copy of which I was unable to obtain) finds, as I do, that Qing extraction faced severe structural limits.

and its low-tax tradition were mutually constitutive. That is to say, by embracing everything from the steppe to the tropics and from the Himalayas to the East China Sea, successive empires eliminated or reduced multistate competition, which made possible a low-tax policy. But by allowing only a superficial administrative penetration, low military demands and light taxation helped the sprawling Chinese state hold together. Only in the absence of sustained large-scale warfare, perhaps, could so improbable an entity have survived.

Some Implications of Size and Pacific Environment

What implications did China's subcontinental extent and modest military engagement have for technological innovation? Economic growth? Military effectiveness? Some have claimed that a slowdown in the rate of technological/economic change in the centuries after 1450 – at the very time such change accelerated in Europe – owed much to the Chinese state's exceptional military and territorial success. I discern two versions of this argument, the "strong state" and "weak state" hypothesis, each with various subthemes.

What may be the least plausible version of the strong state thesis claims that Ming–Qing economic policy retarded Chinese capitalism. In this view, the command economy, in particular hybrid state–merchant enterprises, weakened commercial competition; while unremitting official support, via tax and resettlement policies, for self-reproducing small peasant households, rather than for innovative capitalist farmers, encouraged stasis in the agrarian sector. Imposition of uniform policies across vast continental spaces meant that, in contrast to Europe, there were few pockets where alternate economic and social systems could take root.[321] On the whole, I find this approach of uncertain value because it a) probably exaggerates the domestic economic influence of what we have seen was a rather superficial state structure, b) minimizes the Qing's real, if not always consistent, commitment to free internal markets, to which Rowe and Helen Dunstan have drawn attention,[322] and c) idealizes European *laissez faire*, when in fact European markets

---

[321] For versions of this approach, see Rowe's summary of the literature in "Approaches," 280–82; Etienne Balazs, *Chinese Civilization and Bureaucracy* (New Haven, 1970); Jones, *European Miracle*, 202–22; Xu and Wu, *Chinese Capitalism*, xxv, 383, 390–401; and n. 194 *supra*.

[322] See nn. 175, 176; Dunstan, *State or Merchant*.

sometimes hewed less closely to neoclassical principles than did their 18th-century Chinese counterparts.[323]

A more subtle version of the strong state argument focuses not on economic policy per se, but on the intellectual and technological ramifications of subcontinental unity. However limited its fiscal goals may have been, the Ming–Qing state was quite able to suppress public expression of heterodox views, especially in print. This ability to regulate discourse over an extraordinarily large cultural area contrasted with the inability of individual European states to prevent rival kingdoms from harboring exiled dissenters, or printing and smuggling offensive materials into neighboring territories. If most such European materials were religious and political, the ensuing synergy between intellectually diverse centers also stimulated physics, chemistry, ship construction, and metallurgy.[324] External stimuli too may have fallen victim to Chinese unity. According to Elvin, by impeding maritime trade, post-Yuan rulers in general and the pre-1567 Ming in particular inhibited transmission of Muslim and European technical and scientific ideas. But if China had remained divided, the argument goes, interstate rivalries, and the ensuing need for external trade revenues and alliances, would have opened those lines of communications.[325] In support of such approaches, Valerie Hansen in her aptly titled *The Open Empire* has noted that the three periods of most intense cultural and/or technological innovation in Chinese history – namely, the era of intense interstate warfare from the 6th to 3rd centuries B.C.E., the Age of Division, and the Song Dynasty – were also, by and large, periods of most intense political fragmentation. The first era engendered cities, coinage, labor specialization, and philosophical speculation; the second saw the introduction of Buddhism and other Inner Asian motifs; the third produced the first commercial revolution, Neo-Confucianism, and a full-blooded examination system. In each case, she concludes, disunity, fighting, and chaos were a precondition for experiment and innovation.[326]

---

[323] Pomeranz, *Great Divergence*, 69–91, 196; Elvin, *Pattern of the Past*, 289–94.

[324] Juan Cole, "New Empires in Asia and the Middle East" (ms); Goldstone in n. 197 *supra*. See too Justin Yifu Lin, "The Needham Puzzle," *Economic Development and Cultural Change* 43 (1995): 269–92, blaming China's post-1400 technological slowdown less on overt state repression than on the intellectually stultifying effects of examination culture.

[325] Elvin, *Pattern of the Past*, 215–25.

[326] Hansen, *Open Empire*, 413–14. Actually, she extends the second period to include the Tang, but since that was an era of political unity, her thesis may need modification.

In the weak state hypothesis, the barrier to novelty and growth was not excessive, but inadequate, intervention. Again these failures often were said to be a function of vast size and modest military imperatives. And again, we find a variety of claims of varying credibility. Perhaps the most convincing formulation is the aforementioned thesis, consistent with both Pomeranz and Bayly, that in their enthusiastic support for overseas colonization and maritime trade, West European states provided ghost acreages, market access, and opportunities for core–periphery industrial differentiation unavailable in China. Also plausible is the claim that in Europe, but not China, intensifying warfare encouraged improvements in military technology that had spin-offs for the wider economy. According to Elvin, in part because of Song military desperation, in part because of bureaucratic precocity, technological change in China to c. 1400 depended far more heavily on official patronage than in Europe. But thereafter, as European technology blossomed, in China declining bureaucratic coverage joined waning military threats to eliminate state support, for which private elites failed to compensate. As Perdue has observed, Chinese regimes like the Song that engaged in sustained warfare patronized science and technology far more assiduously than those whose security destroyed incentives.[327]

Other attempts to apply the weak state hypothesis are less persuasive. Partly because of the Skinnerian burden of size, China may have provided less per capita infrastructural aid – roads, standardized weights and measures, commercial laws, uniform coinages – than many European realms. Certainly the failure of successive dynasties to create reliable, standardized coinages must have raised transactions costs.[328] Yet in China as elsewhere, the chief benefits of state action tended to derive from pacification and *laissez faire* market policies; and in these respects – following the collapse of Tang efforts to regulate landowning and urban trade – China does not seem to have been disadvantaged. On the contrary, one could argue, the Smithian benefits of Ming–Qing pacification

---

[327] Elvin, *Pattern of the Past*, chs. 13, 14; Peter Perdue, "Joseph Needham's Problematic Legacy," *Technology and Culture* 47 (2006): 175–78, on the economic benefits of military technology in Europe; idem, *China Marches West*, 184, 447–60. Cf. the more skeptical views of Joel Mokyr, *The Lever of Riches* (Oxford, 1990), chs. 7, 9; and Pomeranz, *Great Divergence*, 194–95. See too Joseph Needham, *The Grand Titration* (Toronto, 1969); Bray, "Towards a Critical History."

[328] Mokyr, *Lever of Riches*, 234; Huang, "The Ming Fiscal System," 169–70; and esp. Kuroda, "Copper Coins Chosen."

were magnified by the extraordinary geographic reach of those commercial, migratory, and diasporic networks that cohered under unified
rule. China was a European Union *avant la lettre*. By the same token, if
size kept infrastructural investment below optimal levels, China's historically low taxes may have had an unusual stimulatory effect, not least
on the undertaxed commercial sector. (One is reminded here of Tokugawa Japan.) When we consider, finally, that the late empire maintained
the chief north–south commercial artery, the Grand Canal; invested in
water control projects, upheld the land tenure system, pursued generally helpful bullionist policies; and, particularly during the Qing, exhibited a strong commitment to markets, its actions do not appear much
less lubricating than those of Eurasian realms with smaller territories
and lower subject-to-official ratios.[329]

Where pacific policy had the most deadening impact, not surprisingly, was in armaments and military tactics. This denouement was
ironic, given that the first true firearms probably appeared in China
in the mid-1100s, 200 years before Europe, and that the Song experimented with bombs and tank-like carts, as well as small cannon. A
taste for innovation continued in varying degrees under the Jin, Yuan,
and early Ming, with the latter deploying naval cannon and equipping
some 10 percent of their infantry with firearms. Quick to recognize the
value of Portuguese and Dutch guns, the Ming tried both to imitate
and to improve upon European designs; and in fact European-style
cannon contributed to Ming success against Japanese forces in Korea in
the 1590s and afforded them a brief respite against Manchu attacks on
urban strongholds in the 1620s. Aided by Chinese prisoners and defectors, the Qing, we saw, promptly developed their own Western-style
artillery and musket corps. In the 1670s the Qing also commissioned a
Flemish Jesuit to design light artillery for use against the Three Feudatories Revolt in the southwest, and two decades later, Qing forces dragged
hundreds of artillery pieces vast distances for its Zunghar campaigns.
In short, Chinese and Manchu leaders were by no means uninterested
in the new technology.[330]

---

[329] Feuerwerker, "State and Economy"; idem, *State and Society*, 88–94; Rowe, "Domestic
Interregional Trade"; idem, *Saving the World*, chs. 5–8; Vries, "Governing Growth";
Pomeranz, *Great Divergence*, esp. ch. 4; Peter Perdue, *Exhausting the Earth* (Cambridge,
MA, 1987), ch. 1.

[330] On Chinese firearms 1100–1800, nn. 65, 221 *supra*, plus Perdue, *China Marches West*, 175,
179–84, 204, 535, 539; Sun Laichen, "Military Technology Transfers from Ming China
and the Emergence of Northern Mainland Southeast Asia (c. 1390–1527)," *JSEAS* 34

Yet two familiar factors ensured that Chinese forces were still using Jesuit-style cannon in the Opium War 200 years after they were designed.[331] First, to repeat, neither the Ming, nor the Qing after vanquishing the Ming, faced armies whose superior technologies had to be mastered. Second, on the steppe, which remained the principal strategic theater, artillery were potentially valuable, but in practice awkward to transport and deploy, while Chinese handheld firearms were too slow to load and insufficiently powerful to stop cavalry charges. Nor could handguns be loaded on horseback.[332] Thus both Ming and Qing tended to relegate firearms to an auxiliary role and for the most part responded to new challenges by increasing force levels and improving logistics. In Keith Krause's terminology, China, like Japan, remained a third-tier power, able to reproduce existing military technologies but not to innovate.[333] Even in regional terms, to judge by China's poor performance in Sino-Burmese wars of 1765–1769, Qing forces could not keep up with the most nimble Southeast Asian armies, for whom (despite growing backwardness by European standards) continuous warfare ensured that firearms and tactical innovation remained vital preoccupations.[334]

A final speculation on the implications of size and pacific environment: I have argued that in some contexts frontier threats led Chinese to regard Inner Asians as a menacing "other." Conquest dynasties like the Jin, Yuan, and Qing outlawed such expressions, but even under the Ming, which freely voiced such views,[335] it is likely that these formulations remained less widespread or influential than in post-1500

(2003): 495–517; Lorge, *War, Politics and Society*, 125, 137 n. 9; Joanna Waley-Cohen, "China and Western Technology in the Late 18th Century," *AHR* 98 (1993): 1525–44, emphasizing technical adaptation; Samuel Hawley, *The Imjin War* (Berkeley, 2005), 5–6, 103, 113–14, 304–305.

[331] Di Cosmo, "Did Guns Matter?" 155; Waley-Cohen, "China and Technology," 1531–32.

[332] See nn. 221, 330, esp. Perdue, *China Marches West*, 535. Why, then, did firearms play a critical role on the southern and eastern Russian frontiers with Inner Asia? Three differences from China may have been responsible: a) From Europe, to which the Qing lacked comparable access, Russia derived continuous improvements in firearms mobility, accuracy, and power. b) The southern Russian frontier, being less arid than the Mongolian steppe, was more suitable for agrarian settlement and the building of locally manned firearms-aided defensive lines. c) In contrast to the steppe, much of Siberia was ill suited for cavalry.

[333] Keith Krause, *Arms and the State* (Cambridge, 1992), 26–32, 48–52; Di Cosmo, "Did Guns Matter?" 160–61, citing Krause.

[334] *SP*, 152–53, 164–67, 167 n. 215, 256–58, 309–10, 454; Michael Chiang, "Burmese-Chinese Relations 1750–1800" (ms), 5–6.

[335] See n. 234 *supra*. Cf. Duara, *Rescuing History*, ch. 2.

European or Southeast Asian states. Imagining oneself part of a political community was difficult enough in *ancien régime* France, but that difficulty can only have been magnified in China by the vast scale of empire and by the relative invisibility of frontier dangers. Until the last years of the Ming, Inner Asian threats remained utterly remote from most people's lives. If they did consider the matter, most literati probably were comforted by the complacent formulaic division between civilized and barbarian, with the former destined to prevail. Notwithstanding the subsequent goad to Chinese consciousness that Manchu dominion provided, such experiences, in combination with strict Qing curbs on nativist expression, must have politicized ethnicity less effectively than European interstate culture, with its public exaltation of political community and its formal division of mankind into juridically equal, but perpetually contending, states and peoples.

CONCLUSION

The most basic similarity between China and other realms under review was a long-term movement toward political and cultural integration. Much as oscillations in mainland Southeast Asia, Russia, and France diminished, interregna in China, albeit from an earlier starting point, grew progressively shorter and less disruptive.

As elsewhere, enhanced stability reflected synergies between economic growth, easier cultural circulation, and rising state capacity. Demographic and economic cycles in China – with expansion particularly notable 800/900–1270, 1470/1500–1640, and 1700–1830 – corresponded to rhythms in much of Europe, Southeast Asia, and (between 1470 and 1720) Japan. Such coordination reflected global climate and epidemics, synchronized adjustments to 14th-century dislocations precipitated in part by the Mongols, and wider maritime trade. Economic growth aided the Chinese state by expanding its resource base and thickening core–periphery linkages. Indirectly, commerce promoted integration by fostering a more mobile, literate social order; strengthening cultural ties between local elites and officialdom, and disseminating Neo-Confucian norms to ever more distant and humble sectors. By "civilizing" popular strata and compensating for the state's limited local presence, Neo-Confucianism represented a particularly potent, if drawn-out version of Gorski's disciplinary revolution. Although Song governance already was more bureaucratic and sophisticated than its protected-zone counterparts at a later date, in China as in much of the protected zone the 10th to 13th centuries and the 16th to 18th centuries saw a quantum leap in economic activity, cultural circulation, and political organization.

But if the state thus drew strength from changes in the local environment, the relation remained thoroughly reciprocal. The Song, the late Ming, and the Qing promoted economic growth via pacification, frontier reclamation, and favorable tax policies. At the same time, through examinations, law codes, village lectures, and support for lineage organizations, the imperial center helped to define and to disseminate normative culture. Naquin and Rawski's summary of these processes to 1800 – "The likelihood that China might dissolve into its component regional units was progressively reduced by the multistranded ties that bound the empire together"[336] – could stand for any of the Eurasian realms we have considered.

Such similarities aside, political and cultural integration in China began by as much as 1,200 years earlier than in the protected zone, in part because North China had easier access to economic artifacts and technologies moving along east–west trade and migration routes.

What is more, the same geographic exposure as favored early civilization accorded Inner Asians a central political role. The China-centered narrative, beloved of the Sinicization School that I just summarized, a narrative of administrative centralization, economic expansion, and thickening cultural circuits, was only one of two grand dynamics, albeit arguably the more important of the two, shaping Chinese history. The second was growing Inner Asian influence. Whether another Chinese dynasty might have succeeded the Ming is sterile speculation, but the decisive character of Inner Asian interventions between 900 and 1800 seems clear. If Inner Asians helped to sunder Chinese territories from the 10th century, it was the Mongols who reassembled them. The Qing then joined China proper and Inner Asia in a stable union for the first time. What is more, the Qing enhanced administrative efficiency, cultural integration, and agrarian prosperity, in effect making the system work better than the Chinese themselves. The growing success of Inner Asian-led states along the steppe–sown interface reflected, most basically, their ability to learn from earlier conquest dynasties and to wed Chinese culture to tribal military power; such acculturation in turn seems to have benefited after c. 900 from expanding Chinese

---

[336] Naquin and Rawski, *Chinese Society*, 216.

settlement and trade along the frontier. In part because of their physical and psychological distance from this creative frontier zone, neither Song nor Ming could resist Inner Asian attacks. Such threats bred defensive Chinese reactions that bore some resemblance to politicized ethnicity elsewhere in Eurasia. But even under the Ming, reactions were muted by the remoteness of the frontier, while under conquest dynasties, such reactions perforce remained subterranean. To preserve their own cohesion, China's Inner Asian rulers fostered ethnic segregation without protected zone parallel and pursued polyethnic imperial strategies distinct from the more unified ethnocentric visions of both Chinese-led dynasties and protected-zone states.

China differed from the protected zone as well in the extraordinary size of imperial territories and population. In part, as I just emphasized, imperial extension reflected Inner Asian power: without the Mongols, a fragmentation that in 1279 was already over 350 years old might have become as permanent as in post-Carolingian Europe. In part, imperial unity reflected a mildly centripetal geography. More basically, unity remained a normative ideal through the influence of civil service examinations, an approved imperial corpus, a nonalphabetic script, and a uniquely prescriptive philosophy of social and political order.

Along with subcontinental dominion came four other signature traits, all mutually dependent: a) weak military imperatives, b) a comparatively low-tax regime, c) a falling post-1500 ratio of centrally appointed officials to subjects, and d) heavy dependence on unremunerated local elites. Dominating territory from the steppe to the tropics, neither the Han, Tang, Yuan, nor Qing Dynasties participated in a competitive interstate system such as we find for most of European and Southeast Asian history. With military imperatives limited, post-Song regimes – like the Tokugawa – could afford the luxury of low taxation, which in turn limited pressure to penetrate society. And because its local ambitions were modest, when the population mushroomed, the state had little trouble reducing its presence in advanced areas. Chinese empires were certainly as effective as any protected-zone state in achieving their goals, but for much of the period after 1450, those goals – focusing more on the reproduction of a stable, moral agrarian order than on maximizing military strength – tended to be *sui generis*.[337] At

---

[337] Wong, *Transforming China*, chs. 4–6 makes a similar argument.

the same time the imperial center relied to an extraordinary degree on informal accommodations and cultural instruments of integration.

To another Eurasian realm subject to growing Inner Asian influence we now turn. South Asia experienced some of the same external pressures as China, but in an environment less favorable to sustained empire.

CHAPTER SIX

Integration Under Expanding Inner Asian Influence, II

South Asia: Patterns Intermediate Between China and the Protected Zone

South Asia as a whole exhibited some of the same developmental features as individual Southeast Asian and European polities, Japan, and China. In familiar, if somewhat languid fashion, intervals between hegemonic polities contracted, the territorial writ of successive polities expanded, while fiscal and military organization grew more efficient. The southward diffusion first of Sanskritic and then of Perso-Islamic culture, the northward movement of "Hindu" devotionalism, and the continuous expansion of agrarian cores encouraged a genuine, if modest, degree of cultural integration across the Indian subcontinent. Political patterns also followed a familiar chronology, including a surge in state formation c. 900 to 1300 and c. 1550 to 1800. As an unprecedentedly powerful state that cohered after an era of fragmentation and that benefited from economic intensification, firearms, new cultural syntheses, and cumulative expertise, the Mughal empire (heyday c. 1560–1707) bears comparison to such contemporaneous realms as Toungoo Burma, Late Ayudhya Siam, Muscovy, Bourbon France, and Tokugawa Japan.

But chronology and geography also set South Asia apart from the protected zone. Most obvious, the North Indian plain, like the North China plain, engendered a charter civilization considerably earlier than more isolated sectors of Eurasia, to which, in the case of Southeast Asia, Tibet, and South India itself, North India served as cultural donor.

Moreover, as this chapter title indicates, postcharter political patterns placed South Asia in a position intermediate between China, on the one hand, and Europe and Southeast Asia, on the other. That is to say, South Asia raised barriers to imperial unification more substantial than in

China, but less formidable than in Europe or mainland Southeast Asia at large. Between 300 B.C.E. and 1800 C.E. northern and north-central India were divided over twice as long as they were unified, but during these same centuries the principal zones of Chinese settlement lay under a single authority some 1.7 times longer than they were divided. If we include southern India in our tabulation of South Asian unity, the discrepancy is far greater. By extension, regional cultures and vernacular literatures in India exhibited a vigor and originality without Chinese parallel. Yet in the end, fusions between regional cultures and regional polities proved far more fragile in South Asia than in individual Southeast Asian or European realms. In a word, South Asia embodied conflicting dynamics. Able to generate neither an enduring pan-South Asian empire nor a stable multistate system of regional kingdoms, its precolonial political fate was, in a sense, Sisyphean.[1]

Why, then, this persistent oscillation? Regional polities were more short lived than their European or Southeast Asian counterparts, in part, because geography provided less secure borders, literacy rates were lower, and ethnicities were less focused. But most basically, regional kingdoms proved more ephemeral because South Asia, unlike the protected zone, lay open to repeated invasions by Inner Asians, chiefly Turkic and allied peoples entering the Indo-Gangetic plain overland from the northwest,[2] and in the 18th century by the British coming by sea. In at least three periods – in the 13th and 14th centuries, in the 16th and 17th centuries, and c. 1765 to 1850 – such interventions overwhelmed Indian regional kingdoms. At the same time as they reconfigured political space, conquest elites introduced more penetrating and efficient administrations and novel cultural and linguistic systems. This succession of imperial formations, which tended to build upon one another, and the fatal barriers they raised to stable *local* fusions of politics and culture, provide our primary justification to treat South Asia, rather than its individual regions, as a unit of historical inquiry. In other words, this chapter's focus on South Asia at large reflects less a retrospective projection of British success than a concern with subcontinental processes

---

[1] Of course, pre-1854 Japan neither participated in an enduring interstate system nor supported one in the home islands.

[2] "What happened in India beginning in the late twelfth century was part of a larger trend occurring throughout much of Eurasia, in which nomadic peoples migrated from the steppes of Inner Asia and became politically dominant over sedentary agrarian societies." *IBE*, 50. Along with Catherine Asher and Cynthia Talbot in *IBE*, I tend to use "South Asia" and "India" interchangeably.

of political and, to a lesser extent, cultural integration that dominated much of the second millennium and indeed had earlier roots.

But in turn, Inner Asian empires remained more fragile in India than in China, because geography, rural militarization, parcelized sovereignty, elite education, caste, alphabetic scripts, and fiscal burdens all were less sympathetic. In addition, the cultural affiliations of Indo-Muslim rulers left them more vulnerable to domestic challenge than their counterparts in China. Whereas in governing China proper, conquest dynasties perforce employed Chinese cultural and administrative systems rather than their own unserviceable preliterate traditions, in South Asia conquest dynasties championed Perso-Islamic norms that, although ever more assimilated to an Indian milieu, still had limited resonance for many provincial elites.

Like Chapter 5, this chapter is divided into two parts. The first considers similarities between South Asia and those areas – individual Southeast Asian and European states, Japan, and China – treated earlier in this volume. Notwithstanding major differences in scale and integrative potential, differences that I make every effort to elucidate, in South Asia at large as in most of those realms we find, as already indicated, progressively shorter eras of polycentrism, ever more penetrating administrations, long-term territorial consolidation, a more rapid circulation of cultural motifs, and economic and demographic cycles that correlated with other sectors of Eurasia. The second part of this chapter explores features that distinguished South Asia from the protected zone but that South Asia shared with China, namely, precocious state formation and Inner Asian conquest. By destroying regional polities, Inner Asians twice prevented South Asia at large from sustaining a competitive network of moderate-sized kingdoms comparable to the multistate systems of mainland Southeast Asia and Europe. The post-1200 divergence between South Asia, on the one hand, and Europe and Southeast Asia, on the other, was particularly notable, because between c. 900 and 1200/1300 we find in all three regions not only increasingly coherent local kingdoms, but a politically pregnant linguistic revolution in which local vernaculars displaced the universal languages of Sanskrit and Latin. In France, England, Burma, and Siam, such trends continued for centuries, but across South Asia the once intimate tie between vernacular languages and political patronage was repeatedly severed or abraded. Part 2 concludes by considering why, despite their initially overwhelming strength, Inner Asians in India failed to consolidate power as effectively as their counterparts in China.

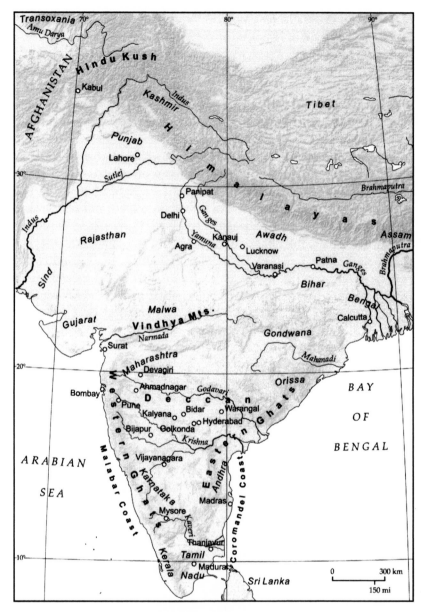

Figure 6.1. South Asia.

1. SIMILARITIES BETWEEN SOUTH ASIA, THE PROTECTED ZONE, AND CHINA

Progressively Shorter Eras of Polycentrism: Overview of South Asian Political History

Let us begin, then, with overarching similarities to realms already examined, starting with the shifting balance between periods of political unification and fragmentation. Because an interregnum suspends *normative* rule while for most of South Asian history polycentrism, not imperial unity, was the norm, it makes little sense to talk about South Asian interregna. Nonetheless, here as in each protected-zone society and in China, intervals between major transregional, that is, imperial, formations did tend to grow shorter.

In India as in China the northern plain gave birth to civilization. But whereas in China economic and, to a lesser extent, political preeminence moved permanently to the Yangzi basin, India saw no such southward shift. With few exceptions, the most extensive precolonial empires remained centered in the Indo-Gangetic plain. With its open expanse and navigable rivers, this region enjoyed easy communications and transport, while reliable rainfall in the central and eastern sectors and rich alluvial soils supported dense populations and early urbanization. In peninsular India, by contrast, intensive agriculture focused on well-watered pockets along river courses and in deltas separated from one another by upland, semi-arid terrain. Particularly in the Deccan, that is, peninsular India between the Narmada and Kaveri Rivers, the rain shadow effect of the Western Ghat mountains creates an extensive dry zone. Although such districts supported powerful warrior lineages and although some southern coastal areas boasted substantial settled populations and maritime trade, by and large South India could not match the demographic or political weight of the north.[3]

During the same period as the Yellow River plain spawned a cultural-cum-territorial charter for China, it was therefore the Ganges basin that generated an imperial template for South Asia. This was the Maurya empire (c. 320–180 B.C.E.), which emerged after a centuries-long competition among clan confederations and local kingdoms. By dominating key agrarian zones and trade routes in parts of India, chiefly the

---

[3] Cf. *IBE*, 9–12; Joseph Schwartzberg, ed., *A Historical Atlas of South Asia* (Chicago, 1978), 3–6, 151–54.

north, and of modern Bangladesh, Pakistan, and Nepal, the Mauryas constructed South Asia's first extensive, if superficial and short lived, empire.[4]

After the Maurya realm collapsed in the early second century B.C.E., victim of overextension aggravated perhaps by an anti-Buddhist brahmanic reaction, a succession of domestic and Inner Asian-led realms sought to refashion the ideal of universal dominion. Among these post-Maurya states the empire of the Guptas (c. 320–550 C.E.) – whose founder Candragupta I seems to have adopted the name of the founder of the Maurya Dynasty – was by far the most influential. New kingdoms along the old Maurya periphery confined Gupta dominion to the Indo-Gangetic plain and the northern peninsula, but none could rival Gupta military power or cultural eclat. By modifying Maurya legacies, in particular by moving toward a more brahmanic social and political order that inspired Indian polities for centuries, the Guptas refined, many would claim generated, India's classical – or to use our term, charter – civilization.[5]

Gupta decline inaugurated a second, yet more extended era of polycentrism, from the mid-500s to at least the early 1200s. This is not to deny during these long centuries the existence of sizeable realms – including the empires of the Pallavas (c. 300–900), Rastrakutas (c. 750–975), Gurjara Pratiharas (c. 725–950), Palas (c. 750–1170), Kalyana Calukyas (c. 960–1200), Yadavas (c. 1000–1296), Hoysalas (c. 1000–1340s), Kakatiyas (c. 1100/1175–1323), and Colas (c. 900–1250). But as these overlapping dates suggest, between c. 500 and 1300 polities with comparable resources and prestige not only coexisted, but competed bitterly.[6]

---

[4] On the Mauryas, Romila Thapar, *Early India* (Berkeley, 2002), chs. 4–6; idem, *Asoka and the Decline of the Mauryas* (rev. ed., Oxford, 1997); M. Bongard-Levin, *Mauryan India* (New Delhi, 1985); Carla Sinopoli, "Imperial Landscapes of South Asia," in Miriam Stark, ed., *Archaeology of Asia* (Malden, MA, 2006), 328–32; David Ludden, *NCHI*, vol. IV, 4: *An Agrarian History of South Asia* (Cambridge, 1999), 62–64; Gerard Fussman, "Central and Provincial Administration in Ancient India," *IHR* 14 (1987/88): 43–72; F. R. Allchin, *The Archaeology of Early Historic South Asia* (Cambridge, 1995), 185–273.

[5] On the Guptas and the concept of classical civilization, Thapar, *Early India*, 282–87; David Ludden, *India and South Asia: A Short History* (Oxford, 2002), 31–34; idem, *NCHI*, 45, 64–76; Hermann Kulke and Dietmar Rothermund, *A History of India* (3rd ed., London, 1998), 6–7, 81–91; Thomas Trautmann, "Indian Civilization to the End of the Mughal Empire" (ms), ch. 4.

[6] On geopolitical configurations c. 550–1300, Kulke and Rothermund, *History*, 8–15, 103–43; Schwartzberg, *Historical Atlas*, 31–32, 40; idem, "The Evolution of Regional Power Configurations in the Indian Subcontinent," in Richard Fox, ed., *Realm and Region in Traditional India* (Durham, NC, 1977),197–233; Thapar, *Early India*, chs. 9–13; Brajadulal

If in Southeast Asia, Russia, France, and Japan, reintegration of the original charter territory in the early or mid-second millennium was entirely the work of indigenous elites, and if in China Sui-Tang reunification benefited from a mix of Chinese and Inner Asian influences, India lay farther in the direction of external agency. Without Turkic conquests, the polycentrism of the post-550 era well might have lasted indefinitely in the manner of Europe or Southeast Asia. In the event, however, after two centuries of raiding, in the late 1100s Turkic cavalry began the systematic reduction of the Indo-Gangetic plain. Founded in 1206, the Delhi Sultanate not only became the first extensive Perso-Islamic state in North India, but between 1296 and 1323 subdued *inter alia* Gujarat, the Deccan, and the southeast. By slicing the Gordian knot of regionalism, Turkic warriors exceeded Gupta conquests and anticipated Mughal reunification.[7]

The Delhi Sultanate declined in the mid- and late 1300s through an array of problems – overextension, patrimonial appropriation of benefices, fresh dangers from the northwest – known to both its non-Muslim Indian predecessors and its Mughal heirs. After the 1398 sack of Delhi by the famed Inner Asian warrior Timur, local kingdoms across the north, the Deccan, and the far south reproduced in crude outline the geopolitical splits of the 6th to 12th centuries.

From the 1450s, however, the Lodi clan of Afghans and more especially the brilliant Indo-Afghan leader Sher Shah Sur (dominant 1538 to 1545) restored some of the authority of the Delhi Sultanate. Coming after prolonged disorder, this halting post-1450 recovery therefore exhibited a chronology similar to that of Toungoo Burma, Ayudhya, Le Vietnam, Muscovy, and Valois France. Moreover, in India as in much of Eurasia, after fresh mid-16th century disorders, consolidation accelerated dramatically. In India this was the work of the Mughals, Turko-Mongols from today's Uzbekistan whose conquests exceeded those of the Delhi Sultanate and whose administrative system proved

---

Chattopadhyaya, *The Making of Early Medieval India* (Delhi, 1994), chs. 1, 8; Hermann Kulke, ed., *The State in India 1000–1700* (Delhi, 1995). My dates generally follow Sheldon Pollock, *The Language of the Gods in the World of Men* (Berkeley, 2006), App. B, and/or Ludden, *India and South Asia*, 45–46, but because some dynasties that later became independent were formerly tributaries in fluctuating degrees of dependence, assigning precise dates can be problematic.

7 Schwartzberg, *Historical Atlas*, 38; Peter Jackson, *The Delhi Sultanate* (Cambridge, 1999); Sunil Kumar, *The Emergence of the Delhi Sultanate 1192–1286* (New Delhi, 2007); *IBE*, 18–45. Ibid., 33 cites 1206 as "the beginning point" of the Sultanate, but Jackson, *Delhi Sultanate*, prefers 1210.

more effective. From c. 1560 to 1605 and c. 1630 to 1690 Mughal armies added territories almost continuously.[8]

Although a Mughal façade endured long thereafter, between 1707 and 1739 the empire disintegrated. As happened after the Delhi Sultanate declined, an intense competition promptly enveloped successor states led in this period by regional warrior alliances, Mughal provincial governors, and the French and English East India Companies – among whom the English Company emerged triumphant. By 1765 the British had secured Bengal and Bihar, to which by 1820 they had added the rest of the Ganges basin, the Deccan, and the southern coasts. With conquests in the northwest, by mid-century British subjugation of South Asia was complete.

To summarize these complex gyrations, note that although political integration remained far more sluggish than in China or in protected-zone states, the long-term balance between regionalism and transregional (imperial) integration clearly favored the latter. Some five centuries passed between the decline of the first great Indian empire of the Mauryas and the emergence of the Guptas. Another 650 years separated Gupta eclipse from the founding of the Delhi Sultanate. But if we follow Peter Jackson in dating Sultanate's eclipse to 1398,[9] only 180 years divided that collapse from the establishment of Mughal authority over all of North India and Bengal. Whether we assign the effective end of Mughal rule to 1707 (when the last formidable emperor, Aurangzeb, died) or 1739 (when the Persian ruler Nadir Shah invaded India), a century or less distinguished that transition from British hegemony. This general trend remains even if we change specific dates, for example, if we date Sultanate decline from 1346 rather than 1398. Or to make the same point, whereas between 300 B.C.E. and 1200 C.E. the lands of northern and north-central India were fragmented three times longer than they were unified, between 1200 and 1830 the disunity-to-unity ratio was less than 1:1.

---

[8] On the Mughals and their ethnolinguistic affiliations, John Richards, *NCHI*, vol. I, 5: *The Mughal Empire* (Cambridge, 1993); Muzaffar Alam and Sanjay Subrahmanyam, eds., *The Mughal State 1526–1750* (Delhi, 1998); Sanjay Subrahmanyam, pers. commun., Aug. 7, 2008; Richard Folz, *Mughal India and Central Asia* (Karachi, 1998); Harbans Mukhia, *The Mughals of India* (Malden, MA, 2004); *IBE*, chs. 5–7. Insofar as they melded Mongol and Turkic elements, Mughals bear comparison to the Mongol-Tatars of the Kipchak khanate discussed in Ch. 2 *supra*.

[9] The year of Timur's sack, after which, notwithstanding Lodi revival, the Sultanate remained "simply one of a number of competing powers" and "a mere shadow of its former self . . . which continued to fragment." Jackson, *Delhi Sultanate*, 321.

Long-Term Improvements in Administrative Coordination and Penetration

In South Asia as elsewhere, an obvious aid to political integration was secular improvement in territorial, military, and fiscal organization. If South Asian hegemons did not form a continuous state tradition to the same degree as in China, from the Gupta period and more especially from c. 1200, we still find progressive refinements in South Asian political culture to which most major states had access.

In the Maurya empire as in Pagan, Angkor, Kiev, Carolingian France, and Heian, extensive influence was possible only because administration remained extremely superficial and uneven. The Maurya polity has been likened to a spider, with a small dense body – the agriculture core of the east central Ganges basin – and long spindly legs extending across the subcontinent. The core supported a system of intensive rule, influenced by Achaemenid Persian models, that included elaborately ranked officers, graded salaries, royal spies, and local agents. To follow Daud Ali, Mauryan "priests and intellectuals" were first to pose political questions – how best to order the royal household and govern the realm – as a concern separate from ancient Vedic religious rituals, which until then had dominated the discourse of kingship.[10] Provincial towns also had a layer of imperial officials, including royal princes. But to control their hinterlands, appointees relied on local lineages and chieftainships that were present when the Mauryas arrived and remained long after they left. Far from being standardized, imperial languages and practices were tailored to local custom. In any case, officials were appointed only in parts of the northern plain, some southern deltaic pockets, and along frontiers and major trade routes, the latter corresponding to the spider's legs. Between these outposts lay forest, pastoral, even agrarian zones inhabited by unvanquished peoples quite outside the imperial orbit.[11]

---

[10] Daud Ali, *Courtly Culture and Political Life in Early Medieval India* (Cambridge, 2004), 29. The Vedas, composed perhaps as early as 1800–1300 B.C.E., were collections of sacred knowledge transmitted orally in archaic Sanskrit by Indo-Aryan tribes of North India. For sharing her extensive knowledge of Harappa and Maurya civilization, I am indebted to Carla Sinopoli, pers. commun., Sept. 4, 2008.

[11] On Maurya administration, n. 4 *supra*, plus Ludden, *India and South Asia*, 28–29, using the spider analogy; Cynthia Talbot, *Precolonial India in Practice* (Oxford, 2001), 6–7, 209–10, like Ludden, taking a jaundiced view of Maurya centralization; and Pollock, *Language of the Gods*, 59, 482, 537 on Achaemenid influence.

The Gupta empire was both less and more powerful than its Maurya predecessor.[12] Officials were appointed only in the central Ganges basin. Beyond lay a sphere of autonomous, but dependent kings who were obliged to pay tribute and attend the imperial court but not necessarily to join the central army. Yet farther afield lay independent rulers who entered into diplomatic relations with the Guptas. The empire, indeed South Asia at large, was conceived as a hierarchy of autonomous powers, as opposed to the more nominally unified system of the Mauryas. Whereas the Maurya ruler Asoka had been "the Beloved of the Gods," the Guptas were "kings of kings." This model of multiple, nested sovereignties and attenuated zones of influence provided a template for all later South Asian – and Indic Southeast Asian – states. It contrasted not only with Maurya aspiration, but with actual practice in China, where the Han, we saw, eliminated independent kings. Within the Ganges basin, however, agrarian reclamation and cultural patronage allowed the Guptas to govern a core – as opposed to an extended imperial sphere – that was apparently larger than that of the Mauryas and to create what some scholars believe were unprecedentedly effective vertical linkages. Key to this success was the royal alliance with brahmans, the priestly and scholarly custodians of Sanskrit culture and the highest category in Vedic social schemas. Whereas the Mauryas had tolerated ancient clan organizations (*janapadas*) and had supported diverse religions, including Buddhism and Jainism, the Guptas displaced *janapadas* and focused patronage on brahmans. By making well-publicized land donations to these ritual specialists, by patronizing temples, and using brahmanic interventions to manage conflict between pastoralists and farmers, the Guptas built more solid local alliances. This new system David Ludden terms "imperial Brahmanism."[13]

From the mid-first millennium Gupta-style brahmanism and administrative technologies radiated from the Ganges basin across northwestern, central, eastern, and southern India. Amidst kaleidoscopic shifts in dynastic fortunes – the 6th and 7th centuries alone saw more than 40 new dynasties – we find outside the North Indian heartland between

---

[12] On Gupta administration, n. 5 *supra*, plus Ashvini Agrawal, *Rise and Fall of the Imperial Guptas* (Delhi, 1989), chs. 5–14; D. N. Jha, *Revenue Systems in Post-Maurya and Gupta Times* (Calcutta, 1967); Ali, *Courtly Culture*, 30, 33 ff.

[13] Ludden, *India and South Asia*, 31.

500 and 1300 an administrative evolution that Hermann Kulke, with heuristic enthusiasm, divides into three stages.[14]

In the first, least well-documented phase, beginning in some cases in the Gupta era and lasting to the 7th century, tribal chieftains, with the aid of brahmans from the Ganges basin, transformed themselves into orthodox princelings, complete with fabricated lineages and sacred paraphernalia. In contrast to earlier historians who saw these developments through a European lens as a form of "feudal decentralization," a decline from classical greatness, scholars like Kulke, Ludden, Cynthia Talbot, and Brajadulal Chattopadhyaya argue that these realms had never been incorporated in any meaningful way into the Gupta system. Rather, they were new political formations that drew strength not from economic contraction, but from the expansion of agrarian cores, from trade and mobility along inland corridors, and from the consequent interplay between Gupta and local traditions. In this early phase, however, each ruler typically controlled only a small domain with a modest administrative apparatus.[15]

In the second stage, c. 650/700 to 850/900, princelings subdued adjacent realms, which were not annexed, but treated as autonomous tributary domains. Tributary rulers (*samantas*), each with his own network of territorial dependencies, occupied an ever more prominent ceremonial and practical role, and royal prestige came to be measured by the size of each king's tributary circle. Thus the Gupta ideal of imperial overlord, king of kings, revived in regional contexts. This stage saw continued agrarian reclamation and commercial exchange, the ongoing

---

[14] In some ways these developments recall state formation in Southeast Asia in the same period and in the Ganges basin during the mid- and late first millennium B.C.E . See Kulke, "The Early and the Imperial Kingdom," in Kulke, *The State*, 233–62; idem, "The Early and the Imperial Kingdom in Southeast Asian History," in David Marr and A. C. Milner, eds., *Southeast Asia in the 9th to 14th Centuries* (Singapore, 1986), 1–22; and discussion of early Java in Ch. 7 *infra*.

[15] For the now unfashionable "feudal" thesis, see R. S. Sharma, "How Feudal Was Indian Feudalism?" in Kulke, *The State*, 48–133, and K. M. Shrimali, "Money, Market, and Indian Feudalism AD 600–1200," in A. K. Bagchi, ed., *Money and Credit in Indian History from Early Medieval Times* (New Delhi, 2002), 1–39. For critiques and alternate approaches, Kulke and Rothermund, *History*, ch. 3; David Ludden, *Peasant History in South India* (Princeton, 1985), 15–41, 204–10; Talbot, *Precolonial India*, 2–7; Chattopadhyaya, *Making*, chs. 1–6, 8; idem, *Aspects of Rural Settlement and Rural Society in Early Medieval India* (Calcutta, 1990); Andre Wink, *Al-Hind*, 2 vols. (Delhi, 1990, 1997), vol. I, 219–334; Nicholas Dirks, *The Hollow Crown* (Cambridge, 1987), 28–32; Ali, *Courtly Culture*, 21–22, 30–37, 101–102.

sedentarization of pastoral and tribal peoples, and more tax-exempt grants to allied brahmans. Also indicative of agrarian settlement and political consolidation was the proliferation of (what are anachronistically termed) "Hindu" temples, now often in stone rather than wood, and the creation of state cults focused on the veneration of an image, usually of Siva or Visnu, who was regarded as the dynasty's cosmic overlord. By the 8th century, states embodying these trends in the Deccan and in the southeast rivaled kingdoms in the Gangetic heartland.[16]

In the third stage, extending from roughly 900 to 1300/1350, kingdoms became regional empires by conquering rival states of similar size, improving revenue extraction within their core territories, displacing chiefly lineages and assemblies in outlying areas with figures more dependent on the throne, and – suitable to an era of intensifying warfare – by promoting military professionalism.[17] Frequently it was warriors from arid and semi-arid zones who encouraged long-distance trade, developed hill forts and cavalry, converted pastoral into arable via new irrigation works, and used these assets to forge new states. Besides making fresh land grants to loyal brahmans in outlying areas, dynasts in this period directed resources to trade caravanserais and, more especially, to royal temples, which could be three to four times larger than earlier edifices. With ritual links to smaller provincial shrines, such

---

[16] Previous notes plus Ronald Inden, *Imagining India* (Bloomington, IN, 2000), 228–62; Richard Eaton, *The Rise of Islam and the Bengal Frontier* (Berkeley, 1993), 14–15. The term "Hindu" originated with Arabs from the 8th century to refer to those living beyond the "Indus" and later was used to identify all followers of indigenous religions in that region. North Indians identified themselves by sectarian labels – Vaisnava or Saiva – or by the narrower labels of Bhagavatas, Pasupatas, etc. rather than by an all-inclusive term. Only from the 1300s, apparently as a direct result of Muslim contacts, did non-Muslims begin referring to themselves as "Hindus," and then only sparingly. Thapar, *Early India*, xxix, 275, 438–40.

[17] On this third stage and its regional variants, Talbot, *Precolonial India*; Kulke and Rothermund, *History*, 123–43; Jos Gommans, "The Silent Frontier of South Asia, c. A.D. 1100–1800," *JWH* 9 (1998): 1–23; Ludden, *Peasant History*, 13–67, 202–203; idem, "History Outside Civilization and the Mobility of South Asia," *South Asia* 27 (1994): 9–11; James Heitzman, "Temple Urbanism in Medieval South India," *JAS* 46 (1987): 791–826; idem, "State Formation in South India, 850–1280," in Kulke, *The State*, 162–94; Burton Stein, *Peasant State and Society in Medieval South India* (Delhi, 1980), introducing his "segmentary state" hypothesis; Wink, *Al-Hind*, vol. I, 219–358 and vol. II, 162–301, 381–84; Sheldon Pollock, "India in the Vernacular Millennium," *Daedalus* 127 (1998): 54–60; idem, *Language of the Gods*, 410–23; Richard Eaton, *NCHI*, vol. I, 8: *A Social History of the Deccan, 1300–1761* (Cambridge, 2005), 9–32, 137–38. For theoretical approaches to the medieval polity, including "feudal" and "segmentary" models (neither, to my mind, satisfactory), see n. 15 *supra*, plus essays in Kulke, *The State*; and Martin Doornbos and Sudipta Kaviraj, eds., *The Dynamics of State Formation* (New Delhi, 1997), pt 1.

temples promoted long-distance and local trade, agricultural investment, technical innovation, and brahmanic social norms, all with centralizing implications. Dedicated to Siva or Visnu whose relation to
local deities mirrored that of the high king to his *samantas*, royal temple
complexes, such as those in Orissa and the Tamil country, came to sym-
bolize ever more dramatically the power and identity of regional states.
Ironically, as their realms expanded, we shall find that such polities
promoted vernacular literatures at the expense of Sanskrit and forsook
universal claims in favor of more realistic territorial goals. Whereas the
Mauryas and Guptas had lasted about 140 and 230 years, respectively,
major medieval dynasties – benefiting from these economic, administrative, and cultural currents – had an average lifespan of over 300 years,
according to Ludden's calculations.[18] Such successes aside, new polities
continued to face recurrent threats from restive tributaries, each with his
own military forces, and in some cases from the flow of resources into
undertaxed temple trusts. Efforts to curb tributaries or raise taxes could
backfire, prompting revolts in *samanta* domains, which then became
new imperial centers.

Most regional states achieved maximum influence at some point
between 1000 and 1330. In these same centuries, recall, Angkor and
Pagan attained their greatest territorial extent, supported extraordinarily grand temple networks that served as foci of agrarian reclamation,
and suffered from strains rooted in the autonomy of temples and of
nominally subordinate tributaries. Such features remind us that extra-
Gangetic South Asia and Southeast Asia both became "Indianized" in
the same period.[19] More broadly, as power radiated from established
agrarian cores across Eurasia, these same centuries saw political flores-
cences in western Europe, Kiev, and South China.

Non-Muslim kingdoms in eastern and southern India remained vigorous through the 15th and much of the 16th centuries. Vijayanagara,
"City of Victory," for example, shortly after its founding in 1346 became
locked in bitter rivalry with a Delhi successor state to its north. To
overcome their foes' initial cavalry superiority, Vijayanagara kings,
although patrons of Siva and Visnu, welcomed Muslim warriors and, in
apparent imitation of Islamic *iqtas* (see below), assigned nonhereditable

---

[18] Ludden, *India and South Asia*, 44 and Table 2, employing the term "medieval" rather
loosely to describe states from the 6th to 16th century, but primarily to 1350 or 1400.

[19] Cf. n. 14 *supra*; Sheldon Pollock, "The Sanskrit Cosmopolis, 300–1300," in Jan E. M.
Houben, ed., *Ideology and Status of Sanskrit* (Leiden, 1996), 197–247; idem, *Language of
the Gods*, 380–97; *SP*, 88–123, 216–42.

lands to nobles who were obliged to provide the crown with stipulated payments and troops.[20] A similar military logic led Vijayanagara to promote cash rather than in-kind taxes, to import horses wholesale from the Mideast, to experiment with brahmans rather than royal kinsmen as garrison commanders, to sponsor agrarian reclamation, and to recruit hardy non-Muslim warriors from throughout the Deccan. With its capital on the strategic frontier between settled and semi-arid zones and thus able to draw resources from both, Vijayanagara by the early 1500s had become the largest, most urbanized, most powerful state in South Indian history.[21] To Vijayanagara's northeast the fellow "Hindu," sometime rival kingdom of the Gajapatis, based on the delta of the Mahanadi River, also demonstrated an insistent creativity and aggressive militarization.[22]

In fact, through imitation and parallel invention, between 1100 and 1600 Muslim and non-Muslim polities across South Asia shared a number of novel features, including more efficient revenue systems, growing reliance on long-distance trade, and expanded military recruitment from foreign lands and dry-zone districts. Extending from the Indus valley through Rajasthan into the Deccan, arid zones had long supplied pastoral warriors and war animals (horses, camels, transport oxen), but from the 11th or 12th century more intense agrarian–pastoral interaction joined improved rainfall (see below) to magnify the influence of these internal corridors.[23]

---

[20] Military prebends in Vijayanagara and Orissa are usually seen as derivative from the Delhi Sultanate. On Vijayanagara history and administration, *IBE*, ch. 3; Burton Stein, *NCHI*, vol. I, 2: *Vijayanagara* (Cambridge, 1989); idem, "State Formation and Economy Reconsidered," *MAS* 19 (1985): 393–400; Eaton, *NCHI*, ch. 4; Talbot, *Precolonial India*, 194–202; Carla Sinopoli, "From the Lion Throne," *JESHO* 43 (2000): 364–98; Carla Sinopoli and Kathleen Morrison, "Economic Diversity and Integration in a Pre-Colonial Indian Empire," *World Archeology* 23 (1992): 335–52; Sinopoli and Morrison, "Dimensions of Imperial Control," *American Anthropologist* 97 (1995): 83–96; Kathleen Morrison, "Naturalizing Disaster," in Garth Bawden and Richard Reycraft, eds., *Environmental Disaster and the Archaeology of Human Response* (Albuquerque, 2000), 21–33; Noboru Karashima, *Toward a New Formation* (Delhi, 1992); Anila Verghese, *Archaeology, Art, and Religion: New Perspectives on Vijayanagara* (New Delhi, 2000); Anna Dallapiccola et al., eds., *Vijayanagara: City and Empire*, 2 vols. (Stuttgart, 1985), vol. I, 1–158.

[21] *IBE*, 54, 56, 63, 83; Eaton, *NCHI*, 90–92.

[22] Kulke and Rothermund, *History*, 172–76, emphasizing imitation of Delhi; *IBE*, 56. On the post-1300 usage of "Hindu" – a term that both of these sources use to characterize the Gajapatis – see n. 16 *supra*.

[23] On the post-1000 role of arid and semi-arid zones, Gommans, "Silent Frontier," 1–23; idem, "The Eurasian Frontier After the First Millennium A.D.," *The Medieval History Jl.* 1 (1998): 125–43; idem, "Warhorse and Gunpowder in India, c. 1000–1850," in Jeremy

Yet the ultimate beneficiaries of new cavalry assets, long-distance trade, and expanding dry-zone influence were not local warriors, but mounted archers from that vast arid domain that extends from today's western Pakistan and Afghanistan through northern Iran to Turkmenistan, Uzbekistan, Tajikistan, and Kazakhstan. As in China, Inner Asian cavalry enjoyed a decisive field advantage magnified by novel organizational and fiscal measures. Andre Wink's claim that Islamic fiscal rationalization "vastly enhanced" the mobilization of Indian agrarian resources[24] finds echoes in Kulke's observation: "[T]here has always been wide agreement among historians that the establishment of the Delhi Sultanate and the Mughal empire initiated a new phase of state formation in Indian history."[25] Likewise Ludden has argued that "the end of the thirteenth century marked the end of an age dominated by ruling elites whose institutional powers had descended from the Guptas."[26]

As a dynamic incubator of military and administrative experiments that would define regional politics for centuries, the interface between arid and arable zones in what is now northern Iran, Afghanistan, northern Pakistan, and northwest India resembled the steppe–arable frontier in North China. Blending Mideastern traditions transmitted through the Ghaznavid (977–1187) and Ghurid (1175–1206) Dynasties of Afghanistan with Iranian and Indian customs, with adaptations of Mongol practice, and with ad hoc improvisation, the Delhi sultans promoted four principal administrative changes.

First, in order to secure access to both the agrarian wealth of Gangetic India and to the warriors, war-animals, and trade of the Inner Asian dry zone from which they themselves hailed, the new rulers set their capital at Delhi, which lay west of the old North Indian capital of Kanauj

---

Black, ed., *War in the Early Modern World* (London, 1999), 105–27; Eaton, *NCHI*, 13–15, 88, 137–38; John Richards, *Mughal Administration in Golconda* (Oxford, 1975), 3–7; Andre Wink, "From the Mediterranean to the Indian Ocean," *CSSH* 44 (2002): 416–45, esp. 435; idem, *Al-Hind*, vol. II, chs. 6–10; *IBE*, 49–52; Sumit Guha, *Environment and Ethnicity in India 1200–1991* (Cambridge, 1999), 47–57; Ludden, "History Outside Civilization." For definitions of arid, semi-arid, and wet, see above works by Gommans, plus Mihir Shah et al., eds., *Indian's Drylands* (Delhi, 1998), 109–27.

[24] Wink, "From the Mediterranean," 435.

[25] Kulke, "Introduction," in Kulke, *The State*, 31–32.

[26] Ludden, *NCHI*, 47. Also John Richards, "Mughal State Finance and the Premodern World Economy," *CSSH* 23 (1981): 295: "Successive Indo-Muslim states were generally more centralized than the conquered indigenous polities... [S]ultans devoted their organizational capacities... toward improving, consolidating, and intensifying the traditional state demand for a fixed share of the produce of the soil."

and closer to the agrarian–dry zone interface. A similar determination to combine sedentary wealth with mobile military power dictated, or would dictate, the siting along ecological borderlands not only of Vijayanagara, but of the Deccan capitals of Devagiri, Warangal, Bidar, Golkonda, and Aurangabad[27] – not to mention Beijing in North China, near the steppe–sown frontier. Second, in keeping with this external orientation, the early sultans relied on deracinated fellow Turks, augmented by Mongols, Khaljis, Persians, Tajiks, and Afghans, all of whom lacked roots in local society. In keeping with Turkic and Mideastern practice, the nucleus of Delhi's 13th-century army in fact were purchased originally as slaves.[28] Third, again influenced by Mideastern conventions, in return for military service, early Delhi sultans awarded their followers land revenue assignments, in principle transferable, known as *iqtas*. Each *iqta*-holder was expected to convert agrarian revenues to cash, remit part to the central treasury, and use the balance to support cavalry at levels specified by the sultan. This was the first time such assignments were used to fund a South Asian army, and, as noted, non-Muslim states seem to have copied this practice. Along with Islamic-cum-alien ethnic loyalties and slave recruitment, *iqta* grants promised to foster an aristocracy with weak local ties, dependent on the throne. Fourth, both because they sought to expand the cavalry and because *iqtas* eventually threatened to become hereditary, in lieu of *iqtas* early-14th-century sultans experimented with military salaries funded by higher land taxes generally payable in cash.[29]

---

[27] Kanauj had dominated since the mid-500s. Gommans, "Silent Frontier," 15–22; Wink, "From the Mediterranean," 435; *EAH*, vol. I, 374–75; vol. II, 270; Kulke and Rothermund, *History*, 105–109, 159.

[28] On Turkic military slavery and Sultanate administration and ethnicity, Wink *Al-Hind*, vol. II, 113–20, 150–61, 170–211; idem, "Al-Hind," *Itinerario* 12 (1988): 36–38; Jackson, *Delhi Sultanate*, 4–6, 41–43, 61–86, 174–85, 271; Clifford Bosworth, *The Ghaznavids* (Edinburgh, 1963), 98–114; *IBE*, 18–52; *EAH*, vol. I, 505–506; Eaton, *NCHI*, 25–26; Irfan Habib, "Formation of the Sultanate Ruling Class of the 13th Century," in Habib, ed., *Medieval India 1* (New Delhi, 1992), 1–21; Iqtidar Husain Siddiqui, "Social Mobility in the Delhi Sultanate," ibid., 22–48; Sunil Kumar, "The Ignored Elites," *MAS* 43 (2009): 45–77; idem, *Emergence*, chs. 2–6. For an incisive historiographic discussion, see ibid., 7–45, 352–61.

[29] Plunder from the Deccan and increased silver bullion flows from China to Bengal may have helped to inspire, or may have reinforced, these reforms. Cf. Akinobu Kuroda, "The Eurasian Silver Century, 1276–1359," *JGH* 4 (2009): 245–69, esp. 250–55; Simon Digby, "The Currency System," in *CEHI*, 93–97; Jackson, *Delhi Sultanate*, 242–49; Irfan Habib, "The Price Regulations of 'Ala'uddin Khalji," in Sanjay Subrahmanyam, ed., *Money and the Market in India 1100–1700* (Delhi, 1994), 85–111.

In the event, few of these innovations proved wholly successful. In part perhaps because bullion supplies and commodification remained inadequate to fund cash taxes on the scale intended, the Sultanate was obliged to return to *iqtas*, many of which became *de facto* fiefs shielded from central supervision. But even where *iqta* controls proved effective, armed chiefs in the countryside, heirs to preconquest traditions, often prevented urban-based Muslim elites from collecting regular taxes. Such vulnerabilities in rural North India were magnified by the Sultanate's ill-judged attempts to conquer the Deccan. Temporary victories aside, southern campaigns diverted attention from the heartland without producing secure ties to the distant, newly annexed provinces. In a mere 13 years, from 1334 to 1347, revolts by Delhi's own governors stripped away control over the entire Deccan, the far south, and Bengal. Retrenchment in the north was only temporarily successful, and well before Timur's sack of Delhi in 1398 the Sultanate was in disarray.[30]

Efforts to revive Delhi's authority, at first under the aforementioned Lodi clan and later Sher Shah Sur, were accompanied by reforms that suggest self-conscious trial and error. Lodi rulers, for example, developed a more uniform system of district jurisdictions (*sarkars*), while Sher Shah Sur laid the foundation for Mughal administration with cadastral surveys, high-quality coinage, demands for annual cash rather than in-kind taxes, and improvements to the trunk road from Bengal to the Punjab.[31] The Turkic-mediated transition from lithic to palm leaf and more especially to paper record-keeping nourished vibrant scribal subcultures that as early as the 1300s circulated handbooks on letter-writing and by the 1500s cherished distinctive norms of education.[32] Such innovations were a further precondition for Mughal administrative success.

---

[30] Jackson, *Delhi Sultanate*, chs. 13–15; Eaton, *NCHI*, 22–26, 37–40; Kulke and Rothermund, *History*, 160–69; Kumar, *Emergence*, ch. 5; and on North Indian provincialism, Simon Digby, "Before Timur Came," *JESHO* 47 (2004): 298–356. On the possible contribution of silver shortages to Sultanate difficulties after 1325/1330, see n. 155 *infra*.

[31] Richards, *NCHI*, 24, 83–84; *CEHI*, 236–37; Burton Stein, *A History of India* (Oxford, 1998), 166–67; Muzaffar Alam and Sanjay Subrahmanyam, "L'etat Moghol et sa fiscalite XVI-XVIIIe siecles," *Annales HSS*, 1994: 189–217; Dirk Kolff, *Naukar, Rajput and Sepoy* (Cambridge, 1990), ch. 2.

[32] Ali, *Courtly Culture*, 269; Eaton, *NCHI*, 150, on paper in Deccan administration; Richard Eaton, pers. commun., 2007; Richards, *NCHI*, 3; Velcheru Narayana Rao, David Shulman, and Sanjay Subrahmanyam, *Textures of Time* (Delhi, 2001), 19–23, 93–139, focusing on South India.

In fact, historians of Mughal administration divide between those who stress uniform, intrusive centralization[33] and those who emphasize patrimonial inefficiency and fluid local contexts. In the latter view, the empire resembled a "wall-to-wall carpet" less than a "patchwork quilt."[34] Yet all accept that until 1700 administration under the Mughals was more effective than under the Delhi sultans or Sher Shah Sur, not to mention pre-Muslim rulers. The Mughals, to whom the term "early modern" is increasingly applied,[35] not only drew on new commercial and technological currents, to which we shall return, but had a broader ethnic base and were less limited by clan organization than the Lodis or Sher Shah Sur. They were also heirs to three centuries of cumulative Indo-Islamic cultural accommodation. Defeated in repeated acts of resistance, by the mid-1550s Rajput, Maratha, Telugu, and other non-Muslim warrior lineages had come to accept the inevitability and legitimacy of Islamic power, which in fact assumed an ever more Indic coloration.[36]

Akbar (r. 1556–1605) – the principal architect of Mughal centralization whose reforms were all the more remarkable in that he, probably because of dyslexia, remained illiterate – expanded Sher Shah Sur's cadastres, but in contrast to that ruler's fixed rates, based taxes on decennial averages of yields and prices for each North Indian district. This pattern of assessments (the *zabt* system) formed the basis for all revenue assignments, now called *jagirs* rather than *iqtas*. To forestall the recreation of territorial fiefs, Akbar also modified the *iqta* system in two respects: first, whereas *iqta*-holders had authority over all aspects of administration, *jagir*-holders, at least in theory, controlled only revenue collections, with police and judicial affairs delegated to separate officials; and second, the Mughals, unlike the Delhi sultans, sought to

---

[33] E.g., Richards, *NCHI*; Stephen Blake, "The Patrimonial-Bureaucratic Empire of the Mughals," *JAS* 39 (1979): 77–99; and members of the so-called Aligarh School, represented by M. Athar Ali, "The Mughal Polity – A Critique of Revisionist Approaches," *MAS* 27 (1993): 699–710.

[34] Alam and Subrahmanyam, *Mughal State*, 57 and 1–71. For similar approaches, Muzaffar Alam, *The Crisis of Empire in Mughal North India* (Delhi, 1986); Chetan Singh, *Region and Empire* (Delhi, 1991); idem, "Centre and Periphery in the Mughal State," *MAS* 22 (1988): 299–318; Andre Wink, *Land and Sovereignty in India* (Cambridge, 1986); Farhat Hasan, *State and Locality in Mughal India* (Cambridge, 2004), 1–34.

[35] E.g., Sanjay Subrahmanyam, *Explorations in Connected History: From the Tagus to the Ganges* (New Delhi, 2005), 3–4, 14–16; *IBE*, 4, 152, 185; Barbara Metcalf and Thomas Metcalf, *A Concise History of India* (Cambridge, 2002), 26–27; Ludden, *India and South Asia*, 42–44, 84–85; John Richards, "Early Modern India and World History," *JWH* 8 (1997): 197–209; Stein, *History*, ch. 4.

[36] Richards, *NCHI*, 3.

rotate and scatter land assignments, to forbid local residence, and to strengthen bars to hereditary transmission.[37]

Between centrally appointed officials in provincial capitals and *jagir*-holders, on the one hand, and local cultivators, on the other, lay a diverse hereditary stratum loosely termed *zamindars*, "landholders," which included non-Muslim lineage heads and military chiefs responsible for collecting taxes directly from the peasantry. Local prestige and armed retainers gave *zamindars* considerable leverage in negotiations with imperial officials over collections and other prerogatives. Yet in the Mughals' heyday, besides concentrating overwhelming force against open opposition, the throne offered a panoply of material and cultural lures that sought to convert *zamindars*, especially the upper ranks, into what John Richards terms "quasi-officials" – men who identified in some degree with imperial culture, accepted incorporation in a central hierarchy, and agreed to surrender stipulated revenues. Thus the Mughals, in Richards' words, tried to crack the "hard cyst" of rural autonomy and to convert miniature tributary kingdoms into petty revenue units.[38] Refined in subsequent reigns, Akbar's tax system in North India is said to have taken from a third to half of agricultural output.[39] The land tax itself provided some 90 percent of royal income, of which over 80 percent went to *jagir* assignments and salaries of military officers, for their personal expenses and support of their troops, and another 9 percent to the central military establishment.[40] Scarcely imagined by

---

[37] On *jagirs*, Richards, *NCHI*, 66–68; Iqtidar Alam Khan, "The Mughal Assignment System During Akbar's Early Years, 1556–1575," in Habib, *Medieval India*, 62–128; *CEHI*, 235–49.

[38] Richards, *NCHI*, 86–93, 191–93, 294–96 focuses on the countryside. For the towns, where merchants could play a role analogous to that of *zamindars*, ibid., 194–96; Hasan, *State and Locality*, 110–25. On *zamindars* and taxes, see too *CEHI*, 244–45; Noman Ahmad Siddiqi, *Land Revenue Administration Under the Mughals (1700–1750)* (Bombay, 1970), 21–40; S. Nurul Hasan, "*Zamindars* Under the Mughals," in Alam and Subrahmanyam, *Mughal State*, 284–98.

[39] *CEHI*, 173, 176, 235, 238, 244–45. Special levies and collection fees could add 25 percent to original charges. Raymond Goldsmith, *Premodern Financial Systems* (Cambridge, 1987), 98, 117 puts the basic land tax at one-third of total rural income and two-fifths of the peasants' gross product. Richards, *NCHI*, 86 says a third of food grains and a fifth of other crops. Om Prakash, "The System of Credit in Mughal India," in Bagchi, *Money and Credit*, 40 says land revenue took "between 40 and 50 percent and perhaps even more of gross agricultural output."

[40] In 1600 the government collected 5,835 million *dams* (a *dam* was one-fortieth of a rupee), which by 1709 had grown to 13,340 million *dams*; but uncertain inflation rates make the real increase problematic. As *jagir*-holders collected their own revenues, the greater part of imperial taxes never actually entered royal coffers. See Richards, *NCHI*, 66–78,

the Delhi sultans, such inflows sustained what Ludden calls "South Asia's first empire of agrarian taxation."[41]

The Mughals strengthened not only fiscality, but broader systems of coordination. To improve provincial control they institutionalized competing jurisdictions, as between provincial governor and treasurer. They also multiplied provincial forts, improved arterial roads, made elaborate ceremonial progresses (in this respect resembling their peripatetic Valois counterparts), sought to standardize titles, weights, and coinage; and curtailed Mughal princely power, albeit without eliminating princely warfare as a basis for succession.[42] *Jagir*-holding military officers were unified in a decimally demarcated hierarchy, the *mansab* system. Because such officials, as heads of private households, bore the immediate burden of pay and recruitment, which in turn relied on clan and kinship ties, and because officials received a personal loyalty from their troops, this system, like those of late-16th-century France, Russia, Japan, and Southeast Asia, fell well short of a centralized standing army.[43] Yet insofar as all *mansab* forces remained at the disposal of the throne and had to meet more or less uniform standards, the Mughal military was more cohesive than its Sultanate predecessor.[44] Especially from the mid-1600s, greater insistence on military and fiscal measurement, efforts at legal standardization, and a torrent of systematized written records intensified trends toward "a paper empire." Complementing these organizational shifts was an enduring emphasis on intense personal devotion to the emperor, or to his princes or high officials, in return for patronage. As embodied in Indo-Persian court ritual, reciprocal obligation underlay aristocratic notions of honor and structured throne–noble relations.[45]

---

186 (note that his figures on 76 and 186 do not agree); Alam and Subrahmanyam, "L'etat Moghol," 194; Siddiqi, *Land Revenue*, 21–59; Shireen Moosvi, "The Zamindars' Share in the Peasant Surplus in the Mughal Empire," *IESHR* 15 (1978): 359–75. On inflation, *CEHI*, 372–81; Sanjay Subrahmanyan, "Precious Metal Flows and Prices in Western and Southern Asia, 1500–1750," *Studies in History* 7 (1991): 79–105.

[41] Ludden, *NCHI*, 6, and 131–35.

[42] Lisa Balabanlilar, "Lords of the Auspicious Conjunction," *JWH* 18 (2007): 1–39, esp. 15–19; Munis Faruqui, "At Empire's End," *MAS* 43 (2009): 9–16. Princely controls were generally less radical than contemporaneous reforms in Burma, Siam, or Russia.

[43] John Lynn, *Battle* (Cambridge, MA, 2003), 152; Seema Alavi, *The Sepoys and the Company* (Delhi, 1995), 13–17.

[44] Richards, *NCHI*, 24–25, 58–64; Jos Gommans, *Mughal Warfare* (London, 2000), 56–64, 81–88, 100–11, 137–38, 197–98.

[45] The phrase "paper empire" is found at Alam and Subrahmanyam, *Mughal State*, 31. On administrative centralization, see Gommans, *Mughal Warfare*, 93–94, 105–106, 137–38;

Spotting differences – in scale, interstate contexts, elite origins – between the Mughal empire and its protected-zone counterparts is easy enough. To such idiosyncrasies we shall return. But for now consider overarching similarities between South Asian, Burmese, Siamese, Russian, French, and Japanese regimes. After mid- or late-16th-century upheavals, in each realm a new dynasty (re)unified extensive territories, reduced provincial autonomy, overhauled the military, worked out new accommodations with hereditary power holders, and thus developed novel tax systems. Differences in efficiency and targeted resources aside, the cadastres of Akbar, Tha-lun's 1630s land inquests in Burma, Romanov enserfment, Richelieu's huge impositions, and the land surveys of Toyotomi Hideyoshi and Tokugawa Ieyasu all sought increases in agrarian extraction in order to support more powerful armies. All these regimes cohered between 1555 and 1630; all built self-consciously on earlier experiments; all founded tax systems that endured at least to the 18th century. As we shall see, all benefited from European-style firearms and growing silver supplies. In each case as well, an early historiographic insistence on central imposition has yielded to a greater appreciation of local powers of negotiation and resistance.

Given early Mughal success, why did the empire collapse in the early and mid-1700s? We shall later treat economic and cultural aspects of this problem, but for now, in keeping with our administrative focus, consider four institutional/political weaknesses, some familiar from the Sultanate. First, despite Mughal power, *zamindar* autonomy carried long-term entropic dangers. Compared to their Tokugawa and Bourbon peers, the Mughals never succeeded in disarming rural elites or in socializing them fully to imperial norms. Unlike *shogun* and *daimyo*, for example, the Mughals rarely dealt directly with individual villages, relations being conducted through *zamindar* intermediaries. As more *zamindars* became imperial military officers (*mansabdars*) without relinquishing local ties, the *mansab* system in effect became an instrument of *zamindar* rather than imperial interests. At the same time, formal prohibitions notwithstanding, many *jagir*-holders began to convert temporary appointments into hereditable lordships, essentially becoming

Richards, *NCHI*, 3, 58–59; and nn. 33, 34 *supra*. On ritualized personal loyalties, John Richards, "Norms of Comportment Among Imperial Mughal Officers," in Barbara Metcalf, ed., *Moral Conduct and Authority* (Berkeley, 1984), 255–89; Hasan, *State and Locality*, 14–17; Gommans, *Mughal Warfare*, 40–41, 56–64; Eaton, *Rise of Islam*, 159–65; Mukhia, *The Mughals*, chs. 1, 2; Rosalind O'Hanlon, "Kingdom, Household and Body History, Gender and Imperial Service Under Akbar," *MAS* 41 (2007): 889–923.

zamindars themselves and accelerating the localization of power. Late-17th-century Mughal efforts to draw up new cadastres and to regulate matters hitherto under regional control often fed *zamindar* resistance, prompting some to form factional alliances with sectors of the imperial elite.

Second, above the level of local *zamindars*, the center had recurrent difficulty controlling regional leaders, both hereditary *rajas* in inaccessible areas and senior provincial appointees in the Deccan and Bengal. When imperial authority faltered in the 1700s, both groups were quick to withhold revenues, to circumvent institutional checks on their power, and to take unauthorized military and diplomatic initiatives.

Third, in a stunning replay of 14th-century problems, the decision of the emperor Aurangzeb (r. 1658–1707) to extend his control over the Deccan overstrained imperial resources. He sought to break the power of Maratha rebels and to annex semi-independent sultanates accused of aiding the Marathas. But the unexpectedly heavy costs of these campaigns, the influx of nobles from the Deccan whom the emperor had to reward with new *jagir* assignments, and his quixotic decision to retain vast Deccan territories as crown lands rather than make them available for *jagirs* created a mismatch between noble expectations and available resources, intensifying factionalism.[46]

Finally, in campaigning against the Marathas and other provincial insurgents, the Mughal army, dependent on imported horses, heavy cavalry, and massive siege trains, failed to adapt organizationally or psychologically to their foes' swift light cavalry, hill forts, infantry, and rustic martial ethos. Likewise the manufacture of crude but effective firearms in the countryside, notwithstanding repeated Mughal prohibitions, eroded the center's technical superiority.[47]

---

[46] M. Athar Ali, *The Mughal Nobility Under Aurangzeb* (Bombay, 1966), 102–11; Richards, *NCHI*, ch. 11; idem, "The 17th-Century Crisis in South Asia," *MAS* 24 (1990): 635–37; Gommans, *Mughal Warfare*, 77–81, 218; *IBE*, 233–36; Satish Chandra, "Review of the Crisis of the Jagirdari System," in Alam and Subrahmanyam, *Mughal State*, 347–60.

[47] On the spread of firearms as a threat to the Mughals, Kulke and Rothermund, *History*, 195. The view that lumbering columns were a Mughal liability is common, but Gommans, "Warhorse and Gunpowder," 109 argues that the Marathas later imitated grand Mughal military processions because they were actually the best way to attract adherents. On Mughal decline generally, nn. 34, 46 *supra*, plus Gommans, *Mughal Warfare*, 68–69, 81, 97–99, 198–99; Alam and Subrahmanyam, *Mughal State*, 1–71, 421–519; Andrea Hintze, *The Mughal Empire and Its Decline* (Aldershot, UK, 1997), chs. 6–11; C. A. Bayly, *NCHI*, vol. II, 1: *Indian Society and the Making of the British Empire* (Cambridge, 1988), 1–44, 79–168; idem, *Rulers, Townsmen and Bazaars* (Cambridge, 1983), 1–73; Stewart

As the empire disintegrated, its heirs and challengers created in the mid-1700s a multistate system whose Darwinian insistence on military and fiscal innovation recalls 18th-century Southeast Asia and, more especially, early modern Europe. Apart from French and British trading companies, the chief players, as noted, were states led by Mughal officers in Bengal, Awadh, and Hyderabad and new or expanding polities under local potentates and warrior-peasant groups. For such contenders a European-inspired military revolution – focusing on field artillery, flintlocks, and intensively drilled infantries – raised substantially the cost and complexity of administration. This in turn mandated closer alliance with banking and commercial interests; wider use of tax farms, monopolies, and cash salaries; a reduction in *zamindar* autonomy; and more elaborate archives – all pointing to more penetrating administrative systems. Whereas, for example, the southern state of Mysore in 1600 had taken as taxes 10 percent of the crop, by the 1790s, it was closer to 40 percent. Post-Mughal regional centralization, we shall find, went hand in hand with the cultivation of regional religious and ethnic identities.[48]

In some ways the English East India Company merely grafted itself onto Indian patterns. The Company continued to acknowledge Mughal suzerainty and until 1835 retained Persian as the chief administrative language. In monopolizing key lines of trade, squeezing *zamindars*, and concentrating funds on trained infantry, the British pursued the same basic strategies as other Mughal successor states. Indian bankers and tax farmers provided the Company with what C. A. Bayly calls "the keys to unlock the wealth of Indian rural society."[49] So too the Company's early adherence to Indo-Persian norms of revenue management won the

Gordon, *NCHI*, vol. II, 4: *The Marathas, 1699–1818* (Cambridge, 1993), chs. 3, 4; J. S. Grewal, *NCHI*, vol. II, 3: *The Sikhs of the* Punjab (Cambridge, 1990), chs. 4–6; *IBE*, chs. 8, 9.

[48] Mysore figures from Bayly, *NCHI*, 25, 96. Recall that after imperial collapse in China, smaller regional regimes also achieved greater administrative penetration. On 18th-century military fiscalism and regional centralization in India, previous note plus Alam and Subrahmanyam, *Mughal State*, 46–55, 68; Alam, *Crisis of Empire*, chs. 6, 7; Norman Peabody, *Hindu Kingship and Polity in Precolonial India* (Cambridge, 2003); Gordon, *NCHI*, 185–95; Stein, "State Formation," 387–413; Ludden, *India and South Asia*, 108–23; idem, *Peasant History*, ch. 3; D. A. Washbrook, "Progress and Problems," *MAS* 22 (1988): 57–96; idem, "South India 1770–1840," *MAS* 38 (2004): 479–516; Wink, *Land and Sovereignty*, ch. 4; Alavi, *Sepoys and the Company*, 11–13, 17–35; Randolph Cooper, *The Anglo-Maratha Campaigns and the Contest for India* (Cambridge, 2003), esp. 15–61.

[49] Bayly, *NCHI*, 44. On pre-Company/Company continuities ibid., chs. 1–5; Washbrook, "Progress and Problems"; idem, "Law, State, and Agrarian Society in Colonial India,"

support of non-Muslim and Muslim notables.[50] Frequently the British sought only indirect influence, as through the "subsidiary alliance system," in which in return for military protection, local princes agreed to pay for Company troops and to accept British advisers. Indeed, outside Bengal, Bihar, and territories around Madras, as late as 1820 there were still few areas that could be described as zones of true colonial rule.[51]

In other respects, however, Company policy was genuinely novel. By joining the revenues of Bengal to North India's military labor market, the Company created a force of indigenous troops (*sepoys*), under European officers, that became not only the largest standing army in Indian history – 155,000 by 1805 – but, through standard arms, regular wages, pensions, and the co-optation of caste loyalties, the most powerful.[52] From the 1780s the Company dismissed all senior Indian office-holders in its employ – "Every native of Hindostan, I verily believe, is corrupt," Governor-General Lord Charles Cornwallis explained[53] – in favor of a cadre of European revenue collectors whose high salaries and rigorous training earned a reputation for incorruptibility. Thus gradually emerged a peculiarly nomothetic, routinized regime, in some ways an extension of the state in Georgian England, manned at top solely by whites and aided by advanced technologies of finance, documentation, and cartography.[54] In order to raise agrarian productivity and secure war finance, the Company also replaced the Bengali system of multiple usufruct land rights with a system in which *zamindars* obtained full proprietary rights subject to fixed revenue assessments. Although the expectation that *zamindars*, their rights secure, would become enterprising English-style farmers was a chimera, these new arrangements met the Company's rising revenue demands. Meanwhile, particularly in the Deccan, by encouraging sedentarization and drying up

---

MAS 15 (1981): 649–721, esp. 661–70; Stein, "State Formation," 404–408; Metcalfs, *Concise History*, 55–90; Bernard Cohn, "The Language of Command and the Command of Language," in Ranajit Guha, ed., *Subaltern Studies IV* (Delhi, 1985), 276–329.

[50] Likewise, on the Company's dialogue with religious and legal authorities, see Thomas Trautmann, *Aryans and British India* (Berkeley, 1997), chs. 1–3.

[51] Susan Bayly, *Caste, Society, and Politics in India* (Cambridge, 1999), 80; Bayly, *NCHI*, 79–105 *passim*; Metcalfs, *Concise History*, 70–74.

[52] Alavi, *Sepoys and the Company*; Lynn, *Battle*, ch. 5; and Stephen Rosen, *Societies and Military Power* (Ithaca, 1996), ch. 5, proposing a different social dynamic than Alavi or Lynn.

[53] Quoted in Metcalfs, *Concise History*, 58.

[54] Cf. Sudipta Sen, *Empire of Free Trade* (Philadelphia, 1998), 17, 40, 89–143, and *passim*.

alternate military employment, the Company curbed hunter-gatherers' and pastoralists' habitual evasion of taxes and eliminated their threat to its military monopoly.[55]

Between 1798 and 1818 an aggressive imperial policy, stimulated by the Napoleonic wars, began to envision British dominion over the entire subcontinent. Some acquisitions required frontal attacks, as against the formidable powers of Mysore and the Maratha confederacy. Other gains evolved from the subsidiary alliance system, which subjected allied states to disintegrative fiscal demands. Although the alliance system lost its *raison d'être* after the Marathas' defeat in 1818, the Company continued to police carefully the remaining princely states, including Awadh, Hyderabad, Mysore, and Rajput domains, some of whose low productivity did not justify the expense of direct rule. But there too independent armies were forbidden and British advisers sought to regulate succession and introduce Western norms. In thus destroying the competitive interstate system and fluid social environment of the 18th century, the British began to construct a fixed sedentary order, based on narrow interpretations of "tradition," which could sustain unprecedentedly heavy taxation. Even in its early days, Bayly concludes, the Company's range of activities, its growing monopoly on force, and its ability to extract resources from a peasantry now increasingly disarmed set it apart from all previous South Asian regimes.[56]

In sum, South Asian administrative culture, benefiting from repeated external interventions and responding most commonly to military exigency, demonstrated a multifaceted, centuries-long improvement in fiscal and military capacity that helps to explain the growing longevity and influence of major states.

---

[55] In parts of the south a revenue scheme that awarded property rights not to landlords, but to peasant cultivators, proved no more successful in stimulating productivity than the Bengal system. See following note plus Guha, *Environment and Ethnicity*, ch. 5; and T. R. Travers, "'The Real Value of the Lands,'" *MAS* 38, 3 (2004): 517–58.

[56] Bayly, *NCHI*, 110. For overviews of early British administration and historiographic emphases ranging from profound continuity to radical dislocation, see n. 49 *supra*, plus Sen, *Empire of Free Trade*, contrasting indigenous and British political economy; C. A. Bayly, *Empire and Information* (New Delhi, 1999); Ian Barrow and Douglas Haynes, "The Colonial Transition: South Asia, 1780–1840," *MAS* 38 (2004): 469–78; P. J. Marshall, *NCHI*, vol. II, 2: *Bengal: The British Bridgehead* (Cambridge, 1987), 93–182; Nicholas Dirks, *Castes of Mind* (Princeton, 2001), and idem, *Hollow Crown*, 309–97, emphasizing political and cultural rupture; Radhika Singha, *A Despotism of Law* (Oxford, 1998); Michael Fisher, *Indirect Rule in India* (Oxford, 1993), chs. 2, 4–7.

Territorial Expansion

Along with shorter periods of polycentrism and more effective administrations, we find a familiar tendency for successive empires to encompass larger territories. The map of British India should not lead us to posit some unwavering *telos* to unify precisely those areas. Not only did most conquerors aspire to rule only a fraction, but from the Achaemenids (522–331 B.C.E.) and the Kusanas (1?–230? C.E.) to the early Mughals, some sought to join North India with lands far to the west. Nonetheless, it is also true that successive polities centered on the North Indian plain not only extended their outer zones of control to embrace more and more of the subcontinent, but reduced India's internal frontiers separating sown from dry pastoral lands and jungle.[57]

The Maurya empire claimed authority over much of the subcontinent, but as noted, its rule was often nominal and its internal frontiers exceptionally long. Beyond the imperial core of the east-central Ganges lay vast areas of forest and pastoral lands – including the Himalayan foothills and much of modern-day Orissa, Madhya Pradesh, Pakistan, Rajasthan, and the Deccan – interspersed with agrarian pockets. Only these latter areas were effectively incorporated into the empire, and even then, only with the help of local intermediaries.

At its height under Candragupta II c. 410 C.E., the Gupta empire, recall, probably held a settled Gangetic core larger than that of the Mauryas, beyond which tributaries controlled most of the subcontinent north of the Narmada. South of that river, however, Gupta influence, via marriage ties to the Vakataka Dynasty, was at best indirect. Meanwhile, notwithstanding a reputed Gupta "Conquest of the Directions" (*digvijaya*) as far as modern Tamil Nadu, extensive eastern and southern areas where the Mauryas had claimed authority were now fully independent.[58]

For almost 700 years after the Guptas declined, that is, from c. 550 to 1236, the subcontinent remained politically divided among four principal spheres: the northern plain west of Bengal, Bengal itself, the western

---

[57] On Achaemenids and Kusanas, Kulke and Rothermund, *History*, 53–54, 74–79. For a fascinating counterfactual account of Indo-Persian empire, Sanjay Subrahmanyam, *Explorations in Connected History: Mughals and Franks* (New Delhi, 2005), 173–209. On external and inner frontiers, n. 23 *supra*, plus J. C. Heesterman, "Warrior, Peasant, and Brahmin," *MAS* 29 (1995): 637–54; Sinopoli, "Imperial Landscapes," 324–49.

[58] Talbot, *Precolonial India*, 7; Kulke and Rothermund, *History*, 82–85, 364, 366; Agrawal, *Rise and Fall*, 95–97, 106–25, 161–70,196–200, 215–16; Ali, *Courtly Culture*, 30.

Deccan, and the southeast. Despite secular improvements in administration and frequent dynastic changes, the same patterns continuously reproduced themselves: each sphere usually had one premier power, no one sphere could dominate any of the other three for any length of time, but within each sphere local *samantas* often challenged their overlord, periodically establishing independent polities.[59]

With Delhi Sultanate conquests, the pendulum again shifted, albeit temporarily. Delhi, we saw, reunited northern and northeastern India and in the 14th century went on to penetrate deep into the peninsula. Thus Delhi, first in a series of what Richard Eaton terms "transregional sultanates," briefly dominated all four previously independent spheres and anticipated Mughal integration.[60] If these southern conquests lasted barely a generation, by smashing existing networks, Delhi facilitated the rise of new polities, including the Bahmani Sultanate, founded 1347 in the northern Deccan, and Vijayanagara, to its south. Under Bahmani, under smaller sultanates that devolved from Bahmani, and to some extent under Vijayanagara, institutional, religious, and ideological systems introduced by Delhi continued. Thus Delhi also brought the culture of North and South India into closer alignment.[61]

Their initial attempt at conquest having been thwarted, the Mughals returned from Persian exile in 1555 and by the end of Akbar's reign in 1605 controlled eastern and central Afghanistan (later lost in part), the entire Indo-Gangetic plain including Bengal, and territories running from Rajasthan, Sind, and Gujarat into the northwest Deccan. Throughout the 17th century, the Mughals pushed farther south to subdue those Deccan sultanates, chiefly Ahmadnagar, Bijapur, and Golkonda, that had devolved from the Bahmani kingdom. As population growth spurred agrarian reclamation (see below), the Mughals also came to dominate interior dry-land and forest districts where the writ of the Delhi sultans had never reached. Except for the far south and humid, malarial areas in Gondwana, Assam, and along the Himalayan foothills and the Western Ghats where imperial cavalry could not easily

---

[59] Kulke and Rothermund, *History*, 8–12, 105–30; Ali, *Courtly Culture*, 30–37; John Keay, *India: A History* (New York, 2000), chs. 8–11.

[60] Eaton, *NCHI*, 9–11, 22–26, 35–40, referring to colonial "direct rule" over the north Deccan. See too idem, *Rise of Islam*, 32–40; Jackson, *Delhi Sultanate*, chs. 10, 13; Kulke and Rothermund, *History*, 159–66. Better to control his conquests, Muhammad Tughluq (r. 1324–1351) shifted his capital from Delhi to the Deccan city of Daulatabad.

[61] *IBE*, 43, 53–54 and 32–50 *passim*; Eaton, *NCHI*, 22, 37–43.

penetrate, by 1700 the subcontinent lay under a nominally unified authority, although as Maratha challenges soon showed, such control could be quite tenuous.[62]

Whereas the Mauryas, Guptas, Delhi sultans, and Mughals all expanded from the Indo-Gangetic plain to the south and from interior to coast, the British, as befit a naval power, advanced from coastal enclaves into the interior. The British acquired Madras, key to the Coromandel textile trade, in 1640, and Bombay from the Portuguese in 1661–1668, but it was Calcutta, founded by the Company in Mughal territory in 1690, that became the centerpiece of British enterprise. Between 1756 and 1765, with the help of local *zamindars* and bankers who prized British ties at a time when trade had shifted from internal routes to the sea, the British seized Bengal from its post-Mughal rulers. Thereafter they used the agrarian wealth of that province, India's richest, to finance expansion across the subcontinent. True, the Company long remained one of several "country powers" – in the 1780s Mysore, with powerful Western-style forces, fought the British to a draw – but from 1798 the Company's new forward policy, as noted, led to the dismemberment of Awadh (1801) and Mysore (1799) and the annexation of Arcot (1801), Maratha territories (1818), Sri Lanka (1815), and coastal Burma (1826). The 1839 death of the Sikh ruler of the Punjab led to the last major subcontinental annexations, namely, Sind, the Punjab, and Kashmir. By 1852 the British controlled a network of directly and indirectly ruled territories from Burma to the frontiers of modern Afghanistan and from the Himalayan foothills to the south coast of Sri Lanka. If their authority in the northwest remained less extensive than that of the early Mughals, it surpassed Mughal dominion in the east and south. So too British control of pastoral and forest lands was unprecedented.[63]

Horizontal and Vertical Cultural Integration Across South Asia

Administrative efficiency and territorial integration had a synergistic relation to, and yet a life independent from, another broadly familiar

---

[62] *IBE*, 117; Richards, *NCHI*, 96–154 *passim*, 282–83; Gommans, *Mughal Warfare*, 34–39; Schwartzberg, *Historical Atlas*, 44–47. For slightly different views of maximum Delhi and Mughal territories, see also Eaton, *NCHI*, 33–35; frontispiece map at Richards, *NCHI*; Stein, *History*, 110; and Schwartzberg, *Historical Atlas*, 46.

[63] On the assemblage of Britain's Indian empire, *IBE*, ch. 9; Bayly, *NCHI*, chs. 3, 4; idem, *Rulers, Townsmen*; Sen, *Empire of Free Trade*, chs. 2–5.

dynamic: long-term cultural integration. Political fragmentation meant that for centuries there was no central authority to define normative culture or promote compliance. This situation joined low literacy, poor communications, and caste constraints to create a far more tenuous link between cultural and political integration in South Asia at large than in China or individual protected-zone realms. And yet for at least part of the Gupta, Delhi Sultanate, and especially the Mughal eras, pan-South Asian cultural currents and imperial projects did support one another. As elsewhere, moreover, cultural integration had both horizontal and vertical components.

I shall consider in turn five major movements of pan-Indian cultural circulation: a) the diffusion of Sanskritic elite practices from North India starting in the mid-first millennium; b) the spread of *bhakti* devotionalism from South India starting in the late first millennium; c) acceptance of more orthodox notions of caste across the subcontinent from the mid-1600s; d) the integrative thrust of Perso-Islamic, or what with time became Indo-Islamic, culture from the 12th century; and e) the intensification across North India after c. 1700 of literate urban-based communications.[64]

The Diffusion of Sanskritic Culture. As elaborated under the Guptas, the charter civilization of North India was preeminently Sanskritic and brahmanic. Essentially a new religion arose under the brahman priesthood, whose ritual credentials derived from Vedic sources of the second and first millennia B.C.E. but who now presided over a devotional culture focused on Siva, Visnu, and the Goddess (Devi). Subsuming local gods and goddesses, these towering deities, Siva and Visnu in particular, were worshipped in royally endowed temples whose land grants were recorded in Sanskrit. Long a sacred ritual language, Sanskrit, the "language of the gods," was itself in the early centuries C.E. reinvented as a code for political and learned expression. By 500 C.E. Sanskrit literature included lawbooks, technical treatises, histories, eulogies, and other forms of verse, prose, and dramatic performance. Sanskrit would retain unchallenged preeminence until the early second millennium when regional languages and then Persian began partially to displace

---

[64] British culture, one could argue, represented a sixth integrative movement, but its impact to 1830 was too limited to justify inclusion in this broad survey. At the other historic extreme, Asokan hagiography aside, too little is known of Mauryan cultural influence across the subcontinent to permit confident discussion.

it.[65] The original region of Sanskrit dominance, North India in general and the Ganges basin in particular, was designated by brahmans as *Aryavarta* – "Land of the Aryans/the Upper Castes/the Noble" – whose privileged relation to benighted outlying lands calls to mind the self-flattering "All Under Heaven" designation that early Chinese elites awarded the North China plain.[66] For centuries the Ganges basin remained the center of Sanskrit culture, and to this day modern Uttar Pradesh, which together with Bihar constituted the Gupta core, has India's largest brahman population.

In the early first millennium southern and central India remained not only too inaccessible, but perhaps too limited demographically and economically to follow northern models in detail. We thus find an array of political, religious, and linguistic forms, as, for example, in the Tamil country where tribal polities and indigenous-language poetry operated independently of northern traditions.[67] However, between c. 300 and 1000 C.E. – a period spanning, in part, all three of Kulke's administrative stages – alongside North Indian political technologies a complex of cultural features oriented toward royal courts spread from the Ganges heartland across northwestern, eastern, and southern India, and indeed parts of Southeast Asia. These features included a Sanskrit monopoly on creative written expression, brahmanic ritual leadership, brahmanically sanctioned social divisions, the notion of *Aryavarta* as a privileged zone, plus Gupta-style court terminology, architecture, and art. Across South Asia we therefore find a composite but increasingly homogeneous elite political culture whose adherents, despite purely local power bases, identified with the Gupta ideal of a supreme ruler presiding over a Sanskrit-sanctified domain. As an expression of this universal ideal, in South India and Southeast Asia alike, cities, mountains, and rivers were named after celebrated sites in the Ganges basin, in *Aryavarta*.[68] By the late first millennium "India" (from the medieval Arabic

---

[65] On first-millennium Sanskrit culture, esp. its relation to the court, Ali, *Courtly Culture*, 78–85; and Pollock, *Language of the Gods*, 1–4, 13–14, 39–44, 77–79, 114–15, 191.

[66] Previous note, plus Madhav Deshpande, *Sociolinguistic Attitudes in India* (Ann Arbor, 1979), 47–50; Pollock, *Language of the Gods*, 58, 191; Eaton, *Rise of Islam*, 118–19; Stein, *History*, 83–86, 96–99; Edward Dimock, Jr. et al., *The Literatures of India* (Chicago, 1974), 16–19, 47–114. Cf. Ch. 5, n. 68 *supra*.

[67] Thapar, *Early India*, 278, 326–62. This, despite the fact that by the first century C.E. elements of Indo-Aryan languages had mixed with Dravidian languages.

[68] Pollock, *Language of the Gods*, 234–36, 245–49, 272–73; Ali, *Courtly Culture*, 33, 37; O. W. Wolters, "Khmer 'Hinduism' in the Seventh Century," in R. B. Smith and W. Watson, *Early South-East Asia* (New York, 1979), 427–42.

"al-Hind") – although its geographic limits were notoriously imprecise, in some accounts restricted to the Indo-Gangetic plain, in others including the peninsula, in yet others embracing the peninsula and much of Southeast Asia – was conceived by Muslim and Chinese observers alike as a coherent civilizational zone. This global culture-power formation Sheldon Pollock terms the "Sanskrit cosmopolis."[69]

Across South Asia, in particular, the dissemination of North Indian Sanskritic norms drew strength from competition among kingdoms eager to partake of Gupta glory as well as from social tensions associated with the agrarian incorporation of pastoral and tribal peoples. According to the fourfold caste (*varna*) system, rulers should come from the *ksatriya* caste, that of warriors, who ranked second below brahmans. But in forested and hilly regions on the agrarian frontier, tribal leaders without proper credentials seeking to carve out kingdoms on the Gupta model invited North India brahmans to provide them with *ksatriya* genealogies and rituals suitable to their new station.[70] Brahmans thus legitimated kingship in the eyes not of commoners – who, of course, were politically invisible – but of royal aspirants themselves, their elite followers, and regional rivals. At the same time the focus on proper language as a necessary correlate of social order and the mastery of intricate codes and protocols must have had a powerful autonomous aesthetic appeal.[71] Once rustic chieftains and their retainers imbibed this "common culture of worldliness," to use Daud Ali's phrase, once they entered the ranks of the *arya*, of "noble society," they left the coarse, vulgar world of villagers, not to mention fierce hill and forest peoples, all of whom were now deemed *adhama* (base). The visible signs, the institutional expressions, of Sanskrit acculturation were the royal court, the brahman educational center (*ghatika*), the seminary (*matha*), the temple, and the Sanskrit poem on copper plate or stone pillar recording royal donations. In short, Sanskrit culture, with its patterned endowments

---

[69] Pollock, *Language of the Gods*, 1, 16–19, 115–61, 177–78, 222, 254–56; idem, "Sanskrit Cosmopolis"; idem, "The Cosmopolitan Vernacular," *JAS* 57 (1998): 6–37; idem, "Literary History, Indian History, World History," *Social Scientist* 23 (1995): 112–42; idem, "Cosmopolitan and Vernacular in History," *Public Culture* 12 (2000): 591–625; idem, "Introduction," in *LCH*, 29, plus Ali, *Courtly Culture*, 15, 20–37, 51, 60–85, 108, 264–65. On the derivation of "India," similar to that of "Hindu," n. 16 *supra*. On early external perceptions of South Asia as a coherent cultural zone, also Wink, *Al-Hind*, vol. I, 5 and *passim*; Subrahmanyam, *Explorations: Tagus to Ganges*, 7–8.

[70] Notes 14–16 *supra*. Nor was this unique to the frontier, as both the Mauryas and Guptas were of non-*ksatriya* origins. Ali, *Courtly Culture*, 37.

[71] See Pollock, *Language of the Gods*, 133, 177–78, 256–58, 524.

and indices of refinement, facilitated both horizontal integration and social differentiation.[72]

As a mid- and late-first-millennium movement exalting a universal elite language with towering claims to expressive superiority, the spread of Sanskrit resembled the contemporaneous dissemination of Latin in early medieval Europe and of Chinese in South China, Vietnam, Korea, and Japan.[73] Yet Sanskrit was unique in that it was a tongue neither of administration nor daily communication; nor, after Gupta eclipse, did its spread depend on a central political or religious organization such as the Carolingian, the Ottonian, or the Chinese empire or the Catholic church. In turn, perhaps because it relied on autonomous processes and independent local actors, Sanskrit, more obviously than Latin and especially Chinese, not only tolerated, but encouraged the writing of local languages (notwithstanding the latter's initial relegation to a documentary role inferior to Sanskrit) and the multiplication of local scripts.[74] Nor did Sanskrit demand religious or cultic conformity, insofar as Jains, Buddhist, Saivas, and Vaisnavas all wrote Sanskrit poetry. In Pollock's formulation, rather than absorb peripheries into the center in the manner of Latin, Sanskrit sought to turn peripheries into new centers. Hence the proliferation across South and Southeast Asia of new rivers Ganges, of new Mount Merus, of new *Aryavartas*.[75]

Essentially Sanskritization, that is, the spread of Sanskritic and brahmanic norms, threw a thin canopy over local practices that remained socially and religiously diverse. By 500 C.E. in long-settled parts of the Ganges basin, rigidly segregated, endogamous social classes may have approximated caste conventions as they were known in 1800. Elsewhere, however, as herders, upland warriors, shifting cultivators, and forest dwellers entered agrarian societies, they assumed identities that were ad hoc, situationally specific, fluid, and usually unconnected to any grand brahmanic schema of caste. Thus in medieval Andhra Pradesh, Talbot shows, public identities stressed local occupations and individual achievement far more than hereditary privilege. The same was probably true of large areas in the western Deccan, Bengal, the Punjab, and other

---

[72] Ali, *Courtly Culture*, 37, 69–70, 101–102, 264.
[73] Or, indeed, of Arabic in North Africa and Southwest Asia.
[74] All derived from Brahmi script.
[75] Sheldon Pollock, "Sanskrit Literary Culture from the Inside Out," in *LCH*, 110 and 39–110 *passim*; idem, *Language of the Gods*, 259–80, 571–72. See too Thapar, *Early India*, chs. 9–11; George Spencer, *The Politics of Expansion* (Madras, 1983), 18–22.

frontiers where people were in short supply and exogamy common.[76] Likewise, if Visnu and Siva became all-India deities, they still presided over idiosyncratic local pantheons, and even Visnu's *avatars* and consorts exhibited remarkable local plasticity. So too, if by 1000 the rituals and basic layout of temples across India were similar, we also find increasingly distinct regional variations.[77]

The Spread of Bhakti *Devotionalism.* A similar interplay between universal and local forms became marked in the second grand movement of cultural diffusion we shall consider, namely the devotional religious tradition known as *bhakti.* Although this included groups as diverse as the antinomian, virulently antibrahman Lingayats and conservative advocates of caste orthodoxy, *bhakti* in general was characterized by intense personal attachment to a deity often expressed in poem-songs. In the Tamil country in the far south, *bhakti* poems or hymns date as early as the 600s C.E. and were collected and established as a canon from the late 11th century. As championed by Tamil Saivite and Vaisnava saints, *bhakti* laid novel stress on emotion, mysticism, and self-effacing submission, all of which promised common people a relation to an iconic deity independent of brahmanic mediation. Tamil *bhakti* poets addressed Visnu, for example, in the language of erotic desire, as if they were lovesick women, or in the idiom of childlike dependence. To reach a mass audience, *bhakti* not only favored poetry in Tamil rather than Sanskrit, but exalted Tamil poet-saints of diverse backgrounds, honored female devotees, and accompanied the singing of poems with music and dance. Here, then, was a powerful challenge to brahman elitism.

Although Tamils were the first to create a corpus of hymns in their own language, from the early second millennium devotees in other regions followed suit, first in other parts of southern and central India and then in the north. Examples included devotees of the aforementioned Lingayat (Virasaiva) cult, an anticaste movement with pastoral roots that cohered in Kannada-speaking areas of the Deccan from the 1160s; Marathi saints who sang in praise of the expressly Marathi cult of Vithoba (Visnu) from the late 1200s; and such North Indian

---

[76] On early support for and indifference to caste, see Talbot, *Precolonial India*, ch. 2, esp. 85–86; Eaton, *NCHI*, 17–18; Ludden, *NCHI*, 74, 85–87; idem, *India and South Asia*, 56–62; Thapar, *Early India*, 389–97, 462–87; Kolff, *Naukar, Rajput*, 181 ff. and *passim*; Dirks, *Hollow Crown*, 247–84; Eaton, *Rise of Islam*, 103, 185–93; Inden, *Imagining India*, 49–84.

[77] Eaton, *NCHI*, 137–41 and n. 234 *infra.*

poet-saints as Kabir (1398?–1448?), an uneducated Benares weaver whose praise-poems to an abstract deity are still cited, and the Bengal brahman Caitanya (c. 1485–1533), whose Krsna devotionalism focused on group singing and ecstatic dancing. All wrote or composed in regional languages, rather than Sanskrit.[78]

But if *bhakti* thus helped to fragment the Sanskrit cosmopolis by encouraging regional forms of devotion and language, in other ways it proved critical to religious integration, both vertical and horizontal, and to the emergence of that loose pan-Indian, post-Gupta religious synthesis we retrospectively term "Hinduism." Consider first *bhakti*'s two-way vertical influence. On the one hand, *bhakti* popularized religious themes that once had been the exclusive preserve of brahmans, kings, and landed elites. It introduced Siva and Visnu to artisans, herders, warriors, shamans, and tribal peoples, and integrated such humble folk more effectively into communities focused on pilgrimage sites and temples. While not necessarily rejecting caste, early *bhakti* made people of low-status, female as well as male, respectable in the eyes of god. In *bhakti* sects solidarities depended less on caste, occupation, or geography than on shared possession by the deity. So too, *bhakti* assimilated tribal and pastoral deities to the great Hindu gods;[79] introduced elements of elite architecture and vocabulary to village shrines; and linked those shrines to subregional and regional temples under brahman control.

On the other hand, folk practices ascended the social hierarchy. Thus folk deities entered official pantheons even at the highest level – a local Tamil god, "King of the Dancers" was adopted by Cola kings as their family deity – and *bhakti* mysticism, originally disdained by brahmans, eventually won an esteemed place in their lofty philosophies.

---

[78] On *bhakti*, *EAH*, vol. I, 154–57, 243, and vol. II, 243; *IBE*, 107–14; Pollock, *Language of the Gods*, 423 ff.; Hermann Kulke, "Royal Temple Policy and the Structure of Medieval Hindu Kingdoms," in Anncharlott Eschmann et al., eds., *The Cult of Jagannath and the Regional Traditions of Orissa* (New Delhi, 1978), 125–37; Karen Prentiss, *The Embodiment of Bhakti* (New York, 1999), 1–77; Susmita Pande, *Birth of Bhakti in Indian Religions and Art* (New Delhi, 1982); idem, *Medieval Bhakti Movement* (Meerut, India, 1989), esp. ix–xxxiii, 73–83, 118–29; Eleanor Zelliott, "The Medieval Bhakti Movement in History," in Bardwell Smith, ed., *Hinduism: New Essays in the History of Religions* (Leiden, 1976), 143–68; Richard Eaton, *Sufis of Bijapur 1300–1700* (Princeton, 1978), 7–13; idem, *NCHI*, 131–41; Cynthia Talbot, pers. commun., July 30, 2007; Subrahmanyam, pers. commun., Aug. 7, 2008.

[79] Cf. Eaton, *NCHI*, 138–41, on the Saivite/Vaisnanva "upgrading" of Vithoba and other pastoral deities in Maharashtra.

Key figures in this philosophical synthesis were the Vedanta theologian Sankara (788–820), who argued that popular devotion and brahmanic orthodoxy represented lower and higher versions of the same truth, and the Vaisnava thinker Ramanuja (1056–1137?), who claimed that the *bhakti* of Vaisnava saints was fully compatible with the Vedic scriptures and that ultimately salvation is possible only through devotion and divine grace. Thus Ramanuja offered an intellectual union between the noniconic, ritual, and metaphysical severity of early Vedic tradition and the idolatrous, emotional intensity of late-first-millennium *bhakti*. In North India in the 15th and 16th centuries the poet-saints known as Sants gained wide social influence, although many were from low castes and, like Kabir, illiterate. In political terms too, by enlisting the authority of local chiefs and lineage heads, not least in frontier zones, *bhakti* helped to forge more inclusive systems of alliance and rank.[80]

At the same time, despite its emphasis on regional languages, *bhakti* promoted horizontal integration. By wedding North Indian Sanskrit texts and caste to Tamil devotional poetry and sectarianism, Ramanuja showed the possibilities of transregional synthesis. From what is now Tamil Nadu, *bhakti* movements, as noted, spread to other parts of the peninsula and then – in reverse of Sanskrit's north-to-south transmission – to the Gangetic plain, the Punjab, Gujarat, and Bengal. By the 1500s many northern districts had become *bhakti* strongholds devoted to worship of Visnu's avatars Krisna (the pastoral lover and nurturer adored by Caitanya) and Rama (the exemplary warrior-king). *Bhakti* therefore was hardly a unified movement, rather a mycelium of sects spread across India with distinctive theologies and organizations but most of which emphasized poet-saints, caste inclusion, vernacular transmission, spiritually charged places, visual fascination with the deity, and personal religious experience rather than ritual punctiliousness. Between 1100 and 1500, as peripatetic brahmans gave *bhakti* an all-India character, the great age of *bhakti* poet-saints in the north was inspired by itinerant teachers from western and southern India, many of whom traced their lineage to Ramanuja. So too, teachers from North India, honoring the custom of "travel and debate," established centers

[80] Ludden, *NCHI*, 80–81; Eaton, *Rise of Islam*, 104–12, describing how forest goddesses ascended the social ladder; essays by Eschmann and by Hermann Kulke in Eschmann et al., *Cult of Jagannath* on the tribal origins of Jagannath; Pande, *Medieval Bhakti Movement*, 1–34. On Sankara and Ramanuja, see too J. B. Carman, *The Theology of Ramanuja* (New Haven, 1974), ch. 2; Pande, *Birth of Bhakti*, 178–89; *EAH*, vol. III, 325, 432–33.

in the south and west. Commerce, easier circulation of texts, and the expansion of regional and all-India pilgrimage routes facilitated such exchanges in the teeth of political fragmentation. Regardless of region, the lives of the saints showed basic similarities, and in fact many teachers were linked by formal sectarian affiliation.[81]

During the 18th century, nourished by Hindi vernacular literature, by popular festivals and popular art, and by armed ascetics who extended protection to the peasantry, *bhakti* devotional cults retained, indeed deepened, the popularity they had acquired during the preaching phase of previous centuries. In particular, warfare seems to have enhanced the influence of the armed ascetic brotherhoods, often quite wealthy, who were associated with these cults and who promoted *bhakti* among new and established peasants, artisans, and traders alike.[82]

The Acceptance of More Orthodox Notions of Caste. However, the late 1600s through the early 1800s also were an era of Hindu institutional consolidation when the egalitarian impulse of early *bhakti* receded and brahmanic ideas of hierarchy and ritual distinction gained ground. After the spread of Sanskrit court culture and of *bhakti*, the post-1650 dissemination of more orthodox notions of caste is the third integrative movement I shall consider.

To be sure, powerful forces still opposed the orthodox emphasis on caste, ritual pollution, and marriage exclusion. This was true not only of recently converted forest tribes, but of large groups of plains-dwellers and martial pastoralists whose social systems were malleable and inclusive and to whose lives brahmans remained peripheral. Among such people boundaries between high and low caste, "pure" and "impure," Hindu and Muslim were hazier in 1830 than they would be in 1930, or indeed 1880. Yet while India remained anything but a homogeneous caste society, it is also true, as Susan Bayly has shown, that by 1830 titles of *varna* (caste in the fourfold brahmanic schema) and *jati* (birth group subordinate to *varna*) were more widely used than in previous centuries; that many tribal and military groups were beginning to precipitate out into something that looked like "traditional" Hindu castes; that principles of purity, pollution, and endogamy had wider purchase; and that

---

[81] On the geographic spread of *bhakti*, previous notes plus Savitri Chandra Shobha, *Social Life and Concepts in Medieval Hindi Bhakti Poetry* (Meerut, India, 1983); Stuart McGregor, "The Progress of Hindi, Part 1," in *LCH*, 912–57, esp. 914–37; Grewal, *NCHI*, 23–27.

[82] Bayly, *NCHI*, 41–42, 159–60; McGregor, "Progress of Hindi," 914–37; Bayly, *Caste*, 46–48.

self-identities and external behaviors therefore conformed more closely to brahmanically defined norms.[83]

This strengthening of caste identification was especially notable because it contrasted sharply with tendencies elsewhere in Eurasia. In Siam, Vietnam, France, Japan, and China most obviously, but also in Burma and to a limited extent Russia, we have seen that commercialization and/or political upheaval in the 18th and early 19th centuries encouraged an erosion – rapid or gradual, sanctioned or veiled – of hereditary social divisions. Post-Mughal South Asia also knew considerable mobility as families sought new market opportunities and as successor states competed for the services of financiers, traders, scribes, and warriors. Yet in South Asia among upwardly mobile, and indeed some downwardly mobile groups, the tendency to define one's status via endogamy and estate segregation proved exceptionally strong.

What factors underlay this movement, that is to say, the wider dissemination of brahmanic social norms between c. 1650 and 1830 (when our inquiry, though not the movement itself, stops)? Of course, textual traditions accorded ascriptive categories exceptional prominence, but since prescriptions were constant and practice varied, one must look to shifting contexts. Of basic import perhaps, in no other realm under review after 1600 was sedentarization of pastorals and semi-agrarians so extensive as in India. Caste allowed settled communities to tame these marginal groups and access their labor, while limiting or prohibiting their access to land. For their part, pastoral and tribal peoples often saw some advantage in acquiring a recognized status, however inferior, for this associated them with sacred norms to which others around them related. These social strategies were particularly attractive in frontier zones where state power was fluid and livelihoods insecure. Among arms-bearing people in such widely separated areas as Tamil Nadu and Gujarat, evidence suggests that *varnas* and *jatis* were of little significance until peasantization was well under way.[84]

---

[83] Bayly, *Caste*, 25, 94–96; idem, "Islam and State Power in Pre-Colonial South India," *Itinerario* 12 (1988): 143–64, esp. 151. On the other hand, Alan Strathern, pers. commun., May 17, 2007 notes that on the Malabar coast 16th-century Portuguese sources already show "reasonably rigid and systemic" "brahmanized caste norms very much in evidence." Clearly, the historical geography of caste orthodoxy remains to be worked out in detail.

[84] Bayly, *Caste*, 31, 39–40; C. A. Bayly, *Origins of Nationality in South Asia* (Delhi, 1998), 43; idem, *NCHI*, 157–58. In Russia too, frontier settlement promoted stratification, seen, for example, in the bifurcation of relatively egalitarian Cossack hosts into landowners and serfs.

Notwithstanding the Mughals' Muslim identity, their alliance with Rajputs and other Hindu warriors led them to endorse the caste pretensions of their lordly allies. Mughal certification of warrior claims joined with emigration of arms-bearing lineages from Rajasthan and other areas to disseminate such usages across the Gangetic plain and deep into central India. Similar processes occurred independently in the south, as under the Telugu-speaking Nayaka dynasts. By the early 1700s a range of standardized social classifications had become central to the discourse of officials and military men in much of the subcontinent.[85]

After the Mughals declined, considerations of prestige and social control attracted Hindu dynasts to brahmanic hierarchy yet more strongly. Eager to assert their legitimacy, parvenu rulers presented themselves as beneficent defenders of *dharma* (cosmic law) and the social divisions that *dharma* prescribed. As self-styled *ksatriyas*, such rulers drew, often selectively, on caste vocabulary and symbols in order to strengthen control over retainers and service providers. In this they were supported not only by brahmans, who could acquire a monopoly on important offices, but by military followers from modest origins who were delighted to be enrolled in honorable *jatis*. In the late 1700s, with administration grown more bureaucratic and brahman scribes yet more indispensable, rough-and-ready warrior ideas of caste yielded to more textually based schemas. Tax records and legal transactions now adjudicated and fixed subjects' *varna* and *jati* statuses. From post-Mughal regional courts, orthodox norms then diffused into the countryside and down the social scale as landholders, court-dependent traders, and well-to-do peasants aped the purity-conscious court ideology in order to buttress their local claims to privilege at the expense of inferior classes.[86] Similar, if less pronounced, patterns could be observed in Muslim-led polities. In brief, in one post-Mughal region after another caste became both a prop of statecraft and – ironically, given the emphasis on hereditary status – a marker of upward mobility. Conceivably, the exceptional duration of South Asia's 18th-century political crisis magnified this yearning for compensatory security and social rigidity compared to other Eurasian realms. In settled cores and agrarian frontiers alike such a climate eroded *bhakti* egalitarianism.[87]

---

[85] Bayly, *Caste*, 26–40.
[86] Cf. Eaton, *NCHI*, 192–93.
[87] Bayly, *Caste*, 25–30, 35–37, 50–79, 94–96; Bayly, *NCHI*, 41–42, 159–60.

Early British rule reinforced orthodox acculturation by speeding the rise of high Hindu kingship and by creating incentives for local groups to police more carefully, even to create, caste boundaries. Shorn of military power, enfeebled British client states turned passionately to Hindu patronage and brahmanic ritualism in the hope of preserving some authority in their relations with both the British and their own subjects. British support for sedentarization enfolded growing numbers of pastoral and forest peoples within caste-oriented societies. By promoting a high-caste identity for its recruits, the British Bengal Army encouraged warrior groups to consolidate claims of community so as to enhance their employment prospects. Most generally, in its enthusiasm for text-based standardization, British law began to dispense to all communities the high brahmanical traditions of Hindu seminaries in Nadia and Tanjore.[88]

Finally, under Muslim, Hindu, and British rule alike, expanding trade, literacy, and travel widened access to supralocal information and raised troubling questions about where to draw social boundaries – even as these same channels provided normative brahmanic answers. Commercial competition, for example, led local traders and commodity producers to protect their skills and credit networks by strengthening bonds of caste. Likewise, traders, artisans, and peasants buffeted by market forces and rising taxes often were drawn to sects that exhorted them to purify their diet, marriage, and domestic practices so as to demonstrate superiority to tribals and humble menials. Benefiting from post-Mughal patronage and from urbanization and commercial expansion, Vaisnava sects like the Ramanandis preached a sober, frugal Hinduism that appealed strongly to town merchants and artisans across North India and even to many low-caste people.[89] Particularly in the cities of North India, proliferating written materials, including cheap vernacular religious tracts, afforded literate and semiliterate groups easier access to written norms of caste organization.

Meanwhile horizontal circulation helped to standardize caste usages across regions. Although pilgrimage networks grew from the 10th century, the density and extent of such routes in the 1700s were unprecedented. An influx of southern brahmans invigorated Gangetic holy

---

[88] Bayly, *Caste*, 80–96, 202–203; Dirks, *Castes of Mind*, pt. 2; Bayly, *NCHI*, 40, 115, 155–58, 136–68 *passim*. So too, having moved from Muslim to British employ, administrative castes like the Kayasthas aspired to a more brahmanical life and discarded what were now seen as degrading Muslim and lower-caste customs.

[89] Bayly, *NCHI*, 66, 159–61.

places, even as Tirupati in the far south became a place of sanctity for merchants from North India. British abolition of pilgrim taxes and better transport swelled this traffic.[90] Artisans and craftsmen also ventured farther afield, while mercantile, scribal, and mercenary castes built all-India networks, often for the first time, in a fashion inconceivable for immobile peasants. Such networks let new arrivals readily establish their honor in unfamiliar settings and capitalize on the growing market for specialized services in finance, commerce, statecraft, and ritual.[91]

Dissemination of Perso-Islamic Culture. Insofar as the first three movements of cultural integration – Sanskritization, *bhakti*, and spreading caste consciousness – originated within South Asia, they may be distinguished from a fourth grand integrative dynamic, the dissemination of Perso-Islamic features across the subcontinent. Providing South Asia with a second charter dispensation comparable to the Sanskrit cosmopolis in its universal codes, north-to-south progression, and pervasive elite influence, Perso-Islamic civilization simultaneously overlay, reinvigorated, and blended with earlier patterns. Yet while Sanskrit civilization arose in the Ganges basin, Perso-Islamic culture entered India, and for generations remained most influential, along those trade and migration corridors that linked Transoxania and the Iranian plateau to Lahore, Delhi, and the Deccan.[92] A flow, far stronger in 1600 than in 1000, of personnel and information along these corridors immersed South Asian elites in a Persian-inflected universe that extended from the Ottoman lands, Transoxania, and Persia around the Indian Ocean littoral as far as Siam.[93]

---

[90] On pilgrimage and the cultural implications of economic change, Bayly, *NCHI*, 39–40, 159–60; idem, *Origins of Nationality*, 43; idem, "Pre-Colonial Indian Merchants and Rationality," in M. Hasan and N. Gupta, eds., *India's Colonial Encounter* (Delhi, 1993), 11; idem, "The Pre-History of 'Communalism'?" *MAS* 19 (1985): 180; Bayly, *Caste*, 68–70, 86; Anne Feldhaus, *Connected Places* (New York, 2003), 185–210.

[91] Bayly, *Caste*, 70–72, 94; Susan Bayly, "Hindu Kingship and the Origin of Community," *MAS* 18 (1984): 177–213, esp. 191; Bayly, *Origins of Nationality*, 43; idem, *NCHI*, 159.

[92] Eaton, *NCHI*, 9. Islam's entry along these land routes must be distinguished from its earlier maritime arrival on the south coasts of India under primarily Arab aegis. Wink, *Al-Hind*, vol. II, 267–68; Sukhdev Singh, *The Muslims of Indian Origin During the Delhi Sultanate* (New Delhi, 2005), 22–31.

[93] Folz, *Mughal India*; Francis Robinson, "Perso-Islamic Culture in India from the 17th to the Early 20th Century," in Robert Canfield, ed., *Turko-Persia in Historical Perspective* (Cambridge, 1991), 104–31; Subrahmanyam, *Explorations: Tagus to Ganges*, 9 ff. and chs. 3, 5. On linguistic usages, esp. Muzaffar Alam, *The Languages of Political Islam: India*

Given their strong external affiliations and modest demographic base, the ability of Muslim elites to transform the culture of the subcontinent may seem surprising. Although from the late 1100s Turkic conquerors founded garrison towns and trade centers whose Muslim population included western immigrants and local artisan and merchant converts, such towns remained islands in a non-Muslim sea.[94] Admittedly, from the late 1500s many indigenes in Sind, Kashmir, the western Punjab, and eastern Bengal assimilated Islamic rituals and cosmologies, eventually producing Muslim majorities in the northwestern and northeastern wings of the subcontinent. But these were exceptions proving the rule about the conservatism of "Hindu" peasants, because before Islamization these had been largely nonagrarian societies, pastoralist in the northwest and forest tribal in the northeast, among whom Hindu gods and brahmanic ideals had yet to penetrate deeply. It was only with the adoption of sedentary agriculture, centered on wheat in the Punjab and wet rice in Bengal, under a Muslim religious leadership – petty *mullahs*, holy men, preachers – that Islamic features began to take root. In the Mughal empire at its height in 1700 people whose primary rituals were Muslim may not have exceeded 15 percent of the total.[95]

Islam's early urban character and association with conquest encouraged, by comparison with Southeast Asia, a militant expression, what Wink terms "an Islamic sanctification" of North India, that included unequivocal statements of Islamic superiority and the desecration of non-Muslim temples linked to political opponents.[96] Official pronouncements, crafted by Persian literati eager to place Delhi within the

1200–1800 (Chicago, 2004), 115–40. Transoxania, also called Transoxiana, lies north and east of the Amu Darya, or Oxus, River.

[94] On Muslim settlement and conversions in North India, M. Habib, "The Urban Revolution in Northern India," in Jos Gommans and Dirk Kolff, eds., *Warfare and Weaponry in South Asia 1000–1800* (New Delhi, 2001), 45–65; Digby, "Before Timur Came"; Singh, *Muslims of Indian Origin*, 31–60; Kumar, *Emergence*, 64, 78, 127, 146 ff., 190–96, 236; idem, "Ignored Elites."

[95] *LCH*, 963, 964 puts Muslims in late-19th-century British India at 14 percent, but Metcalfs, *Concise History*, 7 claims 25 percent. Bayly, *Rulers, Townsmen*, 12 estimates Muslims in "Gangetic north India" c. 1700 at below 15 percent, while Mukhia, *The Mughals*, 27, says 16 percent for the subcontinent as a whole in 1826. On Islam's success in lightly Hinduized frontier zones, Richard Eaton, "Introduction," and "The Political and Religious Authority of the Shrine of Baba Farid," in Eaton, ed., *India's Islamic Traditions, 711–1750* (New Delhi, 2003), 14–22, 263–84; Eaton, *Rise of Islam*, 113–227, 307–308; Wink, *Al-Hind*, vol. II, 4–5, 242, 265–67, 294.

[96] Wink, *Al-Hind*, 265 and 294–333; Richard Eaton, *Temple Desecration and Muslim States in Medieval India* (Delhi, 2004), 37–39, 84. On contrasts with Southeast Asia, Ch. 7 *infra*.

constellation of Muslim sultanates described its rulers as sultans "of the Turks and the Persians," that is, of the Muslim soldiers and scholars who staffed the empire. But with their overwhelmingly non-Muslim subjects, categorized generically in some sources as "Hindus" and dismissed by a leading 14th-century writer as "worshippers of idols and of cow-dung,"[97] there was little identification. Indeed, in early Muslim sources, Peter Hardy noted, Hindus were interesting never in themselves, merely as converts, taxpayers, or corpses.[98] Not only did Islam become the state religion, but Perso-Islamic norms informed Sultanate language, literature, administration, etiquette, dress, music, art, architecture, and cuisine. (Perso-Islamic, or Turko-Persian, culture was a mix of Arabic, Persian, and Turkic elements that melded in the 9th and 10th centuries in Khurasan in eastern Iran and in Transoxania, whence it was carried by Persianized Turks to West and South Asia.)[99] Official use of Persian lost ground under post-Delhi regimes. But the Mughals, who had close ties to Safavid Persia and who regarded North Indian dialects as too aesthetically unappealing and too impractical to build an imperial culture, made Persian the sole language of administration and the premier language of literature. Soon the Persian literary corpus from India vastly outweighed that from Persia itself.[100] As I shall argue shortly, this early tension between imperial and regional cultures never entirely lost its salience and helps to distinguish South Asia from both the protected zone and China.

And yet, despite friction and limits, Perso-Islamic culture became accessible to non-Muslims through the following dynamics: a) Muslim and Hindu warriors implicitly shared basic values. b) Administrative necessity and liberal intellectual currents led Inner Asian rulers to recruit non-Muslims and to promote eclectic, recombinatory cultural

---

[97] Yohanan Friedmann, "Islamic Thought in Relation to the Indian Context," in Eaton, *India's Islamic Traditions*, 60–61, quoting Ziya al-Din Barani, on whom see too Alam, *Languages*, 31–43; Jackson, *Delhi Sultanate*, 21, 50–51, 290–92. Also Kumar, *Emergence*, 228. On the term "Hindu," n. 16 *supra*. On Persian literati who fled the Mongol devastation of Islam in eastern Iran, Kumar, "Ignored Elites," esp. 60–64.

[98] Peter Hardy, *Historians of Medieval India* (London, 1960), 114. See too idem, "Growth of Authority over a Conquered Political Elite," in John Richards, ed., *Kingship and Authority in South Asia* (Delhi, 1998), 216–41.

[99] On the development and spread of Perso-Islamic (Turko-Persian) culture and language, Canfield, *Turko-Persia*, esp. Canfield, "Introduction," 1–34; Carter Vaughn Findley, *The Turks in World History* (Oxford, 2005), chs. 2, 3; Folz, *Mughal India*, xxiii–45; Alam, *Languages*, 143.

[100] Folz, *Mughal India*, 2; Muzaffar Alam, "The Pursuit of Persian," *MAS* 32 (1998): 317–49; idem, *Languages*, 123–44; *IBE*, 141–42, 156.

expressions.[101] c) The enormous prestige and utility of Muslim conventions encouraged imitation by non-Muslim elites. d) At a popular level, Islam also entered into fruitful dialogue with South Asian religions and language.

Muslim and Hindu traditions agreed that society was an organic hierarchy of complementary elements, and that the ruler's task was to preserve social distinctions and to make the world flourish. Because rule under both *sharia* and *dharma* accorded with cosmic principles, in both traditions royal authority was intrinsically universal.[102] Turks and Hindus shared a variety of pre-Islamic courtly practices, including robing ceremonies.[103] More basically, warriors in both cultures – in India, especially the Rajputs – championed a self-sacrificing military ethic, hypergamous marriage alliance, and patron–client reciprocity.[104]

If these implicit understandings offered possibilities for cross-cultural accommodation, pragmatic concerns, above all, the need to ensure a steady flow of revenue from non-Muslim subjects, ensured that Muslim rulers would exploit those openings. This was true to a limited extent under the Delhi sultans, some of whom incorporated Hindu motifs in public rituals, exempted brahman and Jain temples from taxes, and used Hindu scribes, who perforce mastered Persian.[105] In part because successor states, with smaller territories than the Sultanate, were more obliged to enter into close relations with Hindu chiefs; in part because the rural settlement of Afghans encouraged localization; and in part because Persian contacts were temporarily reduced, post-1400 Muslim rulers became more enthusiastic than Delhi sultans about granting non-Muslims posts of authority and patronizing local cults,

---

[101] I use "eclectic" to describe the unsystematic recombination of originally distinct elements, without implying that a) those elements were pure essences, or b) their subsequent fate represented either lamentable dilution or unnatural admixture. On the potential dangers of using "syncretism" – and "eclecticism" (?) – to describe popular practices, Eaton, "Introduction," 18–27; Tony Stewart, "In Search of Equivalence," in Eaton, *India's Islamic Traditions*, 363–92.

[102] Peter Hardy, "The Authority of Muslim Kings in Medieval South Asia," *Purusartha* 9 (1986): 37–55.

[103] Stewart Gordon, ed., *Robes of Honour* (New Delhi, 2003); Ali, *Courtly Culture*, 267–68; Eaton, *NCHI*, 11, 18.

[104] Hardy, "Growth of Authority"; Norman Ziegler, "Rajput Loyalties During the Mughal Period," in Richards, *Kingship and Authority*, 242–84; Stewart Gordon, *Marathas, Marauders, and State Formation in 18th-Century India* (Delhi, 1994), 183–92.

[105] Jackson, *Delhi Sultanate*, 278–95; Hardy, "Growth of Authority"; Muzaffar Alam, "Competition and Co-Existence," *Itinerario* 13 (1989): 37–59; idem, *Languages*, 42; *EAH*, vol. I, 379. Also Kumar, *Emergence*, 101–102 on pre-1206 accommodations.

languages, and architecture. We shall find that regionally specific combinations of Islamic and non-Islamic features flourished from the 14th to 16th centuries.[106]

Notwithstanding Mughal disinterest in local languages, Akbar, in part to reduce his dependence on Transoxanian Turks, patronized not only local Muslims, but Hindu Rajputs, thus for the first time bringing non-Muslims, with whom he formed marriage alliances, into the highest levels of empire, albeit as a still modest proportion of the overall elite.[107] In a similar spirit Akbar abolished discriminatory taxes on non-Muslims, banned cow slaughter, translated Sanskrit texts into Persian, patronized Hindu temples, favored composite styles in painting and architecture, and projected a more inclusive style of kingship that emphasized divine illumination and universal concord, captured in the phrase *sulh-i kull*, "peace with all." Many of these policies continued under Akbar's son Jahangir (r. 1605–1627). A conservative reaction set in under Shah Jahan (r. 1628–1658) and more especially Aurangzeb (r. 1658–1707), but even then pragmatic considerations told heavily. Both Muslim and non-Muslim warriors continued to pride themselves on family traditions of service to the imperial house; and as nobles of Persian and Turkic ancestry made way for more local Muslims and some Hindus, the nobility grew more South Asian in origins and sensibility.[108] Post-Mughal Muslim regimes, not unlike post-Delhi

---

[106] On cultural localization in this period, Muhammed Sadiq, *A History of Urdu Literature* (London, 1964), 44–45, and nn. 257–62 *infra*. On Afghan diasporas, Nile Green, "Tribe, Diaspora, and Sainthood in Afghan History," *JAS* 67 (2008): 171–211.

[107] Rajputs identified the emperor with the cultural hero Rama and regarded him as a Rajput. Ziegler, "Rajput Loyalties," 269; Richards, *NCHI*, 20–24; *IBE*, 125–27. From 1575 to 1595 of Akbar's highest nobles Rajputs and other Hindus were 16 percent, Indian Muslims 16 percent, Persians 28 percent, and Transoxanian Turks (Turanis) 37 percent, according to Iqtidar Alam Khan, "The Nobility Under Akbar and the Development of His Religious Policy, 1560–1580," in Eaton, *India's Islamic Traditions*, 120–32. But Ali, *Mughal Nobility*, 31 puts non-Muslim nobles in 1595 at 23 percent. On ethnic and religious categories among the nobility, see too Ali, *Mughal Nobility*, ch. 1.

[108] From 1679 to 1707, 40 percent of *mansabdars* ranked 1,000 or higher were of known Persian, Turkic, or Afghan ancestry, but fewer than a quarter of these Persians and Turks had immigrated; whereas from 1575 to 1595, recall, 65 percent were Persians or Turks, the vast majority immigrants (I have no 1575–1595 figures for Afghans). Previous note plus Eaton, *Rise of Islam*, 165–66; Ali, *Mughal Nobility*, 14–35. On evolving Mughal policy toward non-Muslim servitors and Indian culture generally, Richards, *NCHI*, 34–47, 148–50; *IBE*, 123–51, 155, 202, 225–31; Muzaffar Alam, "The Mughals, the Sufi Shaikhs and the Formation of the Akbari Dispensation," *MAS* 43 (2009): 135–74; Sri Ram Sharma, *The Religious Policy of the Mughal Emperors* (London, 1940); Satish Chandra, "Jizya and the State in India During the Seventeenth Century," in

successor states, deepened these accommodations. Muzaffar Alam has shown that, although challenged by more orthodox currents, liberal Muslim policies drew continuously on three rich intellectual resources, namely, medieval texts of ethical statecraft (*akhlaq*) that emphasized respect for non-Islamic perspectives, inclusive cultural perspectives in Persian literary tradition, and the *sufi* belief in "unity in multiplicity."[109]

The willingness of Muslim rulers and thinkers to accommodate non-Muslim traditions paralleled the enthusiasm of Hindu elites to embrace Perso-Islamic culture by separating "Islam" the religion from the broader notion of what Marshall Hodgson termed "Islamicate" culture. Such accommodations were motivated, above all, by a desire to share the prestige and benefits of Muslim power. Thus at the same time as Vijayanagara's rulers patronized caste, they imported from Muslim states not only military techniques, but architecture, ceremonies, courtly dress, and political terminology, with successive rulers styling themselves "Sultan among Hindu kings."[110] In the same spirit, during the Mughal period from Kashmir to the Kaveri delta local magnates – non-Muslim and Muslim alike – emulated imperial ritual and aesthetics, the impact of which was magnified by the court's peripatetic character and universal pretensions. Mughals sought to standardize titles and terminology, while panegyrics and art portrayed a center whose authority radiated toward an endless horizon. Indeed, "Jahangir" and "Shah Jahan" meant "World Conqueror" and "King of the World." Two indices of Mughal influence were the way diverse regional architectures yielded to a common aesthetic in forts, palaces, mosques, even Hindu temples,[111] and the spread of Persian language. Imperial scribes gained

---

Eaton, *India's Islamic Traditions*, 133–49; Alam, "Competition and Co-Existence"; idem, *Languages*, 61–78, 91–98.

[109] Alam, *Languages*, chs. 2–4; idem, "*Akhlaqi* Norms and Mughal Governance," in Muzaffar Alam et al., eds., *The Making of Indo-Persian Culture* (Delhi, 2000), 67–95. On Akbar's inclusive, somewhat idiosyncratic notions of kingship, Peter Hardy, "Abul Fazl's Portrait of the Perfect Padshah," in Christian Troll, ed., *Islam in India. Vol. 2: Religion and Religious Education* (Delhi, 1985), 114–37; O'Hanlon, "Kingdom, Household."

[110] On "Islamicate" borrowings, Marshall Hodgson, *The Venture of Islam. Volume III. The Gunpowder Empires and Modern Times* (Chicago, 1974), ch. 2; Canfield, "Introduction," 1; Phillip Wagoner, "Sultan Among Hindu Kings," *JAS* 55 (1996): 851–80; idem, "Harihara, Bukka, and the Sultan," in David Gilmartin and Bruce Lawrence, eds., *Beyond Turk and Hindu* (Gainesville, 2000), 300–26; Eaton, *NCHI*, 102, and 30–32, 41–50, 78–104; Catherine Asher, "Islamic Influence and the Architecture of Vijayanagara," in Dallapiccola, *Vijayanagara*, 188–95; *IBE*, 70–74.

[111] On architecture and art, Metcalfs, *Concise History*, 14, 22; Eaton, *Rise of Islam*, 160, 171–74; Z. A. Desai, "Mughal Architecture in the Deccan," in H. K. Sherwani and P. M.

full Persian proficiency, but even village functionaries usually had to have some knowledge. Among non-Muslim and Muslim literati, Persian thus became a primary linguistic vehicle, so that the divide between those knowledgeable and those ignorant of Persian was less a matter of religion than of class.[112] As we shall see, the failure of imperial culture to penetrate more thoroughly the middle and lower strata of provincial elites limited Mughal vitality, but compared to the Delhi Sultanate, Mughal integration was impressive. Towering prestige and practical value explain why Mughal culture spread even in the far south where no Mughal emperor set foot,[113] and why Mughal usages long outlived Mughal decline.

Below imperial and regional courts, on the level of popular culture, Islam also supported recombinative trends. Arguably this was most pronounced in the Punjab and Bengal, where Islamization and sedentarization of lightly Hinduized people went hand in hand. But even in areas of long-standing brahmanic influence, non-Muslims used *sharia* courts, and *bhakti* devotees listened aptly to *sufis* (Muslim mystics whose leaders guided novices in a search for oneness with God). In North India the aforementioned Sant tradition, yearning for a god without form as in the poetry of Kabir, expressed *sufi* as well as *bhakti* impulses. Often genuinely appreciative of indigenous practices, *sufis* localized Islam by shunning ritual, writing poetry in vernacular languages with Sanskritic Devanagari, rather than Persian, script; adopting yogic practices (breath control, celibacy, vegetarianism), emphasizing the universal power of *sufi* saints' tombs, and grafting the image of those saints onto that of a Vaisnava *avatar*. Attractive to humble people of diverse backgrounds, some Muslim saint cults resembled the followings of *bhakti* teachers. *Sufis*, for whom music and ecstasy were closely linked, also sought to

Joshi, eds., *History of Medieval Deccan, 1295–1724*, 2 vols. (Hyderabad, 1973–74), vol. II, 305–14; *IBE*, 131–51, 186–201, 208–13, 291; Catherine Asher, *NCHI*, vol. I, 4: *Architecture of Mughal India* (Cambridge, 1992), chs. 2–6; Milo Cleveland Beach, *NCHI*, vol. I, 3: *Mughal and Rajput Painting* (Cambridge, 1992). On the ways Mughal universalism accommodated European cartography, Sumathi Ramaswamy, "Conceit of the Globe in Mughal Visual Practice," *CSSH* 49 (2007): 751–82.

[112] Muzaffar Alam, "The Culture and Politics of Persian in Precolonial Hindustan," in *LCH*, esp. 163–71; idem, "Pursuit of Persian'; idem, *Languages*, 129–33; Robinson, "Perso-Islamic Culture," 105–14; Kumkum Chatterjee, "The Persianization of *Itihasa*," *JAS* 67 (2008): 513–43.

[113] *IBE*, 221–22; Robinson, "Perso-Islamic Culture," 113; Bayly, "Islam and State Power."

harmonize Persian and Indian musical traditions. Meanwhile caste, in varying guises, infiltrated Muslim society.[114]

After the Mughals declined, the transition from Persian to Urdu showed the continued power of Muslim-mediated cultural integration. In North India quotidian interaction between Muslim elites and locals gradually engendered after 1200 various *patois* known (to Persian speakers) as Hindi or Hindavi, which were based on local Indo-Aryan dialects and grammar but used many Persian and Arabic loan words. Between 1400 and 1650, similar dynamics in the Deccan produced another *patois*, Dakani, that combined largely North Indian syntax with considerable Perso-Arabic vocabulary. The Mughals treated all vernaculars condescendingly, but with the 18th-century growth of regionalism, northern Muslim literati began to embrace these *patois*, particularly the felicitous register of Delhi, as a literary alternative to Persian, now judged to have exhausted much of its vitality and to have become excessively distant from the Indian context. This new language elites dignified by admitting yet more Persian usages and calling it the language of the imperial "camp"– Urdu. In social terms the transition drew strength from the concentration in Delhi of *nouveaux riches* merchants and service gentry from nonnoble rural backgrounds who lacked extensive training in Persian. Sensitive to claims by established writers that they were ignorant rustics, this new elite sought to demonstrate that Urdu was capable of elegance and refinement. By the late 1700s, Urdu in fact had replaced Persian as the chief vehicle of poetry and public discourse, available to both educated Muslims and Hindus and embraced by the rump Mughal court itself. As political and commercial pressures pushed North Indian forms to Hyderabad and the south, Urdu and related forms began to act, in C. A. Bayly's words, as

---

[114] Muslim patronage of an all-India military culture also favored religious eclecticism insofar as soldiers were typically distant from literate norms. On Muslim/non-Muslim interactions, Alam, "Competition and Co-Existence," 37–40; idem, *Languages*, 81–114, 186; *IBE*, 89, 106–108, 168; Bayly, "Pre-History of Communalism," 181–84; Aditya Behl, "The Magic Doe," in Eaton, *India's Islamic Traditions*, 180–208; Ali Asani, "Creating Tradition Through Devotional Songs and Communal Script," in ibid., 285–310; Juan Cole, "Popular Shi'ism," in ibid., 311–41, esp. 332; Eleanor Zelliott, "A Medieval Encounter Between Hindu and Muslim," in ibid., 64–82; essays by Tony Stewart, Christopher Shackle, Vasudha Narayanan, and Carl Ernst in Gilmartin and Lawrence, *Beyond Turk*, 21–120; Eaton, *Rise of Islam*, 177–83; idem, *Sufis of Bijapur*, 135–74; idem, "Introduction," 27: "[B]y the end of our period Islam had become as Indian as any other religious tradition of the subcontinent."

"a subcontinental link language, crossing regional and religious boundaries."[115]

Urdu's popularity and Muslim–Hindu interaction helped to generate a vaguely protopatriotic consciousness centered on Hindustan. Building on North Indian imperial loyalty and religious inclusiveness stretching back to Akbar, northern literati, chiefly though not exclusively Muslim, began in the 1700s to glorify and sentimentalize Hindustan as the site of uniquely valuable arts, customs, and manners, a luminous domain, home to Hindus and Muslims alike. Most commonly "Hindustan" referred to the area from the Punjab to Bengal. But, as North Indian cultural forms spread to the south, some authors began to identify Hindustan with the greater part of the subcontinent.[116]

The Intensification of Literate, Urban-Based Communications. What is more, C. A. Bayly argues, protopatriotism and Urdu joined with rising literacy to nourish a sphere of public information, a North Indian "ecumene."[117] This illustrated the fifth and, to 1830, the most short-lived movement of cultural integration with which we are concerned, namely, an intensification of literate, urban-based communications.

Now at first sight, Indian literacy seems an unpromising agency of cultural diffusion: some research suggests that only about 6 percent of North Indian adult males, and a far smaller fraction of women, could read or write their names in 1800[118] – compared to 47 percent of French, 40 percent of Japanese, 20–60 percent of Burmese and Siamese, and

---

[115] Bayly, *Origins of Nationality*, 40, 43. Also idem, *Empire and Information*, 42–43, 192–96 (defining Urdu as a refined, Persianized form of Hindustani); Alam, *Languages*, 178–85; idem, "Pursuit of Persian"; *IBE*, 77, 168–69, 247; Robinson, "Perso-Islamic Culture," 118–19; Sadiq, *History of Urdu*, chs. 3–8; Eaton, *Sufis of Bijapur*, 91–94; idem, *NCHI*, 141–45; Shamsur Rahman Faruqi, "A Long History of Urdu Literary Culture, Part 1," in *LCH*, 805–63; Frances Pritchett, "A Long History of Urdu Literary Culture, Part 2," in *LCH*, 864–81; Talbot, pers. commun., July 30, 2007; McGregor, "Progress of Hindi," 912–49. In fact, the dissemination of Hindi across North India from Kanauj was a commercially aided process that long antedated the Delhi Sultanate. Ibid., 946.

[116] Bayly, *Origins of Nationality*, 38–43, 63; idem, *NCHI*, 196–98; Subrahmanyam, *Explorations: Tagus to Ganges*, 1.

[117] Also termed a "public sphere" by analogy to Europe. Bayly, *Empire and Information*, 181–82, 187–89, 368.

[118] Extrapolated, on an assumption of 15 percent urbanization, from Bayly, *Empire and Information*, 37–39; Marshall, *NCHI*, 30; Tirthankar Roy, "Knowledge and Divergence from the Perspective of Early Modern India," *JGH* 3 (2008): 364, n. 14. Rates in Bengal, the Punjab, and South India may have been higher than in North India, but as late as 1901 the Indian census showed a male literacy rate of only 9.8 percent and a female one of 0.6 percent. Gregory Clark, *A Farewell to Alms* (Princeton, 2007), 264–65.

15–50 percent of Chinese males.[119] Why this deficit? India lacked print-ing, but since the same was true of Indic Southeast Asia, this was hardly fatal. Did the larger absolute size of South Asia's rural population pro-duce greater inertia? (In this respect, China's relatively low rates may be significant). But most basic, surely, the link between literacy and upper caste status inhibited schools catering to a broad social cross section on the Theravada, Catholic, or even Tokugawa pattern.

Such impediments aside, during the 1700s and early 1800s record-keeping, sectarianism, and vernacular literatures joined to promote lit-eracy in select groups and what Bayly terms "literacy awareness" in the wider society.[120] As merchant and government records became more elaborate, they required more advanced skills. As vernacular authors democratized their social settings and metrical forms, nonelites accessed the written word in a fashion impossible so long as San-skrit or Persian retained an effective monopoly.[121] In basic outline, of course, this plebeian turn is familiar from Southeast Asia, France, Japan, and China. Symptom and cause of wider literacy, sales of poetry, newsletters, almanacs, horoscopes, medical guides, and religious tracts in Hindi/Urdu, Bengali, and other vernaculars multiplied. Thus, if per capita literacy remained low, by 1800 the "middling sort" did gain easier access to written information. At a lower level, urban illiterates gained indirect exposure through puppet shows, songs, dramas, and discus-sions at temples, mosques, and bazaars. Mughal collapse precipitated among jurists and divines a flurry of political and doctrinal debates, while written materials and poetic assemblies introduced issues of aes-thetics, health, and politics to educated Sunnis, Shiites, and Hindus alike. Also indicative of wider, more politicized communications, in the early 1800s urban commoners of diverse sectarian and caste back-ground supported petitions and mass meetings. To be sure, as an arena of policy review, the North Indian "ecumene" was far less legally secure, politically influential, or ideologically innovative than European public spheres. Yet debate did touch on issues of public concern, breaching, without eliminating, religious and caste divisions, opening a dialogue

---

[119] See *SP*, 189, 314 and Chs. 3–5 *supra*.
[120] Bayly, *Empire and Information*, 36–44, 180–211.
[121] Sudipta Kaviraj, "Writing, Speaking, Being," in Dagmar Hellmann-Rajanayagam and Dietmar Rothermund, eds., *Nationalstaat und Sprachkonflikte in Sud-und-sudostasien* (Stuttgart, 1992), 34–39; idem, "The Two Histories of Literary Culture in Bengal," in *LCH*, 527–29; Velcheru Narayana Rao, "Multiple Literary Cultures in Telugu," in *LCH*, 414–18.

between elite and popular cultures, and spreading common standards of aesthetics and language across the cities of North India, even the Deccan.[122]

In sum, starting with the creation of the Sanskrit cosmopolis and continuing with the northward spread of *bhakti*, the post-1650 dissemination of caste, the post-1200 diffusion of Perso-Islamic culture, and the post-1700 intensification of urban communications, more frequent exchanges knit together many of the subcontinent's principal regions, while encouraging a modest degree of vertical integration.

Admittedly, in 1830 such convergences remained limited, more comparable perhaps to those across all of Europe than in China or individual protected-zone kingdoms, where central authorities defined and promoted cultural norms far more easily than in India. At the elite level not only did Hindu and Muslim traditions remain distinct,[123] but both were internally fragmented by lineage and doctrine. Or, to continue the discussion of language, if Urdu began to link north and south, it never acquired the authority of Parisian French, Russian, Edo Japanese, or Mandarin in their respective realms. Even in the Ganges heartland, Arabic, Persian, Sanskrit, Hindi, and Urdu filled more or less distinctive functional and social niches. If Hindi and Urdu merged into one spoken language, Hindi was typically written in Devanagari script and was more open to Sanskritic associations than Urdu, written in Persian script. In outlying regions other Indo-Aryan (Bengali, Punjabi, Marathi, Gujarati, Oriya) and Dravidian (Tamil, Kannada, Telugu, Malayalam) literatures flourished alongside Persian, Dakani/Urdu, and Sanskrit.[124]

We shall return to South Asia's luxuriant cultural polymorphism. But for now consider the larger point, namely, that by 1830 religious and social practices were more uniform across South Asia than at any time since the decline of the Sanskrit cosmopolis in the early second millennium (see below), possibly than at any time in history. In this sense cultural integration in South Asia paralleled that in other Eurasian realms, and notwithstanding Mughal collapse, drew strength, directly

---

[122] Bayly, *Empire and Information*, 54–55, 180–211, 368; idem, "South Asia and the 'Great Divergence'," *Itinerario* 24 (2000): 89–103; Bayly, *Caste*, 51–52.

[123] See Zelliott, "A Medieval Encounter," for literate 16th-century perceptions of Islamic–Hindu distinctions; and Alam, *Languages*, 163.

[124] Madhav Deshpande, *Sanskrit and Prakrit* (Delhi, 1993), 111; Michael Shapiro and Harold Schiffman, *Language and Society in South Asia* (Delhi, 1981), ch. 3; Rich Freeman, "Genre and Society," in *LCH*, 437–500, esp. 442–43; Bayly, *Empire and Information*, 158, 194, 241, 284; Eaton, *NCHI*, 142, with chart of Deccan language use 1500–1697.

and indirectly, from the legacy of imperial unification. What is more, in 1830 Hindu caste and specifically Indo-Muslim religious practices probably distinguished South Asia as a whole from West Asia, Southeast Asia, and East Asia more clearly than in any previous period.[125]

Economic and Technological Spurs to Integration Synchronized with Other Sectors of Eurasia

A final parallel – on which all others substantially depended – was economic growth loosely coordinated between South Asia and other sectors of Eurasia. Notwithstanding a 17th- and 18th-century record closer to that of Japan than of Europe, China, or Southeast Asia, long-term increases in cultivation, population, and trade, especially c. 850–1300 and c. 1500–1700, provided a familiar spur to both political integration and cultural circulation.

Marxist scholars, I noted, tried to connect India and Europe by arguing that the fall of the Guptas precipitated a "feudal" economic contraction like that which Europe suffered after Rome. Some evidence from North India does point to declining urbanization, money use, and population.[126] However, in areas like Rajasthan, the Deccan, and the southeast between c. 500 and 850 cultivation, temple foundations, and markets seem to have increased markedly, nurturing political rivals to the Gangetic heartland.[127] One is reminded of the shift in authority from North China to the Yangzi basin starting in the mid-first millennium, and from the Mediterranean to northern Europe from the 8th century, the key difference being that whereas South China and North Europe permanently altered regional balances, North India later regained its hegemony.

In familiar fashion, moreover, economic growth in much of South Asia intensified between 800/900 and 1300. We lack Chinese- or

---

[125] This was particularly true with the post-1200/1400 collapse of Hindu-Buddhist-Sanskrit culture across Southeast Asia and with the development of specifically Indo-Muslim traditions. Cf. Bayly, *Caste*, 30, 95; Bayly, *Origins of Nationality*, 43; Richards, "Early Modern India," 204; and Ch. 7 *infra*.

[126] *Supra* n. 15, plus *CEHI*, 45–47; R. S. Sharma, *Urban Decay in India* (New Delhi, 1987). As in Ch. 5, my economic inquiry focuses on the post-500 C.E. era, both because reliable pre-500 data are sparse, and because protected zone syncrhonizations become visible only in the latter half of the first millennium.

[127] Ludden, *NCHI*, 70–73; Dirks, *Hollow Crown*, 28–30; Thapar, *Early India*, chs. 9, 10; Kulke, "Early and Imperial Kingdom"; Ali, *Courtly Culture*, 21–22, 32–37, 60, 101–102; Chattopadhyaya, *Making*, 130–54; Guha, *Environment and Ethnicity*, 47.

European-style agrarian records, but inscriptions, archeology, and foreign accounts point to widening mobility and the accelerated spread of agriculture over pastoralism. "[T]here is broad agreement," Burton Stein has written, that in the latter half of the first and the early centuries of the second millennium "agricultural settlement spread more rapidly th[a]n ever before, from the scattered zones of secure riverine irrigation to ever larger areas."[128] Aided by new crops, tanks, wells, and other water technologies, cultivation advanced along India's inner and outer frontiers to create new irrigated districts, new zones of mixed wet and dry cultivation and of agriculture mixed with herding. In long-settled districts land use became more intensive, while cropping for interregional trade, although modest by post-1600 standards, grew more specialized (e.g., sugar in Bihar and the Punjab, cotton and indigo in Gujarat). After 900 or 1000 mobile warriors, traders, and pastoralists from arid zones in the northwest and the Deccan built wider commercial networks based on camel and ox caravans; stronger polities based on more numerous and powerful warhorses; and more productive dry-zone agriculture (wheat and millet) based on wider use of oxen for manuring, water lifting, threshing, and transport. Although ports in Bengal, Coromandel, and elsewhere also prospered, it was primarily dry-zone lineages (the Yadavas, Hoysalas, Kakatiyas, and Delhi sultans) who founded new kingdoms, locating their capitals, as noted, on the frontier between agrarian and pastoral zones.[129] Whereas from the fourth century the Guptas had revolutionized Indian political economy from the Ganges basin, Ludden terms the rise of warriors and traders from western dry zones starting in the late first millennium "the second medieval

---

[128] Stein, *History*, 114; and ibid., 124, referring to India's third urbanization, after those of Harappa and the mid-first millennium B.C.E. Ludden, *NCHI*, 77 also sees the period c. 550–1250 as a watershed producing the basis for all of South Asia's major agrarian regions. On agrarian and commercial vitality 700/750–1300/1350, see nn. 17, 23 *supra*, Ludden, *NCHI*, 47, 69–77, 113–16; Noboru Karashima, *South Indian History and Society* (Delhi, 1984), 20; Chattopadhyaya, *Making*, 28–29, 159–82; R. J. Barendse, "The Feudal Mutation," *JWH* 14 (2003): 517–24; Thapar, *Early India*, 381–92, 409, 452–61; Talbot, *Precolonial India*, 72–79, 87–106; Digby, "Before Timur Came," 303–304, 318, 350–51; John Deyell, *Living Without Silver* (Delhi, 1990), 233–48; V. K. Jain, *Trade and Traders in Western India (AD 1000–1300)* (New Delhi, 1990), 250–53 and *passim*.

[129] See nn. 17, 23, 27 *supra*; plus Andre Wink, "India and the Turko-Mongol Frontier," in Anatoly Khazanov and Andre Wink, eds., *Nomads in the Sedentary World* (Richmond, UK, 2001), 211–33. On maritime stimuli to agrarian growth, Karashima, *South Indian History*, 20.

revolution."[130] What, then, can South Asia in this period tell us about the recurrent conundrum of Eurasian correlations? What coordinating factors, singly and in combination, were at work?

Elsewhere between c. 850 and 1300 we found growth associated with institutional and/or social reorganization: new temple foundations in Pagan and Angkor, princely colonization in Kiev, feudal manors in France, frontier estates in the Yangzi basin. In South India as well, royal temples played a major role as landlords, centers of production and retail, moneylenders, and investors in irrigation and land reclamation.[131] Yet, as Chapter 5 suggested, however beneficial they may have been, such initiatives alone cannot explain Eurasian coordination because a) To point out that institutional innovation across Eurasia encouraged growth merely reformulates the basic puzzle of simultaneity. Outside India and Indic Southeast Asia, these institutions had no common root. b) Focusing on novel institutions and social forms ignores the degree to which such elements responded to antecedent shifts in the economy. Recall in this connection R. I. Moore's theory that in early medieval Europe and Song China, rapid economic growth embroiled "clerical elites" in crises that demanded more efficient sociopolitical institutions, which favored yet more rapid growth. This same model Moore has invoked to explain the rise of brahman temples in South India c. 900–1250.[132] But, leaving aside the fact that in most of India after 900 political agency resided less with brahmans ("clerical elites") than with dry-zone warriors, we are still left wondering why in the first place "crisis-inducing" growth should have been coordinated between Europe, China, and India, not to mention Southeast Asia and Kiev.

Long-distance trade offers a more direct connection. By most accounts, commerce both within South Asia and with adjacent regions rose markedly from 900 to 1300, and especially in the 13th century. The effects were felt most directly a) in the northwest, where the intersection of Gangetic and Inner Asian land routes transformed Delhi, Lahore, and other administrative centers into more cosmopolitan, market-oriented

---

[130] Ludden, "History Outside Civilization," 9. So too for Gommans, "Eurasian Frontier," 133, 142, the end of the first and start of the second millennia constituted a watershed. There is unexplained slippage between this emphasis on growth from the *late* first millennium and the emphasis on growth from the *mid*-first millennium in Stein and Ludden cited in n. 128 *supra*.

[131] See nn. 16, 17 *supra*, esp. Ludden, *Peasant History*, 33; Heitzman, "Temple Urbanism."

[132] See references to Moore's work in Ch. 5, nn. 138, 139 *supra*.

cities; b) in coastal Gujarat, Coromandel, and Bengal, which – benefiting from new forms of merchant organization, an expanded network of Indian Ocean emporia, and better weaving and dyeing techniques – exchanged Indian cotton textiles and foodstuffs for Mideastern horses, Mideastern and Chinese handicrafts, Southeast Asian spices, and Chinese and Burmese silver; c) along trade and migration corridors in the Deccan. In effect, Ludden and Wink argue, by joining the northwest to the coast, Deccan corridors let South Asia function as a commercial hinge between Inner Asia and the Indian Ocean.[133] Not only did trade revenues aid pacification and agrarian investment, but from Inner Asia and the Persian Gulf derived new technologies for irrigation, construction, and textile and paper production.[134] Furthermore, South Asia, which had meager domestic sources of precious metal, obtained gold and silver from as far as Yunnan, Tibet, Hungary, and Africa. At least until c. 1325 Deccan plunder and bullion imports permitted Delhi sultans to replace billon and copper coins with silver issues, which aided both revenue collection (their initial goal) and commodification.[135]

Yet it is doubtful that trade can explain overall expansion in the agrarian sector, only a small part of which in 1300 produced for distant markets and much of which remained outside the money economy entirely, as Sultanate frustrations with cash taxation suggest. Nor – as with China's silver trade in the 16th century – can external factors explain why domestic demand for bullion rose initially. Wink, a scholar of exogenous linkages, argues that India's pre-1300 commercial

---

[133] Ludden, "History Outside Civilization," 9–10 and *passim*; Wink, "From the Mediterranean"; idem, *Al-Hind*, vol. I, 254–360 and vol. II, 4, 212–93. New textile techniques were in vogue by the 13th century. I rely on sources in nn. 17, 23, 27 *supra*, plus Janet Abu-Lughod, *Before European Hegemony* (New York, 1989), pt. 3; *IBE*, 17–18, 49–52, 77–80; Jan Wisseman Christie, "The Medieval Tamil-Language Inscriptions in Southeast Asia and China," *JSEAS* 129 (1998): 239–68; Sheldon Pollock, "The Transformation of Culture-Power in Indo-Europe, 1000–1300," in Johann Arnason and Bjorn Wittrock, eds., *Eurasian Transformations, Tenth to Thirteenth Centuries* (Leiden, 2004), 266–67; Talbot, pers. commun., July 30, 2007; Kuroda, "Eurasian Silver Century." See too Ch. 1, n. 117 and Ch. 2, n. 40 *supra*.

[134] *IBE*, 49; Beach, *NCHI*, 1; Eaton, *NCHI*, 150; Simon Digby, *Warhorse and Elephant in the Delhi Sultanate* (Oxford, 1971), 13.

[135] See nn. 29, 131 *supra*; Shireen Moosvi, "Numismatic Evidence and the Economic History of the Delhi Sultanate," *Proceedings of the Indian History Congress*, 50 (Delhi, 1989), 207–18; essays by John Richards and John Deyell in Richards, ed., *Precious Metals in the Later Medieval and Early Modern Worlds* (Durham, NC, 1983), 183–227; Wink, *Al-Hind*, vol. II, 214–15; Kuroda, "Eurasian Silver Century."

vitality in general and its favorable trade balance in particular were "primarily a question of population density and agricultural potential"[136] – whose dynamism requires explanation. Long-distance exchange did not descend magically from on high, but reflected evolving complementarities between South Asia and adjacent regions.

In this light, Inner Asian interventions may seem like a viable candidate for economic coordination. Between c. 1000 and 1300 states founded by dry-zone warriors not only advanced the economic fortunes of the Deccan and much of North India by expanding trade, irrigation, and livestock supplies; they also transformed a vast pastoral–sedentary frontier zone extending from Anatolia and Transoxania to Xinjiang and North China. Thus the Yadavas, Hoysalas, and Delhi sultans in India overlapped with the Turkic Seljuk empire (1038–1307) in Anatolia, Iraq, and Iran; with the Turkic Karakhanid empire (999–1212) in Transoxania and Kashgaria; and with the Khitan, Jurchen, and Mongol empires discussed in Chapter 5.[137] If Mongol agrarian policies could be highly destructive, Inner Asian regimes, including the Mongols, commonly promoted long-distance trade and bullion flows, and in some instances aided agriculture with a view to fiscal maximization.[138]

But if we concede Inner Asian economic benefits (and the picture outside India was actually quite mixed), the question then becomes: what led to Inner Asian ascendancy? Three explanations are often provided, but again none satisfies our comparative needs. First, some argue that better cavalry equipment and weapons – sturdier saddles, the stirrup, the martingale and modern harness, the compound bow – enhanced the power of mounted archers and heavy armored horsemen. The problem is that many of these technologies had been known for centuries – the stirrup appeared in China in the 5th century, while the compound bow was used in Mesopotamia by 2350 B.C.E. – so it is unclear why they

---

[136] Wink, *Al-Hind*, vol. I, 360. Cf. Shrimali, "Money, Market," 4–9; Sanjay Subrahmanyam, *The Political Economy of Commerce* (Cambridge, 1990), 361–70, writing of a later period from a similar perspective.

[137] Cf. Gommans, "Silent Frontier," 1–23, referring to changes across "Saharasia"; Michael Chamberlain, *Knowledge and Social Practice in Medieval Damascus, 1190–1350* (Cambridge, 1994), ch. 1; Yuri Bregel, "Turko-Mongol Influences in Central Asia," in Canfield, *Turko-Persia*, 53–77; *EAH*, vol. II, 272 and vol. III, 409–11; Svat Soucek, *A History of Inner Asia* (Cambridge, 2000), chs. 5–7.

[138] See Ch. 5 and this chap., nn. 23, 137 *supra*; Jackson, *Delhi Sultanate*, 37, 251; Nicola Di Cosmo, "State Formation and Periodization in Inner Asian History," *JWH* 10 (1999): 1-40; Kuroda, "Eurasian Silver Century."

should have produced a seismic shift in the 11th and 12th centuries.[139] Second, acceptance of Sunni Islam from the 9th and 10th centuries is said to have enhanced Turkic access to sedentary cultural expertise and to have legitimized Turkic rule in the eyes of Muslim subjects. But this says nothing about coordination with non-Muslim groups on the China/steppe frontier and elsewhere. Third, one can, with good reason, argue that agrarian and urban prosperity c. 900–1300 joined nomadic population growth to intensify sedentary–nomadic social and economic interactions, which accorded Inner Asians the political and cultural skills needed to extract sedentary resources on a sustained basis.[140] In this sense Turkic Islamization was one aspect of a far more general process of nomad acculturation. But this still leaves the initial prosperity a puzzle. What is more, the thesis that Inner Asian warriors assisted growth between 1000 and 1300, even if valid for parts of South and Southwest Asia and North China, hardly explains the dynamism of South China's economy and is utterly irrelevant to western Europe and Southeast Asia. Nor do changes peculiar to the Inner Asian frontier help us understand Tai entry into Southeast Asian lowlands in the 12th and 13th centuries. Of course, Inner Asian and Tai movements may have been unrelated, but chronological overlap and the fact that in both realms mobile warriors suddenly began to dominate nearby agrarian societies raises the possibility of similar dynamics. Such dynamics probably involved intensifying agrarian–tribal interactions during an era of economic expansion. But again, we must explain coordinated prosperity in far-flung areas prior to the breaching of the frontiers.[141]

---

[139] On cavalry technologies, see Chamberlain, *Knowledge and Social Practice*, 28–47; Gommans, "Eurasian Frontier," 129–35; idem, "Warhorse and Gunpowder," 109–11; Digby, *Warhorse and Elephant*, 11–28; Jean Deloche, *Horses and Riding Equipment in Indian Art* (Madras, 1990), 18 and 7–20; idem, *Military Technology in Hoysala Sculpture* (New Delhi, 1989), esp. 48; Catherine Uray-Kuhalmi, "La periodisation de l'histoire des armaments des nomades des steppes," *Etudes Mongoles* 5 (1974): 145–55. On the compound bow, ibid., 146–47; J. R. McNeill and William McNeill, *The Human Web* (New York, 2003), 55 n. 3.

[140] For theories of nomadic state formation emphasizing sedentary stimuli, see Philip Burnham, "External Factors vs. Internal Dynamics in Social Differentiation," in *Pastoral Production and Society* (Cambridge, 1979), 349–60; William Irons, "Political Stratification Among Pastoral Nomads," ibid., 361–75; and esp. Ch. 5, nn. 217–20 *supra*.

[141] On the Tais in Southeast Asia, *SP*, 122–23, 240–46; David Wyatt, *Thailand: A Short History* (2nd ed., New Haven, 2003), chs. 2, 3, explaining Tai inroads in a fashion consistent with my schema of economically generated trans-frontier integration.

Does disease help our inquiry? Smallpox may have reached South Asia from the Mideast by the late second millennium B.C.E., becoming endemic – a locally sustained affliction primarily of children – in the Ganges basin. But in more thinly populated areas like the Deccan, smallpox may have remained more uniformly lethal until the early second millennium C.E., when demographic growth and more regular external contacts allowed local populations to cross the threshold from epidemic to endemic affliction. Hence perhaps the loosely synchronized rise vis-à-vis older Eurasian centers of South India, Europe's northern fringes, Japan, and Southeast Asia. But again disease reconstructions are speculative, and we still must explain antecedent population growth.[142]

A word finally on climate – our usual default coordinating agent – which both Volume 1 and this volume identified as potentially critical during the Medieval Climate Anomaly, 800/850–1250/1300, when enhanced solar radiation and a reduction in volcanism and El Nino events combined to enhance rainfall and improve wet-rice cultivation in mainland Southeast Asia and South China even as those same factors, through atmospheric warming, extended the growing season and raised yields in France and Russia. Because South Asia shares a monsoon and El Nino regime with much of mainland Southeast Asia, one would expect comparable conditions to have aided the subcontinent. In fact, studies show a strong long-term correlation between El Nino events and deficient summer monsoons in northern, central, and peninsular India, which is significant if one remembers that during the entire period 700–1900, El Nino events are thought to have been weakest between c. 820 and 1270 C.E.[143] What is more, paleoclimatic and historical records

---

[142] For what little South Asian data exists, McNeill, *Plagues and Peoples*, 80–127 *passim*; Wink, *Al-Hind*, vol. II, 165–66; F. Fenner et al., *Smallpox and Its Eradication* (Geneva, 1988), 211–15; Mohammed Said, "Diseases of the Premodern Period in South Asia," in Kenneth Kiple, ed., *The Cambridge World History of Human Disease* (Cambridge, 1993), 413–17.

[143] See *SP*, 49–50, 101–12 (esp. Fig. 2.3), 224–27, 363–64. On correlations, strong in the long term but occasionally variable in the short term, between El Nino events and Indian droughts, and between climate in India and extensive parts of Southeast Asia, see Richard Grove and John Campbell, eds., *El Nino – History and Crisis* (Cambridge, 2000), 1–34, 171–90; C. F. Ropelewski and M. S. Halpert, "Global and Regional Scale Precipitation Patterns Associated with the El Nino/Southern Oscillation," *Monthly Weather Review* 115 (1987): 1606–26; David Bachiochi et al., "The Effect of Indian Ocean Warming on the Indian Monsoon," *Mausam* 52 (2001): 151–62, citing Indian–Indonesian correlations; Peter Whetton et al., "Rainfall and River Flow Variability in Africa, Australia and East Asia Linked to El Nino-Southern Oscillation Events,"

point to similar, if imperfectly correlated, long-term shifts in rainfall in Southeast Asia and India between 1400 and 1850,[144] and, more relevant to the present discussion, during the Medieval Climate Anomaly. In normally dry Rajasthan, for example, analyses of lake levels and pollen residues show both a positive correlation between temperatures and summer monsoon strength and major long-term increases in precipitation – of over 100 percent – starting c. 800, peaking between c. 1000–1250, and then trailing off to an historic low in the mid-1600s during the Little Ice Age. Dendrological studies in north Pakistan also point to higher temperatures and heavier precipitation c. 1000–1220, a connection researchers explain in part by noting that warming increases the moisture-holding capacity of the atmosphere.[145] According to dendrological profiles from northwest Karakorum in Pakistan and the southern Tien Shan range of Kirghizia, between 700 and 2000 C.E., the 9th

Geological Society of America Symposium Proceedings 1 (1990): 71–82, also treating South Asia and all of Southeast Asia as a coherent ENSO zone; J. O. Murphy and P. H. Whetton, "A Re-Analysis of a Tree Ring Chronology from Java," *Dendrochronology*, Proceedings B 92 (Sept., 1989): 241–57; Peter Whetton and Ian Rutherford, "Historical ENSO Connections in the Eastern Hemisphere," *CC* 28 (1994): 221–53, arguing for positive rainfall correlations between India and archipelagic Southeast Asia, but negative correlations with central and eastern sectors of the mainland; R. H. Kripalani and S. V. Singh, "Large-Scale Aspects of India-China Summer Monsoon Rainfall," *Advances in Atmospheric Sciences* 10 (1993): 71–84, indicating strong rainfall correlations between India and most of mainland Southeast Asia; R. H. Kripalani and Ashwini Kulkarni, "Rainfall Variability over South-East Asia," *Intl. Jl. of Climatology* 17 (1997): 1155–68, showing rainfall correlations between India, the northwest mainland, North China, and eastern, but not western, Indonesia.

[144] Previous note, plus Morrison, "Naturalizing Disaster"; R. R. Yadav and Won-kyu Park, "Precipitation Reconstruction Using Ring-Width Chronology of Himalayan Cedar from Western Himalaya," *Proceedings of the Indian Academy of Sciences: Earth and Planetary Sciences* 109 (2000): 339–45; R. P. Kane, "El Nino Timings and Rainfall Extremes in India, Southeast Asia and China," *International Jl. of Climatology* 19 (1999): 653–72; Eaton, *NCHI*, 130; Guha, *Environment and Ethnicity*, 48–49, 54–55; Gordon, *NCHI*, 23, 46, 53; Richards, *NCHI*, 163; Grove and Chappell, *El Nino*, 14–22. Drought references in these last five sources and *SP*, 106–107 n. 55 correlate reasonably well. On Indian–Indonesian drought and famine correlations, strong for much of the 17th century but in some years inverse, see too Peter Boomgaard, "Crisis Mortality in 17th-Century Indonesia," in Ts'ui-jung Liu et al., eds., *Asian Population History* (Oxford, 2001), 191–220, esp. 196–97.

[145] R. A. Bryson and A. M. Swain, "Holocene Variations of Monsoon Rainfall in Rajasthan," *Quaternary Research* 16 (1981): 135–45; H. H. Lamb, *Climate, History and the Modern World* (London, 1995), 131, Fig. 45, and 182–85, 207–208. On north Pakistan, Kerestin Treydte et al., "The Twentieth Century Was the Warmest Period in Northern Pakistan over the Past Millennium," *Nature* 440 (2006): 1179–82. The latter series starts only in 1000.

and 10th centuries, at the start of the Medieval Climate Anomaly, saw maximum vegetative growth, the result of warming more pronounced even than in the 20th century. Elevated temperatures and sustained growth continued until c. 1140, when a cooling trend began that would last until the early 1800s.[146] In the western and eastern Himalayas as well, pollen and tree-ring studies point to warmer, wetter, more vegetatively benign conditions during the Medieval Climate Anomaly: the 13th was the warmest century, while monsoons during the cooler 1355–1453 period were among the weakest.[147] Peat bog analyses from the Nilgiri Hills in southwest India show that monsoons strengthened starting c. 900 and climaxing c. 1200–1400.[148] So too palynological studies reveal elevated rainfall in northeast India after c. 1000, and wetter, warmer climate starting between 800 and 950 in Madhya Pradesh in central India.[149] In brief, diverse evidence points to wetter, more agriculturally propitious conditions during the Medieval Climate Anomaly in much of the subcontinent, including the normally dry, agriculturally vulnerable western sector.

If subsequent research confirms these patterns, it would help to explain – along with novel institutions, evolving pastoral–sedentary

---

[146] Jan Esper et al., "1300 Years of Climatic History for Western Central Asia Inferred from Tree-Rings," *The Holocene* 12 (2002): 267–77, concluding that the Medieval Warm Period had a major regional effect.

[147] The series runs from 1167 to 1988. See R. R. Yadav, "Climatic Variations over the Western Himalaya as Deduced from Tree-Rings," *Geological Survey of India Special Publication* 53 (2001) (Proceedings of the Symposium on Snow, Ice, and Glaciers): 157–60, esp. 158; Yadav and Park, "Precipitation Reconstruction," 339–45. Because monsoon and non-monsoon precipitation correlate inversely, the last study's finding of strong non-monsoon precipitation 1355–1453 agrees with mainland Southeast Asian patterns, and with records of severe drought in central India 1396–1408, in Guha, *Environment and Ethnicity*, 48–49. See too Chayya Sharma and M. S. Chauhan, "Late Holocene Vegetation and Climate of Kupup (Sikkim), Eastern Himalaya, India," *Jl. of the Palaeontological Society of India* 46 (2001): 51–58; and M. S. Chauhan et al., "Pollen Analytical Study of Late-Holocene Sediments from Trans-Yamuna Segment of Western Doon Valley of Northwest Himalaya," *The Palaeobotanist* 50 (2001): 403–10.

[148] R. Sukumar et al., "A delta-13 C Record of Late Quaternary Climate from Tropical Peats in Southern India," *Nature* 364 (1993): 703–706; R. Ramesh, "First Evidence for Little Ice Age and Medieval Warming in India," *Eos, Transactions of the American Geophysical Union* 74 (1993), Supplement, 118; Malcolm Hughes and Henry Diaz, "Was There a 'Medieval Warm Period,' and If So, Where and When?," *CC* 26 (1994): 109–42, esp. 132.

[149] Kathleen Morrison, "Oceans of Dharma" (ms), 54–55, citing Mazari; M. S. Chauhan, "Pollen Evidence of Later-Quaternary Vegetation and Climate Change in Northeastern Madhya Pradesh, India," *The Palaeobotanist* 49 (2000): 491–500.

relations, and perhaps reduced smallpox mortality – four critical phenomena between c. 850 and 1300:

a) Why reclamation and population growth accelerated in northern and eastern India, but more particularly in the broad arid expanse (receiving less than 1,000 mm of rain a year) extending from the Indus valley through Rajasthan into central India and the Deccan. On such marginal lands stronger monsoons would have encouraged both rainfed cultivation and the damming of rain-fed streams to create small irrigation reservoirs. In fact, in the central Deccan's dry Telangana area alone between c. 1000 and 1300, an estimated 5,000 such reservoirs were constructed, many still in use.[150] One thinks of proliferating irrigation works in the dry zones surrounding Pagan and Angkor in this same period.[151] In turn, it is conceivable that denser populations in hitherto marginal areas helped smallpox to cross the epidemicity–endemicity threshold.

b) Why in this era the breeding of horses and oxen flourished in marginal, rain-dependent pasturelands in Inner Asia and South Asia, with corresponding benefits for pastoralists, cavalry, and nearby cultivators alike.[152]

c) Why in India as in other sectors of Eurasia frontiersmen became more closely involved with settled society as craftsmen, transporters, dairymen, traders, sorcerers, farmers, and especially warriors. On the one hand, in arid and semi-arid zones, better rainfall and diet and relative freedom from sedentary-zone diseases may have permitted unusually strong population growth. Wink argues that from c. 630 to 1030 the population in dry regions north of Iran and west of the Indus grew by 20 percent a century, appreciably faster than in the Indo-Gangetic basin; and that this imbalance impelled large-scale migrations starting with Ghaznavid and the Ghurid attacks on North India in the 11th and 12th centuries and peaking in the 13th century.[153] On the other hand, to repeat my earlier hypothesis, as prosperity in agrarian and dry zones

---

[150] Eaton, *NCHI*, 14–15, referring to the Kakatiya era and the period after the 11th century. Cf. n. 23 *supra*, and Stein, *NCHI*, 21.

[151] *SP*, 95–112, esp. n. 24, and 224–28; Michael Aung-Thwin, *Pagan: The Origins of Modern Burma* (Honolulu, 1985), chs. 2, 5, 8, 9.

[152] Gommans, "Silent Frontier," 11 suggests that "climatological changes" joined technological and biological shifts to spur "the horse revolution" in the 1100s and 1200s. *IBE*, 50 also refers to "improvements in livestock" in the arid zone.

[153] Wink, *Al-Hind*, vol. II, 50, 66, 168; idem, "India and the Turko-Mongol Frontier," 222–25; Ludden, "History Outside Civilization," 16. Cf. Neville Brown, *History and Climate Change* (London, 2001), 211–17, on Mongol demography.

magnified frontier exchanges, pastoral knowledge of urban societies increased, along with their ability to dominate those societies. Similar dynamics c. 900–1300, I submit, allowed Tai warriors to menace Pagan and Angkor, and Khitans, Jurchens, and Mongols to challenge Song China.[154]

d) Why South Asia's long-distance commerce expanded overland with Inner Asia and by sea with the Mideast, Southeast Asia, and South China. That is to say, as economies across southern Eurasia diversified, they were better able to pursue complementary Smithian exchanges, aided in some cases by Inner Asian political patronage.

As usual, however, climate reconstructions rest on a still modest evidential base, and linkages between climate and other factors need closer study than I, an outsider to South Asian studies, can provide. In sum, although in India as elsewhere the economy showed great vigor between c. 850 and 1300 and although climate may have played a critical role, for now one cannot quantify that contribution.

At various times between 1240 and 1450 Southeast Asia, France, Russia, and China all suffered political and economic upheavals whose severity contrasted with the relative stability and prosperity of previous centuries. Each of mainland Southeast Asia's chief regions and Russia also saw major religious and/or cultural shifts. India was not exempt. Between 1296 and 1323, recall, the chief kingdoms of the Deccan and South India all collapsed under assaults from the Delhi Sultanate, which itself disintegrated in the second half of the 14th century.

In other realms the disorders of 1240 to 1450 were in some degree a function of antecedent growth that overtaxed agrarian resources and aggravated bullion shortages (Southeast Asia, France, Kiev), strengthened provincial elites at the expense of weak central authorities (Pagan, Angkor, Kiev), and/or magnified the danger of invasion by mobile warriors from beyond the frontier (Southeast Asia and China). In most cases climatic deterioration between 1300 and 1450 seriously aggravated these problems. Were similar factors at work in South Asia? From the 1320s North India suffered silver shortages that by mid-century had undermined the monetary system favored by Muslim rulers since the early 1200s. Currency debasements weakened Delhi's military organization and anticipated yet more debilitating scarcities, characterized by wholesale reversion to mixed metal coinages with a scanty admixture

---

[154] See nn. 138–41 *supra*; Ch. 5, nn. 217–21 *supra*; William McNeill, *The Rise of the West* (Chicago, 1963), 486–87.

of silver, that would continue at least to the late 1400s. No doubt this was part of William Atwell's Eurasian "bullion famine" precipitated *inter alia* by falling production and disruption of established currency flows, to which Chapters 2 and 5 referred.[155] The early or mid-1300s also inaugurated a sustained desiccative trend that reversed favorable climate in the Deccan and North India during much of the previous four centuries. Drought contributed to severe famines in 1291, 1333–1341 (years that saw anti-tax revolts), 1396–1408, 1412–1413, 1423–1424, and 1471–1472.[156] This same period, indeed many of these same years, saw serious climatic deterioration in Southeast Asia, France, Russia, and parts of China.[157] More loosely, Delhi's weak provincial controls in Bengal and the Deccan invite comparison to the immature territorial systems of charter Southeast Asia and Kiev. Finally, although from 1299 to 1307 the Delhi Sultanate was one of a very few Eurasian states to thwart land-based Mongol attacks, Delhi's destruction of southern kingdoms, followed by Timur's sack of Delhi in 1398, were themselves instances of severe dislocations by Inner Asians. Delhi's conquests also transformed the ethnic composition and cultural orientation of elites in much of the subcontinent. Again, one thinks of 13th- to 14th-century Tai and Mongol irruptions in Southeast Asia and of Mongol actions in Russia and China.

At least in physical terms, however, the 13th and 14th centuries were kinder to South Asia than to most other realms. There is no convincing evidence of bubonic plague or population collapse on the fearful scale of western Europe, Russia, or China. (In this respect South Asia may have

---

[155] See Ch. 2, n. 160 and Ch. 5, n. 157 *supra*; Digby, "Currency System," 98–99; idem, "Before Timur Came," 300; Subrahmanyan, "Precious Metal Flows," 81–86, 92; William Atwell, "Time, Money, and the Weather," *JAS* 61 (2002): 83–113; Jackson, *Delhi Sultanate*, 255–56, 261–62, 302, 316, 325. On Delhi's 14th-century economic and political woes, ibid., 255–77, 292, 314–21. Recently Kuroda, "Eurasian Silver Century," 256–57 has argued that plummeting Chinese silver exports from c. 1359 reflected less falling mine production than the collapse of paper currency, which suddenly increased domestic Chinese demand for silver. Although Bengali imports of Chinese and Burmese silver remained strong to 1359, monetary trends in Bengal and the western Ganges region did not correlate precisely. Kuroda's article appeared too late for me to incorporate into Chs. 2 or 5, but his findings are consistent with Richard von Glahn's work cited in Ch. 5.

[156] See drought and famine references in Guha, *Environment and Ethnicity*, 48–49, 54–55; Eaton, *NCHI*, 85; Morrison, "Naturalizing Disaster," 30; and Jackson, *Delhi Sultanate*, 169–70, 265–69, 302, 315, treating claims of late-14th-century prosperity with skepticism; and post-1300 climate data in nn. 145–48 *supra*.

[157] *SP*, 121, 253, 370–71; Ch. 1, n. 106; and Chs. 2, 5 *supra*.

resembled mainland Southeast Asia.[158]) Because the Bahmani Sultanate (founded 1347) and Vijayanagara (founded 1346) quickly divided the Deccan between them, disorders attending northern invasions arguably were less disruptive than disorders in 14th-century Southeast Asia, Russia, France, or China. Indeed, for much of the period 1350–1450 the southern Deccan and Tamil country seem to have enjoyed considerable prosperity.[159]

From the late 15th to the late 17th century, moreover, the economy of key regions expanded sharply. Notwithstanding local droughts, rainfall c. 1480–1590 in much of the subcontinent was favorable. In the Tamil country Kannada and Telugu immigrants wedded better irrigation techniques to larger labor inputs and a martial tradition to wrest new agrarian tracts from forest peoples. In the south-central Deccan reservoir construction and coin issues grew rapidly during Vijayanagara's first century, then slowed c. 1450–1500. However, between 1510 and 1580, driven in part by the crown's need for military revenues, Vijayanagara experienced a "phenomenal" increase in settlement, irrigation reservoirs and canals, and agrarian yields, all "far outstripping" earlier advances. Money use rose too, as shown by temple endowments, taxes, and coinage.[160] Across much of South India, Sanjay Subrahmanyam concludes, the agrarian economy entered an expansionary phase c. 1400 that continued for almost 300 years.[161] The Punjab may have experienced a similar rhythm. In eastern Bengal from the late 1500s an eastward shift in the river systems that bore the rich silt and fresh water needed for wet rice joined with Mughal land grants to begin the historic transformation of that jungle terrain into one of Asia's greatest rice granaries.[162]

All told – spurred by state and market incentives, better seeds, improved irrigation techniques, and more readily available iron-shod

---

[158] Cf. *SP*, 169, 369; Wink, *Al-Hind*, vol. II, 164–67.

[159] Ludden, *Peasant History*, 23, 42–59; idem, *NCHI*, 113; Morrison, "Naturalizing Disaster," 25–29; Subrahmanyam, *Political Economy*, 357; Eaton, *NCHI*, 84–86; Stein, *NCHI*, 45–46.

[160] Morrison, "Naturalizing Disaster," 25–30, with quoted phrases p. 27; Ludden, *Peasant History*, ch. 2; Guha, *Environment and Ethnicity*, 46–52; Stein, *History*, 155–59; idem, *NCHI*, 47–54; Eaton, *NCHI*, 84–86.

[161] Subrahmanyam, *Political Economy*, 357. But see ibid., 359 on the 1540s famine in Southeast India, and evidence of monsoon failures in the 15th century in n. 156 *supra*, and in 1594–1597, 1629–1633, 1685–1688 in n. 144 *supra*.

[162] Eaton, *Rise of Islam*, 194–227, 306–308; Grewal, *NCHI*, 9; Ludden, *NCHI*, 95, 119; C. A. Bayly, *The Birth of the Modern World* (Malden, MA, 2004), 60.

plows – cultivated acreage in the lowlands and adjacent hills of the Ganges basin and Bengal increased by some two-thirds between 1600 and 1700 alone. If acreage grew more rapidly than population, the latter probably kept pace with output,[163] so that the subcontinent's total population may have risen – estimates vary – from something like 120,000,000 in 1500 to 145,000,000 in 1600 to 170,000,000–180,000,000 in 1700.[164] In this 17th-century expansion South Asia resembled Japan, as well as Nguyen Vietnam and southern Russia, more closely than France, Upper Burma, or China.

Mughal towns and cities, forming an urban grid approaching Gilbert Rozman's Stage G ("national marketing") and containing 7 to 15 percent of the population, served as centers of finance, crop marketing, and artisanry. Cash cropping, urban and rural handicrafts all grew more specialized.[165] As in East Asia, cotton and silk thus came to depend on complex chains of growers, spinners, weavers, dyers, wholesalers, and retailers. With wealth more liquid, religious donations tended to shift from land to mobile assets – as happened in Burma after 1500.[166] Rents and taxes were commuted to cash, systems of credit and remittance became more sophisticated, money values were used more often to express social relations, and copper and silver coins spread to more

---

[163] Ludden, *NCHI*, 134–36, relying on James Hagen; Richards, *NCHI*, 193.

[164] Estimates from Juan Cole, "New Empires in Asia and the Middle East" (ms), 3; *CEHI*, ch. 6; Wink, *Al-Hind*, vol. II, 163–67; Richards, "Early Modern India," 207; Colin McEvedy and Richard Jones, *Atlas, of World Population History* (New York, 1980), 183; Subrahmanyam, *Political Economy*, 14–15, 358–59; Bayly, *NCHI*, 7.

[165] On urban size, Stephen Blake, "The Urban Economy in Premodern Muslim India," *MAS* 21 (1987): 447–71, esp. 452, and *CEHI*, 168–69, 436, neither of which, unfortunately, defines "urban." Cf. Gilbert Rozman, *Urban Networks in Russia 1750–1800, and Premodern Periodization* (Princeton, 1976), 34–35, 269–70, by which schema India in 1800 would have been at Stage F or G. On towns, domestic trade, cash crop production – which as late as 1840 reportedly claimed only 15 percent of North Indian acreage (Blake, "Urban Economy," 454) – and the social implications of commerce c. 1500–1750, see Bayly, *NCHI*, 9–13; *CEHI*, pt. II; Sanjay Subrahmanyam, ed., *Merchants, Markets and the State in Early Modern India* (Delhi, 1990), esp. essays by Stewart Gordon, Madhavi Bajekal, and Rajat Datta; Ludden, *NCHI*, 74–75, 129–32; Frank Perlin, "Proto-Industrialization and Pre-Colonial South Asia," *PP* 98 (1983): 30–95; Richards, *NCHI*, 185–204; Om Prakash, *NCHI*, vol. II, 5: *European Commercial Enterprise in Pre-Colonial India* (Cambridge, 1998), ch. 4; idem, "System of Credit"; Najaf Haider, "The Monetary Basis of Credit and Banking Instruments in the Mughal Empire," in Bagchi, *Money and Credit*, 58–83.

[166] Victor Lieberman, "The Political Significance of Religious Wealth in Burmese History," *JAS* 39 (1980): 753–69; Talbot, *Precolonial India*, 28.

humble strata. From the late 1500s in South India and somewhat later in the north the portfolio capitalist – an entrepreneur who traded in a host of local and imported goods, farmed revenue, and supplied credit for military operations – became a characteristic feature of the political economy.[167]

Foreign commerce, as ever, reflected and fueled internal growth. By land and sea Southwest and Southeast Asia exchanged bullion, horses, and spices for Indian foodstuffs, industrial crops, and textiles, among which cottons were most popular. The growing specialization in domestic production and marketing and an associated bullion hunger drew foreign merchants to the subcontinent and empowered overseas Indian trade diasporas.[168] In turn foreign contacts from 1450 to 1700 spurred the Indian economy in four familiar ways: a) Maritime demand stimulated handicrafts and commercial reorganization, especially in silk and Bengali cottons.[169] b) New World maize, tobacco, chilies, and tomatoes diversified agriculture. (But according to Sucheta Mazumdar, the demographic impact was less marked than in China, because lower man-to-land ratios rendered peasants less dependent on agrarian intensification.)[170] c) From West Asia came the Persian waterwheel, the dome arch, the draw loom, and novel accounting techniques.[171] d) Most critical, rising bullion production (chiefly silver, but also gold and copper) in central Europe, Japan, Africa, and especially the Americas ended Eurasia's "bullion famine." Although India produced virtually no precious metals, New World silver flowing overland via West Asia

---

[167] Sanjay Subrahmanyam and C. A. Bayly, "Portfolio Capitalists and the Economy of Early Modern India," *IESHR* 25 (1988): 401–24.

[168] *SP*, 145–49, 168, 171, 282; *AC*, vol. II, 23–31; Om Prakash, *The Dutch East India Company and the Economy of Bengal 1630–1720* (Princeton, 1985), 97–112; *IBE*, 77–80, 172–73, 256–64, 275; *CEHI*, ch. 13.

[169] Such demand generated up to 100,000 jobs and 30 percent of the increase in Bengali textile production 1680–1740. Prakash, *Dutch East India Company*, 234–44; Bayly, "South Asia and the Great Divergence," 91. Cf. figures at Markus Vink, "A Match Made in Heaven?," in Ernst van Veen and Leonard Blusse, eds., *Rivalry and Conflict* (Leiden, 2005), 267–314.

[170] Sucheta Mazumdar, "The Impact of New World Food Crops on the Diet and Economy of China and India, 1600–1900," in Raymond Grew, ed., *Food in Global History* (Boulder, 1999), 58–79; *CEHI*, 217; Ludden, *NCHI*, 48.

[171] Cf. n. 134 *supra*; Shobha, *Social Life*, 17; Roy, "Knowledge and Divergence," 367. This receptivity to West Asian influences contrasts with South Asia's substantial pre-1700 indifference to nonmilitary European technology. A. J. Qaisar, *The Indian Response to European Technology and Culture (A.D. 1498–1707)* (Delhi, 1982), 33–60.

and by sea in Iberian and Muslim ships contributed to a tripling of circulating silver rupees from 1591 to 1639 alone.[172]

In short, in South Asia as elsewhere after c. 1500 stronger international linkages joined advances in agrarian and handicraft technique, reclamation, and commercial organization to provide a cushion against climatic deterioration and political upheaval and to permit sustained population increases. Hence the linear-cum-cyclic, rather than purely cyclic, nature of growth.

Furthermore, notwithstanding the depressive effects of heavy taxation, on balance the Mughal state probably aided growth not only by creating a uniform, high-quality trimetallic currency (silver, gold, and copper) to replace adulterated regional issues, but also by ushering in long periods of domestic peace; improving arterial roads, bridges, and caravanserais and thus linking ports and other cities to wider hinterlands; and offering tax incentives and land grants to develop towns, reclaim land, and plant high-value crops. Aurangzeb's "entire elevated attention," a 1665 edict declared, is "devoted to the increase in the population and cultivation of the Empire."[173] By obliging peasants to increase market sales, state demand for cash taxes, payable in imperial coin, acted like a giant pump, sucking foodstuffs from the countryside into towns and cities, whose traders, officials, and landholders provided credit for next year's cultivation. The imperial family and high nobles used their large discretionary incomes to purchase goods and services on the market, but more generally to support private workshops producing everything from household goods to weapons.[174] Mughal nomothesis joined the archival propensities of Hindu traders to foster a

---

[172] On late-15th- to 16th-century world bullion flows, Ch. 2, nn. 226, 295; Ch. 4, nn. 135–36, 250; Ch. 5, n. 162 *supra*. On India's external trade, including bullion flows, *CEHI*, 363–65 (with rupee figures), 382–433; Folz, *Mughal India*, 6–7, 62–64; Subrahmanyan, "Precious Metal Flows," 85–93; Ashin Das Gupta, *The World of the Indian Ocean Merchant 1500–1800* (New Delhi, 2001); Sinnapah Arasaratnam, *Maritime Trade, Society, and European Influence in Southern Asia, 1600–1800* (Aldershot, UK, 1995); Najaf Haider, "Precious Metal Flows and Currency Circulation in the Mughal Empire," *JESHO* 39 (1996): 298–364; Richards, *NCHI*, 196–204, 239–42, 286. But according to Jadunath Sarkar, *Studies in Aurangzib's* (sic) *Reign* (rpt., Hyderabad, 1989), 191, land revenues were 111 times larger than maritime import duties.

[173] Quoted in Ludden, *NCHI*, 96.

[174] On Mughal economic stimuli, John Richards, ed., *The Imperial Monetary System of Mughal India* (Delhi, 1987); idem, *NCHI*, 71–75, 86, 186–90, 204, 285–86; Blake, "Urban Economy," 456–63; Ludden, *NCHI*, 106–107, 137–40; Alam and Subrahmanyam, *Mughal State*, 13–16, 58–59; Bagchi, *Money and Credit*, 41, 61–62; *IBE*, 152.

culture of commercial rationality that Bayly suggests loosely resembled state–capitalist syntheses in early modern Europe.[175]

If South Asian states encouraged economic growth, however, the relation remained thoroughly reciprocal. Not only were the Mughals – through *zabt* assessments, customs revenues, better coinage, *jagir* and *zamindar* controls – able to collect a larger share of the economic pie than their predecessors, but the pie itself in 1700 was substantially larger than in 1450. Although historians debate what fraction of nominal tax claims were realized and how inflation affected the value of collections, all agree that Mughal revenues greatly exceeded those of either the Delhi sultans or Sher Shah Sur. Improved financial and credit systems also lent Mughal taxation a novel resilience. Thus the Mughals got the best of two worlds, amassing cavalry and animals from the dry zones of Inner Asia and the subcontinent, collecting surpluses from agrarian zones, and linking these zones ever more tightly with silver.[176] Meanwhile the more rapid movement of people and goods encouraged that dissemination of brahmanic caste and Perso-Islamic norms that I described.

As we shall see, historians have focused on ways in which economic growth empowered local resistance to Mughal demands. Scholars have shown less interest in the goodwill that state-assisted growth may have engendered. But by analogy with Europe and Southeast Asia, it is reasonable to assume that wider opportunities for cash cropping, moneylending, interregional trade, and tax commissions profited many *zamindars*, aspiring peasants, and traders whose support became a significant source of Mughal strength.[177]

To what extent did Mughal power also rest on firearms? Over 30 years ago Marshall Hodgson called attention to the signal contribution of cannon and matchlocks to consolidation of the Safavid, Ottoman, and Mughal states, his so-called gunpowder empires, whose collective experience he sought to assimilate to post-1500 European patterns.[178] Recent research has qualified his views, at least for India. Jos Gommans, for example, has argued that 16th-century Indian cannon (derived variously from Inner Asia, Persia, Turkey, and Portuguese mercenaries)

---

[175] Bayly, "Pre-Colonial Indian Merchants," 3–24.
[176] See nn. 38–41 *supra*.
[177] No doubt, depending on circumstance, the same groups might support and oppose Mughal power. See n. 47 *supra*, nn. 281–84 *infra*, plus Richards, *NCHI*, 193, 295–96; Alam, *Languages*, 98–99.
[178] Hodgson, *Gunpowder Empires*, esp. 16–30.

were too cumbersome and unreliable to be truly effective for siege warfare; thus India, unlike Europe, never experienced widespread decastel-
lization. Even the Mughal's famed "gunpowder" victories at Panipat
(1526) and Khanua (1527), which opened up North India, were the
work not of heavy guns, but of mounted archers fighting in concert
with light artillery and matchlockmen shielded by a barricade of carts.
The endless availability of cavalry archers removed the incentive to
develop matchlock-wielding infantry able to provide permanent fire
like the infantry squares of Europe; and in fact Indian matchlockmen
never equaled the rate of fire of trained archers.[179] Yet firearms retained
considerable tactical value. Well into the 1700s the practice of combining artillery with flanking cavalry dominated field operations, with
artillery assuming the central role once played by elephants and, in
some cases, by heavy cavalry. Likewise, Mughal forces used small arms
to good effect behind cover or in ambush. Mughal matchlocks proved
more accurate at long range than their European counterparts, while
technical adaptations rendered successive generations of Mughal field
artillery simpler and more mobile. Seventeenth-century artillery and
exploding mines also figured prominently in sieges. The alacrity with
which Mughal forces adopted such weapons, their willingness to innovate in some technical spheres, heavy financial outlays for firearms, the
often enormous burdens Mughal armies bore to deploy siege guns, and
the prominence of cannons in imperial cavalcades, histories, and painting – all suggest that firearms contributed substantially to early Mughal
success, notwithstanding the devolutionary effects that the rural manufacture and diffusion of guns from the mid-1600s may have had.

To sum up, although here as in China, Inner Asians provided a critical
spur to territorial consolidation absent in the protected zone, the benefits
that the Mughals derived from post-1500 agrarian expansion, firearms,

[179] Gommans, "Warhorse and Gunpowder," 112–19; idem, *Mughal Warfare*, 100, 145–62,
185–96; Kolff, *Naukar, Rajput*, 23. Discussion of firearms relies too on Parker, *Military
Revolution*, 128–36; Richards, *NCHI*, 26–28, 142–43, 287–89; Sanjay Subrahmanyam,
"The *Kagemusha* Effect," *Moyen Orient & Ocean Indien* 4 (1987): 97–123; Eaton, *Rise of
Islam*, 151–53, 158; Bruce Lenman, "The Transition to European Military Ascendancy
in India, 1600–1800," in John Lynn, ed., *Tools of War* (Urbana, IL, 1990), 100–30; Iqtidar
Alam Khan, *Gunpowder and Firearms* (New Delhi, 2004), arguing for early localization;
Jos Gommans and Dirk Kolff, "Introduction," in Gommans and Kolff, *Warfare and
Weaponry*, 33–39, noting that Indian military architecture remained far more conservative than European; and Richard Eaton, "'Kiss My Foot,' Said the King," *MAS* 43
(2009): 289–313, analyzing interior India's earliest significant, but far from decisive,
use of cannon and matchlocks, in 1520.

cumulative administrative expertise, rising domestic and global trade, and the accelerated circulation of goods and people are broadly familiar from post-1500 protected-zone realms. These features, together with the Mughals' unprecedented territorial and political success after generations of localism, justify our "early modern" rubric.[180]

The Mughal state resembled its counterparts in France, Burma, Siam, and Vietnam in another respect: it collapsed in the course of the 18th century. Obviously, key French cultural ingredients – secularization, popular sovereignty, an explicitly meritocratic ethos – lacked even vague Indian analogue. Indeed, disintegrating French corporatism ran directly counter to strengthening caste ideology. Obviously too, among the regions so far considered, only in South Asia did the 18th-century state, once fallen, fail to resurrect itself. Yet in India we also find familiar features deriving from the strains of long-term economic growth. Volume 1 argued that between 1752 and 1771 commerce helped to destabilize Southeast Asian states by nurturing landholding and ministerial interests without adequate influence at court and by empowering coastal zones at the expense of the capital. In each case military pressures precipitated collapse.[181] In *ancien régime* France market-based mobility eroded estate identities in favor of a more individualistic ethos and, along with foreign reverses, debased the monarchy's ideological credit.

In Mughal India too, commodification in some instances favored provincial officials, merchants, *zamindars*, and pioneering peasants who accumulated untaxed resources and appropriated income formerly controlled by the state. Although compliant so long as imperial authority was secure, many of these groups were at best weakly assimilated to imperial culture and were quick to exploit Mughal setbacks such as Aurangzeb met in the Deccan. With central control slackening and maritime superseding overland trade, aspiring elites sought alliance with financial cliques, including Europeans, tied to coastal commerce. The waxing influence of Bengal, in particular, recalls that of Lower Burma, the Gulf of Siam, and the Mekong delta, all heavily invested in foreign trade. Some of the most dynamic Mughal provinces and groups – Bengal, the new gentry, revenue farmers, merchant-traders – were first to revolt or quietly to withdraw support.[182] At the same time, to follow

---

[180] On an "early modern," as opposed to "late medieval," designation, see n. 35 *supra*.

[181] *SP*, 182–87, 299–302, 419–23.

[182] C. A. Bayly, *Imperial Meridian* (London, 1989), 29–33; Richards, *NCHI*, 295–96; Alam, *Crisis of Empire*, 35, 41, 130–32, 202; idem, "The Mughals and the 18th-Century Transition in Bengal" (ms); nn. 34, 46, 47 *supra* and nn. 281–83 *infra*. Some sources (*CEHI*, 376;

Rosalind O'Hanlon, the emergence in North India of more commercial, complexly stratified urban societies encouraged an ethos of conspicuous consumption and personal connoisseurship that was in tension with older notions of absolute devotion to the emperor. Associated at first with high nobles, this outlook spread in the late 1600s to lesser officials and gentry. If the attendant sense of aristocratic hauteur was antithetical to a growing French interest in political equality, in a broader sense the devaluation of corporate obligation and government service in favor of a more individualized, consumerist sensibility may have eroded morale in both realms.[183] Finally, although less disastrous than military reverses in 18th-century Southeast Asian realms or France, Aurangzeb's prolonged, ultimately unsuccessful Deccan campaigns diverted attention from the heartland and aggravated factionalism by creating more aspirants for *jagir* awards than could be satisfied.[184]

With the empire fragmenting, successor states battened on the intertwined processes of military innovation and commercialization. As early as the 1660s Maratha insurgents had shown the vulnerability of lumbering Mughal columns, but after 1750 European companies and mercenaries wrought a revolution in South Asian warfare that eclipsed Mughal-style heavy cavalry and revealed the full potential of European firearms and training. European iron-casting, boring, and standardization rendered artillery far more effective and mobile. From the mid-1700s as well, some two generations after being adopted in Europe and at the same time as they spread across Southeast Asia, flintlock muskets – replete with quick-firing cartridges and socket bayonets – gave infantry drilled in European fashion a critical advantage over cavalry, not to mention footsoldiers using crude village manufactures. Quickly mastering the new technology, Indian arsenals began churning out artillery and muskets equal, in some cases superior, to the finest Western arms.[185] To meet the huge cost of new weapons and of training

---

M. Athar Ali, "The Passing of Empire," *MAS* 9, 1975, 385–96) speculate that, as in 18th-century Southeast Asia, price inflation intensified elite disquiet, but Subrahmanyam, "Precious Metal Flows," 93–103 is skeptical.

[183] Rosalind O'Hanlon, "Manliness and Imperial Service in Mughal North India," *JESHO* 42 (1999): 47–93. Cf. Ch. 3, nn. 214–15 *supra*, and Richards, "Norms of Comportment."

[184] See n. 46 *supra*.

[185] On the military balance, Cooper, *Anglo-Maratha Campaigns*, 15–61, 284–312, and *passim*; Gommans, *Mughal Warfare*, 166, 203–206; Gordon, *NCHI*, 149–53, 190–94; Gommans and Kolff, "Introduction," 40–41; Lenman, "Transition to European Ascendancy"; Dirk Kolff, "The End of an *Ancien Regime*," in J. A. de Moor and H. L. Wesserling, eds., *Imperialism and War* (Leiden, 1989), 22–49.

European-style forces, during all or part of the period 1740–1820 the Marathas, Mysore, Awadh, Hyderabad, Bengal, the Sikhs, and smaller Rajput and Indo-Afghan polities pursued thrusting programs of fiscalism and centralization – the "commercialization and scribalization" of power[186] – which in turn rested on monetization of wages and rents and improvements in credit and capital transfer. One is reminded of competitive interstate pressures in Europe, whose outliers, the French and English East India companies, in fact set the pace of South Asian innovation. One is reminded too how synchronization between and within world regions constantly accelerated through trade and technical diffusion. By the 18th century not only had Russia, once hopelessly backward by West European standards, drawn abreast of France in military terms, but western Europe, where charter states arose 800 to 1,300 years later than North India, was setting military terms on the subcontinent.

But if Indian states and European trading companies employed comparable fiscal strategies, and if Indian armies began to approach, even exceed, the technical level of British infantry and artillery, why did the British triumph? The vast wealth of Bengal – which the Company secured by 1765 while its military superiority was yet intact – let it fund, directly or through credit, larger, more durable armies and more efficient administrations than any individual foe could afford.[187] The Company more readily attracted indigenous banking and commercial interests, because its control of maritime routes told heavily in an era when most bullion and textiles entered and left India by sea. The accommodation between British power and indigenous capital was illustrated by the decline of Mughal centers and the spectacular rise of Calcutta, Madras, and Bombay, the first two of which by 1800 probably were the subcontinent's largest cities. These ports became hubs not only for Company operations, but for fleets of private British-owned vessels specializing in intra-Asia exchange, the "country trade."[188] Besides control of specie and external trade, the sea afforded the British two major strategic

---

[186] Phrase from Washbrook, "Progress and Problems," 70.

[187] Whereas Maratha rulers, for example, could maintain their war effort for only a few months, the Company could funnel Bengal resources across the entire subcontinent for years on end. See n. 185 *supra*, plus Metcalfs, *Concise History*, 54; Bayly, *NCHI*, 46–54; 85, 102–103, 106; Subrahmanyam and Bayly, "Portfolio Capitalists," 422. But see Lynne, *Battle*, 176, on British numerical inferiority in key battles.

[188] On British commercial superiority and private trade, Bayly, *NCHI*, 5, 46–78 *passim*; *IBE*, 286; Metcalfs, *Concise History*, 49, 53–54; P. J. Marshall, *East Indian Fortunes* (Oxford, 1976); Leonard Blusse, "The Run to the Coast," *Itinerario* 12 (1988): 195–214; R. J. Barendse, *The Arabian Seas* (Armonk, NY, 2002), ch. 9.

advantages: a) superior communications and logistics, and b) unimpeded access to home country resources. Whereas its opponents were solitary and regional, the Company controlled three states-cum-armies around the Indian perimeter able to cooperate and at critical times to call on the British government, including the royal navy. An island nation, England was prepared to protect its Indian possessions – and their profitable trade with China and Southeast Asia – at enormous cost.[189] Their patriotism fired by the French wars, late-18th-century Englishmen also enjoyed a unique solidarity, refusing to fight against compatriots, as Indians, motivated by more personal loyalties, were wont to do.[190] Finally, British success owed much to the solidity of the Company itself, its global reach, transgenerational character, extensive archives, fusion of military and commercial roles – what D. A. Washbrook terms "armed corporate mercantilism" – all of which lent it a stability that neither Indian traders nor rulers could match.[191]

British consolidation overlapped with a weakening of some sectors of India's economy. If overall economic performance c. 1700–1830 was more dynamic than in the "disaster" scenario once favored by both colonial and nationalist historians, latest research suggests that it also was less rosy than many revisionists assumed.[192] Naturally, conditions varied by subperiod and region, but in the Ganges basin and Bengal, after a sustained increase that began to flag in the late 1600s, the percentage of total land under cultivation stagnated between 1700 and 1800.[193] If South Asia's population in 1700 was in the order of 175,000,000, by century's end it was still only 190,000,000–200,000,000. This lethargy contrasted with India's performance for most of the 16th and 17th centuries, as well as with 18th-century demographic trends in China, which

---

[189] On the strategic implications of seapower, previous note, plus Washbrook, "South India 1770–1840," 511–12, referring to Hyder Ali's ill-fated fleet; Cooper, *Anglo-Maratha Campaigns*, 302.

[190] In dealing even with the Marathas, who exhibited a vaguely patriotic identity, the British repeatedly exploited family and factional tensions.

[191] Washbrook, "South India 1770–1840," 513–14, suggesting that Company features influenced evolution of the British home government; Lynn, *Battle*, 175–76; Metcalfs, *Concise History*, 43.

[192] See historiographic discussion in Bayly, "South Asia and the Great Divergence," 89–92. On the 18th- to early-19th-century economy, idem, *Rulers, Townsmen*; idem, *NCHI*, chs. 1, 2; *CEHI*, ch. 13; Frank Perlin, "Changes in the Production and Circulation of Money in 17th and 18th Century India," in Subrahmanyam, *Money and the Market*, 276–308; *IBE*, ch 9; Prasannan Parthasarathi, "Rethinking Wages and Competitiveness in the Eighteenth Century," *PP* 158 (1998): 70–109.

[193] Ludden, *NCHI*, 134. Also Grewal, *NCHI*, 68–69.

saw a rise of perhaps 90 percent; in France, which saw a 33 percent increase; and in Europe as a whole, whose population rose by some 50 percent.[194] South Asia's post-1700 slowdown, in fact, bears comparison to that of Japan.

Moreover, although India's external trade per se prospered, from the late 1600s European companies and private traders took a growing share until by the third quarter of the next century, non-European shippers and exporters were in irreversible decline. Overall, despite buoyant sectors and communities, the non-European economy had become locked in a zero-sum game, with peoples and resources moving from area to area but little net growth. Revealingly, 18th-century interest rates were usually at least three times higher than in western Europe, skilled wage labor was far less readily available, while market integration, as measured by regional price convergences, lagged well behind China and Japan as well as Europe.[195]

Four causes for economic deterioration merit attention: a) In areas where cultivation had expanded rapidly through the late 1600s, marginal returns may have begun to fall. As we have seen, something like this happened in Japan after 1720 and in Upper Burma and Dong Kinh after 1750/1770. In other words, those Eurasian regions, chiefly Japan and South Asia, that grew most rapidly in the 1600s were among the first to suffer resource constraints in the 1700s. b) Climate during part of the 18th century was less favorable in South Asia than in much of Southeast Asia, China, or Europe (though not Japan). Especially dramatic were droughts in 1769–1771 – when one in three Bengalis starved to death! – and 1789–1793.[196] c) Although stimulating growth in some

---

[194] Note 164 *supra; CEHI*, 167; McEvedy and Jones, *Atlas*, 18, 57, 183; Ch. 3, n. 179 and Ch. 5, n. 166 *supra*.

[195] Overall analysis relies on Bayly, *Birth of the Modern World*, 59; idem, *Rulers, Townsmen*, chs. 2, 3; *IBE*, 277, 282. Data on interest rates, skilled labor, and market integration are from Jan Luiten van Zanden, "The Road to the Industrial Revolution," *JGH* 3 (2008): 343–47. Note too that whereas in 1600 estimated per capita product in Mughal India and Great Britain had been equal, in 1700 the Indian figure was 76 percent, and in 1857 22 percent, of its English counterpart. Goldsmith, *Premodern Financial Systems*, 102.

[196] India also suffered serious droughts in 1710s and 1730s (although less severe than in 1629–1633 and 1685–1688), while summers from 1720 to 1780 were relatively dry. Although generally synchronized by a common monsoon regime, weather in mainland Southeast Asia and South Asia could diverge in the short and medium term. Yadav and Park, "Precipitation Reconstruction," 343–44; Grove and Chappell, *El Nino*, 13–22; Bayly, "South Asia and the Great Divergence," 92–93; idem, *NCHI*, 32; idem, *Rulers, Townsmen*, 85–86; Alam, *Crisis of Empire*, 31–33.

regions, Mughal decline joined widespread warfare to degrade infrastructure, impede famine relief, and undermine the imperial market hubs of Delhi, Agra, and Surat.[197] d) Starting in the 18th century but more especially in the early 1800s, British rule "knocked the stuffing out" of a large part of South Asia's mercantile economy, to cite Washbrook again. This it did by imposing heavy tribute that obviated hitherto vital British imports of bullion, by dismantling royal courts and other foci of elite consumption, and by destroying the market for Indian textiles in favor of British machine-made goods at first in Britain and overseas, and from c. 1820 in India itself.[198]

Lest one exaggerate the potential for indigenous development *sans* colonialism, consider finally those South Asian structural "deficiencies" that, Bayly and others suggest, inhibited long-term growth on the West European, especially the British, model.[199] Indian merchants remained subject to multiple taxes and amercements more like those of late-medieval than of 18th-century Europe, and the state typically offered less security for property rights. Family enterprises lacked either the continuity or the capital-raising capacity of European joint-stock corporations, while Indians, more than Europeans and perhaps Japanese, expected merchants to legitimate their wealth with religious gifts and community largesse.[200] We find fewer economic benefits from warfare than in Europe, whether spin-offs in metallurgy and chemistry or those war-induced financial instruments that allowed Europeans to mobilize capital for domestic investment as well as war. Without naval power

[197] Bayly, "South Asia and the Great Divergence," 93; n. 192 *supra*, and Sanjay Subrahmanyam, "Rural Industry and Commercial Agriculture in Late Seventeenth-Century South-Eastern India," *PP* 126 (1990), 76–114, emphasizing market segmentation and poor transport.

[198] Washbrook, "Progress and Problems," 79, and idem, "South India 1770–1840," 507–508, focusing on the depression of the late 1820s to early 1850s. Also Metcalfs, *Concise History*, 74–77; Om Prakash, "From Negotiation to Coercion," *MAS* 41 (2007): 1331–68, modifying the image of pre-1800 Bengal textile decline; Bayly, *NCHI*, 104–24, 135; C.A. Bayly, "Van Leur and the Indian Eighteenth Century," in Leonard Blusse and Femme Gaastra, eds., *On the Eighteenth Century as a Category of Asian History* (Aldershot, UK, 1998), 289–302; Irfan Habib, "The Eighteenth Century in Indian Economic History," ibid., 217–36; Om Prakash, "Trade and Politics in 18th-Century Bengal," ibid., 237–60.

[199] Bayly, "South Asia and the Great Divergence"; idem, *Birth of the Modern World*, 58–83; Roy, "Knowledge and Divergence"; van Zanden, "Road to Industrial Revolution."

[200] On merchant organization, strengths, and vulnerabilities, n. 192 *supra* plus Bayly, *Birth of Modern World*, 60–62, 81–82; Subrahmanyam and Bayly, "Portfolio Capitalists," esp. 419–20; Irfan Habib, "Merchant Communities in Precolonial India," in James Tracy, ed., *The Rise of Merchant Empires* (Cambridge, 1990), 371–99; Sen, *Empire of Free Trade*, 38–59.

or overseas investments, Indian states could not match the profits that Britain, France, and Holland derived from agricultural intensification in Asia and the Americas. As Chapter 5 noted, up to 90 percent of the value added in the trade of non-European food crops, stimulants, and opium went to Europeans, who in effect appropriated other people's "industrious revolutions." Whereas in Europe printing, high literacy rates, permeable occupational boundaries, and proliferating technical and scientific bodies supported the rapid dissemination of knowledge, Indian technology was the tacit, oral preserve of closed artisan and caste communities. Manufacture thus remained far more conservative, labor intensive, and small scale.

Consider finally differences in consumer culture. In western Europe, and to a lesser extent perhaps Japan and China, the growing availability of porcelains, textiles, and specialty foods seduced producers to intensify their labor. Although, as my comments on noble sensibilities suggest, consumerism in South Asia was by no means absent, inducements to a de Vriesian-style industrious revolution[201] were weaker than in Europe, because a) society was less urbanized and the rural economy, less monetized; b) abundant wood, palms, and clay pottery inhibited consumer innovation; c) religion absorbed a larger share of income; d) caste restrictions on imitative expenditure were more effective than fast fading European sumptuary regulations; e) income distribution was exceptionally unequal.[202]

For all these reasons, although hardly static, Indian economic growth after 1700 was more modest than in Europe.

2. DISTINCTIVE FEATURES: EARLY STATE FORMATION, GROWING INNER ASIAN AND BRITISH INFLUENCE, PERSISTENT OSCILLATIONS

To recapitulate our South Asian discussion thus far: Over some two millennia successive eras of political fragmentation in the subcontinent grew shorter, administrative systems more efficient, empires

---

[201] Cf. Ch. 3, n. 176; Ch. 4, n. 279; and Ch. 5, n. 169 *supra*.

[202] According to Goldsmith, *Premodern Financial Systems*, 105–108, in India in 1600 the top one-ten-thousandth of all families took 5 percent of national income, whereas in England in 1688 the comparable figure was 2 percent. A similar picture emerges from A. J. Qaisar, "Distribution of the Revenue Resources of the Mughal Empire Among the Nobility," in Alam and Subrahmanyam, *Mughal State*, 252–58.

larger, and culture more horizontally, and to some extent vertically, uniform. Although, given South Asia's size and complexity, most integrative tendencies remained relatively weak, these tendencies are recognizable from our study of individual Southeast Asian and European realms, Japan, and China. Moreover, despite a growing post-1700 divergence between India and Europe, from c. 850 to 1800 Indian economic trends – on which political and cultural integration ultimately relied – drew strength from demographic and commercial rhythms and technological changes loosely coordinated across Eurasia. Particularly familiar were South Asia's economic and political vitality between c. 850 and 1300/1350 (which benefited in some uncertain degree from the Medieval Climate Anomaly), its 14th- and early-15th-century disorders, and the characteristically brilliant early modern (Mughal) achievement.

Given these similarities, how did South Asia differ from those protected-zone societies that provided our initial frame of reference? And how far can we push similarities between South Asia and China? The remainder of the chapter will consider these questions.

Early Genesis of Civilization

An obvious feature that the Indo-Gangetic plain shared with North China but that distinguished both regions from Southeast Asia, northern Europe, and Japan was the early genesis of urban, literate, bronze-age culture. The civilization of the Indus valley is conventionally divided into pre-Harappan or Early Harappan (3200–2600 B.C.E.), Mature Harappan (2600–1900 B.C.E.), and Late Harappan (also termed posturban) phases, with the latter said to conclude as early as 1750 or as late as 1250 B.C.E.[203] The third phase thus ended close to or overlapped with the start of China's Shang culture (c. 1600 B.C.E.), but the first two phases essentially coincided with bronze-age civilization in Mesopotamia.[204] In fact, Mesopotamia and the Indus Valley shared basic ecological

---

[203] Cf. Thapar, *Early India*, 80; Allchin, *Archaeology*, 29; Gregory Possehl, *The Indus Civilization* (Walnut Creek, 2002), 40. Discussion of Harappan and early Gangetic civilization (the "second urbanization") relies on ibid; Allchin, *Archaeology*, 1–151; Thapar, *Early India*, chs. 3–6; Michael Cook, *A Brief History of the Human Race* (New York, 2003), 130–33, 149–64; Christopher Scarre and Brian Fagan, *Ancient Civilizations* (Upper Saddle River, NJ, 2003), ch. 5; Charles Maisels, *Early Civilizations of the Old World* (London, 1999), ch. 4; Bruce Trigger, *Understanding Early Civilizations* (Cambridge, 2003), 28–36.

[204] Trigger, *Understanding Early Civilizations*, 28–35.

profiles (a perennial river in an arid zone of rich alluvial soils), traded extensively with one another, had access to the same array of domesticated crops and animals, and evolved more or less in tandem. So far as is known, these interactions did not extend to wholesale cultural or institutional borrowing such as distinguished secondary from primary civilizations.[205] And yet it is hardly accidental that Harappan culture arose in that part of India that lay closest to Mesopotamia and most resembled it – but never spread anywhere else in the subcontinent. The principal crops and animals of Indus civilization, including wheat, barley, lentils, sheep, goats, and cattle, appear to have been domesticated, and metallurgy seems to have begun, at roughly the same time across an area extending from the Mediterranean to the southeast Caspian Sea to the Indus valley. Within this region, which Gregory Possehl terms the "middle Asian interaction sphere," pastoralism, migration, travel, and trade, both overland and by sea, were so intensive even in the prehistoric era that crops, animals, or technical advances in one locality diffused throughout the region with great speed. Likewise, in Shereen Ratnagar's formulation, Harappan civilization was the eastern manifestation of a bronze-age culture typical of the Southwest Asian arid zone.[206] In terms of aridity, easily cleared vegetation, river dependency, and access to critical technologies, crops, and animals moving along east–west Eurasian axes, the Indus valley also resembled North China. But in most of these respects, both North China and North India differed from Eurasia's protected zone. (As a secondary civilization partly dependent on Gangetic inspiration, South India had much in common with the protected zone.)

What caused the breakdown of the Harappan system – theories of climate change, environmental degradation, disease, invasion, and ideological brittleness have been invoked – is unclear, as is the degree to which India's so-called second urbanization, centered on the Ganges

---

[205] See definitions at Ch. 1, n. 63 and Ch. 5, n. 205.

[206] Possehl, *Indus Civilization*, 1–29; Ch. 1, n. 156 *supra*; and Shereen Ratnagar, *Encounters: The Westerly Trade of the Harappa Civilization* (Delhi, 1981), xiv, 78–198, 230–53, detailing trade goods and routes and arguing that trade was critical to Harappan genesis. See too Scarre and Fagan, *Ancient Civilizations*, 150–59, suggesting that roughly simultaneous urbanization in Mesopotamia and the Indus valley benefited from seaborne trade but assigning a priority to Mesopotamian crop and animal domestication at variance with Possehl; Madhav Gadgil and Ramachandra Guha, *This Fissured Land* (Berkeley, 1992), 76–77; Cook, *Brief History*, 149; Maisels, *Early Civilizations*, 257–58. For information on recent advances in Harappa, pre-Maurya, and Maurya archeology, I am grateful to Carla Sinopoli, pers. commun., Sept. 4, 2008.

basin between c. 600 and 400 B.C.E., was influenced by Harappan legacies. (Current research tends to emphasize the autonomy of pre-Mauryan urbanization and state formation in the Ganges basin.) In any case, intertwined processes of agricultural intensification and political consolidation such as led in China to the Qin unification of 221 B.C.E. culminated in North India a century earlier in the Maurya empire (c. 320–180 B.C.E.). Also parallel to China, iron technology intensified economic and political change prior to unification. Whether introduced from points farther west or subject to a degree of independent invention, iron was present in North India by c. 1200 B.C.E., but was widely used for craft and agricultural implements only from the 6th century. Such tools accelerated a much older movement to clear forests along the fertile banks of the Ganges and its tributaries, much of which was now planted in rice. An indigenous crop suitable to the wet ecology of eastern India, rice offered higher yields than the wheat- and barley-based Harappan regime.[207] Aided by new rice strains and improved transplantation methods, the continuous sedentarization of forest and pastoral lands in North India made possible sustained population growth and the appearance of Gangetic cities. Population growth favored too the evolution of lineage societies into more stratified, organizationally complex, territorially cohesive oligarchies, kingdoms, and empires, with some Ganges polities absorbing local rivals by the 6th century B.C.E.[208] Over a century before Maurya consolidation, North India boasted monumental urban architecture, complex religious/philosophical systems (brahmanical, Buddhist, Jain), literacy, law codes, and the basic *varna* system.

Such developments closely paralleled the birth in China of a multi-state system during the late Spring and Autumn and the early Warring States periods (656–221 B.C.E.) and the elaboration of Chinese social philosophies and instruments of governance. But the emergence of imperial charter states in North India by 320 B.C.E. and in China by 221 B.C.E. antedated comparable developments in mainland Southeast

---

[207] Harappa also grew some rice. On debates concerning Harappan "decline," the Harappa–Gangetic transition, iron, rice, and the second urbanization, I rely on Allchin, *Archaeology*, 39, 54–122 *passim*; Possehl, *Indus Civilization*, 237–45, 250–51; Thapar, *Early India*, 52–53, 137–73; Scarre and Fagan, *Ancient Civilizations*, 163–68; Sinopoli, pers. commun., Sept. 4 and Nov. 24, 2008; and Talbot, pers. commun., July 30, 2007, noting that the second urbanization could also be dated 600–150 B.C.E.

[208] Thapar, *Early India*, chs. 4, 5; Allchin, *Archaeology*, 119–22.

Asia by at least 1,000 years, in France by over 700 years, in Kiev by some 1,150 years, and in Japan by over 900 years.

Growing Exposure to Inner Asian Conquest: An Overview

Along with the early date of charter state formation, a second cardinal feature that was shared by South Asia and China but that distinguished both from the protected zone was subjection to ever more insistent external incursions. If in India from the 1760s these were led by the British, for the great bulk of the period with which we are concerned in both South Asia and China, Inner Asians compressed and transformed the options of local actors.

To the extent that Inner Asians entered along the same ancient east–west routes of trade, oases settlement, and pastoral migration as originally favored the spread of domestic animals, crops, metallurgy, and other technologies in North China and the Indus valley, we are again reminded of links between civilizational precocity and exposure to Inner Asian nomads, and of the double contrast between Eurasia's exposed and protected zones. Although, as Chapter 1 noted, not all Eurasian areas open to Inner Asian conquest were sites of primary civilization, all of the latter were vulnerable to Inner Asian occupation. Originating as far afield as Transoxania, Kazakhstan, and Xinjiang, Inner Asian warriors in fact followed those routes across the mountains of modern Pakistan and Afghanistan into the Indo-Gangetic plains along which West Asian agricultural elements are thought to have entered in the third millennium B.C.E. In India, though not China, overland contacts were supplemented by maritime links, as between Mesopotamian and Harappan ports from the third millennium B.C.E., and between Persia and the Deccan.[209]

Moreover, chronologies of Inner Asian advance in South Asia and China were broadly synchronized. The vexed question of Aryan origins aside,[210] early Inner Asian warrior entrants to South Asia included a) the Sakas, nomads originally perhaps from Xinjiang, who crossed the mountains from Transoxania and modern Tajikistan into the Indus

---

[209] On the overland transmission of Mideastern influences via Transoxania, the Iranian plateau, Afghanistan in the third and second millennia B.C.E. and on seaborne contacts in that same period, see n. 206 *supra* and Ch. 1, n. 159 *supra*.

[210] Thomas Trautmann, "The Aryan Debate" (Univ. of Michigan, lecture, Sept. 10, 2004).

plains in the early first century B.C.E.; Saka migrations apparently were set in motion by attacks from the Xiongnu, who formed the first great nomadic confederation north of China and who entered China in force in 166 B.C.E.; b) the Kusanas, originally from Inner Mongolia, Gansu, and Transoxania, who followed the Sakas into northwest India by the first century C.E. to build a tribute-and-trade empire extending from the Oxus to the eastern Ganges; and c) the Hephthalites (White Huns), who, having crossed from Transoxania into the Punjab and Rajasthan, crippled the Guptas in the early 500s not long after apparently related tribes overran North China.[211] Notwithstanding the Sakas' and Kusanas' seminal contributions to the Sanskrit cosmopolis, in South Asia as in China none of these early conquest states could match the stability or prestige of the great indigenous empires they encountered, Han or Gupta.

However, from the late first millennium in China, Southwest Asia, and South Asia alike, Inner Asians – benefiting, I already suggested, from population growth, expanding trade, and more sustained agrarian–pastoral contacts – acquired the manpower, siege technology, and administrative skills needed to build more durable empires straddling frontier and sown. Each Inner Asian polity typically borrowed best practices from its predecessors so as to provide a cumulative expertise no less impressive than that of the agrarian host societies. In China between 907 and 1368 this dynamic produced, in the teeth of Song resistance, the empires of Khitans, Jurchens, and Mongols. In West and South Asia it was Turkic tribesmen, recently incorporated into the world of Islam, who as early as the 11th century provided a majority of Muslim rulers and the cutting edge for Islamic expansion into both Christendom and North India. Like the aforementioned Seljuk and Karakhanid empires, Muslim incursions into India after 986 and the founding of the Delhi Sultanate were disproportionately the work of Persianized Turks, seconded in India by Tajiks (sedentary Persian-speakers of the Iranian plateau and Transoxania) and Afghans (chiefly Turkified Pashtuns). Much as Khitan and Jurchen power in the 11th and 12th centuries anticipated Mongol conquests, attacks on northwest India by Turkic Ghaznavids and Tajik Ghurids in the 11th and 12th centuries paved the way for the famed Delhi Sultanate. In basic chronology, earlier Inner

---

[211] Wink, *Al-Hind*, vol. II, 43–59; Kulke and Rothermund, *History*, 72–81, 89–91; Thomas Barfield, *The Perilous Frontier* (Cambridge, MA, 1989), 98–103; *CIHC*, 68, 89–93; Ali, *Courtly Culture*, 79–80; Pollock, *Language of the Gods*, 67–74, 277, 499–500, 513, 537; *EAH*, vol. II, 87, 376–78; Sinopoli, "Imperial Landscapes," 335–38; Nicolo Di Cosmo, *Ancient China and Its Enemies* (Cambridge, 2002), ch. 6.

Asian debts, and vaunting ambition, the Sultanate thus invites comparison with the contemporary Mongol Yuan Dynasty (1215/1276–1368) in China.[212]

Whereas in China Yuan eclipse opened the way to an indigenous resurgence under the Ming, after the Sultanate fell, South Asia knew no comparable revival. That is to say, post-Delhi regional sultanates, the Sher Shah Sur regime, and the Mughal empire all were dominated by immigrants or their descendants from Transoxania, Afghanistan, and Persia. Between 1250 and 1550 recurrent disorders in the Mideast and Persia acted like a great winnowing fan, sucking fighters from the steppe into the Muslim heartlands, and then driving them pell-mell to find their fortunes on the frontiers of Islam. By virtue of its wealth and size, India was particularly attractive to such adventurers, providing Indo-Muslim dynasts with an endless stream of recruits, usually as freemen but also as military slaves purchased from Inner Asia.[213]

To these dynamics of recruitment East Asia offered no close parallel. Mughal emperors, like Delhi sultans before them, were magnets around which modest groups of military nobles of diverse ethnicity adhered, but the Manchus were a large, ethnically coherent tribal confederation. In 1526 at the battle of Panipat, which opened North India, Babur, the Mughal founder, commanded only 12,000 men, whereas the Manchus (warriors and their families) when they conquered China numbered between 206,000 and 390,000.[214]

In a broader sense, however, both Mughal and Qing empires represented the intersection of two by now familiar grand dynamics: a) a long-term growth in the resources and institutional efficiency of settled societies that provided a substratum for imperial expansion, whether under indigenous or Inner Asian leadership, and b) a long-term rise in Inner Asian administrative and military capacity. In both Chinese and Indian historiography, national pride has emphasized the first dynamic to the neglect of the second, but in Qing studies we found that a corrective movement is now well established, and there are suggestions

---

[212] See n. 2 *supra*. On Turkic and Sultanate history, nn. 28, 99 *supra*, McNeill, *Rise of the West*, 486–94; Chamberlain, *Knowledge and Social Practice*, 33–37; David Christian, *A History of Russia, Central Asia, and Mongolia* (Malden, MA, 1998), 247–326; Soucek, *History*, chs. 5–8.

[213] McNeill, *Rise of the West*, 493–94; Eaton, *NCHI*, 23–24 and 59–128 *passim*; Kumar, "Ignored Elites."

[214] Richards, *NCHI*, 8; Gommans, *Mughal Warfare*, 56–64; Mark Elliott, *The Manchu Way* (Stanford, 2001), 39–88, 363.

that a similar trend may be developing in Mughal studies. Thus Lisa Balabanlilar, among others, has argued against seeing the Mughals as a primarily or singularly Indian polity and in favor of the view that to the late 1600s Mughal identity and ambition were formed chiefly by Inner Asian legacies.[215]

A dynasty of Chaghatai Turks from Samarkand in Transoxania, the Mughals boasted descent from both the Mongol (Mughal) conqueror Chinggis Khan through his son Chaghatai and from the Turkic conqueror Timur. Key elements of Mughal rule – including succession disputes to select the most capable prince (tanistry), constant royal movement, decimal military ranks, reliance on heavy cavalry, military land grants, alliance with the Naqshbandi *sufi* order, particular aesthetic norms, syncretic cultural propensities – derived from Timurid and/or Turko-Mongol practice. Much as the Manchus looked to their ancestral homeland, the Mughals identified strongly with Timurid Transoxania and self-consciously pursued a Timurid renaissance on the Indian subcontinent.[216] As a post-1500 Inner Asian conquest regime that melded Inner Asian skills with sedentary wealth and culture, the Mughal empire bears comparison not only to the Qing, but to the Safavid realm in Persia (1501–1722),[217] the Shaibanid Uzbek state (1500–1599),[218] and the Ottoman empire.

---

[215] Balabanlilar, "Lords of the Auspicious Conjunction," critiquing the India-centered approach to Inner Asian rule of John Richards and others. An emphasis similar to Balabanlilar's appears at Alam and Subrahmanyan, *Mughal State*; Folz, *Mughal India*; and Kumar, "Ignored Elites." On Qing historiography, see Ch. 5 *supra*, esp. Peter Perdue, *China Marches West* (Cambridge, MA, 2005), 536–46, and Elliott, *Manchu Way*, 1–35, 345–61, contrasting the Altaic school of historiography with the Sinicization or Eurasian Similarity school.

[216] Maria Subtelny, "The Timurid Legacy," *Cahiers d'Asie Centrale* 3–4 (1997): 9–19; Stephen Dale, "The Legacy of the Timurids," *JRAS*, ser. 3, 8 (1998): 43–58; Folz, *Mughal India*, 21–45; Ram Prasad Tripathi, "The Turko-Mongol Theory of Kingship," in Alam and Subrahmanyam, *Mughal State*, 115–25; Richards, *NCHI*, 8–9, 110–111, 145–47; M. Athar Ali, "Towards an Interpretation of the Mughal Empire," *JRAS*, 1978: 38–49; Findley, *The Turks*, 122–23, 128–29; Gommans, *Mughal Warfare*, 179–87; Alam, "The Mughals, the Sufi Shaikhs," analyzing early Mughal relations with Chishti and Naqshbandi *sufis*. On identification of the Timurids as "Mughals," i.e., Mongols, a generic Indian term for Inner Asian invaders, Folz, *Mughal India*, 12.

[217] The vast majority of whose early supporters were Turkmen tribesmen from Anatolia, the Armenian highlands, northern Syria, and Iraq. Kathryn Babayan, *Mystics, Monarchs, and Messiahs* (Cambridge, MA, 2002); *EAH*, vol. III, 358–62; Andrew Newman, *Safavid Iran* (London, 2006).

[218] The Shaibanid Dynasty also traced its descent to Chinggis Khan, but through his son Jochi. Soucek, *Inner Asia*, ch. 11; *EAH*, vol. III, 420–21.

The Recurrent Prosperity and Decline of Regional Polities: Why
Were Such States Less Stable Than in the Protected Zone?

How, then, did Inner Asians alter the main lines of South Asian political
development? In a word, they (and later the British) prevented regional
cultures from entering into the sort of centuries-long, continuous synergy with medium-sized polities that we find in mainland Southeast
Asia and Europe.

At the outset, I acknowledge that Inner Asian incursions were not
the sole barrier to regional consolidation. Geography, for example, was
less sympathetic to regional power centers in India than in Southeast
Asia or much of Europe. Compared if not to central and eastern Europe,
then surely to England, France, and each of mainland Southeast Asia's
mountain-edged polities, states in the Indo-Gangetic plain and parts of
the Deccan had less well defined, defensible borders. That Sri Lanka,
the Himalayan foothills, Kerala, and other peripheral enclaves escaped
imperial incorporation argues that if South Asia had a more jagged
coast or fragmented internal geography, it would have sustained a
higher level of polycentrism.[219] (In a sense this confirms the experience of Korea and Taiwan in the Chinese Sphere.) At the same time
the vast Indo-Gangetic plain, with its wealth, population, and riverine transport, provided a base for imperial expansion, that is, for the
destruction of outlying regional kingdoms, that again had no European
or Southeast Asian parallel.[220] And yet, if the plain's enduring superiority explains why the Mauryas, Guptas, Delhi sultans, and Mughals
all based themselves there, it cannot explain why northern-based transregional empires disappeared between c. 550 and 1200, only to revive
suddenly thereafter. Conversely, if ill-defined internal borders imposed
a low ceiling on regional consolidation, these were constant constraints,
whereas regional polities were more robust and long lived before 1200
than in subsequent centuries. Why so?

[219] Cf. S. M. Alam, "The Historic Deccan," in V. K. Bawa, ed., *Aspects of Deccan History*
(Hyderabad, 1975), 16–29; P. M. Joshi, "Historical Geography of Medieval Deccan,"
in Sherwani and Joshi, *History of Medieval Deccan*, vol. I, 1–28. Moreover, in northwest
Indian and Deccan dry zones armed pastoralists able to resist sedentary authority
lacked a European analogue.

[220] As E. L. Jones, *The European Miracle* (Cambridge, 1987), ch. 6 argues, after Rome
fell, Europe was fated to support a multistate system precisely because its dispersed
agrarian cores were of comparable scale.

Similar questions arise from a consideration of political and institutional culture. As we shall see, deeply rooted structures – including overlapping sovereignties, hereditary local office, tributary autonomy, attenuated zones of authority – circumscribed royal power in virtually all Indian states from the 6th to 18th centuries. But since basically the same constraints operated in Indic Southeast Asia,[221] such weaknesses leave us wondering why *no* Indian kingdom approached the continuity or longevity of its Southeast Asian counterparts. No less curious is the contrast between the *increasing* efficiency of administrative and military culture in South Asia at large between c. 500 and 1800 and the *decreasing* longevity of regional dynasties during this same period. I noted Ludden's claim that "major dynasties," primarily regional, between c. 500 and c. 1400 averaged over 300 years.[222] But post-1400 regional dynasties in Delhi, Bengal, Jaunpur, Gujarat, the Deccan, and in Mughal successor states usually lasted only 50 to 200 years, with post-Mughal dynasties among the most short lived.[223] Why this pattern?

Consider, finally, a barrier to state formation noted by Pollock: South Asians expressed consistently less interest in ethnicity than peoples in Europe – and, I would add, in Burma, Siam, Vietnam, and probably Japan. Indeed, in Pollock's view, in India's various regions ethnicity – defined by a common name, ancestry, shared history, vertical solidarity – was feeble to nonexistent.[224] Likewise, South Asians exhibited a relatively weak attachment to kingdoms as enduring personalities. Rarely do we find emotive political evocations comparable to those focused, for example, on "most sweet France" or the Heaven-protected

---

[221] Southeast Asia had higher literacy and lacked caste, but parcelized sovereignty, hereditary office, tributary autonomy, attenuated spheres, and limited rural penetration were similar there and in India.

[222] See n. 18 *supra*; Ludden, *India and South Asia*, 44, and 45–47, referring to "medieval times" and the "medieval millennium," for which, however, he does not provide precise dates. My bracketing dates of 500 and c. 1400 I extrapolate from his text and from Table 2.

[223] Ludden refers to "dynasties," not kingdoms, but this schema of decreasing longevity works equally well for kingdoms, especially when one considers the brevity of most post-Delhi and post-Mughal polities. Talbot, pers. commun., July 30, 2007 takes an agnostic view of Ludden's claim, but see discussion *infra*.

[224] Pollock, *Language of the Gods*, 474–76, 509–11. Alan Strathern, *Kingship and Conversion in Sixteenth–Century Sri Lanka* (Cambridge, 2007); idem, pers. commun., May 17–18, 2007 points to Sri Lanka as a counterfactual. Precisely because it was long sheltered against invasion and entered the 16th century as part of Eurasia's protected zone, Sri Lanka did support a strongly politicized ethnicity linked to language and religion.

"Southern Country" of Vietnam.[225] Surely, this denied Indian realms the sort of affective ties that proved critical to the emergence and vitality of French, Russian, Burmese, and Vietnamese states. But again one must ask: If in South Asia these impediments remained constant, or even relaxed,[226] why did regional dynasties grow *more* short lived? One is tempted to explain ethnic frailty in terms of caste, whose horizontal allegiances were inimical to vertical solidarities. But can caste, which acquired an all-India salience only after c. 1650, adequately explain patterns before that date? Especially in those extra-Gangetic areas where brahmanic notions of caste remained weak well into the 18th century, why did politicized ethnicity make so little headway?

A principal solution to all these conundrums, I submit, is external intervention, generally (though not exclusively) by Inner Asians and, finally, by the British. To illustrate this claim, I shall sketch the development and eclipse of regional kingdoms during three periods of their most promising florescence – namely, c. 550–1206/1334, c. 1350–1560/1687, and c. 1700 to 1800/1850.[227] In each period localism seemed set to vanquish subcontinental integration, but in each era external armies aborted the process. In all three eras, mainland Southeast Asia and more especially Europe (which, although over twice as large as South Asia, contained in 1830 about the same size population) offer apt scalar comparisons. Although ultimately the South Asian system alone collapsed, particularly striking are the parallels between multistate systems in India, Europe, and Southeast Asia during the earliest period c. 550 to 1206/1334.

Phase One: Regional Florescence and Eclipse, c. 550–1206/1334

The Mauryas and Guptas followed an essentially universal or transregional ideal. That is, they sought tribute without serious regard for culture or ecology. *Rajyam*, universal imperium, was in some degree

---

[225] See, e.g., Ch. 2, n. 139 *supra*; *SP*, 132–34, 198–202, 365–67, 405–13, 430–33. True, medieval Tamil writers sought to identify the region of "pure Tamil," while Marathi poets described Maharashtra as a uniquely virtuous land. But these exaltations carried no express political message.

[226] Pollock, *Language of the Gods*, 511 n. 21 suggests that in fact some South Asian ethnicities grew stronger after 1400 and more esp. 1600.

[227] My terminal dates are imprecise, because imperial conquest affected different regions at different times.

the reality as well as the norm.[228] What is more, Pollock has shown, so long as the Sanskrit cosmopolis endured, that is, until the late first or early second millennium, universal rhetoric and geographic imaginaries dominated courtly expression.[229]

Yet even as post-Gupta rulers continued to style themselves sovereigns of the "entire earth,"[230] as a practical matter, with the growing density of economic and political organization, South Asia dissolved into four major spheres, some of which in turn were divided into regions.[231] Persisting to the Delhi Sultanate and beyond, these four spheres, recall from earlier discussion,[232] were a) the northern plain west of Bengal; from 725 until it fragmented in the mid-900s, this area was dominated by the Gurjara-Pratihara Dynasty; b) Bengal, whose humid climate and dense waterways afforded a certain protection against forces from the west; here the chief dynasties were the Palas (c. 750–1170) and Senas (c. 1100–1206); c) the Deccan, with rival foci in the northwest and east-central sectors; the dominant powers were the Rastrakutas (c. 750–975), followed by the Kalyana Calukyas, whose realm devolved in the late 1100s into regional kingdoms of the Yadavas, Hoysalas, and Kakatiyas; d) the southeast coast, whose valleys supported rival centers under the Colas, dominant c. 900–1250, and the Pantiyas, who overthrew Cola power in the 1250s.

Each sphere and often each inferior region, usually with a riverine core, was surrounded by open frontiers, and each combined an expanding agrarian base with pasturage and long-distance trade. Attempts by rulers in each sphere to win control of border districts led to large-scale warfare along substantially the same frontiers century after century; but although spheres themselves might fragment, ambitions to dominate more than one sphere were rarely gratified. This relatively durable balance reflected the fact that in each sphere material resources, military equipment, and strategic concepts were comparable. Moreover, in each sphere or region, interstate warfare joined economic expansion to support increasingly effective administrations.[233] One is reminded of political consolidations during the late first and early second millennia

---

[228] Pollock, "Vernacular Millennium," 54–55.
[229] Pollock, *Language of the Gods*, 234–58 *passim*.
[230] See examples in Inden, *Imagining India*, 230, 258–62.
[231] On enduring geographic divisions, Ali, *Courtly Culture*, 30–32; Kulke and Rothermund, *History*, 105 ff.; Gommans, *Mughal Warfare*, 18, 23–37.
[232] See n. 59 *supra*.
[233] See nn. 16–17, 59 *supra*.

in mainland Southeast Asia's three chief corridors, in Capetian France, and Russia. In India too state building, we saw, drew strength from the economic vigor characteristic of the period c. 850–1300.

Most intriguing for Eurasian perspectives, in India as in the protected zone, political consolidation to 1300 encouraged and reflected a growing regionalization of elite conventions in architecture, art, music, dance, scripts, language, and literature. All Indian temples, for example, derived from a classical template that placed one or more porches before an inner sanctum surmounted by a tall spire, but within that tradition South Indian temples, like the great 11th-century Cola complex at Tanjore with its towering pyramidal spire, diverged notably from North Indian shrines, like that of Kandariya Mahadeva with its reduplicated clusters of small spires lining a central core. Western and eastern India developed variations on the northern style, while in the Deccan the Yadava, Hoysala, and Kakatiya kingdoms produced yet other distinctive traditions.[234]

But it was changing language use that offers the most arresting parallels to Europe and Southeast Asia. If the first millennium saw the creation of the Sanskrit cosmopolis, the late first and early second millennia saw its dissolution during what Pollock terms "the vernacular revolution."[235] Even as they continued to genuflect before Sanskrit's prestige and drew on Sanskrit grammar and vocabulary – much as European cultures continued to honor Latin – across South Asia vernacular languages began to carve out coherent territories. Through royal patronage, "languages of place," as Pollock calls them, now became the preferred vehicle not merely of documentation, a function they had long performed, but of literary and political aesthetics. At the same time dreams of universal dominion shrank to vernacular-language

---

[234] *IBE*, 13–18, 74; Wink, *Al-Hind*, vol. II, 297; Thapar, *Early India*, 477; Shobha, *Social Life*, 1; George Michell, *The Hindu Temple* (Chicago, 1988), 18, 50, 53, 89–92; *EAH*, vol. II, 81; Pollock, *Language of the Gods*, 406–408.

[235] Pollock, "Introduction," 21. Ensuing discussion relies on Pollock, "Vernacular Millennium"; idem, "Cosmopolitan Vernacular"; idem, "Transformation of Culture-Power"; idem, *Language of the Gods*, 1, 6, 13–30, 254, 283–494, 553; plus Thapar, *Early India*, 312–32, 345 ff., 392–96, 414 ff., 432–36, 441, 477 ff., and sources *infra*. For brevity's sake, I telescope what were in fact, according to Pollock, two phases of the vernacular revolution: a) the creation of cosmopolitan vernaculars, which sought to retain the full spectrum of Sanskrit's literary qualities and cultural concerns, and b) the creation of more genuinely local vernaculars, which emphasized regional idioms and demotic traditions over Sanskritic conventions. In effect, cosmopolitan vernaculars were a bridge between Sanskrit and local vernaculars.

territories. Once admitted to an aesthetic role and disseminated via inscriptions and manuscripts, such languages, originally embracing numerous dialects, became more standardized, hence more useful for political integration.

Thus, by way of illustration, although Tamil had been written since the second century B.C.E., not until the vernacular revolution did it rival Sanskrit as a vehicle of poetic and political expression. Following tentative 8th-century efforts, in the 11th century Cola rulers began to inscribe spectacular eulogies in the vernacular; Cola officials disseminated Tamil through inscriptions and charters; and writers, fortified with Sanskrit-derived philologies, sought to map the "region of pure Tamil."[236]

Northeast of the Tamil country, literature in Telugu (like Tamil, a Dravidian language) appeared from the 9th to 11th centuries, but neither of the chief southern powers, the Calukyas of Kalyana or the Colas, privileged Telugu. Only after the Telugu-speaking Kakatiya Dynasty in Andhra broke away from the Calukyas in 1163, did a polity dependent on Telugu develop at the expense of Sanskrit and non-Telugu vernaculars. Not only did the Kakatiyas forge a Telugu-speaking elite community by joining for the first time Telugu-speaking coasts and interior, but the area of Telugu inscriptions doubled as outlying elites who had formerly used Kannada or Tamil self-consciously switched to the royal tongue. By the early 1300s Kakatiya boundaries were largely congruent with the area of Telugu inscriptions.[237]

In the southwestern Deccan the Dravidian language of Kannada underwent a similar evolution. Kannada was first used for poetic royal eulogies in the 9th century, but under the Rastrakuta and Calukya empires, both of which were decidedly transregional and multilingual, it enjoyed no special favor over Sanskrit or other vernaculars. Not until the Hoysala Dynasty threw off Calukya tutelage from the mid-1100s

---

[236] Pollock, *Language of the Gods*, 290–92, 383–86, 398–99, 413–15; idem, "Vernacular Millennium," 51–52; Prentiss, *Embodiment of Bhakti*, 27; Burton Stein, "Circulation and the Historical Geography of Tamil Country," *JAS* 37 (1977): 7–26.

[237] Talbot, *Precolonial India*, 7–10, 24–37, 124–39; idem, "Inscribing the Other, Inscribing the Self," *CSSH* 37 (1995): 692–722, esp. 710–11; Eaton, *NCHI*, 13; Pollock, *Language of the Gods*, 289, 323–24, 380–81, 398, 408–409; Narayana Rao, "Multiple Literary Cultures," 383–400, 425–27; idem, "Coconut and Honey," *Social Scientist* 23 (1995): 23–40; S. Nagaraju, "Emergence of Regional Identity and Beginnings of Vernacular Literature," *Social Scientist* 23 (1995): 8–23. Yet Talbot, pers. commun., July 30, 2007 says that she would "probably tone down" her emphasis on regional identity were she to write the Andhra book afresh.

and took control of Kannada-speaking districts in modern Karnataka, did Kannada assume a position comparable to that of Telugu in the Kakatiya realm. By the 13th century the Hoysala court was patronizing belles lettres and political works in Kannada, together with grammars, prosodies, and dictionaries needed to standardize the language, while Hoysala territorial claims were limited largely to the region of Kannada culture.[238]

In the northwestern Deccan as well, in modern Maharashtra, Marathi language helped to define a political/cultural space distinct from Kannada, Telugu, and Gujarati areas on its borders. First used in a documentary context in 983, Marathi became a literary medium only after 1190 when the Marathi-speaking Yadava Dynasty, like their Hoysala and Kakatiya contemporaries, broke with the Calukyas and promoted their native tongue. Marathi self-identification drew strength too from the *bhakti* sect of Vithoba that ascribed unique religious virtue to Maharashtra and distinguished its followers from Kannada-speaking *bhaktis* attached to the Lingayat cult in the south. A late-13th- or early-14th-century religious text expressly enjoined devotees to avoid the Telugu and Kannada countries.[239]

North India saw vernacular movements as well, but for reasons to be discussed shortly, these generally came later and remained more hesitant than in the south. Nonetheless, by the 1300s literary texts were being written in Hindi and Bangla. The Solanki rulers of Gujarat confined their power to the Gujarati vernacular region, while to the east the domain of the Gajapatis grew coterminous with Oriya speech. Again, court literati, using Sanskrit models, normally took the lead in forging literary vehicles from the vernacular.[240]

During this same period in Europe and Southeast Asia, the partial, tentative displacement of classical languages by vernaculars also was tied to emergent territorial identities. Pioneered often by clerical elites allied to royal courts who valued vernacularization as an expression of

---

[238] Pollock, *Language of the Gods*, 20–27, 288–89, 330–79; idem, "Transformation of Culture-Power," 255–63; idem, "Vernacular Millennium," 49–51; Thapar, *Early India*, 367–69; D. R. Nagaraj, "Critical Tensions in the History of Kannada Literary Culture," in *LCH*, 323–82; *EAH*, vol. II, 81; Eaton, *Sufis of Bijapur*, 5–13.

[239] Eaton, *NCHI*, 13–14, 137–41; idem, *Sufis of Bijapur*, 5–13; Pollock, *Language of the Gods*, 289–90, 324–25, 381–83, 430–36; Feldhaus, *Connected Places*, ch. 6; idem, "Maharashtra as a Holy Land," *BSOAS* 49 (1986): 532–48; Deshpande, *Sociolinguistic Attitudes*, 68–72.

[240] Pollock, "Vernacular Millennium," 53–54, 59; idem, *Language of the Gods*, 292–95, 304–305, 327–28, 390–400, 434, 443–44, 449; Stein, *History*, 123; Grewal, *NCHI*, 13–14.

incipient community, English writings appeared in the 8th and 9th centuries; Bulgarian and Russian in the 10th and 11th centuries; Icelandic, Tuscan, Provencal, Castilian, Norman, and Parisian French from the 12th to 14th centuries. At the other end of Eurasia, Burmese achieved literary status in the 12th and 13th centuries, Tai in the 13th century, Javanese as early as the 10th.[241] In Japan the late Heian and Kamakura periods generated an indigenous literature in *kana*.

To be sure, these far-flung movements differed not only in precise chronology and social contexts, but in political visions. Unlike some early English, French, and Italian writers, South Asian litterateurs did not posit a historic link between language and "people," regarding speech more as a function of ecology than of blood. Some Burmese and Vietnamese authors did link ethnicity to speech. But this tendency was weaker in the Tai world, and in most other respects, including official hyperglossia, Indic Southeast Asia may have resembled South Asia more closely than western Europe.[242]

Differences can be multiplied indefinitely. And yet similarities between Europe, South Asia, and Southeast Asia are more intriguing, if only because they are so unexpected. In all three sectors of Eurasia universal languages (Latin, Church Slavonic, Sanskrit) in the late first and more especially the early second millennia facilitated the birth of vernacular literatures by providing vocabulary, grammars, and aesthetic models. By extension, universal visions yielded, partially and fitfully, to territorial goals more circumscribed by local culture. Thus, as the Latinate Carolingian empire split into Francophone and Germanophone halves, and as Siam and Cambodia carved vernacular-language kingdoms from Sanskritic Angkor, the Calukya empire split into Marathi, Kannada, and Telugu successor states.

Note too that in both South Asia and Europe vernacularization began earlier and was at first more vigorous in outlying areas than in the classical heartlands. Vernacular literatures blossomed in the Tamil country

---

[241] Pollock, *Language of the Gods*, 437–67; NCMH, vol. II, 49–50, 60–61, 683, 840; Simon Franklin, *Writing, Society and Culture in Early Rus, c. 950–1300* (Cambridge, 2002); SP, 114–16, 131–39, 230–32, 264, 266, 269, 271–73.

[242] Pollock, *Language of the Gods*, 399–483 passim, 508–511, 573–74; idem, "Vernacular Millennium," 59–65; idem, "Cosmopolitan and Vernacular," 612–14. However, Pollock tends to collapse medieval and early modern Europe, and his contrasts are most convincing for the latter (post-1450/1500) era. Before c. 1250 French kings may not have differed much from their Deccan counterparts in hyperglossia, classical biases, and still fragile links between linguistic and political identity.

and the Deccan – not to mention the farthest reaches of the Sanskrit cosmopolis, namely, Burma, Tai areas, and Java – earlier than in the *Aryavarta* home of Sanskrit. Unlike southern vernaculars, precolonial North Indian languages never acquired written grammars and, in some cases, lacked even a stable name. Likewise vernacularization occurred notably earlier in Ireland, England, and Russia than in France, Italy, or Spain. In part, surely, this reflected the fact that North Indian Indo-Aryan tongues had greater difficulty distinguishing themselves from Sanskrit, to which they were related, than did Dravidian or Southeast Asian tongues, which had no genetic link to Sanskrit. Similarly, Germanic and Celtic languages found it easier to forge distinct identities than did Romance languages, which separated imperceptibly and hesitantly from Latin.[243] Perhaps too universal ideals inhibited regional identities more readily in North India, home to the imperial Guptas and the Delhi Sultanate, than in areas where imperial legacies were slight. By the same logic, European heartlands of political and religious universalism (the Italian peninsula, the Holy Roman Empire) proved less congenial to regional projects than lands on the periphery.[244] No doubt too, easy transport and communications rendered the Indo-Gangetic plain less sympathetic to localization than the more fragmented Deccan.

Most basic perhaps, the social dynamics of cultural localization suggest broad similarities. In South Asia this issue has not attracted much theorization, but I would suggest that the economic surge of c. 850 to 1300 aided localization in four ways familiar from Europe and Southeast Asia: a) By swelling the ranks of influential *homines novi* who perforce were literate not in the classical tongue but in more easily mastered demotic languages, economic growth fostered a vernacular elite community. Eventually the vernacular achieved sufficient density and prestige to support a self-replicating aesthetic.[245] b) Agrarian and commercial growth enhanced the wealth, hence cultural patronage, of regional courts. c) Economic expansion permitted warfare on a larger scale, which led local elites to identify more closely with the court and

---

[243] I add Bulgarian and Russian, which presumably found it relatively easy to disengage from Greek, to examples in Pollock, *Language of the Gods*, 390–400, 443–44, 472.

[244] Insofar as the Holy Roman Empire was German based, this argument runs counter to the thesis that weak German linguistic affinity to Latin encouraged precocious vernacularization.

[245] Cf. Talbot, *Precolonial India*, 8; Thapar, *Early India*, 470–72; Nagaraju, "Emergence of Regional Identity"; Eaton, *NCHI*, 13–14.

sharpened communal identities.[246] d) Although Pollock has demurred, others claim that by spawning vernacular poetry and hymns as an aid to mass religiosity, *bhakti* – which battened on sedentarization and new pilgrimage networks – instilled pride in regional cultures.[247]

In short, in the early second millennium some Indian territories, particularly in the south, seemed no less likely to fuse vernacular culture with royal authority than comparably sized regions in Europe or Southeast Asia.

Whether in South Asia these fusions would have continued and intensified is impossible to say, of course, for between 1192 and 1323 they were terminated by conquerors from the steppe–sown interface region of Transoxania and Afghanistan. Whereas earlier Ghaznavid raids sought merely booty, the Turkic generals who founded the Delhi Sultanate sought permanent dominion. As in North China in this period, the invaders' most basic advantages were powerful swift mounts and a far higher percentage of males qualified for military service than in agrarian societies. Although most were no longer nomads and although, in contrast to the Chinese steppe, heavy cavalry played a more critical role than light-armed horse archers, their equestrian skills, tactics, and mobility often reflected a nomadic ancestry.[248] Importing horses from afar, in this case West Asia, could not compensate Indian rulers any more than their Song contemporaries for inadequate pasture and insalubrious equine climate. Withal, Indian weapons lacked the penetration of

---

[246] Pollock, "Literary History, Indian History," 126, and Deshpande, *Sanskrit and Prakrit*, 117 offer examples from the 11th-century Deccan.

[247] Cf. Eaton, *Sufis of Bijapur*, 5–12; Feldhaus, *Connected Places*, ch. 6; idem, "Maharashtra as a Holy Land"; Sitamshu Yashaschandra, "From Hemacandra to *Hind Svaraj*," in *LCR*, 576–85; Prentiss, *Embodiment of Bhakti*, ch. 2; and esp. Sudipta Kaviraj, "The Imaginary Institution of India," in Partha Chatterjee and Gyanendra Pandey, eds., *Subaltern Studies VII* (New Delhi, 1992). In "Literary History, Indian History," "Cosmopolitan and Vernacular," and *Language of the Gods*, 423 ff. Pollock argues that in the north vernacular literatures predated *bhakti*, and that as in the Deccan vernacularization was less a popular than a court-dependent phenomenon.

[248] On the imbalance between Muslim and indigenous forces, Wink, *Al-Hind*, vol. II, 79–93, 381–84; idem, "India and the Turko-Mongol Frontier"; Digby, *Warhorse and Elephant*; Gommans, *Mughal Warfare*, 111–20, 141–46; idem, "Warhorse and Gunpowder"; Nicola Di Cosmo, ed., *Warfare in Inner Asian History* (Leiden, 2002), Introduction; Thapar, *Early India*, 434–37; Jackson, *Delhi Sultanate*, 14–19, 213–16. Cf. Talbot, *Precolonial India*, 173 on Deccan developments. Barendse, "Feudal Mutation," seeks to assimilate Inner Asian cavalry ascendancy to a Eurasian "warhorse revolution" c. 900–1300, but Stephen Morillo, "A 'Feudal Mutation'?," *JWH* 14 (2003): 531–50 raises convincing objections.

Turkic compound bows and crossbows, all the more so since only Turkic heavy cavalry, astride sturdy mounts, wore armor. Nor did South
Asians enjoy comparable access to the latest West Asian siege technologies, including huge stone-throwing counter-trebuchets that let Delhi's
forces reduce every notable fort in central and southern India in a single
campaign.[249] Inner Asian recruitment seems to have been more meritocratic than early Indian systems. And whereas Turkic armies had a
professional core accustomed to fighting together, Indian forces were
often ill-coordinated coalitions. Such advantages, in combination with
the wealth of the Indo-Gangetic plain, explain the great blitzkrieg movements of the 13th and early 14th centuries, which subdued not only the
plain, but Bengal, Gujarat, Rajasthan, and the entire south as far as
Madurai.

Sultanate rule, we saw, was accompanied by expanded cash taxes
and *iqtas*. At first these novel features were confined to the plain, while
outlying kingdoms were allowed to continue as tributaries, subject
to Perso-Islamic overlordship, but with local institutions intact. Deccan areas south of the Krisna River remained autonomous, but as had
happened in the Indo-Gangetic plain and Bengal during the previous
century, Delhi imposed direct rule on Gujarat from 1306 and on the
Yadava and Kakatiya kingdoms in the northern and central Deccan from
1314–1323. Governors now displaced local dynasts, who disappeared
from the record. Imperial coinage and mosques proclaimed the sultan's
sovereignty, and a network of *iqtas* integrated newly annexed areas into
the Sultanate politically and economically. If many *iqta*-holders were
local, others were Muslim immigrant warriors. In the northern Deccan, in particular, such newcomers, including *sufis* of the Chishti order,
comprised a large and influential settler community, who deepened
cultural ties to the north and to the wider Muslim world.[250] A transregional formation whose preferred language and cultural heroes were
Persian,[251] the Delhi Sultanate, Eaton argues, would accept from local
cultures, local literary traditions, and local kinship no constraints on
its authority. To non-Muslims Delhi projected an image of intimidating
force. "By conquering the towns of India in every expedition," read

---

[249] On siege technology, previous note, plus Eaton, *NCHI*, 19; *IBE*, 40.
[250] Eaton, *NCHI*, 22–27, 34–40; idem, *Rise of Islam*, 32–40; *IBE*, 35–50; S. C. Misra, *The Rise of Muslim Power in Gujarat* (Bombay, 1963), 59–71.
[251] On Persian models, Alam, *Languages*, 143.

the 1298 inscription on a Bengal mosque, the donor "has destroyed the obdurate among infidels with his sword and spear."[252]

In sum, after generations of promising synthesis between regional cultures and polities on the European and Southeast Asian pattern, Delhi directly challenged that process and collapsed regional kingdoms across India.

Phase Two: Regional Florescence and Eclipse, c. 1350–1560/1687

The second phase of extensive regionalism began with the disintegration of the Delhi Sultanate in the mid- and late 14th century and continued until Mughal conquests, which rolled across the subcontinent from 1555 to 1687. Delhi's unification of much of the subcontinent was as fleeting as it was spectacular. In North India Delhi's territory devolved into *inter alia* the Muslim sultanates of Bengal, Jaunpur, Gujarat, and Malwa. Founded by former Delhi officials, these frequently warring states at first sought to preserve Delhi institutions and ideology, although gradually each developed a more local personality. Delhi itself remained a modest regional polity even under the Afghan Lodi Dynasty (1451–1526). South of Delhi Rajput states, and on the east coast Orissa, remained under non-Muslim dynasties. The Deccan north of the Krisna River came under control of the Bahmani Sultanate, also founded by ex-Delhi officials; while south of the Krisna Vijayanagara absorbed the Hoysala realm, southern Kakatiya lands, and areas as far as Madurai.[253] (See Figure 6.2.) Wedding coastal trade to Delhi military and administrative techniques and benefiting from a sense of Deccan regionalism, the Bahmani Sultanate prospered for over a century. But ultimately it failed to contain poisonous rivalries between Deccanis – Muslim families from the north who had put down local roots – and Westerners, that is, more recent seaborne Arab and Persian immigrants. By the 1510s Bahmani itself had dissolved into the sultanates of Berar, Bidar, Ahmadnagar, Bijapur, and Golkonda. The last four in turn joined forces in 1565 to destroy their southern nemesis Vijayanagara, which henceforth was divided between Bijapur, Golkonda, a rump Vijayanagar, and three

---

[252] Eaton, *Rise of Islam*, 34–38; idem, *NCHI*, 23. Also Alam, "Culture and Politics," 133–42; and Kumar, "Ignored Elites," on unacknowledged tensions between Islamic rhetorical solidarity and the non-Muslim Turkic/Mongol steppe origins of many Sultanate elites.

[253] J. Duncan Derrett, *The Hoysalas* (Oxford, 1957), 143–74, and n. 20 *supra*.

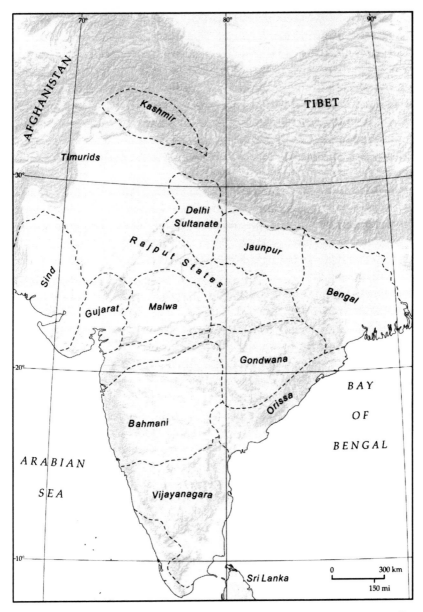

Figure 6.2. South Asian states in the 15th century. *Sources:* John Keay, *India: A History* (New York, 2000), 280 (map by Jillian Luff); Catherine Asher and Cynthia Talbot, *India Before Europe* (Cambridge, 2006), 55, 90.

polities led by Telugu-speaking warrior families who had entrenched themselves in the far south during Vijayanagara's heyday.[254]

Mutatis mutandis, South Asia thus reverted to a political condition no less fragmented than in the pre-1200/1300 era. The unifying promise of Turkic conquest was not fulfilled because of Delhi's internal weaknesses and limited cultural penetration, but also because post-Delhi states were quick to imitate, and thus neutralize, the military and fiscal advantages of the Delhi Sultanate. One is reminded how the post-500 diffusion of Gupta technologies contributed to the rise of regional kingdoms.

In cultural terms as well, pre-Mughal Muslim influences proved double edged. On the one hand, I emphasized, Perso-Islamic culture was a new charter civilization comparable to Sanskrit in its audacious universalism and integrative promise. From the Punjab to the Deccan, Hindu as well as Muslim elites entered a coherent world of aesthetic and literary expression. In the 15th and 16th centuries, as Eaton has emphasized, the entire Deccan, including "Hindu" Vijayanagara, was drawn into the orbit of Persianate culture.[255]

On the other hand, Perso-Islamic influence complicated the landscape by providing fresh stimuli, partly unintentional, to specifically regional cultures. *Sufi* literati were among the first to inscribe and compose literature in the spoken languages of the north (Hindi, Madhyadeshiya, Punjabi, Oriya, Bangla) and later of the Deccan. Various factors have been cited to explain this proclivity. As a practical matter, proselytizers often felt obliged to employ local idioms. The ecstatic, even feminine tone of local religious poetry allegedly appealed to *sufi* sensibility. As Muslims "who did not swim in the Indic sea,"[256] they were more willing than learned Hindus to develop alternate vehicles to Sanskrit, whose center of gravity in fact shifted from Muslim North

---

[254] These three Telugu polities were known as the Nayaka states. On post-Delhi polycentrism, Keay, *India*, ch. 12; *EAH*, vol. II, 438–39; *IBE*, 84–114, 163–85; Eaton, *NCHI*, 22–23, 33–43, 59–104, 112; idem, *Rise of Islam*, 40–50; Misra, *Rise of Muslim Power*, 59–179; Kulke and Rothermund, *History*, 156–72; Haroon Khan Sherwani, *The Bahmanis of the Deccan* (New Delhi, 1985); Engseng Ho, *The Graves of Tarim* (Berkeley, 2006), 103–12 (on Gujarat).

[255] Eaton, *NCHI*, 102; Alam, "Historic Deccan," 25; Yashaschandra, "From Hemacandra," 592–93; and n. 110 *supra*.

[256] Phrase from Pollock, *Language of the Gods*, 392. On *sufi* contributions to vernacularization, ibid., 392–93, 553; idem, "Vernacular Millennium," 53; Alam, "Competition and Co-Existence," 38–40; McGregor, "Progress of Hindi," 914–23; Behl, "Magic Doe"; Grewal, *NCHI*, 13–14; Eaton, *Sufis of Bijapur*, 174, 289.

India to Vijayanagara. Whatever the reasons, literature in Indo-Aryan vernaculars is unthinkable without *sufi* poems, hymns, and romances.

At the same time, regional rulers began to adopt more autochthonous cultural styles than their Delhi predecessors, both because the heirs of Muslim immigrants grew increasingly conversant with local traditions, and because the insecurity of small, relatively weak post-Delhi successor states obliged leaders to cultivate local support regardless of sectarian affiliation. In North India, for example, some Lodi rulers and Sher Shah Sur expanded the use of Hindi alongside Persian for administration,[257] while in Bengal and the Deccan Muslim courts used local vernaculars in lieu of or in addition to Persian for administration and, in some cases, literature. Such trends became particularly marked after 1550 in Golkonda, whose heads, in order to appeal to Telugu warrior lineages,[258] supported Hindu temples, adopted indigenous royal idioms, and patronized Telugu alongside Persian, becoming, in one historian's formulation, "Telugu Sultans."[259] Likewise Bijapur and Ahmadnagar relied on Marathi for local administration.[260] In the same spirit, Muslim rulers patronized local festivals, dress, music, art, and architecture, even Hindu philosophy. In Bengal the new mood transformed mosque architecture, which from the 1420s abandoned Mideastern designs in favor of so-called thatched-hut and Buddhist-temple traditions. In the words of Percy Brown, "the country, originally possessed by the invaders, now possessed them."[261] Bengal's brick mosques in turn had little in common with the almost Gothic wooden

---

[257] Moreover, chancery rescripts transcribed Persian documents in Devanagari, rather than Arabic, script. Alam, "Culture and Politics," 158.

[258] Golkonda's domain coincided with the northern half of the old Telugu-based Kakatiya kingdom.

[259] Laxmi Ranjanam, "Telugu," in Sherwani and Joshi, *History of Medieval Deccan*, vol. II, 147. See also ibid., 161–64; Eaton, *NCHI*, 156–57; Alam, *Languages*, 149; Richards, *Mughal Administration*, 10–11, 17, 75–76. Note too that in Vijayanagara early-16th-century Telugu warriors created a common genealogy stemming from their alleged past service to the Kakatiya kings. Cynthia Talbot, "The Story of Prataparudra," in Gilmartin and Lawrence, *Beyond Turk*, 282–99; Eaton, *NCHI*, 27–30.

[260] Bijapur and Ahmadnagar, however, did not patronize non-Dakani vernacular literature. Cf. n. 115 *supra*.

[261] Percy Brown, *Indian Architecture, Islamic Period* (Bombay, 1968), cited in Eaton, *Rise of Islam*, 70. Discussion of regional cultures relies on Eaton, *Rise of Islam*, 50–70; idem, *Sufis of Bijapur*, 12–18, 40–44, 83–106, 135–74, 285–86; idem, *NCHI*, 59–77, 91, 141–45 (see esp. Table 3); idem, *India's Islamic Traditions*, 185, 232; Alam, "Culture and Politics," 157–58; idem, *Languages*, 113, 149–50; *IBE*, 77, 84–114, 163–75; Kaviraj, "Two Histories," 505–16; Behl, "Magic Doe," 185 ff., 209; Sumit Guha, "Transitions and Translations: Regional Power and Vernacular Identity in the Dakhan, 1500–1800,"

structures of Kashmir, the open and spacious buildings of Gujarat, the massive, pylon-based mosques of Jaunpur, or the pillared halls of Ahmadabad.[262]

Pre-Mughal regionalism drew strength from forces other than *sufi* intervention and local court patronage. Between 1350 and 1555 economic growth continued to swell the ranks of vernacular-language literates, to pull peasant communities into more coherent pilgrimage and marketing networks, to sedentarize tribal and pastoral peoples, and to circulate texts, balladeers, and sectarians, all bearers of vernacular knowledge. Whether in response to *sufi* inspiration, political upheaval, or autonomous shifts in sensibility, between 1400 and 1600 across North India an oral literature of Krisna *bhakti* songs and poetry became enormously popular along with narrative and expository verse, much of it aimed at popular audiences and virtually all in vernacular languages.[263]

In brief, at the same time as South Asia resumed a polycentric political structure, regional cultures grew more distinct. Shall we conclude therefore that with Delhi's fall, the situation reverted to the status quo ante? That Delhi's influence was brief and transient and that South Asia after 1350 or 1400 resumed the same pattern of continuously evolving regional kingdoms and cultures that we find throughout the protected zone?

Such a conclusion would be wrong indeed. Between 1350 and 1600 Burma, Siam, Vietnam, France, Russia, and Japan all supported increasingly coherent polities with continuity of name, territory, institutions, elite religion, court language, and often of dynasty, with growing concordance between elite and popular religious practices, an ever more exclusive role for vernacular languages, closer royal identification with each realm's dominant ethnicity, and the production of myths and histories that invoked the authority of charter states from the late first or early second millennium. In South Asia such elements were far weaker. True, Indian geopolitical alignments sometimes reproduced themselves. Thus, for example, Bengal habitually resisted the Gangetic

---

Comparative Studies of South Asia, Africa and the Middle East 24 (2004): 23–31; Sherwani and Joshi, *History of Medieval Deccan*, vol. II, 17–172, 227–304.

[262] Metcalfs, *Concise History*, 14; *IBE*, 89–96.

[263] These genres stimulated and reflected the growth of Bengali, Hindi, Gujarati, and Oriya cultures. McGregor, "Progress of Hindi," 912–33; Yashaschandra, "From Hemacandra," 576–89; Kaviraj, "Two Histories," 505–25; Achintya Kumar Deb, *The Bhakti Movement in Orissa* (Calcutta, 1984); Asher and Talbot, *India Before Europe*, 108–12.

plain, while the Kalyana Calukya and Bahmani realms controlled substantially the same lands.[264] Yet in South Asia far more often than in the protected zone, external conquests (generally by Turks but in some cases by Telugus, Tamils, and Marathas) meant that kingdoms and dynasties vanished with barely a trace – illustrating Pollock's "law of political entropy"[265] – and that regional fusions between power and culture withered. In vain we search for those enduring linkages typical of the protected zone between, on the one hand, ever more homogenized kingdom-specific cultures and, on the other hand, states with centuries-long continuity in territory and self-identification. In this light, consider briefly the history of some of India's chief regions between c. 1300 and the Mughal conquest.

The Telugu-speaking eastern Deccan. It is true that Telugu cultural vitality hardly ended with the Kakatiyas' 1323 collapse.[266] Yet after 1323 Telugu lost its privileged relation to political authority, and no exclusively Telugu state reappeared. Absorbed first into the Delhi Sultanate, Kakitaya territories were then divided between the Bahmani Sultanate and Vijayanagara – both expressly transregional formations – and still later between Golkonda and Bidar. No two states occupied the same territories, and no ruling house boasted of institutional links to the Kakatiyas.[267] Rather, Delhi and Bahmani systems of revenue, *iqta* assignment, and ceremony provided the primary model. The preferred languages at the Bahmani court were Persian and Dakani; at the Vijayanagara court, Telugu, Kannada, and Sanskrit. If Golkonda's rulers shared more continuities with pre-1300 Deccani society than did any other Bahmani successor state, such accommodations faced definite limits: Golkonda's rulers encouraged not only Telugu, but Persian and Dakani literature, used Arabic on coins, and identified unambiguously as Muslims, distinct from their overwhelmingly non-Muslim

---

[264] Each then split into more linguistically coherent states whose territories, as with the Kakatiyas and Golkonda, also could overlap in different centuries. Cf. maps at Eaton, *NCHI*, 10, 44 93; Keay, *India*, 217; Schwartzberg, *Historical Atlas*, 32.

[265] Pollock, "Transformation of Culture-Power," 259.

[266] Moreover, from the 1400s a heightened sense of Telugu ethnicity was contrasted with other regional identities. Talbot, "Inscribing the Other," 711, and n. 259 *supra*.

[267] Post-1600 Deccan writers sometimes invoked the last Kakatiya king to justify Bahmani rule, but insisted, contrary to fact, that the king had been Muslim. Eaton, *NCHI*, 30–31. On invocations of the Kakatiya dynasty not by Vijayanagara kings, but by local Telugu warriors, see n. 259 *supra*. On Golkonda's cultural lineages, M. A. Nayeem, *The Splendour of Hyderabad* (Hyderabad, 2002), 12–14; idem, *The Heritage of the Qutb Shahis of Golconda and Hyderabad* (Hyderabad, 2006), 2–3.

subjects.[268] In short, whereas France, Burma, and so forth produced an ever closer tie between state and regional culture, in Andhra after 1323 the link eroded.

Marathi- and Kannada-speaking areas of the western Deccan. Here the story was much the same. Vijayanagara identified less with Yadava or Hoysala styles than with the transregional legacies of the old Calukya empire[269] and with Islamicate forms, while Bahmani sultans patronized chiefly Indo-Muslim and Persian forms that derived from North India and the Mideast. After Bahmani dissolved, the new Bijapur and Ahmadnagar Sultanates, as noted, used Marathi for local administration. So too, between 1400 and 1650 military and fiscal networks under a succession of Muslim regimes helped to redefine the social category "Maratha" and assisted a broad-based Marathi cultural flowering that reached maturity under the Maratha confederation of the late 17th and 18th centuries. Yet this was an unintended by-product, not the goal, of policy, for like their counterparts elsewhere, western Deccan sultans had no use for politicized ethnicity. Unfailingly they championed Muslim ritual primacy and made no claim to Yadava or Hoysala heritage. In literature they favored neither Marathi nor Kannada, but Persian and Dakani. Ominously, in the mid-1600s the Bijapur court's policy of religious tolerance changed to open hostility toward Hindus.[270]

The far south. Neither a long-term growth in the size of local empires, nor a shared literary culture and Saivite sensibility, nor a precocious sense of Tamil linguistic space was sufficient to produce among Tamil-speakers a sustained sense of political community or a stable state tradition. Cola rule was regarded by fellow Tamil-speaking Pantiyas as imperial domination; when in the 13th century the Pantiyas triumphed, Colas returned the favor. To a persistent sub-Tamil localism were

---

[268] On the post-1323 relation of politics to Telugu culture, nn. 259, 267 *supra*, plus Talbot, *Precolonial India*, 9, 25, 174–207; Eaton, *NCHI*, 29–30, 43, 63–64, 94–95, 141–45, 155–59; *IBE*, 74–75; Pollock, "Sanskrit Literary Culture," 94–95; idem, *Language of the Gods*, 337; Nagaraj, "Critical Tensions," 368–78; Alam, "Culture and Politics," 157; John Richards and Velcheru Narayana Rao, "Banditry in Mughal India," in Alam and Subrahmanyam, *Mughal State*, 491–94.

[269] On Vijayanagara–Calukya links, Eaton, *NCHI*, 94–99, 103; Stein, *NCHI*, vol. I, 111. Also like the Calukyas, Vijayanagar began to create a pan-southern elite culture by combining Telugu, Kannada, and Tamil elements. *IBE*, 74–75.

[270] Eaton, *Sufis of Bijapur*, 105–34, 190–201, 283–89. See n. 331 *infra*. Precisely because it favored no vernacular, the Bijapur Sultanate took root on the fault line between Kannada, Marathi, and Telugu zones. On culture and politics in the Bahmani Sultanate and its successors, nn. 258, 260 *supra*; Sherwani, *Bahmanis of the Deccan*, 53–65, 76–81, 101–105; Sherwani and Joshi, *History of Medieval Deccan*, vol. II, 35–115.

added the dislocating effects of repeated external conquests, first by Delhi Sultanate armies who destroyed the Pantiya kingdom, then by the Telugu and Kannada warriors of Vijayanagara, later by Telugu warriors who colonized upland sectors of the Tamil country in the early 1500s and whose petty kingdoms devolved from Vijayanagara.[271]

Bengal. Even before Muslim conquest, the connection between vernacular-language use and state power may have been weaker in Bengal than in other parts of the old Sanskrit cosmopolis.[272] After breaking with Delhi in 1342, leaders of the Bengal Sultanate pursued a strategy of legitimation, as evidenced in coinage and architecture, that emphasized pan-Islamic and Persian imperial themes, although it has also been suggested that some architectural features deferred to local sensibilities. Certainly from the 1420s to the late 1500s indigenizing trends became more marked, as sultans patronized Bengali literature as well as architecture, as Muslim–Vaisnava syntheses took root, and as Bengali provided a medium for translated Persian and Arabic texts and for a profusion of Krisna devotional works. Even in this period, however, Bengali sultans maintained a self-consciously Perso-Islamic model at court and made no effort to invoke the glories of Bengal's pre-Muslim Sena Dynasty.[273]

The Indo-Gangetic Plain. The fact that this was the heartland of Indo-Muslim imperial tradition meant that the link between regional culture and politics was yet less secure than in the Deccan or Bengal. The plain supported three closely related, not always distinct indigenous literary languages – Hindi, Brajbhasha, and Avadhi – but none developed a privileged, centuries-long symbiotic relation with a political center. Blending Persian and Arab vocabulary with the speech of the Delhi area, Hindi spread as a language of trade, administration, and military use to towns under Delhi's influence in somewhat the same way that Parisian French radiated from Paris or Burmese spread

---

[271] The aforementioned Nayaka states, n. 254 *supra*. See Ludden, *Peasant History*, 15–22, 43–45, 68–71, 208–12; Dirks, *Hollow Crown*, 28–54; Pollock, "Vernacular Millennium," 50–57; idem, *Language of the Gods*, 383–86; Narayana Rao, "Multiple Literary Cultures," 413–14; *EAH*, vol. IV, 60–62; *IBE*, 175–85, 221–24. Note too that the chief 18th-century Kerala state had shallow historical roots. Bayly, "Hindu Kingship and the Origin of Community," 177–213.

[272] Kaviraj, "Two Histories," 527, n. 31; Pollock, *Language of the Gods*, 220, 292, 391.

[273] Eaton, *Rise of Islam*, 40–70, 95–112; *IBE*, 85–89, 110–11, taking issue with Eaton's emphasis on early sultanate insensitivity to Bengali culture; Pollock, *Language of the Gods*, 312–13; Kaviraj, "Two Histories," 503–28. On indigenizing Bengali architecture from the 1420s, n. 261 *supra*.

from Ava. Unlike those capitals, however, Delhi lacked the power or inclination to promote vernacular usage over many generations; the semi-official status alongside Persian that Hindi enjoyed at Delhi under the Lodis and Sher Shah Sur was not matched under earlier or later regimes. Brajbhasha, the speech of the Agra area south of Delhi, became the chief language of Krisna devotional poetry in the 1500s and of much North Indian court poetry in the 17th century; while Avadhi, the speech of the Lucknow area, became the vehicle of *sufi* narrative poetry and of the Rama-*bhakti* work of Tulsidas (1532?–1623), arguably India's most celebrated religious poet. But again, outside Hindu courts, as literary media Brajbhasha and Avadhi had to share pride of place with Persian. And as usual, Muslim states like Delhi, Agra, and Jaunpur made no effort to identify with preconquest, pre-Muslim dynasties.[274]

Most critical, whatever regional syntheses had taken root to 1555 were severely disrupted by the Mughals, whose influence far exceeded that of the Delhi sultans. Although the Mughals continued to recognize hereditary rulers in many regions and on various levels, and although some governors continued to exercise quasi-royal prerogatives, in realms like Gujarat, Kashmir, Malwa, Bengal, and the Deccan the transition from independent kingdom to dependent province entailed unmistakable rupture. Hereditary dynasts disappeared in favor of temporary appointees, and *mansabdars* from North India replaced many local notables. Northern monetary and fiscal systems were imposed on the Deccan, and provincial jurisdictions and capitals shifted not infrequently.[275] At the same time, the Mughal embrace of Perso-Islamic culture and Persian language bred a novel reserve toward regional cultures. Thus Mughal officers in Bengal contemptuously contrasted their martial heritage with the docility of local "fishermen," and rejected architectural

---

[274] McGregor, "Progress of Hindi," 912–47; Alam, *Languages*, 123–24, 148–50; *EAH*, vol. IV, 147; *IBE*, 115–16, 120. Talbot, pers. commun., July 30, 2007 noted that the relation of Hindi, Brajbhasa, and Avadhi is "very difficult to write about because the situation is so murky." Hindi/Hindavi originally referred to any North Indian vernacular from a Persian-speaker's perspective, and it "was not necessarily (or even in most cases) distinct from the North Indian literary languages of Braj Bhasa and Avadhi."

[275] On new boundaries and capitals, Richards, *Mughal Administration*, 72; Eaton, *Rise of Islam*, 149, 176; Nayeem, *Splendour of Hyderabad*, 1–7, 76, 91; K. Sajun Lal, "The Mughals in the Deccan," in Sherwani and Joshi, *History of Medieval Deccan*, vol. I, 612, 614–15. On administrative changes, ibid., 601–27; Eaton, *Rise of Islam*, 137–93; Richards, *Mughal Administration*, 71–235 *passim*; Richards, *NCHI*, 14–15, 33, 59; Eaton, *NCHI*, 157–59.

traditions patronized by Muslim rulers in Bengal in favor of styles transplanted directly from the North Indian heartland.[276] Akbar's conquest of Gujarat reportedly prompted writers and poets who used regional languages to flee to Deccani courts. Although vernacular literatures continued to develop on the local level, the Mughals until the 18th century refused to patronize them or to use Hindi either at court or for provincial administration. Whereas from 1450–1550 North Indian vernaculars had begun to infiltrate politics, Persian's reemergence under the Mughals, in the words of Muzaffar Alam, "put paid to this trend."[277]

Phase Three: Regional Florescence and Eclipse, c. 1700–1800/1850

Mughal displacements and discontinuities become yet more apparent if we consider how little Mughal successor states owed – or acknowledged owing – to pre-1560 traditions. Insofar as some of these states had an ethnic or religious character, historians have been tempted to see them as a resurfacing of primordial solidarities. But closer inquiry suggests that regional identities arose more basically from conditions specific to the Mughal and post-Mughal periods.[278] In part, regional sentiment reflected the novel prosperity and rising influence of pioneering peasants and low-level *zamindars* who had little knowledge of Persian and were at best poorly assimilated to Mughal norms. In part, Mughal political debility weakened the appeal of imperial culture. In part, warfare in the late 1600s and 1700s encouraged local identities in opposition to an alien "other," often Mughal, but in some cases Maratha, Indo-Afghan, or British. But if regional leaders readily enlisted local idioms and myths, their sense of legitimizing precedent, on present evidence at least, was quite shallow, rarely reaching back before 1560 – compared, for example, to Tokugawa Japanese, whose imperial lineage antedated

---

[276] Eaton, *Rise of Islam*, 169–73.
[277] Alam, "Culture and Politics," 187, 158–89; idem *Languages*, 146–50. In the Deccan Mughal rule devalued not only Telugu, but Dakani literature. Sherwani and Joshi, *History of Medieval Deccan*, vol. II, 30–34, 164. Yet on the continued vitality of vernacular writing *without* official patronage 1550–1750, see McGregor, "Progress of Hindi," 937–46; Deshpande, *Sociolinguistic Attitudes*, 77–83; Kaviraj, "Two Histories," 506; Narayana Rao, "Multiple Literary Cultures," 385–90, 413–18.
[278] I follow Alam and Subrahmanyam, *Mughal State*, 68.

Heian; or to the French, for whom the Franks and Hugh Capet remained relevant to political debates in the late 1700s.[279]

Absent the British, would these states have become ever more cohesive on the European or Southeast Asian pattern? All one can say is that between 1700 and 1850, fresh ideas of moral community fused with attachments to particular landscapes and cultic traditions and with Mughal legacies to foster what C. A. Bayly terms novel regional "patriotisms."[280] This, then, was the third and final period of regional florescence in South Asia.

The Marathas well illustrate these trends. Rooted in modern Maharashtra, from the 1660s, 1705, and 1720 they expanded until by the 1750s they were levying tribute from Bengal to the Punjab to the far south. The Marathas drew on a culturally specific energy generated by a constellation of factors, including Marathi *bhakti* and pilgrimage networks and the associated tradition of Marathi poetry; the expansion of revenue and juridical networks under the Deccan sultanates that brought Marathi-speakers into more regular contact with one another; a buoyant military labor market under the sultanates and the Mughals; and the commercialization of Maharashtra's black soil cotton districts. Early Maratha warbands recruited from hardy, upwardly mobile peasants-cum-warriors and small *zamindars* whose social cohesion mirrored a shared hostility to Mughal elites and their refined urban culture. With reciprocal disdain, Aurangzeb branded the Maratha ruler a "mountain rat." Devotion to a Maratha homeland, to "self-rule"(*swarajya*), and to the primacy of Hindu rituals led some Marathas to cast "Turks" as their natural foe, to reduce Persian in favor of Marathi terms for administration, and to present the Maratha ruler as "Hindu emperor" (*hindu padpadshahi*).[281] As preserved in folksongs and ballads, notions of a relatively egalitarian, specifically Maharashtrian moral order survived

---

[279] Keith Michael Baker, *Inventing the French Revolution* (Cambridge, 1990), 36–57, 80. But Talbot, pers. commun., July 30, 2007 suggests that part of the reason that a sense of legitimizing precedent, of recycling history, in this and perhaps earlier periods seems shallow may be that existing scholarship simply has not explored the issue in adequate depth.

[280] Bayly, *Origins of Nationality*, vii, 26, and 1–62; Alam and Subrahmanyam, *Mughal State*, 68. Cf. Ludden, *NCHI*, 141–45; *SP*, 39–44.

[281] On the Marathas, Alam, "Competition and Co-Existence," 54; Wink, *Land and Sovereignty*, 48–49; esp. Eaton, *NCHI*, 129–54 (incl. n. 64), 177–202, analyzing stimuli to state formation. "Mountain rat" epithet from *IBE*, 238. On state and culture, see too ibid., 232–44, 272–73; Stewart Gordon, "Hindus, Muslims, and the 'Other' in 18th-Century India" (ms); idem, *NCHI*, 10–66, 81, and chs. 5–6 *passim*; Wink, *Land and*

into the 1800s, notwithstanding the post-1720 triumph at the capital Pune of more brahmanic currents. In typical Indic fashion, Marathas insisted not on the exclusivity, but the symbolic primacy of their own religious system; thus they included local Muslims in this moral order and patronized Muslim institutions and holy men. They also retained rituals, fiscal practices, and land rights from the Mughals as well as the sultanates of Ahmadnagar and Bijapur. But Maratha leaders claimed descent from neither of these regional sultanates, seeing their kingdom as an essentially novel creation. Nor, curiously, did they retain much historical memory of Vijayanagara, large parts of whose territories they controlled, or of the fellow-"Hindu," Maharashtra-based Yadava polity.[282] Likewise, their territorial objectives were ad hoc and improvised, rather than the expression of some inherited cultural imperative.

The Sikh polity too should be seen as a regional response to social and cultural forces specific to the Mughal period. Emerging in the Punjab from the Sant tradition that rejected institutionalized religion, Sikhism during the 16th and 17th centuries developed its own scriptures and a relatively egalitarian social ethic that appealed to diverse clienteles. These included urban commercial castes, village artisans, and the great Jat peasant caste, including Jat *zamindars*, whose warlike itinerant qualities reflected their pastoral origins. Although or perhaps because some of these groups had benefited from 17th-century prosperity, they bitterly resented the privileged beneficiaries of Mughal power, chiefly tax-exempt Muslim institutions and the entrenched Muslim aristocracy of the Punjab. Fierce revolts against the Mughals joined internal disputes to forge for the Sikh Panth, or community, an increasingly distinct martial and socioreligious identity. The foe would change and internecine wars would engulf the Punjab, but by 1799 an independent Sikh state had emerged under the warrior Ranjit Singh, who ruled the Punjab and adjacent districts to 1839. Like the Marathas, Sikhs relied closely on Mughal fiscal precedents and retained Persian for administration and literary purposes, while Sikh poets conceived of the Punjab as the common homeland of Muslim, Hindu, and Sikh communities (*aqwam*).

Sovereignty, esp. chs. 1, 2, Bayly, *Origins of Nationality*, 21–26; idem, "Pre-History of Communalism," 181–82, 187; Hintze, *Mughal Empire*, 218–43.

[282] Gordon, *NCHI*, 66, 80–81, 138–39, 143–44, 180, 186; and Sumit Guha, "The Frontiers of Memory," *MAS* (2009): 269–88, discussing weak to nonexistent Maratha–Vijayanagara links.

But the leaders elevated Sikh over Muslim religious symbols, pointedly refused to acknowledge Mughal suzerainty, encouraged Punjabi writing and arts, conceived of their polity as a new entity, and pursued territorial goals that, like those of the Marathas, were novel and opportunistic.[283]

Lying between the Marathas and Sikhs, Rajasthan supported a number of established Hindu polities, some originating as early as the 11th century. Yet there too Mughal pressures, followed by Maratha interventions, joined wider social and cultural links to nurture a more expansive political self-image. By the early 1700s poets were writing vernacular paeans to a Rajput "homeland," reminiscent of Marathi "patriotic" ballads. To the east, Hindu Jats, who supported distinctive dialects and religious practices and whose chieftains carved out modest realms, also exhibited in the 1700s what Bayly does not hesitate to call Jat "territorial patriotism," but with historic precedents that were shallow to nonexistent.[284]

By 1760 Maratha, Sikh, Rajput, and non-Sikh Jat polities covered the greater part of northwestern, western, and central India.[285] In much of the Ganges basin, I argued that easy communications and strong Sanskrit and Persian traditions weakened local expression. Moreover, in contrast to Maratha, Sikh, Rajput, and Jat areas, the central basin and much of the south still were ruled by Muslims (Shiite and Sunni), whose religious identity set lower limits to indigenization. Such was the logic of post-Mughal regionalism, however, that even in Muslim-ruled realms like Awadh and Bengal in the north and Hyderabad and Mysore in the south, localizing trends appeared. Awadh, for example, prided itself as

---

[283] On the Sikhs, Alam, *Crisis of Empire*, 110ff., 134–203, 315–16; Bayly, *Origins of Nationality*, 41–42, 56; idem, "Pre-History of Communalism," 182, 188–89; idem, *Rulers, Townsmen*, 21–22; *IBE*, 265–73; Indu Banga, *The Agrarian System of the Sikhs* (New Delhi, 1978), esp. 1–38, 186–93; Grewal, *NCHI*, chs. 3–6, noting Sikhs were only 12 percent in areas they ruled; *EAH*, vol. III, 463–65, 475; Hintze, *Mughal Empire*, 243–66; Harjot Oberoi, "From Punjab to 'Khalistan,'" *Pacific Affairs* 60 (1987): 26–41; Farina Mir, pers. commun., March 30, 2005.

[284] Bayly, *Origins of Nationality*, 27–28, plus Hiralal Maheshwari, *A History of Rajasthani Literature* (Delhi, 1980), 75–76; Norbert Peabody, "Tod's *Rajast'han* and the Boundaries of Imperial Rule in 19th-Century India," *MAS* 30 (1996): 185–220; *IBE*, 249–50, 265–66. Note too distinctive Rajput painting in Beach, *NCHI*, chs. 5, 6. On the development of an expressly "Afghan" identity among diasporic immigrants under the Mughals and the transmission of that identity to the new Afghan state as the Mughals declined, see Green, "Tribe, Diaspora."

[285] See Bayly, *Caste*, Map 1.

birthplace of Rama and home to Hindu as well as Muslim heroes whose exploits were celebrated in Avadhi. As they disengaged from Mughal control, Awadh's Shiite rulers reinforced the local mystique by patronizing distinctive cultural styles, supporting Hindu shrines, and emphasizing Shiite adherence. Yet Awadh's anomalous political status, as a breakaway province of an empire whose suzerainty it still recognized, kept Awadh from claiming the mantle of independent pre-Mughal regional polities like Jaunpur, much less of pre-Muslim kingdoms.[286] Hyderabad's position was comparable. Occupying the same heartland as the Golkonda Sultanate, Hyderabad could claim a distinguished regional lineage. Yet Hyderabad's rulers lacked dynastic ties to Golkonda, abandoned the old capital for much of the 18th century, and as rulers of a province still nominally loyal to Delhi, derived legitimacy not from Golkonda, but from the Mughals. Of the Kakatiyas, who once held much the same area as Hyderabad and Golkonda, we hear little or nothing.[287] In Mysore in the late 1700s, *parvenu* Muslim dynasts summoned fierce Tamil and Kannada warrior deities and appealed indirectly to a Karnataka identity, but again in a quasi-Muslim idiom and in the service of a territorial vision that, for Mysore at least, was utterly novel.[288]

By protecting princely states like Hyderabad, Mysore, and Rajput polities, the British, one could argue, honored regional traditions. True though this may have been in a technical sense, the British denied these states any dynamism or independent action, circumscribed their territories, and hastened, intentionally or not, the erosion of regional cultures in favor of pan-Indian currents. What is more, princely states were but large islands in a directly-ruled sea. Ultimately therefore, like Delhi and Mughal rulers before them, the British destroyed India's competitive multistate system and weakened incipient regional fusions of culture and power.

[286] Bayly, *Origins of Nationality*, 41, 52–54; idem, *Rulers, Townsmen*, 12, 25–27; idem, "Pre-History of Communalism," 182–86; Richard Barnett, *North India Between Empires* (Berkeley, 1980); Juan Cole, *Roots of North Indian Shi'ism in Iran and Iraq* (Berkeley, 1988), chs. 2, 4, 9; Asher, *NCHI*, 318–24; Rudrangshu Mukherjee, *Awadh in Revolt* (Oxford, 1984); Alam, *Crisis of Empire*, ch. 6.

[287] On early independent Hyderabad, pragmatically recruiting Mughal personnel from the north while cultivating local constituencies, see Faruqui, "At Empire's End," 5–43; Nayeem, *Splendour of Hyderabad*, 2–7, 76, 85–97, 102–105.

[288] Kate Brittlebank, "*Sakti* and *Barakat*," *MAS* 29 (1995): 257–69; Bayly, *Origins of Nationality*, 28. On evolving regional identities in the far south, Susan Bayly, "Islam and State Power in Pre-Colonial South India," *Itinerario* 12 (1988): 143–64.

Why Were Empires Less Durable in South Asia Than in China?

In summary, syntheses between regional polities and cultures proved less stable and enjoyed weaker official sanction in South Asia than in protected-zone states primarily because India, unlike the latter zone, remained subject to externally based military assault. If the British introduced a novel strategic vision, throughout the second millennium and part of the first, the principal threat issued from Inner Asia and Afghanistan. Indeed, this was true as late as 1761.[289] In this basic vulnerability to Inner Asian power, South Asia resembled China.

Yet, as I also have emphasized, imperial unification remained less secure in South Asia than in China, with a functional Mughal empire lasting not much more than half as long the Qing, and with Delhi Sultanate authority yet more tenuous. Conversely, regional kingdoms and cultures in India were far more prominent and durable than in China. Indeed, although China, like South Asia, supported several mutually unintelligible languages, it boasted but one literary language and, in effect, one literary tradition. Having considered the vicissitudes of regional polities, let us now look at the other side of the ledger, as it were. Why were South Asian empires more fragile than their Chinese counterparts? Several factors merit attention.

The implications of geography were mixed, but on balance probably favored Chinese more than Indian unification. South Asia and China had a common physical structure in that the North Indian plain and the North China plain were the largest stretches of level terrain in their respective spheres, both plains supported greater linguistic homogeneity than outlying areas, and both were charter cradles. Yet not only is the North Indian plain considerably larger, but in 1700 it contained some 60 percent of India's population and wealth, compared to 25–30 percent of China's population and a smaller fraction of output in the North China plain.[290] Following G. William Skinner, I define a macroregion as an area whose riverine core concentrates arable land, transport, people, and capital, and whose periphery

---

[289] That year the Afghan leader Ahmad Shah Durrani, who repeatedly invaded the Indian plains, defeated the Marathas – albeit to the ultimate benefit of the British. Kulke and Rothermund, *History*, 210, 215; Gommans, *Mughal Warfare*, 70, 128, 187.

[290] Projecting from earlier and later figures at *CEHI*, 166; Cole, "New Empires," 3; G. William Skinner, ed., *The City in Late Imperial China* (Stanford, 1977), 213; and Susan Naquin and Evelyn Rawski, *Chinese Society in the Eighteenth Century* (New Haven, 1987), 213, Table 3.

suffers a marked thinning out of those same resources.[291] By this definition, whereas in 1700 Mughal India beyond the northern plain had only
five macroregions,[292] China proper outside the North China plain had
seven, almost all of which far exceeded their largest South Asian counterpart in size and population.[293] The improbability of the Qing empire
looms yet larger if we consider that it included vast difficult-to-control
non-Chinese areas – Manchuria, Mongolia, Tibet, Xinjiang – without
close Mughal analogue. All told, the Qing empire in 1800 embraced
320,000,000–350,000,000 people in 11,000,000 square kilometers, compared to a Mughal population in 1700 of c. 175,000,000 in roughly
5,000,000 square kilometers. By these criteria, South Asia should have
been more governable than China.

But other features told a different story. India lacked an integrating
system of water transport as extensive or efficient as China's, primarily
because there was no second great river system parallel to the Ganges
that could be linked by a north–south transverse the way China's
Grand Canal joined the Yellow River and the Yangzi, but also because
local canal and river networks (and perhaps coastal shipping) were
less fine grained and dendritic in South India than in South China.[294]
Withal, arid corridors stretching from Inner Asia through northwest
India and across the Deccan supported warrior lineages and armed
pastoralists without Chinese parallel. Rural militarization was manifest
in the proliferation of hill redoubts and mud forts and in the existence
in 1590 of an estimated 4,400,000 arms-bearing men, roughly 10 percent of the active Indian male population.[295] If some of these groups

---

[291] Skinner, *The City*, 213–16.

[292] Kabul, Bengal, Malwa/north Deccan, the central Deccan, and Arcot, according to
Gommans, *Mughal Warfare*, 17–18. I treat his "nuclear zones of power" as broadly
comparable to Skinner's macroregions.

[293] This is hardly surprising, since China proper had almost twice the population of India
in 1800, and concentrated a far smaller portion of its people on the northern plain.
Skinner, *The City*, 213–16; Naquin and Rawski, *Chinese Society*, Maps. 1, 2 and ch. 5;
Gommans, *Mughal Warfare*, 17–19.

[294] Cf. Schwartzberg, *Historical Atlas*, 3, 151–52; Mark Elvin, *The Pattern of the Chinese Past*
(Stanford, 1973), 131–45, 304–306. South Asia also has a larger ratio of coast to interior
than China, but in the absence of large protected peninsulas and offshore islands, and
with naval power marginal before c. 1760, this was not a consistent centrifugal danger.

[295] Kolff, *Naukar, Rajput*, 3–4 and 1–31 *passim*; idem, "End of *Ancien Regime*"; Gommans
and Kolff, "Introduction," 16; Hardy, "Authority of Muslim Kings," 47. See an early
1700s Awadh governor's complaint about seditious *zamindars* who "possess a strong
fortress in almost every village," Alam, *Crisis of Empire*, 94. But Alavi, *Sepoys and
the Company*, 11–13 questions whether peasants armed largely for self-defense, who

could be recruited into imperial forces, the overwhelming majority were subject not to Mughal appointees, but to autonomous rural notables. This made it impossible for Indian empires even to think about a monopoly on force, as Maratha challenges to the Mughals illustrated all too graphically. Admittedly, bandits also found a natural haven along China's rugged, habitually underadministered provincial frontiers, while forested uplands in the southwest let non-Chinese aboriginals resist imperial troops with stubborn determination. But within China proper, independent armed groups never played so seminal a role as in South Asia because a) aboriginals were even more culturally encapsulated than Indian pastoralists and peasants, b) the semipastoral sector of the Indian rural economy had no analogue in China proper, c) China's inner frontiers lay more distant from key power centers than their South Asian equivalents, d) in theory and substantially in practice, Chinese governments alone insisted on demilitarization of the interior and on uniform provincial administration.

Indeed, a formidable barrier to the stability of all Indian polities, regional as well as transregional, was the irremediably segmented conceptualization of power. Although reinforced by India's dry rugged topography, this pattern must have had an autonomous dynamic, as its reproduction in extremely diverse ecological contexts across both South and Southeast Asia suggests. Here the Sinic–Indic contrast is particularly marked. Now it is true that Chinese emperors, during the opening phase of dynasties and especially along the frontiers, sometimes sanctioned hereditary frontier jurisdictions. Yet these were at best temporary concessions, for the cardinal principle of administration demanded that all officials to the county level be temporary nonlocal appointees. China recognized no local potentates.[296] By contrast, in India under Muslim and Hindu overlords alike, local kings and notables retained irreducible, hereditary rights of taxation, ritual, and coercion comparable to those of the overlord. In this world, sovereignty was not unified and inalienable, but multiple, residual, and nested; and the countryside bristled with petty principalities. Like South Asian rulers since the Guptas, the Mughal emperor therefore was "king of kings" – but without apology, the same title might be used by a Mughal provincial governor in dealing

---

probably represented the vast majority of the 4,400,000, should be seen as part-time soldiers.

[296] See Ch. 5 passim and T'ung-tsu Ch'u, *Local Government in China Under the Ch'ing* (Stanford, 1962), chs. 1, 2. On demilitarization of the interior, Mark Edward Lewis, *The Early Chinese Empires* (Cambridge, MA, 2007), 3, 6, 7.

with his own subordinates.[297] At all levels, the abiding goal was to woo clients through honors and largesse and to prevent defections to one's rivals. Territorial jurisdictions were often imprecise, and hierarchies, based on personal ties, were subject to constant negotiation, dissolution, reintegration. Thus Wink characterizes the Indian state as "a form of institutionalized dissidence."[298] (This same generous acceptance of multiple sources of power, one might argue, underlay India's official hyperglossia and its decidedly non-European toleration of multiform religious practices.)

Despite long-term improvements in coordination, administration in India thus remained less penetrating than in late imperial China. In China proper the Ming and Qing supported, in effect, five levels of nonlocal appointees (those of county, prefecture, and province, with the latter often combined into multiprovince jurisdictions and with subprefects frequently inserted above the county). By contrast, the Mughals normally had two such levels: a) gubernatorial, fiscal, military, and religious officers in the provincial capital, and b) military intendants (*faujdars*) and commanders of military checkpoints (*thanas*) at the subprovincial level. Given the smaller Mughal population, official-to-subject ratios may not have been much smaller in Mughal than in Chinese provinces, but in extensive areas like Rajasthan and much of the pre-1687 Deccan with hereditary tributaries, the capital made no local appointments at all.[299] Although in principle Mughal provincial officials, like Chinese, held office temporarily, in practice Mughal rotations seem to have been far less regular. *Jagir* revenue assignments, potentially devolutionary, had no Chinese analogue, all the more significant in that *jagir* rotations also grew less frequent.[300]

---

[297] *IBE*, 151, and 213, 228, 271–73; Hasan, "*Zamindars* Under the Mughals"; Eaton, *Rise of Islam*, 160.

[298] Wink, *Land and Sovereignty*, 386 and 9–51 *passim*; idem, "Sovereignty and Universal Dominion in South Asia," in Gommans and Kolff, *Warfare and Weaponry*, 99–130. For similar views, Peabody, *Hindu Kingship*, 1–9, 80–91; Hasan, *State and Locality*, ch. 2; Richards, *NCHI*, 79–82; Kolff, *Naukar, Rajput*, 9–16, 30–31; Gommans, *Mughal Warfare*, 74–77, 91; 213, 228, 271–73. Cf. *SP*, Chs. 2, 3.

[299] One might object that these tributary zones, as a proportion of imperial territory, were no more extensive than Mongolia, Tibet, Qinghai, and Xinjiang; but not only did they contain a far larger portion of imperial population than non-Chinese areas in the Qing empire, they also occupied a more critical strategic position and were less culturally insulated. See Richards, *NCHI*, 58–93, 127–31, 179, 282–83; Alam and Subrahmanyan, *Mughal State*, 40–44, 57; Alam, *Crisis of Empire*, 56–91; Singh, "Centre and Periphery"; Gordon, *NCHI*, 22–35.

[300] Alam, *Crisis of Empire*, 5–6, 24–25, 74, 124–30, 302–303, 318.

Entry into the regular Ming and Qing bureaucracy was not hereditary, but sons of Mughal officials routinely entered imperial service, if
not necessarily in their fathers' posts.[301] Chinese bureaucratic norms
(admittedly not the same as practice) proscribed factionalism and clientage, but Mughal culture deemed factionalism natural and personal ties,
highly desirable.[302] Whereas separate civil and military hierarchies let
Chinese magistrates control only petty militias, in South Asia cavalry
and infantry owed *rajas, mansabdars,* and *zamindars* alike a personal loyalty. Mughal authority decayed, in large measure, when armed notables
sought to assert a more complete authority.

In part perhaps because a military, rather than civilian, ethos dominated, in part too because literacy rates were less than half to an eighth
those of China, political socialization remained less widespread and
formal. No South Asian polity sponsored civil service examinations,
much less a literary corpus devoted to problems of governance that
all educated elites as well as would-be officials were expected to study.
Akbar did issue to princes and officials a code of conduct and a working
manual that emphasized notions of justice and toleration sanctioned by
akhlaq statecraft literature.[303] But this was mere exhortation without any
sort of certification; nor is there evidence of such manuals in later reigns.
In China, moreover, because the gentry not only were familiar with
canonical texts but supported official efforts to popularize political and
social norms associated with those texts, Confucianism's homogenizing thrust extended well beyond examination hopefuls. After disasters,
the Chinese empire reformed again and again because it expressed the
unshakeable conviction of sizeable groups that social harmony required
uncontested, unified sovereignty.

For Mughal India the implications of size were therefore ironic. On
the one hand, fewer levels of administration and smaller population
reduced the sort of Skinnerian pressures discussed in Chapter 5. On the
other hand, the insularity and self-sufficiency of innumerable local units

---

[301] Cf. Richards, "Norms of Comportment," 266 and *passim; CEHI,* 241, 243; Alam, *Crisis
of Empire,* 25, 35, 129; Naquin and Rawski, *Chinese Society,* 123; *CIHC,* 145–49, 161,
198–99. By the Qing the *yin* privilege and small examination quotas for officials' sons
and nephews were mere remnants of hereditary advantage.

[302] Cf. Richards, "Norms of Comportment"; Alam, *Crisis of Empire,* 19–20, 34; Naquin and
Rawski, *Chinese Society,* 7, 50–54.

[303] Alam, "*Akhlaqi* Norms," 84, 90. On courtly norms and discipline, also n. 45 *supra;* and
on Indian and Chinese literacy rates, nn. 118, 119 *supra.*

spread across a vast landscape rendered imperial control consistently less secure than in China.[304]

Along with difficult geography, fragmented sovereignty, and limited political indoctrination, a feature often seen as the quintessential Indian institution, namely caste, is sometimes invoked to explain the weakness of empire. Three major charges have been laid at the door of caste, which, we saw, grew more influential toward the end of our period: a) Segregated, endogamous, linguistically differentiated *jatis* and *varnas* – whose resolute particularism contrasted with both the normative Mencian and the practical Qing emphasis on social inclusion and mobility – precluded the vertical cohesion on which successful polities necessarily rely. b) Along with self-regulating religious temples and sects – which also lacked close Chinese analogue – self-replicating castes obviated state regulation. c) The fact that brahmans enjoyed higher status than kings circumscribed royal authority.[305] Though certainly weighty, none of these charges stands uncontested. In some contexts caste not only required royal sanction, but by promoting social discipline, advanced the state's interest in pacification and control. Not infrequently, caste distinctions grew directly from political centralization. What is more, brahmans' ritual, purificatory, and administrative expertise commonly buttressed aspirant rulers.[306]

---

[304] Cf. Ch. 5, nn. 266–72 *supra*.

[305] C. A. Bayly, "State Building in the Shadow of Imperialism" (ms), 14–17 suggests that caste explains the 18th-century weakness of ethnic and political solidarity in Maharashtra compared to Burma. Pollock, *Language of the Gods*, 475–76, 510–11 suggests an inherent opposition between caste and ethnicity; while Eaton, *Rise of Islam*, 103 suggests that by displacing royal regulatory functions to society at large, Turkic destruction of Hindu kingship in Bengal encouraged protomodern caste organizations. On the political implications of caste, see too Inden, *Imagining India*, 56–75, 162–80, 217–20; Stein, *History*, 82–83, 155; idem, *Peasant State and Society*, 264–85; Bayly, *Caste*, 11–23, 29; and Louis Dumont's ahistorical *Homo Hierarchicus* (Chicago, 1980).

[306] See nn. 70, 86 *supra*, plus critiques of Dumont in Dirks, *Castes of Mind*, 54–59, 64–78; the emphasis on royal precedence in idem, *Hollow Crown*; Bayly, *Caste*, 21–24; Bayly, *NCHI*, 13; Declan Quigley, *The Interpretation of Caste* (Oxford, 1999), esp. chs. 6, 7, arguing that caste reflects a historical tension between royal centralization and kinship entropy; Strathern, pers. commun., May 17, 2007. By analogy with Philip Gorski, *The Disciplinary Revolution* (Chicago, 2003), caste might be considered an extreme form of disciplinary control. Another putative anthropological explanation for greater political fissiparousness in India than China, namely marriage patterns, must be discounted, because in both its North Indian and Dravidian variants, elite exogamy was no less integrative than the Chinese imperative to marry into surname lineages other than one's own. Thomas Trautmann, pers. commun., April 5, 2007.

I suggested that South Asia's low literacy rates militated against a Confucian-style system of indoctrination. Yet literacy per se may have been no more politically significant than differences between Indian and Chinese writing systems. Chapter 5 argued that the universal impact of Chinese texts depended on their being written in a nonalphabetic, logographic code, an artificial language, above the cacophonous world of local tongues. Regardless of speech, all readers had access to the same normative concepts. Now insofar as it translated Sanskrit classics, the vernacular revolution in India also disseminated shared visions. But, quite apart from the fact that these visions were less resolutely political than their Confucian counterparts, Indian scripts, by virtue of their phonetic character, supported a plethora of regional literatures – in Punjabi, Gujarati, Hindi, Bengali, Oriya, Marathi, Kannada, Telugu, Tamil, and so forth – far more easily than did Chinese logographs. One simply cannot speak of robust Sichuanese or Hunanese literatures. But we have seen that post-Sanskrit writing in South Asia paralleled the post-Latin development of Germanic, Romance, and Slavic literatures and cultures in Europe, and of Burmese and Tai in Southeast Asia, all dependent on phonetic alphabets. Here, then, was another reason that transregional formations in South Asia, although more durable than in Europe, proved far less stable than in China.

What impact did warfare and fiscal extraction have? In China, I argued, a precondition for imperial longevity was modest taxation – in the 18th century about 5 percent of national income – which in turn required military restraint. Although Chinese warfare was neither inexpensive nor uncommon, both Ming and Qing by and large met this desideratum. By contrast, the Mughals demanded remarkably high taxes, 33 to 50 percent or more of rural output,[307] and constantly sought fresh territories for new *jagir* assignments. The Mughals were more interested in resource maximization than the Qing because a) Operating in an "international" environment in which service at Persian or Transoxanian courts was a live possibility, the Mughals had to attract and retain military nobles. China faced no such competition. b) The system of shared sovereignty and multiple local courts meant that the Mughals also operated in a far more competitive domestic environment. Control over the Deccan, for example, could be secured only by *jagir* grants to both Maratha defectors and nobles fighting the Marathas. c) As professional soldiers from a culture that prized war and

[307] See n. 39 *supra*.

lavish elite remuneration, Mughals lacked a principled commitment to fiscal restraint comparable to that of Neo-Confucian China. By one calculation, in Mughal India wealth was more concentrated at the very top, among *mansabdars*, than in any society in history with the possible exception of pharaonic Egypt.[308]

Insofar as South Chinese peasants in areas of dense population had to pay private rents without close Indian equivalent, the discrepancy between aggregate peasant burdens was less than the bald figures of 5 percent and 33–50+ percent suggest. Nonetheless, not only do overall elite exactions in Mughal India still appear to have been appreciably higher than in Qing China,[309] but in India alone by far the heaviest impositions derived from the state, rather than private landowners. The *jagir* system thus contributed, if indirectly, to two political strains. First, while today few historians accept fully Irfan Habib's thesis that taxes immiserated the North Indian peasantry, from the late 1600s *jagir* demands, by squeezing the income of lower *zamindars* in the Punjab, Maharashtra, and elsewhere, probably did contribute to rural grievance and revolt. Second, once Deccan campaigns failed to yield assignments as lucrative as those enjoyed by earlier *jagir*-holders, resentment and factionalism spread throughout higher levels of administration.[310]

In other words, in South Asia as in China the endurance of empire required either military restraint or constant military success – neither

---

[308] Or ancient Mesopotamia. See n. 202 *supra*.

[309] So far as I can determine, the revenues the government assigned to *jagir*-holders combined what elsewhere would be termed private rents and government taxes; the same lands normally did not pay rents in addition to *jagir* taxes. *CEHI*, 235, 247–60 and n. 39 *supra*. In the 1750 Yangzi delta tenants paid 30–40 percent of annual agricultural output in private rent, but no taxes directly to the state, because these were levied on landlords, not tenants. Thus the total burden for such peasants was at the low end of average Mughal *jagir* taxes. But landholding in the Yangzi delta was more concentrated and onerous than in other regions, with the possible exception of the West River basin, and even in the Yangzi delta rented land comprised only 42 percent of the total. In North China the figure was 18 percent. By definition, although they were liable for taxes of approximately 5 percent, owner-cultivators did not pay any rent. Robert Brenner and Christopher Isett, "England's Divergence from China's Yangzi Delta," *JAS* 61 (2002): 615; Philip Huang, *The Peasant Family and Rural Development in the Yangzi Delta, 1350–1988* (Stanford, 1990), 40–42, 102. By this logic Mughal peasants on average surrendered to elites – in the Mughal case, primarily officials – a considerably larger percentage of total output than their mid-Qing Chinese counterparts.

[310] See n. 46 *supra*, plus Hasan, "Zamindars Under the Mughals," 297–98; *CEHI*, 172–73, 177–78; Irfan Habib, *The Agrarian System of Mughal India* (New York, 1963), esp. 317–51; Bayly, "South Asia and the Great Divergence," 90; Richards, *NCHI*, 75, 290–97; Kulke and Rothermund, *History*, 195–96; Alam, *Crisis of Empire*, 145–46, 303–306.

of which the Mughals after 1689 achieved. Following Mughal collapse, warfare continued, of course, but under successor states whose modest territories and sensitivity to regional idioms allowed them to mobilize local resources more efficiently than the Mughals.[311]

Cohesion and Vulnerability Among Conquest Elites: Turks and Other Overland Immigrants

How did Inner Asian cultural loyalties influence imperial stability? And how did those affiliations compare to elite patterns in the protected zone and in China?

The relation of Inner Asians to South Asian culture has long been, and remains, politically contentious. Although peasants may not have noticed much difference, early Muslim and non-Muslim writers, in order to celebrate or lament the arrival of a new religious system, portrayed Turkic invasions as a decisive break with the past. Centuries later British historians reinscribed Turkic-Hindu opposition by emphasizing Muslim oppression from which Britain graciously rescued the subcontinent. Again, history was neatly divided into Hindu and Muslim periods. With the advent of colonial-era politics, such views gained further traction, as political leaders sought to naturalize their constituencies by claiming that Indian Muslims had always constituted a separate "nation," or that historic Muslim abuses justified Hindu control of the civil service. In the 1990s tensions between the Hindu rightist Bharatiya Janata Party and Muslims gave such narratives a fresh impetus.[312]

Spurred by a deep distaste for this essentialized approach and the violence it engendered, a reaction against communal historiography has gathered strength in recent years. Although this trend itself may have inspired a countermovement, anticommunal views remain dominant, and as such, contrast with Qing historiography, whose early emphasis on Sinicization, we saw, has yielded to a concern with enduring Manchu–Chinese difference and tension.[313]

---

[311] See n. 48 *supra.*

[312] Eaton, "Introduction," 9–14; Barbara Metcalf, "Presidential Address," *JAS* 54 (1995): 953–56; Peter van der Veer, *Religious Nationalism* (Berkeley, 1994), chs. 1, 2; Romila Thapar, "Somanatha and Mahmud," *Frontline* April 23, 1999: 121–27; Gyanendra Pandey, *The Construction of Communalism in Colonial North India* (Delhi, 1992); Metcalfs, *Concise History,* ch. 9.

[313] See n. 215 *supra.*

What, then, does current South Asian historiography offer?[314] First, rejecting the image of all peoples west of modern Pakistan as utterly alien to South Asia, scholars have shown that before 1100 contact between the Punjab and the Iranian plateau was as close as that between the Ganges basin and South India. Moreover, Inner Asian warriors and animal breeders played a role comparable to that of Kannada and Telugu frontiersmen within South Asia itself.[315] Second, Muslims constituted less an overarching religious category than additions to an already rich mosaic. Contemporaries usually identified immigrants not as Muslims, but as members of specific ethnolinguistic groups, Turk, Persian, Afghan, or Arab. Shiites, moreover, were distinguished from Sunnis, Westerners from Deccanis, and members of one *sufi* order from another. Of course, people perceived differences between Muslim and non-Muslim practices, but they saw differences too between Saivas, Saktas, and Vaisnavas. The congeries of sects that for convenience we call "Hindu" lacked a unified catechism or organization; and if boundaries between large religious groupings, like those between castes, grew sharper from the 14th century and more especially in the 1700s and 1800s, most scholars agree that the great majority of South Asians still did not think in terms of Muslim and Hindu blocs. Indeed, to treat brahmans and untouchables as members of a single community would have struck most people as odd, if not repugnant.[316] Third, as noted, patrimonial ties crosscut sectarian identities. Muslim cavalry fought for *ksatriya* kings, and brahman scribes loyally served sultans. All were tied to the

---

[314] See n. 312 *supra*, plus Thapar, *Early India*, 438–41; K. Butler Brown, "Did Aurangzeb Ban Music?" *MAS* 41 (2007): 77–120; and overview in Talbot, "Story of Prataparudra," 282–84.

[315] Wink, "From the Mediterranean," 435; Ludden, *NCHI*, 44–48; Stein, *NCHI*, 66; *IBE*, 7–9.

[316] Talbot, "Inscribing the Other," 701, 719–21; Richard Eaton, "Temple Desecration and Indo-Muslim States," in Gilmartin and Lawrence, *Beyond Turk*, 270; Brajadulal Chattopadhyaya, *Representing the Other?* (New Delhi, 1998), 28–60, 89–91; Thapar, *Early India*, 438–39; idem, "Imagined Communities?" *MAS* 23 (1989): 209–31; Bayly, *Empire and Information*, 27–28, 54–55, 188–89; Eaton, *NCHI*, ch. 3; idem, *Rise of Islam*, 281, describing how Bengali peasants sought supernatural aid from any source at hand; Kumar, *Emergence*, 41–45, 106, 194–95, 202–37, emphasizing diversity in the 13th-century North Indian Muslim community. See too Gommans, *Mughal Warfare*, 41–42, arguing that similarities between Muslim and Hindu military adventurers – or ascetics or literati – exceeded similarities among all Muslims or among all Hindus. Clearly, however, some 16th- to 18th-century sources did use global terms "Muslim" and "Hindu." See Gordon, "Hindus, Muslims, and the Other," 13; Zelliot, "A Medieval Encounter"; n. 318 *infra*.

ruler, or his deputies, by dyadic ties of protection and obedience.[317] Fourth, as a pan-Indian warrior culture took root and Muslims penetrated small towns and rural areas, political culture separated to some extent from religious affiliation. Non-Muslim elites aped Mughal ritual, while Mughals were deeply attracted to Rajput notions of honor. Even as they insisted on the ritual supremacy of Islam, Muslim elites accepted Indian polytheists as *dhimmis,* inferior but protected peoples entitled to their own laws, provided they paid a poll tax. Nowhere do we find efforts to convert, or to impose *sharia* upon, masses of non-Muslims. True, Turkic invaders desecrated Hindu temples, but Eaton sees such acts less as an expression of iconoclastic theology than as an effort, in keeping with pre-Muslim custom, to destroy sources of sacred power with which enemy kings identified. Absent such political motives, Indo-Muslim rulers usually not only protected, but patronized non-Muslim sites.[318] One can draw analogies to 18th-century England where Anglicans extended Catholics and Dissenters a conditional toleration, or to pre-1685 France where Huguenots enjoyed a comparable status. Substituting ethnicity for religion, one thinks too of Kon-baung Burma, where Burmans conceded Mons an inferior but secure position, or Nguyen Vietnam, where Khmers and Chams played the role of Mons. Much as in India, Southeast Asians normally destroyed symbols of dependent cultures only in response to armed provocation.[319]

And yet from a comparative perspective, these analogies hide as much as they reveal. Compare first elite demography in South Asia,

---

[317] See n. 45 *supra.*

[318] Eaton, "Temple Desecration," 246–81; idem, *Temple Desecration,* 67–70, supported by Talbot, "Inscribing the Other," 718–19; Asher, *NCHI,* 253–55; Jackson, *Delhi Sultanate,* 289; Kumar, *Emergence,* 107–108. Yet one wonders whether the categorical refusal of Muslim leaders to destroy mosques, even those linked to their enemies, was simply another way of saying that they regarded fellow Muslims as part of a category intrinsically different from non-Muslims. Did Mughals not also destroy some Hindu temples without political provocation? And if mosques were not politically potent symbols, why did Vijayanagara armies, Rajput chiefs, Hindu *zamindars,* and Sikhs periodically destroy them? – for examples of which see Eaton, *Temple Desecration,* 69 n. 2; Mukhia, *The Mughals,* 26, 27; Bayly, "Pre-History of Communalism," 188; Alam, *Crisis of Empire,* 146; Wink, *Al-Hind,* vol. II, 308; Kulke and Rothermund, *History,* 180. On these patterns of symbolic statement, see too Satish Chandra, *Parties and Politics at the Mughal Court 1707–1740* (Calcutta, 1959), 29–34; idem, "Jizya and the State," 140; Wink, *Al-Hind,* vol. II, 313–33; Richards, *NCHI,* 122, 175; and Mukhia, *The Mughals,* 23–27. On *sharia,* ibid., 39 ff.

[319] *SP,* 202–206; Victor Lieberman, "Ethnic Politics in 18th-Century Burma," *MAS* 12 (1978): 455–82. Cf. Bayly, *Birth of the Modern World,* 75.

where after 1206 small ethnoreligious minorities ruled, to that in protected-zone realms, where leaders invariably championed the major ethnicity and culture. Admittedly, Great Russians in 1800 were only about half of the imperial population, and in Siam Siamese may have been a third, but each group was several times larger than its nearest rival. By contrast, although they dominated every Indo-Muslim polity, immigrants from Transoxania, Afghanistan, and Persia and their offspring may not have been 1 percent of the population.[320] In the Delhi Sultanate, Turks, Khaljis, Mongols, Persians, Afghans, Arabs, and their immediate descendants held virtually all top posts.[321] From 1565 to 1575 Persians and Turks alone constituted 78 percent of Mughal *mansabdars*.[322] From 1679 to 1707, although increasingly assimilated to Indian culture, nobles of Persian, Turkic, or Afghan ancestry still held 40–45 percent.[323] Indo-Muslim rulers sought foreign recruits not merely for their military skill or Persian learning, but also because their alien character isolated them from local society and rendered them heavily dependent on the throne. As Sunil Kumar has argued recently, historians of early Indian Islam need to focus not only on patterns of localization, but on those processes by which Muslim political society was continuously strengthened and reconstituted by fresh immigrant infusions from the Afghan-Punjab frontier. Mughal courtship of the Rajputs, who provided another 10 to 13 percent of the upper nobility, confirmed this theme insofar as Rajputs in Malwa and elsewhere, like Inner Asians, were "foreign" immigrants who fraternized little with local people.[324]

---

[320] Cf. Wink, *Al-Hind*, vol. II, 170.

[321] Chandra, *Parties and Politics*, xxv; Jackson, *Delhi Sultanate*, 184–85, 271, plus 61–85, 171–93, 278–95 *passim*; Singh, *Muslims of Indian Origin*, chs. 2–4; and n. 28 *supra*. On "racial"/ethnic distance from local Muslims, not to mention non-Muslims, demonstrated by the early Delhi Turkic oligarchy, see Singh, *Muslims of Indian Origin*, 69–94, 207, 218; Kumar, *Emergence*, 195–202; Kumar, "Ignored Elites." Ibid., 48, 75 notes further that every Sultanate dynasty from 1290 to 1526 arose on the frontier.

[322] With rank of 500 or higher. Khan, "Nobility Under Akbar," 126, offering no Afghan figures. In 1647–48, Persian, Turk, and Afghan nobles above 500 were 57 percent. Richards, *NCHI*, 145.

[323] That is, 40 percent (232 out of 575) of *mansabdar* posts ranked at 1,000 or higher (Ali, *Mughal Nobility*, 35), and 45 percent (125 out of 277) ranked at 1,500 or higher (Ali, "Towards an Interpretation," 45). I have no figures for ranks 500 and higher in this period. Cf. nn. 107, 108 *supra*.

[324] Kumar's comments, focusing on the pre-Mughal period, appear in "Ignored Elites," 48, 75, and *passim*. On Mughal-Rajput relations, see Ali, "Towards an Interpretation," 45; Hintze, *Mughal Empire*, 240. On the inclination to isolate high-ranking nobles from Indian society, see too Richards, *NCHI*, 66.

The same was true of another indigenous noble component, Indo-Muslims known as *shaikhzadas,* many of whom had lived as itinerant warriors without roots in Indian soil.[325]

Judged in religious, rather than ethnic terms, the Mughal elite remained deeply unrepresentative, albeit less starkly so. Whether recent arrivals or locals, Muslims held 92 percent of *mansabdar* posts from 1565 to 1575 and 70 percent from 1679 to 1707[326] – even though Muslims, recall, may not have exceeded 15 percent of the population.[327] If we seek a true European analogy, non-Muslims in India resembled religious minorities in England or France far less closely than they resembled majority Catholics in Protestant-ruled Ireland.

The ritual counterpart to South Asia's peculiar political demography was Muslim insistence on the ceremonial primacy, the public sovereignty, of what remained a distinctly minority faith. Even under Akbar, a growing desire to accommodate non-Muslims had to be weighed against the opinion of Muslim scholars, the *ulama,* and of *ulama*-allied nobles who feared non-Muslim inroads would threaten their position. Thus, if Akbar respected non-Muslim customs and from the late 1580s sought to create an overarching ideology incorporating fire symbolism and Safavid-style master–disciple relations, he also refused to worship Hindu gods and unambiguously identified the official state cult as Islam.[328] The 17th century saw a revivalist movement among educated Sunnis, leading to sharper boundaries against Shiites and non-Muslims and prompting Shah Jahan to adopt more orthodox positions, symbolic and practical.[329] But it was Aurangzeb who embraced orthodoxy most fervently, both as an expression of personal piety and, Satish Chandra argues, as a response to two political problems, namely, the Deccan military crisis of the 1670s that obliged the

---

[325] Gommans, *Mughal Warfare,* 72: "[E]ven in their policy to recruit an increasing number of Indian warlords, the Mughals always showed a certain preference for military men [like *shaikhzadas*] without roots in Indian soil." For an ethnic and religious overview, Ali, *Mughal Nobility,* 14–37.

[326] Khan, "Nobility Under Akbar," 126; Ali, "Toward an Interpretation," 45. Cf. Ali's earlier figures at *Mughal Nobility,* 31. In 1647–48 Muslims were 80 percent of *mansabdars* above 500 rank. Richards, *NCHI,* 145.

[327] See n. 95 *supra.*

[328] Cf. Khan, "Nobility Under Akbar," 122–27; Sharma, *Religious Policy,* 29, 36, 41, 47–48, 50–51, 58; Mukhia, *The Mughals,* 14–71; Subrahmanyam, *Explorations: Tagus to Ganges,* 123–27 and idem, *Explorations: Mughals and Franks,* 2–5, 54–55, noting that as late as 1586 Akbar defended himself against charges of Muslim laxity by using orthodox, defensive language.

[329] Richards, *NCHI,* 121–23; Sharma, *Religious Policy,* 94–115; Mukhia, *The Mughals,* 17–43.

throne to rally elite Muslim opinion, and growing *ulama* unemploy-
ment. Aurangzeb reimposed (after it had been suspended by Akbar)
the non-Muslim poll tax (*jizya*), whose proceeds now went to support
the *ulama*; doubled taxes on non-Muslim merchants, strove to implement *sharia* more rigorously among Muslims, and sought to build the
Muslim gentry as a barrier against refractory Hindu cultivators and
zamindars (even, ironically, as the number of non-Muslim *mansabdars*
continued slowly to rise).[330] Lest one exaggerate the aleatory element
in these shifts, recall that in Muslim Bijapur the mid- and late 1600s also
saw a turn from religious accommodation to systematic discrimina-
tion against non-Muslims as demanded by the increasingly influential
orthodox establishment.[331] To follow Bayly, Muslim versus non-Muslim
contestation rose after 1700 because political devolution, Islamic revivalism, and social mobility eroded local systems of compromise, even if
this rarely led to a pervasive sense of separation. Communal violence,
in other words, was quite compatible with syncretic practices.[332] Those
inclined to romanticize *sufi* ecumenicism also should consider Alam's
observation that many *sufis* exhibited a competitive spirituality and an
unwavering sense of the superiority of their own faith.[333]

In fact, recurrent, if manageable, religious strains illustrated a broader, more general tension between South Asia's original charter culture,
that of Sanskritic "Hinduism" in all its luxuriant diversity, and the
second charter formation, that of Perso-Islamic (or Turko-Persian) culture. No protected-zone society wrestled with an externally derived second charter dispensation. To recall the argument of previous chapters,
Russia escaped alien settlement and derived administrative and military, but not religious or literary, inspiration from the Mongols during
their relatively brief overlordship. If subsequently Enlightenment and
French culture reconfigured elite sensibilities, Orthodoxy remained the

---

[330] On Aurangzeb's policy, Chandra, "Jizya and the State"; Alam, *Languages*, 98–99; *IBE*,
227–36, Sharma, *Religious Policy*, ch. 5; Bayly, "Pre-History of Communalism," 190–91;
Richards, *NCHI*, 171–84, 194; Mukhia, *The Mughals*, 24–26, 35–41, 64.

[331] See n. 270 *supra*. Eaton explains these shifts in terms of a) the *ulama's* growing institutional power, b) Bijapur's need to deflect Aurangzeb's demand for orthodoxy, c) a
theodictic conviction that political decline could best be averted by enhanced piety.

[332] Bayly, "Pre-History of Communalism"; idem, *Empire and Information*, 188–89, 210–11.
For similar views, Alam, *Crisis of Empire*, 28; Chaudhuri, *Trading World*, 150; Hasan,
State and Locality, 66–70; Cole, *Roots of North Indian Shi'ism*, 228; Subrahmanyam's
sophisticated analysis in *Explorations: Tagus to Ganges*, 82–86.

[333] Alam, "Competition and Co-Existence," 40–51; idem, *Languages*, 151–68; also Eaton,
Sufis of Bijapur, 19–39 on early warrior sufis; and Richards, *NCHI*, 121–23.

official religion, and Russian the language of noble domesticity as well as administration. Though of German origin, Catherine the Great took care to acquire flawless Russian, to embrace her adopted culture with studied enthusiasm, and to style herself "Mother of All the Russias."[334] In the only other protected-zone realm subject to direct external influence, namely Siam, Tai newcomers imbibed Indic traditions and joined Mon and Khmer subjects in a Siamese synthesis so thorough that by 1550 little trace of Tai/pre-Tai difference survived.[335] That Russian and Siamese rulers identified completely with the language, religion, and ethnicity of the imperial core population shows the pull of dominant cultures in protected-zone polities.

Such accommodations Delhi and Mughal elites resolutely refused – a refusal that contributed to both their dramatic success and long-term vulnerability. To follow again Muzaffar Alam, the leading historian of Indo-Persian culture, as it fostered a new imperial ideal, "Persian, being an alien language, also drove, in some ways, a wedge between the Mughals and their subjects."[336] This had been yet more true of the Delhi sultans. Besides prestige and aesthetic grace, Perso-Islamic culture had several political appeals to would-be unifiers. It promised to constrain ethnic rivalry among immigrant warriors, to distinguish them from indigenous subjects, and thus to promote cohesion within the conquest elite.[337] At the same time, Persian offered a lingua franca, an imperial instrument, superior to any of North India's numerous vernacular dialects. Shading off into one another without stable names or standard grammars, the latter not only lacked the eclat of Persian, but seemed an impractical instrument of standardization.[338] Nor was Sanskrit an option, because "the language of the gods" was inextricable from Hinduism and lacked an administrative tradition. However, precisely because Persian culture lacked roots below a relatively thin, primarily urban stratum, the imperial center could not easily enlist local cultural solidarities. And once the empire collapsed, those identities surfaced at the expense of Persian. In a word, if imperial conquest repeatedly disrupted regional cultures, cultural entropy threatened imperial impositions. Hence, in part, India's Sisyphean oscillation.

[334] Ch. 3, n. 107 *supra*.
[335] *SP*, ch. 3.
[336] Alam, *Languages*, 144. Discussion relies on ibid., 98, 142–71, 180–84.
[337] This point receives emphasis at *IBE*, 46; and Chandra, "Jizya and the State," 137.
[338] Cf. Alam, *Languages*, chs. 3, 4; nn. 243, 276, 277 *supra*.

In this light consider again the cultural tensions that successive Turkic conquests engendered. Once can reject communalist historiography and still accept that such tensions lacked protected zone parallel. If non-Muslim pundits bewailing the end of an age were prone to self-pitying exaggeration, as royal patronage waned from the 13th century, North Indian temple construction did languish.[339] Pollock argues that the Turks' alien character led non-Muslim writers and artists to develop the royal cult of Rama precisely because of its divinizing/demonizing worldview.[340] Likewise, although eventually local writers incorporated Muslims into the natural order, Talbot has shown that 14th-century assaults in Andhra spurred anti-Turk polemics.[341] That Persian usage in this early period was less widespread than it would be under the Mughals only magnified the gap between imperial and regional styles.[342] Admittedly, provinces that rebelled against Delhi usually did not enlist indigenous cultures until they had been independent for some time, which argues against the view that cultural centrifugalism weakened Delhi in any direct or immediate sense. But the fact that most Delhi successor states eventually patronized groups not immersed in Perso-Islamic culture – for example, by recruiting Maratha and Telugu warriors and supporting non-Muslim shrines – confirms that such groups retained great influence.[343]

With the Mughals, the pendulum swung back to Turko-Persian norms, propelled by the Mughals' proud Turko-Mongol and Timurid heritage, their early political debt to the Safavids, and the resumption of large-scale western, especially Persian, immigration. As in the Delhi period, boasts of Persian or Inner Asian ancestry bred an inferiority complex among nonimmigrants close to the court. What is

---

[339] Ludden, *NCHI*, 47; Wink, *Al-Hind*, vol. II, 294–333; Chattopadhyaya, *Representing the Other?*, 18, 20, 55–60, 80–91; *IBE*, 45–47.

[340] Sheldon Pollock, "Ramayana and Political Imagination in India," *JAS* 52 (1993): 261–97; idem, *Language of the Gods*, 40, 487–94; idem, "Transformation of Culture-Power," 270–78. See too Aziz Ahmad, "Epic and Counter-Epic in Medieval India," *JAOS* 83 (1963): 470–76; Phyllis Granoff, "Tales of Broken Limbs and Bleeding Wounds," *East-West* 41 (1991): 189–203.

[341] Talbot, "Inscribing the Other," 692–722; idem, "Story of Prataparudra"; idem, *Precolonial India*, 178–79. For similar arguments, Deshpande, *Sanskrit and Prakrit*, 118–21; Narayana Rao, "Multiple Literary Cultures," 419; Gordon, *NCHI*, 13–14, 19; Bayly, *Origins of Nationality*, 29.

[342] Alam, *Languages*, 115–22; Jackson, *Delhi Sultanate*, 278–95.

[343] See nn. 257–62 *supra*.

more, western contacts inhibited the tendency for Persian language and literature to adopt an Indian inflection, for the Mughals were obsessed to "purify" Persian usages. In cultural terms, Mughal India, in Alam's words, thus "emerged as a kind of Iranian colony"[344] – an identity rendered all the more pronounced by Mughal disinterest in vernaculars. Whereas Catherine of Russia realized that her survival depended on mastering Russian, Aurangzeb, although well able to speak Hindavi, pointedly refused to do so unless absolutely unavoidable.[345]

Again I concede that Persian culture under the Mughals circulated well beyond narrow court circles. After the Mughals declined, even Maratha and Sikh polities retained Mughal procedures and Persian language for administration; while Mughal ritual, architecture, painting, and literature continued to inspire regional imitators.[346]

And yet, alongside institutional weakness, territorial overextension, and destabilizing economic growth, a *comparatively* high degree of cultural encapsulation helps to explain not only the Mughals' 18th-century collapse, but also their failure – unique among polities under review – to revive thereafter. The Mughals strove to convert Maratha, Jat, Rajput, and other rural notables into quasi-officials, but without formal systems of acculturation, had limited success.[347] In Maratha and Sikh areas, recall, provincial elites who were oriented toward the Mughal court and its elaborate ceremonial clashed with aspiring lower gentry and peasant-warriors who had little or no grounding in Perso-Islamic culture. Thus social and sectarian distinctions intertwined. Mughal officials disdained provincial insurgents as uncouth outsiders, but Maratha, Sikh, and Afghan warbands scornfully contrasted their egalitarian, masculine ethos with the "effete" urban luxury and hierarchy of the Mughal court.[348] And whereas Mughals insisted not on the exclusivity, but the ritual primacy of Islam, Marathas and Sikhs proudly conferred that honor on their own religious systems. Similar ritual inversions in the mid-1700s let non-Sikh Jat peasants

---

[344] Alam, *Languages*, 147 and 144–47. Reference to "inferiority complex" appears on 144.
[345] Ibid., 148.
[346] See nn. 113, 282, 283 *supra*.
[347] See n. 38 *supra*.
[348] See nn. 281–84 *supra*, esp. *IBE*, 238, 272; plus Rosalind O'Hanlon, "Issues of Masculinity in North Indian History," *Indian Jl. of Gender Studies* 4 (1997): 1–19; Gordon, *Marathas, Marauders*, 182–208, on different zones of military culture.

carve out a Hindu polity south of Agra.[349] If conflict between *arrivistes* and Mughal elites was largely absent in Rajasthan, from 1679 the Mughal–Rajput alliance, a cornerstone of empire since Akbar, also came under strain, in part because Aurangzeb's Muslim orthodoxy antagonized Hindu Rajput ruling houses.[350] In Awadh, Bengal, and Hyderabad, Mughal-appointed officers remained in control, but there too the rise of Hindi, Urdu, and other vernaculars reflected local leaders' determination to supplement or dislodge Persian in favor of regional dialects.[351]

Revealingly, whereas in the 1300s. Delhi sultans had faced revolts by their own governors who were as enamored of Persian norms as Delhi itself, the Mughals, although more powerful militarily than Delhi, faced far more culturally coherent and self-conscious regional challenges. This is not to resurrect an old historiography that claimed that Aurangzeb's Islamic zeal led him to persecute the non-Muslim majority, whose revolts inspired further repression, leading to imperial collapse.[352] Rather, it is to argue, more modestly, that the centripetal pull of imperial culture was insufficient to inhibit new regional expressions, and that this insufficiency hastened, in some difficult-to-calibrate but possibly critical fashion, imperial disintegration.

The weakness of Perso-Islamic strategy becomes more evident if we compare Delhi/Mughal practices to those of the Manchus. This offers a final answer to our query: why were Inner Asian empires less durable in South Asia than in China?

Delhi and Mughal elites differed from the Manchus in three respects. Most basic and obvious, they entered very different worlds. Turkic warriors found in India a resolutely polycentric political and cultural topography. If an empire were to span the subcontinent, Delhi sultans would have to create one. By contrast, the Qing inherited from the Ming a remarkably effective, durable imperial administration and culture. Manchus simply inserted themselves into the top echelons of an established system.

---

[349] And Bhumihar brahmans maintain an independent Hindu state at Benares. On these and Indo-Afghan polities, Bayly, *Rulers, Townsmen*, 17–20, 23–25; O'Hanlon, "Issues of Masculinity."

[350] Richards, *NCHI*, 179–84, 293, and n. 284 *supra*.

[351] Alam, *Languages*, 178–85; nn. 286, 287 *supra*.

[352] Cf. historiographic discussion at Brown, "Did Aurangzeb Ban Music?," 112–16; Alam, *Crisis of Empire*, 2–3.

Second, in part because of these different local inheritances and in part because of different preconquest backgrounds, Turks and Manchus adopted radically different cultural strategies. Had the Turks entered South Asia without an independent literate religious culture, had they not been heirs to a tradition of "transcendentalist intransigence,"[353] one could imagine that they, like Saka and Kusana invaders before them, well might have adopted Sanskritic high culture. So too if Delhi or Mughal elites, anticipating or continuing Sher Shah Sur's experiment, had promoted the Hindi dialect of Delhi, perhaps they could have harnessed long-standing processes of linguistic diffusion to create a locally resonant transregional medium comparable to Parisian French or Edo Japanese, or indeed to Urdu and Hindi in the 18th century.[354] But Delhi and Mughal rulers were committed to Perso-Islamic norms not only for practical and aesthetic reasons. At a deeper level, despite accommodations to non-Muslim traditions, such patronage was circumscribed by commitment to an ultimate truth which was in tension with a corrupt world, which enjoined a moral community to avoid fatal compromise with that world, and which was upheld by a Muslim clerisy devoted to maintaining religious/cultural boundaries.[355] Whether, at the end of the day, this posture yielded higher levels of integration than a Sanskrit or Hindi strategy would have done is impossible to say. But by emphasizing the finality of Islam and the superiority of Perso-Islamic theology, jurisprudence, belles lettres, and arts, imperial culture created tensions with regional cultures that were more pronounced in the early 1700s than in the late 1500s.

By contrast, we have seen that Manchus, like Xianbei, Khitans, Jurchens, and Mongols before them, came from pre-urban, substantially preliterate traditions that could not compete with the conventions of the people they conquered and that had no principled opposition to extensive borrowing. Indeed, if they were to rule so complex a society as China, inner Asians had little choice but to embrace Chinese elite culture wholesale.[356] By defining Neo-Confucianism as

---

[353] Alan Strathern, "Transcendentalist Intransigence," *CSSH* 49 (2007): 358–83 assimilating Indian Islam to a more general category of compromise-resistant faiths.

[354] On Sakas and Kusanas n. 57, and on Hindi's historic progress n. 115 *supra*.

[355] Cf. Strathern, "Transcendentalist Intransigence."

[356] The Mongols' limited political success in China was in part a function of their limited commitment to Sinic administration and culture. Strathern, pers. commun., May 17, 2007 makes the interesting point that although the Romans, unlike the Manchus, boasted a sophisticated literate culture, the Romans were willing to adopt barbarian

the possession of all cultured humans, they created a bond with subject elites far more secure than that which the Turks produced by
introducing a second charter dispensation. In China, one might conclude, Inner Asian political success owed much to Inner Asian cultural
poverty.

This leads to a third difference in Inner Asian profiles, also conducive
to greater stability in China, namely different degrees of elite ethnic
cohesion. Each Delhi sultan and Mughal emperor collected nobles of
diverse background to form, in effect, an ad hoc warband. Absent a single core ethnicity, Sultanate and Mughal courts sought cohesion both
by emphasizing Perso-Islamic norms and personal obligation and by
balancing ethnic factions. That such policies did not always succeed is
shown by ethnically based, at times profoundly destabilizing upheavals
under both the Delhi Sultanate[357] and the Mughals; the latter disturbances started with an Uzbek revolt against Akbar and continued with
Aurangzeb's struggles against Rajputs and Marathas.[358] Recall too that
Westerner versus Deccani splits ripped apart the Bahmani Sultanate and
plagued some of its successors. By contrast, Manchus were an ascriptive, ethnically coherent tribal confederation all of whose members were
subject to close control in the Eight Banners. Even as they patronized
Neo-Confucian culture, their formula for cohesion required that they
retain customs, residence, and speech distinct from those of the Chinese. If some early Manchu princes allied with Chinese bannermen and
literati, the Manchu core, unlike its South Asian counterparts, never
fragmented. Similar commitments to what Mark Elliott terms "ethnic
sovereignty" underlay Khitan and Jurchen policy.[359] In effect, by combining core exclusion with broad cultural assimilation, the Manchus
maximized both central control and local influence.

Cohesion Among Conquest Elites: The British

Such views, finally, allow us to place the British in wider perspective.
If we were to arrange conquest regimes examined in Chapters 5 and 6

gods because they, like Inner Asians in China, did not subscribe to an exclusive
religious tradition.

[357] Jackson, *Delhi Sultanate*, chs. 4, 9; Singh, *Muslims of Indian Origin*, chs. 2–4.
[358] On Mughal ethnic factionalism, Khan, "Nobility Under Akbar"; Richards, *NCHI*,
chs. 8, 10–12; Mukhia, *The Mughals*, 44; Alam, *Crisis of Empire*, 20–23; Chandra, *Parties
and Politics*, xxvii–xxxiv, 9–10, 244 ff.; and n. 350 *supra*.
[359] Elliott, *Manchu Way*, 4–6, 276, 347–57. See Ch. 5 *supra*.

on a continuum ranging from most to least dependent on the culture of the host population, we would start with the Xianbei, Jurchen, and Manchus, move to the Deccan sultans and Mughals, and end with the Mongols and Delhi sultans. The British lay near this latter pole.[360]

To be sure, as I already indicated, the British in some ways continued existing trends and accommodated themselves to local conventions. They claimed the mantle of the Mughals, patronized Hindu and Muslim institutions, pursued policies of military fiscalism similar to those in other Indian states, relied at first on Indian commercial networks and scribal talent, and advanced the trend toward caste distinctions.

Yet, despite or because of their tiny numbers,[361] the British also represented a genuinely novel force not only militarily and economically, as we saw, but in cultural terms. In lieu of an earlier sympathetic appreciation of Indian religion and literature, in the late 1700s and early 1800s British leaders, motivated by a combination of military superiority, moralistic liberalism, and evangelical Christianity, began to treat indigenous customs with ever greater condescension and to follow a logic of racial separation, as Thomas Trautmann's analysis of the turn from "Indomania" to "Indophobia" has shown. Whereas an older generation of British scholars delighted in discovering links between Sanskrit and Greek, and thus between ancient Indian and European civilizations, new biological theories of race dismissed Indians of presumed Aryan ancestry as hopelessly contaminated by having mixed their blood with indigenous peoples. Along with British patriotism, which soared in the aftermath of the Napoleonic wars, this outlook left Britons increasingly insensitive to indigenous aspiration and divorced from local society. Their position thus contrasted with that of Mughal emperors, whose primary criteria of distinction were religiocultural, hence potentially inclusive, and who welcomed strategic marriages with Rajput princesses. For their part, the Manchus never claimed that Chinese were racially inferior and awarded Chinese with posts far more senior than the British allowed Indians, at least in the 19th century. Nonetheless, as a practical matter the British embrace of racial/ethnic cleavage bore some resemblance to Manchu barriers to Manchu–Chinese intermarriage and policies of ethnic and residential apartheid.[362] Whereas English Company

---

[360] Cf. discussion of continua in Ch. 1, n. 168; Ch. 7, and Conclusion *infra*.
[361] Cf. Washbrook, "South India 1770–1840," 492; Marshall, *East Indian Fortunes*, 22–24.
[362] See Ch. 5, n. 249 *supra*.

officials and common soldiers alike once had lived openly with Indian mistresses (*bibis*), in the 19th century such liaisons were increasingly stigmatized, along with their Eurasian offspring. Eurasians in India thus came to comprise a distinct community suspended uneasily between British and Indians – and disdained by both. Bars to Eurasian employment in the Company from 1793 followed the dismissal of all senior Indian officers in Company service. If its full implications would not be felt until later in the century, by 1830 the social, residential, and psychological distance between rulers and ruled, especially in the increasingly segregated British colonial cities, already was formidable.[363]

Along with racial endogamy and derogation of Indian ways arose a British commitment to assimilate educated Indians to British culture and thus to liberate them from their own benighted past – a cultural program whose ambition recalled Perso-Islamic policy but that lacked the latter's openness to intermarriage and that Trautmann therefore terms "one-way asexual assimilation."[364] Well articulated by the 1830s and symbolized by the replacement of Persian by English as the language of government and education, the goal was not merely to create a class of Indians qualified at some uncertain time to help the British run India, but to form an elite that was, in the words of Thomas Babington Macaulay (scion of a famous evangelical family), "Indian in blood and colour, but English in taste, in opinions, in morals, and in intellect."[365] This was to be effected by symbolic impositions like the prohibition of *sati* (widow self-immolation), by private cultural exchanges, and by the founding of government secondary schools in India's major cities (at a time when no government-run schools existed in England itself). For their part, British evangelical Protestants were no less convinced than their Turko-Persian predecessors that they alone could save India from idolatry.

In short, the British mix of racial endogamy, racial monopoly of senior posts, and cultural/religious proselytism – in effect, a third charter dispensation – had elements of both Mughal and Qing policy, but was itself *sui generis*. So too, the pace and direction of British intervention in India responded to forces – the global struggle with France, demands of

---

[363] Metcalfs, *Concise History*, 58–66, 80–88; Trautmann, *Aryans and British India*, chs. 3–7; Bayly, *NCHI*, 69–71, 78, 81; Washbrook, "South India 1779–1840," 489–90; Keay, *India*, 427, with trenchant quotes from Thomas Munro; and n. 53 *supra*.

[364] Trautmann, *Aryans and British India*, 110.

[365] Ibid., 111, text from 1835.

British trade, domestic British political and intellectual currents – that in origin lay even farther afield from South Asia than forces in Inner Asia.

CONCLUSION

South Asia simultaneously illustrated and resisted the move toward sustained integration that we find in other sectors of Eurasia. As such it shared critical features with both protected-zone realms and China, but conformed fully to neither pattern.

As in individual protected-zone realms and in China, so in South Asia at large, intervals between major political formations grew shorter, successive formations controlled larger territories, while administration grew more efficient. As elsewhere, administrative innovations were particularly notable between c. 900 and 1300 and again from 1550 to 1800. An exceptionally intrusive and extensive polity that took root c. 1560 after a period of disorder and that profited from new economic linkages, firearms, and administrative experiment, the Mughal empire was South Asia's equivalent to early modern protected-zone and Qing states. No less familiar, cultural systems – starting with Sanskritic brahmanism and *bhakti* and continuing with Perso-Islamic culture and orthodox caste practices – implicated wider strata and more extensive regions. In accustomed fashion, political and cultural integration drew strength from a synergistic expansion in population, cultivation, and domestic and international trade, with growth particularly vigorous between c. 850 and 1300 during the Medieval Climate Anomaly, and again between c. 1550 and 1700.

Yet if South Asia resembled protected-zone realms and China in these integrative trends, Indian political development was uniquely oscillatory and discontinuous. Between c. 300 and 1300 much of Europe, Southeast Asia, and South Asia alike moved through three stages: a) universal transregional empires (Roman, Angkorian, Gupta), which promoted universal languages/cultures (Latin, Sanskrit); b) imperial fragmentation, albeit with universal languages retaining considerable prestige; c) postimperial regional kingdoms that patronized vernaculars at the expense of universal languages. After the Gupta-inspired Sanskrit cosmopolis of the first millennium fragmented, had South Asia been left to itself, it is conceivable that this third stage would have yielded increasingly stable, culturally distinct kingdoms on the European or Southeast Asian model. The same potential was inherent during two other periods of pronounced regionalism, namely, those that lay between the decline of the Delhi Sultanate and Mughal conquests, and between the Mughal decline and British consolidation.

At the end of the day, however, South Asian regional kingdoms were circumscribed by the Indo-Gangetic plain's physical superiority and by a variety of unsympathetic cultural practices, but most basically, by external invasions. In the 12th to 14th and the 16th and 17th centuries these incursions were preeminently the work of Turks and Turko-Mongols, seconded by Afghans, Tajiks, and Persians; while from 1765 the English East India Company destroyed Mughal successor states. To be sure, even without political patronage, India's regions continued to nourish rich vernacular traditions. But external conquests precluded stable connections between those traditions and regional kingdoms – with self-conscious continuities in name, territory, dynasty, institutions, and religion – such as became ever more secure from 900 to 1830 throughout the protected zone.

In this vulnerability to Inner Asian military power South Asia resembled China (as well as Persia and Southwest Asia). As in China cavalry superiority provided Inner Asians with a critical physical advantage. At the same time they benefited from cumulative administrative expertise and more sustained interactions with prosperous sedentary cultures, especially after c. 900. In dynamics and broad chronology, the two-stage evolution of Inner Asian rule in China, from Khitan, Jurchen, and Mongol states c. 900–1370 to post-1644 Qing dominion, resembled the transition in South Asia from the Delhi Sultanate to the Mughals.

But if South Asia thus resembled China, the fortunes of empire in those two realms also diverged. Most obviously, in India transregional formations suffered from some of the same weaknesses as did Indian regional states, namely, rural militarization, nested sovereignties, weak political indoctrination, caste segmentation, and low levels of literacy. South Asian alphabets also nurtured politically pregnant subimperial cultures more readily than did Chinese logographic scripts, while South Asian warfare, at least under the Mughals, required more destabilizing taxes than we generally find in China. What is more, if Islamic administrative and military traditions promised critical advantages to would-be unifiers, Islamic ritual primacy left Turko-Persian rulers more distant from a segment of provincial elites than did the Manchus' uninhibited embrace of Neo-Confucianism. That is to say, whereas Inner Asians in China inherited demonstrably successful systems that had been cohering since at least the Han, in South Asia they were obliged to try to create such systems *de novo* and to promote a second charter cultural dispensation as an aid to empire. The British resembled Inner Asians in the violence of their assault on Indian polycentrism and the freshness and self-sufficiency of their cultural impositions. In turn, without long-lived imperial structures to define and police cultural boundaries, movements of cultural integration across South Asia at large between c. 900 and 1800 remained less coherent than in China proper, comparable perhaps to those in Europe at large.

Supporting neither a stable multistate system nor long-lived transregional empires, South Asia thus wavered between the experience of Europe and mainland Southeast Asia, on the one hand, and of China, on the other. As we shall find in the next chapter, in island Southeast Asia Iberians and Dutchmen played a role similar to that in India of Inner Asians and the British.

CHAPTER SEVEN

Locating the Islands

OVERVIEW: THE RELATION OF MARITIME
TO MAINLAND SOUTHEAST ASIA

As a historian of mainland Southeast Asia, I began this project in order to compare my region to other sectors of Eurasia. Having considered protected-zone realms and parts of the exposed zone, in this, the final chapter, I return to Southeast Asia to examine its island, or maritime, component.[1] By some yardsticks, mainland and maritime Southeast Asia together constituted a reasonably coherent, distinctive sphere. But while cultural commonalities endured, after 1511 political trends began gradually to assimilate the island world, hitherto part of Eurasia's protected zone, to exposed-zone status. The mainland, by contrast, remained sheltered for another 300 to 350 years, with all that implied for indigenous agency and political continuity. As a region that completes our inquiry into Southeast Asia and bridges both of our main analytical categories, the archipelago, then, seems a particularly fitting area with which to conclude.

---

[1] Whereas mainland Southeast Asia consists of present-day Myanmar, Thailand, Laos, Cambodia, and Vietnam, island – also variously termed "archipelagic" or "maritime" – Southeast Asia comprises the contemporary states of Malaysia, Singapore, Indonesia, Brunei, the Philippines, and Timor Leste (East Timor). Although obviously not an island, peninsular Malaysia is conventionally included in "island" Southeast Asia because a) its economy relied on maritime trade and, along with island areas, attracted sustained European involvement far earlier than the mainland; b) its language is in the same Austronesian family as island languages; c) it helped to generate the Muslim identity that now dominates Malaysia, Indonesia, Brunei, and the southern Philippines.

Consider first cultural and social parallels between mainland and islands. Compared to Europe, China, or India, all of Southeast Asia is fragmented, whether by mountains, jungle, or seas; and stretches of fertile land are modest. Ecological heterogeneity and poor communications ensured that linguistic variety was pronounced and ethnicity was relatively local. Moreover, whether because of limited arable, high mortality, weak immigration, or chronic warfare, population densities in the region at large in 1600 may have averaged only a sixth or seventh those of South Asia and China.[2] By extension, across Southeast Asia labor was usually a more critical resource than land, and far-flung population clusters mandated decentralized state structures in which provincial planets revolved around an imperial sun whose gravitational pull ebbed rapidly with distance. On the farthest margins of each "solar polity"[3] or indeed outside the state's purview entirely, that is to say, in the hills of the mainland, in the interior of most islands, and in many small islands, dwelled tribal peoples whose animism, illiteracy, shifting cultivation, and nonagricultural pursuits distinguished them from settled agrarian populations. If in 1800 such groups still had counterparts in China and South Asia, in western Europe the last holdouts from world religions and state impositions had disappeared centuries earlier.

With some exceptions,[4] kinship across Southeast Asia was cognatic, which meant that descent was reckoned through both male and female lines and that women retained substantial inheritance rights and autonomy, at least compared to China or India. Political authority typically depended less on lineage than personal charisma, what O. W. Wolters termed "soul stuff."[5] Southeast Asians sought security by enlisting influential patrons: in the visible world, men of prowess, and in the invisible world, ancestor and spirit agents of illness, fertility, and wealth. Propitiation rites, central to what Anthony Reid called "Southeast Asian religion," flourished long after the introduction of textual faiths – Theravada Buddhism, Islam, Christianity, Neo-Confucianism – that were

---

[2] An estimated 5.5 people per square kilometer compared to 32 in South Asia and 37 in China, excluding Tibet. *AC*, vol. I, 13–15.

[3] *SP*, 33 and Ch. 1 *supra*. "Solar polity" is more descriptively apt than "galactic polity" or "mandala."

[4] Including Minangkabau, Chams, and elite Vietnamese.

[5] O. W. Wolters, *History, Culture, and Region in Southeast Asian Perspectives* (rev. ed., Ithaca, 1999), 18–19, 93–95. On female roles in Southeast Asia, Barbara Watson Andaya, *The Flaming Womb* (Honolulu, 2006).

concerned more with postdeath status or issues of social harmony than with control of quotidian events.[6] Other region-wide features included tattooing, betel-chewing, cockfighting, debt bondage, a rice–fish diet, and a maritime/riverine orientation.

Of course, such features were not uniformly distributed, while individual traits also could be found in Southeast China, South India, or Oceania. And yet this complex was sufficiently widespread and distinctive to render the area east of modern India, south of China, west of New Guinea, and north of Australia a moderately distinct cultural zone.[7]

Any consideration of Southeast Asian political chronology and agency must enhance this sense of regional coherence. In a word, for much of their history both mainland and islands were protected-zone realms whose rhythms, though hardly in lockstep, remained broadly coordinated. Like northern Europe and Japan, all of Southeast Asia was sufficiently isolated that bronze, iron, and writing appeared quite late. But by importing religious/political complexes from older centers, local peoples compressed a process that, were it to proceed entirely by trial and error, would have been far more leisurely. Thus as in northern Europe and Japan, across Southeast Asia in the mid- and late first millennium C.E., Indian contacts joined local dynamics to engender complex charter states. Between 1300 and 1500 all such polities disintegrated, in part because economic growth overstrained still weak central institutions. In familiar fashion from 1400/1450 to c. 1650 such disorders yielded to a fresh phase of consolidation that drew strength from textual religions, expanding long-distance trade, firearms, intensifying warfare, and local experiment. The formation of Islamic polities in the archipelago after 1400/1450 thus paralleled the consolidation of new mainland states, not to mention Muscovy and Valois France. Until the 16th or 17th century in the islands and until 1824 on the mainland, northern mountains and encompassing seas ensured that political and

---

[6] *AC*, vol. II, 136–40; Anthony Reid, *Charting the Shape of Early Modern Southeast Asia* (Chiang Mai, 1999), 17–22. Also Barbra Watson Andaya and Yoneo Ishii, "Religious Developments in Southeast Asia, c. 1500–1800," in *CHSEA*, 508–13.

[7] Andaya, *Flaming Womb*, 11–41, 226–31, and *passim* offers an articulate formulation of Southeast Asian distinctiveness. Cf. *AC*, vols. I and II, 136–40 and *passim*; Wolters, *History, Culture, and Region*, esp. 11–40, 107–25; and comments by that famed iconoclast Sanjay Subrahmanyam, "Notes on Circulation and Asymmetry in Two Mediterraneans, c. 1400–1800," in Claude Guillot et al., eds., *From the Mediterranean to the China Sea* (Wiesbaden, 1998), 21–43.

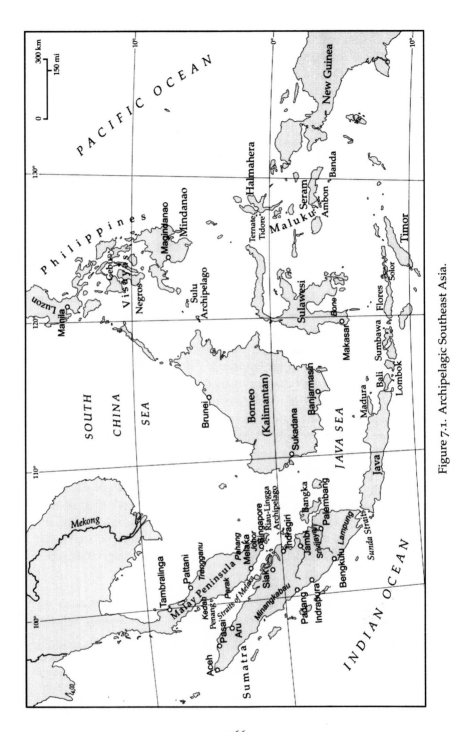

Figure 7.1. Archipelagic Southeast Asia.

766

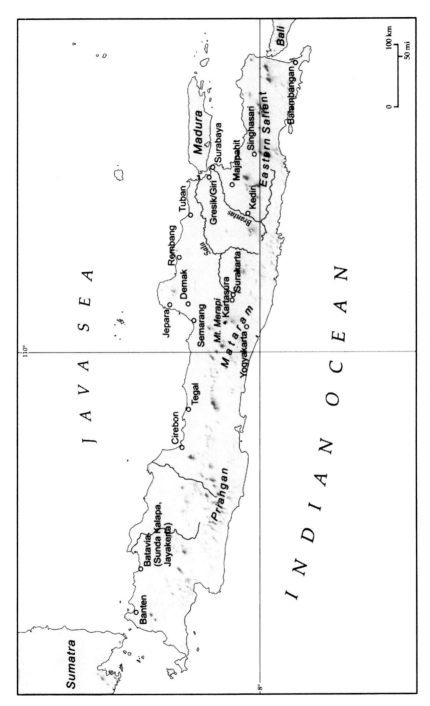

Figure 7.2. Java.

cultural integration remained entirely in the hands of indigenous, not external, agents.

Despite these shared features, mainland and maritime Southeast Asia differed in at least three basic respects, all in part a function of geography. First, the peninsula and archipelago were inherently more fragmented than the mainland's north–south corridors and therefore supported weaker, less historically continuous polities. Because export-producing zones in the islands often lay at considerable physical and cultural distances from ports, far-flung coastal cities could have closer contact, via the sea, with one another than with the interior of their own islands. Moreover, outside Southwest Sulawesi and Central and East Java, easily leached soils and excessive rainfall deprived ports of rich agrarian hinterlands. Nowhere was this more obvious than in the western archipelago, including the Malay peninsula, eastern Sumatra, West Java and West Borneo, an area Reid terms Southeast Asia's "empty center."[8] The core populations of some major archipelagic states did not equal 10 percent of those of Burma or Dong Kinh. Their ensuing reliance on mainland or Javanese rice left such states vulnerable to blockade and precluded those demographic densities that let mainland valleys overawe interior districts and recover from periodic defeat with relative ease. Central and East Java, with rich volcanic soils, did support populations comparable to those of Burma, Siam, or Vietnam.[9] But Java's population was divided into more or less isolated pockets, separated by mountains and swamps; and although the Brantas and Sala were major riverine arteries, neither drained a catchment as large or populous as the Irrawaddy or Chaophraya. In short, whereas Volume 1 traced the progressive consolidation of three overarching political-cum-cultural systems in mainland Southeast Asia, this chapter must consider the kaleidoscopic fortunes of 10 to 15 small polities – which unfortunately makes for a far less tidy narrative. Indeed, continuities in name,

---

[8] Anthony Reid, "*Negeri*," in Mogens Herman Hansen, ed., *A Comparative Study of Thirty City-State Cultures* (Copenhagen, 2000), 417–29. Cf. David Henley, "Population and the Means of Subsistence," *JSEAS* 36 (2005): 337–72; Charles Fisher, *South-East Asia: A Social, Economic and Political Geography* (London, 1964), ch. 7. Much as in the interior mainland, low population densities correlated with high levels of ethnic/linguistic heterogeneity.

[9] This was true also of Bali and Southwest Sulawesi. In parts of Java and Bali demographic densities actually exceeded those on the mainland, but because areas of intense agriculture were limited, the total population of Java and of Bali was smaller than or similar to those of Burma, Siam, or Vietnam. *AC*, vol. I, 14.

territory, dynasty, institutions, and elite culture may have been even less marked in archipelagic Southeast Asia than in India.

Second, again with the chief exception of Central and East Java, which seem to have followed an internal dynamic partly independent of maritime trade, island political economies tended to be more sensitive to international commercial currents than their mainland counterparts. Such receptivity reflected not only the islands' more modest agrarian base, but also the unique presence of pepper and fine spices and the fact that virtually all seaborne traffic between West and East Asia necessarily passed through the western straits and the South China Sea. An orientation to Indian Ocean trade helps to explain archipelagic acceptance of Islam, which in turn favored a more pronounced postcharter cultural rupture in much of the island world than on the mainland.

A third distinction, closely related to the second but more critical for Eurasian perspectives, is that maritime Southeast Asia lay open to European interventions appreciably earlier than the mainland. After several pendulum swings, as Volume 1 suggested, the debate between "externalist" historiography, emphasizing the European impact, and "autonomous" views, which minimize that contribution, now has settled closer to the former position.[10] By seizing the archipelago's key commercial ganglion at Melaka in 1511, the Portuguese provided major, if quite unintended, spurs to local state formation. From 1571 the Spanish began to transform what is now the central and northern Philippines, which to that point had resisted the pull of world religions and had known only local polities. Finally, with episodic but cumulative force, from the early 1600s to 1830 the Dutch emasculated the archipelago's chief Muslim polities.

In other words, from the 16th century the sea, which had protected island Southeast Asia from sustained attack by external actors, became an avenue for such incursions.[11] By subjecting local societies to novel political, and in the Philippines cultural, demands, Iberians and

---

[10] Externalist vs. autonomous debates concern not only the European period, but early Indianization. *SP*, 6–15; M. A. P. Meilink-Roelofsz, *Asian Trade and European Influence in the Indonesian Archipelago Between 1500 and About 1630* (The Hague, 1962), 1–12.

[11] Alan Strathern, "Sri Lanka in the Long Early Modern Period" (ms) argues that Sri Lanka underwent a similar transition in the 16th and 17th centuries. See Ch. 6, n. 224 *supra*. This is to deny neither that the Colas in 1025 and the Mongols in 1293 raided Sumatra and Java, nor that Southeast Asian port cities were constantly subject to seaborne attack from within the region. I claim merely that until the 16th century no actors from outside Southeast Asia launched a sustained, successful seaborne invasion.

Dutch – "white Inner Asians" – became agents of early modern transformation in somewhat the same way that Inner Asians influenced China and South Asia, or the British eventually altered Indian trajectories. The Spanish project began at the same time as Mughal expansion and was even more revolutionary in its cultural and political effects. Dutch interventions started later, were more halting, more commercial, far less culturally ambitious, and less territorially cohesive. Yet by 1830, indeed the late 1600s, the Dutch too had moved beyond a spoiler role to lay the foundations for an unprecedentedly extensive territorial and commercial system. *Mutatis mutandis*, those assemblages begun by alien conquest elites in the 16th and 17th centuries provided a foundation for the contemporary states of the Philippines, Indonesia, China, and India. By contrast, limited vulnerability to naval power, larger populations, and fewer commercial attractions delayed at least until 1824 European penetration of the mainland, where Europeans were obliged to preserve, with only minor modifications, states and ethnicities that had been developing since the 10th century.

1. THE CHARTER ERA IN THE ARCHIPELAGO, C. 650–1350/1500

Early State Formation

Inadequate information about the protohistoric period joined a fascination with the Sanskrit inscriptions and Indic monuments that "suddenly" appeared in the mid- and late first millennium to foster an early scholarly conviction that Southeast Asian state formation depended entirely on Indian initiatives. In curious contrast to the aforementioned debate on early European influence, recent archeology has modified those "externalist" understandings. In the archipelago, for example, it is now appreciated that some areas supported advanced chiefdoms, stratified societies, and complex systems of symbolic legitimation long before the domestication of Indian culture, and that Southeast Asians pioneered trade circuits across the Bay of Bengal and the South China Sea by using vessels built not with foreign, but distinctively local techniques.[12]

---

[12] Including V-shaped dowelled hulls, keels, quarter rudders, and sewn planks. On early archipelagic state formation, Peter Bellwood, *Prehistory of the Indo-Malaysian Archipelago* (rev. ed., Honolulu, 1997), chs. 5, 9; John Miksic, "The Classical Cultures of Indonesia," in Ian Glover and Peter Bellwood, eds., *Southeast Asia from Prehistory to History* (London, 2004), 234–56; Elisabeth Bacus, "The Archaeology of the Philippine Archipelago," ibid., 257–81; Pierre-Yves Manguin, "The Archaeology of Early Maritime Polities of

Such processes notwithstanding, recent studies also point to the archipelago's late civilizational genesis and its reliance on external motifs once rapid development got underway. North China was producing bronze by 2200–1900 B.C.E. and iron by 800–600 B.C.E., while in North India the comparable dates were roughly 2500 B.C.E. and 1200–600 B.C.E. But in the islands we do not find bronze or iron until c. 300–200 B.C.E., and when these metals appeared, they apparently did so together, almost certainly as a result of contacts with mainland Southeast Asia and more especially India.[13] This same combination of historical lag and substantial reliance on South Asia characterized state formation. From at least the early first millennium Indian religious and political motifs began to modify indigenous conceptualizations and to provide them with a prestigious overlay.

Given the islands' trade links to China and China's strong imprint on *ritsuryo* Japan, why did Southeast Asia look to South Asia rather than China for inspiration? Until the early second millennium C.E. Chinese traders were far less active in Southeast Asian waters than Indians. China's logographic script was inherently more difficult to master than Indian alphabets, while Confucianism, as a civil cult, probably was less mobile or sympathetic to local deities than were Hinduism or Buddhism. Prehistoric Southeast Asian cultures also may have been closer to those of coastal India than of South China.[14]

Having become familiar with the work of brahmans, monks, and artisans during visits to India, Southeast Asians either acquired Indian expertise *in situ* or invited specialists to return with them to glorify local courts and temples. Not only Hinayana and Mahayana Buddhism,

---

Southeast Asia," ibid., 282–313; Jan Wisseman Christie, "State Formation in Early Maritime Southeast Asia," *BKI* 151 (1995): 235–88; Himanshu Ray, *The Winds of Change* (Delhi, 1994), chs. 4, 5; Michel Jacq-Hergoualc'h, *The Malay Peninsula* (Leiden, 2002), chs. 3–8; O. W. Wolters, *Early Indonesian Commerce* (Ithaca, 1967), chs. 9–13. On ships, Pierre-Yves Manguin, "Trading Ships of the South China Sea," *JESHO* 36 (1993): 253–80; idem, "The Southeast Asian Ship," *JSEAS* 11 (1980): 266–76; Leonard Andaya, "Interactions with the Outside World and Adaptations in Southeast Asian Society, 1500–1800," in *CHSEA*, 372–76.

[13] Cf. Ch. 5, n. 208 *supra*; *CIHC*, 22; Charles Maisels, *Early Civilizations of the Old World* (London, 1999), 216, 222, 237–38, 252–56, 311–13; Glover and Bellwood, *Southeast Asia*, 36–38, 68-83, 91; Bellwood, *Prehistory*, ch. 9; Charles Higham, *The Bronze Age of Southeast Asia* (Cambridge, 1996), 301–304, 308.

[14] Hermann Kulke, "Indian Colonies, Indianization or Cultural Convergence?," in H. Schulte Nordholt, ed., *Onderzoek in Zuidoost-Azie* (Leiden, 1990), 8–32; idem, "The Early and the Imperial Kingdom in Southeast Asian History," in David Marr and A. C. Milner, eds., *Southeast Asia in the 9th to 14th Centuries* (Singapore, 1986), 1–22.

with their strong commercial sympathies, but Vaisnava and Saivite *bhakti* sects became popular.[15] At the same time, as Wolters emphasized, Southeast Asians constantly reshaped Indic motifs to express local understandings of sacred space, "soul stuff," and spirit propitiation.[16] In substance and broad chronology, these processes of borrowing and localization paralleled the rise of urban, literate societies in Kiev, *ritsuryo* Japan, Burma, and Angkor, and the expansion in India of Sheldon Pollock's "Sanskrit cosmopolis." Or to follow Hermann Kulke, social convergence produced "universal" Indian kingship on both sides of the Bay of Bengal.[17]

An Archipelagic Charter State: Srivijaya

Evidence of Indianized state formation has been found scattered around the archipelago. On Borneo's east coast, for example, 5th-century inscriptions recorded gifts to brahmans by a *maharaja* whose grandfather, without Sanskritic dignity, probably had been a petty chief.[18] One would expect that the Malay peninsula, athwart the route from India to China, also supported early kingdoms, and in fact Chinese sources from the 2nd to 7th centuries refer to at least three harbor polities on the east peninsular coast and another near Kedah on the west. Some of these towns, which sent regular envoys to China and India, reportedly contained hundreds of brahmans and large communities of Indian and Persian traders.[19]

However, the most powerful pre-1400 archipelagic states lay neither on Borneo nor the peninsula, but in Southeast Sumatra and Central and East Java. The former controlled access to the Straits of Melaka, the main chokepoint for Indian Ocean–South China Sea traffic to which peninsular ports served merely as feeders. The great strength of Central and East Java was its ability to combine the archipelago's richest agrarian

---

[15] Ray, *Winds of Change*; Manguin, "Archaeology of Early Polities," 303–305; Wisseman Christie, "State Formation," 279.

[16] Wolters, *History, Culture, and Region*, 58–95; 155–76; idem, "Khmer 'Hinduism' in the Seventh Century," in R. B. Smith and W. Watson, eds., *Early South East Asia* (Oxford, 1979), 427–42.

[17] See Ch. 6, nn. 14, 19, 69 *supra*; Glover and Bellwood, *Southeast Asia*, chs. 3, 5–9; *SP*, 88–119, 216–33, 348–67.

[18] *HM*, 31–32, 60; J. G. de Casparis, *India and Maritime South East Asia* (Kuala Lumpur, 1983), 3–5.

[19] Jacq-Hergoualc'h, *Malay Peninsula*, 100–231; Manguin, "Archaeology of Early Polities," 294–96; Paul Wheatley, *The Golden Khersonese* (Kuala Lumpur, 1961), 14–60.

base with access to specialized east archipelagic products. One could argue that discontinuities associated with the introduction of Islam in the island world after c. 1400 rendered pre-1400 charter legacies weaker than on the mainland. But to the extent that the islands did boast charter legacies, they derived chiefly from the famed thalassocracy of Srivijaya in Southeast Sumatra, whose traditions were recast in 15th-century Melaka, and from Javanese Majapahit (1293–1527?), which adumbrated the last great Javanese state of Mataram (founded c. 1575).

Consider first Srivijaya. Recent research has animated what for long remained a ghostly conjecture. In 1918 George Coedes brought together inscriptions, Chinese and Arab texts, Tamil charters, and a few archeological finds to postulate the existence from c. 650 of a long-lived maritime state known as Srivijaya centered at Palembang, on the Musi River, in Sumatra. The difficulty of interpreting early records and the discovery on the peninsula of archeological remains richer than those around Palembang led many scholars either to doubt the existence of such a polity or to place its capital far from the Musi.[20] But subsequent studies of Chinese sources, including Wolters' work on Srivijayan origins and Billy K. L. So's examination of Fujian records, have joined Franco-Indonesian archeology to confirm, and at the same time greatly to amplify, the basic story provided by Coedes.[21]

Southeast Sumatra's prosperity probably began in the 4th and 5th centuries when political difficulties in North China and the expanding South China market combined to favor the shipment by sea of West Asian luxuries that had been entering China overland via Inner

---

[20] For Coedes' early scholarship, George Coedes and Louis-Charles Damais, *Sriwijaya: History, Religion and Language of an Early Malay Polity*, Pierre-Yves Manguin, ed. (Kuala Lumpur, 1992). For Arab sources, G. R. Tibbetts, *A Study of the Arabic Texts Containing Material on South-East Asia* (Leiden, 1979), 43–60, 100–28; Gabriel Ferrand, ed. and tr., *Relations de Voyages et Textes Geographiques Arabes, Persans et Turks Relatifs a l'Extreme-Orient du VIII au XVIII Siecles*, 2 vols. (Paris, 1913–1914), vol. I, 22–30, 64–66, 78–100 *passim*, 107–11, 144, 175; and vol. II, 297–98, 310, 342.

[21] Major works in the last 40 years of Srivijayan scholarship include Wolters, *Early Indonesian Commerce*; idem, *The Fall of Srivijaya in Malay History* (London, 1970); idem, "Restudying Some Chinese Writings on Sriwijaya," *Indonesia* 42 (1986): 1–41; Billy K. L. So, *Prosperity, Region, and Institutions in Maritime China* (Cambridge, MA, 2000), 220–26; idem, "Dissolving Hegemony or Changing Trade Pattern?," *JSEAS* 29 (1998): 295–309; SEAMEO Project in Archaeology and Fine Arts, *Final Report: Consultative Workshop on Archaeological and Environmental Studies on Srivijaya* (Bangkok, 1985); Pierre-Yves Manguin, "Le programme de fouilles sur les sites de Sriwijaya, " *BEFEO* 79 (1992): 272–77; idem, "Palembang and Sriwijaya," *JMBRAS* 66 (1993): 23–46; Hermann Kulke, "'Kaduatan Srivijaya' – Empire or Kraton of Srivijaya?," *BEFEO* 80 (1993): 159–80.

Asia. Although West Javanese and Malay harbors profited, Sumatran ports drew the lion's share, in part because they were able to dominate the Straits, the most practicable route for east–west bulk trade, but also because they learned to supplement Persian/Arab drugs and fumigants prized in China with similar local products. What is more, because Chinese did not sail oceangoing vessels before the 8th or 9th century and Arab shipping east of Sri Lanka was yet limited, transport from the Straits to China continued to rely on Indian and, more especially, Indonesian ships.[22] By the 500s an Indianized port called Gantoli in Chinese sources and vaguely located in Southeast Sumatra had taken the lead in collecting forest products and transhipping goods to China. Although a subsequent trade slump apparently eclipsed Gantoli, Wolters argues that its policies of commercial coordination and Chinese alliance paved the way for Srivijaya when trade revived in the mid-600s.[23]

Srivijaya, so far as we know, was the first island Southeast Asian polity to command widespread attention outside the region. The wealth of its ruler, who figured in some Mideastern accounts as among the great kings of the world, and its patronage of Buddhism were recognized from Baghdad to Tang and Song China.[24] Like Gantoli before it presumably, and like the Portuguese 800 years later, Srivijaya sought not a territorial empire, but control over strategic points on the main trade routes. Dependencies were obliged to supply specified goods for export and to divert vessels to Srivijaya's harbor. Old Malay inscriptions from the 680s refer to bloody conquests of rival ports. In 695 a Chinese pilgrim reported that Kedah had become a vassal, while a 775 inscription has been interpreted as showing Srivijayan authority over part of the east peninsula as well.[25] An 11th-century Chinese account described

---

[22] Wolters, *Early Indonesian Commerce*, 145–58, 250; Manguin, "Southeast Asian Ship," 275–76; J. V. Mills, "Arab and Chinese Navigators in Malaysian Waters in about A.D. 1500," *JMBRAS* 47 (1974): 7–8.

[23] Wolters, *Early Indonesian Commerce*, chs. 5–14; Manguin, "Archaeology of Early Polities," 303–307; Leonard Andaya, *Leaves of the Same Tree* (Honolulu, 2008), 49–54; and Pierre-Yves Manguin, "City States and City-State Cultures in pre-15th- Century Southeast Asia," in Hansen, *Comparative Study*, 409–16, pointing to Malay city states as early as 500–300 B.C.E. that resembled Srivijaya.

[24] Manguin, "Archaeology of Early Polities," 305; Wolters, *Early Indonesian Commerce*, 16–17, 207–10, 237–41; So, "Dissolving Hegemony"; and Mideastern sources in n. 20 *supra*.

[25] Jacq-Hergoualc'h, *Malay Peninsula*, 240–48; Wolters, *Early Indonesian Commerce*, 15–18, 239–40; Manguin, "Archaeology of Early Polities," 305–308; Andaya, *Leaves*, 54–68.

Srivijaya as "uncontested master of the Straits," receiving tribute from 14 cities, including harbors in North Sumatra.[26] From the 9th through the 11th century, great quantities of Chinese and Mideastern ceramics in the Musi basin also attest to the region's prosperity.[27] More obviously than in Kiev, not to mention Pagan, Angkor, Dai Viet, or Japan, international trade thus provided the primary stimulus to charter state florescence.

Eventually this very prosperity encouraged external powers to challenge Srivijaya's commercial restrictions and vassals to assert a more complete autonomy. Java invaded Southeast Sumatra c. 992. In 1025 the Colas of South India sacked Srivijaya/Palembang, seizing the *maharaja*. The 11th and 12th centuries also may have seen Burmese and Khmer efforts to capture the trade of the Malay isthmus.[28] Meanwhile Palembang began to lose control over planets in what from the start had been a weak solar polity. In 1079–1082 Malayu-Jambi, whose location in the Batang Hari River system offered more direct access than the Musi system to gold from the Minangkabau highlands, displaced Palembang as imperial capital. By the 1370s, if not earlier, Malayu-Jambi and Palembang were sending separate missions to China.[29] From the late 11th century small North Sumatran ports and Kedah also began to trade independently and, in some cases, to send envoys to China.[30]

---

[26] Wolters, *Fall of Srivijaya*, 9–10; *HM*, 24; Nik Hassan Shuhaimi Bin Nik Abd. Rahman, "The Kingdom of Srivijaya as Socio-Political and Cultural Entity," in J. Kathirithamby-Wells and John Villiers, eds., *The Southeast Asian Port and Polity* (Singapore, 1990), 61–82.

[27] Manguin, "Archaeology of Early Polities," 308; Jan Wisseman Christie, "The Medieval Tamil-Language Inscriptions in Southeast Asia and China," *JSEAS* 29 (1998): 239–68, esp. 250–52; Jacq-Hergoualc'h, *Malay Peninsula*, 255; and archeological references in n. 21 *supra*.

[28] On external competition, Wolters, *Early Indonesian Commerce*, 250–51 (erroneously dating the Javanese attack to 922); G. Coedes, *The Indianized States of Southeast Asia* (Honolulu, 1968), 132; Herman Kulke, "Rivalry and Competition in the Bay of Bengal in the 11th Century and Its Bearing on Indian Ocean Studies," in Om Prakash and Denys Lombard, eds., *Commerce and Culture in the Bay of Bengal, 1500–1800* (New Delhi, 1999), 17–35; *HM*, 29.

[29] Malayu-Jambi was later known simply as Jambi. See O. W. Wolters, "A Note on the Capital of Srivijaya During the Eleventh Century," *Essays Offered to G. H. Luce, Artibus Asiae*, vol. I (1966): 225–39; idem, *Fall of Srivijaya*, 2, 90; John Miksic, "Urbanization and Social Change," *Archipel* 37 (1989): 17, discussing Jambi; *HM*, 28–33; Leonard Andaya, "The Search for the 'Origins' of Melayu," *JSEAS* 32 (2001): 315–30; Manguin, "City States," 409–16.

[30] Miksic, "Classical Cultures," 248; Wolters, *Fall of Srivijaya*, 43–44; *HM*, 30–32; So, "Dissolving Hegemony," 297.

Underlying these centrifugal trends was rising post-1050 demand for Indonesian produce in the Indian Ocean and in China, with the latter paying for forest goods and other exotica through massive exports of bronze cash and ceramics. Starting c. 1050 but more especially after 1127, when the Southern Song tried to compensate for its loss of North China by encouraging private overseas trade, the number of Chinese merchants in Southeast Asian waters rose sharply. Rather than operate entirely through Palembang or Malayu-Jambi, many preferred to tap products closer to their source.[31] In short, a single dominant entrepot no longer seemed feasible.

Yet if this dynamic, to which we shall return, promoted devolution, So's recent work shows – *pace* earlier scholars who argued for Srivijaya's terminal illness by 1100 – that it persevered into the 13th century. Not only did Chinese and Arab travelers continue to write glowing accounts, but as late as 1225 "Srivijaya" (foreigners generally retained this term after the capital shifted to Malayu-Jambi) still exercised substantial control over the Straits and reportedly dominated 14 tributary ports from North Sumatra to West Java.[32]

What, then, were the sources of Srivijayan longevity? How, despite frequent oscillations, could the system exhibit some degree of coherence for over 600 years? Srivijaya's strengths were sixfold.

First, geography. Although Southeast Sumatra lay at some distance from the Straits, it was well placed to police the southern approaches. Located at "the end of the monsoons," Palembang and Malayu-Jambi were natural stopping points where merchants from the South China Sea and the Indian Ocean could await the annual change of winds either to continue further or to return homeward. Within Sumatra the Musi and the Batang Hari provided links to interior jungle produce and gold. To the west, moreover, the Sumatran piedmont was relatively fertile, although Srivijaya's dependence on rice from that area and from Java must have represented a strategic liability. To the east, a thick belt of mangrove swamps protected against sudden naval attack, while tidewater bays and inlets offered local collection and transshipment

---

[31] Wolters, *Fall of Srivijaya*, 4, 42–48; idem, "Restudying Chinese Writings"; idem, *Early Indonesian Commerce*, 248–50; John Miksic, "Archaeology, Ceramics, and Coins," *JESHO* 39 (1996): 287–97; idem, "Urbanization"; So, "Dissolving Hegemony," 298–308 and his 298 n. 15; Ch. 5, n. 128 *supra*.

[32] So, *Prosperity, Region*, 220–26; idem, "Dissolving Hegemony," 298–308, incl. tributary list on 302, from which I exclude Ceylon; Tibbetts and Ferrand in n. 20 *supra*.

points easily accessible from the peninsula and the nearby Riau-Lingga archipelago.[33]

Second, the value of these same waterways was dramatically enhanced by the support of local sea and riverine peoples, the *orang laut*. In return for material rewards (including assured markets for their goods) and marks of royal favor, these feared warriors supplied Srivijaya with marine exports (pearls, turtle shells), piloted ships on the treacherous approaches to Palembang or Malayu-Jambi, guarded the Straits, and enforced royal restrictions on chosen lines of trade.[34]

Third, Srivijaya's reputation for cultural refinement attracted both regional elites and foreign visitors, although to different audiences the ruler directed distinct appeals. Pierre-Yves Manguin points to competition between Buddhist and Vaisnava trading networks in the western archipelago, where Mahayana Buddhism won out.[35] Commercial pre-eminence thus may have had a religious component insofar as Srivijaya, which in the late 600s reportedly had over a thousand monks, became a center of Mahayana scholarship and a patron of Buddhist endowments in India.[36] Among tributaries, including *orang laut* leaders, Srivijaya's rulers sought to inculcate loyalty and stigmatize "treason" (*derhaka*) by emphasizing their magical potency (*sakti*), by presenting themselves as Bodhisattvas and Tantric adepts, and by invoking wrathful tutelary deities. Commercial ties and Srivijayan prestige produced widespread imitation of the court's linguistic and ritual practices. Inscribed in Srivijaya as early as the 680s, Old Malay became the lingua franca of inscriptions as far afield as Java and the Philippines, but increasingly "Malayu" referred to the speech and culture of people in the Musi and Batang Hari basins. Perhaps by the late 11th century and more probably by the 13th, Southeast Sumatrans loyal to Srivijaya called themselves *orang Malayu* – "the people of Malayu" (a term derived either from

---

[33] John Miksic, "Traditional Sumatran Trade," *BEFEO* 74 (1985): 423–67, esp. 438–42; Wolters, *Early Indonesian Commerce*, 225–28; idem, *Fall of Srivijaya*, 8–9; HM, 19, 25.

[34] On *orang laut*, Wolters, *Early Indonesian Commerce*, 227, 242; idem, *Fall of Srivijaya*, 11–17; HM, 26; Andaya, *Leaves*, ch. 6.

[35] Manguin, "Archaeology of Early Polities," 303–305. Also J. G. de Casparis and I. W. Mabbett, "Religion and Popular Beliefs of Southeast Asia Before c. 1500," in *CHSEA*, 311, 318–20.

[36] Jacq-Hergoualc'h, *Malay Peninsula*, 238–40, 246, 254, 346. But see Pisit Charoenwongsa, "A Confusing Picture of Srivijaya History," in SEAMEO Project, *Final Report*, App. 5A, 105–12, arguing that self-interest led at least one Chinese monastic visitor to exaggerate Srivijaya's scholarly reputation.

Malayu-Jambi or from a Malayu site near Palembang).[37] From this Srivijayan origin, Malay ethnicity would evolve in later centuries.

A fourth strength, to the 12th century at least, was Srivijaya's use of Chinese diplomacy. Until the Southern Song (1127–1276), imperial refusal to sanction private trade meant that overseas goods could enter China legally only through tribute missions. Other archipelagic polities obviously knew this, but none was so skillful in manipulating the system as Srivijaya, whose missions began in the late 600s and, after an apparent 9th-century break, continued intermittently to the late 1300s. Not only did privileged entrée to the imperial court strengthen the *maharaja*'s commercial position in the archipelago, but tribute missions increased Chinese interest in Srivijayan goods, while raising the prospect of Chinese diplomatic support against local challengers.[38]

But how could Srivijaya survive the post-1127 proliferation of Chinese merchants across the archipelago? According to So, working with hitherto ignored Chinese materials, a policy shift in the late 1000s or early 1100s provided Srivijaya's fifth asset. Recognizing that it could no longer control the export of widely dispersed forest and marine products, Srivijaya, centered now in Malayu-Jambi, decided to concentrate on the purchase and transshipment of only the most valuable Indian Ocean commodities, including frankincense and ivory. *Orang laut* naval power could still enforce these claims, while for their part, tributary ports were willing to cooperate insofar as they could trade freely in unreserved goods, send their own envoys to China, and perhaps share the profits from the *maharaja*'s privileged lines of trade. According to

---

[37] Whereas early Chinese sources associated "Malayu" with Jambi, the *Sejarah Malayu* chronicle identified "Malayu" as a river near a sacred hill Bukit Siguntang in Palembang. In 1515 Tome Pires also identified "the land of the Malays" (*tana Malayu*) as an area near Palembang. *HM*, 47; Armando Cortesao, ed., *The Suma Oriental of Tome Pires and the Book of Francisco Rodrigues*, 2 vols. (London, 1944), vol. I, 158. On Srivijaya's cultural/religious appeals and early Malayu identity, Andaya, *Leaves*, 58–64, 77–79; idem, "Search for Melayu," 319–30; Anthony Reid, "Understanding *Melayu* (Malay) as a Source of Diverse Modern Identities," *JSEAS* 32 (2001): 295–313, esp. 297–98; Kulke, "Kadatuan Srivijaya," 166–67 n. 30, 171; *HM*, 27–28; Wolters, *Fall of Srivijaya*, 11–13, 17. At the same time, Jacq-Hergoualc'h, *Malay Peninsula*, 190, 270, 494–95 is at pains to deny a distinctive Srivijayan style of art.

[38] Wolters, *Early Indonesian Commerce*, 224; idem, *Fall of Srivijaya*, 33–48; *HM*, 20, 25; Jacq-Hergoualc'h, *Malay Peninsula*, 270; Jan Wisseman Christie, "Javanese Markets and the Asian Sea Trade Boom of the 10th to 13th Centuries," *JESHO* 41 (1998): 344–81, esp. 344–46; So, *Prosperity, Region*, 222.

So, this compromise allowed Srivijaya to maintain substantial tributary allegiance well into the 13th century.[39]

Finally, Srivijaya survived in one form or another for over six centuries because its decentralized, gelatinous, minimalist administrative system easily reconstituted itself after recurrent dislocations. In this respect it resembled Angkor, the Frankish kingdom, and Kiev, which were also decentralized but surprisingly durable and, in the case of Angkor and the Franks, remarkably long-lived. In lieu of the once popular image of a unified territorially bounded empire, Kulke has argued that Srivijaya was organized into four zones of increasingly attenuated royal influence: a) the palace area, where the *maharaja*, his wives, and staff resided, b) an extended semi-urban zone around the palace under chiefs often related to the royal family, c) secondary and tertiary centers upriver in the Musi or Batang Hari basin, which, under local lords with their own family networks, served as stapling and trading posts for the capital, d) tributary ports in the peninsula and coastal Sumatra under local families who had been subdued by the capital or, in a few cases, under princes who had been sent from the capital. Although tied to the royal seat through kinship, sacred oaths, trade, and fear of chastisement, these ports, each with its own satellite centers, replicated in miniature the structure of the central basin. Reflecting the irreducible autonomy of small population clusters in a vast forested landscape, such arrangements provided scope for local ambition and rendered Srivijaya's *maharaja* merely *primus inter pares*. Because relations between the capital and the third and fourth zones were continuously renegotiated, and because leaders in those zones lacked collective voice, individual defections rarely threatened the system as a whole. Thus too the system easily survived the shift from Palembang to Malayu-Jambi. In Kulke's words, "the longevity ... of Srivijaya was based on the very non-existence of those structural features which historians regard as a prerequisite of a genuine empire."[40]

---

[39] So, *Prosperity, Region*, 220–26; idem, "Dissolving Hegemony." I have yet to find a direct critique of So's theory, but Leonard Andaya, pers. commun., Sept. 21, 2008 suggests that this policy, roughly coincident with the shift of capital to Malayu-Jambi, was as much a sign of weakness as of flexibility.

[40] Kulke, "Kadatuan Srivijaya," 176. On territorial organization, idem, "Early and Imperial Kingdom," 122; Andaya, *Leaves*, 63–68; Pierre-Yves Manguin, "The Amorphous Nature of Coastal Polities in Insular Southeast Asia," *Moussons* 5 (2002): 73–99; Wolters, "Restudying Chinese Writings"; Jan Wisseman Christie, "Trade and State Formation in the Malay Peninsula and Sumatra, 300 BC.– AD 700," in Kathirithamby-Wells and

We shall find that five of these six features – a location near the Straits, *orang laut* support, Malay cultural appeals, Chinese imperial patronage, and fluid, relatively amorphous political structures – passed intact to Srivijaya's primary heir, Melaka.

Charter States and Civilization in Pre-Muslim Java

We turn now to the second archipelagic zone of charter state formation, Central and East Java. That fertile island, as noted, boasted both active ports and a formidable wet-rice economy. Despite tensions between mercantile coast and agrarian interior reminiscent of conflicts in Burma and Angkor, for long periods before 1500 Java succeeded in wedding the two spheres under a single authority.

Lacking significant deposits of tin or iron, Java from an early date was obliged to seek metals through long-distance trade, which facilitated the entry of Indian scripts and culture. Archeology and Chinese records from the 5th century point to three polities on the north coast, of which at least one eventually seems to have been absorbed into the emergent south-central Javanese state of Mataram.[41]

This latter polity relied on the fertile uplands around modern Yogyakarta, an area suitable for wet-rice cultivation, albeit also favored by trade routes to the north coast.[42] Why in the 8th and, more especially, the 9th and 10th centuries Java's center of gravity came to focus on interior ricelands is an issue I shall defer until we consider agrarian dynamics. Suffice it for now to note: a) The rise of south-central Java coincided with an economic shift from the coast to the interior in Cambodia.[43] b) In Java as in Cambodia, Burma, and Vietnam, the 9th and 10th centuries also inaugurated a phase of demographic and

---

Villiers, *Port and Polity*, 39–60. Outside the "realm" (*bhumi*) of Srivijaya, but economically tied to it, were *swidden* tribesmen and highland chiefs who, in return for salt, metal tools, and cloth, funneled forest goods to riverine collecting centers.

[41] On early ports, Miksic, "Classical Cultures," 237–38; F. H. van Naerssen and R. C. de Iongh, *The Economic and Administrative History of Early Indonesia* (Leiden, 1977), 24–25; Antoinette Barrett Jones, *Early Tenth Century Java from the Inscriptions* (Dordrecht, 1984), 26; Wisseman Christie, "State Formation," 263–74.

[42] Jan Wisseman Christie, "Revisiting Early Mataram," in Marijke Klokke and Karel van Kooij, eds., *Fruits of Inspiration* (Groningen, 2001), 33; idem, "States Without Cities," *Indonesia* 52 (1991): 27. Mataram bore the same name as, and its heartland lay close to that of, the Muslim realm of Mataram, founded c. 1575, but the two were discontinuous. Poor harbors and treacherous seas minimized trade on Java's south coast.

[43] *SP*, 216–18; Glover and Bellwood, *Southeast Asia*, 96–101. Burma may have experienced a similar, if less pronounced, shift.

economic expansion that would continue at least to the early 1300s. c) Southeast Asian vitality to 1300/1350 was part of that great Eurasian upsurge we have encountered in virtually every chapter. d) West Java could rarely compete with more agriculturally well-endowed Central and East Java.[44]

With the rise of Mataram begins what I would designate the charter period, but which is conventionally termed the Classical period, of Javanese history, in turn subdivided into the Early (716–930), Middle (930–1222), and Late Classical (1222–1527?) eras.[45] Clearly, Java's charter civilization survived longer than that of Upper Burma, Angkor, Dai Viet, or indeed Srivijaya, all of which were in serious trouble by 1350 – just as classical Java was entering its period of greatest prosperity. As we shall see, this longevity reflected, in large part, Java's ability to combine maritime with agrarian wealth at a time when surging coastal commerce was tearing apart other polities. And yet, divergent post-1350 chronologies aside, in Java as on the mainland the classical/charter era supported a distinctive Hindu-Buddhist religious culture together with sustained trends toward territorial integration, agrarian expansion, and commercialization. Moreover, insofar as Angkor, despite growing vicissitudes, remained a premier regional center for some 640 years (from 800 to the 1430s or 1440s), it was not dramatically less long-lived than classical Java.

During the Early Classical period (716–930), the center of gravity remained in south-central Java under Mataram. This era is best known for its monumental architecture, including the famed Mahayana step-pyramid of Borobudur and the Hindu complex of Candi Loro Jong-grang at Prambanan.[46] Mataram's grand shrines and smaller temples preceded by two centuries the major phase of Pagan construction, but were coeval with the onset of large-scale temple projects at Angkor. As in mainland Southeast Asia and India, temples were funded though

---

[44] At least in part, because of excessive rains in the west. Naerssen and Iongh, *Economic History*, 28; Mason Hoadley, *Towards a Feudal Mode of Production: West Java, 1680–1800* (Singapore, 1994), 26–29.

[45] Cf. periodization at Jan Fontein, ed., *The Sculptures of Indonesia* (Washington, DC, 1990), 70; Miksic, "Classical Cultures," 234; *CHSEA*, 202–29.

[46] On dynasties, temples, and religious affiliations c. 700–930, Wisseman Christie, "Revisiting Early Mataram," 25–55; Soekmono, "The Archaeology of Central Java Before 800 AD," in Smith and Watson, *Early South East Asia*, 457–71; Luis Gomez and Hiram Woodward, Jr., eds., *Barabudur* (Berkeley, 1981); Fontein, *Sculptures of Indonesia*, 67–95; Mary-Louise Totton, "Weaving Flesh and Blood into Sacred Architecture" (Univ. of Michigan, PhD diss., 2002).

permanent transfers of tax rights on specified lands – known in Java as *sima* grants – awarded by the king or lesser lords. By collecting and marketing produce from these lands and by using bonded labor to build not only new religious edifices, but water control systems, bridges, and roads, Javanese temples, like their counterparts in mainland Southeast Asia and in India, became foci of economic development and agrarian reclamation.[47]

Recall from Chapter 6 Kulke's evolutionary schema for South India from 500 to 1300 that began with tribal chiefs' transforming themselves into petty Hindu kings. Kings then annexed adjacent realms but treated them as self-sufficient tributaries, until finally regional kingdoms reduced tributary states to more closely controlled provinces. In this scenario, which Kulke has extended to Southeast Asia,[48] Srivijaya never became more than a loose assemblage of far-flung tributary ports. But Java's relatively dense markets and population allowed 9th-century Mataram, like Pagan and Angkor (at later dates), to pursue more effective centralization. Mataram grew by absorbing on its flanks tributary kingdoms that were originally comparable to Mataram but that were now converted into *wateks*, or apanages, awarded to middle-tier officials and relatives of the Mataram ruler. Gradually, as Jan Wisseman Christie, the leading authority on early Java, has shown, *watek*-holders were drawn into the status system of the central state, even as *watek* holdings and revenue rights became ever more fragmented. Such fragmentation reflected complex inheritance patterns, but more particularly, royal policy designed to inhibit territorially cohesive challenges. Thus in contrast to Srivijaya, revolts in Mataram rarely sought to revive fallen polities.[49]

---

[47] Jan Wisseman Christie, "Texts and Textiles in 'Medieval' Java," *BEFEO* 80 (1993): 181–211; idem, "Negara, Mandala, and Despotic State," in Marr and Milner, *Southeast Asia*, 65–93; idem, "Raja and Rama," in Lorraine Gesick, ed., *Centers, Symbols, and Hierarchies* (New Haven, 1983), 9–10, defining *sima* grants; Peter Boomgaard, "From Riches to Rags?," in Greg Bankoff and Peter Boomgaard, eds., *A History of Natural Resources in Asia* (New York, 2007), 188–90; and Ch. 6, nn. 17, 131 *supra*. On inscriptions to 898, Jan Wiseman Christie, "Register of the Inscriptions of Java," 2 vols. (ms, 2002).

[48] See Ch. 6, nn. 14–17 *supra* and Kulke's elaboration in Southeast Asian context, "Early and Imperial Kingdom," 1–22. Kulke's three stages prior to 1300 should not be confused with the Early, Middle, and Late Classical eras. See discussion *infra*.

[49] Wisseman Christie, "Negara, Mandala," esp. 69–84; idem, "State Formation," esp. 274–76; idem, "Revisiting Early Mataram." See too J. G. de Casparis, "Some Notes on Relations Between Central and Local Government in Ancient Java," in Marr and Milner, *Southeast Asia*, 49–63; Jones, *Early Tenth Century Java*, ch. 4; Naerssen and Iongh, *Economic History*, 46–52.

In the 930s the royal palace/capital – the *kraton* – moved east from Central Java to the Brantas River basin, where the transplanted dynasty continued this policy of absorbing local statelets. Although massive eruptions of Mt. Merapi in 928–929 may have provided the immediate spur,[50] in a larger sense this shift climaxed decades of growing royal interest in the Brantas basin. That swampy but fertile region, whose wet-rice potential had barely been tapped, promised not only to broaden the kingdom's agrarian base, but to improve its maritime access via ports on the northeast coast. Indeed, Brantas basin rice became Java's major export, and until Chinese merchants arrived in force in the 1100s, Javanese, with Srivijayans, apparently dominated archipelagic trade.[51]

The Middle Classical era (930–1222) thus saw a number of critical reorientations. East Java, focusing on the Brantas and Sala basins and the northeast coast, now rendered Central Java a backwater. As maritime income came to supplement agrarian income, the state became more of a hybrid entity.[52] Commercial ambition sparked conflict with Srivijaya and contributed to the temporary extension of Javanese control over Bali.[53] By 1178 a Chinese writer claimed Java was richer than Srivijaya and in wealth second only to Arab countries.[54] Larger surpluses were now invested in trade and luxury imports than in stone temples, which, Wisseman Christie argues, therefore decreased markedly in size and number.[55] In mainland Southeast Asia as well, a maritime-aided shift in religious donations from land to money and movable goods contributed to the virtual cessation of stone temple construction in Cambodia after c. 1220 and in Burma after c. 1350.[56]

---

[50] Boechari, "Some Considerations on the Problem of the Shift of Mataram's Centre of Government from Central to East Java in the 10th Century," in Smith and Watson, *Early South East Asia*, 473–91; Jan Wisseman Christie, "Money and Its Uses in the Javanese States of the Ninth to Fifteenth Centuries," *JESHO* 39 (1996): 243–86, esp. 249. Some sources continue to refer to the post-930 state as Mataram, but most limit that usage to the pre-930 Central Javanese kingdom.

[51] Wisseman Christie, "Javanese Markets"; idem, *Theatre States and Oriental Despotisms* (Hull, 1985), 34–35; idem, "Revisiting Early Mataram"; idem, "Asian Sea Trade Between the 10th and 13th Centuries and Its Impact on the States of Java and Bali," in Himanshu Ray, ed., *Archaeology of Seafaring* (Delhi, 1999), 221–70.

[52] Wisseman Christie, "Asian Sea Trade," 245–48.

[53] Java's aforementioned attack c. 992 produced a Srivijayan counterattack in 1016. See n. 28 *supra*, and Wisseman Christie, "Asian Sea Trade," 223. As early as the 11th century Javanese had begun to replace Old Balinese as the official court language of Bali.

[54] Wolters, *Early Indonesian Commerce*, 251.

[55] Wisseman Christie, "Javanese Markets," 346.

[56] After c. 1500 South Asia apparently saw similar trends; see Ch. 6, n. 166 *supra*. Moreover, in Burma, Angkor, and Java alike, after the charter/classical period lithic inscriptions

Within the lower Brantas core of the new East Java empire, the *watek* system continued to evolve, providing the same benefits as had aided 9th-century Mataram. Yet despite these features and despite its commercial access, the new realm proved curiously unstable. Whether this represented a retreat in Kulke's evolutionary schema is a definitional problem that need not delay us,[57] but clearly the territorial momentum of the period c. 930–1050 began to falter. After c. 1050 not only did the court lose control over Central Java and Bali, but the East Javanese state itself split, as coastal regions hived off from the agrarian interior.[58]

It was not for another 200 years, at the start of the Late Classical period (1222–1527?), that a sustained countermovement finally took hold. In brief, the kingdom of Singhasari (1222–1292) subdued all rival centers in East Java, reuniting coastal and interior districts, and proceeded to mount successful expeditions against Bali and the Straits of Melaka. But it was only under Singhasari's heir, the celebrated empire of Majapahit (1293–1527?), again centered in the lower Brantas basin, that the residual autonomy of independent East Javanese states was finally extinguished. A massive 1293 Mongol invasion of Java, apparently designed to seize control of the pepper trade to China, unwittingly facilitated this transition from Singhasari to Majapahit. Coinciding with Mongol defeats in Burma, Dai Viet, and Japan, this failed invasion confirmed that the islands remained part of Eurasia's protected zone.[59]

ended or decreased dramatically. See Glover and Bellwood, *Southeast Asia*, 105, 168; *SP*, 109, 121–22, 140–49, 159–60, 240, 254–56; Victor Lieberman, "The Political Significance of Religious Wealth in Burmese History: Some Further Thoughts," *JAS* 39 (1980): 753–69.

[57] Kulke, "Early and Imperial Kingdom," 8 describes Mataram's 9th-century efforts and those of Airlannga (r. 1016–1045) as "temporarily successful attempts" at centralization. Cf. the stronger linear emphasis in Wisseman Christie, "Raja and Rama," 18, 20, and idem, *Theatre States*, 37: "The process of integration and growth of the early [900–1300] states . . . [was] largely linear rather than cyclic. Rights ceded to the centre seem not to have been regained . . . New states picked up where their predecessors left off."

[58] On Middle Classical history, Kulke, "Early and Imperial Kingdom," 9; Wisseman Christie, "Javanese Markets," 346, 368; idem, "States Without Cities," 27; Max Nihom, "Ruler and Realm," *Indonesia* 42 (1986): 78–100; Denys Lombard, *Le Carrefour Javanais*, 3 vols. (Paris, 1990), vol. III, 18–19.

[59] On Mongol motives and impact, Coedes, *Indianized States*, 198–201; Christie, "Tamil-Language," 261; Anthony Reid, "Flows and Seepages in the Long-Term Chinese Interaction with Southeast Asia," in Reid, ed., *Sojourners and Settlers* (St. Leonards, Australia, 1996), 17–21.

Continuing the work of Mataram and Singhasari, but on a grander scale, in the early and mid-1300s the new kingdom of Majapahit replaced tributary rulers with apanage-holders, generally princes and princesses of the central dynasty. Again, the fragmentation of apanage lands and the assimilation of apanage-holders to a central status hierarchy eroded territorial identities in a process that has been termed the "dynastification" of East Java.[60] In its East Java core the court also collected taxes both directly and via tax farms-, awarded *sima* grants, and undertook regular royal tours. Here the network of temples and title-holders dependent on royal certification was most dense. Beyond the core, in Central Java and Java's Eastern Salient, autonomous tributaries replicated on a smaller scale the structure of the Majapahit *kraton*. All were said to be part of *yawadwipamandala*, the "circle of the island of Java." "Over all of Java-land," an inscription declared, "the Illustrious Great King" of East Java was "the one sunshade."[61] But wretched transport meant that to retain outlying dependencies, the center had to combine marriage alliances, spies, supernatural sanctions, and military threats with acceptance of extensive autonomy. Moreover, island-wide claims aside, over West Java Majapahit apparently had no authority.

Beyond Java, again in the footsteps of Singhasari, Majapahit in the mid-1300s subdued Bali and Madura and, by exploiting north coastal shipping and trade restrictions, established a loose, indirect ascendancy, what has been termed "punitive influence," over archipelagic ports ranging from North Sumatra in the west to Sulawesi and Maluku (the Spice Islands) in the east. Courts in the outer islands frequently looked to Majapahit for cultural, even dynastic legitimation. Given 14th-century disarray on the mainland, Majapahit had become Southeast Asia's most brilliant and influential polity, not least because it proved better able than other charter states (with the possible exception of Champa) to combine agrarian with new mercantile sources of wealth. Yet ultimately

---

[60] Term from Kulke, "Early and Imperial Kingdom," 8–11. On Late Classical administration, see *The Legacy of Majapahit* (Singapore, 1995), 7–8; Naerssen and Iongh, *Economic History*, 62–70; Wisseman Christie, "Raja and Rama," 9–44; idem, "Negara, Mandala," 70–74; Slametmuljana, *A Story of Majapahit* (Singapore, 1976), 87–149; Theodore G. Th. Pigeaud, *Java in the 14th Century*, 5 vols. (The Hague, 1960–1963), vol. IV, 3–115, 219–343.

[61] Inscription from 1269 describing King Kertanagara, said to be the prototype for Majapahit rulers. Kulke, "Early and Imperial Kingdom," 15; Wisseman Christie, "Raja and Rama," 32.

its archipelagic dominance proved quite fragile, lasting only to the early 1400s.[62] Pulsating outer zones of authority, of course, were also typical of the mainland.

No less familiar to students of mainland Southeast Asia or indeed of the Frankish kingdom, Kiev, or Heian, was the initially derivative, elitist, socially encapsulated quality of classical Javanese court culture. From an early period Javanese architects looked to South Asia, while Siva, Visnu, Brahma, Durga, and Ganesa images employed standard Indian iconography.[63] Majapahit kings patronized four religious communities – Saivas, Vaisnavas, Mahayana Buddhists, and Rsis – the first three of which were obviously Indic and the last of which included brahmans. Royal consecration and funerary rites also were decidedly Hindu, with many 12th-century kings, for example, described as incarnations of Visnu. Courts endorsed a modified form of the fourfold *varna* system and almost certainly practiced suttee (widow-burning).[64] As part of Sheldon Pollock's "Sanskrit cosmopolis," Java to the early 800s tailored Sanskrit inscriptions to Indian norms of royal eulogy. Thereafter Javanese became the sole language of official texts and literature, but continued to rely on Sanskrit lexicography, meters, and genres.[65] In an overwhelmingly illiterate society where the court made few, if any, religious demands on villagers and where, ascetics aside, there seems to have been little rural religious infrastructure and no centrally approved textual corpus, these practices tended to insulate literate elites from the general population. To the extent that the court's Hindu-Mahayana complex lacked deep local roots and a sense of exclusive orthodoxy such as postcharter Theravada Buddhism and Neo-Confucianism were beginning to develop on the mainland, Javanese – along with Malay – culture may have been particularly open to Islamic penetration.[66]

---

[62] Keith Taylor in *CHSEA*, 179, using the term "punitve influence"; Slametmuljana, *Story*, 59–66, 132–43; Pigeaud, *Java*, vol. III, 16–19 and vol. IV, 29–39; J. Noorduyn, "Majapahit in the Fifteenth Century," *BKI* 134 (1978): 208. "Outer islands" refers to those beyond Java. On Champa, a maritime-oriented polity from the outset that in the late 1300s devastated Dai Viet, *SP*, 348–52, 371–72.

[63] Fontein, *Sculptures of Indonesia*, 67–70 and following note.

[64] Casparis and Mabbett, "Religion," 304–29; Casparis, *India and Maritime*, 16–17; *HMI*, 22; Pigeaud, *Java*, vol. III, 94–95 and vol. IV, 468, 479–93. On *suttee* c. 1510, Cortesao, *Suma Oriental*, vol. I, 167, 176, 198. On court sects, Hariano Santiko, "Early Research on Sivaitic Hinduism During the Majapahat Period," *Legacy of Majapahit*, 55–70.

[65] Sheldon Pollock, *The Language of the Gods in the World of Men* (Berkeley, 2006), 130–32, 387–90.

[66] Cf. *SP*, 135–39, 258–63; Alan Strathern, "Transcendentalist Intransigence," *CSSH* 49 (2007): 358–83, noting shallow pre-Muslim Indic religious roots in Malaya and Sumatra;

It is also obvious, however, that in Java as in other pre-1400 protected-zone realms, elites selectively reinterpreted donor norms, while localization joined economic growth to open a space, however modest by later standards, for elite–mass interaction. Even the earliest Indic architecture and sculpture exhibited idiosyncratic Javanese features that only grew more pronounced in later centuries.[67] Javanese pantheons – including the Goddess of the Southern Ocean and Brahma as volcano deity – reflected visions distinct from those of India. The same was true of ancestor veneration, which provided a principal rationale for royal temple cults, and of the peculiar relation at court between Buddhists, Saivite, and Rsi clerisies. The debt that literary Javanese owed Sanskrit was less remarkable than the development from the 9th to the 15th century of Old Javanese as an independent literary vehicle suitable *inter alia* for epic court poetry (*kakawins*). As such, Java offers an early and lusty example of the vernacular revolution that spread across South Asia, Southeast Asia, and Europe, as discussed in Chapter 6.[68] What is more, if local practices infused royal religion, vertical acculturation cut both ways. Saivite teachings spread from the *kraton* to secondary centers and thence to the countryside. Village music, shadow puppet plays, and masked dances drew on Hindu epics and in some cases may have been sponsored by the court. As such, they helped to disseminate elite understandings of hierarchy, sanctity, and cosmic order. That downward communication occurred is suggested by the large number of Sanskritized personal names in *sima* charter lists – 20 to 25 percent at lower social levels, more at higher levels. From the 11th century *kraton*–village links may be seen as well in the proliferation of court-defined ranks and sumptuary privileges among local officials.[69]

Wisseman Christie, *Theatre States*, 36, on ceremonial distance between village and court; and M. C. Ricklefs, "Six Centuries of Islamization in Java," in Nehemia Levtzion, ed., *Conversion to Islam* (New York, 1979), 100–28, esp. 102, on nonexclusivity. But see too Pigeaud, *Java*, vol. III, 36–37, 64, 94, and Cortesao, *Suma Oriental*, vol. I, 177 on rural ascetic networks.

[67] Fontein, *Sculptures of Indonesia*, 67–108. Borobudur, in particular, had no Indian analogue.

[68] Note 65 *supra* and Ch. 6, n. 235 *supra*; plus Pigeaud, *Java*, vol. IV, 219; P. J. Zoetmulder, *Kalangwan: A Survey of Old Javanese Literature* (The Hague, 1974), pt. 1; Slametmuljana, *Story*, 105–109, 115–32; Thomas Hunter, "The Body of the King," *JSEAS* 38 (2007): 27–54; Helen Creese, "Old Javanese Studies," *BKI* 157 (2001): 3–33. Presumably vernacularization expanded literacy, but I find no data.

[69] Wisseman Christie, "Raja and Rama," 15, 21–22, 33–35; idem, *Theatre States*, 17, 35–36; idem, "Negara, Mandala," 83–84; idem, "*Wanua, Thani, Paraduwan*," in Wolfgang Marschal, ed., *Texts from the Islands* (Berne, 1989): 27–42. On court–local cultural

In short, classical Java exhibited a number of features familiar from other charter polities not only in mainland Southeast Asia but across Eurasia's protected zone during the late first and early second millennia – including unprecedented territorial authority, a novel administrative and ritual integration, an idiosyncratic reworking of religious and literary themes imported from older Eurasian cores, weak notions of religious orthodoxy, and a substantial, if diminishing, cultural gap between court and countryside.

Most basic perhaps, in Java as in much of Eurasia in this period, political/cultural dynamism coincided with a marked economic upsurge. From c. 850 to 1300 legal records, monuments, and *sima* references to forest clearing point to a sustained expansion of cultivation, especially in the Brantas and Sala basins, and of population, which may have exceeded 3,000,000 island-wide.[70] By the early 1400s double-cropping of rice was common in advanced areas of East Java.[71] Recent excavations at Trowulan, Majapahit's probable capital, have unearthed a sophisticated urban commercial complex.[72] But as a general rule, settlement on the fringes of established communities led not to urban hierarchies or larger taxpaying units, but to village fissioning, the multiplication of taxpaying units, reclamation, and population dispersal. With agrarian extension came an increase in periodic and permanent markets, to which pedlars and wholesalers fed rice and other foodstuffs, livestock, local textiles and pottery, along with Chinese and Indian metals and handicrafts. Monetization grew apace. In the 10th century a medley of local exchange media were supplemented by Javanese silver coins. But these yielded to Chinese bronze cash, which, becoming insufficient during the Southern Song and Yuan eras, were supplemented by Javanese imitations.[73]

exchange, see too Casparis and Mabbett, "Religion," 311; Slametmuljana, *Story*, 142–43; Pigeaud, *Java*, vol. IV, 480.

[70] Cf. Wisseman Christie, "States Without Cities," 29, crediting a 5,000,000 "guess" for 1350 by P. MacDonald; *AC*, vol. I, 14, claiming 4,000,000 in 1600 and 5,000,000 in 1800; M. C. Ricklefs, n. 285 *infra*, with an estimate, he considers suspect, that in 1795 the north coast and south-central Java together had not much more than 3,000,000. On agrarian and demographic expansion, Wisseman Christie, "States Without Cities," 23–40; idem, "*Wanua, Thani*"; idem, "The Agricultural Economies of Early Java and Bali" (ms); idem, "Water and Rice in Early Java and Bali" (ms); N. V. van Setten van der Meer, *Sawah Cultivation in Ancient Java* (Canberra, 1979); Lombard, *Carrefour Javanais*, vol. III, 17–25.

[71] Ma Huan, *Ying-yai Sheng-lan*, J. V. G. Mills, tr. (Bangkok, 1970), 91.

[72] *Legacy of Majapahit*, 19–41; Miksic, "Archaeology, Ceramics," 292–93.

[73] On local trade and coinage, previous note, plus Wisseman Christie, "Javanese Markets"; idem, "Weaving and Dyeing in Early Java and Bali," in Wibke Lobo and Stefanie

How did agrarian and commercial vigor aid Javanese charter expansion? Majapahit's wealth let it equip those "expeditionary forces" that a contemporary account boasted "annihilated altogether" "commandment-breakers" in the seas beyond Java, while its rice surplus let it supply food-deficit ports around the archipelago, especially in the east, where it sought to access spices. To follow Wisseman Christie, Majapahit's rich agrarian base also let it weather commercial downturns more easily than Srivijaya, which relied wholly on trade.[74] Within Java, agrarian/manpower superiority undergirded eastern hegemony and, along with trade revenues, magnified royal patronage. In the East Java core itself an "explosive growth of affluence"[75] multiplied economic niches and intermediate social groups. The ambition of many such groups, neither royal nor truly aristocratic, to acquire new status markers and to gain tax exemption for family temples obliged the crown to regulate local ranks, sumptuary privileges, and tax rights. All such measure eroded village autonomy and absorbed local elites in external, *kraton*-defined status systems. Insofar as upwardly mobile groups imbibed court culture and theatrical troupes moved along trade networks, commerce also aided cultural circulation.

But if economic growth was a precondition for charter florescence, what caused economic growth, especially between c. 900 and 1350? This question, of course, has haunted virtually every chapter of this book. Again, none of the usual explanations – state initiatives, foreign trade, or climate – seems entirely satisfactory, at least not by itself.

State and Elite Initiatives. To augment their income, East Javanese kings and subordinate apanage-holders undertook a variety of measures that had the effect, if not also the intent, of raising agrarian output. They decreed severe penalties for anyone impeding reclamation and ratified shifts from communal to private land tenures, thereby

---

Reimann, eds., *Southeast Asian Archaeology 1998* (Hull, 1999), 17–27; idem, "Trade and Value in Pre-Majapahit Java," *Indonesian Circle* 59–60 (1992–1993): 3–17; idem, "Money and Its Uses"; idem, *Theatre States*, 28–35; Lombard, *Carrefour Javanais*, vol. II, 139–41; *Legacy of Majapahit*, 99–105, 158; A. van Aelst, "Majapahit Pisis," *BKI* 151 (1995): 357–93; Robert Wicks, *Money, Markets, and Trade in Early Southeast Asia* (Ithaca, 1992), 243–300; Derek Thiam Soon Heng, "Export Commodity and Regional Currency," *JSEAS* 37 (2006): 179–204; Ma Huan, *Ying-yai*, 96; Pigeaud, *Java*, vol. IV, 496–500.

[74] Wisseman Christie, "Javanese Markets," 346. Cf. *HMI*, 22; Pigeaud, *Java*, vol. IV, 500–503. Quoted references to naval expeditions at ibid., vol. III, 19. Cf. ibid., vol. IV, 39; Slametmuljana, *Story*, 61–63, 139.

[75] Wisseman Christie, "Trade and Value," 5. Discussion also follows nn. 69, 73 *supra*.

perhaps enhancing market involvement.[76] On occasion they endowed lands to maintain dams and flood-barriers. Most critical, kings and apanage-holders awarded agrarian tax rights to temples on the understanding that the latter would convert shifting cultivation (*swidden*) and wasteland to wet rice (*sawah*). Fiscal privileges and bonded labor let temples, as noted, become foci of reclamation, but residual tax claims meant that the crown also benefited. At the same time, the conversion of *swidden* to wet rice and the retreat of jungle promised to reduce brigandage and strengthen royal control over the population.[77] Arguing that wet rice was far less productive per man-hour than *swidden*, Peter Boomgaard suggests that without these coercive interventions by rulers and allied temples, large-scale wet-rice expansion was unlikely to have occurred.[78]

But Robert Hunt claims that wet-rice labor productivity exceeded *swidden*, which presumably weakens the argument for elite coercion.[79] Yet even if we follow Boomgaard's reasoning, state interventions and temple endowments still provide only a partial explanation for economic dynamism, first, because Majapahit saw more vigorous agrarian growth, but far more modest temple endowments, than earlier East Javanese states; and second, because state–temple actions per se say nothing about the problem of coordinated prosperity across Eurasia, or even between Srivijaya, which lacked such landed endowments, and Java.

---

[76] I follow Wisseman Christie, *"Wanua, Thani"*; idem, "Water and Rice," 1–6; Lombard, *Carrefour Javanais*, vol. III, 35.

[77] See Pigeaud, *Java*, vol. IV, 470–71; H. J. de Graaf and Th. G. Th. Pigeaud, *Chinese Muslims in Java*, M. C. Ricklefs, ed. (N. Melbourne, 1984), 185. *Carrefour Javanais*, vol. III, 21–24 identifies five major East Java reclamation projects between 804 and 1486, but does not contradict Wisseman Christie's insistence that waterworks, except in rare circumstances, remained in local, rather than royal hands. Wisseman Christie, *Theatre States*, 25–26; idem, "State Formation," 275; idem, "Water and Rice," 6–12.

[78] Boomgaard, "Riches to Rags?," 188–90, citing Michael Dove, and identifying six factors conducive to wet-rice expansion, of which the first three focus on forms of elite coercion and the latter three are ready availability of work animals, export demand, and enhanced security stemming from concentrated settlement.

[79] Robert Hunt, "Labor Productivity and Agricultural Development: Boserup Revisited," *Human Ecology* 28 (2000): 251–77. I am at a loss to explain the difference with Boomgaard. Hunt defines *swidden* as long-fallow technique with slash and burn, planting by dibble stick, many cultivars, and extensive hand weeding; whereas *sawah* is annual rice cropping on level valley land, with animal-drawn plows and harrows, irrigation, seed beds, and seedling transplantation.

Foreign Trade. Maritime stimuli promise to address the issue of coordination. As Wisseman Christie has shown, the Eurasian trade boom of the 10th to 13th centuries, drawing on an economic surge in Fatimid/early Mamluk Egypt, Cola India, and Song China, stimulated East Javanese agriculture, handicrafts, and monetization alike. To Maluku and archipelagic ports flowed Javanese rice, beans, salt, garlic, and sugar, most of which were collected by itinerant traders through periodic markets. To China went black pepper, safflower dye, coriander, sugar, and medicinal herbs. Java imported archipelagic goods for reshipment to China and Srivijaya, plus Indian textiles and Chinese porcelain and silks for local consumption. Chinese ingots supplied Javanese ironmongery. Chinese and Indian techniques transformed local artisanry, and Chinese cash and local imitation coins revolutionized commodity exchange.[80]

Yet for all this, there is no evidence, even in the Majapahit era, that more than a small fraction of East Java's population depended for their livelihood on foreign markets, which alone therefore seem inadequate to explain a general demographic/agrarian upsurge. If we project David Henley's work on colonial Sulawesi to an earlier era, proliferating markets eroded customary restraints on agrarian productivity while improving food distribution in rice-deficit areas. Better nutrition in turn raised female fertility and lowered child mortality. But again, although Wisseman Christie has shown that foodstuffs and livestock did enter a thickening network of local markets, there is no way to disentangle foreign from domestic stimuli to commodification, much less assess pre-1350 fertility implications.[81] Nor, if archipelagic trade helped to spur region-wide vitality, is it clear why East Java began to flourish only some 300 years after Srivijaya arose.

Conceivably, as in later periods, more regular trade contacts with India and China helped Java to domesticate smallpox and other epidemic diseases, but again this is mere speculation.[82]

---

[80] See n. 73 *supra*, plus Wisseman Christie, "Agricultural Economies"; idem, "Asian Sea Trade, 226–27; *Legacy of Majapahit*, 91–97, 200.

[81] Henley, "Population and Subsistence"; idem, *Fertility, Food, and Fever* (Leiden, 2005), 466–67, 606–10 emphasizes for post-1700 North Sulawesi the role of markets in raising incentives to food production, weakening slave- and kin-based barriers to agrarian productivity and human fertility, and thus breaking open demographic restrictions characteristic of subsistence economies.

[82] Cf. *SP*, 97–98, 224; and evidence that 18th-century smallpox was most devastating in the most isolated areas of Java and Sumatra: Peter Carey, "Waiting for the 'Just King,'"

Climate. In dry years rice yields for Java as a whole now average about one half those of normal years.[83] But because rainfall diminishes as one moves east from Central Java, East Java is significantly more sensitive to fluctuations than the rest of the island. Repeated studies point to strong correlations between El Nino events and Javanese droughts, which tend to correlate with droughts in South Asia, parts of mainland Southeast Asia, and North (but not necessarily South) China. On present evidence, between 700 and 1900 El Nino events were weakest and most infrequent from c. 820 to 1270, during the Medieval Climate Anomaly, which suggests that monsoons in that era were especially strong and contributed to East Java's agricultural expansion. Between 800 and 1300, as the economic center of gravity shifted to the drier eastern part of Java, Cambodia saw a similar shift from the coast to the normally dry interior, while the 10th and 11th centuries also brought rapid agrarian development in dry-zone Burma.[84] Lest one embrace climatic determinism too enthusiastically, however, note that climate necessarily operated in synergy with elite initiatives and foreign trade; that early climatic reconstructions rest largely on proxy records; and that when lower Brantas reclamation took off in the 10th century, the last thing that swampy domain may have needed was more water.[85]

MAS 20 (1986): 106–107; Barbara Watson Andaya, *To Live as Brothers* (Honolulu, 1993), 228.

[83] This is true despite the stabilizing effects of modern chemical fertilizers, pesticides, and scientifically selected seeds. I. Amien et al., "Effects of Interannual Climate Variability and Climate Change on Rice Yield in Java, Indonesia," *Water, Air, and Soil Pollution* 2 (1996): 29–39.

[84] On historic drought-famine links, Peter Boomgaard, "Crisis Mortality in 17th-Century Indonesia," in Ts'ui-jung Liu et al., eds., *Asian Population History* (Oxford, 2001), 191–220; Wisseman Christie, "Water and Rice," 2. On correlations between ENSO-related drought in South Asia, mainland Southeast Asia, and Indonesia, see *SP*, 103–12, 224–27, 362–65; Ch. 6, n. 143 *supra*; Nick Salafsky, "Drought in the Rain Forest," *CC* 27 (1994): 373–96; David Bachiochi et al., "The Effect of Indian Ocean Warming on the Indian Monsoon," *Mausam* I52 (2001): 151–62; Boomgaard, "Riches to Rags?," 193–94. Also R. P. Kane, "El Nino Timings and Rainfall Extremes in India, Southeast Asia and China," *Intl. Jl. of Climatology* 19 (1999): 653–72, acknowledging discrepancies between the incidence of ENSO and drought. See too Ch. 1, nn. 98, 99 and Ch. 2, n. 90 *supra*, pointing to increased solar radiation during the Medieval Climate Anomaly and exploring links between solar radiation and ENSO oscillations.

[85] Note too that to some extent farmers could modify crop types in response to climate shifts. Thus in the 1700s Javanese responded to droughts by planting rice varieties requiring less water. Barbara Andaya, "The Unity of Southeast Asia," *JSEAS* 28 (1997): 167.

Charter State Collapse in the Straits and in Java, c. 1300–1500

If the roots of Java's charter prosperity remain tangled, the dynamics of Srivijaya's and Majapahit's eclipse are somewhat less impenetrable. At various times between 1200 and 1350, recall, sustained economic growth began to destabilize charter polities in both mainland Southeast Asia and Europe. Pagan, Angkor, Dai Viet, and France all suffered from growing shortages of quality arable land. In the first two realms and Kiev we found too a tendency for outlying dependencies to profit from commercial elaboration more than the capitals to which they were nominally subject.[86] Once political devolution began, in both Europe and mainland Southeast Asia 14th-century economic woes dimmed the prospects of reintegration.

Broadly comparable dynamics helped to undermine both of the archipelago's main charter states, starting with Srivijaya. I noted that Song trade expansion stoked local resistance to Srivijaya's commercial claims. Although the decision to refocus on a handful of prized Indian Ocean goods let that maritime polity retain a measure of prosperity into the 13th century, centrifugal pressures continued to mount. By the mid-1200s, with Kedah and North Sumatran ports attracting Chinese and Indian Ocean trade, the northern economic sector of the Melaka Straits effectively separated from the southern sector still focused on Malayu-Jambi. After a Javanese fleet sacked Malayu-Jambi in 1275, a political vacuum opened in the south as well. Java claimed suzerainty over Southeast Sumatra,[87] but with Malayu-Jambi and Palembang disputing preeminence, with rival Sino-Indonesian commercial networks supporting different local rulers, and with Java too distant to exert systematic authority, the Straits no longer had an acknowledged center. Supplying a limited number of products rather than the complete array such as Srivijaya had offered in its heyday, local ports either went their own way or sought protection from whatever power seemed most sympathetic. As if to dramatize centrifugal pulls, in the late 1200s, in order to escape Javanese pressure and to control gold and camphor from

---

[86] Likewise, although Champa was not tributary to Dai Viet, attacks from Champa, which was more commercially oriented than Dai Viet, contributed to the latter's 14th-century collapse. See *SP*, 119–23, 236–42, and Ch. 2 *supra*.

[87] This is a claim that gained credence with the spread to that region of Javanese currency and weights. Heng, "Export Commodity," 193–202; *HM*, 32–33.

the interior, Malayu-Jambi's ruling family moved from the coast to the upper Batang Hari River.[88]

Ironically, if commercial expansion thus helped to fragment Srivijaya, Reid and others argue that by decreasing port revenues, commercial contraction from c. 1280 to 1400 further reduced the chances of recentralization. As manifest in declining Chinese pottery exports, this disruption grew from population losses in China and other key Eurasian markets, the Mongol diversion of traffic across Inner Asia, bullion shortages, and crippling early Ming curbs on private trade. Insofar as the Pax Mongolica contributed to archipelagic localization, we have yet another instance of Mongol-mediated Eurasian rupture.[89]

Despite – or more probably because of – these manifold problems, leaders in Southeast Sumatra drew heart from the 1371 decision by the new Ming Dynasty to expand Chinese tributary trade in lieu of now prohibited overseas private trade. Might the imperial patronage that had nourished early Srivijaya now return? Thus hopeful, from 1371 to 1377 both Malayu (now based in the interior) and Palembang apparently sent envoys to the Ming court. And in 1391, in an effort to revive Palembang's ancient claims, its ruler declared himself independent of

---

[88] In the 1300s their capital would move yet farther inland near the headwaters of the Indragiri and Batang Hari, from where Adityavarman (r. 1347–1375?), the first Minangkabau king, may have exercised some sort of authority over much of central Sumatra. On this interior progression, Andaya, *Leaves*, 83–88, 93; idem, "Unravelling Minangkabau Ethnicity," in Leonard Blusse and Felipe Fernandez Armesto, eds., *Shifting Communities and Identity Formation in Early Modern Asia* (Leiden, 2003), 117–38, esp. 121–23; Wolters, *Fall of Srivijaya*, 57–58, 75, 90, 94, 169; Jane Drakard, *A Kingdom of Words* (Oxford, 1999), 19–24.

[89] The decline in pottery exports is known from its late-14th-century intensification as the early "Ming gap." *AC*, vol. II, 10–53, esp. 13–21; Reid, *Charting the Shape*, 63–64; idem, "Flows and Seepages," 17–37; David Bulbeck et al., comps., *Southeast Asian Exports Since the 14th Century* (Leiden, 1998), 1–106 *passim*. Evidence supporting Reid appears in William Atwell, "Time, Money, and the Weather," *JAS* 61 (2002): 83–114; Geoff Wade, "Ming China and Southeast Asia in the 15th Century," in Wade, ed., *Southeast Asia in the 15th Century* (Singapore, forthcoming); Pierre-Yves Manguin, "New Trends in Shipbuilding and Shipping in the South China Sea Starting in the 15th and 16th Centuries," in ibid.; Roxanna Brown, "A Ming Gap?" in ibid.; Geoff Wade, "An Early Age of Commerce in Southeast Asia: 900–1300 C.E." (ms); Christie, "Tamil-Language," 247, 259–61; Ch. 5, nn. 153, 155, 157 *supra*; Ch. 6, n. 155 *supra*; Richard von Glahn, "Towns and Temples," in *SYMT*, 176–211; Wolters, *Fall of Srivijaya*, 187–90. But note that Miksic, "Archaeology, Ceramics," 287–97; Kenneth Hall, "Local and International Trade and Traders in the Straits of Melaka Region: 600–1500," *JESHO* 47 (2004): 213–60; and Roderich Ptak, "From Quanzhou to the Sulu Zone and Beyond," *JSEAS* 29 (1998): 269–94 argue for a gradual, persistent rise in Sino-Southeast Asian trade from 1100 to 1500.

Java and overlord of Southeast Sumatra. These ambitions ended in utter disaster: the Javanese, now under Majapahit, again invaded Palembang and expelled the ruler. By 1397, Ming records noted tersely, Srivijaya "was a ruined country."[90]

Majapahit thus outlasted Srivijaya. But Majapahit's overseas authority, such as it was, also began to unravel because renewed trade expansion favored independent Muslim ports in the Straits and North Java, and more immediately because the Ming court, whose eunuch admiral Zheng He from 1405 headed seven massive trading expeditions to Southeast Asia, encouraged port-cities to enter into direct relations with China. Thus in the early 1400s erstwhile dependencies from Sumatra to Brunei to Sulu and Maluku sent their own tribute-cum-trade missions to China and left Majapahit's sphere of influence.[91]

Thereafter problems mounted within Java itself. To be sure, the picture of unalloyed 15th-century decline can be overdrawn. Contrary to earlier scholarship, Aoyama Toru has shown that a civil war in 1405–1406 did not pit eastern and western polities against one another, merely factions within a still unified Majapahit kingdom.[92] In the same spirit, J. Noorduyn has argued that putative dynastic upheavals in 1437 and 1453 either did not occur or were less traumatic than was assumed. Likewise, religious patronage, Sanskrit scholarship, and Old Javanese belles lettres flourished for most of the 15th century as they had in the 14th.[93] Such limited materials as survive, however, also point to growing political troubles, if not from the mid-1450s, then surely from 1468, which saw a major princely rebellion. At an uncertain date between 1486 and 1512 the *kraton* shifted to Kediri, possibly under a new dynasty. Denys Lombard speculates that the unchecked economic power of religious institutions reinforced the devolutionary effects of endemic princely competition.[94] To some degree, climatic deterioration in the late 1300s and 1400s

---

[90] *HM*, 33. Thereafter Palembang came under the control of Chinese traders/pirates. I rely too on Wolters, *Fall of Srivijaya*, 39–107, 120, 125, 147; and Anthony Reid, "Hybrid Identities in the 15th-Century Straits" (ms), 10–14, exploring the Sino-Indonesian background to regional rivalries.

[91] AC, vol. II, 15–16; Reid, "Flows and Seepages," 23–25, 31–33; Andaya, *Leaves*, 69–70; Wade, "Ming China and Southeast Asia"; and nn. 62 *supra* and 99 *infra*.

[92] Aoyama Toru, "A New Interpretation of the 'East-West Division of Java' in the Late 14th Century," *Acta Asiatica* 92 (2007): 31–52.

[93] Noorduyn, "Majapahit in the Fifteenth Century," 207–74. Cf. Zoetmulder, *Kalangwan*, 21–24, and an earlier scholarly tradition represented by Slametmuljana, *Story*.

[94] Lombard, *Carrefour Javanais*, vol. III, 26–35. He and Hunter, "Body of the King" also suggest that political devolution encouraged and reflected the rise of *kidung* literature,

aggravated Majapahit's problems.[95] By 1500 the Hindu-Buddhist power of East Java was in an advanced state of decay, beset by internal disputes and subject to attacks by newly risen Muslim trading ports on the north coast. About 1527 the most powerful of these north coast city-states, Demak, captured both Kediri and the kingdom's chief port, Tuban. Thus ended the charter/classical era of Javanese history – even though, as befit a charter polity, Majapahit inspired the rulers of Demak and later Muslim states to preserve its high culture and to depict themselves as Majapahit's legitimate heirs.[96]

In itself, the rise between c. 1400 and 1550 of Demak and other towns on Java's north coast – an area known as the *pasisir* – climaxed a commercially driven process that differed in precise chronology, but not centrifugal thrust from that which weakened Srivijaya and mainland charter states. Rather than attempt to rule directly Javanese port-cities, from the outset Majapahit relied on tax farms run by resident foreign (Malay, South Asian, Chinese) and local traders. Although for generations such arrangements let Majapahit benefit from mercantile expansion more directly than Pagan, Angkor, or Dai Viet, as trade expanded in the mid-1400s, these coastal enclaves, already semidetached, finally became too wealthy and powerful to remain subservient. Even as alien traders in the *pasisir* adopted local clothing, food, and language and aped Majapahit court ritual and aesthetics, Islam reflected and encouraged a growing sense of cultural and political independence from the interior.[97] In short, on present evidence, commercial expansion weakened both Srivijaya and Majapahit, but during different phases of the Asian trade cycle. The first expansion, c. 1050–1280, undermined Srivijaya, but East Java, in part because of its ability to combine agrarian

sympathetic to princely entourage and local autonomy, at the expense of *kakawin* poetry championing royal power. Cf. Zoetmulder, *Kalangwan*, chs. 1, 16.

[95] Noorduyn, "Majapahit in the Fifteenth Century," 208 and n. 84 *supra*.

[96] *HMI*, 22, 41–42, 46; M. C. Ricklefs, *Mystic Synthesis in Java* (Norwalk, CT, 2006), 63; idem, *The Seen and Unseen Worlds in Java, 1729–1746* (Honolulu, 1998), xix–xx.

[97] Previous note, plus Ricklefs, *Mystic Synthesis*, 17–29; idem, "Six Centuries," 104–105; Wisseman Christie, "States Without Cities," 27, 37; idem, "Trade and Value," 16; Pigeaud, *Java*, vol. IV, 501–504, 522–23; Graaf and Pigeaud, *Chinese Muslims*, 183. Although Islam was not a factor on the mainland, these fissures closely paralleled the 14th-century breakaway of the Mon coast from Upper Burma and of Siamese Ayudhya from Angkor. But, as noted, Champa survived longer than Pagan or Angkor, probably because it, like Majapahit, was better able to profit from maritime commercial expansion. See n. 86 *supra*.

with maritime wealth, remained vital. However, the second expansion, 1400/1450–1527, collapsed Majapahit.

To recapitulate the broader argument of Part 1: During their first eight historic centuries, the islands absorbed Indian influences and gave birth to two principal charter realms, Srivijaya, c. 650–1397, and classical Java, c. 716–1527. Overlapping with Pagan, Angkor, Dai Viet, Kiev, Capetian France, and Heian Japan, these polities, like other charter states, benefited from expanding Eurasian trade, easier contacts with older Eurasian centers, local political experiments, and in the case of East Java from agrarian intensification that may have owed something to improved climate. In typical charter fashion, both island realms exercised a superficial, unstable hegemony and patronized a relatively elitist, encapsulated court culture (although in Java *kraton*-rural links seem to have been more ramified in 1400 than in 800). Finally, at various points between 1250 and 1527 long-distance trade empowered dependencies whose waxing strength joined long-standing institutional weaknesses to collapse both Srivijaya and Majapahit.

2. TRADE, NEW STATES, AND ISLAM, C. 1350–1511

Problems of Periodization and Regional Coherence

Convenient though it would be to find political history closely synchronized across Southeast Asia, reality did not always oblige. As we just saw, the unraveling of Pagan, Angkor, Dai Viet, and Srivijaya coincided with Majapahit's glory. Well before Majapahit collapsed, the western archipelago had adjusted to Srivijaya's demise and had entered a fresh phase of consolidation, whose most celebrated pre-1511 example was the city-state of Melaka.

Yet in a wider sense, Melaka symbolized deep postcharter transformations that affected the entire archipelago. Notwithstanding political disjunctures between the Straits and Java, three broad changes gave island development between c. 1350 and 1511 (after which Europeans began to modify its main lines) a reasonably coherent character. First, from the early or mid-1400s, in response to revived demand in China, Europe, Southwest Asia, and India, transit trade and local exports rose notably. Second, quickening commerce nourished a network of essentially new coastal states extending from North Sumatra through Melaka and the *pasisir* to Maluku and the Philippines. Third, through contact with Muslim merchants and preachers, from the late 1200s one city-state after another went over to Islam. Wedding the new faith to Malay language and court rituals, Melaka, in particular, fostered a novel Malayo-Muslim cultural identity.

What is more, the rise of Melaka and the spread of Malayo-Muslim culture again paralleled developments elsewhere in Eurasia. From the mid-1400s as postcharter disorders subsided, we saw that recentralizing movements transformed the western, central, and eastern sectors of mainland Southeast Asia as well as Russia and France. In each case renewed economic growth joined official patronage and provincial imitation to promote capital cultures and textual religions. Because Malayo-Muslim identities spread far more widely than Melakan military power, and because Malay was an archipelago-wide commercial lingua franca, the link between culture and political loyalty in the archipelago was looser than in other areas. Yet, in its basic chronology and integrative potential, the spread of Malayo-Muslim culture between 1350 and 1511 recalls the diffusion of majority ethnicities and state-centered Theravada and Neo-Confucian cults in Burma, Siam, and Vietnam, of Russian ethnicity and Orthodoxy under Muscovy, of the "royal religion" and Parisian culture in France, and of aristocratic/warrior culture in post-1300 Japan.

The Opening Phase of the "Age of Commerce," c. 1400–1511: Rising Global Demand

Reid argued that the early 1400s initiated a politically and culturally transformative surge in Southeast Asian trade that gained strength to the 1640s. This period he famously christened the "Age of Commerce." According to this thesis, as already noted, the antecedent era c. 1280–1400 was less propitious, in part because demographic declines depressed global demand, the Pax Mongolica redirected some exchange overland, and the first Ming emperor issued bans on private overseas shipping that remained in force, at least on paper, to 1567.[98]

Such bans notwithstanding, four factors invigorated Chinese–archipelagic traffic during the 15th and early 16th centuries. First, in lieu of private activity, Zheng He's aforementioned state expeditions from 1405 to 1433 encouraged official tribute-and-trade missions from Southeast Asia. Long after 1433, albeit with declining frequency, such

[98] See n. 89 *supra*.

missions provided an approved vehicle for Ming–Southeast Asian exchange.[99]

Second, after its unification in 1429, the island kingdom of Ryukyu developed a lively official commerce with Java, Sumatra, and the Straits, on the one hand, and with Ming China, Korea, and Japan, on the other. Managed by Chinese traders who had settled in Ryukyu to circumvent Ming restrictions, Ryukyuan court trade helped to link East Asia and Southeast Asia for the better part of a century.[100]

Illegal traffic, particularly from the mid-1400s, provided a third spur to Chinese–archipelagic exchange, with Chinese and Southeast Asian smugglers focusing on Fujian and Guangdong. Repeated government complaints about smuggling, with ever more drastic penalties, show that official channels could not satisfy a growing demand for Southeast Asian exotica, a demand that fed on China's post-1450 demographic recovery, the familiarity with Southeast Asian goods that official trade itself promoted, and a post-Yuan constriction of overland contacts with West Asia. In the 15th century pepper and other products from the Nan-yang – the Southern Ocean – became items of mass consumption in China, so popular, in fact, that soldiers received pepper as part of their salary. In turn smugglers exported the same goods as the Chinese and Ryukyuan courts shipped openly, chiefly cash, ceramics, and silks.[101]

Finally, Chinese living in Southeast Asia expanded their activities to fill the void created by Ming restrictions. But since virtually no Chinese women went overseas and early Ming curbs reduced male emigration,

[99] Zheng He is also credited with introducing or encouraging the cultivation of black pepper in Sumatra for the China market. *AC*, vol. II, 12–16; Reid, *Charting the Shape*, 63–64; idem, "Flows and Seepages," 21–30; Leo Suryadinata, ed., *Admiral Zheng He and Southeast Asia* (Singapore, 2005); n. 101 *infra*. But again John Miksic, "Before and After Zheng He," in Wade, *Southeast Asia in the 15th Century*, is skeptical that Zheng He altered the main lines of trade development.

[100] *AC*, vol. II, 13–14; idem, "Flows and Seepages," 30; Okamoto Hiromichi, "Foreign Policy and Maritime Trade in the Early Ming Period," in Wade, *Southeast Asia in the 15th Century*; A. Kobata and M. Matsuda, *Ryukyuan Relations with Korea and South Seas Countries* (Kyoto, 1969), sects. III–VIII; Ch. 4, nn. 132, 133 *supra*.

[101] On pepper, T'ien Ju-kang, "Cheng Ho's Voyages and the Distribution of Pepper in China," *JRAS* 1981: 186–97; Reid, *Charting the Shape*, 64; Andaya, *Live as Brothers*, 43–44; and n. 104 *infra*. On post-1450 Chinese trade expansion, also Ch. 5 nn. 162–63 *supra*. On illegal trade, Wade, "Ming China and Southeast Asia"; Pin-tsun Chang, "The First Chinese Diaspora in Southeast Asia in the 15th Century," in Roderich Ptak and Dietmar Rothermund, eds., *Emporia, Commodities and Entrepreneurs in Asian Maritime Trade, c. 1400–1750* (Stuttgart, 1991), 13–28; Roderich Ptak, "Ming Maritime Trade to Southeast Asia, 1368–1567," in Guillot et al., *From the Mediterranean*, 157–91.

assimilation to host cultures accelerated.[102] Many, if not most, envoys to the Middle Kingdom were Sino-Malays and Sino-Javanese, as apparently were most Southeast Asians trading illicitly to China. Chinese–local interaction fostered hybrid vocabularies, cuisines, and technologies, including a shipbuilding tradition that melded Chinese techniques (iron nails and clamps, axial rudders, bulkheads) with Southeast Asian traditions (hardwoods, V-shaped dowelled hulls, keels). Using these so-called junks, which carried up to a thousand tons and were built largely under Sino-Southeast Asian auspices in coastal Java, Borneo, and Burma, traders of Chinese ancestry not only expanded trade with China, but helped to develop the archipelago's chief 15th-century axis that ran between Melaka, Java, and Maluku.[103]

Parallel to East Asian demand for archipelagic products, Indian Ocean traders in growing numbers sought goods for South Asia, the Mideast, and ultimately Europe. In these regions as in China, commercial vigor reflected demographic recovery from 14th-century traumas, larger late-15th-century bullion flows, and a decline (whether relative or absolute is unclear) in Inner Asian traffic after the collapse of the Pax Mongolica. Cairo's *karimi* merchants amassed fortunes from Indian Ocean spices, which Venetians, Catalans, and Genoese then funneled to northern Europe. Although spices entering Europe were but a fraction of what remained in India and the Mideast, figures for Europe are more reliable. From 1400 to 1500 European spice imports, including Malukun cloves, nutmeg, and mace, reportedly grew 155 to 177 percent, while less lucrative pepper imports (from both Southeast Asia and Malabar) rose 10 to 45 percent. The biggest increases came after 1470.[104] According

---

[102] A shared Islamic identity often facilitated assimilation, even though Chinese Muslims' legal affiliation was chiefly Hanafi and indigenes' was Shafi'i. On Chinese diasporas, previous note, plus Anthony Reid, "Chinese and Malay Identities in Southeast Asia," *Academic Sinica Program for Southeast Asian Studies, Research Paper No. 34* (Taipei, 2000); idem, "Flows and Seepages," 27–37; idem, "Hybrid Identities"; idem, *Charting the Shape*, 56–76; Ma Huan, *Ying-yai*, 93; *HMI*, 4, 41, 45; Cortesao, *Suma Oriental*, vol. I, 182; Graaf and Pigeaud, *Chinese Muslims*, 171, 183–84 and *passim*.

[103] Manguin, "Trading Ships"; idem, "Southeast Asian Ship"; idem, "New Trends in Shipbuilding"; idem, "The Vanishing *Jong*," in Anthony Reid, ed., *Southeast Asia in the Early Modern Era* (Ithaca, 1993), 197–213; *AC*, 36–43; Andaya, "Interactions," 377–78. Chinese also introduced new technologies for bronze-casting, scales, and gunpowder. Reid, *Charting the Shape*, 23.

[104] C. H. Wake, "The Volume of European Spice Exports at the Beginning and End of the 15th Century," *JEEH* 15 (1986): 621–35, revising idem, "The Changing Pattern of Europe's Pepper and Spice Imports, ca 1400–1700," *JEEH* 8 (1979): 361–403. Wake's fine spice figures are broadly consistent with *AC*, vol. II, 14, Fig. 3 and *CHSEA*, 465,

to the Portuguese apothecary Tome Pires (author of a detailed eyewitness account of Asian trade in 1515), in exchange for spices, pepper, gold, and Chinese manufactures, Muslim merchants supplied Southeast Asians with opium, metals, and diverse Indian textiles and West Asian handicrafts.[105]

Lured by imported commodities, local groups reorganized the provision of forest products and cash crops. The clove plant grew only in North Maluku, principally on five small islands, while the tree whose seed provides nutmeg and whose outer covering provides mace grew only in the tiny South Malukun archipelago of Banda. Cloves were prized in Han China (where courtiers used them as breath sweeteners) and in classical Rome. Yet so modest was demand that the people of Ternate and Tidore may not have appreciated cloves' commercial value until Chinese traders arrived in the 14th century. The late 1300s and more especially the late 1400s and 1500s saw a major increase in the supply of cloves to Javanese and Malay middlemen, from whom the Chinese began to obtain that spice indirectly. Such middlemen provided rice, ironware, and textiles, which allowed aspirant overlords in North Maluku to centralize patronage and thus to systematize the gathering of cloves from wild trees; as yet cloves were not cultivated. Nutmeg and mace followed a similar trajectory, with Muslims from the western archipelago and Java providing a catalyst from the late 1400s for the expanded harvesting of wild trees.[106] In China, India, the Mideast, and Europe by this time these three so-called "fine spices" from Maluku

Fig. 8.1, but in the latter source Anthony Reid suggests a steep rise in pepper exports not to Europe alone, but to Europe and China (by far the largest market), from 25 metric tonnes in 1400 to 250 tonnes in 1500. On Mideast and European spice imports via the Indian Ocean, see too Bulbeck et al., *Southeast Asian Exports*, 9, 23–26, 31, 33, 60; *AC*, vol. II, 10–16, 21; Eliyahu Ashtor, *A Social and Economic History of the Near East in the Middle Ages* (Berkeley, 1976), 325–28; D. S. Richards, ed., *Islam and the Trade of Asia* (Oxford, 1970), 81–157.

[105] Cortesao, *Suma Oriental*, vol. I, 214 and vol. II, 268–73; Paul Wheatley, *Impressions of the Malay Peninsula in Ancient Times* (Singapore, 1964), 160. M. C. Ricklefs, pers. commun., April 26, 2008 informs me that a more reliable Portuguese edition of Pires' work has appeared recently.

[106] *AC*, vol. II, 3–7; Leonard Andaya, *The World of Maluku* (Honolulu, 1993), 77 and ch. 2 passim; idem, "Cultural State Formation in Eastern Indonesia," in Reid, *Southeast Asia in Early Modern Era*, 32–33; Leonard Andaya, pers. commun., Sept. 21, 2008; Roderich Ptak, "China and the Trade in Cloves, circa 960–1435," *JAOS* 113 (1993): 1–13; idem, "From Quanzhou," 287–88; R. A. Donkin, *Between East and West* (Philadelphia, 2003), 4, 56–59, 120–24, 156. Not until the 1600s did the Dutch begin planting clove on Ambon and nutmeg on Banda, and uprooting trees elsewhere.

were widely prized as drugs, aromatics, and condiments.[107] Black pepper (*piper nigrum*), valued as preservative, aphrodisiac, medicine, and flavoring, was less expensive, because unlike clove and nutmeg trees, pepper vines were easily and widely cultivated, producing ten times the annual export volume of fine spices. Introduced probably from Malabar and encouraged by Zheng He, pepper in the early 1400s was concentrated in North Sumatra and West Java. But by 1500, through an array of bonded and free labor systems, it had spread to Lampung and interior Sumatra and to Pahang, Pattani, and Kedah on the peninsula, with China the chief market.[108]

Presumably in some areas, Southwest Sulawesi and North Java most obviously but perhaps also sectors of Sumatra and the peninsula, domestic population growth to 1500 both reflected and encouraged the expansion of international trade. Foreign demand, to recall Henley's thesis, enhanced market efficiency, which stimulated local food production, which raised fertility and depressed child mortality, which expanded the labor force needed to supply export goods. The rapid growth of urban centers, to which we shall turn shortly, presupposes a mobile "surplus" rural population. Volume 1 argued that mainland Southeast Asia between c. 1400 and 1550 benefited from such trends. But, to date at least, archeology and written sources from the archipelago offer little hard information on 15th-century demography.

Clearly, however, with commercial expansion came wider monetization. In the 12th century, recall, Javanese markets relied on Chinese bronze cash and local replicas. By the early 1500s unprecedented quantities of cash – supplemented by local tin and gold coins and lump silver – comprised the chief commercial lubricants not only in Java, but eastern and southern Sumatra, Melaka, Brunei, Sumbawa, and Maluku.[109]

Major Port Polities, c. 1350–1511

Yet the most visible index of prosperity between c. 1350 and 1511 was the expansion and proliferation of port-cities, which, together with their

---

[107] On Eurasian uses and knowledge of fine spices, Donkin, *Between East and West*, chs. 2–5.

[108] *AC*, vol. II, 7–9; Bulbeck et al., *Southeast Asian Exports*, 77; Ma Huan, *Ying-yai*, 118; Andaya, *Leaves*, 110–12, 115, 156–57; Andaya, *Live as Brothers*, 43–44. This geographic expansion is consistent with Reid's figures for sharply rising Southeast Asian pepper exports to Europe and China in n. 104 *supra*.

[109] Wade, "Ming China and Southeast Asia"; *AC*, vol. II, 93–97; Cortesao, *Suma Oriental*, vol. I, 144, 170, 181, 203, 206–207; Heng, "Export Commodity," 202.

immediate hinterlands, were known in Malay as *negeri*. Located as close to a river mouth as security allowed, such towns drew their livelihood by providing entrepot services along with interior crops, metals, and forest products. Because regional population densities were low and residential compounds sprawled haphazardly from the city center, port conurbations often contained a sizeable fraction of a region's total population. Indeed, if we accept a flexible definition of "city," Reid has argued that by 1500 archipelagic Southeast Asia was among the world's most urbanized regions.[110] Typically, as Bennet Bronson and Barbara Watson Andaya have shown, interior products were collected at secondary and tertiary centers at upstream river junctions and funneled downriver to the capital. The latter might try to coerce upstream locales, but for the most part they could be held in orbit only through a mutually profitable exchange of interior goods for coastal salt, iron, and textiles. Even over tributary ports near the mouths of independent river systems, naval control by the capital was so difficult as to mandate a high degree of autonomy.[111]

Moving west to east, here follows a *tour d'horizon* of major *negeri* during the early phase of the Age of Commerce to 1511. The northwest tip of Sumatra was particularly attractive to Indian Ocean merchants because as Indonesia's most westerly point, it let them buy Malukun spices and Chinese goods from Indonesian traders without themselves having to travel deep into the archipelago. Although North Sumatra also supplied local forest products (benzoin, camphor, eaglewood),[112] in the 1400s surging Chinese demand for pepper marginalized those goods, while promoting extensive pepper cultivation in the Sumatran interior. For much of the 14th and 15th centuries the chief beneficiary of these trends was the port-city of Pasai. Close ties to Muslim traders from the west and weaker Hindu-Buddhist legacies than in Southeast Sumatra or Java help to explain why Pasai was one of the earliest archipelagic states to accept Islam. But while it maintained a reputation for Islamic learning and absorbed some polities to which its

---

[110] Anthony Reid, "The Structure of Cities in Southeast Asia: 15th to 17th Centuries," *JSEAS* 11 (1980): 235–50; *AC*, vol. II, 67–77.

[111] Cf. Bennet Bronson, "Exchange at the Upstream and Downstream Ends," in Karl Hutterer, ed., *Economic Exchange and Social Interaction in Southeast Asia* (Ann Arbor, 1977), 39–52; Andaya, *Live as Brothers*, 13–20; idem, "Upstreams and Downstreams in Early Modern Sumatra," *The Historian* 57 (1995): 537–52.

[112] Note 30 *supra*; *The Travels of Marco Polo* (New York, n.d.), 272–80.

rulers had kinship ties, Pasai never achieved extensive territorial influence.[113]

In Southeast Sumatra the old Srivijayan capital cities of Malayu-Jambi (by this period known simply as Jambi) and Palembang retained some importance, but from the late 1400s again fell under Javanese influence.[114] In terms of commercial and cultural influence, Srivijaya's principal heir was neither Jambi nor Palembang, rather Melaka, on the Straits that still bear its name at the intersection of the Bay of Bengal, the South China Sea, and the Java Sea. Indeed, Melaka became the most celebrated city in the precolonial history of maritime Southeast Asia.[115]

European and Malay accounts suggest Melaka was founded c. 1400 by a refugee prince from Palembang who descended from the Srivijayan royal house.[116] The new outpost quickly paid homage to Siam and Majapahit, both to forestall attacks by those powers (Majapahit apparently had driven Melaka's founder from Palembang) and to obtain rice supplies. But Melaka's early success – not unlike that of Srivijaya 750 years earlier – depended more basically on China, which, desiring one strong center in the Straits to avoid trade disruptions, restrained Siamese hostility to Melaka and provided it with invaluable tributary openings. Visited by Ming imperial fleets no less than 10 times in its first quarter century, Melaka became the chief archipelagic collecting center for pepper, marine, and forest goods destined for China both as official tribute and illicit trade, and the main distribution point for Chinese textiles, porcelains, and handicrafts arriving through similar channels.[117] Ryukyuan ships dealt in comparable items.

---

[113] Also known as Samudra-Pasai, this polity fell in 1524 to Aceh, to which we shall return. On North Sumatra 1300–1520, Pigeaud, *Java*, vol. IV, 30–31; Andaya, *Leaves*, 110–16; Miksic, "Urbanization," 3–30; Wolters, *Fall of Srivijaya*, 157–58, 175; Cortesao, *Suma Oriental*, vol. I, 142–45; Amirul Hadi, *Islam and State in Sumatra* (Leiden, 2004), 11–21.

[114] Such influence, from Demak, was more pronounced in Palembang than Jambi. Cortesao, *Suma Oriental*, vol. I, 154–56, 185; *HMI*, 41; Andaya, *Live as Brothers*, 14.

[115] On Melakan history, Wolters, *Fall of Srivijaya*, chs. 2–11; Cortesao, *Suma Oriental*, vol. II, 229–89; *HM*, 33–60; Luis Thomaz, "The Malay Sultanate of Melaka," in Reid, *Southeast Asia in Early Modern Era*, 69–90; Kernial Singh Sandhu and Paul Wheatley, "The Historical Context," in Sandhu and Wheatley, eds., *Melaka* (Kuala Lumpur, 1983), 3–69; C. H. Wake, "Melaka in the 15th Century," in ibid., 127–61; John Bowen, "Cultural Models for Historical Genealogies," in ibid., 162–79. Between Pasai and Jambi the Malay-Batak state of Aru also enjoyed some influence.

[116] On Srivijaya–Melaka links, Cortesao, *Suma Oriental*, vol. II, 229 ff.; *HM*, 21, 28, 33–38; Wolters, *Fall of Srivijaya*.

[117] Meilink-Roelofsz, *Asian Trade*, 74–80; Wolters, *Fall of Srivijaya*, ch. 11.

Other lines of Melakan trade soon supplemented that with China. Arguably the most profitable segment, with the Indian Ocean, was managed by a great throng of Arabs, Persians, Armenians, Jews, Malabaris, Deccanis, Bengalis, Tamils, and Gujaratis. This predominantly Muslim traffic relied heavily on Gujarat, which dominated forward shipments to the Mideast and organized West Asian merchants into companies for the voyage to Melaka. A third line of trade, in volume probably the largest, involved the archipelago and the southern mainland, which together supplied Melaka with foodstuffs, ships, pepper, spices, marine products, and slaves.[118] Thus Melaka, like Srivijaya, concentrated at one entrepot a vast array of goods that, after Srivijaya's decline, had been sold at ports specializing in only a few local items.

To enhance tributary deliveries and to guard against Siam, Melaka from the mid-1400s extended its territorial influence through a mix of force, strategic marriages, and commercial ventures. By the 1480s the city dominated *negeri* throughout the southern peninsula, the central east coast of Sumatra, and the Riau-Lingga archipelago, areas that overlapped substantially with those once loyal to Srivijaya.[119] Thus Melaka – estimates of whose 1511 population range from 10,000 to 200,000, with lower-end figures most plausible[120] – became a major node in a Muslim-dominated trade network running from Maluku to North Java to Melaka to Gujarat to Hormuz, Alexandria, and Venice. "Malacca [sic] is a city that was made for merchandise, fitter than any other in the world," claimed Pires. It "lies in the middle, and the trade and commerce between the different nations for a thousand leagues on every hand must come to Malacca.... Whoever is lord of Malacca has his hand on the throat of Venice."[121] As for Melaka's early regional rival, by 1511 "you could make ten cities like Pase [Pasai] out of the city of Malacca."[122]

---

[118] Indians based in Melaka also brought spices directly from Maluku. On Melaka's trade, n. 105 *supra*; Meilink-Roelofsz, *Asian Trade*, chs. 3, 4; Thomaz, "Malay Sultanate," 74; and Manguin, "City States," emphasizing hinterland exports.
[119] On territorial influence, Wheatley, *Golden Khersonese*, 308–10; *HM*, 52–53, 66–67; Thomaz, "Malay Sultanate," 69–90.
[120] Thomaz, "Malay Sultanate," 71 claims 100,000–200,000, while Reid, "*Negeri*," 419 cites a range of figures, but opts for 100,000 as a peak. However, Ulbe Bosma and Remco Raben, *Being 'Dutch' in the Indies* (Singapore, 2008), 5 suggest 10,000 is more probable. Ricklefs, pers. commun., April 26, 2008, and Leonard Andaya, pers. commun., Sept. 21, 2008 have also expressed great skepticism of the high range estimates; Andaya argues that 20,000–25,000 was most likely.
[121] Cortesao, *Suma Oriental*, vol. II, 286–87.
[122] Ibid., vol. I, 144, apparently referring to population size, but possibly to trade volume. Pires' figures suggest that annual trade at Melaka was 2,400,000 cruzados (cf. 4,000,000

Apart from early Chinese support, how shall we explain Melaka's success? And why after 1400 did commercial expansion favor a uni-centered system in the western archipelago, whereas in the 13th and 14th centuries expansion had undermined Srivijaya? Claims to Srivi-jayan royal ancestry won Melaka's rulers the loyalty of both Malayu (Malay) immigrants from Sumatra and *orang laut* sea peoples who, as in earlier centuries, protected traffic in the Straits. As heirs to Srivijaya, Melaka's kings knew how to foster an attractive mercantile environment with secure storage facilities, codified laws, moderate tolls, and rapid turnover. A minimalist administration accommodated diverse interests not only in tributary *negeri*, but the capital itself, where the heads of powerful Malay kinship networks tended to treat the king as *primus inter pares*.[123]

But if these features were familiar from Srivijaya, Melaka also enjoyed distinct advantages over its charter predecessor. Its harbor was supe-rior to that of Srivijaya, free of mangrove swamps, sheltered, yet with control of the Straits near its narrowest point. High-value, low-volume pepper and Malukun fine spices, which became the chief draws for Indian Ocean merchants, may have encouraged a concentration of sell-ers and buyers at a single point more readily than had pre-1450 trade in which spices figured less prominently. Whereas Srivijaya's rulers had insisted on controlling key items, Melaka sought less to coerce than to attract traders in a basically free market. This policy, together with the lure of spices and a general rise in Eurasian demand, meant that the volume of goods at Melaka almost certainly exceeded that at Srivijaya.[124] Agrarian expansion on the mainland and Java now pro-vided larger surpluses to feed chronic rice-deficit areas like Melaka. The city-state's Islamic environment probably attracted Indian Ocean

at Spain's chief Atlantic port of Seville). *HM*, 46. But Pires must be taken with a grain of salt, since he sought Portuguese royal support for the newly acquired outpost of Melaka.

[123] *HM*, 44–52; Andaya, 71–81; Pierre-Yves Manguin, "The Amorphous Nature of Coastal Polities in Insular Southeast Asia," *Moussons* 5 (2002): 73–99; Liaw Yock Fang, "The *Undang-undang Melaka*," in Sandhu and Wheatley, *Melaka*, 180–94; J. Kathirithamby-Wells, "Forces of Regional and State Integration in the Western Archipelago, c. 1500–1700," *JSEAS* 18 (1987): 41–42.

[124] Thomaz, "Malay Sultanate"; idem, "Malaka et ses communautes marchandes au tour-nant du 16e siecle," in Denys Lombard and Jean Aubin, eds., *Marchands et Hommes d'Affaires Asiatiques* (Paris, 1988), 31–48; M. A. P. Meilink-Roelofsz, "Trade and Islam in the Malay-Indonesian Archipelago Prior to the Arrival of the Europeans," in Richards, *Islam*, 137–57; Kathirithamby-Wells, "Regional and State Integration," 25, 42.

traders more readily than had Srivijayan Buddhism, which was more court centered and esoteric. Likewise Melaka's Islamic modification of Malay culture may have appealed more strongly to regional *negeri*, even if family ties remained the principal determinant of *negeri* loyalties.

Despite these assets, there is reason to suspect that Melaka's position – like that of Srivijaya in the 13th and 14th centuries – was inherently unstable and that over time spreading pepper cultivation and rising demand for other specialized goods again would have broken the system into regional components, with an attendant increase in inter-*negeri* conflict. Indeed, a North Javanese armada tried to seize Melaka in 1513. Although this attack came two years after Melaka had fallen to the Portuguese, it was planned *before* the Europeans arrived. Had Portuguese or *pasisir* warships not taken Melaka in the early 1500s, the rising North Sumatran pepper port of Aceh well might have done so later in the century. Fearing North Sumatran competition, Melaka in fact laid plans to attack that region, but failed to carry through.[125]

Apart from the Melaka Straits, Java's north coast, the *pasisir*, was the most dynamic commercial zone in the 15th century as it had been during the charter era. By sending Indian textiles and Javanese rice to the Spice Islands (Maluku) and local foodstuffs and Malukun spices to Melaka, the *pasisir* linked the archipelago's western and eastern termini. Although religious-cum-commercial interests began to separate the *pasisir* from its suzerain Majapahit and although several ports cooperated for the 1513 attack on Melaka, the coast at large remained quite fragmented. In the far west the Hindu state of Pajajaran held the ports of Banten and Sunda Kalapa (the future Jayakerta/Batavia), both of which specialized in rapidly rising pepper exports to China. Until the 1520s most of this area resisted Islamization.[126] As a self-consciously Muslim town, Demak at its height dominated a second coastal sphere from Cirebon to Rembang. Demak opened as a port in the late 1400s under a Chinese Muslim trader whose son (or younger brother) launched a series of campaigns that extended the city's authority, along with Islam, at the expense of Hindu-Buddhist Majapahit. Yet, as noted, this did not

---

[125] Cortesao, *Suma Oriental*, vol. I, 187–88; *HMI*, 36–37; Meilink-Roelofsz, *Asian Trade*, 138, 147.

[126] Cortesao, *Suma Oriental*, vol. I, 166–73, listing "Bantam" (Banten) and five other ports in the kingdom of Sunda (but cf. Leonard Blusse, *Strange Company*, Dordrecht, 1988, 38, describing Banten as a mere fishing village in 1527), and *HMI*, 42. "Jayakerta," of course, became "Jakarta." But for traditions of early Islamization at Banten, see Ota Atsushi, *Changes of Regime and Social Dynamics in West Java* (Leiden, 2006), 53–54.

prevent Demak's rulers from claiming to be Majapahit's cultural and dynastic heirs.[127] Farther east lay Tuban, whose ruler, at best nominally Muslim in 1515 ("This man does not seem to me to be a very firm believer in Mohammed," Pires noted), was one of the last coastal lords loyal to Majapahit.[128] A fourth area focused on Gresik in the northeast. Also founded by a Chinese immigrant, Gresik specialized in exchanging Indian textiles and local foodstuffs for Malukun spices. Styled by Pires "the jewel of Java,"[129] Gresik too was a major Islamic center, for the nearby site of Giri was home to one of Java's great Muslim apostles (*walis*).

In north Borneo the celebrated port-city of Brunei, like Melaka, responded enthusiastically to early Ming diplomatic overtures and cemented its ties to western traders by accepting Islam.[130] But the islands east of Borneo (and indeed, much of coastal, not to mention interior, Borneo itself) lay quite literally at the end of the world, which meant that state formation and literacy were long delayed, and when states did cohere through expanding commerce, they often assumed an immediate Islamic guise, without those Hindu-Buddhist precursors found farther west.[131] In the Philippines, for example, in order to obtain Chinese ceramics and other prestige-enhancing imports, petty chiefs fought to monopolize key exports and to augment their labor supply. The 15th and early 16th centuries thus saw intensified slave raiding and larger fortified settlements. In Luzon and the Visayas by 1570 such processes had yet to produce stable supralocal structures, but farther south in Sulu and Mindanao, where Islamic influence was more extensive, statelets

---

[127] Although silting now separates Demak from the sea, in the 1500s its naval power extended to Southeast Sumatra. See nn. 96, 114 *supra*; Cortesao, *Suma Oriental*, vol. I, 183–89; Lombard, *Carrefour Javanais*, vol. II, 50–54.

[128] Cortesao, *Suma Oriental*, vol. I, 189–92; quote 191.

[129] Cortesao, *Suma Oriental*, vol. I, 192–93 ff. On the early 16th-century *pasisir*, see too Theodore G. Th. Pigeaud and H. J. de Graaf, *Islamic States in Java 1500–1700* (The Hague, 1976), ch. 1; Meilink-Roelofsz, *Asian Trade*, 103–15.

[130] On early Brunei, *HM*, 60–61; *HMI*, 4–5; Reid, "Flows and Seepages," 34–36; D. E. Brown, *Brunei* (Brunei, 1970), 136–42; Robert Nicholl, "Brunei Rediscovered," *JSEAS* 14 (1983): 32–45.

[131] Conversely, persistent traits in the east – kinship defined by shared substances (blood, milk, ritual food), headhunting, unstable charismatic authority – reflected an Austronesian heritage that had much in common with the prehistoric Pacific. Andaya, *World of Maluku*, 5, 246–49; Barbara Watson Andaya, "History, Headhunting, and Gender in Monsoon Asia," *South East Asia Research* 12 (2004): 13–52; Reid, *Charting the Shape*, 100–25; John Villiers, "Trade and Society in the Banda Islands in the Sixteenth Century," *MAS* 15 (1981): 723–50. The interiors not only of Borneo, but most islands remained removed from Islamic trade.

began to resemble Muslim *negeri* to the west.[132] Similarly, although origin myths sanctioned island-wide and regional identities in Maluku, those eastern islands, Leonard Andaya has shown, remained divided into small, unstable chieftainships until the late 1300s and more especially the 1460s, when demand for cloves began to strengthen would-be overlords by affording them control of imported rice, cloth, and iron implements. Islam also favored emergent hegemons by promoting royal patrilineality and sanctioning the creation of offices dependent on the ruler, as in the new spice-exporting sultanates of Ternate and Tidore.[133]

Negeri *Society, Islamization, and Malay Identity*

From Sumatra to Maluku *negeri* between c. 1300 and 1511 exhibited a number of generic traits. In contrast to agrarian, inland states, coastal elites typically consisted of merchants and wealthy aristocrats – the *orang kaya* ("wealthy men," "powerful men") – whom Reid divides into three occasionally overlapping categories: a) Foreign merchants residing temporarily. b) Merchant-officials who mediated between the court and traders, who themselves were often of foreign descent, but who resided permanently in the port-city or its dependencies. The classic merchant-official was the *syahbandar* (Persian for "port master"), appointed to handle tolls and protocol for particular groups of foreign traders. c) Indigenous aristocrats whose power derived from commercial wealth and the retainers such wealth supported.[134]

To judge from anecdotal evidence, this emphasis on commercial success, alongside or in lieu of pedigree, permitted considerable social mobility, at least by the standards of mainland societies. The future *syahbandar* of Banten arrived in the city with "nothing to live on, so that he busied himself with vile things to earn his living."[135] The grandfather of the lord of Jepara was "a working man [who]...went to Malacca with very little nobility and less wealth."[136] The ruler of Demak

---

[132] Laura Lee Junker, *Raiding, Trading, and Feasting* (Honolulu), 1999), 4–5, 15–28, 373–86 and *passim*; Bacus, "Archaeology of Philippine Archipelago," 266–78. See discussion *infra*.

[133] See n. 106 *supra*, plus John Villiers, "The Cash-Crop Economy and State Formation in the Spice Islands in the 15th and 16th Centuries," in Kathirithamby-Wells and Villiers, *Port and Polity*, 83–105. On the early history of South Sulawesi, see n. 260 *infra*.

[134] *AC*, vol. II, 114–23. Also Denys Lombard, "Le sultanat Malais comme modele socio-economique," in Lombard and Aubin, *Marchands*, 117–24.

[135] Meilink-Roelofsz, *Asian Trade*, 240, citing an early Dutch account.

[136] Cortesao, *Suma Oriental*, vol. I, 187.

descended from a slave, as did the admiral of Melaka.[137] Although all Malay-speaking city-states used slave labor, such bondsmen were readily assimilated to the free population through a mix of Muslim conversion, frequent manumission, and the custom whereby slaves hired themselves out, keeping up to half of the profits for themselves.[138]

If servile origins were not a fatal barrier to elite status, foreign ethnicity was even less so, and in fact, was often an asset. As Manguin has shown, *negeri* foundation myths commonly emphasized the seminal role of foreign shipmasters, while many *pasisir* rulers, to cite Pires again, "are not Javanese of long standing in the country, but they are descended from Chinese, from Parsees and Kling, and from the nations we have already mentioned."[139] Cities typically were organized into discrete, self-administered ethnic quarters. But if cosmopolitanism favored economic dynamism, it also risked factionalism. One reason the Portuguese attack on Melaka succeeded in 1511 is that the city's *orang kaya* split between a pro-Portuguese, anti-Muslim group supported by Chinese and Tamils who hoped Portuguese demand would boost prices for their goods, and an anti-Portuguese, Muslim faction supported by Gujaratis and Malays fearful of European competition and hostile to Christianity. In many *negeri*, Malay-speaking Muslims in the city proper and in hinterland villages (which supplied the city with food and services) constituted the ruler's most reliable base of support.[140]

Even without ethnic splits, *orang kaya* constituted a potential danger, for individual merchants commanded not only their own ships, but great numbers of slaves and dependents, often armed, who were both symbol and guarantee of their high status.[141] Elaborate ritual and an official emphasis on the unspeakable wickedness of treason (*derhaka*) sought to compensate for the monarchy's all-too-fragile reliance on shifting kin and patronage networks. If subjects were exhorted to obedience, rulers were enjoined to consult the great *orang kaya* and to rule in conciliar fashion. The price for ignoring this maxim could be

[137] Cortesao, *Suma Oriental*, vol. I, 184, and vol. II, 249.

[138] Reid, "*Negeri*," 424–26; Anthony Reid, ed., *Slavery, Bondage and Dependency in Southeast Asia* (New York, 1983), 1–43, 156–215; Lombard, *Carrefour Javanais*, vol. II, 131–62.

[139] Pierre-Yves Manguin, "The Merchant and the King," *Indonesia* 52 (1991): 41–54; Cortesao, *Suma Oriental*, vol. I, 182. Kling were Hindu Tamils.

[140] Reid, "*Negeri*," 426; Wheatley, *Impressions*, 187; Thomaz, "Malay Sultanate," 88–90, dissecting ethnically tinged factionalism. Leonard Andaya, pers. commun., Sept. 21, 2008 emphasizes the leavening role of Malay Muslim hinterlands.

[141] Reid, "*Negeri*," 425.

fatal. Thus in Pasai "grandee" factions reportedly elevated no fewer than seven kings in a single day. In Pires' terse conclusion, "kings do not last long in their estate."[142] Banda rejected the monarchic principle entirely in favor of an *orang kaya* oligarchy; while in Manila the ruler explained to Spaniards in 1570, "[T]here is no king and no sole authority in this land; but everyone holds his own view and opinion, and does as he prefers."[143] In Aceh, Pattani, Palembang, Jambi, Ternate, and elsewhere, merchants supported the elevation of female rulers, because – Reid and others have suggested – in at least some cases they sought thereby to reduce the threat of arbitrary policy and vainglorious warfare.[144]

Internally divisive, pre-1511 *negeri* also tended to exert weak territorial claims, again as measured by mainland or post-1511 archipelagic states. Admittedly, this may have begun to change by the late 1400s, to judge from Demak's expansion in Sumatra and Java, from Melaka's conquests, and from the 1513 *pasisir* attack on Melaka. Nonetheless, major *negeri* in the 15th century allowed hereditary succession among rulers in dependent ports, regarded each realm as an assemblage of autonomous kingdoms, required written reports from such dependencies infrequently, if at all; took no direct interest in cash crop production; and rarely sought to monopolize particular goods. Muslim firearms in this period had a surprisingly marginal impact,[145] and military innovation attracted limited attention. Not until after 1511 and more especially 1600, we shall find, did European competition contribute to more

---

[142] Cortesao, *Suma Oriental*, vol. I, 143. Discussion also follows Reid, "Negeri," 422–24; *AC*, vol. II, 251–53; *HM*, 46–52.

[143] Cited in Reid, "Negeri," 422.

[144] Ibid., 422–24; *AC*, vol. I, 171; *AC*, vol. II, 265–66, citing examples from the early 1400s to the late 1600s. But in many cases, Reid also acknowledges, these queens, far from being powerless figureheads, served as a kind of Elizabethan referee among aristocratic factions. Leonard Andaya, pers. commun., Sept. 21, 2008 agrees that queens in Aceh, Pattani, and Sulawesi were politically effective, in some cases precisely because of their moderation. Yet he also points out that foreign accounts of female rule often have an unverifiable air of hearsay. See his "'A Very Good-Natured but Awe-Inspiring Government': The Reign of a Successful Queen in 17th-Century Aceh," in Elsbeth Locher and Peter Riesbergen, eds., *Hof en Handel: Aziatische Machthebbers en de VOC* (Leiden, 2004), 59–84. Andaya, *Flaming Womb*, 165–69, and Barbara Watson Andaya pers. commun., Oct. 9, 2008 also emphasize the competence of female rulers.

[145] Although Melaka's forces reportedly had 3,000 firearms, Meilink-Roelofsz, *Asian Trade*, 38, 63, 123, 357 n. 29 argues that their practical value was very limited. See too Lombard, *Carrefour Javanais*, vol. II, 178–82; Junker, *Raiding, Trading*, 384; Andaya, "Interactions," 379 ff.

"absolutist" states able to repress factionalism, control production, and pursue more militarily professional, territorially ambitious policies.

In sum, as preeminently commercial enterprises, 14th- and 15th-century *negeri* championed a socially mobile, fractious, plutocratic, cosmopolitan, remarkably irenic ethos. They also shared an increasingly self-conscious Muslim identity.

Evidence from graves and local and foreign accounts shows that Islam moved east along the trade routes and that it took root most readily in areas involved in the new international boom. If Muslim traders-cum-proselytizers came from Champa, Chinese coastal cities, even Yunnan, the bulk were South Asian and Mideastern. From North Sumatra we have gravestones for Muslim rulers dated 1211 and 1297 that point to Indian Ocean contacts, and Marco Polo's 1292 claim that the port of Perlak was already Muslim. In Trengganu in northeast Malaya an inscription points to the introduction of Islamic law by 1302 or 1387. Melaka's first three rulers embraced Islam, at least nominally, but Muslim control remained insecure until a Hindu-Buddhist reaction in 1445 inspired a pro-Muslim coup the next year.[146] By the 1470s Pahang also was in transition to Islamic culture. Gaining converts from the mid-1400s, Islam by 1515 was accepted in varying degrees on Java's north coast from Cirebon to Surabaya. From Gresik Muslim preachers in the 1460s helped to proselytize Maluku, although Pires noted that while some Malukun rulers had become Muslim, the majority remained heathen, and even many Muslims were "not very deeply involved in the sect" and were not circumcised.[147] Lest one imagine a vast wave moving uniformly ever eastward, note that some eastern islands were precocious (Sulu had a Muslim "chief," of foreign origin, as early as 1310[148]) and that vast areas – not only Bali and the interior of most islands, but even coastal sectors of Sumatra, Sulawesi, Borneo, Flores, and Timor – remained non-Muslim long after centers farther east had converted.

In part, Islam spread because it strengthened aspiring rulers much as Hindu-Buddhism had empowered first millennium kingdoms. A Muslim *syahbandar* might tell a heathen ruler that he was more likely to

---

[146] For different views of Melaka's conversion, Wolters, *Fall of Srivijaya*, 12, 154–75; Wake, "Melaka in the 15th Century," superseding his 1964 article on conversion. On early Islamization generally, see esp. *HMI*, ch. 1.

[147] Cortesao, *Suma Oriental*, vol. I, 213 and 214–18; Andaya, *World of Maluku*, 57–62. Malukun chiefs with Arabic names and Javanese ties in the 14th century suggest an earlier, yet more superficial Islamization. Reid, *Charting the Shape*, 38 n. 5.

[148] *HMI*, 7; Cesar Majul, *Muslims in the Philippines* (Quezon City, 1999), 11–13, 56–69.

attract Muslim traders if he built a mosque, appointed Muslim judges, and provided a congenial milieu; piecemeal concessions eventually culminated in formal conversion. Thus early Melaka sought to divert trade from its archrival Pasai. In domestic terms as well, Muslim support could be critical, as during the succession dispute at Melaka in 1446. Islam also buttressed royal power by introducing law codes, even literacy; by standardizing royal succession, creating religious and legal posts, invoking the prestige of the Ottomans and later the Mughals, providing scriptural writ for war against Hindu-Buddhists and animists, and elevating the royal person. Novel formulae and theories, including Persian traditions of kingship and the mystical notion of the "Perfect Man," identified the ruler, "God's Shadow on earth," with a cosmic force superior to all local deities.[149]

In these ways self-interest led elites to embrace Islam from above. But surely the new faith had wider social appeal. Identification of foreign Muslims with economic success recommended it to many a local trader. Some Filipinos, for example, avoided pork because they thought such abstinence was the secret to Muslim wealth.[150] In a more subtle psychological sense, Reid has argued that Islam – more emphatically than Hindu-Buddhist cults, but somewhat like Theravada Buddhism and Philippine Christianity – offered not only powerful prophylactic rituals, but a predictable moral universe responsive to individual action. To those facing novel hazards of the market and urbanization, such messages may have been particularly comforting. Likewise, when people seeking work as cash-croppers, pedlars, warriors, or mariners were obliged to leave ancestral shrines and territorial spirits, the universality of the Muslim deity and the portability of the Koran may have provided welcome reassurance.[151] That texts and prayers were written in Arabic, incomprehensible to all but a few, only enhanced their talismanic aura.[152] Moreover, to follow A. H. Johns, many Southeast Asians found this ostensibly austere, monotheistic religion accessible in

[149] A. C. Milner, "Islam and the Muslim State," in Hooker, *Islam in South-East Asia*, 23–49; *AC*, vol. II, 169–73; *HMI*, ch. 1; Andaya, *World of Maluku*, 59–73; Anthony Reid, ed., *The Making of an Islamic Political Discourse in Southeast Asia* (Clayton, 1993), 83–107; n. 133 *supra*.
[150] Majul, *Muslims*, 80–81; *AC*, vol. II, 151.
[151] *AC, vol.* II, ch. 3, esp. 150–61.
[152] For examples, some post-1511, see William Cummings, *Making Blood White* (Honolulu, 2002), 37–41, 154–55; Andaya, *Live as Brothers*, 146; and *AC*, vol. II, 153–54. One is reminded of writing's talismanic function in Kiev. See Ch. 2, n. 124 *supra*.

the first instance, because, as in India, often it was introduced by *sufis*. Peripatetics of diverse ethnicity linked to merchant guilds, *sufis* offered an eclectic, quasi-pantheistic faith that readily accommodated pre-Muslim sensibilities.[153] To judge from Muslim gravestones of Javanese aristocrats near Majapahit's capital in the late 1300s, such mystics may have attracted even sophisticated courtiers knowledgeable in Hinduism and Buddhism far from the coast.[154]

How did Islam influence social and cultural patterns? In interior Java Islam made rapid headway only from the late 1500s – after the period of the present discussion – and not until the 1630s, M. C. Ricklefs argues, can one write of a synthesis between Islam and the Hindu-Buddhist high cultural legacies of Majapahit.[155] Densely populated, with weak maritime links, complex hierarchies, and prestigious Hindu-Buddhist legacies, interior Java offers the best example of vigorous pre-Muslim survivals in an ostensibly Muslim context. Bali, with some of the same characteristics, never made even a nominal conversion.

In coastal regions too, change could come piecemeal. Pires, I just noted, emphasized Malukun Muslims' limited commitment after at least half a century of Islamization. In Melaka as well, it remained far less central to Malay self-images than would be the case in the 16th and 17th centuries. A 1462 account of Melaka by the Arab navigator Ahmad ibn Majid was absolutely scathing:

> [W]hat people. They have no [Muslim] culture at all. The infidel marries Muslim women while the Muslim takes pagans to wife. You do not know whether they are Muslim or not.... [T]heft is rife among them and they do not mind. The Muslim eats dogs for meat for there are no food laws. They drink wine in the markets and do not treat divorce as a religious act.[156]

---

[153] For A. H. Johns' evolving views – supported in part by Azyumardi Azra, *The Origins of Islamic Reformism in Southeast Asia* (Honolulu, 2004), 2–4, 9; and Ricklefs, *Seen and Unseen*, xx – see Johns, "Sufism as a Category in Indonesian Literature and History," *JSEAH* 2 (1961): 10–23; idem, "Islam in Southeast Asia," *Indonesia* 19 (1975): 33–55; idem, "From Coastal Settlement to Islamic School and City," *Hammdad Islamicus* 4 (1981): 3–28; idem, "Islamization in Southeast Asia," *Southeast Asian Studies* 31 (1993): 43–61. *Sufis* were particularly successful transmitting complex theology to unschooled audiences, including women. Andaya, *Flaming Womb*, 87–88.

[154] *HMI*, 5–6.

[155] Ricklefs, *Mystic Synthesis*, ch. 2; idem, *Seen and Unseen*, xxiii.

[156] Tibbetts, *Study of Arabic Texts*, 206 and 189–93. On the shared shamanistic outlook of Hindu and Muslim rulers in 16th-century West Java, see Robert Wessing, "A Change

Such latitude notwithstanding, in many thinly populated coastal states with weak Hindu-Buddhist traditions, particularly in the islands outside of Java, Islam by 1500 had begun to produce paradigmatic cultural shifts. The Muslim calendar and theodicy recast time, while Muslim maps reconfigured space. Perso-Arabic scripts replaced Indic alphabets, novel literary genres and rituals took hold, and Muslim pseudo-sciences gained a following.[157] Muslim short-hair styles, head-cloths, and circumcision also spread among urban males, and if alcohol persisted, pigs disappeared – as did tattooing, penis-inserts, cremation, suttee, and transvestite cults, albeit often more gradually. As Muslim codes began to modify commercial and family law in the direction of a more assertive patriarchy, women's legal status declined, even though Muslim prestige attracted many elite females, and Muslim teachings offered new support to women and infants threatened by illness. Islamic norms were most honored among foreign Muslims, urban traders, and local dynasts, and least honored in rural areas, but everywhere they acquired the prestige of elite endorsement. The link between Islam and multifaceted cultural change is captured in a 1544 report that when Javanese brought Islam to Ternate in the previous century, they intro-duced titles of rank, coinage, the gong, the dagger, the law, "and all the other good things [Ternatens] have."[158]

What is more, Islam joined Melakan prestige to redefine and extend Malay ethnicity. By the 13th century, we saw, people in Southeast Suma-tra loyal to the Srivijaya court probably called themselves *orang Malayu* – "the people of Malayu" – while Melaka's ruling house cited a sacred hill

---

in the Forest," *JSEAS* 24 (1993): 1–17; and on continuities between pre-Muslim and Muslim attitudes to the dead, Reid, *Charting the Shape*, 17–22.

[157] Indic alphabets persisted in Sunda, interior Java, and Southwest Sulawesi. On calendars, scripts, maps, literature, dress, diet, burial, architecture, law, female roles, and other cultural shifts, Ian Proudfoot, *Old Muslim Calendars of Southeast Asia* (Leiden, 2006); Anthony Reid, "Overlapping Communities" (ms), ch. 4; *AC*, vol. I, 35, 40, 57, 67–68, 77, 81–89,142–58, 217–35 and vol. II, 177–78; Peter Riddell, *Islam and the Malay-Indonesian World* (Honolulu, 2001), 101–103; Ricklefs, *Mystic Synthesis*, 22–27; Andaya, *World of Maluku*, 8–9, 61, 194, 217; *HMI*, 4–7; Farish Noor, "From Majapahit to Putrajaya," *SEAR* 8 (2000): 239–79; Andaya *Flaming Womb*, 89–94; Fang, "*Undang-undang Melaka*," 183–93; and Lombard, *Carrefour Javanais*, vol. II, 155, 173–76, 203–207, arguing for novel conceptions of time, history, and the indi-vidual.

[158] Antonio Galvao, *A Treatise on the Moluccas (c. 1544)*, Hubert Jacobs., ed. and tr. (Rome, 1971), 105. On Islamic appeals to women, Andaya, *Flaming Womb*, 86, Barbara Watson Andaya, pers. commun., Oct. 9, 2008.

in Palembang as its place of origin.[159] It was therefore natural that those residents of Melaka, many descended from Sumatran immigrants, who spoke Malay as their first language and who identified with the Melaka ruler as "his loyal people" also should call themselves "the people of Malayu" or, more simply, "Malays" (*malayos*). Thus the *Sejarah Malayu* chronicle has the Melakan king, bloodied in battle, hold up his wounded hand and exclaim to his men, "Hey, Malays, look at this!" In particular, "Malay" was used to contrast the king's followers, their language, and Muslim faith with the customs of Siamese and other foreigners.[160]

Malayo-Muslim culture and Melakan influence thus nourished one another. In coastal areas of Sumatra and the peninsula under its control, Melaka compelled or induced vassals to embrace Islam.[161] More broadly, the middleman role that Melakan traders filled across the archipelago strengthened Malay's long-standing role as a commercial lingua franca and led many traders who would share Melaka's prosperity to adopt its language and religion, in effect, "to become Malays." By the same token, especially in the western archipelago and coastal Borneo but as far away as the Philippines, rulers outside Melaka's political orbit sought to bask in Melaka's glory by adopting Islam and imitating its court structure, music, dance, dress, literature, legal codes, and speech. As Barbara Watson Andaya and Leonard Andaya have observed, so closely joined were Malay speech and culture that the word *bahasa* (language) came to designate refined speech, appropriate behavior, and knowledge of Malay custom generally.[162] Malay ethnicity, defined by religion, language, and these broader traits, was sufficiently assimilative that by 1511 it had incorporated at elite and popular levels not only coastal peoples in the peninsula, in northern and eastern Sumatra, and parts of coastal Borneo, but some marine-based *orang laut* and forest tribesmen (*orang asli*) in the peninsula. The ease with which the

---

[159] The hill of Bukit Siguntang. On the derivation of "Malayu," see Reid, "Understanding *Melayu*," 298, and n. 37 *supra*.

[160] Reid, "Understanding *Melayu*," 298, arguing that the *Sejarah Malayu*, the earliest extant version of which dates from 1612 but which incorporated earlier material, preserved late Melakan usages. Portuguese accounts also equated *"Malayos"* with pro-Sultan Muslims from Melaka.

[161] Farther afield, Sultan Muzaffar Syah (r. 1446–1459) reportedly sent missionaries to the *pasisir*. See Andaya and Ishii, "Religious Developments," 518; *HM*, 39, 45, 53–58; Reid, *Charting the Shape*, 27; idem, "*Negeri*," 418; Andaya, *Leaves*, 70 ff.

[162] *HM*, 39, 57. On Malayness in a later period, A. C. Milner, *Kerajaan* (Tucson, 1982), 1–13.

latter two groups assumed, temporarily or permanently, a Malay identity was crucial in allowing Melaka's immigrant founders to expand their modest ranks.[163]

The language of Melaka was almost certainly a later version of that spoken at the court of Srivijaya.[164] Thus Melaka renewed and intensified that thrust toward Malay cultural hegemony along the coasts of the western archipelago that began under Srivijaya but that probably had waned amidst the turmoil of the late 13th and 14th centuries. At the same time Melaka modified this movement in three critical respects: a) It shifted the locus of authority from southeastern Sumatra to the southern peninsula. b) It extended Malay culture to areas never under substantial Srivijayan influence. c) By wedding Islam to Malay identity, it introduced a novel religious element of enormous popular appeal.

The spread of Malay ethnicity and culture differed in important dimensions from that of Burmese, Siamese, and Vietnamese culture. Malay markers moved along archipelagic sealanes well beyond Melaka's territorial domain, which was ill defined to start. As a result, Malay identity remained hazier at the margins, especially in the central and eastern archipelago, and less closely tied to a political center than its mainland counterparts. The proportion of self-identified Malays who came under Melaka's control must have been far smaller than the proportion of, say, self-identified Burmans ruled by Ava. Without a moving land frontier, Malay acculturation, unlike Burmese or Vietnamese, rarely benefited from colonization. *Sufi* orders relied less on state patronage than did Theravada monastic networks and had more cosmopolitan memberships. If in some locales, including Melaka, Kutai (where an Islamic teacher reportedly arrived on the back of a swordfish!), and especially interior Java, Islam achieved a gradual synthesis and an amicable localization, in other regions it introduced a more profound sense

[163] A Malay identity specifically associated with Melaka thus separated from a proto-Malay identity that also engendered Minangkabau, Acehnese, and Batak ethnicities. On the evolution of these as well as *orang laut* and *orang asli* cultures, Andaya, *Leaves*; idem, "A Reconstruction of Orang Asli and Melayu Relations on the Malay Peninsula prior to the 19th Century," in Edi Sedyawati and Susanto Zuhdi, eds., *Arung Samudera* (Depok, 2001), 391–415; *HM*, 47–49; Jane Drakard, *A Malay Frontier* (Ithaca, 1990), 1–13. Cf. language map at Bellwood, *Prehistory*, 121. Until 1400 most of the peninsular coast probably spoke not Malay, but an Austronesian language related to Mon-Khmer. Leonard Andaya, "Aceh's Contribution to Standards of Malayness," *Archipel* 61 (2001): 32–34; idem, *Leaves*, 78–79.
[164] *HM*, 57.

of rupture, a more marked indifference to pre-1400 culture, than we find typically on the Theravada or Neo-Confucian mainland.[165]

But in other respects the diffusion of Malayo-Muslim culture paralleled changes on the mainland, where Burmese and Siamese ethnicities fused with Theravada Buddhism and where Neo-Confucianism became pivotal to Vietnamese identity. After 1400 or 1450 in all four realms – the western archipelago and the western, central, and eastern mainland – political recentralization drew strength from modified charter legacies, textual religions, and maritime expansion. Melaka, no less than Ava, Pegu, Ayudhya, and Thang Long, became exemplar and patron of cultic and linguistic norms whose acceptance implied support for a central dynasty. Finally, although religious leaders might seek foreign inspiration (Sinhalese, Chinese, Arab), in all four realms elites operated free of extraregional compulsion. From c. 1350 to 1600, Russia, France, and Japan conformed to these same basic patterns of political recentralization, accelerated cultural integration, and autonomous local agency.[166]

How did Islamization in Southeast Asia compare to that in South Asia, the only other area under review with a substantial Muslim population? Islamic chronologies in these two regions were broadly similar, with serious conversion starting in the 13th century. In both regions, Islam sought to displace a Hindu or Hindu-Buddhist charter culture, providing a new theology, script, calendar, architecture, and lexicon. In both regions, *sufi* accommodations tended to preserve substantial pre-Muslim legacies and to facilitate conversion.

Yet South–Southeast Asian differences were at least as significant, and speak directly to the distinction between exposed and protected zones.

---

[165] Sumatran and many peninsular annals, for example, often showed little interest in pre-Muslim history, whereas Burmese chronicles identified with Pagan, and later Vietnamese historians identified with early Dai Viet. *CHSEA*, 176; *SP*, 131–39, 258–63, 365–67, 377–83. Changes in diet, burial, and dress also could be abrupt. On this and other "difficult transitions," *AC*, vol. II, 161–73, and n. 157 *supra*. On the other hand, Javanese Muslim states, as noted, often invoked Majapahit's legacy; while the Melakan chronicle *Sejarah Malayu* recalled pre-Muslim ancestors associated with Bukit Siguntang in Palembang. Leonard Andaya, pers. commun., Sept. 21, 2008. I rely too on Barbara Watson Andaya, pers. commun., Oct. 9, 2008; idem, *Flaming Womb*, 88, emphasizing "amicable localizations." Kutai is in eastern Borneo.

[166] One is also reminded how "Burman" and "Frank" – like "Malay" – originally designated immigrant groups (often warriors), but expanded to provide general ethnic labels. Cf. *SP*, 90–91, 114–15, 131–54, 242–74, 372–96; Ch. 2., nn. 59, 60 *supra*. Although individual foreign traders led some *pasisir* towns (see n. 139 *supra*), their accession was rarely military in origin, and in any case those immigrants assimilated rapidly to Javanese culture.

In India Islam was introduced by Inner Asian warriors who sought to displace indigenous political (and less directly, religious) elites. Notwithstanding Muslim success in poorly sedentarized areas like Bengal and the Punjab, in areas of long-settled agriculture mass conversion foundered on the rocks of brahman resistance and caste resilience. But in archipelagic Southeast Asia, if preachers often were of foreign origin, we find no external Muslim invasions. Rather, as Russell Jones and A. C. Milner emphasize, Islamization commonly proceeded through the voluntary conversion of existing dynasties, with erstwhile pagan rulers themselves becoming the most enthusiastic advocates of the new faith.[167] Both because the islands knew neither an entrenched brahman class nor pervasive caste, and because the peaceful nature of religious change accommodated existing political prerogatives, pre-Muslim traditions offered remarkably weak resistance, and Islam rapidly became the dominant idiom not only in the outer islands, but in interior Java.[168]

To sum up, archipelagic history between 1350 and 1511 often seems fragmented because geography favored a large number of independent port-cities, and because political rhythms in the Straits, where Melaka revived Srivijaya's legacy after 1400, differed from those in Java, where Majapahit's decline still had not run its course by 1511. And yet in the archipelago at large we find three overarching transformations. First, expanding regional and international trade stimulated the marketing of specialized crops and forest products, along with money use and urbanization. Second, trade nourished a chain of new polities, from Pasai through Maluku, which shared a distinctively urban, cosmopolitan, mobile, commercial culture. Third, new trade currents, interstate competition, and Melakan prestige joined to disseminate Malayo-Muslim identities in the western archipelago, and Islam in coastal regions from North Sumatra to the southern Philippines. As was typical of the protected zone, all three of these processes proceeded under indigenous auspices. And yet in 1511 sectors of the archipelago were about to shift from being part of Eurasia's protected zone to being part of the exposed zone. To that transition we now turn.

---

[167] Russell Jones, "Ten Conversion Myths from Indonesia," in Levtzion, *Conversion to Islam*, 129–58; Milner, "Islam and the State," 30–31.

[168] According to Cortesao, *Suma Oriental*, vol. I, 177, far from opposing Islam, some 50,000 ascetics (*tapas*) in Java accommodated themselves to the new faith, and were in turn venerated by Muslims even in the *pasisir*. See Ricklefs, *Mystic Synthesis*, 11, 20, 25, 28. In many locales the rapidity of Islamization was itself responsible for the sense of rupture highlighted in n. 165 *supra*.

3. EUROPEAN INTERVENTIONS IN AN ERA OF MULTISTATE PARITY, 1511–C. 1660

Between 1511 and c. 1660 archipelagic states grew more integrated, militarized, and interventionist. In so doing, they responded to a further strengthening of Eurasian commercial demand, to the arrival of more effective firearms, to the growing influence of Indian Ocean Islam – and most dramatically, to the arrival of West Europeans, whose ambition and techniques altered the rules of regional life. By modifying local political and, in some degree, cultural options, the Spanish and the Dutch, in particular, began to play a role reminiscent of Inner Asians in China and India. However, to the mid-1660s the chief Southeast Asian players, learning rapidly from one another as well as from Christian newcomers, succeeded in holding their own in this ever more combative multistate system.

Archipelagic Prosperity to c. 1640

Consider first economic stimuli to both European intervention and indigenous reorganization. Such data as we have suggest that the expansion in exports and urbanism that we noted for the 15th century accelerated after 1510 and more especially between 1570 and 1640, with the latter decades representing the zenith of Reid's Age of Commerce.

According to C. H. H. Wake, Malukun clove, nutmeg, and mace exports rose as much as 500 percent between 1500 and 1620, with growth particularly notable from 1550.[169] Likewise, Reid and David Bulbeck argue for a 550 percent increase by volume of Southeast Asian pepper exports from the 1510s to the 1670s, and a twelvefold increase by value to the 1640s.[170] Although Sanjay Subrahmanyam has queried some of Reid's figures,[171] the geographic diffusion of pepper cultivation is clear. In 1500 it was grown chiefly along the northern and southeastern coasts and in some interior districts of Sumatra, and in Pahang, Pattani, Kedah,

---

[169] Wake, "Changing Pattern," 393, which is consistent with *CHSEA*, 465, Fig. 8.1, and with estimates of spice exports to Europe at *AC*, vol. II, 14, Fig. 3. After 1620, however, Dutch control depressed fine spice production. On spreading clove cultivation, Meilink-Roelofsz, *Asian Trade*, 153–66.

[170] Calculated in local prices. Bulbeck et al., *Southeast Asian Exports*, 86–87. Cf. figures at *CHSEA*, 465, Fig. 8.1; *AC*, vol. II, 20–23; Andaya, *Live as Brothers*, 44–45.

[171] Sanjay Subrahmanyam, "Writing History 'Backwards,'" *Studies in History* 10 (1994): 131–45.

and northwest Java. By 1600 it had spread to the northeast peninsula and along the West Sumatran coast, as Chinese and European demand shot up and as Portugal's capture of Melaka led Muslim pepper traders to develop alternate routes and sources of supply. By 1680 fresh cultivation had opened in the Malay peninsula, around Banjarmasin in Borneo, in the Minangkabau highlands, and in Southwest Sumatra. All told, in 1650 some 6 percent of the population of Sumatra, the peninsula, and Borneo may have earned a living growing pepper.[172] Exports of Malayan tin and forest and sea products also rose.[173]

In turn, Southeast Asia consumed growing quantities of Indian textiles – by far the largest item of nonessential expenditure – plus Chinese manufactures. Whereas in 1511 the region as a whole imported Indian textiles valued at 12 tons of silver, from 1620 to 1655 annual imports, sufficient to make about 6,000,000 *sarungs*, were worth some 40 tons.[174] What Southeast Asia's trading partners could not pay for in goods, they did so with bullion and specie, substantially enhancing regional money supplies. We lack figures for the archipelago, but for China and Southeast Asia together, from the 1580s to the 1620s New World and Japanese precious metal imports rose from an estimated 43 metric tons of silver equivalent to at least 178 tons. New World silver moved from Acapulco to Manila in Spanish galleons and across the Indian Ocean in Muslim, Dutch, and English ships.[175] What is more, silver's value for large-scale transactions notwithstanding, in the late 16th and 17th centuries vast quantities of cheap Chinese-style lead, bronze, and/or tin coins (*picis*) provided the basic medium of petty trade and an invaluable tool – in Leonard Blusse's phrase, the "Trojan horse of lead" – by which Chinese drew local producers into commercial dependence.[176]

Home to aristocrats, pedlars, artisans, laborers, and foreign traders alike, indigenous cities in the archipelago enjoyed a vitality between

---

[172] *AC*, vol. II, 8–10, 32–36 and Map 2; Bulbeck et al., *Southeast Asian Exports*, ch. 3, esp. Map 4; and n. 108 *supra*.

[173] Previous note, plus Bulbeck et al., *Southeast Asian Exports*, ch. 4.

[174] *AC*, vol. II, 26–31, offering no mainland vs. archipelago breakdown.

[175] See Figures at *AC*, vol. II, 24–27, esp. Table 3, and Ward Barrett, "World Bullion Flows, 1450–1800," in James Tracy, ed., *The Rise of Merchant Empires* (Cambridge, 1990), 224–54, esp. Tables 7.6–7.8. On the galleon trade, Benito Legarda, Jr., *After the Galleons* (Madison, WI, 1999), 32–50. On silver flows generally, *AC*, vol. II, 93–107, and Ch. 5, nn. 162, 173.

[176] Such cash were minted in China or produced locally from lead imported by the Dutch and English. Blusse, *Strange Company*, 35–48; *AC*, vol. II, 107, 312–17; Gerrit Knaap, *Shallow Waters, Rising Tide* (Leiden, 1996), 11–13.

1570 and 1660 that they would not know again until the 20th century. Mataram in 1650 may have held 150,000 people, and Aceh, Makasar, and Banten, from 10,000 to 100,000 each. The high proportion of each kingdom's population residing in and around the capital reflected low rural densities, the availability of Javanese and mainland rice, and trade's prominence in the general economy.[177] In Gilbert Rozman's schema, urbanization in Aceh, Banten, and Makasar in 1650 may have approximated Stage C ("state city"), but Mataram may have approached Stage E ("standard marketing").[178]

Why, then, this prosperity? As usual, external demand was most visible. During China's "second commercial revolution," hunger for imports, especially silver to lubricate the economy, eroded early Ming maritime bans, which were formally abolished in 1567. Whereas 50 junks got licenses to trade that year, by 1616 there were "several hundred" such craft, most headed to the archipelago. In addition, a large, if uncertain number left without permits.[179] The chief attractions were pepper, tin, New World and Japanese silver. Such contacts encouraged a modest resumption of Chinese emigration to Nan-yang portcities.

From about 1580 until Tokugawa authorities halted overseas travel in 1635, Japan – in a phase of commercial and urban growth no less marked than in China – also boosted Southeast Asian contacts. As Chapter 4 noted, Ming bans on direct contact with Japan (designed to curb piracy on the China coast) and the decline of Ryukyuan traffic rendered Southeast Asian ports indispensable rendezvous to exchange Japanese silver for Chinese silks and porcelains.[180]

From Arabia, Persia, Gujarat, Malabar, Coromandel, and Bengal came a stream of merchants seeking to trade *inter alia* New World silver and South Asian cottons for archipelagic spices, forest products, tin, elephants, and Chinese silks. Although the Portuguese reduced the flow

---

[177] See estimates in n. 110 *supra* and caveats in n. 120 *supra*, plus skeptical views on large Banten population claims in Ota, *Changes of Regime*, 18–19, 35, 43.

[178] Stage C had essentially one urban center, but Stage E had at least three urban levels with populations, respectively, of over 30,000; 3,000–10,000; and below 3,000. See Gilbert Rozman, *Urban Networks in Russia 1750–1800* (Princeton, 1976), 34–35, and Ch. 1, n. 78 *supra*.

[179] On Chinese trade and emigration c. 1520–1670, AC, vol. II, 18; Reid, *Sojourners and Settlers*, 35–40; Ptak, "Ming Maritime Trade," 183–91; Bulbeck et al., *Southeast Asian Exports*, 77–79.

[180] AC, vol. II, 17–18; Robert Innes, "The Door Ajar" (Univ. of Michigan, PhD diss., 1980), 51–66; Ch. 4, nn. 128, 129, 132, 247 *supra*.

of fine spices and pepper to Europe via the Levant, the movement of those commodities to the Levant itself rose to the late 1500s, buoyed by rising commercial velocities in the Ottoman empire.[181] As noted, from 1511 to 1620–1655 the annual value in silver of Indian textile imports to Southeast Asia grew an estimated 233 percent.[182]

If European attempts at commercial restriction raised protection costs for Asian merchants and led eventually to a Dutch spice monopoly, on balance Europeans to c. 1650 also stimulated regional trade in the following ways: a) By opening an all-water route around the Cape of Good Hope, the Portuguese and Dutch permitted more efficient trade to Europe, the world's most rapidly growing market for fine spices and pepper. But because between 1530 and 1590 the old Muslim routes to the Red Sea and Persian Gulf revived, the net effect of European intervention to 1650 was to magnify overall demand, especially for pepper, which defied monopoly.[183] b) Similarly, by augmenting the total carrying capacity of ships visiting Southeast Asia and by increasing imports to the region of Indian textiles, Europeans encouraged local cash cropping and market production.[184] c) Via Manila and the Indian Ocean, Europeans, as noted, supplied Southeast Asia with New World silver.

But again a historiographic focus on external agency tends to obscure indigenous actors. The spread of pepper and other cash crops, the forging of links between interior and coast, the provisioning of port-cities, the exchange of Javanese foodstuffs and Indian cloths for Malukun spices, the transport of spices to Melaka and other distribution

---

[181] That is to say, spices reached the Levant in quantities sufficient for local needs, but insufficient for re-export to Europe in competition with Portuguese supplies. See n. 226 *infra*, plus Halil Inalcik with Donald Quataert, eds., *An Economic and Social History of the Ottoman Empire*, 2 vols. (Cambridge, 1994), vol. I, 25–41, 214–16, 325–55, and vol. II, 433–526; *AC*, vol. II, 14, Fig. 3; *CHSEA*, 465, Fig. 8.1.

[182] From 12 to 40 tons silver equivalent. Note 174 *supra*. On Indian-Southeast Asian trade 1510–1660, also *AC*, vol. II, 26–31, esp. Table 4; M. N. Pearson, "India and the Indian Ocean in the 16th Century," in Ashin Das Gupta and M. N. Pearson, eds., *India and the Indian Ocean 1500–1800* (Calcutta, 1987), 71–93; S. Arasaratnam, "India and the Indian Ocean in the 17th Century," in ibid., 94–130; Sanjay Subrahmanyam, *The Political Economy of Commerce* (Cambridge, 1990), 91–251 *passim*; Andaya, "Aceh's Contribution," 40–45.

[183] *AC*, vol. II, 19–23; Wake, "Changing Pattern"; Inalcik, *Economic and Social History*, vol. I, 340–47; *HMI*, 73; discussion *infra*.

[184] Previous notes, plus *AC*, vol. II, 26–31; Meilink-Roelofsz, *Asian Trade*, 180. Cf. Sanjay Subrahmanyam, *The Portuguese Empire in Asia 1500–1700* (London, 1993), 274–76; idem, *Political Economy*, 250.

points – all were primarily the work of Southeast Asians themselves. Rural-to-urban migration and the prosperity of key rice-growing districts suggest that urban expansion was part of a more general demographic surge.[185] To invoke Henley again, rising commercial demand may have removed production ceilings embedded in subsistence economies, improving nutrition and fertility and reducing mortality. In Southwest Sulawesi and Central Java I shall cite indirect evidence of strong demographic and agrarian growth between 1500 and 1650.[186]

Europeans as "White Inner Asians"[187]

In these ways between 1511 and c. 1660 alien Asians, Southeast Asians, and Europeans collaborated, more or less unintentionally of course, to enhance Southeast Asian prosperity. And yet Europeans also stood apart from their Asian contemporaries in critical ways, most obviously by deploying naval power to impose commercial restrictions and to incorporate Southeast Asian enclaves into global empires. By Eurasian standards, such behavior was extremely peculiar.

This is not to say that no Asian power ever sought to coerce maritime trade. The Ottomans occupied commercially attractive islands like Rhodes, Chios, and Cyprus. To guard Egypt's spice revenues, they swept the Portuguese from the Red Sea and dreamed of driving them from the Indian Ocean itself.[188] From 1650 to 1730 Oman dominated parts of the East African coast and the approaches to the Persian Gulf.[189] Early Ming naval expeditions briefly overshadowed Asia's chief maritime routes; while the Ming loyalist regime of Zheng Chenggong, in expelling the Dutch from Taiwan in 1662, again showed the potential of Chinese seapower.[190]

---

[185] *AC*, vol. II, 114–29; Denys Lombard, *Le Sultanat d'Atjeh au Temps d'Iskandar Muda, 1607–1636* (Paris, 1967), 101–25; Subrahmanyam, *Political Economy*, 132–33, 153, 335.

[186] Cf. *HMI*, 46–47; Pigeaud and Graaf, *Islamic States*, 20–23; and nn. 260, 268 *infra*. Recall that according to Henley, in n. 81 *supra*, the chief impediments to rising population were debt-slavery and kin-based systems of production and resource sharing.

[187] I adopt this phrase from the Burmese habit of identifying early Europeans as *kala-pyu*, "white Indians."

[188] Daniel Goffman, *The Ottoman Empire and Early Modern Europe* (Cambridge, 2002), 99, 151–58; Subrahmanyam, *Portuguese Empire*, 65–67; Inalcik, *Economic and Social History*, vol. I, 319–40.

[189] Subrahmanyam, *Portuguese Empire*, 177, 192–94; C. R. Boxer, *The Portuguese Seaborne Empire 1415–1825* (London, 1969), 133–36.

[190] Tonio Andrade, *How Taiwan Became Chinese* (New York, 2006), ch. 11.

However, no Asian polity, with the fleeting exception of early Ming China, moved beyond a purely local maritime hegemony; and none offered an effective long-term barrier to European naval penetration.

Building on the work of Tonio Andrade, I would argue that European naval supremacy grew from the interplay of three factors peculiar to the North Atlantic.[191] First, maritime revenues were far more important to modest-sized Atlantic states, and before them Mediterranean city-states, than to major Asian realms, and maritime affairs assumed a peculiar prominence in Atlantic strategy. Portugal introduced to the Indian Ocean notions of monopoly and militarized trade that had been pioneered by Italian city-states. With virtually no natural resources and a population in 1520 of 1,400,000, Portugal had no access to status and wealth other than through trade. Likewise, the Dutch Republic, with barely 2,000,000 people, relied on freightage and entrepot functions at the intersection of Baltic, Rhine, and Atlantic trade. For Spain and England overseas revenues were also critical. But the Mughals and late imperial China derived an insignificant income from the maritime sector. Zheng He's expeditions ended because Inner Asia diverted Ming attention from the coast, while the Qing conquest of Taiwan grew from strategic, not commercial, concerns. Likewise, the Ottomans in practice never showed more than a desultory interest in Indian Ocean affairs.[192] Japan by the 1630s had forsaken naval power, as had Javanese Mataram. Admittedly, a handful of Asian states with weak agrarian bases – Yemen, Hormuz, Oman, Calicut, as well as Aceh and Banten in Southeast Asia – resembled Atlantic powers in their reliance on coastal revenues and their willingness to use force to control trade. But few could challenge even the Portuguese, whose strength in all of Asia did not exceed 9,000.[193]

---

[191] Cf. Tonio Andrade, "The Rise and Fall of Dutch Taiwan," *JWH* 17 (2006): 429–50; idem, "The Age of Expansion: Europeans in Maritime Asia, 1400–1800" (ms).

[192] For contrasts between European coastal and Asian agrarian states, see John Wills, Jr., "Maritime Asia, 1500–1800," *AHR* 98 (1993): 83–105; M. N. Pearson, "Merchants and States," in James Tracy, ed., *The Political Economy of Merchant Empires* (Cambridge, 1991), 41–116; Sanjay Subrahmanyam and Luiz Thomaz, "Evolution of Empire," in ibid., 298–331; Subrahmanyam, *Portuguese Empire*, 10–20, 177, 191–94; David Abernathy, *The Dynamics of Global Dominance* (New Haven, 2000), pts. 1, 3; David Ringrose, *Expansion and Global Interaction, 1200–1700* (New York, 2001); and n. 191 *supra*.

[193] Francisco Bethencourt, "Political Configurations and Local Powers," in Bethencourt and Diogo Ramada Curto, eds., *Portuguese Oceanic Expansion, 1400–1800* (Cambridge, 2007), 224–25; Bethencourt, "Low Cost Empire," in Ernst van Veen and Leonard Blusse, eds., *Rivalry and Conflict* (Leiden, 2005), 115, claiming 7,000.

What is more, Southeast Asian and Omani maritime belligerence was largely a reaction to Iberian or Dutch assaults.

Second, sustained, centuries-long European warfare between medium-sized states of comparable power created unusually intense pressures toward military and institutional innovation. Whereas Iberians and Dutch strained to improve their cannon, handguns, fortresses, and ships, when Ibérians arrived in the Indian Ocean, Muslim ships rarely even carried arms. Likewise, as Chapter 6 suggested was true of the British, the ability of Iberians and Dutchmen to coordinate affairs across five continents and the transgenerational stability of Iberian kingdoms and of the Dutch United East India Company – the VOC – found few parallels in household-based regimes around the Indian Ocean littoral. It has also been suggested that stoic acceptance of high casualty rates in a single-minded pursuit of victory often let small numbers of Europeans triumph over far larger foes.[194]

Third, their location on the extreme western edge of Eurasia afforded Atlantic powers privileged access to New World resources, silver in particular. In the absence of competitive European manufactures, bullion provided an entrée to that nonmonopolized intra-Asian trade on which Portuguese and Dutch profitability came to rely in large measure.[195]

Iberians and Dutch promptly used such advantages to redraw the economic, political, and in some instances the cultural, map of island Southeast Asia. In so doing, I submit, these itinerant seafarers began to play a role comparable to that of land nomads in China and South Asia.

Now at first blush, this equation may seem bizarre, for in many ways West Europeans and Inner Asians were polar opposites. As maritime peoples, the former established outposts on the other side of the world where the Portuguese and Dutch were long content to control small coastal enclaves and, in the case of the Dutch, to move only fitfully into interior. By contrast, Inner Asians advanced overland to dominate vast agrarian spaces relatively close to their Inner Asian homelands.

---

[194] VOC = Vereenigde Oost-Indische Compagnie. On attitudes to casualties, *AC*, vol. I, 123–24; Anthony Reid, "Europe and Southeast Asia: The Military Balance" (ms); Luc Nagtegaal, *Riding the Dutch Tiger* (Leiden, 1996), 62–63. But those interpretations are contested in Michael Charney, *Southeast Asian Warfare, 1300–1900* (Leiden, 2004), 17–22.

[195] And yet European exports to 1750 were 10 percent commodities, 30 percent bullion, and 60 percent services. Pearson, "Merchants and States," 108. Access to both North Atlantic and Mediterranean shipbuilding also let Iberians create superior vessels in somewhat the same way that Sino-Southeast Asian diasporas combined Chinese and Southeast Asian ship construction techniques.

Only then did they link up to the coast. Whereas Iberians and Dutchmen overseas were an infinitesimal fraction of their home populations, Inner Asians were organized into tribal confederations and warbands whose members sometimes moved en masse into conquered areas. For European agents of nation-states and trading organizations, Europe remained the political, economic, and cultural center of gravity. That is to say, notwithstanding painfully slow communications and extensive autonomy, they took orders from the metropole (or its agents) and relied on the home economy for capital, personnel, and technical innovation. Metropole–colony ties only grew closer from the late 1700s. Inner Asians, however, typically shifted their headquarters to newly conquered territories whose economies framed their fiscal and technical options. Whereas Christianity tended to insulate Iberians and Dutchmen from host cultures, Inner Asians, at least in China, were avid cultural borrowers. Navigational barriers decreed that European inroads in Southeast Asia began only in 1511, but Inner Asian land empires appeared by the third century B.C.E. Accordingly, whereas Iberians and Dutch arrived with virtually no knowledge of Southeast Asia, Inner Asians had long familiarity with their sedentary neighbors.[196]

Set alongside such differences, however, were arresting similarities. Most basic, both Europeans and Inner Asians were extraregional catalysts of early modern integration whose relation to local peoples contrasted with that of leaders in the protected zone. After 1511 Europeans, in effect, converted parts of island Southeast Asia – not to mention coastal West Africa and the New World – from protected- to exposed-zone status. In European enclaves as in Inner Asian-led domains, agency gravitated to alien conquerors. Iberians, Dutch, and Inner Asians all owed their authority to a combination of organizational superiority and military innovation, whether in warships and firearms or cavalry training and tactics. Such advantages allowed them to create political units appreciably larger and better administered than any indigenous antecedent. At the same time self-isolating cultural strategies enhanced the cohesion of conquest elites. Iberians and Dutchmen – like their Khitan, Mongol, Manchu, Delhi Sultanate, and Mughal counterparts – championed an official language, ethnicity, and in most cases an official

---

[196] Cf. comparisons of Qing and European colonialism in Michael Adas, "Imperialism and Colonialism in Comparative Perspective," *IHR*, 20 (1998): 371–88. Of course, most of these Iberian and Dutch characterizations apply as well to the British in India, albeit at a later date.

religion/cult that separated them from indigenes more sharply than did the typical noble–commoner divide in protected-zone societies. So too, although international commerce normally was less central to Inner Asian than to European projects, both Europeans and some Inner Asian empires (e.g., those of the early Turks, Tanguts, Khazars, and Mongols) facilitated trans-Eurasian exchange.

Most curious perhaps, the chronologies of European and Inner Asian expansion were more similar than a first glance suggests. In Southeast Asia, China, and India, alien conquests between 1511 and 1800 actually represented the second phase in a process of resource acquisition and institutional experiment whose first phase began with the great Eurasian economic boom of c. 850/900–1300/1350. Chapters 5 and 6 argued that economic growth in that period favored Inner Asian advance by swelling nomad ranks, magnifying arable–steppe interactions, and expanding the repertoire of Inner Asian skills needed to rule sedentary peoples. Pre-1350 empires in Inner Asia in turn lay the foundations for post-1550 "direct-taxation" successors, to recall Nicola Di Cosmo's terminology.[197] Thus Jurchen and Mongol empires inspired the Manchus, while Delhi Sultans anticipated the Mughals.

Similar continuities, I submit, characterized Iberian conquest. The first major phase of Christian expansion occurred between c. 1000 and 1350. Strengthened by rapid demographic growth, a pan-European crusading ideology, and Frankish knights from beyond the Pyrenees, the beleaguered Christians of northern Iberia began pushing steadily south, taking the central Tagus basin in 1085, followed by the Ebro valley and lands from Oporto to the Algarve in modern Portugal. By the mid-1200s Castile, Aragon, and Portugal between them effectively had crushed Muslim power in the peninsula. These remarkable advances encouraged and reflected a novel mercantile vitality, together with historic movements of agrarian colonization and intensification. From the mid-1300s to the 1460s expansionary momentum ebbed in the face of the Black Death, peasant uprisings, and magnate revolts that crippled Castile and Aragon, in particular. But with the union of those two kingdoms in 1479, the conquest of Granada in 1492, and the creation of Spain's European and New World empires, Spain entered a spectacular era of "universal monarchy" whose prosperity benefited from

---

[197] Nicola Di Cosmo, "State Formation and Periodization in Inner Asian History," *JWH* 10 (1999): 1–40. Indeed, "direct-taxation empires" are said to have begun with the Yuan Dynasty.

post-Black Death demographic recovery and from an explosive growth of colonial trade and tribute. Portugal from the late 1400s proved no less dynamic. Vasco da Gama's 1498 arrival in India initiated Portugal's Indian Ocean empire, while in 1500 the Portuguese made good their claims to Brazil. In short, the 1490s inaugurated a second great phase of Iberian expansion that would continue into the 17th century.

For Iberians as for Inner Asians, these two expansionary phases, pre-1350 and post-1490, were linked geographically, culturally, and institutionally. Indeed, despite 14th- and 15th-century upheavals, Iberian expansion never ceased completely: after capturing Ceuta in Morocco in 1415, Portugal inaugurated those voyages along the African coast that culminated in both da Gama's breakthrough and the discovery of Brazil. In turn Portugal's African voyages built on Genoese-cum-Iberian explorations between 1350 and 1450 of the Azores, Madeira, Cape Verde, and the Canary Islands – from the last of which Columbus set sail. The anti-Muslim *Reconquista* ideology of medieval Iberia directly inspired both Portuguese and Spanish conquests in North Africa and Asia, while military-religious orders, Italian financing, and Italian-style trading posts (*fondachi*) in the medieval Mediterranean anticipated colonial institutions in the Americas and Asia. In other words, Christian reconquest of Iberia led, directly and indirectly, to empire in the African littoral, the New World, and maritime Asia. Or to rephrase my argument, the line from 12th-century to 17th-century conquests was no less, and arguably more, direct for Iberians than for Jurchens and Manchus.[198]

In the Netherlands too, Holland's medieval hegemony north of the Meuse and its 13th- and 14th-century conquests in Friesland and Zeeland benefited from dramatic post-1000 economic growth, including advances in reclamation, rural productivity, fishing, and bulk carriage. Holland's incorporation into Burgundy (1428) and the Habsburg empire

---

[198] On links between pre-1350 and post-1490 Iberian expansion, ideology, and institutions, see Subrahmanyam, *Portuguese Empire*, chs. 1–3; idem and Thomaz, "Evolution," 298–331; Pearson, "Merchants and States," 77–80, 106; Isabel dos Guimaraes Sa, "Ecclesiastical Structures and Religious Action," in Bethencourt and Curto, *Portuguese Oceanic Expansion*, 255–82; Felipe Fernandez-Armesto, "Portuguese Expansion in a Global Context," in ibid., 480–511; David Birmingham, *A Concise History of Portugal* (Cambridge, 1993), 17–31; Peter Russell, *Prince Henry 'The Navigator'* (New Haven, 2001); Simon Barton, *A History of Spain* (New York, 2004), chs. 1–3; Henry Kamen, *Empire: How Spain Became a World Power 1492–1763* (New York, 2003), 9–14, 29–33; Bernard Reilly, *The Medieval Spains* (Cambridge, 1993), chs. 4–7; G. V. Scammell, *The World Encompassed* (Berkeley, 1981), chs. 4–6; Ringrose, *Expansion*, 68–77.

(1477) precluded further independent political action until the anti-Hapsburg, anti-Catholic Revolt of 1568. As in Iberia, however, the 16th century inaugurated an era of intensified political and economic activity that saw the strengthening of Holland's provincial government and urban patriciate – institutions that would undergird the Dutch Republic (1588–1795) – and further innovations in agriculture, shipbuilding, fisheries, and trade. What finally allowed Holland to pursue the anti-Habsburg struggle with growing confidence was the 1584–1585 mass immigration of merchants and craftsmen from the Habsburg south. Thus fortified, the new Republic strode in the 1590s toward European economic supremacy. The Dutch promptly sent fleets to Indonesia to seize Portugal's spice trade, while moving aggressively against Iberian positions in Africa and the New World. If the Dutch pursued more narrowly commercial objectives than the Spanish, Mughals, or Manchus, like forward movements by the latter groups, Dutch colonization in the 17th century may be seen as a hypertrophic elaboration, the second phase, of an economic-cum-political expansion whose roots lay in the early second millennium.[199]

In sum, two great post-1550 pincer movements on agrarian Asia – Europeans arriving by sea and Inner Asians moving overland – benefited from curiously synchronized long-term developments in the societies of those conquest elites.

Creating the Spanish Philippines to c. 1660

Against this Eurasian background, let us examine European interventions in the islands to c. 1660, starting with by far the most transformative, that of Spain in what would become the Philippines.

Compared to archipelagic areas farther west, I argued that state formation in the pre-Hispanic Philippines came late, but clearly it was less secure the farther north one moved. Sulu, recall, had some sort of Muslim ruler by 1310 and a sultanate by the mid-1400s; while by the early 1500s Malay contacts also had helped to establish a sultanate on

---

[199] Symptomatic of Dutch economic vigor, disruptions in Holland and Zeeland between 1348 and 1450 were milder than in most Europeans lands. On the Netherlands c. 1000–1700, Herman Van der Wee, *The Low Countries in the Early Modern World* (Aldershot, UK, 1993); Jonathan Israel, *Dutch Primacy in World Trade 1585–1740* (Oxford, 1989), chs. 1–3; idem, *The Dutch Republic* (Oxford, 1995), chs. 1–12; J. C. Blom and E. Lamberts, eds., *History of the Low Countries* (New York, 2006), 23–140. Conceivably, a similar two-stage model could be applied to British imperial expansion.

Mindanao. A Manila bishop in 1588 reported that the men of that island built mosques, circumcised youths, and taught the Koran.[200] North of Mindanao in Cebu in the Visayas, a chiefly confederation in 1565 reportedly mobilized 2,000 warriors, but Cebu, unlike Mindano, had no stable paramount ruler and its elites were at best very superficially Muslim.[201] Yet farther north Pires reported that Luzon's people were "nearly all heathen; they have no king, but they are ruled by groups of elders."[202] In 1571 a Raja Sulayman in the Manila area was still trying to persuade local chiefs to recognize his authority and to accept Islam.[203]

Had the Spanish, who began a permanent presence in 1565 and the conquest of Luzon in 1571, arrived two generations later, there is every reason to believe they would have found Islam as entrenched in the central and northern islands as it was in Sulu and Mindanao, in which case they well may have failed to implant Spanish culture. Late-16th- and 17th-century efforts to quench the "pestilential fire" of Islam actually strengthened the southern sultanates, whose forces were sufficiently centralized to offer sustained resistance, but not so centralized that the Spanish could deliver a fatal blow.[204] The Visayas and Luzon were a different story entirely. With the likes of Raja Sulayman brushed aside, Hispanization proceeded without large-scale opposition.

The timing of the Spanish venture was fortuitous in two other respects: it gave them some 40 years to consolidate their position before the onslaught of the Dutch War from 1609 to 1648, and it let them draw on over seven decades of evangelizing experience in Latin America. Initially Spain sought the Philippines both to convert the local population and to provide a base for Christianizing Japan and China and conquering Maluku. But by the 1620s Christian prospects in Japan had

---

[200] Majul, *Muslims*, 68–76, plus Ruurdje Laarhoven, "Lords of the Great River," in Kathirithamby-Wells and Villiers, *Port and Polity*, 162; nn. 132, 148 *supra*.

[201] John Villiers, "Portuguese Malacca and Spanish Manila," in Roderich Ptak, *Portuguese Asia* (Stuttgart, 1987), 44; John Phelan, *The Hispanization of the Philippines* (rpt., Manila, 1985), 16–17; Junker, *Raiding, Trading*, 367, 374–75, 388.

[202] Cortesao, *Suma Oriental*, vol. I, 133; Reid, "Flows and Seepages," 34–36. But see Thomaz, "Malay Sultanate," 81, on Luzon Muslims in Melaka. Note too that Manila merchants of Chinese origin traded with Brunei and Melaka.

[203] Majul, *Muslims*, 78–84; John Larkin, *The Pampangans* (Berkeley, 1972), 19–22. On the pre-Spanish Philippines, n. 132 *supra*, plus F. Landa Jocano, *The Philippines at the Spanish Contact* (Quezon City, 1975); William Henry Scott, *Cracks in the Parchment Curtain* (Quezon City, 1982); idem, *Prehispanic Source Materials for the Study of Philippine History* (Quezon City, 1984); idem, *Barangay* (Quezon City, 1994); Vicente Rafael, *Contracting Colonialism* (Ithaca, 1988), 137–46.

[204] Majul, *Muslims*, 74–76 (with quote), 121–89; Phelan, *Hispanization*, 137–43.

collapsed, while in Maluku, although Spanish forces would linger to 1666, Portuguese claims and Dutch opposition crippled Spain's efforts.[205] With these reverses, fear that the Filipinos would revert to paganism, or that Dutch heretics would take over, provided the abiding rationale for continued Philippine involvement. That the colony remained largely a missionary enterprise is suggested by the crown's willingness to accept chronic budget deficits in express deference to the religious orders.[206]

The political structure of the Philippines followed that of New Spain, to whose Mexico City viceroy the islands were subordinate. Aided by a modest staff, the Manila governor-general executed Spanish laws, commanded military forces, exercised legislative authority, and presided over the high court (*real audiencia*). Yet disputes were endemic between the governor and other power centers in Manila, including the high court, the Archbishop, and the religious orders. Beyond Manila the islands were divided into 12 major provinces, each usually under an *alcalde mayor*, who also combined executive, military, and judicial authority. Beneath these jurisdictions lay townships (*pueblos*) and villages under indigenous leaders responsible for organizing those corvées and compulsory sales of rice and timber on which the government relied, especially during the Dutch War. Given minimal monetization, labor and in-kind taxes were the only local resource readily available to the state.[207] The political system as a whole was weakly articulated, territorially uneven, and subject to unchecked patrimonial appropriation at all levels. Yet it was at least as coherent as the reforming monarchies of early-17th-century Burma and Siam, the two most powerful states on the mainland. In local terms, Philippine unification was obviously revolutionary.[208]

As in Latin America, the initial imposition of Spanish authority relied on *encomenderos*, individuals who, in return for control of an extended

---

[205] Andaya, *World of Maluku*, 39–40, 152–56; Meilink-Roelofsz, *Asian Trade*, 155.

[206] Phelan, *Hispanization*, 7–14, 94; CHSEA, 362, 530; Greg Bankoff, pers. commun., June 8, 2008.

[207] Cf. skeptical comments by Subrahmanyam, *Portuguese Empire*, 109–11, which, however, minimize the anemic state of pre-1565 Philippine trade and urbanization compared to the western and central archipelago. At the same time it is probably true that Spanish rule reduced Filipino involvement in international trade from the precolonial period.

[208] On pre-1660 administration, Phelan, *Hispanization*, chs. 7, 8; Nicholas Cushner, *Spain in the Philippines* (Quezon City, 1971), chs. 5–7; Eliodoro Robles, *The Philippines in the Nineteenth Century* (Quezon City, 1966), 15–26.

area, were expected to establish Spanish sovereignty, instruct the people in the rudiments of Christianity, and prepare the way for missionary orders. Also as in New Spain, *encomenderos* and missionaries, with gubernatorial support, sought to deepen Spanish control by resettling the population, hitherto dispersed, into a grid of stable settlements, each with a church and Spanish priest and each surrounded by satellite hamlets.[209] Although without strong commercial incentives, resettlement proved far slower and ultimately less successful than in Latin America, by 1650 virtually the entire lowland population of Luzon, and by the late 1600s of the Visayas, some 500,000–700,000 in total, had accepted baptism. Christianization led local elites to adopt elements of Spanish dress and (as with Islamization) induced the general population gradually to abandon tattooing and penis-inserts.[210]

The European intrusion, recent research suggests, was far more violent than church historians allowed. In some settled parts of Luzon the population may have declined by half from 1565 to 1591 as a result of Spanish exactions, natural or Spanish-precipitated famines, and epidemics. From 1606 to 1655, chiefly because of the Dutch War, the tributary rolls fell another 8 percent. Early Spanish attempts to suppress "devil worship" entailed systematic attacks on animist cults, to which shamans, generally women and transvestites, responded by raiding churches.[211] Escalating tax and labor demands to fend off the Dutch prompted more serious uprisings.[212]

---

[209] Large settlements were termed *cabeceras*. On settlement and *encomiendas* to 1721, Phelan, *Hispanization*, 44–48, 95–98; Rafael, *Contracting*, 87–91.

[210] Bankoff, pers. commun., June 8, 2008 emphasizes the modest success of the *reduccion* process. See conversion figures and dates at T. Valentino Sitoy, Jr., *A History of Christianity in the Philippines*, vol. 1 (Quezon City, 1986), 268; AC, vol. II, 133; Phelan, *Hispanization*, 56, 108; John Schumacher, "Syncretism in Philippine Catholicism," *Philippine Studies* 32 (1984): 251–72; Linda Newson, "Old World Diseases in the Early Colonial Philippines and Spanish America," in Daniel Doeppers and Peter Xenos, eds., *Population and History* (Madison, WI, 1998), 17–36. esp. 20 and 34 n. 31. Perhaps 500,000 non-Christians inhabited mountains and the Muslim south. On sartorial change, tattooing, and penis-inserts, Phelan, *Hispanization*, 64, 185–86; AC, vol. I, 77, 89–90, 150; Rafael, *Contracting*, 58; Carolyn Brewer, *Shamanism, Catholicism and Gender Relations in Colonial Philippines, 1521–1685* (Aldershot, UK, 2004), 74, 152.

[211] Smaller population declines occurred 1606–1655. Newson, "Old World Diseases," esp. 25–27 and Tables 2.1 and 2.2, and Andaya, *Flaming Womb*, 94–95 on animist persecution.

[212] On resistance and accommodation to Hispanization, Phelan, *Hispanization*, chs. 3–6, 10; Rosario Cortes, *Pangasinan 1572–1800* (Quezon City, 1974), chs. 3, 6; Alfred McCoy, "Baylan," *Philippine Quarterly of Culture and Society* 10 (1982): 141–94; Andaya,

And yet it is also clear that the religious orders succeeded in transmitting a substantial measure of Christianity to the settled population. Again adapting lessons from the Americas, from which many hailed, Spanish missionaries gained social entrée by focusing on the children of chiefs and by providing instruction, apart from key terms, in vernacular tongues. Of necessity, this allowed space for selective appropriation and creative revalorization, which in tacit, rarely acknowledged fashion, drew upon pre-Christian beliefs. Filipinos might have difficulty with marriage and penance, but they took enthusiastically to baptism and holy water, which recalled water-centered animist rites. Co-parenthood appealed to kinship traditions, much as saints to whom petitions were addressed were assimilated to the circle of propitiated ancestors. Consuming Christ's body and blood may have echoed ritual feasting and headhunting. Bibles, rosaries, and crosses became new talismans. But at the same time, Reid argues, many Filipino converts (like converts to Islam elsewhere) found deeply comforting the promise – for which animism offered no precedent – that individual moral action could influence life after death. Such was the power of the new faith that even shamans began to appropriate Christian symbols.[213]

Moreover, initial violence notwithstanding, on the whole Spanish conquest proved less socially disruptive than in most of Latin America, because in the Philippines Spaniards remained more physically isolated. In 1650 some 7,300 Spaniards, the vast majority, lived in the Latin American-style walled city of Manila, supported by some 20,000 *indios* (indigenes) and 15,000 Chinese laborers and traders outside the walls. Directly or indirectly, all of Manila relied on the royal galleon trade, which brought Mexican crown silver across the Pacific to exchange primarily for Chinese silks. However, the urban self-sufficiency of this trade, in which Philippine goods played only the most marginal role, obviated the need for Latin American-style, European-directed latifundia and thus kept Spaniards – apart from a handful of officials, soldiers, and friars – from entering the provinces. Left to their own devices,

Flaming Womb, 94–102; Brewer, *Shamanism*, pts. 2, 3; John Larkin, "Philippine History Reconsidered," *AHR* 87 (1982): 604–606.

[213] *AC*, ch. 3, esp. 157–61 (but see n. 220 *infra*). On the cultural/psychological dynamics of early Christianization, two previous notes, plus Phelan, *Hispanization*, chs. 3–6; Horacio de la Costa, *The Jesuits in the Philippines, 1581–1768* (Cambridge, MA, 1961); 70–92; Carolyn Brewer, "From Animist 'Priestess' to Catholic Priest," in Barbara Watson Andaya, ed., *Other Pasts* (Honolulu, 2000), 69–86; and Rafael's highly original *Contracting*, 84–219.

without a substantial European presence, rural *indios* had opportunity to interpret Christianity largely on their own terms.[214]

But perhaps the most critical prop to Spanish hegemony was the benefit that political reorganization conferred on indigenous elites and, in some measure, the wider society. Before 1571 authority on the village level was insecure, subject to the vagaries of clientage and external attack. As seems to have been typical of much of the eastern archipelago, without a stable supralocal power, society had no ready mechanism to quell endemic vendettas and blood feuds.[215] The Spanish, however, organized village chiefs into a hereditary, tax-exempt class, the *principales*, from whose ranks a "petty governor" (*gobernadorcillo*) was chosen to aid the Spanish priest and provincial officials on the superior level of the township (*pueblo*). Although pre-1571 chiefs made hereditary claims, the Spanish-sanctioned oligarchy in general, and *gobernadorcillos* in particular, achieved a level of security, patronage, and wealth – the latter by manipulating tax collections, extending debt-peonage, and converting communal into private land – without pre-1571 analogue. Understandably grateful, they served as cultural brokers between their followers and the Spanish. No less critical to colonial success, as external authorities who were convinced of their own superiority and who often lacked ties to local kin groups, Spanish officials and friars frequently were able to resolve conflicts more or less impartially. To follow Henley, Filipino appreciation of this new dispensation – which was inextricably linked to Christianity but which conceivably fed on pre-Christian notions of beneficent "stranger-kings" – helps to explain how an early occupation force of some 500 could control tens of thousands.[216]

---

[214] Until 1768 laws actually limited Spanish provincial residence. On the conservative political economy and its social implications, see Phelan, *Hispanization*, 11–14, 42, 51–52, 57–61, 84, 105–13, 157; Legarda, *After Galleons*, 32–50; Newson, "Old World Diseases," suggesting population remained too dispersed to sustain endemic infections. See too J. E. Spencer, "The Rise of Maize as a Major Crop Plant in the Philippines," *Jl. of Historical Geography* 1 (1975): 1–16. On the role of the Chinese and the galleon trade, Phelan, *Hispanization*, 12, 178, n. 11; Robert Reed, *Colonial Manila* (Berkeley, 1978), chs. 4–6; Edgar Wickberg, *The Chinese in Philippine Life 1850–1898* (Manila, 2000), 3–20; n. 175 *supra*.

[215] See n. 203 *supra*, and the clever analysis in David Henley, "Conflict, Justice, and the Stranger-King Roots of Colonial Rule in Indonesia and Elsewhere," *MAS* 38 (2004): 85–144.

[216] Because some/many (?) Spanish friars had mistresses and children, it is wrong to claim that they invariably lacked local kin ties, but spiritual and political potency still would have afforded them a unique prestige. On political and economic Hispanization, besides Henley, "Conflict, Justice," 117–18, 125–26, I rely on Cortes, *Pangasinan*, 91–92;

Thus arose not only the Spanish state of the Philippines, but a Christian cultural sphere, which after the Theravada, Neo-Confucian, and Muslim zones, was the last and smallest Southeast Asian cultural zone to cohere. Should we view Hispanic Christianization, then, as a source of solidarity between conquerors and subjects? The idea of Catholic community gained physical expression, one could argue, in shared defense against Dutch and Muslim attacks and in the enthusiasm with which Spaniards, *indios*, and Christian Chinese mestizos cooperated to massacre non-Catholic Chinese at Manila in 1603, 1639, and 1662.[217] But set against such liminal moments were insuperable quotidian barriers to Spanish–*indio* equality. The insularity of the Spaniards was simultaneously spatial – in Manila they walled themselves off quite literally – legal, and racial. Exempt from taxes or corvées to which Chinese and *indios* were subject, Spaniards formed a self-governing commonwealth, with its own courts and laws. But *la republica de los indios*, a commonwealth of legal minors protected by the crown and church, employed a very different set of laws, magistrates, and languages; in 1660 probably over 95 percent of *indios* knew no Spanish.[218] The latter could hold neither lay office above *gobernadorcillo* nor, with very rare pre-1698 exceptions, church office higher than assistant to Spanish friars. Denouncing Filipinos as congenitally unfit for sacerdotal office, a friar asked, "What reverence will the *indios* themselves have for such a priest, when they see he is of their color and race? Especially . . . when his proper station in life should have been that of a convict or a slave."[219] Interracial marriage – as opposed to sex – also was unusual. Not surprisingly, while accepting

Phelan, *Hispanization*, 115–18, 121–35, 157; Larkin, *Pamapangans*, 30–40; idem, *Sugar and the Origins of Modern Philippine Society* (Berkeley, 1993), 29–32; Nicholas Cushner, *Landed Estates in the Colonial Philippines* (New Haven, 1967), 2, 17–20. On Spanish forces, Newson, "Old World Diseases," 25.

[217] Larkin, *Pampangans,*, 27–28; Phelan, *Hispanization*, 11–12, 145–46; Wickberg, *Chinese*, 10, 20, 36.

[218] In 1903, after considerable expansion of Spanish-language education, still less than 10 percent spoke the language. Phelan, *Hispanization*, 121, 129–35, 150; Greg Bankoff, *Crime, Society, and the State* (Quezon City, 1996), 6–7, 11–12, 94–100; Wickberg, *Chinese*, 7–20; Rafael, *Contracting*, 163. On Tagalog self-images and emulation of Spaniards, ibid., 19–83, 163–66.

[219] Phelan, *Hispanization*, 86 (with quote) and 84–89, 160. On clerical racism, see too Luciano Santiago, *The Hidden Light* (Quezon City, 1987), 9–19, 71; John Schumacher, *Readings in Philippine Church History* (Quezon City, 1979), 93–97; Larkin, *Pampangans*, 58–59; Rafael, *Contracting*, 185–86. But on the 18th-century growth of a small Filipino secular clergy, and for a sympathetic view of their achievements based not on hostile foreign sources, but on local archives, see Santiago, *Hidden Light*, esp. chs. 3–5.

the plausibility of heaven, some Visayans doubted that Spanish would ever let them share it.[220]

Their technical and organizational superiority and their role as supralocal arbiters permitted the Spanish a degree of insularity and unilateral imposition more extreme than either the Qing or the Mughals attempted. Indeed, in some ways the relation between Spaniards and *indios* was the reverse of that between Manchus and Chinese. The Manchus retained their own cults and exclusive ethnicity, but, lacking serviceable literary or administrative traditions, adopted Chinese systems more or less *in toto* to govern China proper. The Spanish monopoly on public written codes,[221] complex organizations, and advanced firearms let them reshape local culture, while borrowing little, if anything in return. Mughal–Indian relations lay somewhere between these two extremes.

Portugal's Impact to c. 1660

Despite their common background in anti-Muslim reconquest and Atlantic exploration, Spaniards and Portuguese played very different roles in Southeast Asia. The Spanish subdued large islands with sizeable populations, but the Portuguese held only Melaka, whose population fell from perhaps 20,000 when the Portuguese seized the city in 1511 to 12,000 in 1641,[222] plus outposts in Maluku, Timor, and a few other locales. Whereas the Spaniards sponsored a novel political integration, the Portuguese fragmented the western archipelago's chief political network. The Manila galleon bypassed local products, but the acquisition of local cash crops provided Portugal's commercial *raison d'être*. Nor did Portuguese-affiliated Christian missions approach the success of their Spanish counterparts.

Such differences reflected both historic legacies and local circumstance. Whereas the Spanish entered the Philippines inspired by the territorial exploits of American *conquistadors* and missionaries,

---

[220] Phelan, *Hispanization*, 59. As Ricklefs, pers. commun., April 26, 2009 points out, this qualifies Reid's claim that Filipinos embraced a predictable moral universe. On sexual relations, Phelan, *Hispanization*, 106–107, 134–35; Larkin, *Pampangans*, 35.

[221] The pre-Hispanic Philippines had writing, but it was used for personal, not religious or political, communication. Bienvenido Lumbera, *Tagalog Poetry 1570–1898* (Quezon City, 1986), 25–27; Geoff Wade, "On the Possible Cham Origins of the Philippine Scripts," *JSEAS* 24 (1993): 44–87.

[222] See n. 120 *supra* and *AC*, vol. II, 73–75. In 1641 the Portuguese lost Melaka to the Dutch.

Portugal's pre-1511 colonial experience, focusing on African and South Asian port-cities, predisposed them to a coastal strategy. Whereas the 1529 Treaty of Zaragoza awarded Spain authority over stateless, poorly commercialized Philippine societies, Portugal received archipelagic areas with strong polities and dense trade. And whereas in Luzon and the Visayas animist and proto-Islamic cults offered Christianity minimal resistance, by the time the Portuguese arrived in the western and central archipelago, Islam was far too strong to be dislodged.

Accordingly, Portugal's influence on Southeast Asia was less sustained or territorially focused than that of Spain. It was also less deliberate insofar as some of its principal effects were entirely inadvertent. But an older historiographic emphasis on Portugal's marginality to Southeast Asian history is surely exaggerated.[223]

With melodramatic flair, Afonso de Albuquerque reported to his king in 1513, "At the rumour of our coming, the [native] ships all vanished and even the birds ceased to skim over the water, so overcast was the Red Sea by our coming and so deserted."[224] In fact, as it evolved, Portugal's system of Asian trade had two segments: a) bilateral trade between Europe and India, which was a royal monopoly and which focused on the exchange of European and South American bullion for Asian spices, pepper, cotton and silk textiles; and b) intra-Asian trade, more or less under official supervision, which sought to amass profits sufficient to purchase Asian goods for Europe and thus to minimize Portugal's bullion exports. To the latter end, cottons were purchased in India and exchanged in the archipelago for spices and pepper, which along with bullion were sold at the Portuguese post of Macao for Chinese silks. Silks were then traded in Japan for silver, which sold in China and India for more textiles. As a source of supply for both segments of trade, Southeast Asia thus filled a critical role.

At the outset, superior guns, ships, and navigational aids[225] led the Portuguese to try to dominate Maluku from fortified posts. But neither that strategy nor the allied system of ship passes (*cartazes*) proved adequate to monopolize fine spices, let alone more widely dispersed pepper. From 1539 the Portuguese therefore turned to notionally free

---

[223] See n. 10 *supra*.

[224] Meilink-Roelofsz, *Asian Trade*, 116.

[225] On the Portuguese–Asian military balance, Wills, "Maritime Asia," 93; Meilink-Roelofsz, *Asian Trade*, 9–10, 118–24; Manguin, "Vanishing *Jong*," 205–209; Boxer, *Portuguese Seaborne Empire*, 39–59; Andaya, "Interactions," 378–79.

trade and hefty in-kind tolls on spice sales at Melaka, which from 1511 served as their regional headquarters and stapling point for shipments to Goa and thence Europe. Along with Indian Ocean chokepoints at Goa and Hormuz, these efforts let Portugal profit from Asian spice sales at the expense of Muslim traders, and obtain cargoes for royal vessels rounding the Cape of Good Hope sufficient to supply some 75 percent of Europe's pepper and as much or more of its fine spices. Thus the Portuguese gutted the venerable Levant–Venice spice route.[226] Meanwhile in the islands Portuguese interference joined Gujarati and Chinese competition to eclipse native junks in favor of smaller freight vessels.[227]

If these commercial effects were more or less deliberate, the *Estado da India* (State of India), as the Portuguese termed their Asian collection of forts and settlements, also helped to modify Southeast Asian development in three ways that were not only unintended, but deeply unwelcome to the Portuguese themselves. First, Portuguese interventions unwittingly joined rising prices to accelerate the growth of new Muslim port cities. Earlier I speculated that as global demand increased, Melaka's concentration of trade at a single site was bound to come under strain, with specialized ports and producing zones seeking to carve out independent spheres. By inducing Asian traders, Muslims in particular, to seek spices and pepper outside Melaka and by splitting that city's trade into Indian Ocean and South China Sea segments, Portugal in 1511 ensured precisely such an outcome. As we shall see, the unintended beneficiaries included Aceh, which became the chief western rendezvous for Indian Ocean spice and pepper traders; and Johor, Pattani, Banten, and Brunei, which specialized in exports to China. To supply these new outlets, pepper cultivation expanded along the west coast of Sumatra

---

[226] Subrahmanyam, *Portuguese Empire*, 77–78, 135–36, 142–43; Wake, "Changing Pattern," 394–95. Because Indian Ocean and Chinese demand for spices rose, the Portuguese probably never sent to Europe more than an eighth of total Malukun cloves, and traffic from India to the Levant – but not the Levant to Venice – continued. *AC*, vol. II, 19; Bulbeck et al., *Southeast Asian Exports*, 63; Inalcik, *Economic and Social History*, 340–55. On Portuguese global trade and rule, see too Subrahmanyam, *Portuguese Empire*, chs. 3–6; Boxer, *Portuguese Seaborne Empire*; Subrahmanyam and Thomaz, "Evolution"; Leonard Blusse, "The Run to the Coast," *Itinerario* 12 (1988): 195–214; Meilink-Roelofsz, *Asian Trade*, chs. 6, 7; Stefan Halikowski Smith, "'Profits Sprout Like Tropical Plants,'" *JGH* 3 (2008): 389–418; Andaya, *World of Maluku*, ch. 4.

[227] *AC*, vol. II, 39–42, 281–86; Anthony Reid, "The Rise and Fall of Sino-Javanese Shipping," in V. J. H. Houben et al., eds., *Looking in Odd Mirrors* (Leiden, 1992), 177–211; Knaap, *Shallow Waters*, 156–57, 162; and n. 103 *supra*.

and the northeast peninsula, while the Sunda Straits began to rival the Straits of Melaka as a commercial artery.[228]

Second, again to Portugal's discomfiture, growing warfare with the Portuguese and with one another obliged indigenous states to adopt more militaristic, administratively coherent policies. Pre-1511 *negeri*, recall, tolerated high levels of factionalism, territorial autonomy, and technological inertia. But the more cutthroat post-1511 environment rendered such practices suicidal. Accordingly, although these changes would reach fruition only in the 17th century, from 1520 to 1600 we shall find that several states reduced *orang kaya* and tributary power, promoted cultural conformity as an aid to political centralization, regulated trade far more closely, and improved firearms and naval construction. Often Portuguese guns and ships provided the standard.

Third, in some locales the Portuguese unwittingly spurred Islamization. The Portuguese, it is often said, combined European racial supremacy with greater sympathy for mestizo cultures than the Dutch displayed, not least because the Portuguese relied more heavily on local financial and political support.[229] Official toleration, however, rarely extended to religion, and the Portuguese crown, like the Spanish, energetically promoted evangelization. Starting with St. Francis Xavier, such missions had their greatest archipelagic success among animists in Maluku and the Lesser Sundas, where in fact an enduring Portuguese influence extended beyond religion to language, dress, and music.[230] But Christianizing efforts, and the close link between religious and commercial affiliation, soon led Muslims to intensify their own efforts. Thus Aceh framed its anti-Portuguese struggle in religious terms, and Portugal's 1570 assassination of the ruler of Ternate led his son to seek revenge by championing Islam.[231] On the whole, local

---

[228] Likewise, clove cultivation spread in Maluku. See nn. 169–173 *supra,* plus Manguin, "Vanishing *Jong,*" 202–208; *AC,* vol. II, 65.

[229] Bethencourt, "Low Cost Empire," 108–30. But see an alternate view at Bosma and Raben, *Being Dutch,* 22–23.

[230] Estimates of converts by the 1590s vary from 10,000 to 85,000. Boxer, *Portuguese Seaborne Empire,* 79–80; *HMI,* 28–29; Andaya, *World of Maluku,* 134. The Lesser Sundas extend from Bali to Timor. From 1580 to 1640 the Spanish and Portuguese crowns were joined. On Portuguese legacies, Antonio Pinto da Franca, *Portuguese Influence in Indonesia* (Lisbon, 1985).

[231] On Aceh, discussion *infra;* on Ternate, Andaya, *World of Maluku,* 132–38. That Aceh used Islam as an instrument of state did not preclude fellow Muslim Johor from allying with Christian Melaka against Aceh. Banten was similarly selective in its religious alliances. See n. 259 *infra.* But for further evidence of Christian–Muslim

Muslim traders-cum-missionaries were far more successful, in part, because Islam did not require subordination to an alien military power; in part because *sufis* and individual Muslims could accommodate local beliefs more readily than centrally controlled friar orders; and in part, simply, because Muslim proselytizers were far more numerous than Jesuits and Dominicans.

The Dutch in Southeast Asia to c. 1660

Arguably, however, Portugal's most lasting contribution to Southeast Asian history was to pave the way for the Dutch. The Dutch had retailed Portuguese spices in northern Europe, but by disrupting access to those commodities, the revolt against Spain in 1568 and the Spanish–Portuguese union of 1580 drove the Dutch to obtain spices directly in Asia. Through the Dutch United East India Company – the VOC – which was formed in 1602, the Dutch, like the Portuguese, organized their trade into two main segments: the monopoly trade between Asia and Europe, which focused on the exchange of silver for spices; and intra-Asian exchanges designed to minimize bullion outflows. Within Asia the VOC sought to seize Portuguese forts and to incorporate its trade networks, starting with the spice routes, moving to the exchange of Chinese silks for Japanese silver, and then invading the Indian Ocean trade in cottons and spices. One sees as well basic operational similarities, including a preference for low-volume, high-profit turnover; shipping passes to control Asian rivals; and a mix of free trade and military imposition to maximize market share.[232]

Given these similarities, how do we explain the VOC's 17th-century superiority? Subrahmanyam and Julia Adams warn against opposing Dutch "rationalized modernity" to Portuguese "medievalism," because

religious-cum-commercial rivalry, Andaya, *World of Maluku*, 127–48; Boxer, *Portuguese Seaborne Empire*, ch. 10; Andaya and Ishii, "Religious Developments," 521 ("The arrival of [Iberians]... was paradoxically another stimulus to the spread of Islam in the archipelago."), 542–43; B. Schrieke, *Indonesian Sociological Studies*, 2 vols. (The Hague, 1955–1957), vol. II, 232–37.

[232] On VOC strategies and organization, Gerrit Knaap, "Shipping and Trade in Java, c. 1775," *MAS* 32 (1999): 405–20; idem, *Shallow Waters*, ch. 2; Leonard Blusse and George Winius, "The Origins and Rhythm of Dutch Aggression Against the Estado da India 1601–1661," in T. R. de Souza, ed., *Indo-Portuguese Trade* (New Delhi, 1985), 73–83; Blusse, "Run to the Coast," 200–201; C. R. Boxer, *The Dutch Seaborne Empire 1600–1800* (London, 1965), esp. 187–88; Meilink-Roelofsz, *Asian Trade*, 173–294, esp. 120–21; Reinout Vos, *Gentle Janus, Merchant Prince* (Leiden, 1993).

the VOC, a faithful reflection of the Dutch state that spawned it, sanctioned corporate and patrimonial privilege of all sorts and, in the final analysis, relied on military power to turn a profit no less than the Portuguese.[233] But it is also true that the company drew strength from (and reinforced) the Netherlands' role as 17th-century Europe's premier economic power, home to manufacturing and financial advances without analogy in the smaller, more sluggish Portuguese economy. Obsessively focused on profit, the early VOC emphasized central control and individual competence more consistently than the *Estado*, which reserved key posts for titled aristocrats, kept New Christians (Jews) at arm's length, and awarded segments of royal trade as fiefs to influential concessionaires. As one of the first joint stock companies, the VOC also accumulated a permanent capital far beyond Portugal's means with which to sustain investment, outfit ships, and hire seamen. Portugal's decision from the mid-1600s to concentrate on the defense of Brazil and Africa, not Asia, only reinforced this discrepancy. Thus whereas by 1688 the VOC was sending 24 ships a year to Asia where it employed 22,000 men, the *Estado da India* at its height sent an average of 6 ships and employed but 7,000 to 9,000.[234] Yet because Portugal focused on the Indian Ocean while the VOC focused on the archipelago – in effect, making Portugal's periphery into the Dutch center – the imbalance in Southeast Asia was yet greater. Finally, Dutch ships typically were more maneuverable and better constructed, carried more and larger caliber brass cannon, and had better trained crews; while small arms, siegecraft, and fortresses also tended to favor the Dutch.[235]

In pursuit of intra-Asian profits, the VOC scattered outposts across the archipelago, seeking preferential contracts for everything from pepper to tin. But the VOC's chief commitments were at Batavia and

---

[233] Subrahmanyam, *Portuguese Empire*, 177–82, 212–15, 271–73; Julia Adams, "Trading States, Trading Places," *CSSH* 36 (1994): 319–55. The VOC's critical post-1639 monopoly of Tokugawa silver, which followed Portugal's expulsion from Japan, was also a politically, not commercially acquired asset.

[234] Note 193 *supra*.

[235] For VOC–Portuguese comparisons, Meilink-Roelofsz, *Asian Trade*, 10–11, 118–22, 175–82; M. C. Ricklefs, *War, Culture and Economy in Java 1677–1726* (Sydney, 1993), 20–21; R. J. Barendse, *The Arabian Seas* (Armonk, NY, 2002), 361–400 *passim*; Pearson, "Merchants and States," 77–87; Niels Steensgaard, "The Dutch East India Company as an Institutional Innovation," in Maurice Aymard, ed., *Dutch Capitalism and World Capitalism* (Cambridge, 1982), 235–57; Boxer, *Portuguese Seaborne Empire*, ch. 7; Bethencourt, "Political Configurations," 223–26.

Maluku. In 1619 the Dutch seized the Javanese port of Jayakerta, renamed it Batavia, and promptly made it their commercial and administrative headquarters. It was to Batavia that VOC directors sent personnel, bullion, and directives, and it was Batavia that coordinated intra-Asian trade from Persia to Japan and monopolized the vital spice shipments to Europe. To corner Malukun spices, the Dutch neutralized the Iberians and in 1621 exterminated the population of Banda, the sole source for nutmeg and mace, replacing its people with slave labor under Dutch planters. In 1652 the VOC also imposed on Ternate, the chief Malukun kingdom, a treaty limiting cultivation of cloves to Ambon and of nutmeg to Banda. Admittedly, "smuggling" – as the Dutch termed any traffic not in their hands – continued to supply Muslim ports like Banten and Aceh with clove, nutmeg, and mace. Pepper, as ever, defied monopoly. Yet by the 1650s a monopoly on fine spices – which Portugal had only dreamed of – seemed within the VOC's grasp.[236]

A commercial enterprise, the Company functioned simultaneously as a territorial power, authorized to recruit soldiers, wage war, make treaties, and administer subjects. In the words of a 1644 pamphlet, the VOC was "a sovereign king in its own lands."[237] In addition to coastal forts and factories from the Cape of Good Hope to Nagasaki, by 1670 the VOC exercised nominal lordship over self-governing Malukun realms, with perhaps 150,000 people, and more direct authority over Melaka, Ambon, Banda, and at least 27,000 people in and around Batavia.[238] At Batavia the chief groups by size were Asian slaves, *Mardijkers* (free Asian Christians), Chinese, Europeans, non-Indonesian Muslims, and Indonesian groups. Lack of white women mandated liaisons with Asians and Eurasians; while in principle the Dutch Reformed Church united Dutchmen, Asians, and Eurasians. But at the same time Dutch policy in

---

[236] *HMI*, 31–34, 73–76; Willard Hanna, *Indonesian Banda* (Philadelphia, 1978), chs. 1–4; Andaya, *World of Maluku*, ch. 5; *AC*, II, 19–23; Bulbeck et al., *Southeast Asian Exports*, 9–10, 19–21, 26; Meilink-Roelofsz, *Asian Trade*, 183–84, 195–238.

[237] Barendse, *Arabian Seas*, 383. An emphasis on the VOC's dual commercial–military character also informs Vos, *Gentle Janus*, 1–2, 207–208, and Jurrien van Goor, "A Hybrid State," in Guillot et al., *From the Mediterranean*, 193–214.

[238] Ricklefs, *War, Culture*, 15 says 27,000 in Batavia and its suburb (*voorstad*) in 1674. Blusse, *Strange Company*, 18 shows 70,000 "inside and outside the town" in 1701–1705, which agrees with Goor, "Hybrid State," 196; but *AC*, vol. II, 73 claims 130,000 "inside and outside the walls" in 1670. See too figures on Europeans at Bosma and Raben, *Being Dutch*, 15–16.

this "plural society" *avant la lettre* encouraged separate quarters, dress, and religious structures for each ethnicity. The highest status naturally attached to *Nederlanders* or *blanken* ("whites"), a somewhat flexible category that admitted people of mixed ancestry provided they knew Dutch, dressed in distinctive fashion, and were Calvinist VOC employees or were married to such employees. Although the 17th-century VOC was eager to convert Catholics and to evangelize "heathens" in areas of strategic and economic importance, it forbade proselytism among Muslims and in general showed far less interest in religion than Iberians or Mughals. Moreover, in contrast to Portuguese or Persian, the Dutch language never spread widely.[239]

One must not exaggerate Dutch strength in the archipelago in 1660. On Java the VOC still was only one of three major powers, along with the interior state of Mataram, whose territory and resources dwarfed the VOC, and Banten. To the east Makasar remained defiant. In the west, although the Portuguese bastion of Melaka fell to the Dutch in 1641, the VOC's Malay ally Johor gained as much as the Dutch from that victory.[240] Private Portuguese trade remained lively. Yet by 1660 the VOC had become the islands' foremost naval and commercial power. Save minor posts in Flores and elsewhere, the Portuguese crown had lost all archipelagic holdings, and its official position was in ruins.[241] Dutch naval strength had parried Mataram and had begun to impose a spice monopoly in Maluku.

---

[239] Malay was used for teaching Protestant ideas early on. On VOC subject populations and VOC social and cultural structures, Blusse, *Strange Company*, 5, 78–84, 156–71, using the "plural society" image; Ricklefs, *War, Culture*, 14–19; Anthony Reid, "The Seventeenth-Century Crisis in Southeast Asia," *MAS* 24 (1990): 639–59; Julia Adams, "Principals and Agents, Colonialists and Company Men," *American Sociological Review* 61 (1996): 12–28; Goor, "Hybrid State," 193–214, esp. 193 n. 1; Hanna, *Indonesian Banda*, ch. 4; Jean Gelman Taylor, *The Social World of Batavia* (Madison, WI, 1983), 3–77, esp. 76; Boxer, *Dutch Seaborne Empire*, 133–54, 215–41; Heather Sutherland, "Ethnicity, Wealth and Power in Colonial Makassar," in J. M. Nas, ed., *The Indonesian City* (Dordrecht, 1986), 37–55; Bosma and Raben, *Being Dutch*, 17–38, 46–65. On VOC religious policy, also Barbara Watson Andaya, "Between Empires and Emporia: The Economics of Christianization in Early Modern Southeast Asia" (ms).

[240] On the VOC in the western archipelago to 1660, Barbara Watson Andaya, *Perak: The Abode of Grace* (Kuala Lumpur, 1979), ch. 2; idem, *Live as Brothers*, 38–73; Leonard Andaya, *The Kingdom of Johor, 1641–1728* (Kuala Lumpur, 1975), chs. 1–3; J Kathirithamby-Wells, "Achehnese Control over West Sumatra up to the Treaty of Painan of 1663," *JSEAH* 10 (1969): 453–79; Dianne Lewis, *Jan Compagnie in the Straits of Malacca 1641–1795* (Athens, OH, 1995), 21–23.

[241] Subrahmanyam, *Portuguese Empire*, 209–211; *HMI*, 80–81. From 1702 Lifau in Timor also became a Portuguese base. Barbara Watson Andaya, pers. commun., Oct. 9, 2008.

Major Archipelagic States, c. 1511 to 1660: Centralization, Militarization, and Commercial Controls

How did indigenous states respond to European incursions? Portuguese and Dutch competition joined rising Eurasian market demand, stronger pan-Islamic circuits, and improved firearms to promote trends – modest but unmistakably similar to those in mainland Southeast Asia, Europe, Japan, and India – toward administrative unification, militarization, and commercial regulation. From a score of maritime polities, I shall illustrate these trends between 1511 and c. 1660 by moving again from west to east to consider five major coastal realms – Aceh, Johor, Banten, Makasar, and Maluku[242] – followed by the interior Javanese empire of Mataram. Some of these states had only tenuous links to major pre-1511 polities, which was typical of the islands with their dispersed populations, but which contrasted with substantial continuity in other protected-zone realms and in China.

Located at the northwest tip of Sumatra, **Aceh** rose largely in response to the Portuguese. Pires described Aceh in 1515 as a minor polity, but Portugal's 1511 conquest of Melaka, its disruption of regional trade, and its anti-Muslim policies led disgruntled Muslim shippers to supply money and arms to anyone able to contain the Christians. Aceh proved best suited. From 1519 to 1524 it drove the Portuguese from Pasai and united all of north coastal Sumatra. In a century of diplomatic and military offensives against rival Malay polities as well as Portugal, Aceh went on to subdue east coast centers as far as Siak, west coast pepper- and gold-exporting ports as far as Indrapura, and peninsular pepper and tin zones under Kedah, Perak, and Pahang. Aceh also launched some 10 attacks on Portuguese Melaka itself, including a massive 1629 assault by 19,000 men, albeit without success.[243]

Aceh's contacts were wide ranging. From the Ottomans it sought both Red Sea commercial ties and military help against their common Christian enemy. From 1537 to 1569 Turkey supplied Aceh with bombards and artillery (which supplemented captured Portuguese pieces) as well as hundreds of gunfounders, gunners, military engineers, shipwrights,

---

[242] Palembang, Jambi, Banjarmasin, and Magindanao also might have served. On Palembang and Jambi, see Andaya, *Live as Brothers*, chs. 1–3.

[243] On Acehnese expansion, Cortesao, *Suma Oriental*, vol. I, 138–39; Reid, "*Negeri*," 426–27; Hadi, *Islam and State*, 13–32; Lombard, *Sultanat d'Atjeh*, 91–101; Andaya, *Perak*, 41–44, 79; *HMI*, 37–40; Kathirithamby-Wells, "Achehnese Control."

and elite troops, who transmitted technical skills, albeit generally without equaling European levels.[244] Aceh also traded with Lower Burma for rice, and with Golkonda and Gujarat for munitions and textiles. To the east a new spice route opened from Maluku to North Java, through the Sunda Straits, along Sumatra's west coast to Aceh, and thence to South Asia and the Red Sea. Thus Muslim traders, pivoting on Aceh, bypassed Melaka entirely. Like other post-1511 ports, Aceh pursued a novel specialization. Whereas Melaka had sold an array of goods to both Chinese and Indian Ocean traders, Aceh offered a more narrow range primarily to Indian Ocean merchants.[245] After Aceh's 1629 humiliation at Melaka, the VOC's 1641 conquest of that city, and Dutch inroads into its sources of supply, Aceh weakened, but arguably remained the foremost indigenous coastal power to the 1650s.

Both European competition and internal threats demanded a strengthening of royal authority in Aceh. Probably the most dramatic spur was a phase of *orang kaya* anarchy from 1579 to 1589 that deposed five kings, four of whom died violently. From 1589, with the support of local war leaders and Muslim scholars, a new dynasty imposed an extreme autocracy, including bans on private arms, escheat of *orang kaya* estates, mass executions, and terrorist discipline (failed generals could be castrated or forced to eat a plate of feces in public).[246] To break *orang kaya* power and forestall Dutch monopolies, the crown also developed its own system of managed trade in which no one could purchase Indian textiles or sell pepper until the king had exercised preemption, no one could buy west coast pepper without a license, and tributaries had to surrender 15 percent of their pepper and gold and sell the rest to the crown at fixed prices.

---

[244] On Acehnese arms, Lombard, *Sultanat d'Atjeh*, 83–91; Anthony Reid, *An Indonesian Frontier* (Singapore, 2005), ch. 4; Manguin, "Vanishing *Jong*," 206–208; Rebecca Catz, ed. *The Travels of Mendes Pinto* (Chicago, 1989), 20–30.

[245] Chiefly tin, gold, pepper, spices, forest products, and elephants. In 1638 Aceh reportedly banned Chinese, temporarily it appears, because they reared pigs. On Acehnese trade, Lombard, *Sultanat d'Atjeh*, 101–25; Andaya, "Aceh's Contribution," 36–45; Subrahmanyam, *Portuguese Empire*, 133–37; Meilink-Roelofsz, *Asian Trade*, 140–46; Barbara Watson Andaya, "A People That Range in All the Kingdoms of Asia" (ms).

[246] This titbit from Reid, *Charting the Shape*, 127. On Acehnese administrative and commercial reform, idem, *Indonesian Frontier*, chs. 5, 7; Lombard, *Sultanat d'Atjeh*, 69–84, 101–25; *AC*, vol. II, 251–66, 310–11; Kathirithamby-Wells, "Regional and State Integration"; idem, "Achehnese Control"; idem, "Royal Authority and the *Orang Kaya* in the Western Archipelago, c. 1500–1800," *JSEAS* 17 (1986): 256–67; Andaya, "Good-Natured Government"; n. 144 *supra*.

Commercial controls required territorial reorganization. For much of the 16th century, in venerable *negeri* fashion, Aceh had remained a confederation of autonomous port-states under local dynasts or imperial princes with indefinite tenure. Besides limiting royal revenues, such arrangements allowed tributaries to scheme with court factions and external rivals. Under the famed Sultan Iskandar Muda (r. 1607–1636), key ports were entrusted to non-royal governors, *panglimas*, who were appointed for only three years and who had to visit the capital annually and accept written instructions and unannounced visits by royal inspectors. Aided by specialized deputies, *panglimas* strove to enforce the new royal trade monopolies. After Iskandar Muda and his son died, *orang kaya* power revived to some extent under a succession of female rulers, but without the extreme instability of the late 1500s and with some key innovations, including *panglimas*, intact. This replacement of senior princes by more closely monitored nonroyal governors recalls provincial changes – the shift from what I term decentralized to centralized Indic administration – between c. 1600 and 1650 in Burma, Siam, and as we shall see shortly, Banten and Mataram. Although Burmese influence on Aceh cannot be ruled out, more basically, mainland and archipelagic reforms probably reflected parallel, but independent, responses to intensifying commercial and military pressure.[247]

Political integration at Aceh nourished and drew sustenance from growing cultural coherence among what, even in the core, was originally a polyglot array of communities and traders for whom Malay had been merely a commercial lingua franca. Although Aceh had never been part of Melaka's empire, its ambition to control Malay-speaking regions once subject to Melaka led Aceh to present itself as heir to Melaka's glory and natural leader of the "Malay world" (*alam Malayu*). That Aceh viewed itself, and was regarded by others, as an integral part of that world becomes clear if we consider that Malay (albeit a dialect influenced by Acehnese, Arabic, and Persian) became the main language of the court and of literature; that Aceh produced the largest pre-1700 corpus of Malay theological, historical, and literary works; and that Aceh's rulers claimed descent from Iskandar Zulkarnain (Alexander the Great),

---

[247] Cf. *SP*, 34–36, 160–62, 278–81 and discussion of Banten and Mataram *infra*. On Aceh provinces, previous note, plus Reid, *Indonesian Frontier*, ch. 7; Christine Dobbin, *Islamic Revivalism in a Changing Peasant Economy* (London, 1983), 73–76; Leonard Andaya, "The 17th-Century Acehnese Model of Malay Society" (ms), 22, identifying 11 *panglima* postings.

putative ancestor of Malay rulers.[248] Where Aceh differed from Melaka and some post-1511 Malay rivals was its unusually intense identification with Islamic practices of the Mideast and India. An artifact both of strong Indian Ocean ties and weak Hindu-Buddhist legacies, this identification became manifest in Aceh's Persian- and Arabic-inflected Malay dialect, in Ottoman- and Mughal-style palace organization, in jihads against the Portuguese and pagan Bataks, and in Aceh's receptivity to teachings from Cairo, Mecca, and Yemen. Known as the "Veranda of Mecca," Aceh became the archipelagic center for monistic *sufi* scholarship between c. 1500 and 1636, followed by *sharia*-oriented neo-*sufism*. Under the influence of chronic warfare, Indian Ocean ties, and court patronage of mosques and scholars, Aceh's population thus coalesced into a more or less distinct version of Malay society, with a particularly salient Muslim identity.[249]

As direct descendants of the Melaka dynasty that fled in 1511, the rulers of **Johor** were inordinately proud of their ancestry and correspondingly loath to acknowledge what they viewed as Aceh's upstart pretensions. Leonard Andaya suggests that this rivalry played out, in part, in royal texts. In the early 1600s Johor patronized two histories that affirmed Melaka-Johor's centrality in the Malay world and pointedly located *tanah Malayu* ("land of the Malays") not in Sumatra, but on the peninsula. Perhaps in reply to these assertions, Aceh not only commissioned its own panegyric, but invaded Johor, taking prisoner the sultan.[250] In fact, this was the fourth of seven Acehnese invasions to 1623. Worse yet, to 1587 Johor faced nine often devastating Portuguese attacks.

Johor's vulnerability in this period reflected a fundamentally weak commercial position. Although Johor exported local pepper, tin, and

[248] Reid, *Indonesian Frontier*, 5, 24; Andaya, *Leaves*, 108–109, 123–24; idem, "17th-Century Acehnese Model," 13–20; Riddell, *Islam*, 139–67. The Malay spoken at Aceh was but one of many Malay dialects, with Javanese usages becoming more influential among Malay-speakers as one moved east in the archipelago.

[249] On Acehnese culture to 1660, previous note plus Ann Kumar in Harry Aveling, ed., *The Development of Indonesian Society* (St. Lucia, 1979), 11–19; *HM*, 64; Andaya, *Leaves*, ch. 4; Hadi, *Islam and State*, chs. 2–5; Reid, *Indonesian Frontier*, chs. 6, 7; Riddell, *Islam*, 101–67; Azra, *Origins*, 8–108; Lombard, *Sultanat d'Atjeh*, ch. 5; Schrieke, *Studies*, vol. II, 241–53; William Clarence-Smith, "Elephants, Horses, and the Coming of Islam to Northern Sumatra," *Indonesia and the Malay World* 32 (2004): 271–84.

[250] The two Johor texts were the *Hikayat Hang Tuah* ("Story of Hang Tuah") and the *Sejarah Malayu* ("History of the Malays"), while the Acehnese text was the *Hikayat Aceh* ("Story of Aceh"). Andaya, *Leaves*, 126–27; idem, "Search for Melaya," 327–28; n. 160 *supra*.

forest products, Portuguese Melaka severely restricted its access to Coromandel textiles, the principal draw for most archipelagic traders. Johor tried to compensate by boosting Chinese imports, but poor port facilities and competition from Pattani limited this success.

The eclipse of its two nemeses in the second quarter of the 17th century, however, suddenly transformed Johor's prospects. Aceh's 1629 defeat before Melaka followed by the death of Iskandar Muda reduced the Aceh threat; while in 1641, we saw, Melaka fell to the Dutch. In gratitude for Johor's help in that campaign, the VOC not only offered protection against Aceh, but agreed, in effect, to let Johor replace Melaka as the chief port of the Straits. (Dutch policy reflected both a determination to concentrate trade on Batavia rather than Melaka and reluctance to become embroiled in war with Johor.) Thus empowered, Johor regained access to Indian textiles, retook Pahang from Aceh, increased the flow of regional goods to its capital, sent its own ships to China as well as India, and sought to counter VOC monopolies by underselling, even on occasion blockading, Dutch factories. Like Aceh, Johor had concluded that in a world of European monopoly, traditional statecraft and unadministered trade no longer sufficed. In the late 1600s, as Aceh faltered, Johor reemerged as the principal patron of Malay culture and as Melaka's universally recognized heir. Johor's refined literature, music, dance, and rituals were esteemed throughout the peninsula, in offshore islands, east coast Sumatra, and parts of coastal Borneo, areas that together comprised the Malay world of the late 1600s.[251]

In **Banten** as in most archipelagic ports, Malay traders were active and Malay served as a commercial lingua franca.[252] But unlike Aceh and Johor, Banten neither considered itself a Malay state nor claimed Melaka's mantle. Sundanese, Javanese, and Lampungers were the chief ethnic groups, with Javanese probably the main court language.[253] In a broader sense, however, Banten showed clear affinities to Aceh and

---

[251] On Johor politics, economics, and culture, *HM*, 72–74, 95; Kathirithamby-Wells, "Regional and State Integration" 38–43; idem, "Royal Authority," 260–61; Andaya, *Kingdom of Johor*, chs. 1–6; Mohd Anis Md Nor, "The Zapin Melayu Dance of Johor" (Univ. of Michigan, PhD diss., 1990), 66–75. On the evolving boundaries of the Malay world, Leonard Andaya, "The Bugis-Makassar Diasporas," *JMBRAS* 68 (1995): 120, *HM*, 116, 125; and on Malay cultural geography c. 1800, Milner, *Kerajaan*, 1–13.

[252] Cf. *AC*, vol. I, 7; idem, "Understanding Melayau," 300–301.

[253] Cf. Peter Carey, "Aspects of Javanese History in the 19th Century," in Aveling, *Development*, 46; Ota Atsushi, "Banten Rebellion, 1750–1752," *MAS* 37 (2003): 613–51, esp. 620; idem, *Changes of Regime*, 14–15.

Johor. If Aceh at the tip of Sumatra and Johor on the Straits of Melaka occupied two natural rendezvous, Banten, on the Sunda Straits, controlled a third. Banten funneled Malukun spices to Aceh and local pepper to China.[254] Like Johor and Aceh, Banten countered European threats with more interventionist economic policies; and like Aceh, identified fervently with Indian Ocean Islam.

Banten's political and commercial evolution is also broadly familiar. In 1523 Demak installed in the small Hindu port of Banten a Muslim ruler whose successor became independent. Between 1550 and 1570, while Aceh acquired pepper districts along Sumatra's west coast, Banten annexed the pepper region of Lampung in South Sumatra and coastal areas below Indrapura. As Aceh sought (unsuccessfully) to convert the Bataks of interior Sumatra to Islam, Banten with rather more success promoted Islam among Lampung tribal chiefs. By 1580 Banten also had destroyed its original suzerain, the Hindu kingdom of Pajajaran.[255]

At the turn of the 17th century Banten still operated an essentially free market. But the English East India Company and more especially the VOC sought to monopolize pepper by extending credit to capital-scarce Chinese sellers. Recognizing the threat this posed to its economic, and ultimately political, independence, Banten raised tolls on European ships and decreed that all pepper and textiles must be purchased through the court at fixed prices. After Batavia retaliated with intermittent blockades, Banten's most famous ruler, Sultan Ageng (r. 1651–1683), sought to strengthen his hand by playing other Europeans against the Dutch, by "smuggling" more spices from Maluku, and by involving the court directly in cash-crop production. In the 1660s every male subject in Sunda and Lampung was obliged to plant 500 (later 1,000) pepper vines and to sell the product at fixed rates to crown agents for shipment to the capital, where the sultan monopolized sales. Chiefs providing large quantities of pepper received titles and insignia. To oversee these arrangements and settle disputes, Bantanese officials (*jinang*) – reminiscent of Acehnese *panglima* – were stationed at Sumatran ports. Eager to tap new markets, the sultan also acquired

---

[254] On Banten trade and the prominent Chinese role, *AC*, vol. II, 212–13; Meilink-Roelofsz, *Asian Trade*, 239–49; Kathirithamby-Wells, "Regional and State Integration," 31, 35, idem, "Banten," in Kathirithamby-Wells and Villiers, *Port and Polity*, 107–25.

[255] Kathirithamby-Wells, "Banten," 107–111; idem, "Regional and State Integration," 30–31.

a fleet of Western and Chinese vessels that traded as far as Japan, China, Persia, and Mocha.[256] Profits funded not only new ship construction, but purchase of British and French firearms, used to suppress at least one revolt.[257] Thus the sultan enhanced his authority vis-à-vis not only the Dutch, but district chiefs and *orang kaya*, who, as in Aceh, had been a source of recurrent instability. No less indicative of novel ambition, Ageng settled some 30,000 agriculturalists on new coconut plantations and rice lands, with Dutch-designed windmills providing irrigation.[258] Although we lack statistics, in Banten as in Central Java and Sulawesi such schemes probably reflected and promoted population growth.

Banten advertised its Muslim piety through scholarly contacts with Arabia and India, a vogue for Arab dress, a commitment to *sharia* law, and well-publicized missions to Mecca (whose Grand Mufti authorized Banten's ruler to call himself Sultan in 1638). Islam sanctioned both the ruler's domestic authority and efforts to build anti-Dutch military coalitions. Given its central location in the archipelago, Banten sought allies in Southeast Asia more than in the Indian Ocean. But much as Aceh toyed with an anti-Portuguese Dutch alliance, Banten's willingness to work with English, Portuguese, and Danes against the VOC showed a pragmatic selectivity in its choice of Christian enemies.[259]

Although **Makasar** in Southwest Sulawesi acquired Islam later than Aceh, Johor, or Banten, its political chronology was similar. Makasar arose in the early and mid-1500s from a union between two local kingdoms. Some evidence points to agricultural intensification, including a widespread move from *swidden* to wet rice, between c. 1400 and 1600. To what extent this trend, and an associated increase in population, responded to maritime demand, climatic shifts, or local

---

[256] On Banten administration and trade, *AC*, II, 249–50, 260; *HMI*, 101–102; Kathirithamby-Wells, "Regional and State Integration," 29–36, 42; idem, "Banten"; Meilink-Roelofsz, *Asian Trade*, 239–58; Lombard, *Carrefour Javanais*, vol. II, 52–53; Knaap, *Shallow Waters*, 167–68; Ota, *Changes of Regime*, ch. 2.

[257] Kathirithamby-Wells, "Banten," 116, 118–19.

[258] *HMI*, 101; *AC*, II, 260; Claude Guillot, "Urban Patterns and Polities in Malay Trading Cities, 15th through 17th Centuries," *Indonesia* 80 (2005): 39–5. On Banten history to c. 1750, also Ota, *Changes of Regime*, 13–35.

[259] On Islam at Banten, Azra, *Origins*, ch. 5; *AC*, vol. II, 181–86; Kathirithamby-Wells, "Banten," 115, 118–20; idem, "Regional and State Integration," 29–31, 35–36; Ota, *Changes of Regime*, 32–34, 53–58.

political interventions is difficult to say. Clearly, however, Javanese and Malay traders evicted from Melaka in 1511 were attracted by the availability of rice and local textiles needed to obtain spices from nearby Maluku. Makasar's Indic-style writing system, if not initiated in this period, became more widely used.[260] A more obvious watershed, however, was Makasar's acceptance in 1605 of Islam, propagated from Malaya and the *pasisir*. In the name of the new faith, between 1608 and 1611 Makasar subdued the rest of Southwest Sulawesi, including kingdoms led by the Makasarese' inveterate ethnic rivals, the Bugis. With a core population that probably exceeded half a million and with war fleets of up to a thousand vessels, Makasar then extended its authority to virtually the entire Sulawesi littoral as well as coastal Borneo, Lombok, Sumbawa, Flores, Timor, and Seram.[261] This was the largest tributary domain in eastern archipelagic history. While not controlling cash-crop production in the manner of Aceh or Banten, Makasarese lords sent their own trading ships as far as Maluku and Sumatra. In the early and mid-1600s Dutch efforts to control Malukun spices only strengthened Makasar insofar as those excluded by the VOC – Malays, Javanese, Indians, Chinese, Iberians, Englishmen, a few Danes – joined local rulers to make Makasar the principal mart for "smuggled" cloves, nutmeg, and mace. Rejecting VOC monopoly demands, Makassar's

---

[260] On Makasar writing, which was not in Arabic script and probably appeared in the 1400s, C. C. Macknight, "The Emergence of Civilization in South Sulawesi and Elsewhere," in Anthony Reid and Lance Castles, eds., *Pre-Colonial State Systems in Southeast Asia* (Kuala Lumpur, 1975), 126–35; William Cummings, *Making Blood White* (Honolulu, 2002), 26, 37–58, 74–90, 115–18, 137 and *passim*. On economic and political history to c. 1650, those sources, plus C. C. Macknight, "The Rise of Agriculture in South Sulawesi Before 1600," *Review of Indonesian and Malay Affairs* 17 (1983): 92–115; idem, *The Early History of South Sulawesi* (Clayton, 1993); Reid, *Charting the Shape*, 100–25; David Bulbeck, "The Politics of Marriage and the Marriage of Politics in Gowa, South Sulawesi," in James Fox and Clifford Sather, eds., *Origins, Ancestry, and Alliance* (Canberra, 1996), 280–315; Christian Pelras, "Celebes-sud avant l'Islam selon les premiers temoignages etrangers," *Archipel* 21 (1985): 153–84; *HMI*, 57–58, 77–78; John Villiers, "Makassar," in Kathirithamby-Wells and Villiers, *Port and Polity*, 143–59; and esp. Leonard Andaya, *The Heritage of Arung Palakka* (The Hague, 1981), 17–31.

[261] On the unusually late date of Makasar Islamization and on Makasar population and conquests, Reid, *Charting the Shape*, 142–44; Villiers, "Makassar," 147–54; *AC*, vol. I, 14 and vol. II, 213; Christian Pelras, "Religion, Tradition and the Dynamics of Islamization in South Sulawesi," *Archipel* 29 (1985): 107–35, arguing that the nobility's fear that Islam would undermine their claims to divine descent delayed conversion; and Cummings, *Making Blood White*, 32–39, 154–64 *passim*.

ruler in 1615 explained that God gave the seas to all men. "It is unheard of that anyone should be forbidden to sail the seas."[262]

Because Dutch threats obliged Makasar to strengthen its defenses and also perhaps because rapid urban and commercial growth bred receptivity to innovation, Makasar became an omnivorous consumer of foreign technology and culture. Chancellor Pattingalloang (active 1639–1654) spoke or read Malay, Portuguese, Spanish, French, Latin, and Arabic and amassed European books and scientific instruments. Between 1590 and 1640, in barely two generations, Makasar initiated the minting of coins, the writing of remarkably objective historical chronicles, the construction of advanced ships, the manufacture of cannons, muskets, and gunpowder; a massive expansion of brick fortifications; and the translation of Iberian treatises on gunnery.[263] Termed by the Dutch the "fighting cock of the East," Makasar from 1615 fought a series of spice wars with the VOC and at least until 1637 held its own.[264]

Between 1511 and 1660 the chief **Malukun kingdoms**, Ternate and Tidore, expanded in three stages: as allies/clients of the Portuguese, as fully independent polities, and as clients of the Dutch. Later, of course, other islands also would pass under Dutch suzerainty, but Maluku's precious spices and small populations left them unusually vulnerable.

In discussing pre-1511 *negeri*, I noted that Islam joined the clove trade to empower the rulers of Ternate and Tidore at the expense of local chiefs. The Portuguese intensified those trends, first, by encouraging more unified procedures for clove preparation, and second, by equating Malukun rulers with European kings who were entitled to buy arms, collect duties, and call on external help against "rebels." Although, as noted, Portugal's assassination in 1570 of a Ternaten ruler broke the Iberian tie, in the late 1500s Ternaten expansion continued to draw strength from rising clove sales, now subject to increasing royal control; from Muslim guns; and from Mideastern and Malay Muslim

---

[262] Villiers, "Makassar," 154; Andaya, *Heritage*, 46 and 29–35. By diverting trade, Mataram's bloody 1620s conquest of the *pasisir* (see *infra*) also strengthened Makasar. On Makasar empire and trade, n. 261 *supra*; William Cummings, "Islam, Empire and Makassarese Historiography in the Reign of Sultan Ala'uddin (1593–1639)," *JSEAS* 38 (2007): 197–214; Reid, *Charting the Shape*, chs. 6, 7.

[263] On cultural debts and achievements, Cummings, *Making Blood White*, 30–31, 58–194; Reid, *Charting the Shape*, 126–54; Villiers, "Makassar," 155; J. Noorduyn, "Some Aspects of Makassar-Buginese Historiography," in D. G. E. Hall, ed., *Historians of South-East Asia* (London, 1961), 29–36; *HMI*, 78.

[264] Cummings, "Islam, Empire," 197; *HMI*, 57–58; Andaya, *Heritage*, 135.

teachers preaching anti-Christian unity. Thus Ternate's sultan, "Lord of 72 Islands," extended his hold over northern and western Maluku and parts of eastern Sulawesi. Using many of the same techniques but with Portuguese and then Spanish help, Ternate's rival, Tidore, pursued a less spectacular expansion to the east and south.[265]

After the VOC arrived, Ternate saw the advantage of a fresh European connection, directed this time against Tidore and the now united Spanish–Portuguese crown. But the Dutch imposed more rigorous conditions than had the Iberians. In 1652 Ternate's sultan signed the aforementioned treaty limiting clove and nutmeg cultivation and sanctioning the eradication of "surplus" trees, in return for which he received Dutch protection and larger payments of cloth, iron, cash, and weapons. In theory he was to redistribute much of this to local chiefs, but in practice he tended to ignore local sensibilities. As if to advertise his allegiance, the sultan named his sons Princes Amsterdam and Rotterdam! As VOC power grew, Tidore, hitherto reliant on Spain, also switched to a Dutch alliance, from 1662 receiving some of the same benefits as Ternate. Under the Dutch umbrella, both sultanates continued to tighten their control over outlying dependencies, which accepted the titles, dress, and Muslim rituals of their overlord as a sign of submission.[266]

Whereas all of the foregoing realms were maritime polities, Javanese **Mataram** arose in those south-central ricelands, far from the coast, that had given birth to the charter state of the same name in the 8th century. Given this interior agrarian base, why did Mataram's heyday, c. 1580–1670, coincide with that of maritime Aceh, Johor, Banten, and Makasar? Four coastal–interior linkages merit consideration. First, directly and indirectly, coastal authorities aided interior agriculture. True, rice from south-central Java, as opposed to the *pasisir*, was not a major export in this period.[267] But by precipitating Majapahit's collapse, coastal attacks prompted a shift in the agrarian center of gravity from the Brantas basin to the interior – which then received support from the coastal centers of Demak and Giri.[268] Second, after subduing the coast, Mataram profited

---

[265] On 16th-century Maluku, Andaya, *World of Maluku*, 56–58, 110–50; idem, "Cultural State Formation"; *HMI*, 27–28; Meilink-Roelofsz, *Asian Trade*, 154–59.

[266] On Maluku 1600–1670, *HMI*, 73–76; Andaya, *World of Maluku*, 55–57, 82–112, 151–79, 201–208.

[267] See Ricklefs, *War, Culture*, 5; Schrieke, *Studies*, vol. I, 59–62, 67, 75, 76, 80; *HMI*, 52, 56, 93.

[268] The beneficiaries included Jaka Tingkir of Pajang, a vassal of Demak, and his captain Kyai Gedhe Pamanahan, who recolonized Mataram. *HMI*, 45–48; Pigeaud and

handsomely from *pasisir* tax farms and from the sale of foodstuffs and timber to Batavia, Melaka, Banjarmasin, and other ports. More generally, coastal cash alleviated chronic specie shortages in the interior.[269] Third, like coastal states, Mataram relied on imported military technology. By the 1620s, but possibly long before, the Javanese not only used European and probably Muslims arms, but had adapted European techniques to produce their own matchlocks, gunpowder, and cannon.[270]

Finally, in Mataram as in coastal states, Islam sanctioned domestic claims and external conquests. I suggested that Mideastern culture influenced Aceh and Banten more profoundly than interior Java, where Hindu-Buddhist mysticism and Old Javanese literature retained great prestige. Javanese, unlike Malay, chronicles generally did not see Islam as a watershed.[271] Nonetheless, Mataram court culture borrowed heavily from Muslim centers like Demak, while Mataram's founder Senapati Ingalaga (r. 1584–1601) reportedly seized Mataram because its ruler refused to accept Islam. So too his celebrated grandson Agung (r. 1613–1646) adopted the Javano-Islamic lunar calendar, assumed the title of Sultan with Mecca's blessing, and took other steps to synthesize Majapahit legacies with *sufi* mysticism.[272]

Initiated by Senapati and triumphantly concluded by his grandson, Mataram's wars of expansion created the most powerful Javanese realm since 1400. If the VOC prevented Mataram from reproducing the archipelagic influence of Majapahit, at its height under Sultan Agung Mataram's suzerainty was acknowledged across Central and East Java,

---

de Graaf, *Islamic States*, 20–23; M. C. Ricklefs, *Jogjakarta Under Sultan Mangkubumi 1749–1792* (London, 1974), 11–15; Peter Carey, "Core and Periphery, 1600–1830," in Bernhard Dahm, ed., *Regions and Regional Developments in the Malay-Indonesian World* (Wiesbaden, 1992), 91–103, esp. 92.

[269] On coastal–interior economic relations, Nagtegaal, *Dutch Tiger*, 46–50, 123, 163–92; HMI, 94; Kwee Hui Kian, *The Political Economy of Java's Northeast Coast c. 1740–1800* (Leiden, 2006), 26–28, 34; Schrieke, *Studies*, vol. I, 59–80 passim.

[270] In 1651 perhaps 10–12 percent of Mataram's campaign forces carried firearms. See Ricklefs, *War, Culture*, 14, 143, 171, 175–76. Nagtegaal, *Dutch Tiger*, 61. On military technology and organization, ibid., 59–70; Ricklefs, *War, Culture*, 12–14, 20, 37–38, 78, 215, 223–35, 265; idem, *Mystic Synthesis*, 57; HMI, 111; Schrieke, *Studies*, vol. II, 122–39.

[271] See nn. 155, 165 supra; HMI, 11–12, 59–64; Ricklefs, "Six Centuries," 110–11; idem, *Modern Javanese Historical Tradition* (London, 1978), 2; Reid, *Charting the Shape*, 15–16; Milner, "Islam and the State," 28–29. Much the same applies to Java's Banjar offshoot.

[272] Agung, whose synthesis recalls that of Akbar, thus neutralized Islamically based challenges to his authority. Ricklefs, *Mystic Synthesis*, 33–52; HMI, 47–48, 53–55; idem, *Seen and Unseen*, 339; Reid, *Islamic Political Discourse*, 97–107; Carey, "Core and Periphery," 92–97.

in most of the Eastern Salient, in the *pasisir*, Madura, and overseas in Banjarmasin, Sukadana, Jambi, and Palembang. In Java alone, perhaps 3,000,000 people fell under some degree of Mataramese control.[273] This was in the same order of magnitude as Burmese and Siamese populations and considerably larger than that of any other archipelagic state, including the Spanish Philippines. Mataram's dependencies emulated the rituals, language, dress, and aesthetics of the exemplary center, to which they gained access through aristocratic marriages and court audiences. At the same time Mataram's historic novelty and its fragmented geography precluded a political/cultural identity as coherent, or a sense of inclusion as widespread, as in the chief mainland realms. Ricklefs, the leading historian of Java, finds little evidence of an emotionally charged all-Mataram consciousness.[274]

While remaining in the agrarian interior, Mataram's rulers sought to overhaul administration so as to ensure subordination of the north coast, whose conquest necessitated a series of bitter and destructive campaigns to 1625. Whereas earlier kings had been content to appoint local dynasts and senior princes to outlying centers, Agung's son Amangkurat I (r. 1646–1677) – reminiscent of his Burmese, Siamese, Acehnese, and Bantenese contemporaries – appointed short-term, nonroyal officials whose authority he repeatedly circumscribed and reshuffled. Amangkurat also subjected *pasisir* ports to heavy, often arbitrary fiscal demands, closed them repeatedly, ordered a census, and forbade his subjects to travel outside Java. Mixing rational calculation with paranoid obsession, he thus sought to compel Batavia to buy rice and timber from him directly, to provide the court rather than local regents with the lion's share of coastal profits, and to crush potential opposition.[275] But

---

[273] See population estimates at n. 70 *supra*; Ricklefs, *War, Culture*, 5; idem, *Mystic Synthesis*, 3, 36; Schrieke, *Studies*, vol. II, 139.

[274] Ricklefs, *War, Culture*, 11–12, 173–74, 225–26, 230; idem, *Seen and Unseen*, xix–xxiii, 330–31; and Carey, "Core and Periphery," emphasizing polycentrism and reciprocal regional influences. But on tributary imitation of Mataram culture, see Carey, "Core and Periphery," 97, 100; Andaya, *Live as Brothers*, xv, 16, 29, 65–72, 78, 93, 110–11; Kathirithamby-Wells, "Regional and State Integration," 40–41; *HM*, 65.

[275] Two *pasisir* governorships were created (1651), which divided into four (1657), which in 1669 yielded to representatives sent directly from the court. *HMI*, 49, 50, 55, 91–95; Pigeaud and Graaf, *Islamic States*, chs. 2–4; Ricklefs, *Jogjakarta*, 18–20; Nagtegaal, *Dutch Tiger*, 37; n. 247 *supra*; and comparison of 17th-century Burmese, Siamese, and Mataramese reforms in Victor Lieberman, *Burmese Administrative Cycles* (Princeton, 1984), 280–92.

as we shall see, in contrast to Burma and Siam, Amangkurat's initiatives proved disastrously counterproductive.

In summary, between 1511 and 1660 the archipelago supported an unprecedentedly competitive multistate system, embracing both indigenous and European actors, whose Darwinian insistence on military and administrative experiment bears at least a passing resemblance to contemporary dynamics in mainland Southeast Asia, Europe, Warring States Japan, and South Asia. If rising global commercial demand, improved weapons and ships, and stronger links to Indian Ocean Islam all encouraged state centralization, that trend responded most directly to European, chiefly Dutch, intervention. In 1660, as the title of Part 3 implies, European and indigenous actors remained broadly comparable in commercial ambition and land-based military capacity. Certainly, the Dutch controlled fewer people and smaller territories than their chief Muslim rivals. Yet already the VOC had demonstrated its potential by throwing Makasar, Banten, and Aceh onto the defensive and by achieving a novel control over fine spices.

4. STRENGTHENING THE DUTCH AND SPANISH REALMS, C. 1660–1830

Between c. 1660 and 1830 the VOC state evolved from *primus inter pares* to dominant archipelagic power. Far more convincingly than under Majapahit, by 1830 a single state controlled far-flung regions in terms not merely of titular preeminence, but hard military strength. Yet Dutch advances during this 170-year period were anything but linear or inevitable. Although from c. 1660 to 1784 the Dutch won spectacular victories, by the mid-1700s, at the height of their military success, new currents had begun to erode VOC economic influence. The phoenix-like rebirth of Dutch fortunes in the post-Napoleonic period was in some ways entirely fortuitous. In other words, the Dutch sphere in the Indies (whose boundaries were not finally fixed until c. 1908) cohered in more desultory, aleatory fashion than the Mughal, Manchu, or Spanish realms, and to 1830 remained less territorially coherent. This section seeks first to sketch and explain Dutch territorial acquisitions; second, to analyze the VOC's mounting 18th-century economic woes; third, to recount Napoleonic-era upheavals; and fourth, to describe cultural alignments under the Dutch. We shall close by comparing Dutch fortunes c. 1660–1830 to those of the Spanish Philippines.

A Survey of Dutch Advances to 1784

It is a testament to early Dutch strength that while the VOC regarded the western archipelago as less commercially valuable than areas farther east, it still was able to dominate key Sumatran markets. Joining forces with the Minangkabau ruler in interior Sumatra and local traders, in 1664 the VOC began to expel Acehnese governors from Sumatra's west and east coast ports, thus cornering pepper and gold exports. By declining to retaliate against VOC provocations, by cultivating ties to Coromandel traders and then to British Penang, and by promoting pepper and rice cultivation in the interior, Aceh preserved not only its independence, but a measure of prosperity. From the late 1700s American and British pepper buyers sparked renewed vitality. And yet by the 18th century VOC actions, Johor's revival, and expanding interior cultivation had combined to end Aceh's period of greatness and to encourage a partial retreat from maritime trade toward agrarian self-sufficiency. In political and cultural terms this meant a shift from sultan and *orang kaya* dominance to that of interior war leaders; from literature in Malay, the cosmopolitan language of trade and Islam, to writing in Acehnese; and from an expansive Malay identity to a more localized Acehnese ethnicity.[276]

On Sumatra's southeast coast, after eclipsing Mataram and English rivals, the VOC won preferential pepper contracts from Jambi and Palembang in the mid-1600s, followed in 1722 by a tin monopoly on newly discovered deposits on Palembang's Bangka island. In return the VOC provided Palembang's sultan with military protection against domestic and foreign threats. Despite widespread pepper and tin "smuggling," VOC–Palembang relations remained amicable.[277]

In the Straits of Melaka the Dutch at first sought less to dominate than to prevent any other power from doing so and threatening Batavia's western approaches. Thus at the same time as the VOC let its

---

[276] Even though by the 1820s Aceh was producing over half the world's pepper. Andaya, "A People That Range." On Aceh's fortunes c. 1660–1820, see too Andaya, "Good-Natured Government"; idem, *Leaves*, 15, 109–110, 137–45; Dobbin, *Islamic Revivalism*, 65, 76–87; *AC*, II, 310–11; Reid, *Indonesian Frontier*, 146–49; Andaya, *Perak*, 44–51; Freek Colombijn, "The Volatile State in Southeast Asia," *JAS* 62 (2003): 497–529; Els Jacobs, *Merchant in Asia* (Leiden, 2006), 164–73.

[277] Pepper-exporting Jambi, which experienced recurrent upriver–downriver conflict, was more unstable than Palembang. *HMI*, 84–89; Andaya, *Live as Brothers*; Vos, *Gentle Janus*, ch. 2; *HM*, 73, 90–91; Andaya, "Upstreams and Downstreams"; Jacobs, *Merchant in Asia*, 214–16.

erstwhile ally Johor develop a profitable port at Riau in the Riau-Lingga archipelago, it moved to limit Johor by protecting breakaway dependencies and exploiting splits between Johor's Malay rulers and Bugis from South Sulawesi, with whom Johor's rulers had allied in 1721. In effect, Dianne Lewis argues, by preventing Johor-Riau (as the kingdom became known) from reunifying the Straits, the 18th-century Dutch, like the 16th-century Portuguese, were content to play the role of spoiler. What finally led not the VOC, but the Dutch Republic, to destroy Johor-Riau in 1784 was fear that the British would convert it into a forward base that could endanger Batavia. Dependent for its success not on the VOC fleet but on warships sailing directly from the Netherlands, this campaign led to the seizure of Johor and its dependencies on both sides of the Straits.[278]

Given the unique profitability of Malukun spices, the east naturally attracted a more sustained VOC commitment than Sumatra or the Straits. By 1662, we saw, Maluku already had come under Dutch control, Ambon and Banda directly, Ternate and Tidore through patronage of their sultans. Thereafter VOC pressure to curb "piracy" and "smuggling" eroded local support for Ternate and Tidore, whose rulers periodically had to call on Dutch arms to retain power. The VOC planted fortresses at strategic points around Maluku and, to guard the southern approaches, in Timor.[279] To protect Maluku's western flank and to plug the chief hole in its spice monopoly, from 1666 to 1669 the VOC finally destroyed its nemesis Makasar. Victory reflected Dutch naval/military superiority combined with a Bugis revolt against their Makasarese overlords. The VOC promptly dismembered Makasar's empire, expelled rival merchants, and set a large garrison in the town, whose population fell sharply. Thus ended what was arguably Indonesia's most imaginative early modern political experiment. The VOC also extended its authority in North Sulawesi, although in South Sulawesi itself after 1700 the VOC often could do little more than defend itself and its Bugis allies amidst chronic rivalries.[280]

---

[278] On the VOC in the Straits c. 1660–1795, Lewis, *Jan Compagnie*, 99–132 and *passim*; Vos, *Gentle Janus*, pts. 2, 3; Barbara Watson Andaya, "Melaka under the Dutch, 1641–1795," in Sandhu and Wheatley, *Melaka*, 195–241; idem, *Perak*, chs. 3–11. In 1787 the Dutch also extended their hold on Banjarmasin. Han Knapen, *Forests of Fortune?* (Leiden, 2001), 70–71.

[279] A 1781 messianic-tinged anticentralizing revolt in Tidore outlived the VOC itself. Andaya, *World of Maluku*, chs. 6, 7; *HMI*, 76–77; Jacobs, *Merchant in Asia*, 13–27, 33–40.

[280] On VOC–Sulawesi relations, Leonard Andaya, *Heritage of Arung Palakka*; Gerrit Knaap, "Mannning the Fleet," in Sedyawati and Zuhdi, *Arung Samudera*, 83–103; *HMI*, 78–82;

In 1682–1683 Banten, where many Muslim and European traders had fled from Makasar, also passed under VOC control. Much as Makasarese–Bugis hostility gave the Dutch an entrée to South Sulawesi, they entered Banten during a civil war between the sultan and his son. If Banten's post-1683 commercial decline is often exaggerated, the Dutch did monopolize pepper exports and certain textile imports, and the city's population contracted markedly. A failed revolt in 1750–1751 led to tighter VOC supervision until by century's end the Banten Sultanate had lost virtually all cohesion.[281]

As the VOC neutered Banten and coastal rivals beyond Java, it extended its influence over Java's northeast coast and interior at the expense of once formidable Mataram. The VOC's evolution in Java from a commercial to a territorial power thus anticipated the later transformation of the English East India Company – the EIC – in India. Mataram's dismemberment grew from four dynamics, the second and third of which, in fact, are loosely familiar from British Bengal.[282] First, the VOC needed to secure critical supplies of timber and food for Batavia. Second, in the 18th century as spices became less important and global demand for coffee, sugar, and indigo intensified, the VOC sought more direct access to Java's rich agrarian resources. Third, recognizing the superiority of Dutch arms, Mataram elites – both princes seeking the throne and provincial leaders eager to detach themselves from Mataram – clamored for Dutch help. To such claimants, in return for military costs and/or territorial concessions, the VOC offered protection. But, as Ricklefs shows, these deals only aggravated Mataram's woes – and here lies the fourth dynamic – because the more the court required Christian backing, the less able it was to win elite respect and forge a stable consensus. This enhanced the likelihood of revolt, which obliged the court to rely yet more heavily on the Dutch.[283]

HMI, 80–81; Henley, "Conflict, Justice," 88–95; Jacobs, *Merchant in Asia*, 28–32. See Makasar urban figures at *AC*, vol. II, 72–73; Heather Sutherland, "Eastern Emporium and Company Town," in Frank Broeze, ed., *Brides of the Sea* (Honolulu, 1989), esp. 115.

[281] *AC*, vol. II, 267, 280–81, 303; *HMI*, 102–104, 138–39; Goor, "Hybrid State," 204–205; Ota, *Changes of Regime*, chs. 1–6; idem, "Banten Rebellion" (cf. ibid., 620 and *AC*, vol. II, 72–73, 303, suggesting an urban decline of 75–90 percent); Ann Kumar, *Java and Modern Europe* (Richmond, UK, 1997), 258–85.

[282] Cf. *IBE*, 279–86 and Ch. 6 *supra*, discussing EIC reliance on Bengal agrarian and textile production and its alliance with local powerholders.

[283] My discussion of Java relies on Robert Van Niel, *Java's Northeast Coast 1740–1840* (Leiden, 2005), chs. 1–5; Nagtegaal, *Dutch Tiger*; Kwee, *Political Economy*; Soemarsaid Moertono, *State and Statecraft in Old Java* (Ithaca, 1981); Pigeaud and Graaf, *Islamic*

Propelled by these forces, usually with little long-range planning, from 1676 to 1757 the VOC peeled away successive layers of Mataram's territory. Along with droughts in the 1670s, Amangkurat I's harsh and erratic policies stoked a massive *pasisir* rebellion that championed Islamic themes, with an anti-Christian tinge. The VOC broke that revolt with its first expedition into the interior and put Amangkurat's son on the throne, receiving in return territorial and poorly honored commercial concessions. In 1705 another intervention won concessions, again with disappointing results. After further rounds of fighting, in 1743–1746 the VOC decided to forsake Mataram's unstable coastal rule altogether in favor of outright control over the *pasisir*, Madura, and the Eastern Salient. Thus Mataram was confined to its original heartland. Finally in 1755–1757, unable to defeat a fresh princely revolt and conceding that its 80-year policy of keeping a client ruler over all of interior Mataram had failed, the VOC agreed to split what remained of the kingdom into two main courts, at Yogyakarta and Surakarta. By institutionalizing division and letting the Dutch serve as arbiter between the courts, this solution allowed the VOC to withdraw its armies from the interior (except for small garrisons) and settle down to drawing wealth as best it could from its own sectors of Java.[284] By 1790 the latter represented well over half of Java's territory and perhaps half of the population.[285]

As it cohered, VOC-ruled Java, not unlike other early modern systems, assumed a concentric ring format in which autonomy grew with distance. The Batavia area, home to the governor-general, Asia's largest Dutch population, the chief port, and a large sugar industry, was, of course, the core. To Batavia's west, a Dutch Resident and garrison represented VOC interests in Banten, still a key source of pepper. To the

---

States; and most esp. the superb scholarship of M. C. Ricklefs, *War, Culture*; idem, *Seen and Unseen*; idem, *Mystic Synthesis*; idem, *Jogjakarta*; idem, *Modern Javanese Tradition*, 1–14, 202–22; idem, "Unity and Disunity in Javanese Political and Religious Thought of the 18th Century," *MAS* 26 (1992): 663–78; *HMI*, chs. 8–10.

[284] A minor third principality gained formal recognition by 1790–92.

[285] Some estimates – cited in M. C. Ricklefs, "Some Statistical Evidence on Javanese Social, Economic and Demographic History in the Later 17th and 18th Centuries," *MAS* (1986): 30 and *HMI*, 144 – put the population in the *pasisir* and Madura in 1795 at 1,500,000 and in the princely states at 1,500,000. In addition the VOC ruled a significant population in West Java. But Ricklefs has limited confidence in those estimates. Carey, *Power of Prophecy*, 39 suggests well over 2,000,000 people for the principalities in 1812. On territorial divisions, see maps at Van Niel, *Java's Northeast Coast*, xii; Jacobs, *Merchant in Asia*, 230.

east after c. 1710 the so-called "contingent system," in which peasants discharged labor obligations to local rulers by tending coffee terraces, converted the Cirebon and Priangan highlands into a prized source of coffee exports. Here the VOC hollowed out indigenous authority and Dutch law supplanted local procedures.[286] Although it retained greater autonomy than Cirebon and Priangan, Java's northeast coast from Tegal to Madura supplied rice, timber, sugar, indigo, pepper, and cotton through comparable systems of forced deliveries run by Javanese regents and Dutch Residents.[287] The Eastern Salient, pacified only in 1775, was ruled by a mix of VOC officials, Chinese tax farmers, and Sino-Javanese regents. In Yogyakarta and Surakarta Dutchmen were recognized as the "senior" relatives of Javanese kings – but there the Dutch had no pretensions to sovereignty.[288]

In sum, the Dutch to 1784 redirected island history in two ways. First, they deformed indigenous development. Whereas the Portuguese unwittingly had strengthened local states, the Dutch gravely weakened

---

[286] Hoadley, *Feudal Mode*, esp. 1–8, 97–178; Kumar, *Java and Modern Europe*, 285–321; Carey, "Aspects," 47–48. Originally only the Batavia district, Ambon, Banda, and Melaka were subject to direct rule and Dutch law. But in Cirebon-Priangan VOC administrative interference designed to ensure the smooth flow of coffee, and "self-colonization" by elites eager to advance their careers within the VOC hierarchy, combined to replace Javanese with Dutch law administered by VOC and Javanese officials. By 1800 Dutch norms also had modified legal institutions in the *pasisir* and even, Hoadley suggests, in Yogyakarta and Surakarta. Mason Hoadley, "Periodization, Institutional Change, and 18th-Century Java," in Leonard Blusse and Femme Gaastra, eds., *On the Eighteenth Century as a Category of Asian History* (Aldershot, UK, 1998), 83–105; idem, *Selective Judicial Competence* (Ithaca, 1994), esp. 143–47.

[287] The northeast coast as a whole came under a VOC Governor at Semarang whose work, an Englishman noted wryly in 1811, "was as much of a mystery to . . . Batavia as the Governor . . . wished to make it." Carey, "Aspects," 49. On the northeast coast, see Van Niel, *Java's Northeast Coast*, chs. 1–5; Kwee, *Political Economy*, pts. 3, 4; Jacobs, *Merchant in Asia*, 236–47.

[288] On the Eastern Salient, Peter Boomgaard, *Children of the Colonial State* (Amsterdam, 1989), 13; Ricklefs, *Jogjakarta*, 135–38; Kumar, *Java and Modern Europe*, 207–19. In south-central Java Dutch Residents functioned as ambassadors, not colonial rulers. Yet the Javanese fashioned a mythical justification for their relation to the Dutch, who were portrayed as heirs to the Pajajaran kingdom of West Java and "elder brothers," "grandfathers," and family members "senior" to the rulers of south-central Java. Ricklefs, *Jogjakarta*, 120–22, 365–70, 377–413, esp. 408–12; *HMI*, 144. East of Java, although Bali escaped VOC conquest, it felt Dutch influence in two ways: a) After the paramount Balinese kingdom of Gelgel collapsed in 1651, Batavia's demand for slaves aggravated civil wars that sought in part to obtain human spoils for export. b) The VOC's 1770s conquest of Balambangan deprived Balinese rulers of a dependency to which they had close ties. *HMI*, 82–83, 132; Henk Schulte-Nordholt, *The Spell of Power* (Leiden, 1996), 1–77; Helen Creese, *Women of the Kakawin World* (Armonk, NY, 2004).

them. Again, one is reminded how the Mughals and British, by inhibiting regional regimes, altered the main lines of Indian history. What is more, in combination with Chinese initiatives and 17th-century intra-Indonesian warfare, Dutch monopolies reversed generations of urban growth at Banten, Makasar, Surabaya and other *pasisir* towns. Dutch enclave cities could not compensate, because they had weak sociocultural links to the countryside and often discouraged immigration for security reasons.[289] In Java, Sulawesi, and Maluku, many indigenes thus found their access to markets constricted. These urban shifts joined VOC forced deliveries and monopolies, an expansion of Dutch and Chinese coastal shipping, and Chinese tax farming and commercial enterprise to reduce the relative economic standing of Indonesians at large and perhaps to depress absolute income among certain sectors.[290]

Second, even as they stunted indigenous polities, the Dutch assembled a new archipelagic state centered on Java. The VOC controlled some 23 posts from the Cape of Good Hope to Japan, but the archipelago, North Java in particular, remained the heart of VOC operations.[291] It was Batavia that appointed all local personnel and maintained a correspondence so voluminous that the VOC archive today occupies over a kilometer of shelf space![292] No archipelagic state had ever sought such fine-grained administrative or commercial control, maintained such far-flung outposts, monopolized the spice trade, or ruled simultaneously Maluku, South Sulawesi, and most of Java. None of this is to minimize VOC vulnerabilities (see below), much less conflate its ramshackle, leopard-spot structure with the high colonial edifice. Rather it is to emphasize by pre-1660 standards the novelty of Dutch power and the unusual character of its territorial achievement.

---

[289] *AC*, vol. II, ch. 5, and Reid, "Seventeenth-Century Crisis."

[290] The reduction of Southeast Asian shipping continued trends underway since the 16th century. Economic realignments profited individual Javanese regents, but several of the following sources point to popular immiseration, difficult though such changes are to quantify. See n. 227 *supra*; Knaap, "Shipping and Trade"; idem, *Shallow Waters*, 149–78; Nagtegaal, *Dutch Tiger*, 89–106, 123–41, 231–32; Kumar, *Java and Early Modern Europe*, 258-356, 432–33; Hanna, *Indonesian Banda*, chs. 4, 5; *AC*, vol. II, ch. 5. For other other assessments of Javanese economic prospects, see n. 311 *infra*.

[291] By 1726–1730 the Indonesian archipelago had 14 out of 23 VOC factories in Asia, 62 percent of VOC personnel, and 74 percent of recorded expenditures. Goor, "Hybrid State," 201, Table 2. In 1790, moreover, Indonesians were 86 percent of all Asians under VOC authority. Cf. nn. 238, 285 *supra*; Goor, "Hybrid State," 193, n. 1.

[292] Jacobs, *Merchant in Asia*, 10. On VOC centralization, ibid., 1–11 and *passim*; Knaap, *Shallow Waters*, chs. 2, 8, 12.

Explaining Dutch Advances

This success raises three broad interpretive problems: Why did Dutch inroads accelerate in the mid-1600s? What long-term advantages explain VOC ascendancy? Why did mainland Southeast Asia escape such impositions until well into the 19th century?

If VOC success in Maluku in the early 1600s showed the Company's potential, that potential was not fully realized for another 60 years. Reid's effort, quite plausible to my mind, to explain this quantum leap focuses on connections between the islands and the wider Eurasian economy.[293] The climatic downturn that we found c. 1640 to 1700 in mainland Southeast Asia, Russia, France, and China also affected Java and much of the archipelago. Tree-ring series and historical data show that amidst a generally dry 17th century, the worst droughts came in Java between 1643 and 1686, and in the outer islands beyond Java between 1660 and 1685. These scarcities weakened indigenous states – especially rice-deficit states like Aceh and Banten – and sparked an unusually intense zero-sum contest for resources.[294] At the same time, partly independent of climate, economic strains in mid-17th-century Europe and China joined Tokugawa restrictions to slash global demand for pepper and other Southeast Asian exports. By the 1670s pepper prices were only a quarter of what they had been in the 1640s, and they remained at that depressed level to the 1680s and beyond. Indian textile imports also fell sharply, along with precious metals from Japan and the New World. In this difficult commercial environment, the VOC, with its heavy overheads, had little choice but to pursue monopolies with novel rigor. In short, there was room for only one winner.[295]

---

[293] Reid, "Seventeenth-Century Crisis"; *AC*, vol. II, 286–301. But my discussion differs in emphases and documentation from Reid.

[294] According to Lombard, *Sultanat d'Atjeh*, 60–61, 99–100, Aceh's inability to feed itself was a major long-term cause of decline. On droughts, which often correlated with epidemics and famine, *AC*, vol. II, 291–98; Reid, "Seventeenth-Century Crisis," 654–57; Boomgaard, "Crisis Mortality," 191–204, with a clever discussion of scarcity's political implications; idem, "Riches to Rags," 193–95; Ricklefs, *War, Culture*, 45; *HMI*, 101. But for cautionary views on climate, see Barbara Watson Andaya, "The Unity of Southeast Asia," *JSEAS* 28 (1997): 161–71; Gerrit Knaap, "The Demography of Ambon in the 17th Century," *JSEAS* 26 (1995): 227–41.

[295] I follow n. 293 *supra*; Anthony Reid, "A New Phase of Commercial Expansion in Southeast Asia, 1760–1840," in Reid, ed., *The Last Stand of Asian Autonomies* (New York, 1997), 60 and 57–81; plus Barrett, "World Bullion Flows," 238, 246, 249, 251;

Once the competition was joined, why did the VOC best its European rivals? I have already identified Dutch advantages over Portugal. England shared with the Low Countries certain cultural traits, but until the English company was reorganized as a permanent joint stock in 1658, its trading capital was of no consequence. Hounded by the Dutch from Ambon to Banten to Bengkulu in Sumatra, the English in the archipelago – until the day of the private trader dawned in the 18th century – had to content themselves with crumbs from the Dutch table.[296]

Against indigenous opponents VOC superiority was yet more marked. At sea, the VOC's natural milieu, Makasarese and Javanese ships were regularly outgunned, and although Bugis and Malays acquitted themselves well against a VOC fleet in 1783–1784, I noted that warships from Holland overwhelmed them completely. On land, the VOC's small numbers and Southeast Asian imitation reduced the gap. By the early 1700s Javanese were copying Dutch fortifications, artillery, flintlocks, paper cartridges, mortars, grenades, bayonets, and drill. But even if we assume – a doubtful proposition after 1700 – that local artisans could match the quality of European manufactures, in training, strategy, siegecraft, and in the percentage of troops supplied with firearms, local armies rarely, if ever, equaled the Dutch.[297]

Military superiority explains not only repeated Dutch triumphs over far larger armies, but the enthusiasm, even desperation with which rival factions in Mataram, Palembang, Maluku, and Sulawesi clamored for Dutch help. Arguably, business acumen was far less critical to VOC profitability than their ability to sell protection, to serve as mafia-like enforcers. Military superiority and commercial disadvantage were two sides of the same coin insofar as high military overheads made it difficult for the VOC to compete with petty traders. But in return for

Sinnappah Arasaratnam, "The Coromandel-Southeast Asian Trade 1650–1740," *JAH* 18 (1984): 113–31.

[296] Adams, "Principals and Agents," 16–17; Arasaratnam, "Coromandel-Southeast Asian Trade," 119–20. Cf. K. N. Chaudhuri, *The Trading World of Asia and the English East India Company 1660–1760* (Cambridge, 1978), chs. 1, 3–5. French, Spanish, and Danish rivalry was yet less credible.

[297] On the small percentage wielding firearms, n. 270 *supra*. Drill aside, in lieu of coordinated regimental maneuver, Indonesians tended to emphasize skirmish, feint, and heroic display. Moreover, naval power allowed Dutch land forces to draw on distant reserves with unique facility. On the military balance, which naturally differed by area, see nn. 194, 270 *supra* plus Knaap, *Shallow Waters*, 31–43; Henley, "Conflict, Justice," 94–97; Leonard Andaya, "The Nature of War and Peace Among the Bugis-Makassar People," *SEAR* 12 (2004): 53–80; Ricklefs, *Mystic Synthesis*, 64, 142, 293–305; Peter Carey, *The Power of Prophecy* (Leiden, 2007), 7–8; CHSEA, 378–94.

Dutch protection, local leaders were willing to pay a considerable premium in the form of lower export and higher import prices. Repeatedly, this dynamic sucked the VOC into Javanese politics. Dearly bought VOC military help explains whatever success Mataram enjoyed during the Kartasura period (1680–1746) in reasserting control over the *pasisir*.[298]

In this view, therefore, early Dutch colonialism was not an exclusively predatory imposition. Often it was solicited by local actors for whom the very alien character of the Dutch was their most appealing quality. This was true of arbitrative as well as military services. Precisely because they were seen as a powerful external party without strong local ties, the Dutch were indispensable not only to the 1757 settlement between Yogyakarta and Surakarta – who generally hated one another more than they hated the Dutch – but also to the pacification of stateless societies like those of North Sulawesi. Even more clearly than in the Philippines, in North Sulawesi from the late 1600s chronically feuding tribes and kin groups, influenced by pre-Dutch myths of benevolent stranger-kings, welcomed Europeans as their best hope for impartial justice and supravillage cooperation.[299]

Dutch–Indonesian cooperation extended beyond military affairs and arbitration to commerce itself. Outside Banda, where the Dutch simply exterminated the local population, long-term profits required constantly renegotiated accommodations. Thus in Palembang, although in practice the VOC received only about half of the pepper and tin on which it claimed a monopoly, both sides tacitly accepted the arrangement, and locals fondly remembered the era of VOC alliance as a period of shared prosperity.[300] Similar understandings governed relations with Johor and the Bugis. Even in northeast Java, political economy was never a matter of simple imposition. Rather, Javanese regents – termed "portfolio capitalists and political entrepreneurs" – cooperated enthusiastically with the VOC and Chinese traders to develop systems of cash cropping,

---

[298] Nagtegaal, *Dutch Tiger*, 25, 51–85; Kwee, *Political Economy*, 34–35, 219. An emphasis on the "sale" of VOC military support also informs Vos, *Gentle Janus*, 4, 15–52, 207–208; Henley, "Conflict, Justice."

[299] Henley, "Conflict, Justice." Apparently unbeknownst to Henley, Manguin, "The Merchant and the King" also explores a trope, widespread across the archipelago, which saw foreign merchant benefactors as instrumental to state formation.

[300] Andaya, *Live as Brothers*, 112–27, 177–210 *passim*, 245, supported by Ricklefs, pers. commun., April 26, 2008; Jacobs, *Merchant in Asia*, 283–85.

tax farming, and mercantile extraction that afforded individual regents "immense wealth, status, and power."[301]

And yet in negotiating with local elites, the VOC also benefited from an institutional culture that by local standards was quite peculiar. Batavia's endemic corruption and entrenched family interests notwithstanding,[302] the Company's standardized procedures, laws, and archives – its dense literization, comparable to that of the English EIC – joined an *esprit de corps* and Dutch racial/cultural pride to promote a remarkable level of solidarity.[303] The governor-general's retirement might threaten Batavia with factionalism, but never dissolution. We hear of repeated Javanese wars of succession, but no Dutch wars of succession. If Banten and Makasar courted the VOC's European rivals, they never came close to splitting the VOC hierarchy, whereas internal splits gave the Dutch a *point d'appui* time and again. Indigenous instability reflected fluid rules of succession, personalized loyalties, and hereditary appointments, all of which contrasted with VOC norms. (Ironically, the high death toll among VOC servants further inhibited the development of local ties.) Likewise the VOC's capital resources, massive by local standards,[304] let it weather market downturns, just as its global reach let it gather information and shift resources on a unique scale.

Why did these same advantages not lead the Dutch or other European to dominate mainland Southeast Asia until well into the 19th century? In large part, because the mainland produced no fine spices and little pepper to attract European interest in the first instance. Then too, when Europeans did try to intervene on the mainland, they encountered larger populations, more formidable armies, and more cohesive polities than in most of the island world. If Central and East Java's rich soils

---

[301] Kwee, *Political Economy*, 12, 40 (with quotes), 222–27, 233–34; Van Niel, *Java's Northeast Coast*, 31 ("[the VOC] through the promise of peace and stability, offered the best possibility for the promotion of control...by the local elite."), 94–100; Nagtegaal, *Dutch Tiger*, 163–79, 219.

[302] Patterns that, along with general debauchery, receive emphasis at Boomgaard, *Children*, 14–15; Blusse, *Strange Company*, 172–259; *HMI*, 106, 109, 118–19, 139; Ricklefs, *Seen and Unseen*, 244; Taylor, *Social World*, chs. 1–3.

[303] These factors also are emphasized at Goor, "Hybrid State," 211–14; Hoadley, *Feudal Mode*, 72–79, 93; Blusse, "Batavia, 1619–1740," 171; Andaya, *Live as Brothers*, 74; Bosma and Raben, *Being Dutch*, 53.

[304] On VOC capital, Niels Steensgaard, "The Companies as a Specific Institution in the History of European Expansion," in Leonard Blusse and Femme Gaastra, eds., *Companies and Trade* (Leiden, 1981), 245–64; Van Niel, *Java's Northeast Coast*, 121; Larry Neal, "The Dutch and the English East India Companies Compared," in Tracy, *Rise of Merchant Empires*, 198–99.

supported populations in the same order of magnitude as Burma and Siam, and if Mataram's administrative features recall those of the mainland, Java had no unifying riverine artery comparable to the Irrawaddy or Chaophraya. Thus Mataram, as I indicated, evoked a weak sense of precedent, provincial identification with the throne had shallow cultural roots, and center-periphery tensions, particularly between mercantile coast and agrarian interior, were more severe than in Burma or Siam. One may object that Vietnam's elongated geography also was fissiparous, precipitating the north–south split of 1620 to 1802. Yet not only did maritime transport link population clusters more easily in Vietnam – all of whose chief centers lay near the coast – than in Java, but Vietnam's historic relation to China allowed the Vietnamese to develop a politicized ethnicity, a standardized elite education, and a bureaucratic repertoire that compensated for a centrifugal environment more successfully than Javanese political culture. Finally, because mainland states tended to rely less heavily on trade, whether for food or income, than their island counterparts, and outside Vietnam were less vulnerable to blockade, Europeans' principal asset, naval superiority, was less telling. Portuguese, French, and Dutch interventions on the mainland between 1600 and 1820 not only failed to impose monopolies, but in Burma and Nguyen Vietnam unwittingly strengthened local authorities.[305]

18th-Century Commercial Dynamism: The Dutch as Victim

Despite the VOC's impressive military performance, 18th-century shifts gradually undermined its economic position. Overwhelmed by new commercial currents in general and by English power in particular, by 1800 the VOC had disappeared.

Consider first how Eurasian demand, new trade diasporas, and internal growth reshaped the 18th-century archipelagic economy. By pushing up prices for Southeast Asian raw materials, China's population boom not only spurred junk traffic to procure such goods, but drove impoverished laborers from Guangdong and Fujian to Southeast Asia in order to grow crops (pepper, gambier, sugar) and to mine tin and gold for sale back home. Recruited by resident Chinese merchants in cooperation with local officials, Chinese communities after 1720 grew

---

[305] *SP*, 149–206, 309–10, 406, 426; Lieberman, *Burmese Administrative Cycles*, 44–60, 248, 252, 280–84. Although densely populated, Southwest Sulawesi and Bali also had fatally centrifugal geographies and cultures. See nn. 260–63, 288 *supra*.

rapidly, particularly in Southeast Asia's "empty center" in the western archipelago, where untapped resources were richest and local labor least available.[306]

Intertwined with Chinese trade was an ever more insatiable British demand for tea, part of that growth in European consumer culture discussed in Chapter 3. China was almost the sole supplier of tea, which in the 1700s replaced ale as the English national beverage. But since China had scant interest in European manufactures and the British sought to limit bullion outflows, "country traders" – private intra-Asian merchants – sought Southeast Asian goods, especially pepper and tin, that could vend at the chief Chinese port of Guangzhou. In exchange they sold in the archipelago firearms, gunpowder, Indian cottons, and Indian opium. Country traders were of diverse nationalities, but by the mid-1700s British dominated by virtue of their nautical skills, willingness to sell arms in defiance of VOC bans, and, most critical, their ties to the EIC. As British conquests in India assured control over textiles, opium, and saltpeter, EIC officials funneled those goods to fellow British private traders, whose China sales financed tea purchases.[307] For the Company, this made more sense than fitting out its own vessels to Southeast Asia. At the same time country traders drove a considerable traffic independent of the China leg. Hounded by the VOC in the late 1600s from every archipelagic post but Bengkulu and obliged to fall back on India, the British, basing themselves on India and the country trade, now roared back with a vengeance.

Additional stimuli to archipelagic trade derived from non-Chinese trade diasporas, most notably by Bugis, Sumatran Minangkabau, and Arabs. Starting with the VOC's conquest of South Sulawesi in 1669,

---

[306] On post-1683 Chinese trade and emigration, Reid, "Flows and Seepages," 41–48; Leonard Blusse, "Chinese Century," *Archipel* 58 (1999): 107–29; Carl Trocki, *Prince of Pirates* (Singapore, 1979), 17–24, 30–34; idem, "Chinese Pioneering in 18th-Century Southeast Asia," in Reid, *Last Stand*, 83–101; idem, *Opium and Empire* (Ithaca, 1990), 7–49; idem, "Opium and the Beginnings of Chinese Capitalism in Southeast Asia," *JSEAS* 33 (2002): 297–314; *HM*, 96–97, 142–46; Van Niel, *Java's Northeast Coast*, 101–20.

[307] And to a lesser extent, porcelains and silk. Country traders received EIC bills of exchange payable in London. On the country trade, Ch. 6, n. 188 *supra*, plus Vos, *Gentle Janus*, 123–24; P. J. Marshall, "Private British Trade in the Indian Ocean Before 1800," in Das Gupta and Pearson, *India and the Indian Ocean*, 276–300; Holden Furber, *Rival Empires of Trade in the Orient* (Minneapolis, 1976), ch. 6; Dianne Lewis, "The Growth of the Country Trade to the Straits of Malacca, 1760–1777," *JMBRAS* 43 (1970): 114–30; S. Arasaratnam, "Merchants and Commerce in Coromandel," in Blusse and Gaastra, *On the Eighteenth Century*, 261–88; John Keay, *The Honourable Company* (New York, 1991), 429–30, 444–46, and pts. 3, 4 *passim*.

waves of Bugis refugees were attracted to sparsely populated areas in Sumatra and the Straits, where their commercial and military skills told heavily. Bugis warriors not only carved out their own kingdom in Johor's tin-rich Selangor territory, but from 1721 to 1784 dominated Johor itself. Plentifully supplied with tin, pepper, and forest products, Johor's port of Riau became the chief magnet for country traders.[308] For centuries emigrants had been leaving interior Sumatra for coastal locales, but from the late 1600s new trade openings swelled that diaspora as well. To enhance their prospects in competition with established populations, some emigrants began emphasizing their shared Minangkabau identity, which meant focusing loyalty on the shadowy Minangkabau "emperor" in Sumatra. As with Bugis, emigration thus sharpened ethnic boundaries.[309] In the 18th century Arabs, particularly from the Hadramut, also achieved novel prominence, using Mideastern trade and scholarly contacts and a reputation for piety to win marriage entrée to many an elite Malay family.[310]

Finally, the restoration of peace in Java after 1755 favored in both the *pasisir* and the princely domains rapid reclamation and population growth. The latter, Ricklefs estimates, by the third quarter of the century reached over 1 percent a year. Agrarian intensification meant expanded irrigation, village handicrafts, cash cropping, and money use, which created new openings for Chinese traders and tax farmers as well as some local cultivators.[311] Quite possibly agrarian output rose elsewhere in the archipelago as well, but we have little information.

[308] Leonard Andaya, "The Bugis-Makassar Diasporas," *JMBRAS* 68 (1995): 119–38; idem, *Kingdom of Johor*, 279–323 and *passim*; HM, 76, 83–88, 98–108; Gilbert Hamonic, "Les reseaux marchands Bugis-Makassar," in Lombard and Aubin, *Marchands*, 253–65.

[309] Andaya, *Leaves*, 100–107; idem, "Unravelling Minangkabau Ethnicity"; HM, 83, 95–106, 116, 121; Colombijn, "Volatile State," 508–509; Andaya, *Live as Brothers*, 92–95, 149–65; Drakard, *Malay Frontier*; idem, *Kingdom of Words*. But on Minangkabau and Bugis identifying as Malays, Timothy Barnard, "Texts, Raja Ismail, and Violence," *JSEAS* 32 (2001): 331–42; Jan van der Putten, "A Malay of Bugis Ancestry," ibid., 343–54.

[310] Enseng Ho, *The Graves of Tarim* (Berkeley, 2006), 152–73; idem, "Before Parochialization," in Huub de Jonge and Nico Kaptein, eds., *Transcending Borders* (Leiden, 2002), 11–35; HM, 96.

[311] On economic and demographic growth, Ricklefs, "Statistical Evidence," esp. 30; Carey, *Power of Prophecy*, 33–47, 66; idem, "Waiting for the Just King," 59–137; idem, "Changing Javanese Perceptions of the Chinese Communities in Central Java, 1755–1825," *Indonesia* 37 (1984): 1–47; Van Niel, *Java's Northeast Coast*, chs. 3–5. But on Javanese commercial retardation vis-à-vis other sectors of Eurasia, as measured by interest rates and skilled wage rates, see Jan Luiten van Zanden, "The Road to the Industrial Revolution," *JGH* 3 (2008): 342–49.

For indigenous states and populations, the political implications of this multifaceted expansion were mixed. On the one hand, trade could be profoundly disruptive. In inaccessible interior districts the discovery of gold and tin often fostered suzerainty disputes or encouraged local leaders to defy their overlords, as Selangor, Negeri Sembilan, and Pahang defied Johor. From the latter's standpoint the rise of local polities obviously signaled disorder. In much of the archipelago such shifts joined new ethnic diasporas, slave raids from Sulu, cheap firearms, and Malay succession disputes to feed a sense of insecurity. Tensions between Bugis and Malays in Johor-Riau and between Chinese and Javanese were symptomatic.[312] On the other hand, particularly on the periphery of Dutch power, economic growth could inspire a new political confidence. For much of the 18th century authorities in Johor-Riau, Kedah, Trengganu, and Siak strengthened their position through the China trade. From the 1780s American and British pepper purchases also permitted a modest revival of royal power in Aceh. Likewise after 1750, Sulu, fortified with guns from country traders, raided the archipelago for slaves needed to harvest jungle and marine produce for China; and on the basis of that predatory political economy erected a powerful segmentary state from Mindanao to Borneo.[313] So too, as their strength revived, Yogyakarta and Surakarta treated Batavia with growing disregard to the point where a Dutch governor warned that if the two courts stood together, the VOC would go down to defeat.[314] Although, in fact, no indigenous state defied the VOC successfully, clearly the Dutch momentum of the 17th and early 18th centuries had ebbed.[315]

---

[312] On political devolution, "piracy" (a subjective category), and ethnic tensions, *HM*, 83–116 *passim*, 133–35; Vos, *Gentle Janus*, 55; Andaya, *Perak*, 16, 25, 59–60, 274, 277, 370; Trocki, *Prince of Pirates*, chs. 1–2; Milner, *Kerajaan*, 18–31; Joseph N. F. M. a Campo, "Discourse Without Discussion," *JSEAS* 34 (2003): 199–214; Carey, "Changing Javanese Perceptions"; Trocki, "Chinese Pioneering," 91–93.

[313] On Aceh, Lee Kam Hing, *The Sultanate of Aceh* (Kuala Lumpur, 1995); Reid, "New Phase," 66–67; *HMI*, 184–86; n. 276 *supra*. On Sulu, James Warren, *Iranun and Balangingi* (Singapore, 2002). On 18th-century Siak and other secondary realms, Timothy Barnard, *Multiple Centres of Authority* (Leiden, 2003); Lewis, *Jan Compagnie*, 81–96; J. Kathirithamby-Wells, "The Long 18th Century and the New Age of Commerce in the Melaka Straits," in Blusse and Gaastra, *On the Eighteenth Century*, 57–82.

[314] Ricklefs, pers. commun., April 26, 2008; n. 288 *supra*. Yet gross inefficiency in tapping the new wealth meant that princely strength never grew as rapidly as the economy. Carey, *Power of Prophecy*, 56–67.

[315] As indigenous political strength increased, so – *pace* earlier views that Dutch hegemony impoverished Southeast Asian Islam – did Islamic learning. Between 1690 and

Such shifts were all the more ominous in that the same commercial trends as aided some indigenous states directly weakened the VOC. Dutch economic strategy, recall, preferred restricted markets with high profit margins to open markets with lower unit profit. At Batavia the VOC tried to concentrate all traffic with Europe and other parts of Asia as well as the bulk of nonmonopoly intraregional trade. While recognizing it could not entirely stop its employees from private trading, the VOC also sought to minimize such activities by making repatriation of funds to Holland exceedingly difficult. But with 18th-century trade expansion, these controls broke down. Heavily invested in goods, especially spices, whose relative value was declining, slow to respond to changing European consumer tastes, and now undercapitalized compared to its English rivals, the VOC, despite its promotion of coffee and sugar from Java, failed to match British investment in the main growth areas of world trade, namely, Indian textiles and opium and Chinese tea. As early as the 1670s the British so dominated Indian piece-goods that the Dutch had to travel to London to buy samples to send back to India for reproduction.[316] Burgeoning British country trade at Riau and other archipelagic ports, Chinese junks' growing preference for Riau over Batavia, initiatives by Chinese, Bugis, Minangkabau, and Arab diasporas; ill-controlled smuggling on Java's northeast coast, rampant piracy in much of the archipelago – all signaled the VOC's deteriorating position. Meanwhile, as they developed exchanges outside the VOC network, British country traders hollowed out that network from within by making it easier for VOC employees to trade privately and to repatriate funds to Europe through British channels. Such was the breakdown of cartel discipline that high Batavia officials, themselves

---

1830 exchanges with the Mideast multiplied, local states prided themselves on their Arab-trained scholars, and religious-aided literacy spread. Barbara Watson Andaya, "Adapting to Political and Economic Change," in Reid, *Last Stand,* esp. 199–200; idem, *Live as Brothers,* 14, 240–41; *HM,* 104, 110–12, Azra, *Origins,* 109–47; Riddell, *Islam,* 168–200. The Padri movement in early 1800s Minangkabau drew strength from Mecca pilgrimages and from the export of salt, coffee, gambier, and textiles. Dobbin, *Islamic Revivalism,* chs. 2–4. In Javanese court circles too foreign contacts strengthened Islamic identity. Nancy Florida, *Writing the Past, Inscribing the Future* (Durham, NC, 1995); Ricklefs, *Mystic Synthesis,* chs. 6, 7. On 17- to 18th-century religious-based literacy, ibid., 28–29; Andaya, *Live as Brothers,* 5, 60, 111, 146–47, 172, 235–36, 246; idem, "Southeast Asia, Historical Periodization and Area Studies," *JESHO* 45 (2002): 268–87.

[316] On the EIC vs. VOC, Adams, "Principals and Agents," 23 n. 23 (with erroneous citation); Furber, *Rival Empires,* 243; C. A. Bayly, *The Imperial Meridian* (London, 1989), 66–67; Neal, "Dutch and the English East India Companies," 195–223; Jacobs, *Merchant in Asia,* 293.

involved in illegal trade, frustrated efforts at reform by the VOC direc-
torate in Holland.[317] True, as Reinout Vos has shown, the gross turnover
of VOC trade continued to rise to 1780, while Company size remained
constant. Yet from 1720 to 1780 profits slumped and debt grew rapidly.[318]
With the VOC's share of island trade falling and its overheads for
forts, ships, and personnel ever less sustainable, the VOC concentrated
available resources on Java's north coast at the expense of the outer
islands.[319]

What finally broke the Company's back was the Fourth Anglo-Dutch
War of 1780–1784. Not only did it destroy half of the Company's ships,
70 percent of its assets, and all Dutch factories in India along with access
to critical Indian markets and raw materials, but the peace treaty obliged
the Dutch to grant country traders free navigation.[320] A new Dutch
government (installed by French troops in 1795) finally dissolved the
bankrupt Company on the last day of the 18th century, taking over all
its possessions not yet in English hands.

---

[317] On private trade and failed reform, Adams, "Principals and Agents"; idem, "Trading
States, Trading Places," *CSSH* 36 (1994): 319–55; Arasaratnam, "Merchants and Commerce," 275; Van Niel, *Java's Northeast Coast*, 121–22, 171, 175; Kwee, *Political Economy*,
227–29.

[318] According to Van Niel, *Java's Northeast Coast*, 45–46, VOC operations in Asia, after
turning a steady profit from 1621 to 1688, produced losses that rose from 10,300,000
guilders in 1689–1700 to 50,400,000 in 1780–1790. As early as 1683–1710 only 3 of
the VOC's 23 outposts in Asia normally made a profit. Yet losses in Asia were still
offset by gains in Europe, so that *overall* profits after 1760 recovered to 7–8 percent,
compared to 13 percent for the late 1600s. Vos, *Gentle Janus*, 6. On the contentious
historiography of VOC decline, see *HMI*, ch. 10; Van Niel, *Java's Northeast Coast*, 43–
47, 121–22; Vos, *Gentle Janus*, 5–7; Blusse, *Strange Company*, 97–155; Knaap, *Shallow
Waters*, 16–18; Furber, *Rival Empires*, chs. 2, 3, 6; Israel, *Dutch Primacy*, 330–39, 390–92,
399–404; Kristof Glamann, *Dutch-Asiatic Trade 1620–1740* (Copenhagen, 1958), 244–65;
Boxer, *Dutch Seaborne Empire*, 105–11, 268–94; Hanna, *Indonesian Banda*, 77–94; Neal,
"Dutch and the English East India Companies," 195–223; Julia Adams, "The Familial
State," *Theory and Society* 23 (1994): 503–39, stressing organizational, not economic
deficiencies; and Jacobs, *Merchant in Asia*, 6–11, 79–83, 133–45, 179–294, weighing the
relative contribution to VOC decline of European competition, declining post-1715
supplies of Japanese bullion, sluggish VOC's responses to European consumer tastes,
overly complex accounting procedures, high overheads, and low capitalization vis-à-
vis the EIC.

[319] Yet the VOC retained posts in Timor, Palembang, Makasar, and elsewhere; while in
1787-1790 it confirmed its role as arbiter between the Javanese courts. *HMI*, 126, 129,
135–39; Ricklefs, *Jogjakarta*, ch. 9; Barbara Watson Andaya, pers. commun., Oct. 9,
2008.

[320] Vos, *Gentle Janus*, 5; Kwee, *Political Economy*, 195–96; Kumar, *Java and Modern Europe*,
24–25; *HM*, 108–109; Van Niel, *Java's Northeast Coast*, 47–51; Jacobs, *Merchant in Asia*,
144–45, 282, 293–94.

Vos contends that these shifts in Dutch and English fortune should be seen as a triumph not of free trade over monopoly, but of one coercive system over another: EIC control of Bengal's textiles and opium and the VOC's post-1780 woes both grew from English military triumphs.[321] But one could argue as easily that economics trumped politics insofar as the VOC fell hostage to the Netherlands' deteriorating commercial position in Europe. As early as 1740, to follow Jonathan Israel, the Netherlands had suffered serious losses to the English and others in bulk carriage, the rich trades, and manufacturing, with Holland reverting to its pre-1590 role of mere transit and storage depot. It was, above all, this economic performance that left the VOC undercapitalized, the Dutch navy and merchant marine understrength and technically deficient, and Dutch possessions in Asia easy prey in time of war.[322]

The collapse of VOC controls in the face of commercial expansion recalls Srivijaya's fate. But among Eurasian realms under review, surely the most apt analogies are to mainland Southeast Asia and France in the same period, that is to say, the late 1700s and early 1800s. Differences in scale and structure aside, between 1752 and 1800 Burma, Siam, Vietnam, and the VOC all suffered from rapid commercial growth led by Chinese and country traders, and from intensifying interstate warfare that itself was partly a function of commercial expansion. In each case, 18th-century collapse was the essential precondition for dramatic political recovery by the start of the next century. In France too, we saw that 18th-century commercialization and warfare overstrained political institutions, whose collapse facilitated a brilliant renewal in fresh institutional garb by the early 1800s. The overarching difference, of course, was that whereas in mainland Southeast Asia and France indigenous elites were in charge, Dutch power remained an extraregional intrusion – an intrusion, moreover, whose post-Napoleonic revival depended on English largesse. To this peculiar rebirth of Dutch fortunes we now turn.

Early 19th-Century Upheavals: The Dutch as Phoenix

The VOC's demise precipitated debate within the Netherlands: What was the best way to enhance the value of the Indies, Java in particular, to the home country, and what was the best way to improve the welfare of the Javanese (insofar as this was compatible with the first

---

[321] Vos, *Gentle Janus*, 123–25.
[322] Israel, *Dutch Primacy*, 359–400; Boxer, *Dutch Seaborne Empire*, 105–10, 268–94.

objective)? Conservatives wanted to retain forced deliveries and indirect rule. Liberals, inspired by Enlightenment theory, sought to transfer land to individual cultivators, to replace forced deliveries with cash taxes, and to have Europeans assume local administration. But both sides agreed that Batavia's network of family privilege should yield to "rational" bureaucratic controls, that the home government should strengthen its control over policy, in short, that European modernity should be welcomed in the Indies.[323]

During the first three decades of the 19th century, initially in response to Napoleonic war dislocations, European regimes on Java vacillated between conservative and liberal economic policies, but pursued administrative centralization more or less consistently. To 1811 their need to build Java's defenses against an expected British invasion led French-allied Dutch officials to strengthen supervision of Javanese elites and to recruit a more professional bureaucracy in Holland. In Banten and Central Java, these changes included much bullying of local aristocrats, who responded with a smoldering resentment. After seizing Java from Dutch officials in 1811, in the name of liberal theory the British moved to end corvées and to promote private landholding. All the while, they too sought to Europeanize administration, in effect reducing Javanese regents to salaried officials. In 1812 this policy led the British to sack a defiant Yogyakarta and to seize lands from that kingdom and Surakarta. This humiliation, the only time European-led forces took a Javanese court by storm, eliminated any lingering prospect that the south-central courts might balance European power on Java.[324]

At the end of the Napoleonic Wars some British officials lobbied to retain Java, but Britain's eagerness to strengthen the Netherlands as a barrier to French expansion in Europe told in favor of returning it in 1816, along with other Dutch outposts in the Indies.[325] By a similar exclusionary logic, the British agreed to divide the western archipelago with the Dutch. In 1819 the British secured from Johor-Riau a base at Singapore, whose superb location soon joined its free trade policy and British naval strength to render it the archipelago's most dynamic entrepot. Eager to consolidate its position in the Straits, and at the same time to exclude rivals like France, the British in 1824 struck a deal with

---

[323] Discussion of Java 1800–1825 follows *HMI*, 144–50; Van Niel, *Java's Northeast Coast*, 187–352; Carey, "Aspects," 45–71; and Carey's magnum opus, *Power of Prophecy*.

[324] *HMI*, 149–50; Boomgaard, *Children*, 29–34, 199–200; Carey, *Power of Prophecy*, chs. 5–8.

[325] Blom and Lamberts, *History of Low Countries*, 305; Hanna, *Indonesian Banda*, 95.

the Netherlands. Henceforth peninsular areas including Singapore and Melaka would constitute a British sphere, while Java, Sumatra, and islands south of Singapore would remain the preserve of the Dutch. In effect, the British and Dutch drew a line through the heart of the Malay world.[326]

Thus a British colony, destined to become Southeast Asia's commercial hub, began to cohere, while the venerable Dutch state in the Indies was reborn in a new guise. Obviously, the latter's phoenix-like ascent owed less to inner strength than to British goodwill. Absent the latter, Dutch holdings in the archipelago would have joined South India, Sri Lanka, and the Cape in saluting the Union Jack. In this reliance on external agency, Dutch revival differed fundamentally from revivals in Burma, Siam, Vietnam, and France between 1760 and 1815.

On Java as in mainland Southeast Asia and France, however, wars provided the chief catalyst to reform. This was true of Napoleonic upheavals, as we just saw, and of a far more traumatic local event, the Java War of 1825 to 1830. After Britain returned Java to the Kingdom of the Netherlands in 1816, Dutch officials continued to open the interior to Western and Chinese capital and to constrict the power of Javanese elites. The result was a massive anti-Dutch uprising that reflected the bitterness of aristocrats and Muslim religious leaders after some 20 years of humiliation and exclusion, as well as peasant distress caused by crop failures and by ruinous, vacillating European fiscal practices. Centered in Yogyakarta, which had been seared by the British sack of 1812, the revolt was led by the mystic prince Dipanagara, who proclaimed himself a messianic deliverer (*ratu adil*) and whose forces initially stunned the Dutch. Yet by 1830 this attempt to reestablish the old political order had succumbed to fresh Dutch tactics, to aristocratic versus religious splits within Dipanagara's movement, and to the reluctance of most courtiers, not least in Surakarta, to break openly with the Dutch.[327]

---

[326] Bengkulu passed from British to Dutch control, while Melaka, under British rule from 1794 to 1818, returned to Britain, along with Dutch holdings in India. In 1826 Singapore, Melaka, Penang, and Province Wellesley formed the Straits Settlement. *HM*, 112–28; *HMI*, 184–85. On Penang and Melaka 1780–1830, Nordin Hussin, *Trade and Society in the Straits of Melaka* (Singapore, 2007).

[327] P. B. R. Carey, *Babad Dipanagara* (Kuala Lumpur, 1981), esp. xxxvii–xlvii; idem, "Waiting for the Just King"; idem, "The Origins of the Java War (1825–30)," *English Historical Review* 91 (1976): 52–78; idem, *Power of Prophecy*, chs. 9–11; C. A. Bayly, "Two Colonial Revolts," in Bayly and D. H. A. Kolff, eds., *Two Colonial Empires* (Dordrecht, 1986), 111–35; Ricklefs, *Mystic Synthesis*, 195–217.

In the aftermath of this cataclysm, which killed well over 200,000,[328] having learned at great cost the danger of ignoring local sensibilities, Dutch officials finally developed a successful conservative formula to tap Java's agrarian potential. As implemented by Governor-General Johannes van den Bosch from 1830, the so-called *cultuurstelsel* ("cultivation system") obliged villages to discharge their traditional land tax obligations by devoting a portion of their fields to export crops – chiefly coffee, sugar, indigo – for sale at fixed prices to the government. Using a new trading company but operating much like the old VOC, the state then sold these goods on the world market. Although European officials now began to function at the village level and took ultimate responsibility for the new system, it relied for its legitimacy on Javanese regents and treated the village, rather than individual cultivator, as the basic tax unit. Gone was the liberal shibboleth of private peasant entrepreneur. For both the Netherlands, about a third of whose state revenues by 1855 came from the *cultuurstelsel*,[329] and for the Javanese aristocracy, who exchanged autonomy for a percentage on deliveries and security in office, the system worked remarkably well.

As the new colonial government, now determined to extend and demarcate its sphere of control, secured Java, it also expanded its authority in the outer islands. On Sumatra the Dutch deposed Palembang's last sultan and assumed direct control over that tin- and pepper-rich state from 1825. Nine years later they imposed a protectorate over nearby Jambi. From 1821 to 1838 Dutch armies also fought a grueling, ultimately successful war against the Wahhabi-like Padri Islamic reform movement in Minangkabau, which led to the imposition of Dutch authority over extensive parts of interior Sumatra for the first time. In coastal Borneo and Sulawesi the Dutch accepted a more nominal authority, but Maluku, Ambon in particular, resumed its earlier allegiance. Shorn of African, Sri Lankan, and Indian territories, the Netherlands' Asian holdings, in a development whose outlines had been clear from 1784, now became exclusively Southeast Asian, laying the foundation for the Netherlands East Indies of the early 1900s and, by extension, for

---

[328] Carey, *Power of Prophecy*, 602, 653–54.

[329] *HMI*, 159. Villagers normally received cash payments in excess of their land tax obligation. On the *cultuurstelsel*, ibid., 155–61; Carey, "Aspects," 79–87; Heather Sutherland, *The Making of a Bureaucratic Elite* (Kuala Lumpur, 1979), 1–18; Cornelius Fasseur, *The Politics of Colonial Exploitation* (Ithaca, 1992), esp. 26–55, 239–43.

Indonesia.[330] One thinks of comparably dramatic territorial extensions between 1750 and 1830 in all three mainland states, Russia, Napoleonic France, Qing China, and British India.

Cultural Cleavages in the Dutch Conquest State

Despite Dutch military and economic power, until the late 1800s the full reproduction of metropolitan culture in the Indies was impossible, and a degree of localization inevitable. After unsuccessful efforts to foster a white settler society by providing its servants with Dutch women, the VOC encouraged marriages to Asian women so as to create a Dutch-oriented mestizo population. Female slaves, many Portuguese-speaking, from South India and Sulawesi were particularly in demand. Thus, although wives were obliged to accept the faith of their Dutch Reformed husbands and children were baptized, a Dutch-Calvinist male culture joined itself to an Asian-Portuguese female counterpart. Within the home, the latter ethos tended to govern food, dress, entertainment, and female seclusion. An "official periwigged façade" came to hide a "batik, baggy-trousered domesticity."[331] Eighteenth-century European visitors never tired of denouncing the lasciviousness and ostentation of Batavian society (especially its female component), whose hybrid conventions found echoes in Semarang, Makasar, and Banda, not to mention more isolated outposts, but seemed distant indeed from European Dutch practices.[332]

And yet by maintaining cultural barriers as an aid to elite cohesion, the Dutch resembled Inner Asians in China and India. Indeed, despite domestic hybridity, three factors probably favored greater cultural distancing in the Dutch than in the Qing or Mughal realm. First, the Company's narrow economic goals and Calvinist commitment denied cultural borrowing official sanction. Second, whereas Manchus lacked

---

[330] *HMI*, 171–89; Dobbin, *Islamic Revivalism*; Andaya, *Live as Brothers*, 246–48; Knapen, *Forests*, 73–74; Jacobs, *Merchant in Asia*, 282.

[331] Kees Zandvliet, *The Dutch Encounter with Asia 1600–1950* (Amsterdam, 2002), 199. On Dutch "harems," Boomgaard, *Children*, 15.

[332] The metropolitan–colonial gap fed too on the large non-Dutch element among VOC personnel and on the lowly origins of many Dutch emigrants, described as "all the garbage of Holland." Andaya, *World of Maluku*, 42–43. On mestizo culture in Dutch-controlled areas, Taylor, *Social World*, 33–34, 52–79, 92; Blusse, *Strange Company*, 10, 156–81; Zandvliet, *Dutch Encounter*, 197–263; Boxer, *Dutch Seaborne Empire*, 215–30; Sutherland, "Ethnicity, Wealth"; Hanna, *Indonesian Banda*, 63–82; Andaya, "Melaka"; and esp. Bosma and Raben, *Being Dutch*, chs. 1–2.

a cultural system to rival Confucianism, the Dutch in Indonesia maintained, and from the late 1700s strengthened, ties to a Europe ever
more confident of its superiority over Asia. Third, New World slavery
may have heightened a peculiar Dutch racial sensitivity. Whereas 18th-
century Qing and Mughal elites gradually became more assimilated,
the Dutch – like the British in India – moved in the opposite direction.

Christian society under the VOC in the 17th and 18th centuries
embraced four circles of receding status and Dutch influence. At the core
high-ranking officials almost invariably were men born and schooled in
the Netherlands. Because such newcomers were privileged over locally
born whites, their language, dress, and customs automatically out-
ranked creole and mestizo norms. Among men at least, knowledge
of Dutch thus correlated with social rank. By limiting posts above assistant to men born in Holland, the VOC deliberately tried to combat
assimilation.[333] A second European circle, whose knowledge of Dutch
customs was inferior, comprised lesser whites, including creoles born
in Asia to European parents. Insofar as mestiza wives of Europeans and
legitimate offspring of European men by non-European women normally were included, this category was not strictly racial. Indeed, mestiza women often brought European men into patronage relations with
one another as in-laws. Yet VOC regulations privileging Europeans over
Eurasians, and frequent pejorative references to dark skin and Asian
features, indicated deeply rooted racial attitudes.[334] Eurasians constituted a third circle. If some Eurasian wives of VOC officers achieved
high status, in general VOC policy sought to keep Portuguese-speaking
Eurasians as a buffer between the mass of Asians and the thin layer
of European leaders.[335] The fourth, least Dutchified circle were Asian
Dutch Reform Christians, including Lusophone *Mardijkers* (whose Portuguese plumed hats and bare feet symbolized their mixed origins),
Indonesian dependents of the Dutch, and residents of Maluku. By converting Roman Catholic Malukuns to Calvinism and by trying (albeit

---

[333] Taylor, *Social World*, 25, 28, 45, 85; Blusse, *Strange Company*, 165; Ricklefs, *War, Culture*,
230.

[334] On this second category and racism, Blusse, *Strange Company*, 205; Taylor, *Social World*,
28, 34, 43, 45, 58, 71–76, 83; Boxer, *Dutch Seaborne Empire*, 230–33; Bosma and Raben,
Being Dutch, 22–24, 53–54; Hanna, *Indonesian Banda*, 81–82; Sutherland, "Ethnicity,
Wealth," 39–50; Andaya, "Melaka," 209–12; Bethencourt, "Low Cost Empire," 123.
On the role of creole (born in Asia to European parents), mestiza, even Asian women
as a link between European-born males in the Indies, Taylor, *Social World*, chs. 2, 3;
Sutherland, "Ethnicity, Wealth," 50.

[335] Taylor, *Social World*, 34, 44–45; Blusse, *Strange Company*, chs. 7, 8.

with little success) to promote Dutch language among Asian Christians, the VOC sought to fuse culture and loyalty and to associate Asian Christians with its rule.[336]

Outside these four circles – which probably totaled fewer than 100,000 Christians – perhaps 2,200,000 Javanese and other Indonesians and 100,000 "heathen" Chinese lay under a degree of Dutch control in 1800.[337] Did a sense of vulnerability linked to miniscule Dutch numbers reinforce Calvinist and racial spurs to insularity? Whatever its roots, such insularity, despite Dutch willingness to borrow isolated Asian elements in a domestic context, generated negative stereotypes and behavioral redlines.[338] As Barbara Watson Andaya noted, even in outlying posts VOC agents, unlike Chinese and Muslim traders, generally refused to be incorporated into local kinships networks through titles, privileges, and women. Gifts and treaties aside, few rituals or symbols joined them to indigenes.[339] In those urban settings where most Dutchmen lived, they occupied separate quarters and effectively banned natives from the inner city. Batavia's stone architecture and city grid were in fact transposed from Holland.[340] Nor, it must be emphasized, did Asian Christians and mestizos in Batavia offer a link to *local society* insofar as their lifestyles relied far more heavily on Portuguese, Indian, and Malay usages than on Javanese. If the Dutch of Batavia were a cultural amalgam, this mix owed remarkably little to Central and East Java. In vain we look for Dutch interest in Javanese art, dance, and music or cross-cultural explorations comparable to Akbar's

---

[336] By the late 1700s *Mardijkers* had largely assimilated to the Indonesian urban population. On Asian Christians under the VOC and the political import of language and religion, see nn. 331–33 *supra*, Andaya, *World of Maluku*, 181–82, 188; Sutherland, "Eastern Emporium," 114, 122–23; Andaya, *Flaming Womb*, 97, 101, 102; idem, "Melaka," 210–11, noting relative religious tolerance.

[337] Excluding Surakarta and Yogyakarta. See nn. 238, 239, 285, 291 *supra*; Carey, "Changing Javanese Perceptions," 14; *AC*, vol. I, 14. Yet Boomgaard, *Children*, 166, Table 14, claiming 6,268,000 people in Java in 1824, suggests higher figures than Ricklefs or Carey.

[338] On Dutch and Indonesian stereotypes alongside selective borrowing, see Ricklefs, *War, Culture*, 224–34; Donald Lach and Edwin van Kley, *Asia in the Making of Europe, vol. 3* (Chicago, 1993), 1300–1466, and discussion *infra*. On Dutch vs. Portuguese attitudes to mestizos, Bethencourt, "Low Cost Empire," 124–26.

[339] Andaya, *Live as Brothers*, 243–44. The English in Southeast Asia displayed much the same attitude. Boomgaard, *Children*, 14–15, while suggesting parallels between Dutch and Javanese elite lifestyles, offers no evidence of kinship ties.

[340] Yet Chinese were scattered throughout Batavia. Blusse, *Strange Company*, 84; Sutherland, "Ethnicity, Wealth," 41; Zandvliet, *Dutch Encounter*, 31–75; Jacobs, *Merchant in Asia*, 231.

Hindu-Muslim dialogue or Kangxi's Neo-Confucian patronage. Compared to the Mughals, the Dutch also showed scant interest in religious outreach, because proselytism was largely extraneous to the VOC's commercial raison d'être and they feared Muslim resentment. No Javanese Christians were to be found in the princely domains. In short, the VOC labored to maintain (what they regarded as) a Dutch identity, an enclave of Europeanness, on the fringe of Javanese society.[341]

Ricklefs argues that by multiplying insults and betrayals, the wars of 1677 to 1726 deepened cultural misunderstandings and exacerbated Dutch–Javanese enmity. Neither side felt a need to borrow, for neither in this period felt any sense of inadequacy.[342] From the mid-1700s new European cultural currents only reinforced Dutch detachment, at least among leading circles and especially in Batavia and Semarang. To strengthen identification with the homeland, VOC governors-general founded Dutch-language schools and a newspaper. Immigrant devotees of the Enlightenment promoted masonic lodges and a European academy of arts and sciences. The British interregnum, 1811–1816, brought a frontal assault on Asian-style female seclusion in Batavian high society. The decades following the introduction of Netherlands' direct rule in 1816 further eroded, if not mestizo culture, then mestizo political influence by promoting easier communications with Europe, Dutch-language education, an influx of Dutch-born officials, and civil service professionalism.[343]

Growing Dutch insularity found parallels among the Chinese. Although, in the aftermath of a 1740 Dutch massacre of Batavian Chinese, many upwardly mobile Chinese sought safety by embracing Islam and entering the Javanese aristocracy,[344] over the long term Dutch power encouraged Chinese segregation for three reasons. First,

---

[341] Ricklefs, *War, Culture*, 229–31; nn. 239, 338 *supra*. In some ways the debt Asian Christians and mestizos in Dutch settlements owed to Indian, Malay, and Portuguese culture continued cosmopolitan *pasisir* traditions already in evidence by the 15th century.

[342] Ricklefs, *War, Culture*, 224–34.

[343] Cf. the emphasis on the erosion of mestizo (*indische*) culture in Taylor, *Social World*, 78–128; Carey, "Aspects," 81, with the emphasis on continued *indische* vitality, a function of limited European immigration to c. 1870, in Bosma and Raben, *Being Dutch*, 17, 66–119, 184–229. Yet ibid., 71–76, 87, 90–94, 101, 106, 112, 187–94, 206–15, 220–28 is replete with examples of rising European cultural influence at variance with the book's general thesis.

[344] On changing Chinese attitudes to assimilation, see Reid, "Flows and Seepages," 41–48; Blusse, *Strange Company*, 73–96; Claudine Salmon, "The Han Family of East Java," *Archipel* 41 (1991): 53–87; Carey, "Changing Javanese Perceptions," 12–16.

in some locales the Dutch pursued a deliberate policy of divide and rule, opposing the assimilation of Chinese to Javanese culture, reclassifying partly assimilated (*peranakan*) Chinese as full Chinese, and banning them from local offices.[345] Second, as the prestige of Javanese aristocrats waned under Dutch and British assaults, entry into their ranks lost its allure.[346] (In this respect the islands differed from the mainland, where well into the 1800s the power of local elites rendered assimilation highly attractive.) If they been allowed to become Dutch, many Chinese no doubt would have done so, but this option was closed. Third, as Chinese immigration rose and as Chinese tax farmers and toll-keepers expanded their activities under the Dutch aegis, relations with Javanese peasants deteriorated sharply. Fierce anti-Chinese pogroms during the Java War dramatized and reinforced the growing ethnic divide.[347]

As for indigenous self-images, what information we have again comes from Java. By introducing a host of minatory invaders (Dutch, Madurese, Bugis, Balinese), chronic warfare to 1757 began to generate a pan-Javanese identity that, Ricklefs shows, was defined by Islam (thus distinguishing Javanese from Balinese as well as from Dutchmen), by a common tongue, and in some contexts, by the legacy of Majapahit.[348] According to Peter Carey, in reaction to the Europeanizing influences that had been sweeping over the south-central courts, Dipanagara resolved to elevate Islam and to restore specifically Javanese sartorial and linguistic codes, even to the point of obliging Dutch and Javanese prisoners to learn High Javanese and convert to Islam.[349] In literature Ann Kumar also finds early-19th-century evidence that alien intrusions inspired a more pronounced Javanese ethnic consciousness. But, sadly, this entailed a self-deprecating insistence on the military, commercial, even the moral inferiority of Javanese compared to both

---

[345] Mason Hoadley, "Javanese, Peranakan, and Chinese Elites in Cirebon," *JAS* 47 (1988): 503–18; idem, *Roots of the Chinese Minority "Problem" in Indonesia* (Stockholm, 1986); Blusse, *Strange Company*, 5.

[346] Previous note, and *AC*, vol. II, 311–19.

[347] By raising the barrier to assimilation, Javanese Islamic orthodoxy after c. 1750 had a similar impact. Carey, "Changing Javanese Perceptions," 16, 32–41; idem, *Power of Prophecy*, 617–20; Ricklefs, *Seen and Unseen*, 178–80; Reid, "Flows and Seepages," 45–46; Sutherland, "Eastern Emporium," 123–26; G. William Skinner, "Creolized Chinese Societies in Southeast Asia," in Reid, *Sojourners and Settlers*, 51–93. In coastal Sumatra and Borneo the appearance of large, "indigestible" Chinese mining and agricultural colonies also had an encapsulating effect. Trocki, "Chinese Pioneering."

[348] Ricklefs, *Mystic Synthesis*, 63–68, 77–79, 86–97, 103–25 passim, 143–44, 224–26; idem, *War, Culture*, 11–12, 173–74, 225; idem, *Modern Javanese Tradition*, 219–20.

[349] Carey, *Power of Prophecy*, 588–89, 617–21, 655.

Europeans and Chinese.[350] In any case, without a stable political center to define, promulgate, and monitor cultural boundaries, Javanese identities necessarily remained labile and inchoate.

In short, by the early 19th century, indeed by the 17th century, elements of what in the high colonial era would become known as a "plural society" could be found in Dutch-ruled areas. In such a society the conquest elite sought to insulate themselves culturally, socially, and religiously; overarching pan-ethnic institutions were minimal to nonexistent, and ethnic communities filled specific economic niches.[351] Admittedly, Eurasians played a more critical role in the Dutch Indies than in British India, and racial barriers were probably weaker. Yet in neither colony did the widening cultural and ethnic gap between Europeans and the host population have analogue in protected-zone societies.

Political and Cultural Integration in the Philippines, c. 1660–1830

Spain's Southeast Asia realm after 1660 never approached the dynamism of its Dutch counterpart. Seeking to curb Muslim raids and to prevent southern sultanates from allying with Dutch, French, or English forces, Spanish fleets from the 17th to the early 19th century repeatedly tried to reduce Sulu and Mindanao. In 1749 the Spanish succeeded in getting the (ex-)sultan of Sulu to accept baptism, but without lasting effect: within five years Muslim attacks on the coasts of Luzon and the Visayas had intensified, enslaving thousands each year to produce goods for the China trade. Pejoratively termed "Moros" by the Spanish, Muslim raiders, especially from Sulu, obtained guns and gunpowder from British country traders and, so equipped, maintained their depredations to the 1850s, albeit with diminishing effect from 1818.[352] Nor did Spanish arms to c. 1820 enjoy sustained success in pacifying and Christianizing the mountainous interior of northern Luzon.[353]

[350] Kumar, *Java and Modern Europe*, 88–92, 177–81, 382–420 *passim*, 431–32, 440–42.
[351] On the "plural society," J. S. Furnivall, *Colonial Policy and Practice* (New York, 1956), 303–12; Blusse's comment in n. 239 *supra*. Cf. Bosma and Raben, *Being Dutch*, 18, 215–18.
[352] On Moro Wars and European threats, Majul *Muslims*, chs. 4–7; Warren, *Iranun*, 11–13, 72–85, 101–23, 143–48, 251–52, 385–400; Robles, *Philippines*, 44–49, 149–53; David J. Steinberg, ed., *In Search of Southeast Asia* (Honolulu, 1985), 94–95.
[353] Felix Keesing, *The Ethnohistory of Northern Luzon* (Stanford, 1962), 11–14, 302–43 *passim*.

Notwithstanding this contrast between Dutch territorial expansion at the expense of Muslim powers and Spanish vulnerability to Muslim raids, both the Dutch and Spanish colonies in Southeast Asia, particularly from the mid-1700s, were transformed by European military and political pressures and more especially by rising global demand for cash crops.

European military pressures impacted the Philippines as early as the Dutch War of 1609–1648, which grew out of the Dutch revolt against Spain. Although it is not clear that Manila derived much long-term benefit from its wartime innovations, while the Dutch threat lasted Manila succeeded in imposing unprecedented levels of corvée (*polo*) and compulsory sale (*vandala*) in a generally successful effort to bolster the colony's naval defenses.[354] By temporarily halting the galleon trade and throwing the colony open to European merchants, the British occupation of Manila from 1762 to 1764 – also an artifact of European military conflicts, in this case the Seven Years War – raised the prospect that the islands might begin producing crops for global markets. After the British left, mercantilist thinkers in the Philippines and at the Spanish court, recognizing that near-exclusive reliance on the galleon trade condemned the colony in general and the public sector in particular to chronic poverty, sought to broaden the Philippines' economic base by encouraging new industries and by opening commercial routes to Europe, Latin America, and China. Accordingly, especially from 1770s Philippine governors sponsored cash crops and mining, opened direct trade with Spain, and created – in what turned out to be the only truly successful initiative – a profitable state tobacco monopoly. The loss of most of Spain's Latin American empire by 1824 – an indirect result of Europe's Napoleonic wars – favored further economic openings, both because that loss finally ended the galleon-based silver subsidy from Mexico, and because it brought a modest influx to the Philippines of Spanish refugees and capital. Somewhat as liberal economic theories sanctioned post-VOC experiments on Java, liberal doctrines provided a rationale for the official opening of Manila to foreign trade – in 1790 to European ships carrying Asian goods, and in 1834 to all foreign traffic.[355]

---

[354] Phelan, *Hispanization*, 12–13, 99–102, 146; Larkin, *Pampangans*, 26.
[355] Larkin, "Philippine History," 606–16; idem, *Pampangans*, 41–84; Ed. C. de Jesus, *The Tobacco Monopoly in the Philippines* (Quezon City, 1980); Legarda, *After Galleons*, 46, 51–217 *passim*; Steinberg, *In Search*, 92–94, 160–63; Cushner, *Spain in Philippines*, 186–202.

But most basically, the political economy evolved in the 18th and early 19th centuries because rising global demand eroded formal restrictions and pushed official policy, willy-nilly, toward greater openness. From 1591 to 1735, while the galleon trade still dominated, the Philippine population grew at an utterly anemic annual rate of .16 percent.[356] Even on friar estates near Manila much of the land was either unused or devoted to grazing.[357] However, particularly from the mid-1700s, legal and more especially illegal shipping by British country traders and Chinese merchants created a novel, if by later standards still modest, market for Philippine goods ranging from birds' nests to textiles, with a growing emphasis on sugar, tobacco, and other agrarian products. Inevitably, smuggling raised the price for domestic goods and lowered the cost of imports, which generated pressures for further liberalization.

From the late 1810s to 1830s a fresh constellation of market forces intensified the production of indigo, abaca, rice, sugar, and tobacco for export. These elements included the post-Napoleonic freeing up of Western shipping, a new sweet tooth in Europe and America, the decline of West Indies sugar after the abolition of slavery, and the opening of British and American merchant houses in Manila. In 1818 local goods already comprised 60 percent of all exports, and the number of foreign ships visiting Manila began rising steeply.[358] By providing new sources of income, the export economy in turn joined a post-1818 reduction in Moro raids and a switch from millet to maize in the Visayas to enhance female fertility and to push annual population growth across the Spanish Philippines to 1.06 percent from 1735 to 1818, and 1.7 percent from 1800 to 1850.[359] Especially in those fertile areas of Luzon with easy access to the port of Manila, cultivation became more intensive and landholding more concentrated. From the 1820s growing land scarcities and deteriorating terms of tenancy produced social tensions and increased banditry, along with a novel movement of frontier colonization that would gather pace into the early 20th century.

[356] Larkin, "Philippine History," 602.
[357] Ibid., 603.
[358] Foreign (chiefly British, American, and Chinese) ships rose from 55 in 1818 to 136 in 1832 to 235 in 1844. Legarda, *After Galleons*, 101, 111. On export growth, n. 355 *supra*, plus Larkin, *Sugar*, 23–27. The chief imports were Chinese, Indian, and European manufactures.
[359] Larkin, "Philippine History," 611; Doeppers and Xenos, *Population and History*, 3–6; Spencer, "Rise of Maize."

Pioneering groups of townmates or kinsmen now pushed out from densely populated older centers of settlement into virgin flatlands suitable for sugar, abaca, and commercial rice, areas such as Tarlac and Neuva Ecija in central Luzon and the western Visayas.[360] The development of Philippine export agriculture from the late 1700s therefore represented a delayed version of sugar, indigo, and coffee cultivation in Java, first under the VOC and then under the *cultuurstelsel.*

Commercial and demographic vigor combined with Moro and European military threats to mandate a larger, more activist administration in the Philippines in the same period as Dutch administration in Java sought to extend its influence. Given the immediacy of the Moro danger, not surprisingly some of the most ambitious 18th- and early-19th-century century reforms focused on improving coastal defenses and upgrading military and naval pay and training. To the mid-1800s colonial armed forces continued to swallow over 70 percent of revenues.[361] Yet after 1780 the export economy also began to generate demands for improved civilian infrastructure, including better roads, port facilities, policing, and judicial regulation.[362] At the same time port duties and the tobacco monopoly provided the wherewithal to finance such projects. In Manila between 1800 and 1830 we thus find a proliferation of agencies, including a General Intendancy of finance, along with desultory efforts at functional specialization.[363] The 12 provinces of 1650 had become 32 by 1840, and many *pueblos* were subdivided.[364]

---

[360] On agrarian expansion, Larkin, "Philippine History," 613–22; idem, *Pampangans*, 23–24, 45; idem, *Sugar*, 20–35; Michael Cullinane and Peter Xenos, "The Growth of Population in Cebu During the Spanish Era," in Doeppers and Xenos, *Population and History*, 71–138; Dennis Roth, "Church Lands in the Agrarian History of the Tagalog Region," in Alfred McCoy and Ed. C. de Jesus, eds., *Philippine Social History* (Honolulu, 1982), 131–53; Cushner, *Landed Estates*, 69–70; Bankoff, *Crime, Society*, 16–17, 59–65, 77.

[361] Excluding remittances to Spain. Robles, *Philippines*, 162–65; Steinberg, *In Search*, 92–94. On improved coastal defenses, Warren, *Iranun*, ch. 5.

[362] Criminal cases before the *real audiencia* in Manila mushroomed from 53 in 1779 to 5,125 by 1879. Bankoff, *Crime, Society*, 106. We have no data on civil cases, but as land became more valuable and as communal ownership yielded to individual possession, litigation over land tenures also rose sharply. Ibid., 16.

[363] Bankoff, *Crime, Society*, 116–18; Robles, *Philippines*, 137–66. Discussion of administration 1770–1840 relies on Bankoff, *Crime, Society*; idem, *In Verbo Sacerdotis* (Darwin, 1992); idem, "Big Fish in Small Ponds," *MAS* 26 (1992): 679–700; Robles, *Philippines*, chs. 1–6; Onofre Corpuz, *The Bureaucracy in the Philippines* (Manila, 1957), chs. 2–7; Michael Cullinane, "Accounting for Souls," in Doeppers and Xenos, *Population and History*, 281–346.

[364] Cf. Phelan, *Hispanization*, 128; Robles, *Philippines*, 98, 101.

Proliferating tasks and more regular capital–provincial communications also favored higher educational qualifications for Spanish governors and greater Spanish language competence by *indio gobernadorcillos* and their aides. Because parish records provided the chief data for tax assessments, Manila pressured parish priests to furnish more regular, detailed, and standardized reports. Priests remained the bedrock of Spanish control in the countryside, but from the late 1700s and more especially in the early 1800s the state sought to supplement that instrument with its own expanded police and judicial apparatus. To control banditry, to protect goods moving to market, above all, to enforce its tobacco monopoly, Manila created, with mixed results, a treasury police (1780s) and a new rural constabulary (1807). The law became codified along Napoleonic lines, punishments became more uniform, and the courts more professional. These efforts persisted in the face of predatory official corruption, itself partly a function of chronically inadequate salaries.[365]

If export agriculture thus modified Philippine administration, its impact on Philippine social structure was yet more dramatic. Although Spaniards and Spanish mestizos were active in a few industries and locales,[366] Chinese mestizos became by far the most dynamic and visible agents of change. The expulsion from the Philippines of most full-blooded Chinese in 1766, following their ill-judged support of the British occupation, removed the principal barrier to Chinese mestizo inroads in wholesaling, retailing, crafts, and moneylending. Descended from Chinese merchants and *indio* mothers, the latter often from elite *indio* families, mestizos typically combined their father's commercial orientation with their mothers' Catholic cultural affinity and social access. Having cornered the shipment of sugar and rice from central Luzon to the capital, Chinese mestizos moved on to control rural credit, the introduction of sugar machinery, the distribution of Western imports, the management of estates owned by the friar orders, and landholding itself, which in turn provided a base for entry into law and the professions. Constituting some 5 percent of the population in 1810 but heavily concentrated in the most economically advanced parts of the Philippines, as they became more closely identified with landed wealth,

---

[365] Bankoff, *Crime, Society,* 7–16, 31, 97 and *passim,* and n. 363 *supra.*

[366] See, e.g., Larkin, *Pampangans,* 35, 79–80, 84, 86 n. 45, 90; McCoy and Jesus, *Social History,* 66–67, 258, 261, 274. Friar estates played a larger role, but their management devolved to Chinese mestizos. Cushner, *Landed Estates,* chs. 3–5.

Chinese mestizos infiltrated, displaced, and merged into the old *indio* *principales* class to the point where in many provinces by 1820 it was no longer possible to distinguish native and Chinese mestizo elites.[367]

In the process Chinese mestizos came to embrace Spanish culture ever more enthusiastically. Unlike non-Christian Chinese immigrants, whose periodic expulsion the Spanish justified on religious grounds, early generations of Chinese mestizos identified as Christians. Of course, their early understanding of Catholicism, like *indio* folk Christianity, remained syncretic and idiosyncratic. Early mestizo dress, names, and language also blended *indio*, Spanish, and Chinese elements. But as their income, education, and urban contacts expanded, mestizos began self-consciously to distance themselves from both *indio* culture, which was decidedly low prestige, and Chinese culture, which was "heathen," in favor of elite Spanish practices as displayed in Manila, Cebu, and other urban centers. This came to entail ostentatious religiosity, lavish church endowments, careful imitation of Spanish speech, dress, and manners; and Spanish-language education culminating, when possible, in the study law or theology at Manila. In general, the wealthier, better educated the individual, the stronger his/her identification with Spanish Catholic norms and the greater the distance from indigenous practices.[368]

In varying degrees, self-Hispanization affected the *indio* population as well. Insofar as mestizo and *indio* landholders fused into a new provincial elite, educated *indios* internalized the same values as their mestizo colleagues/relatives and pursued the same Hispanic status markers.[369] But we find evidence of modified sensibilities even at lower levels of *indio* society, among illiterate, ostensibly insulated smallholders, tenants, sharecroppers, and laborers with fewer mestizo connections. Thus in northern and central Luzon and Cebu in the late 1700s and early 1800s, as population rose, as rural–*pueblo* communication became easier, and as religious confraternities extended their influence,

---

[367] On Chinese mestizos, Wickberg, *Chinese*, 17–31 (population figures at 25); Larkin, *Pampangans*, 48–62, 84–88. idem, *Sugar*, 33–34; Bruce Cruikshank, "Continuity and Change in the 19th-Century Economic and Administrative History of Samar," in McCoy and Jesus, *Social History*, 219–49.

[368] Conversely, poorer mestizos in contact with *indios* or Chinese might be reclaimed by either of those communities. Wickberg, *Chinese*, chs. 1, 2, 5; Larkin, *Pampangans*, 58–59, 84–85, 93–94; Michael Cullinane, "The Changing Nature of the Cebu Urban Elite in the 19th Century," in McCoy and Jesus, *Social History*, 251–96.

[369] Previous note, plus Andaya, *Flaming Womb*, 102.

attendance at church festivals increased, Christian names became more common, and communion, marriage, and last rites were observed more widely.[370] According to Vicente Rafael, among Tagalog-speaking *indios* only in the early 1700s did understandings of Christianity finally allow internalization of basic doctrines; only then, imitating the style and substance of Spanish missionaries, did *indio* elites find ways to reorient their followers' fear of malevolent spirits toward Christian notions of heaven and hell and a beautiful death.[371] Significant too was the growing frequency and ostentation with which local shamans, even anti-Spanish rebels in outlying regions, deployed Christian motifs. Thus, for example, Visayan *baylans* ("native priests") combined folk and Catholic beliefs in an idiosyncratic mysticism.[372] With the opening of the agrarian frontier after 1820 the dominance of lowland Christian culture became ever more entrenched throughout Luzon and the Visayas, and the vertical penetration of Spanish culture acquired a fresh horizontal counterpart.[373]

In two respects, one could conclude, Dutch and Spanish colonialism, despite similar military and administrative pressures, were mirror images, that is to say opposite, of one another. First, whereas export agriculture strengthened the Dutch in both their public and private capacities at the expense of local elite autonomy, in the Philippines cash cropping enhanced the economic and social position of Chinese mestizos and some *indio* families, while conferring relatively few benefits on the Spanish. Neither the Spanish government nor Spanish entrepreneurs could match the social networks and low overheads of Chinese mestizos. Likewise, whereas the Dutch government established the Netherlands Trading Company in 1824–1825 in a successful effort to market *cultuurstelsel* products in Europe and so break British and American dominance of shipping in the Dutch Indies, the Philippines continued to rely on British, American, and Chinese shippers, with whose capital, expertise, and connections the Spanish could never compete. By 1879

---

[370] Cortes, *Pangasinan*, 99–128; Cullinane, "Accounting," 291–96; Deirdre Leong de la Cruz, "All His Instruments" (Columbia Univ., PhD diss., 2006), ch. 2 and *passim*.

[371] Rafael, *Contracting*, 211 and 188–209.

[372] Larkin, "Philippine History," 605; Cortes, *Pangasinan*, 175–99, 221; nn. 212, 213 *supra*; and after 1840, Reynaldo Ileto, *Pasyon and Revolution* (Quezon City, 1979).

[373] Larkin, "Philippine History," 613. However, not only did lowland Christianity make little headway with hillpeoples, but as Christians who returned to the hills (*remontados*) showed, cultural currents could flow in the opposite direction. Keesing, *Ethnohistory of Northern Luzon*, 302–43; Larkin, *Sugar*, 38–39; Phelan, *Hispanization*, 140–42.

the Philippines were described as an "Anglo-Chinese colony with a Spanish Flag."[374]

Second and rather ironically in view of the two nations' very different economic and military performance, the Dutch to 1830 had an extremely modest cultural impact. But Spain succeeded in transmitting a substantial degree of Christian culture to the entire lowland population of Luzon and the Visayas, and most especially to the mestizo-cum-*indio arrivistes* who regarded aristocratic Hispanization as a badge of success. As I have emphasized, this discrepancy grew largely from the fact that by 1565 Islam was far more entrenched in the future Dutch than in the future Spanish sphere. In addition, Spain's willingness to commit to an evangelization that (apart from concentrating people for corvée labor and taxes) offered the crown few economic benefits reflected a "civilizing," proselytizing zeal foreign to the VOC and its state successor.[375] The contrast between the growing insularity of Chinese-descended communities in Java and the enthusiastic self-Hispanization of Chinese mestizos in the Philippines well illustrates these divergent paths.

These, then, were major economic and cultural differences between the Dutch and Spanish enterprises. Yet overarching parallels are no less striking and speak to our larger Eurasian concerns. Both the Dutch and Spanish were militarized peoples from outside the region who transformed local political structures and, to maintain cohesion, systematically excluded indigenous elements from official culture. Admittedly, all northern and central Philippine lowlanders shared with the Spanish a nominal faith. Yet this in no way gainsaid Spanish self-segregation or "plural society" divisions. From 1741 laws specifically separated residents into four categories – Spanish and Spanish mestizos, Chinese, Chinese mestizos, and *indios* – each with distinct rights, obligations, and administrative structures. To the end of the colonial period the Spanish language remained unknown to over 90 percent of Filipinos (although admittedly those who did master Spanish enjoyed considerable influence and opportunities for social mobility).[376] Conversely, apart from the friars, few Spaniards spoke local vernaculars or indeed had sustained contact with *indios*. Non-Spaniards remained barred from supralocal office and, in practice, from desirable church positions. An

374 Legarda, *After Galleons*, 93. Cf. *HMI*, 156.
375 Of course, Spanish rule also made possible the galleon trade, but while profitable for individual and institutional ticket-holders, that trade could only function with heavy state subsidies.
376 See n. 218 *supra*.

attempt from 1767 to replace Spanish parish priests with *indio* and Chinese mestizo clerics, many of whom were poorly trained, proved to be a disaster and was eventually abandoned. In a comment on alleged *indio* incompetence, Spaniards quipped that there were no longer any men to row the ferry boats in Manila because the archbishop had ordained them all.[377] The vitality, or at least the self-confidence, of Manila no less than of Batavia required regular infusions of European ideas and personnel. Spaniards born in Spain looked down on those born in the colonies. All Spaniards felt superior to Spanish mestizos, who regarded as inferior Chinese and Chinese mestizos, who felt themselves above *indios*. "The whole fabric of colonial society in the Philippines," Greg Bankoff concludes, "was structured along racial lines."[378]

Therefore, if Eurasians in the Dutch Indies, by virtue of European ancestry, tended to enjoy a higher social status than Chinese mestizos in the Philippines, the caste-like layering of both societies was basically comparable. Again one might invoke Russia to argue that there as in the Philippines hereditary, legal divisions fractured religious community, while elites looked to western Europe for inspiration and knew a language (French) different from that of the peasantry. But Philippine social distinctions, based on race and ethnicity, were far more stark than in Russia, all of whose core population prided themselves on being Great Russians and used Russian as their primary tongue.[379] And while political subordination to a distant metropole was the essence of Spanish and Dutch colonialism, that feature was entirely absent in Eurasia's early modern protected zone, Russia included.

CONCLUSION: THE ISLANDS AND THE MAINLAND

By way of summation, let us return to the chapter's opening theme, the relation of island to mainland Southeast Asia. For much of their history these regions exhibited comparable rhythms. In the late first and early

---

[377] This followed the expulsion of Jesuits from the Spanish empire. Steinberg, *In Search*, 162–63. On racial barriers, ibid., 162–66; Cushner, *Spain in Philippines*, 212–20; Larkin, *Pampangans*, 49–50; Rafael, *Contracting*, 185–86; Robles, *Philippines*, 33–44; and nn. 218–221 *supra*. But for a far more sympathetic portrait of the Filipino clergy, again see Santiago, *Hidden Light*.

[378] Bankoff, *Crime, Society*, 38–39, plus 6–7, 11–12, 95–97, 126–28. The post-1820 influx of Spaniards only heightened tensions.

[379] Cf. discussion of Russia vs. exposed zones in discussion preceding Ch. 5, nn. 256, 260 and Ch. 6, n. 334.

second millennia both supported unprecedentedly expansive charter polities, namely, Pagan, Angkor, Dai Viet, Srivijaya, and Classical Java. All these realms drew strength from South Asian and/or Chinese models, intra-Asian trade, and – except for Srivijaya – from rapid post-900 agrarian and demographic growth. All patronized elitist cultures that stood apart from both village systems and postcharter court traditions. All collapsed between c. 1300 and 1527, in part through the intersection of institutional weaknesses with the centrifugal pull of maritime commerce. East Java's ability to stand on two legs, to combine agrarian with mercantile wealth, helps to explain its superior longevity, but in the end Majapahit too failed to contain coastal extremities.

In mainland river valleys and along archipelagic coasts, the years c. 1350 to 1510 were an era of postcharter experiment and political reorganization. Revived demand for Southeast Asian products and for goods transiting Southeast Asian waters encouraged new cash crops and port-based polities. So too the dissemination of Islam and synergies between Islam and Malay ethnicity recall the spread across the mainland of Theravada Buddhism and Neo-Confucianism, along with Burmese, Siamese, and Vietnamese ethnicity.

After c. 1510 a familiar early modern cast of characters – improved firearms, a further expansion of Eurasian demand, imported cultural models, administrative experiment – continued to promote more efficiently interventionist polities. This characterization applies to states on the mainland as well as in the islands, to indigenous as well as to European colonial regimes. Burma, Ayudhya, Vietnam, Aceh, Johor, Banten, Makasar, Mataram, the VOC state, the Spanish Philippines – all faced broadly similar pressures and entertained a limited set of responses. Aceh, Banten, and Mataram, for example, were quick to adopt and, in some cases improve upon, European military and commercial organization at the same time as they pursued provincial reforms similar to those in Burma and Siam. As a discourse that was privileged over animism by state sanction and literate monopoly and that diffused both vertically and horizontally, Christianity in the Spanish Philippines bears comparison to Theravada Buddhism on the mainland. Late-18th-century crises shattered institutions and demanded reforms no less sweeping in Chakri Siam than in the VOC Indies. The upward mobility of Chinese mestizos in the Philippines recalls commercially driven mobility in defiance of custom and law in 18th- to early-19th-century Burma and Siam.

Finally, both in the islands and on the mainland European interventions in the 1820s and 1830s constituted a watershed between the "early modern" and the "modern" eras, and thus offer a fit ending to the present study. Such interventions included the sudden irruption of European power on the mainland during the First Anglo-Burmese War, Singapore's founding, the Anglo-Dutch Treaty of 1824, the Java War, and the opening of Manila.

But set against these shared traits were three seminal differences between continental and archipelagic Southeast Asia. First, geography – frequently indifferent soils, far-flung ports, limited riverine arteries – imposed a lower ceiling on territorial and administrative consolidation in most archipelagic states, Java included. At any given period, this meant a larger number of contending polities, more pronounced discontinuities, and – without stable centers to maintain kingdom-specific norms – relatively weak politicized ethnicity.

Second, their modest agrarian base, their position athwart the chief east–west trade routes, their extraordinary high ratio of coast to interior, and their fine spices and pepper rendered the islands more dependent on international commercial rhythms than most mainland areas. I say this with some hesitation, because our understanding of agrarian history in areas like Java and South Sulawesi is rudimentary. Yet across the archipelago maritime trade seems to have dominated not only political economy, but religious life, as the rapid penetration of trade-mediated Islam suggests. To the extent that Islam diverged more profoundly from charter-era Hindu-Buddhism than did Theravada Buddhism, Islam reinforced the discontinuity of island culture.

The third critical distinction, also a function of geography and commercial attraction, was the islands' early vulnerability to European power. The Spanish from 1571 initiated a transformation more profound than anything attempted by Europeans in mainland Southeast Asia even after 1824. The Portuguese and the Dutch, pursuing more narrow commercial goals in a more complex universe than Spain encountered, had less immediate impact. And yet over the long term the Dutch also modified some of the main lines of archipelagic development by eclipsing Muslim states, weakening indigenous urbanization, forging a political/commercial network more extensive than anything Srivijaya or Majapahit had attempted, and conferring a unique prestige on their own ethnicity and culture. Obviously the new Dutch and Spanish domains were on a different scale than Inner Asian empires. But as

893

extraregional actors, culturally insulated from their subjects, whose military and organizational superiority allowed them to deform regional politics and to create early modern systems more powerful than any indigenous precedent, "white Inner Asians" in Southeast Asia filled a role analogous to that of Manchus and Mughals in their respective spheres.

Insofar as the islands saw the creation of European-defined zones long before mainland Southeast Asia, one might conclude that the islands were precocious. But viewed from the perspective of the 10th century, the opposite view is more convincing. Such was European power in the archipelago that the territorial creations of the Dutch, Spanish, and eventually the British bore minimal relation to precolonial configurations. By contrast, once they arrived on the mainland the British and French were obliged to accept, with minor modifications, the tripartite political and ethnic division between Burma, Siam, and Vietnam that had been evolving since 900 or 1000. In this sense precolonial changes across the mainland were both more precocious and enduring than in the island world. The difference was essentially between a sphere that remained part of Eurasia's protected zone from 800 to 1824, and a sphere that in the 16th and 17th centuries began to shift, partially, fitfully, and unevenly, from protected- to exposed-zone status.

Conclusion

At Eurasia's northwestern and southeastern extremities, two large peninsulas often have been considered exceptions to the general course of human history, albeit in diametrically opposed fashion. Europe has been seen as a site of a unique economic and political dynamism that distinguished its peoples from the rest of mankind by the 16th, if not the 13th, century. Mainland Southeast Asia frequently has been portrayed as a backwater, a residual region between China and India, easily influenced by external agents, but prone to inertia and lacking its own dynamic.[1]

I argue that in fact both peninsulas followed comparable political and cultural trajectories according to ever more synchronized chronologies. These odd congruences, these "strange parallels," provide my point of departure to consider patterns of political and cultural construction across Eurasia.

My central thesis is that over at least a thousand years vast stretches of Eurasia, including Southeast Asia, Europe, Japan, China, and South Asia, responded in broadly comparable ways to coordinated economic, climatic, and military stimuli. Most regions, for example, saw a great upsurge in economic and political vitality in the late first and early second millennia, and again for much of the 16th and 17th centuries. In every case the latter era generated an unprecedentedly expansive, internally specialized "early modern" political and cultural system whose essential features endured to the early 1800s. At the same time, I argue

---

[1] See my analysis of Eurocentric, autonomous, and Age of Commerce historiography at *SP*, 5–21 and historiographic discussion at Ch. 1, Pt. 1 *supra*.

that in chronology, agency, and scale, Eurasian integration may profitably be subdivided into two moderately distinct patterns, those of the "protected zone," including mainland and (to 1571) island Southeast Asia, most of Europe, and Japan; and the "exposed zone," including China and South Asia.

This approach is not necessarily hostile to European exceptionalism. Clearly, some European traits were uniquely favorable to the accumulation of economic and military power. But I seek to complement that traditional view by showing that Europe embodied idiosyncratic variations on a pattern of cyclic-cum-linear coalescence that operated over several centuries from the English Channel to the Java Sea.

Consider first our six protected-zone case studies: Burma, Siam, Vietnam, Russia and France (which together I take as representative of diverse European experiences), and Japan. Even within this limited category I have been at pains to acknowledge differences in everything from geographic inheritance to charter acculturation, demography, political penetration, and cultural circulation. Such discrepancies are hardly surprising, given the physical and cultural distances at play. What is truly extraordinary, what demands explanation, is the coexistence of such particularities with ever more insistent parallels.

In the second half of the first millennium all six protected-zone realms imported literate cultures from older centers to forge states that provided a territorial, religious, and institutional "charter" for later generations. All six owed their rise to new intra-elite accommodations, new labor systems, perhaps to coordinated disease immunities, and to expanded external contacts, commercial as well as cultural. Yet by later standards charter polities tended to remain superficial, culturally deeply elitist, and dependent on religious institutions to supplement as yet weak lay administrations.

Between 1240 and 1470, moreover, polities in all six regions collapsed through a mix of institutional and economic woes among which the destabilizing effects of centuries of agrarian/commercial expansion may have been most potent. The inadequacy of early institutions now became painfully obvious in Kievan princely disputes, English challenges to Valois suzerainty, and provincial devolution in Pagan, Angkor, Dai Viet, and Ashikaga Japan. In Southeast Asia and Europe the waning of the Medieval Climate Anomaly after 1250/1300 and Mongol actions compounded these problems. Mongol dislocations were both direct, through military assaults; and indirect, through Tai migrations, commercial shifts, and the dissemination of the Black Death, which moved along commercial pathways opened during the previous centuries of high medieval growth.

At various points between c. 1450 and 1560 consolidation resumed in all six realms and continued to the 1820s and beyond. Admittedly, Southeast Asia and parts of Europe experienced two additional periods of breakdown. Yet 18th-century disturbances typically were less prolonged and territorially disruptive than those of the late 1500s, which in turn were less severe than those of the 13th to 15th centuries. The possibility, still very much alive in 1400, that Burma, Muscovy, or France would be fundamentally reconfigured or simply disappear grew increasingly remote. If Japan knew only one prolonged interregnum, the Tokugawa regime – like contemporary states in Southeast Asia, Russia, and France – was by far the most powerful its region had yet produced.

In fact, in each realm between c. 1500 and 1830 consolidation had three dimensions. The justification for labeling these centuries "early modern" resides precisely in the fact that all three features anticipated post-1830 patterns.[2] Most obvious was territorial integration. After 1450 or 1500 in each region we find a continuous reduction in the number of independent political units. Insofar as larger states required more effective provincial controls, while the concentration of resources that issued from improved coordination aided conquest, territorial expansion was symbiotic with the second trend, namely, administrative reform. Typically, outlying zones were assimilated to the status of home provinces, while regulation in the core grew more efficient. Everywhere, too, secular authorities curbed the autonomy of charter-era religious institutions. All six countries had a modest population over which preindustrial technologies could exert progressive control, and with the partial exception of Vietnam, all boasted a natural center of gravity in a privileged economic/demographic core.

Our third integrative trend involved the consolidation of myriad parochial ethnicities, dialects, and religious practices inherited from the charter era to yield cultures that were ever more coherent and polity specific. All six cultures engendered extensive horizontal niche specialization (as in consumer goods and reading material) at the same time as vertical territorial fissures retreated. The ensuing sense of what I term "politicized ethnicity" differed from modern nationalism insofar as it was juridically hierarchic rather than egalitarian, accorded indigestible minorities a secure status, promoted universal religious themes

---

[2] See discussion attending Ch. 1, nn. 19, 93 *supra*.

alongside secular culture, and located sovereignty in the person of the ruler. Like nationalism, however, politicized ethnicity championed a discrete sub-universal culture, elevated particular markers as symbols of allegiance, looked to the capital to define and police cultural boundaries, and was symbiotic with political centralization. If cultural shifts relied on gradual, capillary processes more than did territorial change, they too accelerated after 1500 and more especially 1700.

A fluid mix of material pressures influenced all three integrative processes. Demographic and agrarian growth favored political consolidation by expanding the base for taxation and military recruitment and by multiplying commercial linkages that lubricated state operations. Population growth itself drew strength from enhanced pacification, rising market incentives, novel crops, more productive smallholder regimes, and favorable climate. If improved agrarian technique gradually reduced climate's impact, hemispheric warming – by extending the growing season in northern Europe and by increasing rainfall in Southeast Asia – helped to coordinate agricultural expansion for much of the period from 850 to 1250, from 1470 to 1570, and from 1710 to 1800. The fact that Japanese climate during the Medieval Climate Anomaly was unfavorable and population stagnated reinforces the putative link between climate and demography. Post-1450 demographic compensation for the Black Death in Europe and for major losses in China also synchronized expansion through its impact on settlement, bullion flows, and market linkages. Most critical perhaps, maritime trade after 1500 boosted output around the Eurasian perimeter by disseminating new crops, technologies, consumer goods, and bullion.

No less conducive to political integration than rising population and output was Smithian specialization, which was simultaneously local, regional, and international. In all six realms, albeit to varying degrees, urban markets encouraged a long-term shift from unwieldy in-kind levies to cash taxes, from devolutionary land grants to more easily controlled salaries and commercial favors, and from administrative generalists to technical specialists. Everywhere too the rising importance of market access led local elites to support a coordinating agency that could protect trade, unify legal jurisdictions, improve transport, control coinage, share revenues, and underwrite privilege. In other words, centralization often reflected local initiatives as much as, if not more than, capital demands. We thus find a virtuous circle in which commercialization in privileged cores aided political centralization, which facilitated economic growth. By empowering the wealthiest, most innovative principalities, the introduction of firearms in Europe by the mid-1400s, and in Southeast Asia and Japan a century later, dramatically reinforced this circularity.

Of course, as repeated breakdowns suggest, economic growth could destabilize society by creating shortages of land, offices, or currency, and by opposing market demands to social ascription. Eighteenth-century tensions in France between market mobility and hereditary restriction were only the most acute illustration of a trend roiling all six societies. But over the long run, particularly in response to military crises, governments in all six realms succeeded in harnessing the new wealth.

On balance, economic expansion also favored cultural circulation. By boosting literacy, widening avenues of communication, and encouraging frontier settlement, such growth disseminated the cultural norms of capital elites, while reducing the charter-era chasm between elite and popular sensibilities. Symptom and cause of cultural integration, provincial dialects eroded, textual religions penetrated the countryside, literacy rose sharply, and vernacular literatures and/or demotic writing systems grew at the expense of elite charter languages. To the extent that cultural integration enhanced identification with the capital and disciplined rural society without a commitment of scarce central resources, such shifts were inherently sympathetic to political centralization. Likewise, insofar as imitation of capital norms responded to local dynamics – snobbery, patronage, autonomous movements of religious reform – cultural integration, like political centralization, expressed bottom-up initiatives as much as top-down imposition.

As states became more powerful, warfare grew in scale, duration, and cost. At the same time territorial expansion amplified the danger of foreign-assisted provincial revolt. To surmount such challenges, Southeast Asian and European states were compelled systematically to reform their militaries and to improve provincial and fiscal controls. Parallel reforms in different regions often involved independent responses to antecedent breakdowns whose simultaneity in turn reflected coordinated economic pressures. Japan confirmed the tie between competition and innovation insofar as that country's most intense era of civil war, 1467–1603, saw the most ambitious administrative experiments. More broadly, enhanced size and technical competence allowed ambitious polities to modify a) their economic environment so as to magnify agrarian and commercial revenues, and b) their cultural environment so as to promote local identification with capital norms. To such deliberate interventions must be added inadvertent state stimuli to the economy and to cultural circulation.

Moreover, as state capacities improved, as firearms spread more widely, and as economies interpenetrated, cycles of construction and collapse across the protected zone meshed more closely. Thus whereas the French kingdom arose over 400 years earlier than those of Russia or Burma and experienced its first interregnum while the latter were still in their heyday, thereafter all three regions – along with central and eastern mainland Southeast Asia – experienced breakdowns in three increasingly narrow time spans, between 1240 and 1390, 1562 and 1613, and 1752 and 1793. After 1500 Japanese development also paralleled more closely that of other rimlands.

Finally, as befit our definition of the protected zone, all six polities, especially after 1400, remained immune to occupation by alien conquest elites. In Russia, Mongol-Tatars never attempted direct rule, and in any case, lost power in the 15th century. Sustained Tai migrations halted in the 14th century. Usual class markers aside, capital elites in all six realms embraced the same ethnicity and religion as the majority of their subjects and vigorously sought to disseminate those identities among outlying populations.

Turning to the exposed zone, represented by China and South Asia, we find many of the same patterns, dynamics, and rhythms. In distinguishing between protected and exposed zones, it was never my intention to replace the traditional Europe versus Asia dichotomy with a new all-encompassing binary.

In China, for example, although sustained political integration began at least 700 years earlier than in post-Roman Gaul, the Han empire was a charter equivalent to the Frankish kingdom, Angkor, Kiev, *ritsuryo* Japan, and so forth, and its collapse ushered in the longest, most disruptive of successive interregna. Between that breakdown and the short-lived passage from Ming to Qing lay dynastic transitions of intermediate duration and rupture, thus anticipating the pattern of progressively shorter interregna that we encounter in Southeast Asian realms, France, and Russia. In China as in the protected zone, administrative experiment both reflected and facilitated a growing political and cultural solidity. Adumbrated in some respects under the Han Dynasty, bureaucratic governance matured during the Song and reached fullest expression under the Qing, whose achievement coincided with the epitome of protected-zone statecraft. The Qing, moreover, doubled Ming territories. From Han to Qing, aided by frontier colonization, proliferating markets, printing, lineage organizations, examinations, and other forms of state patronage, we see as well a more or less continuous horizontal extension and redefinition of Chinese ethnicity, family norms, and written culture; and from the late Tang to Qing, a substantial narrowing of the once vast gap between elite and mass cultural practices. A final similarity that in varying degrees shaped all other trends was economic growth coordinated between China and other sectors of Eurasia, with vitality particularly notable c. 800/900 to 1270, 1470 to 1640, and 1700 to 1830. China's first commercial revolution and the onset of Song bureaucracy thus coincided with charter-era reorganization in the protected zone, while the second commercial revolution, 1500/1550–1800/1830, coincided with the maturation of early modern social, cultural, and political forms in that same zone. Those complex feedback loops between economic, political, and cultural integration that we find in protected-zone realms had obvious Chinese parallels.

But consider three defining differences between China and the protected zone. Most obvious, whereas protected-zone societies imported institutions wholesale from China, India, and the Mediterranean, China itself was a site of primary civilization, which meant that processes of state and culture formation not only began earlier, but in the absence of external blueprints, necessarily remained more hesitant and drawn out.

Second, in China, political development, especially from c. 900 to 1800, was heavily influenced by nomadic and seminomadic peoples from Inner Asia. Along with the growing cohesion and complexity of the Chinese sociopolitical order, this was one of two grand motors of Chinese history. Inner Asian capacity drew strength from cumulative experience and from more sustained contacts with sedentary peoples, not least during the economic upsurge of 850–1300. Yet if Inner Asians, Manchus in particular, embraced Neo-Confucianism as a supra-ethnic doctrine, conquest elite cohesion also required that they erect ethnic barriers between themselves and their subjects, proscribe nativist writings, and regard the empire as a horizontal system in which the Chinese were but one of several ethnic blocs. Such policies contrasted with the assimilative, integrationist thrust of cultural policy in protected-zone states and in China itself under Chinese-led dynasties. Far from impeding Inner Asian effectiveness, by sustaining an *esprit de corps*, this posture contributed to the remarkable success of conquest dynasties in China and allowed Manchus to serve as critical agents of early modern integration.

These two features – civilizational precocity and Inner Asian dominance – seem to have been related in that the same physical openness as
afforded ancient North China access to pan-Eurasian technologies later
left North China vulnerable to Inner Asian incursions.

A third difference between China and protected-zone realms (Russia
aside) was the enormous size of Chinese imperial territories. Immense
Yuan and Qing conquests testified to the power of Inner Asian cavalry.
But more basically, the expanse and solidity of empire under Chinese
and Inner Asian dynasties alike benefited from a moderately centripetal
geography and continuous frontier migration, in combination with four
nonpareil cultural instruments that Inner Asians merely appropriated –
namely, genuine bureaucracy, logographic scripts, the Neo-Confucian
educational corpus, and civil service examinations. Immense size and
population, however, set stricter limits to progressive centralization
than in more easily managed protected-zone realms and help to explain
why Chinese authorities were less interested than their protected-zone
counterparts (Japan being the obvious exception) in fiscal maximization. Because their subcontinental expanse tended to preclude serious
military threats, Chinese empires, the Ming and Qing in particular, could
afford a low-tax regime. Conversely, by minimizing local resistance,
light taxes helped the empire hold together. This hardly means that
governance in China was less effective than in protected-zone realms:
cultural instruments joined political controls to foster exceptional levels
of stability over unusually large areas for remarkably long periods. Yet a
singular interstate context ensured that for much of the period c. 1400 to
1800 the Chinese state followed a developmental logic and a regressive
bureaucratic trajectory distinct from protected-zone patterns.

In South Asia at large we also meet substantial, if less sustained,
similarities to individual protected-zone realms and indeed to China.
Periods of polycentricity between successive Indian empires grew
shorter and, in some ways, less disruptive. Indian administrative culture became more efficient, especially between c. 800 and 1300, which
coincided with protected-zone charter polities and the Song commer-
cial/bureaucratic revolution; and again between c. 1550 and 1750/1800,
when China, India, and the protected rimlands all fashioned unprecedentedly effective early modern states. From the Guptas through the
British Raj, we see as well a sustained expansion of imperial territories.
Loosely familiar too were long-term trends toward horizontal cultural
integration across South Asia as represented by the southward spread
of Sanskritic culture, the northward penetration of *bhakti*, the integrative

thrust of Perso-Islamic culture, and growing acceptance of brahmanic notions of caste. Finally, integration in South Asia responded to familiar economic stimuli according to well-known rhythms.

But chronology and geography also set South Asia apart from the protected zone. For one thing, the Indo-Gangetic plain, much like the North China plain, supported a charter state at least 800 years earlier than any protected-zone realm, as well as a primary civilization by the early third millennium B.C.E.

Second, again like China, South Asia after c. 1000 C.E. lay open to ever more insistent Inner Asian incursions, which pivoted on long-term cavalry superiority but which also seem to have benefited from sustained agrarian–pastoral contacts during the post-900 boom. Inner Asians entered South Asia along some of the very routes by which new crops, animals, and technologies had entered in the third and second millennia B.C.E.

In many ways Inner Asians in India were more ambitious than their counterparts in China. Whereas in China Inner Asian regimes, lacking an independent literate tradition, necessarily embraced Neo-Confucianism, Delhi sultans and Mughal emperors accorded primacy to Perso-Islamic norms. Thus, in effect, they sponsored a second charter dispensation comparable to imperial brahmanism. In China Inner Asians sought to perfect, without fundamentally altering, local administration, but in India from c. 1200 to 1700 Inner Asians introduced quite novel Perso-Islamic systems of military finance and provincial control that were widely imitated. Territorially, moreover, both the Delhi sultans and the Mughals extinguished regional kingdoms that, absent Inner Asian incursions, well might have engendered a stable multistate system such as took root in Europe and mainland Southeast Asia. Admittedly the Mongols, by reuniting North and South China, and the Manchus, by joining China proper to Inner Asia, also modified territorial patterns. But the Manchus inherited, rather than created, China proper as a political unit. The British in effect reproduced Inner Asian achievements, while introducing fundamentally new cultural and political arrangements.

And yet, compared to China, in India from 1200 to 1800 empires remained fragile and fleeting, while regional regimes and cultures proved surprisingly vital. In this sense India's historic profile was intermediate between those of protected-zone realms and of China. Indian empires remained vulnerable because South Asian terrain was less centripetal than its Chinese counterpart, and frequent warfare precluded a low-tax regime on the Ming and Qing model. Less favorable too were South Asian cultural features, including pervasive rural militarization, nested sovereignties, weak instruments of political acculturation, caste, low literacy rates, and alphabetic, rather than logographic, scripts. Finally, *pace* an anticommunal historiography stressing Mughal localization, the Mughals' Perso-Islamic identity proved to be a double-edged sword. On the one hand, Perso-Islamic culture was marvelously well suited to create a transregional empire and to maintain conquest elite cohesion. But on the other, Perso-Islamic affiliations left the Mughals vulnerable to challenge by regional leaders who were weakly assimilated to imperial culture and who now insisted on the ritual primacy of their own religious/cultural traditions. In China, where a common Neo-Confucian commitment precluded this sort of confessional cleavage, one could argue that Inner Asian cultural limitations contributed to Inner Asian political vitality.[3]

If South Asia's oscillation between regional and transregional formations gave it something of a hybrid character, archipelagic Southeast Asia was a yet more curious amalgam of protected- and exposed-zone experiences. From c. 700 to 1571, island trajectories paralleled those of mainland Southeast Asia, and both regions should be seen as part of the protected zone. Although archipelagic states were unusually numerous and small scale, the rise of Melaka, Aceh, Makasar, Mataram, and so forth paralleled post-1450/1500 revivals on the mainland. So too the spread of Malayo-Islamic culture recalls the contemporaneous expansion of Burmese, Siamese, Vietnamese – not to mention Russian, French, and Japanese – ethnicity and the dissemination of textual religions. Above all, in the archipelago as in all protected-zone realms, political and cultural change long remained under local auspices.

In the 16th century, however, Europeans – "white Inner Asians" – began to modify archipelagic development in a fashion reminiscent of Manchus and Mughals. To be sure, the territorial scale, global ties, commercial objectives, and numerical strength of Europeans and Inner Asians were incomparable. But both conquest elites used superior military and organizational skills to overwhelm local opponents and to forge novel territorial entities and ethnically stratified social systems.

---

[3] Although I focus only on China and South Asia, much of Southwest Asia exhibited the same defining features of the exposed zone – precocious civilizations, vulnerability to Inner Asian domination, and challenges to progressive, long-term centralization – as did China and South Asia. Cf. Ch. 1, n. 151.

Chronologically too, both Inner Asian and European advances after 1500/1550 represented the second wave of an imperial expansion whose first wave occurred during the Eurasian economic boom of 900–1300.[4]

The Philippines' pre-1571 unfamiliarity with supralocal organization or administrative literacy left them particularly vulnerable to European interference. Indeed, Hispanization constituted the most radical transformation anywhere in Southeast Asia between 1500 and 1830. If Manchus and Mughals represented successive points in a series extending from accommodation of indigenous traditions to external imposition, the Spanish represented a point well beyond the Mughals.

Although Dutch commercial goals and Muslim self-sufficiency meant that the Dutch at first had a weaker cultural impact than the Spanish, the Dutch influenced the archipelago's political economy more decisively, because they boasted larger resources and concentrated on the most profitable lines of trade. By 1683 the Dutch had monopolized fine spices and by 1757 had subdued or fragmented the archipelago's most powerful states. Thereafter, in a version of that commercially generated crisis that convulsed France and mainland kingdoms, Dutch fortunes declined – only to revive brilliantly in the early 1800s thanks to British support. The commercial-cum-territorial system that cohered by 1830 bore no obvious relation to any pre-Dutch entity. By creating ever more powerful, encapsulated European enclaves on the fringe of Indonesian society and by inhibiting Chinese assimilation, the Dutch eventually also modified regional cultural patterns. In these ways, between 1570 and 1830 Spanish and Dutch conquest elites decoupled early modern trajectories in the archipelago from those in mainland Southeast Asia.

What, then, is the ultimate value of this study for global history? Ironically, given its breadth, one major benefit is an ability to enrich local understandings. That is to say, by multiplying case studies, Eurasian comparisons make it easier to identify factors influential across a range of societies and to isolate such factors from forces that were truly *sui generis*. Without reliable case studies, comparativists can have no confidence in their grand theories. But without comparative perspectives, self-referential encapsulation goes unchallenged.

Let me be more specific. Between c. 900 and 1250/1300 Southeast Asia, Russia, France, China, and South Asia all experienced exceptionally

---

[4] The chief difference was that whereas Inner Asians operated in the same geographic theater during both waves, Europeans to 1300 focused on their own continent.

rapid economic growth, in explanation of which I used secondary literature to suggest synergies between climate, disease, trade, new social forms, and so forth. Between secondary and primary research, however, we need more sustained dialogue. As regards climate, for example, a scholar of country A would be well advised to combine local primary sources with secondary accounts of climate–social interactions in countries B and C subject to the same climatic regime as country A. Such an exercise could enhance sensitivity to easily ignored, but potentially critical patterns, while permitting more confident discussion of local singularity.

So too with Inner Asian and Tai expansion. I argued that Inner Asian conquests in China between c. 900 and 1350 and in India between c. 1150 and 1350, and Tai inroads in mainland Southeast Asia between c. 1100 and 1350, all drew strength during an era of rapid growth from thickening sown–nomadic interactions that gave frontier peoples the cultural skills needed to rule sedentary populations. But again, this is a hypothesis awaiting *in situ* testing.

Nor are economic and political events the only patterns to profit, potentially, from comparative analysis. In any given Eurasian realm, how did niche specialization relate to generic cultural convergence? How did people address tensions between market mobility and hereditary status? How did they reconcile a growing emphasis on discrete secular cultures with loyalty to universal religious norms? How did social hierarchy accommodate the horizontal community implicit in Burmese, Siamese, Vietnamese, Russian, and French mobilizations? Again, insofar as far-flung peoples struggled with similar quandaries at roughly the same time, imaginative studies from ostensibly unrelated regions can invigorate local inquiry with novel hypotheses and perspectives.

However, if Eurasian comparisons can enrich local understandings, surely the larger benefit is a modified view of Eurasia itself. As Chapter 1 indicated, comparativists to date have focused either on explaining European versus Asian differences or on compressing those differences through the discovery of institutional or protoindustrial similarities. While naturally I value such approaches, my concern with synchronized integration yields rather different classifications. So far as I know, no one has advanced any of the central themes of this study, including the following: the distinction between protected and exposed zones; the concept of coordinated charter states; South Asia as intermediate between protected zone and Chinese patterns; progressively milder interregna across both Asia and Europe; politicized ethnicity as a common European and Southeast Asian mobilizing device; sustained synergies between political, cultural, and commercial integration; the essential isomorphism of ever more complex commercial, political, and cultural structures; and the coordinating role of the Medieval Climate Anomaly and of parallel institutional experiments. But if my criteria of classification are novel, I seek to answer the same broad and abiding questions, the first explicit, the second generally implicit, as earlier historical inquiries: What forces shaped the life options, the self-images of earlier generations? How did those patterns condition the world in which we live? My goal is not to replace, rather to supplement and to complicate earlier understandings.

The picture of Europe that emerges from this inquiry is therefore both familiar and jarring. It is familiar in the sense that in terms of centralization, military and industrial potential, France in 1830 was the most successful realm under review. Western Europe boasted a combination of traits – dense information and commercial networks, an intensely competitive interstate system, a protected public sphere, a unique commitment to the marriage of warfare and maritime trade – that awarded it a grossly disproportionate share of global wealth and power. And yet by other criteria – criteria that arguably impacted common people no less than centralization or military power – Europe and Asia are not especially serviceable categories. For example, in terms of charter acculturation and the dynamics and geography of postcharter collapse, among the realms under review Vietnam and France were by far the most similar. On the other hand, in urbanization and publishing France and Japan had most in common. Bureaucratic forms were most developed in France, Japan, and Vietnam. Russia's post-1650 political economy, based on hereditary bound labor, resembled those of Burma and Siam more closely than that of France. Elites in 18th-century Russia and Vietnam looked to foreign cultural models far more readily than did their French or Southeast Asian contemporaries. Politicized ethnicity in Burma, Vietnam, France, and Russia was more salient than in Japan. And so on.

Precisely because Southeast Asia has long been marginalized, conversations between Southeast Asian and Eurasian studies hold particular promise. The region's marginality can become a source of creativity in three ways. First, by reducing the danger of external contamination, Southeast Asia's relative insularity makes it easier to isolate genuinely universal factors behind Eurasian-wide transitions. All of the large comparative issues that I have identified – Eurasian prosperity between

c. 900 and 1250, Eurasian turmoil between c. 1250 and 1450, external irruptions between c. 900 and 1300, long-term changes in the relation between local and kingdom-wide loyalties – can profit from a consideration of Southeast Asian experiences. Second, once we concede common concerns, information can flow more easily in the opposite direction as well, and scholars of Southeast Asia can more easily breach a tedious encapsulation. Finally, realization that one of the most distant, seemingly conservative sectors of Eurasia actually participated in wider rhythms for at least a thousand years must strengthen our confidence in Eurasia as a interactive sphere. As European exceptionalism and its corollary, Southeast Asian encapsulation, recede, we sense that two peninsulas on Eurasia's farthest extremities were, in fact, idiosyncratic representations of an increasingly coherent ecumene.

Index

Abbasid caliphate, 86, 130, 131, 134, 140
absolutism, 318–19, 438
Abu-Lughod, Janet, 146, 159
Aceh: claims legacy of Melaka, 847; and
    Dutch, 843, 846, 857; early commercial
    and territorial expansion of, 807, 839,
    845; external alliances of, 845–46; female
    rulers in, 811, 847; firearms at, 845–46;
    Malay and Muslim identity of, 847–48;
    opposes Johor, 848–49; opposes
    Portuguese, 825–26, 839, 840, 845–46,
    848; *panglimas* under, 847; political,
    commercial, and cultural centralization
    at, 846–48; post-1650 shift to less
    mercantile, less Malay orientation in,
    849, 858, 864, 871; urban population of,
    822
Achaemenid empire, 107, 639, 656
Adams, Julia, 841
administrative centralization: in China,
    504–19, 524, 562; in France, 57–63,
    169–70, 177–79, 251–56, 323–29, 340–41,
    353–55; in island Southeast Asian
    realms, 832–37, 841–57, 861–63, 875–78,
    886–87; in Japan, 57–63, 382–85,
    404–406, 438–48, 467–68, 470–71; in
    mainland Southeast Asian realms,
    22–25, 240–41, 269, 274; in Russia, 57–63,
    224–28, 299–306; in South Asia, 639–55
administrative cycles: 94–95; in Chinese
    and Southeast Asian historiography, 94,
    118, 123; defined, 55, 125 n.2; in France,
    94 n.131, 125, 205, 376; in Japan, 55–56

and n.68, 376–77, 491–92; in mainland
    Southeast Asia, 205, 376; in Russia, 125,
    205, 376. *See also* interregna
Adolphson, Mikael, 406
Afghanistan, 97, 102, 109, 645, 657, 709,
    711, 722, 738, 749
Afghans, 637, 646, 673, 701, 710, 733, 749,
    754, 761
Africa, 49, 97, 116, 188, 207, 684, 838,
    842
Age of Commerce in Southeast Asia, 798,
    803, 820
Age of Division in China, 94, 102, 499–500,
    502, 504–509, 538–39, 557, 616, 623
Ageng, sultan of Banten, 850–51
Agra, 704, 732, 755
agrarian expansion and intensification: in
    China, 526–30, 550; in France, 156–65,
    333–34; in Iberia, 828; in island
    Southeast Asia, 780–81, 783, 788–92, 797,
    824, 851, 870, 885–86; in Japan, 71,
    381–82, 395, 423–27, 449, 460; in
    mainland Southeast Asia, 16, 33–35, 42,
    46–48, 69, 71, 318, 335; in Russia, 69, 71,
    134, 140–47, 187, 214, 218, 220, 239, 291,
    294–98, 317–18; in South Asia, 641–42,
    644, 681–91, 693–94, 702, 708
agrarian tenures: in China, 568, 608, 615
    n.296, 625; in Europe, 160–61, 165, 291,
    330; in Japan, 75, 424–25, 452–53; in
    South Asia, 654; in Southeast Asia, 45,
    75, 423
Agung, sultan of Mataram, 855, 856

909

933